City of Smithville Continuous Computerized Problem

A great way to understand the GASB *Statement No. 34* financial reporting model is to be actively engaged in learning through this "hands-on" continuous problem for a small governmental entity. The City of Smithville CD that is included with this text is a general ledger software package in which students record transactions into the appropriate general journals of a city. Transaction analysis, of course, is the first and most important step in the accounting cycle of any organization. After journal entries have been recorded, the City of Smithville software conveniently posts changes to all accounts in general and subsidiary ledgers. From this point, students can preview trial balances, export them to a Microsoft ® Excel file, and then prepare financial statements from that data.

This instructional supplement substantially aids student learning by requiring them to decide whether each transaction has an effect on the *fund financial statements,* the *government-wide financial statements,* or both. The City of Smithville is built on the *dual-track approach* described on the adjacent page. Students can apply the conceptual framework that connects the government-wide financial statements (that report on the flow of total economic resources of the government using the accrual basis of accounting) and the fund financial statements (that report on the flow of current financial resources using the modified accrual or near-cash basis of accounting).

STUDENTS

Several examples are provided to show how the software facilitates learning. When a government sends out property tax bills for the year, this transaction is recorded in the General Fund general journal because it impacts the governmental funds statement of revenues, expenditures and changes in fund balance and in the governmental activities general journal because it has an impact on the government-wide statement of activities. The student can easily toggle among the journals for each fund and governmental activity. Drop down menus make it easy to decide which revenues account should be increased or decreased. Journal entries must balance before one can proceed. When the government records its budget or encumbers items related to purchase orders, however, these journal entries affect only the governmental funds. Budgetary account titles are available for selection in the governmental funds general journals but not in the governmental activities general journal because funds, not governmental activities, capture information to show compliance with the short-term, legally approved budget. Conversely, depreciation expense of general capital assets is recorded in the general journal of governmental activities because the accrual basis of accounting captures and matches the cost of using up the utility of capital assets with the time period in which the assets generate revenues.

INSTRUCTORS

This software can be used in several ways. You can project it each day as part of the classroom experience and discuss transactions that are keyed to the chapter under discussion. Depending on your objectives, you can require a small set of the transactions be recorded for each fund or governmental activity or you can assign the full problem as a semester-long case. Regardless of how you choose to use the case, we recommend that students work on the City of Smithville problem as they are studying the related chapter in the text and turn in each chapter as they go along. You may find that small student work groups provide an efficient way for students to learn from each other.

We continue to be encouraged by our students' positive reaction as they *learn by doing* the City of Smithville Continuous Computerized Problem. Many improvements were made in the software for this 14th edition of the text based on the constructive comments of users.

Accounting for Governmental and Nonprofit Entities

Fourteenth Edition

Earl R. Wilson, Ph.D., CPA

Professor Emeritus
University of Missouri–Columbia

Susan C. Kattelus, Ph.D., CPA, CGFM

Professor and Department Head
Eastern Michigan University

Jacqueline L. Reck, Ph.D., CPA

Associate Professor and James E. Rooks
Distinguished Professor in Accounting
University of South Florida

McGraw-Hill Irwin

Boston   Burr Ridge, IL   Dubuque, IA   Madison, WI   New York   San Francisco   St. Louis
Bangkok   Bogotá   Caracas   Kuala Lumpur   Lisbon   London   Madrid   Mexico City
Milan   Montreal   New Delhi   Santiago   Seoul   Singapore   Sydney   Taipei   Toronto

McGraw-Hill
Irwin

ACCOUNTING FOR GOVERNMENTAL AND NONPROFIT ENTITIES

American Institute of Certified Public Accountants, Inc. materials reproduced are copyright © 2005 by AICPA, reproduced with permission.

Portions of various GASB documents, copyright by the Governmental Accounting Standards Board, 401 Merritt 7, PO Box 5116, Norwalk, CT 06856-5116, U.S.A., are reproduced with permission. Complete copies of these documents are available from the GASB.

International City/County Management Association (ICMA) materials are reprinted with permission of the International City/County Management Association, 777 North Capitol Street, NE, Suite 500, Washington, DC 20002. All rights reserved.

Published by McGraw-Hill/Irwin, a business unit of The McGraw-Hill Companies, Inc., 1221 Avenue of the Americas, New York, NY, 10020.

Some ancillaries, including electronic and print components, may not be available to customers outside the United States.

This book is printed on acid-free paper.

3 4 5 6 7 8 9 0 VNH/VNH 0 9 8 7

ISBN-13:   978-0-07-310095-1
ISBN-10:   0-07-310095-1

Editorial director: *Stewart Mattson*
Sponsoring editor: *Steve DeLancey*
Editorial assistant: *Megan McFarlane*
Executive marketing manager: *Rhonda Seelinger*
Senior media producer: *Elizabeth Mavetz*
Project manager: *Bruce Gin*
Senior production supervisor: *Sesha Bolisetty*
Designer: *Cara David*
Senior media project manager: *Rose M. Range*
Cover design: *Chris Bowyer*
Typeface: *10.5/12 Times New Roman*
Compositor: *GTS – New Delhi, India Campus*
Printer: *Von Hoffmann Corporation*

Library of Congress Cataloging-in-Publication Data
Wilson, Earl R., 1939-
    Accounting for governmental and nonprofit entities / Earl R. Wilson, Susan C. Kattelus,
Jacqueline L. Reck. -- 14th ed.
        p. cm.
    Includes bibliographical references and index.
    ISBN-13: 978-0-07-310095-1 (alk. paper)
    ISBN-10: 0-07-310095-1 (alk. paper)
    1. Finance, Public--Accounting. 2. Nonprofit organizations--Accounting. 3. Nonprofit
organizations--United States--Accounting. I. Kattelus, Susan C. II. Reck Jacqueline L. III.
Title.
HJ9733. W48 2007
657′.825--dc22   2005056189

www.mhhe.com

About the Authors

Earl R. Wilson

Is Professor Emeritus of the School of Accountancy at the University of Missouri–Columbia. He received his BA and MBA from Chapman University and his MA and Ph.D. in Accountancy from the University of Missouri–Columbia. He is a certified public accountant (Missouri).

Professor Wilson has contributed substantially to standards setting in governmental accounting and auditing, having served as an academic fellow with the Governmental Accounting Standards Board (GASB) and as a member of the Governmental Accounting Standards Advisory Council, the U.S. Comptroller General's Advisory Council on Governmental Auditing Standards, the American Institute of CPAs Government Accounting and Auditing Committee, and as chair of the Missouri Society of CPAs (MSCPA) Government Accounting Committee and president of the American Accounting Association Government and Nonprofit (AAA-GNP) Section. In addition, he has served on several GASB task forces and conducted financial reporting research for the GASB.

Dr. Wilson has published numerous research articles in journals such as *The Accounting Review; Journal of Accounting Research; Contemporary Accounting Research; Journal of Accounting and Public Policy; Journal of Accounting, Auditing, and Finance; Research in Governmental and Nonprofit Accounting; Public Budgeting and Finance,* and others. Many of these articles are frequently cited as influential studies of the municipal bond market. He has been an author of this text since the ninth edition in 1992. He has extensive experience teaching governmental and nonprofit accounting, including online courses.

Professor Wilson has received a number of awards for his teaching and research, including the Enduring Lifetime Contribution Award from the AAA-GNP section, the Cornelius Tierney/Ernst & Young Research Award for 2003 from the Association of Government Accountants, Outstanding Teacher of the Year for 2002 from the Kansas City MU Business Alumni Association, and the 2000 Outstanding Educator of Year Award from the MSCPA. He has chaired or served as reader of more than 30 doctoral dissertations, many in the area of governmental accounting.

Susan C. Kattelus

Is a professor of accounting and head of the Department of Accounting and Finance at Eastern Michigan University. She received her BBA and Ph.D. from Michigan State University and MSA from Eastern Michigan University. Professor Kattelus is a certified public accountant (Michigan) and a certified government financial manager.

Professor Kattelus has served on the Governmental Accounting Standards Advisory Council as the academic representative of the American Accounting Association (AAA), president of the Government and Nonprofit Section of the AAA, and chair of the Nonprofit Task Force of the Michigan Association of CPAs (MACPA). She is currently a board member of the MACPA. She has taught the public and nonprofit accounting course for accounting majors and currently teaches the financial management for nonprofit organizations course in the Nonprofit Management Graduate Certificate program at Eastern Michigan University.

Dr. Kattelus has published articles in *The Accounting Review; Research in Governmental and Nonprofit Accounting; Journal of Government Financial Management; Public Budgeting and Finance; Issues in Accounting Education; Journal of Accounting Education; and Journal of Public Budgeting, Accounting and Financial Management,* among others. She joined as an author on the 11th edition in 1999.

Jacqueline L. Reck

Is an associate professor and the James E. Rooks Distinguished Professor in Accounting for the School of Accountancy at the University of South Florida. She received a BS degree from North Dakota State University, BS and MAcc degrees from the University of South Florida, and her Ph.D. from the University of Missouri–Columbia. She is a certified public accountant (Florida).

Dr. Reck worked for state government for several years before joining academia. Currently, she is active in several professional associations. In addition to teaching governmental and not-for-profit accounting, Dr. Reck frequently presents continuing professional education workshops and sessions. She has provided workshops on governmental and not-for-profit accounting for local accounting firms and the state auditor general's staff. Dr. Reck has received several teaching and research awards, is currently the doctoral program coordinator for the School of Accountancy, and has chaired or served on several doctoral dissertation committees.

Dr. Reck has published articles in *The Journal of Accounting and Public Policy; Research in Governmental and Nonprofit Accounting; Journal of Public Budgeting, Accounting and Financial Management;* and the *Journal of Information Systems,* among others. She joins as author on the current edition.

Preface

Welcome to the 14th edition of *Accounting for Governmental and Nonprofit Entities*. This book continues to be the leading governmental and not-for-profit accounting text, in part because of the tremendous contributions of Dr. Leon E. Hay, now retired. Dr. Hay joined Professor R. M. Mikesell of Indiana University–Bloomington in 1961 on the third edition of this book, which was first published in 1951. Dr. Earl R. Wilson joined with the ninth edition (1992) and Dr. Susan Kattelus with the 11th edition (1999) of the text. Dr. Jacqueline Reck joins this edition of the text. Dr. Wilson and Dr. Kattelus have followed Dr. Hay's example by serving as president of the Government and Nonprofit (GNP) Section of the American Accounting Association and as members of the Governmental Accounting Standards Advisory Council, among other councils and boards. Professors Wilson, Kattelus, and Reck are active in many professional organizations. Professors Kattelus and Reck regularly teach a GNP course at their universities. Drs. Wilson and Hay are two of only eight people who have received the Enduring Lifetime Contribution Award from the Government and Nonprofit Section of the American Accounting Association.

ORGANIZATION AND CONTENT

Chapters 1 through 9 of this text focus on accounting and financial reporting issues of governmental entities at the state and local levels that follow the reporting model prescribed by GASB *Statement No. 34* (*GASBS 34*). Chapters 10 and 11 are similar in that they describe how decision makers can use audited annual financial statements to analyze the financial performance of an entity. Chapter 13 focuses on budgeting and costing of services provided by government. In Chapters 12 and 14 through 17, readers will examine the accounting and financial reporting issues of federal government agencies, the federal government as a whole, and not-for-profit organizations as they demonstrate accountability for financial and operational performance and compliance with regulations to resource providers and other interested parties. Chapters 14 and 15 describe nongovernmental, not-for-profit organizations. Chapters 16 and 17 pay particular attention to the higher education and health care industries, respectively, encompassing entities that have governmental, commercial, and not-for-profit legal structures.

KEY CHANGES IN THIS EDITION

In this edition, users will find significant revisions to the text and several new or revised illustrations that will enhance readability and understanding. The City and County of Denver's financial information is used to provide real-world examples of financial statements, schedules, and management discussion and analysis. More emphasis has been placed on accounting for internal service funds, new information is provided on reconciling modified accrual and accrual statements, and information is provided on how users can convert from a modified basis of accounting to an accrual basis. In addition, several new cases have been added to the end-of-chapter materials, two versions of the Smithville computerized project are provided, and revisions and additions have been made to the exercises and problems at the end of the chapters.

As always, readers can count on this edition to include authoritative changes from the Financial Accounting Standards Board, Governmental Accounting Standards

Board, Federal Accounting Standards Advisory Board, American Institute of Certified Public Accountants, Office of Management and Budget, and Government Accountability Office. Update bulletins will be provided periodically on the text Web site as new authoritative statements are issued.

INNOVATIVE PEDAGOGY

For state and local government accounting, the authors have found that *dual-track* accounting is an effective approach in showing the juxtaposition of government-wide and fund financial statements in *GASBS 34*'s integrated model of basic financial statements. It allows students to see that each transaction has an effect on the fund financial statements (that are designed to show fiscal compliance with the annual budget), on the government-wide financial statements (that demonstrate accountability for operational performance of the government as a whole), or both. This approach better serves students who will design and use accounting information systems, such as enterprise systems, to allow information to be captured once and used for several purposes. Accounting for federal agencies as well as non-governmental, not-for-profit entities closely parallels this approach as traditional fund accounting may be appropriate for keeping track of resources with restricted purposes, but citizens and donors also need to see the larger picture provided by the entity as a whole.

Governments may continue to prepare fund-based statements throughout the year and convert to accrual-based government-wide statements at the end of the year until they invest in information systems that can deliver real-time information for decision making. We want students to think beyond being transaction-bookkeepers and aspire to design and use the systems that will make government-wide financial information available when managers and citizens need it. The City of Smithville Computerized Continuous Problem is a teaching tool that develops these skills and perspective. The authors feel so strongly that this general ledger software tool helps students understand the material that we again provide it with the text. Students have enthusiastically told us that they like "learning by doing" and that the City of Smithville problem helped them to understand the concepts in the book.

TARGET AUDIENCE

The text continues to be best suited for senior and graduate accounting majors who plan to sit for the certified public accountant (CPA) exam and then audit governmental or not-for-profit entities. Public administration and other students who plan to provide financial management or consulting services to government and not-for-profit entities report that the text provides a more comprehensive set of competencies than traditional public budgeting texts. Students in not-for-profit management education programs find that the coverage of accounting, financial reporting, auditing, taxation, and information systems for both governmental and not-for-profit entities provides the exposure they need to work across disciplines and sectors. Finally, students preparing for the certified government financial manager (CGFM) exam will also find Chapters 1 through 12 useful for Examination 2. We encourage all students who use this book to consider the challenge and rewards of careers in public service—in federal, state, and local governments as well as not-for-profit organizations.

SUPPLEMENT PACKAGE

These ancillary materials are prepared by the authors and are available on the Instructor's Resource CD-ROM and/or the textbook's Web site, www.mhhe.com/business/accounting/wilson14e.

- Instructor's Guide and Solutions Manual (including teaching and case analysis tips).
- PowerPoint lecture presentations.
- Test Bank (including a computerized version using Diploma software).
- The City of Smithville Continuous Computerized Problem—a general ledger practice set—packaged free with each new copy of the textbook.
- City of Smithville Instructors' Version software, Instructors' Utility Manual for the City of Smithville, solution data files for Cases A and B, and solution page image (.pdf) files for Cases A and B.

Acknowledgments

We are thankful for the encouragement, suggestions, and counsel provided by many instructors, professionals, and students in writing this book. They include the following professionals and educators who read portions of this book and previous editions in various forms and provided valuable comments and suggestions:

Mr. Robert Bramlett
Federal Accounting Standards Advisory Board
retired

Dr. Kenneth W. Brown
Southwest Missouri State University
emeritus

Dr. Barbara Chaney
University of Montana

Mr. Jeremy Craig
Chesterfield, Missouri

Ms. Rebecca Craig
St. Charles County, Missouri

Mr. Michael Crawford
Crawford & Associates

Ms. Mary Foelster
American Institute of Certified Public Accountants

Mrs. Kristen Hockman
University of Missouri—Columbia

Ms. Marie Hunniecutt
University of South Florida

Mr. J. Thomas Luter
formerly, U.S. Department of the Treasury

Ms. Johanna Lyle
Kansas State University

Mr. Bruce K. Michelson
U.S. Government Accountability Office

Mr. Roger P. Murphy
Iowa State University
retired

Ms. Melanie Nelson
California State University–San Marcos

Dr. David O'Bryan
Pittsburgh State University

Dr. Suzanne M. Ogilby
California State University–Sacramento

Dr. James Patton
Federal Accounting Standards Advisory Board and University of Pittsburgh

Dr. Terry K. Patton
Governmental Accounting Standards Board

Ms. Janet Prowse
University of Nevada, Las Vegas

Dr. Walter A. Robbins
University of Alabama

Mr. Lawrence Roman
Cuyahoga Community College–East Campus

Dr. Relmond P. Van Daniker
Association of Government Accountants

Mr. Jay Wahlund
Minot State University

Mr. James F. White
Harvard Extension School

Dr. William T. Wrege
Ball State University

We acknowledge permission to quote pronouncements and reproduce illustrations from the publications of the Governmental Accounting Standards Board, American Institute of Certified Public Accountants, International City/County Management Association, and Crawford and Associates. Special thanks go to our spouses, Florence J. Wilson and Albert F. Hohenstein, for their patience, understanding, and inspiration in completing this book, and we dedicate it to them.

Although we are extremely careful in checking the text and end-of-chapter material, it is possible that errors and ambiguities remain in this edition. As readers encounter such, we urge them to let us know so that corrections can be made. We also invite every user of this edition who has suggestions or comments about the material in the chapters to share them with one of the authors, either by regular mail or e-mail. The authors will continue the service of issuing Update Bulletins to adopters of this text that describe changes after the book is in print. These bulletins can be downloaded from the text Web site at www.mhhe.com/business/accounting/wilson14e or either of the author's Web sites:

Dr. Earl R. Wilson
School of Accountancy
University of Missouri–Columbia
303 Cornell Columbia, MO 65211
wilsonea@missouri.edu
http://www.missouri.edu/~accterw

Dr. Susan C. Kattelus
Department of Accounting and Finance
Eastern Michigan University
406 Owen Ypsilanti, MI 48197
susan.kattelus@emich.edu
http://people.emich.edu/skattelus

Dr. Jacqueline L. Reck
School of Accountancy
University of South Florida
4202 East Fowler Avenue, BSN 3403
Tampa, FL 33620
jreck@coba.usf.edu
http:www.coba.usf.edu/departments/
accounting/faculty/reck

December 2005

Brief Contents

Preface v

1   Introduction to Accounting and Financial Reporting for Governmental and Not-for-Profit Entities   1

2   Principles of Accounting and Financial Reporting for State and Local Governments   33

3   Governmental Operating Statement Accounts; Budgetary Accounting   59

4   Accounting for Governmental Operating Activities—Illustrative Transactions and Financial Statements   103

5   Accounting for General Capital Assets and Capital Projects   163

6   Accounting for General Long-Term Liabilities and Debt Service   207

7   Accounting for the Business-Type Activities of State and Local Governments   253

8   Accounting for Fiduciary Activities—Agency and Trust Funds   303

9   Financial Reporting of State and Local Governments   347

10   Analysis of Governmental Financial Performance   395

11   Auditing of Governmental and Not-for-Profit Organizations   433

12   Accounting and Reporting for the Federal Government   467

13   Budgeting and Costing of Government Services   515

14   Accounting for Not-for-Profit Organizations   555

15   Not-for-Profit Organizations—Regulatory, Taxation, and Performance Issues   601

16   Accounting for Colleges and Universities   627

17   Accounting for Health Care Organizations   667

GLOSSARY   707

GOVERNMENTAL AND NOT-FOR-PROFIT ORGANIZATIONS   736

INDEX   740

Table of Contents

Preface   v

Chapter 1

Introduction to Accounting and Financial Reporting for Governmental and Not-for-Profit Entities   1

What Are Governmental and Not-for-Profit Organizations?   2
Distinguishing Characteristics of Governmental and Not-for-Profit Entities   2
Sources of Financial Reporting Standards   4
Determining Whether a Not-for-Profit Organization Is Governmental   5
Objectives of Financial Reporting   6
Financial Reporting of State and Local Governments   8
Comprehensive Annual Financial Report   9
Expanding the Scope of Accountability Reporting   24
Overview of Chapters 2 through 17   25
GASB Statement No. 34 Principles and Standards   25
Analysis of Governmental Financial Statements; Financial Statement and Performance Audits   25
Accounting and Financial Reporting for the Federal Government and Not-for-Profit Organizations   26
A Caveat   26
Key Terms   27
Questions   27
Cases   28
Exercises and Problems   29

Chapter 2

Principles of Accounting and Financial Reporting for State and Local Governments   33

Activities of Government   34
Governmental Financial Reporting Entity   34
Integrated Accounting and Financial Reporting Model   36
Government-wide and Fund Financial Statements   36
Fiscal Accountability and Fund Accounting   37
Fund Categories   39

Appendix: Summary Statement of Governmental Accounting and Financial Reporting Principles   47
Key Terms   51
Selected References   51
Questions   51
Cases   52
Exercises and Problems   54

Chapter 3

Governmental Operating Statement Accounts; Budgetary Accounting   59

Classification and Reporting of Revenues and Expenses at the Government-wide Level   60
Reporting Direct and Indirect Expenses   60
Program Revenues and General Revenues   62
Reporting Special Items and Transfers   63
Structure and Characteristics of the General Fund; Classification and Description of Operating Statement Accounts   64
Governmental Fund Balance Sheet and Operating Statement Accounts   64
Budgetary Accounts   68
Terminology and Classification for Governmental Fund Budgets and Accounts   72
Classification of Appropriations and Expenditures   72
Classification of Estimated Revenues and Revenues   74
Budgetary Accounting   79
Recording the Budget   80
Budgetary Control of Revenues   81
Budgetary Control of Encumbrances and Expenditures   82
Accounting for Allotments   85
Accounting Information Systems   86
Accounting for Government-wide Operating Activities   88
Appendix: Accounting for Public School Systems   89
Key Terms   92
Selected References   92
Questions   92

Cases   94
Exercises and Problems   95

Chapter 4

Accounting for Governmental Operating Activities—Illustrative Transactions and Financial Statements   103

Illustrative Case   104
   Measurement Focus and Basis of Accounting   104
Dual-Track Accounting Approach   106
Illustrative Journal Entries   107
   Recording the Budget   107
   Interfund Transfer to Create a New Fund   108
   Encumbrance Entry   108
   Payment of Liabilities   111
   Payrolls and Payroll Taxes   112
   Revenues Recognized as Received in Cash   114
Accounting for Property Taxes   115
   Recording Property Tax Levy   115
   Collection of Current Taxes   116
   Collection of Delinquent Taxes   118
   Tax Anticipation Notes Payable   119
   Repayment of Tax Anticipation Notes   120
   Other Taxes   121
Interim Financial Reporting   121
Special Topics   124
   Correction of Errors   124
   Receipt of Goods Ordered in Prior Year   125
   Revision of the General Fund Budget   126
   Internal Exchange Transactions   127
   Adjusting Entries   129
   Pre-Closing Trial Balance   132
   Closing Entries   133
   Year-end Financial Statements   133
Special Revenue Funds   137
   Accounting for Operating Grants   137
   Financial Reporting   138
Interfund Activity   138
   Reciprocal Interfund Activity   138
   Nonreciprocal Interfund Activity   141
   Intra- versus Inter-Activity Transactions (Government-wide Level)   142
   Intra-Entity Transactions   142
Permanent Funds   142
   Budgetary Accounts   142

   Illustrative Case   143
   Journal Entries—Permanent Fund   143
Appendix: Concepts and Rules for Recognition of Revenues and Expenses (or Expendituress)   147
Key Terms   150
Selected References   150
Questions   150
Cases   151
Exercises and Problems   153

Chapter 5

Accounting for General Capital Assets and Capital Projects   163

Accounting for General Capital Assets   164
   Required Disclosures about Capital Assets   165
   Classification of General Capital Assets   166
   General Capital Assets Acquired under Capital Lease Agreements   172
   Costs Incurred after Acquisition   174
   Reduction of Cost   174
   Asset Impairments and Insurance Recoveries   175
Illustrative Entries   175
Accounting for Capital Projects   177
   Legal Requirements   178
Illustrative Transactions—Capital Projects Funds   178
   Illustrative Financial Statements for a Capital Projects Fund   184
   Alternative Treatment of Residual Equity or Deficits   184
   Bond Premium, Discount, and Accrued Interest on Bonds Sold   185
   Retained Percentages   187
   Claims and Judgments Payable   188
   Bond Anticipation Notes Payable and the Problem of Interest Expenditures   188
   Investments   190
   Multiple-Period and Multiple-Project Bond Funds   190
   Reestablishment of Encumbrances   191
   Capital Projects Financed by Special Assessments   192
   Financial Reporting for Capital Projects Funds   193
Key Terms   194
Selected References   194
Questions   194
Cases   195
Exercises and Problems   198

Chapter 6
Accounting for General Long-Term Liabilities and Debt Service 207

General Long-Term Liabilities   207
Schedule of Future Debt Service Requirements   209
Debt Limit and Debt Margin   209
Overlapping Debt   213
General Long-Term Liabilities Arising from Capital Lease Agreements   216
Debt Service Funds   217
Number of Debt Service Funds   217
Use of General Fund to Account for Debt Service   217
Budgeting for Debt Service   218
Types of Serial Bonds   218
Debt Service Accounting for Regular Serial Bonds   219
Second-Year Transactions   222
Debt Service Accounting for Term Bonds   224
Financial Reporting   228
Deposit and Investment Disclosures   228
Valuation of Debt Service Fund Investments   231
Debt Service Accounting for Special Assessment Debt   232
Use of Debt Service Funds to Record Capital Lease Payments   233
Accounting for Debt Refunding   234
Advance Refunding of Debt   235
Disclosures about Advance Refundings   236
Key Terms   236
Selected References   236
Questions   236
Cases   237
Exercises and Problems   240

Chapter 7
Accounting for the Business-Type Activities of State and Local Governments 253

Proprietary Funds   254
Financial Reporting Requirements   254
Internal Service Funds   256
Illustrative Case—Supplies Fund   259
Internal Financial Reporting—Management Use   263
Illustrative Statements   263
External Financial Reporting of Internal Service Funds   264
Assets Acquired under Lease Agreements   266
Internal Service Funds with Manufacturing Activities   267
Internal Service Funds as Financing Devices   267
Dissolution of an Internal Service Fund   268
Enterprise Funds   269
Illustrative Case—Water Utility Fund   270
Current and Accrued Assets   270
Restricted Assets   271
Utility Plant   271
Current Liabilities   273
Liabilities Payable from Restricted Assets   273
Long-Term Liabilities   273
Net Assets   274
Illustrative Accounting for a Water Utility Fund   274
Illustrative Statements   279
External Financial Reporting of Enterprise Funds   283
Regulatory Accounting Principles (RAP)   283
Accounting for Nonutility Enterprises   285
Accounting for Municipal Solid Waste Landfills   285
Required Segment Information   287
Key Terms   288
Selected References   288
Questions   288
Cases   288
Exercises and Problems   291

Chapter 8
Accounting for Fiduciary Activities—Agency and Trust Funds 303

Agency Funds   304
Agency Fund for Special Assessment Debt Service   304
Tax Agency Funds   305
Illustration of Composition of Total Tax Rates   306
Accounting for Tax Agency Funds   308
Entries Made by Funds and Governments Participating in Tax Agency Funds   310
"Pass-Through" Agency Funds   311
Financial Reporting of Agency Funds   312
Trust Funds   312
Investment Pools   313
Creation of an Investment Pool   313
Operation of a Cash and Investment Pool   317
Withdrawal of Assets from the Pool   321
Closing Entry   321
Illustrative Financial Statements   322

Private-Purpose Trust Funds   323
Pension Accounting   324
  Required Financial Reporting for Defined Benefit
  Pension Plans   325
  Statement of Plan Net Assets   327
  Statement of Changes in Plan Net Assets   327
  Schedule of Funding Progress   328
  Schedules of Employer Contributions   328
  Alternative Reporting and Disclosure   328
  Illustrative Transactions for a Defined Benefit Pension
  Plan   328
  Employer's Pension Accounting   331
  Employer Recording and Reporting of Pension
  Expenditure/Expense   334
Other Postemployment Benefits (OPEB)   335
Termination Benefits   335
Key Terms   336
Selected References   336
Questions   336
Cases   336
Exercises and Problems   338

Chapter 9
Financial Reporting of State and Local Governments   347

The Governmental Reporting Entity   347
  Entity Definition Criteria   348
Governmental Financial Reports   351
  Need for Periodic Reports   351
  Interim Financial Reports   352
  Annual Financial Reports   352
Preparation of Basic Financial Statements   365
  Fund Financial Statements   372
  Required Reconciliations   372
Current Financial Reporting Issues   375
  Communication Methods   376
  Elements of Financial Statements   376
  Popular Reporting   377
  Other Comprehensive Basis of Accounting
  (OCBOA)   377
Appendix: Converting Accounting Information from
the Modified Accrual to the Accrual Basis of
Accounting   378
Key Terms   382
Selected References   382
Questions   382
Cases   383
Exercises and Problems   387

Chapter 10
Analysis of Governmental Financial Performance   395

The Need to Evaluate Financial Performance   395
Government Financial Performance Concepts   396
  Financial Position versus Financial Condition   398
  Economic Condition   399
Internal Financial Trend Monitoring   399
  Environmental Factors   402
  Organizational Factors   404
  Financial Factors   405
Analyzing Government-wide Financial
Statements   407
Use of Benchmarks to Aid Interpretation   410
  Sources of Governmental Financial Data   411
  Credit Analyst Models   413
Key Terms   417
Selected References   417
Questions   418
Cases   418
Exercises and Problems   424

Chapter 11
Auditing of Governmental and Not-for-Profit Organizations   433

Financial Audits by Independent CPAs   434
  Generally Accepted Auditing Standards   434
  Types of Audit Reports   435
  Types of Opinion   437
  Materiality   440
  Required Supplementary Information   441
Government Auditing Standards   441
  Types of Audits and Engagements   442
  Independence Standards   445
Single Audits   446
  History of the Single Audit   447
  Single Audit Act Amendments of 1996   447
  Who Must Have a Single Audit?   448
  What Does the Single Audit Require?   450
  How Are Programs Selected for Audit?   452
  What Reports Are Required for the Single
  Audit?   454
  Other Single Audit Requirements   456
Impact of SOX on Governments   *456*
Key Terms   458
Selected References   458
Questions   458

Cases   459
Exercises and Problems   461

Chapter 12
Accounting and Reporting for the Federal Government   467

Federal Government Financial Management Structure   468
  Comptroller General   470
  Secretary of the Treasury   470
  Director of the Office of Management and Budget   471
  Director of the Congressional Budget Office   471
Generally Accepted Accounting Principles for Federal Agencies   472
  Hierarchy of Accounting Principles and Standards   472
Conceptual Framework   473
  Concept Statements   473
  Objectives   473
  Reporting Entity   474
  Management's Discussion and Analysis   475
  Target Audience   475
  Funds Used in Federal Accounting   475
Required Financial Reporting—U.S. Government-wide   477
Required Financial Reporting—Government Agencies   478
  Management's Discussion and Analysis   478
  Basic Financial Statements   479
  Required Supplemental Information   489
  Accounting for Social Insurance   489
Dual-Track Accounting System   491
  Illustrative Transactions and Entries   491
  Adjusting Entries   497
  Illustrative Financial Statements   498
Summary of Accounting and Reporting for Federal Government Agencies   503
Key Terms   505
Selected References   505
Questions   505
Cases   506
Exercises and Problems   507

Chapter 13
Budgeting and Costing of Government Services   515

Objectives of Budgeting   516
  Implications of GASBS 34 for Public Budgeting   516
  Interrelation of Planning, Budgeting, and Performance Measurement   517

Budgeting Approaches   518
  Types of Budgeting   519
Budgeting Procedures   521
  Budgeting Governmental Appropriations   521
  Budgeting Governmental Revenues   524
  Budgeting Capital Expenditures   524
  Budgeting Cash Receipts   525
  Budgeting Cash Disbursements   526
Budgeting for Performance   528
  Total Quality Management   528
  Customer Relationship Management   529
  Service Efforts and Accomplishments (SEA)   530
Costing of Government Services   533
  Federal Grants and Sponsored Agreements   534
  Activity-Based Costing   537
Conclusion   541
Key Terms   541
Selected References   541
Questions   542
Cases   543
Exercises and Problems   545

Chapter 14
Accounting for Not-for-Profit Organizations   555

Defining the Not-for-Profit Sector   555
GAAP for Nongovernmental NPOs   558
Financial Reporting and Accounting   558
  Financial Reporting   559
  Accounting for Revenues, Gains, and Support   564
  Accounting for Expenses   568
  Accounting for Assets   570
Financially Interrelated Entities   572
  Investments in For-Profit Entities   573
  Financially Interrelated NPOs   573
  Funds Received as an Intermediary   573
  Funds Held in Trust by Others   574
  Combinations of NPOs   574
  Component Units of Governmental Entities   574
Optional Fund Accounting   575
Accounting Information Systems for Not-for-Profit Organizations   576
Illustrative Transactions—Voluntary Health and Welfare Organizations   579
  End-of-the-Year Adjusting Journal Entries   584
  End-of-the-Year Reclassification Journal Entries   584
  End-of-the-Year Closing Journal Entries   586
Key Terms   589

Selected References 589
Questions 589
Cases 590
Exercises and Problems 591

Chapter 15
Not-for-Profit Organizations—Regulatory, Taxation, and Performance Issues 601

Oversight Authority 601
State Regulation 602
  Nonprofit Incorporation Laws 602
  Registration, Licenses, and Tax Exemption 603
  Lobbying and Political Influence 604
Federal Regulation 605
  Tax-Exempt Status 605
  Unrelated Business Income Tax 609
  Political Activity 610
  Intermediate Sanctions 611
  Reorganization and Dissolution 612
  Emerging Issues 612
Governance 613
  Incorporating Documents 613
  Board Membership 614
Benchmarking and Performance Measures 614
Summary 616
Key Terms 617
Selected References 617
Questions 617
Cases 618
Exercises and Problems 619

Chapter 16
Accounting for Colleges and Universities 627

Accounting and Financial Reporting Standards 628
  Public Colleges and Universities 629
  Private Colleges and Universities 629
  Fund Accounting 633
Accounting and Reporting Issues 633
  Statement of Net Assets or Financial Position 633
  Statement of Revenues, Expenses, and Changes in Net Assets 637
  Statement of Cash Flows 641
  Segment Reporting 641
Illustrative Transactions for Private Colleges and Universities 641
  Adjusting Entries 646
  Closing Entries 647
Other Accounting Issues 648

  Performance Measures 648
  Auditing Colleges and Universities 650
  Federal Financial Assistance 652
  Related Entities 652
Key Terms 653
Selected References 653
Questions 654
Cases 654
Exercises and Problems 658

Chapter 17
Accounting for Health Care Organizations 667

Health Care Industry 667
GAAP for Health Care Providers 668
Financial Reporting 670
  Balance Sheet or Statement of Net Assets 671
  Operating Statement 674
  Statement of Changes in Net Assets 675
  Statement of Cash Flows 675
Accounting and Measurement Issues 676
  Revenues 676
  Assets 677
  Expenses 678
  Liabilities 678
Illustrative Case for a Not-for-Profit Health Care Organization 679
Financial Reporting for a Governmental Health Care Organization 687
Related Entities 689
Other Accounting Issues 689
  Budgeting and Costs 689
  Auditing 690
  Taxation and Regulatory Issues 690
  Prepaid Health Care Plans 691
  Continuing Care Retirement Communities 691
Financial and Operational Analysis 691
Conclusion 692
Key Terms 692
Selected References 692
Questions 693
Cases 693
Exercises and Problems 695

Glossary 707

Governmental and Not-for-Profit Organizations 736

Index 740

Chapter **One**

Introduction to Accounting and Financial Reporting for Governmental and Not-for-Profit Entities

Learning Objectives

After studying this chapter, you should be able to:

1. Identify and explain the characteristics that distinguish governmental and not-for-profit entities from for-profit entities.
2. Identify the authoritative bodies responsible for setting financial reporting standards for (1) state and local governments, (2) the federal government, and (3) not-for-profit organizations.
3. Contrast and compare the objectives of financial reporting for (1) state and local governments, (2) the federal government, and (3) not-for-profit organizations.
4. Explain how management's discussion and analysis (MD&A), basic financial statements, and required supplementary information of state and local governments relate to their comprehensive annual financial reports.
5. Explain the different objectives, measurement focus, and basis of accounting of the government-wide financial statements and fund financial statements of state and local governments.

Welcome to the strange new world of accounting for governmental and not-for-profit organizations! Initially, you may find it challenging to understand the many new terms and concepts you will need to learn. Moreover, if you are like most readers, you will question at the outset why governmental and not-for-profit organizations find it necessary to use accounting practices that are very different from those used by for-profit entities.

As you read this first chapter of the text, the reasons for the marked differences between governmental and not-for-profit accounting and for-profit accounting should become apparent. Specifically, governmental and not-for-profit organizations serve entirely different purposes in society than do business entities. Furthermore, because

1

such organizations are largely financed by taxpayers, donors, and others who do not expect benefits proportional to the resources they provide, management has a special duty to be accountable for how those resources are used in providing services. Thus, the need to report on management's accountability to citizens, creditors, oversight bodies, and others has played a central role in shaping the accounting and reporting practices of governmental and not-for-profit organizations.

This first chapter will give you a basic conceptual foundation for understanding the unique characteristics of these organizations and how their accounting and financial reporting concepts and practices differ from those of for-profit organizations. By the time you finish subsequent chapters assigned for your course, you should have an in-depth practical knowledge of governmental and not-for-profit accounting and financial reporting.

WHAT ARE GOVERNMENTAL AND NOT-FOR-PROFIT ORGANIZATIONS?

Governmental and not-for-profit organizations are vast in number and range of services provided. In the United States, governments exist at the federal, state, and local levels and serve a wide variety of functions. The most recent census of governments reports 87,525 local governmental units, in addition to the federal government and 50 state governments. These 87,525 local governments consist of 3,034 counties, 19,429 municipalities, 16,504 towns and townships, 13,506 independent school districts, and 35,052 special district governments that derive their power from state governments.[1]

States, counties, municipalities (for example, cities and villages), and townships are **general purpose governments**—governments that provide many categories of services to their residents (such as police and fire protection; sanitation; construction and maintenance of streets, roads, and bridges; and health and welfare). Independent school districts, public colleges and universities, and special districts are **special purpose governments**—governments that provide only a single function or a limited number of functions (such as education, drainage and flood control, irrigation, soil and water conservation, fire protection, and water supply). Special purpose governments have the power to levy and collect taxes and to raise revenues from other sources as provided by state laws to finance the services they provide.

Not-for-profit organizations also exist in many forms and serve many different functions. Estimates of the number of not-for-profit organizations range from several hundred thousand to more than 1 million.[2] These include private colleges and universities, various kinds of health care organizations, certain libraries and museums, professional and trade associations, fraternal and social organizations, and religious organizations.

DISTINGUISHING CHARACTERISTICS OF GOVERNMENTAL AND NOT-FOR-PROFIT ENTITIES

Governmental and not-for-profit organizations differ in important ways from business organizations. Not surprisingly then, accounting and financial reporting for governmental and not-for-profit organizations are markedly different from accounting and financial

[1] U.S. Department of Commerce, Bureau of the Census, *2002 Census of Governments,* vol. 1, no. 1 (Washington, DC: U.S. Government Printing Office), p. v.

[2] The Independent Sector and Urban Institute estimate that there are 1.6 million organizations in the not-for-profit sector. (Urban Institute, *The New Nonprofit Almanac & Desk Reference,* Washington, D.C., 2002).

reporting for businesses. An understanding of how these organizations differ from business organizations is essential to understanding the unique accounting and financial reporting principles that have evolved for governmental and not-for-profit organizations.

In its *Statement of Financial Accounting Concepts No. 4,* the **Financial Accounting Standards Board (FASB)** noted the following characteristics that it felt distinguished governmental and not-for-profit entities from business organizations:

a. Receipts of significant amounts of resources from resource providers who do not expect to receive either repayment or economic benefits proportionate to the resources provided.

b. Operating purposes that are other than to provide goods or services at a profit or profit equivalent.

c. Absence of defined ownership interests that can be sold, transferred, or redeemed, or that convey entitlement to a share of a residual distribution of resources in the event of liquidation of the organization.[3]

The **Governmental Accounting Standards Board (GASB)** further distinguishes governmental entities in the United States from not-for-profit entities and from businesses by stressing that governments exist in an environment in which the power ultimately rests in the hands of the people. Voters delegate that power to public officials through the election process. The power is divided among the executive, legislative, and judicial branches of the government so that the actions, financial and otherwise, of governmental executives are constrained by legislative actions, and executive and legislative actions are subject to judicial review. Further constraints are imposed on state and local governments by the existence of the federal system in which higher levels of government encourage or dictate activities by lower levels and finance the activities (partially, at least) by an extensive system of intergovernmental grants and subsidies that require the lower levels to be accountable to the entity providing the resources, as well as to the citizenry. Revenues raised by each level of government come, ultimately, from taxpayers. Taxpayers are required to serve as providers of resources to governments even though they often have very little choice about which governmental services they receive and the extent to which they receive them.

Since governments may have a monopoly on the services they provide to the public, the lack of a competitive marketplace makes it difficult to measure efficiency in the provision of the services. It is also extremely difficult to measure optimal quantity or quality for many of the services rendered by government—for example, how many police are "enough"? The Governmental Accounting Standards Board notes the determination of optimal quantity or quality of government services is complicated by the involuntary nature of the resources provided. "A consumer purchasing a commercial product can determine how much to purchase and may choose among 'good,' 'better,' or 'best' quality and pay accordingly. A group of individuals paying for governmental services (and paying in different proportions for services that some of them may or may not use or desire) presents a far more complex situation."[4] For example, two homeowners may pay the same amount of property taxes but consume different amounts of government services if one does not drive and use the roads or has no children in public schools.

---

[3] Financial Accounting Standards Board, *Statement of Financial Accounting Concepts No. 4,* "Objectives of Financial Reporting by Nonbusiness Organizations" (Norwalk, CT, 1980), p. 3. In 1985 the FASB replaced the term *nonbusiness* with the term *not-for-profit.* Other organizations use the term *nonprofit* as a synonym for *not-for-profit.* The term *not-for-profit* is predominantly used in this text.

[4] Governmental Accounting Standards Board, *Codification of Governmental Accounting and Financial Reporting Standards as of June 30, 2005* (Norwalk, CT, 2005), Appendix B, *Concepts Statement No. 1,* par. 17-e.

SOURCES OF FINANCIAL REPORTING STANDARDS

Illustration 1–1 shows the primary sources of accounting and financial reporting standards for business and not-for-profit organizations, state and local governments, and the federal government. Specifically, the FASB sets standards for for-profit business organizations and nongovernmental not-for-profit organizations; the GASB sets standards for state and local governments, including governmental not-for-profit organizations; and the Federal Accounting Standards Advisory Board (FASAB) sets standards for the federal government and its agencies and departments.

Authority to establish accounting and reporting standards for not-for-profit organizations is split between the FASB and the GASB because a sizeable number of not-for-profit organizations are governmentally owned, particularly public colleges and universities and government hospitals. The FASB is responsible for setting accounting and reporting standards for the great majority of not-for-profit organizations, those that are independent of governments. Governmental not-for-profit organizations follow standards established by the GASB.

The GASB and the FASB are parallel bodies under the oversight of the Financial Accounting Foundation. The foundation appoints the members of the two boards and supports the boards' operations. The federal Sarbanes-Oxley Act greatly enhanced financial support for the FASB by mandating an assessed fee on corporate security offerings. In 2004, financial support for the GASB took an important step when a voluntary assessment on municipal bond offerings was initiated. Still, the GASB relies substantially on contributions from state and local government organizations and sales of publications for financial support of its operations.

Because of the breadth of support and the lack of ties to any single organization or governmental unit, the GASB and the FASB are referred to as "independent standards-setting boards in the private sector." Before the creation of the GASB and the FASB, financial reporting standards were set by groups sponsored by professional

ILLUSTRATION 1–1 **Primary Sources of Accounting and Financial Reporting Standards for Businesses, Governments, and Not-for-Profit Organizations**

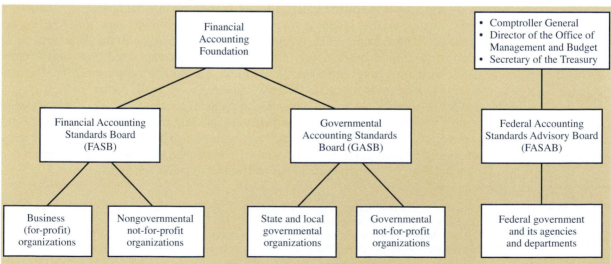

Source: Statement on Auditing Standards (SAS) 69, amended by SAS 91, April 2000, AICPA *Professional Standards,* v.1, Au Sec. 411.

organizations: The forerunners of the GASB (formed in 1984) were the National Council on Governmental Accounting (1973–84), the National Committee on Governmental Accounting (1948–73), and the National Committee on Municipal Accounting (1934–41). The forerunners of the FASB (formed in 1973) were the Accounting Principles Board (1959–73) and the Committee on Accounting Procedure (1938–59) of the American Institute of Certified Public Accountants.

Federal statutes assign responsibility for establishing and maintaining a sound financial structure for the federal government to three officials: the Comptroller General, the Director of the Office of Management and Budget, and the Secretary of the Treasury. In 1990, these three officials created the **Federal Accounting Standards Advisory Board (FASAB)** to recommend accounting principles and standards for the federal government and its agencies. It is understood that, to the maximum extent possible, federal accounting and financial reporting standards should be consistent with those established by the GASB and, where applicable, by the FASB.

In Rule 203 of its Code of Professional Conduct, the American Institute of Certified Public Accountants (AICPA) has formally designated the GASB, the FASAB, and the FASB as the authoritative bodies to establish **generally accepted accounting principles (GAAP)** for state and local governments, the federal government, and business organizations and nongovernmental not-for-profit organizations, respectively. "Authority to establish accounting principles" is interpreted in practice to mean "authority to establish accounting and financial reporting standards."[5]

Determining Whether a Not-for-Profit Organization Is Governmental

Illustration 1–1 suggests that the kinds of organizations for which the FASB and GASB are responsible for setting standards are clearcut. Unfortunately, this is sometimes not the case. In practice, it may be difficult to determine whether some types of not-for-profits are governmental in nature or not, and thus which standards-setting body to look to for authoritative guidance.

The U.S. Bureau of the Census defines a *government* as:

> An organized entity which, in addition to having governmental character, has sufficient discretion in the management of its own affairs to distinguish it as separate from the administrative structure of any other governmental unit.[6]

This definition, though helpful, provides insufficient guidance because it fails to explain the meaning of "having governmental character." In order to provide additional guidance for auditors on this issue, two audit and accounting guides of the AICPA, with the tacit approval of both the FASB and the GASB, state:

> Public corporations and bodies corporate and politic are governmental organizations. Other organizations are governmental organizations if they have one or more of the following characteristics:
>
> *a.* Popular election of officers or appointment (or approval) of a controlling majority of the members of the organization's governing body by officials of one or more state or local governments,

---

[5] *Statement on Auditing Standards (SAS) 69,* as amended by *SAS 91,* April 2000, specifically establishes the FASB, the GASB, and the FASAB as the bodies to establish GAAP for their respective organizations. Other literature, such as AICPA Audit and Accounting Guides, are afforded secondary status as sources of authoritative guidance. These sources are discussed more fully in the "GAAP Hierarchy" section of Chapter 11.

[6] U.S. Department of Commerce, Bureau of the Census, *2002 Census of Governments,* p. ix.

b. the potential for unilateral dissolution by a government with the net assets reverting to a government, or

c. the power to enact *and* enforce a tax levy.[7]

Furthermore, organizations are presumed to be governmental if they have the ability to issue directly (rather than through a state or municipal authority) debt that pays interest exempt from federal taxation. However, organizations possessing only that ability (to issue tax-exempt debt) and none of the other governmental characteristics may rebut the presumption that they are governmental if their determination is supported by compelling, relevant evidence. Colleges and universities, hospitals, museums, and social service agencies are examples of organizations that may be either governmental or nongovernmental.

OBJECTIVES OF FINANCIAL REPORTING

In its *Concepts Statement No. 1,* "Objectives of Financial Reporting," the Governmental Accounting Standards Board stated that "**Accountability** is the cornerstone of all financial reporting in government. . . . Accountability requires governments to answer to the citizenry—to justify the raising of public resources and the purposes for which they are used."[8] The board elaborated:

> Governmental accountability is based on the belief that the citizenry has a "right to know," a right to receive openly declared facts that may lead to public debate by the citizens and their elected representatives. Financial reporting plays a major role in fulfilling government's duty to be publicly accountable in a democratic society.[9]

Illustration 1–2 shows several ways that state and local governmental financial reporting is used in making economic, social, and political decisions and assessing accountability. Closely related to the concept of accountability as the cornerstone of governmental financial reporting is the concept the GASB refers to as **interperiod equity.** The concept and its importance are explained as follows:

> The Board believes that interperiod equity is a significant part of accountability and is fundamental to public administration. It therefore needs to be considered when establishing financial reporting objectives. In short, *financial reporting should help users assess whether current-year revenues are sufficient to pay for services provided that year and whether future taxpayers will be required to assume burdens for services previously provided.* (Emphasis added.)[10]

Accountability is also the foundation for the financial reporting objectives the Federal Accounting Standards Advisory Board (FASAB) has established for the federal government. The FASAB's *Statement of Accounting and Reporting Concepts Statement No. 1* identifies four objectives of federal financial reporting (see Illustration 1–2) focused on evaluating budgetary integrity, operating performance, stewardship, and adequacy of systems and controls.

[7] American Institute of Certified Public Accountants, Audit and Accounting Guide, *Health Care Organizations* (New York, 2004), par. 1.02c; and American Institute of Certified Public Accountants, Audit and Accounting Guide, *Not-for Profit Organizations* (New York, 2004), par. 1.03.

[8] GASB, *Codification,* Appendix B, *Concepts Statement No. 1,* par. 56.

[9] Ibid.

[10] Ibid., par. 61.

ILLUSTRATION 1–2 **Comparison of Financial Reporting Objectives—State and Local Governments, Federal Government, and Not-for-Profit Organizations**

State and Local Governments[a]	Federal Government[b]	Not-for-Profit Organizations[c]
Financial reporting is used in making economic, social, and political decisions and in assessing accountability primarily by: • Comparing actual financial results with the legally adopted budget • Assessing financial condition and results of operations • Assisting in determining compliance with finance-related laws, rules, and regulations • Assisting in evaluating efficiency and effectiveness	Financial reporting should help to achieve accountability and is intended to assist report users in evaluating: • Budgetary integrity • Operating performance • Stewardship • Adequacy of systems and controls	Financial reporting should provide information useful in: • Making resource allocation decisions • Assessing services and ability to provide services • Assessing management stewardship and performance • Assessing economic resources, obligations, net resources, and changes in them

[a]Source: *GASB Concepts Statement No. 1*, par. 32.
[b]Source: *FASAB Statement of Federal Accounting Concepts No. 1*, par. 134.
[c]Source: *FASB Concepts Statement No. 4*, pp. 19–23.

Unlike the FASB and the GASB, which base their standards on *external* financial reporting, the FASAB and its sponsors in the federal government are concerned with *both* internal and external financial reporting. Accordingly, the FASAB has identified four major groups of users of federal financial reports: citizens, Congress, executives, and program managers. Given the broad role the FASAB has been assigned, its standards focus on cost accounting and service efforts and accomplishment measures, as well as on financial accounting and reporting.

Financial reports of not-for-profit organizations—voluntary health and welfare organizations, private colleges and universities, private health care institutions, religious organizations, and others—have similar uses. However, as Illustration 1–2 shows, the reporting objectives for not-for-profit organizations emphasize decision usefulness over financial accountability needs, presumably reflecting the fact that the financial operations of not-for-profit organizations are generally not subject to as detailed legal restrictions as those of governments.

Note that the objectives of financial reporting for governments and not-for-profit entities stress the need for the public to understand and evaluate the financial activities and management of these organizations. Readers will recognize the impact on their lives, and on their bank accounts, of the activities of the layers of government they are obligated to support and of the not-for-profit organizations they voluntarily support. Since each of us is significantly affected, it is important that we be able to read intelligently the financial reports of governmental and not-for-profit entities. In order to make informed decisions as citizens, taxpayers, creditors, and donors, readers should make the effort to learn the accounting and financial reporting standards developed by authoritative bodies. This chapter is intended to set forth the distinguishing characteristics of governmental and not-for-profit entities and to provide an overview of accounting and financial reporting for these entities. The standards are further explained and illustrated in Chapters 2 through 17 of this text.

FINANCIAL REPORTING OF STATE AND LOCAL GOVERNMENTS

Like the FASB, the GASB continues to develop concepts statements that communicate the framework within which the Board strives to establish consistent financial reporting standards for entities within its jurisdiction. The GASB, as well as the FASB, is concerned with establishing standards for financial reporting to *external* users—those who lack the authority to prescribe the information they want and who must rely on the information management communicates to them. The Board does not intend to set standards for reporting to managers and administrators or others deemed to have the ability to enforce their demands for information.

Illustration 1–3 displays the minimum requirements for general purpose external financial reporting under the governmental financial reporting model specified by GASB *Statement No. 34 (GASBS 34).*[11] Central to the model is the **management's discussion and analysis (MD&A).** The MD&A is **required supplementary information (RSI)** designed to communicate in narrative, easily readable form the purpose of the basic financial statements and the government's current financial position and results of financial activities compared with those of the prior year.

As shown in Illustration 1–3, *GASBS 34* prescribes two categories of **basic financial statements,** government-wide and fund. **Government-wide financial statements** are intended to provide an aggregated overview of a government's net assets and changes in net assets. The government-wide financial statements report on the government as a whole and assist in assessing *operational* **accountability**—whether the government has used its resources efficiently and effectively in meeting operating objectives. The GASB concluded that reporting on operational accountability is best achieved by using essentially the same basis of accounting and measurement focus used by business organizations: the accrual basis and flow of economic resources measurement focus.

Fund financial statements, the other category of basic financial statements, assist in assessing *fiscal* **accountability**—whether the government has raised and spent financial resources in accordance with budget plans and in compliance with pertinent laws and regulations. Certain funds, referred to as *governmental funds,* focus on the short-term flow of current financial resources rather than on the flow of economic resources.[12] Other funds, referred to as *proprietary* and *fiduciary funds,* account for the business-type and certain fiduciary activities of the government. These funds follow accounting and reporting principles similar to those of business organizations, although a number of GASB standards applicable to these funds differ substantially from FASB standards applicable to business organizations. These differences will be discussed in later chapters.

As shown in Illustration 1–3, the notes to the financial statements are considered integral to the financial statements. In addition, governments are required to disclose certain RSI other than MD&A. These additional information disclosures are discussed in several of the following chapters.

---

[11] GASB *Statement No. 34,* "Basic Financial Statements—and Management's Discussion and Analysis—for State and Local Governments" (Norwalk, CT, 1999). Hereafter, *Statement No. 34* is abbreviated as *GASBS 34.*

[12] The definition of *fund* is given in Chapter 2. For now, you can view a fund as a separate set of accounts used to account for resources segregated for particular purposes.

ILLUSTRATION 1–3 **Minimum Requirements for General Purpose External Financial Reporting—GASB** *Statement No. 34* **Reporting Model**

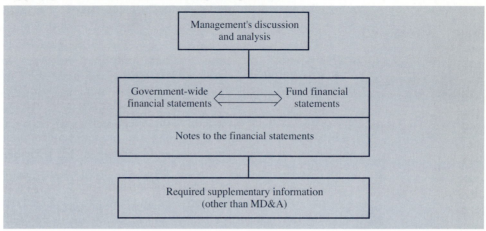

Source: GASB *Codification*, Sec. 2200.103.

Comprehensive Annual Financial Report

Serious users of governmental financial information need much more detail than is found in the MD&A, basic financial statements, and RSI (other than MD&A). For state and local governments, much of that detail is found in the governmental reporting entity's **comprehensive annual financial report (CAFR).** Although governments are not required to prepare a CAFR, most do so as a matter of public record and to provide additional financial details beyond the minimum requirements shown in Illustration 1–3. As such, the GASB provides standards for the content of a CAFR in its annually updated publication *Codification of Governmental Accounting and Financial Reporting Standards.* A CAFR prepared in conformity with these standards should contain the following sections.[13]

Introductory Section[14]

The introductory section typically includes items such as a title page and contents page, a letter of transmittal, a description of the government, and other items deemed appropriate by management. The letter of transmittal may be literally that—a letter from the chief financial officer addressed to the chief executive and governing body of the governmental unit—or it may be a narrative over the signature of the chief executive. In either event, the letter or narrative material should cite legal and policy requirements for the report.

Financial Section

The financial section of a comprehensive annual financial report should include (1) an auditor's report, (2) management's discussion and analysis (MD&A), (3) basic financial statements, (4) required supplementary information (other than MD&A), and

---

[13] GASB, *Codification*, Sec. 2200.104–193.

[14] For a view of the introductory section, as well as the other sections of the CAFR, you may wish to look at the City and County of Denver, Colorado's CAFR at *http://www.denvergov.org/auditor/.* Click on "End-of-Year Audited Financial Statements." Portions of Denver's CAFR for 2004 are included for illustrative purposes in various places in this text.

(5) other supplementary information, such as combining statements and individual fund statements and schedules. Items (2), (3), and (4) represent the minimum requirements for general purpose external financial reporting, as depicted in Illustration 1–3. So, it should be apparent that a CAFR provides additional supplementary financial information beyond the minimum amount required by generally accepted accounting principles.

Laws regarding the audit of governmental units vary from state to state. Some states have laws requiring that all state agencies and all local governments be audited by an audit agency of the state government. In other states, local governments are audited by independent public accounting firms. In still other states, some local governments are audited by the state audit agency and some by independent public accounting firms. In any event, the auditor's opinion should accompany the financial statements reproduced in the report.

The financial section should contain sufficient information to disclose fully and present fairly the financial position and results of financial operations during the fiscal year. Laws of higher jurisdictions, actions of the legislative branch of the governmental unit itself, and agreements with creditors and others impose constraints over governments' financial activities and create unique financial accountability requirements.

As mentioned at the beginning of this chapter, governmental financial reporting has evolved to meet the unique needs of citizens and other financial statement users. It should not be surprising that these financial statements are quite different from those prepared by business organizations. Real-world examples of local government financial statements—the basic financial statements of the combined City and County government of Denver, Colorado—are provided as Illustrations 1–4 through 1–14 and are described briefly in the remainder of this chapter.[15] These basic financial statements, which are reported in the financial section of Denver's CAFR, consist of

Government-wide Financial Statements

1. Statement of net assets (see Illustration 1–4).
2. Statement of activities (see Illustration 1–5).

Fund Financial Statements

1. Balance sheet—governmental funds (see Illustration 1–6).
2. Statement of revenues, expenditures, and changes in fund balances—governmental funds (see Illustration 1–8).
3. Statement of net assets—proprietary funds (see Illustration 1–10).
4. Statement of revenues, expenses, and changes in fund net assets—proprietary funds (see Illustration 1–11).
5. Statement of cash flows—proprietary funds (see Illustration 1–12).
6. Statement of fiduciary net assets (see Illustration 1–13).
7. Statement of changes in fiduciary net assets (see Illustration 1–14).

---

[15] The City and County of Denver's financial statements provided in Chapter 1, and various required and other supplementary information that are presented in later chapters, are intended for illustrative educational purposes only. Omitted in this text are the auditor's report on the financial statements, the notes to the financial statements, and other required supplementary information. Moreover, depending on the time since this text was released, more current financial statements may be available. Those who have a need for financial information for credit analysis or other evaluative or decision purposes should refer to the City and County of Denver's audited financial statements in the comprehensive annual financial report.

ILLUSTRATION 1–4

CITY AND COUNTY OF DENVER
Statement of Net Assets
December 31, 2004
(amounts expressed in thousands)

	Primary Government			Component Units
	Governmental Activities	Business-type Activities	Total	
ASSETS				
Cash on hand	$ 523	$ —	$ 523	$ 57
Cash and cash equivalents	395,843	311,344	707,187	15,609
Investments	—	217,910	217,910	165,675
Receivables (net of allowances):				
Taxes	237,886	—	237,886	5,765
Special assessments	1,607	—	1,607	—
Notes	88,240	—	88,240	—
Accounts	3,982	26,320	30,302	29,997
Accrued interest	1,470	4,104	5,574	106
Other	—	—	—	16,389
Due from other governments	37,531	—	37,531	
Internal balances	17,474	(17,474)	—	—
Inventories	1,751	5,628	7,379	6,096
Prepaid items and other assets	29,290	5,059	34,349	31,048
Restricted assets:				
Cash and cash equivalents	28,887	344,653	373,540	21,800
Investments	—	398,329	398,329	386,588
Accrued interest	—	815	815	—
Other receivables	—	34,570	34,570	—
Restricted net assets held by third party	—	—	—	157,655
Capital assets:				
Land and construction in progress	383,165	467,757	850,922	298,118
Buildings, improvements, infrastructure, collections, and equipment, net of accumulated depreciation	1,643,350	3,342,920	4,986,270	1,346,538
Long-term receivables (net of allowances)	31,024	—	31,024	7,150
Bond issue cost and other assets (net of accumulated amortization)	9,425	90,095	99,520	2,669
Assets held for disposition	4,719	24,500	29,219	—
TOTAL ASSETS	2,916,167	5,256,530	8,172,697	2,491,260
LIABILITIES				
Vouchers payable	52,182	34,347	86,529	23,291
Accrued liabilities	22,472	63,853	86,325	20,923
Deferred revenue	188,572	35,519	224,091	6,489
Advances	1,797	—	1,797	31,412
Due to other governments	—	—	—	1,780
Liabilities payable from restricted assets	—	70,303	70,303	
Noncurrent liabilities:				
Due within one year	94,442	130,058	224,500	36,378
Due in more than one year	1,267,796	3,816,881	5,084,677	1,086,739
TOTAL LIABILITIES	1,627,261	4,150,961	5,778,222	1,207,012
NET ASSETS				
Invested in capital assets, net of related debt	869,239	149,591	1,018,830	898,464
Restricted for:				
Capital projects	42,883	94,783	137,666	288,824
Emergency use	26,173	—	26,173	417
Debt service	85,625	401,754	487,379	47,676
Donor restrictions:				
Expendable	15,810	—	15,810	94,402
Nonexpendable	3,359	—	3,359	82,992
Unrestricted	245,817	459,441	705,258	(128,527)
TOTAL NET ASSETS	$1,288,906	$1,105,569	$2,394,475	$1,284,248

ILLUSTRATION 1–5

CITY AND COUNTY OF DENVER
Statement of Activities
For the year ended December 31, 2004
(amounts expressed in thousands)

Function/Program	Expenses	Program Revenues — Charges for Services	Program Revenues — Operating Grants and Contributions	Program Revenues — Capital Grants and Contributions	Net (Expense) Revenue and Change in Net Assets — Primary Government — Governmental Activities	Net (Expense) Revenue and Change in Net Assets — Primary Government — Business-type Activities	Net (Expense) Revenue and Change in Net Assets — Primary Government — Total	Net (Expense) Revenue and Change in Net Assets — Component Units
Primary Government								
Governmental Activities								
General government	$ 187,616	$ 58,075	$ 15,862	$ 549	$ (113,130)	$ —	$ (113,130)	$ —
Public safety	365,856	52,738	24,311	1,150	(287,657)	—	(287,657)	—
Public works	92,968	38,094	22,023	12,485	(20,366)	—	(20,366)	—
Human services	100,488	1,302	64,459	—	(34,727)	—	(34,727)	—
Health	46,132	1,052	5,921	—	(39,159)	—	(39,159)	—
Parks and recreation	61,025	4,890	305	6,958	(48,872)	—	(48,872)	—
Cultural activities	73,912	11,475	2,544	16,646	(43,247)	—	(43,247)	—
Community development	38,013	17,660	36,991	—	16,638	—	16,638	—
Economic opportunity	19,417	6,458	12,352	—	(607)	—	(607)	—
Interest on long-term debt	54,572	—	—	—	(54,572)	—	(54,572)	—
Total governmental activities	1,039,999	191,744	184,768	37,788	(625,699)	—	(625,699)	—
Business-type Activities								
Wastewater management	70,260	67,091	24	13,509	—	10,364	10,364	—
Denver airport system	588,126	477,665	62,280	62,205	—	14,024	14,024	—
Environmental services	9,315	5,958	—	—	—	(3,357)	(3,357)	—
Golf course	6,856	7,332	—	—	—	476	476	—
Total business-type activities	674,557	558,046	62,304	75,714	—	21,507	21,507	—
Total primary government	$1,714,556	$749,790	$247,072	$113,502	(625,699)	21,507	(604,192)	—
Component Units	$ 385,463	$166,085	$ 67,201	$ —				(152,177)
General revenues:								
Taxes:								
Property					179,497	—	179,497	5,155
Sales and use					381,891	—	381,891	—
Other					117,162	—	117,162	50,626
Investment and interest income					14,449	24,982	39,431	8,446
Miscellaneous					48,428	7,932	56,360	37,246
Transfers					340	(340)	—	—
Total general revenues and transfers					741,767	32,574	774,341	101,473
Change in net assets					116,068	54,081	170,149	(50,704)
Net assets—January 1					1,172,838	1,051,488	2,224,326	1,334,952
Net assets—December 31					$1,288,906	$1,105,569	$2,394,475	$1,284,248

Government-wide Financial Statements   Denver's government-wide financial statements (see Illustrations 1–4 and 1–5) follow the *GASBS 34* recommended formats; financial information is presented in separate columns for governmental activities and business-type activities of the primary government and its discretely presented component units (i.e., legally separate organizations for which the City and County of Denver is deemed financially accountable). Governmental and business-type activities are discussed in Chapter 2. Essentially, governmental activities encompass the executive, legislative, and judicial functions of the government as well as major service functions such as public safety, public works, parks and recreation, health and human services, and cultural activities. Business-type activities are largely self-supporting activities of a government that provide services to the public for a fee. Typical examples are electric, sewer, and water utilities; transportation systems; airports; toll roads and bridges; and parking facilities.

Because the financial statements display information in multiple columns, they are not fully consolidated in the manner of corporate financial statements. Receivables and payables between activities reported in the same activities column or between component units are eliminated in preparing the financial statements. However, receivables/payables between activities reported in different columns are not eliminated. For example, Denver's statement of net assets shows a receivable of $17,474 under the line item *internal balances* in the Governmental Activities column with an equal contra-asset (payable) in the Business-type Activities column. These two amounts represent the *net* receivables and payables between these two activity categories.

As mentioned earlier and discussed more fully in Chapter 2, the two government-wide financial statements are intended to report on the government's *operational accountability.* As such, the government-wide financial statements are prepared using essentially the same basis of accounting and measurement focus that are used in business accounting—that is, the accrual basis of accounting and measurement of total economic resources.

Fund Financial Statements   By contrast, governmental fund financial statements (see Illustrations 1–6 and 1–8) report on *fiscal accountability.* Therefore, these statements report only information that is useful in assessing whether financial resources were raised and expended in compliance with budgetary and other legal provisions. Thus, governmental fund statements focus on the flow of current financial resources—cash and near-cash resources that are available for expenditure. Since long-term obligations do not have to be paid in the current budgetary period, nor do noncurrent assets such as land, buildings, and equipment provide resources to pay current period obligations, neither is reported in the governmental funds. Both are reported in the Governmental Activities column of the government-wide statement of net assets, however, as shown in Illustration 1–4.

Modified accrual is the basis of accounting that has evolved for governmental funds. Under this basis, revenues are recorded only if they are measurable and available for paying current period obligations. Expenditures are generally recognized when incurred. As shown in Illustration 1–8, the governmental fund statement of revenues, expenditures, and changes in fund balances reports expenditures, since outlays to acquire goods or services are more relevant than expenses in measuring the outflow of current financial resources. Expenses, however, are more relevant at the government-wide level, as they measure the cost of services provided. Consequently, expenses, classified by program or function, are reported for both governmental and

ILLUSTRATION 1–6

CITY AND COUNTY OF DENVER
Balance Sheet
Governmental Funds
December 31, 2004
(amounts expressed in thousands)

	General Fund	Human Services	Bond Projects	Other Governmental Funds	Total
ASSETS					
Cash on hand	$ —	$ 313	$ —	$ 210	$ 523
Cash and cash equivalents	77,031	9,932	48,007	245,734	380,704
Restricted assets:					
Cash and cash equivalents	17,989	2,043	—	8,841	28,873
Receivables (net of allowances):					
Taxes	121,778	40,357	—	75,751	237,886
Special assessments	—	—	—	1,607	1,607
Notes	—	—	—	88,240	88,240
Accounts	3,633	126	—	31,194	34,953
Accrued interest	552	1	201	671	1,425
Due from other funds	14,613	—	—	1,488	16,101
Due from other governments	88	9,180	—	28,263	37,531
Prepaid items and other assets	28,500	—	—	790	29,290
Assets held for disposition	—	—	—	4,719	4,719
TOTAL ASSETS	$264,184	$61,952	$48,208	$487,508	$861,852
LIABILITIES AND FUND BALANCE					
Liabilities:					
Vouchers payable	$ 10,814	$ 2,878	$ 7,492	$ 29,126	$ 50,310
Accrued liabilities	7,590	341	—	245	8,176
Due to other funds	1,935	1,579	14	3,575	7,103
Deferred revenue	77,884	42,155	—	101,939	221,978
Advances	—	320	—	800	1,120
TOTAL LIABILITIES	98,223	47,273	7,506	135,685	288,687
FUND BALANCE					
Reserved for emergency use	17,989	—	—	8,184	26,173
Reserved for encumbrances	12,349	7,410	23,557	68,885	112,201
Reserved for prepaid items and other assets	28,500	—	—	790	29,290
Reserved for construction	—	2,043	—	449	2,492
Reserved for notes receivable	—	—	—	88,240	88,240
Reserved for debt service:					
Long-term debt	—	—	—	36,020	36,020
Interest	—	—	—	21,184	21,184
Unreserved:					
Designated for net unrealized gain, reported in:					
Bond projects fund	—	—	347	—	347
Capital projects funds	—	—	—	166	166
Designated for subsequent years' expenditures, reported in:					
Capital projects funds	—	—	—	38,161	38,161
Undesignated, reported in:					
General Fund	107,123	—	—	—	107,123
Special revenue funds	—	5,226	16,798	65,170	87,194
Capital projects funds	—	—	—	21,215	21,215
Permanent fund	—	—	—	3,359	3,359
TOTAL FUND BALANCE	165,961	14,679	40,702	351,823	573,165
TOTAL LIABILITIES AND FUND BALANCE	$264,184	$61,952	$48,208	$487,508	$861,852

ILLUSTRATION 1–7

CITY AND COUNTY OF DENVER
Reconciliation of the Balance Sheet—Governmental Funds
to the Statement of Net Assets
December 31, 2004
(amounts expressed in thousands)

Amounts reported for governmental activities in the statement of net assets are different because:

Total fund balance-governmental funds	$ 573,165
Capital assets used in governmental activities, excluding internal service funds of $4,521, are not financial resources, and therefore, are not reported in the funds.	2,021,994
Accrued interest payable not included in the funds.	(14,001)
Other long-term assets are not available to pay for current-period expenditures and, therefore, are deferred in the funds.	33,406
Bonds issuance costs, net of accumulated amortization.	9,425
Internal service funds are used by management to charge the cost of these funds to their primary users-governmental funds. The assets and liabilities of the internal service funds are included in governmental activities in the statement of net assets.	(4,761)
Long-term liabilities, including bonds payable, are not due and payable in the current period and therefore are not reported in the governmental funds (this excludes internal service liabilities of $31,916).	(1,330,322)
Net assets of governmental activities.	$1,288,906

business-type activities, as shown in Denver's statement of activities (see Illustration 1–5).

Readers may be confused by the fact that the same underlying financial information for governmental activities is reported in two different ways: (1) using accrual basis accounting with an economic resources measurement focus in the government-wide financial statements and (2) using modified accrual with a current financial resources focus in the fund statements. To ensure integration of these statements, GASB standards require that the total fund balances reported on the balance sheet—governmental funds (Illustration 1–6) be reconciled to total governmental activities net assets reported in the statement of net assets (Illustration 1–4). The reconciliation can be displayed on the face of the balance sheet—governmental funds or, as Denver has done, separately as a stand-alone schedule (see Illustration 1–7). Similarly, GASB requires that operating statement results be reconciled for governmental activities. Accordingly, Denver presents a reconciliation (see Illustration 1–9) of the net changes in fund balances—total governmental funds reported on its statement of revenues, expenditures, and changes in fund balances—governmental funds (Illustration 1–8) to the change in net assets of governmental activities reported on its statement of activities (Illustration 1–5). For now, it is sufficient to just be aware that such reconciliations are required; you will learn to prepare reconciliations later in the text.

Proprietary fund financial statements present financial information for enterprise funds and internal service funds. Both types of funds operate essentially as self-supporting entities and, therefore, follow accounting and reporting practices similar to those of business organizations. Enterprise funds and internal service funds are distinguished primarily by the kinds of customers they serve. Enterprise funds provide

ILLUSTRATION 1–8

CITY AND COUNTY OF DENVER
Statement of Revenues, Expenditures, and Changes in Fund Balance
Governmental Funds
For the year ended December 31, 2004
(amounts expressed in thousands)

	General Fund	Human Services	Bond Projects	Other Governmental Funds	Total
REVENUES					
Taxes:					
Property	$ 71,600	$ 39,104	$ —	$ 68,793	$ 179,497
Sales and use	361,988	—	—	19,903	381,891
Other	71,235	—	—	45,272	116,507
Special assessments	—	—	—	655	655
Licenses and permits	23,439	—	—	228	23,667
Intergovernmental revenues	29,212	63,973	—	99,071	192,256
Charges for services	103,878	1,302	203	25,505	130,888
Investment and interest income	3,994	28	1,550	8,877	14,449
Fines and forfeitures	31,159	—	—	2,353	33,512
Contributions	116	38	—	18,797	18,951
Other revenue	12,328	1,503	1	23,688	37,520
TOTAL REVENUES	708,949	105,948	1,754	313,142	1,129,793
EXPENDITURES					
Current:					
General government	137,838	—	—	28,537	166,375
Public safety	338,000	—	—	26,355	364,355
Public works	67,212	—	—	745	67,957
Human services	9	98,225	—	—	98,234
Health	40,145	—	—	5,622	45,767
Parks and recreation	40,932	—	—	7,908	48,840
Cultural activities	28,815	—	—	25,411	54,226
Community development	16,217	—	—	28,056	44,273
Economic opportunity	—	—	—	19,130	19,130
Principal retirement	355	2,315	—	64,114	66,784
Interest	6,764	2,582	—	46,691	56,037
Bond issue costs	—	—	—	297	297
Capital outlay	1,705	—	100,904	108,573	211,182
TOTAL EXPENDITURES	677,992	103,122	100,904	361,439	1,243,457
Excess (deficiency) of revenues over expenditures	30,957	2,826	(99,150)	(48,297)	(113,664)
OTHER FINANCING SOURCES (USES)					
Sale of capital assets	—	—	—	1,038	1,038
Developer advance	—	—	—	92	92
GID bonds issued	—	—	—	2,411	2,411
Payment to refunding escrow	—	—	—	(2,287)	(2,287)
Capital leases	1,705	—	—	2,103	3,808
Transfers in	18,175	105	—	62,920	81,200
Transfers out	(38,183)	—	—	(51,677)	(89,860)
TOTAL OTHER FINANCING SOURCES (USES)	(18,303)	105	—	14,600	(3,598)
Net change in fund balance	12,654	2,931	(99,150)	(33,697)	(117,262)
Fund balance—January 1	153,307	11,748	139,852	385,520	690,427
FUND BALANCE—December 31	$165,961	$ 14,679	$ 40,702	$351,823	$ 573,165

ILLUSTRATION 1–9

CITY AND COUNTY OF DENVER
Reconciliation of the Statement of Revenues
Expenditures and Changes in Fund Balance—Governmental Funds
to the Statement of Activities
For the year ended December 31, 2004
(amounts expressed in thousands)

Amounts reported for governmental activities in the statement of activities are different because:

Net change in fund balance—total governmental funds	$(117,262)

Governmental funds report capital purchases as expenditures. However, in the statement of activities the cost of those assets is allocated over their estimated useful lives and reported as depreciation expense. This is the amount by which capital expenditures exceed depreciation in the current period:

Capital outlay	232,446
Depreciation expense	(82,025)

Revenues in the statement of activities that do not provide current financial resources are not reported as revenue in the funds:

Revenues from long-term receivables	2,741

The issuance of long-term debt and other obligations (e.g., bonds, certificates of participation, and capital leases) provides current financial resource to governmental funds, while the repayment of the principal of long-term debt consumes the current financial resources of governmental funds. Neither transaction, however, has any effect on net assets. Also, governmental funds report the effect of issuance cost, premiums, discounts, and similar items when debt is first issued, whereas these amounts are deferred and amortized in the statement of activities. These differences in the treatment of long-term debt and related items consist of:

General improvement district bonds issued	(2,411)
Capital leases	(3,808)
Principal retirement on bonds	62,541
Issuance costs, premium, and discounts	1,041
Certificates of participation principal payments	9,360
Capital lease principal payments	1,930

Some expenses reported in the statement of activities do not require the use of current financial resources and, therefore, are not reported as expenditures in governmental funds:

Compensated absences (excluding internal service)	1,032
Accrued interest payable	2,260
Legal liability	1,222
Note payable	6,494

Internal service funds are used by management to charge their cost to individual funds. The net revenue of certain activities of internal service funds is reported within governmental activities.

	507
Change in net assets of governmental activities.	$ 116,068

goods or services to the public, whereas internal service funds mainly serve departments of the same government. For most governments, the information reported in the Business-type Activities column of the government-wide statements is simply the total of all enterprise funds information. Because internal services funds predominantly serve governmental activities, financial information for internal service funds is typically reported in the Governmental Activities column at the government-wide level.

ILLUSTRATION 1–10

CITY AND COUNTY OF DENVER
Statement of Net Assets Proprietary Funds
December 31, 2004
(amounts expressed in thousands)

| | Business-type Activities-Enterprise Funds | | | | Governmental Activities— Internal Service Funds |
	Wastewater Management	Denver Airport System	Other Enterprise Funds	Total Enterprise Funds	
ASSETS					
Current assets:					
Cash and cash equivalents	$128,092	$ 161,221	$22,031	$ 311,344	$15,139
Investments	—	217,910		217,910	—
Receivables (net of allowance for uncollectibles of $1,378):					
Accounts	10,583	14,684	1,053	26,320	53
Accrued interest	238	3,789	77	4,104	45
Due from other funds	53	416	119	588	2,041
Inventories	—	5,505	123	5,628	1,751
Prepaid items and other assets	275	4,784	—	5,059	—
Restricted assets:					
Cash and cash equivalents	—	343,805	848	344,653	14
Investments	—	398,329	—	398,329	—
Accrued interest receivable	—	812	3	815	—
Other receivables	—	34,219	351	34,570	—
Total Current Assets	139,241	1,185,474	24,605	1,349,320	19,043
Capital assets:					
Land and construction in progress	27,862	431,651	8,244	467,757	—
Buildings and improvements	14,207	1,669,551	9,076	1,692,834	4,107
Improvements other than buildings	396,336	1,907,899	8,556	2,312,791	82
Machinery and equipment	12,310	681,753	3,691	697,754	7,277
Accumulated depreciation	(145,314)	(1,200,725)	(14,420)	(1,360,459)	(6,945)
Net Capital Assets	305,401	3,490,129	15,147	3,810,677	4,521
Bonds issue costs and other assets, net	354	89,741	—	90,095	—
Assets held for disposition	—	24,500	—	24,500	—
TOTAL ASSETS	$444,996	$4,789,844	$39,752	$5,274,592	$23,564

ILLUSTRATION 1–10 (Continued)

LIABILITIES

Current liabilities:					
Vouchers payable	$ 8,103	$ 24,507	$ 1,737	$ 34,347	$ 1,872
Revenue bonds payable	1,050	106,250	—	107,300	295
Accrued liabilities	899	62,854	100	63,853	1,104
Due to other funds	2,268	7,084	1,171	10,523	182
Capital lease obligations	—	—	—	—	—
Compensated absences	371	810	71	1,252	108
Advances-capital replacement	—	—	—	—	677
Deferred revenue	10,628	24,891	—	35,519	—
Current liabilities (payable from restricted assets):					
Vouchers payable	—	16,350	—	16,350	—
Retainage payable	—	14,825	—	14,825	—
Notes payable	—	19,450	—	19,450	—
Capital lease obligations	—	2,056	—	2,056	—
Accrued interest and other liabilities	—	27,537	—	27,537	—
Other accrued liabilities	—	11,591	—	11,591	—
Total Current Liabilities	23,319	318,205	3,079	344,603	4,238
Notes payable	—	56,763	—	56,763	—
Revenue bonds payable	27,738	3,980,405	—	4,008,143	—
Deferred loss on refunding	—	(244,015)	—	(244,015)	—
Unamortized discounts	—	(12,880)	—	(12,880)	—
Capital lease obligation	—	1,058	—	1,058	220
Other accrued liabilities	1,634	5,548	630	7,812	883
Claims reserve	—	—	—	—	30,523
TOTAL LIABILITIES	52,691	4,105,084	3,709	4,161,484	35,864
NET ASSETS					
Invested in capital assets, net of related debt	277,055	(142,611)	15,147	149,591	4,119
Restricted for:					
Capital projects	—	94,783	—	94,783	—
Debt service	—	401,754	—	401,754	—
Unrestricted	115,250	330,834	20,896	466,980	(16,419)
TOTAL NET ASSETS	$392,305	$ 684,760	$36,043	$1,113,108	$(12,300)
Adjustment to reflect consolidation of internal service fund activities related to enterprise funds				(7,539)	
Net assets of business-type activities				$1,105,569	

ILLUSTRATION 1–11

CITY AND COUNTY OF DENVER
Statement of Revenues, Expenses, and Changes in Fund Net Assets
Proprietary Funds
For the year ended December 31, 2004
(amounts expressed in thousands)

	Business-type Activities-Enterprise Funds				Governmental Activities— Internal Service Funds
	Wastewater Management	Denver Airport System	Other Enterprise Funds	Total Enterprise Funds	
OPERATING REVENUES					
Charges for services	$ 67,091	$467,433	$12,627	$ 547,151	$ 24,644
Other revenue	—	10,232	663	10,895	39
Change in claims reserve	—	—	—	—	865
TOTAL OPERATING REVENUES	67,091	477,665	13,290	558,046	25,548
OPERATING EXPENSES					
Personnel services	17,404	90,005	5,498	112,907	8,775
Contractual services	14,297	117,091	6,686	138,074	503
Supplies and materials	1,318	14,118	810	16,246	9,552
Depreciation and amortization	8,888	148,386	826	158,100	958
Metropolitan Wastewater Reclamation District	24,818	—	—	24,818	—
Claims payments	—	—	—	—	9,944
Other operating expenses	—	—	2,723	2,723	12,117
TOTAL OPERATING EXPENSES	66,725	369,600	16,543	452,868	41,849
Operating income (loss)	366	108,065	(3,253)	105,178	(16,301)
NONOPERATING REVENUES (EXPENSES)					
Investment and interest income	2,040	22,486	456	24,982	300
Other revenue	24	62,040	—	62,064	—
Gain on disposition of assets	—	—	7,932	7,932	—
Grants	—	240	—	240	—
Interest expense	(2,027)	(221,296)	—	(223,323)	(47)
Other expense	—	(2,050)	—	(2,050)	—
TOTAL NONOPERATING REVENUES (EXPENSES)	37	(138,580)	8,388	(130,155)	253
Income (loss) before contributions and transfers	403	(30,515)	5,135	(24,977)	(16,048)
Capital grants and contributions	13,509	62,205	—	75,714	—
Transfers in	—	—	—	—	9,000
Transfers out	(340)	—	—	(340)	—
Change in net assets	13,572	31,690	5,135	50,397	(7,048)
Net assets—January 1	378,733	653,070	30,908	1,062,711	(5,252)
NET ASSETS—December 31	$392,305	$684,760	$36,043	$1,113,108	$(12,300)

Change in net assets of enterprise funds	$ 50,397
Adjustment to reflect consolidation of internal service fund activities related to enterprise funds	3,684
Change in net assets of business-type activities	$ 54,081

As required by GASB standards, the City and County of Denver reports proprietary funds financial information in three financial statements: a statement of net assets—proprietary funds (Illustration 1–10), a statement of revenues, expenses, and changes in fund net assets—proprietary funds (Illustration 1–11), and a statement of cash flows—proprietary funds (Illustration 1–12). An astute reader will note that these are very similar to the three financial statements required for business organizations, although there are important differences, as will be discussed in later chapters.

The final two required financial statements are those for the fiduciary funds. By definition, fiduciary funds account for resources that the government is holding or managing for an external private party, that is, an individual, organization, or other government. Because these resources may not be used to support the government's own programs, GASB standards require that financial information about fiduciary activities be omitted from the government-wide financial statements; however, the information must be reported in two fund financial statements: a statement of fiduciary net assets—fiduciary funds and a statement of changes in fiduciary net assets—fiduciary funds. Both statements are prepared using accrual accounting with the economic resources measurement focus. These two statements for the City and County of Denver are presented in Illustrations 1–13 and 1–14.

Both governmental funds and proprietary funds financial statements must provide separate columns for each **major fund** (see Chapter 2 for the definition of a major fund). The aggregate of nonmajor governmental and enterprise funds is reported in a single column of the corresponding statements. In addition to the General Fund, which is always considered a major fund, Denver identifies its Human Services and Bond Projects funds as major governmental funds and its Wastewater Management and Denver Airport System funds as major enterprise funds. Major fund reporting is not applicable to internal service funds or fiduciary funds.

Reporting by major fund meets the information needs of citizens and other report users having a specific interest in the financial condition and operations of a particular fund. To meet the needs of individuals having an interest in particular *nonmajor* funds, governments should provide separate combining financial statements for nonmajor governmental and proprietary funds, as well as for discretely presented component units. Combining and individual fund statements are not ordinarily audited unless the engagement letter with the auditor extends the scope of the audit to include these statements. Other supplementary information that may be presented in the financial section of the CAFR includes schedules necessary to demonstrate compliance with finance-related legal and contractual provisions and schedules to present comparative data on items such as tax collections and long-term debt.

Statistical Section

In addition to the introductory and financial sections of the CAFR, which were just described, a CAFR should contain a statistical section. The statistical section typically presents tables and charts showing social and economic data, financial trends, and the fiscal capacity of the government in detail needed by readers who are more than casually interested in the activities of the governmental unit. The GASB *Codification* suggests the content of the statistical tables usually considered necessary for inclusion in a CAFR. The statistical section is discussed at greater length in Chapter 9 of this text.

ILLUSTRATION 1–12

CITY AND COUNTY OF DENVER
Statement of Cash Flows
Proprietary Funds
For the year ended December 31, 2004
(amounts expressed in thousands)

| | Business-type Activities-Enterprise Funds | | | | Governmental Activities— |
	Wastewater Management	Denver Airport System	Other Enterprise Funds	Total Enterprise Funds	Internal Service Funds
CASH FLOWS FROM OPERATING ACTIVITIES					
Receipts from customers	$70,024	$498,050	$13,310	$581,384	$22,275
Payments to suppliers	(40,346)	(147,595)	$ (8,164)	(196,105)	(14,561)
Payments to employees	(17,496)	(89,674)	(5,494)	(112,664)	(8,172)
Sale of salvage	—	—	—	—	35
Claims paid	—	—	—	—	(9,944)
Remediation revenue	—	6,459	—	6,459	—
Other payments	—	—	(911)	(911)	—
Net cash provided (used) by operating activities	12,182	267,240	(1,259)	278,163	(10,367)
CASH FLOWS FROM NONCAPITAL FINANCING ACTIVITIES					
Transfers in	—	—	—	—	9,000
Transfers out	(340)	—	—	(340)	—
Passenger facility charges	—	60,670	—	60,670	—
Operating grants	—	266	—	266	—
Net cash provided (used) by noncapital financing activities	(340)	60,936	—	60,596	9,000
CASH FLOWS FROM CAPITAL AND RELATED FINANCING ACTIVITIES					
Issuance of long-term debt	—	57,974	—	57,974	—
Issuance of notes payable	—	33,000	—	33,000	—
Bond issue costs	—	(2,235)	—	(2,235)	—
Passenger facility charges	—	20,122	—	20,122	—
Principal payments	(1,015)	(120,718)	—	(121,733)	(513)
Acquisition and construction of capital assets	(14,939)	(111,446)	(2,970)	(129,355)	(223)
Sale of capital assets	35	14,324	3,986	18,345	—
Interest paid	(2,033)	(216,437)	—	(218,470)	(47)
Contributions and advances	2,676	37,922	—	40,598	—
Payments to escrow for current refunding of debt	—	(10,171)	—	(10,171)	—
Net cash provided (used) by capital and related financing activities	(15,276)	(297,665)	1,016	(311,925)	(783)

ILLUSTRATION 1–12 (*Continued*)

	Business-type Activities-Enterprise Funds				Governmental Activities—Internal Service Funds
	Wastewater Management	Denver Airport System	Other Enterprise Funds	Total Enterprise Funds	
CASH FLOWS FROM INVESTING ACTIVITIES					
Purchases of investments	—	(7,690,760)	—	(7,690,760)	—
Proceeds from sale of investments	—	7,627,938	—	7,627,938	—
Interest received	2,201	31,671	448	34,320	255
Net cash provided (used) by investing activities	2,201	(31,151)	448	(28,502)	255
Net increase (decrease) in cash and cash equivalents	(1,233)	(640)	205	(1,668)	(1,895)
Cash and cash equivalents—January 1	129,325	505,666	22,674	657,665	17,048
Cash and cash equivalents—December 31	$128,092	$ 505,026	$22,879	$ 655,997	$ 15,153
Reconciliation of Operating Income (Loss) to Net Cash Provided (Used) by Operating Activities					
Operating income (loss)	$ 366	$ 108,065	$ (3,253)	$ 105,178	$(16,301)
Adjustments to reconcile operating income to net cash provided by operating activities:					
Depreciation and amortization	8,888	148,386	826	158,100	958
Decrease in accounts receivable, net of allowance	1,217	11,349	20	12,586	5,546
Decrease (increase) in due from other funds	361	—	—	361	(153)
Decrease (increase) in inventories	—	(1,135)	30	(1,105)	(54)
Decrease in prepaid items	20	808	644	1,472	—
Increase (decrease) in vouchers payable	781	989	229	1,999	(58)
Increase in deferred revenue	1,354	12,258	—	13,612	—
Increase (decrease) in accrued and other liabilities	(7)	(4,260)	5	(4,262)	(22)
Increase (decrease) in due to other funds	(91)	(9,220)	240	(9,071)	582
Decrease in claims reserve	—	—	—	—	(865)
Decrease in payables from designated assets	(707)	—	—	(707)	—
Net cash provided (used) by operating activities	$ 12,182	$ 267,240	$ (1,259)	278,163	$(10,367)
NONCASH ACTIVITIES					
Assets acquired through capital contributions	$ 10,833	$ —	$ 3,945	$ 14,778	$ —
Refunded bond proceeds deposited into irrevocable trust for defeasance of debt	—	91,762	—	91,762	—

ILLUSTRATION 1–13

CITY AND COUNTY OF DENVER
Statement of Fiduciary Net Assets
Fiduciary Funds
December 31, 2004
(amounts expressed in thousands)

	Pension Trust Fund	Private-Purpose Trust Funds	Agency Funds
ASSETS			
Cash on hand	$ —	$265	$ 2,000
Cash and cash equivalents	42,452	467	12,916
Receivables (net of allowance for uncollectibles of $5,231):			
Taxes	—	—	394,891
Accounts	5,015	14	886
Accrued interest	5,538	—	—
Investments, at fair value:			
U.S. Treasury securities	175,133	—	—
Domestic stocks and bonds	974,992	—	—
International stocks	311,058	—	—
Mutual funds	372,770	—	—
Real estate	151,898	—	—
Other	38,349	—	—
Total investments	2,024,200	—	—
Capital assets, net of accumulated depreciation	1,309	—	—
TOTAL ASSETS	2,078,514	746	410,693
LIABILITIES			
Vouchers payable	19,457	364	2,455
Other accrued liabilities	—	—	105
Due to taxing units	—	265	408,133
TOTAL LIABILITIES	19,457	629	410,693
NET ASSETS			
Held in trust for pension benefits and other purposes	$2,059,057	$117	$ —

EXPANDING THE SCOPE OF ACCOUNTABILITY REPORTING

Some governments publish highly condensed popular reports. These reports usually contain selected data from the audited financial statements, statistical data, graphic displays, and narrative explanations, but the reports themselves are not audited. In addition, many state and local governments have begun to identify and report nonfinancial performance measures. For more than a decade, the GASB has encouraged state and local governments to experiment with reporting **service efforts and accomplishments (SEA)** measures to provide more complete information about a governmental entity's performance than can be provided by basic financial statements, budgetary comparison statements, and schedules. Indicators of service efforts include inputs of nonmonetary resources as well as inputs of dollars. Indicators of service accomplishments include both outputs and outcomes; outputs are quantitative measures of work done, such as the number of juvenile cases handled, and outcomes are the impacts of outputs on program objectives, such as a reduction in the high school dropout rate or incidence of juvenile crime. Chapter 13 provides additional discussion of SEA measures.

ILLUSTRATION 1–14

CITY AND COUNTY OF DENVER
Statement of Changes in Fiduciary Net Assets
Fiduciary Funds
For the year ended December 31, 2005
(amounts expressed in thousands)

	Pension Trust Funds	Private-Purpose Trust Funds
ADDITIONS		
Contributions:		
Employer	$ 33,108	$ —
Denver Health and Hospital Authority	5,702	—
Plan members	45,736	—
Total contributions	84,546	—
Investment income:		
Net appreciation in fair value of investments	157,799	—
Interest and dividends	50,426	—
Total investment income	208,225	—
Less investment expense	(7,606)	
Net investment income	200,619	—
Other additions	—	85
TOTAL ADDITIONS	285,165	85
DEDUCTIONS		
Benefits	107,305	—
Refunds of contributions	86	—
Administrative expenses	2,467	—
TOTAL DEDUCTIONS	109,858	—
Change in net assets	175,307	85
Net assets—January 1	1,883,750	32
Net assets—December 31	$2,059,057	$117

OVERVIEW OF CHAPTERS 2 THROUGH 17

GASB *Statement No. 34* Principles and Standards

The principles that underlie GASB accounting and financial reporting standards are introduced and discussed briefly in Chapter 2. Chapters 3 through 9 explain and illustrate in depth the standards applicable to general purpose external financial reporting of state and local governments, including the measurement focus and basis of accounting utilized for the government-wide and fund financial statements. Chapter 2 also identifies the types of funds and characteristics of each fund type, and distinguishes between major and nonmajor funds. Chapter 9 provides an extensive discussion of the financial reporting entity and *GASBS 34* financial reporting requirements.

Analysis of Governmental Financial Statements; Financial Statement and Performance Audits

The characteristics that distinguish governmental and not-for-profit entities from business entities are identified in the section of this chapter headed "Distinguishing

Characteristics of Governmental and Not-for-Profit Entities." Consideration of those characteristics should make it obvious that many of the ratios used in the analysis of the financial statements of business organizations have little relevance to the analysis of the financial statements of a governmental reporting entity or a not-for-profit entity. Similarly, the section on distinguishing characteristics and the section headed "Objectives of Financial Reporting" should indicate that the objectives of independent audits of governmental financial statements are broader than the objectives of independent audits of profit-seeking businesses. Governmental auditing objectives may also include reviews of the economy and efficiency with which governmental agencies manage and utilize resources, determination of whether results intended by those who authorized programs or activities are being achieved, as well as audits (similar to those of businesses) to determine whether financial statement presentations are in conformity with GAAP. In all cases, auditors of governmental entities should ascertain that the entity has complied with relevant laws and regulations. Chapter 10 discusses financial ratios useful for the analysis of governmental financial statements. Chapter 11 explains government auditing standards established by the Comptroller General of the United States and related publications issued by the AICPA for the guidance of auditors of governmental and not-for-profit entities.

Accounting and Financial Reporting for the Federal Government and Not-for-Profit Organizations

Accounting and financial reporting standards for the federal government differ significantly from those for state and local governments. An introduction to accounting and reporting standards for the federal government and illustrative financial statements for federal departments or agencies is provided in Chapter 12. Similarly, accounting and financial reporting standards for not-for-profit organizations differ from those for both state and local governments and the federal government. Although logic would suggest that entities in the same specialized industries, such as public and private colleges and universities, should follow similar accounting and reporting practices, the fact is that their practices are quite different. The reasons, of course, are the different standards-setting bodies for governmental and nongovernmental not-for-profit organizations and different information needs of financial statement users, as discussed previously and depicted in Illustrations 1–1 and 1–2.

Budgeting for improved performance and determining the costs of government services are covered in Chapter 13. Chapters 14 and 15 discuss accounting for not-for-profit organizations and related regulatory and taxation issues. Specific accounting and reporting requirements applicable to colleges and universities and health care organizations are discussed in Chapters 16 and 17.

A CAVEAT

The first edition of this text was written by the late Professor R. M. Mikesell more than 55 years ago in 1951. Some words of his bear thoughtful rereading from time to time by teachers and students in all fields, not just those concerned with accounting and financial reporting for governmental and not-for-profit entities:

> Even when developed to the ultimate stage of perfection, governmental accounting cannot become a guaranty of good government. At best, it can never be more than a valuable tool for promotion of sound financial management. It does not offer a panacea for all the ills that beset representative government; nor will it fully overcome the influence of

disinterested, uninformed citizens. It cannot be substituted for honesty and moral integrity on the part of public officials; it can help in resisting but cannot eliminate the demands of selfish interests, whether in the form of individual citizens, corporations, or the pressure groups which always abound to influence government at all levels.

Source: Mikesell, R. M. *Governmental Accounting,* rev. ed., Homewood, IL: Richard D. Irwin, 1956, p. 10.

Key Terms*

Accountability, *6*
Basic financial statements, *8*
Comprehensive annual financial report (CAFR), *9*
Federal Accounting Standards Advisory Board (FASAB), *5*
Financial Accounting Standards Board (FASB), *3*
Fiscal accountability, *8*

Fund financial statements, *8*
General purpose governments, *2*
Generally accepted accounting principles (GAAP), *5*
Governmental Accounting Standards Board (GASB), *3*
Government-wide financial statements, *8*
Interperiod equity, *6*

Major fund, *21*
Management's discussion and analysis (MD&A), *8*
Operational accountability, *8*
Required supplementary information (RSI), *8*
Service efforts and accomplishments (SEA), *24*
Special purpose governments, *2*

Questions

1–1. What, in your judgment, justifies the markedly different accounting and financial reporting practices of government and not-for-profit organizations as compared with business organizations?

1–2. Describe the principal differences that distinguish governmental and not-for-profit organizations from business organizations.

1–3. How do *general purpose governments* differ from *special purpose governments?*

1–4. Which standard-setting bodies have responsibility for establishing accounting and reporting standards for (1) state and local governments, (2) business organizations, (3) not-for-profit organizations, and (4) the federal government and its agencies and departments?

1–5. "Interperiod equity is the cornerstone of all financial reporting in government." Do you agree with this statement? Why or why not?

1–6. Distinguish between *fiscal accountability* and *operational accountability* and explain which basic financial statements are intended to assist financial statement users in assessing each type of accountability.

1–7. What are the three sections of a comprehensive annual financial report (CAFR)? What kinds of information are contained in each section? How do the minimum requirements for general purpose external financial reporting relate in scope to the CAFR?

1–8. Why is it necessary to provide schedules to reconcile certain financial information reported in the governmental fund financial statements to that reported in the Governmental Activities column of the government-wide financial statements?

*See the glossary at the back of the text for a definition of each term and concept.

1–9. Which fund financial statements use the same basis of accounting and measurement focus as the government-wide financial statements? Explain why.

1–10. Why do the governmental fund financial statements report revenues and expenditures on the *modified accrual basis of accounting* rather than reporting revenues and expenses on the accrual basis, as do the proprietary and fiduciary funds and the government-wide financial statements?

Cases

1–1 Research Case—Governmental or Not-for-Profit Entity? Deadwood Western Heritage Museum is located in Calumet City, a small western city. The museum is open to the general public at no charge; however, signs at the information desk in the entry lobby encourage gifts of $5.00 for adults and $2.00 for children 12 and under. Many visitors make the recommended contribution, some contribute larger amounts, and some do not contribute at all. Such contributions comprise 35 percent of the museum's total annual revenues, with net proceeds from fund-raising events and governmental grants comprising the remaining 65 percent. The museum shares a building with the local post office, for which it pays fair rental. Except for a part-time director, the museum is staffed exclusively by unpaid volunteers. Duly organized as a tax-exempt not-for-profit organization, the museum is governed by a six-member board of trustees, each appointed for a three-year term. Four of the trustees are appointed by the Calumet City Council, one is appointed by the Jackson County Commission, and one is appointed by the Calumet Arts Commission. The museum's original charter provides that in the event the museum ceases to operate, two-thirds of its net assets will revert to the city and the remaining one-third will revert equally to the county and the Arts Commission.

Although the museum has never been audited, the board of trustees has decided to initiate annual audits in response to state government grant sources. Grantors have indicated that grants will not continue in the future unless the museum receives an unqualified (clean) audit opinion stating that its financial statements are presented fairly in conformity with generally accepted accounting principles.

Required:

Assume you are the CPA who has been engaged to conduct this audit. To which standards-setting body (or bodies) would you look for accounting and financial reporting standards to assist you in determining whether the museum's financial statements are in conformity with generally accepted accounting principles? Explain how you arrived at this conclusion.

1–2 Internet Case—FASB. Go to the Financial Accounting Standards Board's Web site at *www.fasb.org.* Prepare a list and brief description of all FASB statements that specifically provide accounting and reporting guidance for not-for-profit organizations. Can you obtain a copy of the full-text of these statements from this Web site? Does the FASB charge for its statements, or are they provided free of charge?

1–3 Internet Case—FASAB. Examine the Federal Accounting Standards Advisory Board's Web site at *www.fasab.gov* and prepare a brief report about its mission, structure, due-process documents, and current technical agenda, and a list of organizations represented on its Accounting and Auditing Policy Committee. Can you obtain a copy of the full-text of FASAB statements from this Web site? If not, how would you obtain a copy of a statement pertinent to federal agencies? What is the cost to purchase a statement?

1–4 Internet Case—GASB. Examine the Governmental Accounting Standards Board Web site (*www.gasb.org*) and prepare a brief report about its mission, structure, due-process documents, current technical agenda, and representative organizations on its Advisory Council? Can you get a copy of the full text of a GASB statement from this Web site? If not, how would you obtain a copy of GASB *Statement No. 34,* for example? What is the cost to purchase a statement?

Exercises and Problems

1–1 Examine the CAFR. Download a copy of the most recent comprehensive annual financial report (CAFR) for the City and County of Denver from its Web site: *http://www.denvergov.org/auditor/* (click on "End-of-Year Audited Financial Statements"), or that of another city or county if you wish.* Familiarize yourself with the organization by scanning the report and reread the section in this chapter entitled "Financial Reporting of State and Local Governments." Be prepared to discuss in class the items suggested below.

a. Introductory Section.

Read the letter of transmittal or any narrative that accompanies the financial statements. Does this material define the governmental reporting entity and name the primary government and all related component units included in the report? (*Note:* The reporting entity may be discussed in the notes to the financial report rather than in the transmittal letter.) Does the introductory section discuss the financial condition of the reporting entity at the balance sheet date? Does it discuss the most significant changes in financial condition that occurred during the year? Does it alert the reader to forthcoming changes in financial condition that are not as yet reflected in the financial statements? Do the amounts reported in the letter of transmittal or other narrative agree with amounts in the statements and schedules in the financial section? Does the introductory section include a list of principal officials? An organization chart? A reproduction of a Certificate of Achievement for Excellence in Financial Reporting from the Government Finance Officers Association (GFOA)? Assuming the government follows *GASBS 34,* compare the information in the letter of transmittal with that in the management discussion & analysis (MD&A).

b. Financial Section.

(1) *Audit Report.* Are the financial statements in the report audited by an independent CPA, state auditors, or auditors employed by the governmental unit being audited? Does the auditor indicate who is responsible for preparing the financial statements? Does the auditor express an opinion that the statements are "in accordance with generally accepted accounting principles applicable to governmental entities in the United States" or

---

*GASB's Web site, *http://www.gasb.org* provides a sizeable list of local governments that early adopted the *GASBS 34* reporting model and indicates whether their CAFRs can be downloaded. You can usually obtain a hardcopy of the CAFR of any city by sending an e-mail request to the city's director of finance (or other appropriate title of the chief financial officer). Be sure to mention that you are a student and need the CAFR for a class project. Contact information for the finance director can usually be obtained by doing a search on "City of (name)" and looking for a link to the city's departments. At that link, select Finance Department or a department with a similar function, such as Accounting and Budgeting. Before you request a CAFR by e-mail, check to see if one is accessible at the department's Web site.

some other phrase? Is the opinion qualified in some manner, disclaimed, or adverse? Does the auditor indicate that the opinion covers the basic financial statements or that plus combining statements?

(2) *Basic Financial Statements.* Does the CAFR contain the two government-wide financial statements and seven fund statements and required reconciliation?

(3) *Notes to the Financial Statements.* How many notes follow the required basic financial statements? Is there a phrase at the bottom of the basic financial statements indicating that the notes are an integral part of the financial statements?

(4) *Individual Fund and Combining Statements.* Following the notes to the financial statements, does the CAFR provide combining and individual fund statements? Do these combining statements aggregate all the funds of a given fund type or all the nonmajor funds?

(5) *Management's Discussion and Analysis (MD&A).* Does the CAFR contain an MD&A? If so, where is it located and what type of information does it contain?

c. Statistical Tables.

Examine these tables so that you can refer to them in discussions accompanying subsequent chapters. For example, is information about long-term debt requirements over time, property assessed values and tax rates over time, and demographic information, such as population, provided?

1–2 Multiple Choice. Choose the best answer.

1. A distinguishing difference between governments and not-for-profit organizations is:
   a. Lack of a profit motive.
   b. Absence of owners.
   c. Taxation as a significant source of funding.
   d. Receipt of significant amounts of funding through nonexchange transactions (i.e., resource providers do not get proportional benefits for what they pay in to the organization).

2. Which of the following is a true statement about accounting standard-setting bodies?
   a. The Financial Accounting Standards Board (FASB) sets accounting and reporting standards for all not-for-profit organizations, but the Governmental Accounting Standards Board (GASB) may also prescribe standards for governmental not-for-profit organizations provided they do not conflict with FASB standards.
   b. The GASB sets accounting and reporting standards for all governmental organizations; the FASB sets standards for all business and not-for-profit organizations.
   c. Only the FASB and GASB enjoy AICPA Ethics Rule 203 coverage as recognized standard-setting authoritative bodies, not the FASAB.
   d. The FASB and GASB are administratively supported by the Financial Accounting Foundation; the FASAB draws its support from the federal government.

3. Which of the following organizations would *least* likely meet the criteria to be classified as a *governmental* not-for-profit organization?
   a. A religion-affiliated university.
   b. A museum.

    c. A public hospital.

    d. A social service agency.

4. The concept of "interperiod equity" means that financial reporting should help report users assess whether:

    a. Revenues equaled or exceeded expenditures for the year.

    b. Current year revenues were sufficient to pay for services provided that year.

    c. Future taxpayers can expect to receive the same or higher level of services as current taxpayers.

    d. Total assets (current and noncurrent) were sufficient to cover total liabilities (current and noncurrent).

5. Which of the following is (are) included in the minimum requirements for general purpose external financial reporting of a government?

    a. Comprehensive Annual Financial Report.

    b. Management's Discussion and Analysis (MD&A) and basic financial statements.

    c. Combining fund financial statements.

    d. Statistical section.

6. Under *GASBS 34,* the basic financial statements are:

    a. MD&A, government-wide statements, fund financial statements, and notes.

    b. MD&A, government-wide statements, fund financial statements, and other required supplementary information.

    c. Transmittal letter, government-wide statements, fund financial statements, notes, and required supplementary information.

    d. Government-wide statements, fund financial statements, and notes.

7. Which of the following is a true statement regarding the *GASBS 34* reporting model?

    a. Fund financial statements are optional if government-wide financial statements are provided.

    b. Government-wide statements provide information about the aggregate assets, liabilities, and net assets of the governmental and business-type activities of the entity and its component units, as well as the results of its activities for the reporting period.

    c. Fund financial statements are intended to provide information to demonstrate operational accountability.

    d. Government-wide statements are intended to provide information to assess fiscal accountability.

8. The modified accrual basis of accounting is used to account for revenues and expenditures reported in the financial statements of:

    a. Governmental activities at the government-wide level.

    b. Business-type activities at the government-wide level.

    c. Governmental funds.

    d. Proprietary funds.

9. Under *GASBS 34,* financial information related to fiduciary activities are reported in which financial statements?

	Government-wide Financial Statements	Fund Financial Statements
a.	No	Yes
b.	Yes	No
c.	Yes	Yes
d.	No	No

10. Separate columns for individual *major funds* are provided in which of the following financial statements?
    a. Statement of net assets—government-wide, balance sheet—governmental funds, statement of net assets—proprietary funds.
    b. Statement of net assets—government-wide, balance sheet—governmental funds, statement of fiduciary net assets—fiduciary funds.
    c. Statement of net assets—government-wide, statement of net assets—proprietary funds, statement of fiduciary net assets—fiduciary funds.
    d. Balance sheet—governmental funds, statement of net assets—proprietary funds.

1–3 Matching. Place the abbreviations corresponding to appropriate reporting attribute(s) in the spaces provided for each financial statement. Include all that apply.

Activities or Funds
Governmental activities—GA
Business-type activities—BTA
Governmental Funds—GF
Proprietary Funds—PF
Fiduciary Funds—FF

Basis of Accounting
Accrual—A
Modified accrual—MA

Measurement Focus
Economic resources—ER
Current financial resources—CFR

Financial Statements	Activities or Funds Reported	Basis of Accounting	Measurement Focus
Statement of net assets—government-wide			
Statement of activities—government-wide			
Balance sheet—governmental funds			
Statement of revenues, expenditures, and changes in fund balances—governmental funds			
Statement of net assets—proprietary funds			
Statement of revenues, expenses, and changes in fund net assets—proprietary funds			
Statement of cash flows—proprietary funds			
Statement of fiduciary net assets			
Statement of changes in fiduciary net assets			

Principles of Accounting and Financial Reporting for State and Local Governments

Learning Objectives

After studying this chapter you should be able to:

1. Explain the nature of the three major activity categories of a state or local government: governmental activities, business-type activities, and fiduciary activities.
2. Explain the components of GASB's integrated accounting and financial reporting model, including:

   The reporting entity

   Government-wide financial statements

   Fund financial statements

   Definition of *fund* and principles of fund accounting

   Major fund reporting

   Types of funds in each fund category and characteristics of each fund type.

Chapter 1 presented a brief overview of the minimum requirements for general purpose external financial reporting under the *GASBS 34* financial reporting model. This chapter expands on the previous discussion and focuses primarily on principles of accounting and financial reporting within the integrated reporting model framework set forth in *GASBS 34.*

When the GASB was formed in 1984, it adopted 12 accounting and financial reporting principles that had been established by its predecessor standards-setting body, the National Council on Governmental Accounting (NCGA). *GASBS 34* modifies several of the original 12 principles and adds one principle for reporting long-term liabilities. A summary of these principles is presented in the appendix to this chapter. Certain of the principles are also discussed in this chapter.

ACTIVITIES OF GOVERNMENT

Chapter 1 explained that the characteristics of governmental organizations differ from those of for-profit business organizations. One key difference is that governments are not profit seeking but exist to meet citizens' demand for services, consistent with the availability of resources to provide those services. Although the types and levels of services vary from government to government, most general purpose governments provide certain core services: those related to protection of life and property (e.g., police and fire protection), public works (e.g., streets and highways, bridges, and public buildings), parks and recreation facilities and programs, and cultural and social services. Governments must also incur costs for general administrative support such as data processing, finance, and personnel. Core governmental services, together with general administrative support, comprise the major part of what GASB *Concepts Statement No. 1* refers to as governmental-type activities.[1] In its more recent pronouncements, GASB refers to these activities as simply **governmental activities.** Chapters 3 through 6 of the text focus on various aspects of accounting for governmental activities.

Some readers may be surprised to learn that governments also engage in a variety of **business-type activities.** These activities include, among others, public utilities (e.g., electric, water, gas, and sewer utilities), transportation systems, toll roads, toll bridges, hospitals, parking garages and lots, liquor stores, golf courses, and swimming pools. Many of these activities are intended to be self-supporting by charging users for the services they receive. Operating subsidies from general tax revenues are not uncommon, however, particularly for transportation systems. Accounting for business-type activities is covered in Chapter 7 of the text.

A final category of activity in which governments are involved is **fiduciary activities.** Governments often act in a fiduciary capacity, either as an agent or trustee, for parties outside the government. For example, a government may serve as agent for other governments in administering and collecting taxes. Governments may also serve as trustee for investments of other governments in the government's investment pool, for **escheat properties** that revert to the government when there are no legal claimants or heirs to a deceased individual's estate, and for assets being held for employee pension plans, among other trustee roles.

Under *GASBS 34,* only *private-purpose* agency and trust relationships—those that benefit individuals, private organizations, and other governments—are reported as fiduciary activities. *Public-purpose* agency and trust activities, those that primarily benefit the general public and the government's own programs, are treated as governmental activities for accounting and financial reporting purposes. Accounting for fiduciary activities is covered in Chapter 8 of the text.

GOVERNMENTAL FINANCIAL REPORTING ENTITY

The notion of financial accountability is basic to the definition of a governmental reporting entity. A **reporting entity** consists of the primary government and certain other organizations, identified as component units, for which the primary government

---

[1] Governmental Accounting Standards Board, *Codification of Governmental Accounting and Financial Reporting Standards as of June 30, 2005.* (Norwalk, CT, 2005), Appendix B, *Concepts Statement No. 1,* par. 10.

is financially accountable.[2] According to GASB standards, the "financial statements of the reporting entity should provide an overview of the entity, yet allow users to distinguish between the primary government and its component units."[3] The government-wide financial statements meet this objective very well.

GASB defines a **primary government** as a state government or general purpose local government, or a special purpose government that has a separately elected governing body, is legally separate, and is fiscally independent of other state and local governments. General purpose local governments are organizations such as cities, towns, villages, counties, and townships. In many states, public school systems are legally and fiscally independent special purpose governments that are primary governments in their own right.

Component units are legally separate organizations, including organizations such as governmental hospitals, library districts, and public building authorities, for which the elected officials of the primary government are financially accountable. In addition, a component unit can be another organization for which the nature and significance of its relationship with the primary government, including its ongoing financial support of the primary government or its other component units, is such that exclusion would cause the reporting entity's financial statements to be misleading or incomplete.

Reporting the financial information of component units in a separate column of the government-wide financial statements, as shown in Illustrations 1–4 and 1–5 in Chapter 1 and Illustration 2–1, is referred to as a **discrete presentation.** Discrete presentation is the most common method used to report component units and should be used unless the financial activities of the component unit are so intertwined with those of the primary government that they are, in substance, the same as the primary government. In such cases the component unit's financial information should be reported in the same columns as the financial information of the primary government itself. This method of inclusion is known as **blending.** Criteria for identification and methods of component unit reporting are covered in greater detail in Chapter 9.

The notes to the financial statements should contain a brief description of the component units of the financial reporting entity and their relationships to the primary government. This disclosure should also describe the criteria for including the component units and for reporting the component units. Information about major component units may be presented in condensed financial statements within the notes or in combining statements that provide a separate column for each component unit, along with a total column for all component units.[4] If there are only a few major component units, their financial information can be reported in separate columns of the government-wide financial statements. Under this option, aggregate financial information for all nonmajor component units is reported in an additional column of the government-wide financial statements. The notes should also include information about how separate financial statements for individual component units may be obtained.

---

[2] GASB, *Codification,* Sec. 2100.111.

[3] Ibid., Sec. 2100.142 Note: All definitions in this section of the text are quoted or paraphrased from GASB *Codification,* Sec. 2100.501.

[4] What constitutes a *major* component unit is a matter of professional judgment, considering each component unit's significance in relation to the other component units and to the primary government. GASB, *Codification,* Sec. 2600.109.

INTEGRATED ACCOUNTING AND FINANCIAL REPORTING MODEL

The minimum requirements for general purpose external financial reporting for state and local governments, as well as a discussion of the contents of a comprehensive annual financial report (CAFR), were briefly discussed in Chapter 1. As shown in Illustration 1–3, every state and local government should provide, in addition to its basic financial statements, a *management's discussion and analysis* (MD&A) and certain other required supplementary information. To understand the basic principles of accounting and financial reporting for state and local governments, one must first understand the *GASBS 34* integrated accounting and financial reporting model. This model is depicted in Illustration 2–1. As shown in Illustration 2–1, the primary aspect of the integrated model is the requirement to provide two kinds of basic financial statements, government-wide and fund, each kind intended to achieve different reporting objectives. These two kinds of statements are integrated in the sense that the total fund balances of governmental funds and changes in fund balances must be reconciled to total net assets and changes in net assets of governmental activities reported in the government-wide financial statements. The necessity for these reconciliations was touched on in Chapter 1 and is further explained in the following discussion.

Government-wide and Fund Financial Statements

The government-wide financial statements report on the governmental reporting entity as a whole but focus on the primary government. As shown in Illustrations 1–4 and 1–5, as well as in Illustration 2–1, the government-wide financial statements present the financial information of the governmental activities and business-type activities of the primary government in separate columns, although there is a total column for the primary government.

The government-wide financial statements present all financial information using the **economic resources measurement focus** and the **accrual basis** of accounting—essentially the same measurement focus and basis of accounting used in the financial statements of for-profit business organizations. Thus, as discussed in Chapter 1, the government-wide financial statements report on the *operational accountability* of the government and help to assess whether the government is covering the full cost of services provided in the long run.

Governments must also present *fund* financial statements or, more precisely, three subsets of fund financial statements, one subset for each of the three fund categories: governmental, proprietary, and fiduciary (see the lower half of Illustration 2–1). These categories correspond closely to the governmental, business-type, and fiduciary activities described earlier in this chapter. An observant reader will note, however, that although internal service funds are included in the proprietary funds category, they are included as part of *governmental activities* in the government-wide financial statements. Thus, in most cases, only enterprise funds are reported as business-type activities in the government-wide statements. Internal service fund financial information is reported as part of governmental activities in the government-wide financial statements because these funds, though businesslike in operation, predominantly serve departments of the same government rather than the general public. If an internal service fund predominantly serves one or more enterprise funds, its financial information is reported in the Business-type Activities column of the government-wide financial statements. Financial reporting of internal service funds is discussed in depth in Chapter 7.

Another interesting aspect of the integrated accounting and reporting framework is that fiduciary activities are reported only in the two *fund* financial statements shown in Illustration 2–1 (examples of these statements are presented in Illustrations 1–13 and

ILLUSTRATION 2–1 **GASB *Statement No. 34* Integrated Accounting and Financial Reporting Model**

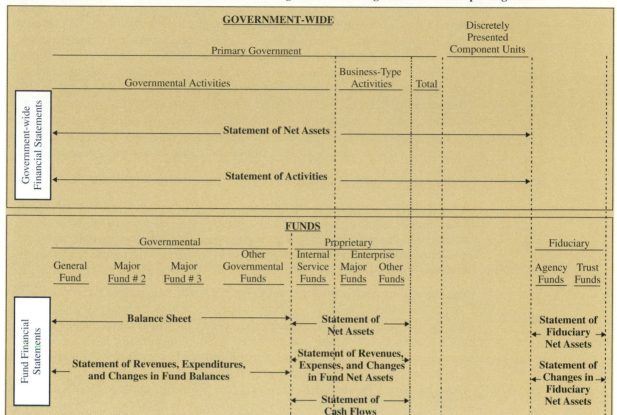

1–14). Fiduciary activities are not reported at all in the government-wide financial statements because the resources held by these activities (funds) belong to private parties and cannot be used to support the services provided by the primary government or its component units.

The discussion to this point has provided a brief overview of the integrated reporting model, which requires both government-wide and fund financial statements. As the following few chapters will make clear, *governmental activities* are reported quite differently in the two types of financial statements. To fully comprehend these differences, one must first become familiar with the concept of a *fund* and the accounting characteristics associated with each fund and activity category. Fund accounting for governmental activities focuses on *fiscal accountability*—reporting on whether current financial resources were obtained from authorized sources and expended only for authorized purposes.

Fiscal Accountability and Fund Accounting

GASB's first accounting and financial reporting principle states:

> A governmental accounting system must make it possible both: (a) to present fairly and with full disclosure the funds and activities of the governmental unit in conformity with generally accepted accounting principles, and (b) to determine and demonstrate compliance with finance-related legal and contractual provisions.[5]

[5] GASB *Codification,* Sec. 1100.101.

In the governmental environment, legal and contractual provisions often conflict with the requirements of generally accepted accounting principles (GAAP). As the first principle states, however, the accounting system must make it possible to present financial information that meets *both* requirements. Legal provisions related to budgeting revenues and expenditures, for example, often differ from GAAP accounting requirements regarding revenues and expenditures. Furthermore, revenues may be legally or contractually restricted for a particular purpose.

The necessity to report on fiscal accountability creates a need for governments to account for restricted-use revenues and expenditures made from such revenues separately from unrestricted revenues and expenditures. The mechanism that has developed for segregating accountability for the inflows and outflows of restricted-use financial resources is the fund.

A **fund** is formally defined as:

> A fiscal and accounting entity with a self-balancing set of accounts recording cash and other financial resources, together with all related liabilities and residual equities or balances and changes therein, which are segregated for the purpose of carrying on specific activities or attaining certain objectives in accordance with special regulations, restrictions, or limitations.[6]

The concept of *fund* is fundamental to governmental accounting and reporting. As the definition states, a *fund* is a separate fiscal entity with its own resources and reporting its own liabilities for obligations incurred by the fund and the results of its operations for the fiscal period. Furthermore, a fund conceptually has its own set of accounting records (e.g., journals and ledgers) and can have prepared for it separate financial statements. Thus, it is a separate accounting entity as well.

The latter part of the definition of fund is also worth noting: Specifically, a fund assists in *carrying on specific activities or attaining certain objectives in accordance with special regulations, restrictions, or limitations.* As this sentence implies, different funds are intended to achieve different objectives. Funds may be established by grant or contract provisions imposed by external resource providers, by state or local laws or regulations, or by the discretionary action of governing bodies. The variety of purposes that may be served by different fund categories and types will become apparent in the discussion that follows.

Although it may be desirable for internal management purposes to prepare statements for a particular fund, *GASBS 34* requires that financial statements prepared for the governmental and proprietary fund categories provide separate columns only for **major funds.**[7] So, for example, in the balance sheet prepared for governmental funds (see Illustrations 1–6 and 2–1), separate columns are provided only for the General Fund, which is always considered a major fund, and other governmental funds that meet the major fund criteria or that are designated as major funds by management. The financial information for all nonmajor governmental funds is reported in a single Other Governmental Funds column. Optionally, the government can provide as

---

[6] Ibid., Sec. 1100.102.

[7] In relation to each fund category or type, discussed on the following pages, a fund is classified as *major* if its (1) total assets, liabilities, revenues, or expenditures/expenses of the individual governmental or enterprise fund are at least 10 percent of the corresponding total of assets, liabilities, revenues, or expenditures/expenses for all funds of that category or type (total governmental or total enterprise funds) *and* (2) total assets, liabilities, revenues, or expenditures/expenses of the individual governmental fund or enterprise fund are at least 5 percent of the corresponding total for all governmental and enterprise funds combined. GASB standards require that the same element, such as assets, meet both criteria. GASB *Codification,* Sec. 2200.153.

supplementary information a separate combining balance sheet. A combining balance sheet contains columns of financial information for each nonmajor fund and a column for total nonmajor governmental funds. An example of a combining balance sheet for the nonmajor governmental funds of the City and County of Denver is presented in Illustration 2–2.

Fund Categories

Three categories of activities in which governments engage were described early in this chapter: governmental, business-type, and fiduciary. There are three closely related categories of funds: governmental, proprietary, and fiduciary (see Illustration 2–1). Except for the fact that most internal service funds are treated as part of governmental activities rather than as part of business-type activities for purposes of government-wide financial reporting, the activity and fund categories are the same. Accounting characteristics and principles unique to each fund category are discussed in the sections that follow.

Governmental Funds

The **governmental funds** category contains five types of funds: the General Fund, special revenue funds, debt service funds, capital projects funds, and permanent funds. Every state and local government has one and only one **General Fund,** although it may be called by a different name such as *general revenue fund, general operating fund,* or *current fund.* Other governmental funds will be created as needed. Most departmental operating activities, such as those of police and fire, public works, parks and recreation, culture, education, and social services, as well as general government support services, such as the city manager's office, finance, personnel, and data processing, are typically accounted for in the General Fund. Unless a financial resource is required to be accounted for in a different fund type, it is usually accounted for in the General Fund.

When tax or grant revenues or private gifts are legally restricted for particular operating purposes, such as the operation of a library or maintenance of roads and bridges, a **special revenue fund** is created. The number of special revenue funds used by state and local governments varies greatly, ranging from a few to many. Nevertheless, GASB standards recommend that governments establish only the minimum number of funds needed to comply with legal requirements and to provide sound management. An excessive number of funds creates undue complexity and contributes to inefficient financial administration.

Governments that have bond obligations outstanding and certain other types of long-term general liabilities may be required by law or bond covenants to create a **debt service fund.** The purpose of a debt service fund is to account for financial resources segregated for the purpose of making principal and interest payments on general long-term debt.[8] Some governments account for all debt service on general long-term debt in their General Fund, but governments ordinarily create one or more debt service funds if they have general long-term debt.

Governments often engage in capital projects to accommodate a growing population or to replace existing capital assets. These projects typically involve major construction of items such as buildings, highways or bridges, or parks. To account for tax or grant revenues, or bond proceeds earmarked for a capital project, as well as payments to

[8] General long-term debt is distinguished from long-term debt issued and serviced by a proprietary or fiduciary fund. Because those funds follow accounting principles similar to those of for-profit entities, interest and principal on debt issued by proprietary or fiduciary funds and payable from the revenues of those funds is accounted for in those funds rather than in a debt service fund.

ILLUSTRATION 2–2

CITY AND COUNTY OF DENVER
Combining Balance Sheet
Nonmajor Governmental Funds
December 31, 2004
(amounts expressed in thousands)

	Special Revenue	Debt Service	Capital Projects	Cableland Trust	Total
ASSETS					
Cash on hand	$ 210	$ —	$ —	$ —	$ 210
Cash and cash equivalents	91,401	54,663	96,364	3,306	245,734
Restricted assets:					
Cash and cash equivalents	8,392	—	449	—	8,841
Receivables (net of allowances for uncollectibles of $54,962):					
Taxes	—	72,756	2,995	—	75,751
Special assessments	—	399	1,208	—	1,607
Notes	88,240	—	—	—	88,240
Accounts	28,975	—	2,219	—	31,194
Accrued interest	247	112	259	53	671
Due from other funds	925	—	563	—	1,488
Due from other governments	20,915	—	7,348	—	28,263
Prepaid items and other assets	140	—	650	—	790
Assets held for disposition	4,719	—	—	—	4,719
TOTAL ASSETS	$244,164	$127,930	$112,055	$3,359	$487,508
LIABILITIES AND FUND BALANCES					
LIABILITIES					
Vouchers payable	$ 13,819	$ —	$ 15,307	$ —	$ 29,126
Payroll liabilities	245	—	—	—	245
Due to other funds	3,350	—	225	—	3,575
Deferred revenue	29,797	70,934	1,208	—	101,939
Advances	800	—	—	—	800
TOTAL LIABILITIES	48,011	70,934	16,740	—	135,685
FUND BALANCE					
Reserved for emergency use	8,184	—	—	—	8,184
Reserved for encumbrances	34,211	—	34,674	—	68,885
Reserved for prepaid items and other assets	140	—	650	—	790
Reserved for construction	—	—	449	—	449
Reserved for notes receivable	88,240	—	—	—	88,240
Reserved for debt service:					
Long-term debt	208	35,812	—	—	36,020
Interest	—	21,184	—	—	21,184
Unreserved:					
Designated for net unrealized gain	—	—	166	—	166
Designated for subsequent years' expenditures	—	—	38,161	—	38,161
Undesignated:					
Special revenue funds	65,170	—	—	—	65,170
Capital projects funds	—	—	21,215	—	21,215
Permanent fund	—	—	—	3,359	3,359
TOTAL FUND BALANCE	196,153	56,996	95,315	3,359	351,823
TOTAL LIABILITIES AND FUND BALANCE	$244,164	$127,930	$112,055	$3,359	$487,508

architects, engineers, construction contractors, and suppliers, a **capital projects fund** is typically created. Multiple capital projects funds may be created if a government has multiple capital projects.

The final type of governmental fund is the *permanent fund.* A **permanent fund** is used to account for permanent endowments created when a donor stipulates that the principal amount of a contribution must be invested and preserved but earnings on amounts so invested can be used for some public purpose. Public purposes include activities such as maintenance of a cemetery or aesthetic enhancements to public buildings. If the earnings from a permanent fund can be used to benefit only *private* individuals, organizations, or other governments, rather than supporting a program of the government and its citizenry, a private-purpose trust fund—a fiduciary fund—is used instead of a permanent fund.

Accounting and financial reporting for the governmental funds category, the five fund types just described, have evolved to meet the budgetary and financial compliance needs of government, as stated earlier, to achieve and report on the government's *fiscal accountability.* Thus, it is hardly surprising that accounting for governmental funds focuses on the inflows and outflows of **current financial resources.** Current financial resources are cash or items such as receivables that will be converted into cash during the current fiscal period or that will be **available** soon enough after the end of the period to pay current-period liabilities. With the lone exception of property tax revenues, which GASB standards require to be collectible within 60 days of the end of the current fiscal year to be deemed available, governments are free to establish their own definition of *available* and, therefore, which items to recognize in their financial statements as current financial resources and revenues.[9] In practice, the definition of *available* may range anywhere from 30 days to one year, but generally does not exceed 120 days.

Because governmental funds account for the inflows and outflows of current financial resources, the balance sheet for governmental funds reports only current assets and current liabilities and **fund balances** (or **fund equity**), the difference between current assets and current liabilities. One can readily see, for example, that no long-lived assets, such as land, buildings, and equipment, nor any long-term liabilities, such as bonds payable, are reported on the City and County of Denver's governmental funds balance sheet shown in Illustration 1–6.

Similarly, Illustrations 1–8 and 2–1 show that inflows and outflows of current financial resources of the governmental funds are reported in a statement of revenues, expenditures, and changes in fund balances. As explained previously, financial resources must be *available* to pay current-period obligations (that is, they must be expected to be received during the current period or soon thereafter) before they can be reported as a revenue of the current period. Recognizing as revenues only those inflows that are measurable and available to pay current-period obligations and recognizing as expenditures only obligations that will be paid from currently available financial resources is referred to as the **modified accrual** basis of accounting.

Accounting for financial resource inflows and outflows in the governmental funds on the modified accrual basis is much different than accounting for the corresponding *economic resource* inflows and outflows for governmental activities on the accrual basis, as they are reported in the government-wide financial statements. As puzzling as this may seem at this early point in the course, the reason for the differential accounting treatment is simple: The governmental fund financial statements report on short-term fiscal

[9] GASB standards require that governments disclose in the notes to their financial statements the length of time used to define *available* for purposes of revenue recognition in the governmental funds financial statements; see GASB *Codification*, Sec. 2300.106, par. a(5).

accountability; the government-wide financial statements report on long-term operational accountability. Thus, governmental activities at the government-wide level are accounted for using principles similar to those used by for-profit business organizations.

In the next few chapters, you will become familiar with the "dual-track" approach the authors have developed to account for the different effects of certain transactions on the governmental fund financial statements and the Governmental Activities column of the government-wide financial statements. The following example illustrates how certain transactions affect the fund and government-wide financial statements differently and thus require different accounting treatment.

The City of Princeton issued a two-year note in the amount of $2,000,000 to finance the acquisition of five new fire trucks. The proceeds of the note and the expenditure for the fire trucks are to be accounted for in the General Fund. The city maintains a general journal and general ledger for the General Fund and a separate general journal and general ledger to record the effect of certain transactions on governmental activities at the government-wide level.

The issuance of the two-year note by the City of Princeton has a very different effect on the General Fund than it does on governmental activities, as shown in journal entries 1a and 1b.

	General Ledger	
	Debits	**Credits**
General Fund:		
1a. Cash	2,000,000	
Other Financing Sources—		
Proceeds of Two-Year Note		2,000,000
Governmental Activities, Government-wide:		
1b. Cash	2,000,000	
Notes Payable		2,000,000

The credit account Other Financing Sources—Proceeds of Two-Year Note in Entry 1a is a temporary account indicating that additional financial resources (cash in this instance) have been added to the fund balance of the General Fund. Thus, the $2,000,000 proceeds of the note have the same effect on the balance of financial resources in the fund that receiving $2,000,000 of tax revenues would have. As you will learn later, other financing sources are reported in a different section of the statement of revenues, expenditures, and fund balances (see Illustration 1–8) than are revenues, but beyond that, the distinction is of little importance; the resources in the fund are all available to spend regardless of their source.[10] Note that Entry 1b is identical to the journal entry

---

[10] Some governmental accounting teachers use the example of a cookie jar or other container to illustrate the operation of a governmental fund. For example, you can visualize the General Fund, and each of the other governmental funds, as being a cookie jar. As revenues or other financing sources (cash and near-cash financial resources) flow into the cookie jar, it causes the balance of financial resources (the fund balance) in the cookie jar to rise. As financial resources (cash) are removed from the jar (or obligations are incurred to use cash later in the period or soon thereafter)—that is, as expenditures are made—the fund balance drops. It is necessary, of course, to keep an accounting record of (journalize) the inflows and outflows of financial resources as well as to maintain ledger accounts that indicate the nature of the financial resources (cash, short-term investments, receivables, and other near-cash assets), current liabilities owed by the fund, and the current fund balance. Although this is not a perfect analogy to the actual operation of a fund, it may help you to visualize its short-term, spending focus.

that a business entity would make for this transaction, reinforcing the fact that transactions affect government-wide financial statements in essentially the same manner as they do business accounting. Note also that the two-year liability is recorded only at the government-wide level since only current assets and current liabilities are recorded in governmental funds.

Journal entries 2a and 2b illustrate the dual effects on the integrated reporting model when the five fire trucks are purchased:

	General Ledger	
	Debits	Credits
General Fund:		
2a. Expenditures—Capital Outlay	2,000,000	
Cash		2,000,000
Governmental Activities, Government-wide:		
2b. Equipment	2,000,000	
Cash		2,000,000

Entry 2a shows that long-lived assets, fire trucks in this example, are not accounted for in the General Fund because governmental funds are used only to account for the inflow and outflows (expenditures) of current financial resources used to provide services or purchase equipment and supplies that have been approved in the budget. In the Governmental Activities column of the government-wide statement of net assets (see Illustration 1–4), the long-term effects of transactions must be reported, including general capital assets such as fire trucks that will provide service benefits in the future. Entry 2b accomplishes this objective by recording the purchase of the fire trucks in the same manner that a business entity would account for the purchase.

In addition, depreciation expense will be recognized on the fire trucks over the next several years in the government-wide financial statements. Thus, the fire trucks and all other depreciable assets used in carrying out governmental activities will be reported net of accumulated depreciation in the Governmental Activities column of the statement of net assets. Additional distinctions between expenditures and expenses will be made in Chapter 3. For now, the essential difference to note is that an **expenditure** is the amount of financial resources used to acquire an asset (i.e., the cost), and an **expense** is how much of that cost expired or was used up in producing services of the period. In the example of the City of Princeton, the expenditure was $2,000,000. If the fire trucks are being depreciated over 10 years, the expense (the portion of the cost that expired) for the year is $200,000. Note that the concept of expense, particularly depreciation expense, has no relevance in accounting for the General Fund because depreciation expense does not require the use of current financial resources.

Proprietary Funds

Proprietary funds of a government follow accounting and financial reporting principles that are similar to those for commercial business entities. As in business, if a government intends to charge users for the goods or services provided, its officials need to know the full cost of those goods and services in order to determine appropriate prices or fees. Determining the full cost is also essential in deciding whether the government should continue to produce or provide particular goods or services or to contract for them with an outside vendor. Accrual accounting, including depreciation of capital assets, is essential for governments to determine the full cost of providing business-type services and to report on the extent to which each such activity is covering its full cost of operation.

As Illustration 2–1 shows, there are two types of proprietary funds: *internal service funds* and *enterprise funds*. Legislative approval is ordinarily required to establish proprietary funds, although they may be required by law or contractual provisions such as debt covenants. The two funds differ primarily in terms of their objectives and the way the financial information of each type of fund is reported in the fund and government-wide financial statements. Accounting and financial reporting requirements for proprietary funds are covered in depth in Chapter 7 of this text. Thus, only a brief overview is provided in this chapter.

Internal service funds are created to improve the management of resources and generally provide goods or services to departments or agencies of the same government and sometimes to other governments on a cost-reimbursement basis. Examples of services typically accounted for by internal service funds include central purchasing and warehousing of supplies, motor pools, centralized data processing, and self-insurance pools.

Enterprise funds *may* be used to account for activities in which goods or services are provided to the public for a fee that is the principal source of revenue for the fund. GASB standards *require* the use of an enterprise fund if:

1. The activity is financed with debt that is secured solely by a pledge of the net revenues from fees and charges of the activity.
2. Laws or regulations require that the activity's costs of providing services, including capital costs (such as depreciation or debt service), be recovered with fees and charges rather than with taxes or similar revenues.
3. The pricing policies of the activity establish fees and charges designed to recover its costs, including capital costs.[11]

As noted earlier, financial reporting differs for internal service funds and enterprise funds. *Major* (as defined in footnote 7) enterprise funds are reported in separate columns of the three proprietary fund financial statements: statement of net assets; statement of revenues, expenses, and changes in fund net assets; and statement of cash flows. As shown in Illustrations 1–10, 1–11, and 1–12, the City and County of Denver has two major enterprise funds, the Wastewater Management Fund and the Denver Airport System Fund. Major fund reporting does not apply to internal service funds. Instead, these funds are all reported in a single column of the proprietary fund financial statements.

To reinforce a point made previously, all internal service fund financial information is generally reported in the Governmental Activities column of the government-wide financial statements, unless an internal service fund predominantly serves a proprietary fund, in which case it is reported in the Business-type Activities column of the government-wide financial statements. Thus, for most governments the information reported in the business-type activities column of the government-wide financial statements will be the same as the enterprise fund totals reported in the proprietary fund financial statements. Furthermore, since the business-type activity financial information is reported using the same measurement focus and basis of

---

[11] GASB *Codification*, Sec. 1300.109.

accounting in the proprietary fund and government-wide financial statements, there is no need to reconcile any differences between the statements or to use a dual-track approach.

Fiduciary Funds

Fiduciary activities of a government are reported using the same principles as proprietary fund and government-wide financial statements: the economic resources measurement focus and accrual basis of accounting. It is worth mentioning again that fiduciary activities are reported *only* in the fiduciary fund financial statements (statement of fiduciary net assets and statement of changes in fiduciary net assets) and not in the government-wide financial statements (see Illustration 2–1). Examples of the two fiduciary fund statements for the City and County of Denver are provided in Illustrations 1–13 and 1–14. These statements present financial information for the City and County pension trust funds, private-purpose trust fund, and agency funds.

The fiduciary fund category consists of agency funds and three types of trust funds: investment trust funds, pension trust funds, and private-purpose trust funds. **Agency funds** generally are used when the government holds cash on a custodial basis for a private party (individual, organization, or government). Examples are taxes or fees collected by a government on behalf of other governments. There are no net assets in agency funds, since for every dollar of assets held there is a dollar of liability to the private party (total assets in the fund always equal total liabilities).

Trust funds differ from agency funds primarily in the length of time and the manner in which resources are held and managed. In most cases, trust fund assets include investments whose earnings add to the net assets of the fund and which can be used for a specified purpose. Examples of trust funds are funds that hold assets in trust to provide retirement benefits for employees (**pension trust funds**), **investment trust funds** used to report the equity of external participants (typically other governments) in a sponsoring government's investment pool, and **private-purpose trust funds** created to benefit private individuals, such as a fund to provide scholarships for the children of firefighters and police officers killed in the line of duty.

Accounting for trust funds is typically much more complex than just accounting for investments. For example, a large, legally separate state pension plan usually has significant capital assets such as land, buildings, and equipment to report in its financial statements. The expenses of the plan include personnel, supplies, utilities, depreciation, and other items, in addition to investment-related expenses. Accounting for fiduciary funds is discussed in depth in Chapter 8 of the text.

Summary of Government-Wide and Fund Characteristics

Illustration 2–3 summarizes the characteristics and principles of accounting and reporting for government-wide and fund categories, as discussed in this chapter. One topic not discussed in this chapter is budgetary accounting, which is a main topic of Chapter 3. As shown in Illustration 2–3, budgetary accounts are integrated into the accounts of certain governmental funds, primarily the General Fund and special revenue funds, but often other governmental funds as well. Chapter 3 also covers other important subjects such as how governmental activity revenues and expenses are classified in the government-wide financial statements and how revenues and *expenditures* are classified in the governmental funds. In addition, Chapter 3 distinguishes other financial resource inflows and outflows, such as other financing sources and uses, from revenues and expenditures.

ILLUSTRATION 2–3   Summary of Government-wide and Fund Characteristics

Characteristics	Government-wide	Governmental Funds	Proprietary Funds	Fiduciary Funds[c]
Types of funds	NA[a]	General, special revenue, debt service, capital projects, permanent	Enterprise, internal service[b]	Agency, investment trust, pension trust, private-purpose trust
Accountability focus	Operational accountability	Fiscal accountability	Operational accountability	Operational accountability
Measurement focus	Economic resources	Current financial resources	Economic resources	Economic resources
Basis of accounting	Accrual	Modified accrual	Accrual	Accrual
Required financial statements	Statement of net assets; statement of activities	Balance sheet; statement of revenues, expenditures, and changes in fund balances	Statement of net assets; statement of revenues, expenses, and changes in fund net assets; statement of cash flows	Statement of fiduciary net assets, statement of changes in fiduciary net assets
Balance sheet/statement of net assets accounts	Current and noncurrent assets, current and noncurrent liabilities, net assets	Current assets, current liabilities, fund balances (equity)	Current and noncurrent assets, current and noncurrent liabilities, net assets	Current and noncurrent assets, current and noncurrent liabilities, net assets[d]
Operating or change statement accounts	Revenues, expenses	Revenues, expenditures, other financing sources/uses	Revenues, expenses	Additions, deductions[e]
Budgetary accounting	Not formally integrated into the accounts	Formally integrated into accounts of certain funds	Not formally integrated into the accounts	Not formally integrated into the accounts

[a]Funds are not applicable to the government-wide financial statements.
[b]Financial information for internal service funds is usually reported in the Governmental Activities column of the government-wide financial statements, unless the funds predominantly benefit enterprise funds. In that case, internal service fund information would be reported in the Business-type Activities column.
[c]Fiduciary activities are reported only in the fund financial statements, not in the government-wide financial statements.
[d]Agency funds have no net assets since total assets equal total liabilities for these funds.
[e]Because fiduciary fund resources benefit private parties and cannot be used to provide governmental services, increases in fiduciary fund net assets are not revenues of the government, nor are decreases expenses of the government. Instead, increases in fiduciary net assets are reported as *additions* and decreases are reported as *deductions*. Since, agency funds have no net assets, they cannot have additions or deductions.

Summary Statement of Governmental Accounting and Financial Reporting Principles

Following is a summary statement of accounting and financial reporting principles for state and local governments, as modified by GASB *Statement No. 34*.[A1] Principles summarized here that have not been discussed in Chapters 1 and 2 will be covered in depth in following chapters.

1. **Accounting and Reporting Capabilities**

   A governmental accounting system must make it possible both: (a) to present fairly and with full disclosure the funds and activities of the government in conformity with generally accepted accounting principles, and (b) to determine and demonstrate compliance with finance-related legal and contractual provisions.

2. **Fund Accounting Systems**

   Governmental accounting systems should be organized and operated on a fund basis. A fund is defined as a fiscal and accounting entity with a self-balancing set of accounts recording cash and other financial resources, together with all related liabilities and residual equities or balances, and changes therein, which are segregated for the purpose of carrying on specific activities or attaining certain objectives in accordance with special regulations, restrictions, or limitations. Fund financial statements should be used to report detailed information about the primary government, including its blended component units. The focus of governmental and proprietary fund financial statements is on major funds.

3. **Types of Funds**

   The following types of funds should be used by state and local governments to the extent that they have activities that meet the criteria for using those funds.

   a. **Governmental Funds**

      (1) *The General Fund*—to account for all financial resources except those required to be accounted for in another fund.

      (2) *Special Revenue Funds*—to account for the proceeds of specific revenue sources (other than private-purpose trusts or for major capital projects) that are legally restricted to use for specified purposes.

      (3) *Capital Projects Funds*—to account for financial resources to be used for the acquisition or construction of major capital facilities (other than those financed by proprietary funds and trust funds).

      (4) *Debt Service Funds*—to account for the accumulation of resources for, and the payment of, general long-term debt principal and interest.

      (5) *Permanent Funds*—to account for legally restricted resources provided by trust in which the earnings but not the principal may be used for purposes that support the primary government's programs (those that benefit the government or its citizenry). [Note: Similar permanent trusts that benefit private individuals, organizations, or other governments—that is, private-purpose trust funds—are classified as fiduciary funds, as shown below.]

   b. **Proprietary Funds**

      (6) *Enterprise Funds*—to account for operations (*a*) that are financed and operated in a manner similar to private business enterprises—where the intent of the gov-

---

[A1] Source: GASB *Codification*, Sec. 1100.101–114.

erning body is that the costs (expenses, including depreciation) of providing goods or services to the general public on a continuing basis be financed or recovered primarily through user charges; or (*b*) where the governing body has decided that periodic determination of revenues earned, expenses incurred, and/or net income is appropriate for capital maintenance, public policy, management control, accountability, or other purposes.

    (7) *Internal Service Funds*—to account for the financing of goods or services provided by one department or agency to other departments or agencies of the governmental unit, or to other governmental units, on a cost-reimbursement basis.

  c. **Fiduciary Funds** (and similar component units). These are *trust* and *agency funds* that are used to account for assets held by a governmental unit in a trustee capacity or as an agent for individuals, private organizations, and other governmental units. These include:

    (8) Agency funds.

    (9) Pension (and other employee benefit) trust funds.

    (10) Investment trust funds.

    (11) Private-purpose trust funds.

4. **Number of Funds**

Governmental units should establish and maintain those funds required by law and sound financial administration. Only the minimum number of funds consistent with legal and operating requirements should be established, however, because unnecessary funds result in inflexibility, undue complexity, and inefficient financial administration.

5. **Reporting Capital Assets**

A clear distinction should be made between general capital assets and capital assets of proprietary and fiduciary funds. Capital assets of proprietary funds should be reported in both the government-wide and fund financial statements. Capital assets of fiduciary funds should be reported in only the statement of fiduciary net assets. All other capital assets of the governmental unit are general capital assets. They should not be reported as assets in governmental funds but should be reported in the Governmental Activities column in the governmental-wide statement of net assets.

6. **Valuation of Capital Assets**

Capital assets should be reported at historical cost. The cost of a capital asset should include capitalized interest (not applicable to general capital assets) and ancillary charges necessary to place the asset into its intended location and condition for use. Donated capital assets should be reported at their estimated fair value at the time of the acquisition plus ancillary charges, if any.

7. **Depreciation of Capital Assets**

Capital assets should be depreciated over their estimated useful lives unless they are either inexhaustible or are infrastructure assets using the modified approach as set forth in *GASBS 34*, pars. 23–26. Inexhaustible assets such as land and land improvements should not be depreciated. Depreciation expense should be reported in the government-wide statement of activities; the proprietary fund statement of revenues, expenses, and changes in fund net assets; and the statement of changes in fiduciary net assets.

8. **Reporting Long-Term Liabilities**

A clear distinction should be made between fund long-term liabilities and general long-term liabilities. Long-term liabilities directly related to and expected to be paid from proprietary funds should be reported in the proprietary fund statement of net assets and in the government-wide statement of net assets. Long-term liabilities directly related to and expected to be paid from fiduciary funds should be reported in the statement of fiduciary net assets. All other unmatured general long-term liabilities of the governmental unit should not be reported in governmental funds but should be reported in the Governmental Activities column in the government-wide statement of net assets.

9. **Measurement Focus and Basis of Accounting in the Basic Financial Statements**
   a. Government-wide Financial Statements
   The government-wide statement of net assets and statement of activities should be prepared using the economic resources measurement focus and the accrual basis of accounting. Revenues, expenses, gains, losses, assets, and liabilities resulting from the exchange and exchange-like transactions should be recognized when the exchange takes place. Revenues, expenses, assets, and liabilities resulting from nonexchange transactions should be recognized in accordance with [*Codification*] Section N50, "Nonexchange Transactions."
   b. Fund Financial Statements
   In fund financial statements, the modified accrual or accrual basis of accounting, as appropriate, should be used in measuring financial position and operating results.
   (1) Financial statements for governmental funds should be presented using the current financial resources measurement focus and the modified accrual basis of accounting. Revenues should be recognized in the accounting period in which they become available and measurable. Expenditures should be recognized in the accounting period in which the fund liability is incurred, if measurable, except for unmatured interest on general long-term liabilities, which should be recognized when due.
   (2) Proprietary fund statements of net assets and revenues, expenses, and changes in fund net assets should be presented using the economic resources measurement focus and the accrual basis of accounting.
   (3) Financial statements of fiduciary funds should be reported using the economic resources measurement focus and the accrual basis of accounting, except for the recognition of certain liabilities of defined benefit pension plans and certain postemployment healthcare plans.
   (4) Transfers between funds should be reported in the accounting period in which the interfund receivable and payable arise.

10. **Budgeting, Budgetary Control, and Budgetary Reporting**
    a. An annual budget(s) should be adopted by every governmental unit.
    b. The accounting system should provide the basis for appropriate budgetary control.
    c. Budgetary comparison schedules should be presented as required supplementary information (RSI) for the General Fund and each major special revenue fund that has a legally adopted annual budget.

11. **Transfer, Revenue, Expenditure, and Expense Account Classification**
    a. Transfers should be classified separately from revenues and expenditures or expenses in the basic financial statements.
    b. Proceeds of general long-term debt issues should be classified separately from revenues and expenditures in the governmental fund financial statements.
    c. Governmental fund revenues should be classified by fund and source. Expenditures should be classified by fund, function (or program), organization unit, activity, character, and principal classes of objects.
    d. Proprietary fund revenues should be reported by major sources, and expenses should be classified in essentially the same manner as those of similar business organizations, functions, or activities.

e. The statement of activities should present *governmental* activities at least at the level of detail required in the governmental fund statement of revenues, expenditures, and changes in fund balance—at a minimum by *function*. Governments should present *business-type* activities at least by *segment*.

12. **Common Terminology and Classification**

A common terminology and classification should be used consistently throughout the budget, the accounts, and the financial reports of each fund.

13. **Annual Financial Reports**

a. A comprehensive annual financial report (CAFR) should be prepared and published, covering all activities of the primary government (including its blended component units) and providing an overview of all discretely presented component units of the reporting entity—including introductory section, management's discussion and analysis (MD&A), basic financial statements, required supplementary information other than MD&A, combining and individual fund statements, schedules, narrative explanations, and statistical section. The reporting entity is the primary government (including its blended component units) and all discretely presented component units presented in accordance with [*Codification*] Section 2100, "Defining the Financial Reporting Entity."

b. The minimum requirements for MD&A, basic financial statements, and required supplementary information other than MD&A are:

(1) Management's discussion and analysis.

(2) Basic financial statements. The basic financial statements should include:

(a) Government-wide financial statements.

(b) Fund financial statements.

(c) Notes to the financial statements.

(3) Required supplementary information other than MD&A.

c. As discussed in [*Codification*] Section 2100, the financial reporting entity consists of (1) the primary government, (2) organizations for which the primary government is financially accountable, and (3) other organizations for which the nature and significance of their relationship with the primary government are such that exclusion would cause the reporting entity's basic financial statements to be misleading or incomplete. The reporting entity's government-wide financial statements should display information about the reporting government as a whole distinguishing between the total primary government and its discretely presented component units as well as between the primary government's governmental and business-type activities. The reporting entity's fund financial statements should present the primary government's (including its blended component units, which are, in substance, part of the primary government) major funds individually and nonmajor funds in the aggregate. Funds and component units that are fiduciary in nature should be reported only in the statements of fiduciary net assets and changes in fiduciary net assets.

d. The nucleus of a financial reporting entity usually is a primary government. However, a governmental organization other than a primary government (such as a component unit, joint venture, jointly governed organization, or other stand-alone government) serves as the nucleus for its own reporting entity when it issues separate financial statements. For all of these entities, the provisions of [*Codification*] Section 2100 should be applied in layers "from the bottom up." At each layer, the definition and display provisions should be applied before the layer is included in the financial statements of the next level of the reporting government.

Key Terms

Accrual basis, *36*
Agency funds, *45*
Available, *41*
Blending, *35*
Business-type
   activities, *34*
Capital projects funds, *41*
Component units, *35*
Current financial
   resources, *41*
Debt service funds, *39*
Discrete presentation, *35*
Economic resources
   measurement focus, *36*

Enterprise funds, *44*
Escheat properties, *34*
Expenditure, *43*
Expense, *43*
Fiduciary activities, *34*
Fund, *38*
Fund balances, *41*
Fund equity, *41*
General Fund, *39*
Governmental
   activities, *34*
Governmental funds, *39*
Internal service funds, *44*

Investment trust funds, *45*
Major funds, *38*
Modified accrual, *41*
Pension trust funds, *45*
Permanent funds, *41*
Primary government, *35*
Private-purpose trust
   funds, *45*
Proprietary funds, *43*
Reporting entity, *34*
Special revenue
   funds, *39*

Selected References

Governmental Accounting Standards Board. *Codification of Governmental Accounting and Financial Reporting Standards as of June 30, 2005.* Norwalk, CT, 2005.

Governmental Accounting Standards Board, *Statement No. 34.* Norwalk, CT, 1999.

Questions

2–1. Describe the governmental activities of a state or local government and identify the measurement focus and basis of accounting used in accounting and financial reporting for these activities.

2–2. Describe the business-type activities of a state or local government and explain how and why accounting and financial reporting for business-type activities differ from those for governmental activities.

2–3. Describe the fiduciary activities of a state or local government and explain how accounting and financial reporting for fiduciary activities differ from those for governmental and business-type activities.

2–4. What organizations does the governmental reporting entity include? Define *primary* government. How does the primary government differ from a *component* unit?

2–5. "If a discrete presentation is used for the financial data of a component unit in the statement of net assets of a governmental financial reporting entity, there is no need for the component unit to issue a separate financial report." Is this statement true or false? What other method may be allowed to include a component unit's financial information with the reporting entity's?

2–6. What alternatives are acceptable under GASB standards for reporting financial information of major component units in the reporting entity's CAFR?

2–7. "If legal or regulatory compliance requires different accounting information than is required by generally accepted accounting principles (GAAP), a government should comply with legal or regulatory requirements and disregard GAAP requirements." Do you agree with this statement? Why or why not?

2–8. What is the distinction between fund long-term liabilities and general long-term liabilities? Between fund capital assets and general capital assets?

2–9. Explain the measurement focus and basis of accounting used in preparing the two government-wide financial statements and the two governmental fund financial statements? Why do these differ?

2–10. Explain in your own words what makes up the *GASBS 34* integrated accounting and financial reporting model.

Cases

2–1 Defining the Reporting Entity. Use the comprehensive annual financial report (CAFR) obtained for Exercise/Problem 1–1, or else locate one for a local government using either the government's own Web site or the Governmental Accounting Standards Board's Web site under the link "GASB 34." Review the notes to the financial statements to find the note that describes the government's reporting entity. Prepare a brief written report summarizing the legally separate organizations that are included as component units of the governmental reporting entity and those that were excluded, and the reasons given for inclusion or exclusion. Also, indicate whether each component unit is reported by blending or by discrete presentation. How and where is financial information for individual component units reported? Describe any legally separate organizations identified as "related organizations" and why they are accorded this treatment.

2–2 Activities and Funds. Using the CAFR accessed for Exercise 1–1 or Case 2–1, prepare a brief report describing the governmental, business-type, and fiduciary activities of the governmental unit, and a listing of the names of the funds used to account for these activities. Which funds are identified as *major funds?* Are nonmajor governmental and enterprise funds reported in combining financial statements?

2–3 Accounting and Reporting Principles. For more than 100 years, the financial statements of the Town of Brookfield have consisted of a statement of cash receipts and a statement of cash disbursements prepared by the town treasurer for each of its three funds: the General Fund, the Road Tax Fund, and the Sewer Fund. As required by state law, the town submits its financial statements to the Office of the State Auditor; however, its financial statements have never been audited by an independent auditor.

Because of its growing population (nearing 2,000) and increasing financial complexity, the town has hired Emily Eager, who recently obtained her CPA certificate, to supervise all accounting and financial reporting operations. Having worked two years for a CPA firm in a nearby town, Ms. Eager gained limited experience auditing not-for-profit organizations, as well as compiling financial statements for small businesses. Although she has little knowledge of governmental accounting, she is confident that her foundation in business and not-for-profit accounting will enable her to handle the job.

For the year ended December 31, 2008, Ms. Eager has prepared the following unaudited financial statements for the Town of Brookfield. Study these financial statements and answer the questions that follow.

TOWN OF BROOKFIELD
BALANCE SHEET
December 31, 2008
(unaudited)

Assets

Cash	$ 1,740
Taxes receivable	18,555
Investments	7,468
Due from other governments	28,766
Land, buildings, and equipment (net of accumulated depreciation of $132,640)	287,580
Total assets	$344,109

Liabilities and Net Assets

Accounts payable	$ 3,892
Due to other governments	11,943
Total liabilities	15,835
Net assets—unrestricted	299,893
Net assets—restricted	28,381
Total net assets	328,274
Total liabilities and net assets	$344,109

TOWN OF BROOKFIELD
STATEMENT OF ACTIVITIES
Year Ended December 31, 2008
(unaudited)

Revenues	
Property taxes	$124,870
Sewer fees	6,859
Investment income	239
Total revenues	131,968
Expenses	
Government services	115,958
Sewer services	7,227
Miscellaneous	8,462
Total expenses	131,647
Increase in net assets	321
Net assets, January 1, 2008	327,953
Net assets, December 31, 2008	$328,274

Required

a. Assume that you are a CPA whom Ms. Eager has contacted about the possibility of performing an audit of the Town of Brookfield's financial statements. Based on your preliminary review, what concerns would you have about these financial statements? Do the statements appear to conform to GAAP? In what respects, if any, do the financial statements depart from GAAP?

b. Assume, instead, that you are a member of the town council or a citizen; what concerns would you have with these financial statements?

Exercises and Problems

2–1 Examine the CAFR. Utilizing the CAFR obtained for Exercise/Problem 1–1, examine the financial statements included in the financial section and answer the following questions. If the CAFR you have obtained does not conform to GAAP, it is recommended that you obtain one that does.

a. Government-wide Statements. What are the titles of the two government-wide statements? Are total assets larger for governmental activities or business-type activities? Which function or program has the highest net cost? What kinds of general revenues are available to cover the net cost of governmental activities? Were business-type activities "profitable"? That is, is the excess of revenues over expenses positive? Are there any component units that are discretely presented as a column on the government-wide financial statements?

b. General Fund. What title is given to the fund that functions as the General Fund of the reporting entity? Does the report state the basis of accounting used for the General Fund? What types of assets are included on the governmental funds balance sheet? Do current and noncurrent assets appear on the balance sheet? Do current and noncurrent liabilities appear on the balance sheet? Is this reporting consistent with the basis of accounting being followed?

c. Other Governmental Fund Types. List the names of governmental funds other than the General Fund that are included as major funds in the fund financial statements. Identify which of the major funds, if applicable, are special revenue funds, debt service funds, capital projects funds, and permanent funds.

d. Proprietary Funds. List the names of the proprietary fund types included in the financial statements. Do the financial statements provide evidence that all proprietary funds use full accrual accounting?

e. Fiduciary Funds. List the names of the fiduciary funds included in the fund financial statements. Identify whether each of these is an agency fund, investment trust fund, pension trust fund, or private-purpose trust fund. Do the financial statements provide evidence as to what basis of accounting these funds use?

Notes to the Financial Statements. Read the notes to the financial statements so that you can refer to them as needed in subsequent chapters. What kinds of significant accounting policies are discussed in the first note? Does the note describe the entities that are included as component units in the reporting entity? Does it list entities that are not considered component units? Are there any notes that disclose (1) any material violations of legal provisions, (2) deficit fund balances or net assets, or (3) significant commitments or contingencies?

2–2 Multiple Choice. Choose the best answer.

1. Which of the following statements is true regarding the *GASBS 34* financial reporting model?
   a. Governmental activities are reported in both fund and government-wide financial statements, using a different measurement focus and basis of accounting for each set of statements.
   b. Business-type activities are reported in both fund and government-wide financial statements, using the same measurement focus and basis of accounting for each set of statements.
   c. Fiduciary activities are reported only in fund financial statements.
   d. All of the above statements are true.

2. Which of the following would be included as part of a governmental reporting entity?
   a. A primary government and any legally separate organization located within the geographic boundaries of the primary government.

b. A primary government and any legally separate organization for which the primary government is financially accountable.

c. A primary government and any legally separate organization that requests to be included.

d. None of the above; a reporting entity consists of only a primary government.

3. In reporting *governmental activities,* operational accountability is demonstrated by:

   a. Fund financial statements.

   b. Government-wide financial statements.

   c. Both fund and government-wide financial statements.

   d. Neither fund nor government-wide financial statements.

4. Which of the following statements is true regarding the government-wide statements?

   a. Governmental activities, business-type activities, and fiduciary activities should be reported in separate columns.

   b. Blended component units should be reported as a separate column on the statements.

   c. All current and noncurrent assets and liabilities are reported in the government-wide statements.

   d. Government-wide statements are considered required supplementary information and not part of the basic financial statements.

5. Which of the following statements is true regarding the definition of a fund?

   a. A fund is a fiscal and accounting entity.

   b. A fund has a self-balancing set of accounts recording cash and other financial resources, together with all related liabilities and residual equities or balances and changes therein.

   c. Resources, related liabilities and residual equities or balances and changes therein are segregated for the purpose of carrying out specific activities or attaining certain objectives.

   d. All of the above.

6. Which of the following fund types would recognize revenues and expenditures on the modified accrual basis of accounting?

   a. An internal service fund.

   b. A permanent fund.

   c. A private-purpose trust fund.

   d. All of the above.

7. Legally restricted resources provided by trust agreements in which both principal amount and earnings thereon may only be used to support a program of the government are accounted for in:

   a. Special revenue funds.

   b. Private-purpose trust funds.

   c. Permanent funds.

   d. Pension trust funds.

8. Capital assets of proprietary funds should be reported in:

   a. Proprietary fund financial statements only.

   b. Government-wide financial statements only.

   c. Neither proprietary fund nor government-wide financial statements.

   d. Both proprietary fund and government-wide financial statements.

9. Long-term liabilities that arise from transactions of a governmental fund and are expected to be repaid from the government's general revenues are called:
   a. Noncurrent liabilities.
   b. Fund long-term liabilities.
   c. General long-term liabilities.
   d. None of the above.

10. Exhaustible general capital assets, such as buildings and equipment used by governmental activities, should:
   a. Be depreciated and reported in the Governmental Activities column of the government-wide statement of net assets.
   b. Be depreciated and reported in either the Business-type Activities column or the Governmental Activities column of the government-wide financial statements, as appropriate.
   c. Be depreciated and reported in the Governmental Activities column of the government-wide statement of net assets and the governmental funds balance sheet.
   d. Not be depreciated.

2–3 True or False. Write T if the corresponding statement is true. If the statement is false, write F and state what changes should be made to make it a true statement.

1. Activities of a general purpose government that provide the basis for GASB's financial accounting and reporting framework consist of governmental, business-type, fiduciary, and political.

2. The permanent fund is one of the several types of fiduciary funds.

3. Government-wide financial statements report financial transactions related to the governmental and business-type activities of the government, but exclude its fiduciary activities.

4. A statement of revenues, expenditures, and changes in fund balances is used to report the inflows and outflows of current financial resources of governmental funds.

5. The accounting system for proprietary funds should provide for integration of budgetary accounts.

6. Financial information for component units can be reported by blending or by discrete presentation.

7. All assets, both current and noncurrent, and all liabilities, both current and noncurrent, are reported in the government-wide financial statements.

8. Depreciation should be reported in the financial statements of the General Fund for general capital assets accounted for in the General Fund.

9. In addition to the General Fund, in governmental and proprietary fund financial statements, the only individual funds for which financial information is reported in separate columns are major funds.

10. All proprietary fund financial information is reported in the Business-type Activities column of the government-wide financial statements.

2–4 Identification of Government-wide and Fund Financial Reporting Characteristics. On the line to the right of each of the 10 fund types or characteristics listed below, insert the appropriate abbreviations for *all* government-wide or fund categories that apply to that item, using the following codes.

Government-wide governmental activities   GWGA
Government-wide business-type activities   GWBTA
Governmental funds   GF
Proprietary funds   PF
Fiduciary funds   FF

Fund Types or Characteristics

1. Fiscal accountability   _____
2. Debt service funds   _____
3. Revenues and expenses   _____
4. Operational accountability   _____
5. Modified accrual   _____
6. Statement of cash flows   _____
7. Current and noncurrent
   assets and liabilities   _____
8. Additions and deductions   _____
9. Agency funds   _____
10. Integrated budgetary accounts _____

2–5 Matching Funds with Transactions. Choose the letter of the sample transaction in the right-hand column that would most likely be reported in the fund listed in the left-hand column.

Funds	Example
1. Agency	*a.* Construction of highways, bridges, or parks.
2. Capital projects	*b.* Administrative expenses of the city manager's office.
3. Debt service	*c.* Gifts in which the principal must be invested and preserved but the investment earnings must be used to provide scholarships to children of police officers who died in the line of duty.
4. Enterprise	*d.* Costs of a central purchasing and warehouse function.
5. General	*e.* Assets held for external government participants in the government's investment pool for the purpose of earning investment income.
6. Internal service	*f.* Gifts in which the principal must be invested and preserved but the investment earnings can be used for public purposes.
7. Investment trust	*g.* Costs of operating a municipal swimming pool.
8. Pension trust	*h.* Grant revenues restricted for particular operating purposes.
9. Permanent	*i.* Assets held in trust to provide retirement benefits for municipal workers.
10. Private-purpose trust	*j.* Principal and interest payments on general long-term debt.
11. Special revenue	*k.* Taxes collected on behalf of another governmental unit.

2–6 **Determination of Major Funds.** The Village of Manchester has adopted GAAP for the current year and, therefore, is busy implementing *GASBS 34*. The village accountant is attempting to determine which of the following special revenue funds might be considered "major funds" that will be reported as a separate column on its balance sheet and statement of revenues, expenditures, and changes in fund balances for the governmental funds. She has been asked by the village manager to provide a rationale for either including or excluding each of the following funds as a major fund. Selected information is provided below.

Village of Manchester
As of (for the year ended) June 30, 2008

	Gas Tax Revenue	Housing and Urban Development Grant	Forfeitures Act	All Governmental Funds	All Governmental and Enterprise Funds
Total assets	$321,496	$350,222	$203,098	$3,127,734	$6,994,796
Total liabilities	145,102	170,866	0	1,735,066	2,974,450
Total revenues	276,672	339,928	241,178	3,074,798	5,974,974
Total expenditures	268,450	261,166	239,624	2,992,446	5,369,062

Additional information: The Forfeitures Act requires that any assets of persons convicted of drug related offenses must be forfeited to the government responsible for the arrest and subsequently sold and used for drug education programs for children. This law has been quite controversial and the subject of recent news stories in the local press.

2–7 **General Long-Term Debt and General Capital Asset Transactions.** The City of Berkeley recently issued a three-year note to finance the purchase of four police vehicles at a cost of $30,000 each.

Required

Record the issuance of the $120,000, 5 percent note and the subsequent purchase of the police vehicles in the general journals of the General Fund and governmental activities at the government-wide level. Explain why the accounting treatment is different in each journal. Is it a GAAP violation to record the issuance of the note and the purchase of the police vehicles in the General Fund?

Chapter **Three**

Governmental Operating Statement Accounts; Budgetary Accounting

Learning Objectives

After studying this chapter, you should be able to:

1. Explain how operating revenues and expenses related to governmental activities are classified and reported in the government-wide financial statements.
2. Distinguish, at the fund level, between Revenues and Other Financing Sources and between Expenditures and Other Financing Uses.
3. Explain how revenues and expenditures are classified in the General Fund.
4. Explain how budgetary accounting contributes to achieving budgetary control over revenues and expenditures, including such aspects as:

   Recording the annual budget.

   Accounting for revenues.

   Accounting for encumbrances and expenditures.

   Accounting for allotments.

   Reconciling GAAP and budgetary amounts.
5. Describe computerized accounting systems.
6. Explain the classification of revenues and expenditures of a public school system.

As discussed in Chapters 1 and 2, the GASB *Statement No. 34* financial reporting model is designed to meet the diverse needs of financial statement users and achieve the broad reporting objectives set forth in GASB *Concepts Statement No. 1*. The fund-based reporting model used for decades by state and local governments meets reasonably well the *fiscal accountability* needs of users for information about the current financial position and flows of current financial resources through the governmental funds. That model falls far short of meeting users' needs for information about the medium- to long-term impacts of the government's current operating and capital decisions, as well as information about the costs of conducting the government's functions and programs.

To meet users' broader needs for *operational accountability* information, the *GASBS 34* reporting model requires—in addition to traditional fund-based financial statements—a management's discussion and analysis (MD&A) and two government-wide financial statements: a statement of net assets or a balance sheet (a statement of financial position) and a statement of activities (an operating statement).[1] This chapter focuses on the latter statement as well as on the operating statement prepared for governmental funds.

CLASSIFICATION AND REPORTING OF REVENUES AND EXPENSES AT THE GOVERNMENT-WIDE LEVEL

The format prescribed for the government-wide statement of activities (see Illustration 3–1) displays the net expense or revenue of each function or program reported for the governmental activities of the government. As shown in Illustration 3–1, the net expense (reported in parentheses if net expense) or net revenue for each function or program is reported in the right-hand column of the top portion of the statement. One will note from the mathematical operators between column headings that the format of the top portion of the statement is as follows:

$$\text{Expenses} - \text{Program Revenues} = \text{Net (Expense) Revenue}$$

According to the GASB, reporting in the net expense or revenue format "identifies the extent to which each function of the government draws from the general revenues of the government or is self-financing through fees and intergovernmental aid."[2] The sum of general revenues and any special or extraordinary items is then added to Net (Expense) Revenue to obtain the change in net assets for the period (see Illustrations 1–5 and 3–1).

Reporting Direct and Indirect Expenses

Except for extraordinary or special item expenses, described later in this section, expenses generally are reported by function or program (see Illustration 3–1). **Direct expenses**—those that are specifically associated with a function or program—should be reported on the line for that function or program. **Indirect expenses**—those that are not directly linked to an identifiable function or program—can be reported in a variety of ways. A typical indirect expense is interest on general long-term liabilities. In most cases, interest on general long-term liabilities should be reported as a separate line item rather than being allocated to functions or programs (observe, for example, how it is reported as the last line before total government activities in Illustration 3–1).

Functions and programs are discussed in more detail later in this chapter. Governments should report *at a minimum* major functions such as those described on page 72 of this chapter or those depicted in Illustration 1–5 for the City and County of Denver. The GASB encourages governments to provide additional information for more detailed programs if such information is useful and does not detract from readers' understanding of the statement.

Some readers might find it surprising that depreciation expense often is reported as a direct expense. Depreciation expense for capital assets that are clearly identified with

---

[1]See Chapters 1 and 2 for definitions and discussions of fiscal and operational accountability.
[2]GASB *Codification*, Sec. 2200.126.

ILLUSTRATION 3–1 Format of Government-wide Statement of Activities, Governmental Activities

Functions/Programs	Expenses		Charges for Services	Program Revenues Operating Grants and Contributions	Capital Grants and Contributions	=	Net (Expense) Revenue
Primary Government:							
Function/Program 1	$ xxx,xxx		$ xxx,xxx	$ xxx,xxx	$ xxx,xxx		$ (xxx,xxx)
Function/Program 2	xxx,xxx		xxx,xxx		xxx,xxx		(xxx,xxx)
Function/Program 3	xxx,xxx		xxx,xxx	xxx,xxx			(xxx,xxx)
Function/Program 4	xxx,xxx			xxx,xxx	xxx,xxx		(xxx,xxx)
Function/Program 5	xxx,xxx		xxx,xxx	xxx,xxx	xxx,xxx		(xxx,xxx)
Interest on long-term debt	xx,xxx						(xx,xxx)
Total governmental activities	$x,xxx,xxx		$x,xxx,xxx	$x,xxx,xxx	$x,xxx,xxx		$(x,xxx,xxx)
General Revenues:							
Taxes:							
Property taxes							xxx,xxx
Sales taxes							xxx,xxx
Other taxes							xx,xxx
Grants and contributions not restricted to particular programs							xx,xxx
Investment earnings							xx,xxx
Special item—Gain on sale of government land							xx,xxx
Extraordinary item—Loss due to volcanic eruption							(xx,xxx)
Total general revenues, special items, and extraordinary items							x,xxx,xxx
Change in net assets							xx,xxx
Net assets—beginning							xxx,xxx
Net assets—ending							$ xxx,xxx

a function or program should be included in the expenses of that function or program. Similarly, depreciation expense for infrastructure assets should be reported as a direct expense of the function responsible for the infrastructure assets (for example, public works or transportation). Depreciation expense for shared assets should be allocated to functions on an appropriate basis (for example, square footage of building use). If a government opts to report unallocated depreciation expense as a separate line item, it should indicate that the amount reported on that line does not include depreciation expense reported as part of direct expense of functions or programs.[3]

To achieve full costing, some governments allocate to service functions or programs certain central administrative costs that other governments may report in the general government function. If such expenses are allocated to service functions, the allocated expenses should be reported in a separate column from the direct expenses, so the direct expenses will be more comparable with the direct expenses of similar functions of other governments. On the other hand, if a government regularly assigns administrative overhead costs to functions through an internal service fund, it is not required to eliminate these costs from the direct expenses of functions or to report them in a separate column. Rather, the government should disclose in the notes to the financial statements that such overhead charges are included as part of function/program direct expenses.[4]

The foregoing discussion should make it clear that governments find it necessary to allocate depreciation and other expenses to particular functions or programs. Allocation methods are discussed in Chapters 13 and 14 of this text and in most managerial accounting texts. In addition to classification by function or program, governmental accounting computer systems typically provide classifications of expenses/expenditures in a variety of ways. These classifications are discussed later in this chapter.

Program Revenues and General Revenues

Reporting in the net (expense) revenue format requires a government to distinguish carefully between **program revenues** and **general revenues.** As shown in Illustrations 1–5 for the City and County of Denver and 3–1, *program revenues* are reported in the functions/programs section of the statement of activities, where they reduce the net expense of each function or program or produce a net revenue. *General revenues* are not directly linked to any specific function or program and thus are reported in a separate section in the lower portion of the statement.

Three categories of *program revenues* are reported in the statement of activities (see Illustrations 1–5 and 3–1): charges for services, operating grants and contributions, and capital grants and contributions. Charges for services include charges to customers or others for both governmental and business-type activities. Charges for services within the governmental activities category include items such as licenses and permits (for example, business licenses and building permits), fines and forfeits, and operating special assessments sometimes charged for services provided outside the normal service area or beyond the normal level of services. A typical example of the latter is snow removal for or maintenance of private lanes or roads that connect with public roads normally maintained by the government. Charges to other

[3]Ibid., Sec. 2200.132.
[4]Ibid., Sec. 2200.130–131.

governments for services such as incarceration of prisoners also are reported in the Charges for Services column.

Grants and contributions restricted by other governments, organizations, or individuals for the *operating* purposes of a particular function or program should be reported in a separate column from those restricted for *capital* purposes. GASB requires that multipurpose grants and contributions be reported as *program revenues* if "the amounts restricted to each program are specifically identified in either the grant award or grant application."[5] Otherwise, multipurpose grants and contributions should be reported as *general revenue.*

Earnings from permanent funds, endowments that are restricted for a specific purpose in the endowment contract or agreement, should be reported as program revenue in the appropriate grants and contributions category. Unrestricted earnings from such sources should be reported as general revenue. In addition, all taxes, even those specified by law for a particular use (for example, motor vehicle fuel taxes that can be used only for road and bridge purposes), should be reported as general revenue.

Reporting Special Items and Transfers

In the *GASBS 34* reporting model, extraordinary items and special items must be reported as separate line items below General Revenues in the statement of activities to distinguish these nonrecurring items from normal recurring general revenues, as shown in Illustration 3–1. Separate reporting of such items serves to inform citizens and other report users when governments engage in the unusual practice of balancing their budget by selling government assets or other similar practices. **Extraordinary items** are defined in the same manner as in business accounting: "transactions or other events that are both unusual in nature and infrequent in occurrence."[6] **Special items** are items *within management's control* that may be either unusual in nature or infrequent in occurrence but not both. An example would be one-time revenues from the sale of a significant governmental asset. Extraordinary items should be reported as the last item on the statement of activities; special items should be reported before extraordinary items. Special items that are beyond management's control but are unusual or infrequent in nature (such as a loss due to civil riot) should be recorded as normal expenses expenditures or revenue, as appropriate, and be disclosed in the notes to the financial statements.

Other items that should be reported on separate lines below General Revenues (see Illustrations 1–5 and 3–1) are contributions to the principal amounts of endowments and permanent funds and transfers between funds reported as part of governmental activities and funds reported as part of business-type activities. Interfund transactions between governmental and business-type activities that involve the sale of goods or services (such as the sale of water from a water utility enterprise fund to the General Fund) are reported as program revenue and expenses, not as transfers. The reader should note that when transfers are reported, as shown in Illustration 1–5, they are reported as an inflow in one activities column and as an outflow in the other activities column, but are eliminated from the Primary Government Total column.

The preceding discussion covers the major points relating to the government-wide operating statement—the statement of activities. Some of the unique aspects of governmental fund accounting are discussed next, focusing on the General Fund.

[5]Ibid., Sec. 2200.138.
[6]Ibid., Sec. 2200.143.

STRUCTURE AND CHARACTERISTICS OF THE GENERAL FUND; CLASSIFICATION AND DESCRIPTION OF OPERATING STATEMENT ACCOUNTS

The General Fund has long been the accounting entity of a state or local government that accounts for current financial resources raised and expended for the core governmental services provided to the citizenry. The General Fund is sometimes known as an *operating fund* or *current fund;* the purpose, not the name, is the true test of identity. A typical government now engages in many activities that for legal and historical reasons are financed by sources other than those available to the General Fund. Whenever a tax or other revenue source is authorized by a legislative body to be used for a specified purpose only, a governmental unit availing itself of that source may create a special revenue fund in order to demonstrate that all revenue from that source was used for the specified purpose only. A common example of a special revenue fund is one used to account for state gasoline tax receipts distributed to a local government; in many states, the use of this money is restricted to the construction and maintenance of streets, highways, and bridges. The accounting structure specified for special revenue funds by GASB standards is identical with that specified for the General Fund.

For the sake of simplicity, and to avoid excessive repetition, the term *General Fund* will be used in the remainder of this chapter and Chapter 4 to denote all *revenue funds,* a generic name sometimes used to describe the General Fund and special revenue funds. As discussed in Chapter 2, there are three other fund types besides the General Fund and special revenue funds that are classified as governmental funds. Those other fund types are *debt service funds, capital projects funds,* and *permanent funds.* The essential characteristics of all governmental fund types were described in Chapter 2. This chapter illustrates in greater depth the manner in which generally accepted accounting principles (GAAP) are applied to the General Fund and special revenue funds. Although permanent funds obtain their revenues from permanent investments in financial securities, rather than taxes and other typical sources of governmental revenues, accounting for these funds is essentially the same as that for the General Fund and special revenue funds. Illustrative accounting transactions for a permanent fund are provided in Chapter 4. Accounting and reporting for capital projects funds and debt service funds are discussed in Chapters 5 and 6, respectively.

Governmental Fund Balance Sheet and Operating Statement Accounts

It should be emphasized that the General Fund and all other funds classified as governmental funds account for only current financial resources (cash, receivables, marketable securities, and, if material, prepaid items and inventories). Economic resources, such as land, buildings, and equipment utilized in fund operations, are not recorded by these funds because they are not normally converted into cash. Similarly, governmental funds account for only those liabilities incurred for normal operations that will be liquidated by use of fund assets. As discussed in Chapter 2, however, general capital assets and general long-term liabilities are reported in the Governmental Activities column of the statement of net assets at the government-wide level.

The arithmetic difference between the amount of financial resources and the amount of liabilities recorded in the fund is the *fund equity*. Residents of the governmental entity have no legal claim on any excess of liquid assets over current liabilities; therefore, the fund equity is not analogous to the capital accounts of an investor-owned entity. Accounts in the fund equity category of the General Fund include reserve accounts established to disclose that portions of the equity are, for reasons explained later, not available for spending, and an account called *Fund Balance* (also referred to as *Unreserved Fund Balance*), which is the portion of fund equity available for spending.

In addition to the balance sheet accounts just described, the General Fund accounts for financial transactions during a fiscal year in operating statement accounts classified as Revenues, Other Financing Sources, Expenditures, and Other Financing Uses. *Revenue* is defined as increases in fund financial resources other than from interfund transfers and debt issue proceeds. Transfers into a fund and debt issue proceeds received by a fund are classified as **other financing sources** of the fund.

Expenditure is a word that represents the cost to purchase a good or service, whereas *expense* represents the cost of a good or service consumed during the period. Recall that governmental funds are concerned only with flows of current financial resources, not with determination of income or cost of services. Thus, governmental funds report expenditures, not expenses. In the case of employee payroll, utilities, professional travel, and other similar items, expenditures and expenses are essentially the same. In other cases, such as the purchase of equipment using General Fund resources, an expenditure is recorded in the General Fund for the full cost of the equipment which differs greatly from depreciation expense, the cost of the utility of the equipment deemed to have been consumed during the year. Depreciation expense is not recorded in the General Fund because it does not represent the use of current financial resources. At the time of the purchase, the cost of the equipment is also recorded as a capital asset of government activities at the government-wide level, and the related depreciation expense is recorded as an adjusting entry at year-end.

Other financing uses, or transfers of financial resources from one fund to another fund, have the same effect on fund balance as expenditures: Both decrease the fund balance at year-end when the temporary accounts are closed. In fact, the word *expenditure* is defined as a decrease in a fund's current financial resources other than from interfund transfers. As an example, interfund transfers occur in those jurisdictions where a portion of the taxes recognized as revenue by the General Fund is transferred to a debt service fund that will recognize an expenditure for the payment of interest and principal on general long-term debt. The General Fund would debit Other Financing Uses—Interfund Transfers Out in the appropriate amount and credit Cash. The debt service fund would debit Cash in the same amount and credit Other Financing Sources—Interfund Transfers In. Thus, the use of transfer accounts achieves the desired objective that revenues be recognized in the fund that raises the taxes and expenditures be recognized in the fund that expends the revenue. Illustrative journal entries are provided in Chapter 4.

Total inflows and outflows for the operating statement accounts of the governmental funds are reported each period in a statement of revenues, expenditures, and fund balances, such as the one presented in Illustration 1–8. Illustration 3–2 presents the format for such a statement in somewhat simpler form. As discussed above, both revenues and other financing sources are temporary accounts that *increase* fund balance at year-end when closing entries are made. Similarly, expenditures and other financing uses are temporary accounts that *decrease* fund balance when closing entries are made. GASB standards emphasize, however, that other financing sources (uses) should be distinguished from revenues and expenditures. The format of the

ILLUSTRATION 3–2   **Format of Governmental Funds Statement of Revenues, Expenditures, and Changes in Fund Balances**

	General	Major Fund #2	Major Fund #3	Other Governmental Funds	Total Governmental Funds
Revenues					
Property taxes	$ xxx,xxx			$ xx,xxx	$ xxx,xxx
Sales taxes	xxx,xxx	$ xx,xxx			xxx,xxx
Fines and forfeits	xx,xxx			xx,xxx	xx,xxx
Licenses and permits	xx,xxx				xx,xxx
Other revenue sources	xx,xxx	xx,xxx	$ xx,xxx	xx,xxx	xxx,xxx
Total revenues	x,xxx,xxx	xxx,xxx	xx,xxx	xxx,xxx	x,xxx,xxx
Expenditures					
General government	xx,xxx	xx,xxx		xx,xxx	xxx,xxx
Public safety	xxx,xxx				xxx,xxx
Health and welfare	xx,xxx			xx,xxx	xxx,xxx
Other functions	xxx,xxx	xxx,xxx	xxx,xxx	xx,xxx	xxx,xxx
Total expenditures	x,xxx,xxx	xxx,xxx	xxx,xxx	xxx,xxx	x,xxx,xxx
Excess (deficiency) of revenues over expenditures	(xx,xxx)	x,xxx	(xx,xxx)	x,xxx	xx,xxx
Other financing sources (uses)					
Capital-related debt issued			xxx,xxx		xxx,xxx
Transfers in	xxx,xxx				xxx,xxx
Total other financing sources (uses)	xxx,xxx		xxx,xxx		xxx,xxx
Net changes in fund balances	x,xxx	x,xxx	x,xxx	x,xxx	xx,xxx
Fund balances—beginning	xx,xxx	xx,xxx	xx,xxx	x,xxx	xxx,xxx
Fund balances—ending	$ xx,xxx	$ xx,xxx	$ xx,xxx	$ x,xxx	$ xxx,xxx

operating statements shown in Illustrations 1–8 and 3–2 accomplishes this objective by reporting other financing sources (uses) in a separate section below the revenues and expenditures sections.

GASB standards require that the operating statement accounts of a governmental fund, such as the General Fund, be recognized on the modified accrual basis of accounting. Under this basis, revenues and other financing sources are recognized if they are *measurable* and *available*. Available means that the revenue or other financing source is expected to be collected during the current period or soon enough thereafter to pay current period obligations. In the case of property taxes, GASB requires expected collection within 60 days after the end of the current fiscal year for the taxes to be recognized as a current-period revenue.[7] Thus, if a portion of the current tax levy is not expected to be collected within 60 days, it would be recorded in the current period as a credit to Deferred Revenues (a current liability). In the following year, Deferred Revenues would be debited and Revenues would be credited. For all other

---

[7]GASB *Codification*, Sec. P70.104.

ILLUSTRATION 3–3   **Comparison of Balance Sheet, Operating Statement, and Budgetary Accounts**

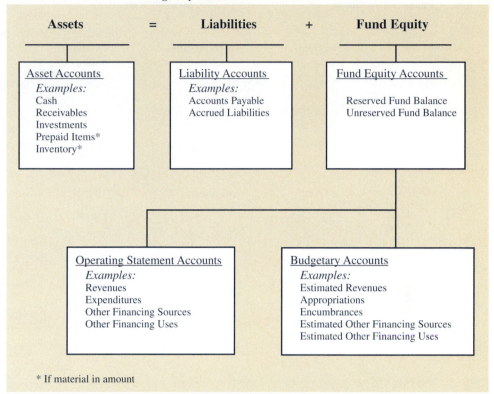

categories of revenues, as well as for other financing sources, governmental units have the discretion to determine the length of time used to define *available* (generally not more than 90 days after the current fiscal year-end) but must disclose their policy in the notes to the financial statements.[8]

The next section introduces the use of budgetary accounts in the General Fund and certain other governmental fund types that may be included in the governmental unit's formal budget. Before beginning the discussion, it is recommended that you review Illustration 3–3, which displays the relationship between budgetary accounts and the balance sheet and operating statement accounts of the General Fund. Two points should be noted in reviewing Illustration 3–3: (1) Both the operating statement accounts and the budgetary accounts are sub-fund equity temporary accounts that are closed to Fund Balance at year-end. (2) Each operating statement account has a budgetary counterpart: Revenues and Estimated Revenues; Expenditures and both Appropriations and Encumbrances (defined in the next section); Other Financing Sources and Estimated Other Financing Sources; and Other Financing Uses and Estimated Other Financing Uses. A tip that may prove useful in understanding budgetary accounting is that, with the exception of Encumbrances, the **budgetary accounts** have normal balances that are the opposite of the corresponding operating statement accounts. For example, since the Revenues account has a normal credit balance, the Estimated Revenues account has a normal debit balance. The use of opposite account balances facilitates budgetary

[8]GASB *Codification,* Sec. 1600.106.

ILLUSTRATION 3–4   **Relationship between Budgetary and Operating Statement Accounts**

Budgetary Accounts		Operating Statement Accounts		Budgetary Status
Account Title	**Normal Balance**	**Account Title**	**Normal Balance**	
Estimated Revenues	Debit	Revenues	Credit	Net balance indicates deficit (excess) of operating (actual) vs. budgeted revenues
Estimated Other Financing Sources	Debit	Other Financing Sources	Credit	Net balance indicates deficit (excess) of actual OFS vs. budgeted OFS*
Appropriations	Credit	Expenditures	Debit	Appropriations minus the sum of Expenditures and Encumbrances indicates remaining or overspent expenditure authority
Estimated Other Financing Uses	Credit	Other Financing Uses	Debit	Net balance indicates the amount of remaining or overspent interfund transfer authority
Encumbrances	Debit	NA	NA	See Appropriations line above. An encumbrance has a normal debit balance because it is a commitment to make an expenditure and often is considered the same as an expenditure for budgetary purposes

NA = Not applicable, since there is no corresponding operating statement account.
*OFS = Other Financing Sources.

comparisons and makes it easy to determine whether actual amounts are under or over the budgeted amounts. Illustration 3–4 shows the normal balances of each budgetary account and its corresponding operating statement account.

BUDGETARY ACCOUNTS

The fact that budgets are legally binding upon administrators has led to the integration of budgetary accounts into the general ledgers of the General Fund and special revenue funds, and all other funds required by state laws to adopt a budget. *GASBS 34* requires that a budget to actual comparison schedule be provided for the General Fund and for each *major* special revenue fund for which a budget is legally adopted.[9] *GASBS 34*

---

[9]Ibid., Sec. 2200.182. See the glossary for the definition of *major fund*.

recommends that these schedules be provided as required supplementary information (RSI), which should be placed immediately following the notes to the financial statements. *GASBS 34* provides the option, however, for governments to report the budgetary comparison information in a budgetary comparison *statement,* a statement of revenues, expenditures, and changes in fund balances—budget and actual, which would then be part of the basic financial statements.[10]

Illustration 3–5 presents an example of a budgetary comparison schedule for the General Fund and Human Services Special Revenue Fund of the City and County of Denver. GASB standards require, at a minimum, the presentation of both the originally adopted and final amended budgets and actual amounts of inflows, outflows, and balances. A variance column, such as that included in the City and County of Denver's budgetary comparison schedule, is encouraged but not required since a financial statement user could calculate the variances himself or herself. Of particular note in this schedule is the row caption *Budget Basis Expenditures.* In a note to the required supplementary information, the City and County of Denver explains that budgets for appropriation in the general, special revenue, and capital projects funds are not adopted on a basis consistent with GAAP, as encumbrances outstanding at year-end are treated as expenditures. As explained in the following paragraph, the budget basis of some governments departs even further from GAAP.

In order to achieve meaningful budgetary comparisons, the actual amounts in the schedule should be reported using the government's budgetary basis. Some governments, for example, budget their revenues on the cash basis. If the Actual Amounts column of the budgetary comparison schedule (or statement) uses a non-GAAP budgetary basis, such as the cash basis, either the schedule captions or column heading for actual amounts should so indicate, as in Illustration 3–5.

Budgetary practices of a government may differ from GAAP accounting practices in respects other than basis. GASB standards identify timing, entity, and perspective differences. Discussion of these differences is beyond the scope of this text; it is sufficient to emphasize that GASB standards require that the amounts shown in the Actual Amounts column of the budgetary comparison schedule conform in all respects with practices used to develop the amounts shown in the Budgeted Amounts columns of the schedule so that there is a true comparison. Standards further require that either on the face of the budgetary comparison schedule or on a separate schedule, the amounts reported in the Actual Amounts column of the budgetary comparison schedule must be reconciled with the GAAP amounts shown in the statement of revenues, expenditures, and changes in fund balances. The City and County of Denver provides its reconciliation at the bottom of the budgetary comparison schedule (see Illustration 3–5).

In order to achieve budgetary control, only three general ledger budgetary control accounts are needed in the General Fund (and other funds for which a budget is adopted): **Estimated Revenues, Appropriations,** and **Encumbrances.** Subsidiary ledger accounts should be provided in whatever detail is required by law or for sound financial administration to support each of the three control accounts. Budgeted interfund transfers and debt proceeds may be recorded in two additional budgetary control accounts: **Estimated Other Financing Sources** and **Estimated Other Financing Uses.** Again, these control accounts should be supported by subsidiary detail accounts as needed.

---

[10]Ibid., footnote 35.

Illustration 3–5

CITY AND COUNTY OF DENVER
Required Supplementary Information
Budgetary Comparison Schedule
General Fund and Human Services Special Revenue Fund
For the year ended December 31, 2004
(amounts expressed in thousands)

| | General Fund | | | | Human Services Special Revenue Fund | | | |
| | Budget | | | | Budget | | | |
	Original	Final	Actual	Variance with Final Budget	Original	Final	Actual	Variance with Final Budget
REVENUES								
Taxes	$500,937	$500,937	$504,823	$ 3,886			$ 39,104	
Licenses and permits	16,618	16,618	23,439	6,821			—	
Intergovernmental revenues	30,319	30,319	29,212	(1,107)			63,973	
Charges for services	97,728	97,728	103,878	6,150			1,302	
Investment and interest income	3,000	3,000	3,994	994			28	
Fines and forfeitures	33,479	33,479	31,159	(2,320)			—	
Contributions	—	—	116	116			38	
Other revenue	12,063	12,063	12,328	265			1,503	
TOTAL REVENUES	694,144	694,144	708,949	14,805			105,948	
BUDGET BASIS EXPENDITURES								
General government	154,021	154,690	144,383	10,307	$ —	$ —	—	$ —
Public safety	333,836	339,913	338,224	1,689	—	—	—	—
Public works	70,422	69,330	67,951	1,379	—	—	—	—
Human services	—	—	—	—	116,866	123,339	110,032	13,307
Health	40,517	40,649	40,415	234	—	—	—	—
Parks and recreation	41,705	41,986	40,879	1,107	—	—	—	—
Cultural activities	28,009	28,981	28,954	27	—	—	—	—
Community development	16,617	16,830	16,152	678	—	—	—	—
TOTAL BUDGET BASIS EXPENDITURES	685,127	692,379	676,958	15,421	$116,866	$123,339	110,032	$13,307

Illustration 3-5 (Continued)

	General Fund				Human Services Special Revenue Fund			
	Budget				Budget			
	Original	Final	Actual	Variance with Final Budget	Original	Final	Actual	Variance with Final Budget
Excess (deficiency) of revenues over budget basis expenditures	9,017	1,765	31,991	30,226			(4,084)	
OTHER FINANCING SOURCES (USES)								
Capital leases	—	—	1,705	1,705				
Transfers in	19,000	19,000	18,175	(825)			105	105
Transfers out	(29,746)	(38,183)	(38,183)	—			—	—
TOTAL OTHER FINANCING SOURCES (USES)	(10,746)	(19,183)	(18,303)	880			105	105
Excess of revenues and other financing sources over budget basis expenditures and other financing uses	$ (1,729)	$ (17,418)	13,688	$31,106			(3,979)	
Add outstanding encumbrances			12,349				7,410	
Less prior year encumbrances, as adjusted			(11,678)				(6,573)	
Add grantor expenditures			—				6,073	
Less capital outlay			(1,705)				—	
Net change in fund balances			12,654				2,931	
Fund balance—January 1			153,307				11,748	
FUND BALANCE—December 31			$165,961				$14,679	

TERMINOLOGY AND CLASSIFICATION FOR GOVERNMENTAL FUND BUDGETS AND ACCOUNTS

Budgets may be described as legally approved plans of financial operations embodying the authorization of expenditures for specified purposes to be made during the budget period and the proposed means of financing them. The sequence of budget preparation in practice is often the same as the sequence in the preceding sentence: Expenditures are planned first; then plans are made to finance the expenditures. For that reason, the discussion in this chapter follows the same sequence. Governmental budgeting is discussed in more detail in Chapter 13.

Classification of Appropriations and Expenditures

An appropriation, when enacted into law, is an authorization to incur on behalf of the governmental unit liabilities for goods, services, and facilities to be used for purposes specified in the appropriation ordinance, or statute, in amounts not in excess of those specified for each purpose. When liabilities authorized by an appropriation have been incurred, the appropriation is said to be *expended*. Thus, budgeted appropriations are sometimes called *estimated expenditures*. Expenditures, then, are expended appropriations. According to the GASB Transfer, Revenue, Expenditure, and Expense Account Classifications Principle (see Chapter 2, Appendix), expenditures should be classified by (1) fund, (2) function or program, (3) organization unit, (4) activity, (5) character, and (6) object. The GASB Common Terminology and Classification Principle should also be reviewed at this time. It provides that a common terminology and classification should be used consistently throughout the budget, the accounts, and the financial reports of each fund.

Classification by Fund

The primary classification of governmental expenditures is by fund, since a fund is the basic fiscal and accounting entity of a governmental unit. Within each fund, the other five classifications itemized in the preceding paragraph are used to facilitate the aggregation and analysis of data to meet the objectives of financial reporting set forth in Chapter 1.

Classification by Function or Program

The GASB distinguishes between functions and programs in the following manner:

> **Functions** group related activities that are aimed at accomplishing a major service or regulatory responsibility. **Programs** group activities, operations, or organizational units that are directed to the attainment of specific purposes or objectives.[11] [Emphasis added.]

Examples of common functional classifications are the following:

General Government   Health and Welfare
Public Safety   Culture and Recreation
Highways and Streets

A good example of program classification is found in the City of Oakland, California's FY 2003–05 Adopted Policy Budget, which classifies numerous operating objectives and programs under seven broad goals:

---

[11]GASB, *Codification*, Sec. 1800.117.

Make Oakland a Safe City

Develop a Sustainable City

Improve Oakland's Neighborhoods

Ensure that All Oakland Youth
and Seniors Have the Opportunity
to Be Successful

Model Best Practices to Improve
Customer Services and to Be a Fiscally
Sound and Efficiently Run City

Maintain and Enhance Oakland's
Physical Assets

Inspire Creativity and Civic Engagement

Classification by Organization Unit

Classification of expenditures by **organization unit** is considered essential to management control, assuming the organizational structure or given governmental unit provides clear lines of responsibility and authority. Some examples of organization units that might be found in a city are these:

Police Department

Fire Department

Building Safety Department

Public Works Department

City Attorney

City Clerk

Personnel Department

Parks and Recreation Department

The key distinction between classification of expenditures by organization unit and classification by program or function is that responsibility for a department is fixed, whereas a number of departments may be involved in the performance of a program or a function. Both management control within a department and rational allocation of resources within the governmental unit require much more specific identification of expenditures (and costs and expenses) than is provided by the major classifications illustrated thus far. The next step needed is classification by activity.

Classification by Activity

An **activity** is a specific and distinguishable line of work performed by an organization unit. For example, within the public works department, activities such as the following may be performed:

Solid waste collection—residential

Solid waste collection—commercial

Solid waste disposal—landfill

Solid waste disposal—incineration

Activity classification is more meaningful if responsibility for the performance of each activity is fixed, performance standards are established, and a good management accounting system is installed to measure input of resources consumed (dollars, personnel time, equipment, and facilities used) relative to units of service outputs. Such information is useful to those interested in assessing the efficiency of government operations.

The GASB recommends that expenditures also be classified by character.

Classification by Character

Classification by **character,** as defined by the GASB, is based on the fiscal period that benefits from a particular expenditure. A common classification of expenditures by character recognizes three groups:

Current expenditures

Capital outlays

Debt service

Current expenditures are expected to benefit the period in which the expenditure is made. Capital outlays are expected to benefit not only the period in which the capital assets are acquired but as many future periods as the assets provide service. Debt service includes payment of interest on debt and payment of debt principal; if the debt was wisely incurred, residents received benefits in prior periods from the assets acquired by use of debt financing, are receiving benefits currently, and will continue to receive benefits until the service lives of the assets expire.

Character classification of expenditures is potentially of great significance to taxpayers and other citizens. Properly used, it could give them valuable information for appraising the cost of government during a given period. Generally speaking, expenditures for debt service relate to actions incurred by previous administrations. Capital outlays are current expenditures expected to provide benefits in future periods; however, as discussed earlier in this chapter, GASB standards do not allow depreciation expense to be recorded in governmental funds, but require that depreciation expense on general capital assets be reported in the government-wide statement of activities (see GASB, "Depreciation of Capital Assets Principle" in Chapter 2). It appears that expenditures in the *current* expenditures class are the most influential on the public mind, strongly influencing popular attitudes toward responsible officials.

A fourth character class, *intergovernmental,* is suggested by the GASB for use by governmental units that act as an intermediary in federally financed programs or that transfer "shared revenues" to other governmental units.

Classification by Object

The **object** of an expenditure is the thing for which the expenditure was made. Object classes may be viewed as subdivisions of character classifications. One scheme of object classification includes the following major classes:

Personal services	Capital outlays
Supplies	Debt service
Other services and charges	

Many other object classifications are encountered in practice, generally more detailed than those listed above. Greater detail can, of course, be achieved by the utilization of subclasses under the major titles. Thus personal services may be subdivided on the basis of permanence and regularity of employment of the persons represented; and each subclass may be further subdivided to show whether the services performed were regular, overtime, or temporary. Employee benefits may be recorded in as much detail as desired as subclasses of the personal services class. "Other services and charges" obviously must be subdivided if the class is to provide any useful budgeting and control information. Professional services, communication, transportation, advertising, printing and binding, insurance, public utility services, repairs and maintenance, rentals, aid to other governments, and miscellaneous are possible subdivisions.

Debt service, also listed as both an object of expenditure and a character class, should be subdivided in as much detail as needed to provide evidence that all interest payments and principal payments that should have been made in a certain fiscal period were actually made (or the appropriate liability recorded).

Classification of Estimated Revenues and Revenues

In order for administrators to determine that proposed expenditures presented in the operating budget can be financed by resources available under the laws of the budgeting jurisdiction and higher jurisdictions, revenue forecasts must be prepared. *Revenue,* in the sense in which it is customarily used in governmental budgeting, includes all financial resource inflows—all amounts that increase the net assets of a fund—interfund transfers and debt issue proceeds, as well as taxes, licenses and permit fees, fines, forfeits, and other revenue sources described in the following sections of this chapter.

It should be emphasized that a governmental unit and the funds thereof may raise revenues only from sources available to them by law. Often, the law that authorizes a governmental unit to utilize a given revenue source to finance general governmental activities, or specific activities, also establishes the maximum rate that may be applied to a specified base in utilizing the source or establishes the maximum amount that may be raised from the source during the budget period.

The primary classification of governmental revenue is by *fund.* Within each fund, the major classification is by *source.* Within each major source class, it is desirable to have as many secondary classes as needed to facilitate revenue budgeting and accounting. Secondary classes relating to each major source are discussed below under each source caption. Major revenue source classes commonly used are these:

Taxes	Charges for Services
Special Assessments	Fines and Forfeits
Licenses and Permits	Miscellaneous Revenues
Intergovernmental Revenues	

The operating budget and the accounting system for each governmental fund should include all revenue sources available to finance activities of that fund. The General Fund of most governmental units will ordinarily need all seven major classes itemized above; in some units, additional major classes may be needed. Each special revenue fund will need to budget and account for only those revenues legally mandated for use in achieving the purpose for which the special revenue fund was created. Similarly, debt service funds budget and account for those sources of revenue that are to be used for payment of interest and principal of tax-supported and special assessment long-term debt. Revenues and other financing sources earmarked for construction or acquisition of general capital assets are budgeted and accounted for by capital projects funds.

In order to determine during a fiscal year that revenues are being realized from each budgeted source in amounts consistent with the budget, actual revenues should be accounted for on the same classification system used for estimated revenues in the operating budget.

Taxes

Taxes are of particular importance because (1) they provide a large portion of the revenue of governmental units on all levels and (2) they are compulsory contributions to the cost of government, whether the affected taxpayer approves or disapproves of the taxes.

Ad valorem (based on value) **property taxes** are a mainstay of financing for many local governments but are not used as a source of revenue by many state governments or by the federal government. Ad valorem taxes may be levied against real property and personal property. Some property taxes are levied on a basis other than property values, one illustration being the tax on some kinds of financial institutions in relation to the deposits at a specified date. Other kinds of taxes are sales taxes, income taxes, gross receipts taxes, death and gift taxes, and interest and penalties on delinquent taxes.

The valuation of each parcel of taxable real property, and of the taxable personal property owned by each taxpayer, is assigned by a process known as **property assessment.** The assessment process differs state by state, and in some states by jurisdictions within the state. The tax rate is set by one of two widely different procedures: (1) the government simply multiplies the assessed valuation of property in its jurisdiction by a flat rate—either the maximum rate allowable under state law or a rate determined by policy—or (2) the property tax is treated as a residual source of revenue. In the latter event, revenues to be recognized from all sources other than property taxes must be budgeted; the total of those sources must be compared with the total proposed appropriations in order to determine the amount to be raised from property taxes, subject, of course, to limits set by law or legislative policy. Illustration 3–6 shows the computation of the total amount of revenues to be raised from property taxes under the assumption that property taxes are a residual source of revenues. The heading of Illustration 3–6 indicates that it is for the Town of Merrill's General Fund. A similar computation would be made for each fund for which property taxes are levied. It is common for an elected county official to serve as collector for all property taxes levied for all funds of all of the governmental units within the county (and, of course, for all of the funds of the county government itself). As discussed in Chapter 8, in such cases the county official serves as an agent for all jurisdictions for which property taxes have been levied; the taxes receivable are properly accounted for as assets of the funds for which they are levied, and those funds recognize revenues from the taxes to the extent that the taxes are expected to be collectible.

Note that Illustration 3–6 is a computation of the amount of revenue to be raised from property taxes six months before the beginning of the next fiscal year. This is one step in determining the tax levy for the year. A second step is the determination from historical data and economic forecasts of the percentage of the tax levy expected to be collectible. (Even though property taxes are a lien against the property, personal

ILLUSTRATION 3–6

TOWN OF MERRILL
General Fund
Calculation of Amount to Be Raised by Property Taxes
for Fiscal Year Ending December 31, 2008
As of Current Date—July 31, 2007

Estimated resource requirements:		
Estimated expenditures, remainder of FY 2007		$ 4,200,000
Appropriations proposed for FY 2008		8,460,000
Estimated working balance needed at beginning of FY 2009		510,000
Total estimated resource requirements		13,170,000
Estimated resources available and to be raised, other than from property taxes:		
Actual current balance (July 31, 2007)	$ 654,000	
From second installment of FY 2007 taxes	2,430,000	
From miscellaneous resources, remainder of FY 2007	1,960,000	
From all non-property tax sources in FY 2008	4,544,000	
Total estimated resources other than FY 2008 property taxes		9,588,000
Amount required from FY 2008 property taxes		$ 3,582,000

property may be removed from the taxing jurisdiction and some parcels of real property may not be salable or valuable enough for the taxing jurisdiction to recover accumulated taxes against the property.) Therefore, the levy must be large enough to allow for estimated uncollectible taxes. For example, assume the Town of Merrill can reasonably expect to collect only 96 percent of the year 2008 property tax levy for its General Fund. Thus, if tax revenue is to be $3,582,000 (per Illustration 3–6), the gross levy must be $3,582,000 ÷ 0.96, or $3,731,250.

When the gross levy is known, the tax rate may be computed on the basis of the assessed valuation of taxable property lying within the taxing jurisdiction. The term **taxable property** is used in the preceding sentence in recognition of the fact that property owned by governmental units and property used by religious and charitable organizations are often not taxable by the local government. In addition, senior citizens, war veterans, and others may have statutory exemption from taxation for a limited portion of the assessed valuation of property. Continuing the example, assume the net assessed valuation of property taxable by the General Fund of the Town of Merrill is $214,348,000. In that case, the gross property tax levy ($3,731,250) is divided by the net assessed valuation ($214,348,000) to determine the property tax rate. The rate would be expressed as "$1.75 per $100 assessed valuation," or "$17.41 per $1,000 assessed valuation"—rounding up the actual decimal fraction (0.017407) to two places to the right of the decimal, as is customary. The latter rate is typically referred to as 17.41 mills.

Interest and Penalties on Delinquent Taxes

A **penalty** is a legally mandated addition to a tax on the day it becomes delinquent (generally, the day after the day the tax is due). Penalties should be recognized as revenue when they are assessed. *Interest* at a legally specified rate also must be added to delinquent taxes for the length of time between the day the tax becomes delinquent until the day it is ultimately paid or otherwise discharged; interest revenue should be accrued at the time financial statements are to be prepared.

Sales Taxes, Income Taxes, and Gross Receipts Taxes

GASB standards provide that revenue from sales taxes, income taxes, and gross receipts taxes be recognized, net of estimated refunds, in the accounting period in which underlying transactions (e.g., sales and earnings) occur.

Special Assessments

Special assessments differ from ad valorem real property taxes in that the latter are levied against all taxable property within the geographic boundaries of the government levying the taxes, whereas the former are levied against certain properties. The purpose of a special assessment is to defray part or all of the cost of a specific improvement or service that is presumed to be of particular benefit to the properties against which the special assessments are levied. Briefly, when routine services (street cleaning, snow plowing, and so on) are extended to property owners outside the normal service area of the government or are provided at a higher level or at more frequent intervals than for the general public, "service-type" special assessments are levied. Service-type special assessments are accounted for by the fund that accounts for similar services rendered to the general public—usually the General Fund or a special revenue fund. Special assessments for capital improvements should be accounted for by a capital projects fund during the construction phase and by a debt service or agency fund during the debt service phase if debt financing is used. (See Chapter 6 for additional details about capital improvement special assessments.)

Licenses and Permits

Licenses and permits include those revenues collected by a governmental unit from individuals or business concerns for various rights or privileges granted by the government. Some licenses and permits are primarily regulatory in nature, with minor consideration to revenue derived, whereas others are not only regulatory but also provide large amounts of revenue, and some are almost exclusively revenue producers. Licenses and permits may relate to the privilege of carrying on business for a stipulated period, the right to do a certain thing that may affect the public welfare, or the right to use certain public property. Vehicle and alcoholic beverage licenses are found extensively on the state level and serve both regulatory and revenue functions. States make widespread use of professional and occupational licenses for purposes of control. Local governments make extensive use of licenses and permits to control the activities of their citizens; and from some they derive substantial amounts of revenue. Commonly found among licenses and permits are building permits, vehicle licenses, amusement licenses, business and occupational licenses, animal licenses, and street and curb permits. Regardless of the governmental level or the purpose of a license or permit, the revenue it produces is ordinarily accounted for when cash is received.

Intergovernmental Revenue

Intergovernmental revenues include grants and other financial assistance. These may be government-mandated nonexchange transactions (for example, certain state sales taxes required by law to be shared with local governments) or voluntary nonexchange transactions (for example, federal or state grants for which local governments compete). In either case, the recipient government does not provide significant value to the grantor government for value received. GASB defines *grants and other financial assistance* as

> transactions in which one governmental entity transfers cash or other items of value to [or incurs a liability for] another governmental entity, an individual, or an organization as a means of sharing program costs, subsidizing other governments or entities, or otherwise reallocating resources to the recipients.[12]

Governmental funds should recognize grants and other financial assistance as revenues in the period in which all time restrictions and eligibility requirements (such as a matching requirement) imposed by the grantor government have been met and the resources are available to pay current period obligations. Revenue recognition rules and the complexities of accounting for intergovernmental revenues are discussed in more detail in Chapter 4.

Charges for Services

As discussed earlier in this chapter, charges for services of the governmental funds (and governmental activities at the government-wide level) include all charges for goods and services provided by a governmental fund to enterprise funds, individuals and organizations, and other governments. A few of the many revenue items included in this category are court costs; special police service; solid waste collection charges; street, sidewalk, and curb repairs; receipts from parking meters; library use fees (but not fines); and tuition.

Classification of expenditures by function is discussed earlier in this chapter. The grouping of Charges for Services revenue may be correlated with the functional

[12]GASB *Codification*, Sec. N50.504.

classification of expenditures. For example, one functional group of expenditures is named General Government, another Public Safety, and so on. A governmental unit, in connection with providing general government service, collects some revenue such as court cost charges, fees for recording legal documents, and zoning and subdivision fees, and should relate the revenues to the expenditures. Charges for services should be recognized as revenue when measurable and available if that is prior to the collection of cash.

Fines and Forfeits

Revenue from fines and forfeits includes fines and penalties for commission of statutory offenses and for neglect of official duty; forfeitures of amounts held as security against loss or damage, or collections from bonds or sureties placed with the government for the same purpose; and penalties of any sort, except those levied on delinquent taxes. Library fines are included in this category. If desired, Fines and Forfeits may be the titles of two accounts within this revenue class, or they may be subgroup headings for more detailed breakdowns.

Revenues of this classification should be accrued to the extent practicable. In direct contrast with general property taxes, neither rates nor base or volume may be predetermined with any reasonable degree of accuracy for this type of revenue. Because of these uncertainties, revenues from fines and forfeits may be recognized when received in cash if accrual is not practicable.

Miscellaneous Revenues

Although the word *miscellaneous* is not informative and should be used sparingly, its use as the title of a revenue category is necessary. It (1) substitutes for other possible source classes that might have rather slight and infrequent usage and (2) minimizes the need for forcing some kinds of revenue into source classifications in which they do not generically belong. While miscellaneous revenues in itself represents a compromise, its existence aids in sharpening the meanings of other source classes. The heterogeneous nature of items served by the title is indicated by the following listing: interest earnings (other than on delinquent taxes); rents and royalties; sales of, and compensation for loss of, capital assets; contributions from public enterprises (utilities, airports, etc.); **escheats** (taking of property in default of legally qualified claimants); contributions and donations from private sources; and "other."

Some items of miscellaneous revenues, such as interest earnings on investments, might well be accrued, but mostly they are accounted for when received in cash. Also, interest earnings that are significant in amount may be reported as a separate classification.

BUDGETARY ACCOUNTING

Budgetary accounts were defined earlier in this chapter. Their use in journal entries and ledgers is described here. At the beginning of the budget period, the Estimated Revenues control account is debited for the total amount of revenues expected to be recognized, as provided in the operating budget. The amount of revenue expected from each source specified in the operating budget is recorded in a subsidiary ledger account (see Illustration 3–7) so that the total of subsidiary ledger detail agrees with the debit to the control account, and both agree with the adopted budget. If a separate entry is to be made to record Estimated Revenues, the general ledger debit to the Estimated Revenues control account is offset by a credit to Fund Balance. Recall that

ILLUSTRATION 3–7

			NAME OF GOVERNMENTAL UNIT Revenues Ledger General Fund		

Class: Licenses and Permits   Number: 351.1

Date	Item	Reference	Estimated Revenues DR.	Revenues CR.	Balance DR. (CR.)
2008 January 1	Budget estimate	J1	$195,000		$195,000
31	Collections	CR6		$13,200	181,800

the Fund Balance account, before the budget is recorded, would normally have a credit balance representing the excess of fund assets over the total of liabilities and reserved fund equity. (If fund liabilities and reserved fund equity exceed fund assets, the Fund Balance account would have a debit balance—referred to as a *deficit.*) After the budgeted revenues are recorded, Fund Balance represents the excess of fund assets *plus* the estimated revenues and other financing sources for the budget period over liabilities and reserves.[13] The credit balance of the Fund Balance account, therefore, is the total amount available to finance appropriations. Consequently, the accounting entry to record legally approved appropriations is a debit to Fund Balance and a credit to Appropriations for the total amount appropriated for the fund's activities. The Appropriations control account is supported by a subsidiary ledger (see Illustration 3–8) kept in the same detail as provided in the appropriations ordinance so that the total of the subsidiary ledger detail agrees with the credit to the Appropriations control account, and both agree with the adopted budget. The use of the Encumbrances account is explained in a later section of this chapter.

As explained earlier in this chapter, the use of budgetary accounts permits comparison of actual revenues and expenditures to budgeted amounts. Budgetary control is further enhanced by clear and logical classification of revenues and expenditures and by formally recording the budget in the accounts of the General Fund and other funds for which a budget is approved. The use of subsidiary ledgers, which permit recording revenues and expenditures—both actual and budgeted amounts—in the same level of detail as the budget, also helps to achieve sound budgetary control. Each of these topics is discussed in the remainder of this chapter.

Recording the Budget

The use of budgetary accounts is described earlier in this chapter. In order to illustrate entries in journal form to record a budget, assume the following are the amounts that have been legally approved as the budget for the General Fund of a certain governmental unit for the fiscal year ending December 31, 2008. As of January 1, 2008, the first day of the fiscal year, the total Estimated Revenues should be recorded in the General Fund general ledger control account, and the amounts expected to be recognized during 2008 from each revenue source specified in the

[13]For simplicity, we assume that a single Fund Balance account is used to record both budgetary (estimated) and actual amounts. In practice, most governments utilize a separate Budgetary Fund Balance account to record the net effects of estimated revenues and appropriations.

budget should be recorded in subsidiary ledger accounts. An appropriate entry would be:

		General Ledger		Subsidiary Ledger	
		Debits	*Credits*	*Debits*	*Credits*
1.	Estimated Revenues	1,277,500			
	Fund Balance		1,277,500		
	Estimated Revenues Ledger:				
	Taxes			882,500	
	Intergovernmental Revenues			200,000	
	Licenses and Permits			195,000	

The total Appropriations and Other Financing Uses legally budgeted for 2008 for the General Fund of the same governmental unit should also be recorded in the General Fund general ledger control accounts, and the amounts appropriated for each function itemized in the budget should be recorded in subsidiary ledger accounts. An appropriate entry using assumed budget amounts would be:

2.	Fund Balance	1,636,500			
	Appropriations		1,362,000		
	Estimated Other Financing Uses		274,500		
	Appropriations Ledger:				
	General Government				1,150,000
	Public Safety				212,000
	Estimated Other Financing Uses Ledger:				
	Interfund Transfers Out to				
	Other Funds				274,500

It would, of course, be acceptable to combine the two entries illustrated above and make one General Fund entry to record Estimated Revenues, Appropriations, and Estimated Other Financing Uses; in this case there would be a debit to Fund Balance for $359,000 (the amount by which Appropriations and Estimated Other Financing Uses exceed Estimated Revenues). Even if a single combined entry is made in the General Fund general ledger accounts, that entry must provide for entry of the budgeted amounts in each individual subsidiary ledger account as shown in the illustrations of the two separate entries.

Budgetary Control of Revenues

To establish accountability for revenues and permit budgetary control, actual revenues should be recognized in the general ledger accounts of governmental funds by credits to the Revenues account (offset by debits to receivable accounts for revenues that are accrued or by debits to Cash for revenues recognized when received in cash). The general ledger Revenues account is a control account supported by Revenues subsidiary ledger accounts kept in exactly the same detail as kept for the Estimated Revenues subsidiary ledger accounts. For example, assume the General Fund of the governmental unit for which budgetary entries are illustrated in the preceding section collected revenues in cash during the month of January from Licenses and Permits, $13,200, and Intergovernmental Revenues, $61,900. In an actual case, entries should be made on a current basis and cash receipts should be deposited each working day; however, for the purpose of this chapter, the following entry illustrates the effect on the General Fund accounts of collections during the month of January 2008:

		General Ledger		Subsidiary Ledger	
		Debits	*Credits*	*Debits*	*Credits*
3.	Cash	75,100			
	Revenues		75,100		
	Revenues Ledger:				
	Licenses and Permits				13,200
	Intergovernmental Revenues				61,900

Comparability between Estimated Revenues subsidiary accounts and Revenues subsidiary accounts is necessary so that periodically throughout the fiscal year actual revenues from each source can be compared with estimated revenues from that source. Material differences between estimated and actual revenues should be investigated by administrators to determine whether (1) estimates were made on the basis of assumptions that may have appeared realistic when the budget was prepared but are no longer realistic (in that event, the budget needs to be revised so that administrators and legislators have better knowledge of revenues to be realized during the remainder of the fiscal year) or (2) action needs to be taken so that revenues estimated with reasonable accuracy are actually realized (i.e., one or more employees may have failed to understand that certain revenue items are to be collected). Illustration 3–7 shows a form of Revenues subsidiary ledger in which the Debit column is subsidiary to the Estimated Revenues general ledger control account and the Credit column is subsidiary to the Revenues general ledger control account.

A Statement of Actual and Estimated Revenues is illustrated in Chapter 4. Normally, during a fiscal year, the amount of revenue budgeted from each source will exceed the amount of revenue from that source realized to date; consequently, the Balance column will have a debit balance and may be headed Estimated Revenues Not Yet Realized. This amount is a *resource* of the governmental unit—legally and realistically budgeted revenues that will be recognized as assets before the end of the fiscal year.

Budgetary Control of Encumbrances and Expenditures

When enacted into law, an appropriation is an authorization for administrators to incur on behalf of the governmental unit liabilities in the amounts specified in the appropriation ordinance or statute, for the purposes set forth in that ordinance or statute, during the period of time specified. An appropriation is considered *expended* when the authorized liabilities have been incurred. Because penalties are imposed by law on an administrator who incurs liabilities for any amount in excess of that appropriated, or for any purpose not covered by an appropriation, or who incurs liabilities after the authority to do so has expired, prudence dictates that each purchase order and each contract be reviewed before it is signed to determine that a valid and sufficient appropriation exists to which the expenditure can be charged when goods or services are received. If the review indicates that a valid appropriation exists and it has an available balance sufficient to cover the amount of the purchase order or contract being reviewed, the purchase order or contract legally may

ILLUSTRATION 3–8

NAME OF GOVERNMENTAL UNIT
Appropriations, Expenditures, and Encumbrances Ledger

Code No.: 0607-03
Fund: General
Year: 2008   Function: General Government

Month and Day	Reference	Encumbrances			Expenditures		Appropriations	
		Debits	Credits	Open	Debits	Cumulative Total	Credits	Available Balance
Jan. 2	Budget (Entry 2)						$1,150,000	$1,150,000
3	Purchase orders issued (Entry 4)	$38,000		$38,000				1,112,000
17	Invoices approved for payment (Entries 5a, 5b)		$35,000	3,000	$35,100	$35,100		1,111,900

be issued. When a purchase order or contract has been issued, it is important to record the fact that the appropriation has been *encumbered* in the amount of the purchase order or contract. The word *encumbered* is used, rather than the word *expended,* because the amount is only an estimate of the liability that will be incurred when the purchase order is filled or the contract executed. It is reasonably common for quantities of goods received to differ from quantities ordered, and it is not uncommon for invoice prices to differ from unit prices shown on purchase orders. The use of appropriation authority may be somewhat tentative inasmuch as some suppliers are unable to fill orders or to perform as stipulated in a contract; in such cases, related purchase orders or contracts must be canceled.

Note that the issuance of purchase orders and/or contracts has two effects: (1) the encumbrance of the appropriation(s) that gave the governmental unit the authority to order goods or services and (2) the starting of a chain of events that will result in the government incurring a liability when the purchase orders are filled and the contracts executed. Both effects should be recorded in order to help administrators avoid overexpending appropriations and plan for payment of liabilities on a timely basis. The accounting procedure used to record the two effects is illustrated by Entry 4. The first effect is recorded by the debit to the general ledger account *Encumbrances.* Encumbrances is a control account that is related to the *Appropriations* control account discussed previously and to the *Expenditures* control account discussed in relation to Entries 5a and 5b. In order to accomplish the matching of Appropriations, Expenditures, and Encumbrances necessary for budgetary control, subsidiary account classifications of all three must correspond exactly (see Illustration 3–8). The general ledger account credited in Entry 4, *Reserve for Encumbrances,* is used to record the second effect of issuing purchase orders and contracts—the creation of an expected liability. Reserve for Encumbrances, sometimes called *Outstanding Encumbrances,* is not a control account; the balance of the account at the balance sheet date is reported as a reservation of fund balance, as illustrated in Chapter 4.

Entries 4, 5a, and 5b illustrate accounting for encumbrances and expenditures for the General Fund of the governmental unit for which entries are illustrated in previous sections of this chapter. Entry 4 is made on the assumption that early in January purchase orders are issued pursuant to the authority contained in the General Fund appropriations;

assumed amounts chargeable to each function for which purchase orders are issued on this date are shown in the debits to the Encumbrances subsidiary accounts.

		General Ledger		Subsidiary Ledger	
		Debits	Credits	Debits	Credits
4.	Encumbrances—2008	45,400			
	Reserve for Encumbrances—2008		45,400		
	Encumbrances Ledger:				
	General Government			38,000	
	Public Safety			7,400	

When goods or services for which encumbrances have been recorded are received and the suppliers' invoices are approved for payment, the accounts should record the fact that appropriations have been *expended,* not merely encumbered, and that an actual liability, not merely an expected liability, exists. Entry 5a reverses Entry 4 to the extent that purchase orders are filled (ordinarily some of the purchase orders recorded in one encumbrance entry will be filled in one time period, and some in other time periods); it is important to note that since estimated amounts were used when encumbrances were recorded, the reversing entry must also use the estimated amounts. Thus, the balance remaining in the Encumbrances control account and in the Reserve for Encumbrances account is the *total* estimated dollar amount of purchase orders and contracts outstanding. The estimated dollar amount of purchase orders outstanding against each appropriation is disclosed by the subsidiary accounts, as shown in Illustration 3–8.

		General Ledger		Subsidiary Ledger	
5a.	Reserve for Encumbrances—2008 .	42,000			
	Encumbrances—2008		42,000		
	Encumbrances Ledger:				
	General Government				35,000
	Public Safety				7,000
5b.	Expenditures—2008	42,400			
	Vouchers Payable		42,400		
	Expenditures Ledger:				
	General Government			35,100	
	Public Safety			7,300	

Expenditures and the liability account must both be recorded at the actual amount the governmental unit agrees to pay the vendors who have filled the purchase orders (see Entry 5b). The fact that estimated and actual amounts differ causes no accounting difficulties as long as goods or services are received in the same fiscal period as ordered. The accounting treatment required when encumbrances outstanding at year-end are filled, or canceled, in a following year is illustrated in Chapter 4.

The encumbrance procedure is not necessary for every type of expenditure transaction. For example, although salaries and wages of governmental employees must be chargeable against valid and sufficient appropriations in order to give rise to legal expenditures, many governmental units do not find it necessary to encumber the departmental personal services appropriations for estimated payrolls of recurring, relatively constant amounts. Departments having payrolls that fluctuate greatly from one season to another may follow the encumbrance procedure to make sure the personal service appropriation is not overexpended.

From the foregoing discussion and illustrative journal entries, it should be apparent that administrators of governmental units need accounting systems designed to provide at any given date during a fiscal year comparisons for each item in the legal appropriations budget of (1) the amount appropriated, (2) the amount of outstanding encumbrances, and (3) the cumulative amount of expenditures to this date. The net of the three items is accurately described as *Unencumbered Unexpended Appropriations* but can be labeled more simply as *Available Appropriations* or *Available Balance.* Classification of appropriations, expenditures, and encumbrances was discussed in a preceding section of this chapter. In order to provide needed comparisons, classification of expenditures and encumbrances must agree with the classifications of appropriations mandated by law. In many jurisdictions, good financial management may dictate all three elements be classified in greater detail than required by law.

At intervals during the fiscal year, a Statement of Budgeted and Actual Expenditures and Encumbrances should be prepared to inform administrators and members of the legislative branch of the data contained in the subsidiary ledger records. An example of such a statement is illustrated in Chapter 4 (see Illustration 4–4). Also in Chapter 4, the entries needed at year-end to close budgetary and nominal accounts are illustrated (Entries 25a and 25b, Chapter 4).

Accounting for Allotments

In some jurisdictions, it is necessary to regulate the use of appropriations so only specified amounts may be used from month to month or from quarter to quarter. The purpose of such control is to prevent expenditure of all or most of the authorized amount early in the year without providing for unexpected requirements arising later in the year. A common device for regulating expenditures is the use of allotments. An **allotment** may be described as an internal allocation of funds on a periodic basis usually agreed upon by the department heads and the chief executive.

Allotments may be formally recorded in ledger accounts. This procedure might begin with the budgetary entry, in which Unallotted Appropriations would replace Appropriations. If this is desired, a combined entry to record the budget would be (using the numbers given in Entries 1 and 2, omitting entries in subsidiary accounts—which would be as illustrated previously with one exception—the subsidiary ledger credit accounts in Entry 2 would be designated as Unallotted Appropriations instead of Appropriations):

	General Ledger		Subsidiary Ledger	
	Debits	Credits	Debits	Credits
Estimated Revenues	1,277,500			
Fund Balance	359,000			
Unallotted Appropriations		1,362,000		
Estimated Other Financing Uses ..		274,500		

If it is assumed that $342,000 is the amount formally allotted for the first period, the following entry could be made (amounts allotted for each function are shown in the subsidiary ledger entries):

	General Ledger		Subsidiary Ledger	
	Debits	Credits	Debits	Credits
Unallotted Appropriations	342,000			
Allotments		342,000		
Allotments Ledger:				
General Government				289,000
Public Safety				53,000

Expenditures should be recorded periodically as invoices are received by using departments or divisions. Under this procedure, Expenditures, Allotments, and unexpended Unallotted Appropriations are all closed to Fund Balance at year-end.

Accounting Information Systems

In a computerized accounting system, an account number structure provides for appropriate classification of revenues and expenditures, as well as for the desired classification of assets, liabilities, and fund equities. Many alternative governmental accounting software systems are available. The general ledger module of most systems can easily accommodate all of the revenue and expenditure detail accounts needed for effective budgetary control.

Instead of using general ledger control accounts and related subsidiary ledgers, computerized systems often use separate files or ledgers for proprietary and budgetary reporting. For example, the general ledger module of one leading fund accounting software system includes both a general ledger and a budget ledger. Actual revenues and expenditures are posted to the general ledger, and budget amounts are posted to the budget ledger. Of course, the same account numbers and titles used in the budget ledger are used in the general ledger to permit budgetary comparison reporting. In addition, the system provides a separate encumbrance ledger to record encumbered amounts and monitor budgetary compliance. Selecting the type of transaction from a menu on the screen determines in which ledger (or ledgers) a particular transaction is posted. All such systems must provide transaction detail reports and other documentation of entries and postings in order to provide an adequate "audit trail."

In an accounting information system, the account number structure is an important design feature—one that affects the ease of financial operation and preparation of financial statements. Most account number structures provide for the multiple expenditure classifications prescribed by the GASB or similar classifications. Consider, for example, the following five-segment account number structure used by one Midwest city:

$$\text{XXX} - \text{XXXX} - \text{XXX} - \text{XX} - \text{XX}$$
$$(1) \qquad (2) \qquad (3) \qquad (4) \quad (5)$$

The five segments of numbers represent the following classifications:

Segment	Represents
1	Fund (e.g., 110 = General Fund; 224 = Library Operating Fund; 550 = Water Fund, etc.)
2	First two positions of the segment represent department; other two positions represent divisions within a department (e.g., 2120 = Police Operations; 2125 = Police Major Crimes; 2127 = Narcotics, etc.)
3	First two positions of segment represent activity; third position represents subactivity (Note: This city uses segment 3 to indicate type of account rather than activity and subactivity. For example, 100–199 = Assets; 200–299 = Liabilities; 300–399 = Equity; 400–499 = Revenues; and 500–699 = Operating Expenses, etc.)
4	Element (broad object of expenditure category) (e.g., 01 = Personnel Services; 12 = Supplies and Materials; 75 = Debt Service, Interest; etc.)
5	Detailed object of expenditure (e.g., some detailed objects associated with Personnel Services are 01 = Salaries and Wages, Permanent Positions; 05 = Salaries and Wages, Temporary Positions; and 41 = Salaries and Wages, Overtime, etc.)

Even though the classification scheme just described does not agree precisely with the expenditure classifications required by the GASB, it conforms in all essential respects with the GASB classifications. Segment (1) accomplishes classification by fund. Segment (2) permits classification by department and division, where divisions, in most cases, represent particular activities, for example, operations, major crimes, narcotics, and other activities of the police department. Because the *Division* classification in segment (2) meets the GASB activity classification requirement, the city uses segment (3) to indicate what kind of account (asset, liability, and so forth) is being used for a particular transaction. Segments (4) and (5) permit adequate object of expenditure detail. Although the account structure provides no specific classification for functions or programs, it is relatively easy to aggregate appropriate departmental accounts to provide totals by function or program for financial reporting or management purposes. Similarly, the lack of a specific character classification is of little concern since object of expenditure accounts are provided for debt service, capital outlays, and intergovernmental.

To illustrate the use of this account number structure in practice to code an actual transaction, consider how the purchase of diesel fuel by the Public Works Department, Street Cleaning activity would be coded for entry into the computer:

110	—	6023	—	534	—	12	—	40
General Fund		Public Works— Street Cleaning		Operating Expenses		Supplies and Materials		Other Supplies— Fuel, Oil, and Lubricants

If, as is likely, the diesel fuel is purchased from an internal service fund of the city, a liability account, Due to Other Funds, would also be credited. In this case, the transaction must also be recorded as a sale (Billings to Departments) and a receivable (Due from General Fund) in the internal service fund. If the fuel is purchased from an external source, either Accounts Payable or Vouchers Payable would be credited.

In actual practice, the interface programs used for most computerized accounting systems make it relatively simple to move around within the account number structure. Though systems differ markedly, department or finance personnel or accounting clerks usually enter the appropriate numbers for funds, department, activity, type of account, expenditure object, and dollar amount or choose these items from drop-down help menus. Function keys are often programmed to produce help menus for account number segments, particularly for expenditure objects.

For transactions that can be entered by department personnel, such as purchase requisitions, internal control considerations usually restrict entry and data access to only certain funds and types of accounts. For these transactions, the fund and department/division information often defaults to that applicable to a particular department or division. In addition to the information imbedded in the account number, purchasing and accounts payable programs also must provide lists of vendor numbers and names, usually in drop-down menu form. Some systems automatically complete the vendor identification information as soon as a few distinguishing keystrokes are entered. Vendor detail records usually permit instant display of vendor account status, including outstanding purchase orders, invoices received, due dates, invoices paid, and payments pending. As is common in computerized accounting environments, whether business, not-for-profit, or government, the accounting clerk often has little knowledge of the actual accounting processes occurring within the information system.

Generally, any account number segments not needed for a transaction have zeros inserted or, in some systems, may be masked. For example, for the city whose account number structure was illustrated earlier, recording revenues or paying vouchers payable requires no data to be entered for segments (4) and (5), so zeros are automatically inserted for those segments. Data classified according to an entity's account number structure can easily be aggregated within any segment, or group of segments, to provide a wide variety of custom financial reports, in addition to predefined reports and financial statements.

ACCOUNTING FOR GOVERNMENT-WIDE OPERATING ACTIVITIES

The illustrative journal entries shown in this chapter to record the budget have no impact on the government-wide statement of activities. Operating transactions, however, may be treated differently at the government-wide level than in the General Fund. Because the illustrative transactions presented in this chapter were intended to illustrate budgetary control over revenues and expenditures, the possible effects of those transactions at the government-wide level were ignored. In Chapter 4, the dual effects of accounting transactions are analyzed and appropriate journal entries are made in both the general journal for the General Fund and the general journal used to record government activities at the government-wide level.

Finally, the discussion of computerized accounting systems in this chapter focused on the systems that have evolved to meet the *fund* accounting needs of government. Governments now face the challenge of redesigning their existing systems or acquiring new systems that will accommodate government-wide accounting and financial reporting requirements, as well as preparing the fund financial statements required by *GASBS 34*. Many governments may continue for an extended period to use their present fund accounting computer systems, supplemented by spreadsheet interfaces that permit the reclassifications of fund-based information needed to prepare government-wide financial statements. The disadvantage of this approach is that government-wide statements are not available for the use of citizens and other users until the end of the reporting period when the reconciling worksheets are prepared.

Appendix

Accounting for Public School Systems

There are about 13,500 independent public school systems in the United States. Although they are classified as special purpose governments, these school systems follow the same generally accepted accounting principles as state and local governments—the accounting and reporting standards issued by GASB.[14] The approximately 1,500 "dependent" school systems are accounted for as part of their parent general purpose government, either a state, county, municipality, or township. Public school systems, both independent and dependent, often follow specialized accounting and reporting procedures prescribed by a state oversight department or agency. Further, all state oversight departments or agencies collect revenues and expenditures data for all pre-kindergarten through grade 12 public schools in their state and provide these data to the National Center for Educational Statistics (NCES) so the NCES can prepare the annual "National Public Education Financial Survey."[15] For sake of uniformity, most school systems follow the system of classification for revenues and expenditures recommended by the NCES. This system of classification is discussed next. In addition, independent public school systems must prepare the MD&A and basic financial statements required by *GASBS 34*.

CLASSIFICATION OF EXPENDITURES OF PUBLIC SCHOOL SYSTEMS

The NCES system of expenditure classifications expands on the GASB classifications discussed in this chapter, reflecting the standardized national data collection and reporting requirements imposed by the NCES on all states. Specifically, the NCES account code structure provides for nine expenditure classification categories: fund, program, function, object, project, level of instruction, operational unit, subject matter, and job class.[16] Generally, school systems need to report data for the classifications required by the education oversight body in their state, which may vary from state to state.

The *program* classification is critically important for effective management of public education at the local, state, and federal levels. The NCES identifies several broad classes of programs, including regular elementary/secondary education programs, special programs, vocational and technical programs, other instructional programs—elementary/secondary, nonpublic school programs, adult/continuing education programs, community/junior college education programs, community service programs, and co-curricular and extracurricular activities. Numerous detailed program classifications are possible within each broad category. For example, *special programs* may include service programs related to mental retardation, physical impairment, emotional disturbance, and developmental delay, among many other services. Similarly, *vocational and technical programs* include programs intended to prepare students for careers in 16 broad-based career areas, such as agriculture and natural resources, architecture and construction, information technology, and law and public safety.

The NCES *function* classification relates to the activity for which goods or services are acquired. Functions are classified into the five broad areas of instruction, support services,

---

[14]Dean Michael Mead, *What You Should Know about Your School District's Finances: A Guide to Financial Statements* (Norwalk, CT: GASB, 2000).

[15] An extensive list of NCES reports and resources is available on the Internet at *http://www.NCES.ed.gov.*

[16] The following discussion of expenditure and revenue classifications is based on the account classification codes provided in National Center for Education Statistics, *Financial Accounting for Local and State School Systems: 2003 Edition* (Washington, DC: U.S. Department of Education, Core Finance Data Task Force, The National Forum on Education Statistics, 2003).

operation of noninstructional services, facilities acquisition and construction, and debt service. In addition, the NCES provides account codes for 61 subfunctions, of which 14 are required for reporting to NCES. The required subfunctions are instruction; support services—students; support services—instruction; support services—general administration; support services—school administration; central services, operation and maintenance of plant; student transportation; other support services; food service operations; enterprise operations; community services operations; facilities acquisition and construction; and debt service.

Consistent with GASB standards, the NCES *object* classification describes the service or goods acquired by a particular expenditure. The NCES provides for nine major object categories: personal services—salaries; personal services—employee benefits; purchased professional and technical services; purchased property services; other purchased services; supplies; property; debt service and miscellaneous; and other items. As with programs and functions, numerous detailed object accounts are provided for each major object category, although only certain of those are identified for mandatory use and reporting to the NCES.

The *project* classification provides coding for projects that are funded from local, state, or federal sources, plus an additional code for projects that do not require specialized reporting to a local, state, or federal funding source. To meet reporting requirements imposed by some states on public school systems, the NCES provides a *level of instruction* classification, consisting of such categories as elementary, middle, secondary, postsecondary, and programs for adult/continuing. Finally, there are three optional-use expenditure classifications for *operational unit, subject matter,* and *job-class.* The operational unit classification provides the option of reporting by separate attendance centers, budgetary units, or cost centers. Subject matter could include such categories as agriculture, art, business, and science. Job-class relates to classifications used for personnel, such as administrative, professional, clerical, and technical.

CLASSIFICATION OF REVENUES OF PUBLIC SCHOOL SYSTEMS

Revenues of public school systems, both those dependent upon a general purpose government and independent school systems, should be classified in the manner prescribed by the NCES, as refined by the appropriate state oversight body. Generally, public school revenues should be classified by fund, source, and project/reporting code. The NCES publication cited in footnote 16 provides the following revenue classifications:

1000	Revenue from local sources	
	1100	Taxes levied/assessed by the school system
	1200	Revenue from local governmental units other than school districts
	1300	Tuition
	1400	Transportation fees
	1500	Investment income
	1600	Food services
	1700	District activities
	1800	Community services activities
	1900	Other revenue from local sources
2000	Revenue from intermediate sources	
	2100	Unrestricted grants-in-aid
	2200	Restricted grants-in-aid
	2800	Revenue in lieu of taxes
	2900	Revenue for/on behalf of the school district

3000   Revenue from state sources
    3100   Unrestricted grants-in-aid
    3200   Restricted grants-in-aid
    3800   Revenue in lieu of taxes
    3900   Revenue for/on behalf of the school district
4000   Revenue from federal sources
    4100   Unrestricted grants-in-aid direct from the federal government
    4200   Unrestricted grants-in-aid from the federal government through the state
    4300   Restricted grants-in-aid direct from the federal government
    4500   Restricted grants-in-aid from the federal government through the state
    4700   Grants-in-aid from the federal government through intermediate governments
    4800   Revenue in lieu of taxes
    4900   Revenue for/on behalf of the school district
5000   Other financing sources
    5100   Issuance of bonds
    5200   Fund transfers in
    5300   Proceeds from the disposal of real or personal property
    5400   Loan proceeds
    5500   Capital lease proceeds
    5600   Other long-term debt proceeds
6000   Other items
    6100   Capital contributions
    6200   Amortization of premium on issuance of bonds
    6300   Special items
    6400   Extraordinary items

Additional detail provided in the NCES revenue classification structure has been omitted from the foregoing list. For example, under classification 1100, taxes levied/assessed by the school district, are additional detail classifications for ad valorem taxes, sales and use taxes, income taxes, among others.

"Intermediate" sources of revenue are administrative units or political subdivisions between the local school system and the state. "Grants-in-aid" from intermediate, state, or federal governments are contributions from general revenue sources of those governments, or, if related to specific revenue sources of those units, are distributed on a flat grant or equalization basis. "Revenue in lieu of taxes," analogous to payment from an enterprise fund to the General Fund discussed in Chapter 7, are payments made out of general revenues of intermediate, state, or federal governments to a local school system because the higher level governmental units own property located within the geographical boundaries of the local school system that is not subject to taxation. "Revenue for/on behalf of the local school system" includes all payments made by intermediate, state, or federal governments for the benefit of the local system; payments to pension funds, or a contribution of fixed assets, are examples.

GASBS 34 financial reporting provides information that has not been readily available to users of public school financial statements in the past. As do other state and local governments, public school systems prepare basic financial statements, which include "district-wide" and fund financial statements, a management discussion & analysis (MD&A), and other required supplementary information. Users are thus better able to assess how much the school owns and owes, its present financial status and future outlook, what it costs to educate students, and the tax burden placed on citizens and businesses to finance education.[17] District-wide

[17]Ibid.

statements report on traditional governmental activities of a public school district, essentially the activities related to educating students, as well as business-type activities, for example, food services or after-school latchkey programs. Accountants and auditors need to be aware of state laws and regulations affecting public schools' commercial activities, such as the sale of products, direct advertising, corporate-sponsored education materials, and exclusivity agreements with soft drink companies.[18]

Key Terms

Activity, *73*
Ad valorem property taxes, *75*
Allotment, *85*
Appropriations, *69*
Budgetary accounts, *67*
Character, *73*
Direct expenses, *60*
Encumbrances, *69*
Escheats, *79*

Estimated other financing sources, *69*
Estimated other financing uses, *69*
Estimated revenues, *69*
Extraordinary items, *63*
Functions, *72*
General revenues, *62*
Indirect expenses, *60*
Object, *74*

Organization unit, *73*
Other financing sources, *65*
Other financing uses, *65*
Penalty, *77*
Program revenues, *62*
Programs, *72*
Property assessment, *75*
Special items, *63*
Taxable property, *77*

Selected References

American Institute of Certified Public Accountants. *Audit and Accounting Guide. Audits of State and Local Governments.* New York, 2005.

Governmental Accounting Standards Board. *Codification of Governmental Accounting and Financial Reporting Standards as of June 30, 2005.* Norwalk, CT, 2005.

Mead, Dean Michael. *What You Should Know about Your School District's Finances: A Guide to Financial Statements.* Norwalk, CT: Governmental Accounting Standards Board, 2000.

U.S. Department of Education, National Center for Education Statistics. *Financial Accounting for Local and State School Systems: 2003 Edition* (NCES 2004–318). Core Finance Data Task Force, The National Forum on Education Statistics. Washington, DC, 2003.

Questions

3–1. Explain how the *GASBS 34* reporting model meets financial report users' needs for *operational accountability* information about governmental activities.

3–2. What benefit do financial statement users derive from the net (expense) revenue format used for the government-wide statement of activities?

3–3. Define *direct expenses* and *indirect expenses*. Why can depreciation expense usually be considered a direct expense, while interest on long-term debt is considered an indirect expense?

3–4. Indicate whether the following revenues would most likely be classified as *program revenues* or *general revenues* on the government-wide statement of activities.

[18]General Accounting Office, *Public Educational Commercial Activities in Schools,* GAO/HEHS-00-156, September 2000.

a. Unrestricted operating grants that can be used at the discretion of the city council.

b. Capital grants restricted for highway construction.

c. Charges for building inspections.

d. Special assessment for snow removal.

e. Contractor forfeit of a construction deposit.

f. Motor vehicle fuel taxes restricted for road repair.

g. Unrestricted investment earnings.

3–5. Define *fund equity* and explain the types of accounts included in the fund equity category. How does *fund equity* compare to net assets? What is the relationship of *fund equity* and *net assets* to the operating statement accounts?

3–6. Distinguish between each account in the following pairs:

a. Expenditures and Encumbrances.

b. Revenues and Estimated Revenues.

c. Reserve for Encumbrances and Encumbrances.

d. Reserve for Encumbrances and Fund Balance.

e. Appropriations and Expenditures.

f. Expenditures and Expenses.

3–7. Indicate whether each expenditure item should be classified as a function, program, organization unit, activity, character, or object.

a. Mayor's Office.

b. Public Safety.

c. Residential trash disposal.

d. Accident investigation.

e. Salaries and wages.

f. Debt service.

g. Environmental protection.

h. Health and welfare.

i. Police Department.

j. Printing and postage.

3–8. State whether each item should be classified as taxes, licenses and permits, intergovernmental revenues, charges for services, fines and forfeits, or miscellaneous revenue in a governmental fund.

a. Sales and use taxes levied by the governmental unit.

b. Receipts from citizens in payment for library services.

c. Building permits to construct a garage at a residence.

d. Traffic violation penalties.

e. Federal community development block grant.

f. Royalties from an exclusivity contract with a soft drink company.

g. Charges to a local university for extra city police protection during sporting events.

h. Barbers and hairdressers' registration fees.

3–9. Why do GASB standards specify that the amounts in the Actual Amounts column of a budgetary comparison statement be reported on the basis required by law for budget preparation—even if that basis differs from GAAP?

3–10. Explain how expenditure and revenue classifications for public school systems differ from those for state and local governments.

Cases

3–1 Internet Case—Revenue and Expense/Expenditure Classification. Locate a comprehensive annual financial report (CAFR) using a city's Web site, or one from the "GASB 34" link of the GASB's Web site, *www.gasb.org*. Examine the city's government-wide statement of activities and statement of revenues, expenditures, and changes in fund balances—governmental funds and prepare a brief report responding to the following questions.

a. Referring to the government-wide statement of activities, explain how the *program revenues* and *expenses* are classified. Are expenses and program revenues reported using a function or program classification? Do any function or program categories show net revenues, or do they all show net expenses? Is the fact that most, if not all, functions or programs show a net expense a problem? Why or why not?

b. Explain how *revenues* are classified and reported on the statement of revenues, expenditures, and changes in fund balances. Compare the amount reported for property taxes in this statement to the amount reported as general revenue on the statement of activities. Do the two amounts agree? If not, can you think of a reasonable explanation for the difference?

c. Explain how *expenditures* are classified and reported on the statement of revenues, expenditures, and changes in fund balances. Compare these amounts to the amounts reported as expenses for the same functions or programs on the statement of activities. Do the amounts agree? If not, can you think of a reasonable explanation for the differences?

3–2 Internet Case—Budgetary Comparison Statements; Budget Basis Compared with GAAP. Refer to Case 3–1 for instructions about how to obtain the CAFR for a city of your choice. Using that CAFR, go to the required supplementary information (RSI) section, immediately following the notes to the financial statements, and locate the *budgetary comparison schedule* (note: this schedule may be titled *schedule of revenues, expenditures, and changes in fund balances—budget and actual*) for the General Fund and major special revenue funds. If this schedule is not included in the RSI, then the city you have selected is one that elects to prepare an audited statement of revenues, expenditures, and changes in fund balances—budget and actual as part of the basic financial statements. Also, locate the GAAP operating statement for governmental funds called the statement of revenues, expenditures, and changes in fund balances—governmental funds in the basic statements (note: this statement does not contain any budgetary information). Examine the schedule and/or statements, as the case may be, and prepare a brief report that responds to the following questions.

a. Are revenues and/or expenditures presented in greater detail in the budgetary comparison schedule (or statement) than in the GAAP operating statement? If so, why, in your judgment, is this the case?

b. Do actual revenues on the budgetary comparison schedule agree in amount with those on the GAAP operating statement? If they differ, is there an explanation provided either in the notes to the financial statements or notes to the RSI to explain the difference? What explanations are provided, if any?

c. Do actual expenditures on the budgetary comparison schedule agree in amount with those on the GAAP operating statement? If they differ, is there an explanation provided either in the notes to the financial statements or notes to the RSI to explain the difference? What explanations are provided, if any?

    d. If no differences were noted in either *b* or *c* above, go to item *e.* If differences were noted, was there a notation in the heading of the budgetary comparison schedule/statement indicating "Non-GAAP Budgetary Basis" or an indication of budget basis in the column heading for actual revenues and expenditures?

    e. Does the budgetary comparison schedule/statement contain a variance column? If so, is the variance the difference between actual and original budget or the difference between actual and final budget?

3–3 Internet Case—Charter Schools. You are an accountant in a state that allows charter schools, or public school academies, to educate kindergarten through 12th grade students and receive public funds to do so. A group of parents and teachers is forming such a school and has asked for your help in establishing an accounting system. Use the Internet to identify resources that may help you in this task. For example, use your favorite search engine to look for information on "charter schools" and "accounting systems," and answer these questions:

    a. Would you expect an accounting system for this type of school to be any different than that used by traditional public schools?

    b. Should you incorporate budgetary accounting? (*Hint:* Try *http://www.uscharterschools.org* and look for "Budgets and Fiscal Management" under "Resources" and "Starting a Charter School.")

Exercises and Problems

3–1 Examine the CAFR. Utilizing the CAFR obtained for Exercise 1–1, review the governmental fund financial statements and related data and government-wide financial statements. Note particularly these items:

    a. **Statement of Activities at the Government-wide Level.** Has the government prepared statements in compliance with the *GASBS 34* financial reporting model? Does the statement of activities appear on one page or across two pages? What is the most costly governmental function or program operated by the government? How much of the cost of governmental activities was borne by taxpayers in the form of general revenues? Did the entity increase or decrease its governmental activities unrestricted net assets this year? Did the entity increase or decrease its business-type activities unrestricted net assets this year?

    b. **Statement of Revenues, Expenditures, and Changes in Fund Balances for Governmental Funds.**

        (1) *Revenues and Other Financing Sources.* What system of classification of revenues is used in the governmental fund financial statements? List the three most important sources of General Fund revenues and the most important source of revenue for each major governmental fund. Does the reporting entity depend on any single source for as much as one-third of its General Fund revenues? What proportion of revenues is derived from property taxes? Do the notes clearly indicate recognition criteria for primary revenue sources?

            Are charts, graphs, or tables included in the CAFR that show the changes over time in reliance on each revenue source? Are interfund transfers reported in the same section of the statement as revenues, or are they reported in other financing sources?

        (2) *Expenditures and Other Financing Uses.* What system of classification of expenditures is used in the governmental fund financial statements? List the three largest categories of General Fund expenditures; list the largest category of expenditure of each major governmental fund.

Are charts, tables, or graphs presented in the CAFR (most likely in the statistical section) to show the trend of General Fund expenditures, by category, for a period of 10 years? Is expenditure data related to nonfinancial measures such as population of the government unit or workload statistics (e.g., tons of solid waste removed or number of miles of street constructed)?

c. **Budgetary Comparison Schedule or Statement.** Does the government present budgetary comparisons as a basic governmental fund financial statement, or as required supplementary information (RSI) immediately following the notes to the financial statements? Is the budgetary comparison title a *schedule* rather than a *statement?* Does the budgetary comparison present the original budget and the final amended budget? Does the budgetary schedule present actual data using the budgetary basis of accounting? Has the government presented one or more variance columns? Do all blended component units use the same budgetary practices as the primary government of the reporting entity? Does the CAFR state this explicitly, or does it indicate that budgetary practices differ by disclosures in the headings of statements, the headings of columns within statements, or by narrative and schedules within the notes to the financial statements?

3–2 Multiple Choice. Choose the best answer.

1. Which of the following is *not* a budgetary account?
   a. Appropriations.
   b. Encumbrances.
   c. Reserve for Encumbrances.
   d. Estimated Revenues.

2. The statement of activities in the government-wide financial statements is designed to provide information to assess:
   a. Functional accountability.
   b. Political accountability.
   c. Fiscal accountability.
   d. Operational accountability.

3. Depreciation expense related to general capital assets should generally be reported as a (an):
   a. Direct expense of appropriate functions or programs.
   b. Indirect expense.
   c. Nonoperating expense.
   d. None of the above; depreciation expense is not reported on general capital assets.

4. One of the primary differences between a *special item* and an *extraordinary item* is that a special item is:
   a. Unusual in nature.
   b. Infrequent in occurrence.
   c. Within management's control.
   d. Reported on a separate line below General Revenues.

5. One characteristic that distinguishes *other financing sources* from *revenues* is that other financing sources:
   a. Arise from debt issuances or interfund transfers in.
   b. Increase fund balance when they are closed at year-end.

    c. Provide financial resources for the recipient fund.

    d. Have a normal credit balance.

6. Under the *modified accrual* basis of accounting, revenues should not be recognized until they are:

    a. Collected in cash.

    b. Earned.

    c. Measurable and available for spending.

    d. Approved for expenditure by the legislative body.

7. Under the requirements for external financial reporting specified by the GASB, one would find the budgetary comparison schedule (or statement) in the:

    a. Required supplementary information (RSI).

    b. Basic financial statements.

    c. Either *a* or *b,* as elected by the governmental unit.

    d. Neither *a* nor *b.*

8. If supplies that were ordered by a department financed by the General Fund are received at an actual price that is less than the estimated price on the purchase order, the department's available balance of appropriations for supplies will be:

    a. Decreased.

    b. Increased.

    c. Unaffected.

    d. Either *a* or *b,* depending on the department's specific budgetary control procedures.

9. The Finance Department of the City of Ocean Beach recorded the recently enacted General Fund budget at the beginning of the current fiscal year, which approved estimated revenues of $2,000,000 and appropriations of $2,100,000. Which of the following is the correct journal entry to record the budget?

	Debits	Credits
a. Appropriations	2,100,000	
Fund Balance		100,000
Estimated Revenues		2,000,000
b. Revenues Receivable	2,000,000	
Budgetary Deficit	100,000	
Appropriations		2,100,000
c. Estimated Revenues	2,000,000	
Fund Balance	100,000	
Appropriations		2,100,000
d. Memorandum entry only.		

10. Which of the following sequences represents the typical sequence of activities for budgetary control over expenditures?

    a. Encumbrance, expenditure, appropriation, disbursement of cash.

    b. Appropriation, encumbrance, expenditure, disbursement of cash.

    c. Expenditure, appropriation, encumbrance, disbursement of cash.

    d. Appropriation, expenditure, encumbrance, disbursement of cash.

3–3 Budgets. Johnson City has budgeted the following General Fund estimated revenues and appropriations for the fiscal year 2008.

Estimated revenues:	
Taxes	$6,000,000
Licenses and permits	800,000
Fines and forfeits	500,000
Intergovernmental revenues	2,000,000
Total estimated revenues	$9,300,000
Appropriations:	
General government	$1,900,000
Public safety	4,000,000
Health and welfare	1,800,000
Public works	1,900,000
Total appropriations	$9,600,000

a. Assuming a reasonably responsible level of financial management, what is the minimum figure the administration of Johnson City expects to have as the fund balance of the General Fund at the conclusion of fiscal year 2007? Explain.

b. Show in general journal form the entry, or entries, that would be necessary to record the budget, assuming it is legally approved, at the beginning of the budget year, 2008. Show entries in subsidiary ledger accounts as well as general ledger accounts.

3–4 Appropriations. Assume purchase orders and contracts in the following estimated amounts were issued by Johnson City (Problem 3–3), chargeable against these 2008 appropriations:

General government	$100,000
Public safety	400,000
Public works	150,000
Total	$650,000

a. Show the necessary entry in general journal form to record the issuance of purchase orders and contracts. (Show entries in subsidiary ledger accounts as well as general ledger accounts.)

b. Explain why GASB standards for state and local governmental units require that the estimated amount of purchase orders issued be recorded in the accounts of governmental fund types, whereas FASB standards for business organizations do not have a similar requirement.

3–5 General Fund Trial Balance and Closing Entries. The following is a preclosing trial balance for Bates City's General Fund as of June 30, 2008.

	Debits	**Credits**
Cash	261,400	
Taxes Receivable—Current	888,500	
Estimated Uncollectible Current Taxes		62,000
Accounts Payable		325,700
Due to Other Funds		16,000
Tax Anticipation Notes Payable		520,000
Reserve for Encumbrances		112,000
Fund Balance		122,500
Estimated Revenues	1,556,200	

Revenues		1,457,300
Appropriations		1,551,600
Encumbrances	112,000	
Expenditures	1,349,000	
Totals	4,167,100	4,167,100

a. After all closing entries are made on June 30, 2008, what is the amount in Fund Balance? Show your calculations, T-account for Fund Balance, or closing journal entries.

b. What was the ending Fund Balance at June 30, 2007?

3–6 **Subsidiary Ledgers.** The printout of the Estimated Revenues and Revenues subsidiary ledger accounts for the General Fund of the City of Warren as of February 28, 2008, appeared as follows:

PROPERTY TAXES

Date	Folio	Estimated Revenues	Revenues	Balance
01 01	45 1	9,600,000		9,600,000
02 28	45 6	(20,000)	9,580,000	0

LICENSES AND PERMITS

Date	Folio	Estimated Revenues	Revenues	Balance
01 01	45 1	1,600,000		1,600,000
01 31	27 4		640,000	960,000
02 27	27 7		200,000	760,000

INTERGOVERNMENTAL REVENUE

Date	Folio	Estimated Revenues	Revenues	Balance
01 01	45 1	3,200,000		3,200,000
02 28	27 7		1,500,000	1,700,000

CHARGES FOR SERVICES

Date	Folio	Estimated Revenues	Revenues	Balance
01 01	45 1	600,000		600,000
02 28	27 7		160,000	440,000

Assuming that this printout is correct in all details and that there are no other General Fund revenue classifications, answer the following questions. *Show all necessary computations in good form.*

a. What should be the balance of the Estimated Revenues control account?

b. What was the original approved budget for Estimated Revenues for 2008?

c. (1) Was the FY 2008 Estimated Revenues budget adjusted during the year?
   (2) If so, when?
   (3) If so, by how much?
   (4) If so, was the original budget increased or decreased?

d. What should be the balance of the Revenues control account?

e. If in the Folio column of the accounts the numerals 45 stand for general journal and the numerals 27 stand for cash receipts journal, what is the most likely reason that revenues from Property Taxes are first recognized in a general journal entry, whereas revenues from the other three sources are first recognized in cash receipts journal entries?

3–7 Appropriations, Encumbrances, Expenditures. The finance director of the Town of Liberty has asked you to determine whether the appropriations, expenditures, and encumbrances comparison for Office Supplies for a certain year (reproduced as follows) presents the information correctly. You determine that the General Fund chart of accounts describes office supplies as "tangible items of relatively short life to be used in a business office." You also determine that the transfer of stationery, at cost, to the town water utility was properly authorized; the Water Utility Fund is to pay the General Fund $330 for the supplies. The transfer of $46,000 from Office Supplies to Personal Services was made by an accounting clerk without the knowledge of superiors to avoid reporting that the Personal Services appropriation had been overexpended.

Required

To determine whether the following budgetary comparison is correct, you need to compute each of the following. Organize and label your computations so the finance director can understand them.

a. The final amended amount of the appropriation for Office Supplies for the year.

b. The valid amount of encumbrances outstanding against this appropriation at the end of the year.

c. The net amount of expenditures made during the year that were properly chargeable to this appropriation.

d. The unencumbered unexpended balance of this appropriation.

TOWN OF LIBERTY
General Fund
Appropriation, Expenditures, and Encumbrances

Purchase No.	Explanation	Appropriations	Encumbrances Debits	Encumbrances Credits	Expenditures	Available Balance
	Budget legally approved	62,200				62,200
350	Purchase order—computer paper		600			61,600
356	Purchase order—stationery			420		62,020
	Refund of prior year expenditure	30				62,050
370	Purchase order—filing supplies		400			61,650
350	Invoice			605	605	61,045
378	Purchase order—computer		3,160			57,885
380	Contract for washing office windows		2,000			55,885
356	Invoice			420	420	55,885
	Cost of stationery issued to town's water utility	330				56,215
	Refund on P.O. 350	10				56,225
370	Invoice			400	425	55,800
380	Invoice				2,000	53,000
385	Purchase order—furniture		7,000			46,000
	Transfer to Personal Services appropriation	(46,000)				0

3–8 Recording General Fund Operating Budget and Operating Transactions.
The Town of Woods Falls approved a General Fund operating budget for the fiscal year ending June 30, 2008. The budget provides for estimated revenues of $2,700,000 as follows: Property taxes, $1,900,000; licenses and permits, $350,000; fines and forfeits, $250,000; and intergovernmental (state grants), $200,000. The budget approved appropriations of $2,650,000 as follows: General government, $500,000; Public Safety, 1,600,000; Public Works, $350,000, Parks and Recreation, $150,000, and Miscellaneous, $50,000.

Required

a. Prepare the journal entry (or entries), including subsidiary ledger entries, to record the Town of Woods Falls' General Fund operating budget on July 1, 2007, the beginning of the Town's 2008 fiscal year.

b. Prepare journal entries to record the following transactions that occurred during the month of July 2007.

   1. Revenues were collected in cash amounting to $31,000 for licenses and permits and $12,000 for fines and forfeits.
   2. Supplies were ordered by the following functions in early July 2007 at the estimated costs shown:

General government	$ 7,400
Public Safety	11,300
Public Works	6,100
Parks and Recreation	4,200
Miscellaneous	900
Total	$29,900

   3. During July 2007, supplies were received at the actual costs shown below and were paid in cash. General Government, Parks and Recreation, and Miscellaneous received all supplies ordered. Public Safety and Public Works received part of the supplies ordered earlier in the month at estimated costs of $10,700 and $5,900, respectively.

	Actual Cost	Estimated Cost
General government	$ 7,300	$ 7,400
Public Safety	10,800	10,700
Public Works	6,100	5,900
Parks and Recreation	4,100	4,200
Miscellaneous	900	900
Total	$29,200	$29,100

c. Calculate and show in good form the amount of budgeted but unrealized revenues in total and from each source as of July 31, 2007.

d. Calculate and show in good form the amount of available appropriation in total and for each function as of July 31, 2007.

3–9 Government-wide Statement of Activities. The following alphabetic listing displays selected balances in the governmental activities accounts of the City of Nokomis as of June 30, 2008. Prepare a (partial) statement of activities in good form. For simplicity, assume that the city does not have business-type activities or component units.

CITY OF NOKOMIS
Governmental Activities
Selected Account Balances (in thousands)
For the Year Ended June 30, 2008

	Debits	Credits
Expenses—Culture and Recreation	11,532	
Expenses—General Government	9,571	
General Revenues—Property taxes		56,300
General Revenues—Unrestricted Grants and Contributions		1,200
Expenses—Health and Sanitation	6,738	
Expenses—Interest on Long-Term Debt	6,068	
General Revenues—Investment Earnings		1,958
Unrestricted Net Assets		126,673
Expenses—Public Safety	34,844	
Program Revenue—Culture and Recreation—Charges for Services		3,995
Program Revenue—Culture and Recreation—Operating Grants		2,450
Program Revenue—General Government—Charges for Services		3,146
Program Revenue—General Government—Operating Grants		843
Program Revenue—Health and Sanitation—Charges for Services		5,612
Program Revenue—Public Safety—Capital Grants		62
Program Revenue—Public Safety—Charges for Services		1,198
Program Revenue—Public Safety—Operating Grants		1,307
Special item—Gain on Sale of Park Land		2,653

Chapter Four

Accounting for Governmental Operating Activities—Illustrative Transactions and Financial Statements

Learning Objectives

After studying this chapter, you should be able to:

1. Analyze typical operating transactions for governmental activities and prepare appropriate journal entries at both the government-wide and fund levels.
2. Prepare and explain interim financial statements and schedules.
3. Distinguish between exchange and nonexchange transactions, and define the classifications used for nonexchange transactions.
4. Prepare adjusting entries at year-end and a pre-closing trial balance for the General Fund.
5. Prepare closing journal entries and year-end General Fund financial statements.
6. Account for interfund and intra- and inter-activity transactions.
7. Account for transactions of a permanent fund.

In Chapter 3, the use of general ledger budgetary control accounts (Estimated Revenues, Estimated Other Financing Sources, Appropriations, Estimated Other Financing Uses, and Encumbrances) and related operating statement accounts (Revenues, Other Financing Sources, Expenditures, and Other Financing Uses) was discussed and illustrated. The necessity for subsidiary ledgers, or equivalent computer files or ledgers, supporting the budgetary control accounts and related operating statement accounts was also discussed. In this chapter, common transactions and events, as well as related recognition and measurement issues, arising from the operating activities of a hypothetical local governmental unit, the Town of Brighton, are discussed, and appropriate accounting entries and financial statements are illustrated.

ILLUSTRATIVE CASE

The Town of Brighton's partial government-wide statement of net assets, showing only the governmental activities, and its General Fund balance sheet, both at the end of the 2007 fiscal year, are presented in Illustration 4–1. Because this chapter focuses on *governmental* operating activities, only the financial information for the Governmental Activities column is presented at this time. The Town of Brighton does have business-type activities, but those activities are discussed in Chapter 7 of the text. Although the Town has no discretely presented component units, the column is shown in the statement of net assets simply to illustrate the recommended financial statement format.

Measurement Focus and Basis of Accounting

As discussed at several points in the earlier chapters, the government-wide statement of net assets reports financial position using the economic resources measurement focus and the accrual basis of accounting—in short, using accounting principles similar to those used by business entities. In contrast, the General Fund balance sheet reports financial position using the current financial resources measurement focus and the modified

ILLUSTRATION 4–1

TOWN OF BRIGHTON
Statement of Net Assets
December 31, 2007

	Primary Government			
	Governmental Activities	Business-Type Activities	Total	Component Units (None)
Assets				
Cash	$ 257,500	(Omitted		
Investments	40,384	intentionally)		
Receivables (net)	619,900			
Inventory of supplies	61,500			
Capital assets (net)	19,330,018			
Total Assets	20,309,302			
Liabilities				
Vouchers payable	320,000			
Accrued interest payable	37,500			
Due to federal government	90,000			
Bonds payable	1,500,000			
Total Liabilities	1,947,500			
Net Assets				
Invested in capital assets, net of related debt	17,830,018			
Restricted for:				
Debt service	77,884			
Unrestricted	453,900			
Total Net Assets	$18,361,802			

ILLUSTRATION 4–1 (*Continued*)

TOWN OF BRIGHTON
General Fund Balance Sheet
December 31, 2007

Assets

Cash		$220,000
Taxes receivable-delinquent	$660,000	
Less: Estimated uncollectible delinquent taxes	50,000	610,000
Interest and penalties receivable on taxes	13,200	
Less: Estimated uncollectible interest and penalties	3,300	9,900
Inventory of supplies		61,500
Total Assets		$901,400

Liabilities and Fund Balances

Liabilities:		
Vouchers payable		$320,000
Due to federal government		90,000
Total Liabilities		410,000
Fund Balances:		
Reserved for inventory of supplies	$ 61,500	
Reserved for encumbrances—2007	127,000	
Fund balance	302,900	
Total Fund Balances		491,400
Total Liabilities and Fund Balances		$901,400

accrual basis of accounting. Although both of these statements represent financial position at the same point in time, even a casual comparison reveals significant differences.

Perhaps the most striking difference between the two statements is that the statement of net assets reports both capital assets and long-term liabilities, whereas the General Fund balance sheet reports only current financial resources and current liabilities to be paid from current financial resources. *Current financial resources* include cash and items (such as marketable securities and receivables) expected to be converted into cash in the current period or soon enough thereafter to pay current period obligations. Prepaid items and inventories of supplies, if material, are also included in current financial resources.

Another major difference is that the information reported in the Governmental Activities column of the statement of net assets includes financial information for *all* governmental activities, not just for the General Fund. For example, the Town of Brighton also has debt service funds whose cash and receivables are combined with those of the General Fund in the Assets section of the statement of net assets. The investments reported in the statement of net assets belong to the debt service funds. In fact, it will be noted that $77,884 of net assets are restricted for purposes of paying debt service (principal and interest) on long-term debt. (*Note:* The debt service funds are discussed in Chapter 6.)

There are some other less important but still noteworthy differences. One noteworthy difference involves format. The Town's statement of net assets is in the GASB-recommended net assets format (that is, assets minus liabilities equals net assets) rather than the traditional balance sheet format (assets equals liabilities plus fund equity). This is not a *necessary* condition, however, as *GASBS 34* permits governments the option of preparing a government-wide *balance sheet* rather than statement of net assets, if they prefer.

An alert reader may have noted that the statement of net assets reports financial information in a more condensed manner than does the General Fund balance sheet. The primary reason for reporting more aggregated financial information is that the government-wide financial statements, along with the required management's discussion and analysis (MD&A), are intended to provide a broad overview of the government's financial position. Additional detail is provided in the notes to the financial statements (not provided in this chapter for sake of brevity), as well as in the fund financial statements.

In the case of the Town of Brighton the $453,900 reported for unrestricted net assets in the government-wide statement of net assets is only $37,500 less than the $491,400 reported as the total fund equity of the General Fund. In practice these amounts may be markedly different as many governments will have financial information for other governmental fund types that will be reported as part of the governmental activities unrestricted net assets. At any rate, neither the net assets at the government-wide level nor the fund equity at the fund level are analogous to the stockholders' equity of an investor-owned entity. Residents have no legal claim on any net assets or fund equity of the government.

A few final points should be noted about the General Fund balance sheet before we continue with illustrative budget and operating transactions. The arithmetic difference between total financial resources and total liabilities of the General Fund is the fund equity. The Town of Brighton's General Fund balance sheet illustrates that at December 31, 2007, a portion of fund equity (captioned as Fund Balances) is reserved because the $61,500 inventory of supplies included in the fund's assets cannot be spent or used to pay current liabilities. In addition, some purchase orders issued in fiscal year 2007 were not filled by the end of that year. The estimated $127,000 liability that will result when these goods or services are received in early 2008 represents a prior budgetary claim on available financial resources, as shown by the reserved for encumbrances—2007 on the balance sheet presented in Illustration 4–1. The portion of fund equity not reserved is shown as a fund balance of $302,900 on the balance sheet. An alternate and more descriptive designation would be *available for appropriation,* but it is more commonly called *unreserved fund balance.*

DUAL-TRACK ACCOUNTING APPROACH

As governments have adopted the *GASBS 34* reporting model, most have continued to use their traditional fund accounting software systems, reclassifying the fund accounting information at year-end as needed to prepare the government-wide financial statements. In the authors' view, the reclassification approach reflects a temporary deficiency in governments' financial accounting systems that will likely be corrected as software vendors develop general ledger systems capable of classifying transactions and events to meet the dual needs of both government-wide and fund financial statements. Among other problems, the reclassification approach limits the preparation of government-wide financial statements to once a year and may present audit trail and accounting record retention problems.

In a computerized accounting system, the dual effects of transactions can be accomplished either through an extensive classification coding scheme or using report writer software to aggregate information in different ways, for example, by major fund and government-wide. In contrast, this text adopts a *dual-track* approach to analyzing and recording transactions based on manual accounting procedures. This approach is designed to facilitate ease of learning; however, as will be apparent in Chapter 9, the dual-track approach also facilitates preparation of both government-wide and fund financial statements.

Operating activities and transactions affect the Town of Brighton's government-wide financial statements and fund financial statements differently. Certain activities (e.g., those relating to the General Fund budget) have no effect on the government-wide financial statements. Most operating activities or transactions affect both the General Fund and governmental activities at the government-wide level, although differently. Still other activities, such as recording depreciation expense or accruing interest on general long-term debt, affect only the government-wide financial statements and are not recorded at all in the General Fund or in any other governmental fund. Examples of the latter journal entries are provided in Chapters 6 and 9.

ILLUSTRATIVE JOURNAL ENTRIES

For the illustrative journal entries that follow, if the account titles or amounts differ in any respect, *separate* journal entries are illustrated for the General Fund general journal and the governmental activities (government-wide) general journal. For activities or transactions in which the entries would be identical, only a single journal entry is illustrated. In these cases, the heading for the entry indicates that it applies to both journals.

Recording the Budget

As discussed in Chapter 3, the budget should be recorded in the accounts of each fund for which a budget is legally adopted. For purposes of review, Entry 1, which follows, illustrates an entry to record the budget in the general journal for the General Fund of the Town of Brighton for fiscal year 2008. (The entry is shown in combined form to illustrate that format. The detail shown is assumed to be the detail needed to comply with laws applicable to the Town of Brighton. Since the Estimated Revenues, Appropriations, and Estimated Other Financing Uses accounts refer only to the fiscal year 2008 budget and will be closed at the end of the year, it is not necessary to incorporate "2008" in the title of either.)

		General Ledger		Subsidiary Ledger	
		Debits	**Credits**	**Debits**	**Credits**
	General Fund:				
1.	Estimated Revenues	3,986,000			
	Fund Balance	285,500			
	Appropriations		4,180,000		
	Estimated Other Financing Uses		91,500		
	Estimated Revenues Ledger:				
	Property Taxes			2,600,000	
	Interest and Penalties on Delinquent Taxes			13,000	
	Sales Taxes			480,000	
	Licenses and Permits			220,000	
	Fines and Forfeits			308,000	
	Intergovernmental Revenue			280,000	
	Charges for Services			70,000	
	Miscellaneous Revenues			15,000	

	General Ledger		Subsidiary Ledger	
	Debits	Credits	Debits	Credits
Appropriations Ledger:				
General Government				660,000
Public Safety				1,240,000
Public Works				910,000
Health and Welfare				860,000
Parks and Recreation				315,000
Contributions to Retirement and				
Other Postemployment				
Benefits Plans				180,000
Miscellaneous Appropriations				15,000
Estimated Other Financing Uses Ledger:				
General Government				91,500

Interfund Transfer to Create a New Fund

The town council approved the creation of a new Supplies Fund, an internal service fund, effective January 1, 2008, to provide most operating and office supplies used by departments accounted for in the General Fund. The new fund was created by transferring the current inventory of supplies and $30,000 in cash from the General Fund, general government function. Appropriate journal entries are provided in Chapter 7 to create the new internal service fund. The effect on the General Fund is reflected in Entries 2 and 2a below. The transfer has no effect on governmental activities at the government-wide level since financial information for both the General Fund and the new Supplies Fund is reported in the Governmental Activities column.

		Debits	Credits
	General Fund:		
2.	Other Financing Uses—Interfund		
	Transfers Out	91,500	
	Inventory of Supplies		61,500
	Cash		30,000
	Other Financing Uses Ledger:		
	General Government		91,500
	General Fund:		
2a.	Reserve for Inventory of Supplies	61,500	
	Fund Balance		61,500

Entry 2a is necessary since the General Fund no longer possesses the supplies for which the reservation of fund balance was established. Although the General Fund will order most operating and office supplies from the new Supplies Fund, certain special-use operating and office supplies will continue to be ordered from external vendors.

Encumbrance Entry

Interdepartmental requisitions for supplies with an estimated cost of $247,360 were submitted to the Supplies Fund, and purchase orders for certain other supplies and contracts for services were placed with outside vendors in the amount of $59,090. Entry 3 below shows the journal entry required to record the estimated cost of supplies ordered and service contracts. Since some encumbrance documents issued in 2008 may not be filled until early 2009, sound budgetary control dictates that "2008" be added to the Encumbrances general ledger control account and the corresponding Reserve for Encumbrances. The amounts chargeable to specific appropriations of 2008 are debited to detail accounts in the Encumbrances Subsidiary Ledger. (Recall that budgetary entries affect only funds for which a budget is legally adopted; they have no effect at the government-wide level.)

		General Ledger		Subsidiary Ledger	
		Debits	Credits	Debits	Credits
	General Fund:				
3.	Encumbrances—2008	306,450			
	Reserve for Encumbrances				
	—2008		306,450		
	Encumbrances Ledger:				
	General Government			28,000	
	Public Safety			72,000	
	Public Works			160,000	
	Parks and Recreation			36,000	
	Health and Welfare			10,000	
	Miscellaneous Appropriations			450	

When supplies and services ordered during the current year have been received and found to be acceptable, the suppliers' or contractors' billings or invoices should be checked for agreement with the original interdepartmental requisitions, purchase orders, or contracts as to prices and terms, as well as for clerical accuracy. If all details are in order, the billing documents are approved for payment. If, as is usual practice, the estimated liability for each order had been previously recorded in the Encumbrances control account in the general ledger, as well as in subsidiary Encumbrance Ledger accounts, entries must be made to reverse the encumbrances entries for the originally estimated amounts. In addition, entries are required to record the actual charges in the Expenditures control account and subsidiary Expenditures Ledger accounts. Expenses and/or assets must also be recorded in governmental activities accounts at the government-wide level, as appropriate.

Assume that goods and services ordered during 2008 by departments financed by the Town of Brighton General Fund (see Entry 3) were received as follows: All supplies ordered from the internal service fund (Supplies Fund) were received at an actual cost of $249,750; however, only a portion of the supplies and contracts with outside vendors were filled or completed during the year at an actual cost of $19,700, for which the estimated cost had been $22,415. For purposes of illustration, the appropriations assumed to be affected are shown in Entries 4 and 4a for the General Fund.

		General Ledger		Subsidiary Ledger	
		Debits	Credits	Debits	Credits
	General Fund:				
4.	Reserve for Encumbrances—2008	269,775			
	Encumbrances—2008		269,775		
	Encumbrances Ledger:				
	General Government				12,250
	Public Safety				72,000
	Public Works				150,900
	Parks and Recreation				30,000
	Health and Welfare				4,175
	Miscellaneous Appropriations				450
4a.	Expenditures—2008	269,450			
	Due to Other Funds		249,750		
	Vouchers Payable		19,700		
	Expenditures Ledger:				
	General Government			12,300	
	Public Safety			72,000	
	Public Works			150,600	
	Parks and Recreation			30,000	
	Health and Welfare			4,100	
	Miscellaneous Appropriations			450	

Although the Town of Brighton records the purchase of supplies from the Supplies Fund at the amount billed, the expenses recorded in the governmental activities accounts at the government-wide level should be the cost of the goods to the Supplies Fund. In other words, the cost to the government as a whole is what the internal service fund paid for the goods to external parties, and does not include the markup charged to departments by the Supplies Fund. As shown in Chapter 7, Entries 5a and b, the cost of the $249,750 of supplies issued to the General Fund was $185,000, so the markup is 35 percent on cost. Accordingly, the total direct expenses recorded at the government-wide level (see Entry 4b) is the $185,000 cost of supplies purchased from the Supplies Fund plus the $19,700 of goods and services purchased from external vendors, or a total of $204,700, distributed to functions based on assumed purchase patterns. It is the town's policy to include miscellaneous expenses as part of the General Government function at the government-wide level. (Note that the account credited at the government-wide level for the supplies purchased from the Supplies Fund is Inventory of Supplies since $185,000 represents supplies issued that are no longer in the Supplies Fund's inventory and thus are no longer in inventory from a government-wide perspective, assuming that substantially all supplies purchased by General Fund departments will be consumed during the year. Immaterial amounts of year-end inventory in the General Fund should be ignored.)

		General Ledger		Subsidiary Ledger	
		Debits	Credits	Debits	Credits
	Governmental Activities:				
4b.	Expenses—General Government	9,885			
	Expenses—Public Safety	54,889			
	Expenses—Public Works	114,148			
	Expenses—Parks and Recreation	22,741			
	Expenses—Health and Welfare	3,037			
	Vouchers Payable		19,700		
	Inventory of Supplies		185,000		

In addition to supplies, General Fund departments will make expenditures (capital outlays) for equipment or other general capital assets during the year. Although capital outlay expenditures are not illustrated in this chapter, they are recorded in the same manner as were supplies in Entries 3, 4, and 4a. At the government-wide level, an entry similar to Entry 4b would be required, except that the debit would be to Equipment (or other capital asset account as appropriate).

Payment of Liabilities

Checks were drawn to pay the $339,700 balance of vouchers payable ($320,000 balance at the end of 2007 plus the $19,700 amount from Entry 4a) and the 2007 year-end amount due to the federal government. In addition, the General Fund paid the Supplies Fund $249,750 for supplies purchased in Entry 4a. The following entries would be made for the General Fund and governmental activities at the government-wide level:

		Debits	Credits
	General Fund:		
5a.	Vouchers Payable	339,700	
	Due to Other Funds	249,750	
	Due to Federal Government	90,000	
	Cash		679,450
	Governmental Activities:		
5b.	Vouchers Payable	339,700	
	Due to Federal Government	90,000	
	Cash		429,700

Note that the entry to Due to Other Funds is omitted from Entry 5b as the transfer of cash between a governmental fund and an internal service fund has no effect on the amount of cash available within governmental activities at the government-wide level. Also, entries to subsidiary appropriation or expenditure accounts in the General Fund are unnecessary since those entries were made previously when the goods and services were received.

Some readers may question how more cash can be disbursed in Entries 5a and 5b than is available. This is no cause for concern, as the examples in this chapter are summarized transactions. Throughout the year revenues are also being collected, as illustrated in a later section. Should tax revenues be received later than needed to pay vendors on a timely basis, governments typically issue *tax anticipation notes* to meet those short-term cash needs, as discussed later in this chapter.

Payrolls and Payroll Taxes

The gross pay of employees of General Fund departments for the month of January 2008 amounted to $252,000. The Town does not use the encumbrance procedure for payrolls. Deductions from gross pay for the period amount to $19,278 for employees' share of FICA tax; $25,200, employees' federal withholding tax; and $5,040, employees' state withholding tax. The first two will, of course, have to be remitted by the Town to the federal government, and the last item will have to be remitted to the state government. The gross pay is chargeable to the appropriations in the General Fund as indicated by the Expenditures Ledger debits. Assuming that the liability for net pay is vouchered, the entry in the General Fund is:

		General Ledger		Subsidiary Ledger	
		Debits	Credits	Debits	Credits
	General Fund:				
6a.	Expenditures—2008	252,000			
	Vouchers Payable		202,482		
	Due to Federal Government		44,478		
	Due to State Government		5,040		
	Expenditures Ledger:				
	General Government			35,040	
	Public Safety			156,120	
	Public Works			29,160	
	Health and Welfare			19,080	
	Parks and Recreation			12,600	

In addition, the following entry would be required to record the payroll transaction in the governmental activities general journal at the government-wide level, using the accrual basis (expenses rather than expenditures):

	Governmental Activities:		
6b.	Expenses—General Government	35,040	
	Expenses—Public Safety	156,120	
	Expenses—Public Works	29,160	
	Expenses—Health and Welfare	19,080	
	Expenses—Parks and Recreation	12,600	
	Vouchers Payable		202,482
	Due to Federal Government		44,478
	Due to State Government		5,040

Recording the salaries and wages expenses in the manner shown in Entry 6b permits reporting direct expenses by function, as shown in Illustration 1–5 and as described in Chapter 3 in the discussion on expense classification in the government-wide statement of activities. If a government prefers to also record the expenses by natural classification (that is, as salaries and wages expense), it will be necessary to add additional classification detail; for example, Expenses—General Government—Salaries and Wages.

Payment of the vouchers for the net pay results in the following entry in both the General Fund and governmental activities journals:

		General Ledger		Subsidiary Ledger	
		Debits	Credits	Debits	Credits
	General Fund and Governmental Activities:				
7.	Vouchers Payable	202,482			
	Cash		202,482		

Inasmuch as the town is liable for the employer's share of FICA taxes ($19,278) and for contributions to additional retirement plans established by state law (assumed to amount to $5,400 for the pay period ended), it is necessary that the town's liabilities for its contributions be recorded, as shown in Entry 8a. These obligations were provided for in the Appropriations budget under the account Contributions to Retirement Plans.

	General Fund:				
8a.	Expenditures—2008	24,678			
	Due to Federal Government		19,278		
	Due to State Government		5,400		
	Expenditures Ledger:				
	Contributions to Retirement Plans				24,678

Entry 8b is also required to record the payroll expense on the accrual basis at the government-wide level.

	Governmental Activities:				
8b.	Expenses—General Government	3,430			
	Expenses—Public Safety	15,289			
	Expenses—Public Works	2,856			
	Expenses—Health and Welfare	1,869			
	Expenses—Parks and Recreation	1,234			
	Due to Federal Government		19,278		
	Due to State Government		5,400		

The expenses in Entry 8b relate directly to payroll; hence, it is assumed that a pro rata allocation of these items to functions is appropriate. For each function, that function's pro rata share is multiplied by the $24,678 total expense to obtain the amount of allocated expense. For example, the share allocated to General Government is $35,040/ $252,000, or 13.9 percent, multiplied by $24,678, yielding an allocated expense of $3,430 (rounded to nearest whole dollar).

Revenues Recognized as Received in Cash

Revenues from sources such as licenses and permits, fines and forfeits, charges for services, and certain other sources are often not measurable until received in cash. However, under the modified accrual basis of accounting, if such revenues are measurable in advance of collection and available for current period expenditure, they should be accrued by recording a debit to a receivable and a credit to Revenues. During fiscal year 2008, the Town of Brighton has collected revenues in cash from the sources shown in Entry 9a.

		General Ledger		Subsidiary Ledger	
		Debits	**Credits**	**Debits**	**Credits**
	General Fund:				
9a.	Cash	259,200			
	Revenues		259,200		
	Revenues Ledger:				
	Licenses and Permits				100,000
	Fines and Forfeits				151,000
	Charges for Services				7,000
	Miscellaneous Revenues				1,200

Of the preceding revenues, licenses and permits, fines and forfeits, and charges for services are appropriately recorded as *program revenues* at the government-wide level. Licenses and permits are attributed to the general government function. Fines and forfeits were assessed by the Public Safety function in the amount of $91,000 and by the Public Works function in the amount of $60,000. Charges for services were received from customers of the Parks and Recreation function. Miscellaneous revenues cannot be identified with a specific program and thus are recorded as *general revenues* at the government-wide level. Based on this information the entry that should be made in the journal for governmental activities is shown as Entry 9b.

		Debits	Credits
	Governmental Activities:		
9b.	Cash	259,200	
	Program Revenues—General Government—Charges for Services		100,000
	Program Revenues—Public Safety—Charges for Services		91,000
	Program Revenues—Public Works—Charges for Services		60,000
	Program Revenues—Parks and Recreation—Charges for Services		7,000
	General Revenues—Miscellaneous		1,200

Readers may be confused by classifying Fines and Forfeits as Charges for Services since generally we associate Charges for Services with **exchange** or **exchange-like transactions** in which value is given for value received. In issuing *Statement No. 37,* GASB considered this issue and decided that Charges for Services does not preclude a nonexchange transaction such as Fines and Forfeits. Furthermore, Fines and Forfeits is not appropriately classified as either Operating Grants and Contributions or Capital Grants and Contributions (see program revenue classifications in Illustration 1–5 and Illustration 3–1). Thus, in substance, the GASB decided to classify Fines and Forfeits as Charges for Services to avoid the need to add a fourth category of program revenues in the government-wide statement of activities.[1]

ACCOUNTING FOR PROPERTY TAXES

Entry 1 of this chapter shows that the estimated revenue for fiscal year 2008 from property taxes levied for the Town of Brighton General Fund is $2,600,000. If records of property tax collections in recent years, adjusted for any expected changes in tax collection policy and changes in local economic conditions, indicate that approximately 4 percent of the gross tax levy will never be collected, the **gross tax levy** must be large enough so that the collectible portion of the levy, 96 percent, equals the needed revenue from this source, $2,600,000. Therefore, the gross levy of property taxes for the General Fund of the Town of Brighton must be $2,708,333 ($2,600,000 ÷ 0.96). In an actual situation, property situated in the Town of Brighton also would be taxed for other funds of that town; for various funds of other general purpose governmental units, such as the township and the county in which the property in the Town of Brighton is located; the various funds of special purpose governmental units that have the right to tax the same property, such as one or more independent school districts or a hospital district; and perhaps the state in which the town is located.

Recording Property Tax Levy

The gross property tax levies for each fund of the Town of Brighton, and for each other general purpose and special purpose governmental unit, must be aggregated, and the aggregate levy for that unit divided by the assessed valuation of property within the geographical limits of that unit, in order to determine the **tax rate** applicable to property within the unit. In many states, a county official prepares bills for all taxes levied on property within the county; the same official, or another, acts as collector of all property taxes levied for the county and all governmental units within the county. Although the billing and collecting functions may be centralized, the taxes levied for each fund must be recorded as an asset of that fund. If the accounts are to be kept in conformity with generally accepted accounting principles, the portion of the taxes expected to be collectible (0.96 of the total levy, in this example) must be recorded as revenues of that fund, and the portion expected to be uncollectible (0.04 of the total levy, in this example) recorded in a "contra-asset" account, as illustrated by Entries 10a and 10b.

---

[1] GASB *Statement No. 37,* "Basic Financial Statements—and Management's Discussion and Analysis—for State and Local Governments: Omnibus" (Norwalk, CT, 2001), pars. 50–54.

	General Ledger		Subsidiary Ledger	
	Debits	**Credits**	**Debits**	**Credits**
General Fund:				
10a. Taxes Receivable—Current	2,708,333			
Estimated Uncollectible				
Current Taxes		108,333		
Revenues		2,600,000		
Revenues Ledger:				
Property Taxes				2,600,000
Governmental Activities:				
10b. Taxes Receivable—Current	2,708,333			
Estimated Uncollectible				
Current Taxes		108,333		
General Revenues—Property Taxes . .		2,600,000		

As Entry 10a shows, since in the General Fund the general ledger control account, Revenues, is credited, an entry must also be made in the Revenues Subsidiary Ledger. Taxes Receivable—Current is also a control account, just as is the Accounts Receivable account of a business entity; each is supported by a subsidiary ledger that shows how much is owed by each taxpayer or customer. Ordinarily, the subsidiary ledger supporting the real property taxes receivable control is organized by parcels of property according to their legal descriptions, since unpaid taxes are liens against the property regardless of changes in ownership. Because of its conceptual similarity to accounting for business receivables, taxes receivable subsidiary ledger accounting is not illustrated in this text.

Property tax revenue is an example of a **nonexchange revenue**—one in which the government receives value without directly giving equal value in exchange. More specifically, it is classified under GASB standards as an **imposed nonexchange revenue.** For imposed nonexchange revenues, a receivable should be debited when there is an enforceable claim, as in the case of a property tax levy, and a revenue should be credited in the year for which the tax was levied. The $2,600,000 credit to Revenues in Entry 10a indicates that the Town of Brighton expects to collect that amount during 2008 or within 60 days after the end of fiscal year 2008.[2] If the Town expected to collect a portion of the $2,600,000 later than 60 days after fiscal year-end, it should credit that portion to Deferred Revenues (a current liability account) and reclassify it to Revenues in the period in which the deferred revenues are collected. Note, however, that even if a portion of revenues is deferred in the General Fund because of the availability criterion, the full $2,600,000 is recognized as General Revenues—Property Taxes in the governmental activities journal at the government-wide level. This is so because availability to finance current expenditures is not a revenue recognition criterion under the accrual basis used at the government-wide level.

Collection of Current Taxes

Collections of property taxes levied in 2008 for the General Fund of the Town of Brighton amount to $2,042,033. Since the revenue was recognized at the time of the

[2] Governmental Accounting Standards Board, *Codification of Governmental Accounting and Financial Reporting Standards as of June 30, 2005* (Norwalk, CT, 2005), Sec. P70.104.

levy (see Entry 10a), the following entry is made in both the General Fund and governmental activities journal.

		General Ledger		Subsidiary Ledger	
		Debits	**Credits**	**Debits**	**Credits**
	General Fund and Governmental Activities:				
11.	Cash	2,042,033			
	Taxes Receivable—Current		2,042,033		

Reclassification of Current Property Taxes

Assuming that all property taxes levied by the Town of Brighton in 2008 were legally due before the end of the year, any balance of taxes receivable at year-end is properly classified as **delinquent taxes** rather than current. The related allowance for estimated uncollectible taxes should also be transferred to the delinquent classification. The entry to accomplish the reclassification, using amounts assumed to exist in the accounts at year-end, is:

	General Fund and Governmental Activities:				
12.	Taxes Receivable—Delinquent	666,300			
	Estimated Uncollectible Current Taxes	108,333			
	Taxes Receivable—Current		666,300		
	Estimated Uncollectible Delinquent Taxes		108,333		

Accrual of Interest and Penalties on Delinquent Taxes

Delinquent taxes are subject to interest and penalties as discussed previously. If the amount of interest and penalties earned in 2008 by the General Fund of the Town of Brighton but not yet recognized is $13,320, and it is expected that only $10,800 of that can be collected, the following entries are necessary:

	General Funds:				
13a.	Interest and Penalties Receivable				
	on Taxes	13,320			
	Estimated Uncollectible Interest				
	and Penalties		2,520		
	Revenues		10,800		
	Revenues Ledger:				
	Interest and Penalties on				
	Delinquent Taxes				10,800
	Governmental Activities:				
13b.	Interest and Penalties Receivable on Taxes	13,320			
	Estimated Uncollectible Interest				
	and Penalties		2,520		
	General Revenues—Interest and				
	Penalties on Delinquent Taxes		10,800		

Collection of Delinquent Taxes

Delinquent taxes are subject to interest and penalties that must be paid at the time the tax bill is paid. It is possible for a government to record the amount of penalties at the time the taxes become delinquent. Interest may be computed and recorded periodically to keep the account on the accrual basis; it must also be computed and recorded for the period from the date of last recording to the date when a taxpayer pays delinquent taxes. Assume that taxpayers of the Town of Brighton have paid delinquent taxes totaling $440,000, on which interest and penalties of $8,800 had been recorded as receivable at the end of 2007; further assume that $600 additional interest was paid for the period from the first day of 2008 to the dates on which the delinquent taxes were paid. Since it is common for the cashier receiving the collections to be permitted to originate source documents that result in credits only to Taxes Receivable—Current, Taxes Receivable—Delinquent, or Interest and Penalties Receivable on Taxes, it is necessary to record the $600 interest earned in 2008 in a separate entry, such as the following:

		General Ledger		Subsidiary Ledger	
		Debits	*Credits*	*Debits*	*Credits*
	General Fund:				
14a.	Interest and Penalties Receivable				
	on Taxes	600			
	Revenues		600		
	Revenues Ledger:				
	Interest and Penalties				
	on Delinquent Taxes				600

The corresponding entry at the government-wide level is:

	Governmental Activities:				
14b.	Interest and Penalties Receivable				
	on Taxes	600			
	General Revenues—Interest and				
	Penalties on Delinquent Taxes		600		

Collection of the delinquent taxes as well as interest and penalties thereon is summarized in Entry 15, which is the entry that should be made in both the General Fund and governmental activities journals. Note that these collections during 2008 are from the delinquent taxes receivable reported on the 2007 General Fund balance sheet and the Governmental Activities column of the government-wide statement of net assets (see Illustration 4–1).

	General Fund and Governmental Activities:				
15.	Cash	449,400			
	Taxes Receivable—Delinquent		440,000		
	Interest and Penalties Receivable				
	on Taxes		9,400		

Write-off of Uncollectible Delinquent Taxes

Just as officers of profit-seeking entities should review aged schedules of receivables periodically to determine the adequacy of allowance accounts and authorize the write-off of items judged uncollectible, so should officers of a governmental unit review aged trial balances of taxes receivable and other receivables. Although the levy of property taxes creates a lien against the underlying property in the amount of the tax, accumulated taxes may exceed the market value of the property, or, in the case of personal property, the property may have been removed from the jurisdiction of the governmental unit. When delinquent taxes are deemed uncollectible, the related interest and penalties must also be written off. If the treasurer of the Town of Brighton receives approval to write off delinquent taxes totaling $26,300 and related interest and penalties of $1,315, the entry in both the General Fund and governmental activities would be:

		General Ledger		Subsidiary Ledger	
		Debits	Credits	Debits	Credits
	General Fund and Governmental Activities:				
16.	Estimated Uncollectible Delinquent Taxes	26,300			
	Estimated Uncollectible Interest and Penalties	1,315			
	Taxes Receivable—Delinquent		26,300		
	Interest and Penalties Receivable on Taxes		1,315		

When delinquent taxes are written off, the tax bills are retained in the files in case it becomes possible to collect the amounts in the future. If collections of written-off taxes are made, it is highly desirable to return the tax bills to general ledger control by making an entry that is the reverse of the write-off entry, so that the procedures described in connection with Entries 14 and 15 can be followed.

Tax Anticipation Notes Payable

In the December 31, 2007, Statement of Net Assets and General Fund Balance Sheet of the Town of Brighton, two items, Vouchers Payable and Due to Federal Government, are current liabilities. Assuming there was a need to pay these in full within 30 days after the date of the Balance Sheet, the Town Treasurer would need to do some cash forecasting because the balance of Cash in the General Fund is not large enough to pay the $410,000 debt. In addition to this immediate problem, the treasurer, and most governmental treasurers, face the problem that cash disbursements during a fiscal year tend to be approximately level month by month, whereas cash receipts from major revenue sources are concentrated in just a few months. For example, property tax collections are concentrated in two separate months, such as May and November, when the installments are due; a local government's receipt from the state or federal government of revenues collected by superior jurisdictions for distribution to a local government are also usually concentrated in one or two months of the year.

Knowing these relationships, the treasurer of the Town of Brighton may, for example, forecast the need to disburse approximately one-fourth of the budgeted appropriations before major items of revenue are received; one-fourth of $4,180,000 is $1,045,000. This amount plus current liabilities at the beginning of the year, $410,000 and a $30,000 interfund transfer to create the new Supplies Fund equals $1,485,000 expected cash disbursements in the period for which the forecast is made. The town's experience suggests that a conservative forecast of collections of delinquent taxes and interest and penalties thereon during the forecast period will amount to $425,000. Furthermore, assume the treasurer's review of the items in the Estimated Revenues budget indicates that at least $140,000 will be collected in the forecast period. Therefore, total cash available to meet the $1,485,000 disbursements is $785,000 ($220,000 cash as of the beginning of the period, plus the $425,000 and $140,000 items just described), leaving a deficiency of $700,000 to be met by borrowing. The taxing power of the government is ample security for short-term debt; local banks customarily meet the working capital needs of a governmental unit by accepting a **tax anticipation note** from the unit. Additional discussion of cash budgeting is provided in Chapter 13. If the amount of $700,000 is borrowed at this time, the necessary entries in both the General Fund and governmental activities are:

		General Ledger		Subsidiary Ledger	
		Debits	Credits	Debits	Credits
	General Fund and Governmental Activities:				
17.	Cash	700,000			
	Tax Anticipation Notes Payable		700,000		

Repayment of Tax Anticipation Notes

As tax collections begin to exceed current disbursements, it becomes possible for the Town of Brighton to repay the local bank for the money borrowed on tax anticipation notes. Just as borrowing the money did not involve the recognition of revenue, the repayment of the principal is merely the extinguishment of debt of the General Fund and is not an expenditure. Payment of interest, however, must be recognized as the expenditure of an appropriation because it requires a reduction in the fund balance of the fund. Assuming the interest to be $13,500, and the amount is properly chargeable to Miscellaneous Appropriations, the entry is:

	General Fund:				
18a.	Tax Anticipation Notes Payable	700,000			
	Expenditures—2008	13,500			
	Cash		713,500		
	Expenditures Ledger:				
	Miscellaneous Appropriations				13,500

Procedures of some governmental units would require the interest expenditures to have been recorded as an encumbrance against Miscellaneous Appropriations at the time the notes were issued, and the liability for the principal and interest to have been vouchered before payment. Even if these procedures were followed by the Town of Brighton, the net result of all entries is achieved by Entry 18a.

A similar entry, shown as Entry 18b, is made at the government-wide level except that an expense rather than expenditure is recorded for the interest charged on the note. This expense is deemed to be an indirect expense that benefits no single function.

		General Ledger		Subsidiary Ledger	
		Debits	**Credits**	**Debits**	**Credits**
	Governmental Activities:				
18b.	Tax Anticipation Notes Payable	700,000			
	Expenses—Interest on Tax Anticipation Notes .	13,500			
	Cash		713,500		

Other Taxes

In addition to property taxes, many state and local governments receive sales and use taxes, income taxes, motor fuel taxes, and various other kinds of taxes, including those on businesses. These taxes, like property taxes, are **nonexchange transactions** in which one party (taxpayers in this case) does not receive (give) value proportionate to the value given (received). However, these taxes derive their valuation from underlying exchange transactions, such as selling goods, earning wages and salaries, and purchasing fuel. Thus, the GASB refers to taxes such as sales and income taxes as **derived tax revenues.**

Generally, derived tax revenues should be recognized in the period in which the underlying exchange has occurred. In practice, collections of sales and income taxes may not occur in the same period in which the underlying sales or earning transactions occurred. For example, local governments often experience delays in collecting sales taxes because in most states these taxes are collected by state governments. Moreover, businesses may only be required to file a sales tax return and remit taxes on a monthly basis. Income taxes are subject to even less frequent filings and collections. Consequently, at the end of a fiscal period governmental units generally will need to estimate the amount of sales or income taxes that have accrued but have not yet been reported. Such entries will require a debit to a taxes receivable account and a credit to the Revenues control account and the appropriate Revenues Subsidiary Ledger accounts.

INTERIM FINANCIAL REPORTING

Periodically during a year it is desirable to prepare financial statements for the information of administrators and members of the legislative branch of the governmental unit. Illustration 4–2 shows how an interim balance sheet would look for the Town of Brighton if it were prepared at March 31, 2008, assuming various additional transactions had been recorded by this date.

The interim balance sheet, Illustration 4–2, reflects the balances of both actual and budgetary accounts. Instead of Assets, which those familiar with accounting for profit-seeking entities would expect, the caption must be Assets and Resources because the excess of Estimated Revenues over Revenues is not an asset as of the balance sheet date but does indicate the amount that will be added to assets when legally budgeted revenues are recognized. Similarly, the caption is not Equities, or Liabilities and Capital, or another title commonly found in financial reports of profit-seeking entities but Liabilities and Budgeted Fund Equity. The Liabilities section is consistent with that of profit-seeking entities, but the next section discloses the three subdivisions of the Fund Equity. The first presents the amount appropriated for the year, less the amount of appropriations that have been expended during the year to date and less the amount of appropriations that have been encumbered by purchase orders and contracts outstanding at balance sheet date; the net is the amount that legally may be expended or encumbered during the remainder of the budget year. In Illustration 4–2 only one item,

ILLUSTRATION 4–2   **Interim Balance Sheet**

TOWN OF BRIGHTON
General Fund Balance Sheet
As of March 31, 2008

Assets and Resources

Assets:		
Cash		$ 513,660
Taxes receivable—current	$2,707,969	
Less: Estimated uncollectible current taxes	108,333	2,599,636
Taxes receivable—delinquent	220,000	
Less: Estimated uncollectible delinquent taxes	50,000	170,000
Interest and penalties receivable on taxes	4,400	
Less: Estimated uncollectible interest and penalties	3,300	1,100
Total Assets		3,284,396
Resources:		
Estimated revenues	3,986,000	
Less: Revenues	2,859,436	1,126,564
Total Assets and Resources		$4,410,960

Liabilities and Budgeted Fund Equity

Liabilities:			
Vouchers payable			$ 581,450
Due to federal government			51,520
Due to state government			10,800
Tax anticipation notes payable			700,000
Total Liabilities			1,343,770
Fund Equity:			
Appropriations		$4,180,000	
Less: Expenditures—2008	$1,191,710		
Encumbrances—2008	36,675	1,228,385	
Available appropriations		2,951,615	
Reserve for encumbrances—2008		36,675	
Fund balance		78,900	
Total Budgeted Fund Equity			3,067,190
Total Liabilities and Budgeted Fund Equity			$4,410,960

Reserve for Encumbrances, is shown in the second subdivision. This subdivision discloses the portion of budgeted fund equity that is not available for appropriation because expected liabilities exist (or because, as discussed later in the Town of Brighton example, certain assets will not be converted into cash in the normal operations of the fund). The remaining subdivision, Fund Balance, discloses that portion of the budgeted fund equity available for appropriation. Accordingly, in financial statement presentation, the word *Unreserved* or the phrase *Available for Appropriation* is sometimes used in place of *Fund Balance.* Fund Balance, in an interim balance sheet such as this, is the excess of the sum of actual assets and budgeted resources over the sum of actual liabilities, available appropriations, and reserves for assets not available for appropriation; in short, it has both actual operating and budgetary aspects at an interim point in time.

ILLUSTRATION 4–3

TOWN OF BRIGHTON
General Fund
Schedule of Budgeted and Actual Revenues
For the Three Months Ended March 31, 2008

Sources of Revenues	Estimated	Actual	Estimated Revenues Not Yet Realized
Taxes:			
Property taxes	$2,600,000	$2,599,636	$ 364
Interest and penalties on taxes	13,000	600	12,400
Sales taxes	480,000	—	480,000
Total taxes	3,093,000	2,600,236	492,764
Licenses and permits	220,000	100,000	120,000
Fines and forfeits	308,000	151,000	157,000
Intergovernmental revenue	280,000	—	280,000
Charges for services	70,000	7,000	63,000
Miscellaneous revenues	15,000	1,200	13,800
Total General Fund Revenue	$3,986,000	$2,859,436	$1,126,564

ILLUSTRATION 4–4

TOWN OF BRIGHTON
General Fund
Schedule of Budgeted and Actual Expenditures and Encumbrances
For the Three Months Ended March 31, 2008

Function	Appropriations	Expenditures of 2008 Appropriations	Outstanding Encumbrances	Available Appropriations
General government	$ 660,000	$ 129,100	$15,750	$ 515,150
Public safety	1,240,000	592,400	—	647,600
Public works	910,000	247,800	9,100	653,100
Health and welfare	860,000	67,700	5,825	786,475
Parks and recreation	315,000	72,000	6,000	237,000
Contributions to retirement plans	180,000	82,260	—	97,740
Miscellaneous appropriations	15,000	450	—	14,550
Total General Fund	$4,180,000	$1,191,710	$36,675	$2,951,615

   Interim schedules should be prepared to accompany the interim balance sheet to disclose other information needed by administrators and members of the legislative body; a schedule comparing the detail of budgeted and actual revenues is shown as Illustration 4–3, and a schedule comparing appropriations, expenditures, and encumbrances in detail is shown as Illustration 4–4. (Note: The amounts of revenues, expenditures, and encumbrances shown in these schedules are the amounts assumed to exist through March 31, 2008). Interim budget and actual comparison schedules, such as those shown in Illustrations 4–3 and 4–4, are essential to sound budgetary control, and are more commonly used than is the interim balance sheet.

SPECIAL TOPICS

This section of the chapter presents several special topics that result in additional journal entries, either in the General Fund or governmental activities journals, or both. Many additional transactions are assumed to have occurred during 2008, the recording of which would have been redundant of the transactions already illustrated.

Correction of Errors

No problems arise in the collection of current taxes if they are collected as billed; the collections are debited to Cash and credited to Taxes Receivable—Current. Sometimes, even in a well-designed and well-operated system, errors occur and must be corrected. If, for example, the assessed valuation of a parcel of property were legally reduced but the tax bill erroneously issued at the higher valuation, the following correcting entry would be made when the error was discovered, assuming the corrected bill to be $364 smaller than the original bill. (The error also caused a slight overstatement of the credit to Estimated Uncollectible Current Taxes in Entry 10, but the error in that account is not considered material and, for that reason, does not require correction.)

		General Ledger		Subsidiary Ledger	
		Debits	**Credits**	**Debits**	**Credits**
	General Fund:				
19.	Revenues	364			
	Taxes Receivable—Current		364		
	Revenues Ledger:				
	Property Taxes				364

An entry similar to Entry 19 would also be made at the government-wide level to correct the overstatement of General Revenues and Taxes Receivable—Current.

Postaudit may disclose errors in the recording of expenditures during the current year or during a prior year. If the error occurred during the current year, the Expenditures account and the proper Expenditures subsidiary account can be debited or credited as needed to correct the error. If it occurred in a prior year, however, the Expenditures account in error would have been closed to Fund Balance at the end of the prior year, so the correcting entry should be made to the Fund Balance account. Technically, overpayment errors of prior periods should also result in corrections to Fund Balance. However, as a practical matter, collections from suppliers of prior years' overpayments may be budgeted as Miscellaneous Revenues and recorded as credits to the Revenues account.

Receipt of Goods Ordered in Prior Year

As noted earlier in this chapter under the heading "Measurement Focus and Basis of Accounting," purchase orders and other commitment documents issued in 2007 and not filled or canceled by the end of that year total $127,000. This amount is designated as Reserve for Encumbrances—2007 in the December 31, 2007, General Fund Balance Sheet of the Town of Brighton. As stated previously, budgetary accounting has no effect on the government-wide financial statements; thus, no encumbrance is recorded at the government-wide level when goods or services are ordered or contracted for. When the goods on order at the end of fiscal year 2007 are received in 2008, their actual cost is considered an expenditure of the 2007 appropriations to the extent of the amount encumbered in 2007; any additional amount must be charged to the 2008 appropriations. The Appropriations account for 2007, however, was closed at the end of that year to Fund Balance, as were the other budgetary accounts for that year.

Although other procedures may be used, the authors prefer to reestablish the Encumbrances account at the beginning of fiscal year 2008, as shown in Entry 20, assuming that the goods were ordered by the Parks and Recreation function.[3] When goods or services ordered in 2007 are received in 2008, it is convenient to debit the Expenditures—2007 account when the liability account is credited and eliminate the encumbrance in the normal manner. At year-end, the Expenditures—2007 account is closed to Fund Balance, along with Expenditures—2008 and all other operating statement and budgetary accounts.

		General Ledger		Subsidiary Ledger	
		Debits	**Credits**	**Debits**	**Credits**
	General Fund:				
20.	Encumbrances—2007	127,000			
	Fund Balance		127,000		
	Encumbrances Ledger:				
	Parks and Recreation—2007				127,000

Assuming that all goods and services for which encumbrances were outstanding at the end of 2007 were received in 2008 at a total invoice cost of $127,250, Entries 21 and 21a are necessary in the General Fund, and Entry 21b is made in the governmental activities journal. Notice that only the estimated amount, $127,000, is charged to Expenditures—2007 since this was the amount of the encumbrance against the 2007 appropriation; the difference between the amount encumbered in 2007 and the amount approved for payment in 2008 must be charged against the 2008 appropriation for Parks and Recreation.

[3] State laws vary considerably regarding the treatment of appropriations and encumbrances at year-end. In some states, appropriations do not lapse at year-end. In others, appropriations lapse and goods encumbered at year-end require a new appropriation in the next year's budget or must be charged to the next year's normal appropriation. Discussion of the methods of accounting for the various alternative laws and practices is beyond the scope of this text.

		General Ledger		Subsidiary Ledger	
		Debits	Credits	Debits	Credits
	General Fund:				
21.	Reserve for Encumbrances—2007	127,000			
	Encumbrances—2007		127,000		
	Encumbrances Ledger:				
	Parks and Recreation—2007				127,000
21a.	Expenditures—2007	127,000			
	Expenditures—2008	250			
	Vouchers Payable		127,250		
	Expenditures Ledger:				
	Parks and Recreation—2007			127,000	
	Parks and Recreation—2008			250	
	Governmental Activities:				
21b.	Expenses—Parks and Recreation	127,250			
	Vouchers Payable		127,250		

Revision of the General Fund Budget

Comparisons of budgeted and actual revenues, by sources, comparisons of departmental or program appropriations with expenditures and encumbrances, and interpretation of information that was not available at the time the budgets were originally adopted could indicate the desirability or necessity of legally amending the budget during the fiscal year. For example, the schedule of actual and estimated revenues for the three months ended March 31, 2008 (Illustration 4–3), shows that more than 70 percent of the revenues budgeted for the General Fund of the Town of Brighton for 2008 have already been realized—almost entirely—because revenue from property taxes was accrued when billed, whereas in this illustrative case revenues from all other sources were recognized when collected during the three-month period for which entries are illustrated. Consequently, administrators of the town must review the information shown in Illustration 4–3 and determine whether the budget that was legally approved before the beginning of 2008 appears realistic or whether changes should be made in the Revenues budget in light of current information about local economic conditions; possible changes in state or federal laws relating to grants, entitlements, or shared revenues; or other changes relating to license and permit fees, fines, forfeits, and charges for services. Similarly, revenue collection procedures and revenue recognition policies should be reviewed to determine whether changes should be made in the remaining months of the year. Assume that the Town of Brighton's General Fund revenues budget for 2008 has been reviewed as described and that the budget is legally amended to reflect that revenues from Charges for Services are expected to be $5,000 more than originally budgeted, and that Miscellaneous Revenues are expected to be $10,000 more than originally budgeted; revenues from other sources are not expected to be materially different from the original 2008 budget. Entry 22 records the amendment of the Revenues budget, as well as the amendment of the appropriations budget, as will be discussed.

Information shown in Illustration 4–4 should be reviewed by administrators of the Town of Brighton to determine whether the appropriations legally approved before the beginning of 2008 appear realistic in light of expenditures of the 2008 budget incurred in the first three months of 2008 and encumbrances outstanding on March 31 of that year. Illustration 4–4 shows that total cumulative expenditures and outstanding encumbrances exceed 29 percent of the total appropriations for 2008, which can be related to the fact that as of March 31, the year is almost 25 percent over. By function, however, cumulative expenditures and outstanding encumbrances range from 3 percent of the Miscellaneous appropriation to almost 48 percent of the Public Safety appropriation. Therefore, each appropriation should be reviewed carefully in whatever detail is available in light of current information about expenditures needed to accomplish planned services during the remainder of 2008. Assume that the Town of Brighton's General Fund appropriations for 2008 have been reviewed and are legally amended to reflect a $50,000 decrease in the appropriation for Public Works and an $80,000 increase in the appropriation for Public Safety. Entry 22 reflects the legal amendment of appropriations for 2008, as well as the amendment of the revenues budget. Note the net increase in Appropriations of $30,000 is more than the net increase in Estimated Revenues of $15,000, requiring a decrease in Fund Balance.

		General Ledger		Subsidiary Ledger	
		Debits	**Credits**	**Debits**	**Credits**
	General Fund:				
22.	Estimated Revenues	15,000			
	Fund Balance	15,000			
	Appropriations		30,000		
	Estimated Revenues Ledger:				
	Charges for Services			5,000	
	Miscellaneous Revenues			10,000	
	Appropriations Ledger:				
	Public Works			50,000	
	Public Safety				80,000

Comparisons of budget and actual should be made periodically during each fiscal year. Generally, monthly comparisons are appropriate. In the Town of Brighton case, it is assumed that comparisons subsequent to the ones illustrated disclosed no further need to amend either the revenues budget or the appropriations budget for 2008.

Internal Exchange Transactions

Water utilities ordinarily provide fire hydrants and water service for fire protection at a flat annual charge. A governmentally owned water utility accounted for by an enterprise fund should be expected to support the cost of its operations by user charges. Fire protection is logically budgeted for as an activity of the Fire Department, a General Fund department. Assuming the amount charged by the water utility to the General Fund for hydrants and water service is $30,000, and the fire department budget is a part of the Public Safety category in the Town of Brighton example, the General Fund should record its liability as:

	General Fund:				
23a.	Expenditures—2008	30,000			
	Due to Other Funds		30,000		
	Expenditures Ledger:				
	Public Safety				30,000

The corresponding entry to record the inter-activities transaction (between the governmental activities and business-type activities) at the government-wide level is given as Entry 23b.

		General Ledger		Subsidiary Ledger	
		Debits	Credits	Debits	Credits
	Governmental Activities:				
23b.	Expenses—Public Works	30,000			
	Internal Balances		30,000		

Governmental utility property is not assessed for property tax purposes, but it is common for governmental utilities to make an annual "in lieu of taxes" contribution to the General Fund in recognition of the fact the utility does receive police and fire protection and other services. In fact, an amount in lieu of taxes is sometimes billed to the utility's customers; the aggregate amount so collected is simply passed on to the General Fund.

If the water utility of the Town of Brighton agrees to contribute $25,000 to the General Fund in lieu of taxes and that amount fairly represents the value of services received from the general government, the required journal entries for the General Fund and governmental activities are:

		General Ledger		Subsidiary Ledger	
	General Fund:				
24a.	Due from Other Funds	25,000			
	Revenues		25,000		
	Revenues Ledger:				
	Miscellaneous Revenues				25,000
	Governmental Activities:				
24b.	Internal Balances	25,000			
	General Revenues—Payments				
	in Lieu of Taxes		25,000		

Internal exchange transactions of the nature illustrated in Entries 23 and 24, and earlier in this chapter by the purchase of supplies by General Fund departments from the Supplies Fund (an internal service fund), affect both the fund and government-wide financial statements. Though the GASB refers to these transactions as *interfund services provided and used,* the authors believe that *internal exchange transactions* is a more precise term. *Internal exchange transactions* better captures the fact that these are reciprocal exchange transactions, but they occur *internally* between funds and activities rather than between the government and an external entity or person.

The funds that participate in internal exchange transactions should recognize revenues and expenditures or expenses, as appropriate, as if the transaction involved each fund and an external entity. Other types of internal transactions between funds, between governmental and business-type activities, and between the primary government and its discretely presented component units are discussed in a later section of this chapter.

Adjusting Entries

Inventories of Supplies

If a governmental unit is large enough to have sizeable inventories of consumable supplies that are used by a number of departments, it is generally recommended that the purchasing, warehousing, and distribution functions be centralized and managed by an internal service fund. This was the motivation for the Town of Brighton to create its Supplies Fund at the beginning of this year, as discussed earlier in this chapter. As is typical of small cities and towns, the town previously determined its inventories at year-end by taking a physical count of supplies on hand; for example, by periodic inventory procedures. Since establishing the Supplies Fund, the town maintains these inventories on a perpetual basis, but will take a physical count at year-end to confirm inventory balances and adjust the inventory accounts accordingly.

Governments that account for their supplies within the General Fund can use either the *purchases method* or the *consumption method*. Using the **purchases method,** expenditures for supplies equals the total amount purchased for the year, even if the amount of supplies consumed is less than or greater than the amount purchased. Thus, the purchases method is consistent with the modified accrual basis of accounting used by the General Fund and other governmental funds. The purchases method is generally associated with a periodic inventory system, so the balance of the Inventory of Supplies account is increased or decreased as necessary at year-end to agree with the valuation based on a physical count. In addition, a Reserve for Inventory of Supplies account, having a credit balance equal in amount to the balance of the inventory account, is required to indicate that the inventory reported on the balance sheet is not available for spending.

The **consumption method** is consistent with the accrual basis of accounting, as resources (i.e., supplies) consumed in providing services is the essence of an expense. Thus, GASB standards require the use of the consumption method for government-wide and proprietary fund reporting. Using this method, the General Fund recognizes expenditures equal to the amount of supplies consumed during the year rather than the amount purchased. Accordingly, budgetary appropriations for supplies are based on estimated consumption rather than estimated purchases. When using the consumption method, reporting of a reservation of fund balance is optional, though recommended.[4]

To illustrate and contrast the consumption and purchases methods, assume the following information for supplies purchases and usage of a certain city for its 2008 fiscal year.

Balance of inventory, January 1, 2008	$ 55,000
Purchases during 2008	260,000
Supplies available for use	315,000
Less: Balance of inventory, December 31, 2008	65,000
Supplies consumed during 2008	$250,000

Consumption Method

Generally, the consumption method is used with a perpetual inventory system; however, because the purchases method is commonly used for General Fund accounting, many governments must convert their purchases information to the consumption basis for governmental activities at the government-wide level. Accordingly, the following

---

[4] American Institute of Certified Public Accountants, Audit and Accounting Guide, *State and Local Governments* (New York: 2004), par. 10.14.

examples show consumption method journal entries using both perpetual and periodic inventory control procedures, omitting subsidiary detail for simplicity.

Assuming a *perpetual inventory system* is used, the summary entry to record purchases for the year in the accounts of the General Fund and governmental activities at the government-wide level is:

	General Ledger		Subsidiary Ledger	
	Debits	Credits	Debits	Credits
General Fund and Governmental Activities:				
Inventory of Supplies	260,000			
Cash		260,000		

The actual consumption (usage) is recorded by the following entries:

General Fund:		
Expenditures	250,000	
Inventory of Supplies		250,000
Governmental Activities:		
Expenses—(function or program detail omitted)	250,000	
Inventories of Supplies		250,000

Observe that these two entries result in expenditures/expenses equal to the amount of supplies consumed ($250,000) and a net increase of $10,000 in the balance of the Inventory of Supplies account during 2008. In addition, if the General Fund opts to report a reserve of fund balance, it would make the following entry:

General Fund:		
Fund Balance	10,000	
Reserve for Inventory of Supplies		10,000

Unless a physical inventory reveals inventory loss (or gain), no adjusting entry is required at year-end at the government-wide level.

If the city uses a *periodic inventory system,* but reports inventories under the consumption method in both the General Fund and governmental activities, the following entries are required. To record purchases of supplies for the year, assuming that for budgetary control purposes the city records expenditures for each purchase of supplies (encumbrance entries and subsidiary detail omitted for simplicity):

General Fund:		
Expenditures	260,000	
Cash		260,000

At year-end, the city's General Fund adjusting entries will be:

	General Ledger		Subsidiary Ledger	
	Debits	*Credits*	*Debits*	*Credits*
Inventory of Supplies	10,000			
Expenditures		10,000		
Fund Balance	10,000			
Reserve for Inventory				
of Supplies		10,000		

The appropriate year-end adjusting entry at the government-wide level depends upon the way inventories are recorded during the year. If purchases during the year are debited to Inventory of Supplies, then the adjusting entry will require a debit to expenses and credit to the inventory account. If, on the other hand, the city records expenses at the government-wide level during the year as purchases are made, the adjusting entry will require a debit to inventory and a credit to expenses for the $10,000 increase in inventory that occurred in 2008. Assuming purchases are recorded initially as expenses, the entries that would be required for governmental activities at the government-wide level are:

To record purchases during the year:

Governmental Activities:		
Expenses (function or program		
detail omitted)	260,000	
Cash		260,000

The required governmental activities adjusting entry is:

Inventory of Supplies	10,000	
Expenses (function or program		
detail omitted)		10,000

Purchases Method

Under the purchases method, the summary entry in the General Fund to record supplies purchased during the year, assuming all supplies are purchased from external vendors and all invoices have been paid, is (encumbrance entries and subsidiary detail omitted for simplicity):

General Fund:		
Expenditures	260,000	
Cash		260,000

At year-end, a physical inventory revealed that $65,000 of inventory remained on hand. The entry to record the $10,000 increase in inventory and the corresponding reservation of fund balance is given as:

General Fund:		
Inventory of Supplies	10,000	
Reserve for Inventory		
of Supplies		10,000

(Note: Reservation of fund balance for inventory and other reasons applies only to governmental funds that are subject to legal budgetary control. Thus, this entry is unnecessary at the government-wide level.)

In all of these examples, the entries in the General Fund are somewhat more complex because of the need to adjust the Reserve for Inventory of Supplies account at the fund level. One can expect that the *GASBS 34* requirement to report inventories using the consumption method at the government-wide level may lead to increased use of this method for the General Fund as well.

Pre-Closing Trial Balance

Assume that all illustrated journal entries for the transactions and events pertaining to the Town of Brighton's 2008 fiscal year have been posted to the general and subsidiary ledgers. In addition, a number of other transactions and events were journalized and posted during the year but were not shown in this chapter because they were similar to those that were illustrated. As a result of all transactions and events recorded for the year (both those that were illustrated and those that were not), the balances of all balance sheet, operating statement, and budgetary accounts before closing entries are presented in the following trial balance.

TOWN OF BRIGHTON
General Fund
Pre-Closing Trial Balance
as of December 31, 2008

	Debits	Credits
Cash	$ 145,800	
Taxes Receivable—Delinquent	701,813	
Estimated Uncollectible Delinquent Taxes		$ 123,513
Interest and Penalties Receivable on Taxes	13,191	
Estimated Uncollectible Interest and Taxes		3,091
Due from Other Funds	25,000	
Estimated Revenues	4,001,000	
Revenues		4,015,000
Vouchers Payable		405,800
Due to Federal Government		126,520
Due to State Government		39,740
Due to Other Funds		30,000
Appropriations		4,210,000
Estimated Other Financing Uses		91,500
Expenditures—2007	127,000	
Expenditures—2008	4,130,760	
Other Financing Uses—Interfund Transfers Out	91,500	
Encumbrances—2008	70,240	
Reserve for Encumbrances—2008		70,240
Fund Balance		190,900
	$9,306,304	$9,306,304

Closing Entries

At fiscal year-end, all temporary accounts, both operating and budgetary, must be closed to Fund Balance. As mentioned in Chapter 3, many state and local governments record the difference between budgeted inflows and outflows to a *Budgetary Fund Balance* account. As a result, the closing process typically involves a simple reversal of the budgetary entry, as amended, with a separate closing entry to close temporary operating accounts to the *Unreserved Fund Balance* account. Since we use a single Fund Balance account for the sake of simplicity, any sequence of entries and combination of accounts should yield the desired result that all temporary accounts have their balances transferred to the balance sheet account, Fund Balance. For illustrative purposes, Entries 25a and 25b show separate closing entries for the budgetary and operating accounts.

		General Ledger		Subsidiary Ledger	
		Debits	**Credits**	**Debits**	**Credits**
	General Fund:				
25a.	Appropriations	4,210,000			
	Estimated Other Financing Uses	91,500			
	Estimated Revenues		4,001,000		
	Fund Balance		300,500		
25b.	Revenues	4,015,000			
	Fund Balance	404,500			
	Expenditures—2008		4,130,760		
	Expenditures—2007		127,000		
	Other Financing Uses—Interfund Transfers Out		91,500		
	Encumbrances—2008		70,240		

Although Entries 25a and 25b affect several General Fund general ledger control accounts, it is not considered necessary to make closing entries in their subsidiary ledger accounts because in a manual system separate subsidiary ledgers are kept for each budget year.

It is important to notice that the closing entry has the effect of reversing the entry made to record the budget (Entry 1) and the entry made to amend the budget (Entry 22). Therefore, after the closing entry is posted, the Fund Balance account is purely a balance sheet account, not one in which historical and expected effects are mixed, as is true during a year. That is, it again represents the net amount of financial resources available for appropriation for fund purposes.

Year-end Financial Statements

The balance sheet for the General Fund of the Town of Brighton as of the end of 2008 is shown as Illustration 4–5. Since only balance sheet accounts are open, the captions "Assets" and "Liabilities and Fund Balances" are used instead of the captions in the interim balance sheet, Illustration 4–2. The amount due from the Water Utility Fund is offset against the amount due to the same fund, and only the net liability is shown in the balance sheet, in conformity with GASB standards. It should be emphasized that it is *not* acceptable to offset a receivable from one fund against a payable to a different fund. The General Fund balance sheet would be presented in columnar form in the

ILLUSTRATION 4–5

TOWN OF BRIGHTON
General Fund Balance Sheet
As of December 31, 2008

Assets

Cash		$145,800
Taxes receivable—delinquent	$701,813	
Less: Estimated uncollectible delinquent taxes	123,513	578,300
Interest and penalties receivable on taxes	13,191	
Less: Estimated uncollectible interest and penalties	3,091	10,100
Total Assets		$734,200

Liabilities and Fund Balances

Liabilities:		
Vouchers payable	$405,800	
Due to federal government	126,520	
Due to state government	39,740	
Due to other funds	5,000	
Total Liabilities		$577,060
Fund Balances:		
Reserved for encumbrances—2008	70,240	
Fund balance	86,900	
Total Fund Balances		157,140
Total Liabilities and Fund Balances		$734,200

Balance Sheet—Governmental Funds, one of the several basic financial statements required for conformity with generally accepted accounting principles (see Illustrations 1–4 through 1–14). In addition, GASB standards require disclosures in the notes to the financial statements of a number of details regarding deposits with financial institutions, investments, property taxes, receivables, and other assets.

A second financial statement should be presented for the General Fund in the year-end comprehensive annual financial report, a statement of revenues, expenditures, and changes in fund balance (see Illustration 4–6). Illustration 4–6 presents the actual revenues and actual expenditures that resulted from transactions illustrated in this chapter and other transactions not illustrated because they were similar in nature. Note that the General Fund of the Town of Brighton reports the financial outflow resulting from the interfund transfer out as an Other Financing Use.

The Other Financing Sources (Uses) section in Illustration 4–6 shows a common means of disclosure of nonrevenue financial inflows and nonexpenditure financial outflows. Information shown as Illustration 4–6 would be presented in columnar form in the Statement of Revenues, Expenditures, and Changes in Fund Balances—Governmental Funds (see Illustration 1–8).

GASBS 34 requires a budgetary comparison schedule, as shown previously in Illustration 3–4, or, alternatively, a statement of revenues, expenditures, and changes in fund balance—budget and actual for the General Fund, as well as for each *major* special revenue fund for which a budget is legally adopted. Illustration 4–7 presents a budgetary comparison schedule for the Town of Brighton General Fund. Note that columns must be provided for both the legally adopted budget amounts and final amended amounts.

ILLUSTRATION 4–6

TOWN OF BRIGHTON
General Fund
Statement of Revenues, Expenditures, and Changes in Fund Balance
For the Year Ended December 31, 2008

Revenues:		
Property taxes	$2,599,636	
Interest and penalties on delinquent taxes	11,400	
Sales taxes	485,000	
Licenses and permits	213,200	
Fines and forfeits	310,800	
Intergovernmental revenue	284,100	
Charges for services	82,464	
Miscellaneous revenues	28,400	
Total Revenues		$4,015,000
Expenditures:		
2008:		
General government	649,400	
Public safety	1,305,435	
Public works	839,800	
Health and welfare	850,325	
Parks and recreation	292,500	
Contributions to retirement plans	179,100	
Miscellaneous appropriations	14,200	
Expenditures—2008	4,130,760	
2007:		
Parks and recreation	127,000	
Total Expenditures		4,257,760
Excess of Expenditures Over Revenues		(242,760)
Other financing sources (uses):		
Interfund transfers in	–0–	
Interfund transfers out	(91,500)	
Total Other Financing Sources		(91,500)
Change (Decrease) in Fund Balances		(334,260)
Fund Balances, January 1, 2008		491,400
Fund Balances, December 31, 2008		$ 157,140

The amounts in the Revenues section of the Actual column in Illustration 4–7 present the same information as shown in the Revenues section of Illustration 4–6 because in the Town of Brighton example, the General Fund revenues budget is on a GAAP basis, the same as actual revenues. However, the amounts in the Expenditures section of the Actual column of the budgetary comparison schedule (Illustration 4–7) differ from the expenditures shown in Illustration 4–6 because under GAAP expenditures chargeable to 2007 appropriations of $127,000 and expenditures of the 2008 appropriations of $4,130,760 are reported in Illustration 4–6. Also, in the GAAP operating statement, Illustration 4–6, encumbrances are not reported in the Expenditures section of the statement. In contrast, GASB standards require the amounts in the Actual column

ILLUSTRATION 4–7

TOWN OF BRIGHTON
General Fund
Schedule of Revenues, Expenditures, and Changes in Fund Balance—Budget and Actual
(Non-GAAP Presentation)
For the Year Ended December 31, 2008

	Budgeted Amounts		Actual Amounts Budgetary Basis	Variance with Final Budget Over (Under)
	Original	Final		
Revenues:				
Taxes:				
Property taxes	$2,600,000	$2,600,000	$2,599,636	$ (364)
Interest and penalties on taxes	13,000	13,000	11,400	(1,600)
Sales taxes	480,000	480,000	485,000	5,000
Total taxes	3,093,000	3,093,000	3,096,036	3,036
Licenses and permits	220,000	220,000	213,200	(6,800)
Fines and forfeits	308,000	308,000	310,800	2,800
Intergovernmental revenue	280,000	280,000	284,100	4,100
Charges for services	70,000	75,000	82,464	7,464
Miscellaneous revenues	15,000	25,000	28,400	3,400
Total Revenues	3,986,000	4,001,000	4,015,000	14,000
Expenditures and encumbrances:				
General government	660,000	660,000	658,850	(1,150)
Public safety	1,240,000	1,320,000	1,318,500	(1,500)
Public works	910,000	860,000	859,200	(800)
Health and welfare	860,000	860,000	858,650	(1,350)
Parks and recreation	315,000	315,000	312,500	(2,500)
Contributions to retirement plans	180,000	180,000	179,100	(900)
Miscellaneous appropriations	15,000	15,000	14,200	(800)
Total Expenditures	4,180,000	4,210,000	4,201,000	(9,000)
Excess of Expenditures over Revenues	(194,000)	(209,000)	(186,000)	23,000
Other financing sources (uses)	(91,500)	(91,500)	(91,500)	–0–
Decrease in Reserve for Encumbrances	—	—	(56,760)	(56,760)
Decrease in Fund Balance for year	(285,500)	(300,500)	(334,260)	(33,760)
Fund Balances, January 1, 2008	491,400	491,400	491,400	–0–
Fund Balances, December 31, 2008	$ 205,900	$ 190,900	$ 157,140	$(33,760)

of Illustration 4–7 to conform with budgetary practices; therefore, in that statement, encumbrances outstanding at the end of fiscal 2008 are added to 2008 expenditures because both are uses of the 2008 appropriation authority.

Note that expenditures for 2007 are excluded from the budget and actual schedule because that schedule relates only to the 2008 budget. GASB standards require differences between the amounts reported in the two statements (Illustrations 4–6 and 4–7) to be reconciled in a separate schedule or in the notes to the required supplementary information. For example, the notes to the budgetary comparison schedule for the Town of Brighton might include the following reconciliation of General Fund Expenditures reported in the two operating statements illustrated:

Expenditures for 2008, budgetary basis	$4,201,000
Less: Reserve for encumbrances as of December 31, 2008	(70,240)
Expenditures for 2008, GAAP basis	$4,130,760

The presentation of Reserve for Encumbrances in Illustrations 4–5, 4–6, and 4–7 and in the illustrative reconciliation is based on the assumption that amounts encumbered at year-end do not need to be appropriated for the following year. The amounts shown in Illustration 4–7 in the Expenditures section in the Variance with Final Budget column, however, disclose the portion of each appropriation for 2008 that was neither expended nor encumbered during that year; those amounts, totaling $9,000, are said to *lapse,* that is, become unavailable for expenditure or encumbrance, in the year following 2008.

SPECIAL REVENUE FUNDS

As noted in Chapters 2 and 3, special revenue funds are needed when legal or policy considerations require separate funds to be created for current purposes other than those served by proprietary or fiduciary funds. An example of a special revenue fund created to demonstrate legal compliance is a Street Fund, which is largely financed by a local government's share of the motor fuel tax levied by the state to be used only for maintenance and construction of streets, roads, and bridges. A second example of a special revenue fund is a Library Operating Fund created to account for a special tax levy or simply the desire of the governing board to have a separate fund to account for an activity that differs from other governmental activities. A third example is a fund to account for grants received from a higher jurisdiction, such as a federal Community Development Block Grant. Grant accounting is discussed briefly in the following paragraph. A final example is a trust fund in which both the investment principal and the investment earnings are available to support a government program or the citizenry. A common example of the latter is a gift received under a trust agreement that can be used only to purchase works of art for public buildings.

Accounting for Operating Grants

Grants received by a local government from the state or federal government—or received by a state from the federal government—are often restricted for specified operating purposes. Consequently, a special revenue fund is frequently used to account for the revenues of such grants. A number of grants provide that the grantor will pay the grantee on a reimbursement basis. In such instances, GASB standards require that the grant revenue not be recognized until the expenditure has taken place.[5] As an example of appropriate accounting procedures, assume that a local government has been awarded a state grant to finance a fine arts program, but the state will provide reimbursement only after the grantee has made expenditures related to the fine arts

[5] GASB *Codification,* Sec. N50.112. See the appendix to this chapter for a more detailed discussion of revenue and expense/expenditure recognition for both exchange and nonexchange transactions.

program. This is an example of a **voluntary nonexchange transaction** in which an **eligibility requirement** (incurrence of allowable costs) must be met before the local government can recognize an asset and revenue. Assuming that the grantee government creates a special revenue fund to account for the fine arts program and has incurred qualifying expenditures, or expense at the government-wide level, the required entries in both the special revenue fund and the governmental activities journals would be:

	Debits	Credits
Special Revenue Fund and Governmental Activities:		
Expenditures (or expense)	50,000	
Vouchers Payable (or Cash)		50,000
Cash	50,000	
Revenues		50,000

The latter entry, of course, records the reimbursement, which presumably would be a short time after the expenditures are incurred. If the grant provided instead that a specified amount would be available for the current accounting period, regardless of whether qualifying expenditures are incurred, there would be no eligibility requirement (except that the grantee be an authorized recipient). In this case, it would be appropriate for the special revenue fund to recognize an asset (Due from Federal [or State] Government) and Revenues upon notification by the state grantor agency. If the grant imposes a **time requirement,** such as specifying that the amount is intended for a future accounting period, a liability account, Deferred Revenues, would be credited upon notification of the grant rather than Revenues. In the period for which the grant is intended, an entry would be made in the special revenue fund and governmental activities journals to debit Deferred Revenues and credit Revenues.

Financial Reporting

Special revenue fund accounting and financial reporting are essentially the same as for the General Fund, as described in depth in this chapter. In addition to amounts for the General Fund, amounts for *major* special revenue funds would be included in the balance sheet and statement of revenues, expenditures, and changes in fund balances prepared for the governmental funds. A budgetary comparison schedule is also provided as required supplementary information for each major special revenue fund. Elsewhere in the financial section of the government's CAFR, a combining balance sheet and combining operating statement should be provided for all *nonmajor* governmental funds, including nonmajor special revenue funds. An example of a combining statement of revenues, expenditures, and changes in fund balances for nonmajor governmental funds is presented in Illustration 4–8 for the City and County of Denver. Because the City and County of Denver has numerous nonmajor governmental funds, it also provides combining financial statements for each governmental fund type; that is, special revenue, debt service, and capital projects.

INTERFUND ACTIVITY

Reciprocal Interfund Activity

Internal exchange transactions—those involving the sales and purchases of goods and services in a reciprocal exchange transaction between two funds—were discussed earlier in this chapter. These transactions are termed *interfund services*

ILLUSTRATION 4–8

CITY AND COUNTY OF DENVER
Combining Statement of Revenues, Expenditures, and Changes in Fund Balance
Nonmajor Governmental Funds
For the year ended December 31, 2004 (amounts expressed in thousands)

	Special Revenue	Debt Service	Capital Projects	Cableland Trust	Total
REVENUES					
Taxes:					
Property	$ —	$ 68,793	$ —	$ —	$ 68,793
Sales and use	175	19,728	—	—	19,903
Other	3,509	16,716	25,047	—	45,272
Special assessments	—	59	596	—	655
Licenses and permits	228	—	—	—	228
Intergovernmental revenues	77,603	—	21,468	—	99,071
Charges for services	22,616	—	2,889	—	25,505
Investment and interest income	3,648	1,387	3,453	389	8,877
Fines and forfeitures	2,353	—	—	—	2,353
Contributions	17,352	—	1,445	—	18,797
Other revenue	22,467	—	1,221	—	23,688
TOTAL REVENUES	149,951	106,683	56,119	389	313,142
EXPENDITURES					
Current:					
General government	28,537	—	—	—	28,537
Public safety	26,355	—	—	—	26,355
Public works	—	—	745	—	745
Health	5,622	—	—	—	5,622
Parks and recreation	7,908	—	—	—	7,908
Cultural activities	25,411	—	—	—	25,411
Community development	28,056	—	—	—	28,056
Economic opportunity	19,130	—	—	—	19,130
Principal retirement	6,446	54,693	2,975	—	64,114
Interest	8,876	37,313	502	—	46,691
Bond issue costs	—	297	—	—	297
Capital outlay	2,103	—	106,470	—	108,573
TOTAL EXPENDITURES	158,444	92,303	110,692	—	361,439
Excess (deficiency) of revenues over expenditures	(8,493)	14,380	(54,573)	389	(48,297)
OTHER FINANCE SOURCES (USES)					
Sale of capital assets	—	—	1,038	—	1,038
Developer advance	—	—	92	—	92
GID bonds issued	—	2,411	—	—	2,411
Payment to refunding escrow	—	(2,287)	—	—	(2,287)
Capital leases	2,103	—	—	—	2,103
Transfers in	32,467	26,713	3,740	—	62,920
Transfers out	(2,849)	(40,374)	(8,277)	(177)	(51,677)
TOTAL OTHER FINANCING SOURCES (USES)	31,721	(13,537)	(3,407)	(177)	14,600
Net change in fund balance	23,228	843	(57,980)	212	(33,697)
Fund balance—January 1	172,925	56,153	153,295	3,147	385,520
FUND BALANCE—December 31	$196,153	$ 56,996	$ 95,315	$3,359	$351,823

provided and used in *GASBS 34.* Other transactions between funds are discussed in this section.

Interfund Loans

Interfund loans are sometimes made from one fund to another with the intent that the amount be repaid. If the loan must be repaid during the current year or soon thereafter, the lending fund should record a current receivable, and the borrowing fund should record a current liability. This is illustrated by the following journal entries, assuming that the General Fund makes a short-term loan in the amount of $100,000 to the Central Stores Fund, an internal service fund.

	General Ledger		Subsidiary Ledger	
	Debits	**Credits**	**Debits**	**Credits**
General Fund:				
Interfund Loans Receivable—Current	100,000			
Cash		100,000		
Internal Service Fund:				
Cash	100,000			
Interfund Loans Payable—Current		100,000		

If this interfund loan did not require repayment for more than one year, the word "Noncurrent" should be used rather than "Current" to signify the noncurrent nature of the loan.[6] As shown in the following entries, *Noncurrent* is added to each of the interfund loan receivable/payable accounts to indicate that the loan is not payable during the current year or soon thereafter.

General Fund:		
Interfund Loans Receivable—Noncurrent . .	100,000	
Cash		100,000
Internal Service Fund:		
Cash	100,000	
Interfund Loans Payable—Noncurrent . .		100,000

Because the noncurrent interfund loan receivable represents assets that are not available for the current year's appropriation in the General Fund, the Fund Balance account should be reserved for this amount, as was done for encumbered amounts and ending inventories of supplies.

---

[6] Governments also use the accounts "Due to (from) Other Funds" and "Advances from (to) Other Funds" to record current and noncurrent interfund loans, respectively. The authors prefer to reserve the use of "Due to (from) Other Funds" for operating transactions only, that is, interfund transfers and internal exchange transactions. Although used for decades, the term "Advances" is somewhat vague.

	General Ledger		Subsidiary Ledger	
	Debits	*Credits*	*Debits*	*Credits*
General Fund:				
Fund Balance	100,000			
Reserve for Noncurrent Interfund				
Loans Receivable		100,000		

An interesting question is whether the illustrated interfund loans require journal entries at the government-wide level. The answer is no since *GASBS 34* requires that internal service fund amounts be reported in the Governmental Activities column of the government-wide financial statements. Interfund receivables and payables between two funds that are both included in governmental activities have no effect on the amounts reported in the government-wide statement of net assets.

Nonreciprocal Interfund Activity

Interfund Transfers

The former reporting model identified two types of interfund transfers: *operating transfers* and *residual equity transfers,* which were reported in two different ways in governmental fund operating statements. Under *GASBS 34,* both types of transfers are described simply as **interfund transfers** and reported in the same manner—as other financing sources by the receiving fund and as other financing uses by the transferring fund. Some interfund transfers are periodic, routine transfers. For example, state laws may require that taxes be levied by a General Fund or a special revenue fund to finance an expenditure to be made from another fund (such as a debt service fund). Since the general rule is that revenues should be recorded as such only once, the transferor records the transfer of tax revenue to the expending fund as an Other Financing Use—Interfund Transfer Out, and the transferee records it as an Other Financing Source—Interfund Transfer In.

Other interfund transfers, those formerly called *residual equity transfers,* are non-routine transactions often made to establish or liquidate a fund, such as the Town of Brighton example (Entries 2 and 2a earlier in this chapter) in which the General Fund transferred cash and inventory to create a supplies internal service fund. The creation of a fund by transfer of assets and/or resources from an existing fund to a new fund, or transfers of residual balances of discontinued funds to another fund, results in the recognition of an other financing source rather than a revenue by the new fund and an other financing use rather than an expenditure by the transferor fund.

Reimbursements

Internal exchange transactions for interfund services provided and used, described earlier in this chapter, represent the only form of interfund transactions that result in the recognition of revenue by the receiving fund. In certain instances, one fund may record as an expenditure an item that should have been recorded as an expenditure by another fund. Often this is the result of an accounting error. When the second fund reimburses the first fund, the first fund should recognize the reimbursement as a reduction of its Expenditures account, not as an item of revenue. The second fund should debit Expenditures and credit Cash, as should have been done when the transaction initially occurred. Reimbursements are not reported in the financial statements except for reporting expenditures/expenses in the correct fund.

Intra- versus Inter-Activity Transactions (Government-wide Level)

In all the preceding examples, if the interfund transaction occurs between two governmental funds (or between a governmental fund and an internal service fund) or between two enterprise funds, that is, an **intra-activity transaction,** then neither the Governmental Activities column nor the Business-type Activities column is affected at the government-wide level. Interfund loans or transfers between a governmental fund (or internal service fund) and an enterprise fund results in an **inter-activity transaction.** These transactions are reported as "Internal Balances" on the government-wide statement of net assets (see Illustration 1–4) and "Transfers" in the statement of activities (see Illustration 1–6). Except for internal exchange transactions between governmental funds and internal service funds, for which any element of profit or loss is eliminated prior to preparing the government-wide financial statements, other internal exchange transactions should be reported as Revenues and Expenses in the statement of activity.

Intra-Entity Transactions

Intra-entity transactions are exchange or nonexchange transactions between the primary government and its blended or discretely presented component units. Transactions between the primary government and *blended* component units follow the same standards as for reciprocal and nonreciprocal interfund activity discussed in preceding paragraphs. Transactions between the primary government and *discretely presented* component units are treated as if the component units are external entities, and thus should be reported as revenues and expenses in the statement of activities. Amounts receivable and payable resulting from these transactions should be reported on a separate line in the statement of net assets.

PERMANENT FUNDS

Governments often receive contributions under trust agreements in which the principal amount is not expendable but earnings are expendable. Most of these trusts are established to benefit a government program or function, or the citizenry, rather than an external individual, organization, or government. Trusts of the first type are called **public-purpose trusts;** trusts of the second type are **private-purpose trusts.**

The *GASBS 34* model requires that public-purpose trusts for which the earnings are expendable for a specified purpose but the principal amount is not expendable (also referred to as *endowments*) be accounted for in a governmental fund called a **permanent fund.** Public-purpose trusts for which both principal and earnings thereon can be expended for a specified purpose are accounted for in a special revenue fund, again a governmental fund type. Accounting issues involving private-purpose trusts are discussed in Chapter 8.

Budgetary Accounts

Budgetary accounts generally should not be needed for permanent funds because transactions of the fund result in changes in the fund principal only incidentally; by definition, the principal cannot be appropriated or expended. However, public-purpose expendable trust funds may be required by law to use the appropriation procedure to ensure adequate budgetary control over the expenditure of fund assets since they are accounted for in special revenue funds. If the appropriation procedure is required, the use of the other budgetary accounts discussed earlier in this chapter is also recommended. The following paragraphs illustrate a public-purpose nonexpendable trust that is accounted for as a permanent fund.

Illustrative Case

As an illustration of the nature of accounting for permanent fund trust principal and expendable trust revenue, assume on November 1, 2007, Wilma Wexner died, having made a valid will that provided for the gift of marketable securities to the City of Concordia to be held as a nonexpendable trust. For purposes of income distribution, the net income from the securities is to be computed on the full accrual basis but does not include increases or decreases in the fair value of investments. Income, so measured, is to be transferred to the City's Library Operating Fund, a special revenue fund. Accounting for the Library Operating Fund is not illustrated here because it would be very similar to General Fund accounting already covered in depth in this chapter. For sake of brevity, corresponding entries in the general journal for governmental activities at the government-wide level are also omitted.

The gift was accepted by the City of Concordia, which established the Library Endowment Fund (a permanent fund) to account for operation of the trust. The following securities were received by the Library Endowment Fund:

	Interest Rate per Year	Maturity Date	Face Value	Fair Value as of 11/1/07
Bonds of AB Company	6%	1/1/12	$640,000	$652,000

	Number of Shares	Fair Value as of 11/1/07
Stocks:		
M Company, common	5,400	$282,000
S Company, common	22,000	214,000
Total		$496,000

Journal Entries—Permanent Fund

The Library Endowment Fund's receipt of the securities is properly recorded at the fair value of the securities as of the date of the gift because this is the amount the trustees are responsible for. Although the face value of the bonds will be received at maturity (if the bonds are held until maturity), GASB standards require that investments in bonds maturing more than one year from receipt be reported at fair value.[7] Thus the entry in the Library Endowment Fund to record the receipt of the securities at initiation of the trust on November 1, 2007 is:

		Debits	Credits
	Permanent Fund:		
1.	Investment in Bonds	652,000	
	Investment in Stocks	496,000	
	Accrued Interest Receivable	12,800	
	Revenues—Contributions for Endowment		1,160,800
	[Interest accrued on the bonds of Company AB ($640,000 × 6% × 4/12 = $12,800), assuming semiannual interest was last received on July 1, 2007]		

[7] GASB *Codification*, Sec. 150.105.

As of January 1, 2008, semiannual interest of $19,200 is received on the AB Company bonds, of which only one-third of the total corresponding to the two months of interest earned since the endowment was created can be transferred to the Library Operating Fund. The entry for the receipt of bond interest on January 1, 2008, and the revenue earned for transfer to the Library Operating Fund is:

		Debits	Credits
	Permanent Fund:		
2.	Cash	19,200	
	Accrued Interest Receivable		12,800
	Revenues—Bond Interest		6,400

Dividends on stock do not accrue. They become a receivable only when declared by the corporation issuing the stock. Ordinarily the receivable is not recorded because it is followed in a reasonably short time by issuance of a dividend check. Assuming dividends on the stock held by the Library Endowment Fund were received early in January 2008 in the amount of $9,800, Entry 3 is appropriate:

	Permanent Fund:		
3.	Cash	9,800	
	Revenues—Dividends		9,800

As the bond interest and dividends on stock were received in cash, the Library Endowment Fund has sufficient cash to pay the amount owed to the Library Operating Fund for interest and dividends earned since the endowment was created. Assuming that cash is transferred as of January 3, 2008, Entry 4 is:

	Permanent Fund:		
4.	Other Financing Uses—Interfund Transfers Out	16,200	
	Cash		16,200

On the advice of an investment manager, 1,800 shares of M Company stock were sold for $99,000; this amount and cash of $7,000 were invested in 4,000 shares of LH Company common stock. The M Company stock sold was one-third of the number of shares received when the trust was established; therefore, the shares sold had a carrying value of one-third of $282,000, or $94,000. The difference between the stock's carrying value and the proceeds at the time of sale is considered in this trust to belong to the corpus and does not give rise to a gain or loss that would adjust the net income to be transferred to the Library Operating Fund. Therefore, the sale of M Company stock and the purchase of LH Company stock should be recorded in the Library Endowment Fund as shown in Entries 5a and 5b:

		Debits	Credits
Permanent Fund:			
5a.	Cash	99,000	
	Investment in Stocks		94,000
	Revenues—Change in Fair Value of Investments		5,000
5b.	Investment in Stocks	106,000	
	Cash		106,000

Assuming there were no further purchases or sales of stock and that dividends received on April 1, 2008, amounted to $10,800, Entry 6a is necessary, as well as Entry 6b to make the required interfund transfer to the Library Operating Fund.

Permanent Fund:			
6a.	Cash	10,800	
	Revenues—Dividends		10,800
6b.	Other Financing Uses—Interfund Transfers Out	10,800	
	Cash		10,800

Interest accrued on June 30, 2008, amounted to $19,200, the same amount received early in January 2008. The fair value of the Library Endowment Fund investments as of June 30, 2008, the last day of the City of Concordia's fiscal year, is given below.

		Fair Value as of 11/1/07	Fair Value as of 6/30/08	Change in Fair Value
Bonds of AB Company		$652,000	$674,000	$22,000
Stocks	**No. of Shares**			
M Company	3,600	$188,000	$194,400	$ 6,400
S Company	22,000	214,000	220,600	6,600
LH Company	4,000	106,000*	104,500	(1,500)
Total		$508,000	$519,500	$11,500

*As of date of transaction 5 for LH Company.

Entry 7a records the accrual of interest earned for transfer to the Library Operating Fund. Entry 7b records the adjusting entry to record the change in fair value of investments at the end of the fiscal year, compared with the prior fair value recorded for the investments. Entry 7c records the liability to the Library Operating Fund.

		Debits	Credits
	Permanent Fund:		
7a.	Accrued Interest Receivable	19,200	
	Revenues—Bond Interest		19,200
7b.	Investment in Bonds	22,000	
	Investment in Stocks	11,500	
	Revenues—Change in Fair Value of Investments		33,500
7c.	Other Financing Uses—Interfund		
	Transfers Out	19,200	
	Due to Library Operating Fund		19,200

The closing entry at the end of the fiscal year, June 30, 2008, is shown in Entry 8.

	Permanent Fund:		
8.	Revenues—Contributions for Endowment	1,160,800	
	Revenues—Bond Interest	25,600	
	Revenues—Dividends	20,600	
	Revenues—Change in Fair Value of Investments	38,500	
	Other Financing Uses—Interfund Transfers Out		46,200
	Fund Balance—Reserved for Endowment		1,199,300

In Entry 8, one can see that $46,200, the total interest earned on bonds and dividends received on investments in stocks, was transferred during the year to the Library Operating Fund; the net change (increase) in fair value of investments, $38,500, and the original contribution are added to the Fund Balance. If the net increase in the value of investments were permitted under the trust agreement to be used for library operating purposes, the entire $84,700 (sum of earnings and increase in fair value) would have been transferred out, and the addition to Fund Balance would have been just the $1,168,300 original contribution.

At year-end, financial statements for the Library Endowment Fund would be presented in essentially the same formats as the General Fund balance sheet and General Fund statement of revenues, expenditures, and changes in fund balance shown in Illustrations 4–5 and 4–6. If the Library Endowment Fund meets the criteria for a major fund, its balance sheet and operating statement information will be included as a column in the balance sheet—governmental funds and statement of revenues, expenditures, and changes in fund balances—governmental funds, examples of which are presented in Illustrations 1–6 and 1–8 in Chapter 1. If the fund is determined to be a nonmajor fund, it would be reported in the combining balance sheet and operating statement presented in the CAFR for the nonmajor governmental funds (see Illustration 4–8 for an example of the latter type of financial statement).

As indicated previously, entries in the Library Operating Fund are omitted for the sake of brevity since accounting for special revenue funds is similar to that for the General Fund. Thus, at the beginning of the 2008 fiscal year (July 1, 2007) a budgetary entry would have been recorded; that entry would have been amended on November 1, 2007, the date the Library Endowment Fund was created, to reflect the Estimated Other Financing Sources (interfund transfers in) expected from the endowment and to authorize expenditures of all or a portion of those resources in the Library Operating Fund. Each time Other Financing Uses—Interfund Transfers Out are recorded in the Library Endowment Fund, Other Financing Sources—Interfund Transfers In would be recorded in the same amount in the Library Operating Fund.

Chapters 3 and 4 have focused on operating activities that are recorded in the General Fund, special revenue funds, permanent funds, and in governmental activities at the government-wide level. Chapter 5 discusses accounting for general capital assets and capital projects funds, while general long-term debt and debt service funds are discussed in Chapter 6.

Appendix

Concepts and Rules for Recognition of Revenues and Expenses (or Expenditures)

EXCHANGE TRANSACTIONS

Current GASB standards provide guidance for the accounting recognition of revenues and expenses on the accrual basis in the government-wide financial statements and revenues and expenditures on the modified accrual basis in the governmental fund financial statements.[1A] Recognition rules for *exchange transactions* and *exchange-like transactions,* those in which each party receives value essentially equal to the value given, are generally straightforward; for operating transactions, the party selling goods or services recognizes an asset (for example, a receivable or cash) and a revenue when the transaction occurs and the revenue has been earned. The party purchasing goods or services recognizes an expense or expenditure and liability (or reduction in cash). As discussed in Chapter 2, under the *modified accrual* basis of accounting, if a governmental fund provides goods or services to another party or fund, it should recognize an asset (receivable or cash) and a revenue if the assets (financial resources) are deemed *measurable* and *available.* If a governmental fund *receives* goods or services from another party or fund, it should recognize expenditures (not expense) when the fund liability has been incurred. In most cases, exchange transactions of governmental funds result in measurable and available assets being received or a fund liability being incurred when the transaction occurs, and thus result in immediate recognition of revenues and expenditures. For example, the General Fund should recognize a revenue immediately when a citizen is charged a fee for a building permit and an expenditure when a purchase order for supplies has been filled.

NONEXCHANGE TRANSACTIONS

Nonexchange transactions are defined as external events in which a government gives or receives value without directly receiving or giving equal value in exchange.[2A] Accounting for nonexchange transactions raises a number of conceptual issues, some of which are

---

[1A] GASB *Codification of Governmental Accounting and Financial Reporting Standards as of June 30, 2005* (Norwalk, CT, 2005), Sec. 1600, and GASB *Statement No. 33,* "Accounting and Financial Reporting for Nonexchange Transactions" (Norwalk, CT, 1998).

[2A] GASB *Codification,* Sec. N50.104.

explored in this chapter and some in later chapters. Two key concepts that affect a resource recipient's recognition of revenues (or a resource provider's recognition of expenses/expenditures) are *time requirements* and *purpose restrictions.*[3A]

Time requirements relate either to the period when resources are required to be used or to when use *may* begin. Thus, time requirements determine the *timing* of revenue or expense (expenditure) recognition—that is, whether these elements should be recognized (recorded in the accounts) in the current period or deferred to a future period. **Purpose restrictions** refer to specifications by resource providers of the purpose or purposes for which resources are required to be used. For example, a grant may specify that resources can be used only to provide transportation for senior citizens. The *timing* of revenue recognition is unaffected by purpose restrictions. Rather, the purpose restrictions should be clearly reported as restrictions of net assets in the government-wide statement of net assets or as reservations of fund balance in the governmental funds balance sheet (see Illustrations 1–4 and 1–6 in Chapter 1 for examples).

For certain classes of nonexchange transactions, discussed later in this section, revenue and expense recognition may be delayed until program *eligibility requirements* are met. Eligibility requirements may include, in addition to time requirements, specified characteristics that program recipients must possess or reimbursement provisions and contingencies tied to required actions by the recipient. GASB *Statement No. 33,* Appendix C, provides the example of state-provided reimbursements to school districts for special education. To meet the specified eligibility requirements, (1) the recipient must be a school district, (2) the applicable school year must have started, and (3) the district must have incurred allowable costs. Only when all three conditions are met can a school district record a revenue and the state record an expense. The school district would record an asset and deferred revenue if the resources are received in advance of meeting eligibility requirements. Otherwise, the school district would not record an asset nor would the state record a liability to provide the resources until all the eligibility requirements have been met.

Nonexchange transactions are subdivided into four classes: (1) *derived tax revenues* (e.g., income and sales taxes), (2) *imposed nonexchange revenues* (e.g., property taxes and fines and penalties), (3) **government-mandated nonexchange transactions** (e.g., certain education, social welfare, and transportation services mandated and funded by a higher level of government), and (4) *voluntary nonexchange transactions* (e.g., grants and entitlements from higher levels of government and certain private donations).[4A]

RECOGNITION OF NONEXCHANGE TRANSACTIONS

Illustration 4–9 provides a summary of the recognition criteria applicable to each class of nonexchange transactions, both for the accrual basis of accounting and for modified accrual. Assets and revenues in the *derived tax revenues* category are generally recognized in the period in which the underlying exchange occurs; the period in which income is earned for income taxes and when sales have occurred for sales taxes.

For *imposed nonexchange revenues,* an asset (receivable or cash) is recognized when there is an enforceable legal claim or when cash is received, whichever is first. Revenues should be recognized in the period in which the resources are required to be used or the first period when their use is permitted. For property taxes, revenues usually are recognized in the period for which the taxes are levied. In governmental funds, the additional criterion of availability for use must be met. Current standards, as interpreted, define

[3A] Ibid., par. 109.
[4A] Ibid., par. 104.

ILLUSTRATION 4–9   **Summary Chart—Classes and Timing of Recognition of Nonexchange Transactions**

Class	Recognition
Derived tax revenues Examples: sales taxes, personal and corporate income taxes, motor fuel taxes, and similar taxes on earnings or consumption	**Assets*** Period when *underlying exchange has occurred* or when resources are received, whichever is first. **Revenues** Period when *underlying exchange has occurred*. (Report advance receipts as deferred revenues.) When modified accrual accounting is used, resources also should be "available."
Imposed nonexchange revenues Examples: property taxes, most fines and forfeitures	**Assets*** Period when an *enforceable legal claim has arisen* or when resources are received. whichever is first. **Revenues** Period when *resources are required to be used* or first period that use is permitted (for example, for property taxes, the *period for which levied*). When modified accrual accounting is used, resources *also* should be "available." (For property taxes, apply NCGA Interpretation 3, as amended.)
Government-mandated nonexchange transactions Examples: federal government mandates on state and local governments **Voluntary nonexchange transactions** Examples: certain grants and entitlements, most donations	**Assets* and Liabilities** Period when *all eligibility requirements have been met* or (for asset recognition) when resources are received, whichever is first. **Revenues and expenses or expenditures** Period when *all eligibility requirements have been met*. (Report advance receipts or payments for use in the following period as deferred revenues or advances, respectively. However, when a provider precludes the sale, disbursement, or consumption of resources for a specified number of years, until a specified event has occurred, or permanently [for example, permanent and term endowments], report revenues and expenses or expenditures when the resources are, respectively, received or paid and report resulting net assets, equity, or fund balance as restricted.) When modified accrual accounting is used for revenue recognition, resources *also* should be "available."

*If there are purpose restrictions, report restricted net assets (or equity or fund balance) or, for governmental funds, a reservation of fund balance.

Source: GASB *Statement No. 33* (Norwalk, CT, 1998), Appendix C.

available in the context of property taxes as meaning "collected within the current period or expected to be collected soon enough thereafter to be used to pay liabilities of the current period."[5A] *Soon enough thereafter* means not later than 60 days after the end of the current period.[6A]

A common set of recognition rules applies to the remaining two classes of nonexchange transactions: *government-mandated* and *voluntary exchange.* An asset (a receivable or cash) is recognized when all eligibility requirements have been met or when cash is received, whichever occurs first. For example, although cash has not been received from a grantor, when a program recipient meets matching requirements imposed by the grantor agency in order to become eligible for a social services grant, a receivable (Due from [Grantor]) would be recorded. Revenues should be recognized only when all eligibility criteria have been met. If cash is received in the period prior

[5A] GASB, *Codification*, Sec. P70.104.

[6A] Ibid.

to intended use (that is, there is a time restriction) or before eligibility requirements have been met, deferred revenues should be reported rather than revenues. In the period when the time restriction expires, the account Deferred Revenues will be debited and Revenues will be credited.

It should be apparent that a particular nonexchange transaction may lead to recognition of revenues in one period in the government-wide statement of activities, but be reported as deferred revenues in a governmental fund because it is deemed not to be *available* to pay current period obligations. These recognition timing differences are illustrated in later chapters.

Key Terms

Consumption method, *129*
Delinquent taxes, *117*
Derived tax revenues, *121*
Eligibility requirements, *138*
Exchange transaction, *115*
Exchange-like transaction, *115*
Government-mandated nonexchange transactions, *148*
Gross tax levy, *115*
Imposed nonexchange revenue, *116*

Inter-activity transactions, *142*
Interfund loans, *140*
Interfund transfers, *141*
Internal exchange transaction, *128*
Intra-activity transactions, *142*
Intra-entity transactions, *142*
Nonexchange revenue, *116*
Nonexchange transactions, *121*

Permanent fund, *142*
Private-purpose trusts, *142*
Public-purpose trusts, *142*
Purchases method, *129*
Purpose restrictions, *148*
Tax anticipation note, *120*
Tax rate, *115*
Time requirements, *138*
Voluntary nonexchange transactions, *138*

Selected References

American Institute of Certified Public Accountants. Audit and Accounting Guide. *Audits of State and Local Governments.* Revised. New York, 2005.
Governmental Accounting Standards Board. *Codification of Governmental Accounting and Financial Reporting Standards as of June 30, 2005.* Norwalk, CT, 2005.

Questions

4–1. Why do certain transactions of a government require an entry in the general journal of the General Fund as well as an entry in the general journal of governmental activities at the government-wide level? Give some examples.

4–2. Explain why it is often necessary to reserve a portion of the fund equity of the General Fund or a special revenue fund.

4–3. Identify some of the key differences between the government-wide statement of net assets and the balance sheet for governmental funds.

4–4. If the General Fund of a certain city needs $6,790,000 revenue from property taxes to finance estimated expenditures of the next fiscal year and historical experience indicates 3 percent of the gross levy will not be collected, how much should the gross levy for property taxes be? Show all computations in good form.

4–5. If a budget is prepared on the cash basis in order to comply with state law, it should be adjusted to the accrual basis so that the budget and actual schedule or statement may be prepared in conformity with generally accepted accounting principles. Do you agree? Why or why not?

4–6. How does the use of encumbrance procedures improve budgetary control over a department's expenditures?

4–7. Why are operating outflows for governmental activities reported as expenditures in governmental funds but as expenses in the Governmental Activities column of the government-wide statement of activities?

4–8. Explain the primary differences between *ad valorem* taxes, such as property taxes, and other taxes that generate *derived tax revenues,* such as sales and income taxes. How does accounting differ between these classes of taxes?

4–9. If interim financial reporting to external parties is not required, why should a government bother to prepare interim financial statements and schedules? Give some examples of interim financial statements or schedules that a government should consider for internal management use.

4–10. How does a *permanent fund* differ from public-purpose trusts that are reported in special revenue funds? How does it differ from private-purpose trust funds?

Cases

4–1 **Analyzing Results of Operations.** Using either a city's own Web site or the *GASB 34* link of the GASB's Web site, download either the city's entire comprehensive annual financial report (CAFR) or, if possible, just the portion of the CAFR that contains the basic financial statements. Print a copy of the government-wide statement of activities and a copy of the statement of revenues, expenditures, and changes in fund balances—governmental funds, along with the reconciliation between these two statements and respond to the requirements below. The city manager is concerned that some recently elected members of the city council will get a mixed message since the change in net assets reported for governmental activities is noticeably different from the change in fund balances reported on the governmental funds statement of revenues, expenditures, and changes in fund balances. The city manager has requested that you, in your role as finance director, explain to the city council in clear, easy-to-understand terms for what purposes each operating statement is intended and how and why the operating results differ.

Required
a. Examine the two operating statements in detail, paying particular attention to the lines on which changes in net assets and changes in fund balances are reported.
b. Develop a list of reasons why the two numbers are not the same.
c. Prepare a succinct and understandable explanation of the results of operations of this government, in terms that a non-accountant Council member can understand.

4–2 **Policy Issues Relating to Property Taxes.** Property owners in Trevor City were shocked when they recently received notice that assessed valuations on their homes had increased by an average 35 percent, based on a triennial reassessment by the County Board of Equalization. Like many homeowners in the city, you have often complained about the high property taxes in Trevor City, and now you are outraged that your taxes will apparently increase another 35 percent in the coming year.

After stewing all weekend about the unreasonable increase in assessed valuation, you decide to visit the county tax assessor on Monday to find out why your assessed valuation has increased so rapidly. When you finally reach the counter, the customer service representative explains that reassessment considers such factors as actual property sales in particular neighborhoods, trends in building costs, and home improvements. He also explains that heavy demand for both new and previously owned homes had skyrocketed in the Trevor City area in recent years. Moreover, you learn that the reassessment on your home was only average, with some being higher and some lower. Although this information calms you down somewhat, you ask: "But how can we possibly afford a 35 percent increase in our taxes next year?" The representative explains that actual tax rates are set by each jurisdiction having taxing authority over particular properties (in your case, these are the county government, Trevor City, the Trevor City Independent School District, the Trevor City Library, and the Trevor City Redevelopment Authority), so he cannot say how much property taxes will actually increase.

Required

a. When you have regained your composure, prepare a brief written analysis *objectively* evaluating the probability that your property taxes will actually increase by 35 percent next year. In doing so, consider factors that you feel may mitigate against such a large increase. What would have to happen to the tax rates for your taxes to remain at their current level or increase only slightly?

b. Put yourself in the position of the city manager of Trevor City. Does she view the rapid growth in property values as a windfall for the city? What are the potential economic and political risks involved with a hot real estate market such as Trevor City is experiencing?

4–3 **Reporting Internal Service Fund Financial Information at the Government-wide Level.** During the current fiscal year, the City of Manchester created a Printing and Sign Fund (an internal service fund) to provide custom printing and signage for city departments, predominantly those financed by the General Fund. As this is the city's first internal service fund, finance officials are uncertain how to account for the activities of the Printing and Sign Fund at the government-wide level. After much discussion, they have approached you, the audit manager, with the following questions:

1. In governmental activities at the government-wide level, should expenses for printing and signage within the various functions be the amount billed to departments or the Printing and Sign Fund's cost to provide the printing and signage service? Please explain.

2. What about the Printing and Sign Fund's operating revenues from billings to departments? Should these revenues be reported as program revenues, specifically charges for services of the functions receiving the services? Why or why not?

3. The Printing and Sign Fund obtains about 10 percent of its revenues from the City Electric, Sewage, and Water Fund, an enterprise fund. Should the financial information related to these transactions be reported in the Business-type Activities column of the government-wide financial statements, rather than the Governmental Activities column? Please explain in detail.

Required

a. Evaluate these questions and provide a written response for each question to the city's finance director.

b. How would your response to question 3 differ if the Printing and Sign Fund provided 60 percent of its total services to the enterprise fund?

Exercises and Problems

4–1 Examine the CAFR. Utilizing the comprehensive annual financial report obtained for Exercise 1–1, follow these instructions.

a. **Governmental Activities, Government-wide Level.** Answer the following questions. (1) Are governmental activities reported in a separate column from business-type activities in the two government-wide financial statements? (2) Are assets and liabilities reported either in the relative order of their liquidity or on a classified basis on the statement of net assets? (3) Is information on expenses for governmental activities presented at least at the functional level of detail? (4) Are program revenues segregated into (a) charges for services, (b) operating grants and contributions, and (c) capital grants and contributions on the statement of activities?

b. **General Fund.** Answer the following questions. (1) What statements and schedules pertaining to the General Fund are presented? (2) In what respects (headings, arrangements, items included, etc.) do they seem similar to the year-end statements illustrated or described in the text? (3) In what respects do they differ? (4) What purpose is each statement and schedule intended to serve? (5) How well, in your reasoned opinion, does each statement and schedule accomplish its intended purpose? (6) Are any noncurrent or nonliquid assets included in the General Fund balance sheet? If so, are they offset by "Reserve" accounts in the Fund Equity section? (7) Are any noncurrent liabilities included in the General Fund balance sheet? If so, describe them. (8) Are revenue classifications sufficiently detailed to be meaningful? (9) Has the government refrained from reporting expenses rather than expenditures?

c. **Special Revenue Funds.** Answer the following questions. (1) What statements and schedules pertaining to the special revenue funds are presented? (2) Are these only combining statements, or are there also statements for individual special revenue funds? (3) Are expenditures classified by character (i.e., current, intergovernmental, capital outlay, and debt service)? (4) Are current expenditures further categorized at least by function?

d. **Examine Again.** Refer to part *b.* Answer each question again, now from the perspective of the special revenue funds. Review your answers to Exercises 1–1, 2–1, and 3–1 in light of your study of Chapter 4. If you now believe your earlier answers were not entirely correct, change them to conform with your present understanding of GASB financial reporting standards.

4–2 Multiple Choice. Choose the best answer.

1. When equipment was purchased with General Fund resources, which of the following accounts would have been increased in the General Fund?
   a. Appropriations.
   b. Expenditures.
   c. Due from Capital Projects Fund.
   d. No entry should be made in the General Fund.

2. The City of Marshall uses the *consumption method* for recording its inventory of supplies in the General Fund. Rather than using a perpetual inventory system, inventories are updated at year-end based on a physical count. Physical inventories were $85,000 and $75,000 at December 31, 2007 and 2008, respectively. The adjusting journal entry on December 31, 2008, will include a:
   a. Debit to Inventory of Supplies for $75,000.
   b. Debit to Expenditures for $10,000.
   c. Credit to Reserve for Inventory of Supplies for $10,000.
   d. Credit to Expenditures for $10,000.

3. Which of the following items would be reported as a *program revenue* on the government-wide statement of activities?
   a. Sales taxes.
   b. Interest and penalties on taxes.
   c. Unrestricted federal grants.
   d. Fines and Forfeits.

4. Of Victor Township's General Fund property tax levy for the fiscal year ending December 31, 2008, $2,500,000 is expected to be collected during 2008 and January and February of 2009, but $400,000 of the levy is not expected to be collected until after February 2009. The amount of property tax revenues to be recognized in FY 2008 is:
   a. $2,900,000 in governmental activities at the government-wide level and $2,500,000 in the General Fund.
   b. $2,900,000 in governmental activities at the government-wide level and $2,900,000 in the General Fund.
   c. $2,500,000 in governmental activities at the government-wide level and $2,900,000 in the General Fund.
   d. $2,500,000 in governmental activities at the government-wide level and $2,500,000 in the General Fund.

5. Which of the following sources of revenues derives from underlying exchange transactions?
   a. Property taxes.
   b. Fines and forfeits.
   c. Federal and state grants.
   d. Income taxes.

6. Goods for which a $750 purchase order had been placed were received at an actual cost of $740. The journal entry to record the receipt of the goods will include a (an):
   a. Debit to Reserve for Encumbrances for $750.
   b. Debit to Expenditures for $740.
   c. Credit to Vouchers Payable for $740.
   d. All of the above are correct.

7. Internal exchange transactions between governmental funds and an internal service fund are:
   a. Reported as expenditures by governmental funds and as revenues by the internal service fund.
   b. Reported as expenses by governmental funds and as revenues by the internal service fund.
   c. Reported as interfund transfers out by governmental funds and as interfund transfers in by the internal service fund.
   d. Either *a* or *c*, depending on local policy.

8. A special revenue fund that administers a program funded by a reimbursement-type (expenditure driven) federal grant should recognize revenue:
   a. When notified of grant approval.
   b. When qualifying expenditures have been made.
   c. When cash is received.
   d. When the special revenue fund has paid for all services rendered.

9. Which of the following transactions is reported on the government-wide financial statements?
   a. An interfund loan from the General Fund to a special revenue fund.

  b. Equipment used by the General Fund is transferred to an internal service fund that predominantly serves departments that are engaged in governmental activities.
  c. The City Airport Fund, an enterprise fund, transfers a portion of boarding fees charged to passengers to the General Fund.
  d. An interfund transfer is made between the General Fund and the debt service fund.

10. A city receives a $10,000,000 cash contribution under a trust agreement in which investment earnings but not the principal amount can be used to purchase art for city buildings. This contribution should be recorded in a (an):
  a. Fiduciary fund.
  b. Permanent fund.
  c. Special revenue fund.
  d. Internal service fund.

4–3 Property Tax Calculations and Journal Entries. The Village of Darby's budget calls for property tax revenues for the fiscal year ending December 31, 2008, of $2,660,000. Village records indicate that, on average, 2 percent of taxes levied are not collected. The county tax assessor has assessed the value of taxable property located in the village at $135,714,300.

Required
  a. Calculate to the nearest penny what tax rate per $100 of assessed valuation is required to generate a tax levy that will produce the required amount of revenue for the year.
  b. Record the tax levy for 2008 in the General Fund. (Ignore subsidiary detail and entries at the government-wide level. Record credits to Revenues of $2,660,000 and Estimated Uncollectible Current Taxes of $54,286.)
  c. Assume by December 31, 2008, $2,540,000 of the current property tax levy had been collected. Record the amounts collected and reclassify the uncollected amount as delinquent. Interest and penalties of 6 percent were immediately due on the delinquent taxes, but the finance director estimates that 10 percent will not be collectible. Record the interest and penalties receivable. (Round all amounts to nearest dollar.)

4–4 Special Revenue Fund, Voluntary Nonexchange Transaction. The Town of Thornton applied for a grant from the state government for providing an after-school recreational program for at-risk children from low-income families. On January 15, 2008, Thornton was notified that it had been awarded $100,000 for the program. Children are eligible for this program if their family income is less than $25,000. The program provides up to $1,000 per child served. The grant provides twice-monthly reimbursement of all allowable costs of conducting the program, upon notification of program services provided and related expenditures incurred. No time limit is imposed for completion of the program. Any unused grant award can be carried forward to the next fiscal year. By December 31, 2008, its fiscal year-end, Thornton had expended $78,000 in providing services for eligible beneficiaries. Reimbursements of $72,000 had been received by this date.

Required
  a. Provide the appropriate journal entries in both the special revenue fund and governmental activities journals, if any, that would be made upon notification of the grant award.
  b. What are the eligibility requirements for this grant?

c. Provide the appropriate journal entries for FY 2008 in both the special revenue fund and governmental activities journals, assuming that the program expenses are incurred in the Parks and Recreation function.

4–5 Closing Journal Entries. At the end of a fiscal year, budgetary and operating statement control accounts in the general ledger of the General Fund of Jane City had the following balances: Appropriations, $6,224,000; Estimated Other Financing Uses, $2,776,000; Estimated Revenues, $7,997,000; Encumbrances, $0; Expenditures, $6,192,000; Other Financing Uses, $2,770,000; and Revenues, $8,022,000. Appropriations included the authorization to order a certain item at a cost not to exceed $64,700; this was not ordered during the year because it will not be available until late in the following year.

Required

Show in general journal form the entry needed to close all of the preceding accounts that should be closed as of the end of the fiscal year.

4–6 Interfund and Interactivity Transactions. The following transactions affected more than one fund in Brady City.

1. The Fire Department, a governmental activity, purchased $70,000 of water from the Water Utility Fund, a business-type activity.

2. The General Fund made a long-term loan in the amount of $50,000 to the Central Stores Fund, an internal service fund that services City departments.

3. The Municipal Golf Course, an enterprise fund, reimbursed the General Fund $1,000 for office supplies that the General Fund had purchased on its behalf and that were used up in the course of the fiscal year.

4. The General Fund recognizes its annual contribution of $80,000 to the debt service fund for the payment of interest and principal on general obligation bonds that will be paid during the year.

5. The $4,000 balance in the capital projects fund at the completion of construction of a new City Hall was transferred to the General Fund.

Required

a. Make the required journal entries in the general journal of the General Fund and any other fund(s) affected by the interfund transactions described. Also make entries in the governmental activities journal for any transaction(s) affecting a governmental fund. Do not make entries in the subsidiary ledgers.

b. Why is it unnecessary to make entries in a business-type activities journal for any transaction(s) affecting proprietary funds? Are internal service funds any different?

4–7 Transactions and Budgetary Comparison Schedule. The following transactions occurred during the 2008 fiscal year for the City of Stoney Creek. For budgetary purposes, the City reports encumbrances in the Expenditures section of its budgetary comparison schedule for the General Fund but excludes expenditures chargeable to a prior year's appropriation.

1. The budget prepared for the fiscal year 2008 was as follows:

Estimated Revenues:	
Taxes	$1,943,000
Licenses and permits	372,000
Intergovernmental revenue	297,000
Miscellaneous revenues	62,000
Total estimated revenues	2,674,000

Appropriations:	
General government	471,000
Public safety	786,000
Public works	650,000
Health and welfare	600,000
Miscellaneous appropriations	86,000
Total appropriations	2,593,000
Budgeted increase in fund balance	$ 81,000

2. Encumbrances issued against the appropriations during the year were as follows:

General government	$ 58,000
Public safety	201,000
Public works	392,000
Health and welfare	160,000
Miscellaneous appropriations	71,000
Total	$882,000

3. The current year's tax levy of $2,005,000 was recorded; uncollectibles were estimated as $62,000.

4. Tax collections from prior years' levies totaled $132,000; collections of the current year's levy totaled $1,459,000.

5. Personnel costs during the year were charged to the following appropriations in the amounts indicated. Encumbrances were not recorded for personnel costs. (Since no liabilities currently exist for withholdings, you may ignore any FICA or federal or state income tax withholdings.)

General government	$ 411,000
Public safety	584,000
Public works	254,000
Health and welfare	439,000
Miscellaneous appropriations	11,100
Credit to Vouchers Payable	$1,699,100

6. Invoices for all items ordered during the prior year were received and approved for payment in the amount of $14,470. Encumbrances had been recorded in the prior year for these items in the amount of $14,000. The amount chargeable to each year's appropriations should be charged to the Public Safety appropriation.

7. Invoices were received and approved for payment for items ordered in documents recorded as encumbrances in Transaction (2) of this problem. The following appropriations were affected. (*Note:* Expenditures charged to Miscellaneous Appropriations should be treated as General Government expenses in the governmental activities general journal at the government-wide level.)

	Actual Liability	Estimated Liability
General government	$ 52,700	$ 52,200
Public safety	187,800	189,700
Public works	360,000	357,000
Health and safety	130,600	130,100
Miscellaneous appropriations	71,000	71,000
	$802,100	$800,000

8. Revenue other than taxes collected during the year consisted of licenses and permits, $373,000; intergovernmental revenue, $299,000; and $66,000 of miscellaneous revenues. For purposes of accounting for these revenues at the government-wide level, the intergovernmental revenues were operating grants and contributions for the public safety function. Miscellaneous revenues are not identifiable with any function and therefore are recorded as General Revenues at the government-wide level.

9. Payments on Vouchers Payable totaled $2,475,000.

   Additional information follows: The General Fund Fund Balance account had a credit balance of $82,900 as of December 31, 2007; no entries other than the one at the beginning of 2008 to record the budgeted increase have been made in the Fund Balance account during 2008.

   Required
   a. Record the preceding transactions in the appropriate entries in general journal form for fiscal year 2008 in both the General Fund and governmental activities general journal.
   b. Prepare a budgetary comparison schedule for the General Fund of the City of Stoney Creek for the fiscal year ending December 31, 2008, as shown in Illustration 4–7. Do not prepare a government-wide statement of activities since other governmental funds would affect that statement.

4–8 **Part A. Operating Transactions and Interim General Fund Balance Sheet.** The City of Macon's General Fund had the following post-closing trial balance at April 30, 2007, the end of its fiscal year:

	Debits	Credits
Cash	$ 97,000	
Taxes Receivable—Delinquent	583,000	
Estimated Uncollectible Delinquent Taxes		$189,000
Interest and Penalties Receivable	26,280	
Estimated Uncollectible Interest and Penalties		11,160
Inventory of Supplies	16,100	
Vouchers Payable		148,500
Due to Federal Government		59,490
Reserve for Inventory of Supplies		16,100
Fund Balance		298,130
	$722,380	$722,380

During the six months ended October 31, 2007, the following transactions, in summary form, with subsidiary ledger detail omitted, occurred:

1. The budget for FY 2008 provided for General Fund estimated revenues totaling $3,140,000 and appropriations totaling $3,100,000.

2. The County Council authorized a temporary loan of $300,000 in the form of a 120-day tax anticipation note. The loan was obtained from a local bank at a discount of 6 percent per annum (debit Expenditures for discount).

3. The property tax levy for FY 2008 was recorded. Net assessed valuation of taxable property for the year was $43,000,000, and the tax rate was $5 per hundred. It was estimated that 4 percent of the levy would be uncollectible. Classify this tax levy as current.

4. Purchase orders and contracts in the amount of $1,027,000 were issued to vendors and others.

5. Current taxes of $1,034,000, delinquent taxes of $340,000, and interest and penalties of $13,240 were collected. Because of taxpayers' delinquencies in payment of the first installment of taxes, additional penalties of $15,230 were levied but had not yet been collected.

6. Total payroll for the first six months of the year was $481,070. Of that amount, the following amounts were withheld: $36,800 for employees' FICA tax liability, $61,200 for employees' federal income tax liability, and $20,000 for state taxes; the balance was paid in cash.

7. The employer's FICA tax liability amounted to $36,800.

8. Revenues from sources other than taxes were collected in the amount of $353,000.

9. Amounts due to the federal government as of April 30 and amounts withheld for federal and state withholding taxes during the year were vouchered.

10. Purchase orders and contracts encumbered in the amount of $890,800 were filled at a net cost of $894,900, which was vouchered.

11. Cash of $1,099,060 was paid on vouchers payable, and credit for purchases discount earned was $8,030 (credit Expenditures).

12. The tax anticipation note of $300,000 was repaid.

Required

a. Record in general journal form the effect of the transactions for the six months ended October 31 on the General Fund and governmental activities. You need not record subsidiary ledger debits and credits.

b. Prepare a General Fund interim balance sheet in the format of Illustration 4–2 as of October 31, 2007.

4–8 Part B. Additional Operating Transactions, Special Topics, and End-of-Year General Fund Balance Sheet. Part B continues transactions of the City of Macon's General Fund. The following transactions occurred during the last half of the fiscal year.

1. Because of a change in a state law, the City of Macon has been informed that it will receive $80,000 less in state revenue than was budgeted.

2. Purchase orders and other commitment documents in the amount of $1,032,000 were issued during the six months ended April 30, 2008.

3. Property taxes of $6,500 and interest and penalties receivable of $1,340, which had been written off in prior years, were collected. Additional interest of $250 that had accrued since the write-off was collected at the same time.

4. Personnel costs, excluding the employer's share of the FICA tax, totaled $338,420 for the second six months. Withholdings amounted to $25,890 for FICA, $42,510 for employees' federal income tax liability, and $14,400 for state withholding tax. The balance was paid to employees in cash.

5. The employer's FICA tax of $25,890 was recorded as a liability.

6. The County Board of Review discovered unassessed properties of a total taxable value of $500,000 located within the City of Macon. The owners of these properties were charged taxes at the City's General Fund rate of $5 per hundred dollars of assessed value. (You need not adjust the Estimated Uncollectible Current Taxes account.)

7. The following were collected in cash: Current taxes of $927,000, delinquent taxes of $43,270, interest and penalties of $7,330, and revenues of $593,700 from a number of sources. (No part of any of these amounts is included in any other transaction given.)

8. Accrued interest and penalties, estimated to be 30 percent uncollectible, was recorded in the amount of $23,200.

9. All unpaid current year's taxes became delinquent. The balances of current tax receivables and related estimated uncollectibles were transferred to the delinquent classification.

10. All amounts due to the federal government and state government were vouchered.

11. Invoices and bills for goods and services that had been encumbered at $1,097,240 were received and vouchered at an actual cost of $1,092,670.

12. Personal property taxes of $39,940 and interest and penalties of $4,180 were written off because of the inability to locate the property owners.

13. A physical inventory of materials and supplies at April 30, 2008, showed a total of $19,100. Inventory is recorded using the consumption method.

14. Payments made on vouchers during the second half-year totaled $1,202,600.

Required

a. Record in general journal form the effect on the General Fund and governmental activities for the second half of fiscal year 2008.

b. Record in general journal form entries to close the budgetary accounts and operating statement accounts.

c. Prepare a General Fund balance sheet as of April 30, 2008.

d. Prepare a statement of revenues, expenditures, and changes in fund balance for the fiscal year ended April 30, 2008. Do not prepare the government-wide financial statements.

4–9 Permanent Fund and Related Special Revenue Fund Transactions. Annabelle Benton, great-granddaughter of the founder of the Town of Benton, made a cash contribution in the amount of $500,000 to be held as an endowment. To account for this endowment, the town has created the Alex Benton Park Permanent Fund. Under terms of the agreement, the town must invest and conserve the principal amount of the contribution in perpetuity. Earnings, measured on the full accrual basis, must be used to maintain Alex Benton Town Park in an "attractive manner." All changes in fair value are treated as adjustments of fund balance of the permanent fund and do not affect earnings. Earnings are transferred periodically to the Alex Benton Park Maintenance Fund, a special revenue fund. Information pertaining to transactions of the endowment and special revenue funds for the fiscal year ended June 30, 2008, follows:

1. The contribution of $500,000 was received and recorded on December 31, 2007.

2. On December 31, 2007, bonds having a face value of $400,000 were purchased for $406,300, plus three months of accrued interest of $6,000. A certificate of deposit with a face and fair value of $70,000 was also purchased on this date. The bonds mature on October 1, 2016 (105 months from date of purchase), and pay interest of 6 percent per annum semiannually on April 1 and October 1. The certificate of deposit pays interest of 4 percent per annum payable on March 31, June 30, September 30, and December 31.

3. On January 2, 2008, the Town Council approved a budget for the Alex Benton Park Maintenance Fund, which included estimated revenues of $13,400 and appropriations of $13,000.

4. On March 31, 2008, interest on the certificate of deposit was received by the endowment fund and transferred to the Alex Benton Park Maintenance Fund.

5. The April 1, 2008, bond interest was received by the endowment fund and transferred to the Alex Benton Park Maintenance Fund.

6. On June 30, 2008, interest on the certificate of deposit was received and transferred in cash to the Alex Benton Park Maintenance Fund.

7. For the year ended June 30, 2008, maintenance expenditures from the Alex Benton Park Maintenance Fund amounted to $2,700 for materials and contractual services and $10,150 for wages and salaries. All expenditures were paid in cash except for $430 of accounts payable as of June 30, 2008. Inventories of materials and supplies are deemed immaterial in amount.

8. On June 30, 2008, bonds with face value of $100,000 were sold for $102,000 plus accrued interest of $1,500. On the same date, 2,000 shares of ABC Corporation's stock were purchased at $52 per share.

Required

a. Prepare in general journal form the entries required in the Alex Benton Park Endowment Fund to record the transactions occurring during the fiscal year ending June 30, 2008, including all appropriate adjusting and closing entries. (*Note:* Ignore related entries in the governmental activities journal at the government-wide level.)

b. Prepare in general journal form the entries required in the Alex Benton Park Maintenance Fund to record Transactions 1–8.

c. Prepare the following financial statements:

   (1) A balance sheet for both the Benton Park Endowment Fund and the Benton Park Maintenance Fund as of June 30, 2008.

   (2) A statement of revenues, expenditures, and changes in fund balance for both the Alex Benton Park Endowment Fund and the Alex Benton Park Maintenance Fund for the year ended June 30, 2008.

Chapter **Five**

Accounting for General Capital Assets and Capital Projects

Learning Objectives

After studying this chapter, you should be able to:

1. Describe the nature and characteristics of general capital assets.
2. Account for the acquisition, maintenance, and disposition of general capital assets.
3. Account for depreciation of general capital assets including the modified approach for infrastructure assets.
4. Explain the purpose and characteristics of a capital projects fund.
5. Explain the typical sources of financing for capital projects.
6. Prepare journal entries for a typical capital project, both within the capital projects fund and within the governmental activities category at the government-wide level.
7. Explain the concepts and accounting procedures for special assessment capital projects.
8. Prepare financial statements for capital projects funds.

Chapters 3 and 4 illustrate that long-lived assets such as office equipment, police cruisers, and other items may be acquired by expenditure of appropriations of the General Fund or one or more of its special revenue funds. Long-lived assets used by activities financed by the General Fund or other governmental funds are called **general capital assets (GCA).** General capital assets should be distinguished from capital assets that are specifically associated with activities financed by proprietary and fiduciary funds. Capital assets acquired by proprietary and fiduciary funds are accounted for by those funds.

Acquisitions of general capital assets that require major amounts of money ordinarily cannot be financed from General Fund or special revenue fund appropriations. Major acquisitions of general capital assets are commonly financed by issuance of long-term debt to be repaid from tax revenues or by special assessments against property deemed to be particularly benefited by the long-lived asset. Other sources for financing the acquisition of long-lived assets include grants from other governments, transfers from other funds, gifts from individuals or organizations, capital leases, or a combination of several of these sources. If money received from these sources is restricted, legally or morally, to the purchase or construction of specified capital assets, it is recommended that a **capital projects fund** be created to account for resources to be used for such projects. When deemed useful, capital projects funds may also be used to account for the acquisition of major general capital assets, such as buildings, under a capital lease agreement. Leases involving equipment are more commonly accounted for by the General Fund.

Illustration 5–1 summarizes the interrelationships among fund types and activities at the government-wide level as they relate to general capital asset acquisition. It shows that general capital assets may be acquired from expenditures of the General Fund, special revenue funds, or capital projects funds. The cost or other carrying value of general capital assets and long-term debt related to their acquisition is recorded in the general ledger for the governmental activities category at the government-wide level.[1] This chapter focuses on capital projects fund accounting and financial reporting. Chapters 3 and 4 discuss accounting and financial reporting for the General Fund, special revenue funds, and permanent funds.

ACCOUNTING FOR GENERAL CAPITAL ASSETS

Only enterprise and internal service funds routinely account for capital assets (property, plant, and equipment) used in their operations. Fiduciary funds that use capital assets for the production of income also account for property, plant, and equipment. Since governmental funds account only for current financial resources, these funds do not account for capital assets acquired by the funds. Rather, general capital assets purchased or constructed with governmental fund resources are recorded in the governmental activities general ledger at the government-wide level. (See Illustration 5–1.)

ILLUSTRATION 5–1   **General Capital Asset Acquisition: Governmental Funds and Government-wide Governmental Activities**

General Fund and/or Special Revenue Funds	Capital Projects Funds	Government-wide Governmental Activities
Used to account for capital outlay expenditures from annual budget appropriations. General capital assets acquired are recorded in the governmental activities general ledger at the government-wide level.	Used to account for construction or other major capital expenditures from debt proceeds, capital grants, special assessments, and other sources restricted for capital asset acquisition. General capital assets acquired and related long-term debt to be serviced from tax revenues or from special assessments are recorded in the governmental activities general ledger at the government-wide level.	Used to account for the cost and depreciation of general capital assets (GCA) acquired by expenditures of the General Fund, special revenue funds, and capital projects funds. Also used to account for GCA acquired under capital leases and for GCA acquired by gift. Used to account for all unmatured long-term debt except debt being repaid from revenues of enterprise funds.

[1] Under the financial reporting model that was superseded by the *GASBS 34* reporting model, general capital assets were accounted for in a set of accounting records called the *General Fixed Assets Account Group,* and general long-term liabilities were accounted for in a second set of accounting records called the *General Long-Term Debt Account Group.* Both account groups were eliminated by the *GASBS 34* model, but some governments may continue to use these records until their accounting systems have been redesigned to accommodate *GASBS 34.*

As indicated in most intermediate financial accounting texts, records of individual assets that exceed the minimum value threshold established for capitalization or groups of related assets of lesser unit value should include all information needed for planning an effective maintenance program, preparing budget requests for replacements and additions, providing for adequate insurance coverage, and fixing the responsibility for custody of the assets.

GASB standards require that general capital assets be recorded at historical cost or fair value at time of receipt if assets are received by donation. **Historical cost** includes acquisition cost plus ancillary costs necessary to put the asset into use.[2] Ancillary costs may include items such as freight and transportation charges, site preparation costs, and set-up costs. If the cost of capital assets was not recorded when the assets were acquired and is unknown when accounting control over the assets is established, it is acceptable to record them at estimated cost.

Prior to *GASBS 34,* depreciation was not recorded on general capital assets in any governmental fund, but accumulated depreciation could optionally be reported in the General Fixed Assets Account Group (see footnote 1). Few governments opted to report depreciation since it was not required. Under the *GASBS 34* reporting model, general capital assets are reported in the Governmental Activities column of the statement of net assets, net of accumulated depreciation, when appropriate, using any rational and systematic depreciation method. Depreciation is not reported for inexhaustible assets such as land and land improvements, noncapitalized collections of works of art or historical treasures, and infrastructure assets that are accounted for using the *modified approach.*[3] The modified approach is explained later in this chapter. Even though general capital assets are acquired for the production of general governmental services rather than for the production of services that are sold, reporting depreciation on general capital assets may provide significant benefits to users and managers alike. Reporting depreciation expense as part of the direct expenses of functions and programs in the Governmental Activities column of the government-wide statement of activities (see Illustration 1–5) helps to determine the full cost of providing each function or program. Depreciation expense on capital assets used in the operations of a government grant–financed program is often an allowable cost under the terms of a grant. In addition, depreciation expense may provide useful information to administrators and legislators concerned with the allocation of resources to programs, departments, and activities. To a limited extent, a comparison of the accumulated depreciation on an asset with the cost of the asset may assist in budgeting outlays for replacement of capital assets. For these reasons, some observers view the *GASBS 34* requirement to report depreciation on general capital assets in the government-wide financial statements as a significant improvement in governmental financial reporting.

Required Disclosures about Capital Assets

GASB standards require certain disclosures about capital assets in the notes to the basic financial statements, both the general capital assets reported in the Governmental Activities column and those reported in the Business-type Activities column of the government-wide financial statements.[4] In addition to disclosure of their general policy for capitalizing assets and for estimating the useful lives of depreciable assets, governments should provide certain other disclosures in the notes to the financial

[2] GASB *Codification,* Sec. 1400.102.

[3] Ibid., par. 104.

[4] GASB *Codification,* Sec. 2300.111–112.

statements. These disclosures should be divided into major classes of capital assets of the primary government (as discussed in the following section) and should distinguish between general capital assets and those reported in business-type activities. Capital assets that are not being depreciated should be disclosed separately from those assets that are being depreciated. Required disclosures about each major class of capital assets include these:

1. Beginning-of-year and end-of-year balances showing accumulated depreciation separate from historical cost.
2. Capital acquisitions during the year.
3. Sales or other dispositions during the year.
4. Depreciation expense for the current period with disclosure of the amounts charged to each function in the statement of activities.
5. For collections of works of art or historical treasures that are not capitalized, disclosures should describe the collections and explain why they are not capitalized.[5] If collections are capitalized, they should be included in the disclosures described in items 1 through 4.

Illustration 5–2 presents capital asset note disclosures for the City and County of Denver. These disclosures conform in all respects to required items 1–4 above. In addition, the City and County of Denver capitalizes and depreciates certain collections of works of art or historical treasures. The first three sections of the city and county's capital asset disclosures essentially correspond to the three major columns of the government-wide statement of net assets—Governmental Activities, Business-type Activities, and Discretely Presented Component Units. Within each section, capital assets not being depreciated (land and land rights and construction in progress) are reported separately from those that are being depreciated, as required by GASB standards.

The information contained in the first three sections of the disclosure should be useful for both internal and external decision makers as it reports on beginning balances for each major class of capital assets, additions to and deletions from each class, and ending balance of each class. The same information is provided for accumulated depreciation for each major asset class. Section 4 of the disclosures presents the amount of depreciation expense that was charged to each function of governmental activities at the government-wide level. Section 5 provides details of construction commitments, both for governmental activities and business-type activities.

Classification of General Capital Assets

The capital asset classifications shown in Illustration 5–2 are typical of those used by state and local governments. Additional or similarly named accounts may be needed to better describe the asset classes of any given governmental entity. As discussed previously in this chapter, general capital assets typically are those acquired using the financial resources of a governmental fund. Many of these assets, however, are not

[5] Even though the GASB encourages capitalization of all collections of works of art or historical treasures, governments can opt *not* to capitalize if the collection is (1) held for public exhibition, education, or research in furtherance of public service rather than for financial gain; (2) protected, kept unencumbered, cared for, and preserved; and (3) subject to an organizational policy that requires the proceeds from sales of collection items to be used to acquire other items for collections (GASB, *Codification,* Sec. 1400.109). These criteria, all of which must be met in order not to capitalize, are identical to those in FASB *Statement No. 116* for nongovernmental nonprofit organizations (see Chapter 14 for discussion).

ILLUSTRATION 5–2 **Illustrative Capital Assets Disclosure**

CITY AND COUNTY OF DENVER, COLORADO
Capital Assets Disclosure
For the Year Ended December 31, 2004

Capital asset activity for the year ended December 31, 2004, was as follows (amounts expressed in thousands):

	January 1	Additions	Deletions	December 31
1. Governmental Activities				
Capital assets not being depreciated:				
Land and land rights	$ 224,638	$ 1,330	$ (46)	$ 225,922
Construction in progress	289,810	172,595	(305,162)	157,243
Total capital assets not being depreciated	514,448	173,925	(305,208)	383,165
Capital assets being depreciated:				
Buildings and improvements	930,807	338,790	—	1,269,597
Equipment and other	178,676	14,177	(8,034)	184,819
Collections	72,758	4,607	(1,267)	76,098
Infrastructure	864,325	21,945	(2,907)	883,363
Total capital assets being depreciated	2,046,566	379,519	(12,208)	2,413,877
Less accumulated depreciation for:				
Buildings and improvements	(208,709)	(26,929)	—	(235,638)
Equipment and other	(107,017)	(22,958)	6,830	(123,145)
Collections	(39,723)	(4,260)	1,267	(42,716)
Infrastructure	(344,057)	(27,878)	2,907	(369,028)
Total accumulated depreciation	(699,506)	(82,025)	11,004	(770,527)
Total capital assets being depreciated, net	1,347,060	297,494	(1,204)	1,643,350
Governmental Activities Capital Assets, net	$1,861,508	$471,419	$ 306,412	$2,026,515
2. Business-type Activities				
Capital assets not being depreciated:				
Land and land rights	$ 302,218	$ 6,997	$ —	$ 309,215
Construction in progress	110,516	129,151	(81,125)	158,542
Total capital assets not being depreciated	412,734	136,148	(81,125)	467,757
Capital assets being depreciated:				
Buildings and improvements	1,613,615	79,219	—	1,692,834
Improvements other than buildings	2,362,610	33,182	(83,001)	2,312,791
Machinery and equipment	669,435	104,879	(76,560)	697,754
Total capital assets being depreciated	4,645,660	217,280	(159,561)	4,703,379
Less accumulated depreciation for:				
Buildings and improvements	(415,711)	(47,813)	—	(463,524)
Improvements other than buildings	(509,721)	(53,114)	—	(562,835)
Machinery and equipment	(312,276)	(92,837)	71,013	(334,100)
Total accumulated depreciation	(1,237,708)	(193,764)	71,013	(1,360,459)
Total capital assets being depreciated, net	3,407,952	23,516	(88,893)	3,342,920
Business-type Activities Capital Assets, net	$3,820,686	$159,664	$(169,673)	$3,810,677

ILLUSTRATION 5–2 *(continued)*

3. Discretely Presented Component Units. Capital asset activity for the DURA, Water Board, Denver Convention Hotel Authority and the Denver Museum of Nature and Science component units for the year ended December 31, 2004, was as follows (amounts expressed in thousands):

	January 1	Additions	Deletions	December 31
Capital assets not being depreciated:				
Land and land rights	$ 97,526	$ 525	$ (23)	$ 98,028
Construction in progress	258,787	90,652	(151,679)	197,760
Total capital assets not being depreciated	356,313	91,177	(151,702)	295,788
Capital assets being depreciated:				
Buildings and improvements	125,887	34,549	(134)	160,302
Improvements other than buildings	1,314,851	168,206	(2,592)	1,480,465
Machinery and equipment	140,152	20,617	(10,374)	150,395
Total capital assets being depreciated	1,580,890	223,372	(13,100)	1,791,162
Less accumulated depreciation for:				
Buildings and improvements	(350,342)	(22,563)	1,100	(371,805)
Improvements other than buildings	(36,345)	(2,547)	111	(38,781)
Machinery and equipment	(40,799)	(9,310)	7,344	(42,765)
Total accumulated depreciation	(427,486)	(34,420)	8,555	(453,351)
Total capital assets being depreciated, net	1,153,404	188,952	(4,545)	1,337,811[1]
Discretely Presented Component Units Capital Assets, net	$1,509,717	$280,129	$(156,247)	$1,633,599

4. Depreciation Expense. Depreciation expense was charged to governmental activities' functions as follows (amounts expressed in thousands):

General Government	$14,542
Public Safety	8,504
Human Services	797
Public Works, including depreciation of general infrastructure	36,220
Health	187
Parks and Recreation	6,864
Culture and Recreation	13,815
Community Development	140
Economic Opportunity	19
Capital assets held by internal service funds	937
TOTAL	$82,025

5. Construction Commitments. The City's governmental and business-type activities have entered into construction and professional services contracts having remaining commitments under contract as of December 31, 2004, as follows (amounts expressed in thousands):

Governmental Activities:	
Bond Projects	$32,103
Entertainment and Culture	204
Total Governmental Activities	$32,307

ILLUSTRATION 5–2 (*continued*)

Business-type Activities:	
Wastewater Management	$ 18,630
Denver Airport System	177,079
Total Business-type Activities	$195,709
Component Units:	
Denver Convention Center Hotel Authority	$133,062
Water Board	114,200
Total Component Units	$247,262

The commitments for these funds are not reflected in the accompanying financial statements. Only the unpaid amounts incurred to date for these contracts are included as liabilities in the financial statements.

[1] Excludes net capital assets of $11,057 of Other Component Units.
Source: City and County of Denver, Colorado, Notes to Basic Financial Statements, Year Ended December 31, 2004, Section III, Note D.

used exclusively in the operations of any one fund, nor do they belong to a fund. Consider, for example, that general capital assets include courthouses and city halls, public buildings in general, the land on which they are situated, highways, streets, sidewalks, storm drainage systems, equipment, and other tangible assets with a life longer than one fiscal year. The following paragraphs present a brief review of generally accepted principles of accounting for each category of capital assets based on applicable GASB and FASB standards.

Land

The cost of land acquired by a government through purchase should include not only the contract price but also such other related costs as taxes and other liens assumed, title search costs, legal fees, surveying, filling, grading, draining, and other costs of preparing for the use intended. Governments are frequently subject to damage suits in connection with land acquisition, and the amounts of judgments levied are considered capital costs of the property acquired. Land acquired through forfeiture should be capitalized at the total amount of all taxes, liens, and other claims surrendered plus all other costs incidental to acquiring ownership and perfecting title. Land acquired through donation should be recorded on the basis of appraised value at the date of acquisition; the cost of the appraisal itself should not be capitalized, however.

Buildings and Improvements Other than Buildings

The nature of assets classified as buildings is a matter of common knowledge, but if a definition is needed, they may be said to consist of those structures erected above ground for the purpose of sheltering persons or property. Improvements other than buildings consists of land attachments of a permanent nature, other than buildings, and includes, among other things, walks, walls, and parking lots.

The determination of the cost of buildings and improvements acquired by purchase is relatively simple, although some peripheral costs may be of doubtful classification.

The price paid for the assets constitutes most of the cost of purchased items, but legal and other costs plus expenditures necessary to put the property into acceptable condition for its intended use, are proper additions. The same generalizations may be applied to acquisitions by construction under contract; that is, purchase or contract price plus positively identified incidentals, should be capitalized. The determination of the cost of buildings and improvements obtained through construction by some agency of the government (sometimes called **force account construction**) poses slightly more difficulty. In these cases, costs should include not only all direct and indirect expenditures of the fund providing the construction but also materials and services furnished by other funds as well.

The valuation of buildings and improvements acquired by donation should be established by appraisal. As in the case of land, one reason for setting a value on donated buildings and improvements is to aid in determining the total value of capital assets used by the government and for reports and comparisons. However, more compelling reasons exist for setting a value on buildings and certain improvements: the need for obtaining proper insurance coverage and the need to substantiate the insurance claim if loss should occur. Last, of course, one should not lose sight of the fact that the cost of general capital assets is also required to be reported in the Governmental Activities column of the government-wide financial statements.

Equipment, or Machinery and Equipment

Machinery and equipment are usually acquired by purchase. Occasionally, however, machinery and equipment may be constructed by the government, perhaps financed by an internal service fund. In such cases, the same rules will apply as for buildings and improvements constructed by governmental employees. The cost of machinery and equipment purchased should include items conventional under business accounting practice: purchase price, transportation costs if not included in purchase price, installation cost, and other direct costs of readying for use. Cash discounts on machinery and equipment purchased should be treated as a reduction of costs. Donated equipment should be accounted for in the same manner and for the same reasons as donated buildings and improvements.

Construction Work in Progress

Construction Work in Progress is the account needed to record construction expenditures accumulated to the end of the fiscal year on projects financed by capital projects funds. As described later in this chapter, construction expenditures by capital projects funds are ordinarily closed to Fund Balance at the end of each year, but the amounts are not capitalized in the funds financing the construction. Instead, the amounts to be capitalized are debited to the account Construction Work in Progress in the governmental activities general journal at the government-wide level.

Infrastructure Assets

Infrastructure assets are capital assets, such as highways, streets, sidewalks, storm drainage systems, and lighting systems, that are stationary in nature and normally can be preserved for a longer life than most other capital assets. The *GASBS 34* reporting model ushered in a new era in infrastructure accounting and reporting by requiring that all state and local governments report the cost of their infrastructure assets in the government-wide statement of net assets. Unless a government adopts the so-called *modified approach* discussed below, it must also report depreciation expense for infrastructure assets in its government-wide statement of activities. Under the previous standards, most governments opted not to report their investment in infrastructure assets because they believed the immovable and nontransferable nature of such assets made financial information about them of limited value for stewardship or decision-making purposes. In its *basis for conclusions* in *GASBS 34,* the GASB argued that failure to recognize the benefits in the statement of net assets associated with investment in capital assets (including infrastructure), while recognizing the long-term debt incurred to acquire the capital assets, would result in a misleading net assets deficit.[6] Moreover, the cost of using capital assets (in the form of a depreciation) should properly be included in determining the full costs of conducting governmental programs.

Modified Approach

Under the **modified approach,** a government can elect not to depreciate certain *eligible* infrastructure assets, provided that two requirements are met.[7] The two requirements that must be met to avoid depreciation reporting are that:

(1) The government manages the eligible infrastructure assets using an asset management system that includes (a) an up-to-date inventory of eligible assets, (b) condition assessments of the assets and summary of results using a measurement scale, and (c) estimates each year of the annual amount needed to maintain and preserve the eligible assets at the condition level established and disclosed by the government, and

(2) The government documents that the eligible infrastructure assets are being preserved approximately at (or above) the condition level established and disclosed (see item 1, (c) above).

What constitutes adequate documentation requires professional judgment. At a minimum, the government must provide documentation that (1) complete condition assessments are made at least every three years and (2) the three most recent condition assessments provide reasonable assurance that the eligible infrastructure assets are being preserved at or above the established condition level.

If the preceding requirements are met and adequate documentation is maintained, all expenditures incurred to preserve the eligible infrastructure assets should be expensed in the period incurred. Additions and improvements to the eligible assets should be capitalized. As long as the conditions are met, there is evidence that the eligible assets have an indefinite useful life and thus do not need to be depreciated. If the government subsequently fails to maintain the assets at or above the established and disclosed condition level, it must revert to reporting depreciation for its infrastructure assets and discontinue its use of the modified approach.

Transition Reporting of Infrastructure Assets

As mentioned previously, most governments did not have a comprehensive inventory of infrastructure assets as they implemented *GASBS 34. GASBS 34* permits governments considerable time to develop an inventory of infrastructure assets and determine applicable costs during the transition to the new model. Governments must report all infrastructure assets acquired subsequent to their implementation of *GASBS 34.* In

---

[6] *GASBS 34*, Appendix B, Part I, pars. 274–276.

[7] Eligible assets are those that are part of a network of infrastructure assets or a subsystem of a network. For example, all roadways in a state might be considered a network, and interstate highways and state highways could be considered subsystems of that network.

addition to this *prospective* reporting, governments must retroactively report all *major* infrastructure assets,[8] with the amount of time allowed for retroactive reporting dependent on the size of the government. Retroactive reporting of *nonmajor* infrastructure assets is encouraged but not required. The amount initially capitalized for retroactive reporting should be based on historical cost. However, if inadequate records make it infeasible to determine historical cost, estimated historical cost can be used. *GASBS 34* provides examples of methods that can be used to estimate historical costs.

GASBS 34 allows governments considerable time to begin retroactive reporting of major infrastructure assets. Large governments (those with $100 million or more in total revenues) and mid-sized governments (those with at least $10 million but less than $100 million in total revenues) have until fiscal years beginning after June 15, 2005 and 2006, respectively, to begin retroactive reporting of all major infrastructure assets. Governments with less than $10 million in total revenues, because of their relatively small size, are exempted from retroactive reporting of major general infrastructure assets.

General Capital Assets Acquired under Capital Lease Agreements

As explained in some detail in Chapter 6, state and local governments generally are subject to constitutional or statutory limits on the amount of long-term debt they may issue. Consequently, governments that have reached their legal debt limit or have nearly done so often acquire the use of capital assets through a lease agreement. A brief example is given of the computation of the amount to be recorded in a governmental fund under the provisions of GASB standards if a general capital asset is acquired under a capital lease. For equipment leases, an entry is made in the General Fund or other appropriate governmental fund to debit an expenditure offset by a credit to Other Financing Sources in the amount of the present value at the inception of the lease of the stream of lease payments.[9] That amount (or the fair value of the leased property, if less) is also recorded in the governmental activities ledger at the government-wide level as the cost of the leased property.

FASB *SFAS No. 13* defines and establishes accounting and financial reporting standards for a number of forms of leases, only two of which, operating leases and capital leases, are of importance in governmental accounting. GASB standards accept the *SFAS No. 13* definitions of these two forms of leases and prescribe accounting and financial reporting for lease agreements of state and local governments.[10] If a particular lease meets any one of the following classification criteria, it is a **capital lease.**

1. The lease transfers ownership of the property to the lessee by the end of the lease term.
2. The lease contains an option to purchase the leased property at a bargain price.
3. The lease term is equal to or greater than 75 percent of the estimated economic life of the leased property.

---

[8] *Major* infrastructure assets are determined at the network or subsystem (see footnote 7) level and consist of those in which (1) the cost or estimated cost of the subsystem is expected to be at least 5 percent of the total cost of general capital assets reported in the first fiscal year ending after June 15, 1999, or (2) the cost or estimated cost of the network is expected to be at least 10 percent of the total cost of all general capital assets reported in the first fiscal year ending after June 15, 1999.

[9] Intermediate accounting texts generally discuss at length the computation of amounts to be capitalized under capital lease agreements.

[10] GASB, *Codification,* Sec. L20.103.

4. The present value of rental or other minimum lease payments equals or exceeds 90 percent of the fair value of the leased property less any investment tax credit retained by the lessor.

If no criterion is met, the lease is classified as an **operating lease** by the lessee. Rental payments under an operating lease for assets used by governmental funds are recorded by the using fund as expenditures of the period. In many states, statutes prohibit governments from entering into obligations extending beyond the current budget year. Because of this legal technicality, governmental lease agreements typically contain a "fiscal funding clause," or cancellation clause, which permits governmental lessees to terminate the agreement on an annual basis if funds are not appropriated to make required payments. GASB standards specify that lease agreements containing fiscal funding or cancellation clauses should be evaluated. If the possibility of cancellation is judged remote, the lease should be disclosed in financial statements and accounts in the manner specified for capital leases.[11]

As an example of accounting for the acquisition of general capital assets under a capital lease agreement, assume that a government signs a capital lease agreement to pay $10,000 on January 1, 2007, the scheduled date of delivery of certain equipment to be used by an activity accounted for by a special revenue fund. The lease calls for annual payments of $10,000 at the beginning of each year thereafter; that is, January 1, 2008, January 1, 2009, and so on, through January 1, 2016. There will be 10 payments of $10,000 each, for a total of $100,000, but GASB standards require entry in the accounts of the present value of the stream of annual payments, not their total. Since the initial payment of $10,000 is paid at the inception of the lease, its present value is $10,000. The present value of the remaining nine payments must be calculated using the borrowing rate the lessee would have incurred to obtain a similar loan over a similar term to purchase the leased asset. Assuming the rate to be 10 percent, the present value of payments 2 through 10 is $57,590. The present value of the 10 payments is, therefore, $67,590. GASB standards require a governmental fund (including, if appropriate, a capital projects fund) to record the following entry at the inception of the capital lease:

	Debits	Credits
Special Revenue Fund:		
Expenditures	67,590	
Other Financing Sources—Capital Lease Agreements		67,590

The corresponding entry in the governmental activities general journal at the government-wide level to record the equipment and long-term liability under the capital lease is as follows:

	Debits	Credits
Governmental Activities:		
Equipment	67,590	
Capital Lease Obligations Payable.		67,590

[11]Ibid., pars. 115–118.

Costs Incurred after Acquisition

Governmental accounting procedures should include clear-cut provisions for classifying costs incurred in connection with capital assets after the acquisition cost has been established. Outlays closely associated with capital assets will regularly occur in amounts of varying size, and responsible persons will be charged with deciding whether these should be recorded as additions to assets. In general, any outlay that definitely adds to the utility or function of a capital asset or enhances the value of an integral part of it may be capitalized as part of the asset. Thus, drainage of land, addition of a room to a building, and changes in equipment that increase its output or reduce its cost of operation are clearly recognizable as additions to assets. Special difficulty arises in the case of large-scale outlays that are partly replacements and partly additions or betterments. An example would be replacement of a composition-type roof with a roof of some more durable material. To the extent that the project replaces the old roof, outlays should not be capitalized unless the cost of the old roof is removed from the accounts, and to the extent that the project provides a better roof, outlays should be capitalized. The distribution of the total cost in such a case is largely a matter for managerial determination. Consistent with policy in recording original acquisition costs, some outlays unquestionably representing increases in permanent values may not be capitalized if the amount is less than some specified minimum or on the basis of any other established criterion.

Outlays that are partly replacements and partly additions or betterments occasion some accounting difficulty. The distribution of the outlay having been decided, the estimated amount of addition or betterment might be added to the asset. Better results are sometimes obtained by crediting the appropriate asset account for the cost of the replaced part, thus removing the amount, and then debiting the asset account for the total cost of the replacing item.

Reduction of Cost

Reductions in the cost of capital assets may relate to the elimination of the total amount expended for a given item or items, or they may consist only of removing the cost applicable to a specific part. Thus, if an entire building is demolished, the total cost of the structure should be removed from the appropriate accounts; but if the separation applies only to a wing or some other definitely identifiable portion, the cost eliminated should be the amount estimated as applying thereto. Reductions in the recorded cost of capital assets may be brought about by sale, retirement from use, destruction by fire or other casualty, replacement of a major part, theft or loss from some other cause, and possibly other changes. The cost of capital assets recorded in the governmental activities ledger may sometimes be reduced by the transfer of a unit to an enterprise fund, or vice versa.

Accounting for cost reductions consisting of entire units is a relatively simple matter if adequate asset records have been kept. If the reduction is only partial, the cost as shown by the capital assets record must be modified to reflect the change with a complete description of what brought about the change.

Since depreciation is recorded on general capital assets, the removal of a capital asset from the governmental activities general ledger may be accomplished by crediting the ledger account recording its cost and debiting Accumulated Depreciation and Cash if the item was sold. Gains or losses should be recognized if the value received differs from the book value of the assets removed. The gains and losses are reported on the government-wide statement of activities.

Governments sometimes trade used capital assets for new items. In the governmental activities general ledger, the total cost of the old item should be removed and the total cost (not merely the cash payment) of the new one set up.

Asset Impairments and Insurance Recoveries

GASB standards provide accounting and reporting guidance for impairment of assets, as well as for insurance recoveries. The GASB defines an **asset impairment** as a *significant, unexpected decline in the service utility of a capital asset.*[12] Impairments occur as a result of unexpected circumstances or events, such as physical damage, obsolescence, enactment of laws or regulations or other environmental factors, or change in the manner or duration of use.[13] Unless an impairment is judged to be temporary, the amount of impairment should be measured using one of three approaches: *restorative cost approach*, the estimated cost to restore the utility of the asset (appropriate for impairments from physical damage); *service units approach,* the portion of estimated service utility life of the asset that has been estimated lost due to impairment (appropriate for impairments due to environmental factors or obsolescence); and *deflated depreciated replacement cost approach,* the estimated current cost of a replacement asset with similar depreciation and deflated for the effects of inflation (appropriate for impairment due to change in the manner or duration of use).[14] Barring evidence to the contrary, asset impairments should be considered permanent.

When an asset impairment has occurred, the estimated amount of impairment is reported as a write-down in the carrying value of the asset and as a program expense in the government-wide statement of activities of the function using the asset, and as an operating expense in the statement of revenues, expenses, and changes in fund net assets of proprietary funds, if applicable. If the impairment is significant in amount and results from an event that is unusual in nature or infrequently occurring, or both, then the loss should be reported as either a special item or extraordinary item, as appropriate.

GASBS 42 requires that impairment losses be reported net of any insurance recoveries that occur during the same fiscal year. Insurance recoveries occurring in a subsequent year should be reported as other financing sources in governmental fund operating statements, as program revenues in the government-wide statement of net assets, and as nonoperating revenues in proprietary fund operating statements. Finally, restorations and replacements of impaired capital assets should be reported as a separate transaction from both the impairment loss and any insurance recovery.

ILLUSTRATIVE ENTRIES

Acquisition of general capital assets requires a debit to the appropriate governmental activities asset account and a credit to Cash or a liability account. Thus, if office equipment is purchased for the treasurer's office from General Fund resources, the following journal entries would be made in the general journals for the General Fund (ignoring encumbrances) and governmental activities at the government-wide level:

	Debits	Credits
General Fund:		
Expenditures	450	
Vouchers Payable		450
Governmental Activities:		
Equipment	450	
Vouchers Payable		450

[12] *GASBS 42,* par. 5.
[13] Ibid, par. 6.
[14] Ibid, par. 12.

Assuming Vouchers Payable is paid shortly after the equipment acquisition, Vouchers Payable will be debited and Cash will be credited, both in the General Fund and the governmental activities journal at the government-wide level. General capital assets acquired by use of capital projects fund resources would be recorded in essentially the same manner as if they had been acquired by the General Fund. If construction of a general capital asset is in progress at the end of a fiscal year, construction expenditures to the date of the financial report should be capitalized in the governmental activities ledger. These capital asset entries will be illustrated later in this chapter in the discussion of capital projects fund transactions.

Accounting for the disposal of general capital assets is relatively simple unless cash or others assets are involved in the liquidation. Accounting for an asset disposal requires elimination of the capital asset and accumulated depreciation accounts and recognition of a gain or loss, as appropriate. Assuming a building that cost $100,000 and with $80,000 of accumulated depreciation is retired without revenue or expenditure to the General Fund, the following entry in the governmental activities general journal would be required:

	Debits	Credits
Governmental Activities:		
Loss on Disposal of Building	20,000	
Accumulated Depreciation—Buildings.	80,000	
Buildings		100,000

Property records for the building should receive appropriate notations about the transaction and thereafter be transferred to an inactive file.

In the event that cash is disbursed or received in connection with the disposal of general capital assets, the Cash account would be debited or credited as part of the entry to remove the book value of the capital asset, and a gain or loss would be recorded, as appropriate. Assuming that in the preceding example the General Fund incurred $3,000 for the demolition of the building, an entry in the following form should be made on the General Fund books:

General Fund:		
Expenditures.	3,000	
Vouchers Payable.		3,000

The corresponding entry at the government-wide level is:

Governmental Activities:		
Loss on Disposal of Building	23,000	
Accumulated Depreciation—Buildings.	80,000	
Buildings		100,000
Vouchers Payable.		3,000

If cash is received from the disposal of a general capital asset, some question may arise as to its disposition. Theoretically, the cash should be directed to the fund that provided the asset, but this may not always be practicable. If the asset was provided by a capital projects fund, the contributing fund may have been liquidated before the sale occurs. Unless otherwise prescribed by law, disposition of the results of a sale will be handled as decided by the legislative body having jurisdiction over the asset and will be recorded in the manner required by the accounting system of the recipient fund. Commonly, proceeds of sales of general capital assets are budgeted as Estimated Other Financing Sources in the General Fund. In such cases, when sales actually occur, the General Fund debits Cash (or a receivable) for the selling price and credits Other Financing Sources—Proceeds of Sales of Assets.

ACCOUNTING FOR CAPITAL PROJECTS

The reason for creating a fund to account for capital projects is the same as the reason for creating special revenue funds—to provide a formal mechanism to enable administrators to ensure revenues and other financing sources dedicated to a certain purpose are used for that purpose and no other, as well as to enable administrators to report to creditors and other grantors of capital projects fund resources that their requirements regarding the use of the resources were met.

Capital projects funds differ from the General Fund and special revenue funds in that the latter categories have a year-to-year life, whereas capital projects funds have a project-life focus. In some jurisdictions, governments are allowed to account for all capital projects within a single capital projects fund. In other jurisdictions, laws are construed as requiring each project to be accounted for by a separate capital projects fund. Even in jurisdictions that permit the use of a single fund, managers may prefer to use separate funds in order to enhance control over each project. In such cases a fund is created when a capital project or a series of related projects is legally authorized; it is closed when the project or series is completed. Appropriation accounts need not be used because the legal authorization to engage in the project is in itself an appropriation of the total amount that may be obligated for the construction or acquisition of the capital asset specified in the project authorization. Estimated revenues need not be recorded because few contractors will start work on a project until financing is ensured through the sale of bonds or the receipt of grants or gifts. To provide control over the issuance of contracts and purchase orders, which may be numerous and which may be outstanding for several years in construction projects, it is recommended that the encumbrance procedure described in Chapter 3 be used. Since the purpose of the capital projects fund is to account for the receipt and expenditure of financial resources earmarked for capital projects, it contains balance sheet accounts for only financial resources and for the liabilities to be liquidated by those resources. Neither the capital assets acquired nor any long-term debt incurred for the acquisition is recorded in a capital projects fund; these items are recorded in the governmental activities general ledger at the government-wide level, as discussed earlier in this chapter and in Chapter 6.

Some jurisdictions raise annual revenues for the specific purpose of financing major repairs to existing capital assets or for replacement of components of those assets (e.g., furnaces, air conditioning systems, roofs). A **capital improvements fund,** sometimes called a *cumulative building fund,* is used to account for such revenues. The specific repairs and replacements to be undertaken by the capital improvement fund in a given year are not necessarily known at the time the revenues are budgeted. The appropriation process described in previous chapters is used to authorize expenditures from capital improvement funds when the nature and approximate cost of needed repairs and replacements become known. Necessary expenditures that cannot be financed by appropriation of the fund balance of a capital improvement fund or from the General Fund or special revenue funds may occasion the establishment of a capital projects fund.

Legal Requirements

Since a governmental entity's power to issue bonds constitutes an ever-present hazard to the welfare of its property owners in particular[15] and its taxpayers in general, the authority is ordinarily limited by legislation. The purpose of legislative limitation is to obtain a prudent balance between public welfare and the rights of individual citizens. In some jurisdictions, most bond issues must be approved by referendum; in others, by petition of a specified percentage of taxpayers. Not only must bond issues be approved according to law but the government must comply with other provisions, such as method and timing of payments from the proceeds and determination of validity of claims for payment. A knowledge of all details related to a bond issue is prerequisite to the avoidance of difficulties and complications that might otherwise occur.

Participation of state and federal agencies in financing capital acquisitions by local government adds further complications to the process. Strict control of how such grants are used is imperative for ensuring proper use of the funds. This more or less dictates that accounting and reporting procedures be established that can provide information showing compliance with terms of the grants. Details of the fund structure and operation should ensure that all required information is provided when it is needed and in the form in which it is needed.

The successful accomplishment of a capital acquisition project may be brought about in one or more of the following ways:

1. Outright purchase from fund cash.
2. By construction, utilizing the government's own workforce.
3. By construction, utilizing the services of private contractors.
4. By capital lease agreement.

ILLUSTRATIVE TRANSACTIONS—CAPITAL PROJECTS FUNDS

GASB standards require the use of the same basis of accounting for capital projects funds as for the other governmental fund types. Proceeds of debt issues should be recognized by a capital projects fund at the time the issue is sold rather than the time it is authorized because authorization of an issue does not guarantee its sale. Proceeds of debt issues should be recorded as Proceeds of Bonds or Proceeds of Long-Term Notes rather than as Revenues, and they should be reported in the Other Financing Sources section of the statement of revenues, expenditures, and changes in fund balance. Similarly, tax revenues raised by the General Fund or a special revenue fund and transferred to a capital projects fund are recorded as Interfund Transfers In and reported in the Other Financing Sources section of the operating statement.

---

[15] An issue of bonds to be repaid from tax revenues in essence places a lien on all taxable property within a government's jurisdiction. Responsibility for payments of principal and interest on general bonded debt provides for no consideration of a property owner's financial condition and ability or inability to pay.

Taxes raised specifically for a capital projects fund would be recorded as revenues of that fund, as would special assessments to be used for the construction of assets deemed to be of particular benefit to certain property owners. Grants, entitlements, or shared revenues received by a capital projects fund from another government are considered revenues of the capital projects fund, as would be interest earned on investments of the capital projects fund if the interest is available for expenditure by the capital projects fund (if, by law, the interest must be used for service of long-term capital debt, the interest should be transferred to the appropriate debt service fund).

In the following illustration of accounting for representative transactions of a capital projects fund, it is assumed that the town council of the Town of Brighton authorized an issue of $1,200,000 of 6 percent bonds as partial financing of a fire station expected to cost approximately $1,500,000; the $300,000 additional financing was to be contributed by other governments. The project, to utilize land already owned by the town, was completed partly by a private contractor and partly by the town's own workforce. Completion of the project was expected within the current year. Transactions and entries related to the project are shown here, all of which are assumed to occur in fiscal year 2008. For economy of time and space, vouchering of liabilities is omitted.

The $1,200,000 bond issue, which had been approved by voter referendum, was officially approved by the town council. No formal entry is required to record voter and town council approval. A memorandum entry may be made to identify the approved project and the means of financing it.

The sum of $50,000 was borrowed on a short-term basis from the National Bank for defraying engineering and other preliminary expenses. Because this transaction affects both the Fire Station Capital Projects Fund and governmental activities at the government-wide level, the following entry is made in both journals:

		Debits	Credits
	Fire Station Capital Projects Fund and Governmental Activities:		
1.	Cash	50,000	
	Short-Term Notes Payable		50,000

Total purchase orders and other commitment documents issued for supplies, materials, items of minor equipment, and labor required for the part of the project to be performed by the town's employees amounted to $443,000. (Since the authorization is for the project, not for a budget year, it is unnecessary to include 2008, or any other year, in the account titles.) The following budgetary control entry is made in the capital projects fund but is not recorded at the government-wide level.

	Fire Station Capital Projects Fund:		
2.	Encumbrances	443,000	
	Reserve for Encumbrances		443,000

A contract was signed for certain work to be done by a private contractor in the amount of $1,005,000. As with Entry 2, only the capital projects fund is affected.

		Debits	Credits
	Fire Station Capital Projects Fund:		
3.	Encumbrances..	1,005,000	
	Reserve for Encumbrances		1,005,000

Special engineering and miscellaneous costs that had not been encumbered were paid in the amount of $48,000. These costs are deemed to be properly capitalized as part of the fire station.

		Debits	Credits
	Fire Station Capital Projects Fund:		
4a.	Construction Expenditures.............................	48,000	
	Cash		48,000
	Governmental Activities:		
4b.	Construction Work in Progress	48,000	
	Cash		48,000

Entries 4a and 4b highlight a major difference between accounting for a governmental fund and governmental activities at the government-wide level. Accounting for a governmental fund focuses on the inflows and outflows of current financial resources on the modified accrual basis; accounting for governmental activities focuses on the inflows and outflows of economic resources, including capital assets, on the accrual basis used in accounting for business organizations.

When the project was approximately half finished, the contractor submitted a billing requesting payment of $495,000.

		Debits	Credits
	Fire Station Capital Projects Fund:		
5a.	Reserve for Encumbrances.............................	495,000	
	Encumbrances.....................................		495,000
5b.	Construction Expenditures.............................	495,000	
	Contracts Payable		495,000
	Governmental Activities:		
5c.	Construction Work in Progress	495,000	
	Contracts Payable		495,000

Entries 5a and 5b record conversion of an estimated liability to a firm liability eligible for payment upon proper authentication. Contracts Payable records the status of a claim under a contract between the time of presentation and verification for vouchering or payment.

Payment in full was received from the other governments that had agreed to pay part of the cost of the new fire station.

		Debits	Credits
	Fire Station Capital Projects Fund:		
6a.	Cash.	300,000	
	Revenues		300,000
	Governmental Activities:		
6b.	Cash.	300,000	
	Program Revenues—Capital Grants and Contributions—Public Safety.		300,00

The National Bank loan was repaid with interest amounting to $1,000.

		Debits	Credits
	Fire Station Capital Projects Fund:		
7a.	Interest Expenditures	1,000	
	Short-Term Notes Payable.	50,000	
	Cash.		51,000
	Governmental Activities:		
7b.	Expenses—Interest on Notes Payable	1,000	
	Short-Term Notes Payable.	50,000	
	Cash.		51,000

The reader will note that the $1,000 of interest expenditure (expense) recorded in Entries 7a and 7b is not capitalized as part of the total cost of the new fire station. GASB standards prohibit capitalization of interest incurred during construction as part of the cost of *general capital assets*. However, as is illustrated and discussed in Chapter 7, interest is capitalized as part of self-constructed capital assets recorded in proprietary funds.

On June 15, 2008, the Town of Brighton issued at par bonds with a par value of $1,200,000 and dated June 15, 2008. Thus, there was no accrued interest as of the date of issue. Entries 8a and 8b show the contrast between how the bond issue is recorded in the general journals for the capital projects fund and governmental activities at the government-wide level. Since the bond issue increases current financial resources in the capital projects fund, the credit in Entry 8a is to Other Financing Sources—Proceeds of Bonds rather than to a liability account. As shown in Entry 8b, the long-term liability is recorded in the governmental activities general journal as a credit to Bonds Payable, reflecting the economic resources measurement focus used at the government-wide level.

		Debits	Credits
	Fire Station Capital Projects Fund:		
8a.	Cash.	1,200,000	
	Other Financing Sources—Proceeds of Bonds		1,200,000
	Governmental Activities:		
8b.	Cash.	1,200,000	
	Bonds Payable.		1,200,000

The contractor's initial claim was fully verified and paid (see Entries 5b and 5c).

		Debits	Credits
	Fire Station Capital Projects Fund and Governmental Activities:		
9.	Contracts Payable	495,000	
	Cash		495,000

Total disbursements for all costs encumbered in Entry 2 amounted to $440,000. Although the encumbrances entry only affects the capital projects fund, the disbursement affects both the capital projects fund and governmental activities at the government-wide level.

	Fire Station Capital Projects Fund:		
10a.	Reserve for Encumbrances	443,000	
	Encumbrances		443,000
10b.	Construction Expenditures	440,000	
	Cash		440,000
	Governmental Activities:		
10c.	Construction Work in Progress	440,000	
	Cash		440,000

Billing for the balance owed on the construction contract was received from the contractor.

	Fire Station Capital Projects Fund:		
11a.	Reserve for Encumbrances	510,000	
	Encumbrances		510,000
11b.	Construction Expenditures	510,000	
	Contracts Payable		510,000
	Governmental Activities:		
11c.	Construction Work in Progress	510,000	
	Contracts Payable		510,000

Inspection revealed only minor imperfections in the contractor's performance, and on correction of these, the liability to the contractor was paid.

	Fire Station Capital Projects Fund and Governmental Activities:		
12.	Contracts Payable	510,000	
	Cash		510,000

All requirements and obligations related to the project having been fulfilled, the operating statement accounts were closed in the capital projects fund. Governmental activities general ledger accounts will be closed in Chapter 9.

		Debits	Credits
	Fire Station Capital Projects Fund:		
13.	Revenues......................................	300,000	
	Other Financing Sources—Proceeds of Bonds..............	1,200,000	
	Construction Expenditures		1,493,000
	Interest Expenditures		1,000
	Fund Balance		6,000

Since the project has been completed, it is appropriate to terminate the capital projects fund. The only remaining asset of the fund after the 13 transactions illustrated is Cash in the amount of $6,000. State laws often require that assets no longer needed in a capital projects fund be transferred to the fund that will service the debt incurred for the project, a debt service fund. Transfers of this nature are called **interfund transfers** and are reported as other financing uses by the transferor fund and other financing sources by the transferee fund in the statement of revenues, expenditures, and changes in fund balance (see Illustration 5–3). The entries to record the transfer and termination of the Town of Brighton Fire Station Capital Projects Fund accounts are:

	Fire Station Capital Projects Fund:		
14a.	Other Financing Uses—Interfund Transfers Out	6,000	
	Cash		6,000
14b.	Fund Balance....................................	6,000	
	Other Financing Uses—Interfund Transfers Out		6,000

Similar entries would be required to record the interfund transfers in by the debt service fund. No entry is required at the government-wide level since the transfer occurs *within* the governmental activities category.

The cost of the fire station constructed by the Town of Brighton is recorded in the governmental activities general journal at the government-wide level. Because all capitalizable costs have previously been recorded as construction work in progress during the period of construction, the only entry required is to reclassify the amount in that account to the Buildings account, as shown in the following entry.

	Governmental Activities:		
15.	Buildings.......................................	1,493,000	
	Construction Work in Progress.......................		1,493,000

ILLUSTRATION 5–3

TOWN OF BRIGHTON
Fire Station Capital Projects Fund
Statement of Revenues, Expenditures, and Changes in Fund Balance
For the Year Ended December 31, 2008

Revenues:		
From other governments		$ 300,000
Expenditures:		
Construction	$1,493,000	
Interest	1,000	1,494,000
Excess of revenues over (under) expenditures		(1,194,000)
Other financing sources (uses):		
Proceeds of bonds	1,200,000	
Interfund transfer out	(6,000)	1,194,000
Excess of revenues and other financing sources/		
uses over expenditures		–0–
Fund balance, January 1, 2008		–0–
Fund balance, December 31, 2008		$ –0–

Illustrative Financial Statements for a Capital Projects Fund

Inasmuch as all balance sheet accounts of the Town of Brighton Fire Station Capital Projects Fund are closed in the case illustrated in the preceding section of this chapter, there are no assets, liabilities, or fund equity to report in a balance sheet. The operations of the year, however, should be reported in a statement of revenues, expenditures, and changes in fund balance, as shown in Illustration 5–3. Since it is assumed that the Town of Brighton is not required to adopt a legal budget for its capital projects funds, it does not need to prepare a budgetary comparison schedule or statement for the capital projects fund type.

At the government-wide level, the completed fire station is reported as a capital asset, net of accumulated depreciation (if any depreciation expense is recorded in the first year in which the asset is placed into service), in the Governmental Activities column of the statement of net assets (see Illustration 1–4). The $1,200,000 of tax-supported bonds issued for the project is reported as a long-term liability in the Governmental Activities column of the statement of net assets. If any depreciation expense is recorded for the portion of a year that the fire station has been in service, it would be reported as a direct expense of the Public Safety function in the statement of activities (see Illustration 1–5).

Alternative Treatment of Residual Equity or Deficits

In the example just presented, a modest amount of cash remained in the Fire Station Capital Projects Fund after the project had been completed and all liabilities of the fund were liquidated. If necessary expenditures and other financing uses are planned carefully and controlled carefully so that actual does not exceed plans, revenues and other financing sources of the capital projects fund should equal, or slightly exceed, the expenditures and other financing uses, leaving a residual fund equity. If, as in the example presented, long-term debt had been incurred for the purposes of the capital projects fund, the residual equity is ordinarily transferred to the fund that is to service the debt. If the residual equity were deemed to have come from grants or shared revenues restricted for capital acquisitions or construction, legal advice may indicate that any residual equity must be returned to the source(s) of the restricted grants or restricted shared revenues.

Even with careful planning and cost control, expenditures and other financing uses of a capital projects fund may exceed its revenues and other financing sources, resulting in a negative fund balance, or a deficit. If the deficit is a relatively small amount, the legislative body of the government may be able to authorize transfers from one or more other funds to cover the deficit in the capital projects fund. If the deficit is relatively large, and/or if intended transfers are not feasible, the government may seek additional grants or shared revenues from other governments to cover the deficit. If no other alternative is available, the government would need to finance the deficit by issuing debt in whatever form is legally possible and feasible under market conditions then existing.

Bond Premium, Discount, and Accrued Interest on Bonds Sold

Governments that issue bonds or long-term notes to finance the acquisition of capital assets commonly sell the entire issue to an underwriter or a syndicate of underwriters on the basis of bids or negotiated terms. The underwriters then "retail" the bonds or notes to institutions or individuals who often have agreed in advance to purchase a specified amount of bonds should the underwriters be successful in tendering the winning bid. Statutes in some states prohibit the initial sale of an issue of local government bonds at a discount. Accordingly, it is usual to set the interest rate high enough to enable the underwriters to pay the issuer at least the par, or face, value of the bonds; it is not unusual for underwriters to pay issuers an amount in excess of par, known as a *premium.* State statutes, local ordinances, or bond indentures often require that initial issue premiums be used for debt service. In such cases only the par value of the bonds is considered as an other financing source of the capital projects fund; the premium is considered as an other financing source of the debt service fund. Therefore, the sale of bonds at a premium would require an entry in the capital projects fund for the face of the bonds (as shown in Entry 8a of this chapter) and an entry in the debt service fund for the premium. At the government-wide level, a premium would be recorded as an additional component of the general long-term liability for the bonds. As in accounting for business organizations, the premium should be amortized, using the effective-interest method, over the life of the bonds, the amount of amortization being the difference between the actual cash paid for interest and the calculated amount of effective interest expense for the period.

Similarly, when bonds are sold between interest payment dates, the party buying the bonds must pay up front the amount of interest accrued from the date of the bonds (the starting date for purposes of calculating interest) to the date the bonds are actually sold as part of the total price of the bonds. Thus, assuming two months of interest have already accrued by the sale date, the two months of interest that bondholders pay at the sale date yields the equitable result that they earn a *net* four months of interest, although they will receive a full six months of interest only four months after the sale date. In a governmental fund, accrued interest sold should conceptually be credited to Interest Expenditure and be offset against the six-month interest expenditure recorded on the first interest payment date following the sale of the bonds. In practice, however, accrued interest sold is generally recorded as a revenue of the debt service fund. This practice simplifies budgetary control by permitting the government to budget appropriations for and record an expenditure for the full six months of interest that must be paid on the first interest payment date. At the government-wide level, however, cash received on the sale date for accrued interest would be credited either as Accrued Interest Payable or Interest Expense, as in business accounting.

It may happen that the issuing government receives one check from the underwriters for the total amount of the par plus the premium. If procedures of that government indicate that it is desirable to record the entire amount in the capital projects fund, the following entries are appropriate (using assumed amounts) (*Note:* This entry and the one that follows are not part of the Town of Brighton Fire Station Capital Projects Fund example):

	Debits	Credits
Capital Projects Fund:		
Cash	1,509,000	
Other Financing Sources—Proceeds of Bonds		1,500,000
Due to Other Funds		9,000

This entry accounts for the bond premium as a liability of the capital projects fund because it must be remitted to the debt service fund. In the debt service fund, an entry would be made to debit Due from Other Funds and credit Other Financing Sources—Premium on Bonds. Some accountants prefer to credit Other Financing Sources—Premium on Bonds rather than Due to Other Funds in the capital projects fund, particularly if the disposition of the premium is still to be determined on the sale date. Some accountants also include the amount of the premium as part of the credit to Other Financing Sources—Proceeds of Bonds in the capital projects fund. If either of these alternative procedures is used, it is necessary to make a second entry in the Capital Projects Fund debiting Other Financing Uses—Interfund Transfers Out and crediting Due to Other Funds.

In those jurisdictions in which it is legal for bonds to be sold initially at a discount, using the same face amount as the bonds in the entry above, except the debt proceeds are less than the face amount of the bonds, the entry might be:

Capital Projects Fund:		
Cash	1,491,000	
Other Financing Uses—Discount on Bonds	9,000	
Other Financing Sources—Proceeds of Bonds		1,500,000

Crediting Other Financing Sources—Proceeds of Bonds for $1,500,000 carries the implication that, if necessary, the discount is expected to be counterbalanced at a future date by receipt of money from another source, perhaps the General Fund. If it has been determined that no money from another source will be provided, the discount would be written off against Proceeds of Bonds. When the money from another source is received, the capital projects fund should debit Cash and credit either Revenues or Other Financing Sources, depending on the source of the money. When it is known in advance that the discount will not be made up by transfers from other sources, an entry debiting Cash and crediting Other Financing Sources—Proceeds of Bonds, each for par value less discount, should be made.

Retained Percentages

It is common to require contractors on large-scale contracts to give performance bonds, providing for indemnity to the government for any failure on the contractor's part to comply with terms and specifications of the agreement. Before final inspection of a project can be completed, the contractor firm may have moved its workforce and equipment to another location, thus making it difficult to remedy possible objections to the firm's performance. Also, the shortcoming alleged by the government may be of a controversial nature with the contractor unwilling to accede to the demands of the government. Results of legal action in such disagreements are not predictable with certainty.

To provide more prompt adjustment on shortcomings not large or convincing enough to justify legal action and not recoverable under contractor's bond, as well as those the contractor may admit but not be in a position to rectify, it is common practice to withhold a portion of the contractor's remuneration until final inspection and acceptance have occurred. The withheld portion is normally a contractual percentage of the amount due on each segment of the contract.

In the Town of Brighton illustration, the contractor submitted a bill for $495,000, which, on preliminary approval, was recorded previously in Entry 5b in the Fire Station Capital Projects Fund as follows:

	Debits	Credits
Capital Projects Fund:		
Construction Expenditures	495,000	
Contracts Payable		495,000

Assuming that the contract provided for retention of 5 percent, current settlement on the billing would be recorded as follows:

	Debits	Credits
Capital Projects Fund:		
Contracts Payable	495,000	
Cash		470,250
Contracts Payable—Retained Percentage		24,750

This same entry would also be made in the governmental activities general journal at the government-wide level. Alternatively, the intention of the government to retain the percentage stipulated in the contract could be recorded at the time the progress billing receives preliminary approval. In that event, the credit to Contracts Payable in the first entry in this section would be $470,250, and the credit to Contracts Payable—Retained Percentage in the amount of $24,750 is made at that time. The second entry, therefore, would be a debit to Contracts Payable and a credit to Cash for $470,250.

On final acceptance of the project, the retained percentage is liquidated by a payment of cash. In the event that the government that recorded the retention finds it necessary to spend money on correction of deficiencies in the contractor's performance, the payment is charged to Contracts Payable—Retained Percentage. If the cost of correcting deficiencies exceeds the balance in the Contracts Payable—Retained Percentage account, the excess amount is debited to Construction Expenditures in the

Fire Station Capital Projects Fund and to Buildings (or other appropriate capital asset account) in the governmental activities general journal.

Claims and Judgments Payable

Claims and judgments often, although not always, relate to construction activities of a government. If a claim has been litigated and a judicial decision adverse to the government has been rendered, there is no question as to the amount of the liability that should be recorded. If claims have not been litigated or judgments have not been made as of balance sheet date, liabilities may be estimated through a case-by-case review of all claims, the application of historical experience to the outstanding claims, or a combination of these methods.[16]

GASB standards specify that the amount of claims and judgments recognized as expenditures and liabilities of governmental funds is limited to the amount that would normally be liquidated with expendable resources then in the fund; however, the full known or estimated liability should be reported in the Governmental Activities column of the government-wide statement of net assets.

Bond Anticipation Notes Payable and the Problem of Interest Expenditures

Bond Anticipation Notes Payable is a liability resulting from the borrowing of money for temporary financing before issuance of bonds. Delay in perfecting all details connected with issuance of bonds and postponement of the sale until a large portion of the proceeds is needed are the prevailing reasons for preliminary financing by use of **bond anticipation notes.** The "bond anticipation" description of the debt signifies an obligation to retire the notes from proceeds of a proposed bond issue. If two conditions specified in FASB *Statement No. 6* are met, then the liability for bond anticipation notes should be treated as a long-term liability:[17]

1. All legal steps have been taken to refinance the bond anticipation notes.
2. The intent is supported by an ability to consummate refinancing the short-term notes on a long-term basis.

In cases in which the bond anticipation notes are secured by approved but unissued bonds and the intent is to repay the notes from the proceeds of the bond issue, it would appear that the two criteria are met and, thus, bond anticipation note issues in such cases would be reported as a long-term liability in the Governmental Activities column of the government-wide statement of net assets and as an other financing source (Proceeds of Bond Anticipation Notes) in the capital projects fund.

As an example of a bond anticipation note that meets the two criteria provided, assume that a particular city issued $500,000 of 6 percent bond anticipation notes under a written agreement that the notes will be retired within six months from the proceeds of a previously approved $5,000,000 bond issue. When the bond anticipation notes are issued, the journal entries for the capital projects fund and governmental activities would be as follows:

[16] GASB standards (GASB *Codification*, Sec. C50.110–111) require governmental entities to use the criteria of FASB *SFAS No. 5* as guidelines for recognizing a loss liability. That is, if information available prior to issuance of the financial statements indicates that it is probable that an asset has been impaired or a liability has been incurred at the date of the financial statements and the amount of the loss can be estimated with a reasonable degree of accuracy, the liability should be recognized.

[17] GASB *Codification*, Sec. B50.101.

	Debits	Credits
Capital Projects Fund:		
Cash	500,000	
Other Financing Sources—Proceeds of Bond Anticipation Notes . .		500,000
Governmental Activities:		
Cash	500,000	
Bond Anticipation Notes Payable		500,000

Six months later, the bonds are issued at par and the bond anticipation notes are retired using a portion of the bond proceeds. Cash from other sources is assumed to be used to pay interest on the bond anticipation notes. The required journal entries are as follows:

Capital Projects Fund:		
Cash	5,000,000	
Other Financing Sources—Proceeds of Bonds		5,000,000
Other Financing Uses—Retirement of Bond Anticipation Notes	500,000	
Interest Expenditures	15,000	
Cash		515,000
Governmental Activities:		
Cash	5,000,000	
Bonds Payable		5,000,000
Bond Anticipation Notes Payable	500,000	
Expenses—Interest on Long-Term Debt	15,000	
Cash		515,000
(*Note:* Interest expense is $500,000 $\times$ .06 $\times$ 6/12 = $15,000)		

As indicated in the preceding example, interest almost always must be paid on bond anticipation notes. Both practical and theoretical problems are involved in the payment of interest on liabilities. Practically, payment of interest by the capital projects fund reduces the amount available for construction or acquisition of the assets, so the administrators of the capital projects fund would wish to pass the burden of interest payment to another fund. Logically, the debt service fund set up for the bond issue should bear the burden of interest on bond anticipation notes and possibly on judgments, but at the time this interest must be paid, the debt service fund may have no assets. It would also appeal to the capital projects fund's administrators that interest on the bond anticipation notes and judgments should be paid by the General Fund (or any other fund with available cash). If such interest payments had been included in the appropriations budget by the General Fund (or other fund), the payment would be legal; if not, the legislative body might authorize the other fund to pay the interest.

If the capital projects fund bears the interest on bond anticipation notes or other short-term debt, either initially or ultimately, an expenditure account must be debited. In Entry 7a in the series of Fire Station Capital Projects Fund and governmental activities entries illustrated earlier in this chapter, interest paid on bond anticipation notes was debited to Interest Expenditures rather than to Construction Expenditures, reflecting the requirements of *GASBS 37*. Entry 7b showed that the $1,000 paid for interest also was not capitalized as part of the cost of the assets for the fire station project.

Investments

Interest rates payable on general long-term debt have typically been lower than interest rates that the government can earn on temporary investments of high quality, such as U.S. Treasury bills and notes, bank certificates of deposit, and government bonds with short maturities. Consequently, there is considerable attraction to the practice of selling bonds as soon as possible after a capital project is legally authorized and investing the proceeds to earn a net interest income. (This practice also avoids the problems and costs involved in financing by bond anticipation notes, described in the preceding section.) However, arbitrage rules under the Internal Revenue Code constrain the investment of bond proceeds to securities whose yield does not exceed that of the new debt. Application of these rules to state and local governments is subject to continuing litigation and legislative action, so competent legal guidance must be sought by governments wishing to invest bond proceeds in a manner that will avoid incurring an **arbitrage rebate** and possible difficulties with the Internal Revenue Service.

Interest earned on temporary investments is available for use by the capital projects fund in some jurisdictions; in others, laws or local practices require the interest income to be transferred to the debt service fund or to the General Fund. If interest income is available to the capital projects fund, it should be recognized on the modified accrual basis as a credit to Revenues. If it will be collected by the capital projects fund but must be transferred to another fund, an additional entry is required to record an interfund transfer out. If the interest will be collected by the debt service fund, or other fund that will recognize it as revenue, no entry by the capital projects fund is necessary.

Multiple-Period and Multiple-Project Bond Funds

Thus far, discussion of capital projects fund accounting has proceeded on the tacit assumption that initiation and completion of projects occur in the same fiscal year. Many projects large enough to require a capital projects fund are started in one year and ended in another. Furthermore, a single comprehensive authorization may legalize two or more purchase or construction projects as segments of a master plan of improvements. Both multiple-period and multiple-project activities require some deviations from the accounting activities that suffice for one-period, one-project accounting.

The first difference appears in the budgeting procedure. Whereas for a one-period operation a single authorization might adequately cover the project from beginning to end, annual budgets, in one form or another, may be desirable or even required for those extending into two or more periods. This practice is used as a means of keeping the project under the legislative body's control and preventing the unacceptable deviations that might result from lump-sum approval, in advance, of a long-term project. Likewise, a large bond issue, to be supplemented by grants from outside sources, may be authorized to cover a number of projects extending over a period of time but not planned in detail before initiation of the first project. Such an arrangement requires the fund administration to maintain control by giving final approval to the budget for each project only as it comes up for action.

For a multiple-projects fund, it is necessary to identify encumbrances and expenditures in a way that will indicate the project to which each encumbrance and expenditure applies in order to check for compliance with the project budget. This can be accomplished by adding the project name or other designation (e.g., City Hall or Project No. 75) to the encumbrance and expenditure account titles. This device is almost imperative for proper identification in the recording of transactions, and it facilitates preparation of cash and expenditure statements for multiproject operations.

In accounting for encumbrances for multiperiod projects, there is some difference of opinion as to the desirable procedure to follow in relation to encumbrances outstanding at the end of a period. In the management of the General Fund, for example, operations in terms of amounts of revenues and expenditures during a specified standard period of time (quarter, half year, etc.) provide measures of budgetary accomplishment. Because capital projects are rarely of the same size and may be started and ended at any time of year, periodic comparisons are of little significance. Furthermore, although the personnel of a legislative body may change at the beginning of a year during which a capital project is in progress, the change is unlikely to affect materially the project's progress. Although the operations of a capital projects fund are project-completion oriented, with slight reference to time, GASB standards require Encumbrances, Expenditures, Proceeds of Bonds, and Revenues accounts to be closed to Fund Balance at year-end to facilitate preparation of capital projects fund financial statements for inclusion in the governments annual report on a basis consistent with year-end statements of other funds.

The required procedure does produce year-end capital projects fund balance sheets that appear similar to those of the General Fund and special revenue funds illustrated in preceding chapters. The similarity of appearance and terminology may be misleading, however. The Fund Balance account of the General Fund or a special revenue fund represents net financial resources available for appropriation, whereas the Fund Balance account of a multiple-period capital projects fund represents net assets already set aside for the acquisition of specified capital facilities. The Fund Balance of a multiple-period capital projects fund is comparable to the unexpended unencumbered appropriation item on an interim balance sheet of the General or a special revenue fund; it is not comparable to the year-end Fund Balance of such funds.

Reestablishment of Encumbrances

The year-end closing procedure required by GASB standards for use by capital projects funds artificially chops the construction expenditures pertaining to each continuing project into fiscal-year segments, rather than allowing the total cost of each project to be accumulated in a single construction expenditures account. Similarly, closing the Encumbrance account of each project to Fund Balance at year-end creates some procedural problems in accounting in the subsequent year. The procedure illustrated for the General Fund and special revenue funds (using separate Encumbrances, Reserve for Encumbrances, and Expenditures accounts for each year) could be followed. The procedure illustrated for the General Fund and special revenue funds is logical in that case because each appropriation expires at year-end, and yearly Expenditure and Encumbrance accounts are needed to match with the yearly Appropriations account. The authorization (appropriation) for a capital project, however, does not expire at the end of a fiscal year but continues for the life of the project. Accordingly, it is necessary to reestablish the Encumbrances account at the beginning of each year in order to facilitate accounting for expenditures for goods and services ordered in one year and received in a subsequent year. Reestablishment of the Encumbrances account may be accomplished as shown by the following entry in the capital projects fund (amount assumed):

	Debits	Credits
Capital Projects Fund:		
Encumbrances	210,000	
Fund Balance		210,000

If the Encumbrances account is reestablished, subsequent receipt of goods or services entered as encumbrances in a prior year may be recorded in the same manner as if they had been ordered in the current year:

	Debits	Credits
Capital Projects Fund:		
Reserve for Encumbrances	210,000	
Construction Expenditures	210,000	
Contracts Payable		210,000
Encumbrances		210,000

Capital Projects Financed by Special Assessments

The second paragraph of this chapter noted that one common source of financing construction of general capital assets is by issuance of long-term debt to be repaid by special assessments. A **special assessment** is a compulsory levy made against certain property to defray part or all of the cost of a specific improvement or service that is presumed to be of general benefit to the public and of particular benefit to the property against which the special assessment is levied. Special assessment financing is allowed under the laws of many states. Generally, a majority of owners of the property that will be assessed must agree to the formation of a special assessment district, sometimes called a *local improvement district.* A special assessment district may be an independent special purpose government created under the laws of the state in which it is located, or a component unit of a county, city, or other general governmental unit. In some cases, special assessment transactions are administered directly by a general purpose government.

If a special assessment district is an independent special purpose governmental unit, it will need to account for the construction phase of a capital project in the manner described in this chapter, the debt service phase of the project in the manner described in Chapter 6, and the resulting general capital assets and related long-term debt as described in this chapter and Chapter 6, respectively. The same observations apply to a special assessment district that is a component unit of a primary government, which should be reported in a discrete presentation in the basic financial statements of the governmental financial reporting entity, as discussed in relation to Illustration 2–1.

If the financial activities of a special assessment district are so intertwined with those of the primary government that the balances and transactions meet the criteria for blending (see discussion related to Illustration 2–1), it is logical that special assessment transactions be administered directly by the primary government. In that event the accounting and reporting standards set forth in this chapter apply to capital projects financed in whole or in part by special assessments with the following modifications and additions.

The total dollar amount of a capital project to be financed by special assessments must be paid by owners of real property within the special assessment district. Accordingly, the portion of the total to be borne by each parcel of property within the district must be determined in whatever manner is specified by laws of the relevant jurisdiction. It is often true that the amount to be paid by each owner is large enough so that laws will provide that the total special assessment against each parcel may be paid in equal installments over a specified period of years. Commonly, the first installment is due within a relatively short period of time (say, 60 days after the assessment is levied) and, if paid by the due date, is noninterest bearing. The remainder of the installments are due annually thereafter and are interest bearing. Assume, for example, that the final installment is due five years after the levy of the special assessment. Contractors cannot be expected to wait five years to be paid for work done on the project; therefore, an issue of long-term debt is authorized in the amount of installments due in future years. The first installment and the proceeds of the long-term debt would be used to finance the capital project and would be recorded by a capital projects fund. GASB standards provide that the first installment should be recognized as revenue of the capital projects fund and governmental activities at the government-wide level at the time of the levy—providing, of course, for any estimated uncollectibles. The deferred installments would be reported as Deferred Revenues, a liability account.

Long-term debt proceeds would be considered an Other Financing Source—Proceeds of Bonds (or Notes) of the capital projects fund, and as a long-term liability at the government-wide level if the primary government has an obligation to assume debt service in the event that collections of remaining installments are insufficient. If the primary government has no obligation for debt service and the creditors are payable solely from collections of the special assessment installments and interest thereon, the proceeds of special assessment long-term debt should be credited to a capital projects other financing sources account such as Contribution from Property Owners rather than as Proceeds of Bonds (or Notes).

Installments of special assessments and interest thereon, which are to be used to service long-term debt and are not available for expenditure by a capital projects fund, should be recorded as described in the discussion of debt service funds in Chapter 6. General capital assets financed wholly or partially through collections of special assessments are recorded in the same manner as any other general capital assets in the governmental activities category at the government-wide level.

Financial Reporting for Capital Projects Funds

Each capital projects fund that meets the definition of a *major fund* (see the Glossary for a definition) must be reported in a separate column of the balance sheet—governmental funds (see Illustration 1–6) and the statement of revenues, expenditures, and changes in fund balances—governmental funds (see Illustration 1–8). Nonmajor capital projects funds would be reported in the same column as other nonmajor governmental funds in these two basic financial statements.

Governments are also encouraged but not required to provide as supplementary information combining financial statements for all nonmajor funds. Combining financial statements present each nonmajor fund as a separate column. These statements usually would not be included within the scope of the auditor's examination other than indirectly as part of the audit of the basic financial statements.

The required basic financial statements and notes thereto, along with the recommended combining financial statements, should meet most external report users' needs for information about capital projects funds. Internal management and those with oversight responsibility for capital projects may need additional information, however, of a more detailed nature. Additional information that may be useful for internal management or oversight purposes includes information about whether the amount and quality of work accomplished to date is commensurate with resources expended to date and project plans and whether the remaining work can be accomplished within the established deadlines with remaining resources.

Key Terms

Arbitrage rebate, *190*	Capital leases, *172*	Historical cost, *165*
Asset impairment, *175*	Capital projects funds, *164*	Infrastructure assets, *170*
Bond anticipation	Force account	Interfund transfers, *183*
notes, *188*	construction, *170*	Modified approach, *171*
Capital improvements	General capital assets	Operating leases, *173*
fund, *177*	(GCA), *163*	Special assessments, *192*

Selected References

Financial Accounting Standards Board. *Statement of Financial Accounting Standards No. 5,* "Accounting for Contingencies." Norwalk, CT, 1975.

——*Statement of Financial Accounting Standards No. 13,* "Accounting for Leases as Amended and Interpreted through April 2002." Norwalk, CT, 2002.

Governmental Accounting Standards Board. *Codification of Governmental Accounting and Financial Reporting Standards as of June 30, 2005.* Norwalk, CT, 2005.

Questions

5–1. What distinguishes *general capital assets* from capital assets recorded in proprietary or fiduciary funds? Explain fully.

5–2. Explain what disclosures the GASB requires for capital assets in the notes to the financial statements.

5–3. What are the essential requirements of the *modified approach* to accounting for infrastructure assets? What happens under the modified approach if the government fails to maintain its infrastructure assets at or above the established and disclosed condition level?

5–4. How does one determine whether a particular lease is a capital lease or an operating lease? What entries are required in the general journals of a governmental fund and governmental activities at the government-wide level to record a capital lease at its inception?

5–5. "Governments are not concerned with measuring the value of *general capital assets;* therefore, capital assets whose value might have become impaired should be ignored in preparing government-wide financial statements." Do you agree with this statement? Explain.

5–6. For what kinds of capital outlays is it advisable to use a capital projects fund?

5–7. If a capital project is incomplete at the end of a fiscal year, why is it considered desirable to close Encumbrances and all operating statement accounts at year-end? Why is it desirable to reestablish the Encumbrances account as of the first day of the following year?

5–8. Which expenditures of a capital projects fund should be capitalized to Construction Work in Progress? Is Construction Work in Progress included in the chart of accounts of a capital projects fund? If not, where would it be found?

5–9. If one capital projects fund is used to account for multiple capital projects, what procedures can be used to maintain adequate control and accountability for individual projects?

5–10. How does the accounting for capital projects that are financed by special assessment bonds differ when a government assumes responsibility for debt service should special assessment collections be insufficient compared to a case in which the government assumes no responsibility whatsoever?

Cases

5–1 Using the Modified Approach or Depreciation. You are an auditor in a regional public accounting firm that does a large volume of governmental audits and consulting engagements. A large metropolitan city has asked you for assistance in determining whether it should use the modified approach or depreciate its infrastructure assets. The city is particularly interested in which accounting approach other large metropolitan cities have chosen.

Required

a. Examine several comprehensive annual financial reports (CAFRs) of large cities prepared following *GASBS 34.* (Note: The GASB provides a list of *GASBS 34* implementers classified by type of government with links to the governments' CAFRs, if available, at its Web site, *www.gasb.org*.) Create a table that lists the cities and the methods they have chosen to report their general infrastructure assets.

b. Prepare a memo to your client summarizing the results of your research. Be sure to address the city's specific concern about what other large cities are doing with respect to reporting of infrastructure assets.

c. Your client has heard that the Government Finance Officers Association (GFOA) may still award a Certificate of Achievement for Excellence in Financial Reporting if a government decides that the costs of capitalizing and depreciating (or of using the modified approach for) infrastructure assets outweighs the benefits, assuming that all other criteria are met. What other consequences can you point out to your client if it decides not to capitalize and report infrastructure assets?

5–2 Options for Financing Public Infrastructure. Desert City is a rapidly growing city in the Southwest, with a current population of 200,000. To cope with the growing vehicular traffic and the need for infrastructure expansion (e.g., streets, sidewalks, lighting, storm water drains, and sewage systems) to stay abreast of the pace of residential and commercial development, members of the city council have recently engaged in debate about the merits of alternative mechanisms for financing infrastructure expansion. The two alternatives the council is exploring are: (1) a sales tax referendum to increase an existing one-half cent capital improvement tax by one-quarter cent on every dollar of sales, and (2) a development fee of $0.50 per square foot imposed on real estate developers for new residential and commercial buildings.

Public debate at recent city council meetings has been contentious, with developers arguing that the burden for infrastructure improvements would be disproportionately placed on homeowners and businesses, whereas reliance on a sales tax increase would permit part of the infrastructure burden to be borne by nonresidents who shop in and otherwise enjoy the benefits of Desert City. Developers have also argued that more of the existing one-half-cent capital improvement tax should be spent for street and sidewalk improvements and less should be spent for improvement of public buildings, parks, and hiking trails.

Proponents of the proposed real estate development fee argue that new residential and commercial building is the main factor driving the growing demand for infrastructure development. Thus, they argue, it is most appropriate that new residents and new businesses shoulder much of the burden for expanding infrastructure. They further argue that the development fee will result in only a modest, largely invisible increase in the cost of each new building. Moreover, the incremental cost of the development fee should be recaptured as property values increase as a result of enhanced infrastructure. Finally, they argue that Desert City citizens enjoy better health and a generally higher quality life as a result of park and hiking trail improvements and that the existing one-half cent sales tax should continue to support recreational facilities.

Required
a. Evaluate the advantages and disadvantages of each potential financing option from the viewpoint of (1) a city council member, (2) the city manager, (3) current homeowners and business owners, and (4) potential new homeowners or new business owners.
b. Would accounting for infrastructure construction be impacted by the choice of financing method? Yes or No? Explain.

5–3 **Political versus Economic Factors in Financing Capital Improvements.** The case described here illustrates how political factors can be as important as or even more important than economic factors in planning and financing major capital projects. Often the political dimension clouds the issues and makes it difficult for even knowledgeable citizens to determine the best course of action. After reading the case, you will be asked to cast your vote on the proposed financing plan and explain why you voted as you did. Although the names of the governments described in the case are fictitious, the case is adapted from an actual case that came to the authors' attention. Similar jurisdictional tax disputes are not uncommon.

Background. Brown County is a rural county with a well-diversified economy, mainly institutional (educational and medical), commercial and light manufacturing, and agricultural. Brown County has a population of about 125,000, which for the last decade has been growing at nearly 5 percent a year. The county's largest city and county seat is Brownville, with a population of about 75,000. Three elected commissioners govern the county, and elected officials manage most key county functions. Brownville has a council-manager form of government under which the chief executive officer, the city manager, is appointed by and serves at the pleasure of the city council. The governments are "overlapping" in the sense that taxpayers who reside in Brownville pay property and sales taxes to both the city and county. However, except for the court system, the county mainly provides services for persons who live outside incorporated cities and towns. Historically, relationships between the county and city governments have been strained, with each government being suspicious of the motives of the other. As a result, regional planning has generally suffered and agreements, when they have occurred, have related to narrow issues or projects rather than long-range plans.

Situation and Facts. To cope with rapid population growth, Brown County has developed a five-year plan that includes paving and upgrading 55 miles of heavily traveled roads at a cost of $7,000,000; upgrading about 150 miles of substandard roads using "chip-and-seal overlay," $2,000,000; eliminating 10 "safety hazard areas," $210,000; and acquiring right of way, $500,000. The total estimated cost is $9,710,000 over five years. Financing for the plan would come from the following sources:

Half-cent sales tax	$5,400,000
Increase in property tax of 5 cents per $100 of assessed valuation	400,000
Gasoline taxes	500,000
Motor vehicle sales tax	200,000
Annual Revenues	$6,500,000

The gasoline taxes and motor vehicle sales taxes are already being collected and distributed to localities by the state government. The property tax increase requires no special approval since the road and bridge property taxes are currently below the limit imposed by state statutes. The half-cent sales tax, however, requires approval by a simple majority of registered voters in the county, including those who reside in Brownville and other incorporated cities and towns. Accordingly, a special election has been called to schedule a vote on the proposed sales tax.

Even a casual look at the financing plan shows that $6,500,000 $\times$ 5 years will produce at least $32,500,000 in revenues (excluding probable investment earnings), whereas the required capital outlay will be only $9,710,000 over the five years. The remainder is intended to provide for expanded operations of the County Road and Bridge Department.

In the weeks before the special election, the Brownville City Council members and the finance director have strongly opposed the proposed sales tax on the grounds that it is unfair to expect taxpayers in the cities and towns to pay for road improvements that mainly benefit rural county residents. They argue that special assessment debt financing should be used, and the debt should be repaid by residents receiving the benefit. They also complain that the county's planning process is flawed and that joint planning with the city is needed to coordinate the five-year plan of both governments. City officials are also concerned that the county's proposed sales tax increase would eliminate the city's ability to raise sales taxes during the next five years if a need should arise. To mute some of the opposition, the county has amended the original plan and proposes to cut in half the road and bridge property taxes paid by taxpayers in the cities and towns. The property tax rollback would reduce revenues from $32.5 million to about $27 million over the next five years. However, since property in that state is assessed at different levels for different classes of property (32 percent of market value for commercial and manufacturing property, 19 percent for residential property, and 12 percent for agricultural property), only the larger (mainly commercial and manufacturing) property owners stand to gain if the proposed sales tax increase is approved. For most taxpayers, the sales tax increase will still be more than the property tax decrease. Thus, some large property owners might now support the sales tax, but the majority of Brownville voters view the proposed rollback as regressive and only worsening the inequity for most property owners in the cities and towns.

Advocates for the sales tax argue that the cities and towns will benefit from improved transportation throughout the county. Furthermore, nearly a quarter of the people who work in Brownville live in the unincorporated subdivisions surrounding the city. Advocates also note that Brownville is a regional shopping center that draws shoppers from a 50-mile radius. Thus, one attractive feature of the proposed sales tax is that it would be borne, in part, by people who neither live nor work in the county.

Required

After weeks of heavy media coverage, both for and against the proposed sales tax, voters have become extremely interested in this issue but thoroughly confused. Election day has finally arrived, and turnout is expected to be heavy. Imagine yourself as a voter in the City of Brownville and answer the following questions.

a. Would you vote *yes* for the proposed half-cent sales tax or *no* in opposition? Explain the rationale for your vote; be sure to analyze factors pertinent to your voting decision.

b. Would your vote have changed under different assumed scenarios (e.g., if you were a large commercial or manufacturing property owner versus a residential or agricultural property owner, or renter)?

    c. Do you think special assessment financing would be more appropriate than general sales taxes for the proposed projects? Explain.

    d. Are there any significant accounting issues related to the financing alternatives? Explain.

Exercises and Problems

5–1 Examine the CAFR. Utilizing the CAFR obtained for Exercise 1–1, answer these questions.

  a. **General and Other Capital Assets:**

    (1) **Reporting of Capital Assets.** Are capital assets reported as a line-item in the government-wide statement of net assets? Are nondepreciable capital assets reported on a separate line from depreciable capital assets, or are they separately reported in the notes to the financial statements? Do the notes include capital asset disclosures, such as those for the City and County of Denver shown in Illustration 5–2? Does the disclosure show beginning balances, increases and decreases, and ending balances for each major class of capital assets, as well as the same information for accumulated depreciation for each major class? Are these disclosures presented separately for the capital assets of governmental activities, business-type activities, and discretely presented component units? Do the notes specify capitalization thresholds for all capital assets, including infrastructure? Do the notes show the amounts of depreciation expense assigned to each major function or program for governmental activities at the government-wide level? Are the depreciation policies and estimated lives of major classes of depreciable assets disclosed? Do the notes include the entity's policies regarding capitalization of collections of works of art and historical treasures? Are accounting policies disclosed for assets acquired under capital leases?

    (2) **Other.** Is the accumulated cost of construction work in progress recorded as an asset anywhere? In your opinion, is the information disclosed about construction work in progress and construction commitments adequate? Which fund, or funds, account for cash received, or receivables created, from sales of general capital assets? Are the proceeds of sales of general capital assets reported as an other financing source or as revenue?

  b. **Capital Projects Funds:**

    (1) **Title and Content.** What title is given to the funds that function as capital projects funds, as described in this chapter? (Street Improvement Funds and Capital Improvement Funds are common titles, although these titles also are often used for special revenue funds that account for ongoing annual maintenance of roadways.) Where does the report state the basis of accounting used for capital projects funds? Is the basis used consistent with GASB standards discussed in this chapter? Are there separate capital projects funds for each project, are there several funds, each of which accounts for related projects, or is only one fund used for all projects?

    (2) **Statements and Schedules.** What statements and schedules pertaining to capital projects funds are presented? In what respects (headings, arrangement, items included, etc.) do they seem similar to statements illustrated or described in the text? In what respects do they differ? Are any differences merely a matter of terminology or arrangement, or do they represent

significant deviations from GASB accounting and reporting standards for capital projects funds?

(3) **Financial Resource Inflows.** What is the nature of the financial resource inflows utilized by the capital projects funds? If tax-supported bonds or special assessment bonds are the source, have any been sold at a premium? At a discount? If so, what was the accounting treatment of the bond premium or discount?

(4) **Fund Expenditures.** How much detail is given concerning capital projects fund expenditures? Is the detail sufficient to meet the information needs of administrators? legislators? creditors? grantors? interested residents? For projects that are incomplete at the date of the financial statement, does the report compare the percentage of total authorization for each project expended to date with the percentage of completion? For those projects completed during the fiscal year, does the report compare the total expenditures for each project with the authorization for each project? For each cost overrun, how was the overrun financed?

(5) **Assets Acquired Under Capital Leases.** Were any general capital assets acquired by the primary government or one or more component units under a capital lease agreement during the year for which you have statements? If so, was the present value of minimum lease rentals recorded as an Expenditure and as an Other Financing Source in a capital projects fund (or in any other governmental fund)? If the primary government or one or more component units leased assets from another component unit, how are the assets, related liabilities, expenditures, and other financing sources reported in the basic financial statements or in another section of the CAFR of the reporting entity?

5–2 Multiple Choice. Choose the best answer.

1. General capital assets are:
   a. Reported in the Governmental Activities column of the statement of net assets, net of accumulated depreciation.
   b. Capitalized in the General Fund.
   c. Recorded at fair value.
   d. Reported as noncurrent assets on both the governmental funds balance sheet and the government-wide statement of net assets.

2. Four new desktop computers, for which the cost exceeded the city's capitalization threshold, were purchased for use in the city clerk's office using General Fund resources. Which of the following entries would be required to completely record this transaction?

	Debits	**Credits**
a. General Fund:		
Expenditures	8,000	
Vouchers Payable		8,000
b. Governmental Activities:		
Expenses	8,000	
Vouchers Payable		8,000
c. General Fund:		
Expenditures	8,000	
Vouchers Payable		8,000

	Debits	Credits
Governmental Activities:		
Expenses	8,000	
Vouchers Payable		8,000
d. General Fund:		
Expenditures	8,000	
Vouchers Payable		8,000
Governmental Activities:		
Equipment	8,000	
Vouchers Payable		8,000

3. Which of the following classes of capital assets would generally **not** be depreciated?
   a. Collections.
   b. Infrastructure.
   c. Construction work in progress.
   d. Improvements other than buildings.

4. Which of the following is a correct statement regarding the use of the *modified approach* for accounting for eligible infrastructure assets?
   a. Depreciation on eligible infrastructure assets need not be recorded if the assets are being maintained at or above the established condition level.
   b. Depreciation on eligible infrastructure assets must still be recorded for informational purposes only.
   c. The government must document that it is maintaining eligible infrastructure assets at the condition level prescribed by the GASB.
   d. All of the above are correct statements.

5. General capital assets acquired under a capital lease:
   a. Should not be capitalized.
   b. Should be capitalized at the lesser of (1) the present value of rental and other minimum lease payments, or (2) the fair value of the leased property.
   c. Should be capitalized under the same rules as proprietary fund capital assets acquired under an operating lease.
   d. Should be capitalized at the lower of cost or market.

6. A governmental entity experienced significant loss of certain roadways and bridges as a result of major flooding. Which of the following estimation approaches would be most useful in estimating the amount of asset impairment that has occurred?
   a. Deflated depreciated replacement cost approach.
   b. Service units approach.
   c. Restorative cost approach.
   d. None of the above; each of these three approaches would be equally useful.

7. Callaway County issued $10,000,000 in bonds at 101 for the purpose of constructing a new County Recreation Center. State law requires that any premium on bond issues be deposited directly in a debt service fund for eventual repayment of bond principal. The journal entry to record issuance of the bonds will require a (an):
   a. Credit to Bonds Payable in the capital projects fund.
   b. Credit to Other Financing Sources—Proceeds of Bonds in the capital projects fund.
   c. Credit to Other Financing Sources—Premium on Bonds in the debt service fund.
   d. Both *b* and *c* are correct.

8. Temporary financing in the form of bond anticipation notes should be recorded in the capital projects fund as a debit to Cash and a:
    a. Credit to Bond Anticipation Notes Payable.
    b. Credit to Other Financing Sources—Proceeds of Bond Anticipation Notes.
    c. Either *a* or *b*, depending on whether legal steps have been taken to refinance the bond anticipation notes and there is management intent supported by ability to refinance.
    d. None of the above.

9. The primary reason for reestablishing the Encumbrance account balance at the beginning of the second and subsequent years of a multiple-year capital project is that:
    a. The project continues beyond a single year; thus it is important that the Encumbrances account show the amount of contractual commitment remaining on the project.
    b. This procedure allows the accountant to record a normal reversal of encumbrances when the next project billing is received.
    c. This procedure corrects for an erroneous closure of the Encumbrances account at the end of the preceding year.
    d. Failure to reestablish the Encumbrances account balance is a violation of GASB standards.

10. Recording the proceeds of special assessment bonds in the capital projects fund as Other Financing Sources—Contribution from Property Owners indicates that:
    a. Property owners in a special assessment district have constructed capital assets and transferred them to the government.
    b. The government is obligated in some manner to provide debt service for the bonds in the event of default by assessed property owners.
    c. The government is not obligated under any circumstances for the special assessment bonds.
    d. The government has used its power of eminent domain to convert private property to government ownership.

5–3 General Capital Assets. Make an entry or entries for each transaction as it should be recorded in the government-wide activities journal and journal of the appropriate governmental fund(s) for the current year.

1. During the year, a capital projects fund completed a building project initiated in the preceding year. The total cost of the project was $7,620,000, of which $5,240,000 had been expended in the two preceding years. Current-year expenditures on the project were reported to have consisted of $580,000 from a federal grant to the Public Works Department, with the balance coming from proceeds of a tax-supported bond issue, both of which were received in the current year.

2. A tract of land held for future development as a city park was, by resolution of the city council, transferred to the City Water Utility. The utility paid the City General Fund $100,000 for the land, which was carried at its estimated cost of $50,000. The land had been purchased with General Fund resources.

3. A personal computer used by the police chief was traded in on a new laptop computer. List price of the laptop computer was $2,500; $300 allowance was received for the old computer. The old computer had been purchased from General Fund revenue for $1,000 and was fully depreciated. Cash for the new computer was furnished by a special revenue fund.

4. The Street Fund, a special revenue fund, purchased a piece of heavy equipment. The catalog price of the equipment was $250,000. Terms of payment quoted by the manufacturer were 1/10, n/30. Payment for the equipment was made within the cash discount period.

5. The cost of remodeling of the interior of the city hall was $623,700; $49,400 of this amount was classified as maintenance chargeable to the public works function rather than improvement. Included in the total cost of $623,700, walls, partitions, floors, and so on, estimated to have cost $84,600, and with an estimated accumulated depreciation of $21,700, were removed and replaced. Cost of the remodeling was financed by a current appropriation of the General Fund.

6. A subdivision annexed by the city contained privately financed streets and sidewalks and a system of sewers. The best available information showed a cost of $1,700,000 for the sewer system and $1,650,000 for the streets and sidewalks, of which $200,000 was the estimated cost of the land. The developers provided both types of improvements. In conformity with *GASBS 34*, the city records infrastructure assets.

5–4 Capital Asset Disclosures. Information in the CAFR of the Town of Lynnwood reported general capital assets in the following amounts as of April 30, 2007.

	Cost	Accumulated Depreciation
Land	$1,326,780	$ –0–
Buildings	7,282,680	1,439,200
Improvements other than buildings	3,027,790	922,600
Equipment	1,733,820	837,500
Construction work in progress	401,130	–0–
Infrastructure assets	3,500,000	1,000,000

During the fiscal year (FY) 2008, the following changes in general capital assets took place:

1. A project started during FY 2008 was being financed by a tax-supported bond issue of $3,000,000 sold at par during the year and a federal grant of $1,000,000. By the end of FY 2008, $80,000 of the federal grant had been received and expended for planning and engineering for a project in progress. Bond proceeds expended during the year totaled $900,000 ($300,000 for land and $600,000 for the building under construction).

2. Records of capital projects funds reported that construction work in progress at the end of FY 2007 was completed during FY 2008 at a total cost of $799,066, which included an additional cost of $397,936 in the current period. All of the construction resulted in additions to the Improvements Other than Buildings account.

3. Special revenue fund expenditures during the year added equipment costing $152,700.

4. General Fund expenditures during the year for equipment amounted to $438,000.

5. Annexation added buildings for which the estimated cost was $301,600 and land for which the estimated cost was $75,000.

6. Land having an appraised value of $750,000 was donated to the city, and additional land with an appraised value of $15,000 was received in settlement of delinquent General Fund property taxes.

7. Land acquired at an estimated cost of $12,000 on which an $80,000 building was located was sold to the State Highway Department for a right-of-way at a price of $119,700.

8. Construction activities during FY 2008 required demolition of a building that had cost $33,600 and a bridge (infrastructure) for which the estimated cost was $119,200. Equipment that had cost $20,000 could not be located and was presumed to have been stolen.

9. No additions of infrastructure assets occurred this year.

10. Depreciation expense for the year was as follows: buildings $440,000; improvements, $320,000; equipment $210,000; and infrastructure assets, $105,000. Accumulated depreciation related to retired assets was buildings, $51,000; improvements, $102,000; and equipment, $5,000.

Required

Prepare in good form a schedule of capital asset disclosures for governmental activities similar to Illustration 5–2 for the fiscal year ended April 30, 2008. Ignore the related schedule showing how current depreciation expense is charged to governmental functions.

5–5 **Capital Assets Acquired under Lease Agreements.** Crystal City signed a lease agreement with East Coast Builders, Inc., under which East Coast will construct a new office building for the city at a cost of $12 million and lease it to the city for 30 years. The city agrees to make an initial payment of $847,637 and annual payments in the same amount for the next 29 years. An assumed borrowing rate of 6 percent was used in calculating lease payments. Upon completion the building had an appraised market value of $13 million and an estimated life of 40 years.

Required

a. Using the criteria presented in this chapter determine whether Crystal City should consider this lease agreement a capital lease. Explain your decision.

b. Provide the journal entries Crystal City should make for both the capital projects fund and governmental activities at the government-wide level to record the lease at the date of inception.

5–6 **Asset Impairment.** On July 20, 2008, the building occupied by Sunshine City's Parks and Recreation Department suffered severe structural damage as a result of a hurricane. It had been 48 years since a hurricane had hit the Sunshine City area, although hurricanes in Sunshine City's geographic area are not uncommon. The building had been purchased in 1998 at a cost of $2,000,000 and had accumulated depreciation of $500,000 as of July 2008. Based on a restoration cost analysis, city engineers estimate the impairment loss at $230,000; however, the city expects during the next fiscal year to receive insurance recoveries of $120,000 for the damage.

Required

a. Should the estimated impairment loss be reported as an extraordinary item? As a special item? Explain.

b. Record the estimated impairment loss in the journal for governmental activities at the government-wide level.

c. How should the insurance recovery be reported in the following fiscal year? (You need not provide the journal entry or entries here.)

5–7 **Capital Assets Acquired with Special Assessment Bonds.** The proceeds of the sale of special assessment bonds issued to finance the acquisition of capital facilities amounted to $5,075,000. The face amount of the bond issue was $5,000,000; $25,000 of the proceeds represented interest accrued on the bonds to the date of sale.

Required

a. Assuming that both the premium on bonds sold and the interest accrued on the bonds to date of sale must be recorded directly in a debt service fund, show in general journal form the entries made by the capital projects fund and in the governmental activities journal for the receipt of the $5,000,000 face amount.

b. If several months are expected to elapse between receipt of bond proceeds and payment for the capital assets being acquired, what action should be taken by the government's finance officer?

c. What are the accounting and financial implications of the course of action you recommended in part *b*?

5–8 **Statement of Revenues and Expenditures.** The post-closing trial balance of the City of Pineville's Capital Projects Fund, as of December 31, 2007, listed Fund Balance in the amount of $1,500,000. The project had been authorized early in 2007 in the total amount of $5,000,000, to be financed $800,000 by the federal government, $200,000 by the state government, and the remainder by a bond issue. The federal and state grants require expenditure in the year received. Most of the work was to be done by various private contractors. Although it is generally regarded as good practice, the city does not use encumbrance accounting procedures for its capital projects funds.

Cash from the state grant was received in full during 2007 and $200,000 was received from the federal government. The entire bond issue was sold at par early in 2007. The federal government is expected to pay the remainder of its grant in full before March 1, 2008. Cash not disbursed during 2007 was invested on December 31, 2007.

Required

a. Assume that GASB standards discussed in this chapter were followed.

(1) How much revenue did the City of Pineville's capital projects fund recognize in 2007? How much should this fund report as other financing sources for 2007?

(2) How much did 2007 expenditures total?

(3) What was the balance of the Investments account on December 31, 2007, assuming that all 2007 expenditures were paid in cash?

b. Prepare a statement of revenues, expenditures, and changes in fund balance for the year ended December 31, 2008, assuming that the following events occurred during 2008:

(1) Expenditures of the fund totaled $1,350,000 on construction contracts.

(2) Interest on temporary investments totaled $16,000.

5–9 **Construction Fund.** During FY 2008, the voters of the Town of Dexter approved constructing and equipping a recreation center to be financed by tax-supported bonds in the amount of $3,000,000. During 2008, the following events and transactions occurred.

1. Preliminary planning and engineering expenses in the amount of $60,000 were incurred. No money was immediately available for paying these costs (credit Vouchers Payable).

2. Supplies to be used by the town's own workforce in connection with the project were ordered in the amount of $30,600.

3. A contract was let under competitive bids for a major segment of the construction project in the amount of $2,500,000.

4. All the supplies referred to in item 2 were received at a net cost of $30,500. This amount was approved for payment.

5. An interfund invoice (not encumbered) was received from the Water Utility Fund (an enterprise fund) for work done on the project in the amount of $40,000. The invoice was approved for payment.
6. An invoice for $1,600,000 was received from a contractor for a portion of work that had been completed under the general contract.
7. The bond issue was sold at par plus accrued interest of $25,000 (the accrued interest was deposited in the fund that will service the bonded debt).
8. The amount due the Water Utility Fund was paid.
9. The contractor's bill, less a 4 percent retention, was vouchered for payment.
10. All vouchers payable, except $1,300 (about which there was some controversy), were paid.
11. Cash in the amount of $1,300,000 was invested in short-term marketable securities.
12. Fiscal year-end closing entries were prepared.

Required

a. Prepare journal entries to record the preceding information in the Town of Dexter Recreation Center Construction Fund and the governmental activities general journal at the government-wide level.
b. Prepare a Town of Dexter Recreation Center Construction Fund balance sheet for the year ended December 31, 2008.
c. Prepare a Recreation Center Construction Fund statement of revenues, expenditures, and changes in fund balance for the year ended December 31, 2008.
d. How would these capital expenditures for the recreation center appear on the Town of Dexter's government-wide statements of net assets and activities?

5–10 **Capital Project Transactions.** In 2008, Falts City began work to improve certain streets to be financed by a bond issue and supplemented by a federal grant. Estimated total cost of the project was $4,000,000; $2,500,000 was to come from the bond issue, and the balance from the federal grant. The capital projects fund to account for the project was designated as the Street Improvement Fund. The following transactions occurred in 2008:

1. Issued $100,000 of 6 percent bond anticipation notes to be repaid from the proceeds of bonds in 180 days.
2. The federal grant was recorded as receivable; half of the grant is to be paid to Falts City in 2008 and the remainder late in 2009. The grantor specifies that the portion to be received in 2009 is not available for use until 2009 because there is no guarantee that the federal government will appropriate the 2009 portion.
3. A contract was let to Appel Construction Company for the major part of the project on a bid of $2,700,000.
4. An invoice received from the City's Stores and Services Fund for supplies provided to the Street Improvement Fund in the amount of $60,000 was approved for payment. (This amount had not been encumbered.)
5. Preliminary planning and engineering costs of $69,000 were paid to the Mid-Atlantic Engineering Company. (This cost had not been encumbered.)
6. A voucher payable was recorded for an $18,500 billing from the local telephone company for the cost of moving some of its underground properties necessitated by the street project.
7. An invoice in the amount of $1,000,000 was received from Appel for progress to date on the project. The invoice was consistent with the terms of the contract, and a liability was recorded in the amount of $1,000,000.

8. Cash received during 2008 was as follows:

From federal government	$ 750,000
From sale of bonds at par	2,500,000

9. The bond anticipation notes and interest thereon were repaid (see Transaction 1). Interest is an expenditure of the capital projects fund and, per GASB standards, will *not* be capitalized as part of the cost of street improvements.
10. The amount billed by the contractor (see Transaction 7) less 5 percent retainage was paid.
11. Temporary investments were purchased at a cost of $1,800,000.
12. Closing entries were prepared as of December 31, 2008.

Required
a. Prepare journal entries to record the preceding information in the general ledger accounts for the Street Improvement Fund. (You may ignore the entries that would also be required in the governmental activities general journal at the government-wide level.)
b. Prepare a balance sheet for the Street Improvement Fund as of December 31, 2008.
c. Prepare a statement of revenues, expenditures, and changes in fund balance for the period, assuming that the date of authorization was July 1, 2008.

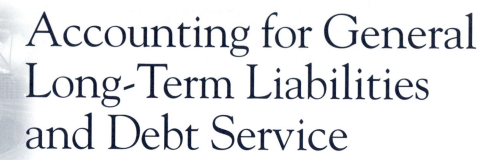

Chapter **Six**

Accounting for General Long-Term Liabilities and Debt Service

Learning Objectives

After reading this chapter you should be able to:

1. Explain what types of liabilities are classified as general long-term liabilities.
2. Make journal entries in the governmental activities general journal to record the issuance and repayment of general long-term liabilities.
3. Prepare note disclosures for general long-term liabilities.
4. Describe the reasons for and nature of statutory debt limits and explain the meaning of *debt margin* and *overlapping debt*.
5. Explain the purpose and types of debt service funds.
6. Describe the budgeting requirements for debt service funds and make appropriate journal entries to account for debt service transactions.

GENERAL LONG-TERM LIABILITIES

The use of long-term debt is a traditional part of the fiscal policy of state and local governments, particularly for financing the acquisition of general capital assets. Although some governments have issued taxable debt, the interest earned on most debt issued by state and local governments is exempt from federal taxation and, in some states, from state taxation. The tax-exempt feature enables governments to raise large amounts of capital at relatively low cost. For example, from 2000 to 2004 total long-term debt outstanding of state and local governments increased by 40.5 percent to $1.67 trillion.[1] Because of the relative ease with which governments can issue debt, most states have acted in the public interest to impose statutory limits on the debt that can be incurred by state and local governments. Consequently, effective management of state and local governmental debt requires good legal advice and a sound understanding of public finance.

This chapter describes the types of debt and other long-term liabilities that are termed "general long-term liabilities." **General long-term liabilities** are those that arise from activities of governmental funds and that are not reported as fund liabilities

---

[1]U.S. Federal Reserve, *Federal Reserve Statistical Release,* "Flow of Funds Accounts of the United States," Washington, D.C., Federal Reserve, June 9, 2005, Table D-3, p. 8.

of a proprietary or fiduciary fund. General long-term liabilities are reported as liabilities in the Governmental Activities column of the government-wide statement of net assets but are *not* reported as liabilities of governmental funds. This chapter also discusses the concepts of direct and overlapping debt, statutory debt limit, and debt margin. It also provides illustrative journal entries at the government-wide level to record increases and decreases in general long-term liabilities. Finally, the chapter explains the nature and types of debt service funds and debt service accounting for various types of general long-term liabilities, as well as accounting for refunding of debt.

In studying this chapter, the reader should recall that the governmental fund types (General, special revenue, capital projects, debt service, and permanent funds) account for only short-term liabilities to be paid from fund assets.[2] Although, as described in Chapter 5, the proceeds of long-term debt may be placed in one of these fund types (usually a capital projects fund), the long-term liability itself must be recorded in the governmental activities accounting records at the government-wide level.[3] Proprietary funds and perhaps certain private-purpose trust funds account for both long-term debt serviced by the fund and short-term debt to be repaid from fund assets.

As discussed in subsequent chapters, the liabilities of enterprise funds should be displayed on the face of the statement of the issuing fund if that fund may realistically be expected to finance the debt service; however, if the liability also is secondarily backed by the full faith and credit of the government, the contingent general obligation liability of the government should be disclosed in a note to the financial statements. The contingent obligation to assume debt service of long-term debt backed primarily by special assessments is acknowledged by reporting such debt in the government-wide financial statement as "special assessment debt with governmental commitment."[4] Any portion of such debt that will be repaid directly by the government (for example, to finance the portion of a special assessment project deemed to have public benefit) should be reported like any other general long-term liabilities of the government.

Bonds and other debt of enterprise funds issued with covenants that give the debt the status, even contingently, of **tax-supported debt** may affect the government's ability to issue additional tax-supported debt. The reason for this is discussed under the heading "Debt Limit and Debt Margin" in this chapter. If the contingency clause becomes effective because resources of the enterprise fund are insufficient for debt service, the unpaid portion of the debt is recorded as a liability of the governmental activities at the government-wide level. The enterprise fund that is relieved of the liability then removes the unpaid debt from its liability accounts and recognizes an

[2]Conceivably a permanent fund could have a long-term liability, for example, if a permanent fund consisted of a gift of income-producing real property that the government accepted subject to a long-term mortgage note. In establishing the permanent fund as a governmental fund type, the GASB cited its belief that most such funds hold only financial resources (for example, investments in financial securities and cash). Thus, it is not clear whether any permanent funds in practice hold assets other than financial assets. If not, the probability is low that any permanent funds have long-term liabilities. Moreover, *GASBS 34* provides no guidance on how income-producing real property and long-term liabilities could be accounted for as a governmental fund.

[3]As discussed in Chapter 5, the *GASBS 34* reporting model eliminates for external financial reporting purposes the General Long-Term Debt Account Group long used by state and local governments to account for their general long-term liabilities and the General Fixed Assets Account Group used to account for general capital assets. Both general long-term liabilities and general capital assets are now reported in the Governmental Activities column of the government-wide statement of net assets (see Illustration 1–4 for an example of this statement).

[4]GASB *Codification*, Sec. 1500.109.

interfund transfer, which is reported after the nonoperating revenues (expenses) section of the proprietary funds statement of revenues, expenses, and changes in fund net assets.

From the discussions earlier in this section and in Chapter 5, it should be evident that entries are ordinarily made in the governmental activities general journal at the government-wide level to reflect increases or decreases in general long-term liabilities that also require entries in the accounts of one or more governmental funds. As shown in illustrative Entries 8a and 8b in Chapter 5, most increases in general long-term liabilities arising from debt issuances are recorded as an other financing source in a governmental fund and as a general long-term liability at the government-wide level. Increases in long-term liabilities that arise from operating activities, such as estimated losses from long-term claims and judgments, for example, are recorded at the government-wide level by debiting an expense and crediting a liability. Except for certain defeasances, as discussed later in this chapter, most general long-term liabilities are settled by the payment of cash from a governmental fund. As one would expect, the entry in the governmental activities journal at the government-wide level to record the decrease in general long-term liabilities is straightforward: debit the liability account and credit Cash. At the same time the governmental fund paying the liability should debit Expenditures and credit Cash. Retirement of matured debt principal using a debt service fund is illustrated later in this chapter.

In any given year, it is common for new debt issues to be authorized, for previously authorized debt to be issued, and for older issues to be retired. When a combination of liability events takes place, a schedule detailing changes in long-term debt is needed to inform report users of the details of how long-term liabilities changed. The general long-term liability disclosures required by *GASBS 34* effectively meet these needs by providing detail of beginning of period long-term liabilities, additions to and reductions of those liabilities, ending liabilities, and the portion of the liabilities payable within one year. Illustration 6–1 presents this disclosure schedule for the City and County of Denver.

Schedule of Future Debt Service Requirements

In addition to the disclosures about long-term liabilities presented in Illustration 6–1, information about the amount of debt principal and interest that will be due in future years is useful information to financial managers, bond analysts, and others having an interest in assessing a government's requirements for future debt service expenditures. One form of such a schedule, representing a disclosure from the notes to the financial statements for the City and County of Denver, prepared in conformity with GASB standards, is shown in Illustration 6–2. The reader should note that the interest portion of the scheduled future debt service payments is *not* a present liability and should not be presented as such. To do so would not be in conformity with generally accepted accounting principles.

Debt Limit and Debt Margin

The information provided in the debt schedules already illustrated in this chapter is primarily useful to administrators, legislative bodies, credit analysts, and others concerned with the impact of long-term debt on the financial condition and activities of the government, particularly with reference to the resulting tax rates and taxes. Another matter of importance is the legal limit on the amount of long-term indebtedness that may be outstanding at a given time, in proportion to the assessed value of property within the jurisdiction represented. This type of restriction is important as a protection of taxpayers against possible confiscatory tax rates. Even though tax-rate limitation

ILLUSTRATION 6–1   Illustrative Long-Term Liabilities Disclosure

CITY AND COUNTY OF DENVER, COLORADO
Long-Term Liabilities Disclosure
For the Year Ended December 31, 2004

Long-term liability activity for the year ended December 31, 2004, was as follows (amounts expressed in thousands):

	January 1	Additions	Deletions	December 31	Due within one year
Governmental Activities:					
Legal liability	$ 3,972	$ 2,677	$ 3,899	$ 2,750	$ 423
Line of credit	11,915	—	—	11,915	—
Compensated absences:					
Classified service employees—3,060	57,982	19,104	23,745	53,341	5,816
Career service employees—6,713	34,577	31,972	28,324	38,225	3,975
Claims payable	31,388	10,120	10,985	30,523	8,350
Other accrued liabilities	3,775	—	1,850	1,925	1,925
General obligation bonds[1]	431,889	794	49,538	383,145	51,310
GID general obligation bonds	3,045	2,411	2,348	3,108	184
Excise tax revenue bonds	343,840	—	8,635	335,205	9,600
Certificates of participation	217,970	—	9,360	208,610	9,700
Capitalized lease obligations	256,034	3,808	2,443	257,399	1,473
Special assessment bonds	460	—	170	290	30
Unamortized premium	21,557	—	1,656	19,901	1,656
Other governmental funds—note payable	22,395	—	6,494	15,901	—
Total Governmental Activities	$1,440,799	$70,886	$149,447	$1,362,238	$94,442

The legal liability, compensated absences, claims payable and other accrued liabilities in the governmental activities are generally liquidated by the General Fund. The other governmental funds—note payable is liquidated by the Community Development special revenue fund. The amount available for long-term debt in the debt service funds for bonds payable and in the special revenue fund was $57,204,000.

[1] Additions to general obligation bonds include accretion of $794.

ILLUSTRATION 6–1 (continued)

	January 1	Additions	Deletions	December 31	Due within one year
Business-type Activities:					
Wastewater Management:					
Revenue bonds (includes unamortized bond premium of $88)	$ 29,808	$ —	$ 1,020	$ 28,788	$ 1,050
Compensated absences	1,920	685	600	2,005	371
Total Wastewater Management	31,728	685	1,620	30,793	1,421
Denver Airport System:					
Revenue bonds	4,128,550	150,000	191,895	4,086,655	106,250
Unamortized discount and deferred loss on refunding	(266,045)	(4,735)	(13,885)	(256,895)	—
Note payable	60,000	33,000	16,787	76,213	19,450
Capitalized lease obligations	5,105	—	1,991	3,114	2,056
Compensated absences	6,004	1,836	1,482	6,358	810
Total Denver Airport System	3,933,614	180,101	198,270	3,915,445	128,566
Nonmajor enterprise funds:					
Compensated absences	694	811	804	701	71
Total Business-type Activities	$3,966,036	$181,597	$200,694	$3,946,939	$130,058
Component Units:					
Revenue bonds[1]	$ 533,655	$ 43,655	$ 17,774	$ 559,536	$ 7,060
General obligation bonds[2]	157,239	—	38,902	118,337	16,490
Capitalized lease obligations[3]	29,620	—	1,029	28,591	1,100
Certificates of participation[4]	58,645	—	4,546	54,099	4,800
Increment bonds and notes payable[5]	87,338	275,000	6,818	355,520	5,111
Compensated absences	6,999	35	—	7,034	1,817
Total Component Units	$ 873,496	$318,690	$ 69,069	$1,123,117	$ 36,378

[1]Includes unamortized premium of $26,877, deferred loss on refunding of ($2,331), and revenue bonds of $8,000 for nonmajor component units.
[2]Includes unamortized premium of $1,372 and deferred loss on refunding of ($410).
[3]Includes capitalized lease obligations of $30 for nonmajor component units.
[4]Includes unamortized premium of $868 and deferred loss on refunding of ($1,324).
[5]Includes deferred loss on refunding of ($1,205) and note payable of $700 for nonmajor component units.

Source: City and County of Denver, Colorado, Notes to Basic Financial Statements, 2004, Section III, Note G.10.

ILLUSTRATION 6–2   **Future Debt Service Requirements**

CITY AND COUNTY OF DENVER, COLORADO
Future Debt Service Requirements
December 31, 2004

Annual debt service requirements to maturity for general obligation bonds are as follows (amounts expressed in thousands):

Year	Governmental Activities				Component Unit—Water Board	
	General Government		General Improvement District			
	Principal[1]	Interest	Principal[2]	Interest	Principal[3]	Interest
2005	$ 51,310	$ 18,854	$ 40	$112	$ 16,490	$ 5,670
2006	49,979	19,834	80	110	13,345	4,869
2007	55,745	13,733	205	107	22,935	4,225
2008	41,460	10,825	230	100	19,230	3,086
2009	27,480	8,581	415	92	12,020	2,141
2010–2014	86,138	31,091	1,570	224	14,855	6,443
2015–2019	66,865	7,351	305	47	5,100	4,137
2020–2024	—	—	—	—	1,850	3,430
2025–2029	—	—	—	—	11,550	3,232
TOTAL	$378,977	$110,269	$2,845	$792	$117,375	$37,233

[1]Does not include $4,168 of compound interest on the series 1990B and 1999A various purposes bonds, respectively.
[2]Does not include deferred loss on refunding of ($263).
[3]Does not include unamortized premium of $1,372 and deferred loss on refunding of ($410).
The City issued $2,411,000 of Series 2004, General Improvement District general obligation bonds, with interest rates of 6.0% to 7.0%, to advance refund $1,040,000 of Series 1998 GID bonds and $970,000 of Series 1999 GID bonds. The transaction resulted in an economic gain of $150,000.

Source: City and County of Denver, Colorado, Notes to Basic Financial Statements, 2004, Section III, Note G.1.

laws may be in effect for a government, the limitation on bonded indebtedness is usually needed because the prevailing practice is to exempt the claims of bondholders from the barrier of tax-rate restrictions. This is to say that, even though a law establishing maxima for tax rates is in the statutes, it will probably exclude debt service requirements from the restrictions of the law. This exclusion may be reiterated, in effect, in the bond covenants.

Before continuing a discussion of debt limitation, it seems appropriate to clarify the meaning of the terms *debt limit* and *debt margin*. **Debt limit** means the total amount of indebtedness of specified kinds that is allowed by law to be outstanding at any one time. The limitation is likely to be in terms of a stipulated percentage of the assessed valuation of property within the government's jurisdiction. It may relate to either a gross or a net valuation. The latter is logical but probably not prevalent because debt limitation exists as a device for protecting property owners from confiscatory taxation. For that reason, tax-paying property *only* should be used in regulating maximum indebtedness. In many governmental jurisdictions, certain property is legally excluded even from *assessment*. This includes property owned by governments, churches, charitable organizations, and some others, depending on state laws. Exemptions, which apply to property subject to assessment, are based on homestead or mortgage exemption laws, military service, and economic status, among others. Both exclusions and exemptions reduce the amount of tax-paying property.

ILLUSTRATION 6–3

CITY AND COUNTY OF DENVER
Computation of Legal Debt Margin
December 31, 2004
(amounts expressed in thousands)

Total Estimated Actual Valuation	$62,867,794
Maximum general obligation debt, limited to 3% of total valuation[1]	$ 1,886,034
Outstanding bonds chargeable to limit	378,977
Less: amount reserved for long-term debt	23,485
Net chargeable to bond limit	355,492
Legal Debt Margin—December 31	$ 1,530,542

[1]Section 7.5.2, Charter of the City and County of Denver: The City and County of Denver shall not become indebted for general obligation bonds, to any amount which, including indebtedness, shall exceed three percent of the actual value as determined by the last final assessment of the taxable property within the City and County of Denver.

Source: City and County of Denver, Colorado, Comprehensive Annual Financial Report, Statistical Section, 2004, p. 154.

Debt margin, sometimes referred to as *borrowing power,* is the difference between the amount of debt limit calculated as prescribed by law and the net amount of outstanding indebtedness subject to limitation. The net amount of outstanding indebtedness subject to limitation differs from total general long-term indebtedness because certain debt issues may be exempted from the limitation by law, and the amount available in debt service funds for debt repayment is deducted from the outstanding debt in order to determine the amount subject to the legal debt limit. Total general long-term indebtedness must, in some jurisdictions, include special assessment debt and debt serviced by enterprise funds if such debt was issued with covenants that give the debt tax-supported status in the event that collections of special assessments or enterprise fund revenues are insufficient to meet required interest or principal payments. Debt authorized but not issued as of the end of a fiscal year should be considered in evaluating debt margin, as it may be sold at any time. Although it would be in keeping with the purpose of establishing a legal debt limit to include the present value of capital lease obligations along with bonded debt in the computation of legal debt margin, state statutes at present generally do not specify that the liability for capital lease obligations is subject to the legal debt limit. The computation of legal debt margin for the City and County of Denver is shown in Illustration 6–3. The upper portion of Illustration 6–4 shows a schedule that presents the City and County of Denver's debt burden for the past 10 years, a statistic closely watched by bond rating analysts and others.

Overlapping Debt

Debt limitation laws ordinarily establish limits that may not be exceeded by each separate governmental entity affected by the laws. This means the county government may incur indebtedness to the legal limit, a township within that county may do likewise, and a city within the township may become indebted to the legal limit, with no restriction because of debt already owed by larger territorial units in which it is located. As a result, a given parcel of real estate or object of personal property may be the basis of debt beyond the legal limit and also may be subject at a given time to assessments for the payment of taxes to retire bonds issued by two or more governments. When this situation exists, it is described as **overlapping debt.**

ILLUSTRATION 6–4

CITY AND COUNTY OF DENVER
Ratio of Net General Bonded Debt to Estimated Actual Value and Net Bonded Debt per Capita
Last Ten Years

	1995	1996	1997	1998	1999	2000	2001	2002	2003	2004
Population*	486,350	492,650	497,625	501,700	507,500	554,636	564,606	562,657	567,526	572,862
Estimated actual valuation (in millions of dollars)	$ 25,797	$ 26,317	$ 31,283	$ 31,562	$ 39,280	$ 40,422	$ 52,322	$ 53,269	$ 61,738	$ 62,868
Gross general obligation bonded debt (in thousands of dollars)	$321,270	$296,160	$269,260	$234,316	$303,114	$295,740	$268,226	$280,505	$424,524	$378,977
Less amount reserved for long-term debt (in thousands of dollars)	14,407	11,539	17,654	21,187	28,608	28,607	25,469	22,029	18,450	23,485
Net general bonded debt (in thousands of dollars)	$306,863	$284,621	$251,606	$213,129	$274,506	$267,133	$242,757	$258,476	$406,074	$355,492
Net general bonded debt to estimated actual valuation	.0119	.0108	.0080	.0068	.0070	.0066	.0046	.0049	.0066	.0057
Per capita net general bonded debt	$630.95	$577.73	$505.61	$424.81	$540.90	$481.64	$429.96	$459.38	$715.52	$620.55

*Population estimates for 1995 through 1999 are not adjusted for the 2000 census.

ILLUSTRATION 6–4 (*continued*)

Computation of Net Direct and Overlapping Debt
December 31, 2004
(amounts expressed in thousands)

	Debt Outstanding	Percentage Applicable	City and County of Denver Share of Debt
NET DIRECT DEBT			
General long-term debt	$ 717,580		
Denver Airport System bonds	3,829,760		
Wastewater Management bonds	28,700		
Water Board bonds	290,216		
Gross Bonded Debt	4,866,256		
Less Self-supporting bonds:			
Gateway Village bonds	3,108		
Special Assessment bonds	290		
Excise Tax Revenue bonds	335,205		
Denver Airport System bonds	3,829,760		
Wastewater Management bonds	28,700		
Water Board bonds	290,216		
Less amount reserved for long-term debt	23,485		
TOTAL NET DIRECT DEBT	355,492	100.0%	$ 355,492
OVERLAPPING DEBT			
Denver Metropolitan Football Stadium District	315,870	28.1%	88,759
Regional Transportation District	467,250	28.1%	131,297
Metro Wastewater Reclamation District	118,901	42.6%	50,652
School District #1	703,857	100.0%	703,857
TOTAL OVERLAPPING DEBT	1,605,878		974,565
TOTAL NET DIRECT AND OVERLAPPING DEBT	$1,961,370		$1,330,057

Source: City and County of Denver, Colorado, Comprehensive Annual Financial Report, Statistical Section, 2004, p. 153.

The extent to which debt may overlap depends on the number of governments represented within an area that are authorized to incur long-term indebtedness. These may include the state, county, township, city, and various special purpose governments. To show the total amount of indebtedness being supported by taxable property located within the boundaries of the reporting government, a statement of direct and overlapping debt should be prepared. Direct debt is the debt that is being serviced by the reporting government. To this direct debt should be added amounts owed by other governmental entities that levy taxes against the same properties on which the direct debt is based. A statement of direct and overlapping debt for the City and County of Denver is presented in the lower portion of Illustration 6–4. Note that the overlapping debt applies to four special purpose governmental entities, including the school district, that levy taxes on certain properties within the boundaries of the City and County of Denver.

General Long-Term Liabilities Arising from Capital Lease Agreements

In Chapter 5, under the heading "General Capital Assets Acquired under Lease Agreements," a brief example is given of the computation of the present value of rentals under a capital lease agreement. The entry necessary in a governmental fund at the inception of the lease is illustrated in Chapter 5. The corresponding entry in the governmental activities general journal at the government-wide level is also given in Chapter 5 to show the capitalization of the asset acquired under the lease. That entry is reproduced here to illustrate how the liability is recorded.

	Debits	Credits
Governmental Activities:		
Equipment	67,590	
Capital Lease Obligations Payable		67,590

As shown in this entry, at the inception of the lease an obligation is recognized at the government-wide level in an amount equal to the present value of the stream of annual payments. Although the lease agreement calls for a $10,000 initial lease payment on January 1, 2007, the full present value should be recorded as the liability until the initial payment has been recorded. Accounting for the initial payment in the debt service fund is illustrated later in this chapter. When the initial payment is recorded in the debt service fund, it will be accompanied by the following entry at the government-wide level to record the reduction of the capital lease obligation.

Governmental Activities:		
Capital Lease Obligations Payable	10,000	
Cash		10,000

On January 1, 2008, the second lease rental payment of $10,000 is made. As the table given later in this chapter shows, only $4,241 of that payment applies to reduction of the principal of the lease obligation (the remaining $10,000 − $4,241, or $5,759, represents interest on the lease). Thus, the following entry is required at the government-wide level to further reduce the balance of the lease principal and to recognize the related interest expense.

	Debits	Credits
Governmental Activities:		
Capital Lease Obligations Payable	4,241	
Interest Expense on Capital Leases	5,759	
Cash		10,000

DEBT SERVICE FUNDS

When long-term debt has been incurred for capital or other purposes, revenues must be raised in future years to make debt service payments. Debt service payments include both periodic interest payments and the repayment of debt principal when due. Revenues from taxes that are restricted for debt service purposes are usually recorded in a *debt service fund,* as are subsequent expenditures for payments of interest and principal. A debt service fund is used only for debt service activities related to *general* long-term liabilities—those reported in the Governmental Activities column of the government-wide statement of net assets. Debt service related to long-term liabilities reported in proprietary and fiduciary funds is reported in those funds, not in a debt service fund.

Number of Debt Service Funds

In addition to debt service for bond liabilities, debt service funds may be required to service debt arising from the use of notes or warrants having a maturity more than one year after date of issue. Debt service funds may also be used to make periodic payments required by capital lease agreements. Although each issue of long-term or intermediate-term debt is a separate obligation and may have legal restrictions and servicing requirements that differ from other issues, GASB standards provide that, if legally permissible, a single debt service fund be used to account for the service of all issues of tax-supported and special assessment debt. Subsidiary records of that fund can provide needed assurance that budgeting and accounting meet the restrictions and requirements relating to each issue. If legal restrictions do not allow for the debt service of all issues of tax-supported and special assessment debt to be accounted for by a single debt service fund, as few additional debt service funds as is consistent with applicable laws should be created. In this chapter, a separate debt service fund for each bond issue is illustrated simply as a means of helping the reader focus on the different accounting procedures considered appropriate for each type of bond issue encountered in practice.

Use of General Fund to Account for Debt Service

In some jurisdictions, laws do not require accounting for the debt service function by a debt service fund. Unless the debt service function is very simple, it may be argued that good financial management would dictate the establishment of a debt service fund even though not required by law. If neither law nor sound financial administration requires the use of debt service funds, the function may be performed within the accounting and budgeting framework of the General Fund. In such cases, the accounting and financial reporting standards discussed in this chapter should be followed for the debt service activities of the General Fund.

Budgeting for Debt Service

Whether or not additions to debt service funds are required by a bond indenture to be approximately equal year by year, good politics and good financial management suggest that the burden on the taxpayers be spread reasonably evenly rather than lumped in the years that issues or installments happen to mature. If taxes for payment of interest and principal on long-term debt are to be recorded directly in the debt service fund, they are recognized as *revenues* of the debt service fund. If the taxes are to be raised by another fund and transferred to the debt service fund, they must be included in the revenues budget of the fund that will raise the revenue (often the General Fund) and be budgeted by that fund as *interfund transfers* to the debt service fund, and reported as an other financing use by the General Fund. The transfers-in are reported as other financing sources by the debt service fund. Since the debt service fund is a budgeting and accounting entity, a revenues and other financing sources budget should be prepared for it that includes interfund transfers from other funds as well as revenues that will be recorded directly or earned on investments. Although the items may be difficult to budget accurately, debt service funds can often count on receiving premiums on debt issues sold and accrued interest on debt issues sold. Accrued interest on debt sold is commonly considered as revenue of the recipient debt service fund; premium on debt sold is an other financing source. Similarly, as illustrated in Chapter 5, if capital projects are completed with expenditures less than revenues and other financing sources, the residual equity may be transferred to the appropriate debt service fund. Persons budgeting and accounting for debt service funds should seek competent legal advice on the permissible use of both premiums on debt sold and interfund transfers of the residual equity of capital projects funds. In some cases, one or both of these items must be held for eventual debt repayment and may not be used for interest payments; in other cases, both premiums and transfers-in of equity may be used for interest payments.

The appropriations budget of a debt service fund must provide for the payment of all interest on general long-term debt that will become legally due during the budget year and for the payment of any principal amounts that will become legally due during the budget year. GASB standards require debt service fund accounting to be on the same basis as is required for general and special revenue funds. One peculiarity of the modified accrual basis used by governmental fund types (which is not discussed in Chapter 3 because it relates only to debt service funds) is that interest on long-term debt is not accrued in the debt service fund but is accrued at the government-wide level. For example, if the fiscal year of a governmental entity ends on December 31, 2007, and the interest on its bonds is payable on January 1 and July 1 of each year, the amount payable on January 1, 2008, would not be considered a liability in the balance sheet of the debt service fund prepared as of December 31, 2007. The rationale for this recommendation is that the interest is not legally due until January 1, 2008. (See Illustration 6–5.) The same reasoning applies to principal amounts that mature on the first day of a fiscal year; they are not liabilities to be recognized in statements prepared as of the day before. In the event 2007 appropriations include January 1, 2008, interest and/or principal payment, the appropriations and expenditures (and resulting liabilities) should be recognized in 2007.

Types of Serial Bonds

Several decades ago, governmental issues of long-term debt commonly matured in total on a given date. In that era, bond indentures often required the establishment of a "sinking fund," sometimes operated on an actuarial basis. Some sinking fund term tax-supported bond issues are still outstanding, but they are dwarfed in number and

ILLUSTRATION 6–5   **Modified Accrual Basis of Recognition of Expenditures for Long-Term Debt Interest and Principal**

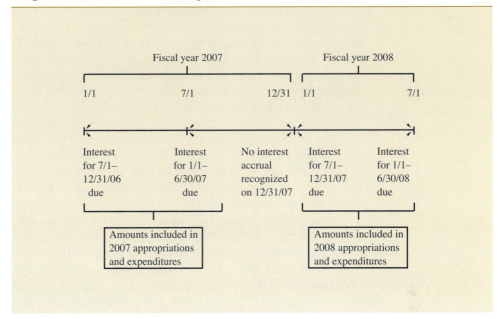

amount by serial bond issues in which the principal matures in installments. Four types of serial bond issues are found in practice: regular, deferred, annuity, and irregular. If the total principal of an issue is repayable in a specified number of equal annual installments over the life of the issue, it is a **regular serial bond issue.** If the first installment is delayed for a period of more than one year after the date of the issue but thereafter installments fall due on a regular basis, the bonds are known as **deferred serial bonds.** If the amount of annual principal repayments is scheduled to increase each year by approximately the same amount that interest payments decrease (interest decreases, of course, because the amount of outstanding bonds decreases) so that the total debt service remains reasonably level over the term of the issue, the bonds are called **annuity serial bonds. Irregular serial bonds** may have any pattern of repayment that does not fit the other three categories.

Debt Service Accounting for Regular Serial Bonds

Accounts recommended for use by debt service funds created to account for resources segregated for the payment of interest and principal of serial bonds are similar to but not exactly the same as those recommended for use by the General Fund and special revenue funds. However, because the number of sources of revenues and other financing sources is relatively small in a typical debt service fund, as is the number of purposes for which expenditures are made, it is generally not necessary to use control and subsidiary accounts such as those used by the General Fund. Moreover, because debt service funds do not issue purchase orders or contracts for goods and services, the use of encumbrance accounting is unnecessary. Thus, the budgetary accounts typically used for a debt service fund are Estimated Revenues, Estimated Other Financing Sources, Appropriations, and Estimated Other Financing Uses. The actual operating accounts usually include only a few revenue accounts, Other Financing Sources (for interfund transfers in and bond issue premiums),

Expenditures—Bond Interest, Expenditures—Bond Principal, and, in the case of certain bond refunding transactions, Other Financing Uses. Similarly, relatively few balance sheet accounts are found in a debt service fund. Accounts typically include current asset accounts such as Cash, Investments, Taxes Receivable (and related estimated uncollectible accounts), and Due from Other Funds. Liability accounts might include Matured Bond Interest Payable and Matured Bond Principal Payable. Fund equity typically consists of a single Fund Balance account. For the convenience of bondholders, the payment of interest and the redemption of matured bonds is ordinarily handled through the banking system. Usually the government designates a bank as paying agent or fiscal agent to handle interest and principal payments for each issue, whether the issue is in registered or bearer form. The assets of a debt service fund often, therefore, include "Cash with Paying (or Fiscal) Agent" and the appropriations, expenditures, and liabilities may include amounts for the service charges of paying agents. Investment management may be performed by governmental employees or by banks, brokers, or others who charge for the service; investment management fees are a legitimate charge against investment revenues. For the sake of simplicity, the debt service examples in this chapter assume that the issuing government issues checks directly to bondholders for interest and redemption of principal.

Accounting for debt service of regular serial bonds furnishes the simplest illustration of recommended debt service fund accounting. Assume the bonds issued by the Town of Brighton as partial financing for the fire station construction project (discussed in Chapter 5, under the heading "Illustrative Transactions—Capital Projects Funds") are regular serial bonds maturing in equal annual amounts over 20 years and are registered as to interest and principal. The total face value of the issue was $1,200,000; all bonds in the issue bear interest of 6 percent per year, payable semiannually on June 15 and December 15. The bonds were dated June 15, 2008, and sold on that date at par. During 2008 the only expenditure the debt service fund will be required to make will be the interest payment due December 15, 2008, in the amount of $36,000 ($1,200,000 × 0.06 × ½ year). Assuming that revenues to pay the first installment of bonds due on June 15, 2009, and both interest payments due in 2009 will be raised in 2009 from a special sales tax, the budget for 2008 need only provide resources in the amount of the 2008 interest expenditure. The entry to record the budget for the year ended December 31, 2008, including $6,000 residual equity to be transferred from the Fire Station Capital Projects Fund, is:

		Debits	Credits
	Serial Bond Debt Service Fund:		
1.	Estimated Revenues	30,000	
	Estimated Other Financing Sources	6,000	
	Appropriations		36,000

If sales tax revenues in the amount of $31,200 were collected in cash for debt service, the entry is:

	Serial Bond Debt Service Fund:		
2a.	Cash	31,200	
	Revenues		31,200

The corresponding entry in the governmental activities general ledger at the government-wide level is (Note: Entry 1 has no effect at the government-wide level since budget entries are made only in governmental funds):

		Debits	Credits
	Governmental Activities:		
2b.	Cash	31,200	
	General Revenues—Sales taxes—		
	Restricted for Debt Service		31,200

As illustrated in Chapter 5, the $6,000 residual equity of the Fire Station Capital Projects Fund was transferred to the debt service fund. The entry required in the latter fund is:

	Serial Bond Debt Service Fund:		
3.	Cash	6,000	
	Other Financing Sources—Interfund Transfers In		6,000

(Note: Governmental activities at the government-wide level are unaffected since the transfer is between two funds within the governmental activities category.)

On December 15, 2008, when the first interest payment is legally due, the debt service fund records the expenditure of the appropriation and the corresponding entry is made to record interest expense at the government-wide level:

	Serial Bond Debt Service Fund:		
4a.	Expenditures—Bond Interest	36,000	
	Interest Payable		36,000
	Governmental Activities:		
4b.	Expenses—Interest on Long-Term Debt	36,000	
	Interest Payable		36,000

Checks totaling $36,000 are written to the registered owners of these bonds. The entries to record the payment in the debt service fund and governmental activities general journals are:

	Serial Bond Debt Service Fund and Governmental Activities:		
5.	Interest Payable	36,000	
	Cash		36,000

As of December 31, 2008, an adjusting entry would be made to accrue one-half of a month's interest expense on the accrual basis at the government-wide level, as would be the case in accounting for business organizations. As was discussed earlier, interest expenditure is recognized in the period when due in the debt service fund and is not accrued at the end of the accounting period.

		Debits	Credits
	Governmental Activities:		
6.	Expenses—Interest on Long-term Debt	3,000	
	Accrued Interest Payable		3,000

All budgetary and operating statement accounts are closed by the following entry:

		Debits	Credits
	Serial Bond Debt Service Fund:		
7.	Revenues	31,200	
	Other Financing Sources—Interfund Transfers In	6,000	
	Appropriations	36,000	
	Estimated Revenues		30,000
	Estimated Other Financing Sources		6,000
	Expenditures—Bond Interest		36,000
	Fund Balance		1,200

In addition, all temporary accounts of the governmental activities general ledger would be closed at year-end. Because that ledger has many temporary accounts besides those related to debt service, its closing entry is not illustrated here.

Second-Year Transactions

In the second year of the Serial Bond Debt Service Fund, the fiscal year ending December 31, 2009, the following journal entries would be required.

The special sales tax for debt service is estimated to produce revenues of $135,000 for the year. From these revenues, two interest payments (the interest due on June 15, 2009, and December 15, 2009) of $36,000 and $34,200, respectively, and a principal redemption payment of $60,000 due on June 15, 2009, must be paid. Entry 8 shows the entry required at January 1, 2009, to record the budget for FY 2009.

		Debits	Credits
	Serial Bond Debt Service Fund:		
8.	Estimated Revenues	135,000	
	Appropriations		130,200
	Fund Balance		4,800

During the year, actual revenues from the special sales tax were $134,100. Entries 9a and 9b summarize these collections.

		Debits	Credits
	Serial Bond Debt Service Fund:		
9a.	Cash	134,100	
	Revenues		134,100
	Governmental Activities:		
9b.	Cash	134,100	
	General Revenues—Sales Taxes—Restricted for Debt Service		134,100

On June 15, 2009, interest of $36,000 and the first redemption of principal in the amount of $60,000 ($1,200,000 ÷ 20 years) were paid to bondholders of record, as shown in Entries 10a and 10b.

		Debits	Credits
	Serial Bond Debt Service Fund:		
10a.	Expenditures—Bond Principal	60,000	
	Expenditures—Bond Interest	36,000	
	Cash		96,000
	Governmental Activities:		
10b.	Bonds Payable	60,000	
	Expenses—Interest on Long-Term Debt	33,000	
	Accrued Interest Payable	3,000	
	Cash		96,000

The semiannual interest payment due on December 15, 2009, was paid on schedule, as reflected in Entries 11a and 11b, based on a remaining principal of $1,140,000 at 6 percent interest per annum.

		Debits	Credits
	Serial Bond Debt Service Fund:		
11a.	Expenditures—Bond Interest	34,200	
	Cash		34,200
	Governmental Activities:		
11b.	Expenses—Interest on Long-Term Debt	34,200	
	Cash		34,200

On December 31, 2009, interest expense and interest payable were accrued in the amount of $2,850 ($1,140,000 \times .06 \times 1/12 \times 1/2$):

		Debits	Credits
	Governmental Activities:		
12.	Expenses—Interest on Long-Term Debt	2,850	
	Accrued Interest Payable		2,850

All temporary accounts of the debt service fund were closed on December 31, 2009, as shown in Entry 13. Closing entries for governmental activities are presented in Chapter 9 for fiscal year 2008.

		Debits	Credits
	Serial Bond Debt Service Fund:		
13.	Revenues	134,100	
	Appropriations	130,200	
	Fund Balance	900	
	Estimated Revenues		135,000
	Expenditures—Bond Interest		70,200
	Expenditures—Bond Principal		60,000

In subsequent years, the pattern of journal entries will be the same as that of the preceding entries, except that actual sales taxes realized will vary from year to year and the amount of interest will decline each year as the principal is reduced. If revenues are insufficient in any year to meet debt service requirements, available fund balance can be used to augment current year revenues. If fund balance is insufficient to cover the shortfall, then an interfund transfer from the General Fund would likely be used. Making all interest and principal redemption payments by their due date is critically important as a missed or late payment could adversely impact the entity's bond rating and significantly increase future borrowing costs.

Debt Service Accounting for Term Bonds

Term bond issues mature in their entirety on a given date, in contrast to serial bonds, which mature in installments. Required revenues of term bond debt service funds may be determined on an "actuarial" basis or on less sophisticated bases designed to produce approximately level contributions during the life of the issue. In order to illustrate the use of an actuarial basis, the following example assumes that the Town of Brighton has a term bond issue amounting to $1,500,000 with a 20-year life. The term bonds bear semiannual interest at a nominal (or stated) annual rate of 5 percent, payable on January 1 and July 1. Revenues and other financing sources of this particular debt service fund are assumed to be property taxes levied directly for this debt service fund and earnings on investments of the debt service fund. The amount of the tax levy is computed in accord with annuity tables on the assumption that revenues for principal repayment will be invested and will earn 6 percent per year, compounded semiannually. (Actuaries are usually conservative in their assumptions because they are concerned with a long time span.) Using either the annuity tables found in most intermediate accounting texts or a calculator, one will find that the future amount of $1 invested at the end of each period will amount to $75.4012597 at the end of 40 periods, if the periodic compound interest is 3 percent (as specified in this example). Since the amount needed for bond repayment at the end of 40 six-month periods is $1,500,000, the tax levy for bond principal repayment must yield $1,500,000 divided by 75.4012597, or $19,893.57, at the end of each six-month period throughout the life of the bonds. Tax revenue must be sufficient to cover each bond interest payment of $37,500 ($1,500,000, the face of the bonds, × 5 percent, the annual nominal interest rate, × ½ year) plus the two required additions of $19,893.57 for sinking fund investment, for a total revenue of $114,787.14 per year.

Assuming the bonds were issued in the preceding fiscal year on January 1, 2007, and actual additions and actual earnings were both exactly as budgeted, the Term Bonds Debt Service Fund of the Town of Brighton would have the following trial balance as of December 31, 2007.[5]

	Debits	*Credits*
Cash	$37,500.00	—
Investments	40,383.95	—
Fund balance	—	$77,883.95
Totals	$77,883.95	$77,883.95

[5]The computation is (all amounts rounded to nearest cent):

Year	Period	Addition at End of Period	3 Percent per Period	Balance at End of Period
2007	1	$19,893.57	$ –0–	$19,893.57
	2	19,893.57	596.81	40,383.95
2008	3	19,893.57	1,211.52	61,489.04
	4	19,893.57	1,844.67	83,227.28

The balance at the end of Period 2 is the total of investments and the total of fund balance in this case since actuarial assumptions were met exactly in 2007. The sum of the interest for Period 3 and Period 4 is $3,056.19, the required earnings for the second year.

For every year of the life of the issue, the budget for the Term Bonds Debt Service Fund of the Town of Brighton, reflecting the conditions just described above, will include two required additions of $19,893.57 each for investment for eventual principal repayment, and two amounts of $37,500 each for interest payment, for a total of $114,787.14. The budget will also include earnings on debt service fund investments computed in accord with actuarial requirements. For 2008, the second year of the Term Bonds Debt Service Fund's operation, the actuarial assumption is that the fund will earn 6 percent per year, compounded semiannually; the required earnings for the year amount to $3,056.19 (see footnote 5 for calculation). Therefore, Estimated Revenues is debited for $117,843.33 ($114,787.14 + $3,056.19). The appropriations budget would include only the amounts becoming due during the budget year, $75,000 (two interest payments, each amounting to $37,500). The entry to record the budget for fiscal year 2008 follows.

		Debits	Credits
	Term Bond Debt Service Fund:		
1.	Estimated Revenues	117,843.33	
	Fund Balance		42,843.33
	Appropriations		75,000.00

If the debt service fund is to accumulate the amount needed to retire the term bond issue at maturity, both additions and earnings must be received, and invested, in accord with the actuarial assumptions. Therefore, the tax levy for this fund must yield collections in the first six months totaling $57,393.57, at least, so that $19,893.57 can be invested and $37,500 can be paid in interest to bondholders, both as of the end of the first six-month period. Collections during the second six months must also total $57,393.57, for the same reason. Realistically, it is unlikely that collections would ever total $57,393.57, to the penny, in either six-month period. If collections are less than that amount in either period, it should be obvious that this fund would have to borrow enough to make the required investments; there is no question that the interest would have to be paid when due, as discussed earlier in this chapter. Assuming that collection experience of the Town of Brighton indicates that a tax levy in the amount of $120,000 is needed in order to be reasonably certain that collections during each six-month period will equal the needed amount, the entries to record the levy and the expected uncollectibles amounting to $3,000 are as follows:

		Debits	Credits
	Term Bond Debt Service Fund:		
2a.	Taxes Receivable—Current	120,000.00	
	Estimated Uncollectible Current Taxes		3,000.00
	Revenues—Property Taxes		117,000.00
	Governmental Activities:		
2b.	Taxes Receivable—Current	120,000.00	
	Estimated Uncollectible Current Taxes		3,000.00
	General Revenues—Property Taxes—Restricted for Debt Service		117,000.00

The required interest payment was made on January 1, 2008, as reflected in Entries 3a and 3b.

		Debits	Credits
	Term Bond Debt Service Fund:		
3a.	Expenditures—Bond Interest	37,500.00	
	Cash		37,500.00
	Governmental Activities:		
3b.	Accrued Interest Payable	37,500.00	
	Cash		37,500.00

(Note: Interest expense and interest payable were accrued at the government-wide level for the second six months of FY 2007, but not in the debt service fund as the interest was not yet due on December 31, 2007.)

Actual tax collections during the first six months of FY 2008 were $57,400. Entries 4 and 5 would be required in the journals of both the debt service fund and governmental activities to record the collections and subsequent addition to sinking fund investments at June 30, 2008.

	Term Bond Debt Service Fund and Governmental Activities:		
4.	Cash	57,400.00	
	Taxes Receivable—Current		57,400.00
5.	Investments	19,893.57	
	Cash		19,893.57

Entries 6a and 6b record the addition of $1,261.99 of interest on June 30, 2008, which is added to the Investments account. Note that the actual interest earned during this six-month period is $50.47 more than the estimated earnings of $1,211.52 for the period because the actual earnings rate for the period was slightly higher than the 6 percent per annum rate used in actuarial computations.

	Term Bond Debt Service Fund:		
6a.	Investments	1,261.99	
	Revenues—Investment Earnings		1,261.99
	Governmental Activities:		
6b.	Investments	1,261.99	
	General Revenues—Investment Earnings—Restricted for Debt Service		1,261.99

The interest payment of $37,500 due on July 1, 2008, was made as scheduled, as shown in Entries 7a and 7b.

	Term Bond Debt Service Fund:		
7a.	Expenditures—Bond Interest	37,500.00	
	Cash		37,500.00
	Governmental Activities:		
7b.	Expenses—Interest on Long-Term Debt	37,500.00	
	Cash		37,500.00

During the second six months of the year, property tax collections for debt service on the term bonds totaled $58,000 and the required addition to the sinking fund Investments account was made on December 31, 2008, as shown in Entries 8 and 9.

		Debits	Credits
	Term Bond Debt Service Fund and Governmental Activities:		
8.	Cash	58,000.00	
	Taxes Receivable—Current		58,000.00
9.	Investments	19,893.57	
	Cash		19,893.57

At December 31, 2008, interest of $37,500 on the term bonds was accrued at the government-wide level for the second six months of the year.

	Governmental Activities:		
10.	Expenses—Interest on Long-Term Debt	37,500.00	
	Acrued Interest Payable		37,500.00

Interest earnings on sinking fund investments for the second six-months of the year was recorded in the amount of $1,883.10, as shown in Entries 11a and 11b.

	Term Bond Debt Service Fund:		
11a.	Investments	1,883.10	
	Revenues—Investment Earnings		1,883.10
	Governmental Activities:		
11b.	Investments	1,883.10	
	General Revenues—Investment Earnings—Restricted for Debt Service		1,883.10

Taxes levied for 2008 but not collected during the year become delinquent as of December 31; the balance of the Estimated Uncollectible Current Taxes account is reviewed and determined to be reasonable. Entry 12 is made in the journals of both the Term Bond Debt Service Fund and governmental activities at the government-wide level to record the reclassification of the property tax accounts as delinquent.

	Term Bond Debt Service Fund and Governmental Activities:		
12.	Taxes Receivable—Delinquent	4,600.00	
	Estimated Uncollectible Current Taxes	3,000.00	
	Taxes Receivable—Current		4,600.00
	Estimated Uncollectible Delinquent Taxes		3,000.00

All budgetary and operating statement accounts of the Term Bond Debt Service Fund were closed at December 31, 2008, as shown in Entry 13. Related closing entries for governmental activities are made in Chapter 9.

		Debits	Credits
	Term Bond Debt Service Fund:		
13.	Revenues—Property Taxes.	117,000.00	
	Revenues—Investment Earnings	3,145.09	
	Appropriations	75,000.00	
	Estimated Revenues		117,843.33
	Expenditures—Bond Interest		75,000.00
	Fund Balance		2,301.76

Although not illustrated in this chapter, accounting for deferred serial bonds has elements of both serial and term bond debt service fund accounting, reflecting the hybrid nature of deferred serial bonds. Illustrative debt service fund journal entries are not provided for these bonds, as they are similar to those provided for serial and term bonds.

Financial Reporting

Debt service activities are reported as part of governmental activities at the government-wide level. In addition, if a debt service fund qualifies as a major fund (see Glossary for definition), the financial information for that fund is reported in a separate column of the balance sheet—governmental funds and the statement of revenues, expenditures, and changes in fund balances—governmental funds. Financial information for debt service funds that do not qualify as a major fund is reported along with that for all other nonmajor governmental funds (i.e., special revenue, capital projects, and permanent funds) in an "Other Governmental Funds" column of the two financial statements just mentioned. Financial information for each nonmajor debt service fund is also reported in a separate column of the supplemental combining financial statements for nonmajor governmental funds in the financial section of the comprehensive annual financial report. For internal management purposes, it may also be desirable to prepare combining financial statements for the debt service funds only. A combining statement of revenues, expenditures, and changes in fund balances and a combining balance sheet for the debt service funds of the Town of Brighton are presented in Illustrations 6–6 and 6–7. Illustration 6–8 presents a schedule of revenues, expenditures, and changes in fund balances—budget and actual for the debt service funds.

Deposit and Investment Disclosures

Bond issuances and subsequent debt service activities typically result in significant deposits in financial institutions and long-term investments for principal redemption. In addition, excess cash of the General Fund and other funds, pension plan assets, self-insurance pool reserves, and investment pools are also common sources of deposits and investments. Among other concerns, deposits and investments held in the custody of financial institutions impose risks such as exposure to loss due to interest rate increases, custodial credit risk related to the underlying creditworthiness of the financial institution, credit risk related to the creditworthiness of debt security issuers, and concentration risk from holding substantial portions of investment securities of a single issuer.

Interest rate risk may be reduced by holding fixed income securities with lower term to maturity (duration) and avoiding highly interest-rate-sensitive derivative investments. Derivative securities are financial instruments or contracts whose value is dependent upon some other underlying security or market measure such as an in-

ILLUSTRATION 6–6

TOWN OF BRIGHTON
Debt Service Funds
Combining Statement of Revenues, Expenditures,
and Changes in Fund Balances
For the Year Ended December 31, 2008
(Amounts reported in whole dollars)

	Serial Bonds	Term Bonds	Total Debt Service Funds
Revenues:			
Taxes	$31,200	$117,000	$148,200
Investment earnings	–0–	3,145	3,145
Total revenues	31,200	120,145	151,345
Expenditures:			
Interest on bonds	36,000	75,000	111,000
Excess of revenues over (under)			
expenditures	(4,800)	45,145	40,345
Other financing sources (uses):			
Interfund transfers in	6,000	–0–	6,000
Increase in fund balance	1,200	45,145	46,345
Fund balance, January 1, 2008	–0–	77,884	77,884
Fund balance, December 31, 2008	$ 1,200	$123,029	$124,229

ILLUSTRATION 6–7

TOWN OF BRIGHTON
Debt Service Funds
Combining Balance Sheet
December 31, 2008
(Amounts reported in dollars)

	Serial Bonds	Term Bonds	Total Debt Service Funds
Assets:			
Cash	$1,200	$ 38,113	$ 39,313
Investments	–0–	83,316	83,316
Taxes receivable (net)	–0–	1,600	1,600
Total assets	$1,200	$123,029	$124,229
Fund Balances:			
Fund balances	$1,200	$123,029	$124,229

dex or interest rates.[6] Custodial credit risk for deposits may be reduced by holding other securities as collateral. Such risk may be eliminated entirely if covered by depository insurance (e.g., Federal Deposit Insurance Corporation). Credit risk can be reduced by investing in bonds with high-quality ratings or that are backed by insurance. Concentration risk can be minimized through diversification of investments

[6]For a formal definition of *derivative,* see GASB *Codification,* Sec. 2300.601, Response to Question 1.

ILLUSTRATION 6–8

TOWN OF BRIGHTON
Debt Service Funds
Combining Schedule of Revenues, Expenditures,
and Changes in Fund Balances—Budget and Actual
for the Year Ended December 31, 2008
(Amounts reported in dollars)

	Serial Bonds			Term Bonds			Total Debt Service Funds		
	Budget	Actual	Actual Over (Under) Budget	Budget	Actual	Actual Over (Under) Budget	Budget	Actual	Actual Over (Under) Budget
Revenues:									
Taxes	$30,000	$31,200	$1,200	$114,787	$117,000	$2,213	$144,787	$148,200	$3,413
Investment earnings	–0–	–0–	–0–	3,056	3,145	89	3,056	3,145	89
Total revenues	30,000	31,200	1,200	117,843	120,145	2,302	147,843	151,345	3,502
Expenditures:									
Interest on bonds	36,000	36,000	–0–	75,000	75,000	–0–	111,000	111,000	–0–
Excess of revenues over (under) expenditures	(6,000)	(4,800)	1,200	42,843	45,145	2,302	36,843	40,345	3,502
Other Financing Sources (Uses):									
Interfund transfers in	6,000	6,000	–0–	–0–	–0–	–0–	6,000	6,000	–0–
Increase in fund balance	–0–	1,200	1,200	42,843	45,145	2,302	42,843	46,345	3,502
Fund balance, January 1, 2008	–0–	–0–	–0–	77,884	77,884	–0–	77,884	77,884	–0–
Fund balance, December 31, 2008	$ –0–	$1,200	$1,200	$120,727	$123,029	$2,302	$120,727	$124,229	$3,502

by avoiding investing in securities of a single issuer that exceed 5 percent of total investments.

GASB standards require certain disclosures about *external investment pools,* as discussed in Chapter 8. For other investments, the government should describe in its notes to the financial statements (1) legal and contractual provisions for deposits and investments, including types of investments authorized to be held and any significant violations of legal or contractual provisions and (2) investment policies related to the kinds of risks described in the preceding paragraph.[7] Investment disclosures should be organized by type of investment. Additionally, the government should provide disclosures about specific risks. These disclosures include information about:[8]

1. Interest rate risk of investments in debt securities, using one of five approved methods described in the standards.
2. Credit quality ratings of investments in debt securities, such as those of the major national bond rating services (e.g., Moodys Investor Service, Standard & Poor's, and FitchRatings). A recommended format is to present aggregated amounts of investments by quality rating category.
3. Custodial credit risk; specifically investment securities or deposits that are not insured, deposits that are not collateralized, investments that are not registered in the name of the government, and both deposits and investments that are held by either (a) the counterparty (e.g., financial institution) or (2) the counterparty's trust department or agent but not in the government's name.
4. Concentration of credit risk, including disclosure of amount and issuer for investments in the securities of any one issuer that exceed 5 percent or more of total investments.

In addition, the government should disclose any deposits or investments that are exposed to foreign currency risk.

Valuation of Debt Service Fund Investments

As shown in the term bond debt service fund example in this chapter, financial resources typically are accumulated in these types of debt service funds for eventual repayment of principal. Such resources should be invested prudently until they are needed for principal repayment. Interest earnings on investments in bonds and other securities purchased at a premium or discount generally would not be adjusted for amortization of any premiums or discounts. Current GASB standards require fair value accounting and reporting for most investments except for certain money market investments with maturities of less than one year.[9] The latter *may* be accounted for at amortized cost (interest earnings adjusted for amortization of premium or discount).[10]

---

[7]GASB *Codification,* Sec. I50.123–126.

[8]Ibid. pars. 127–131.

[9]GASB standards define **fair value** as "the amount at which an investment could be exchanged in a current transaction between willing parties, other than in a forced or liquidation sale." GASB, *Codification,* Sec. I50.105.

[10]The reader should note that this discussion refers to amortization of premium and discount on investments purchased with the expectation of holding them until maturity. A premium or discount on bonds payable sold by a government is *not* amortized in the debt service fund but should be amortized at the government-wide level so that effective interest expense is reported in the government-wide statement of activities. Premium on bonds sold is considered as an other financing source of the debt service fund if it must be used for debt service, as discussed in Chapter 5. Accrued interest on bonds sold should be recorded as revenue of the debt service fund.

Often, however, premiums and discounts are not amortized for short-term investments. All long-term investments in debt and equity securities held for repayment of general long-term debt principal are reported at fair value in the debt service fund balance sheet. All *changes* in the fair value of investments during the period, both realized and unrealized, are reported as revenue in the statement of revenues, expenditures, and changes in fund balances.

Debt Service Accounting for Special Assessment Debt

Special assessment projects, as discussed in Chapter 5, typically follow the same pattern as transactions of other capital projects. Specifically, construction activities are usually completed in the first year or so, using either interim financing from the government or proceeds of special assessment debt issuances (bonds or notes) to pay construction costs to contractors. Either at the beginning of the project or, more commonly, when construction is completed, assessments for debt service are levied against property owners in the defined special benefit district. Annual assessment installments receivable and interest on the balance of unpaid installments usually approximate the amount of debt principal and interest payable during the same year. If the government is obligated in some manner to make the debt service payments in the event that amounts collected from benefited property owners are insufficient, the debt should be recorded in the governmental activities journal at the government-wide level and a debt service fund should be used to account for debt service activities. If the government is not obligated in any manner for special assessment debt, the debt should *not* be recorded in any accounting records of the government. In the latter case, which is relatively rare, debt service transactions should be recorded in an *agency fund,* as explained in Chapter 8.

Assume that special assessment bonds, secondarily backed by the general taxing authority of a certain city, were issued to complete a street-widening project. Upon completion of the project the city levied assessments amounting to $480,000, payable in 10 equal installments with 5 percent interest on unpaid installments, on owners of properties fronting on the improved streets. As shown in Entry 1, all receivables are recorded at the time of the levy, but Revenues is credited only for the amount expected to be collected within one year from the date of the levy; Deferred Revenues is credited for the amount of deferred installments. Because the entries at the government-wide level would be similar, except that interest expense would be reported rather than expenditures, those entries are omitted for the sake of brevity. Required budgetary entries, as shown earlier in this chapter for serial bond and term bond debt service funds, are omitted.

		Debits	Credits
1.	Assessments Receivable—Current	48,000	
	Assessments Receivable—Deferred	432,000	
	Revenues		48,000
	Deferred Revenues		432,000

All current assessments receivable due at year-end were collected along with interest of $24,000 (see Entry 2). Any amounts not collected by the due date should be reclassified by a debit to Assessments Receivable—Delinquent and a credit to Assessments Receivable—Current.

		Debits	Credits
2.	Cash	72,000	
	Assessments Receivable—Current		48,000
	Revenues		24,000

Matured special assessment bond principal in the amount of $48,000 and matured bond interest payable of $24,000 were recorded and paid on schedule.

3a.	Expenditures—Bond Principal	48,000	
	Expenditures—Bond Interest	24,000	
	Bonds Payable		48,000
	Interest Payable		24,000
3b.	Bonds Payable	48,000	
	Interest Payable	24,000	
	Cash		72,000

The second installment of assessments receivable was reclassified from the deferred category to the current category. A corresponding amount of Deferred Revenues was reclassified as Revenues.

4a.	Assessments Receivable—Current	48,000	
	Assessments Receivable—Deferred		48,000
4b.	Deferred Revenues	48,000	
	Revenues		48,000

This pattern of journal entries will be repeated during each of the remaining nine years until all special assessment bonds have been retired.

Use of Debt Service Funds to Record Capital Lease Payments

In Chapter 5, under the heading "General Capital Assets Acquired under Capital Lease Agreements," an example is given of the computation of the amount to be recorded in a governmental fund at the inception of a capital lease. The example illustrates the entry required at the government-wide level when an asset is acquired by a capital lease agreement. The example presented in Chapter 5 specified that the first payment of $10,000 was due on January 1, 2007, the inception of the lease. Governments may use a debt service fund to record capital lease payments because the annual payments are merely installment payments of general long-term debt. The first payment, since it is on the first day of the lease, is entirely a payment on the principal of the lease obligation. Accordingly, the payment would be recorded as follows:

Expenditures—Principal of Capital Lease Obligation	10,000	
Cash		10,000

The expenditures detail record would show that the entire amount of the first payment was a payment on the principal. The payment due on January 1, 2008, and the payment due each year thereafter, however, must be considered a partial payment on the lease obligation and a payment of interest on the unpaid balance of the lease obligation. GASB standards are consistent with the FASB's *SFAS No. 13;* both specify that a constant periodic rate of interest must be used. In the example started in Chapter 5, the present value of the obligation is computed using the rate of 10 percent per year. It is reasonable to use the same interest rate to determine what part of the annual $10,000 payment is payment of interest and what part is payment of principal. The following table shows the distribution of the annual lease rental payments:

Payment Date	Amount of Payment	Interest on Unpaid Balance at 10 Percent	Payment on Principal	Unpaid Lease Obligation
				$67,590
1/1/07	$10,000	$ –0–	$10,000	57,590
1/1/08	10,000	5,759	4,241	53,349
1/1/09	10,000	5,335	4,665	48,684
1/1/10	10,000	4,868	5,132	43,552
1/1/11	10,000	4,355	5,645	37,907
1/1/12	10,000	3,791	6,209	31,698
1/1/13	10,000	3,170	6,830	24,868
1/1/14	10,000	2,487	7,513	17,355
1/1/15	10,000	1,736	8,264	9,091
1/1/16	10,000	909	9,091	–0–

Although the total expenditure recorded each year, January 1, 2007, through January 1, 2016, is $10,000, the detail records for each year should show how much of the expenditure was for interest on the lease obligation and how much was payment on the obligation itself. As noted earlier in this chapter, the unpaid balance of the capital lease obligation is carried in the governmental activities general ledger at the government-wide level.

Accounting for Debt Refunding

If debt service fund assets accumulated for debt repayment are not sufficient to repay creditors when the debt matures, or if the interest rate on the debt is appreciably higher than the government would have to pay on a new bond issue, or if the covenants of the existing bonds are excessively burdensome, the governmental unit may issue refunding bonds.

The proceeds of refunding bonds issued at the maturity of the debt to be refunded are accounted for as other financing sources of the debt service fund that is to repay the existing debt. The appropriation for debt repayment is accounted for as illustrated in the Town of Brighton Serial Bond Debt Service Fund second-year example (see entry 1 under the heading "Second-Year Transactions" and related discussion).

If a government has accumulated no assets at all for debt repayment, it is possible that no debt service fund exists. In such a case, a debt service fund should be created to account for the proceeds of the refunding bond issue and the repayment of the old debt. When the debt has been completely repaid, the debt service fund relating to the liquidated issue should be closed, and a debt service fund for the refunding issue should be created and accounted for as described in this chapter. If the refunding bond issue is not sold but is merely given to the holders of the matured issue in an even exchange, the transaction does not require entries in a debt service fund or at the government-wide level but should be disclosed adequately in the notes to the financial statements.

Advance Refunding of Debt

Advance refundings of tax-exempt debt are common during periods when interest rates are falling sharply. Complex accounting and reporting issues have surfaced relating to legal issues such as whether both issues are still the debt of the issuer. If the proceeds of the new issue are to be held for the eventual retirement of the old issue, how can the proceeds be invested to avoid conflict with the Internal Revenue Service over the taxability of interest on the debt issue? (Compliance with the arbitrage rules under the Internal Revenue Code Sec. 148 and related regulations is necessary for the interest to be exempt from federal income tax and, possibly, from state and local taxes.) Full consideration of the complexities of accounting for advance refundings resulting in defeasance of debt is presented in the GASB *Codification* Section D20. Defeasance of debt can be either "legal" or "in substance." **Legal defeasance** occurs when debt is legally satisfied based on certain provisions in the debt instrument, even though the debt is not actually paid. **In-substance defeasance** occurs when debt is considered settled for accounting and financial reporting purposes, even though legal defeasance has not occurred. GASB *Codification* Section D20.103 sets forth in detail the circumstances for in-substance defeasance. Briefly, the debtor must irrevocably place cash or other assets in trust with an escrow agent to be used solely for satisfying scheduled payments of both interest and principal of the defeased debt. The amount placed in escrow must be sufficiently large so that there is only a remote possibility that the debtor will be required to make future payments on the defeased debt. The trust is restricted to owning only monetary assets that are essentially risk free as to the amount, timing, and collection of interest and principal.

To illustrate accounting for advance refundings resulting in defeasance of debt reported in the governmental activities ledger at the government-wide level, assume that the proceeds from the sale of the refunding issue amount to $2,000,000 and that debt defeased amounted to $2,500,000. The proceeds are recorded in the fund receiving the proceeds (normally, a *debt service fund*) by an entry such as follows:

	Debits	Credits
Cash	2,000,000	
Other Financing Sources—Proceeds of Refunding Bonds		2,000,000

Payments to the escrow agent from resources provided by the new debt should be recorded in the debt service fund as an other financing use; payments to the escrow agent from other resources are recorded as debt service expenditures. Therefore, assuming $500,000 has previously been accumulated in the debt service fund for payment of the $2,500,000 bond issue, the entry to record the payment to the escrow agent is as follows:

	Debits	Credits
Other Financing Uses—Payment to Refunded Bond Escrow Agent	2,000,000	
Expenditures—Payment to Refunded Bond Escrow Agent	500,000	
Cash		2,500,000

Disclosures about Advance Refundings

The *disclosure* guidance on debt refunding in GASB *Codification* Section D20 is applicable to state and local governments, public benefit corporations and authorities, public employee retirement systems, and governmental utilities, hospitals, colleges and universities, and to all funds of those entities.

Detailed disclosure guidance is set forth in Section D20.111–.114. Briefly, all entities subject to GASB jurisdiction are required to provide in the notes to the financial statements in the year of the refunding a general description of any advance refundings resulting in defeasance of debt. At a minimum the disclosures must include (1) the difference between the cash flows required to service the old debt and the cash flows required to service the new debt and complete the refundings and (2) the economic gain or loss resulting from the transaction. Economic gain or loss is the difference between the *present value* of the old debt service requirements and the *present value* of the new debt service requirements, discounted at the effective interest rate and adjusted for additional cash paid. Section D20.901–.917 provides examples of effective interest rate and economic gain calculations and of note disclosures.

Key Terms

Annuity serial bonds, *219*
Debt limit, *212*
Debt margin, *213*
Deferred serial bonds, *219*
Fair value, *231*

General long-term
   liabilities, *207*
In-substance
   defeasance, *235*
Irregular serial bonds, *219*

Legal defeasance, *235*
Overlapping debt, *213*
Regular serial bonds, *219*
Tax-supported debt, *208*
Term bonds, *224*

Selected References

American Institute of Certified Public Accountants. Audit and Accounting Guide. *Audits of State and Local Governments*. Revised. New York, 2005.
Governmental Accounting Standards Board. *Codification of Governmental Accounting and Financial Reporting Standards, as of June 30, 2005*. Norwalk, CT, 2005.

Questions

6–1. How are *general long-term liabilities* distinguished from other long-term liabilities of the government? How does the financial reporting of general long-term liabilities differ from the financial reporting of other long-term liabilities?

6–2. What disclosures about long-term liabilities are required in the notes to the financial statements?

6–3. *a.* When general obligation bonds are issued at a premium that is recorded in a debt service fund and is to be used for eventual retirement of that bond issue, what is the effect on the amount of liability to be shown in the statement of net assets?

   b. If a general obligation bond issue were sold at a premium that is required to be set aside for payment of bond interest, what is the effect on the accounts in the statement of net assets?

6–4. If a bond ordinance provides for regular and recurring payments of interest and principal payments on a general obligation bond issue of a certain government to be made from earnings of an enterprise fund and these payments are being made by the enterprise fund, how should the bond liability be disclosed in the comprehensive annual financial report of the government?

6–5. Define the terms *debt limit* and *debt margin,* and explain how each is typically calculated. Why do many states impose a statutory debt limit on local governments?

6–6. "Debt service funds are established to account for all long-term debt issued by state or local governments and for assets held to pay interest and matured debt principal." Is this statement true or false? Explain.

6–7. "If a certain city has six tax-supported bond issues and three special assessment bond issues outstanding, it would be preferable to operate nine separate debt service funds or, at a minimum, one debt service fund for tax-supported bonds and one for special assessment bonds." Do you agree? Explain.

6–8. Explain the essential differences between regular serial bonds and term bonds and how debt service fund accounting differs for the two types of bonds.

6–9. "Premiums and discounts on bond investments of the debt service fund should not be amortized since the debt service fund is not a profit-seeking entity." Do you agree or disagree? Explain your answer.

6–10. During periods of low interest rates, governments often refund outstanding bonds in advance of their maturity. Explain the different ways of treating advance refundings that will permit, under GASB standards, removal of the liability for the refunded bonds from the general long-term liabilities at the government-wide level.

Cases

6–1 Policy Issue: Who Should Pay for Neighborhood Improvements? Related Accounting Issues.

Facts: Pursuant to its capital improvement plan, the City of Kirkland decided to make certain improvements to Oak Ridge Street, a residential thoroughfare located in the northern part of the city. Specifically, the project entailed purchasing 20 feet at the front of all private properties fronting the street to facilitate widening of the street from two lanes to four lanes and adding sidewalks. The project was expected to cost $5 million.

After extensive and often contentious hearing presentations by property owners, the public works director, city planners, and the city attorney, the city council decided that property owners fronting on Oak Ridge Street would be the primary beneficiaries of the street-widening project. Accordingly, as permitted by state law, the city council formed the Oak Ridge Special Improvement District and approved the issuance of $5 million in special assessment bonds to be repaid from special assessment levies on the Oak Ridge Street property owners. To reduce interest rates on the debt, the city agreed to make the bonds general obligations of the city should property owners default on debt service payments.

After the bonds had been issued and the project was well underway, all Oak Ridge Street property owners retained a local law firm and sued the City of Kirkland to make the street-widening project a publicly funded project of the city rather than a special assessment project. Attorneys for property owners argued in briefs filed with the court that (1) the property owners will not benefit from the street improvements and, in fact, had fought the project for years since they would lose valuable property and the street would be transformed from a quiet, low-density, mainly local traffic street to a noisy, high-density public thoroughfare, and

(2) property owners were not adequately informed about the special assessment financing for the project before the financing was approved and the bonds were issued.

The city attorney has filed a brief with the court laying out the city's reasoning for financing the street-widening project with special assessment bonds, essentially arguing that the Oak Ridge Street Project is no different from many past city neighborhood improvement projects that have been financed with special assessments. According to the city attorney, there is strong legal precedent for requiring property owners who receive private benefit to pay for such improvements.

Required

a. Assume you are the judge in this case. After analyzing the facts of this case, decide what remedies, if any, you will order for the plaintiffs (the property owners). Prepare a written brief explaining your reasoning and verdict.

b. How would accounting for the bond issuance, street construction, and debt service differ if you (the judge) rule for the plaintiffs and require the city to repay the project bonds from tax revenues rather than from special assessments? How would accounting differ if you rule against the plaintiffs *and* assuming the city had not pledged to be secondarily liable for the bonds?

6–2 Financial Statement Impact of Incurring General Long-Term Debt on Behalf of Other Governments.

Facts: The Bates County government issued $2.5 million of tax-supported bonds to finance a major addition to the Bates County Hospital, a legally separate organization reported as a discretely presented component unit of the county. At the end of the fiscal year in which the debt was issued and the project completed, the county commission was shocked to see a deficit of more than $2 million reported for unrestricted net assets in the Governmental Activities column of the government-wide statement of net assets, compared with a surplus of over $400,000 the preceding year. The commission is quite concerned about how creditors and citizens will react to this large deficit and have asked you, in your role as county finance director, to explain how the deficit occurred and what actions should be taken to eliminate it.

Required

a. Write a brief memo to the county commission explaining how the $2.5 million bond issue for the addition to the Bates County Hospital resulted in the large and apparently unexpected deficit in unrestricted net assets. (Hint: Refer to Illustration 1–4, the City and County of Denver statement of net assets, and evaluate whether the bonds issued by Bates County would affect net assets—invested in capital assets, net of related debt or net assets—unrestricted. For additional insight, you may also wish to read the portion of Chapter 9 of this text that relates to preparation of government-wide financial statements for the Town of Brighton.)

b. In your memo, explain what actions can be taken, if any, to eliminate the deficit in governmental activities unrestricted net assets, or at least make it less objectionable.

6–3 The Case of the Vanishing Debt.

Facts: A county government and a legally separate organization—the Sports Stadium Authority—entered into an agreement under which the authority issued revenue bonds to construct a new stadium. Although the intent is to make debt service payments on the bonds from a surcharge on ticket sales, the county agreed to annually advance the Sports Stadium Authority the required amounts to make up any debt service shortfalls and has done so for several years. Accordingly, the county has recorded a receivable from the authority and the authority has recorded a liability to the county for all advances made under the agreement.

Ticket surcharge revenues that exceed $1,500,000 are to be paid to the county and be applied first toward interest then toward principal repayment of advances. Both parties acknowledge, however, that annual ticket surcharge revenues may never exceed $1,500,000, since to reach that level would require an annual paid attendance of 3,000,000. Considering that season ticket holders and luxury suite renters are not included in the attendance count, it is quite uncertain if the required trigger level will ever be reached.

The authority has twice proposed to raise the ticket surcharge amount, but the county in both cases vetoed the proposal. Thus, the lender in this transaction (the county) has imposed limits that appear to make it infeasible for the borrower (the authority) to repay the advances. Consequently, the authority's legal counsel has taken the position that the authority is essentially a pass-through agency with respect to the advances in that the authority merely receives the advances and passes them on to a fiscal agent for debt service payments. Moreover, they note that the bonds could never have been issued in the first place without the county's irrevocable guarantee of repayment, since all parties knew from the beginning that the authority likely would not have the resources to make full debt service payments.

Based on the foregoing considerations, the authority's legal counsel has rendered an opinion that the liability for the advances can be removed from the authority's accounts. The county tacitly agrees that the loans (advances) are worthless, since it records an allowance for doubtful loans equal to the total amount of the advances. Still, the county board of commissioners refuses to remove the receivable from its accounts because of its ongoing rights under the original agreement for repayment.

Required

a. Assume you are the independent auditor for the authority, provide a written analysis of the facts of this case and indicate whether or not you concur with the authority's decision to no longer report the liability to the county for debt service advances.

b. Alternatively, assume you are the independent auditor for the county, based on the same analysis you conducted for requirement *a,* indicate whether or not you concur with the county continuing to report a receivable for debt service advances on its General Fund balance sheet and government-wide statement of net assets.

6–4 Assessing General Obligation Debt Burden. This case focuses on the analysis of a city's general obligation debt burden. After examining the accompanying table that shows the general obligation (tax-supported) debt for Southwest City's last five fiscal years, answer the following questions.

Required

a. What is your initial assessment of the trend of the city's general obligation debt burden?

b. Complete the table by calculating the ratio of Net General Bonded Debt to Estimated Actual Value of taxable property and the ratio of Net General Bonded Debt per Capita. In addition, you learn that the average ratio of Net General Bonded Debt to Actual Value for comparable-size cities in the southwestern United States in 2008 was 2.13, and the average net general bonded debt per capita was $1,256. Based on time series analysis of the ratios you have calculated and the benchmark information provided in this paragraph, is your assessment of Southwest City's general obligation still the same as it was in part *a,* or has it changed? Explain.

SOUTHWEST CITY
Ratio of Net General Bonded Debt to Estimated Actual Value and Net Bonded Debt per Capita
(Last Five Fiscal Years)

Fiscal Year	Estimated Population	Estimated Actual Value of Taxable Property	Gross General Bonded Debt	Less: Amount in Debt Service Fund	Net General Bonded Debt	Net General Bonded Debt to Actual Value	Net General Bonded Debt per Capita
2004	95,050	$5,116,156,651	$ 97,455,624	$3,943,987	$ 93,511,637	_____	_____
2005	97,200	5,423,815,321	97,596,890	4,727,595	92,869,295	_____	_____
2006	102,350	5,799,206,379	104,343,051	4,271,471	100,071,580	_____	_____
2007	105,800	6,332,268,731	109,007,745	4,578,799	104,428,946	_____	_____
2008	111,400	7,045,371,795	123,097,884	4,706,700	118,391,184	_____	_____

Exercises and Problems

6–1 Examine the CAFR. Utilizing the CAFR obtained for Exercise 1–1, follow the instructions below.

a. **General Long-Term Liabilities.**

(1) *Disclosure of Long-Term Debt.* Does the report contain evidence that the government has general long-term liabilities? What evidence is there? Does the report specify that no such debt is outstanding, or does it include a list of outstanding tax-supported debt issues; capital lease obligations; claims, judgments, and compensated absence payments to be made in future years; and the unfunded pension obligations?

Refer to the enterprise funds statement of net assets as well as note disclosures for long-term liabilities. Are any enterprise debt issues backed by the full faith and credit of the general government? If so, how are the primary liability and the contingent liability disclosed?

(2) *Changes in Long-Term Liabilities.* How are changes in long-term liabilities during the year disclosed? Is there a disclosure schedule for long-term liabilities similar to Illustration 6–1? Does the information in that schedule agree with the statements presented for capital projects funds and debt service funds and the government-wide financial statements?

Are interest payments and principal payments due in future years disclosed? If so, does the report relate these future payments with resources to be made available under existing debt service laws and covenants?

(3) *Debt Limitations.* Does the report contain information as to legal debt limit and legal debt margin? If so, is the information contained in the report explained in enough detail so that an intelligent reader (you) can understand how the limit is set, what debt is subject to it, and how much debt the government might legally issue in the year following the date of the report?

(4) *Overlapping Debt.* Does the report disclose direct debt and overlapping debt of the reporting entity? What disclosures of debt of the primary government are made in distinction to debt of component units? Is debt of component units reported as "direct" debt of the reporting entity or as "overlapping debt"?

b. **Debt Service Funds.**

(1) *Debt Service Function.* How is the debt service function for tax-supported debt and special assessment debt handled—by the General Fund, by a special revenue fund, or by one or more debt service funds? If there is more than one debt service fund, what kinds of bond issues or other debt instruments are serviced by each fund? Is debt service for bonds to be retired from enterprise revenues reported by enterprise funds?

Does the report state the basis of accounting used for debt service funds? If so, is the financial statement presentation consistent with the stated basis? If the basis of accounting is not stated, analyze the statements to determine which basis is used—full accrual, modified accrual, or cash basis. Is the basis used consistent with the standards discussed in this chapter?

(2) *Investment Activity.* Compare the net assets reserved for debt service, if any, in the Governmental Activities column of the government-wide statement of net assets and the fund balance of each debt service fund at balance sheet date with the amount of interest and the amount of debt principal the fund will be required to pay early in the following year (you may find debt service requirements in the notes to the financial statements or in supplementary schedules following the individual fund statements in the Financial Section of the CAFR). If debt service funds have accumulated assets in excess of amounts needed within a few days after the end of the fiscal year, are the excess assets invested? Does the CAFR contain a schedule or list of investments of debt service funds? Does the report disclose increases or decreases in the fair value of investments realized during the year? Does the report disclose net earnings on investments during the year? What percentage of revenue of each debt service fund is derived from earnings on investments? What percentage of the revenue of each debt service fund is derived from taxes levied directly for the debt service fund? What percentage is derived from transfers from other funds? List any other sources of debt service revenue and other financing sources, and indicate the relative importance of each source.

Are estimated revenues for term bond debt service budgeted on an actuarial basis? If so, are revenues received as required by the actuarial computations?

(3) *Management.* Considering the debt maturity dates as well as the amount of debt and apparent quality of debt service fund investments, does the debt service activity appear to be properly managed? Does the report disclose whether investments are managed by a corporate fiduciary, another outside investment manager, or governmental employees? If outside investment managers are employed, is the basis of their fees disclosed? Are the fees accounted for as additions to the cost of investments or as expenditures?

Is one or more paying agents, or fiscal agents, employed? If so, does the report disclose whether the agents keep track of the ownership of registered bonds, write checks to bondholders for interest payments and matured bonds or, in the case of coupon bonds, pay matured coupons and matured bonds presented through banking channels? If agents are employed, does the balance sheet or the notes to the financial statements disclose the amount of cash in their possession? If so, does this amount appear reasonable in relation to interest payable and matured bonds payable? Do the statements, schedules, or narratives disclose for how long a period of time debt service funds carry a liability for unpresented checks for interest on registered bonds, for matured but unpresented interest coupons, and for matured but unpresented bonds?

(4) *Capital Lease Rental Payments.* If general capital assets are being acquired under capital lease agreements, are periodic lease rental payments accounted for as expenditures of a debt service fund (or by another governmental fund)? If so, does the report disclose that the provisions of *SFAS No. 13* are being followed (see the "Use of Debt Service Funds to Record Capital Lease Payments" section of this chapter) to determine the portion of each capital lease payment considered as interest and the portion considered as payment on the principal.

6–2 Multiple Choice. Choose the best answer.

1. The following obligations were among those reported by Grant City at December 31, 2007:

Vendor financing with a term of 10 months when incurred, in connection with a capital asset acquisition that is not part of a long-term financing plan	$ 150,000
Long-term bonds for financing of capital asset acquisition	3,000,000
Bond anticipation notes due in six months, issued as part of a long-term financing plan for capital purposes	400,000

What aggregate amount should Grant City report as general long-term liabilities at December 31, 2007?

a. $3,000,000
b. $3,150,000
c. $3,400,000
d. $3,550,000

Items 2 through 5 are based on the following information:

On March 2, 2007, the Town of Jonesburg issued 20-year, 6 percent, general obligation serial bonds at the face amount of $3,000,000 to construct a new recreation center, with construction to begin April 1, 2007, and to be completed by March 31, 2008. Interest of 6 percent per annum is due semi-annually on March 1 and September 1 and the first payment of $150,000 for redemption of principal is due on March 1, 2008. During the fiscal year ended June 30, 2007, construction expenditures amounted to $900,000. As of June 30, 2007, no resources had yet been provided to the debt service fund for payment of principal and interest.

2. Proceeds from the bond issue should be recorded in the journal of the:
a. Debt service fund.
b. Capital projects fund.

    c. General fund.

    d. Internal service fund.

3. The long-term liability for the bond issue should be recorded in the journal of:

    a. The debt service fund.

    b. The General Fund.

    c. The capital projects fund.

    d. Governmental activities at the government-wide level.

4. At June 30, 2007, accrued interest payable should be recorded in the journal of:

    a. The debt service fund.

    b. Governmental activities at the government-wide level.

    c. Both the debt service fund and governmental activities at the government-wide level.

    d. None of the above. Interest should not be accrued on general obligation bonds.

5. At June 30, 2007, the amount to be reported as bonds payable on the balance sheet for the debt service fund is:

    a. $0.

    b. $150,000.

    c. $2,850,000.

    d. $3,000,000.

6. Debt service funds may be used to account for all of the following *except:*

    a. Repayment of debt principal.

    b. Lease payments under capital leases.

    c. Amortization of premiums on bonds payable.

    d. The proceeds of refunding bond issues.

7. Expenditures for redemption of principal of tax-supported bonds payable should be recorded in a debt service fund

    a. When the bonds are issued.

    b. When the bond principal is legally due.

    c. When the redemption checks are written.

    d. Any of the above, if consistently followed.

8. Which of the following items would be reported in the Governmental Activities column of the government-wide financial statements?

	Premium on Bonds Payable	Noncurrent Portion of General Long-Term Liabilities Payable
a.	Yes	Yes
b.	Yes	No
c.	No	No
d.	No	Yes

9. Interest on general long-term debt would be recorded as an expenditure in which of the following financial statements?

    a. Statement of revenues, expenditures, and changes in fund balances—governmental funds.

    b. Statement of activities.

    c. Both *a* and *b* are correct.

    d. None of the above; interest is recorded as an expense not an expenditure.

10. Which of the following accounts is unlikely to appear in the chart of accounts of a debt service fund?
    a. Matured Bonds Payable.
    b. Estimated Revenues.
    c. Appropriations.
    d. Encumbrances.

6–3 **Long-Term Liability Transactions.** Following are stated a number of unrelated transactions for the Town of Treadway, some of which affect governmental activities at the government-wide level. None of the transactions has been recorded yet.

 1. The tax levy for the General Fund included $650,000 to be transferred to the debt service fund; $425,000 of this amount is designated for eventual retirement of outstanding serial bonds; the remainder is to be expended for interest on long-term debt. All taxes were collected, the transfer was made as planned, and the interest was paid.

 2. A $5,000,000 issue of serial bonds to finance a capital project was sold at 102 plus accrued interest in the amount of $50,000. The accrued interest was recorded as revenue of the debt service fund and the premium was recorded as an other financing source of the debt service fund. Accrued interest on bonds sold must be used for interest payments; premium is designated by state law for eventual payment of bond principal.

 3. A summary of debt service fund operations during the year showed receipt of interest on investments in the amount of $180,000; this amount is to be used for payment of interest on long-term debt.

 4. $2,800,000 par value of tax-supported serial bonds was issued in cash to permit partial refunding of a $3,500,000 par value issue of term bonds. The difference was settled with $700,000 that had been accumulated in prior years in a debt service fund. Assume that the term bonds had been issued several years earlier at par.

Required

Prepare in general journal form the necessary entries in the governmental activities and appropriate fund journals for each transaction. Explanations may be omitted. For each entry you prepare name the fund in which the entry should be made.

6–4 **Statement of Legal Debt Margin.** In preparation for a proposed bond sale, the city manager of the City of Appleton requested you to prepare a statement of legal debt margin for the city as of December 31, 2007. You ascertain that the following bond issues are outstanding on that date:

Convention center bonds	$3,600,000
Electric utility bonds	2,700,000
General obligation serial bonds	3,100,000
Tax increment bonds	2,500,000
Water utility bonds	1,900,000
Transit authority bonds	2,000,000

You obtained other information that included the following items:

1. Assessed valuation of real and taxable personal property in the city totaled $240,000,000.

2. The rate of debt limitation applicable to the City of Appleton was 8 percent of total real and taxable personal property valuation.

3. Electric utility, water utility, and transit authority bonds were all serviced by enterprise revenues, but each carries a full-faith-and-credit contingency provision. By law such self-supporting debt is not subject to debt limitation.

4. The convention center bonds and tax increment bonds are subject to debt limitation.

5. The amount of assets segregated for debt retirement at December 31, 2007, is $1,800,000.

6–5 Direct and Overlapping Debt. At April 30, 2007, all property inside the limits of the City of Marksville was situated within four additional governmental units, each authorized to incur long-term debt. At that date, net long-term debt of the five was as follows:

Florence County	$40,000,000
Florence Library District	2,000,000
City of Marksville	8,000,000
Marksville School District	17,000,000
Marksville Hospital District	13,600,000

Assessed values of property at the same date were county and library district, $900,000,000; city, $360,000,000; school district, $450,000,000; and hospital district, $720,000,000.

Required

a. Prepare a statement of direct and overlapping debt for the City of Marksville. (Carry percentages to tenths.)

b. Compute the actual ratio (in percentage carried to tenths) of total debt applicable to the City of Marksville property to assessed value of property within the city limits.

c. Compute the share of the city's direct and overlapping debt that pertained to the Reliable Manufacturing Company, having assessed valuation of $3,600,000 at April 30, 2007.

6–6 Capital Lease. The City of Jamestown has agreed to acquire a new city maintenance building under a capital lease agreement. At the inception of the lease, a payment of $100,000 is to be made; nine annual lease payments, each in the amount of $100,000, are to be made at the end of each year after the inception of the lease. The total amount to be paid under this lease, therefore, is $1,000,000. The town could borrow this amount for nine years at the annual rate of 8 percent; therefore, the present value of the lease at inception, including the initial payment, is $724,689. Assume that the fair value of the building at the inception of the lease is $750,000.

a. Show the entry that should be made in a capital projects fund at the inception of the lease after the initial payment has been made.

b. Show the entry that should be made at the inception of the lease in the government activities journal.

c. Show the entry that should be made in the debt service fund and governmental activities journal to record the second lease payment.

6–7 Serial Bond Debt Service Fund Journal Entries and Financial Statements.
The Village of Vandalia Serial Bond Debt Service Fund balance sheet as of December 31, 2007, is presented below:

VILLAGE OF VANDALIA **Serial Bond Debt Service Fund** **Balance Sheet As of December 31, 2007**			
Assets		**Fund Balance**	
Cash	$253,000		
Investments	50,000		
Interest receivable on investments	2,000		
Total assets	$305,000	Fund balance	$305,000

Additional information: The bonds were issued on January 1, 2007. During FY 2007 the General Fund transferred sufficient cash to the debt service fund to finance the July 1, 2007, interest payment and to provide sufficient resources for timely payment of the January 1, 2008, interest and principal payments, plus an additional $50,000 that was invested as a financial cushion should tax collections be insufficient for future debt service. Beginning in FY 2008, property taxes will be levied in sufficient amounts each year to cover all future debt service payments. (Note: Do not record any of the FY 2007 transactions and events. Rather, proceed to the requirements listed below.)

Required

a. Prepare debt service fund entries in general journal form to reflect, as necessary, the following information and transactions for FY 2008 (ignore entries at the government-wide level):

(1) The operating budget for FY 2008 consists of estimated revenues from property taxes of $360,000 and from interest on investments of $6,000. Appropriations must be provided for a bond principal redemption payment of $150,000 and a semiannual interest payment of $100,000 due on January 1, 2008, and an interest payment of $96,250 due on July 1, 2008.

(2) Property taxes are levied in the amount of $372,000, of which $12,000 is estimated to be uncollectible.

(3) Checks are written and mailed for the principal redemption and interest payment due on January 1, 2008.

(4) Collections of current year property taxes during the year amount to $352,000.

(5) Interest receivable as of December 31, 2007, is collected in cash.

(6) Checks are written and mailed for the interest payment due on July 1, 2008.

(7) Interest on investments is collected in the amount of $4,300.

(8) Accrued interest receivable on investments at year-end is $1,800.

(9) Budgetary and operating statement accounts are closed, and the uncollected taxes receivable and the related estimated uncollectible account balance are reclassified as delinquent.

b. Prepare a balance sheet for the Village of Vandalia's Serial Bond Debt Service Fund as of December 31, 2008.

c. Prepare a statement of revenues, expenditures, and changes in fund balances for the debt service fund for the year ended December 31, 2008.

d. Prepare a schedule of revenues, expenditures, and changes in fund balance—budget and actual for the fund for the year ended December 31, 2008.

6–8 Term Bond Debt Service Fund Transactions and Advance Refunding. The City of Henderson had outstanding 8 percent term bonds scheduled to mature July 1, 2013, in the amount of $5,000,000. The bonds were issued several years ago at par. At the beginning of FY 2008, only $1,000,000 had been accumulated as sinking fund investments in a term bond debt service fund. The bonds pay interest of 4 percent per annum semiannually on January 1 and July 1.

a. During 2008, the following transactions occurred. Record the transactions in the term bond debt service fund and the governmental activities general journals. Ignore all entries that would be made in the General Fund.

(1) The budget for FY 2008 provided for an interfund transfer from the General Fund in the amount needed for two semiannual interest payments plus $53,000 on June 30 and December 31 for sinking fund investments. The budget also provides for estimated investment revenues of $161,000. Investment revenues are added to the sinking fund investment principal semiannually on June 30 and December 31. Appropriations were approved for the two semiannual interest payments. An entry was made to accrue the interfund transfer from the General Fund.

(2) The interest payment due on January 1, 2008, was made on schedule.

(3) On June 30, 2008, cash was transferred from the General Fund in the amount required for the July 1 interest payment and the semiannual addition to the sinking fund. The addition to the sinking fund was immediately invested.

(4) The city received notice that sinking fund investments earned interest of $79,160 on June 30, 2008.

(5) The interest payment due on July 1, 2008, was made on schedule.

(6) On December 31, the General Fund transferred the remaining budgeted amount to the term bond debt service fund. This included the amount required for the January 1, 2009, interest payment and the semiannual addition to the sinking fund. The addition to the sinking fund was immediately invested.

(7) The city received a notice that sinking fund investments earned interest of $81,300 for the last six months of the fiscal year.

(8) Because interest rates have dropped dramatically since these bonds were issued, the city's finance director obtained approval from the Henderson City Council in late 2008 to issue $4,000,000 of new 5 percent serial bonds to refund and retire the old term bond issue. The remaining $1,000,000 required to redeem the term bonds was obtained by cashing in all investments. The excess of cash from investments will be transferred to a new serial bond debt service fund and held for principal repayment of the serial bonds. The new serial bonds were issued at par on December 31, 2008, the end of the fiscal year, and the old term bonds were redeemed on the same date. Semiannual interest was also paid on the term bonds on December 31, 2008, because of the early redemption.

(9) All accounts in the term bond debt service fund were closed after the bonds were redeemed.

6–9 Comprehensive Capital Assets/Serial Bond Problem. Transaction data related to the City of Chambers' issuance of serial bonds to finance street and park improvements follows. Utilizing worksheets formatted as shown at the end of the problem, prepare all necessary journal entries for these transactions in the city's capital projects fund, debt service fund, and governmental activities at the government-wide level. You may ignore related entries in the General Fund. Round all amounts to the nearest whole dollar.

   a. On July 1, 2007, the first day of its fiscal year, the City of Chambers issued serial bonds with a face value totaling $5,000,000 and having maturities ranging from one to 20 years to make certain street and park improvements. The bonds were issued at 102 and bear interest of 5 percent per annum, payable semiannually on January 1 and July 1, with the first payment due on January 1, 2008. The first installment of principal in the amount of $250,000 is due on July 1, 2008. Premiums on bonds issued must be deposited directly in the debt service fund and be used for payment of bond interest. Premiums are amortized using the straight-line method in the governmental activities journal but are not amortized in the debt service fund. Debt service for the serial bonds will be provided by a one-quarter-cent city sales tax imposed on every dollar of sales in the city.

      (1) Record the FY 2008 budget for the Serial Bond Debt Service Fund, utilizing worksheets formatted as shown at the end of this problem. The city estimates that the sales tax will generate $440,000 in FY 2008. An appropriation needs to be provided for only the interest payment due on January 1, 2008.

      (2) Record the issuance of the bonds, again utilizing your worksheets.

   b. On August 2, 2007, the city entered into a $4,800,000 contract with Central Paving and Construction. Work on street and park improvement projects is expected to begin immediately and continue until August 2008.

   c. On August 10, 2007, the capital project fund paid the city's Utility Fund $42,000 for relocating power lines and poles to facilitate street widening. No encumbrance had been recorded for this service.

   d. On August 20, 2007, the city's Public Works Department billed the capital projects fund $30,000 for engineering and other design assistance. This amount was paid.

   e. Street and park improvement sales taxes for debt service of $248,000 were collected in the six months ending December 31, 2007.

   f. On January 1, 2008, the city mailed checks to bondholders for semiannual interest on the bonds.

   g. On January 15, 2008, Central Paving and Construction submitted a billing to the city for $2,500,000. The city's public works inspector agrees that all milestones have been met for this portion of the work.

   h. On February 2, 2008, the city paid Central Paving and Construction the amount it had billed, except for 4 percent that was withheld as a retained percentage per terms of the contract.

   i. During the six months ended June 30, 2008, sales tax collections for debt service amounted to $194,600.

   j. Make all appropriate adjusting and closing entries at June 30, 2008, the end of the fiscal year. Based on authorization from the Public Works Department,

$1,650,000 of construction work in progress was reclassified as infrastructure and another $250,000 was reclassified as improvements other than buildings. (Ignore closing entry for governmental activities.)

k. Reestablish the Encumbrances account balance in the capital projects fund effective July 1, 2008.

l. Record the FY 2009 budget for the debt service fund, assuming sales revenues are estimated at $492,000.

m. On July 1, 2008, the city mailed checks totaling $125,000 to all bondholders for semiannual interest and $250,000 to holders of record for bonds being redeemed.

n. On August 14, 2008, Central Paving and Construction submitted a final billing to the city for $2,300,000.

o. On August 23, 2008, the city paid the August 14 billing, except for a 4 percent retained percentage.

p. Upon final inspection by the Public Works Department, it was discovered that the contractor had failed to provide all required landscaping and certain other work for the street and park improvements. Public works employees completed this work at a total cost of $210,000. This amount was transferred to the General Fund using all retained cash and other cash of the capital projects fund.

q. The balance of the Construction Work in Progress account was reclassified as $150,000 to Improvements Other Than Buildings and the remainder to Infrastructure.

r. All remaining cash in the capital projects fund was transferred to the debt service fund and all accounts of the capital projects fund were closed.

Capital Projects Fund		Capital Projects Fund	Governmental Activities
Example:			
Cash	5,000,000		
OFS—Proceeds			
of Bonds	5,000,000		

Debt Service Fund	Debt Service Fund	Governmental Activities

(Label as needed)	(Label as needed)	(Label as needed)

6–10   Comprehensive Capital Assets/Term Bond Liabilities Problem. Following are transaction data for related capital assets and capital liabilities of the City of Stevens. Utilizing worksheets formatted as shown at the end of the problem, prepare all necessary entries for these transactions in the city's capital projects fund, debt service fund, and governmental activities journals at the government-wide level. You may ignore related entries in the General Fund. Round all amounts to the nearest whole dollar.

a. On July 1, 2007, the first day of its 2008 fiscal year, the City of Stevens issued at par $2,000,000 of 6 percent term bonds to construct a new city office building. The bonds mature in five years on July 1, 2012. Interest is payable semiannually on January 1 and July 1. A sinking fund is to be established with equal semiannual additions made on June 30 and December 31, with the first addition to be made on December 31, 2007. Cash for the sinking fund additions and the semiannual interest payments will be transferred from the General Fund shortly before the due dates. Assume a yield on sinking fund investments of 6 percent per annum, compounded semiannually. Investment earnings are added to the investment principal. Based on this information:

   (1) Prepare a schedule in good form showing the required additions to the sinking fund, the expected semiannual earnings, and the end-of-period balance in the sinking fund for each of the 10 semiannual periods. (*Note:* The future amount of an ordinary annuity of $1 for 10 periods at 3 percent per period is $11.4638793.)

   (2) Record the issuance of the bonds. (Utilize worksheets formatted as shown at the end of the problem.)

   (3) Create a term bond debt service fund and record its budget for the fiscal year ended June 30, 2008. An appropriation should be provided only for the interest payment due on January 1, 2008. Also record an accrual for all interfund transfers to be received from the General Fund during the year.

b. On July 17, 2007, the city entered into a construction contract with Jones Construction Company for $1,950,000 to construct the new city office building.

c. On December 28, 2007, the General Fund transferred $234,461 to the debt service fund. The addition to the sinking fund was immediately invested in 6 percent certificates of deposit.

d. On December 28, 2007, the city issued checks to bondholders for the interest payment due on January 1, 2008.

e. On June 1, 2008, Jones Construction billed the city in the amount of $1,000,000 for construction work to date on the city office building project.

f. On June 15, 2008, the city paid the $1,000,000 partial billing from Jones Construction except for 5 percent that was retained pending final inspection at the conclusion of the project.

g. On June 27, 2008, the General Fund transferred $234,461 to the debt service fund. The addition for the sinking fund was invested immediately in 6 percent certificates of deposit.

h. Actual interest earned on sinking fund investments at year-end (June 30, 2008) was the same as the amount budgeted [see *a*(1) and *a*(3)]. This interest adds to the sinking fund balance.

i. All appropriate adjusting and closing entries were made at June 30, 2008. (Ignore closing entries for governmental activities.)

j. On July 1, 2008, the city paid the interest payment due that date. (*Note:* As discussed in this chapter, it is important that all principal and interest be paid by the due date. Usually a city does not directly pay the bondholders but uses a paying (fiscal) agent to pay the bondholders of record. Furthermore, the use of electronic funds transfer permits same-day transfer of cash to the fiscal agent.)

k. On July 1, 2008, the encumbrances were reestablished in the capital projects fund.

  l. The budgetary entry for fiscal year 2009 was recorded on July 1, 2008.

 m. On September 10, 2008, Jones Construction completed the city office building project and billed the city for the remaining $950,000 due on the contract.

  n. On September 14, 2008, the city paid the $950,000 partial billing from Jones, except for 5 percent, which was retained pending final inspection of the project.

  o. Following final inspection, the city incurred $125,000 for additional exterior and interior refinishing and site cleanup. Public works (General Fund) employees were used for the refinishing and cleanup, which was completed on October 1, 2008. On October 5, 2008, the $125,000 due to the city's General Fund was paid.

  p. The balance of cash in the capital projects fund was transferred to the term bond debt service fund. This amount was deemed available for eventual repayment of the principal of the 6 percent term bonds and was invested immediately in 6 percent CDs. Record the transfer and close all accounts in the capital projects fund.

  q. Ignoring all other transactions in fiscal years 2009 and those for 2010 and 2011, prepare the journal entries in the term bond debt service fund for the transfer of cash from the General Fund on June 27, 2012. None of this amount is invested.

  r. On June 30, 2012, all sinking fund investments in the term bond debt service fund were redeemed for cash in the amount of $1,825,539. Of this amount, $99,712 represented interest earned during fiscal 2012. Of the interest earned, $46,541 had been recorded on December 31, 2011, but the June 30, 2012, interest of $53,171 has not yet been recorded.

  s. Prepare the closing entry for the term bond debt service fund at the end of fiscal year 2012.

  t. Prepare the budgetary entry for the term bond debt service fund at July 1, 2012, the beginning of fiscal year 2013.

  u. Record the payment of bond principal and interest on July 1, 2012. Close all accounts of the term bond debt service fund.

Capital Projects Fund	**Capital Projects Fund**	**Governmental Activities**
Example:		
Cash 2,000,000		
OFS—Proceeds		
of Bonds 2,000,000		

Debt Service Fund	**Debt Service Fund**	**Debt Service Fund**

Governmental Activities	**Governmental Activities**	**(Label this column as needed)**

Chapter Seven

Accounting for the Business-Type Activities of State and Local Governments

Learning Objectives

After reading this chapter, you should be able to:

1. Distinguish between the purposes of internal service funds and enterprise funds.
2. Describe the characteristics of proprietary funds, including those unique to internal service and enterprise funds.
3. Explain the financial reporting requirements, including the differences in reporting of internal service and enterprise funds in the government-wide and fund financial statements.
4. Describe accounting procedures and prepare journal entries and financial statements for an internal service fund.
5. Describe accounting procedures and prepare journal entries and financial statements for an enterprise fund.

Chapters 3–6 addressed accounting and reporting for governmental funds. This chapter addresses accounting and reporting for proprietary funds. Governmental funds owe their existence to legal constraints placed on the raising of revenues and the use of resources. In contrast to the governmental funds, proprietary funds rely primarily on exchange transactions, specifically charges for services, to generate revenues. As a result, proprietary funds follow accounting principles that are similar to those of investor-owned businesses.

The focus on exchange transactions with parties outside of government is the reason that the enterprise funds are reported in a separate Business-type Activities column at the government-wide level, whereas governmental funds and internal service funds are reported as governmental activities at the government-wide level.

PROPRIETARY FUNDS

As shown in Illustration 2–1, there are two types of proprietary funds, internal service funds and enterprise funds. Traditionally, the reason for the creation of proprietary funds was to improve the management of resources. More recently, with increased citizen resistance to tax increases, many governmental entities have turned to user charges as a means of financing operations formerly financed by tax revenues and intergovernmental revenues. Thus, proprietary funds are now frequently used to account for activities formerly found in governmental funds.

In order to determine whether user charges are commensurate with operating costs and to improve the ability of administrators and governing bodies to determine that costs are reasonable in relation to benefits, it is desirable that the accounting and operations of the activities be conducted in a businesslike manner. As a result, proprietary funds focus on the economic flow of resources through use of the accrual basis of accounting, as is done in business.

As governments become more complex, efficiencies can be gained by combining or centralizing services that are commonly found in several departments or funds of government. Doing so meets one of the primary objectives of proprietary funds, improved management of resources. An example of a common service that is frequently centralized is purchasing. Another example is a central motor pool. *Internal service funds* are used to account for the production and distribution of centralized goods and services that are provided to departments or agencies of the government, or to other governments, on a cost-reimbursement basis. (Internal service funds are sometimes called *intragovernmental service funds, working capital funds,* or *revolving funds*.) Although internal service funds are accounted for *internally* as business-type activities, their transactions predominantly involve sales of goods or services to, or interfund transactions with, the General Fund and other funds that compose the governmental activities of government. For this reason, *GASBS 34* requires that the financial balances of most internal service funds be reported in the Governmental Activities column at the government-wide level rather than the Business-type Activities column. At the fund level, internal service funds are reported in a separate column of the proprietary fund financial statements. (See Illustrations 1–10, 1–11, and 1–12 for examples of proprietary fund statements for the City and County of Denver.)

Enterprise funds account for activities that produce goods or services to be sold to the general public. Activities of enterprise funds are referred to as *business-type activities* for purposes of accounting and financial reporting at the government-wide level (see the City and County of Denver's statement of activities presented in Illustration 1–5). Similar to governmental funds, *major* enterprise funds must be identified and reported in separate columns of the fund financial statements, while nonmajor enterprise fund information is aggregated and reported in an Other Enterprise Funds column (see Illustrations 1–10, 1–11, and 1–12).

Financial Reporting Requirements

Accounting for proprietary funds is similar to that of investor-owned business enterprises of the same type. An enterprise fund established to account for a government-owned electric utility, for example, should follow accounting principles similar to those of investor-owned electric utilities. Accordingly, proprietary funds focus on the flow of economic resources recognized on the accrual basis, both within the fund and at the government-wide level. Thus, these funds account for all capital assets used in their operations and for all long-term liabilities to be paid from the revenues generated from their operations, as well as for all current assets and current liabilities. Because proprietary funds follow business-type accounting principles, one should not be surprised that these funds prepare essentially the same financial statements that businesses do: a balance sheet (called either a statement of net assets or a balance sheet); a statement of revenues, expenses, and changes in fund net assets (equivalent to an income statement); and a statement of cash flows. These statements are prepared according to GASB standards, which differ in some respects from the equivalent statements prescribed by FASB standards for business organizations.

Statement of Net Assets

As one would expect when the accounting for funds is similar to that of profit-seeking businesses, the statement of net assets (or a traditional balance sheet) for proprietary funds is classified; that is, current assets are segregated from capital assets and other assets, and current liabilities are segregated from long-term debt. Additionally, current assets are listed in the order of liquidity. However, unlike businesses, there is no owners' or stockholders' equity section on the statement of net assets. Instead *GASBS 34* requires the reporting of net assets (assets minus liabilities), which is divided into three components: invested in capital assets, net of related debt; restricted; and unrestricted. Invested in capital assets, net of related debt is calculated as the total of gross capital assets, net of accumulated depreciation, less any outstanding debt related to the acquisition or construction of capital assets. If debt has been incurred for construction or acquisition of a capital asset, but the proceeds of the debt have not been spent by year-end, that debt is excluded in calculating invested in capital assets, net of related debt. Restricted net assets are those net assets with restrictions on use imposed by law or external parties. For example, if a bond is issued for construction of a capital asset, but is unspent at year-end, the proceeds from the bond would be considered restricted net assets. Unrestricted net assets represent the residual amount of net assets after segregating investment in capital assets, net of related debt, and restricted net assets.

Operating Statement

The period results of operations for a proprietary fund should be reported in a statement of revenues, expenses, and changes in net assets, which is similar to the income statement of a profit-seeking business. *GASBS 34* requires that the statement identify operating revenues and expenses and nonoperating revenues and expenses, and that the statement provide separate subtotals for operating revenues, operating expenses, and operating income. Operating revenues and expenses are those related to the primary function of the proprietary fund. Management judgment is necessary when defining which revenues and expenses are primary to the operations of the fund. However, the distinction is important for achieving effective management control, as well as for complying with the GASB requirement to separately report operating and nonoperating revenues and expenses.

Statement of Cash Flows

GASB financial reporting standards require the preparation of a statement of cash flows as a part of the full set of financial statements for all proprietary funds. The statement is required to be prepared using the direct method of presentation. Additionally, categories of cash flows provided by FASB *Statement No. 95* were deemed insufficient to meet the needs of users of governmental financial reports. Consequently, GASB standards provide four categories of cash flows: operating, noncapital financing, capital and related financing, and investing. In each category, the term *cash* also includes **cash equivalents** (defined as short-term, highly liquid investments).

Cash flows from operating activities include receipts from customers, receipts from sales to other funds, payments to suppliers of goods or services, payments to employees for services, payments for purchases from other funds (including payments in lieu of taxes), and other operating cash receipts and payments.

Cash flows from *noncapital financing* activities include proceeds from debt not clearly attributable to acquisition, construction, or improvement of capital assets; receipts from grants, subsidies, or taxes other than those specifically restricted for capital purposes or those for specific operating activities; payment of interest on and repayment of principal of noncapital financing debt; grants or subsidies paid to other governments, funds, or organizations except payments for specific operating activities of the grantor government.

Cash flows from *capital and related financing* activities include proceeds of debt and receipts from special assessments and taxes specifically attributable to acquisition, construction, or improvement of capital assets; receipts from capital grants; receipts from the sale of capital assets; proceeds of insurance on capital assets that are stolen or destroyed; payments to acquire, construct, or improve capital assets; payment of interest on and repayment or refunding of capital and related financing debt.

Cash flows from *investing* activities include receipts from collection of loans; interest and dividends received on loans, debt instruments of other entities, equity securities, and cash management and investment pools; receipts from the sales of debt or equity instruments; withdrawals from investment pools not used as demand accounts; disbursements for loans; payments to acquire debt or equity instruments; and deposits into investment pools not used as demand accounts.

Budgetary Comparison Schedule

Unlike the General Fund and other major governmental funds for which a budget is legally adopted, proprietary funds are not required by GASB standards to record budgets in their accounting systems, nor to present a budgetary comparison schedule. Some governments do, however, require all funds to operate under legally adopted budgets. In such cases GASB standards permit but do not require the integration of budgetary accounts in the manner described in Chapters 3 and 4 for General and special revenue funds.

Illustrative financial statements for internal service funds and enterprise funds are presented later in this chapter, using the Town of Brighton as an example.

INTERNAL SERVICE FUNDS

Although the reason for the establishment of an internal service fund is to improve financial management of scarce resources, it should be stressed that a fund is a fiscal entity as well as an accounting entity; consequently, establishment of a fund is ordinarily subject to legislative approval. The ordinance or other legislative action that authorizes the establishment of an internal service fund should also specify the source or sources of financial resources to be used for fund operations. The original allocation of resources to the fund may be derived from a transfer of assets of another fund, such as the General Fund or an enterprise fund, intended as a *contribution* not to be repaid, or a transfer in the nature of a long-term interfund loan to be repaid by the internal service fund over a period of years. Alternatively, the resources initially allocated to an internal service fund may be acquired from the proceeds of a tax-supported bond issue or by transfer from other governments that anticipate utilizing the services to be rendered by the internal service fund. Since internal service funds are established to improve the management of resources, it is generally considered that their accounting and operations should be maintained on a business basis.

Application of this general truth to a specific case can lead to conflict between managers who wish the freedom to operate the fund in accord with their professional judgment and legislators who wish to exercise considerable control over the decisions of the internal service fund managers. For example, assume that administrators request the establishment of a fund for the purchasing, warehousing, and issuing of supplies used by a number of funds and departments. At the time of the request, since no internal service fund exists, each fund or department must include in its budget its requested appropriation for supplies, its requested appropriation for salaries and wages of personnel engaged in purchasing and handling the supplies, and its requested appropriation for any operating expense or facility costs associated with the supply function. Accordingly, legislators tend to believe that through their control over budgets, they are controlling the investment in supplies and the use of supplies by each fund and department. Legislators may believe that if they approve the establishment of an internal service fund with authority to generate operating revenues sufficient to perpetuate the fund without annual appropriations, the supply function would no longer be subjected to annual legislative budget review and the legislature would "lose control" after the initial allocation of resources to the fund. Administrators are more likely to believe that if an internal service fund did not have authority to generate operating revenues sufficient to perpetuate the fund and to spend those revenues at the discretion of fund management, rather than at the discretion of persons possibly more concerned with reelection than with financial management, little would be gained by establishing the internal service fund.

The two opposing views should be somewhat balanced by the fact that, as shown in Illustration 7–1, the customers of an internal service fund are, by definition, other

ILLUSTRATION 7–1   **Relationship between Appropriations and Internal Service Funds**

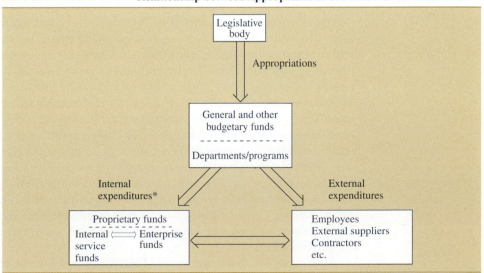

*Internal expenditures are more formally referred to as *interfund services provided and used,* or the term the authors prefer, *internal exchange transactions.*

funds and departments of the government or of other governments. Therefore, each using fund and department must include in its appropriations budget request the justification for the amount to be spent (i.e., paid to the internal service fund) for supplies, so the legislative branch continues to exercise budgetary review over the amount each fund and department budgets for supplies. As shown in Illustration 7–1, departments and programs that require legislative appropriations to expend resources for goods and services should account for purchases of goods or services from internal suppliers (i.e., internal service funds or enterprise funds) in essentially the same manner as goods and services purchased from external suppliers. By setting pricing policies for the internal service fund and policies governing the use and retention of current earnings, the legislature can maintain considerable control over the function performed by the internal service fund but leave the fund managers freedom to operate at their discretion within the policies set by the legislative branch.

One of the more difficult problems to resolve to the satisfaction of persons with opposing views is the establishment of a pricing policy. "Cost" is obviously an incomplete answer: Historical cost of the supplies themselves, whether defined as first-in-first-out, last-in-first-out, average, or specific identification, will not provide sufficient revenue to replace supplies issued if replacement prices have risen since the last purchase or to increase the inventory quantities if the scale of governmental operations is growing. Payroll and other cash operating expenses of the internal service fund must be met; if the internal service fund has received a loan from another fund or another government, prices must be set at a level that will generate cash needed for debt retirement. If the internal service fund is to be operated on a true business basis, it must also be able to finance from its operations the replacement, modernization, and expansion of plant and equipment used in fund operations. Prices charged by the internal service fund, however, should be less than the using funds and departments would have to pay outside vendors for equivalent products and services if the existence and continued operation of the internal service fund is to be justified.

Because of the considerations mentioned in preceding paragraphs, many different approaches to internal service fund operations are found in practice. The illustrations given in the following sections of this chapter assume that the financial objective of an internal service fund is to recover from operating revenues the full cost of operations with enough net income to allow for replacement of inventories in periods of rising prices and enough increase in inventory quantities to meet the needs of using funds and departments whose scale of operations is increasing. The illustrations also assume that net income should be sufficient to allow for replacement of capital assets used by the internal service fund but that expansion of the facilities must be financed through contributions from other funds authorized in their appropriations budgets. Managers of internal service funds must prepare operating plans—budgets—as a management tool. The illustrations assume that the budgets of internal service funds are submitted to the legislative body, or bodies, and to the public for information but not for legal action. Therefore, the budget is not formally recorded in internal service fund accounts. Similarly, managers of businesses must be kept informed of the status of outstanding purchase orders and contracts, but encumbrances need not be recorded in the accounts to accomplish this.

Accounting for an internal service fund concerned with the functions of purchasing, warehousing, and issuing supplies is illustrated in the following section.

ILLUSTRATIVE CASE—SUPPLIES FUND

In prior chapters a "dual track" approach captured transactions using both the modified accrual (governmental funds) and the full accrual (government-wide) basis of accounting. Because the internal service fund uses full accrual accounting, the "dual track" approach is not needed to capture the different basis of accounting, since the basis is the same at the fund level and the government-wide level. However, the internal service fund is generally reported as a part of the Governmental Activities column of the government-wide financial statements. To ensure that double counting of revenues, expenses, and other transactions does not occur, *GASBS 34* requires the elimination of the effect of transactions between governmental funds and internal service funds.[1] For this reason, the "dual track" approach is used in recording the following internal service fund transactions, thus ensuring that double counting does not occur at the government-wide level.

Assume that the administrators of the Town of Brighton obtain approval from the town council to centralize the purchasing, storing, and issuing functions as of January 1, 2008, and to administer and account for these functions in a Supplies Fund. The town's General Fund is to transfer to the new fund its December 31, 2007, inventory of supplies totaling $61,500 and $30,000 in cash to be used for working capital; these transfers are intended as contributions to the Supplies Fund and are not to be repaid (see Chapter 4, illustrative Entry 2). Transfers of this nature are initially recorded by the recipient fund as interfund transfers in, as shown in Entry 1. Since the transaction involves two funds reported in the Governmental Activities column of the government-wide financial statements, no journal entry is made at the government-wide level.

		Debits	Credits
	Supplies Fund:		
1.	Cash	30,000	
	Inventory of Supplies	61,500	
	Interfund Transfers In		91,500

In order to provide cash to be used for acquisition of a building and the equipment needed to handle the supply function efficiently, the town's Water Utility Fund is to provide a long-term interest-free interfund loan of $130,000 to the Supplies Fund. The loan is to be repaid by the Supplies Fund in 20 equal annual installments. Entry 2 illustrates the entry to be made by the Supplies Fund for the receipt of the interfund loan; Water Utility Fund entries for this transaction are illustrated later in this chapter.

	Supplies Fund:		
2a.	Cash	130,000	
	Interfund Loan from Water Utility Fund—Current		6,500
	Interfund Loan from Water Utility Fund—Noncurrent		123,500
	Governmental Activities:		
2b.	Cash	130,000	
	Internal Balances		130,000

[1]GASB *Codification of Governmental Accounting and Financial Reporting Standards, as of June 30, 2005* (Norwalk, CT: GASB, 2005), Sec. 1800.107.

Assume that a satisfactory warehouse building is purchased for $95,000; $25,000 of the purchase price is considered the cost of the land. Necessary warehouse machinery and equipment are purchased for $25,000. Delivery equipment is purchased for $10,000. If the purchases are made for cash, the acquisition of the assets would be recorded in the books of the Supplies Fund as follows:

		Debits	Credits
	Supplies Fund:		
3a.	Land	25,000	
	Buildings	70,000	
	Machinery and Equipment—Warehouse	25,000	
	Equipment—Delivery	10,000	
	Cash		130,000
	Governmental Activities:		
3b.	Land	25,000	
	Buildings	70,000	
	Equipment	35,000	
	Cash		130,000

Additional supplies would be ordered to maintain inventories at a level commensurate with expected usage. During 2008, it is assumed supplies are received and related invoices are approved for payment in the amount of $192,600; the entry needed to record the asset and the liability follows:

		Debits	Credits
	Supplies Fund and Governmental Activities:		
4.	Inventory of Supplies	192,600	
	Vouchers Payable		192,600

The Supplies Fund should account for its inventories on the perpetual inventory basis since the information is needed for proper performance of its primary function. Accordingly, when supplies are issued, the inventory account must be credited for the cost of the supplies issued. Since the using fund will be charged an amount in excess of the inventory carrying value, the receivable and revenue accounts must reflect the selling price. The markup above cost should be determined on the basis of budgeted expenses and other items to be financed from net income, in relation to expected requisitions by using funds. If the budget for the Town of Brighton's Supplies Fund indicates a markup of 35 percent on cost is needed, issues to General Fund departments (see Chapter 4, illustrative Entry 4a) of supplies costing $185,000 would be recorded by the following entries:

		Debits	Credits
	Supplies Fund:		
5a.	Cost of Supplies Issued	185,000	
	Inventory of Supplies		185,000
5b.	Due from General Fund	249,750	
	Billings to Departments		249,750

For the effect of this transaction at the government-wide level see Chapter 4, Entry 4b.

If collections from the General Fund (see Chapter 4, illustrative Entry 5a) during 2008 totaled $249,750, the entry is as follows:

		Debits	Credits
	Supplies Fund:		
6.	Cash	249,750	
	Due from General Fund		249,750

No entry is required at the government-wide level since this transaction is between two funds that are both part of governmental activities.

Assuming that payroll and fringe benefits totaling $55,000 during the year were all paid in cash and distributed to the functional expense accounts in the amounts shown, Entry 7 is appropriate.

	Supplies Fund:		
7a.	Administrative Expenses	11,000	
	Purchasing Expenses	19,000	
	Warehousing Expenses	12,000	
	Delivery Expenses	13,000	
	Cash		55,000
	Governmental Activities:		
7b.	Expenses—General Government	55,000	
	Cash		55,000

If payments on vouchers during the year totaled $164,000, the entry is as follows:

	Supplies Fund and Governmental Activities:		
8.	Vouchers Payable	164,000	
	Cash		164,000

The interfund loan from the Water Utility Fund is to be repaid in 20 equal annual installments; repayment of one installment at the end of 2008 and reclassification of the next installment are recorded:

	Supplies Fund:		
9a.	Interfund Loan from Water Utility Fund—Current	6,500	
	Cash		6,500
9b.	Interfund Loan from Water Utility Fund—Noncurrent	6,500	
	Interfund Loan from Water Utility Fund—Current		6,500
	Governmental Activities:		
9c.	Internal Balances	6,500	
	Cash		6,500

The building used as a warehouse was estimated at the time of purchase to have a remaining useful life of 20 years; the warehouse machinery and equipment were estimated to have useful lives of 10 years, and the delivery equipment to have a useful life of 5 years. If the administrative and clerical office space occupies 10 percent of the area of the warehouse, 10 percent of the depreciation of the warehouse, $350, may be considered administrative expense. Similarly, if the purchasing office occupies 10 percent of the space in the warehouse building, 10 percent of the building depreciation, $350, may be considered purchasing expense. The remainder of the building is devoted to warehousing; therefore, 80 percent of the total building depreciation, $2,800, is to be charged to Warehousing Expenses. This account is also charged $2,500 for machinery and equipment depreciation expense. Delivery Expense is charged $2,000 for depreciation of equipment during the year.

		Debits	Credits
	Supplies Fund:		
10a.	Administrative Expenses	350	
	Purchasing Expenses	350	
	Warehousing Expenses	5,300	
	Delivery Expenses	2,000	
	Allowance for Depreciation—Building		3,500
	Allowance for Depreciation—Machinery and Equipment—Warehouse		2,500
	Allowance for Depreciation—Equipment—Delivery		2,000
	Governmental Activities:		
10b.	Expenses—General Government	8,000	
	Accumulated Depreciation—Building		3,500
	Accumulated Depreciation—Equipment		5,500

Organizations that keep perpetual inventory records must adjust the records periodically to reflect shortages, overages, or out-of-condition stock disclosed by physical inventories. Adjustments to the inventory account are also considered adjustments to the warehousing expenses of the period. This illustrative case assumes that no adjustments were found necessary at year-end.

Assuming that all revenues and expenses applicable to 2008 have been properly recorded by the preceding entries, the operating statement accounts should be closed as of December 31, 2008:

	Supplies Fund:		
11.	Billings to Departments	249,750	
	Cost of Supplies Issued		185,000
	Administrative Expenses		11,350
	Purchasing Expenses		19,350
	Warehousing Expenses		17,300
	Delivery Expenses		15,000
	Excess of Net Billings to Departments over Costs		1,750

The government-wide revenue and expense accounts related to the Supplies Fund will be closed, along with all other governmental activities revenue and expense accounts, in Chapter 9.

Excess of Net Billings to Departments over Costs (or Excess of Costs over Net Billings to Departments, if operations resulted in a loss) is the account title generally considered more descriptive of the fund's results than Income Summary or Current Earnings, the titles commonly found in profit-seeking businesses. No matter the title used for the account summarizing the results of operations for the period, the account should be closed at year-end. The title of the account that records earnings retained in an internal service fund, as well as contribution to equity, are recorded in the account Net Assets—Unrestricted.

		Debits	Credits
	Supplies Fund:		
12.	Excess of Net Billings to Departments over Costs	1,750	
	Net Assets—Unrestricted		1,750

The Interfund Transfers In account is also closed to Net Assets—Unrestricted as shown in Entry 13:

		Debits	Credits
	Supplies Fund:		
13.	Interfund Transfers In	91,500	
	Net Assets—Unrestricted		91,500

The interfund transfer is reported after the Nonoperating Revenues/Expenses section of the statement of revenues, expenses, and changes in fund net assets.

Internal Financial Reporting—Management Use

To ensure sound financial management, each government should prepare a statement of net assets (or balance sheet), a statement of revenues, expenses, and changes in fund net assets, and a statement of cash flows for each internal service fund.

Illustrative Statements

Statement of Net Assets

The statement of net assets for the Supplies Fund of the Town of Brighton as of December 31, 2008, is shown as Illustration 7–2. As of December 31, 2008, the Supplies Fund investment in capital assets of $122,000 is less than the balance of the interfund loan of $123,500 ($117,000 long-term liability plus $6,500 current portion due within one year). Thus, there is no investment in capital assets to report. There also are no assets restricted as to use by external resource providers or legislative action. As a result, the Supplies Fund has only unrestricted net assets as of December 31, 2008.

Statement of Revenues, Expenses, and Changes in Fund Net Assets

Illustration 7–3 presents a statement of revenues, expenses, and changes in fund net assets for the year ended December 31, 2008, for the Town of Brighton Supplies Fund. Since interfund transfers are not a part of the primary activity of the Supplies Fund, they are shown below operating income.

ILLUSTRATION 7–2

TOWN OF BRIGHTON SUPPLIES FUND
Statement of Net Assets
As of December 31, 2008

Assets			
Current assets:			
Cash			$ 54,250
Inventory of supplies, at average cost			69,100
Total current assets			123,350
Capital assets:			
Land		$25,000	
Building	$70,000		
Less: Allowance for depreciation	3,500	66,500	
Machinery and equipment—warehouse	25,000		
Less: Allowance for depreciation	2,500	22,500	
Equipment—delivery	10,000		
Less: Allowance for depreciation	2,000	8,000	
Total capital assets			122,000
Total assets			245,350
Liabilities			
Current liabilities:			
Vouchers payable			28,600
Current portion of long-term liabilities			6,500
Total current liabilities			35,100
Long-term liabilities:			
Interfund loan from water utility			117,000
Total liabilities			152,100
Net Assets			
Unrestricted			$ 93,250

Statement of Cash Flows

For the statement of cash flows (Illustration 7–4), the transactions of the Supplies Fund recorded in Entries 6, 7a, and 8 are classified as operating activities and are reported in the first section of the statement of cash flows. As required by GASB standards, the statement of cash flows is accompanied by a reconciliation of operating income with the net cash flow from operating activities. The contribution from the General Fund to the Supplies Fund (see Entry 1) is reported in the cash flows from noncapital financing activities section of the statement of cash flows. The transactions recorded in Entries 2a, 3a, and 9a are classified as capital and related financing activities and are reported in that section of the statement of cash flows. During 2008 there were no transactions that would be classified as investing activities.

External Financial Reporting of Internal Service Funds

The financial statements presented in Illustrations 7–2, 7–3, and 7–4 are prepared for internal management purposes. As indicated earlier, for external reporting purposes the Supplies Fund financial information would be reported as a separate column of the

ILLUSTRATION 7–3

TOWN OF BRIGHTON SUPPLIES FUND
Statement of Revenues, Expenses, and Changes in Fund Net Assets
For the Year Ended December 31, 2008

Operating revenues:		
Billings to departments		$249,750
Less: Cost of supplies issued		185,000
Gross margin		64,750
Operating expenses:		
Purchasing expenses	$19,350	
Administrative expenses	11,350	
Warehousing expenses	17,300	
Delivery expenses	15,000	
Total operating expenses		63,000
Operating income		1,750
Interfund transfers in		91,500
Change in net assets		93,250
Net assets—January 1, 2008		–0–
Net assets—December 31, 2008		$ 93,250

statement of net assets—proprietary funds; statement of revenues, expenses, and changes in net assets—proprietary funds; and statement of cash flows—proprietary funds, each of which is prepared for all proprietary funds (see Illustrations 1–10, 1–11, and 1–12 for examples). In the government-wide statement of net assets and statement of activities, internal service fund financial information is, in most cases, "collapsed" into and reported in the Governmental Activities column of both government-wide financial statements.

As shown by the journal entries for the Supplies Fund, collapsing information requires eliminating any interfund activity between a governmental fund and an internal service fund. Thus, under the dual track approach those activities involving a transaction between a governmental fund (General Fund in the Town of Brighton illustration) and an internal service fund (Supplies Fund in the Town of Brighton illustration) are not recorded for governmental activities at the government-wide level.

If a portion of an internal service fund's operating income results from billings to enterprise funds, the *GASBS 34* requirement to report internal service fund financial information in the governmental activities category tends to overstate unrestricted net assets in that category and understate unrestricted net assets in the business-type category. Usually this effect should not be material, particularly if the internal service fund pricing is set to cover approximately the full cost of its operations.

Because internal service fund financial information is reported in most cases in the Governmental Activities column of the government-wide financial statements, the financial information reported in the Business-type Activities column will usually be that for enterprise funds only. If this is the case, there is no need to maintain a separate set of accounting records for the business-type activities at the government-wide level. Rather, the financial records of the enterprise funds can simply be added together for

ILLUSTRATION 7–4

TOWN OF BRIGHTON SUPPLIES FUND
Statement of Cash Flows
For the Year Ended December 31, 2008

Cash Flows from Operating Activities:		
Cash received from customers	$249,750	
Cash paid to employees for services	(55,000)	
Cash paid to suppliers	(164,000)	
Net cash provided by operating activities		$30,750
Cash Flows from Noncapital Financing Activities:		
Interfund transfer from General Fund	30,000	
Net cash provided by noncapital financing activities		30,000
Cash Flows from Capital and Related Financing Activities:		
Advance from water utility fund	130,000	
Partial repayment of advance from water utility fund	(6,500)	
Acquisition of capital assets	(130,000)	
Net cash used for capital and related activities		(6,500)
Net increase in cash and cash equivalents		54,250
Cash and cash equivalents, 1/1/2008		–0–
Cash and cash equivalents, 12/31/2008		$54,250
Reconciliation of Operating Income to Net Cash		
Provided by Operating Activities		
Operating income		$ 1,750
Adjustments:		
Depreciation expense		8,000
Increase in inventory	$ 69,100	
Less contributed inventory	61,500	(7,600)
Increase in vouchers payable		28,600
Net cash provided by operating activities		$30,750

financial reporting purposes at the government-wide level. Any interfund transactions between enterprise funds would be eliminated because they would have no net effect on the overall business-type activities. Enterprise fund accounting and financial reporting are discussed later in this chapter.

Assets Acquired under Lease Agreements

The acquisition of general capital assets under lease agreements is discussed in Chapter 5. Assets for use by proprietary funds may also be acquired under lease agreements. The criteria set forth in *SFAS No. 13* (itemized in Chapter 5) are used to determine whether the lease is an operating lease or a capital lease.

Assets acquired under an operating lease belong to the lessor, not to the internal service fund; accordingly, the annual lease payment is recorded as a rental expense of the internal service fund,[2] and there is no depreciation expense on the assets acquired

---

[2] GASB, *Codification*, Sec. L20.104–108 establishes measurement criteria and recognition criteria for revenues and expenditures/expenses relating to operating leases with scheduled rent increases. This situation is beyond the scope of this text.

under an operating lease agreement. Assets acquired under a capital lease agreement by an internal service fund, or an enterprise fund, should be capitalized by that fund. The amount to be recorded by a proprietary fund as the *cost* of the asset acquired under a capital lease is the lesser of (1) the present value of the rental and other minimum lease payments or (2) the fair value of the leased property. The amount recorded as the cost of the asset is amortized in a manner consistent with the government's normal depreciation policy for owned assets of proprietary funds. The amortization period is restricted to the lease term, unless the lease (1) provides for transfer of title or (2) includes a bargain purchase option, in which case the economic life of the asset becomes the amortization period.

During the lease term, each minimum lease payment by an internal service fund is to be allocated between a reduction of the obligation under the lease and an interest expense in a manner that produces a constant periodic rate of interest on the remaining balance of the obligation. This allocation and other complexities that arise in certain events are described and illustrated in various paragraphs of *SFAS No. 13* and in many intermediate accounting texts. These complexities are beyond the scope of this text.

Internal Service Funds with Manufacturing Activities

The Supplies Fund of the Town of Brighton, for which journal entries and statements are illustrated in a preceding section of this chapter, is responsible for purchasing, storing, and issuing supplies used by other funds and departments of the town. Many states and local governments have funds similar to that of the Town of Brighton. It is also common to find that funds and departments use printing shops, asphalt plants, and other service units that produce a physical product or that facilitate the operations of the other funds and departments by performing maintenance or repair jobs or even performing a temporary financing function.

If an internal service fund performs a continuous process manufacturing operation, its accounting system should provide process cost accounts. If a service fund performs a manufacturing, maintenance, or repair operation on a job-order basis, the fund's accounting system should provide appropriate job-order cost accounts. To the extent that operations, processes, or activities are capable of being standardized, cost standards for materials, direct labor, and overhead should be established; in such cases, the accounting system should provide for the routine measurement and reporting of significant variances from the standards. Cost determination for government services is discussed in Chapter 13 of this text.

Internal Service Funds as Financing Devices

Governments may utilize internal service funds as devices to finance risk management, equipment purchases and operations (including centralized computer operations), and other functions that are facilitated by generating revenues from user charges to cover costs and expenses computed on a full accrual basis. In the case of funds to finance equipment purchases and operations, including the operations of computers owned by the government, an internal service fund can include depreciation and, perhaps, expected increases in the cost of replacing assets, in the charge to the using funds, thus incorporating these costs in current appropriations of governmental funds, rather than budgeting the estimated cost of equipment expected to be replaced. If internal service funds are used to finance equipment purchases and operations, the appropriations and expenditures of governmental funds more nearly approximate costs that would be reported by entities using full accrual accounting than is true under the procedures discussed in Chapters 3 and 4.

GASB has issued accounting and financial reporting standards for risk financing and related insurance activities.[3] Government entities that use internal service funds to account for risk financing activities are required to recognize revenues, claims expenses, and liabilities in essentially the same manner as do public entity risk pools (cooperative groups of government entities joined together to finance risks of loss to property, workers' compensation, employee health care, and similar risks or exposures). Briefly, the internal service fund should recognize a claims expense and a liability when a claim is asserted, it is probable that an asset has been impaired or a liability has been incurred, and the amount of the loss is reasonably estimable; or if an estimable loss has been incurred and it is probable that a claim will be asserted. Reasonably possible (but not probable) loss contingencies, probable losses that are not reasonably measurable, and loss exposure in excess of the accrued liability should be disclosed in the notes to the financial statements. The disclosure should explain the nature of the contingency and an estimate of the possible loss, range of the loss, or that the amount is not estimable.

Internal service fund charges to other funds for risk financing activities should be sufficient to recover the total amount of claim expenses recognized for the period or, alternatively, may be based on an actuarial method so that internal service fund revenues and expenses over time are approximately equal. Charges to other funds may also include a reasonable provision for expected future catastrophe losses. Internal service fund charges to other funds are recognized as revenues by the internal service fund and as expenditures by governmental funds or expenses by proprietary funds. Internal service fund charges in excess of the full cost amount should be reported as a nonoperating transfer by the internal service fund and an other financing use by the other funds. If the internal service fund fails to recover the full cost of claims over a reasonable period of time, the accumulated fund deficit should be charged to the other funds and reported by the other funds as an expenditure or expense, as appropriate.

Dissolution of an Internal Service Fund

When an internal service fund has completed the mission for which it was established or its activity is terminated for any other reason (such as outsourcing the activity to an outside vendor), dissolution must be accomplished. Liquidation may be accomplished in any one of three ways or in combinations thereof: (1) transfer the fund's assets to another fund that will continue the operation as a subsidiary activity, for example, a supply fund becoming a *department* of the General Fund; (2) distribute the fund's assets in kind to another fund or to another government; or (3) convert all its noncash assets to cash and distribute the cash to another fund or other funds. Dissolution of an internal service fund, as for a private enterprise, would proceed by first paying outside creditors, followed by repayment of long-term interfund loans not previously amortized, and, finally, liquidation of remaining net assets. The entire process of dissolution should be conducted according to pertinent law and the discretion of the appropriate legislative body. Net assets contributed by another fund or government logically would revert to the contributor fund or government, but law or other regulations may dictate otherwise. If net assets have been built up from charges in excess of costs, liquidation will follow whatever regulations may govern

[3] GASB, *Codification*, Sec. Po20.

the case; if none exist, the appropriate governing body must decide on the recipient or recipients.

ENTERPRISE FUNDS

Enterprise funds and internal service funds are both classified by the GASB as proprietary funds, although only the enterprise funds are generally reported as part of the Business-type Activities column of the government-wide financial statements. As discussed in the prior section of the chapter, internal service funds are generally reported as part of the Governmental Activities column. Enterprise funds are used by governments to account for services provided to the *general public* on a user charge basis. Under the *GASBS 34* model, a government must report certain activities in an enterprise fund if the following criteria are met.[4]

1. The activity is financed with debt that is secured *solely* by a pledge of the revenues from fees and charges of an activity. [Emphasis added by authors.]
2. Laws or regulations require that the activity's costs of providing services, including capital costs (such as depreciation or debt service), be recovered with fees and charges, rather than with taxes or similar revenues.

These criteria are quite specific regarding when an enterprise fund *must* be used. For example, if debt issued is also backed by the full faith and credit of the government entity, even though it is intended to be repaid from revenues of a particular activity, that activity need not be reported in an enterprise fund. Similarly, if an activity is subsidized by a government's General Fund rather than fully covering its costs of providing services with fees or charges, that activity need not be reported in an enterprise fund. In either of these examples, the government could opt to report the activities in an enterprise fund. However, if governments support the activities *primarily* with general or special revenue sources rather than user charges, accounting for the activities is more appropriate in the General Fund or a special revenue fund.

Since the word *enterprise* is often used as a synonym for "business-type activity," it is logical that enterprise funds should use full accrual accounting and account for all assets used in the production of goods or services offered by the fund. Similarly, if long-term debt is to be serviced by the fund, the fund does the accounting for the debt.

The most common examples of governmental enterprises are public utilities, notably water and sewer utilities. Electric and gas utilities, transportation systems, airports, ports, hospitals, toll bridges, produce markets, parking lots, parking garages, liquor stores, and public housing projects are other examples frequently found. Services of the types mentioned are generally accounted for by enterprise funds because they are intended to be largely self-supporting.

Almost every type of enterprise operated by a government has its counterpart in the private sector. In order to take advantage of the work done by regulatory agencies and trade associations to develop useful accounting information systems for the investor-owned enterprises, *it is recommended that governmentally owned enterprises use the accounting structures developed for investor-owned enterprises of the*

---

[4] GASB *Codification*, Sec. 1300.109.

same nature.[5] Budgetary accounts should be used only if required by law. The accounting for debt service and construction activities of a governmental enterprise occur within the enterprise fund rather than by separate debt service and capital projects funds. Thus, the financial statements of enterprise funds are self-contained, and creditors, legislators, or the general public can evaluate the performance of a governmental enterprise on the same bases as they can the performance of investor-owned enterprises in the same industry.

By far the most numerous and important enterprise services rendered by local governments are public utilities. In this chapter, therefore, the example used is that of a water utility fund.

ILLUSTRATIVE CASE—WATER UTILITY FUND

The statement of net assets as of December 31, 2007, for the Town of Brighton Water Utility Fund is shown in Illustration 7–5. The statement appears fairly conventional, but terminology peculiar to utilities warrants discussion prior to proceeding to the illustrative transactions for the year ending December 31, 2008. Part of the difference in terminology relates to the fact that the Water Utility Fund is part of a regulated industry. As such, the primary regulatory bodies, the National Association of Regulatory Utility Commissioners (NARUC) and Federal Energy Regulatory Commission (FERC), influence the accounting for utilities.

Current and Accrued Assets

Cash, and Materials and Supplies shown in Illustration 7–5 in the Current and Accrued Assets section are not peculiar to utilities and need not be discussed here. The other two asset accounts in this section—Customer Accounts Receivable and Accrued Utilities Revenues—are related. The former represents billings to customers that are outstanding at year-end (and are reduced, as one would expect, by an accumulated provision for uncollectibles). The latter results from the fact that utilities generally prepare billings to customers on the basis of meter readings, and it is not practical for utilities to read all meters simultaneously at year-end and bill all customers as of that time. Utilities that meter their service make extensive use of cycle billing, which, in substance, consists of billing part of their customers each day instead of billing by calendar months. Under this plan, meter reading is a continuous day-by-day operation, with billings following shortly after the filing of the meter readers' reports. Individual

[5] *GASBS 20* and *GASBS 34* provide guidance on business-type accounting and financial reporting for proprietary activities. This guidance clarifies the authoritative status of FASB pronouncements in determining generally accepted accounting principles (GAAP) for proprietary activities given the GAAP hierarchy provided in *Statement on Auditing Standards No. 69*, "The Meaning of 'Present Fairly in Conformity with Generally Accepted Accounting Principles' in the Independent Auditor's Report" (AICPA, 1992). *GASBS 20* gives governments an option between two accounting and financial reporting approaches for proprietary funds. The first approach requires consistent use of all GASB pronouncements and applicable pronouncements of FASB and its predecessors (Accounting Principles Board and Committee on Accounting Procedure) issued on or before November 30, 1989, unless those pronouncements conflict with or contradict GASB pronouncements. The second approach requires consistent use of all GASB pronouncements and all applicable pronouncements (both before and after November 30, 1989) of FASB and its predecessors unless those pronouncements conflict with or contradict GASB pronouncements. Thus, under the first approach, unless GASB directs otherwise, governments are not required to change their accounting procedures if FASB issues a standard that supersedes or amends a standard issued on or before November 30, 1989. This date (November 30, 1989) is significant as the date the Financial Accounting Foundation resolved a conflict over jurisdiction of the FASB and GASB.

meters are read on approximately the same day each month, or every other month, so that each bill covers approximately the same number of days of usage. Cycle billing eliminates the heavy peak load of accounting and clerical work that results from uniform billing on a calendar month basis. It does, however, result in a sizeable amount of unbilled receivables on any given date. Thus, in order to state assets and sales properly, accrual of unbilled receivables (Accrued Utilities Revenues, in regulatory terminology) is required as of the financial statement date.[6]

Restricted Assets

The section following Current and Accrued Assets in Illustration 7–5 is captioned Restricted Assets, the caption most commonly used when the use of assets is restricted by contractual agreements or legal requirements. Some governments that use regulatory terminology report restricted assets of utilities under the broader caption, Other Property and Investments. Other Property and Investments may include, in addition to restricted assets, the carrying value of property not being used for utility purposes or being held for future utility use.

Cash and Investments are the only two items reported under the Restricted Assets caption of the balance sheet shown in Illustration 7–5. Those items are restricted for return of customer deposits and for retirement of revenue bonds pursuant to the bond covenants. The amount of assets segregated, $562,600, is offset by liabilities currently payable from restricted assets (in the case of the Town of Brighton, customer deposits of $23,700) and restrictions of net assets (in this case, restricted for payment of debt service, $538,900). This *fund within a fund* approach permits segregation of assets, related liabilities, and restricted net assets within a single enterprise fund. Net assets should be restricted in the amount of the net assets of each restricted "fund" within the enterprise fund, as shown in Illustration 7–5. Other items commonly reported in the Restricted Assets section include assets set aside to fund depreciation for capital improvements or grants and contributions restricted for capital acquisition or improvement.

Utility Plant

Utility Plant in Service

Utility Plant in Service is a control account, supported in whatever detail is required by regulatory agencies and by management needs. For example, water utilities commonly have six subcategories of plant assets: intangible plant, source of supply plant, pumping plant, water treatment plant, transmission and distribution plant, and general plant. Each of the six subcategories is supported by appropriate subsidiary accounts. For example, intangible plant consists of the costs of organization, franchises and consents, and any other intangible costs necessary and valuable to the conduct of utility operations. Source of supply plant consists of land and land rights; structures and improvements; collecting and impounding reservoirs; lake, river, and other intakes; wells and springs; infiltration galleries and tunnels; supply mains; and other water source plant. Each of the accounts within each subcategory is supported by necessary subsidiary records for each individual asset detailing its description, location, cost, date of acquisition, estimated useful life, salvage value, depreciation charges, and any other information

[6] Some governments use the same or a similar chart of accounts for utilities as those of regulated profit-seeking enterprises in the same industry. The principal regulatory bodies are the National Association of Regulatory Utility Commissioners (NARUC), an association of state regulatory utility commissioners, and the Federal Energy Regulatory Commission (FERC), which has jurisdiction over certain utilities in interstate commerce.

ILLUSTRATION 7–5

TOWN OF BRIGHTON WATER UTILITY FUND
Statement of Net Assets
As of December 31, 2007

Assets

Current and accrued assets:

Cash		$ 126,000
Customer accounts receivable	$69,000	
Less: Accumulated provision for uncollectibles	2,900	66,100
Accrued utilities revenues		14,800
Materials and supplies		28,700
Total current and accrued assets		$ 235,600
Restricted assets:		
Cash	6,600	
Investments	556,000	562,600
Utility plant:		
Utility plant in service	3,291,825	
Less: Accumulated depreciation	440,325	
Utility plant—net	2,851,500	
Construction work in progress	125,000	
Net utility plant		2,976,500
Total assets		3,774,700

Liabilities

Current liabilities:		
Accounts payable	33,200	
Customer advances for construction	21,000	
Total current liabilities		54,200
Liabilities payable from restricted assets:		
Customer deposits		23,700
Long-term liabilities:		
Revenue bonds payable (net of unamortized discount of $5,300)		1,744,700
Total liabilities		1,822,600

Net Assets

Invested in capital assets, net of related debt	1,231,800
Restricted for payment of debt service	538,900
Unrestricted	181,400
Total net assets	$1,952,100

needed for management planning and control, regulatory agency reports, financial statements, or special reports to creditors.

Construction Work in Progress

The other utility plant item shown on the statement of net assets, Illustration 7–5, is Construction Work in Progress. This account represents the accumulated costs of work orders for projects that will result in items reportable as utility plant when completed and is supported by the work orders for projects in progress. Each work order, in turn, is supported by documents supporting payments to contractors and to suppliers or supporting charges for materials, labor, and overhead allocable to the project. Unlike self-constructed general capital assets, GASB requires interest capitalization for self-constructed assets of proprietary funds, except those constructed with general long-term debt that will be repaid from resources of governmental activities.[7]

Current Liabilities

Items commonly found in the Current Liabilities section of a utility statement of net assets are shown under that caption in Illustration 7–5. Accounts Payable needs no comment here. The other item, **Customer Advances for Construction,** results from utilities' practice of requiring customers to advance to the utility a sizeable portion of the estimated cost of construction projects to be undertaken by the utility at the request of the customer. If the advances are to be refunded, either wholly or in part or applied against billings for service rendered after completion of the project, they are classified as shown in Illustration 7–5. When a customer is refunded the entire amount to which he or she is entitled according to the agreement or rule under which the advance was made, the balance retained by the utility, if any, is reported as Contributions from Customers in the statement of revenues, expenses, and changes in net assets. Other items commonly reported under Current Liabilities include accrued expenses, amounts due to other funds, and current portions of long-term liabilities. Some governments also report customer deposits under the Current Liabilities caption.[8]

Liabilities Payable from Restricted Assets

Liabilities payable from restricted assets should be displayed separately from current liabilities as shown in Illustration 7–5. In addition to customer deposits, the current portion of revenue bonds payable, if any, would be reported here since restricted assets have been set aside for that purpose. The Town of Brighton follows the common practice of most utilities and requires all new customers to deposit a sum of money with the utility as security for the payment of bills. In many, but not all, jurisdictions, utilities are required to pay interest on customer deposits at a nominal rate. Regulatory authorities or local policy may require utilities to refund the deposits, and interest, after a specified period of time if the customer has paid all bills on time. The utility may be required, as was the Town of Brighton Water Utility Fund, to segregate cash or investments in an amount equal to the liability for Customer Deposits. Customer Advances for Construction are contractually different from Customer Deposits and are less likely to be reported separately as restricted assets and liabilities unless agreements with developers make it necessary to restrict assets for this purpose.

Long-Term Liabilities

Bonds are the customary form of long-term liabilities. Bonds issued by a utility are usually secured by the pledge of certain portions of the utility's revenue, the exact terms of the pledge varying with individual cases; bonds of this nature are called **revenue bonds.** Some utility bonds are secured not only by a pledge of a certain portion of the utility's revenues but also by an agreement on the part of the town's or city's general government to subsidize the utility in any year in which its normal revenue is

---

[7] GASB requires application of FASB *Statement No. 34,* "Capitalization of Interest Cost," as amended.
[8] Generally, customer deposits should be reported as Liabilities Payable from Restricted Assets, a special category of current liabilities, as explained in the following section.

inadequate for compliance with the terms of the bond indenture. Other utility bonds carry the pledge of the government entity's full faith and credit, although the intent is to service them from utility revenues rather than general taxes. The latter are, therefore, technically **general obligation bonds.** GASB standards require that general obligation bonds intended to be serviced from utility revenues be reported as a liability of the enterprise fund. Similarly, special assessment debt may be assumed by an enterprise fund if the assets constructed by special assessment financing are used in enterprise fund operations.

Governmentally owned utilities may have received long-term interfund loans from the government's General Fund or other funds. Also, enterprises may acquire assets under a capital lease arrangement. The portion of interfund loans, required lease payments, or bond or other debt issues to be paid within one year from the statement of net assets date should be reported as a current liability; the remainder is properly reported in the Long-Term Liabilities section of the utility statement of net assets. Long-term bonds payable should be reported net of unamortized discount or premium, as shown in Illustration 7–5, or the unamortized discount or premium can be reported as an offset against bonds payable at par on the statement of net assets.

Net Assets

As discussed earlier in the chapter, proprietary funds report using three net asset categories: invested in capital assets, net of related debt; restricted; and unrestricted. The three categories of net assets for the utility fund are shown in Illustration 7–5. Restrictions may be placed by law, regulation, or contractual agreement with creditors or other outside parties. Illustration 7–5 shows a typical restriction: a sinking fund created pursuant to a bond indenture for repayment of revenue bond principal. Unrestricted net assets represent the residual amount of net assets after segregating investment in capital assets, net of related debt, and restricted net assets.

ILLUSTRATIVE ACCOUNTING FOR A WATER UTILITY FUND

The discussion in preceding pages concerning the statement of net asset accounts of a water utility includes by implication the essential characteristics of accounting necessary for both governmentally owned utilities and investor-owned utilities. In this section, accounting for characteristic transactions of a utility fund is illustrated in general journal entry format for the year following the statement of net assets presented in Illustration 7–5.

It is assumed that the Town of Brighton is located in a state that permits enterprise funds to operate without formal legal approval of their budgets. Utility or other enterprise management must prepare operating budgets and capital expenditure budgets as management tools. For the illustrative case, it is assumed that the budgets are submitted to the town administrators, the town legislative body, and the public for information, not for legal action. Accordingly, the budget is not formally recorded in enterprise fund accounts. While utility management must be informed periodically of the status of outstanding construction contracts and purchase orders, encumbrances need not be recorded in the accounts in order to accomplish this.

The nature of the Accrued Utilities Revenues account was explained previously in the section "Current and Accrued Assets." In the year following the one for which the statement of net assets is shown, it is not feasible when customers' bills are prepared to determine whether a portion of the bill has been accrued and, if so, in what amount. The simplest procedure, therefore, is to reverse the accrual entry as of the start of the

new fiscal year. Assuming that the entire December 31, 2007, Town of Brighton Water Utility Fund revenues accrual has been credited to Sales of Water, the following entry is appropriate as of January 1, 2008:

		Debits	Credits
1.	Sales of Water	14,800	
	Accrued Utility Revenues.		14,800

Earlier in this chapter, the establishment of a Supplies Fund by the Town of Brighton as of January 1, 2008, was illustrated. The Water Utility Fund advanced $130,000 to the Supplies Fund as a long-term loan. The entry by the Supplies Fund is illustrated in Entry 2a in the "Illustrative Case—Supplies Fund" section earlier in this chapter; the corresponding entry in the Water Utility Fund would be:

2.	Interfund Loan to Supplies Fund—Noncurrent	130,000	
	Cash		130,000

When utility customers are billed during the year, appropriate revenue accounts are credited. Assuming that during 2008 the total bills to nongovernmental customers amounted to $696,000, bills to the Town of Brighton General Fund amounted to $30,000, and all revenue was from the sale of water, the following entry summarizes the events:

3.	Customer Accounts Receivable.	696,000	
	Due from General Fund	30,000	
	Sales of Water		726,000

If collections on receivables from nongovernmental water customers totaled $680,000, Entry 4 is needed:

4.	Cash	680,000	
	Customer Accounts Receivable.		680,000

Materials and supplies in the amount of $138,000 were purchased during the year by the Water Utility Fund. The liability is recorded as:

5.	Materials and Supplies	138,000	
	Accounts Payable		138,000

Materials and supplies chargeable to the accounts itemized in the following entry were issued during the year.

		Debits	Credits
6.	Source of Supply Expenses	18,000	
	Pumping Expenses	21,000	
	Water Treatment Expenses	24,000	
	Transmission and Distribution Expenses	13,000	
	Construction Work in Progress	66,000	
	Materials and Supplies		142,000

Payrolls for the year were chargeable to the accounts shown in the following entry. Tax Collections Payable is the account provided in the NARUC and FERC systems to report the amount of taxes collected by the utility through payroll deductions or otherwise pending transmittal of such taxes to the proper taxing authority. Taxes Accrued is the account provided in the NARUC and FERC systems to report the liability for taxes that are the expense of the utility, such as the employer's share of social security taxes. The following entry assumes that the employer's share of social security taxes is charged to the same accounts that the employees' gross earnings are; it also assumes that checks have been issued for employees' net earnings.

7.	Source of Supply Expenses	8,200	
	Pumping Expenses	15,700	
	Water Treatment Expenses	17,500	
	Transmission and Distribution Expenses	76,250	
	Customer Accounts Expenses	96,550	
	Sales Expenses	17,250	
	Administrative and General Expenses	83,150	
	Construction Work in Progress	30,400	
	Taxes Accrued		13,800
	Tax Collections Payable		51,750
	Cash		279,450

Bond interest in the amount of $105,000 was paid; the bonds were issued to finance the acquisition of utility plant assets. Amortization of debt discount amounted to $530.

8.	Interest on Long-Term Debt	105,530	
	Unamortized Discount		530
	Cash		105,000

Bond interest in the amount of $12,900 was properly capitalized as part of construction work in progress during the year. (The Town of Brighton does not impute interest on its own resources during construction.)

9.	Construction Work in Progress	12,900	
	Interest on Long-Term Debt		12,900

Construction projects on which costs totaled $220,000 were completed and the assets placed in service are recorded:

		Debits	Credits
10.	Utility Plant in Service.	220,000	
	Construction Work in Progress		220,000

Collection efforts on bills totaling $3,410 were discontinued. The customers owing the bills had paid deposits totaling $2,140 to the water utility; the deposits were applied to the bills, and the unpaid remainder was charged to Accumulated Provision for Uncollectible Accounts (Entry 11a). Restricted assets (cash) is reduced by $2,140, the amount of the decrease in Customer Deposits (Entry 11b).

		Debits	Credits
11a.	Customer Deposits.	2,140	
	Accumulated Provision for Uncollectible Accounts	1,270	
	Customer Accounts Receivable		3,410
11b.	Cash	2,140	
	Cash—Customer Deposits		2,140

Customers' deposits amounting to $1,320 were refunded by check to customers discontinuing service (see Entry 12a). Deposits totaling $2,525 were received from new customers (see Entry 12b).

		Debits	Credits
12a.	Customer Deposits.	1,320	
	Cash—Customer Deposits		1,320
12b.	Cash—Customer Deposits	2,525	
	Customer Deposits		2,525

Customers' advances for construction in the amount of $14,000 were applied to their water bills; in accord with the agreement with the customers and NARUC recommendations, the remainder of the advances was transferred to Capital Contributions from Customers.

		Debits	Credits
13.	Customers Advances for Construction	21,000	
	Customer Accounts Receivable		14,000
	Capital Contributions from Customers		7,000

Payments of accounts payable for materials and supplies used in operations totaled $67,200, and payment of accounts payable for materials used in construction totaled $66,000. Payments of taxes accrued amounted to $13,500, and payments of tax collections payable amounted to $50,000.

		Debits	Credits
14.	Accounts Payable..................	133,200	
	Taxes Accrued	13,500	
	Tax Collections Payable..........	50,000	
	Cash..........................		196,700

The Water Utility Fund agreed to pay $25,000 to the town General Fund as a payment in lieu of property taxes. The entry in the General Fund is illustrated in Chapter 4 (see Chapter 4, illustrative Entry 24a). The following entry records the event in the accounts of the Water Utility Fund:

		Debits	Credits
15.	Payment in Lieu of Taxes..........	25,000	
	Due to General Fund		25,000

During the year, interest amounting to $44,500 in cash was received on restricted investments. The amount $1,375 is allocable to investments of customer deposit assets and is unrestricted as to use; the remaining $43,125 adds to the amount restricted for revenue bond repayment.

		Debits	Credits
16a.	Cash	1,375	
	Cash—Bond Repayment......................	43,125	
	Interest and Dividend Income		44,500
16b.	Net Assets—Unrestricted	43,125	
	Net Assets—Restricted for Bond Repayment..............		43,125

At year-end, entries to record depreciation expense, the provision for uncollectible accounts, and unbilled customer accounts receivable should be made as illustrated by Entry 17. In accord with regulatory terminology, Customer Account Expenses instead of Bad Debts Expense is debited for the amount added to Accumulated Provision for Uncollectible Accounts. Amounts are assumed.

		Debits	Credits
17.	Depreciation Expense	102,750	
	Customer Accounts Expenses...........................	3,980	
	Accrued Utility Revenues	15,920	
	Accumulated Provision for Depreciation of Utility Plant........		102,750
	Accumulated Provision for Uncollectible Accounts		3,980
	Sales of Water		15,920

In accord with the revenue bond indenture, $100,000 of unrestricted cash was invested in U.S. government securities for eventual retirement of revenue bonds. Net assets are restricted in an amount equal to the increase in restricted assets. In addition, investments totaling $40,000 were made from restricted cash for eventual bond repayment.

		Debits	Credits
18a.	Investments—Bond Repayment	140,000	
	Cash		100,000
	Cash—Bond Repayment		40,000
18b.	Net Assets—Unrestricted	100,000	
	Net Assets—Restricted for Bond Repayment		100,000

Toward the end of 2008, the supplies fund paid its first installment of $6,500 to the water utility fund as a partial repayment of the long-term advance. Entry 9a of the illustrative entries for the supply fund shown earlier in this chapter illustrates the effect of the supplies fund on the accounts. The effect on the accounts of the water utility fund is recorded by the following entry:

19.	Cash	6,500	
	Interfund Loan to Supplies Fund—Noncurrent		6,500

Nominal accounts for the year were closed:

20.	Sales of Water	727,120	
	Capital Contributions from Customers	7,000	
	Interest and Dividend Income	44,500	
	Source of Supply Expenses		26,200
	Pumping Expenses		36,700
	Water Treatment Expenses		41,500
	Transmission and Distribution Expenses		89,250
	Customer Account Expenses		100,530
	Sales Expenses		17,250
	Administrative and General Expenses		83,150
	Interest on Long-Term Debt		92,630
	Payment in Lieu of Taxes		25,000
	Depreciation Expense		102,750
	Net Assets—Unrestricted		163,660

In addition, Net Assets—Invested in Capital Assets, Net of Related Debt, would be decreased for depreciation and amortization of the debt discount and increased or decreased, as appropriate, for the net change in utility plant during the year. Decreases are recorded as a debit to Net Assets—Invested in Capital Assets, Net of Related Debt and as a credit to Net Assets—Unrestricted. The reverse entry would be required for increases in capital asset balances.

Illustrative Statements

Statement of Net Assets

The statement of net assets for a water utility, and definitions of certain statement of net assets categories and items peculiar to regulated utilities, are explained at length in the sections of this chapter preceding the illustrative entries. The statement of net

ILLUSTRATION 7–6

TOWN OF BRIGHTON WATER UTILITY FUND
Statement of Net Assets
As of December 31, 2008

Assets

Current and accrued assets:

Cash		$ 4,865	
Customer accounts receivable	$67,590		
Less: Accumulated provision for uncollectibles	5,610	61,980	
Accrued utilities revenues		15,920	
Due from General Fund		5,000	
Materials and supplies		24,700	
Total current and accrued assets			$ 112,465
Restricted assets:			
Cash		8,790	
Investments		696,000	704,790
Utility plant:			
Utility plant in service		3,511,825	
Less: Accumulated depreciation		543,075	
Utility plant—net		2,968,750	
Construction work in progress		14,300	
Net utility plant			2,983,050
Other noncurrent assets:			
Interfund loan to supplies fund			123,500
Total assets			3,923,805

Liabilities

Current liabilities:			
Accounts payable		38,000	
Taxes accrued		300	
Tax collection payable		1,750	
Total current liabilities			40,050
Liabilities payable from restricted assets:			
Customer deposits			22,765
Long-term liabilities:			
Revenue bonds payable (net of unamortized discount of $4,770)			1,745,230
Total liabilities			1,808,045

Net Assets

Invested in capital assets, net of related debt			1,237,820
Restricted for payment of debt service			682,025
Unrestricted			195,915
Total net assets			$2,115,760

assets of the Town of Brighton Water Utility Fund as of December 31, 2008, is shown as Illustration 7–6. Note the amount due to the General Fund is offset against the amount due from that fund, and only the net amount of the receivable, $5,000, is shown as an asset.

ILLUSTRATION 7–7

TOWN OF BRIGHTON WATER UTILITY FUND
Statement of Revenues, Expenses, and Changes in Net Assets
For the Year Ended December 31, 2008

Utility operating revenue:		
Sales of water (net of $3,980 provision for bad debt)		$ 723,140
Operating expenses:		
Source of supply expenses	$ 26,200	
Pumping expenses	36,700	
Water treatment expenses	41,500	
Transmission and distribution expenses	89,250	
Customer account expenses	96,550	
Sales expenses	17,250	
Administrative and general expenses	83,150	
Depreciation expense	102,750	
Payment in lieu of taxes	25,000	
Total operating expenses		518,350
Utility operating income		204,790
Nonoperating income and deductions:		
Interest and dividend revenue	(44,500)	
Interest on long-term debt	92,630	
Total nonoperating income and deductions		48,130
Income before contributions		156,660
Capital contributions from customers		7,000
Change in net assets		163,660
Total net assets, January 1, 2008		1,952,100
Total net assets, December 31, 2008		$2,115,760

Operating Statement

The results of the operations of the Town of Brighton's Water Utility Fund for the year ended December 31, 2008, are shown in Illustration 7–7, the statement of revenues, expenses, and changes in net assets. The classifications used in the statement are consistent with NARUC and FERC recommendations.

Statement of Cash Flows

GASB standards require that a statement of cash flows be prepared for all proprietary funds as part of a full set of annual financial statements. As discussed earlier in this chapter, GASB standards for preparation of a cash flow statement differ from FASB standards, the main difference being that GASB standards specify four major categories of cash flows rather than three. The statement of cash flows for the Town of Brighton for the year ended December 31, 2008 (Illustration 7–8), utilizes only three of the four categories of cash flows since the town had no cash flows from noncapital financing activities. The section *Cash Flows from Operating Activities* (Illustration 7–8) was provided by receipts from customers (Entry 4) and the net increase in refundable customer deposits (Entries 12a and 12b). Note that the application of customer deposits to pay overdue bills (Entries 11a and 11b) has no effect on total cash and cash equivalents. Cash from operating activities was used to pay employees

ILLUSTRATION 7–8

TOWN OF BRIGHTON WATER UTILITY FUND
Statement of Cash Flows
For the Year Ended December 31, 2008

Cash Flows from Operating Activities:

Cash received from customers	$680,000
Cash provided from customer deposits	1,205
Cash paid to employees for services	(312,550)
Cash paid to suppliers	(67,200)
Net cash provided by operating activities	301,455

Cash Flows from Capital and Related Financing Activities:

Acquisition and construction of capital assets	(96,400)
Interest paid on long-term bonds	(105,000)
Net cash used for capital and related financing activities	(201,400)

Cash Flows from Investing Activities:

Interest and dividend income	44,500
Purchases of restricted investments	(140,000)
Interfund loan	(123,500)
Net cash used for investing activities	(219,000)
Net decrease in cash and cash equivalents	(118,945)
Cash and cash equivalents—January 1, 2008	132,600
Cash and cash equivalents—December 31, 2008	$ 13,655

Reconciliation of Cash and Cash Equivalents to the Balance Sheet

	End of Year	Beginning of Year
Cash and cash equivalents in current and accrued assets	$ 4,865	$126,000
Restricted cash and cash equivalents	8,790	6,600
Total cash and cash equivalents	$ 13,655	$132,600

Reconciliation of Utility Operating Income to Net Cash Provided by Operating Activities

Utility operating income		$204,790
Adjustments:		
Depreciation expense	$102,750	
Increase in accounts payable	4,800	
Increase in accrued liabilities	2,050	
Decrease in customer deposits	(935)	
Decrease in inventories	4,000	
Increase in interfund receivables	(5,000)	
Increase in accrued receivables	(1,120)	
Decrease in customer accounts receivable	4,120	
Customer advances applied to customer receivables	(14,000)	
Total adjustments		96,665
Net cash provided by operating activities		$301,455

(Entries 7 and 14). As suggested in the GASB *Implementation Guide* on reporting cash flows,[9] all employee-related items (in this case Taxes Accrued and Tax Collections Payable) have been added to the amount actually paid to employees. Payroll taxes and fringe benefits may be included in a separate line, called cash payments for taxes, duties, fines, and other fees or penalties, if significant in amount. Cash paid to employees for services in the amount of $312,550 is calculated as the net cash paid directly to employees, $279,450, less $30,400 capitalized as Construction Work in Progress (Entry 7) plus $63,500 paid for Taxes Accrued and Tax Collections Payable (Entry 14). Finally, cash from operating activities was used to pay suppliers (Entry 14). Although suppliers were paid $133,200 in total, only $67,200 of this amount applied to operating activities.

The section *Cash Flows from Capital and Related Activities* in Illustration 7–8 shows two uses of cash. The first item, acquisition and construction of capital assets, is calculated as the sum of $30,400 (Entry 7) and $66,000 (Entry 14). The other item, interest paid on long-term bonds, reflects bond interest in the amount of $105,000 paid in cash (Entry 8).

The *Cash Flows from Investing Activities* section shows cash provided by interest and dividend income (Entry 16a), cash used to purchase investments (Entry 18a), and cash used to acquire an interfund loan (Entries 2 and 19).

As shown in Illustration 7–8, two reconciliations are required. The first reconciliation is necessary because the Town of Brighton's Statement of Cash Flows reports changes in *total* cash and cash equivalents, whereas the balance sheet shows two components of cash and cash equivalents: that included in Current and Accrued Assets and that included in Restricted Assets, respectively.[10] GASB standards also require a reconciliation of operating income to net cash provided by operating activities.

External Financial Reporting of Enterprise Funds

As shown in Illustrations 1–4 and 1–5, the totals for all enterprise funds, with interfund transactions between enterprise funds eliminated, are reported in the Business-type Activities columns of the government-wide financial statements. Governments must also prepare three fund financial statements for their major enterprise funds (see the Glossary for a definition of major funds) and the total of their internal service funds. These statements are the statement of net assets (or balance sheet), statement of revenues, expenses, and changes in fund net assets, and statement of cash flows. Illustrative proprietary fund statements are presented in Illustrations 1–10, 1–11, and 1–12. As those statements show, a separate column is provided for internal service funds. The amounts shown in this column are the totals for all internal service funds, since major fund reporting does not apply to the internal service funds.

Regulatory Accounting Principles (RAP)

Investor-owned utilities, as well as governmentally owned utilities in some states, are required to report in a prescribed manner to state regulatory commissions. Electric and certain other utilities subject to the Federal Power Act must also file reports with the FERC. As mentioned in footnote 6, both NARUC and FERC prescribe charts of accounts and uniform financial statement formats for reporting to regulatory agencies. Even though the Town of Brighton follows GAAP rather than **regulatory accounting**

---

[9] Governmental Accounting Standards Board, *Comprehensive Implementation Guide—2004* (Norwalk, CT, 2004), p. 105.

[10] Ibid., p. 28.

principles (RAP) in preparing its financial statements, the town uses some of the chart of accounts and some of the financial statement captions provided in regulatory publications. The illustrative financial statements shown earlier in this chapter are typical of those for water funds included in comprehensive annual financial reports.

For utilities that are required to report to a state rate regulatory commission or the FERC, accounting and reporting procedures under RAP are quite different from GAAP. Because plant assets and long-term debt are customarily a dominant share of the total assets and total debt of utilities and current assets and current liabilities are relatively insignificant in amount, the regulatory balance sheet format displays plant assets before current assets and long-term debt before current liabilities. In Illustration 7–5, for example, Utility Plant—Net amounts to almost 79 percent of total assets, and long-term debt is almost 96 percent of total debt.

Under regulatory reporting, Utility Plant in Service is stated at original cost. Original cost is a regulatory concept that differs from historical cost, a concept commonly used in accounting for assets of nonregulated businesses. In essence, **historical cost** is the amount paid for an asset by its present owner. In contrast, **original cost** is *the cost to the owner who first devoted the property to public service*. When a regulated utility purchases plant assets from another utility, it must record in its accounts the amounts shown in the accounts of the seller for the utility plant purchased and for the related accumulated depreciation. Any premium paid by the present owner over and above such cost less depreciation is in the general nature of payments for goodwill by nonutility enterprises. But utilities enjoy monopoly privileges and are subject to corresponding restrictions. One of the restrictions is that earnings shall not exceed a fair rate of return. Since goodwill is the capitalized value of excess earnings, utilities can have no goodwill (in the accounting sense). Premium on plant purchased is therefore accounted for as **Utility Plant Acquisition Adjustments.** The amount of acquisition adjustment capitalized is amortized over a period of time determined by the appropriate regulatory body; accumulated amortization is disclosed in the Accumulated Provision for Amortization of Utility Plant Acquisition Adjustments account.

For construction work in progress the Uniform System of Accounts for water, sewer, gas, and electric utilities published by NARUC contains a section on Utility Plant Instructions that, among other items, specifies the components of construction cost. Generally, the components are in agreement with those listed in any intermediate accounting text. One item long recognized in utility accounting and accepted by the FASB is the Allowance for Funds Used during Construction (AFUDC).[11]

AFUDC includes the net cost for the period of construction of borrowed funds used for construction purposes *and a reasonable rate on other funds so used*. Thus, interest paid, accrued, or imputed during the period of construction of a utility plant asset is included as a cost of the asset. Interest paid or accrued, known as the *debt component* of AFUDC, is deducted from Interest on Long-Term Debt in the Other Income and Deductions section of the utility's operating statement. This practice accomplishes two things: (1) It discloses to financial statement readers the amount of interest that was capitalized during the year and (2) it reduces the reported interest expense, thus increasing reported net income for the period (presumably slowing down utilities' requests for rate increases). If construction is financed, in part, by use of resources

---

[11] Financial Accounting Standards Board, *Statement of Financial Accounting Standards No. 71*, "Accounting for the Effects of Certain Types of Regulation" (Norwalk, CT, 1982), par. 15, as amended by *Statement of Financial Accounting Standards No. 90* (Norwalk, CT, 1986), par. 8, and *Statement of Financial Accounting Standards No. 92* (Norwalk, CT, 1987), pars. 8 and 9.

generated by operations of the utility, regulatory authorities allow interest to be imputed on these "equity" funds and capitalized. Since imputed interest is not viewed by accountants as an expense, it is offset by reporting the *equity component* of AFUDC as nonoperating income.

Other asset sections of balance sheets prepared in the regulatory format are Other Property and Investments and Deferred Debits. One item usually reported in the former section is Special Funds, which is similar to the Restricted Assets section of the GAAP–format statement of net assets shown in Illustrations 7–5 and 7–6. Thus, as mentioned previously, Other Property and Investments is broader in scope than Restricted Assets and may contain items other than restricted assets. One item typically reported under the Deferred Debits caption is Unamortized Debt Discount and Expense, which under GAAP is reported as an offset to the related long-term debt.

Accounting for Nonutility Enterprises

Early in this chapter it was stressed that each governmentally owned enterprise should follow the accounting and financial reporting standards developed for investor-owned enterprises in the same industry. Generally, the standards developed by the Financial Accounting Standards Board and its predecessors have been accepted by the GASB as applying to internal service funds and enterprise funds.[12] Consequently, sections earlier in this chapter that discuss generally accepted accounting principles applicable to internal service funds (such as "Assets Acquired under Lease Agreements") apply equally to enterprise funds accounting for activities other than utilities.

One item not covered in the earlier discussion of internal service funds is a provision for uncollectible accounts. Because internal service funds deal with receivables and payables within the same government, uncollectibility of accounts is generally not a problem. However, if an internal service fund or a nonutility enterprise fund estimates that there will be uncollectible accounts, a debit should be recorded in a contra-revenue account such as Provision for Bad Debts. The related credit would be to a contra-receivable account such as Allowance for Uncollectible Accounts. The GASB requires that revenues be reported net of any provisions for bad debt in both the statement of revenue, expenses, and changes in fund net assets and the government-wide statement of activities.

Accounting for Municipal Solid Waste Landfills

According to Environmental Protection Agency (EPA) estimates, there are approximately 6,000 municipal solid waste landfills (MSWLFs) in the United States, of which about 80 percent are owned by state or local general purpose or special purpose governments.[13] An EPA Rule, "Solid Waste Disposal Facility Criteria" (40 *Code of Federal Regulations,* parts 257 and 258), establishes certain closure requirements for MSWLFs and imposes stringent criteria for location, design, and operation of landfills, groundwater monitoring and corrective action, postclosure care, and financial assurance. State governments are assigned primary responsibility for implementing and enforcing the EPA rule and may increase or reduce its provisions based on site conditions existing within their states.

MSWLF owners and operators may incur a variety of costs both during the period of operation and after closure. These costs include the equipment and facilities

---

[12] See footnote 5.

[13] Governmental Accounting Standards Board, *Statement of Governmental Accounting Standards No. 18,* "Accounting for Municipal Solid Waste Landfill Closure and Postclosure Costs" (Norwalk, CT, 1993), par. 24.

(including final covering of the MSWLF upon closure) and services for such items as postclosure maintenance and monitoring for a period of 30 years after closure. The EPA requires owners and operators to estimate in detail the current dollar cost of hiring a third party to close the largest area of an MSWLF expected to require a final cover and to care for the MSWLF over the 30-year postclosure period. Each year the closure and postclosure cost estimates must be adjusted for inflation and revised as necessary to reflect changes in plans or conditions. Owners and operators of MSWLFs must provide assurances that adequate financial resources will be available to cover the estimated costs of closure, postclosure care, and remediation or containment of environmental hazards when the landfill has been filled to capacity. Several forms of financial assurance are acceptable, including third-party trusts, surety bonds, letters of credit, insurance, or state-sponsored plans.

GASB standards provide guidance both for measuring and reporting estimated total closure and postclosure costs. Although the detailed cost estimation procedures are beyond the scope of this chapter, reporting requirements for MSWLFs that use proprietary fund accounting are described briefly. An expense and a liability should be recognized each period for a portion of the estimated total current cost of MSWLF closure and postclosure care. The portion of total cost to be recognized is based on the units-of-production method so that estimated total current cost is assigned to periods on the basis of landfill usage rather than the passage of time. Recognition begins in the period in which the MSWLF first accepts solid waste and continues each period until closure. For example, a town opens a landfill and estimates that the capacity of the landfill is 4,000,000 cubic yards. Once capacity is reached, the town currently estimates that it will cost $9,500,000 to close and care for the landfill after closure. Based on the GASB guidance, the estimated closure and postclosure cost for the first year would be $190,000, if 80,000 cubic yards of capacity is used in the first year. The journal entry to record the estimated cost would be:

	Debits	Credits
Provision for Landfill Closure and Postclosure	190,000	
Accrued Landfill Closure and Postclosure Liability		190,000

Estimated total closure and postclosure costs should be reevaluated each year during operation of the landfill, and the cumulative effect of changes in the estimated costs, if any, should be reported in the period of the change. Costs of equipment, facilities, services, or final cover acquired during the period are reported as a reduction of the accrued liability, not as capital assets. Equipment and facilities installed prior to commencement of operation of the landfill should be fully depreciated by the closure date.

Assets held by third-party trustees or in surety standby trusts to meet financial assurance requirements should be reported as "amounts held by trustee" in the Restricted Assets section of the statement of net assets and as net assets restricted for closure and postclosure costs. Earnings on such investments should be reported as revenue.

GASB standards also provide guidance for reporting of MSWLFs in governmental fund types or by other entities such as colleges and universities. Accounting for MSWLFs in the General Fund, for example, requires that an expenditure and a fund liability be reported for the current closure and postclosure costs to the extent that an accrued liability would be settled with available fund resources; any remaining liability would be reported in the Governmental Activities column at the government-wide level, as discussed in Chapter 6. Regardless of the fund type or entity reporting the MSWLF activities, GASB standards require the following note disclosures.[14]

1. The nature and source of landfill closure and postclosure care requirements (federal, state, or local laws or regulations).
2. The recognition of a liability for closure and postclosure care costs based on landfill capacity used to date.
3. The reported liability for closure and postclosure care at the balance sheet date (if not apparent from the financial statements) and the estimated total current cost of closure and postclosure care remaining to be recognized.
4. The percentage of landfill capacity used to date and approximate remaining landfill life in years.
5. How closure and postclosure care financial assurance requirements, if any, are being met. Also, any assets restricted for payment of closure and postclosure care costs (if not apparent from the financial statements).
6. The nature of the estimates and the potential for changes due to inflation or deflation, technology, or applicable laws or regulations.

While municipal solid waste landfills may seem to be a dull topic, the costs of improving landfills to meet increased EPA standards, providing financial assurance, and complying with accounting and reporting requirements may be significant for many governments.

Required Segment Information

As with investor-owned enterprises, governments are required to disclose segment information related to certain enterprise funds.[15] The GASB defines a segment as an identifiable activity or group of activities within the enterprise fund. Within an enterprise fund, only those segments with one or more bonds or other debt instruments outstanding, and with a revenue stream pledged to support the debt, are subject to segment disclosure requirements. Additionally, segment disclosure is not required if the enterprise fund is both a segment (only one identifiable activity or group of activities) and is reported as a major fund.

In reporting segment information, emphasis is placed on identifiable streams of revenues pledged for the support of revenue bonds along with related expenses, gains, losses, assets, and liabilities of the same activity. Disclosure requirements for segments are met by presenting condensed financial information in the notes. The condensed statement of net assets should provide information on total assets, total liabilities, and total net assets (by net asset type). The condensed statement of revenues, expenses and changes in net assets should identify major sources of operating revenues, operating expenses, operating net income, nonoperating revenues and expenses, along with any capital contributions, special or extraordinary items, and transfers. At the bottom of the condensed statement of revenues, expenses, and changes in net assets, the change in net assets should be shown, along with beginning and ending net asset balances. The GASB's format for the statement of cash flows should be followed when presenting the required condensed statement of cash flows for the segment.

---

[14] GASB, *Codification,* Sec. L10.115.

[15] Segment reporting is also required for a stand-alone entity that has one or more bonds or other debt instruments outstanding, with a revenue stream pledged to support the debt. (GASB, *Codification,* Sec 2500.101.)

Key Terms	Cash equivalents, *256* Historical cost, *284* Revenue bonds, *273*

Key Terms

Cash equivalents, *256*
Customer Advances for Construction, *273*
General obligation bonds, *274*

Historical cost, *284*
Original cost, *284*
Regulatory accounting principles, *283*

Revenue bonds, *273*
Utility Plant Acquisition Adjustment, *284*

Selected References

Financial Accounting Standards Board. *Statement of Financial Accounting Standards No. 71,* "Accounting for the Effects of Certain Types of Regulation." Norwalk, CT, 1982.

Governmental Accounting Standards Board. *Codification of Governmental Accounting and Financial Reporting Standards, as of June 30, 2005.* Norwalk, CT, 2005.

Questions

7–1. Explain the reporting requirements for internal service funds and enterprise funds.

7–2. When would a city establish an internal service fund? An enterprise fund?

7–3. "Since the reason for the establishment of internal service funds is to facilitate management of resources, not primarily to demonstrate compliance with law, they may be established at the discretion of governmental administrators." Comment.

7–4. What are some of the more important considerations in establishing a pricing policy for an internal service fund?

7–5. What is the purpose of the Restricted Assets section of an enterprise fund statement of fund net assets? Provide examples of items that might be reported in the Restricted Assets section.

7–6. Explain how capitalization of interest costs differs for enterprise funds as opposed to governmental funds.

7–7. How does the statement of cash flows under GASB standards differ from the statement of cash flows under FASB standards?

7–8. Explain why utilities customarily need to present an Accrued Utilities Revenues account in their statement of fund net assets. How should the amount of the accrual be determined?

7–9. Explain the difference between operating revenue/expenses and nonoperating revenue/expenses. Why does the GASB require that operating revenues/expenses be separately reported on proprietary statements of revenues, expenses, and changes in fund net assets?

7–10. What is meant by "segment information for enterprise funds"? When is segment information required to be disclosed?

Cases

7–1 Building Maintenance Fund. The balance sheet and statement of revenues, expenditures, and changes in fund balance for the building maintenance fund, an internal service fund of Coastal City, are reproduced here. No further information about the nature or purposes of this fund is given in the annual report.

COASTAL CITY BUILDING MAINTENANCE FUND
Balance Sheet
As of December 31, 2008

Assets

Assets:	
Cash and investments	$152,879
Accounts receivable	2,116
Inventory	779,000
Prepaid expenses	19,854
Total assets	$953,849

Liabilities and Fund Equity

Liabilities:	
Accounts payable	$ 35,675
Other accrued liabilities	109,099
Accrued annual leave	227,369
Total liabilities	372,143
Fund equity:	
Fund balance	581,706
Total liabilities and fund equity	$953,849

COASTAL CITY BUILDING MAINTENANCE FUND
Statement of Revenues, Expenditures,
and Changes in Fund Balance
Year Ended December 31, 2008

Revenues:	
Billings to departments	$10,774,781
Miscellaneous	100,344
Total billings	10,875,125
Expenditures:	
Salaries and employee benefits	3,353,413
Supplies	3,409,096
Operating services and charges	495,143
Maintenance and repairs	3,536,443
Total expenditures	10,794,095
Excess of revenues over expenditures	81,030
Fund balance—January 1, 2008	500,676
Fund balance—December 31, 2008	$ 581,706

Required

a. Assuming that the building maintenance fund is an internal service fund, discuss whether the financial information is presented in accordance with *GASBS 34*.

b. If you were the manager of a city department that uses the services of the building maintenance fund, what would you want to know in addition to the information disclosed in the financial statements?

7–2 Internal Service Fund Policies. The formal financial objectives and funding policies for the internal service funds of the City of Columbia, Missouri, are presented here and on the next page. Read these policies and respond to the questions that follow.

A Resolution

establishing a formal policy with respect to the financial objectives for internal service funds; and establishing a policy regarding generation of funds required for capital outlay.

BE IT RESOLVED BY THE COUNCIL OF THE CITY OF COLUMBIA, MISSOURI, AS FOLLOWS:

SECTION 1. That internal service funds such as Data Processing, Vehicle Maintenance, Utilities Accounts and Billing, Public Buildings, and Printing are funds whose financial objective should be to only recover the complete cost of operations without producing any significant amount of profit in excess of the fund's requirements.

SECTION 2. That Section 1 is consistent with practices of "Governmental Accounting, Auditing, and Financial Reporting."

SECTION 3. That in computing an internal service fund's revenue requirement for rate setting purposes, the rate base should include such items as debt expense, interest expense, operating expense, prorated reserve (accumulated over time to allow for purchase option under lease/purchase arrangements), and either depreciation expense or estimated capital outlay, either of which are usually financed 100% internally through rates.

SECTION 4. That since working capital in different funds varies because of many factors it should be reviewed more closely with the budgetary process to assure captive users that the cash account is not a result of billings in excess of revenue requirements.

SECTION 5. That if it appears that cash buildup has occurred in excess of reasonable revenue requirements, rates should be adjusted in the budgetary process; cost recoveries, either over or under, should be rolled forward.

SECTION 6. That generation of funds for capital outlay be allowed either 100% internally through rates or through budgeted depreciation expense when lease/purchase agreements are used, in which case, an amount should be included in the rate base for a prorated reserve which, accumulated over time, will enable purchase of such capital outlay at some future date.

Allowable costs used in determining revenue requirements for the City of Columbia's internal service funds are diagrammed in the next box.

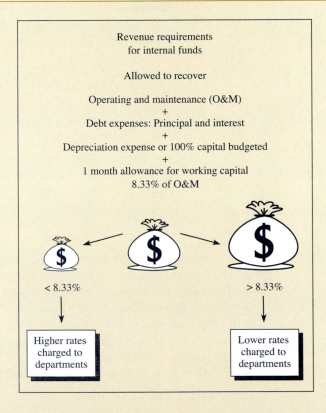

Required

a. Do the City of Columbia's financial objectives and funding policies appear to promote sound resource management?

b. Evaluate the reasonableness of the factors used to determine billing rates/revenue requirements from the viewpoint of

(1) A city council member.

(2) The mayor or city manager.

(3) A department head.

c. Is having a uniform policy for all internal service funds optimal, or would it be better to tailor the revenue requirements to the needs of each individual fund? Explain.

7–3 **Mass Transit System.** The City of Dixon operates a mass transit system (DTS) consisting of a network of bus and trolley routes. The following information is provided about the operations and financing of the mass transit system.*

1. Operating revenues for the most recent fiscal year amounted to $549,420; operating expenses for the same year amounted to $1,011,843. Operating revenues have covered only 45 to 50 percent of operating expenditures since DTS was established five years ago.

2. The operating deficit (from part 1) of $462,423 was financed jointly by $362,423 from the city's General Fund and $100,000 in operating grants from the Urban Mass Transit Administration (UMTA). Capital contributions over the past five years have amounted to $3,334,286 divided about evenly between the city and capital grants from the UMTA.

3. Transit system managers have been pressured at times by city officials to increase bus and trolley fares but are strongly opposed because they believe DTS ridership would drop significantly. Advocates for disadvantaged groups have also lobbied hard to keep the current fares. Thus, for at least the next several years, the city plans to provide an annual operating subsidy to DTS to cover its operating deficit, less any operating grants received from UMTA or other sources.

4. Until now the accounting and reporting for DTS has been as an enterprise fund of the city. The city finance director and the head of the mass transit system would like to continue to use enterprise fund accounting; however, influential members of the finance committee of the city council are insisting that, since DTS is never expected to break even, it should use special revenue fund accounting. Changing to a special revenue fund also means that DTS will require council-approved appropriations for its expenditures.

Required

a. Develop an argument for retaining enterprise fund accounting.

b. Develop an argument for adopting special revenue fund accounting.

c. How would GASB require the transit system be reported?

Exercises and Problems

7–1 **Examine the CAFR.** Utilizing the annual report obtained for Exercise 1–1, follow these instructions:

a. **Internal Service Funds.**

(1) *Use of Funds.* What activities of the government are reported as being administered by internal service funds (working capital funds, revolving

*The authors are indebted to Charles M. Hicks for providing the information from which this case was adapted.

funds, rotary funds, industrial funds, and intragovernmental service funds are other names used for funds of the type discussed in Chapter 7)? If internal service funds are not used by the reporting entity, does the report disclose how financing and accounting for activities such as purchasing, motor pools, printing, data processing, and other activities commonly used by more than one fund are handled? Does the report state the basis of accounting used for the internal service funds? Is the accounting for all funds in this category on the same basis? If so, is the financial statement presentation consistent with the stated basis? If the basis of accounting is not stated, analyze the statements to determine which basis is used—full accrual, modified accrual, or cash basis.

(2) *Fund Disclosure.* In the balance sheet(s) or statement(s) of net assets displaying information for the internal service fund(s), are assets classified in accord with practices of profit-seeking businesses, or are current, capital, and other assets not separately displayed? If there are receivables other than from other funds or other governments, are allowances for estimated uncollectibles provided? Are allowances for depreciation deducted from related capital asset accounts?

Are current liabilities and long-term debt properly distinguished in the balance sheet? Are long-term loans from other funds properly distinguished from capital contributions received from other funds?

Are budgetary accounts (Estimated Revenues, Appropriations, Encumbrances) used by the internal service funds? From what sources were revenues actually obtained by each internal service fund? How are costs and expenses of each fund classified? Are noncash expenses, such as depreciation, separately disclosed? Do the revenues of each fund exceed the costs and expenses of the period? Compute the net income (or net loss) of each fund in this category as a percentage of its operating revenue for the period. Does the net income (or net loss) for any fund exceed 5 percent of operating revenues? If so, do the statements or the accompanying text explain how the excess is being used or how the deficiency is being financed?

(3) *Statement of Cash Flows.* Is a statement of cash flows presented for internal service funds? If so, how does the cash provided by operations shown in this statement relate to the revenues and expenses shown in the statement of revenues, expenses, and changes in net assets, or other similarly titled operating statement? Are cash flows from financing activities presented separately for noncapital- and capital-related activities? Is there a section for cash flows from investing activities?

(4) *Government-wide Financial Statements.* Is there a column for business-type activities on the statement of net assets and statement of activities? Is there any evidence that the internal service fund account balances were collapsed into the Governmental Activities column? If enterprise funds are the predominant participants in the internal service fund, do you see evidence that the internal service fund balances are reported in the Business-type Activities column of the government-wide statements?

b. **Enterprise Funds.**

(1) *Use of Funds.* What activities of the government are reported as being administered by enterprise funds? Does the government own and operate

its water utility? Electric utility? Gas utility? Transportation system? Are combining statements presented in the financial section of the CAFR for all enterprise funds, or are separate statements presented for each enterprise fund? Do all enterprise funds use full accrual accounting? Are all funds in this category earning revenues at least equal to costs and expenses? If not, how is the operating deficit being financed? What sources furnished the original investment in fund assets? Do the notes include segment information on individual enterprise funds where applicable (see "Required Segment Information" section of this chapter)?

Are sales to other funds or other governments separately disclosed? Are there receivables from other funds or other governments? How are receivables from component units, if any, disclosed? Is there any evidence that enterprise funds contribute amounts to the General Fund in lieu of taxes to help support services received by the enterprise? Is there any evidence that enterprise funds make excessively large contributions to the General Fund or any other funds?

(2) *Utility Funds.* Is it possible to tell from the report whether utilities of this government are subject to the same regulations as investor-owned utilities in the same state? (If the utility statements follow the format of the NARUC and the FERC, as described in this chapter, there is a good chance that the governmentally owned utilities are subject to at least some supervision by a state regulatory agency.) What rate of return on sales (or operating revenues) is being earned by each utility fund? What rate of return on total assets is being earned by each utility fund?

Is depreciation taken on utility plant? Are accounting policies and accounting changes properly disclosed? If so, what method of depreciation is being used? Does each utility account for its own debt service and construction activities in the manner described in this chapter? What special funds or restricted assets are utilized by each utility?

(3) *Nonutility Enterprise Funds.* Is the accounting for nonutility enterprise funds the same as investor-owned enterprises in the same industries? (In order to answer this, you may need to refer to publications of trade associations or to handbooks or encyclopedias of accounting systems found in business libraries.) If you cannot find information about investor-owned counterparts of the governmental nonutility enterprise funds, do the statements of the latter provide evidence that generally accepted accounting principles devised for profit-seeking businesses were used?

(4) *Government-wide Financial Statements.* What proportion of the net assets of the business-type activities are reported as invested in capital assets, restricted, and unrestricted? Were the business-type activities profitable; that is, did revenues exceed expenses?

7–2 Multiple Choice. Choose the best answer.
1. Which of the following correctly states the role of budgeting in proprietary funds?
   a. Proprietary fund managers should ensure that a valid appropriation exists before providing goods or services to other funds or departments of the same government.
   b. Proprietary fund managers should have discretion to operate within a flexible budget consistent with pricing and other policies established by the legislative body.

   c. To ensure that appropriations are not overspent, all proprietary funds should use encumbrance procedures.
   d. Expenditures from proprietary funds should not be made unless there is a valid appropriation authorizing the expenditure.

2. Which of the following is an appropriate reason to establish an internal service fund?
   a. To improve the management of resources.
   b. To determine a reasonable level of user charges relative to operating costs.
   c. To analyze the costs in relation to the benefits of providing a service.
   d. All of the above are appropriate.

3. According to *GASBS 34,* an interfund transfer from the General Fund to a proprietary fund would increase which component of net assets when closing entries are posted for the proprietary fund?
   a. Restricted net assets.
   b. Unrestricted net assets.
   c. Contributed capital.
   d. Retained earnings.

4. The City of Jenkins operates a central motor pool as an internal service fund for the benefit of the city's other funds and departments. In 2008, this fund billed the Community Services Department $30,000 for vehicle rentals. What account should the internal service fund use to record these billings?
   a. Interfund Transfers In.
   b. Interfund Exchanges.
   c. Billings to Departments.
   d. Cost of Providing Rentals to Other Funds and Units.

5. Which of the following events would generally be classified as nonoperating on an enterprise fund's statement of revenues, expenses, and changes in net assets?
   a. Billing other funds of the same government for services.
   b. Loss on the sale of a piece of equipment.
   c. Depreciation expense.
   d. Administrative expense.

6. During 2008 Darden City reported the following operating receipts from self-sustaining activities paid by users of the services rendered:

Operations of water supply plant	$4,000,000
Operations of transit system	800,000

   What amounts should be reported as operating revenues of Darden's enterprise funds?
   a. $4,800,000.
   b. $4,000,000.
   c. $800,000.
   d. $0.

7. Under GASB standards, which of the following events would be classified as an investing activity on a proprietary fund's statement of cash flows?
   a. Interest earned on certificates of deposit held by the proprietary fund.
   b. Purchase of equipment for use by the proprietary fund.
   c. Grant received to construct a building that will be used by the proprietary fund.
   d. All of the above would be considered investing activities for reporting purposes.

8. The proceeds of tax-supported bonds issued for the benefit of an enterprise fund and being serviced by a debt service fund:
   a. Should not be reported by the enterprise fund at all.
   b. Should be reported in the notes to enterprise fund statements but not in the body of any of the statements.
   c. Should be reported in the enterprise fund as long-term debt.
   d. Should be reported in the enterprise fund as a contribution or interfund transfer in the statement of revenues, expenses, and changes in net assets.
9. Under GASB standards, capital assets received by gift or contribution by a proprietary fund or acquired from grants, entitlements, and shared revenues restricted for acquisition of capital assets should:
   a. Not be depreciated.
   b. Be depreciated only in the government-wide statements.
   c. Be depreciated or not be depreciated at the option of the government, provided a consistent policy is followed.
   d. Be depreciated in the normal manner in both the Business-type Activities column in the government-wide statements and in the proprietary fund statements.
10. The financial statements required by *GASBS 34* for a proprietary fund are:
   a. Balance sheet and statement of revenues, expenditures, and changes in net assets.
   b. Balance sheet; statement of revenues, expenditures, and changes in fund balance; statement of cash flows.
   c. Statement of net assets; statement of revenues, expenses, and changes in net assets; statement of cash flows.
   d. Balance sheet and statement of revenues, expenses, and changes in retained earnings.

7–3 Central Duplicating Internal Service Fund. As of September 30, 2007, the Central Duplicating Fund of the Town of Frederick had the following post-closing trial balance:

	Debits	Credits
Cash	$ 15,000	
Due from Other Funds	20,200	
Service Supplies Inventory	35,300	
Machinery and Equipment	300,000	
Allowance for Depreciation		$ 90,000
Due to Federal Government		1,500
Due to Other Funds		800
Accounts Payable		12,700
Net Assets—Invested in Capital Assets		210,000
Net Assets—Unrestricted		55,500
	$370,500	$370,500

During the fiscal year ended September 30, 2008, the following transactions (summarized) occurred:

1. Employees were paid $290,000 wages in cash; additional wages of $43,500 were withheld for federal income and social security taxes. The employer's share of social security taxes amounted to $23,375.

2. Cash remitted to the federal government during the year for withholding taxes and social security taxes amounted to $65,500.
3. Utility bills received from the Town of Sanders' Utility Fund during the year amounted to $23,500.
4. Office expenses paid in cash during the year amounted to $10,500.
5. Service supplies purchased on account during the year totaled $157,500.
6. Parts and supplies used during the year totaled $152,300 (at cost).
7. Charges to departments during the fiscal year were as follows:

General Fund	$308,700
Street Fund	279,300

8. Unpaid balances at year-end were as follows:

General Fund	$10,000
Street Fund	20,000

9. Payments to the utility fund totaled $21,800.
10. Accounts Payable at year-end amounted to $13,250.
11. Annual depreciation rate for machinery and equipment is 10%.
12. Revenue and expense accounts for the year were closed.

Required

a. Prepare a statement of revenues, expenses, and changes in net assets for the year. Classify expenses as to direct and indirect costs. Wages and payroll taxes are considered to be 90 percent direct and 10 percent indirect. Utility services are estimated to be 80 percent direct and 20 percent indirect. Parts and supplies used and depreciation of machinery and equipment are considered direct costs; all other costs are considered indirect costs.

b. Comment on the evident success of the pricing policy of this fund, assuming that user charges are intended to cover all operating expenses, including depreciation, but are not expected to provide a net income in excess of 3 percent of billings to departments.

c. Prepare a statement of net assets for the Central Duplicating Fund as of September 30, 2008.

d. Prepare a statement of cash flows for the Central Duplicating Fund for the year ended September 30, 2008.

7–4 Central Garage Internal Service Fund. The City of Ashville operates an internal service fund to provide garage space and repairs for all city-owned-and-operated vehicles. The Central Garage Fund was established by a contribution of $300,000 from the General Fund on July 1, 2005; at which time the land and building were acquired. The post-closing trial balance at June 30, 2007, was as follows:

	Debits	Credits
Cash	$110,000	
Due from Other Funds	9,000	
Inventory of Supplies	90,000	
Land	50,000	
Building	250,000	
Allowance for Depreciation—Building		$ 20,000
Machinery and Equipment	65,000	

Allowance for Depreciation—		
Machinery and Equipment	12,000	
Vouchers Payable	31,000	
Net Assets—Invested in Capital Assets	333,000	
Nets Assets—Unrestricted	178,000	
	$574,000	$574,000

The following information applies to the fiscal year ended June 30, 2008:

1. Supplies were purchased on account for $92,000; the perpetual inventory method is used.
2. The cost of supplies used during the year ended June 30, 2008, was $110,000. A physical count taken as of that date showed materials and supplies on hand totaled $72,000 at cost.
3. Salaries and wages paid to employees totaled $235,000, including related costs.
4. Billings totaling $30,000 were received from the enterprise fund for utility charges. The Central Garage Fund paid $27,000 of the amount owed.
5. Depreciation of the building was recorded in the amount of $10,000; depreciation of the machinery and equipment amounted to $9,000.
6. Billings to other departments for services provided to them were as follows:

General Fund	$270,000
Special revenue fund	37,000
Water and Sewer Utility Fund	90,000

7. Unpaid interfund receivable balances were as follows:

	6/30/07	*6/30/08*
General Fund	$2,500	$3,000
Special revenue fund	3,500	7,000
Water and Sewer Utility Fund	3,000	2,000

8. Vouchers payable at June 30, 2008 were $16,000.
9. For June 30, 2008, closing entries were prepared for the Central Garage Fund (ignore government-wide closing entry).

Required

a. Assume all expenses at the government-wide level are charged to the General Government function. Prepare journal entries to record all of the transactions for this period in the Central Garage Fund accounts and in the governmental activities accounts.

b. Prepare a statement of revenues, expenses, and changes in net assets for the Central Garage Fund for the period ended June 30, 2008.

c. Prepare a statement of net assets for the Central Garage Fund as of June 30, 2008.

d. Explain what the Central Garage Fund would need to report at the governmental activities level, and where the information would be reported.

7–5   Net Assets. During the past year Oak City had a number of transactions that impacted net asset classifications of its produce market, which is operated as an enterprise fund. All nominal accounts for the period have been closed to unrestricted net assets. For reporting purposes, the city's finance director is trying to update the net asset categories to properly reflect current balances in each of the three net asset categories based on the following transaction information.

1. For the year, depreciation expense totaled $534,000.
2. During the year a piece of equipment with a carrying value of $2,610 was sold for its carrying value.
3. During the year $1,000,000 in deferred serial bonds were issued to construct a building to house the produce market. At the end of the year, construction work in progress for the building totaled $948,000. It is expected the building will be completed at the beginning of the next year.
4. To retire the $1,000,000 deferred serial bonds, $25,000 cash was placed in a sinking fund.
5. A $5,000 principal payment was made on a capital lease.

Required

To assist the finance director you have been asked to provide a journal entry for each of the above five items. Your journal entries should indicate the effect of each item on the net asset categories—invested in capital assets, net of related debt; restricted and unrestricted.

7–6 Parking Facilities Fund. The City of Dalton accounts for its parking facilities as an enterprise fund. For the year ended December 31, 2008, the pre-closing trial balance for the Parking Facilities Fund is provided.

Accounts	Debits	Credits
Cash & Cash Equivalents	$ 869,168	
Accounts Receivable	3,607	
Allowance for Doubtful Accounts		$ 72
Restricted Cash & Cash Equivalents	993,322	
Land	3,021,637	
Buildings and Equipment	23,029,166	
Accumulated Depreciation		5,623,315
Accounts & Accrued Payables		312,830
6-month Note Payable		360,000
Bonds Payable		15,579,325
Net Assets—Invested in Capital Assets, Net of Related Debt		4,931,749
Net Assets—Restricted		951,996
Net Assets—Unrestricted		765,893
Charges for Services		1,640,261
Interest Income		251,480
Personnel Expense	852,380	
Utilities Expense	100,726	
Repairs & Maintenance Expense	64,617	
Supplies Expense	17,119	
Depreciation Expense	578,861	
Interest Expense	874,909	
Transfer Out	11,409	
	$30,416,921	$30,416,921

Additional information concerning the Parking Facilities Fund is as follows:
1. All bonds payable were used to acquire property, plant, and equipment.
2. During the year, a principal payment of $500,000 was made to retire a portion of the bonds payable.
3. Equipment with a carrying value of $4,725 was sold for its carrying value.

4. Total cash received from customers was $1,640,155 and cash received for interest and dividends was $251,480; $150,000 of this amount is restricted cash. (*Hint:* this was the only change to restricted cash during the year.)
5. Cash payments included $750,828 to employees, $365,137 to vendors, $874,909 for interest on bonded debt, and $11,409 to subsidize public works (the General Fund).
6. The beginning balance in Accounts Receivable was $3,501, and Accounts & Accrued Payables was $393,953.
7. The net asset categories have not been updated to reflect correct balances as of the December 31, 2008, year-end.

Required

a. Prepare the statement of revenues, expenses, and changes in fund net assets for the Parking Facilities Fund as of December 31, 2008.
b. Prepare the statement of net assets for the Parking Facilities Fund as of December 31, 2008.
c. Prepare the statement of cash flows for the Parking Facilities Fund as of December 31, 2008.

7–7 Water Utility Fund. The council of the City of Templeton directed that $1,000,000 cash be transferred from its General Fund as a permanent contribution to a newly created water utility fund. The water utility fund is *not* regulated by a state regulatory agency. The cash is intended to cover the purchase price of the Southland Water Company plus an additional amount to serve as initial working capital for the new activity. At June 30, 2007, the effective date of purchase, Southland Water Company had the following post-closing trial balance:

	Debits	Credits
Utility Plant in Service	$2,195,000	
Allowance for Depreciation—Utility Plant		$1,357,000
Cash	29,000	
Accounts Receivable	64,000	
Estimated Uncollectible Receivables		26,000
Materials and Supplies	66,000	
Vouchers Payable		99,000
Miscellaneous Accruals		28,000
Capital Stock		1,000,000
Retained Earnings	156,000	
	$2,510,000	$2,510,000

The acquisition occurred as follows:

1. The General Fund contribution was received on June 27, 2007.
2. As of June 30, 2007, the City of Templeton Water Utility Fund acquired the assets of the Southland Water Company, excluding cash. Receivables were purchased at half of their gross value. When the purchased assets were recorded, the allowance for uncollectible receivables was increased to establish the new book value of receivables. The vendor's liabilities were assumed. A cash payment of $900,000 was made for the net assets of the water utility. (*Hint:* Record Accounts Receivable, Materials and Supplies, Accounts Payable, and Miscellaneous Accruals at the amounts shown in the trial balance. Increase Estimated Uncollectible Receivables to $32,000. Amounts shown for Southland Water Company's Cash, Capital Stock, and Retained Earnings accounts should not be recorded by the Water Utility Fund.)

Required

a. Record in general journal form the entries that should be made in the Water Utility Fund for the events of June 27 and June 30, 2007.

b. Prepare in conformity with GAAP a statement of net assets for the City of Templeton Water Utility Fund as of June 30, 2007.

7–8 **Water Utility Fund.** This problem continues the preceding problem. During the year ended June 30, 2008, the following transactions and events occurred in the City of Templeton Water Utility Fund:

1. On July 1, 2007, to finance needed plant improvements, the Water Utility Fund borrowed $500,000 from a local bank on notes secured by a pledge of water utility revenues. The notes mature in five years and bear interest at the annual rate of 8 percent.

2. Accrued expenses at June 30, 2007, were paid in cash.

3. Billings to nongovernmental customers for water usage during the year totaled $632,000; billings to the General Fund totaled $40,000.

4. Liabilities for the following were recorded during the year:

Materials and supplies	$88,000
Source of supply expenses	32,000
Pumping expenses	40,500
Water treatment expenses	51,500
Transmission and distribution expenses	68,000
Customer accounts expenses	93,000
Administrative and general expenses	76,000
Construction work in progress	357,000
Total	$806,000

5. Materials and supplies were used by the following departments in the stated amounts: Source of Supply, $10,800; Pumping, $6,500; Treatment, $34,500; Transmission and Distribution, $32,200; total, $84,000.

6. On July 2, 2007, utility plant assets that had a historical cost of $25,000 were sold for $15,000 cash.

7. $28,000 of old accounts receivable were written off.

8. During fiscal 2008, the utility instituted a program of deposits to reduce meter damage and customer defaults on water bills. Cash amounting to $15,000 was collected during the year (debit Cash—Customer Deposits).

9. Accounts receivable collections totaled $460,000 for the fiscal year from nongovernmental customers and $38,000 from the General Fund.

10. $800,000 of accounts payable were paid in cash.

11. $500 was recorded as interest expense accumulated on customers' deposits (credit Customer Deposits).

12. Depreciation expense of $47,050 was recorded for the year.

13. Bills for materials and supplies, $7,000, were received and recorded as payables on June 30, 2008.

14. One year's interest on notes payable was paid.

15. Interest on long-term notes was charged to Construction Work in Progress.

16. The provision for uncollectible accounts was increased by an amount equal to 1 percent of the sales of water to nongovernmental customers for the year.

17. Cash in the amount of $100,000 was restricted for eventual redemption of five-year notes. As required by the loan agreement, net assets in the same amount were recorded as restricted.
18. Operating statement accounts for the year were closed.

Required

a. Record the transactions for the year in general journal form.
b. Prepare a statement of net assets as of June 30, 2008.
c. Prepare a statement of revenues, expenses, and changes in net assets for the year ended June 30, 2008.
d. Prepare a statement of cash flows for the City of Templeton Water Utility Fund for the fiscal year ended June 30, 2008, assuming that cash outflows for operating activities included $310,000 for wages and salaries.
e. On the basis of your analysis of the financial statements, comment on any matters that should be brought to the attention of the management of the City of Templeton Water Utility Fund. What actions do you suggest management should take?

Chapter Eight

Accounting for Fiduciary Activities—Agency and Trust Funds

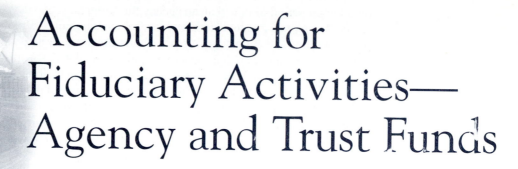

Learning Objectives

After reading this chapter, you should be able to:

1. Explain how fiduciary funds are used to report on the fiduciary activities of a government.
2. Distinguish among agency funds and trust funds (private-purpose, investment, and pension).
3. Describe the uses for and characteristics of agency funds.
4. Explain the operations of and accounting and financial reporting for commonly used agency funds.
5. Explain the creation, operation, accounting, and financial reporting for:

    A cash and investment pool (including an investment trust fund).

    A private-purpose trust fund.

    A pension trust fund.
6. Describe accounting for Other Post-Employment Benefits.

Fiduciary activities benefit other individuals, organizations, or governments, rather than the reporting government. For this reason, *GASBS 34* excludes the reporting of fiduciary activities in the government-wide financial statements. However, fiduciary activities are reported in the fiduciary fund financial statements, the focus of this chapter.

Fiduciary funds, under the *GASBS 34* reporting model, are used to account only for those activities in which a government holds assets as an agent or trustee. To account for these private-purpose fiduciary activities agency funds, investment trust funds, private-purpose trust funds, and pensions trust funds are used. Resources that are held in trust for the benefit of the government's own programs or its citizenry should be accounted for using a governmental fund rather than a fiduciary fund. Such public-purpose trusts should be accounted for as special revenue funds (see Chapter 4) if the resources are expendable for the trust purpose. A permanent fund, as illustrated in Chapter 4, should be used to account for trusts in which the trust principal is permanently restricted, but earnings may be used for the specified *public* purpose.

In law, there is a clear distinction between an agency relationship and a trust relationship. In accounting practice, the legalistic distinctions between trust funds and agency funds are not of major significance. The important and perhaps the sole consideration from an accounting standpoint is what can and what cannot be done with the fund's assets in accordance with laws and other pertinent regulations. The name of a particular fund is not a reliable criterion for determining the correct accounting basis for trust and agency funds.

Trust funds differ from agency funds principally in degree: Trust funds often exist over a longer period of time than an agency fund, represent and develop vested interests of a beneficiary to a greater extent, and involve more complex administration and financial accounting and reporting. Agency funds are used only if a government holds resources in a purely custodial capacity for others. As noted, specific accounting procedures and limitations depend on the enactment that brought about creation of a particular trust or agency fund, plus all other regulations under which it operates. Regulations include pertinent statutes, ordinances, wills, trust indentures, and other instruments of endowment, resolutions of the governing body, statements of purposes of the fund, kinds and amounts of assets held, and others. This aggregate of factors or those applicable to a given fund determine the transactions in which it may and should engage.

AGENCY FUNDS

GASB standards identify *agency funds* as one of the four types of fiduciary funds. **Agency funds** are used to account for assets held by a government acting as an agent for one or more other governments or for individuals or private organizations. Similarly, if a fund of a government regularly receives assets that are to be transmitted to other funds of that government, an agency relationship exists. Assets that are held in an agency fund belong to the party or parties for which the government acts as agent. Therefore, *agency fund assets are offset by liabilities equal in amount; no fund equity exists. GASBS 34* requires agency fund assets and liabilities to be recognized on the accrual basis. Revenues and expenses are not recognized in the accounts of agency funds, however.

Unless use of an agency fund is mandated by law, by GASB standards, or by decision of the governing board, an agency relationship may be accounted for within governmental and/or proprietary funds. For example, local governments must act as agents of the federal and state governments in the collection of employees' withholding taxes, retirement contributions, and social security taxes. In the absence of contrary legal requirements or administrative decisions, it is perfectly acceptable to account for the withholdings, and the remittance to federal and state governments, within the funds that account for the gross pay of the employees, as is shown by the illustrative entries in Chapter 4. In general, if an agency relationship is incidental to the primary purposes for which a given fund exists, the relationship is ordinarily discharged on a current basis, and the amounts of assets held as agent tend to be small in relation to fund assets, there is no need to create an agency fund unless required by law or administrative decision.

Agency Fund for Special Assessment Debt Service

Readers of Chapters 5 and 6 of this text should recall that GASB standards specify that a government that has *no* obligation to assume debt service on special assessment debt in the event of property owners' default but does perform the functions of billing property owners for the assessments, collecting installments of assessments and interest on the assessments, and *from the collections,* paying interest and principal on the special assessment debt, should account for those activities by use of an agency fund.

To illustrate *agency fund* accounting for special assessment debt service activities, assume the same information as used in Chapter 6 except that the government is not obligated in any manner for the special assessment debt. When the assessments in the amount of $480,000, payable in 10 equal installments, were levied on benefited property owners, the following journal entry was made in the agency fund.

		Debits	Credits
1.	Assessments Receivable—Current	48,000	
	Assessments Receivable—Deferred	432,000	
	Due to Special Assessment Bondholders—Principal		480,000

All current assessments receivable were collected (see Entry 2) along with $24,000 of interest (5 percent on the previous unpaid receivable balance). As indicated in Chapter 6, any amounts not collected by the due date should be reclassified as Assessments Receivable—Delinquent.

		Debits	Credits
2.	Cash	72,000	
	Assessments Receivable—Current		48,000
	Due to Special Assessment Bondholders—Interest		24,000

Special assessment bond principal in the amount of $48,000 and interest in the amount of $24,000 were paid during the current year.

		Debits	Credits
3.	Due to Special Assessment Bondholders—Principal	48,000	
	Due to Special Assessment Bondholders—Interest	24,000	
	Cash		72,000

The second installment of assessments receivable was reclassified at year-end from the deferred category to the current category.

		Debits	Credits
4.	Assessments Receivable—Current	48,000	
	Assessments Receivable—Deferred		48,000

This pattern of journal entries will be repeated during each of the remaining nine years until all special assessment bonds are retired.

Tax Agency Funds

An agency relationship that does, logically, result in the creation of an agency fund is the collection of taxes or other revenues by one government for several of the funds it operates and for other governments. State governments commonly collect sales taxes, gasoline taxes, and many other taxes that are apportioned to state agencies and to local governments within the state. At the local government level, it is common for an elected county official to serve as collector for all property taxes owed by persons or corporations owning property within the county. Taxes levied by all funds and governments within the county are certified to the county collector for collection. The county collector is required by law to make periodic distributions of tax collections for each year to each fund or government in the proportion that the levy for that fund or government bears to the total levy for the year. In many jurisdictions, the law provides that governments may request advances or "draws" from the tax agency fund prior to regular distributions; advances are usually limited by law to a specified percentage, often 90 percent, of collections for the period from the last distribution until the date of the advance.

Tax agency fund accounting would be quite simple if all taxes levied for a given year were collected in that year. It is almost always true, however, that collections during any year relate to taxes levied in several prior years as well as taxes levied for the current year, and sometimes include advance collections of taxes for the following year. In many jurisdictions, not only does the total tax rate vary from year to year but the proportion that the rate of each government (and each fund) bears to the total rate also varies from year to year. Additionally, interest and penalties on delinquent taxes must be collected at statutory rates or amounts at the time delinquent taxes are collected; interest and penalties collected must be distributed to participating funds and governments in the same manner that tax collections are distributed.

Illustration of Composition of Total Tax Rates

Assume that the county collector of Campbell County is responsible for collecting the taxes due in 2008 for the funds and governments located within the county. Ordinarily, the taxes levied for each fund and government within the county are shown in columnar form in a newspaper advertisement as legal notice to taxpayers. In order to keep the illustrations in this text legible and comprehensible, Illustration 8–1 shows two columns of a legal advertisement. Real property tax statements are prepared for each parcel of property located within the jurisdiction for which the tax agency fund is operated. Whether each statement discloses the amount of tax that will be distributed to all of the tax agency fund's participants that levy taxes on that parcel, or shows only the total tax payable to the county collector, the collector's office must be able to compute and appropriately distribute all taxes collected to the appropriate funds and governments.

For example, Illustration 8–1 shows that a parcel of property located in Washington Township outside the City of Washington would be taxed at the rate of $7.10 per $100 of assessed valuation; if the parcel were inside the city limits, however, the tax rate would be $10.06. Therefore, if a parcel of property located in Washington Township outside the city had an assessed valuation of $10,000, the total real property tax payable in 2008 would be $710, but a parcel with the same assessed valuation located within the city would be taxed at $1,006. The subtotals in each column represent the taxes levied for each tax agency fund participant, as shown in Illustration 8–1. In turn, the taxes levied for each government are broken down into the taxes levied for funds of that government, as also shown in Illustration 8–1. The relationship between direct and overlapping debt is discussed in Chapter 6. Note that Illustration 8–1 shows that a person or organization owning property within the City of Washington is required to pay 66 cents of the total rate for debt service (20 cents to Campbell County, 38 cents to the school district, and 8 cents to the City of Washington). Illustration 8–2 summarizes the composition of each tax statement by government.

ILLUSTRATION 8–1

Composition of Taxes to Be Collected by County Collector of Campbell County for the County Funds and other Taxing Authorities for the Year 2008		
	Washington Township	**City of Washington**
Total state rate	$0.01	$ 0.01
County funds:		
General	1.08	1.08
Capital projects	0.09	0.09
Debt service	0.20	0.20
Welfare	0.11	0.11
Total county rate	1.48	1.48
Library Fund	0.25	0.25
Township funds:		
General	0.07	0.07
Fire protection	0.23	—
Total township	0.30	0.07
School funds:		
General	4.50	4.50
Capital projects	0.18	0.18
Debt service	0.38	0.38
Total school rate	5.06	5.06
City funds:		
General		2.53
Street		0.33
Pension		0.25
Debt service		0.08
Total city rate		3.19
Total tax rates per $100 assessed valuation	$7.10	$10.06

In those states in which taxes are levied on personal property, the funds and governments that levy the personal property taxes are generally assumed to be the ones that levy taxes on the residence of the owner unless there is convincing evidence that the legal location of the personal property is elsewhere. Inasmuch as the tax rate levied for each tax agency fund participant often varies from year to year, it is necessary that all tax collections be identified with the year for which the taxes were levied as well as with the particular parcels for which taxes were collected.

Operation of the collector's office often requires the use of substantial administrative, clerical, and computer time and provision of extensive building and computer facilities. Accordingly, it is common for the collector to be authorized to withhold a certain percentage from the collections for each government, and to remit to the county General Fund (or other fund bearing the expenditures for operating the tax agency fund) the total amount withheld from the collections of other governments.

ILLUSTRATION 8–2

<table>
<tr><td colspan="3" align="center">**2008 Taxes Payable
to Campbell County Collector for Parcel
with Assessed Valuation of $10,000**</td></tr>
<tr><td></td><td colspan="2" align="center">**Parcel Located**</td></tr>
<tr><td>**Amount Levied by**</td><td align="center">**Outside City**</td><td align="center">**In City**</td></tr>
<tr><td>State</td><td align="right">$ 1.00</td><td align="right">$ 1.00</td></tr>
<tr><td>County</td><td align="right">148.00</td><td align="right">148.00</td></tr>
<tr><td>Library</td><td align="right">25.00</td><td align="right">25.00</td></tr>
<tr><td>Township</td><td align="right">30.00</td><td align="right">7.00</td></tr>
<tr><td>School</td><td align="right">506.00</td><td align="right">506.00</td></tr>
<tr><td>City</td><td align="right">—</td><td align="right">319.00</td></tr>
<tr><td>   Total</td><td align="right">$710.00</td><td align="right">$1,006.00</td></tr>
</table>

Accounting for Tax Agency Funds

Taxes levied each year should be recorded in the accounts of the appropriate funds of each government in the manner illustrated in preceding chapters. Although an allowance for estimated uncollectible current taxes would be established in each fund, the *gross* amount of the tax levy for all funds should be recorded in the Tax Agency Fund as a receivable. Note the receivable is designated as belonging to other funds and governments, and the receivable is offset in total by a liability. Assuming total real property taxes certified for collection during 2008 amounted to $10,516,400, the entry would be as follows:

		Debits	**Credits**
	Tax Agency Fund:		
1.	Taxes Receivable for Other Funds and Governments—Current	10,516,400	
	Due to Other Funds and Governments		10,516,400

It would be necessary for the county collector to keep records of the total amount of 2008 taxes to be collected for each of the funds and governments in the Tax Agency Fund in order to distribute tax collections properly. Assume that the 2008 taxes were levied for the following governments (to reduce the detail in this example, a number of the governments are combined):

State	$ 10,400
Campbell County	1,480,000
Washington School District	5,060,000
City of Washington	2,400,000
Other governments (should be itemized)	1,566,000
	$10,516,400

If collections of 2008 taxes during a certain portion of the year amounted to $5,258,200, the Tax Agency Fund entry would be:

		Debits	Credits
	Tax Agency Fund:		
2.	Cash	5,258,200	
	Taxes Receivable for Other Funds and Governments—Current		5,258,200

The tax collections must in an actual case be identified with the parcels of property against which the taxes were levied because the location of each parcel determines the funds and governments that should receive the tax collections. Assuming for the sake of simplicity that the collections for the period represent collections of 50 percent of the taxes levied against each parcel in Campbell County and that the County General Fund is given 1 percent of all collections for governments other than the county as reimbursement for the cost of operating the Tax Agency Fund, the distribution of the $5,258,200 collections would be:

	Taxes Collected (50% of Levy)	Collection Fee (Charged) Received	Cash to Be Distributed
State	$ 5,200	$ (52)	$ 5,148
Campbell County	740,000	45,182	785,182
Washington School District	2,530,000	(25,300)	2,504,700
City of Washington	1,200,000	(12,000)	1,188,000
Other governments (should be itemized)	783,000	(7,830)	775,170
	$5,258,200	$ –0–	$5,258,200

If cash is not distributed as soon as this computation is made, the entry by the Tax Agency Fund to record the liability would be:

	Tax Agency Fund:		
3.	Due to Other Funds and Governments	5,258,200	
	Due to State		5,148
	Due to Campbell County		785,182
	Due to Washington School District		2,504,700
	Due to City of Washington		1,188,000
	Due to Other Governments		775,170

If, as is likely, collections during 2008 include collections of taxes that were levied for 2007, 2006, and preceding years, computations must be made to determine the appropriate distribution of collections for each tax year to each fund and government that levied taxes against the property for which collections have been received.

When cash is distributed by the Tax Agency Fund, the liability accounts shown in Entry 3 should be debited and Cash credited. If cash is advanced to one or more funds or governments prior to a regular periodic distribution, the debits to the liability accounts may precede the credits. By year-end, all advances should be settled, all distributions computed and recorded, and all cash distributed to the funds and governments for which the Tax Agency Fund is being operated. Therefore, if all those events have taken place, the year-end balance sheet for the Tax Agency Fund would consist of one asset: Taxes Receivable for Other Funds and Governments—Delinquent, and one liability, Due to Other Funds and Governments.

Entries Made by Funds and Governments Participating in Tax Agency Funds

Each fund or government that receives a distribution must record the appropriate portion of it in each of the funds it maintains. In each fund it must also record the fact that cash received differs from the amount of taxes collected by the fee paid to the county General Fund. The fee paid is recorded as an expenditure. For example, the computation for the entries to be made by the various funds of Washington School District would be (using the rates shown in Illustration 8–1) as follows:

	2008 Rate	Collections of 2008 Taxes	Collection Fee Paid	Cash Received
School Funds:				
General	$4.50	$2,250,000	$22,500	$2,227,500
Capital projects	0.18	90,000	900	89,100
Debt service	0.38	190,000	1,900	188,100
Total	$5.06	$2,530,000	$25,300	$2,504,700

From the computations it can be seen that the entry made in the Washington School District General Fund for the 2008 collections distributed should be:

	Debits	Credits
Washington School District General Fund:		
Cash	2,227,500	
Expenditures	22,500	
Taxes Receivable—Current		2,250,000

Similar entries would be made in the other two funds of the Washington School District and in all the funds of governments that paid a tax collection fee to the county General Fund. Collection by the county General Fund of taxes collected for it and the fee collected for it is computed as follows.

	2008 Rate	Collections of 2008 Taxes	Collection Fee	Cash Received
County Funds:				
General	$1.08	$540,000	$45,182	$585,182
Capital Projects	0.09	45,000	–0–	45,000
Debt Service	0.20	100,000	–0–	100,000
Welfare	0.11	55,000	–0–	55,000
Total	$1.48	$740,000	$45,182	$785,182

The entry to be made in the General Fund of Campbell County for the 2008 collections distributed should be:

	Debits	Credits
Campbell County General Fund:		
Cash	585,182	
Taxes Receivable—Current		540,000
Revenues		45,182

"Pass-Through" Agency Funds

Grants, entitlements, or shared revenues from the federal or a state government often pass through a lower level of government (primary recipient) before distribution to a secondary recipient. Accounting for such "pass-through" grants depends on whether the primary recipient government is deemed to have *administrative involvement* or *direct financial involvement* in the grants. According to GASB standards:

> A recipient government has administrative involvement if, for example, it (a) monitors secondary recipients for compliance with program-specific requirements, (b) determines eligibility of secondary recipients or projects, even if using grantor-established criteria, or (c) has the ability to exercise discretion in how the funds are allocated. A recipient government has direct financial involvement if, for example, it finances some direct program costs because of a grantor-imposed matching requirement or is liable for disallowed costs.[1]

More often than not, the criteria for administrative or direct financial involvement are met, in which case the primary recipient government must recognize a revenue for the receipt and an expenditure or expense for the transfer in a governmental fund, private-purpose trust fund, or proprietary fund. If, however, neither administrative nor financial involvement is deemed to exist, then a pass-through agency fund must be used and no revenue or expenditure/expense is recognized.

To illustrate accounting for a pass-through agency fund, assume that $5 million of federal financial assistance is received by a state government from the federal government, the full amount of which must be passed to local governments according to predetermined eligibility requirements and in amounts according to a predetermined

[1] GASB *Codification of Governmental Accounting and Financial Reporting Standards of June 30, 2005* (Norwalk, CT: GASB, 2005), Sec. N50.128.

formula. Since the state government is serving merely as a "cash conduit" in this case, the use of a pass-through agency fund is deemed appropriate. The entry to record receipt of the $5 million in the pass-through agency fund would be:

	Debits	Credits
Cash	5,000,000	
Due to Other Governments		5,000,000

Assuming that all monies were disbursed to the secondary recipients during the current fiscal year, the pass-through agency fund entry would be:

	Debits	Credits
Due to Other Governments	5,000,000	
Cash		5,000,000

Accounting for the receipt of cash or other assets from a pass-through agency fund by the recipient should be in conformity with GASB standards discussed previously: Governmental funds are to recognize all grants as revenue when the grant proceeds are available for use for the purposes of the fund and eligibility requirements have been met. If grant proceeds are available immediately, the Revenues account is credited; if some eligibility requirement must be met, the Deferred Revenues account should be credited at the time the grant proceeds are recognized as assets, and amounts should be transferred from Deferred Revenues to Revenues as eligibility requirements are met. Proprietary funds recognize as nonoperating revenues the proceeds of grants for operating purposes or grants that may be expended at the discretion of the recipient government; if the terms of the grant restrict the use of the proceeds to the acquisition or construction of capital assets, the proceeds must be recorded as capital contributions (see Chapter 7).

Financial Reporting of Agency Funds

As mentioned earlier in this chapter, fiduciary activities are reported only in the fiduciary fund financial statements; they have no effect on the governmental or business-type activities of the primary government reported in the government-wide financial statements. As shown in Illustration 1–13, agency fund financial information is reported in a separate column of the statement of fiduciary net assets. Agency funds are not included in the statement of changes in fiduciary net assets (see Illustration 1–14) because they have no net assets (assets minus liabilities equals zero net assets) and therefore cannot have *changes* in net assets. GASB standards do not require disclosure of the assets and liabilities of individual agency funds, but a government may optionally include in its comprehensive annual financial report a combining statement of net assets displaying the assets and liabilities of each agency fund in separate columns.

TRUST FUNDS

In addition to agency funds, the fiduciary fund classification includes investment trust funds, private-purpose trust funds, and pension trust funds.

Historically, trust funds have been created to account for assets received by the government in a trust agreement in which the assets are to be invested to produce income to be used for specified purposes (generally cultural or educational). The majority of such trusts benefit the government's own programs or its citizenry. As discussed and illustrated in Chapter 4, under *GASBS 34,* trusts that benefit the government's own programs or citizens at large are accounted for as either special revenue funds or *permanent funds*. The type of fund used depends on whether the principal of the gift can be spent for the specified purposes or is permanently restricted for investment, with only the earnings therefrom available to spend for the specified purposes. As discussed in Chapter 4, both special revenue funds and permanent funds are governmental fund types. Under the provisions of *GASBS 34* fiduciary funds are used when trusts benefit others, such as individuals, organizations, or other governments. Examples of trust funds are shown in the following sections.

INVESTMENT POOLS

Effective management of investments (and in some cases, idle cash) often is enhanced by placing the investments of the funds in a pool under the control of the treasurer or a professional investment manager, either within the treasurer's office or in a financial institution such as a bank or investment firm. If the investment pool is an *internal* investment pool (participating funds are all within the same government) an agency fund may be used to account for the investments in the pool. However, each participating fund is required, for financial reporting purposes, to report its proportionate share of pooled cash and investments as fund assets, and the assets and liabilities of the agency fund are not reported in the government's external financial statements.[2] For internal management purposes, it may be useful for participating funds to use the account title *Equity in Pooled Cash and Investments,* the account title used in the illustrative journal entries shown later in this section.

If the investment pool has external participants (other governments or organizations outside the government administering the pool), an **external investment pool** is used. GASB standards require that an **investment trust fund** be used to account for the assets, liabilities, net assets, and changes in net assets corresponding to the equity of the *external* participants.[3] The accounting for investment trust funds uses an economic resources measurement focus and the full accrual basis of accounting.

Typically, the administering government also participates in the pool; however, its equity is considered *internal* and is not reported in the financial statements of the investment trust fund. Instead, the net assets and changes in net assets relating to the internal portion of the pool are presented in the financial statements of each participating fund and in the governmental activities and business-type activities of the sponsoring government's government-wide financial statements. Recall that the financial information for investment trust funds is reported only in the fiduciary fund financial statements (see Illustrations 1–13 and 1–14) and is not reported in the government-wide financial statements.

Accounting for an external investment pool is presented in the remainder of this section.

Creation of an Investment Pool

Earnings on pooled investments and changes in fair value of investments are allocated to the participants having an equity interest in the pool in proportion to their relative

---

[2] GASB, *Codification,* Sec. I50.112.
[3] Ibid., par. 116.

contributions to the pool. To ensure an equitable division of earnings and changes in fair value it is necessary to do revaluations whenever contributions to the pool or distributions from the pool occur. The revaluation involves adjusting to **fair value** all investments in the pool, and all investments being brought into the pool or removed from the pool.[4] Each fund of the sponsoring government and external participant that contributes investments to the pool should debit Equity in Pooled Investments, or some similar account, for the fair value of the investments, credit the Investments account for the carrying value (cost or fair value at the time the investments were previously marked to fair value), and credit or debit Revenues—Change in Fair Value of Investments, depending on whether the current fair value is higher or lower than carrying value, respectively. Note that a net debit balance in the Revenues—Change in Fair Value of Investments account would be reported as a contra-revenue item in the operating statement of the appropriate fund, and as a component of investment income, not as an expenditure or expense.

Illustration of the Creation of an Investment Fund

On January 10, 2008, Drew County decided to create a new investment pool to be accounted for as an *investment trust fund*. Operating expenses of the pool, primarily for personnel time, office supplies, computer, telephone, and postage, are considered nominal and will not be charged to the pool. The initial participants in the pool are the county's own debt service fund and two external participants, the Town of Calvin's Debt Service Fund and the Calvin Independent School District's Capital Projects Fund. The equity pertaining to the Drew County Debt Service Fund represents an *internal* investment pool, so its proportionate equity share of the investment pool's assets are reported in the debt service fund for financial reporting purposes, not as part of the investment trust fund net assets. The proportionate share of assets allocated to *external* participants, however, is properly reported in the financial statements of the investment trust fund.

Illustration 8–3 shows the specific cash and investments that were transferred on January 10, 2008, to create the Drew County Investment Pool.

At the time the Drew County Investment Pool is created, journal entries are required in the accounts of the Drew County Debt Service Fund and Town of Calvin Debt Service Fund, the Calvin Independent School District Capital Projects Fund, and the investment trust fund to record creation of the fund. The journal entries in the Drew County Debt Service Fund and Drew County Investment Pool (the investment trust fund) to create the investment pool are shown in Entries 1a and 1b. Entries in the funds of the external participants would be similar to those for the Drew County Debt Service Fund and therefore are omitted for the sake of brevity.

		Debits	Credits
	Drew County Debt Service Fund:		
1a.	Equity in Pooled Investments	14,850,000	
	Cash		1,000,000
	Investments—U.S. Agency Obligations		13,373,000
	Revenues—Change in Fair Value of Investments		52,000
	Revenues—Investment Earnings		425,000

[4] GASB standards define *fair value* as the amount at which an investment could be exchanged in a current transaction between willing parties, other than in a forced liquidation sale. GASB, *Codification,* Sec. 150.105.

ILLUSTRATION 8–3 **Assets Transferred to Create Drew County Investment Pool**

Assets Transferred	Fair Value at 12-31-07	Fair Value at 1-10-08	Change in Fair Value	Accrued Interest
Drew County Debt Service Fund:				
Cash	$ 1,000,000	$ 1,000,000	$ –0–	$ –0–
U.S. agency obligations	13,373,000	13,425,000	52,000	425,000
Town of Calvin Debt Service Fund:				
U.S. Treasury notes	9,568,000	9,545,000	(23,000)	192,000
U.S. agency obligations	158,700	160,000	1,300	3,000
Calvin Independent School District Capital Projects Fund:				
U.S. agency obligations	2,789,000	2,800,000	11,000	76,900
Repurchase agreements	2,060,000	2,060,000	–0–	13,100
Totals	$28,948,700	$28,990,000	$ 41,300	$710,000

		Debits	Credits
	Drew County Investment Pool:		
1b.	Cash	1,000,000	
	Investments—U.S. Treasury Notes	9,545,000	
	Investments—U.S. Agency Obligations	16,385,000	
	Investments—Repurchase Agreements	2,060,000	
	Accrued Interest Receivable	710,000	
	Due to Debt Service Fund		14,850,000
	Additions—Deposits in Pooled Investments— Town of Calvin		9,900,000
	Additions—Deposits in Pooled Investments— Calvin Independent School District		4,950,000

A trial balance, prepared for the Drew County Investment Pool immediately after Entry 1b has been posted to the pool's general ledger, is presented in Illustration 8–4.

On February 1, 2008, Drew County sold tax-supported bonds in the amount of $15,000,000 to finance the construction of roads and bridges. The proceeds of the bonds are added to the pool for investment until such time as they are needed for capital projects fund disbursements. As of February 1, 2008, the U.S. Treasury notes in the pool have a current fair value of $9,535,000 ($10,000 less than the carrying value reported in the trial balance shown in Illustration 8–4), and the U.S. agency obligations in the pool have a fair value of $16,695,000 ($310,000 more than the carrying value reported in the trial balance); the fair value of the repurchase agreement is the same as reported in the trial balance. The balance of the Cash account was still $1,000,000 as of February 1, 2008. Therefore, total assets of the pool, revalued to fair value as of February 1, 2008, amount to $30,000,000 (a net increase of $300,000 over the carrying values previously reported).

In the investment pool accounts, the $300,000 increase in carrying value of assets should be credited to a liability account for the share of the internal participant (Drew County's Debt Service Fund) and to "additions" accounts (addition to net assets, similar to revenue) for the shares of the external participants, based on their equitable proportions in the pool just prior to the asset revaluation. The liability to the debt service

ILLUSTRATION 8–4

DREW COUNTY
Investment Pool
Trial Balance
As of January 10, 2008

Account Title	Debits	Credits
Cash	$ 1,000,000	
Investments—U.S. Treasury Notes	9,545,000	
Investments—U.S. Agency Obligations	16,385,000	
Investments—Repurchase Agreements	2,060,000	
Accrued Interest Receivable	710,000	
Due to Debt Service Fund		$14,850,000
Additions—Deposits in Pooled Investments— Town of Calvin		9,900,000
Additions—Deposits in Pooled Investments— Calvin Independent School District		4,950,000
Totals	$29,700,000	$29,700,000

fund, therefore, is increased by $150,000 (300,000 × 14,850/29,700); Additions—Change in Fair Value—Town of Calvin is credited for $100,000 (300,000 × 9,900/29,700); and Additions—Change in Fair Value—Calvin Independent School District is credited for $50,000 (300,000 × 4,950/29,700). Note that the equity of each participant in the pool remains proportionately the same (i.e., the amount due to the Town of Calvin is $10,000,000 after revaluing the investments to current fair value; total liabilities and net assets [if the Additions accounts were closed] of the pool are $30,000,000; 10,000/30,000 = 9,900/29,700, etc.). The journal entry in the investment pool summarizing the revaluation of investments and the capital projects entry into the investment pool is given as follows:

		Debits	Credits
	Drew County Investment Pool:		
2.	Cash	15,000,000	
	Investments—U.S. Agency Obligations	310,000	
	Investments—U.S. Treasury Notes		10,000
	Due to Debt Service Fund		150,000
	Due to Capital Projects Fund		15,000,000
	Additions—Change in Fair Value of Investments— Town of Calvin		100,000
	Additions—Change in Fair Value of Investments— Calvin Independent School District		50,000

After revaluation of investments in the pool and receipt of $15,000,000 cash from proceeds of bonds sold to finance road and bridge construction, the Drew County Trial Balance of the Investment Pool becomes as shown in Illustration 8–5.

ILLUSTRATION 8–5

<table>
<tr><th colspan="3">DREW COUNTY
Investment Pool
Trial Balance
As of February 1, 2008</th></tr>
<tr><th>Account Title</th><th>Debits</th><th>Credits</th></tr>
<tr><td>Cash</td><td>$16,000,000</td><td></td></tr>
<tr><td>Investments—U.S. Treasury Notes</td><td>9,535,000</td><td></td></tr>
<tr><td>Investments—U.S. Agency Obligations</td><td>16,695,000</td><td></td></tr>
<tr><td>Investments—Repurchase Agreements</td><td>2,060,000</td><td></td></tr>
<tr><td>Accrued Interest Receivable</td><td>710,000</td><td></td></tr>
<tr><td>Due to Debt Service Fund</td><td></td><td>$15,000,000</td></tr>
<tr><td>Due to Capital Projects Fund</td><td></td><td>15,000,000</td></tr>
<tr><td>Additions—Deposits in Pooled Investments—Town of Calvin</td><td></td><td>9,900,000</td></tr>
<tr><td>Additions—Deposits in Pooled Investments—
  Calvin Independent School District</td><td></td><td>4,950,000</td></tr>
<tr><td>Additions—Change in Fair Value of Investments—
  Town of Calvin</td><td></td><td>100,000</td></tr>
<tr><td>Additions—Change in Fair Value of Investments—
  Calvin Independent School District</td><td></td><td>50,000</td></tr>
<tr><td>   Totals</td><td>$45,000,000</td><td>$45,000,000</td></tr>
</table>

Operation of a Cash and Investment Pool

Although the capital projects fund invested $15,000,000 cash, upon admission to the pool, that fund no longer has a specific claim on the cash of the pool; rather, it (and each other fund or government that is a member of the pool) has a proportionate interest in the total assets of the pool and will share in earnings, gains, and losses of the pool in that proportion. Ordinarily, it is inconvenient and unnecessary to apportion to liability accounts and additions to net asset accounts for each receipt of dividends or interest and each revaluation of the portfolio to fair value (some pools revalue to fair value daily). It is simpler to accumulate the earnings in the *Undistributed Earnings on Pooled Investments* account and the unrealized and realized gains and losses in the *Undistributed Change in Fair Value of Pooled Investments* account (both of these accounts are clearing accounts) and to make periodic distributions from these accounts to the specific liability and additions to net asset accounts for pool participants.

The frequency of distributions depends on whether all cash of all participants is pooled along with investments or whether each participant retains an operating cash account. In the former case, the pool would have frequent receipts attributable to collections of revenues and receivables of the participants and would have daily disbursements on behalf of the participants; in this case, the interest of each participant in the pool would have to be recomputed each day. If, however, a working cash balance is retained by each participant, the receipts and disbursements of pool cash would be much less frequent, and the distribution of gains and losses and earnings, as well as the recomputation of the interest of each participant in the pool could be correspondingly less frequent.

As an example of accounting for earnings on investments of a pool, assume the pool shown in Illustration 8–5 collects interest of $1,610,000, including the $710,000 accrued interest receivable. An appropriate entry would be:

		Debits	Credits
	Drew County Investment Pool:		
3.	Cash	1,610,000	
	Accrued Interest Receivable		710,000
	Undistributed Earnings on Pooled Investments		900,000

By the time the earnings are to be distributed, the fair value of all investments may have changed. Even if this is true, the proportionate interest of each participant will not have changed because each participant continues to bear gains and losses in the same proportion until a participant changes all participants' proportionate interest in the pool by contributing additional assets to the pool or taking assets out of the pool. Therefore, in this example, when earnings are distributed, the shares apportioned to the participants are Drew County Debt Service Fund, 15/45 or 3/9; Drew County Capital Projects Fund, 15/45 or 3/9; Town of Calvin, 10/45 or 2/9; and Calvin Independent School District, 5/45 or 1/9. The entry in the Drew County Investment Pool to distribute $900,000 of earnings follows:

	Drew County Investment Pool:		
4a.	Undistributed Earnings on Pooled Investments	900,000	
	Due to Debt Service Fund		300,000
	Due to Capital Projects Fund		300,000
	Additions—Investment Earnings—		
	Town of Calvin		200,000
	Additions—Investment Earnings—		
	Calvin Independent School District		100,000

After the distribution, each participant has the same proportionate interest in the assets of the pool as it had before the distribution.

As noted previously, internal management of the pool is enhanced if each participant that is a member of the pool maintains an asset account with a title such as Equity in Pooled Investments. The balance of this account in each member's fund should be the reciprocal of the pool's account that reports the pool's liability or net asset balance to that participant (depending on whether the participant is an internal member or external member). Thus, in the Drew County example, the Drew County Debt Service Fund's Equity in Pooled Investments account had a debit balance of $15,000,000 as of March 31, 2008, before the earnings distribution. Upon notification of the earnings distribution on the pooled investments, the Drew County Debt Service Fund would make the following entry:

	Drew County Debt Service Fund:		
4b.	Equity in Pooled Investments	300,000	
	Revenues—Investment Earnings		300,000

Interest and dividends earned on pooled investments would increase the participants' equity in the pool, as would realized gains on the sales of investments (excess of fair value on date of sale over carrying value) and unrealized gains resulting from periodic revaluation of the pooled investment portfolio to fair value in times of rising market values of securities held in the portfolio. Both realized losses on securities sold (deficit of fair value at prior revaluation date compared with fair value at the sale date) and unrealized losses resulting from periodic revaluation of the portfolio in times of falling market values decrease the equity of members of the pool. In the Drew County Investment Pool example, each member maintains an operating cash account. Consequently, the pool does not need to distribute gains and losses daily, so it accumulates realized and unrealized gains and losses in the *Undistributed Change in Fair Value of Pooled Investments* account. This procedure allows a netting of gains and losses in each account so that only the net realized and unrealized gain (or loss) need be distributed to pool participants, thus saving some clerical or computer time.

GASB standards require that realized and unrealized gains and losses be reported as a single amount, "Change in Fair Value of Investments," as a component of investment income rather than being reported as separate amounts in the financial statement. However, realized and unrealized gains and losses can be disclosed in the notes to the financial statements, if desired.[5] If a government intends to disclose realized and unrealized gains or losses or needs such information for internal management purposes, it may be useful to maintain a separate *Allowance for Changes in Fair Value of Pooled Investments* (a contra-asset account) to record all changes in fair value rather than increasing and decreasing the balance of the investment accounts. This technique permits the investment accounts to be carried at cost.

Assume that during fiscal 2008, the realized gains on sales of pooled investments of the Drew County Investment Pool, all credited to the Undistributed Change in Fair Value of Pooled Investments, amounted to $235,000 (measured as excess of fair value at the sale dates over prior fair value). During the year, realized losses, all debited to the undistributed change account, totaled $50,000 (measured as the deficit of fair value at the sale dates under prior fair value). Thus, there was a net credit of $185,000 for realized gains and losses for the period. Similarly, assume the net effect of marking the portfolio to fair value is an unrealized gain of $265,000, which is credited to the undistributed change account. The net effect of recognizing these gains and losses in the accounts of the Drew County Investment Pool, pending distribution, is summarized in Entry 5.

		Debits	Credits
	Drew County Investment Pool:		
5.	Investments (specific investments should be debited or credited here)	450,000	
	Undistributed Change in Fair Value of Investments		450,000

Assuming that no participants have joined the pool or withdrawn from the pool and that the four participants that have continued to be members of the pool have not transferred assets to or withdrawn additional assets from the pool, the realized and unrealized net gains of $450,000 should be distributed to the participants in the proportions

[5]GASB, *Codification*, Sec. 150.111. If the entity opts, however, to disclose realized gains and losses, they must be measured independently of the basis used for accounting recognition in the pool. That is, the realized gains and losses reported in the notes must be measured as the fair value at the sale date of the investments over (under) cost rather than over (under) fair value at the prior revaluation date.

used for the distribution of earnings in Entry 4a (3/9, 3/9, 2/9, and 1/9). The distribution is shown in the following entry:

		Debits	Credits
	Drew County Investment Pool:		
6.	Undistributed Change in Fair Value of Investments	450,000	
	Due to Debt Service Fund		150,000
	Due to Capital Projects Fund		150,000
	Additions—Change in Fair Value of Investments—Town of Calvin		100,000
	Additions—Change in Fair Value of Investments—Calvin Independent School District		50,000

At December 31, 2008, interest earnings of $720,000 had accrued and were recorded, as shown in Entry 7:

	Drew County Investment Pool:		
7.	Accrued Interest Receivable	720,000	
	Undistributed Earnings on Pooled Investments		720,000

Assuming that the accrued interest was immediately distributed to pool participants in the same proportions listed for Entry 6, the following entry would be made to record the distribution:

	Drew County Investment Pool:		
8.	Undistributed Earnings on Pooled Investments	720,000	
	Due to Debt Service Fund		240,000
	Due to Capital Projects Fund		240,000
	Additions—Investment Earnings—Town of Calvin		160,000
	Additions—Investment Earnings—Calvin Independent School District		80,000

Both Entries 6 and 8 would lead to entries to recognize an increase in each participant's Equity in Pooled Investments and revenue accounts. Those entries would be similar to Entry 4b and thus are not shown here.

After all earnings and changes in fair value have been recorded as in the entries illustrated, the equities and proportionate interests of the participants follow:

Debt service fund	$15,690,000, or 3/9 of total
Capital projects fund	15,690,000, or 3/9 of total
Town of Calvin	10,460,000, or 2/9 of total
Calvin Independent School District	5,230,000, or 1/9 of total
Total	$47,070,000

Withdrawal of Assets from the Pool

If a participant in a pool withdraws part of its equity from a pool, that participant's proportionate interest is decreased and all other participants' proportionate interest is increased. Before a withdrawal is made, there should be an apportionment of earnings, gains, and losses to date. The same is true in the event of complete withdrawal of one or more participants from the pool.

Continuing with the Drew County Investment Pool example, assume that the debt service fund needs to withdraw $5,000,000 from the pool to retire matured bonds. Ignoring the fact that in most practical cases it would be necessary to first sell some investments, the entry in the investment trust fund for the withdrawal is given as follows:

		Debits	Credits
	Drew County Investment Pool:		
9a.	Due to Debt Service Fund	5,000,000	
	Cash		5,000,000

The corresponding entry in the debt service fund follows:

	Drew County Debt Service Fund:		
9b.	Cash	5,000,000	
	Equity in Pooled Investments		5,000,000

After withdrawal of $5,000,000 by the debt service fund, the proportionate interests in the pool become:

Debt service fund	$10,690,000, or 25.4% of total
Capital projects fund	15,690,000, or 37.3% of total
Town of Calvin	10,460,000, or 24.9% of total
Calvin Independent School District	5,230,000, or 12.4% of total
Total	$42,070,000

Closing Entry

To assist in preparing financial statements, the additions accounts (see Entries 1b, 2, 4a, 6, and 8), which reflect changes in the external participants' proportionate interest due to net new deposits/withdrawals, investment earnings, and changes in fair value, must be closed to the appropriate net asset accounts, as shown in Entry 10 below:

	Debits	Credits
Drew County Investment Pool:		
10. Additions—Deposits in Pooled Investments—Town of Calvin	9,900,000	
Additions—Deposits in Pooled Investments— Calvin Independent School District	4,950,000	
Additions—Investment Earnings—Town of Calvin	360,000	
Additions—Investment Earnings— Calvin Independent School District	180,000	
Additions—Change in Fair Value of Investments— Town of Calvin	200,000	
Additions—Change in Fair Value of Investments— Calvin Independent School District	100,000	
Net Assets Held in Trust for Participants—Town of Calvin		10,460,000
Net Assets Held in Trust for Participants— Calvin Independent School District		5,230,000

Illustrative Financial Statements

Illustrative fiduciary fund statements, prepared for internal management purposes, are presented in Illustrations 8–6 and 8–7. These statements are prepared as of, or for the year ended, December 31, 2008, Drew County's fiscal year-end. These statements also provide the information to be reported in a column of the statement of fiduciary fund net assets (see Illustration 1–13) and statement of changes in fiduciary fund net assets (see Illustration 1–14). All assets of the pool are reported in the statement of net assets although the external participants' equity in the assets of the investment pool amounts to only the $15,690,000 reported as net assets, about 37.3 percent of the total assets. The other $26,380,000 is reported as a liability owed to the two participating funds of the Drew County government. Those funds would report their share of the investment pool as Equity in Pooled Investments rather than specific assets.

ILLUSTRATION 8–6

DREW COUNTY
Investment Pool
Statement of Net Assets
As of December 31, 2008

Assets		
Cash		$12,610,000
Investments		28,740,000
Accrued interest receivable		720,000
Total assets		42,070,000
Liabilities		
Due to internal participants		26,380,000
Total liabilities		26,380,000
Net Assets		
Held in trust for participants—		
Town of Calvin	$10,460,000	
Calvin Independent School District	5,230,000	
Total net assets		$15,690,000

ILLUSTRATION 8–7

DREW COUNTY
Investment Pool
Statement of Changes in Net Assets
for the Year Ended December 31, 2008

Additions

Deposits of participants	$14,850,000
Investment earnings	540,000
Increase in fair value of investments	300,000
Total additions	15,690,000
Deductions	
Total deductions	–0–
Change in net assets	15,690,000
Net assets, January 1, 2008	–0–
Net assets, December 31, 2008	$15,690,000

PRIVATE-PURPOSE TRUST FUNDS

The fair value of assets placed in trust under a trust agreement is referred to as the *principal* or *corpus* of the trust. If the principal of the trust must be held intact (nonexpendable) to produce income, the trust is often called an *endowment*. The income from the assets of an endowment may be used only for the purposes specified by the trustor. Not all trusts require that the principal be held intact. Some trusts allow the principal to be spent (expended) for the purpose specified by the trust. Additionally, not all trusts make distinctions between the use of principal and income. For example, loan funds operated as trust funds usually require that both the principal and income be held intact, whereas, public retirement systems are trusts whose principal and income are both expended for specified purposes.

Trust funds are also classified as public or private. *Public trust funds* are those whose principal or income, or both, must be used for some public purpose. The beneficiaries of *private trust funds* are private individuals, organizations, or other governments. A fund established for the purpose of holding performance deposits of licensees under a government's regulatory activities is an example of a private trust fund. A fund used to account for escheat property arising from the estate of persons who die intestate without any known heirs is another example of a private trust fund.

Because most trusts administered by governments are created for public purposes (for example, to maintain parks and cemeteries or to acquire art for public buildings), they are considered governmental rather than fiduciary activities under *GASBS 34*. Thus, nonexpendable public-purpose trusts are accounted for as permanent funds and expendable public-purpose trusts are accounted for as special revenue funds. These governmental fund types were discussed and illustrated in Chapter 4.

Private-purpose trust funds are relatively few compared with public-purpose trust funds. Further, private-purpose trust funds follow accounting and financial reporting practices that are quite similar to those illustrated in the previous section on investment trust funds. The accounting for a private-purpose trust fund whose principal is permanently restricted for investment, with earnings available for a specified private purpose, is similar to that for the City of Concordia Library Endowment Fund illustrated in Chapter 4 as a permanent fund. The principal difference is that financial information for a private-purpose trust is reported in the statement of fiduciary net assets and statement of changes in fiduciary net assets, whereas that for a permanent fund is reported in the balance sheet—governmental funds and statement of revenues, expenditures, and changes in fund balances—governmental funds. Even though a private-purpose trust reports additions and deductions from net assets (see Illustration 8–7 for an example), those items are measured in essentially the same manner as revenues and expenditures of a permanent fund. Because there is little difference in accounting and reporting for private-purpose trusts, permanent funds, and investment trust funds, already illustrated, no journal entries or financial statements are provided in this chapter for private-purpose trust funds.

PENSION ACCOUNTING

Cash and investments held by state and local pension plans for fiscal year 2002–03 amounted to nearly $2.2 trillion.[6] Thus, it is not surprising that the GASB has devoted substantial effort to improving accounting and financial reporting for pension plans. This section provides an overview of the accounting and reporting requirements for pension plans, as well as the governmental employers that sponsor such plans.

Pension plans are of two general types, *defined contribution plans* and *defined benefit plans.* A **defined contribution plan** specifies the amount or rate of contribution, often a percentage of covered salary, that the employer and employees must contribute to the members' accounts in the pension plan. The level of benefits payable upon retirement is determined by the total amount of contributions to a member's account, earnings on investments, and allocations of forfeited contributions of other members credited to the account.[7] Because future benefits are neither formula based nor guaranteed, the risk associated with defined contribution plans rests primarily with employees; the employer's responsibility essentially ends once the required contribution is made. Such plans ordinarily are *not* administered on an actuarial basis; therefore, accounting and financial reporting requirements for both the plan and the employer are straightforward and present few complications. Essentially, the plan reports the fair value of pension assets and any liability for accrued plan benefits; the employer reports expenditures/expenses for the amount contributed to the plan. Both the plan and the employer are required to provide in the notes to the financial statements a brief description of the plan, classes of employees covered, plan provisions, contribution requirements, significant accounting policies for the plan, and concentrations of investments in any one organization that exceed 5 percent or more of plan net assets.[8]

A **defined benefit plan** provides a specified amount of benefits based on a formula that may include factors such as age, salary, and years of employment.[9] Determining the present value of projected pension benefits involves numerous factors, such as employee mortality, employee turnover, salary progression, and investment earnings. To ensure that plan assets will be adequate to cover future benefits, professional actuaries

[6] U.S. Bureau of the Census, *National Summary of State and Local Government Employee-Retirement System Finances: Fiscal Year 2002–2003,* Table 1.

[7] GASB, *Codification,* Sec. Pe5.525.

[8] GASB, *Codification,* Sec. Pe6.104.

[9] GASB, *Codification,* Sec. Pe5.524.

are engaged to calculate the present value of benefits and the required contributions that must be made by employers and, in some cases, employees. Of course, the basic assumptions underlying actuaries' projections may change over time, giving rise to periodic revisions in the required contributions. Because of the need to rely extensively on actuaries' estimates, it is not surprising that accounting for defined benefit plans is much more complex than for defined contribution plans. The remainder of this section provides a summary overview of the accounting and financial reporting requirements for defined benefit pension plans; a complete discussion of these plans is considerably beyond the scope of this text.

The illustrative transactions for defined benefit pension plan accounting discussed in this section are based on a "single-employer plan," that is, a single plan administered by a single governmental employer. Readers should be aware, however, that many governments sponsor several employer pension plans for different classes of employees (for example, a plan for general employees and one or more separate plans for public safety employees). Furthermore, in some states, some or all local government employees participate in a statewide defined benefit pension plan rather than one sponsored by the local government. Such plans or groups of plans are often referred to as **Public Employee Retirement Systems** (PERS). The GASB standards that apply to a single-employer plan apply as well to multiple-employer plans.

Until 1996, governments had considerable latitude regarding the choice of accounting method for pension plans. However, after several years of effort, the GASB implemented two standards that provide comprehensive guidance on pension accounting and financial reporting. These standards differ from FASB standards for accounting and reporting of pension plans. GASB *Statement No. 25* provides accounting and reporting guidance for defined benefit pension plans and GASB *Statement No. 27* provides the same guidance for the sponsor/employer. The authoritative portions of these standards can be found in the GASB's *Codification of Governmental Accounting and Financial Reporting Standards,* Sections Pe5 and P20, respectively. Most observers agree that the standards have helped to achieve more uniform reporting of governmental pension plans. More recently, under *GASBS 34,* pension plans are required to be reported in the basic fiduciary fund statements for the sponsoring government (see Illustrations 1–13 and 1–14). For those plans administered as legally separate entities that publish "stand-alone" financial statements, *GASBS 34* also requires the reporting of the separate entities' pension fund financial information in the fiduciary funds statements of the sponsoring governments.

Required Financial Reporting for Defined Benefit Pension Plans

GASB standards establish a financial reporting framework for defined benefit pension plans that includes both required financial statements and required schedules of historical trend information. The schedules are *required supplementary information* (RSI) that should follow immediately after the financial statements.[10] Two financial statements and two supplementary schedules of historical trend data are required. These requirements are described as follows:

   a. *A statement of plan net assets* showing plan assets, liabilities, and net assets. Plan assets should be reported at fair value. (See Illustration, 8–10 and 8–11.)

[10] Ibid., par. 111. GASB, *Codification*, Sec. Pe5.125, note 18 alternatively allows for presentation of the required information in the notes to the financial statements.

ILLUSTRATION 8–8   **Required Supplementary Information**

		Johnson County Employee Retirement System Schedule of Funding Progress (in thousands)				
Actuarial Valuation Date	Actuarial Value of Assets (a)	Actuarial Accrued Liability (AAL)— Entry Age (b)	Unfunded or (Overfunded) AAL (b − a)	Funded Ratio (a/b)	Covered Payroll (c)	Unfunded or (Overfunded) AAL as a Percentage of Covered Payroll ((b − a)/c)
12/31/2002	$ 86,320	$ 80,302	($6,018)	107.49%	$59,584	(10.10)%
12/31/2003	71,756	69,436	(2,320)	103.34	59,487	(3.90)
12/31/2004	79,887	77,704	(2,183)	102.81	64,206	(3.40)
12/31/2005	88,452	88,450	(2)	100.00	50,000	0.00
12/31/2006	92,887	92,885	(2)	100.00	51,282	(0.00)
12/31/2007	111,246	111,304	58	99.95	86,567	0.07

    b. A statement of changes in plan net assets showing additions to plan net assets, deductions from plan net assets, and net increase (decrease) in plan net assets. (See Illustration 8–12.)

    c. A schedule of funding progress showing historical trend data about the actuarially determined status of plan funding "from a long-term, ongoing perspective and the progress made in accumulating sufficient assets to pay benefits when due." (See Illustration 8–8.)

    d. A schedule of employer contributions showing historical trend data about the *annual required contributions of the employer* (ARC) and employer contributions in relation to ARC.[11] (See Illustration 8–9.)

In addition, the plan is required to provide notes to the financial statements *and* notes to the required schedules. The notes to the financial statements should disclose the following information:

    a. Plan description, including:
        1. Identification of the type of plan.
        2. Classes of employees covered.
        3. Brief description of benefit provisions.

    b. Summary of significant accounting policies.

    c. Description of contributions and reserves, including:
        1. The authority under which contributions are made.
        2. Funding policies.
        3. Required contribution rates of active plan members.
        4. Brief description of any long-term contracts for contributions.
        5. Balances of the plan's legally required reserves at the reporting date.[12]

The notes to the required schedules should provide:

    a. Identification of actuarial methods used and significant actuarial assumptions for the most recent year covered by the required supplementary schedules.

---

[11] Ibid., par. 111.

[12] Ibid., par. 124.

ILLUSTRATION 8–9

Johnson County Employee Retirement System Schedule of Employer Contributions (in thousands)		
Year Ended December 31,	Annual Required Contribution	Percentage Contributed
2002	$ 2,814	100%
2003	1,702	100
2004	2,609	100
2005	5,063	100
2006	7,352	100
2007	13,615	100

b. Factors such as changes in benefit provisions, employees covered by the plan, or actuarial methods or assumptions used that significantly affect the trends reported in the schedules.[13]

Statement of Plan Net Assets

Illustrations 8–10 and 8–11 present the statement of plan net assets for the hypothetical Johnson County Employee Retirement System for fiscal years 2007 and 2008, respectively. Johnson County administers one pension plan. As shown, plan investments should be reported at fair value (last reported sales price) for all investments in securities that trade on active exchanges. Investments in mortgages should be based on the discounted present value of future interest and principal payments to be received. Investments in real estate should be reported at fair value based on independent appraisals. All other investments should be reported at estimated fair value, including institutional price quotes for debt securities for which trade prices are unavailable.

Depreciable assets of a pension fund, that is, capital assets held for use by the fund, should be reported at cost less accumulated depreciation. Cash, short-term investments (reported at cost), and receivables typically represent a minor part of the total assets of a pension fund. The assets of a pension fund are not classified as current and noncurrent; the distinction not being important since short-term liabilities typically are immaterial in relation to available plan assets. Fund liabilities, usually short-term (e.g., benefits due but unpaid, refunds for terminated employees, vouchers payable, accrued expenses, and payroll taxes payable), are reported as a deduction from assets; the difference is typically captioned *net assets held in trust for pension benefits.*

Statement of Changes in Plan Net Assets

The Johnson County Employee Retirement System Statement of Changes in Net Plan Assets is presented in Illustration 8–12. This statement reports employer and employee contributions and investment income as additions to net assets rather than as revenues. Similarly, benefits paid, refunds of contributions, and administrative expenses are reported under the caption deductions from net assets rather than as expenses. The net increase (decrease) in net assets is added to beginning-of-period net assets to calculate end-of-period net assets. Additions and deductions are recognized on the accrual basis.

[13] Ibid., par. 132.

Schedule of Funding Progress

An example of a *schedule of funding progress* for Johnson county is presented in Illustration 8–8. This schedule shows funding progress of the plan in relation to *actuarial* requirements. A key measure of how well the plan is funded is the *funded ratio*. The **funded ratio** is the ratio of *actuarial value of assets* to *actuarial accrued liability* (AAL). **Actuarial value of assets** is the value of plan assets used by the actuary; the methods of determination for the various assets should be disclosed in the notes.[14] **Actuarial accrued liability** is determined by using any of several generally accepted actuarial methods (consistently applied) and is the present value of projected benefits other than normal costs (benefits earned from current and future employee service). Thus, AAL arises primarily from past underfunding and ad hoc changes in plan provisions. Both the schedule of funding progress and the other required schedule, the *schedule of employer contributions,* should present information for the current year and five prior years (six years in total).

Schedule of Employer Contributions

The key information the reader should note in the *schedule of employer contributions* shown in Illustration 8–9 is the *annual required contribution* (ARC) and what percentage of the ARC the employer has contributed. **Annual required contribution** is an actuarially determined amount that the employer should contribute each year to ensure full actuarial funding of the plan. Calculation of the ARC is discussed later in the section headed "Employer's Pension Accounting."

Alternative Reporting and Disclosure

While the two financial statements and two schedules discussed previously illustrated the employer government's financial statements and schedules, stand-alone entities or Public Employee Retirement Systems (PERS) would also issue similar types of statements, schedules, and note disclosures.[15]

Illustrative Transactions for a Defined Benefit Pension Plan

Assume that the Johnson County Employee Retirement Plan started the fiscal year beginning July 1, 2007, with the statement of plan net assets presented in Illustration 8–10. During fiscal year 2008, the following transactions occurred that require journal entries as shown.

Accrued interest receivable as of June 30, 2007, was collected:

		Debits	Credits
1.	Cash	2,507,612	
	Accrued Interest Receivable		2,507,612

Member contributions in the amount of $8,009,400 and employer contributions in the amount of $14,126,292 were received in cash:

		Debits	Credits
2.	Cash	22,135,692	
	Additions—Member Contributions		8,009,400
	Additions—Employer Contributions		14,126,292

[14] The definitions paraphrased here and following are based on those provided in GASB, *Codification,* Sec. Pe5.572.A-1 through A-6.

[15] GASB *Statement No. 34* (Norwalk, CT: GASB, 1999), par. 106.

ILLUSTRATION 8–10

JOHNSON COUNTY EMPLOYEE RETIREMENT SYSTEM
Statement of Plan Net Assets
June 30, 2007

Assets	
Cash	$ 51,213
Accrued interest receivable	2,507,612
Investments (at fair value):	
Bonds	71,603,976
Common stocks	31,957,205
Commercial paper and repurchase agreements	12,570,401
Total assets	118,690,407
Liabilities	
Accounts payable and accrued expenses	401,581
Net assets held in trust for pension benefits	**$118,288,826**

Annuity benefits in the amount of $3,134,448 and disability benefits in the amount of $287,590 were recorded as liabilities:

		Debits	Credits
3.	Deductions—Annuity Benefits	3,134,448	
	Deductions—Disability Benefits	287,590	
	Accounts Payable and Accrued Expenses		3,422,038

Accounts payable and accrued expenses paid in cash amounted to $3,571,969:

4.	Accounts Payable and Accrued Expenses	3,571,969	
	Cash		3,571,969

Terminated employees whose benefits were not vested were refunded $2,057,265 in cash:

5.	Deductions—Refunds to Terminated Employees	2,057,265	
	Cash		2,057,265

Investment income received in cash amounted to $9,440,769; $4,882,076 of interest income was accrued at year-end. In addition, the fair value of investments in bonds decreased during the year by $5,626,382 and the fair value of investments in common stocks increased by $3,427,600.

		Debits	Credits
6a.	Cash	9,440,769	
	Accrued Interest Receivable	4,822,076	
	Additions—Investment Income		14,262,845
6b.	Investment in Common Stock	3,427,600	
	Deductions—Change in Fair Value of Investments	2,198,782	
	Investment in Bonds		5,626,382

Commercial paper and repurchase agreements carried at a cost of $1,354,568 matured, and cash in that amount was received:

		Debits	Credits
7.	Cash	1,354,568	
	Commercial Paper and Repurchase Agreements		1,354,568

Common stocks carried at fair value of $6,293,867 were sold for that amount; $1,536,364 was reinvested in common stocks and the remainder in bonds. An additional amount of $29,229,967 was also invested in bonds:

		Debits	Credits
8a.	Cash	6,293,867	
	Investment in Common Stocks		6,293,867
8b.	Investment in Bonds	33,987,470	
	Investment in Common Stocks	1,536,364	
	Cash		35,523,834

Administrative expenses for the year totaled $568,219, all paid in cash:

		Debits	Credits
9.	Deductions—Administrative Expenses	568,219	
	Cash		568,219

Nominal accounts for the year were closed:

		Debits	Credits
10.	Additions—Member Contributions	8,009,400	
	Additions—Employer Contributions	14,126,292	
	Additions—Investment Income	14,262,845	
	Deductions—Annuity Benefits		3,134,448
	Deductions—Disability Benefits		287,590
	Deductions—Refunds to Terminated Employees		2,057,265
	Deductions—Administrative Expenses		568,219
	Deductions—Change in Fair Value of Investments		2,198,782
	Net Assets Held in Trust for Pension Benefits		28,152,233

Entries 1 through 10 result in the financial statements shown as Illustrations 8–11 and 8–12, when applied to the accounts existing at the beginning of the period as shown in Illustration 8–10.

ILLUSTRATION 8–11

JOHNSON COUNTY EMPLOYEE RETIREMENT SYSTEM
Statement of Plan Net Assets
June 30, 2008

Assets	
Cash	$ 62,434
Accrued interest receivable	4,822,076
Investments (at fair value):	
Bonds	99,965,064
Common stocks	30,627,302
Commercial paper and repurchase agreements	11,215,833
Total assets	146,692,709
Liabilities	
Accounts payable and accrued expenses	251,650
Net assets held in trust for pension benefits	**$146,441,059**

Employer's Pension Accounting

GASB standards for the employer's accounting for defined benefit pension plans provide guidance for measurement, recognition, and display of the employer's pension information. In addition to general purpose government employers, the standards apply also to governmental public benefit corporations and authorities, utilities, hospitals, and other health care providers, colleges and universities, and, if they are employers, to public employee retirement systems.

Many of the note and statistical disclosures applicable to defined benefit pension plans, discussed in the preceding paragraphs, apply as well to the employer. If the plan (or PERS) is deemed to be part of the government's reporting entity, many of the employer's required disclosures are redundant of those required of the plan (a pension trust fund). In this case, the employer need not make disclosures that would duplicate those made by the plan. If the plan issues a stand-alone financial report, however, the employer will have to make many of the same disclosures in the CAFR that the plan makes in its stand-alone report. Because of the similarity of the disclosures and supplementary information required of the employer to those enumerated previously for the plan, the reader is referred to GASB *Codification,* Sec. P20.117, for specific disclosure requirements applicable to the employer.

Whether a government employer accounts for payroll in a governmental fund or proprietary fund, or both, there are three primary measures to be calculated and reported: (1) *annual required contribution* (ARC), (2) *net pension obligation* (NPO), and (3) *annual pension cost.*

Annual Required Contribution

Annual pension cost must be calculated and disclosed in the notes to the employer's financial statements. As shown in Illustration 8–13, the *annual required contribution*

ILLUSTRATION 8–12

JOHNSON COUNTY EMPLOYEE RETIREMENT SYSTEM
Statement of Changes in Plan Net Assets
for the Fiscal Year Ended June 30, 2008

Additions:	
Contributions:	
Employer	$ 14,126,292
Plan members	8,009,400
Total contributions	22,135,692
Investment income:	
Net decrease in fair value of investments	(2,198,782)
Interest and dividends	14,262,845
Total investment income	12,064,063
Total additions	34,199,755
Deductions:	
Annuity benefits	3,134,448
Disability benefits	287,590
Refunds to terminated employees	2,057,265
Administrative expenses	568,219
Total deductions	6,047,522
Net increase	28,152,233
Net assets, July 1, 2007	118,288,826
Net assets, June 30, 2008	$146,441,059

(ARC) is the starting point for understanding the calculation of annual pension cost. A discussion of the detailed procedures for calculating ARC is well beyond the scope of this text; therefore, only the components of ARC are discussed here.

ARC is calculated in accordance with certain parameters provided in GASB standards. The parameters require that for financial reporting purposes an actuarial valuation be performed at least biennially and that ARC be based on an actuarial valuation as of a date not more than 24 months prior to the beginning of the current fiscal year. A component of ARC is the **actuarial present value of total projected benefits,** allowing for projected salary increases and additional statutory or contractual agreements such as ad hoc cost-of-living increases and other types of postemployment benefit increases.

The parameters used to calculate ARC also provide broad guidance regarding actuarial and economic assumptions, even though any of six actuarial methods is permitted, subject to the limitation that in most cases the same actuarial method should be used both for funding and financial reporting purposes. Further, both the plan and the employer should use the same actuarial method.

An employer's ARC should include **normal cost** (i.e., the actuarial present value of benefits allocated to the current year by the actuarial cost method being used) and amortization of any **unfunded actuarial liability** (same as *actuarial accrued liability* defined previously in the discussion of the required schedule of funding progress). The provision for amortization can be determined using either level dollar amounts each year or a level percentage of the projected payroll. The amortization period must fall

ILLUSTRATION 8–13

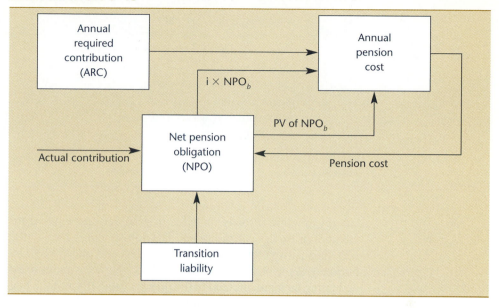

between defined maximum and minimum amortization periods. The maximum amortization period after 2006 is 30 years.[16] If there is a significant decrease in the total unfunded actuarial liability caused by a change in actuarial cost method or a change in asset valuation method, the decrease must be amortized over a period of not less than 10 years.

Once ARC is calculated, it becomes an input to the calculation of annual pension cost (see Illustration 8–13). If there is no *net pension obligation* (NPO), the annual pension cost is the same as ARC, and that is the amount the employer should contribute during the period to the plan in order to fully fund current-period accrued benefits. If the employer has undercontributed in the past, then ARC will contain an amount for the amortization of the unfunded actuarial liability. Moreover, if actual contributions have been less than annual pension cost, NPO will have a positive balance. Thus, annual pension cost will be affected by the existence of an NPO in addition to ARC. Before discussing the precise calculation of annual pension cost in the presence of an NPO, it will be useful to first examine the components of NPO.

Net Pension Obligation

Net pension obligation (NPO) has two components: (1) the transition pension liability (or asset), if any, existing at the date GASB *Statement No. 27* was implemented and (2) the cumulative difference from the implementation date of *Statement No. 27* to the current balance sheet date between annual pension cost (the amount that should be contributed) and the employer's actual contributions. These inputs to NPO (actual contribution, annual pension cost, and transition liability) are shown clearly in Illustration 8–13.

Annual Pension Cost

When an employer has an NPO, **annual pension cost** is equal to (1) the ARC, plus (2) one year's interest on the beginning-of-year NPO, and minus or plus (3) an adjustment

---

[16]GASB, *Codification,* Sec Pe5.128.

ILLUSTRATION 8–14   **Calculation of Annual Pension Cost and Net Pension Obligation**

Annual required contribution (ARC)	$ 165,485
Interest on net pension obligation ($i \times NPO_b$)	5,070
Adjustment to annual required contribution (PV of NPO_b)	(3,692)
Annual pension cost	166,863
Contributions made during the year	(157,982)
Increase in net pension obligation	8,881
Net pension obligation, January 1, 2008	67,594
Net pension obligation, December 31, 2008	$ 76,475

Source: Based on example shown in GASB, *Codification,* Sec. P20.902.

for any amounts already included in ARC for past amortization of contribution deficiencies or excess contributions. The adjustment is minus if the beginning balance of NPO is positive (contribution deficiencies) and plus if NPO is negative (excess contributions). As shown in Illustration 8–13, the adjustment to ARC is approximated by deducting an amount equal to the present value (PV) of the beginning balance of NPO. Illustration 8–14 provides a numerical example of how annual pension cost and NPO are related and how each is calculated.

Employer Recording and Reporting of Pension Expenditure/Expense

Referring to Illustrations 8–13 and 8–14, a governmental employer that reports pension expenditures in a governmental fund should recognize the expenditures on the modified accrual basis. Thus, the amount recognized will be the actual amount contributed to the plan during the year. Assuming that the calculation in Illustration 8–14 is recognized by the General Fund of a city, the following transaction would be appropriate.

	Debits	Credits
General Fund:		
Expenditures—Contribution to Pension Fund	157,982	
Cash		157,982

The governmental activities journal at the government-wide level would recognize the pension cost on an accrual basis. Therefore, if the amount contributed to the pension fund for the year is less than the annual pension cost, the difference should be added to NPO. Referring to Illustration 8–14, the appropriate journal entry for governmental activities at the government-wide level would allocate the pension cost to the various functions of government by debiting expenses.

	Debits	Credits
Governmental Activities:		
Expenses—(various government functions)	166,863	
Cash		157,982
Net Pension Obligation		8,881

If the contribution is greater than the annual pension cost, the difference should be deducted from the NPO. Any cumulative positive balance of NPO, including a transition liability should be reported in the statement of net assets at the government-wide level. A negative NPO balance should be used to reduce any other liability to the plan to zero but should not be reported as an asset. Annual pension cost should be disclosed in the notes to the financial statements. Under- or overfunding by a proprietary fund employer should be reported in the same manner except the NPO should be reported in the statement of net assets of the proprietary fund. The amount of pension expense recognized in the proprietary fund should be the same as the annual pension cost. This amount would also be recognized as program expenses in the government-wide statement of activities for business-type activities.

OTHER POSTEMPLOYMENT BENEFITS (OPEB)

Since unfunded **other postemployment benefits** (OPEB), such as health care benefits for retirees, can represent a material liability, the GASB has addressed the need to report information related to such benefits through the issuance of two standards, GASB *Statement No. 43* and *Statement No. 45*. For large governments, *GASBS 43* is effective for periods beginning after December 15, 2005, and *GASBS 45* is effective for periods beginning after December 15, 2006. Medium and small governments will have additional time to implement the statements. Until the required implementation dates, GASB *Statement No. 26* remains in effect.

GASB *Statement No. 26* was issued as interim guidance, and as a result it only relates to one type of postemployment benefit—health care plans. Under *GASBS 26* the reporting and disclosure requirements for health care plans administered by defined benefit plans is similar to that discussed in the section on pension plans.

GASBS 43 and *GASBS 45* relate to all types of OPEB (e.g., health care and life insurance). The statements provide information on accounting and reporting for plans (*GASBS 43*) and the sponsor/employer (*GASBS 45*) in a manner similar to that for pension plans. Under the standards, governments are required to measure expenses and the liability associated with the annual cost of OPEB on the accrual basis of accounting. Additionally, the standard requires several note disclosures related to OPEB.

One major difference between pension and OPEB accounting and reporting does exist for the employer. Under *GASBS 45* the employer will set the net pension obligation to zero as of the beginning of the transition year. That is, *GASBS 45* is applied on a prospective basis. The employer need not retroactively apply the standard, unless the employer has retrospective information and elects to compute the net pension obligation retroactively. However, since accounting for OPEB has been on a pay-as-you-go basis, it is anticipated that even without retrospective application, governments will experience a dramatic impact on unrestricted net assets once a liability for future benefits must be recorded.

TERMINATION BENEFITS

In addition to the standards on pensions and OPEB, GASB has issued a standard relating to accounting for **termination benefits** (GASB *Statement No. 47*). This standard provides guidance on expense and liability recognition for voluntary and involuntary termination benefits. Voluntary termination benefits occur when employers provide an incentive to hasten an employee's voluntary termination of employment, such as a one-time cash payout. An involuntary termination benefit could relate to layoffs or reductions in force, and include such items as career counseling and severance pay.

Key Terms

Actuarial accrued
   liability, *328*
Actuarial present value of
   total projected
   benefits, *332*
Actuarial value of
   assets, *328*
Agency funds, *304*
Annual pension cost, *333*
Annual required
   contributions, *328*

Defined benefit pension
   plan, *324*
Defined contribution
   pension plan, *324*
External investment
   pool, *313*
Fair value, *314*
Funded ratio, *328*
Investment trust fund, *313*
Net pension obligation, *333*

Normal cost, *332*
Other post-employment
   benefits *335*
Public Employee
   Retirement System, *325*
Termination benefits *335*
Unfunded actuarial
   liability, *332*

Selected References

American Institute of Certified Public Accountants. Audit and Accounting Guide, *State and Local Governments,* revised. New York, 2005.

Governmental Accounting Standards Board. *Codification of Governmental Accounting and Financial Reporting Standards, as of June 30, 2005.* Norwalk, CT, 2005.

Governmental Accounting Standards Board, *Statement No. 43.* Norwalk, CT, 2004.

Governmental Accounting Standards Board, *Statement No. 45.* Norwalk, CT, 2004.

Governmental Accounting Standards Board, *Statement No. 47.* Norwalk, CT, 2005.

Questions

8–1. Explain the distinction(s) between *agency funds* and *trust funds.*

8–2. Why are *fiduciary funds* used by governmental units?

8–3. Must an agency fund be used to account for withholding taxes, retirement contributions, and (if applicable) social security taxes of General Fund employees? Explain.

8–4. Why do agency funds have no fund equity?

8–5. Under what circumstances should a government use an agency fund to account for special assessment debt service? What is the rationale for using an agency fund for these transactions?

8–6. How does accounting for an internal investment pool differ from the accounting for an external investment pool?

8–7. Why would pooled investments be revalued to fair value when a fund is added to the pool or when a fund withdraws from the pool?

8–8. Explain the difference between a private purpose trust and a public purpose trust. How does the reporting for the two types of trusts differ?

8–9. Explain the essential differences between a *defined benefit pension plan* and a *defined contribution pension plan.* Which involves the more complex accounting and reporting requirements? Why?

8–10. What are the required financial statements and supplementary schedules that must be reported by a defined benefit pension plan in its stand-alone financial report or in the CAFR of the employer (sponsor government), if applicable?

Cases

8–1 Internet Case—CalPERS. While the examples in this chapter of the text have focused on a single-employer plan, many states operate statewide plans, referred to as Public Employee Retirement Systems (PERS), to which multiple employers contribute. One of the largest PERS plans in the nation is operated in the State of California.

Required

To answer the following questions use the Web site found at www.calpers.org. The answers to the questions can be found in CalPERS' annual report or in the general information section provided on the site.

a. When was CalPERS established?

b. What types of employers contribute to CalPERS?

c. How many individuals are served by CalPERS?

d. How many and what types of funds are administered by CalPERS?

e. For the most recent reporting period, what is the value of total fiduciary assets?

f. For the most recent reporting period, what was the change in pension fund net assets?

g. What are the funded ratios from the schedule of funding progress and what do the funded ratios tell you?

h. What is the reporting relationship between CalPERS and the State of California?

8–2 Identification of Fiduciary Funds. Following is a list of fund names and descriptions of funds from comprehensive annual financial reports (CAFRs).

Required

For each fund, indicate which type of fund should be used to account for the activities and explain why that fund is most appropriate.

a. Tri-Centennial Fund. Accounts for money raised or contributed by several local area governments and other organizations. The purpose is to ensure availability of resources to celebrate the United States Tri-Centennial in 2076.

b. Perpetual Care Fund. Accounts for endowed gifts and investment earnings dedicated to perpetual care of the city's cemeteries.

c. Debt Service Trust Fund. The city collects special assessments from citizens in designated special benefit districts that is intended for debt service on bonds issued for projects within the district. The city bears no responsibility for this debt.

d. Charitable Gambling Fund. The city manages money received from taxes on gambling establishments that is earmarked for certain restricted purposes in the community.

e. School Impact Fee Fund. The city collects school impact fees as part of the cost of building permits issued. Money must be remitted periodically to the local school district, a legally separate government that is not a component unit of the city.

f. Housing Rehabilitation Fund. Accounts for several revolving funds that provide low interest loans for housing. The collection of the loans is used to run the program and make new loans to qualified citizens. Several government sources provided the start-up funds.

g. Payroll Fund. The city has established a fund in which all payroll deductions are reported.

h. Telephone Commissions Fund. The city collects commissions on pay telephones used by jail inmates. The funds are used to provide inmates such benefits as library resources and fitness equipment.

i. Block Grant Fund. The state receives federal funds for the homeless which it passes through to local not-for-profit organizations. The only responsibility the state has is to contribute an additional amount of funds (match) to the federal grant.

8–1 Examine a CAFR. Utilizing the annual report obtained for Exercise 1–1, follow these instructions:

a. Agency Funds. Are employees' and employers' FICA tax contributions and contributions to other retirement funds reported in the General Fund, an agency fund, or in some other manner (describe)? Does the government operate a tax agency fund or participate in a tax agency fund operated by another government? Does the government act as agent for owners of property within a special assessment district and for the creditors of those property owners? Does the government operate one or more pass-through agency funds? If so, describe.

b. Investment Trust Funds. Does the government operate, or participate in, a cash and investments pool? If so, is the pool operated as an investment trust fund? If there is a cash and investment pool and it is not reported as an investment trust fund, how is it reported? Explain.

c. Private-purpose Trust Funds. Does the government operate one or more private-purpose trust funds? If yes, explain the purpose(s).

d. Pension Trust Funds. Are the government employees covered by a retirement fund operated by the government, by the state, by the federal Social Security Administration, or by two or more of these? If the government operates one or more pension plans, or retirement systems, are the plan statements accompanied by an actuary's report, or is a reference made to the actuary's report in the notes to the financial statements? Is a net pension obligation (NPO) reported in the government-wide statement of net assets and/or in a proprietary fund? Is all the pension information specified by GASB standards and discussed in Chapter 8 presented in the notes to the financial statements? Are all required supplementary schedules and related notes reported in the comprehensive annual financial report?

e. Fiduciary Fund Financial Statements. Are all fiduciary funds shown in a statement of fiduciary net assets and a statement of changes in fiduciary net assets? Does the financial report state the basis of accounting used for trust and agency funds? Are agency funds properly disclosed in the financial statements? Does the report contain a schedule or list of investments of trust funds? Are investments reported at fair value? Is the net increase (decrease) shown separately from interest and dividend income? If trust funds own depreciable assets, is depreciation taken? If so, is depreciation considered a charge against principal or against income?

8–2 Multiple Choice. Choose the best answer.

1. Which of the following is *not* a fiduciary fund?
   a. Permanent fund.
   b. Agency fund.
   c. Investment trust fund.
   d. Pension trust fund.

2. Which of the following fiduciary fund types is likely to require formal legislative approval (appropriation procedures) for expenditures?
   a. Investment trust funds.
   b. Pension trust funds.
   c. Agency funds.
   d. None of the above.

3. Which of the following financial statements is prepared by fiduciary funds?
   a. Statement of net assets.

      b. Statement of activities.

      c. Statement of cash flows.

      d. All of the above.

4. At the government-wide level, how are fiduciary funds reported?

      a. In the Governmental Activities column.

      b. In the Business-type Activities column.

      c. As a part of component units.

      d. Fiduciary funds are not reported at the government-wide level.

5. Which of the following funds would be used to account for taxes collected by the county collector for distribution to other funds of the county and/or other governments within the county?

      a. Investment trust fund.

      b. Internal service fund.

      c. Agency fund.

      d. Private-purpose trust fund.

6. An investment trust fund is used to report the net assets available to the:

      a. Sponsoring government only.

      b. External participants only.

      c. Financial institution that acts as custodian for the fund's investments.

      d. All of the above.

7. Which of the following fiduciary funds would account for an endowment (i.e., the principal must remain intact)?

      a. Investment trust fund.

      b. Private-purpose trust fund.

      c. Pension trust fund.

      d. Permanent fund.

8. If a county incurs the cost of monitoring grant recipients, which of the following funds would most likely account for pass-through grants to a not-for-profit organization assisting low-income individuals?

      a. Private-purpose trust fund.

      b. Agency fund.

      c. Special revenue fund.

      d. Permanent fund.

9. Arkmo City has a single pension plan for its employees, all of whose salaries and wages are paid from the General Fund. Ordinarily, the city's General Fund should report an expenditure for its annual pension contribution to a defined benefit pension plan in an amount equal to the:

      a. Annual required contribution.

      b. Annual pension cost.

      c. Net pension obligation.

      d. Actual contribution.

10. Which of the following is required supplementary information under GASB's pension standards?

      a. Schedule of funding progress.

      b. Schedule of employer contributions.

      c. Schedule of net pension obligation.

      d. Both *a* and *b*.

8–3 Multiple Choice. Choose the best answer.

    Items 1 through 3 relate to the following information.

The county administers a tax agency fund that collects taxes on behalf of the county, city, and a special purpose district. For 2008, the taxes to be levied by the government are:

County	$ 632,000
City	917,000
Special purpose district	26,000
Total	$1,575,000

1. On the date the taxes are levied, the city would debit which of the following accounts?
    a. Due from Tax Agency Fund.
    b. Equity in Tax Agency Fund.
    c. Taxes Receivable.
    d. No journal entry is recorded since the city is not collecting the taxes.
2. On the date the taxes are levied the tax agency fund would credit which of the following accounts?
    a. Due to Other Funds and Governments.
    b. Revenues—Taxes.
    c. Additions—Other Funds and Governments.
    d. Accrued Taxes.
3. If the tax agency fund assessed a 1 percent administrative fee, it would be recorded by the agency fund as a credit to:
    a. Revenue.
    b. Transfer In.
    c. Additions—Fund Equity.
    d. Due to County.

Items 4 through 7 relate to the following information:

The city council of the City of Cadillac decided to pool the investments of its General Fund with that of Cadillac School District and Cadillac Township, each of which carried its investments at fair value as of the prior balance sheet date. All investments are revalued to current fair value at the date of the creation of the pool. At that date, the prior and current fair value of the investments of each of the participants were as follows:

	Investments	
	Prior Fair Value	Current Fair Value
General Fund	$ 600,000	$ 590,000
Cadillac School District	3,600,000	3,640,000
Cadillac Township	1,800,000	1,770,000
Total	$6,000,000	$6,000,000

4. At the date of the creation of the investment pool, each of the participants should:
    a. Debit its Fund Balance account and credit its Investments account for the prior fair value of the assets transferred to the pool.
    b. Debit or credit its Investments account as needed to adjust its carrying value to current fair value. The offsetting entry in each fund should be to Fund Balance.

    c. Debit Equity in Pooled Investments for the current fair value of investments pooled, credit Investments for the prior fair value of investments pooled, and credit or debit Revenues—Change in Fair Value of Investments for the difference.

    d. Make a memorandum entry only.

5. At the date of creation of the pool, the City of Cadillac should account for all the pooled investments in:

    a. An investment trust fund at fair value at the date the pool is created.

    b. An agency fund at fair value as of the prior balance sheet date.

    c. Its General Fund at fair value at the date the pool is created.

    d. Its General Fund at fair value as of the prior balance sheet date.

6. One day after creation of the pool, the investments that had belonged to Cadillac Township were sold by the pool for $1,760,000.

    a. The loss of $40,000 is borne by each participant in proportion to its equity in the pool.

    b. The loss of $10,000 is borne by each participant in proportion to its equity in the pool.

    c. The loss of $40,000 is considered to be a loss borne by Cadillac Township.

    d. The loss of $10,000 is considered to be a loss borne by Cadillac Township.

7. One month after creation of the pool, earnings on pooled investments totaled $59,900. It was decided to distribute the earnings to the participants, rounding the distribution to the nearest dollar. The Cadillac School District should receive:

    a. $36,000.

    b. $35,940.

    c. $36,339.

    d. $37,000.

Items 8 through 10 are based on the following information:

    The City of Mapleton contributes to and administers a single-employer defined benefit pension plan on behalf of its covered employees. The plan prepares its own stand-alone financial report and is accounted for as a pension trust fund. The annual pension cost and actual contributions made for the past three years, along with the percentage of annual covered payroll, were as follows:

	Actual Contribution		Annual Pension Cost	
	Amount	Percent	Amount	Percent
2008	$25,000	26	$25,000	26
2007	7,500	12	15,000	24
2006	–0–	—	9,000	20

8. What account should be credited by the pension plan to record the year 2008 employer contribution of $25,000?

    a. Revenues—Employer Contributions.

    b. Other Financing Sources—Interfund Transfers In.

    c. Due from General Fund.

    d. Additions—Employer Contributions.

9. To record the year 2008 pension contribution of $25,000, what account would be debited in the General Fund for the employer pension contributions?

    a. Other Financing Uses—Interfund Transfers Out.

    b. Expenditures.

     c. Pension Expense.

     d. Due to Pension Fund.

10. By what amount did the net pension obligation increase in 2008?

     a. $0.

     b. $16,500.

     c. 74% of the annual covered payroll.

     d. None of the above.

8–4 Tax Agency Fund. The county collector of Lincoln County is responsible for collecting all property taxes levied by funds and governments within the boundaries of the county. To reimburse the county for estimated administrative expenses of operating the tax agency fund, the agency fund deducts 1 percent from the collections for the town, the school district, and the townships. The total amount deducted is added to the collections for the county and remitted to the Lincoln County General Fund.

    The following events occurred in 2008:

1. Current-year tax levies to be collected by the agency fund were:

County General Fund	$ 2,752,000
Town of Smithton General Fund	4,644,000
Lincoln Co. Consolidated School District	7,912,000
Various townships	1,892,000
Total	$17,200,000

2. $8,400,000 of current taxes was collected during the first half of 2008.
3. Liabilities to all funds and governments as the result of the first half-year collections were recorded. (A schedule of amounts collected for each participant, showing the amount withheld for the county General Fund and net amounts due the participants, is recommended for determining amounts to be recorded for this transaction.)
4. All money in the tax agency fund was distributed.

Required

a. Make journal entries for each of the foregoing transactions that affected the tax agency fund.

b. Make journal entries for each of the foregoing transactions that affected the Lincoln County General Fund. Begin with the tax levy entry, assuming 3 percent of the gross levy will be uncollectible.

c. Make journal entries for each of the foregoing entries that affected the Town of Smithton General Fund. Begin with the tax levy entry, assuming 3 percent of the gross levy will be uncollectible.

d. Which financial statements would be prepared by the tax agency fund?

8–5 Special Assessment Agency Fund. The City of Fayette agreed to bill the owner of each parcel of property within Special Assessment District No. 21 for each installment of the owner's share of the total assessment for the construction project being undertaken by Special Assessment District No. 21. The city agreed to collect the installments and interest thereon and to use the collections to pay interest and principal due on debt incurred for the construction project, although the city is not obligated in any manner for the special assessment debt.

Required

a. Name the fund type that should be used by the City of Fayette to record the activities described. Explain the reason for your answer.

    b. If the total assessment for the project to be undertaken by Special Assessment District No. 21 is $3,600,000, to be collected in three equal annual installments, show in general journal form the entry that should be made by the fund for the total assessment, assuming that all installments are to be used for service of debt incurred for this project.

    c. Show in general journal form the entry that should be made for collections from owners of property within Special Assessment District No. 21 of the first installment amounting to $1,276,000 ($1,160,000 for principal and $116,000 for interest).

    d. Show in general journal form the entry that should be made to record the payment of interest amounting to $110,000 and principal amounting to $1,150,000 on debt incurred for the Special Assessment District No. 21 project.

    e. Assuming that all transactions described occurred in the fiscal year ended June 30, 2008, and that the City of Fayette had no other transactions during that year with the property owners or creditors of Special Assessment District No. 21, name the basic financial statement, or statements, of the City of Fayette in which the results of the transactions described above should be reported, and state which information about the transactions should be reported in each statement you name.

8–6 Pass-Through Agency Fund. Marshall County customarily receives from various federal government agencies resources that are designated for the use of the governments within the county. A pass-through agency fund is used to account for the resources.

Required

Show in general journal form the entries in the pass-through fund for the following events and transactions, which occurred in 2008.

    a. The county received in cash a grant of $40,000,000, which is to be distributed to various governments within the county in a manner not yet specified.

    b. Official notice was received that $17,000,000 of the grant in (*a*) is to be distributed to the City of Pittsfield for public improvements. The distribution was made.

    c. Official notice was received that $16,000,000 was to be distributed to Marshall Schools. The distribution was made. Remaining cash was invested in marketable securities.

    d. The county received in cash a grant of $3,000,000 to be distributed to law enforcement agencies throughout the county in a manner yet to be specified. The cash was invested in marketable securities.

8–7 Investment Trust Fund. The Albertville City Council decided to pool the investments of its General Fund with Albertville Schools and Richwood Township in an investment pool to be managed by the city. Each of the pool participants had reported its investments at fair value as of the end of the last fiscal year. At the date of the creation of the pool, the fair value of the investments of each pool participant was as follows:

	Investments	
	Prior Fair Value	Current Fair Value
City of Albertville General Fund	$ 890,000	$ 900,000
Albertville Schools	4,200,000	4,230,000
Richwood Township	3,890,000	3,870,000
Total	$8,980,000	$9,000,000

Required

a. Show the entry that should be made by (1) the City of Albertville, (2) Albertville Schools, and (3) Richwood Township to do the following: open a new asset account, Equity in Pooled Investments, in the amount of the current fair value of the investments transferred to the pool; close the existing investments account; and debit or credit the revenues account of each participant as needed to adjust for changes in fair value.

b. Show in general journal form the entries to be made in the accounts of the investment pool trust fund to record the following transactions of the first year of its operations:

  (1) Record at current fair value the investments transferred to the pool; assume that the investments of the city's General Fund were in U.S. Treasury notes and the investments of both the schools and the township were in certificates of deposit.

  (2) Certificates of deposit (CDs) that had been recorded at a fair value of $1,000,000 matured. The pool received $1,050,000 in cash ($1,000,000 for the face of the CDs and $50,000 interest). The entire amount was reinvested in a new issue of certificates of deposit.

  (3) Interest on Treasury notes in the amount of $50,000 was collected.

  (4) Interest on certificates of deposit accrued at year-end amounted to $28,250.

  (5) At the end of the year, it was decided to compute and record the pool's liability or net assets held for each of the three participants for its proportionate share of earnings on the pooled investments. Assume that there were no changes in the fair value of investments since the investment pool was created. Carry your computation of each participant's proportionate share to two decimal places. Round the amount of the distribution to each fund or participant to the nearest dollar.

c. Record in each of the participant's funds the increase in its Equity in Pooled Investment account.

d. The City of Albertville General Fund decided to withdraw $100,000 from the investment pool to obtain the cash it needed to acquire general capital assets. The investment pool trust fund sold $50,000 of its investments in U.S. Treasury notes (no interest had accrued on these investments) to obtain the cash needed for the withdrawal. Record the sale of U.S. Treasury notes. Record the cash withdrawal in the investment pool trust fund and the City of Albertville General Fund. Recalculate each participant's proportionate share of pooled investments after the withdrawal is made.

e. Explain how the investment trust fund would report the General Fund's interest in the investment pool and the Albertville School's interest in the investment pool.

8–8 **Pension Plan Calculation.** The Village of Vandover administers a defined benefit pension plan for its police and fire personnel. Employees are not required to contribute to the plan. The village received from the actuary and other sources the following information about the Public Safety Employees' Pension Fund as of December 31, 2008.

Item	Amount
Annual required contribution	$ 49,600
Net pension obligation, 1/1/2008	147,300
Present value of net pension obligation as of 1/1/2008	12,400
Interest rate applicable to beginning net pension obligation	8%
Transition liability	–0–

Required

Assuming that the Village of Vandover contributes $45,000 cash to the plan on December 31, 2008, calculate the employer's

a. Annual pension cost.

b. Net pension obligation, as of December 31, 2008.

8–9 **Pension Plan Financial Statements.** The State of Nodak operates a Public Employee Retirement System (PERS) for all employees of the state. The pre-closing trial balance of the PERS as of June 30, 2008, follows (in thousands of dollars):

	Debits	Credits
Cash	$ 16,000	
Accrued Interest Receivable	33,200	
Investments	2,002,000	
Equipment and Fixtures	25,200	
Accumulated Depreciation–Equipment and Fixtures		$ 3,100
Accounts Payable and Accruals		33,400
Net Assets Held in Trust for Pension Benefits, July 1, 2007		1,577,000
Member Contributions		112,100
Employer Contributions		197,800
Interest and Dividend Income		199,700
Net Change in Fair Value of Investments		58,800
Annuity Benefits	53,900	
Disability Benefits	14,000	
Refunds to Terminated Employees	28,800	
Administrative Expenses	8,800	
Total	$2,181,900	$2,181,900

Required

a. Prepare a statement of changes in plan net assets for the State of Nodak Public Employees Retirement System for the year ended June 30, 2008, in as much detail as possible.

b. Prepare a statement of plan net assets as of June 30, 2008, for the State of Nodak Public Employees Retirement System.

c. Explain how the State of Nodak (the employer) would report its participation in the state PERS at the fund level and at the government-wide level.

8–10 **Fiduciary Financial Statements.** Ray County administers a tax agency fund, an investment trust fund and a private-purpose trust fund. The tax agency fund acts as an agent for the county, a city within the county and the school district within the county. Participants in the investment trust fund are the Ray County General Fund, the city and the school district. The private-purpose trust is maintained for the benefit of a private organization located within the county. Ray County has prepared the following statement of fiduciary net assets.

RAY COUNTY
Statement of Fiduciary Net Assets
Fiduciary Funds
June 30, 2008
(in thousands)

	Trust Funds	Agency Funds	Total
Assets			
Cash and cash equivalents	$ 104,747	$ 788	$ 105,535
Receivables	12,166	87,858	100,024
Investments:			
Short-term investments	241,645		241,645
Bonds, notes, and stock	992,226		992,226
Total assets	1,350,784	88,646	1,439,430
Liabilities			
Accounts Payable	61,447		61,447
Net Assets			
Held in trust for:			
Organizations	193,400		193,400
County	219,187	10,638	229,825
City of Leetown	383,578	23,048	406,626
Leetown School District	493,172	54,960	548,132
Total net assets	$1,289,337	$88,646	$1,377,983

Required

The statement as presented is not in accordance with *GASBS 34*. Using Illustration 1–14 as an example identify the errors (problems) in the statement and explain how the errors should be corrected.

Chapter **Nine**

Financial Reporting of State and Local Governments

Learning Objectives

After studying this chapter, you should be able to:

1. Describe the financial reporting requirements of the *GASBS 34* reporting model.
2. Explain the key concepts and terms used in describing the governmental reporting entity.
3. Apply the GASB criteria used to determine whether a potential component unit should be included in the reporting entity and when included, the manner of reporting component units.
4. Identify and describe the contents of a comprehensive annual financial report (CAFR).
5. Understand how to reconcile governmental fund financial statements to governmental activity in the government-wide financial statements.
6. Identify and explain contemporary financial reporting issues.

Chapters 2 through 8 present extended discussions of the principles of accounting for governmental, proprietary, and fiduciary funds, and governmental and business-type activities at the government-wide level. Chapters 1 and 2 provide overviews of *GASBS 34* financial reporting requirements, and financial reporting requirements for specific fund types are discussed in several chapters. This chapter presents the *GASBS 34* reporting requirements in more depth and discusses contemporary financial reporting issues.

THE GOVERNMENTAL REPORTING ENTITY

The objectives of accounting and financial reporting for governments set forth in the GASB's *Concepts Statement No. 1* are discussed in Chapter 1. *Concepts Statement No. 1* does not deal with the practical problem of deciding what a "government" is. The average citizen—including accountants whose only experience has been with business organizations—has only a vague knowledge and little understanding of the overlapping layers of general purpose and special purpose governmental organizations that have some jurisdiction over us wherever we may live and work. Illustration 8–1, for example, shows a few layers of general purpose governments that can levy taxes on property. The school funds in that illustration show that taxes are also levied by special purpose governments (an independent school district in that illustration). Omitted from the illustration, for the sake of brevity, are taxes levied by any *special districts.* Special districts are defined by the Bureau of the Census as "independent special-purpose governmental units (other than school districts) that exist as separate entities with substantial administrative and fiscal independence from general-purpose local governments."[1] About 40 percent of the local governments in the United States are classified as special districts.[2]

Although the Census definition stresses the independence of special districts, in many instances they were created to provide a vehicle for financing services demanded by residents of a general purpose government that could not be financed by the general purpose government because of constitutional or statutory limits on the rates or amounts it could raise from taxes, other revenue sources, and debt. Building authorities are examples of special districts created as a financing vehicle.

In addition to independent special districts, certain governmental activities are commonly carried on by commissions, boards, and other agencies that are not considered as independent of a general purpose government by the Bureau of the Census but that may have some degree of fiscal and administrative independence from the governing board of the general purpose government. In past years, some governments included in their annual reports the financial statements of such semi-independent boards and commissions and even certain of the special districts, whereas other governments excluded them.

To reduce disparity in reporting and to promote the preparation of financial reports consistent with GASB *Concepts Statement No. 1,* GASB *Codification* Section 2100 provides authoritative guidance on defining the reporting entity, and Section 2600 presents guidance on reporting entity and component unit presentations and disclosure. GASB *Codification* Section 2100 also provides guidance for reporting certain affiliated organizations, such as fund-raising foundations.

Entry Definition Criteria

GASB *Codification* Section 2100 notes that all government organizations are ultimately responsible to elected governing officials at the federal, state, or local level. Elected officials of the primary government are accountable to the citizens for those organizations that financially depend on the primary government or on which the primary government can impose its will. Thus, Section 2100 takes the position that governmental financial reporting should report the elected officials' accountability for such organizations. It should be emphasized that Section 2100 deals only with criteria for defining a governmental reporting entity; it does not establish standards for the incorporation of financial data of component units in the financial statements of the reporting entity. Standards for the incorporation of financial data are set forth in Section 2600.

Definitions of key terms and concepts needed to understand and apply reporting entity criteria are given in Section 2100.501, as amended by *GASBS 34,* from which selected terms and concepts are provided in the remaining paragraphs of this section.

A **financial reporting entity** is *a primary government,* organizations for which the primary government is *financially accountable,* and other organizations for which the

[1] U.S. Department of Commerce, Bureau of the Census, *2002 Census of Governments,* vol. 1, no. 1 (Washington, D.C.: U.S. Government Printing Office), p. vii.
[2] Ibid.

nature and significance of their relationship with the primary government are such that exclusion would cause the reporting entity's basic financial statements to be misleading or incomplete. The nucleus of a financial reporting entity usually is a primary government. However, a governmental organization other than a primary government (such as a *component unit,* a *joint venture,* a *jointly governed organization,* or *other stand-alone government*) serves as the nucleus for its own reporting entity when it issues separate financial statements.

A **primary government** is a state government or general purpose local government. Also, it is a special purpose government that has a separately elected governing body, is legally separate, and is fiscally independent of other state or local governments. A legally separate organization has an identity of its own as an "artificial person" with a personality and existence distinct from that of its creator and others. A *fiscally independent* organization has the authority to determine its budget; levy its own taxes and set rates or charges; and issue bonded debt without approval of another government.

A primary government is **financially accountable** for another organization if the primary government appoints a voting majority of the organization's governing board and is either able to impose its will on the organization or there is a potential for the organization to provide specific financial benefits to, or impose specific financial burdens on, the primary government. The ability of the primary government to impose its will on an organization exists if the primary government can significantly influence the programs, projects, or activities of, or the level of services performed or provided by, the organization. A financial benefit or burden relationship exists if the primary government *(a)* is entitled to the organization's resources; *(b)* is legally obligated or has otherwise assumed the obligation to finance the deficits of, or provide financial support to, the organization; or *(c)* is obligated in some manner for the debt of the organization. Additionally, a primary government may be financially accountable for organizations with separately elected governing boards, governing boards appointed by other governments, or a jointly appointed board that is fiscally dependent on the primary government.

Component units are legally separate organizations for which the elected officials of the primary government are financially accountable. In addition, a component unit can be another organization for which the nature and significance of its relationship with the primary government are such that exclusion would cause the reporting entity's financial statements to be misleading or incomplete. Because the reporting entity must include the component unit's financial information in its financial statements, the GASB has provided that the information can be included by blending the information or discretely presenting the information. These two methods of presentation are discussed in greater detail later in this section.

A **joint venture** is a legal entity or other organization that results from a contractual arrangement and that is owned, operated, or governed by two or more participants as a separate and specific activity subject to joint control, in which the participants retain *(a)* an ongoing financial interest or *(b)* an ongoing financial responsibility.

A **jointly governed organization** is a regional government or other multigovernmental arrangement that is governed by representatives from each of the governments that create the organization, but that is not a joint venture because the participants do not retain an ongoing financial interest or responsibility.

An **other stand-alone government** is a legally separate governmental organization that *(a)* does not have a separately elected governing body and *(b)* does not meet the definition of a component unit. Other stand-alone governments include some special purpose governments, joint ventures, jointly governed organizations, and pools.

ILLUSTRATION 9–1   Decision Process for Inclusion or Exclusion of Potential Component Unit (PCU)

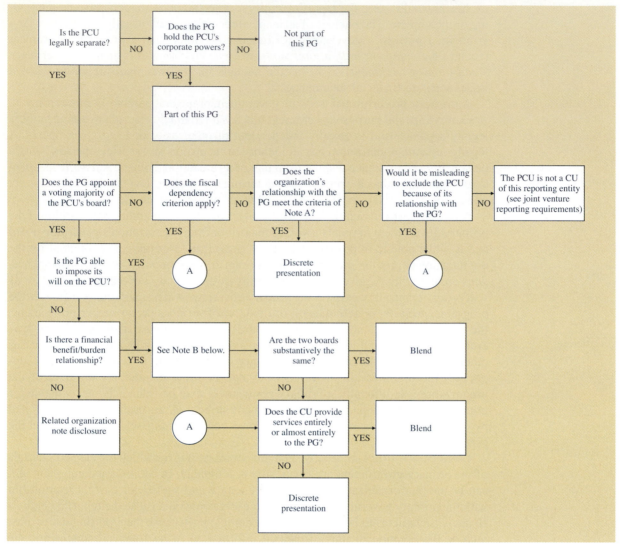

Notes:

A. A legally separate, tax-exempt organization should be reported as a component unit of a reporting entity if *all* of the following criteria are met: (a) The economic resources received or held by the separate organization are entirely or almost entirely for the direct benefit of the primary government, its component units, or its constituents; (b) the primary government or its component units is entitled to or has the ability to otherwise access a majority of the economic resources received or held by the separate organization; (c) the economic resources received or held by an *individual* organization that the specific primary government or its component unit, is entitled to or has the ability to otherwise access are significant to that primary government.

B. A potential component unit (PCU) for which a primary government (PG) is financially accountable may be fiscally dependent on another government. An organization should be included as a component unit (CU) of only one reporting entity. Professional judgment should be used to determine the most appropriate reporting entity. A primary government that appoints a voting majority of the governing board of a component unit of another government should make the disclosures required for related organizations.

Source: GASB, *Codification,* Sec. 2100.901.

As indicated earlier, in determining the reporting entity an analysis must be made of all organizations for which the primary government is financially accountable. To assist in determining whether an organization is financially dependent on the primary government, that is, potentially a component unit of the reporting entity, the GASB has developed the flowchart in Illustration 9–1. In addition to assisting in determining whether a component unit should be included in the financial statements of the reporting entity, the flowchart also assists in determining whether the component unit information should be blended or discretely presented.

Blended presentation is when the component unit's financial data for its funds and activities are reported with the same fund types and activities of the primary government. For example, if a component unit has special revenue funds the funds should be reported in the same manner as special revenue funds for the primary government. A separate column should be used in the governmental funds financial statements if the fund is considered major; if the fund is not major it should be aggregated with other nonmajor funds. At the government-wide level the component unit special revenue fund data should be reported in the Governmental Activities column. One exception is that the General Fund data of a component unit cannot be combined with the General Fund data of the primary government. Instead, the component unit General Fund data should be reported as a special revenue fund (major or nonmajor).[3] As shown in the flowchart, blending is required when the component unit is, in substance, a part of the primary government. An example of such an occurrence is a building authority that was specifically established to finance and construct capital assets for the primary government, with the debt service for the capital assets provided by lease payments from the primary government.

Discrete presentation is when financial data of the component unit is reported in a column(s) separate from the financial data of the primary government. An integral part of this method of presentation is that major component unit supporting information is required to be provided in the reporting entity's basic financial statements by *(a)* presenting each major component unit in a separate column in the reporting entity's statements of net assets and activities, *(b)* including combining statements of major component units in the reporting entity's basic statements after the fund financial statements, or *(c)* presenting condensed financial statements in the notes to the reporting entity's basic financial statements.

GOVERNMENTAL FINANCIAL REPORTS

Once the reporting entity has been determined in accord with the criteria discussed in the preceding section, persons responsible for preparing financial reports for the reporting entity should follow the guidance given in currently effective authoritative literature to determine the content of financial reports to be issued for external users. Chapter 2 contains a summary of the standards *GASBS 34* sets forth for the content of the comprehensive annual financial report (CAFR) of a state or local governmental reporting entity. Chapters 3 through 8 elaborate on the application of those standards to accounting and financial reporting for each of the funds and government-wide activities. Although much of the discussion in preceding chapters concerns general purpose external financial reporting, the needs of administrators, legislators, and other users not properly classifiable as "external" have been given some attention. In the following paragraphs, the discussion in preceding chapters is briefly summarized and placed in perspective.

Need for Periodic Reports

Individuals concerned with the day-to-day operations and activities of governmental funds should be familiar with much of the data processed by the accounting information

---

[3]GASB, *Codification*, Sec. 2600.114.

system because it results from the events and transactions with which they are involved. However, it is easy for these individuals to become overconfident of their understanding of the data with which they are daily involved. Past events are not always as remembered, and the relative significance of events changes over time. Similarly, administrators at succeedingly higher levels in the organization may feel that participation in decision making and observation of the apparent results of past decisions obviate the necessity for periodic analysis of accounting and statistical reports prepared objectively and with neutrality. The memory and perceptions of administrators at higher levels are also subject to failure. Therefore, it is generally agreed that it is useful for financial reports to be prepared and distributed at intervals throughout a fiscal period as well as at period-end.

Interim Financial Reports

Government administrators have the greatest need for interim financial reports, although members of the legislative branch of the government (particularly those on its finance committee) may also find interim reports useful. Other users of interim reports are news media and residents who are particularly concerned with aspects of the government's financial management.

Although the particular statements and schedules that should be prepared on an interim basis are a matter of local management preference, the authors believe the following interim statements and schedules are useful for budgetary and cash management purposes.

1. Statement of actual and estimated revenue (for the General Fund and special revenue funds and other funds for which budgets have been legally adopted).
2. Statement of actual and estimated expenditures (for the General Fund and special revenue funds and other funds for which budgets have been legally adopted).
3. Comparative statement of revenue and expense (for each enterprise and internal service fund).
4. Combined statement of cash receipts, disbursements, and balances—all funds.
5. Forecast of cash positions—all funds.

Other statements and schedules, in addition to those just listed, may be needed, depending on the complexity and scope of a government's activities. A statement of investments held and their cost and fair values is an example of an additional statement that may be useful. Schedules of past-due receivables from taxes, special assessments, and utility customers may also be needed at intervals.

Complete interim reports should be prepared and distributed at regular intervals throughout a fiscal period, generally monthly, although small governments that have little financial activity may find a bimonthly or quarterly period satisfactory. Partial interim reports dealing with those items of considerable current importance should be prepared and distributed as frequently as their information would be of value. For example, reports of the fair values of investments and of purchases and sales may be needed by a relatively small number of users on a daily basis during certain critical periods.

Annual Financial Reports

Governmental annual financial reports are needed by the same individuals and groups receiving interim reports. They are also often required to be distributed to agencies of higher governmental jurisdictions and to major creditors. Other users include financial underwriters; debt insurers; debt rating agencies; debt analysts; libraries; other governments; associations of governmental administrators, accountants, and finance officers; and college professors and students.

Most larger governments prepare a comprehensive annual financial report (CAFR). The CAFR is the government's official annual report prepared and published as a matter of public record. GASB standards make it clear that a primary government is the nucleus of a financial reporting entity for which a CAFR is prepared. However, a governmental organization other than a primary government (e.g., a component unit, joint venture, jointly governed organization, or other stand-alone government) serves as the nucleus of its own reporting entity. The separately issued financial statements of such a reporting entity should follow the same reporting entity standards as those for a primary government and its component units.

In addition to the required management's discussion and analysis (MD&A), basic financial statements and related notes (government-wide and fund), and required supplementary information other than the MD&A, the CAFR should contain individual fund and combining financial statements, schedules, narrative explanations, a statistical section and other material management deems relevant. For CAFRs containing audited financial statements, the auditor's report should also be included.

Introductory Section

As discussed in Chapter 1, the introductory section of a CAFR generally includes the table of contents, a letter of transmittal, and other material deemed appropriate by management.

The letter of transmittal should cite legal and policy requirements for the report. The introductory section may also include a summary discussion of factors relating to the government's service programs and financial matters. Matters discussed in the introductory section should not duplicate those discussed in the MD&A. Because the MD&A is part of the information reviewed (but not audited) by the auditor, it presents information based only on facts known to exist as of the reporting date. Since the introductory section is generally not covered by the auditor's report, it may present information of a more subjective nature, including prospective information such as forecasts or expectations.

Financial Section

The financial section should contain sufficient information to disclose fully and present fairly the financial position and results of financial operations during the fiscal year. GASB *Codification* Section 2200 identifies the minimum content for the financial section of a CAFR as consisting of the:

1. Auditor's report (discussed in Chapter 11)
2. MD&A
3. Basic financial statements
   a. Government-wide financial statements
      (1) Statement of net assets (see Illustration 1–4)
      (2) Statement of activities (see Illustration 1–5)

   b. Fund financial statements
      (1) Governmental funds
          (a) Balance sheet (see Illustration 1–6)
          (b) Statement of revenues, expenditures, and changes in fund balances (see Illustration 1–8)

    (2) Proprietary funds

        (a) Statement of net assets (see Illustration 1–10)

        (b) Statement of revenues, expenses, and changes in fund net assets (see Illustration 1–11)

        (c) Statement of cash flows (see Illustration 1–12)

    (3) Fiduciary funds (including component units that are fiduciary in nature)

        (a) Statement of fiduciary net assets (see Illustration 1–13)

        (b) Statement of changes in fiduciary net assets (see Illustration 1–14)

  c. Notes to the financial statements

4. Required supplementary information other than MD&A, including, but not limited to, the budgetary comparison schedule (see Illustration 3–5)

5. Combining statements and individual fund statements and schedules

State and local governments may provide in the financial section of the CAFR combining financial statements for nonmajor funds of each fund type and individual fund statements for the General Fund or for a nonmajor fund that is the only fund of a given type (for example, a debt service fund that is the only fund of that type). The GASB requires that all "lower" level statements, such as combining statements, be prepared and displayed in the same manner as "higher" level statements, such as the governmental funds financial statements.

Examples of all required basic financial statements were provided in Chapter 1; however, no example is provided in Chapter 1 for an MD&A. An example of an MD&A from the City and County of Denver is presented in Illustration 9–2. As shown in Illustration 9–2, the MD&A should provide an overview of the government's financial activities and financial highlights for the year. The MD&A should provide a narrative explanation of the contents of the CAFR, including the nature of the government-wide and fund financial statements, and the distinctions between those statements. The remainder of the MD&A should describe the government's financial condition, financial trends of the government as a whole and of its major funds, budgetary highlights, and activities affecting capital assets and related debt. Finally, the MD&A should discuss economic factors and budget and tax rates for the next year.

Statistical Section

In addition to the output of the accounting information system presented in the financial section of the governmental annual report, statistical information reflecting social and economic data, financial trends, and the fiscal capacity of the government are needed by users interested in better understanding the activity and condition of the government. GASB *Statement No. 44* indicates that generally the statistical section should present information in five categories to assist the user in understanding and assessing a government's economic condition.[4] To be most useful, the 10 most recent years of data should generally be included (unless otherwise indicated) in the schedules used to meet the requirements of the five categories defined by the GASB. The five categories are:

1. **Financial trends information,** which provides the user with information that is helpful in understanding and assessing how a government's financial position has changed over time. Schedules in this category are prepared at both the fund level

---

[4] GASB *Statement No. 44*, "Economic Condition Reporting: The Statistical Section" (Norwalk, CT, 2004), effective for periods beginning after June 15, 2005.

ILLUSTRATION 9–2   City and County of Denver—Management's Discussion and Analysis (MD&A)

Management of the City and Country of Denver (City) offers readers of the basic financial statements this narrative overview and analysis of the financial activities of the City for the fiscal year ended December 31, 2004. Readers are encouraged to consider the information presented here in conjunction with additional information that is furnished in the letter of transmittal. The focus of the information herein is on the primary government.

Financial Highlights

- The City's assets exceeded its liabilities at the close of the fiscal year by $2,394,475,000 (net assets). Of this amount $705,258,000 (unrestricted net assets) may be used to meet the City's ongoing obligations.
- The City's total net assets increased by $170,149,000.
- As of close of the current fiscal year, the City's governmental funds reported combined ending fund balances of $573,165,000, a decrease of $117,262,000 from the prior year. This overall decrease is attributable to reductions in fund balances of several capital projects funds. Approximately 44.9% of the fund balance (unreserved fund balance) is available for spending at the government's discretion.
- At the end of the current fiscal year, unreserved/undesignated fund balance of the General Fund was $107,123,000, or 15.8% of total General Fund expenditures.
- The City's total bonded debt decreased by $100,371,000 during the year. Decreases were seen in all categories of bonded debt: general obligation bonds, special assessment bonds, and revenue bonds.

Overview of the Financial Statements

This discussion and analysis is intended as an introduction to the City's basic financial statements. The basic financial statements comprise three components: 1) government-wide financial statements, 2) fund financial statements, and 3) notes to the basic financial statements. In addition to the basic financial statements, also provided is other supplementary information.

Government-wide financial statements

The government-wide financial statements are designed to provide readers with a broad overview of the City's finances, in a manner similar to a private-sector business.

The Statement of Net Assets (the "Unrestricted Net Assets") is similar to a bottom line for the City and its governmental and business-type activities. This statement reports all of the governmental fund's current financial resources (short-term spendable resources) with capital assets and long-term obligations. Over time, increases or decreases in net assets may serve as a useful indicator of whether the financial position of the City is improving or deteriorating.

The Statement of Activities reports how the City's net assets changed during the most recent year. All changes in net assets are reported as soon as the underlying event giving rise to the change occurs, regardless of the timing of related cash flows. Thus, revenues and expenses are reported in this statement for some items that will only result in cash flows in future fiscal periods (e.g., uncollected taxes and earned but unused vacation and sick leave).

The governmental activities reflect the City's basic services, including police, fire, public works, sanitation, economic development, and culture and recreation. Sales and property taxes finance the majority of these services.

The business-type activities reflect private sector type operations, such as Wastewater Management; the Denver Airport System, including Denver International Airport (DIA); and Golf Courses, where fees for services typically cover all or most of the cost of operations, including depreciation.

The government-wide financial statements include not only the City itself (referred to as the primary government), but also other legally separate entities for which the City is financially accountable. Financial information for most of these component units is reported separately from the financial information presented for the primary government itself. A few component units, although legally separate, function essentially as an agency of the City and therefore are included as an integral part of the City.

Fund financial statements

A fund is a grouping of related accounts used to maintain control over resources that have been segregated for specific activities or objectives. The City uses fund accounting to ensure and demonstrate compliance with finance-related legal requirements. All of the funds of the City can be divided into three categories: governmental funds, proprietary funds, and fiduciary funds.

Governmental funds are used to account for essentially the same functions reported as governmental activities in the government-wide financial statements. Governmental fund financial statements focus on near term inflows and outflows of spendable resources, as well as on the balances left at year end that are available for spending. Consequently, the governmental fund financial statements provide a detailed short-term view that helps the reader determine whether there are more or fewer financial resources that can be spent in the near future to finance the City's programs. Because this information does not encompass the long-term focus of the government-wide statements, additional information is provided that

ILLUSTRATION 9–2   Continued

reconciles the governmental fund financial statements to the government-wide statements explaining the relationship (or differences) between them.

The City maintains 23 individual governmental funds. Information is presented separately in the governmental fund balance sheet and in the governmental fund statement of revenues, expenditures, and changes in fund balances for the General Fund, Human Services special revenue fund, Bond Projects capital projects fund, each of which are considered to be major funds. Data from the other 20 governmental funds are combined into a single aggregated presentation. Individual fund data for these nonmajor governmental funds is provided in the form of combining statements elsewhere in this report.

The City adopts an annual appropriated budget for the General Fund and Human Services special revenue fund. A budgetary comparison schedule has been provided to demonstrate compliance with these budgets.

The City maintains two different types of *proprietary funds:* enterprise funds and internal service funds. Enterprise funds are used to report the same functions presented as business-type activities in the government-wide financial statements. The City uses enterprise funds to account for its Wastewater Management, Denver Airport System, Environmental Services, and Golf Course funds. Internal Service funds are an accounting device used to accumulate and allocate costs internally among the City's various functions. The City uses internal service funds to account for its fleet of vehicles, workers' compensation self insurance, paper and printing supplies inventory, and asphalt plant operations. The internal service funds provide services which predominantly benefit governmental rather than business-type functions; therefore they have been included within governmental activities in the government-wide financial statements.

Proprietary funds provide the same type of information as the government-wide financial statements, only in more detail. The proprietary fund financial statements provide separate information for Wastewater Management and the Denver Airport System, both of which are considered to be major funds of the City. Data for the other two enterprise funds and all of the internal service funds are combined into their respective single aggregated presentations. Individual fund data for the nonmajor enterprise funds and all of the internal service funds is provided in the form of combining statements elsewhere in this report.

The City uses *fiduciary funds* to account for assets held on behalf of outside parties, including other governments. When these assets are held under the terms of a formal trust agreement, a private-purpose trust fund is used.

Agency funds generally are used to account for assets that the City holds on behalf of others as their agent. Pension trust funds account for the assets of the City's employee retirement plans.

Fiduciary funds are not reflected in the government-wide financial statements because the resources of those funds are not available to support the City's own programs. The accounting used for fiduciary funds is much like that used for proprietary funds.

The *notes to the basic financial statements* provide additional information that is essential to a full understanding of the data provided in the government-wide and fund financial statements.

Other information in addition to the basic financial statements and accompanying notes is presented in the form of certain required supplementary information concerning the City's progress in funding its obligation to provide pension benefits to its employees and budgetary comparison schedules.

The combining statements referred to earlier in connection with nonmajor funds, internal service funds, and nonmajor component units are presented immediately following the required supplementary information on pensions.

Government-wide Financial Analysis

As noted earlier, net assets may serve over time as a useful indicator of a government's financial position. In the case of the City, assets exceeded liabilities by approximately $2,394,475,000 at the close of the most recent fiscal year.

A portion of the City's net assets $705,258,000 (29.5%) is unrestricted and may be used to meet the City's ongoing financial obligations. These are net assets that are not restricted by external requirements nor invested in capital assets.

Of the City's $2,394,475,000 in net assets, $1,018,830,000 (42.5%) reflects investment in capital assets (e.g. land, buildings, infrastructure, machinery, and equipment) less any related debt used to acquire those assets that is still outstanding. The City uses these capital assets to provide services to citizens; consequently, these assets are not available for future spending. Although the City's investment in its capital assets is reported net of related debt, it should be noted that the resources need to repay this debt must be provided from other sources, since the capital assets themselves cannot be used to liquidate these liabilities.

Net assets of the City also include $670,387,000 of restricted net assets. These are assets representing resources subject to external restrictions as to how they may be used by the City.

ILLUSTRATION 9–2   Continued

The following reflects the City's net assets (amounts expressed in millions):

	Governmental Activities		Business-type Activities		Total Primary Government	
	2004	2003	2004	2003	2004	2003
Current and other assets	$ 889	$1,057	$1,446	$1,393	$2,335	$2,450
Capital assets	2,027	1,861	3,811	3,821	5,838	5,682
Total assets	2,916	2,918	5,257	5,214	8,173	8,132
Long-term liabilities outstanding	1,362	1,441	3,947	3,950	5,309	5,391
Other liabilities	265	304	204	213	469	517
Total liabilities	1,627	1,745	4,151	4,163	5,778	5,908
Net assets:						
Invested in capital assets, net of related debt	869	744	150	93	1,019	837
Restricted	174	85	497	459	671	544
Unrestricted	246	344	459	499	705	843
Total net assets	$1,289	$1,173	$1,106	$1,051	$2,395	$2,224

At December 31, 2004, the City reported positive balances in all three categories of net assets for both the government as a whole and the separate governmental and business-type activities.

The following reflects the City's Changes in Net Assets (amounts expressed in millions):

	Governmental Activities		Business-type Activities		Total Primary Government	
	2004	2003	2004	2003	2004	2003
Revenues:						
Program revenues:						
Charges for services	$ 192	$ 185	$ 558	$ 516	$ 750	$ 701
Operating grants and contributions	185	188	62	64	247	252
Capital grants and contributions	38	14	76	56	114	70
General revenues:						
Property tax	180	148	—	—	180	148
Sales and use tax	382	385	—	—	382	385
Other taxes	117	117	—	—	117	117
Investment income	14	13	25	27	39	40
Other revenues	48	29	8	20	56	49
Total Revenues	1,156	1,079	729	683	1,885	1,762
Expenses:						
General government	188	186	—	—	188	186
Public safety	366	364	—	—	366	364
Public works	93	99	—	—	93	99
Human services	100	108	—	—	100	108
Health	46	194	—	—	46	194
Parks and recreation	61	63	—	—	61	63
Cultural activities	74	82	—	—	74	82
Community development	38	67	—	—	38	67
Economic opportunity	19	23	—	—	19	23
Interest on long-term debt	55	45	—	—	55	45
Wastewater management	—	—	70	66	70	66

ILLUSTRATION 9–2   **Continued**

Denver airport system	—	—	588	588	588	588
Other enterprise funds	—	—	16	17	16	17
Total Expenses	1,040	1,231	674	671	1,714	1,902
Increase (decrease) in net assets						
before transfers	116	(152)	55	12	171	(140)
Special item—loss on revised capital lease	—	(28)	—	—	—	(28)
Transfers	—	1	—	(1)	—	—
Increase (decrease) in net assets	116	(179)	55	11	171	(168)
Net assets—January 1	1,173	1,354	1,051	1,040	2,224	2,394
Prior period adjustment	—	(2)	—	—	—	(2)
Net assets—December 31	$1,289	$1,173	$1,106	$1,051	$2,395	$2,224

Governmental activities increased the City's net assets by $116,068,000 for the year ended December 31, 2004. Key elements of the increase are as follows:

- Tax revenues are comprised of property tax, sales and use tax, franchise tax, facilities development tax, occupational privilege tax and other miscellaneous taxes. Property tax and sales and use taxes totaled 82.7% of all tax revenues and 48.6% of all governmental activities' revenue.
- Property tax recorded in the General Fund, special revenue funds and debt service funds totaled $179,497,000 for an increase of $31,284,000 or 21.1%. Property taxes are not recorded in the capital projects funds. Sales and use tax revenues of $381,891,000 were down $3,470,000 or 0.9% compared to 2003.
- General government expenses in 2004 were $187,616,000 or 18.0% of total expenses. Public safety expenses were $365,856,000 or 35.2% of total expenses. Public works' expenses were $92,968,000 or 8.9% of total expenses.
- Human services' expenses were $100,488,000 or 9.7% of total expenses. The remaining areas of health $46,132,000 or 4.4%, parks and recreation $61,025,000 or 5.9%, cultural activities $73,912,000 or 7.1%, community development $38,013,000 or 3.7%, economic opportunity $19,417,000 or 1.9%, and interest on long-term debt $54,572,000 or 5.2%, comprise the remainder of the governmental activities expenses for 2004.

Intergovernmental revenues are grants and other revenues received from the state and federal government. Licenses and permits include amounts collected from the issuance of licenses and permits required by the City for various purposes. Revenues from fees collected by the City for a variety of services provided to the public are recorded as charges for services. Investment income reflects revenues from investment activity. Other revenue includes amounts collected from the sale of property at auction, land, salvage, surplus and scrap materials, and reimbursements.

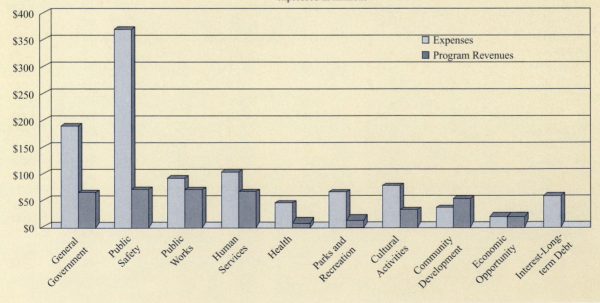

EXPENSES AND PROGRAM REVENUES—GOVERNMENTAL ACTIVITIES
expressed in millions

ILLUSTRATION 9–2   Continued

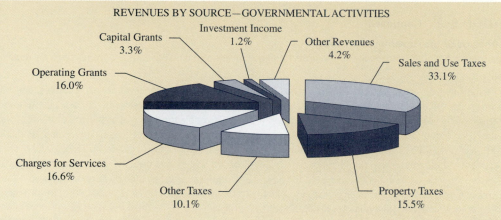

REVENUES BY SOURCE—GOVERNMENTAL ACTIVITIES

Capital Grants 3.3%

Investment Income 1.2%

Other Revenues 4.2%

Operating Grants 16.0%

Sales and Use Taxes 33.1%

Charges for Services 16.6%

Other Taxes 10.1%

Property Taxes 15.5%

Business-type activities increased the City's net assets by $54,081,000. Key elements of this increase are as follows:

- Total revenues of $728,978,000 were $46,166,000, or 6.8%, higher compared to prior year amounts primarily due to higher capital grants to the Denver Airport System for construction projects and increased charges for services in all of the enterprise funds.
- Total expenses of $674,557,000 increased by $3,705,000, or 0.6%, when compared to the prior year; mostly due to higher expenses in the Wastewater Management fund of $4,787,000 during 2004. Wastewater Management expenses in 2004 totaled $70,260,000, or 10.4%, of total business-type activities. Denver Airport System expenses totaled $588,126,000, or 87.2%, of business-type activities. The remaining $16,171,000, or 2.4%, of expenses in business-type activities were related to Environmental Services and Golf activities.

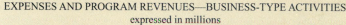

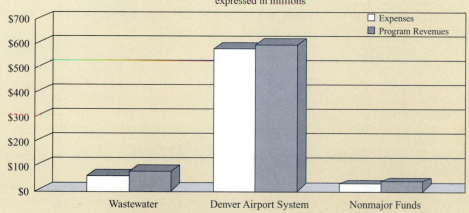

EXPENSES AND PROGRAM REVENUES—BUSINESS-TYPE ACTIVITIES
expressed in millions

Expenses
Program Revenues

Wastewater   Denver Airport System   Nonmajor Funds

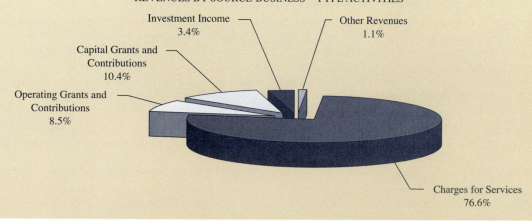

REVENUES BY SOURCE-BUSINESS—TYPE ACTIVITIES

Investment Income 3.4%

Other Revenues 1.1%

Capital Grants and Contributions 10.4%

Operating Grants and Contributions 8.5%

Charges for Services 76.6%

ILLUSTRATION 9–2 Continued

Financial Analysis of the Government's Funds

As noted earlier, the City uses fund accounting to ensure and demonstrate compliance with finance-related legal requirements.

Governmental funds

The focus of the City's governmental funds is to provide information on current year revenue, expenditures, and balances of spendable resources. Such information is useful in assessing the City's financing requirements. In particular, unreserved fund balance may serve as a useful measure of a government's net resources available for spending at the end of the fiscal year.

As of the year ended December 31, 2004, the City's governmental funds reported combined ending fund balances of $573,165,000, a decrease of $117,262,000 in comparison with the prior year. Approximately 44.9% ($257,565,000) of the total fund balance amount constitutes unreserved fund balance, which is available for spending at the City's discretion. The remainder of fund balance is reserved to indicate that it is not available for new spending because it has already been committed 1) to liquidate contracts and purchase orders of the prior period ($112,201,000), 2) to pay debt service ($57,204,000), 3) for emergency use ($26,173,000), 4) for a variety of other purposes ($120,022,000).

The General Fund is the chief operating fund of the City. For the year ended December 31, 2004, unreserved fund balance of the General Fund was $107,123,000 while total fund balance was $165,961,000. As a measure of the General Fund's liquidity, it may be useful to compare both unreserved fund balance and total fund balance to total fund expenditures. Unreserved fund balance represents 15.8% of total General Fund expenditures, while total fund balance represents 24.5% of the same amount.

The total fund balance of the City's General Fund increased by $12,654,000, or 8.3%, during the year ended December 31, 2004. Key factors in this increase are as follows:

- Expenditures from the construction fund for the Wellington E. Webb Municipal Office Building decreased total fund balance by $6,338,000. This portion of the fund balance is restricted for costs related to the building and is not available for general operations of the City.
- Total revenues including other financing sources collected in 2004, less the proceeds from capital leases, decreased by $5,202,000 from 2003. Total expenditures including transfers out decreased by $48,928,000 from 2003.

Certain revenues in the General Fund that increased from 2003 to 2004 include:

- Property tax revenues increased by $3,338,000. The TABOR amendment to the state constitution limits municipal property tax revenue growth to the sum of prior year inflation plus growth in the current year.
- Other tax revenues increased by $1,528,000. The major component of the increase was a $1,430,000 increase in Xcel Energy franchise revenue resulting from higher than anticipated energy costs. Other increases include $1,179,000 increase in Auto A&B and $286,000 in Lodger's tax.
- Licenses and permits increased by $2,038,000, or 9.5%, due to continued strength in construction activity in the northeast areas of Denver.
- Charges for services increased by $3,025,000, or 3.0%, due to higher internal service and indirect charges and various fees, including docket fees, probation fees, and motor vehicle fees.
- Miscellaneous other revenues increased by $2,380,000 primarily due to the receipt of a refund of prior year expenditure. Also included in the 2004 miscellaneous revenue is the effect of the write-off of an outstanding liability account from prior years.

Significant revenues in the General Fund that decreased from 2003 to 2004 include:

- Sales and use taxes collected were lower by $4,639,000. The telecommunications' industry, which provided much of Denver's economic strength in the late 1990's, has yet to recover. In 2003, sales and use tax revenue contained $8,000,000 of collections from a one-time sales tax amnesty and unanticipated audits. If the one-time amnesty and audit revenue is removed from 2003, sales and use tax collections were higher by $3,371,000 for 2004.
- Transfers in to the General Fund decreased by $13,386,000 due to the closeout of a number of dormant funds in 2003 including the Y2K Equipment Special Revenue fund and the Unplanned Fleet Replacement fund.
- Investment income decreased by $216,000 due primarily to continued low interest rates.

Due to the continued recession in Denver's economy and its impact on revenues, the City made across-the-board reductions in 2004 to reduce both personnel and non-personnel costs. Personnel cost reductions included a planned five days leave without pay for most City employees (three of the days were cancelled), having employees contribute 2 percent of pension cost and paying a larger share of their health insurance premiums. Non-personnel reductions included reducing capital equipment purchases by

ILLUSTRATION 9–2   **Continued**

two-thirds, reducing the fleet replacement program by 40 percent, and refinancing some debt. Other areas of change in the General Fund included:

- Public safety expenditures increased by $9,775,000 due primarily to collective bargaining increases averaging 3 percent for uniformed officers.
- General government expenditures decreased by $8,365,000, due in part to a continued freeze on hiring and non-critical spending.
- Other areas experiencing decreases included: public works by $6,763,000, parks and recreation by $2,162,000, cultural activities by $2,057,000, and community development by $2,112,000.
- Transfers out of the General Fund to other funds decreased by $2,140,000 including: a reduction of $2,955,000 in the transfer for fleet replacement and a reduction of $880,500 in the transfer to Information Technology projects. These decreases were partially offset by increases in the transfer to Theaters and Areas of $717,000 and an increase of $450,000 in the transfer to the Housing Trust project.
- A decrease in capital outlay of $32,256,000 due to the one-time adjustment in 2003 for the capital lease of the Wellington E. Webb Municipal Office Building.

The Human Services' special revenue fund had a total fund balance of $14,679,000, of which $9,453,000 is reserved for encumbrances and construction. The net increase in fund balance of $2,931,000 during the current year in the Human Services special revenue fund was due primarily to a decrease in state funding of $9,248,000 and an increase in property taxes for the Developmental Disabilities fund. To offset the decline in State funding the Department of Human Services continued a hiring freeze and reduced actual expenditures by $7,370,000.

A decrease in fund balance in the Bond Projects fund of $99,150,000 primarily reflects the construction outlays for the Colorado Convention Center Expansion, funded with excise bonds, and construction outlays for the Art Museum Expansion, funded with 1999 General Obligation bonds. Other capital outlays included completion of police district station improvements, intersection improvements, recreation center improvements, general parks improvements, and intersection and street improvements funded by 1998 General Obligation Bonds. Additionally, a portion of the decrease in fund balance represents spending of the 2003 A general obligation bonds for the Auditorium Theatre renovation of $25,000,000.

Proprietary funds

The City's proprietary funds provide the same type of information found in the government-wide financial statements, but in more detail.

Total net assets of Wastewater Management amounted to $392,305,000 and those for the Denver Airport System were $684,760,000. The total growth in net assets for all enterprise funds was $50,397,000. Other significant factors concerning the finances of the enterprise funds can be found in the discussion of the City's business-type activities.

General Fund Budgetary Highlights

Differences between the General Fund original budget and the final amended budget include significant changes in the expenditure amounts.

Original revenue estimates for 2004 were based on a slowly recovering economy but were still less than 2003 actual amounts by $11,939,000 due to a number of one-time revenues received in 2003. This forecast was revised upward by a total amount of $10,390,000 during 2004. A significant amount of the revision resulted from an increase of $3,967,000 in estimated sales and use tax revenue.

Individual significant upward revisions in the revenue estimates were due to:

- An increase in Xcel franchise of $2,046,000 due to projected rate increases as a result of higher natural gas prices.
- An increase for licenses and permits revenue from increases in restaurant licenses, construction and excavation permits, construction application permits, electrical permits, elevator and plumbing permits, and street occupancy permits. These increases were partially offset by a decrease in revenue from meter sacking permits.
- Revenue from fees were increased by $2,855,000 due to expected increases in recorder fees, construction services plan review fees, foreclosure fees, public trustee release fees, inspection fees, recognizant bond fees, and sheriff's fees.
- An increase in miscellaneous general governmental revenue of $2,084,000 was primarily due to a one-time release of insurance reserves.
- All of the following revenue categories were increased: Auto A&B by $600,000, interest income by $773,000, and internal service indirect costs by $1,626,000.

ILLUSTRATION 9–2   Continued

Reductions to the 2004 revenue estimates were made for:

- A reduction in property taxes of $751,000 to account for increases in bankruptcy filings.
- A reduction in Occupational Privilege taxes of $1,183,000 due to continued unemployment rates higher than surrounding cities.
- A reduction in the Highway Users Trust Fund (HUTF) revenue of $939,000 due to the weakness in the Denver economy, a reduced municipal share, and more jurisdictions sharing the HUTF proceeds.
- A reduction in use charges revenue of $2,221,000 due to decreases in parking lot revenue and parking meter revenue. The City reduced the hourly rates for downtown meters and instituted free parking on Sunday.

In 2004 our original projection was a use of fund balance of $4,547,000. Because revenues increased slightly, combined with strong internal restrictions on spending, the projected fund balance for 2004 was revised to show an increase of $2,443,000.

Differences between the final amended budget and actual revenues and expenditures are briefly summarized in the following paragraphs.

General Fund revenues, including transfers in, were $5,216,000 or 0.7 percent more than the revised budget due primarily to miscellaneous general governmental revenue receipts, which were $1,610,000 above the revised forecast, and licenses and permits, which were $1,614,000 above the revised forecast due to continued strength in the residential construction industry, especially in the northeast part of Denver.

Specific revenue variances to budget included:

- Property tax was $1,290,000 ahead of forecast due to fewer bankruptcy filings than expected.
- Intergovernmental revenues were above forecast by $1,173,000 due primarily to increases in state grant revenue for the county-wide cost allocation.
- Revenues from charges for services were $1,542,000 more than budgeted due to increases in internal service charges and indirect cost reimbursement, recorder fees, construction services plan review fees, foreclosure fees, public trustee release fees, inspection fees, recognizant bond fees, and sheriff's fees.
- Transfers in was $825,000 lower than budgeted due primarily to reductions in the amount of excess excise bond revenues transferred to the General Fund.

General Fund budget basis expenditures in total were $15,421,000 less than the final amended budget amount due to the across the board cuts made during 2004. In addition to the amounts unspent in agency budgets, the unspent reserves, including the general contingency reserve at year-end, totaled $7,193,000. The City continued the hiring freeze and stopped all non-critical spending including requiring all non-civil service employees to take a two-day furlough during 2004.

Capital Asset and Debt Administration

Capital Assets

The City's capital assets for its governmental and business type activities as of December 31, 2004, amounted to $5,837,192,000 (net of accumulated depreciation). This investment in capital assets includes land, buildings and improvements, equipment and other, park facilities, and infrastructure (including streets, alleys, traffic signals and signs, and bridges) of governmental activities. Infrastructure type assets of business-type activities are reported as buildings and improvements. The City's capital assets by activity at December 31, 2004 and 2003, were as follows (amounts expressed in thousands):

	Governmental Activities		Business-type Activities		Total Primary Government	
	2004	2003	2004	2003	2004	2003
Land and construction in progress	$ 383,165	$ 514,448	$ 467,757	$ 412,734	$ 850,922	$ 927,182
Buildings and improvements	1,269,597	930,807	4,005,625	3,976,225	5,275,222	4,907,032
Equipment and other	184,819	178,676	697,754	669,435	882,573	848,111
Collections	76,098	72,758	—	—	76,098	72,758
Infrastructure	883,363	864,325	—	—	883,363	864,325
Less accumulated depreciation	(770,527)	(699,506)	(1,360,459)	(1,237,708)	(2,130,986)	(1,937,214)
Total	$2,026,515	$1,861,508	$3,810,677	$3,820,686	$5,837,192	$5,682,194

ILLUSTRATION 9–2 Continued

Major capital asset activity during the year ended December 31, 2004 included the following:
Governmental Activities:

- Completion of the Police District 2 Station Replacement—$9,449,000.
- Completion of the Police District 3 Station Replacement—$8,672,000.
- Completion of the Predator Ridge at the Denver Zoo—$8,961,000.
- Renovation of the Auditorium Theatre—$61,714,000.
- Completion of the Cherry Creek North Parking Garage—$5,445,000.
- Completion of the Colorado Convention Center Expansion—$221,489,000.
- Completion of the Minori Yasui Office Building Remodel—$16,401,000.
- Completion of Parkfield Fire Station—$3,454,500.
- Construction of the Denver Art Museum Expansion—$23,920,000.

Business-type Activities:

- Additions to the Storm Collection system—$12,000,000.
- Additions to the Sanitary Collection system—$9,000,000.
- The Denver Airport System checked baggage explosive detection system—$92,000,000.

Additional information on the City's capital assets can be found in Note III-D beginning on page 66 of this report.

Bonded debt

At December 31, 2004, the City had total bonded indebtedness of $4,834,083,000. Of this amount, $383,145,000 comprises debt backed by the full faith and credit of the City and $290,000 is special assessment debt for which the City is liable in the event of default by the property owners subject to the assessment. The remainder of the City's debt, $4,450,648,000, represents bonds and commercial notes secured by specified revenue sources (i.e. revenue bonds of the Denver Airport System, Wastewater Management, and excise tax revenue bonds). Outstanding debt by activity at December 31, 2004 and 2003, was as follows (amounts expressed in thousands):

	Governmental Activities		Business-type Activities		Total Primary Government	
	2004	2003	2004	2003	2004	2003
General obligation bonds	$383,145	$431,889	$ —	$ —	$ 383,145	$ 431,889
Special assessment debt	290	460	—	—	290	460
Revenue bonds	335,205	343,840	4,115,443	4,158,265	4,450,648	4,502,105
Total	$718,640	$776,189	$4,115,443	$4,158,265	$4,834,083	$4,934,454

The City's general obligation debt is rated AA+ by Standard & Poor's and Fitch rating agencies and Aa1 by Moody's Investors Service. The Denver Airport System's senior lien debt is rated by Standard & Poor's, Moody's, and Fitch at A, A2 and A, respectively. During the first quarter of 2004, in response to the Airports' strong operational and financial performance, Standard & Poor's and Fitch upgraded their outlooks on the airport from negative to stable.

During 2004, the City took advantage of favorable interest rates and issued $150,000,000 of Airport System Revenue Bonds, Series 2004A and 2004B used to refund prior debt ($92,655,000 of Airport System Revenue Bonds, Series 1994A).

Additional information on the City's bonded debt can be found in Note III-G beginning on page 70 of this [CAFR] report.

Economic Factors and Next Year's Budget

The 2005 budget continues the City's attempt to maintain core basic services and a sufficient fund balance during the current economic downturn. The Denver area's economy is showing signs of recovery. With these assumptions in mind, the 2005 forecast for General Fund revenues are to increase by $15,524,000, or 2.1 percent, from 2004 estimated revenues. Highlights of the 2005 General Fund budget are as follows:

- Total 2005 General Fund expenditures are budgeted at $748,959,000, which is $27,868,000 more than the revised 2004 expenditures.
- Sales and use tax revenue is projected to grow 2.9 percent from 2004. This includes $1,600,000 for the City's share of the Stapleton Tax Increment Financing District.

ILLUSTRATION 9–2 Continued

- Most revenue estimates were held flat with the exception of miscellaneous general governmental revenue which was reduced by $5,062,000 for one-time revenue received in 2004 for insurance proceeds and reimbursement for Undersheriff regional services.
- Personnel costs included restoring 5 furlough days and an estimated 2.25 percent salary increase for most Career Service employees for 2005 at the time of their performance evaluation.
- The 2005 budget also includes restoring collective bargaining pay and benefits that were conceded by the Fire and Sheriff's unions as part of the 2004 budget.
- Personnel costs also include increases in funding for the increase in effective strength of the Police Department. This includes $2,500,000 in accelerated Police training to replace vacancies more quickly and $1,400,000 to pay for unused sick leave instead of requiring officers to take time off.

During 2004, unreserved and undesignated fund balance in the General Fund increased to $107,296,000. The City anticipates using $9,902,000 of the unreserved fund balance for General Fund operations in 2005.

At Denver International Airport (DIA), United Airlines is the dominant air carrier. DIA is United's second largest connecting hub in its route system. On December 9, 2002, United filed for bankruptcy protection under Chapter 11 of the Bankruptcy Code. The Chapter 11 filing permits United to continue operations while developing a plan of reorganization.

Following months of good faith negotiations, the City and United reached agreement regarding the affirmation of United's use and lease agreement. The conditions of the affirmation were memorialized in a stipulated order that was filed with and accepted by the bankruptcy court on November 11, 2003. The full text of the stipulated order is available on the DIA website, www.flydenver.com. The City cannot predict the ultimate outcome of United's bankruptcy proceedings; however, the affirmation of United's lease at DIA is nonetheless a signal of United's commitment to its Denver hub operations.

Requests for Information

This financial report is designed to provide a general overview of the City's finances for all those with an interest in the government's finances. Questions concerning the information provided in this report or requests for additional financial information should be addressed to the Denver City Auditor's Office, 201 West Colfax Avenue, Dept. 705, Denver, CO 80202.

and government-wide level. The focus is on showing the trend in fund balances and net asset categories, including changes in net asset and fund balances.

2. **Revenue capacity information,** which assists the user with understanding and assessing the government's ability to generate its own revenues (own-source revenues), such as property taxes and user charges. The schedules presented should focus on the government's most significant own-source revenues. Suggested schedules provide information on the revenue base (sources of revenue), revenue rates (including overlapping tax rate information), the principal revenue payors, and property tax levy and collection information.

3. **Debt capacity information,** which is useful in understanding and assessing the government's existing debt burden and its ability to issue additional debt. Four types of debt schedules are recommended—ratios of outstanding debt to total personal income of residents, information about direct and overlapping debt, legal debt limitations and margins, and information about pledged revenues.

4. **Demographic and economic information,** which assists the user in understanding the socioeconomic environment in which the government operates, and provides information that can be compared over time and across governments. Governments should present demographic and economic information that will be most relevant to users, such as information on personal income, unemployment rates, and employers.

5. **Operating information,** which is intended to provide a context in which the government's operations and resources can be better understood. This information is also intended to assist users of financial statements in understanding and assessing the government's financial condition. At a minimum, three schedules of operating

information should be presented—number of government employees, indicators of demand or level of service (*operating indicators*), and capital asset information.

Some of the information in the statistical section has been discussed previously. For example, reporting the ratio of debt per capita, as well as the computation of legal debt limit, legal debt margin, and direct and overlapping debt and future debt service requirements, are all illustrated and discussed in Chapter 6. Other information listed by the GASB as recommended for presentation in the statistical section of the CAFR is generally self-explanatory.

PREPARATION OF BASIC FINANCIAL STATEMENTS

The basic financial statements that must be presented to meet minimum general purpose financial reporting requirements were described earlier in this chapter. Although examples of the basic statements of the City and County of Denver are provided in Chapter 1, it will be instructive to illustrate preparation of those statements for the Town of Brighton, the hypothetical town used for illustrative purposes in several of the preceding chapters. The prior chapters provided illustrative journal entries for fund and government-wide activities for the fiscal year ending December 31, 2008, as follows:

Chapter	Illustrative Entries for
4	General Fund/governmental activities
5	Capital projects fund/governmental activities
6	Serial bond debt service fund/governmental activities
	Term bond debt service fund/governmental activities
7	Supplies fund (an internal service fund)
	Water utility fund (an enterprise fund)

Recall from Chapter 7 that the Business-type Activities column of the government-wide statements simply reports information for the enterprise funds (internal service fund information is reported in the Governmental Activities column). Further, enterprise funds report using the same measurement focus (flow of economic resources) and basis of accounting (accrual) as the government-wide financial statements. Thus, unlike governmental activities, which use a different measurement focus and basis of accounting than governmental funds, there is no need for a separate set of accounting records to record government-wide business-type transactions. The accounting information reported in enterprise funds can easily be aggregated for reporting at the government-wide level. Since, in the case of the Town of Brighton, the water utility fund is the only enterprise fund, its financial information will simply be reported in the Business-type Activities column of the government-wide financial statements. Internal service funds also use the same measurement focus and basis of accounting as the government-wide financial statements. However, internal service funds are generally reported in the Governmental Activities column. Recall that in Chapter 7 entries were made at both the fund level and the government-wide level to simplify reporting and to avoid double counting transactions (recording in the governmental fund and internal service fund) when reporting at the government-wide level.

The Governmental Activities column of the government-wide financial statements for the Town of Brighton, presented later in this section, includes all pertinent financial information, other than budget related, arising from transactions of the General Fund, the capital projects fund the two debt service funds and the internal service fund. In addition, the direct expenses of the functions reported in the statement of activities include depreciation on the general capital assets assigned to those functions or allocated to the functions on a rational basis, such as square footage of usage for functions that share public buildings.

All changes in government-wide net assets that occurred due to transactions during fiscal year 2008 in the General Fund, capital projects fund, serial bond debt service fund, term bond debt service fund, and internal service fund are reflected in the pre-closing general ledger trial balance for governmental activities presented in Illustration 9–3. The amounts shown for certain accounts are assumed amounts that reflect many transactions that were not illustrated in Chapter 4.

Before preparing the government-wide financial statements, an adjusting entry should be made to record fiscal year 2008 depreciation expense for the general capital assets, as well as other appropriate adjusting entries. Using assumed amounts for depreciation and assuming that depreciation is assigned to functions in the amounts shown, the journal entry to record the adjusting entry for depreciation in the governmental activities general journal is as follows:

	Debits	Credits
Governmental Activities:		
Expenses—General Government	114,746	
Expenses—Public Safety	229,493	
Expenses—Public Works	672,288	
Expenses—Health and Welfare	95,622	
Expenses—Parks and Recreation	133,871	
Accumulated Depreciation—Buildings		527,240
Accumulated Depreciation—Equipment		428,980
Accumulated Depreciation—Improvements Other than Buildings		289,800

The pre-closing trial balance presented in Illustration 9–3 provides all of the information needed for the Governmental Activities column of the government-wide financial statements, including the effects of the preceding adjusting entry for depreciation.

ILLUSTRATION 9-3

TOWN OF BRIGHTON **Pre-Closing Trial Balance** **Governmental Activities General Ledger** **December 31, 2008**		
	Debits	**Credits**
Cash	$ 239,363	
Taxes Receivable—Delinquent	706,413	
Estimated Uncollectible Delinquent Taxes		$ 126,513

ILLUSTRATION 9-3   Continued

Interest and Penalties Receivable	13,191	
Estimated Uncollectible Interest and Penalties		3,091
Inventory of Supplies	69,100	
Investments	83,316	
Land	1,239,600	
Buildings	15,545,248	
Accumulated Depreciation—Buildings		10,971,847
Equipment	6,404,477	
Accumulated Depreciation—Equipment		4,063,944
Improvements Other than Buildings	16,693,626	
Accumulated Depreciation—Improvements Other than Buildings		5,148,162
Vouchers Payable		434,400
Accrued Interest Payable		40,500
Due to Federal Government		126,520
Due to State Government		39,740
Internal Balances		128,500
Current Portion of Long-Term Debt		60,000
Bonds Payable		2,640,000
Net Assets—Invested in Capital Assets, Net of Related Debt		17,830,018
Net Assets, Restricted for Debt Service		77,884
Net Assets, Unrestricted		453,900
Program Revenues—Charges for Services—General Government		213,200
Program Revenues—Charges for Services—Public Safety		186,480
Program Revenues—Charges for Services—Public Works		124,320
Program Revenues—Charges for Services—Parks and Recreation		82,464
Program Revenues—Operating Grants and Contributions— Public Safety		100,000
Program Revenues—Operating Grants and Contributions— Health and Welfare		184,100
Program Revenues—Capital Grants and Contributions—Public Safety		300,000
General Revenues—Property Taxes		2,599,636
General Revenues—Sales Taxes		485,000
General Revenues—Interest and Penalties on Delinquent Taxes		11,400
General Revenues—Miscellaneous		28,400
General Revenues—Property Taxes—Restricted for Debt Service		117,000
General Revenues—Sales Taxes—Restricted for Debt Service		31,200
General Revenues—Investment Earnings—Restricted for Debt Service		3,145
Expenses—General Government	773,409	
Expenses—Public Safety	1,646,321	
Expenses—Public Works	1,546,874	
Expenses—Health and Welfare	959,564	
Expenses—Parks and Recreation	562,362	
Expenses—Interest on Tax Anticipation Notes	13,500	
Expenses—Interest on Notes Payable	1,000	
Expenses—Interest on Long-Term Debt	114,000	
Totals	$46,611,364	$46,611,364

Illustrative closing entries for the temporary accounts of the governmental activities were deferred in earlier chapters. The complete closing entry to close all temporary accounts of the governmental activities general ledger follows the pre-closing trial balance.

The governmental activities closing entry is given as follows:

	Debits	Credits
Governmental Activities:		
Program Revenues—Charges for Services— General Government	213,200	
Program Revenues—Charges for Services— Public Safety	186,480	
Program Revenues—Charges for Services— Public Works	124,320	
Program Revenues—Charges for Services— Parks and Recreation	82,464	
Program Revenues—Operating Grants and Contributions—Public Safety	100,000	
Program Revenues—Operating Grants and Contributions—Health and Welfare	184,100	
Program Revenues—Capital Grants and Contributions—Public Safety	300,000	
General Revenues—Property Taxes	2,599,636	
General Revenues—Sales Taxes	485,000	
General Revenues—Interest and Penalties on Delinquent Taxes	11,400	
General Revenues—Miscellaneous	28,400	
General Revenues—Property Taxes— Restricted for Debt Service	117,000	
General Revenues—Sales Taxes— Restricted for Debt Service	31,200	
General Revenues—Investment Earnings— Restricted for Debt Service	3,145	
Net Assets—Unrestricted	1,150,685	
Expenses—General Government		773,409
Expenses—Public Safety		1,646,321
Expenses—Public Works		1,546,874
Expenses—Health and Welfare		959,564
Expenses—Parks and Recreation		562,362
Expenses—Interest on Tax Anticipation Notes		13,500
Expenses—Interest on Notes Payable		1,000
Expenses—Interest on Long-Term Debt		114,000

In addition to the closing entry just shown, entries are required to reclassify the three net asset accounts to their correct amounts as of December 31, 2008. By comparing the pre-closing trial balance (see Illustration 9–3) to the Governmental Activities column of the statement of net assets as of December 31, 2007 (see

Illustration 4–1), one can verify that the balances of the two accounts Net Assets—Invested in Capital Assets, Net of Related Debt and Net Assets—Restricted for Debt Service in the pre-closing trial balance are the same as those reported at the end of the prior year. That is, these accounts have not yet been updated to reflect changes in either general capital asset transactions and related debt or changes in net assets restricted for debt service.

From the information in the trial balance, the total amount of capital assets, net of accumulated depreciation, as of December 31, 2008, is calculated as $19,698,998. Therefore, the correct balance of Net Assets—Invested in Capital Assets, Net of Related Debt is $16,998,998 ($19,698,998, less related debt of $2,700,000), a decrease of $831,020 during the year. Since capital debt increased by $1,200,000 (from $1,500,000 to $2,700,000) during the year and accumulated depreciation increased $1,254,020 (including $8,000 on internal service fund depreciable assets), capital asset acquisitions during the year must have exceeded dispositions by $1,623,000 ($1,200,000 + $1,254,020 − $831,020). The Town of Brighton Fire Station (see Entry 15 on page 183 in Chapter 5) was completed during the year at a cost of $1,493,000, which together with $130,000 of capital assets reported by the internal service fund accounts in full for capital asset acquisitions during 2008.

Based on the assets reported in the combined debt service funds balance sheet presented in Illustration 6–7, assets reported in the governmental activities trial balance must include amounts totaling $124,229 for cash, investments, and taxes receivable that are restricted for debt service. However, accrued interest payable of $40,500 will be paid from these assets. Thus, the correct balance for Net Assets—Restricted for Debt Service as of December 31, 2008, must be $83,729 ($124,229 less $40,500), an increase of $5,845 from its current balance of $77,884.

Based on the foregoing analysis, the journal entry to reclassify the governmental activities net asset accounts to the appropriate amounts is given as:

	Debits	Credits
Governmental Activities:		
Net Assets—Invested in Capital Assets, Net of Related Debt	831,020	
Net Assets—Restricted for Debt Service		5,845
Net Assets—Unrestricted		825,175

The Town of Brighton's government-wide statement of net assets and statement of activities are presented in Illustrations 9–4 and 9–5. Compared with the trial balance shown in Illustration 9–3, it is apparent that the financial statements are highly condensed. For example, taxes receivable, interest and penalties receivable, and interest receivable are reported as a single receivables amount, net of related estimated uncollectible amounts. Detail of the receivables and uncollectibles should be disclosed in the notes to the financial statements. Similarly, because the detail of capital assets, including depreciation expense and accumulated depreciation, should be disclosed in the notes to the financial statements, it is acceptable to report the aggregate net amount for capital assets on a single line. The town has also decided to report all current liabilities, except for the current portion of long-term debt, as a single amount for vouchers payable and accrued liabilities. Such highly condensed reporting is consistent with the

ILLUSTRATION 9–4

TOWN OF BRIGHTON
Statement of Net Assets
December 31, 2008

| | Primary Government | | | |
	Governmental Activities	Business-type Activities	Total	Component Units (None)
Assets				
Cash	$ 239,363	$ 13,655	$ 253,018	
Receivables (net)	590,000	77,900	667,900	
Investments	83,316	696,000	779,316	
Inventory of supplies	69,100	24,700	93,800	
Capital assets (net)	19,698,998	2,983,050	22,682,048	
Total assets	20,680,777	3,795,305	24,476,082	
Liabilities				
Vouchers payable and accrued liabilities	641,160	62,815	703,975	
Internal balances	128,500	(128,500)	–0–	
Current portion of long-term debt	60,000		60,000	
Bonds payable	2,640,000	1,745,230	4,385,230	
Total liabilities	3,469,660	1,679,545	5,149,205	
Net Assets				
Invested in capital assets, net of related debt	16,998,998	1,237,820	18,236,818	
Restricted for debt service	83,729	682,025	765,754	
Unrestricted	128,390	195,915	324,305	
Total net assets	$17,211,117	$2,115,760	$19,326,877	

GASB's objective to "enhance the understandability and usefulness of the general purpose external financial reports of state and local governments" by providing an overview of the financial condition and results of activities of the government as a whole, in addition to more detailed fund financial statements and detailed disclosures in the notes to the financial statements.[5]

As shown in Illustrations 9–4 and 9–5, the two government-wide financial statements should also report amounts for discretely presented component units. Because the Town of Brighton has no component units, only primary government information is presented. To minimize line-item detail in the financial statements and thus make the financial statements easier to understand, immaterial amounts for specific items may be reported with the amounts for broadly similar items. For example, in the Town of Brighton's Statement of Activities, it would have been acceptable to report the relatively small amount of revenue from interest and penalties on delinquent taxes as part of revenues from property taxes.

[5]*GASBS 34,* par. 1.

Illustration 9–5

TOWN OF BRIGHTON
Statement of Activities
For the Year Ended December 31, 2008

Functions/Programs	Expenses	Program Revenues			Net (Expenses) Revenues and Changes in Net Assets			
		Charges for Services	Operating Grants and Contributions	Capital Grants and Contributions	Primary Government			Component Units (None)
					Governmental Activities	Business-Type Activities	Total	
Primary government:								
Governmental activities:								
General government	$ 773,409	$ 213,200			$ (560,209)		$ (560,209)	
Public safety	1,646,321	186,480	$100,000	$300,000	(1,059,841)		(1,059,841)	
Public works	1,546,874	124,320			(1,422,554)		(1,422,554)	
Health and welfare	959,564		184,100		(775,464)		(775,464)	
Parks and recreation	562,362	82,464			(479,898)		(479,898)	
Interest on long-term debt	114,000				(114,000)		(114,000)	
Interest on notes	14,500				(14,500)		(14,500)	
Total governmental activities	5,617,030	606,464	284,100	300,000	(4,426,466)		(4,426,466)	
Business-type activities:								
Water	614,960	727,120		7,000		119,160	119,160	
Total primary government	$6,231,990	$1,333,584	$284,100	$307,000	(4,426,466)	119,160	(4,307,306)	
General revenues:								
Taxes:								
Property taxes levied for general purposes					2,599,636		2,599,636	
Property taxes levied for debt service					117,000		117,000	
Sales taxes					485,000		485,000	
Sales taxes for debt service					31,200		31,200	
Investment earnings for debt service					3,145	44,500	47,645	
Interest and penalties on delinquent taxes					11,400		11,400	
Miscellaneous					28,400		28,400	
Total general revenues					3,275,781	44,500	3,320,281	
Increase (decrease) in unrestricted net assets					(1,150,685)	163,660	(987,025)	
Net assets, January 1, 2008					18,361,802	1,952,100	20,313,902	
Net assets, December 31, 2008					$17,211,117	$2,115,760	$19,326,877	

Fund Financial Statements

In addition to the MD&A and government-wide financial statements, the Town of Brighton would prepare several required fund financial statements. The latter include a balance sheet—governmental funds and a statement of revenues, expenditures, and changes in fund balances—governmental funds. The town would also prepare proprietary fund financial statements for the Supply Fund and the Town of Brighton Water Utility Fund. The statement of net assets; statement of revenues, expenses, and changes in net assets; and statement of cash flows for the funds were provided in Chapter 7 as Illustrations 7–6, 7–7, and 7–8, and thus are not shown again in this chapter.

Illustration 9–6 presents the Balance Sheet—Governmental Funds for the Town of Brighton. The Fire Station Capital Projects Fund meets the criteria of a *major fund* established by *GASBS 34* (see the glossary for the definition of this term and the criteria for determining whether a fund is a major fund). Since the Fire Station Capital Projects Fund has no assets or liabilities at December 31, 2008, it does not appear in the Town of Brighton Balance Sheet—Governmental Funds shown in Illustration 9–6. Therefore, no major funds are shown on the balance sheet, other than the General Fund. The nonmajor funds are combined in a single column headed Other Governmental Funds. The Town of Brighton's Statement of Revenues, Expenditures, and Changes in Fund Balances is shown in Illustration 9–7. Because all governmental funds had activity during the year, they are all included in the operating statement. The two nonmajor funds (the Serial Bond Debt Service Fund and the Term Bond Debt Service Fund) are combined in the column headed Other Governmental Funds.

Required Reconciliations

GASBS 34 requires that the financial information reported in the governmental funds balance sheet be reconciled to that reported in the Governmental Activities column of the government-wide statement of net assets. Similarly, the information reported in the governmental funds statement of revenues, expenditures, and changes in fund balances must be reconciled to that reported as governmental activities in the government-wide statement of activities. The need for reconciliation arises from the use of different measurement focuses and bases of accounting, as discussed at several points in prior chapters. Because enterprise funds are reported on the accrual basis, using the economic resources measurement focus, usually there will be no need for a reconciliation between the enterprise fund financial information and that of business-type activities at the government-wide level.

Items that typically differ between governmental fund statements and governmental activities at the government-wide level, and thus should be reconciled, include:

1. Capital outlays that are reported as expenditures in governmental funds but as capital assets at the government-wide level.
2. Disposition of capital assets that are reported as other financing sources in governmental funds but as reduction of capital assets and gains/losses at the government-wide level.
3. Depreciation on capital assets that is not reported in governmental funds but is reported as expenses and contra-assets at the government-wide level.
4. Issuance of long-term debt that is reported as other financing sources in governmental funds but as an increase in general long-term liabilities at the government-wide level.

ILLUSTRATION 9–6

	TOWN OF BRIGHTON **Balance Sheet** **Governmental Funds** **December 31, 2008**		
	General Fund	Other Governmental Funds	Total Governmental Funds
Assets			
Cash	$145,800	$ 39,313	$185,113
Receivables (net)	588,400	1,600	590,000
Investments		83,316	83,316
Total assets	734,200	124,229	858,429
Liabilities and Fund Balances			
Liabilities:			
Vouchers payable	405,800		405,800
Due to other governments	166,260		166,260
Due to other funds	5,000		5,000
Total liabilities	577,060		577,060
Fund Balances:			
Reserved for encumbrances	70,240		70,240
Unreserved reported in:			
General Fund	86,900		86,900
Debt service		124,229	124,229
Total fund balances	157,140	124,229	281,369
Total liabilities and fund balances	$734,200	$124,229	$858,429

5. Retirement of long-term debt that is reported as an expenditure in governmental funds but as a reduction of general long-term liabilities at the government-wide level.

6. Some revenues that do not provide current financial resources are not recognized in governmental funds but are recognized at the government-wide level.

7. Reporting expenses on an accrual basis at the government-wide level.

8. Interfund transfers between governmental funds, which are not reported at the government-wide level.

9. Adjusting for internal service funds' assets, liabilities, operating income (loss), and transfers.

Illustration 1–7 reconciles the City and County of Denver's total fund balance for governmental funds to the net assets of governmental activities, while Illustration 1–9 reconciles changes in governmental fund balances to changes in governmental activities net assets. *GASBS 34* permits reconciliations to be provided on the face of the governmental fund basic financial statements or in accompanying schedules.

The reconciliation for the Town of Brighton's balance sheet of governmental funds (Illustration 9–6) to the statement of net assets (Illustration 9–4) is presented in

ILLUSTRATION 9–7

TOWN OF BRIGHTON
Statement of Revenues, Expenditures, and Changes in Fund Balances
Governmental Funds
For Year Ended December 31, 2008

	General Fund	Fire Station Capital Projects Fund	Other Governmental Funds	Total Governmental Funds
Revenues				
Property taxes	$2,599,636		$117,000	$2,716,636
Interest and penalties	11,400			11,400
Sales taxes	485,000		31,200	516,200
Licenses and permits	213,200			213,200
Fines and forfeits	310,800			310,800
Intergovernmental	284,100	$ 300,000		584,100
Charges for services	82,464			82,464
Investment earnings			3,145	3,145
Miscellaneous	28,400			28,400
Total revenues	4,015,000	300,000	151,345	4,466,345
Expenditures				
Current:				
General government	649,400			649,400
Public safety	1,305,435			1,305,435
Public works	839,800			839,800
Health and welfare	850,325			850,325
Parks and recreation	419,500			419,500
Contributions to retirement plans	179,100			179,100
Miscellaneous	14,200			14,200
Debt service:				
Interest		1,000	111,000	112,000
Capital outlay		1,493,000		1,493,000
Total expenditures	4,257,760	1,494,000	111,000	5,862,760
Excess (deficiency) of revenues over expenditures	(242,760)	(1,194,000)	40,345	(1,396,415)
Other Financing Sources (Uses)				
Proceeds of long-term capital debt		1,200,000		1,200,000
Interfund transfers in (out)	(91,500)	(6,000)	6,000	(91,500)
Total other financing sources (uses)	(91,500)	1,194,000	6,000	1,108,500
Net change in fund balances	(334,260)	0	46,345	(287,915)
Fund balances, January 1, 2008	491,400	0	77,884	569,284
Fund balances, December 31, 2008	$ 157,140	$ 0	$124,229	$ 281,369

Illustration 9–8. Illustration 9–9 presents the reconciliation of the statement of revenues, expenditures, and changes in fund balance for the governmental funds (Illustration 9–7) to the statement of activities (Illustration 9–5).

ILLUSTRATION 9–8

TOWN OF BRIGHTON
Reconciliation of the Balance Sheet—Governmental Funds to the Statement of Net Assets
December 31, 2008

Total fund balances—governmental funds	$ 281,369
Amounts reported for governmental activities in the statement of net assets are different because:	
Capital assets used in governmental activities are not financial resources and therefore are not reported in the funds.	19,698,998
Long-term liabilities, including bonds payable, are not due and payable in the current period and therefore are not reported in the funds.	(2,700,000)
The assets and liabilities of the internal service fund are included in governmental activities in the statement of net assets.	(28,750)
Accrued interest payable is not due in the current period and therefore not included in the funds.	(40,500)
Net assets of governmental activities	$17,211,117

ILLUSTRATION 9–9

TOWN OF BRIGHTON
Reconciliation of the Statement of Revenues, Expenditures, and Changes in Fund Balances—Governmental Funds to the Statement of Activities
For the Year Ended December 31, 2008

Net change in fund balances—governmental funds	$ (287,915)
Amounts reported for governmental activities in the statement of activities are different because:	
Governmental funds report capital outlays as expenditures. However, in the statement of activities the cost of those assets is allocated over their estimated useful lives as depreciation expense. This is the amount by which capital outlays exceeded depreciation.	246,980
Bond proceeds provide current financial resources to governmental funds, but issuing debt increases long-term liabilities in the statement of net assets. This is the amount of proceeds.	(1,200,000)
Some expenses reported in the statement of activities do not require the use of current financial resources and therefore are not reported as expenditures in governmental funds.	(3,000)
Interfund transfers between the governmental funds and the internal service fund is reported in governmental funds.	91,500
Internal service funds are used by management to charge the costs of certain activities to individual funds. The net revenue of the internal service fund is reported with governmental activities.	1,750
Change in net assets of governmental activities	$(1,150,685)

CURRENT FINANCIAL REPORTING ISSUES

GASB reporting objectives emphasize the role of accountability in external financial reporting. Indeed, accountability is considered to be "the paramount objective from which all other objectives must flow."[6] GASB *Concepts Statement No. 1* expands the definition of accountability beyond the traditional notion of accountability for expenditures of financial resources in conformity with the legally adopted budget. GASB's concept of accountability also includes accountability for the efficient and effective use of resources in providing government services and for interperiod equity or the extent to which current-year revenues are sufficient to pay for current-year services. The *GASBS 34* reporting model, upon which the first nine chapters of the text are based, represents a step toward meeting broader accountability objectives. Recently, the GASB added a concept statement on communication methods and is currently working on a statement that will identify and define the elements of the financial statements. In addition, the GASB has on its technical agenda projects dealing with reporting issues such as intangible assets, derivatives, pollution remediation obligations, and fund balance reporting.[7]

Communication Methods

Concepts Statement No. 3, issued in April 2005, provides the GASB and users with guidance concerning where information should be placed in general purpose financial reports. This statement is particularly beneficial to the GASB as it deliberates how information related to a new standard should be communicated, or presented, in the general purpose financial reports.

The statement recognizes that information can be communicated to external users of financial reports through one of four placement methods—recognition in the financial statements, disclosure in the notes, presentation as required supplementary information, or presentation as supplementary information. If an information item meets the definition of an element of the financial statement and can be measured with sufficient reliability, the item should be recognized in the financial statements. Notes to the financial statements should be used when the information item has a relationship to information presented in the financial statements and is essential to the user's understanding of the financial statements. Required supplementary information and supplementary information methods of communication are used when disclosures are either essential or useful, respectively, for putting financial statements and the related notes into context.

Elements of Financial Statements

The objective of the concept statement on elements of financial statements is to define the key elements of financial statements and define or describe any related concepts that will help guide future standard setting. As with the FASB conceptual framework, the GASB's intent is to develop a conceptual framework that will be useful in future standard-setting, allowing for more consistent development of standards that can be accomplished in a more timely manner.

The GASB had made considerable progress on the elements concept statement prior to the development of the reporting model (*GASBS 34*). However, since 1995 time and effort has been diverted to the development of the reporting model, and as a result work on the elements concept statement was slowed between 1995 and 2004. Since the beginning of 2004, the GASB has tentatively decided that the elements should be defined using a flow-of-resources approach. With this focus, the GASB

---

[6] GASB, *Codification,* Appendix B, *Concepts Statement No. 1,* par. 76.
[7] As new standards are issued in these areas, the publisher will provide updates to adopters of this edition of the text.

believes the statement of activities will provide more useful information concerning management performance than would a focus on increases or decreases in asset and liability accounts. It is the intent that the elements of the financial statements be defined by their inherent (or basic) characteristics, thus allowing the definitions to apply regardless of measurement focus or basis of accounting (i.e., modified accrual or accrual).

Popular Reporting

Although the CAFR has evolved to meet the diverse information needs of financial report users (i.e., citizens, legislative and oversight bodies, and investors and creditors), it is widely recognized that most citizens are unable to read and comprehend the CAFR. To better communicate financial results to citizens, a growing number of governments prepare and distribute **popular reports** that provide highly condensed financial information, budget summaries, and narrative descriptions. They are usually short in length and employ a variety of graphical techniques to enhance understandability. Popular reports are intended to supplement the CAFR, not replace it. Since they do not present minimum data required for complete and fair presentation, popular reports are considered "summary data" and are unaudited.[8] Both the GASB and the Government Finance Officers Association (GFOA), however, recognize the value of popular reports. The GASB has published a commissioned research report on popular reporting,[9] and the GFOA has established an award program for excellence in popular reporting. The award for excellence in popular reporting focuses on report characteristics such as reader appeal, understandability, distribution, and the ability of the popular report to achieve an overall goal of usefulness and quality.

Other Comprehensive Basis of Accounting (OCBOA)

Chapters 1–9 of the textbook have focused on GAAP for state and local governments. However, a large number of state and local governments do not maintain internal accounting records on a GAAP basis and many do not report using GAAP. One individual indicates that he believes that up to 75 percent of state and local governments do not use GAAP for internal and/or external reports.[10] In place of GAAP, many of these governments use an **other comprehensive basis of accounting (OCBOA).** As defined by Statement of Auditing Standards No. 62, OCBOA includes five bases of accounting other than GAAP.[11] The OCBOA most commonly used by state and local governments are cash basis, modified cash basis, and regulatory basis of accounting.

Some of the reasons given for using OCBOA instead of GAAP include: OCBOA accounting records are easier to understand and maintain, the financial statements are easier to prepare and may be easier for users to understand, and the accounting and reporting is less costly than GAAP. However, use of OCBOA does not preclude the need

---

[8] Audit standards issued by the American Institute of Certified Public Accountants permit auditors to express their opinion that a popular report (and other forms of summary data) is fairly stated *in relation to* the basic financial statements from which it is derived. Current AICPA guidance does not permit auditors to express an opinion on popular reports that they are fairly presented in conformity with GAAP.

[9] Frances H. Carpenter and Florence C. Sharp, *Research Report,* "Popular Reporting: Local Government Financial Reports to the Citizenry" (Norwalk, CT: GASB, 1992).

[10] Michael A. Crawford, AICPA Practice Aid Series, *Applying OCBOA in State and Local Governmental Financial Statements,* edited by Leslye Givarz (New York, NY: AICPA, 2003).

[11] American Institute of Certified Public Accountants, *Professional Standards,* AU section 623 (New York: AICPA, 2005).

to present information similar to that reported under GAAP. For example, if a government is using a cash or modified cash basis of accounting, it is expected to comply with presentation of financial statement requirements set forth in GAAP, including presentation of government-wide and fund financial statements, notes to the financial statements, and required supplementary information, such as management's discussion and analysis.[12] Readers interested in a more comprehensive discussion of OCBOA are referred to the following resources: AICPA's *Professional Standards; Applying OCBOA in State and Local Governmental Financial Statements;* and the Auditing and Accounting Guide, *State and Local Governments.*

Appendix

Converting Accounting Information from the Modified Accrual to the Accrual Basis of Accounting

As mentioned in Chapter 4, there are two basic approaches to obtaining the information necessary to prepare the government-wide financial statements. The first method is the dual-track approach used in this textbook, which requires an accounting information system capable of capturing two bases of accounting, the modified accrual basis and the accrual basis. The second approach, not as conceptually desirable, is to maintain one set of records on the modified accrual basis and at the end of the reporting period analyze all transactions occurring over the period and prepare a worksheet that converts the modified accrual basis transactions to the full accrual basis. It is this second approach that is used by a number of governments, since most existing accounting information systems only provide for reporting governmental funds on a modified accrual basis. To familiarize readers with the worksheet process, a brief introduction is provided.

The point of the worksheet is to take account balances derived under the modified accrual basis of accounting and convert the account balances to an accrual basis. Converting and extending the account balances provides management with the balances needed to prepare the government-wide statement of activities and statement of net assets. The conversion is accomplished through a series of adjustments to a total governmental funds pre-closing trial balance. The types of adjustments made to the modified accrual balances are similar to the adjustments found in the reconciliation process shown in Illustrations 9–8 and 9–9. Some of the transactions requiring adjustments include:

1. Converting capital acquisitions from expenditures to capital assets.
2. Recording sales of capital assets.
3. Accounting for the depreciation of capital assets.
4. Converting issuance of debt from an operating statement account to a liability.
5. Converting payment of debt from an operating statement account to a liability adjustment.
6. Recording any accruals for expenses that are deferred under modified accrual, since the payment is not legally due (e.g., interest due on long-term debt).
7. Adjusting assets and liabilities, and including the change in net assets for internal service funds.

[12] American Institute of Certified Public Accountants, Audit and Accounting Guide, *State and Local Governments* (New York: AICPA, 2005).

8. Eliminating interfund receivables and payables among governmental funds (such as a special revenue fund and the General Fund) and between governmental funds and internal service funds. Any remaining balance represents activity between the governmental funds and enterprise funds (business-type activities) and is transferred to an account titled Internal Balances. Internal Balances may have a debit or credit balance. When reported in the actual *financial statement,* Internal Balances between governmental and business-type activities are offsetting.

9. Interfund transfers in and interfund transfers out occurring among governmental funds, and between governmental funds and internal service funds must be eliminated. Any remaining balance represents the transfers between governmental and business-type activities. When reported in the actual *financial statement,* transfers between governmental and business-type activities are offsetting.

A worksheet conversion example, using the Town of Brighton, is presented in Illustration 9–10. Since Brighton uses the dual track approach to record keeping, it would not need to prepare a worksheet. However, the reader's familiarity with the Town of Brighton makes it easier to see how a worksheet conversion would work for a government that does not keep records on both the modified and accrual basis of accounting. The top portion of the worksheet presents the pre-closing trial balances for all governmental funds as of December 31, 2008. At the bottom of the worksheet are those accounts that would not appear in the governmental funds using the modified accrual basis but would appear under the accrual basis used by governmental activities. Examples of such accounts include capital asset and long-term debt accounts. Under the worksheet approach, the governmental activities accounts are only adjusted once a year, at the time the annual financial statements are prepared; thus the balances in the worksheet represent the beginning balances, unadjusted for any activity during the 2008 fiscal year. For ease of explanation the following liberties have been taken with the worksheet—revenue information has been consolidated since no adjustments need to be made to revenues, and capital asset accounts have been consolidated into a single capital assets (net) account. The reader should keep in mind the following points concerning the worksheet:

1. Through the conversion process expenditures are adjusted to expenses.
2. Adding the fund balance (top portion) and the net asset balance (bottom portion) yields the total net asset balance needed for the statement of net assets.
3. The total net asset balance is separated into the three components for reporting in the statement of net assets.
4. Revenues are identified as general or program for reporting in the statement of activities.
5. No worksheet entries are made in the fund journals. However, entries should be made in the worksheet to update account balances for governmental activities.

The following key provides information concerning the figures presented in the adjustment column. An identification (ID) letter is used for tracing purposes.

a. Adjusts the capital projects expenditure into a capital asset (Chapter 5).
b. Records the annual depreciation on capital assets (Chapter 9).
c. Adjusts the other financing source—bond proceeds to a long-term liability (Chapter 5).
d. Records the accrual of interest on serial bond debt (Chapter 6).
e. Incorporates the internal service fund activity (Chapter 7, Illustrations 7-2 and 7-3).
f. Transfers net Due from Other Funds and Due to Other Funds balances to Internal Balances (Chapter 4).
g. Eliminates interfund transfers between governmental funds (Chapters 4 and 6) and between governmental funds and internal service funds (Chapters 4 and 7).

Illustration 9–10

TOWN OF BRIGHTON
Conversion Worksheet
For the Year Ended December 31, 2008

Fund Accounts	Fund Balances Debit	Fund Balances Credit	Adjustments ID	Adjustments Debit	Adjustments ID	Adjustments Credit	Statement of Activities Debit	Statement of Activities Credit	Statement of Net Assets Debit	Statement of Net Assets Credit
Cash	185,113		e	54,250					239,363	
Taxes Receivable—Delinquent	706,413								706,413	
Estimated Uncollectible Delinquent Taxes		126,513								126,513
Interest and Penalties Receivable	13,191								13,191	
Estimated Uncollectible Interest and Penalties		3,091								3,091
Due from Other Funds	25,000				f	25,000				
Inventory of Supplies				69,100	e				69,100	
Investments	83,316								83,316	
Vouchers Payable		405,800			e	28,600				434,400
Due to Federal Government		126,520								126,520
Due to State Government		39,740								39,740
Due to Other Funds		30,000	f	30,000						
Fund Balance		569,284								569,284
Revenues		4,463,200						4,463,200		
Revenues—Interest		3,145						3,145		
Other Financing Sources—Bond Proceeds		1,200,000	c	1,200,000						
Other Financing Sources—Interfund Transfers In		6,000	g	97,500	g	91,500				
Expenditures—General Government	649,400		b	114,746	e	1,750	762,396			
Expenditures—Public Safety	1,305,435		b	229,493			1,534,928			
Expenditures—Public Works	839,800		b	672,288			1,512,088			
Expenditures—Health and Welfare	850,325		b	95,622			945,947			
Expenditures—Parks and Recreation	419,500		b	133,871			553,371			
Expenditures—Contributions to Retirement	179,100						179,100			
Expenditures—Miscellaneous	14,200						14,200			
Expenditures—Construction	1,493,000				a	1,493,000				
Expenditures—Interest	112,000		d	3,000			115,000			
Other Financing Uses—Interfund Transfers Out	97,500				g	97,500				
Total	6,973,293	6,973,293								

Illustration 9–10 Continued

Government-Wide Accounts	Government-wide Beginning Balances					
Capital Assets (net)	19,330,018	a,b,e	368,980			19,698,998
Accrued Interest Payable	37,500			d	3,000	40,500
Bonds Payable	1,500,000			c	1,200,000	2,700,000
Net Assets	17,792,518					17,792,518
Total	19,330,018					
Interfund Loan Payable				e	123,500	123,500
Internal Balances				f	5,000	5,000
Total			3,068,850		3,068,850	21,961,066
					5,617,030	20,810,381
Change in Net Assets					1,150,685	1,150,685
Total					5,617,030	21,961,066
					4,466,345	

Key Terms

Blended presentation, *351*
Component units, *349*
Discrete presentation
  (discretely
  presented), *351*
Financial accountability
  (financially
  accountable), *349*

Financial reporting
  entity, *348*
Joint venture, *349*
Jointly governed
  organizations, *349*
Other comprehensive
  basis of accounting, *377*

Other stand-alone
  government, *349*
Popular reports (or
  reporting), *377*
Primary government, *349*

Selected References

American Institute of Certified Public Accountants, *Professional Standards,* New York, 2005.

American Institute of Certified Public Accountants, Audit and Accounting Guide. *State and Local Governments.* New York, 2005.

Crawford, Michael A. AICPA Practice Aid Series, *Applying OCBOA in State and Local Governmental Financial Statements,* edited by Leslye Givarz. New York: AICPA, 2003.

Governmental Accounting Standards Board. *Codification of Governmental Accounting and Financial Reporting Standards, as of June 30, 2005.* Norwalk, CT, 2005.

Governmental Accounting Standards Board. *Concepts Statement No. 3,* "Communication Methods in General Purpose External Financial Reports That Contain Basic Financial Statements." Norwalk, CT, 2005.

Questions

9–1. *a.* State the principal reasons for the use of funds in accounting for governments.
  b. List five types of funds frequently found in the accounting system of a municipality, and briefly discuss the content of each.

9–2. What is the minimum number of funds a government could keep if it were attempting to adhere to GASB standards? Explain.

9–3. Describe some of the reasons that a government should prepare periodic interim reports.

9–4. What are the three major sections of a CAFR and what are the contents of each?

9–5. The mayor of a city contends that since he is the elected head of all city activities, he has authority to transfer assets from one fund to another on a temporary basis because "it is all in the family." What is the merit, if any, of the mayor's contention?

9–6. Explain the difference between a primary government and a component unit.

9–7. Explain the difference between a *discrete* presentation of a component unit's financial information and a *blended* presentation.

9–8. What additional steps must be taken to convert fund financial information statements to government-wide statements at the end of the year?

9–9. Give examples of items (transactions) that would require reconciliation of total governmental fund balances to net assets of governmental activities.

9–10. What is OCBOA and why would a government choose to use OCBOA rather than GAAP?

Cases

9–1   Reporting Entity. The following example of application of reporting entity criteria is based on an example contained in GASB *Codification* Section 2100.

The Greater Metropolis Urban Development Authority (GMUDA) was authorized as a not-for-profit corporation by the state legislature and created by the City of Metropolis Council to attract new industry and participate in long-range planning of the city. Although the city council appoints GMUDA's governing board, the board has complete authority to hire management and all other employees. The city has no role in monitoring or participating in the day-to-day operating activities of GMUDA.

Per its state charter, GMUDA has separate taxing powers and levies taxes on all commercial and industrial properties located within the designated development district. GMUDA's tax levies are completely independent of the city's, other than they are levied on some of the same taxpayers. GMUDA performs some services for the Chamber of Commerce and other local business organizations for a fee. However, its primary source of revenues is property taxes. GMUDA receives no financial subsidies of any kind from the city and the city is not obligated in any manner for the authority's debt. Even though GMUDA does not require the city's approval of its operating budget, it routinely sends the budget to the city council for review. The city attorney has ruled that the city council has no option but to approve the budget as submitted.

Required

a. Using the reporting entity flow chart presented in Illustration 9–1, and the reporting entity definitions and criteria discussed in Chapter 9, determine whether the Greater Metropolis Urban Development Authority should be included in the reporting entity of which the City of Metropolis is the primary government. If so, should GMUDA be reported by blending or discrete presentation? Explain your rationale for the inclusion/exclusion decision and, if applicable, method of display.

b. Assume the same facts as in Part *a* except that the city council has the power to remove members of GMUDA's board for cause. Also, the city must approve all debt issuances and all expenditures in excess of $100,000. Do your conclusions made in Part *a* above change in light of the different facts in Part *b?* Explain fully.

9–2   Letter of Transmittal. The letter of transmittal to the mayor and council accompanying the annual financial statements of the Town of Stevens follows. (*Note:* This case is based on an actual letter of transmittal and financial statements obtained quite some time ago; however, the name of the town and certain other facts have been changed.)

Letter of Transmittal

To the Honorable Mayor and Town Council
Town of Stevens

Gentlemen:

We are attaching the financial report for the Town of Stevens for the year 2008. The statements and organization of this report are designed to conform to generally accepted principals [*sic*] and standards of government accounting and reporting. A review of this report will reveal much information about the financial position and movements of the Town, some of which it is hoped will be valuable and some of which we fear will be tiresome and redundant.

Plans and performance for 2008 did not exactly match. Hopes for major street repair and water line replacement on Castle Avenue were frustrated by the need to follow the county engineering and road department on its Jones Street relocation project. This meant relocating 300 feet of 6-inch main line, the rebuilding of two laterals, 12 services and the digging out and adjusting of 10 valve covers a number of times. This work, which was not anticipated, occupied most of the summer and partly explained why the water line maintenance cost was $97,418 for 2008 as compared with $46,554 for last year. It is hoped that this deferred work can be accomplished next year.

For the first time in a number of years the streets were hand-cleaned of old dirt and the remains of the winter debris. Although a new and richer layer of gum wrappers, beer cans, and cigarette packs corrected this condition, the Town's purchase of a Wayne sweeper in August puts the Town temporarily one up in its long struggle for clean streets. An additional help is that a tough antilitter ordinance was passed.

The new Town Hall was purchased on a contract for $90,900 payable at $30,000 per year, the first installment of which was met in 2008. We thus own outright the Town Hall from the front door to the west end of the fireplace. A new roof was installed and arrangements made to have part of the interior repaired next year.

At the moment the Town's financial position is not too grim. This may be changed in attempting to solve the remaining problems of sewage disposal and providing additional water to the areas the Town is required to serve.

/s/ Treasurer-Clerk

THE TOWN OF STEVENS
General Fund
Balance Sheet—December 31, 2008   Form A–1

Assets	
Petty cash	500
Cash on deposit with treasurer	(16,405)
Temporary investments	100,000
Inventory of supplies	3,800
Total assets	87,895
Liabilities, Reserves, and Surplus	
Warrants payable	8,587
Contract payable—new town hall	60,900
Cumulative reserve fund	53,298
Deficit (A–2)	(34,890)
	87,895

Analysis of Changes in Fund Balance	Estimated	Actual	Form A–2 Excess or Deficiency
Surplus—Jan. 1, 2008	43,030	43,030	
Add: Revenues (A–3)	288,200	303,880	15,680
Total	331,230	346,910	15,680
Less: Town Hall contract		90,900	(90,900)
Expenditures (A–4)	310,200	290,900	19,300
Deficit—Dec. 31, 2008	21,030	(34,890)	55,920

Statement of Revenues—Estimated and Actual   Form A–3

	Estimated	Actual	Difference
General property tax	140,000	94,636	45,364
Special tax—utilities	33,000	31,400	1,600
Licenses and permits	10,000	8,146	1,854
Fines and penalties	9,000	21,275	(12,275)
Rental income	7,200	6,700	500
Revenue from other agencies:			
Aid to cities	7,000	23,457	(16,457)
State liquor tax	39,000	38,795	205
Motor vehicle excise tax	35,000	38,374	(3,374)
Expense sharing—Fire District 2	8,000	4,853	3,147
Interest income		4,750	(4,750)
Other income		31,494	(31,494)
	288,200	303,880	15,680

Statement of Expenditures Compared with Authorizations   Form A–4

	Appropriated	Expended	Actual Under (Over) Estimate
Police:			
Salaries	123,000	123,482	(482)
FICA tax	5,500	5,495	4
Retirement	7,400	7,228	171
Industrial insurance	3,000	1,666	1,333
Hospital insurance	3,000	2,644	355
Vehicle care	1,500	4,763	(3,263)
Police bond	700	550	150
Motor fuel	8,000	11,641	(3,641)
Supplies	2,000	2,892	(892)
Total	154,100	160,364	(6,264)
Clerk:			
Salaries	21,000	21,335	(335)
FICA tax	1,000	1,067	(67)
Retirement	2,300	2,345	(45)
Hospital	1,200	529	671
Bond	150	140	10
Office supplies	2,500	2,997	(497)
Total	28,150	28,413	(263)
Fire Department:			
Salaries	12,000	8,120	3,880
Pensions	6,000	2,655	3,345
Hydrant rental	12,000	12,000	–0–
Vehicle care	2,000	242	1,758
Equipment repair		511	(511)
Heat and lights		5,102	(5,102)

	Appropriated	Expended	Actual Under (Over) Estimate
Motor fuel	1,500	274	1,226
Supplies	1,000	1,252	(252)
Total	34,500	30,156	4,344
General Government:			
Census	1,000	897	103
Elections	800		800
Attorney fees	10,000	1,500	8,500
Police judge	9,000	6,000	3,000
Councilmen:			
Salaries (Ord. #581)		3,666	(3,666)
Retirement		374	(374)
FICA tax		171	(171)
Heat and lights	8,000	4,762	3,238
Telephone	1,500	1,687	(187)
Building repair	5,000	6,356	(1,356)
Audit fee	4,000		4,000
Printing	2,000	302	1,698
Advertising	2,850	2,256	594
Postage	500	469	31
Surety bonds and insurance	15,000	12,850	2,150
Janitor service	1,800	1,441	359
Library	19,000	15,110	3,890
Travel and subsistence	2,000	1,976	24
Association dues	2,000	1,876	124
Planning commission	3,000		3,000
Miscellaneous	3,500	3,948	(448)
Supplies	1,000	1,030	(30)
Household supplies	1,500	526	974
Driver education		4,770	(4,770)
Total	93,450	71,967	21,483
Combined totals—General Fund	310,200	290,900	19,300

Required

The remainder of the report deals with other funds of the Town of Stevens; those statements are not reproduced because they are similar to the General Fund statements above. On the basis of the material given you, prepare a written evaluation of the information produced by the town's accounting system from the standpoint of its usefulness to:

a. Town administrators.

b. The town council (the legislative body).

c. Taxpayers and citizens of the town.

d. Creditors of the town.

9–3 **Internet Case—Popular Reports.** You have just been hired as an accountant for a large metropolitan city in the eastern part of the country. Your first assignment is to assist the finance director in the preparation of a "popular report." The city has long been concerned with the difficulty that most citizens have in understanding its comprehensive annual financial report. The finance director tells you that she saw Hillsborough County, Florida's popular report at a conference and was quite impressed.

Required

a. Obtain a copy of Hillsborough County's popular report by going to www.hillsclerk.com (*Hint:* it is identified as the Annual Report Summary.) Also, try to obtain popular reports of other local governments by using an Internet search engine.

b. Evaluate the usefulness of the popular reports you are able to obtain from the perspective of a citizen. In particular, focus on financial accounting information. Do you have adequate information to determine whether the government has a strong financial position and condition? Does the government report any nonfinancial performance information? Explain.

Exercises and Problems

9–1 Examine the CAFR. Utilizing the CAFR obtained for Exercise 1–1 and your answers to the questions asked in Exercise 1–1 and the corresponding exercises in Chapters 2 through 8, comment on the following:

a. *Analysis of Introductory Section.* Does the report contain all of the introductory material recommended by the GASB? Is the introductory material presented in such a manner that it communicates significant information effectively—do you understand what the government is telling you? On the basis of your study of the entire report, list any additional information you believe should have been included in the introductory section and explain why you believe it should have been included. On the basis of your study of the entire report, do you think the introductory material presents the information fairly? Comment on any information in the introductory section you feel is superfluous, and explain why.

b. *Analysis of Financial Statements.*

1. Do the statements, notes, and schedules in the financial section present the information required by the GASB? Are Total columns provided in the basic financial statements and schedules for the primary government and the reporting entity? If so, are the Total columns for the current year compared with Total columns for the prior year? Are the basic financial statements and notes cross-referenced to each other? Are they cross-referenced to the statements and schedules of individual funds?

2. Review your answers to the questions asked in Exercises 3–1 and 4–1 in light of your study of subsequent chapters of the text and your analysis of all portions of the annual report. If you believe your earlier answers were not entirely correct, change them in accord with your present understanding of generally accepted accounting principles and proper disclosure of the financial position and financial operations of a governmental reporting entity.

3. Review your answers to Exercise 5–1 and all subsequent exercises in this series in light of knowledge you have gained since you prepared the answers. If any of your earlier answers should be changed, change them.

c. *Analysis of Statistical Section.* Does the statistical section present information in the five categories defined by the GASB? What tables and schedules are presented for each category? Does the information provided in each category appear to meet the purpose of the category? Explain your response.

    d. GFOA Certificate of Achievement. Does the report include a copy of a GFOA Certificate of Achievement for Excellence in Financial Reporting or refer to the fact that the government has received one? If the report has been awarded a certificate, does your review indicate it was merited? If the report has not been awarded a certificate, does your review indicate that the report should be eligible for one?

    e. Service Potential of the CAFR. Specify the most important information needs that a governmental annual report should fulfill for each of the following:

      1. Administrators.
      2. Members of the legislative branch.
      3. Interested residents.
      4. Creditors or potential creditors.

    In what ways does the CAFR you have analyzed meet the information needs you have specified for each of the four groups, assuming that members of each group make an effort to understand reports equivalent to the effort you have made? In what way does the report fail to meet the information needs of each of the four groups?

9–2 Multiple Choice. Choose the best answer.

  1. Which of the following fund type(s) uses the accrual basis of accounting?
    a. Permanent.
    b. Enterprise.
    c. Pension trust.
    d. Both *b* and *c*.

  2. Which of the following items would generally be reported as a program revenue in the Governmental Activities column of the government-wide statement of net assets?
    a. Fines and forfeits.
    b. Property taxes.
    c. Sales taxes.
    d. All of the above.

  3. Which of the following fund type(s) utilizes the modified accrual basis of accounting?
    a. Special revenue.
    b. Permanent.
    c. Internal service.
    d. Both *a* and *b*.

  4. When a general obligation bond is sold at a premium, the premium should be reported:
    a. In the Governmental Activities column of the government-wide statement of net assets.
    b. In the balance sheet for governmental funds.
    c. In the Business-type Activities column of the government-wide statement of net assets.
    d. Premium on bonds sold is not reported in the financial statements of a government.

  5. A building in general governmental service for which the construction had been recorded in a capital projects fund was sold at a gain for $1,000,000. Which of the following is true regarding proper reporting of the transaction under the *GASBS 34* reporting model?

a. The full proceeds of the sale would be reported as an other financing source in the General Fund.

b. The gain on the sale would be reported in the Governmental Activities column of the government-wide financial statements.

c. The full proceeds of the sale would be reported in the Governmental Activities column of the government-wide statement of activities.

d. Both *a* and *b*.

6. The members of the Library Board of the City of Fayetteville are appointed by the City of Fayetteville City Council, which has agreed to finance any operating deficits of the library. Under these conditions:

a. The city is a primary government.

b. The library is a component unit.

c. Financial information of the library should be reported as part of the reporting entity by discrete presentation.

d. All of the above.

7. Ordinarily debt service for a revenue bond would be reported in a (an):

a. Enterprise fund.

b. Private-purpose trust fund.

c. Debt service fund.

d. Permanent fund.

8. The comprehensive annual financial report (CAFR) of a governmental reporting entity should contain a statement of revenues, expenditures, and changes in fund balances for:

	Governmental Funds	Proprietary Funds
a.	Yes	No
b.	Yes	Yes
c.	No	Yes
d.	No	No

9. The comprehensive annual financial report (CAFR) of a governmental reporting entity should contain a statement of cash flows for:

	Governmental Funds	Proprietary Funds
a.	Yes	No
b.	Yes	Yes
c.	No	Yes
d.	No	No

10. The activities of a central data processing department that offers data processing services at a discount to other departments of a certain city should be recorded in:

a. An enterprise fund.

b. A special revenue fund.

c. The General Fund.

d. An internal service fund.

9–3 Multiple Choice. Choose the best answer.

1. Some governments have begun to provide highly condensed financial information, budget summaries, and narrative descriptions, in addition

to their traditional CAFR. This type of report is generally referred to as a (an):

a. Popular report.

b. MD&A.

c. Operating budget.

d. General purpose financial report.

2. The City of Gourman's employee pension fund would be included in which of the following financial statements?

a. Government-wide statement of net assets.

b. Statement of fiduciary net assets.

c. Statement of cash flows.

d. Both *a* and *b*.

3. Which of the following terms would be used when describing a primary government?

a. Fiscally independent.

b. Legally separate organization.

c. Separately elected governing body.

d. All of the above.

4. Which of the following criteria regarding the relationship between a legally separate, tax-exempt organization and a primary government would lead to the separate organization being reported as a component unit?

a. Economic resources received or held by the separate organization are entirely or almost entirely for the direct benefit of the primary government.

b. The primary government is entitled to or has the ability to otherwise access a majority of the economic resources received or held by the separate organization.

c. The economic resources received or held by an individual organization that the specific primary government is entitled to or has the ability to otherwise access are significant to that primary government.

d. All of the above criteria must be met.

5. Which of the following is *not* part of the minimum requirements for general purpose external financial reporting?

a. Combining financial statement for nonmajor funds.

b. Basic financial statements.

c. Management's discussion and analysis (MD&A).

d. Required supplementary information, other than MD&A.

6. A comprehensive annual financial report (CAFR) generally would include all of the following sections except:

a. Financial section.

b. Audit section.

c. Statistical section.

d. Introductory section.

7. In a balance sheet, governmental funds, prepared in conformity with GAAP, a separate column is provided for each:

a. Fund type.

b. Major fund.

c. Government.

d. Significant fund.

8. Which of the following might be included as a reconciling item in reconciling governmental fund financial statements to the government-wide financial statements?
   a. Bond issuances are reported as an other financing source in a governmental fund but as a long-term liability in the government-wide financial statements.
   b. Acquisition of capital assets is reported as an expenditure in the governmental fund financial statements but as capital assets in the government-wide financial statements.
   c. Some expenses reported in the government-wide financial statements are not reported as expenditures in the governmental fund financial statements.
   d. All of the above.
9. Which of the following is *not* one the categories of the statistical section recommended by the GASB?
   a. Demographic and economic information.
   b. Operating information.
   c. Pro forma financial information.
   d. Debt capacity information.
10. Which of the following is generally considered an other comprehensive basis of accounting (OCBOA) acceptable for governments?
    a. Cash.
    b. Budgetary.
    c. Accrual.
    d. Reserve cash.

9–4 Independent Transactions. Following are five independent transactions or events that relate to a local government. All events occurred within the same fiscal year.
   1. $25,000 was disbursed from the General Fund for the cash purchase of new equipment.
   2. An unrestricted operating grant of $100,000 was received from the state.
   3. Listed common stock with a total carrying value of $100,000 was sold by the permanent fund for $105,000 before any dividends were declared on the stock. There are no restrictions on the gain.
   4. General obligation bonds with a face amount of $1,000,000 sold at 101. The face amount is required to be used solely for construction of a new building, while the premium must be used to retire the debt. This building was completed at a total cost of $1,000,000, which was paid.
   5. The General Fund transferred $25,000 for payment of interest on a general obligation bond.

Required

Prepare journal entries to properly record each of the above transactions or events in the appropriate fund(s) and/or governmental activities journal. No explanations are needed.

9–5 Comprehensive Set of Transactions. The City of Lynnwood was recently incorporated and had the following transactions for the fiscal year ended December 31, 2008.
   1. The city council adopted a General Fund budget for the fiscal year. Revenues were estimated at $2,000,000 and appropriations were $1,990,000.

2. Property taxes in the amount of $1,940,000 were levied. It is estimated that $9,000 of the taxes levied will be uncollectible.
3. A General Fund transfer of $25,000 in cash and $300,000 in equipment (with accumulated depreciation of $65,000) was made to establish a central duplicating internal service fund.
4. A citizen of Lynnwood donated marketable securities with a fair value of $800,000. The donated resources are to be maintained in perpetuity with the city using the revenue generated by the donation to finance an after school program for children, which is sponsored by the parks and recreation function. Revenue earned and received as of December 31, 2008, was $40,000.
5. The city's utility fund billed the city's General Fund $125,000 for water and sewage services. As of December 31, the General Fund had paid $124,000 of the amount billed.
6. The central duplicating fund purchased $4,500 in supplies.
7. Cash collections recorded by the general government function during the year were as follows:

Property taxes	$1,925,000
Licenses and permits	35,000
User charges	28,000

8. During the year the internal service fund billed the city's general government function $15,700 for duplicating services and it billed the city's utility fund $8,100 for services.
9. The city council decided to build a city hall at an estimated cost of $5,000,000. To finance the construction, 6 percent bonds were sold at the face value of $5,000,000. A contract for $4,500,000 has been signed for the project, however no expenditures have been incurred as of December 31, 2008.
10. The general government function issued a purchase order for $32,000 for computer equipment. When the equipment was received, a voucher for $31,900 was approved for payment and payment was made.

Required

Prepare all journal entries to properly record each transaction for the fiscal year ended December 31, 2008. Use the following funds and government-wide activities, as necessary:

General Fund	GF
Capital projects fund	CPF
Internal service fund	ISF
Permanent fund	PF
After School Fund (a special revenue fund)	SRF
Enterprise fund	EF
Governmental activities	GA

Each journal entry should be numbered to correspond with each transaction. Do *not* prepare closing entries.

Your answer sheet should be organized as follows:

Transaction Number	Fund or Activity	Account Title	Amounts	
			Debits	Credits

9–6 General Fund Adjustments. The City of Allenton has engaged you to examine its June 20, 2008, financial statements. You are the first CPA ever engaged by the city and you find that the city's accounting staff is unfamiliar with GAAP accounting and reporting requirements. Following is the pre-closing trial balance of the General Fund as of June 30, 2008.

	Debits	Credits
Cash	$ 460,000	
Taxes Receivable—Current	169,200	
Estimated Uncollectible Taxes—Current		$ 18,000
Taxes Receivable—Delinquent	38,000	
Estimated Uncollectible Taxes—Delinquent		30,200
Equipment	66,000	
Donated Land	120,000	
Estimated Revenues	1,320,000	
Appropriations		1,378,000
Expenditures—Principal	90,000	
Expenditures—Other	1,152,000	
Bonds Payable		200,000
Revenues		1,384,000
Accounts Payable		76,000
Fund Balance		329,000
	$3,415,200	$3,415,200

Additional information is as follows:
1. The estimated uncollectible amount of $18,000 for current-year taxes receivable was determined to be adequate. The tax year coincides with the fiscal year.
2. The city purchased $66,000 of equipment during the year.
3. The Expenditures—Principal account reflects the annual retirement of general obligation bonds issued in 2007. Interest payments of $12,000 for this bond issue are included in the Expenditures—Other account.
4. The General Fund's outstanding purchase orders as of June 30, 2008, totaled $11,300. These purchase orders were not recorded in the books.
5. The balance in the Revenues account included a credit of $100,000 for a note issued to a bank to obtain cash in anticipation of property tax collections, and a credit of $120,000 for donated land to be used by public works. As of June 30, 2008, the note was still outstanding.

Required

The foregoing information disclosed by your examination was recorded only in the General Fund even though a debt service fund is used to account for debt, using resources provided by the General Fund. Prepare the adjusting journal entries necessary to correct the General Fund and to record information for the debt service fund, assuming the financial statements are to be prepared in conformity with GAAP.

9–7 Matching. Section A provides a list of transactions or events that occurred during the year, followed Section B by a list of the possible effects each transaction or event has on adjusting net asset accounts at year-end, assuming that all temporary accounts have already been closed to Net Assets-Unrestricted.

Section A
_____1. Depreciation for the year.
_____2. A vehicle was purchased.

_____3. Interest on bonds issued to construct city hall.

_____4. An operating grant was received with the purpose restriction that it be used for a summer youth program (half of the grant remains unexpended at fiscal year-end).

_____5. Bonds payable were issued to construct a new fire station.

Section B

a. Restricted Net Assets is **increased** and Unrestricted Net Assets is **decreased.**
b. Restricted Net Assets is **decreased** and Unrestricted Net Assets is **increased.**
c. Invested in Capital Assets, Net of Related Debt is **increased** and Unrestricted Net Assets is **decreased.**
d. Invested in Capital Assets, Net of Related Debt is **decreased** and Unrestricted Net Assets is **increased.**
e. None of the above.

Required

Identify how the net asset categories would need to be adjusted for each of the transactions. For the statement in section A, select the appropriate answer from section B.

9–8 **Change in Net Assets of Governmental Activities.** You have been provided with the following information concerning operating activity for Leetown. For the year ended June 30, 2008, the net change in total governmental fund balances was $106,600. During the year, Leetown issued $2,000,000 in general obligation bonds for capital construction projects. Capital outlays for the period totaled $1,500,000. Relative to the beginning of the period, the increase in accrued interest expense on bonds payable was $470,000. For the year depreciation on capital assets totaled $625,000, and at the end of the year there was revenue accrued but not available for use totaling $560,000.

Required

Using the information provided, prepare a schedule that calculates the change in net assets of governmental activities.

Chapter **Ten**

Analysis of Governmental Financial Performance

Learning Objectives

After studying this chapter, you should be able to:

1. Explain the importance of evaluating governmental financial performance.
2. Distinguish among and describe key financial performance concepts, such as:

   Financial position

   Financial condition

   Economic condition
3. Explain the relationships among environmental factors, organizational factors, and financial factors in determining governmental financial condition.
4. Identify, calculate, and interpret key ratios that measure financial performance.
5. Analyze financial performance using government-wide statements.
6. Describe how benchmarks can aid financial analysis.

THE NEED TO EVALUATE FINANCIAL PERFORMANCE

Over the past four decades, many large cities have been profiled in the press for financial crises or fiscal mismanagement on the part of managers. In the 1970s New York City defaulted on several billions of short-term debt[1] and Cleveland, Ohio, was near bankruptcy in the 1980s. In the 1990s Orange County, California did file for bankruptcy after suffering investment losses of $1.7 billion related to derivatives,[2] while the cities of Miami, Florida and Washington D.C. were in a state of public receivership—the financial management of both cities had been handed over to public boards until fiscal integrity was restored.[3]

[1] Virginia E. Soybel, "Municipal Financial Reporting by General Purpose Local Governments," in *Objectives of Accounting and Financial Reporting for Governmental Unit: A Research Study,* vol. 11 (Chicago: NCGA, 1981), p. 2-1.

[2] David Reyes, "Orange County Renews Its Ties with Merrill Lynch," *Los Angeles Times,* August 14, 2002, part 2, p. 1.

[3] Carlos A. Gimenez, "Transmittal Letter of the 2001 Comprehensive Annual Financial Report of the City of Miami," p. ix; Sewell Chan, "After 6 Years of Recovery, Still No Cure; Control Board Leaves a Legacy of Questions," *Washington Post,* October 1, 2001, p. B01.

Despite increased public scrutiny and higher than ever expectations of accountability for the use of scarce public resources, in the first decade of the 21st century there is no shortage of governments in fiscal crisis. The City of Detroit faces a financial disaster as it struggles to adjust the size of its government to a population that, at 911,000, is half of what it was at its peak in the 1950s.[4] For FY 2004 the city reported a $31.6 million deficit in unrestricted net assets (net of a $315.2 million deficit in governmental activities and $283.6 million surplus in business-type activities), as well as a $248.4 million deficit in unrestricted net assets for its component units.[5] The City of San Diego's public-employee pension fund is running a billion-dollar deficit, and officials are under investigation for awarding generous new benefits to retirees while the pension fund is severely underfunded. These conditions led to the city's credit rating being below investment grade and officials considering municipal bankruptcy.[6] Large cities and high-profile cases such as these may get most of the ink in the national press, but financial crises in small governments are just as devastating to its citizens, who often band together and demand the recall of whole city councils, county and township boards, and school boards.

The cause for concern in these news stories varies widely, from political corruption and imprudent management practices to intractable environmental factors. Too often a combination of causes lead to financial factors that affect the overall financial health of the government. A common thread in these reports, however, is deficient financial reporting and a lack of transparency in how government financial decisions are made. Disclosures are deemed to be inadequate, liabilities and costs understated, or assets and revenues overvalued. Citizens appear to be caught by surprise and wonder why there were not early warning signals of financial distress.

The good news is that most governments survive financial crises and build stronger systems of internal controls to prevent them from slipping down that slope again. The combined efforts on the part of user, preparer, attestor, and bond rating groups who have a stake in government financial reporting have led to higher quality governmental accounting principles, government auditing standards, and programs to recognize excellence in financial reporting. The purpose of this chapter is to examine some of those efforts and the analytical tools for measuring governmental financial performance that have evolved since the 1980s. Chapter 11 on auditing of governmental organizations explores the role of an independent public accountant in providing assurance that the data used in financial analysis are reliable and relevant.

GOVERNMENT FINANCIAL PERFORMANCE CONCEPTS

Preventing financial crises such as those just discussed requires an early-warning system to identify trends or practices that may adversely impact the long- and short-term solvency of a government. To be useful, early-warning systems and other analytical tools must be built on a comprehensive, conceptual framework of government financial management that includes performance indicators that can be tracked over time and compared to targeted goals. Although, arguably, all users of government financial

---

[4] Wilgoren, Jodi and Jeremy W. Peters, "Shrinking, Detroit Faces Fiscal Nightmare," *New York Times,* February 2, 2005, National Desk.

[5] City of Detroit, *Comprehensive Annual Financial Report for the Fiscal Year Ended June 20, 2004*, p. 29.

[6] John R. Broder, Mary Williams Walsh, "Mayor of Scandal-Plagued San Diego Says He Will Quit," *New York Times,* National Desk, April 26, 2005.

statements need a full set of information about the entity, user groups usually focus on just the indicators and concepts that most closely correspond to their areas of interest or responsibility.

Ensuring that the government has the financial capacity to sustain desired services is the primary reason for managers to monitor financial performance. Bond investors and creditors have an interest in evaluating financial health, namely, to assess the government's ability to make future interest and principal payments, even in the face of adverse economic trends or other events (for example, natural disasters). Knowing that managers are employing a system to track financial trends provides investors and creditors with added confidence in the quality of the government's financial management, particularly if such trend data are shared with credit analysts. Credit analysts also have more than a passing interest in the government's ability to provide services in the long run since experience has shown that, in times of fiscal crisis, expenditures for vital services often take priority over debt service payments.

Legislative bodies have responsibility for helping formulate sound fiscal policies for the government they serve, whereas oversight bodies have responsibility for monitoring and in some cases establishing the fiscal policies of governments for which they have oversight responsibility. Some states, for example, impose uniform financial accounting and reporting systems that all municipalities within the state must follow. Municipalities may also be required to submit annual financial reports to a state oversight body. Finally, legislative and oversight bodies typically have responsibilities to monitor executives' compliance with laws and regulations.

Although citizens should have an interest in the government's overall financial performance, often their interests lie more narrowly with a particular program, or rising tax rates or service fees. Moreover, citizens' interests usually are represented through intermediaries such as the media, taxpayer *watchdog* groups, special interest groups, and groups that serve the public interest. Thus, citizen groups typically have not been involved in evaluating the overall financial condition of government, even though they may suffer severe cutbacks in governmental services in the event of a financial crisis.

In an effort to meet the needs of financial statement users, such as citizens and taxpayers, the GASB produced a set of guides to financial statements.[7] In the first guide *What You Should Know about Your Government's Finances,* the GASB points out that government managers need to demonstrate to citizens that they are financially accountable for raising enough resources to remain financially viable and to spend those resources responsibly. The unique relationship between involuntary tax financing and the provision of public goods and government services requires special care to assess whether government has met its duties to be accountable to citizens. In a related outreach effort to the analyst user community (broadly defined), the GASB produced a user guide titled *An Analyst's Guide to Government Financial Statements* (2001)[8] in which it points out that the process of drawing meaning from financial statement data is an art form, not a science. As indicated by these user guides, different people are interested in different aspects of financial health, and those doing the analyzing must focus on the concepts that are most relevant for their purposes.

---

[7] Dean M. Mead, *What You Should Know about Your Local Government's Finances: A Guide to Financial Statements* (Norwalk, CT: GASB, 2000). Related guides, also by Dean M. Mead, include *What You Should Know about Your School District's Finances: A Guide to Financial Statements* (2001) and *What Else You Should Know about a Government's Finances* (2005).

[8] Dean M. Mead, *An Analyst's Guide to Government Financial Statements* (Norwalk, CT: GASB, 2001), p. 105.

Prior to examining systems for evaluating financial performance, it is important to distinguish among key terms related to accountability: financial position, financial condition, and economic condition.

Financial Position versus Financial Condition

Various definitions have been developed for the terms *financial position* and *financial condition*. A GASB research study notes that **financial position** "tends to be a shorter-run concept compared with financial condition."[9] The GASB study further notes that "*financial position* for governmental funds focuses on assets and liabilities that require cash or are normally converted to cash in the near future and can generally be determined from the financial statements alone."[10] Thus, *financial position* is closely related to the concept of liquidity. By contrast, the GASB study defines **financial condition** as follows:

> The probability that a government will meet both its financial obligations to creditors, consumers, employees, taxpayers, suppliers, constituents, and others as they become due and its service obligations to constituents, both currently and in the future.[11]

Another view of financial condition is provided by the International City/County Management Association (ICMA). In the aftermath of New York City's debt default in the 1980s, the ICMA published in 1980 a set of five handbooks that dealt with evaluating financial condition. These handbooks resulted from a three-year research project funded by a National Science Foundation grant. The 2003 update of a subsequent handbook that consolidates the concepts from the original handbooks provides an excellent discussion of the concepts that comprise their use of the term "financial condition."[12] The 2003 handbook's definition of financial condition incorporates four types of solvency: **cash solvency**—a government's ability to generate enough cash over a 30- or 60-day period to pay its bills; **budgetary solvency**—a government's ability to generate enough revenue over its normal budgetary period to meet its expenditures and not incur deficits; **long-run solvency**—a government's ability in the long-run to pay all the costs of doing business such as expenditures in the annual budget and those that appear only in the years in which they must be paid; and **service-level solvency**—a government's ability to provide services at the level and quality that are required for the health, safety, and welfare of the community and that its citizens desire (p. 1).

The ICMA's term *cash solvency* is the component of financial condition that is most closely related to the GASB's definition of financial position; that is, both terms focus on the shorter-term, balance sheet concept addressing whether the government is able to meet its current obligations. Definitions of both the GASB study and the ICMA handbook make it clear that *financial condition* includes the ability to maintain existing or provide increasing service levels. This concept is related to the accountability concept of *interperiod equity*, a term the GASB defines as determining "whether current-year revenues are sufficient to pay for the services provided that year and whether future taxpayers will be required to assume burdens for services previously

---

[9] Robert Berne, *Research Report,* "The Relationship between Financial Reporting and the Measurement of Financial Condition" (Norwalk, CT: GASB, 1992), pp. 16–17.

[10] Ibid., p. 17.

[11] Ibid.

[12] Karl Nollenberger, *Evaluating Financial Condition: A Handbook for Local Government,* 4th ed. (Washington, DC: International City/County Management Association, 2003); a revision of the original 1980 text by Sanford M. Groves and Maureen G. Valente.

provided."[13] Excessive shifting of the burden to pay for current services to future tax-payers may threaten the government's ability to sustain the current level of services or to expand services to meet future population growth.

Economic Condition

In its long-term economic condition project that builds on the work of the 1992 Berne study on financial condition, the GASB has tentatively decided to replace the term *financial condition* with a broader concept—**economic condition**—defined as

> a composite of a government's financial health and its ability and willingness to meet its financial obligations and its commitments to provide services.[14]

Conceptually, economic condition includes three components: *financial position*—the status of a government's asset, liability, and net asset accounts, as displayed in its basic financial statements; **fiscal capacity,** a government's ongoing ability and willingness to raise revenues, incur debt, and meet its financial obligations as they come due; and **service capacity,** a government's ongoing ability and willingness to supply the capital and human resources needed to meet its commitments to provide services.

These definitions are part of Phase I of GASB's economic condition project. Phase II resulted in *GASBS 44, Economic Condition Reporting: The Statistical Section,*[15] the first comprehensive look at the statistical section of the comprehensive annual financial report (CAFR) since NCGA Statement No. 1 was issued in 1979. This statement is expected to improve the understandability, comparability and, hence, usefulness of the financial statements by incorporating new information resulting from *GASBS 34;* providing guidance to all types of governments, not just general purpose governments; and restructuring the amount and type of information from 15 required schedules to five categories of information. The scope of Phase III of the economic condition project is to consider whether any additional information should be required or encouraged for inclusion in a government's financial report, as well as what information should be included in a separately issued document.[16]

This project is certain to elicit different opinions on whether financial and economic performance information should be included in CAFRs. Issues include the demand for such information, the level of auditor's review of information, comparability across similar entities, and the role of the GASB in setting standards on the inclusion of economic performance indicators in financial reports. GASB's service efforts and accomplishments (SEA) project is discussed in more detail in Chapter 13 on budgeting of governmental services.

INTERNAL FINANCIAL TREND MONITORING

As mentioned earlier in this chapter, the ICMA developed a set of handbooks in the wake of the New York City default for internal financial managers to use in tracking the financial performance of their own governments. They called the tool described in those handbooks (and the 2003 version of the consolidation of the handbooks) the

[13] Governmental Accounting Standards Board, *Concepts Statement No. 1,* "Objectives of Financial Reporting" (Norwalk, CT: GASB, 1987), par. 61.

[14] Governmental Standards Accounting Board, *Action Report* (Norwalk, CT: GASB, January 2002), p. 2.

[15] Governmental Accounting Standards Board, Statement No. 44, *Economic Condition Reporting: The Statistical Section, an amendment of NCGA Statement 1* (Norwalk, CT: GASB, May 2004).

[16] Governmental Standards Accounting Board, *Action Report* (Norwalk, CT: December 2004), pp. 3 and 7.

financial trend monitoring system. Credit market analysts, particularly analysts with the major rating agencies, have developed proprietary (in-house) approaches for evaluating the general obligation creditworthiness of governments that issue bonds. Although evaluation objectives differ slightly between internal and external evaluation systems and among the approaches used by external users, both types of systems focus on many of the same kinds of factors. Presumably, these systems can be useful as well for legislative and oversight bodies and citizen groups.

Both the 1992 GASB study and the revised ICMA handbook point out that financial condition is a complex, multidimensional concept whose measurement requires analysis of a multitude of factors. The GASB study identifies the major categories of factors as economy and demographics; revenue base; current and capital expenditures; debt, pensions, and other postemployment benefits; internal resources; management capabilities; infrastructure; and willingness to raise revenues and to provide needed public services.[17] Perusal of this list suggests that evaluation of some categories such as management capabilities, infrastructure, and willingness to raise revenues and provide services are largely qualitative judgments. Thus, unlike the rather straightforward evaluation of the financial condition of a business entity based on analysis of profitability and well-understood financial ratios, evaluation of governmental financial condition involves subjective judgments about the interplay of complex environmental, organizational, and financial factors.

Illustration 10–1 shows the framework the ICMA developed for internal managers to use in evaluating financial condition. The Financial Trend Monitoring Systems (FTMS) is comprised of environmental, organizational, and financial factors that influence a government's financial condition, and that are measured by various indicators. Environmental factors such as community needs and resources, intergovernmental constraints, disaster risk, political culture, and external economic conditions largely determine revenue capacity and demand for services. How fiscal policy within the government responds to environmental demand and changes in the environment is a major factor determining how environmental factors are translated into financial factors. Financial factors (identified in Illustration 10–1 as revenues, expenditures, operating position, debt structure, unfunded liabilities, and condition of capital plant) are the result of management practices and legislative policies in response to environmental demands and resources. Measures of financial condition include ratios consisting of one financial amount divided by another financial amount (such as fund balance divided by revenues,) and ratios consisting of financial amounts divided by demographic or economic measures (such as debt divided by population).

The ICMA provides a large number of potentially useful indicators grouped into the factors corresponding to the environmental, organizational, and financial dimensions shown in Illustration 10–1. Some local governments that participated in field testing, as well as other governments, continue to use the financial trend monitoring system (FTMS) developed in the handbooks to monitor their financial condition. The FTMS, together with various publications of the municipal credit market, have long been the main sources of guidance for monitoring and evaluating governmental financial condition, including how to use financial and other information for these purposes. Examining changes in indicators over time and relationships among indicators can yield useful information on financial issues, such as whether revenue trends are adequate to meet expenditure trends, the adequacy of financial reserves to withstand revenue shortfalls or unforeseen expenditure requirements, current

[17] Berne, *Research Report,* p. 25.

ILLUSTRATION 10–1   Factors Affecting Financial Condition

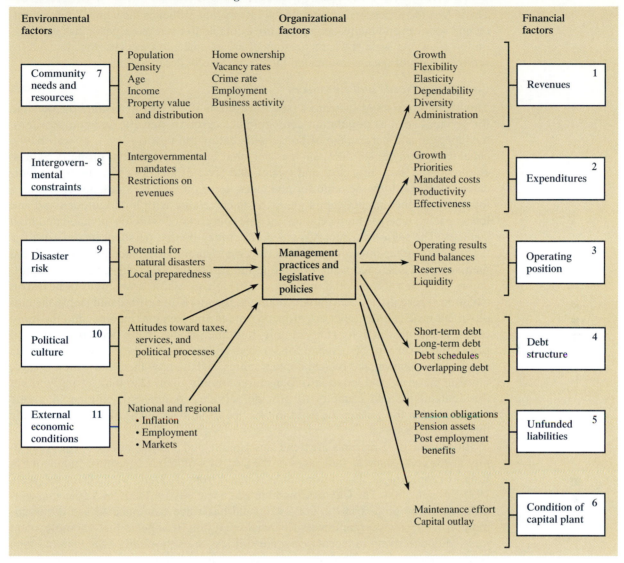

Source: Karl Nollenberger, *Evaluating Financial Condition: A Handbook for Local Government,* 4th ed. (Washington, DC: International City/County Management Association, 2003), p. 5.

debt burden and future debt capacity, future service demands and the ability of the government to meet those demands, adequacy of enterprise fund revenues to meet debt covenant requirements, and what portions of operating costs could be met by user charges rather than by taxes. However, making a reasonable judgment about the financial condition of a particular entity requires a sound understanding of how environmental factors influence the demand for and capacity to supply services, how organizational factors influence fiscal policy given a particular level or trend in the demand for and capacity to supply services, and how to measure the financial outcomes of the entity's fiscal policy. Each of these sets of factors is discussed at some length prior to moving to the identification, calculation, and interpretation of financial ratios.

Environmental Factors

The ICMA identifies five environmental factors that influence the demand for governmental services and the resources that are available to meet those demands (see Illustration 10–1). At issue is whether resources are adequate to meet citizens' demand for services. Each of the environmental factors are briefly described next.

Community Needs and Resources

This factor consists of indicators (see Illustration 10–1) that determine the demand for services such as population demographics (growth, density, and composition), median age, and percentage of households below the poverty level, as well as the capacity to provide services, such as personal income per capita, property values, employment (level, diversity, and types), and level of business activity. Some indicators affect both the demand for and capacity to provide services; for example, a low personal income per capita generally is correlated with both high demand and low capacity, whereas high personal income is correlated with low demand and high capacity. The reason for this two-sided effect may be that personal income itself is the result of other indicators such as the employment base, educational level, and median age. Thus, even when evaluating indicators within a single factor, the indicators are often interrelated, making it difficult to assess any single indicator in isolation. These difficulties notwithstanding, the more diversified and stable the employment base is, the higher are property values and personal income, and the more robust is business activity (for example, building permits, bank deposits, and retail sales), the lower will be demand for services and the higher the capacity to provide services. Population and related demographics such as growth, composition by age, housing patterns, and location (urban, rural, or suburban) also may strongly affect the demand for and capacity to provide services. A constant enigma in public finance is that the greater the need for services, the lower is the capacity to provide them, and vice versa.

Illustration 10–2 presents the trend, description, and analysis of one of the community needs and resources indicators of the City of Columbia, Missouri: Indicator 35, Rate of Employment. This information is taken from its Trend Manual for the years 1995 through 2004. The City of Columbia was a test city for the ICMA financial condition research project in the late 1970s and has since continued to use the trend-monitoring system to monitor its financial condition. It appears that unemployment rates, although rising in recent years, are still less than one-third of the national rate. Based on the city's own analysis, since manufacturing jobs comprise less than 10 percent of the city's workforce, they should pay particular attention to employment trends in the service industry.

Intergovernmental Constraints

Most local governments operate under various legal constraints imposed by the state government. Moreover, the federal government imposes constraints as a condition for receiving federal financial assistance. Among the state-imposed constraints may be legal limitations on the ability of local governments to raise revenues and issue debt. If such limitations exist, the current levels of revenues and debt subject to such limits should be compared to the authorized limits. Of particular importance is consideration of the extent to which legal limits may impede needed acquisition of capital assets and future growth in services. In addition to revenue raising constraints and debt limits, local governments are often burdened with unfunded mandates by higher level governments to provide specified services.

ILLUSTRATION 10–2   **Indicator 35—Rate of Employment**

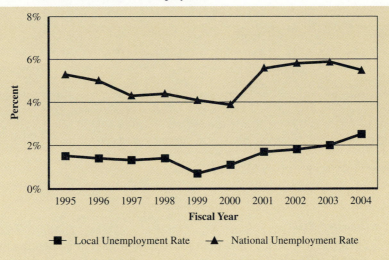

Warning Trend:

Increasing rate of unemployment or a decline in number of jobs provided within a community.

Formulation:

Unemployment rate and number of jobs in the community.

Fiscal Year	Unemployment Rate Local	Unemployment Rate National	Jobs In Community— Civilian Labor Force
1995	1.5%	5.3%	75,684
1996	1.4%	5.0%	78,470
1997	1.3%	4.3%	73,726
1998	1.4%	4.4%	78,108
1999	0.7%	4.1%	83,257
2000	1.1%	3.9%	81,453
2001	1.7%	5.6%	83,744
2002	1.8%	5.8%	85,452
2003	2.0%	5.9%	89,315
2004	2.5%	5.5%	88,800

Description:

Unemployment and jobs in the community are considered together because they are closely related; and for purposes of this discussion are referred to as "employment base." In addition, for comparative purposes, the national unemployment rate is included. Employment base is important because it is directly related to the levels of the business activity and personal income. Changes in the number of jobs provided by the community are a measure of and an influence on business activity. Changes in rate of employment of the community's citizens are related to changes in personal income and thus, are a measure of and an influence on the community's ability to support its local business sector.

   If the employment base is growing, if it is sufficiently diverse to provide against short-run economic fluctuation, or downturn in one sector, and if it provides sufficient income to support the local business community, then it will have a positive influence on the city's financial condition. A decline in employment base as measured by the number of jobs, or the lack of employment, can be an early warning sign that overall economic activity will decline and thus, that governmental revenues may decline (or at least not increase at the expected rate), particularly sales tax revenues.

ILLUSTRATION 10–2 Continued

Analysis:

The unemployment rate for Columbia has varied significantly from a high of 2.5% to a low of 0.7% while the number of jobs have increased 17.33% for the period shown. This compares to a national unemployment rate in the same period ranging from a high of 5.9% to a low of 3.9%. The City of Columbia's unemployment rate is generally less than one-third of the national unemployment rate.

Although the unemployment base has been sufficiently diverse to cushion against temporary economic downfalls in any particular sector, most employment fluctuations have been associated with national manufacturing firms located in Columbia. Such jobs comprise slightly less than 10% of the City's total work force. However, in future years the City should pay particular attention to its increases in the services industry as any economic downturn could affect that area.

Source: City of Columbia, Missouri, *1995–2004 Trends Manual*, 352–53.

Disaster Risk

The need to consider and plan for natural disasters is incumbent on all top governmental officials. Certainly, no place is immune from such events, although some locations are more vulnerable than others. The question that should be asked is: What would happen if a major earthquake or hurricane were to strike or a terrorist attack were to occur? Related questions that need to be asked are these: (1) Does the city have sufficient insurance and reserves to cover possible losses? (2) Does the government have sufficient resources (and a plan) for evacuation, protection against looting, and cleanup? In addition to natural disasters, it can be equally difficult to prepare and budget for man-made disasters, for example, chemical spills from industry, or labor strikes.

Political Culture

This perhaps is the most difficult of all factors to measure but is certainly critically important to determining how the administration will react to the other environmental factors in shaping the government's fiscal policy. Political culture includes such factors as form of government (e.g., mayor-council—weak or strong, council-manager, commission) and the entity's economic, political, and social history. The entity's history may reveal underlying community philosophies regarding willingness to support higher taxes, issuances of long-term debt, and increased social services.

External Economic Conditions

Obviously, no local or state government operates independently of the regional and national economy. Regional economic activity affects local business activity, employment, and income by influencing the demand for manufactured, agricultural, and service products as well as the levels of wholesale and retail sales. Similarly, inflation at the national level influences regional and local prices, including wages and the cost of debt financing. Although consideration of external economic conditions is essential to assessing the local economy, the linkages are generally difficult to pinpoint and quantify.

Organizational Factors

Management Practices and Legislative Policies

As indicated by their pivotal location in Illustration 10–1, *management practices and legislative policies* play a crucial role in determining fiscal policy in response to the environmental factors just discussed. Sound financial management and the political will to resist easy solutions can minimize financial problems that might otherwise result from factors such as economic downturns, plant closings, or natural disasters. Financial crises often build over a number of years during economic recessions. Politicians may be either unwilling or unable to curtail expenditures for services in response to revenue shortfalls. Results of past policies, such as heavy reliance on debt or an excessive labor force, may make it difficult or infeasible to reduce expenditures sufficiently in the short run. Short-run solutions, such as deferring needed maintenance, curtailing capital expenditures, or underfunding pensions, may lead to even more serious problems in the future. Thus, sound financial management means planning for adverse environmental conditions or events and devising long-run solutions when problems do occur. Although management practices and legislative policies are critical determinants of financial condition, they are among the most difficult factors to measure. Evidence of mismanagement or management practices that sustain an operating deficit include using reserves, short-term borrowing, internal borrowing, sale of assets, or one-time accounting changes to balance the budget. Other signs of deficient fiscal policies include deferring pension liabilities, deferring maintenance expenditures, failing to fund employee benefits, and ignoring full-life costs of capital assets.[18]

Financial Factors

Examples of governmental fund financial ratios typically used in assessing financial condition in the ICMA trend monitoring system are shown in Illustration 10–3. Although the ratios contained in Illustration 10–3 represent what the authors consider key ratios, they are not intended to represent *all* ratios that might be useful in evaluating financial condition. In fact, the ICMA handbook provides for a total of 27 financial indicators across the six financial factors. The ratios given in Illustration 10–3 cover each of the financial factors shown on the right-hand side of Illustration 10–1. Of course, these ratios were developed before *GASBS 34* and, as such, focus on information available from the fund financial statements. As described later in the chapter, information about the condition of general capital assets, including infrastructure, and general long-term liabilities is now more readily available in government-wide financial statements and related notes.

The data to calculate the financial ratios shown in Illustration 10–3 are readily obtainable from most CAFRs. Except for population, which is usually disclosed in the statistical section, data for most of the ratios can be obtained from the statement of revenues, expenditures, and changes in fund balances—governmental funds (see Illustration 1–8) and the balance sheet—governmental funds (see Illustration 1–6). Data for the remaining ratios usually can be found in the notes to the financial statements.

In calculating most of the ratios, some analysts prefer to utilize General Fund data only, whereas others utilize combined data for all governmental fund types. This decision depends, in part, on how large the General Fund is relative to all governmental fund types. In calculating operating revenues, capital project fund revenues should be excluded since the capital project fund is not an operating fund. For purposes of calculating revenues and expenditures in these ratios, other financing sources are often added to revenues and other financing uses are often added to

[18] Nollenberger, *Evaluating Financial Condition*, pp. 147–54.

ILLUSTRATION 10–3   **Selected Financial Ratios Based on CAFR Governmental Funds Information**

Indicator	Computation[1]	Suggestions for Analysis
Revenues Measures:		
Revenues per capita	$\dfrac{\text{Operating revenues}^2}{\text{Population}}$	If per capita operating revenues are decreasing, the government may not be able to maintain existing service levels unless it finds new sources of revenue.
One-time revenues	$\dfrac{\text{One-time revenues}}{\text{Operating revenues}^2}$	Continual use of one-time revenues, such as grants, interfund transfers or use of reserves, can disguise an imbalance between operating revenues and expenditures.
Expenditures Measures:		
Expenditures by function	$\dfrac{\text{Operating expenditures for one function}}{\text{Operating expenditures}}$	Determine which functions are increasing and if the increase represents increased services or new services. Are there sufficient revenues to pay for these?
Employees per capita	$\dfrac{\text{Number of municipal employees}}{\text{Population (or households)}}$	If personnel costs (as measured by the number of employees) are increasing at a greater rate than the population base, determine why this is happening.
Operating Position Measures:		
Fund balances	$\dfrac{\text{Unreserved fund balances}}{\text{Operating revenues}^2}$	Declining unreserved fund balances as a percentage of net operating revenues can affect a government's ability to withstand financial emergencies.
Liquidity	$\dfrac{\text{Cash and short-term investments}}{\text{Current liabilities}}$	If this measure of a government's cash position is less than one then determine if this is a temporary situation or whether causes, such as receivables, may persist leading to long-term solvency concerns.
Debt Indicators:		
Long-term debt	$\dfrac{\text{Net direct bonded long-term debt}}{\text{Assessed valuation (or population or personal income)}}$	An increase in this ratio may be an indication that the government's ability to repay the debt is diminishing, assuming the government depends on property taxes from the population to repay the debt.
Debt service	$\dfrac{\text{Net direct debt service}}{\text{Operating revenues}^2}$	Debt service on net direct debt that exceeds 20 percent of operating revenues is considered a potential problem.
Unfunded Liability Measures:		
Pension obligations	$\dfrac{\text{Pension obligations}}{\text{Salaries and wages}}$	An increasing amount of net pension obligation is a negative signal that should be investigated to determine if the trend of not funding annual pension cost is expected to continue.
Post-employment benefits	$\dfrac{\text{Liability for post-employment benefits}}{\text{Number of municipal employees}}$	An increasing ratio over time indicates the potential difficulty for a government to be able to cover the cost of promises made to retirees for benefits other than pensions.

ILLUSTRATION 10–3 **Continued**

Capital Plant Indicators:		
Maintenance effort	$$\frac{\text{Expenditures for maintenance of general capital assets}}{\text{Quantity of assets}}$$ (e.g., miles of sidewalks or square feet of buildings)	If maintenance expenditures per unit of general capital assets is not relatively stable over time, this may be a sign that the capital assets are deteriorating.
Capital outlay	$$\frac{\text{Capital outlay from operating funds}}{\text{Operating expenditures}}$$	If a decline in the relationship between expenditures for general capital assets to operating expenditures persists over three years, the government may be deferring the replacement of capital assets which adversely affects delivery of government services.

Source: Adapted from Karl Nollenberger, *Evaluating Financial Condition: A Handbook for Local Government* (Washington, DC: ICMA, 2003). This handbook provides worksheets and an electronic spreadsheet that guides the user in defining the terms used in these ratios.
[1] Express amounts in constant dollars; that is, adjusted for inflation using the consumer price index (CPI). See the U.S. Bureau of Labor Statistics Web site at www.bls.gov/cpi for how to access and use the CPI.
[2] Operating revenues are those that are available for general government operations, such as tax revenues, revenues from fees and user charges, and other local revenues, but excluding revenues restricted to capital improvements and special purpose revenues. Nollenberger suggests that when presenting this indicator in a report, you should define the terms used for the reader (p. 17).

expenditures. The government-wide financial statements prescribed by *GASBS 34* offer additional opportunities for analysis of financial factors relating to the governmental entity as a whole and are discussed next.

ANALYZING GOVERNMENT-WIDE FINANCIAL STATEMENTS

Introduced in 1999, *GASBS 34* provides information about the government as a whole that should assist citizens, bond analysts, governing boards, and other financial statement users to answer questions that are not easily answered with disaggregated fund financial statements. The management's discussion and analysis and two accrual-based government-wide financial statements that focus on the flow of total economic resources in and out of the government offer a level of analysis about the real cost of government services, the means of financing them, and the financial condition of the government as a whole.

One firm that stepped up to describe and report ratios designed to take advantage of aggregated information was Crawford & Associates, P.C., a public accounting firm that developed a financial analysis and rating tool to use in measuring a government's financial health and success. The firm suggests 17 performance indicators that measure financial position, financial performance, and financial capability (Illustration 10–4) from basic financial statements. A brief description of the questions best answered by these ratios is presented here, along with Crawford & Associates' "plain English" statement of the questions to be addressed by the performance measure.[19]

[19] Crawford & Associates, P.C., *The Performeter*® (Oklahoma City, OK, 2005). See its Web site at crawfordcpas.com.

Financial Position Ratios:

1. *Unrestricted Net Assets.* How do our rainy days funds look?
2. *General Fund Budgetary Fund Balance.* How does our budgetary carryover look?
3. *Debt to Assets.* Who really owns our government?
4. *Capital Asset Condition.* How much useful life do we have left in our capital assets?
5. *Current Ratio.* Will our vendors and employees be pleased with our ability to pay them on time?
6. *Quick Ratio.* How is our short-term cash position?
7. *Pension Plan Funding.* Will we be able to pay our employees when they retire?

Financial Performance Ratios:

8. *Change in Net Assets.* Did our overall financial condition improve, decline, or remain steady over the past year?
9. *Interperiod Equity.* Who paid for the cost of operating the government this year?
10. *BTA Self-Sufficiency.* Did current year utility services and other business-type activities (BTA) pay for themselves?
11. *Debt Service Coverage.* Can we pay our bond investors on time?

Financial Capability Ratios:

12. *Revenue Dispersion.* How heavily are we relying on revenue sources we cannot directly control?
13. *Debt Service Load.* How much of our annual budget is loaded with disbursements to pay off long-term debt?
14. *Financing Margin—Bonded Debt per Capita.* What is the current debt burden on our taxpayers?
15. *Financing Margin—Legal Debt Limit.* Will we be able to issue more bonded debt, if needed?
16. *Financing Margin—Property Taxes per Capita.* What is our property tax burden on our taxpayers?
17. *Financing Margin—Sales Tax Rate.* Will our citizens be likely to approve an increase in sales tax rates, if needed?

Other ratios can capture the dimensions presented in Illustration 10–4. For example, Chaney, Mead, and Schermann suggest that change in overall financial position be reported as a percentage of total net assets and that levels of reserves or deficits employ expenses as a denominator instead of revenues. They develop additional ratios, such as general revenues minus transfers as a percentage of expenses to measure financial performance, and an additional solvency measure that is change in net assets plus interest expense as a percentage of interest expense.[20]

Despite the complexity of evaluating government-wide financial condition, there are recognizable signals of fiscal stress. These include (1) a decline or inadequate growth in revenues relative to expenses, (2) decline in property values, (3) a decline in

---

[20] Barbara A. Chaney, Dean M. Mead, and Kenneth R. Schermann, "The New Governmental Financial Reporting Model," *Journal of Government Financial Management,* Spring 2002, pp. 27–31. In this article, the authors calculate and compare these ratios for two cities with similar population size.

ILLUSTRATION 10–4 **Financial Indicators using *GASBS 34* Government-wide and General Fund Statements**

Performance Measures	Description	Ratio
Financial Position:		
1. Unrestricted net assets	A measure of the adequacy of the amount of the government's total unrestricted net assets or level of deficit at the measurement date.*	$$\frac{\text{Unrestricted net assets}}{\text{Total revenue}}$$
2. General Fund budgetary fund balance	A measure of the adequacy of the amount of the government's General Fund (GF) budgetary basis fund balance (deficit) at the measurement date.	$$\frac{\text{Unreserved GF balance}}{\text{GF revenue (net of internal transfers and excluding special and extraordinary items)}}$$
3. Debt to assets	A measure of the degree to which the government's total assets have been funded with debt as of the measurement date.*	$$\frac{\text{Total liabilities}}{\text{Total assets}}$$
4. Capital asset condition	A measure of the extent to which the government's total depreciable capital assets, on average, are reaching the end of their useful lives, and, therefore, may need replacement.*	$$\frac{\text{Accumulated depreciation}}{\text{Average cost of depreciable capital assets}}$$
5. Current ratio	A measure of the government's ability to pay its short-term obligations as they become due.*	$$\frac{\text{Current assets}}{\text{Current liabilities}}$$
6. Quick ratio	A more conservative measure of the government's liquidity that focuses on unrestricted cash and cash equivalents.	$$\frac{\text{Unrestricted cash and cash equivalents}}{\text{Current liabilities}}$$
7. Pension plan funding	A measure of the funding status of a single employer or agent multi-employer pension plan of the government.	$$\frac{\text{Fair value of plan assets}}{\text{Actuarial accrued liability}}$$
Financial Performance:		
8. Change in net assets	A measure of the change in the overall financial condition of the government that includes governmental and business-type activities (BTA) but not fiduciary activities or discretely presented component units.	Total ending net assets (governmental and BTA) − total beginning net assets
9. Interperiod equity	A measure of whether the government has lived within its means for the year.*	$$\frac{\text{Net revenues (gross revenues plus/minus internal transfers/special/extraordinary items)}}{\text{Total expenses}}$$
10. BTA self-sufficiency	A measure of the extent to which the government's business-type activities (BTA) are funded with current-year service charge revenues, rather than prior year resources or subsidies from other funds.	$$\frac{\text{BTA service charge revenues}}{\text{BTA total expenses}}$$
11. Debt service coverage	A measure of the extent the government met its debt service requirements from net operating revenues available for such debt service.	$$\frac{\text{Net revenues (or cash flows from operations)}}{\text{Principal and interest payment on debt}}$$
Financial Capability:		
12. Revenue dispersion	A measure of the exposure to potential financial difficulties resulting from reliance on revenue sources beyond the direct control of the government.	$$\frac{\text{Non-tax revenue sources}}{\text{Total revenue (excluding special or extraordinary items)}}$$

*Calculate for governmental activities and business-type activities separately and then for the total.

ILLUSTRATION 10–4   Continued

13. Debt service load	A measure of the extent to which the government's noncapital expenditures or cash flows are comprised of payment of principal and interest on long-term debt.*	$$\frac{\text{Principal and interest payment on debt}}{\text{Total noncapital cash outlays}}$$
14. Financing margin— bonded debt per capita	A measure of the government's bonded debt burden on its taxpayers.	$$\frac{\text{General bonded debt}}{\text{Population}}$$
15. Financing margin— legal debt limit	A measure of the government's capacity to issue general bonded debt.	$$\frac{\text{General bonded debt}}{\text{Legal debt limit}}$$
16. Financing margin— property taxes per capita	A measure of the government's property tax burden on its taxpayers.	$$\frac{\text{Property tax levy}}{\text{Population}}$$
17. Financing margin— sales tax rate	A measure of the government's capacity to raise additional sales tax if needed.	$$\frac{\text{Sales and use tax revenue current year} - \text{sales and use tax revenue prior year}}{\text{Prior year sales and use tax revenue}}$$

*Calculate for governmental activities and business-type activities separately and then for the total.

Source: Crawford & Associates, P. C. *The Performeter.*® 2005. See www.crawfordcpas.com.

economic activity (such as increasing unemployment, declining retail sales, and declining building activity), (4) erosion of capital plant, particularly infrastructure, (5) increased levels of unfunded pension and other postemployment obligations, and (6) inadequate capital expenditures. Warning signals such as these, particularly if several exist simultaneously, may indicate a potential fiscal crisis unless the government takes action to increase revenues or decrease spending.

USE OF BENCHMARKS TO AID INTERPRETATION

Regardless of how the ratios are calculated, the more difficult task is how to interpret the ratios to make an informed judgment about a government's financial condition. Checking each ratio in Illustration 10–3 and 10–4 against a target or acceptable range is a critical step in the process of analyzing financial performance. **Benchmarking** is a very useful tool in the continual process of monitoring performance of "the plan," allowing for identification of needed improvements in the delivery of government services. Chapter 13 further develops the concept of continuous improvement and presents tools for comparing actual to budgeted performance of a government.

A benchmark, broadly defined, is any target, range, or "red-flag" that provides an analyst with a basis for comparison in order to draw conclusions about whether performance indicators suggest good news or bad news. Appropriate benchmarks for comparisons can be found inside or outside of the government. Internal monitoring of trends over time within an organization is the most common method of assessing whether the government has performed better or worse than prior years. The Government Finance Officers' Association (GFOA) recommends that a government's past performance is usually the most relevant context for analyzing current-year financial data.[21] The ICMA's Financial Management Trend System is a good example of a tool

[21] Government Finance Officers' Association, *Recommended Practice: The Use of Trend Data and Comparative Data for Financial Analysis* (2003). Available at www.gfoa.org

that has been used by many governments since its development in the 1980s as a way to compare current-period ratios to those of prior years for a variety of performance indicators. Illustration 10–5 shows the use of time-series trend monitoring by the City of Columbia, Missouri, for one indicator of financial condition—Excess of Revenues over Expenditures for the General Fund over a 10-year period. A narrative description of the ratio is provided as well as the mathematical formulation of the ratio. Graphical display of the trend in addition to data tables assists the analyst in drawing conclusions about the government's performance. Providing a "warning trend" helps the reader understand whether increasing or decreasing trends are positive or negative signals.

Illustration 10–5 also presents benchmark information from outside the government. A section called "Credit Industry Benchmarks" provides metrics and ranges that reflect credit analysts' assessment of what is appropriate for a government of this type. More information about the process used by municipal bond analysts is provided in the next section.

Illustration 10–6 presents a comprehensive look at all the financial and economic indicators the City of Columbia, Missouri, tracks over time with a rating of whether that indicator is reflecting a positive trend, a negative trend, or whether it needs to be closely monitored. These qualitative labels, positive or negative, are drawn from the ICMA FTMS authors' experience with many governments over time. A caveat to keep in mind in using external benchmarks is that comparison groups may not always be appropriate. A good example is that in a few states, local school districts are legally part of the government of the city in which they are located, whereas in most states school districts are independent governments. In some governments population may be the best denominator for a per capita ratio and in others households are more appropriate.

In addition to analyzing ratios, one should evaluate the stability, flexibility, and diversity of revenue sources; budgetary control over revenues and expenditures; adequacy of insurance protection; level of overlapping debt; and growth of unfunded employee-related benefits. Socioeconomic and demographic trends should also be analyzed, including trends in employment, real estate values, retail sales, building permits, population, personal income, and welfare. Much of this information is contained in the statistical section of the CAFR; the remainder can be obtained from the U.S. Bureau of the Census publications available in most university libraries and from its Web site www.census.gov.

Sources of Governmental Financial Data

Until 1999, a benchmarking source was Dr. Kenneth Brown's *Comparative Ratios for Cities* and 10-point test, which was discussed in earlier editions of this text. On occasion, Brown's 10-point test is referenced by those who strive to compare one government's fiscal health to that of a similar government.[22] However, there are no benchmark values with up-to-date data using *GASBS 34* financial statements available for easy-to-use comparisons. Raw data, such as that compiled by the GFOA in its *Financial Indicators Database* from CAFRs submitted to the Certificate of Excellence in Financial Reporting program, must be converted to useful geographic and population strata benchmarks. Benchmark data can be expected to become more readily available as demand increases and suppliers with resources to process raw data into useful information step up to meet that demand for comparative information.

---

[22] Robert Kleine, Philip Kloha, and Carol S. Weissert, "Monitoring Local Government Fiscal Health," *Government Finance Review,* June 2003; Ken W. Brown, "The 10-Point Test of Financial Condition: Toward an Easy-to-Use Assessment Tool for Smaller Cities," *Government Finance Review* 9 (December 1993), pp. 21–26.

ILLUSTRATION 10–5   **Indicator 16—Excess of Revenues over Expenditures: General Fund**

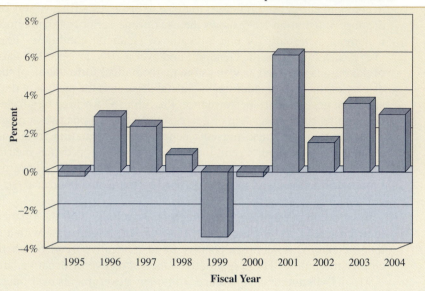

Warning Trend:

Increasing amount of General Fund operating deficits as a percent of operating revenues and transfers

Formulation:

General Fund operating (deficits)/surpluses
    Operating revenues and transfers

Fiscal Year	General Fund Operating Surplus/(Deficit)*	Operating Revenues & Transfers†	General Fund Operating Surplus/(Deficit) as a Percentage of Operating Revenues & Transfers
1995	$ (122,256)	$36,945,336	−0.33%
1996	$1,122,324	$38,794,027	2.89%
1997	$1,005,174	$41,207,631	2.44%
1998	$ 323,804	$43,532,800	0.74%
1999	($1,431,390)	$43,416,652	−3.30%
2000	$ (122,068)	$43,891,836	−0.28%
2001	$3,011,397	$48,665,665	6.19%
2002	$ 803,846	$51,593,618	1.56%
2003	$1,891,263	$54,210,002	3.49%
2004	**$1,745,541**	**$58,238,591**	**3.00%**

*Not including encumbrances.
†Operating revenues and transfers: General Fund revenues plus operating transfers from other funds and increase in obligations under capital leases and appropriated fund balance where applicable.

Description:

An operating deficit will occur as operating expenditures exceed operating revenues. However, this does not necessarily mean the budget will be out of balance. Reserves (fund balances) and transfers are sometimes used to cover the difference. Continuing use of reserves and the unjustifiable transfer of funds to balance the deficit may indicate a revenue/expenditure problem.

The existence of an operating deficit in one year is not cause for concern, but frequent and increasing deficits can indicate that current revenues are not supporting current expenditures, and that serious problems may lie ahead.

ILLUSTRATION 10–5 Continued

Credit Industry Benchmarks:

A current year operating deficit would be considered a minor warning signal, and the reasons and manner of funding would be carefully examined before it was even considered a negative factor. However, the following situations would be looked at with considerably more attention and would probably be considered negative factors:

1. Two consecutive years of operating fund deficits.
2. A current year deficit greater than the previous year's deficit.
3. A current operating fund deficit in two or more of the last five years.
4. An abnormally large deficit (5% to 10% of operating revenues) in any one year.

Analysis:

For the period shown, there have been three years (FY 1995, FY 1999 and FY 2000) where there was a deficit. In FY 1999 there was a planned use of accumulated appropriated fund balance. While the deficit is significant, it should be noted that the amount is still considerably below the amount budgeted for appropriated fund balance ($2,378,624). For FY 2001 management worked toward keeping the deficit at a minimum. The appropriated fund balance for FY 2004 is $3,587,694. Therefore, a deficit in one year and a decrease to a smaller deficit amount in the next year is not, in and of itself, considered to be a negative factor. Management and the City Council will continue to closely monitor this indicator. The City is exploring additional avenues for increasing the revenue base.

According to Fiscal and Budget Policies adopted by Council, the City will calculate an unreserved, undesignated fund balance equal to 16% of expenditures for the adopted budget. These funds will be used to avoid cash flow interruptions, generate interest income, reduce need for short-term borrowing and assist in maintaining what is considered an investment grade bond rating capacity.

Source: City of Columbia, Missouri, *1995–2004 Trends Manual,* pp. 286–87. Full report available at http://www.gocolumbiamo.com/finance/services/financial_reports.

The Performeter® tool developed by Crawford & Associates to assist governments in building a composite reading of their financial health each year can be used not only to compare the government to itself over time, but also to other governments. External information already reflected in the tool includes suggested ratings and weights based on the firm's experience with governmental clients primarily in Oklahoma. The value of these variables can change as more data on these performance measures by various governmental entities is available. Illustration 10–7 shows an evaluation of the financial performance of a sample city. A value for each performance measure is computed based on the government-wide financial statements and fund statements, where applicable (underlying data not presented here). A rating is assigned to that performance measure with reference to the suggested ratings at levels 1–5–10. That rating is weighted by a factor of 1, 2, or 3 to arrive at a score for each performance measure. Those scores are totaled and divided by the maximum possible points (maximum rating of 10 times the suggested weights = 330 for this illustration) and expressed as a rating from 1 to 10, again with 10 being the highest overall reading available. As more governments make performance measures accessible to citizens on government Web sites, it is likely comparisons to similar governments will be made. Clearly, there is danger in attaching too much importance to a single measure of financial performance for a government; however, the attraction of a single measure is in enticing the reader or analyst to investigate the underlying factors and indicators that make up that signal.

Credit Analyst Models

As discussed earlier in this chapter, credit analysts are concerned with assessing a government's ability to pay interest and principal when due. Credit analysts typically examine the same kinds of information that internal managers use in evaluating financial

ILLUSTRATION 10–6   **Columbia Financial Trend Monitoring System: Summary FY 1995–FY 2004**

Indicator	Description of Indicator	State of Indicator* General Fund/ Governmental Funds	Enterprise/Internal Service Funds	Community Needs and Resources
Chart A	Columbia Financial Trend Monitoring System: Warning Trends/Factors			
Revenues:				
Chart B	Impact of Inflation on City Revenues	+		
1	Revenues per Capita: General Fund	+		
2-A	Restricted Revenues: Governmental Funds	+		
2-B	Restricted Revenues: Enterprise Funds		+	
3	Intergovernmental Revenues: General Fund	+		
4	Elastic Tax Revenues: General Fund	+		
5	Operating Transfers from Other Funds: General Fund	+		
6	Temporary Revenues: Governmental Funds	+		
7	Property Tax Revenues: General Fund	+		
8	Uncollected Property Taxes: General Fund	+		
9	Service Charges Coverage: General Fund	+		
10	Revenues—Budgeted vs. Actual: General Fund	+		
Expenditures:				
Chart C	Impact of Inflation on City Expenditures	+	+	
11-A	Expenditures per Capita: General Fund	+		
11-B	Expenses per Capita: Enterprise Funds		+	
12-A	Employees per Capita: General Fund	+		
12-B	Employees per Capita: Enterprise Funds and Internal Service Funds		+	
13	Fixed Costs: All Funds	Monitor	Monitor	
14	Fringe Benefits	+	+	
15	Expenditures: General Fund Over/Under Budget	+		
Operating Position:				
16	Excess of Revenues over Expenditures: General Fund	+		
17	Enterprise Retained Earnings/Loss		+	
18	General Fund Balances	+		
19-A	Liquidity: General Fund	+		
19-B	Liquidity: Enterprise Funds		+	
20-A	Revenues to Expenditures: Governmental Funds & Expendable Trust Funds	+		
20-B	Revenues to Expenses: Proprietary Funds & Nonexpendable Trust Funds		+	
21-A	Current Liabilities: General Fund	+		
21-B	Current Liabilities: Enterprise Fund		+	
22-A	General Obligation Long-Term Debt: per Assessed Valuation	+		
22-B	General Obligation Long-Term Debt: per Capita	+		

*State of Indicator: + Positive trend; − Negative trend; Monitor − Needs to be closely monitored.

ILLUSTRATION 10–6 Continued

23-A	Debt Service: General Obligation Bonds	+		
23-B	Debt Service: Revenue Bonds		+	

Unfunded Liabilities:

24	Pension Assets	+	+	
25	Accumulated Employee Leave	+	+	
26-A	Maintenance Effort: Streets & Sidewalks	+		
26-B	Maintenance Effort: Water & Electric Utilities		+	
27	Capital Outlay: General, Internal Service, & Enterprise Funds	Monitor	Monitor	
28	Depreciation: Enterprise & Internal Service Funds		+	

Community Needs & Resources:

29	Population		+
30	Median Age		+
31	Household Effective Buying Income		+
32	Public Assistance Recipients		Monitor
33	Property Value		+
34	Residential Development		+
35	Employment Base		+
36-A	Business Activity: Business License Accounts		+
36-B	Business Activity: Retail Sales		+

Source: City of Columbia, Missouri, *1995–2004 Trends Manual*, pp. 233–34.

condition. Of course, internal managers have access to *all* information generated by the government for as far back as data have been retained, whereas credit analysts have access only to what management provides or what they require from management. Thus, internal managers have an informational advantage with respect to their own government. Credit analysts with the major bond rating agencies (Moody's Investors Service, Standard & Poor's, and Fitch, Inc.) or with companies that insure bonds against default may have an informational advantage with respect to *benchmark* information, in that they have data from thousands of entities whose bonds are rated or insured. Moreover, these analysts develop extensive multiple-year libraries, including budgets and CAFRs, for the entities whose bonds are rated or insured, and they often visit the entity for discussions with management. Analysts with investment firms (underwriters and brokers) tend to collect and process much less information than do bond rating and insurer organizations. Rather, these analysts rely in part on agency ratings to help them properly determine the credit risk of municipal bonds.

The rating agencies are recognized as one of the primary groups of users of governmental financial reports, particularly, comprehensive annual financial reports (CAFR). They use financial measures discussed earlier in the chapter built on audited numbers in the government-wide and fund financial statements, management's discussion and analysis, notes to the financial statements, and statistical information in the last section of the CAFR. Five factors that Moody's Investor's Service considers important in assessing current financial condition and long-term solvency of a government are: (1) debt, (2) finances, (3) the debt's legal security, (4) economy and demographics, and (5) management strategies. Signals that management is strong include conservative budgeting techniques, fund balance policies, debt planning, succession and contingency

ILLUSTRATION 10–7 Performeter® Evaluation—Sample City

Performance Measures	Suggested Rating 1	Suggested Rating 5	Suggested Rating 10	Computation	Rating	Suggested Weight	Score
Financial Position:							
1. Unrestricted net assets	0%	30%	50%	32.7%	5.5	3	16.5
2. GF budgetary fund balance	0%	10%	30%	8.7%	4.5	2	9
3. Debt to assets	>90%	50%	<10%	25.6%	8	1	8
4. Capital asset condition	25%	50%	75%	54%	6.5	1	6.5
5. Current ratio	1.00	2.00	3.00	11.39	10	3	30
6. Quick ratio	0.5	1.00	2.00	1.90	9.5	2	19
7. Pension plan funding	85%	95%	105%	97%	6	1	6
Financial Performance:							
8. Change in net assets	−10%	0%	10%	5.9%	8	3	24
9. Interperiod equity	90%	95%	100%	120.8%	10	2	20
10. BTA self-sufficiency	85%	95%	105%	90.6%	3	3	9
11. Debt service coverage	<0.75	1.25	2.00	3.35	10	3	30
Financial Capability:							
12. Revenue dispersion	10%	50%	90%	37.9%	4	1	4
13. Debt service load	>35%	20%	<5%	29.3%	4	2	8
14. Financing margin— bonded debt per capita	$1,000	$500	$0	$523	5	1	5
15. Financing margin— legal debt limit	0%	50%	100%	55%	5.5	2	11
16. Financing margin— property taxes per capita	$100	$50	$0	$47	5.5	1	5.5
17. Financing margin— sales tax rate	5.00%	3.50%	2.00%	3.5%	5	2	10
Total:					Total	33	221.15
					Max. Possible		330
					Reading:		**6.71**

Source: Special thanks to Michael Crawford of Crawford & Associates, PC, Oklahoma City, OK for permission to use this example from *The Performeter* ® for educational purposes.

planning, strategic planning for economic development, and timely disclosure of audited financial information.[23]

Raters form their initial assessment of the financial worthiness of the government based on these factors and signals, then compare them to similar governments in arriving at a rating for a municipal bond (e.g., Aaa, Aa, A, Baa, Ba). Each rating agency, of course, has its own strategies and may emphasize different factors in its analysis based on its experience. Moody's Investors Service makes some benchmark data, such

[23] Moody's Investors Service, *The Six Critical Components of Strong Municipal Management: Managerial Methods to Promote Credit Enhancement,* March 2004, p. 1.

as medians of selected ratios categorized by type of government (e.g., city, county, school district) and size (e.g., population), available in Special Comment reports published by Moody's Public Finance Group.[24]

It should be noted that bond ratings are often viewed, particularly by investors, as crude indicators of long-term financial condition. For example, a Moody's Aaa rating indicates a city is likely in better financial condition than a city with a Baa rating (the lowest *investment grade* rating) but a user is unable to tell how much better from the ratings. Furthermore, ratings assigned to general obligation (GO) bonds often apply to all GO bonds of the same issuer, although, GO bonds issued with state credit backing or other credit enhancement may carry a higher rating than the ordinary GO bonds of the same issuer.

This chapter describes the evaluation of financial condition. Continued sound financial condition indicates quality financial management and good financial performance. Achieving strong financial performance, however, does not ensure efficient and effective operating performance. Although it is difficult to provide an adequate level of services without sufficient financial resources, achieving efficient and effective use of *productive* resources requires innovative budgeting and management techniques. We defer discussion of these techniques until Chapter 13. In reading Chapter 13, keep in mind the importance of maintaining sound financial condition if service levels are to be sustained.

---

[24] Moody's Investors Service, "Moody's Public Finance Group 2004 Regional Ratings National Medians," (September 2004).

Key Terms

Benchmarking, *410*	Financial condition, *398*	Service capacity, *399*
Budgetary solvency, *398*	Financial position, *398*	Service-level
Cash solvency, *398*	Fiscal capacity, *399*	solvency, *398*
Economic condition, *399*	Long-run solvency, *398*	

Selected References

Berne, Robert. *Research Report,* "The Relationship between Financial Reporting and the Measurement of Financial Condition." Norwalk, CT: GASB, 1992.

Chaney, Barbara A., Dean M. Mead, and Kenneth R. Schermann. "The New Governmental Financial Reporting Model," *Journal of Government Financial Management,* Spring 2002, pp. 27–31.

Governmental Accounting Standards Board. *Concepts Statement No. 1,* "Objectives of Financial Reporting." Norwalk, CT: GASB, 1987.

_____. *Concepts Statement No. 3,* "Communication Methods in General Purpose External Financial Reports That Contain Basic Financial Statements." Norwalk, CT: GASB, 2005.

Mead, Dean M. *What You Should Know about Your Local Government's Finances: A Guide to Financial Statements.* Norwalk, CT: GASB, 2000.

_____. *An Analyst's Guide to Government Financial Statements.* Norwalk, CT: GASB, 2001.

_____. *What You Should Know about Your School District's Finances: A Guide to Financial Statements.* Norwalk, CT: GASB, 2001.

————. *What* Else *You Should Know about a Government's Finances: A Guide to Notes to the Financial Statements and Supporting Information.* Norwalk, CT: GASB, 2005.

Nollenberger, Karl. *Evaluating Financial Condition: A Handbook for Local Government,* 4th ed. Washington, DC: ICMA, 2003.

Temelo, Judy W., and The Bond Market Association. *Fundamentals of Municipal Bonds,* 5th ed. New York: John Wiley and Sons, 2001.

Questions

10–1. Describe some typical causes of municipal financial crises. How could an effective monitoring system reduce the risk of a financial crisis?

10–2. Discuss the differences among the concepts of *financial position, financial condition,* and *economic condition.*

10–3. Describe how managers can use the Financial Trend Monitoring System of the International City/County Management Association (ICMA) to demonstrate accountability to citizens.

10–4. "Citizens regularly evaluate their city's financial condition." Do you agree with this statement? Why or why not?

10–5. Describe how a taxpayer might assess the financial solvency and viability of a government using government-wide financial statements prepared in accordance with *GASBS 34?*

10–6. Explain what assessment can be made from the ratio *unrestricted net assets as a percent of total revenue* that cannot be made from the ratio *unreserved fund balances as a percent of total revenues.*

10–7. Explain how environmental factors influence a city's management practices and legislative policies.

10–8. Explain how organizational factors, such as management practices and legislative policies, affect a government's financial condition.

10–9. Identify some financial indicators or ratios that are designed to measure short-term financial position of a governmental entity. Why are these measures not as useful in assessing long-term financial or economic condition?

10–10. How can a government use benchmarks to demonstrate accountability for the use of taxpayers' dollars?

Cases

10–1 Comparative Ratios. The government-wide financial statements for Catalpa City for a three-year period are presented on the following pages.

Additional information follows:
Population: Year 2008: 30,420, Year 2007: 28,291, Year 2006: 26,374. Debt limit remained at $20,000,000 for each of the three years. Net cash from operations is generally 80 percent of total revenues each year.

Required
a. Which of the financial performance measures in Illustration 10–4 can be calculated for Catalpa City based on the information that is provided?
b. Calculate those ratios identified in part a. for FY 2008. Show your computations.
c. Provide an overall assessment of Catalpa City's financial condition using all the information provided, both financial and nonfinancial. Use information from the prior years to form your assessment.

CATALPA CITY
Statements of Net Assets
As of December 31
(in thousands)

	2008			2007			2006		
	Governmental Activities	Business-type Activities	Total	Governmental Activities	Business-type Activities	Total	Governmental Activities	Business-type Activities	Total
Assets									
Current assets:									
Cash	$ 5,540	$ 1,800	$ 7,340	$ 4,531	$ 1,663	$ 6,194	$ 3,452	$ 1,487	$ 4,939
Investments	733	291	1,024	638	181	819	769	179	948
Receivables (net)	2,747	1,809	4,556	2,947	1,608	4,555	1,865	1,472	3,337
Prepaid expenses	253	8	261	251	6	257	171	5	176
Inventories	26	58	84	101	48	149	167	49	216
Total current assets	9,299	3,966	13,265	8,468	3,506	11,974	6,424	3,192	9,616
Capital assets:									
Land	2,180	2,101	4,281	2,070	1,804	3,874	1,971	1,604	3,575
Depreciable assets	37,600	14,455	52,055	37,183	17,775	54,958	39,347	14,801	54,148
Accumulated depreciation	(15,039)	(3,681)	(18,720)	(16,732)	(9,776)	(26,508)	(19,680)	(7,402)	(27,082)
Total capital assets (net)	24,741	10,774	35,515	22,521	9,803	32,324	21,638	9,003	30,641
Total assets	34,040	14,740	48,780	30,989	13,309	44,298	28,062	12,195	40,257
Liabilities									
Accounts payable	1,580	467	2,047	412	376	788	1,633	295	1,928
Deferred revenue	32		32	30		30	42		42
Other, current	1,754	200	1,954	1,443	190	1,633	1,489	170	1,659
Total current liabilities	3,366	667	4,033	1,885	566	2,451	3,164	465	3,629
Bonds payable	15,900	6,500	22,400	16,900	7,500	24,400	15,900	6,500	22,400
Total liabilities	19,266	7,167	26,433	18,785	8,066	26,851	19,064	6,965	26,029
Net Assets									
Invested in capital assets, net of related debt	9,104	4,027	13,131	7,945	3,065	11,010	5,366	2,067	7,433
Restricted for:									
Capital projects	140	—	140	151	—	151	130	—	130
Debt service	933	—	933	1,033	—	1,033	818	—	818
Unrestricted (deficit)	4,597	3,546	8,143	3,075	2,178	5,253	2,683	3,163	5,846
Total net assets	$14,774	$ 7,573	$22,347	$12,204	$ 5,243	$17,447	$ 8,997	$ 5,230	$14,227

CATALPA CITY
Statement of Activities
For the Year Ended December 31, 2008
(in thousands)

Functions/Programs	Expenses	Program Revenues			Net (Expense) Revenue and Changes in Net Assets		
		Charges for Services	Operating Grants and Contributions	Capital Grants and Contributions	Governmental Activities	Business-type Activities	Total
Governmental Activities:							
General government	$ 5,716	$ 531	$ —	—	$ (5,185)	—	$ (5,185)
Judicial	1,926	716	99	—	(1,111)	—	(1,111)
Public safety	7,958	1,530	168	—	(6,260)	—	(6,260)
Health and sanitation	2,804	524	—	—	(2,280)	—	(2,280)
Culture and recreation	2,166	554	—	$495	(1,117)	—	(1,117)
Road maintenance	2,455	5	1,619	—	(831)	—	(831)
Interest on long-term debt	948	—	—	—	(948)	—	(948)
Total governmental activities	23,973	3,860	1,886	495	(17,732)	—	(17,732)
Business-type activities	2,895	5,218	—	7	—	$ 2,330	2,330
Total government	$26,868	$9,078	$1,886	$502	(17,732)	2,330	(15,402)

General Revenues:		
Property taxes	17,296	17,296
Grants and contributions not restricted to specific programs	2,190	2,190
Investment earnings	716	716
Special item—gain on sale of land	100	100
Total general revenues and special items	20,302	20,302
Change in net assets	2,570	2,330	4,900
Net assets—January 1	12,204	5,243	17,447
Net assets—December 31	$14,774	$ 7,573	$ 22,347

CATALPA CITY
Statement of Activities
For the Year Ended December 31, 2007 (in thousands)

Functions/Programs	Expenses	Program Revenues			Net (Expense) Revenue and Changes in Net Assets		
		Charges for Services	Operating Grants and Contributions	Capital Grants and Contributions	Governmental Activities	Business-type Activities	Total
Governmental Activities:							
General government	$ 4,133	$ 148	—	—	$ (3,985)	—	$ (3,985)
Judicial	1,737	209	$ 17	—	(1,511)	—	(1,511)
Public safety	5,239	1,943	30	—	(3,266)	—	(3,266)
Health and sanitation	2,129	147	—	—	(1,982)	—	(1,982)
Culture and recreation	3,762	322	—	$350	(3,090)	—	(3,090)
Road maintenance	1,055	—	501	—	(554)	—	(554)
Interest on long-term debt	804	—	—	—	(804)	—	(804)
Total governmental activities	18,859	2,769	548	350	(15,192)	—	(15,192)
Business-type activities	4,287	4,290	—	10	—	$ 13	13
Total government	$23,146	$7,059	$548	$360	(15,192)	13	(15,179)

General Revenues:

	Governmental Activities	Business-type Activities	Total
Property taxes	13,619		13,619
Grants and contributions not restricted to specific programs	3,664		3,664
Investment earnings	916		916
Special item—gain on sale of land	200		200
Total general revenues and special items	18,399	—	18,399
Change in net assets	3,207	13	3,220
Net assets—January 1	8,997	5,230	14,227
Net assets—December 31	$12,204	$5,243	$17,447

CATALPA CITY
Statement of Activities
For the Year Ended December 31, 2006
(in thousands)

		Program Revenues			Net (Expense) Revenue and Changes in Net Assets		
Functions/Programs	Expenses	Charges for Services	Operating Grants and Contributions	Capital Grants and Contributions	Governmental Activities	Business-type Activities	Total
Governmental Activities:							
General government	$ 3,922	$ 109	$ —	—	$ (3,813)	—	$ (3,813)
Judicial	1,601	198	57	—	(1,346)	—	(1,346)
Public safety	4,113	1,723	10	—	(2,380)	—	(2,380)
Health and sanitation	2,096	216	—	—	(1,880)	—	(1,880)
Culture and recreation	3,484	364	—	$ 320	(2,800)	—	(2,800)
Road maintenance	1,438	—	460	—	(978)	—	(978)
Interest on long-term debt	948	—	—	—	(948)	—	(948)
Total governmental activities	17,602	2,610	527	320	(14,145)	—	(14,145)
Business-type activities	2,637	3,708	—	20	—	$1,091	1,091
Total government	$20,239	$6,318	$527	$ 340	$(14,145)	1,091	(13,054)

General Revenues:		
Property taxes	13,100	13,100
Grants and contributions not restricted to specific programs	2,990	2,990
Investment earnings	681	681
Special item—gain on sale of land	150	—	150
Total general revenues and special items	16,921	—	16,921
Change in net assets	2,776	1,091	3,867
Net assets—January 1	6,221	4,139	10,360
Net assets—December 31	$ 8,997	$5,230	$14,227

10–2 **Internet Case—Municipal Credit Analysts.** Use any of the several Internet search engines to locate the Web sites for Moody's Investors Service, Standard & Poor's, and Fitch Investors Service. Locate and print their bond rating categories. Do they provide any information on how they perform municipal (tax-backed) bond rating evaluations? If so, summarize those procedures and compare them to the procedures described in this chapter.

10–3 **Financial Trends.** You are a new city council person for the City of Scottsdale, Arizona. You are aware that several cities have been in the news recently for financial crises for which the council or board is being held accountable. The governing bodies have been criticized for not being aware of the negative signals and trends that obviously led to the cities in challenging financial situations. Although you were assured at the first few council meetings that the city was overall in good financial shape, you want to be sure you "do your homework" and assess the financial condition of the city for yourself.

You know that the City of Scottsdale, Arizona, prepares a *Financial Trends* report each year based on the ICMA's Financial Trends Monitoring System and that it posts this on its Web site at www.scottsdaleaz.gov.

Required

a. Go to the city's Web site and print a copy of the *Financial Trends* report. Hint: Look in the Finance, Demographics, Economics areas of the Web site under Budget and Finance. Examine the five-year trend information and make a list of any indicators that are negative.

b. Prepare a list of questions for the next city council meeting that you can ask of the finance manager that will help you understand whether you and the council should be concerned about these negative trends.

10–4 **Analysis of Overall Performance.** The City of Okemah, Oklahoma, uses the Crawford Performeter® as a financial analysis tool and presents the results of this analysis in its Management Discussion and Analysis in the annual audited financial statements. For the year ended June 30, 2004, values for the following indicators were presented for the city as a whole:

	Performeter Rating Benchmark		Computation for 2004
Rating:	10	5	
Unrestricted net assets as a percentage of annual revenue	50%	30%	32%
Percentage of assets funded with outstanding debt	10%	50%	36%
Change in net assets	10%	0%	3.4%
Interperiod equity—percentage of current year expenses funded by current year revenues	100%	95%	114%

Required

a. Use Illustration 10–7 in the text and assign a rating to each of the ratios provided (with 1 = lowest or worst to 10 = highest or best), calculate a score using the suggested weights provided, and compute an overall rating of the financial health and performance of this city for FY 2004.

  b. Describe in your own words whether this city is in good shape or bad shape based on these indicators. Do the ratios point to areas where the city should pay particular attention to in the future?

  c. What other information would you find useful in analyzing the financial performance of this city for this year?

Exercises and Problems

10–1 **Examine the CAFR.** Utilizing the CAFR obtained for Exercises and Problems 1–1 and your answers to the questions asked in Chapters 1 through 8, assess the financial condition of the government. For purposes of this project, *financial condition* is broadly defined as a city's ability to provide an adequate range of services on a continuing basis. Specifically, it refers to a city's ability to (1) maintain existing service levels, (2) withstand major economic disruptions, and (3) meet the demands of a changing society in a changing economy. Examine the following issues and questions.

 a. Analysis of revenues and revenue sources.

  (1) How stable and flexible are the city's revenue sources in the event of adverse economic conditions?

  (2) Is the revenue base well diversified, or does the city rely heavily on one or two major sources?

  (3) Has the city been relying on intergovernmental revenues for an excessive portion of its operating expenditures?

  (4) What percentage of total expenses of governmental activities is covered by program revenues? By general revenues?

  (5) Do any extraordinary or special items reported in the statement of activities deserve attention?

 b. Analysis of reserves.

  (1) Are the levels of financial reserves (i.e., fund balances, contingency funds, and unrestricted net assets) adequate to meet unforeseen operational requirements or catastrophic events?

  (2) Is insurance protection adequate to cover losses due to lawsuits or damage to property?

  (3) Is an adequate amount of cash and securities on hand, or could the city borrow quickly to cover short-term obligations?

 c. Analysis of expenditures and expenses.

  (1) Do any components of expenditures and, at the government-wide level, expenses exhibit sharp growth?

  (2) Is adequate budgetary control being exercised over expenditures?

  (3) How does the growth pattern of operating expenditures and expenses over the past 10 years compare with that of revenues?

 d. Analysis of debt burden.

  (1) What has been the 10-year trend in general obligation long-term debt relative to trends in population and revenue capacity?

  (2) Are significant debts of other governments (e.g., a school district, a county) supported by the same taxable properties? What has been the trend for this "overlapping" debt?

  (3) Are there significant levels of short-term operating debt? If so, has the amount of this debt grown over time?

  (4) Are there any significant debts (e.g., lease obligations, unfunded pension liabilities, accrued employee benefits) or contingent liabilities?

     (5) Are any risky investments such as derivatives disclosed in the notes to the financial statements? Are the types of investments adequately explained, and are their risks adequately disclosed?

   e. Socioeconomic factors.

   What have been the trends in demographic and economic indicators, such as real estate values, building permits, retail sales, population, income per capita, percent of population below the poverty level, average age, average educational level, employment and unemployment, and business licenses? (*Note:* Many of these items and other potentially useful information can be obtained from the *City and County Data Book* published by the U.S. Bureau of the Census. See your university library or get selected data from the Census Bureau's Web site www.census.gov.)

   f. Potential "red flags" or warning signs.

     (1) Decline in revenues.

     (2) Decline in property tax collection rate.

       (a) Less than 92 percent of current levy collected?

       (b) Property taxes more than 90 percent of the legal tax limit?

       (c) Decreasing tax collections in two of the last three years?

     (3) Expenditures increasing more rapidly than revenues.

     (4) Declining balances of liquid resources and fund balances.

       (a) General fund deficit in two or more of the last five years?

       (b) General fund balance less than 5 percent of general fund revenues and other financial sources?

     (5) Reliance on nonrecurring (i.e., special item) revenues to support current-period operations.

     (6) Growing debt burden

       (a) Short-term debt more than 5 percent of operating revenues?

       (b) Two-year trend of increasing short-term debt?

       (c) Short-term interest and current-year debt service on general obligation debt more than 20 percent of operating revenues?

       (d) Debt per capita ratio 50 percent higher than four years ago?

     (7) Growth of unfunded pension and other employee-related benefits such as compensated absences and postemployment health care benefits.

     (8) Deferral of needed maintenance on capital plant.

     (9) Decrease in the value of taxable properties, retail sales levels, or disposable personal income.

   (10) Decreasing revenue support from federal or state government.

   (11) Increasing unemployment.

   (12) Unusual climatic conditions or the occurrence of natural disasters.

   (13) Ineffective management and/or dysfunctional political circumstances.

Required

a. Calculate, insofar as possible, the financial ratios in Illustrations 10–3 and 10–4 of the text. Evaluate the ratios in terms of the red flags and benchmarks provided in Illustrations 10–6 and 10–7 and long-term trend data for each ratio, if available.

b. Locate any additional data that you think may be useful in assessing the financial condition of this city; for example, see the U.S. Census Bureau's Web site at www.census.gov and the Web sites of cities you consider comparable in size or other attributes to this city.

c. Prepare a report providing the results of your analysis. The report should have an appendix providing a few graphs and/or tables to support your analysis. In particular, graphs showing revenues, expenditures, and key debt ratios for the past 10 years and selected demographic and socioeconomic trends are helpful. You may want to include some of the ratios calculated in Part *b* in an appendix. Be succinct and include only data relevant to your analysis. Organize your report along the lines of the ratios evaluated in Part *a*.

10–2 Multiple Choice. Choose the best answer.

1. Which of the following groups or parties generally has taken the most initiative to evaluate the financial condition of a city?
   a. Citizens.
   b. Credit market analysts.
   c. Managers.
   d. Legislative and oversight bodies.

2. Which of the following terms or concepts focuses primarily on assets and liabilities that require cash or are normally converted to cash, or require the use of cash in the near future and can generally be determined from fund-based financial statements alone?
   a. Interperiod equity.
   b. Financial condition.
   c. Financial position.
   d. Solvency.

3. Which of the following environmental factors reveals the entity's underlying philosophies regarding willingness to support higher taxes, issuances of long-term debt, and increased social services?
   a. Intergovernmental constraints.
   b. Community needs and resources.
   c. Political culture.
   d. Management policies and legislative policies.

4. The group of factors that largely determines how fiscal policy is influenced by environmental factors is:
   a. Natural disasters and emergencies.
   b. Unfunded liabilities.
   c. External economic conditions.
   d. Management practices and legislative policies.

5. Which of the following would be an effective means of benchmarking?
   a. Comparing the city's key ratios to those of special purpose governments in the area.
   b. Comparing current-period ratios to published medians of the same ratios for cities of similar size or in the same geographic region.
   c. Comparing key ratios to published medians of the same ratios for larger cities in other parts of the country.
   d. Comparing current-period ratios to estimates for future periods.

6. Which of the following conditions *could* signal impending fiscal stress?
   a. Decreasing unemployment.
   b. Increasing property values.
   c. Increasing revenues relative to expenditures.
   d. Increasing levels of unfunded pension obligations and other postemployment retirement benefits.

7. Credit rating agencies such as Moody's, Standard & Poor's, and Fitch examine factors in which of the following four major groups when assessing creditworthiness for purposes of rating tax-supported bonds?
   a. Economic, financial, administrative/political, education.
   b. Economic, scope of services, financial, debt.
   c. Economic, financial, debt, administrative/political.
   d. Economic, financial, debt, education.

8. Which of the following statements is correct regarding the relationship between financial condition and operating performance?
   a. Sound financial condition ensures efficient and effective operating performance.
   b. Sound financial condition may be a necessary but not sufficient condition for achieving efficient and effective operating performance.
   c. Efficient and effective operating performance ensures sound financial condition.
   d. None of the above.

9. Which of the following most suggests a government that is relying heavily on revenue sources it cannot directly control?
   a. Property taxes, 20%; charges for services, 70%; grants and contributions, 5%; investment income, 5%.
   b. Property taxes, 20%; charges for services, 60%; grants and contributions, 10%; investment income, 10%.
   c. Property taxes, 40%; charges for services, 40%; grants and contributions, 10%; investment income, 10%.
   d. Property taxes, 60%; charges for services, 5%; grants and contributions, 30%; investment income, 5%.

10. The following description that best defines *economic condition* is:
    a. The probability that a government will meet its financial obligations and sustain services in the future.
    b. Current-year revenues are sufficient to pay for the services provided this year.
    c. A composite of a government's financial health and its ability and willingness to provide services.
    d. A government's ongoing ability to supply the capital and human resources needed to meet its commitments to provide services.

10–3 **Financial Condition.** Write the letters *a* through *j* on a sheet of paper. Beside each letter, put a plus (+) if a high or increasing value of the item is generally associated with *stronger* financial condition, a minus (−) if a high or increasing value of the item is generally associated with a *weaker* financial condition, and NE if the item generally has *no effect* on the financial condition or the direction of the effect cannot be predicted.

a. Personal income per capita.

b. Inflation rate.

c. Percentage of households below the poverty level.

d. Bank deposits.

e. Property values.

f. Population growth.

g. Political party of the mayor.

    h. Unfunded pension liability.

    i. Level of overlapping debt.

    j. Reserves for self-insurance.

10–4 **Benchmarks.** Examine the following tables from the 2003 Financial Trend Monitoring Report for the Town of Brookline, Massachusetts, that reports on fiscal year 2002. The performance indicators selected are *total revenue* and *revenue per capita.* The town provides three reference groups with which to compare Brookline: Aaa-rated municipalities, comparison municipalities, and the state median. Since local government budgeting in Massachusetts is driven by the property tax levy cap, this is a key variable in comparing municipalities.

Aaa-Rated Municipality	FY02 Total Revenue	FY02 Rev per Cap	State Rank	Comparison Municipality	FY02 Total Revenue	FY02 Rev per Cap	State Rank
Weston	49,794,904	4,342	12	Cambridge	356,895,723	3,521	27
Lexington	111,784,312	3,683	21	**Brookline**	**175,058,152**	**3,065**	**45**
Wayland	47,219,656	3,605	24	Belmont	71,477,390	2,954	51
Cambridge	356,895,723	3,521	27	Newton	245,812,303	2,932	53
Andover	103,338,507	3,307	33	Wellesley	76,196,553	2,863	63
Brookline	**175,058,152**	**3,065**	**45**	Winchester	59,310,311	2,850	65
Hingham	59,373,338	2,986	48	Waltham	161,444,163	2,726	80
Belmont	71,477,390	2,954	51	Braintree	89,441,958	2,644	97
Newton	245,812,303	2,932	53	Framingham	169,322,957	2,531	116
Concord	49,726,361	2,926	55	Arlington	99,100,870	2,338	168
Wellesley	76,196,553	2,863	63	Medford	120,977,460	2,169	210
Winchester	59,310,311	2,850	65	Weymouth	116,134,368	2,151	217

Aaa-Rated Median	73,836,972	3,026	Aaa-Rated LQ	2.37	1.01
Comparison RG Median	118,555,914	2,788	Comparison RG LQ	1.48	1.10
State Median	23,487,291	2,314	State LQ	7.45	1.32

where RG = reference group

    LQ = location quotient showing how much above or below the median this government is.

Required

    a. Prepare a histogram or bar graph that shows Brookline in relation to the three reference groups, Aaa-rated median, comparison reference group, and state median for FY02 total revenue and a separate graph for FY02 revenue per capita.

    b. Evaluate the financial performance of Brookline for FY02. Use information from the tables and the graph you prepared for Part *a* to support your analysis.

    c. What other performance measures would you like to see before you conclude the town is in good shape or bad shape for the fiscal year shown?

10–5 **Financial Trend Monitoring System—Reserves.** The City of Scottsdale, Arizona, has prepared the following report about its reserve policies that appears on page 13 of its October 2004 financial trends booklet.

Required

a. Refer to Illustration 10–1. To which categories of factors affecting financial condition do you believe this statement belongs?

b. Assess the adequacy of this note. Do you need more information to understand how the reserve financial policy affects the city's financial condition? Explain.

Reserve Policies

37. All fund designations and reserves will be evaluated annually for long-term adequacy and use requirements in conjunction with development of the City's balanced five year financial plan.

38. General Fund Stabilization Reserve of 10 percent of annual general governmental (General/HURF funds) operating expenditures will be maintained for unforeseen emergencies or catastrophic impacts to the City. Funds in excess of 10 percent, but not to exceed $5 million, may be used for economic investment in the community when justified by the financial return to the City.

39. Debt Service Reserve will be funded with secondary property taxes, levied by City Council, sufficient to pay the bonded indebtedness for General Obligation bond principal and interest. A debt service sinking fund will be maintained to account for these restricted revenues and debt payments, as well as any additional debt amounts deemed to be advisable and necessary for any public or municipal purposes.

40. Water and Sewer Fund Reserves will be maintained to meet three objectives: 1) ensure adequate funding for operations; 2) to ensure infrastructure repair and replacement; and, 3) to provide working capital to provide level rate change for customers.

    a. An Operating Reserve will be funded not to exceed 90 days of budgeted system operating expenditures to provide sufficient expenditure flexibility during times of unusual weather resulting in variations in average consumption and associated operating expenses.

    b. A Replacement and Extension Reserve will be maintained, per bond indenture requirements, to meet the minimum requirement of 2% of all tangible assets of the system to ensure replacement of water and sewer infrastructure.

    c. In addition, Working Capital will be funded based upon a multi-year financial plan to provide adequate cash for water and sewer capital improvements and to level the impact of rate increases upon our customers.

41. Solid Waste Management Fund Reserve will be funded not to exceed 90 days of budgeted system operating expenditures to provide contingency funding for costs associated with solid waste disposal. Costs may include site purchase, technology applications, or inter-governmental investment to maximize the value of waste disposal activities.

42. Aviation Fund Reserve will be funded not to exceed 90 days of budgeted system operating expenditures to provide contingency funding for costs associated with airport operations. Costs may include site purchase, technology applications, or inter-governmental investment to maximize the value of airport activities.

43. Self-Insurance Reserves will be maintained at a level, which, together with purchased insurance policies, will adequately indemnify the City's property, liability, and health benefit risk. A qualified actuarial firm shall be retained on an annual basis in order to recommend appropriate funding levels, which will be approved by Council.

44. Fleet Management Reserve will be maintained based upon lifecycle replacement plans to ensure adequate fund balance required for systematic replacement of fleet vehicles and operational contingencies. Operating departments will be charged for fleet operating costs per vehicle class and replacement costs spread over the useful life of the vehicles.

45. Contingency Reserves to be determined annually will be maintained to offset unanticipated revenue shortfalls and/or unexpected expenditure increases. Contingency reserves may also be used for unanticipated and/or inadequately budgeted events threatening the public health or safety. Use of contingency funds should be utilized only after all budget sources have been examined for available funds, and subject to City Council approval.

Source: City of Scottsdale AZ Financial Trends, October 2004, pp. 13–14

10–6 Factors Affecting Financial Condition. The transmittal letter from the chief financial officer to the mayor and city council of Detroit that accompanies the City of Detroit's Comprehensive Annual Financial Report for the Year Ended June 30, 2004, includes the following:

Economic Considerations

This is not an easy time for Detroit. But, we are not alone. The latest numbers tell us that around the world, a quarter of the world's urban centers are declining in population—twice the number of just a decade ago.

Nationally, the economy continues to be troubled. We are fighting two foreign wars that have diverted billions of dollars away from domestic programs at a time when the need for those programs have grown. Gasoline prices are reaching record levels that could seriously impact the auto industry. The federal government is running record deficits.

The federal government is systematically cutting assistance to local units of government across a broad range of programs such as community development block grants, homeless assistance, and others. For example, the funding under the federal COPS program to hire new police declined from $2.5 million to under $150,000 in three years.

Closer to home, Michigan's economy continues to be one of the weakest in the nation, ranking 49th out of 50 states in unemployment. For Detroit, this has meant deep cuts in income taxes and state revenue sharing.

In Detroit, rising health care and pension costs are costing the City $200 million more than they did just three years ago at a time when our revenues are falling. In the past three years—

- Health care costs have risen $78 million or 46%
- Pension costs have risen by $120 million

Source: City of Detroit, MI 2004 Comprehensive Annual Financial Report, pp. I 6–7.

Required

a. Which of the environmental, organizational, and financial factors from the ICMA's Financial Trend Monitoring System (see Illustration 10–1) are identified in this excerpt from the City of Detroit's letter of transmittal?

b. Take the perspective of a taxpayer and member of a citizen watchdog agency in the city. Prepare a memo to the chief financial officer of the city in which you request specific financial ratios to be calculated and presented so you can better assess the financial condition of the city. Use the transmittal letter provided to guide your choice of ratios.

10–7 **Government-wide Financial Analysis.** Condensed government-wide financial information from the Comprehensive Annual Financial Report for the Commonwealth of Pennsylvania for the fiscal year ended June 30, 2004, is provided below.

Required

a. Identify significant trends that appear in the condensed statement of net assets and statement of activities that are useful in analyzing the financial condition of the commonwealth (or state). Comment on whether these trends appear to be positive, negative, or neutral.

b. Write a brief memo to a state legislator from the perspective of a staff assistant that discusses the financial position and results of operations for FY03 and FY04 for the commonwealth based on these two government-wide financial statements. Use ratios in your memo to support your positions where appropriate given the limited set of information provided in this problem. Note: the full CAFR is available at the commonwealth's Web site at www.state.pa.us under "Budget."

The following presents condensed financial statement information from the statement of net assets (amounts in billions):

	Governmental Activities			Business-type Activities			Total		
	2004	2003	Change	2004	2003	Change	2004	2003	Change
Assets:									
Cash and investments	$10.5	$ 8.5	$2.0	$4.8	$4.7	$ 0.1	$15.3	$13.2	$2.1
Capital assets (net)	20.8	19.8	1.0	—	—	—	20.8	19.8	1.0
All other assets	5.7	5.4	0.3	1.1	1.0	0.1	6.8	6.4	0.4
Total assets	**37.0**	**33.7**	**3.3**	**5.9**	**5.7**	**0.2**	**42.9**	**39.4**	**3.5**
Liabilities:									
Accounts payable	4.0	3.3	0.7	0.4	0.5	(0.1)	4.4	3.8	0.6
All other current liabilities	4.3	3.6	0.7	1.3	0.9	0.4	5.6	4.5	1.1
Total current liabilities	**8.3**	**6.9**	**1.4**	**1.7**	**1.4**	**0.3**	**10.0**	**8.3**	**1.7**
Bonds payable	6.7	6.6	0.1	—	—	—	6.7	6.6	0.1
All other long-term liabilities	2.3	2.0	0.3	2.1	1.8	0.3	4.4	3.8	0.6
Total long-term liabilities	**9.0**	**8.6**	**0.4**	**2.1**	**1.8**	**0.3**	**11.1**	**10.4**	**0.7**
Total liabilities	**17.3**	**15.5**	**1.8**	**3.8**	**3.2**	**0.6**	**21.1**	**18.7**	**2.4**

(continued)

Net assets:

	Governmental 2004	Governmental 2003	Governmental Change	Business-type 2004	Business-type 2003	Business-type Change	Total 2004	Total 2003	Total Change
Invested in capital assets, net of related debt	16.9	16.1	0.8	—	—	—	16.9	16.1	0.8
Restricted	3.0	2.5	0.5	2.1	2.5	(0.4)	5.1	5.0	0.1
Unrestricted	(0.2)	(0.4)	0.2	—	—	—	(0.2)	(0.4)	0.2
Total net assets	**$19.7**	**$18.2**	**$1.5**	**$2.1**	**$2.5**	**$(0.4)**	**$21.8**	**$20.7**	**$1.1**

The following presents condensed financial statement information from the statement of activities (amounts in billions):

	Governmental Activities 2004	Governmental Activities 2003	Governmental Activities Change	Business-type Activities 2004	Business-type Activities 2003	Business-type Activities Change	Total 2004	Total 2003	Total Change
Revenues:									
Program revenues:									
Charges for sales and services	$ 4.5	$ 4.2	$ 0.3	$5.6	$5.1	$ 0.5	$10.1	$ 9.3	$ 0.8
Operating grants and contributions	16.5	14.6	1.9	0.8	1.2	(0.4)	17.3	15.8	1.5
Capital grants and contributions	—	0.1	(0.1)	—	—	—	—	0.1	(0.1)
Total program revenues	**21.0**	**18.9**	**2.1**	**6.4**	**6.3**	**0.1**	**27.4**	**25.2**	**2.2**
General revenues:									
Taxes and investment income	23.5	21.6	1.9	—	—	—	23.5	21.6	1.9
Total general revenues	**23.5**	**21.6**	**1.9**	—	—	—	**23.5**	**21.6**	**1.9**
Total revenues	**44.5**	**40.5**	**4.0**	**6.4**	**6.3**	**0.1**	**50.9**	**46.8**	**4.1**
Expenses:									
Governmental activities:									
Direction and supportive services	2.0	1.0	1.0	—	—	—	2.0	1.0	1.0
Protection of persons and property	3.9	3.9	—	—	—	—	3.9	3.9	—
Public education	10.6	10.2	0.4	—	—	—	10.6	10.2	0.4
Health and human services	21.7	20.5	1.2	—	—	—	21.7	20.5	1.2
Economic development	1.3	1.4	(0.1)	—	—	—	1.3	1.4	(0.1)
Transportation	3.2	3.0	0.2	—	—	—	3.2	3.0	0.2
Recreation and cultural enrichment	0.4	0.4	—	—	—	—	0.4	0.4	—
Interest	0.3	0.4	(0.1)	—	—	—	0.3	0.4	(0.1)
Business-type activities:									
State lottery	—	—	—	2.1	1.8	0.3	2.1	1.8	0.3
Unemployment compensation	—	—	—	2.6	3.5	(0.9)	2.6	3.5	(0.9)
Liquor control	—	—	—	1.0	0.9	0.1	1.0	0.9	0.1
Worker's compensation	—	—	—	0.4	0.2	0.2	0.4	0.2	0.2
Tuition payment	—	—	—	0.3	0.3	—	0.3	0.3	—
Total expenses	**43.4**	**40.8**	**2.6**	**6.4**	**6.7**	**(0.3)**	**49.8**	**47.5**	**2.3**
Excess/(deficiency) before transfers	1.1	(0.3)	1.4	—	(0.4)	(0.4)	1.1	(0.7)	1.8
Transfers	0.4	0.6	(0.2)	(0.4)	(0.6)	0.2	—	—	—
Increase (decrease) in net assets	1.5	0.3	1.2	(0.4)	(1.0)	0.6	1.1	(0.7)	1.8
Net assets, beginning	18.2	17.7	.5	2.5	3.5	1.0	20.7	21.2	.5
Net assets, ending, before restatement	19.7	18.0	1.7	2.1	2.5	0.4	21.8	20.5	1.3
Restatement related to implementation of GASB Technical Bulletin 2004-1	—	0.2	0.2	—	—	—	—	0.2	0.2
Net assets, ending (restated)	**$19.7**	**$18.2**	**$1.5**	**$2.1**	**$2.5**	**$0.4**	**$21.8**	**$20.7**	**$1.1**

Auditing of Governmental and Not-for-Profit Organizations

Learning Objectives

After studying this chapter, you should be able to:

1. Explain the essential elements of financial audits by independent CPAs, including:
   The objective(s) of financial audits.
   The source and content of generally accepted auditing standards (GAAS).
   The types of audit reports that can be rendered.
   The contents of an unqualified and a qualified audit report.
   Materiality.
   GAAP hierarchy.
   Required supplementary information.
2. Explain what is meant by generally accepted government auditing standards (GAGAS), the source of GAGAS, and why GAGAS are much broader than GAAS.
3. Explain the types of audits performed under GAGAS, including:
   Financial audits.
   Attestation engagements.
   Performance audits.
4. Explain the characteristics of a single audit, including:
   The purpose.
   Which entities must have a single audit.
   What auditing work is required.
   How major programs are selected for audit.
   What reports must be rendered, when, and to whom.
5. Describe the implications of the Sarbanes-Oxley Act of 2002 on governments and not-for-profit organizations.

The auditing profession has been in the news as a result of high-profile corporate accounting scandals in the 1990s and early 2000s. Despite a variety of causes behind the crises experienced by businesses (e.g., Enron, WorldCom, Tyco), governmental entities (e.g., Orange County, California; Miami, Florida; Washington, D.C.), and not-for-profit entities (e.g., United Way and American Red Cross), a common refrain on the part of those who lost money or trust in these organizations was "Where were the auditors?"

The public accounting profession tackled this question on several fronts. It took responsibility for lapses when warranted. It educated the public about the value added to financial statements when independent auditors provide assurance that the statements fairly present the financial position, changes in financial position, and cash flows of an entity. It clarified what it means to be independent, as well as the auditor's role in detecting fraud. The American Institute of Certified Public Accountants established Audit Quality Centers (for governmental, employee benefits, and public company audits) to provide resources to auditors for enhancing the quality of audits. In this chapter, the unique aspects of auditing public and not-for-profit sector entities are discussed along with fundamental auditing concepts that apply to audits of any organization.

FINANCIAL AUDITS BY INDEPENDENT CPAs

Financial statements of governmental entities, colleges and universities, health care organizations, voluntary health and welfare organizations, and other not-for-profit organizations are the representations of the officials responsible for the financial management of the entity. In order for users of the financial statements to have the assurance that the statements are prepared in conformity with accounting and financial reporting standards established by authoritative bodies, and that all material facts are disclosed, the statements should be accompanied by the report of an independent auditor. Audits for this purpose are called **financial audits.** Audits or engagements conducted for other purposes are discussed later in this section.

The auditor's objective in performing a financial audit is to render a report expressing his or her opinion that the financial statements present fairly the financial position, changes in financial position, and, where applicable, cash flows of the organization. "Present fairly" means in conformity with generally accepted accounting principles. Auditing standards prescribe standard wording of audit reports to ensure that report users clearly understand the responsibilities of management and those of the auditor, what was audited, the scope of audit, and the nature of the audit opinion. Auditors provide opinions on financial statements that are based on *reasonable assurance* that the financial statements are free from material misstatements, which is not the same as ensuring or guaranteeing that the statements are free of errors and all fraud was detected.[1]

Generally Accepted Auditing Standards

In the case of state and local governments, audits may be performed by independent certified public accountants (CPAs) or by state or federal audit agencies. Generally, not-for-profit organizations electing or required to have an audit are audited by CPAs. In performing audits, CPAs are professionally and ethically obligated by Rule 202 of the American Institute of Certified Public Accountants' (AICPA) *Code of Professional Conduct* to follow **generally accepted auditing standards (GAAS)**—standards set by the AICPA and promulgated in *Statements on Auditing Standards.* State or federal auditors, whether or not they are CPAs, will also be required to follow GAAS if GAAS is prescribed by law or policy for the audits they conduct.

---

[1] American Institute of Certified Public Accountants, Audit and Accounting Guide, *State and Local Governments* (New York: AICPA, 2005), par. 4.63.

ILLUSTRATION 11–1   Generally Accepted Auditing Standards (GAAS)—AICPA

General Standards

1. The audit is to be performed by a person or persons having adequate technical training and proficiency as an auditor.
2. In all matters relating to the assignment, an independence in mental attitude is to be maintained by the auditor or auditors.
3. Due professional care is to be exercised in the performance of the audit and the preparation of the report.

Standards of Field Work

1. The work is to be adequately planned and assistants, if any, are to be properly supervised.
2. A sufficient understanding of internal control is to be obtained to plan the audit and to determine the nature, timing, and extent of tests to be performed.
3. Sufficient competent evidential matter is to be obtained through inspection, observation, inquiries, and confirmations to afford a reasonable basis for an opinion regarding the financial statements under audit.

Standards of Reporting

1. The report shall state whether the financial statements are presented in accordance with generally accepted accounting principles (GAAP).
2. The report shall identify those circumstances in which such principles have not been consistently observed in the current period in relation to the preceding period.
3. Informative disclosures in the financial statements are to be regarded as reasonably adequate unless otherwise stated in the report.
4. The report shall contain either an expression of opinion regarding the financial statements, taken as a whole, or an assertion to the effect that an opinion cannot be expressed. When an overall opinion cannot be expressed, the reasons therefore should be stated. In all cases where an auditor's name is associated with financial statements, the report should contain a clear-cut indication of the character of the auditor's work, if any, and the degree of responsibility the auditor is taking.

Source: AICPA, *Professional Standards,* 2005 AU 150.02.

GAAS have been summarized by the AICPA in the three general standards, three standards of field work, and four standards of reporting shown in Illustration 11–1. These 10 standards are amplified by numerous *Statements on Auditing Standards* published in codified form in the AICPA's *Professional Standards*. Failure to follow GAAS can result in severe sanctions, including, in some instances, loss of the auditor's license to practice as a CPA and expulsion from the AICPA. It is the auditor's duty to adhere to auditing standards, and it is his or her technical qualifications and independence from the entity being audited that add credibility to reported financial information and increase financial statement users' confidence in the information.[2]

In addition to the obligation to follow GAAS, auditors may be engaged to perform an audit that requires they follow generally accepted government auditing standards (GAGAS). Audits conducted under GAGAS are discussed later in this chapter.

Types of Audit Reports

Illustration 11–2 shows the standard audit report wording for an unqualified audit opinion on the basic financial statements of a state or local government that reports under the *GASBS 34* reporting model. The first paragraph of the auditor's report is

[2] The *Public Company Accounting Reform and Investor Protection Act* (the Sarbanes-Oxley Act of 2002, H.R. 3763, July 25, 2002) creates a federal oversight board with the authority to set and enforce generally accepted auditing standards for auditors of public companies.

ILLUSTRATION 11–2 Unqualified Opinions on Basic Financial Statements Accompanied by Required Supplementary Information and Supplementary Information

---

Independent Auditor's Report

We have audited the accompanying financial statements of the governmental activities, the business-type activities, the aggregate discretely presented component units, each major fund, and the aggregate remaining fund information of the City of Example, Any State, as of and for the year ended June 30, 20X1, which collectively comprise the City's basic financial statements as listed in the table of contents. These financial statements are the responsibility of the City of Example's management. Our responsibility is to express opinions on these financial statements based on our audit.

We conducted our audit in accordance with auditing standards generally accepted in the United States of America. Those standards require that we plan and perform the audit to obtain reasonable assurance about whether the financial statements are free of material misstatement. An audit includes examining, on a test basis, evidence supporting the amounts and disclosures in the financial statements. An audit also includes assessing the accounting principles used and significant estimates made by management, as well as evaluating the overall financial statement presentation. We believe that our audit provides a reasonable basis for our opinions.

In our opinion, the financial statements referred to above present fairly, in all material respects, the respective financial position of the governmental activities, the business-type activities, the aggregate discretely presented component units, each major fund, and the aggregate remaining fund information of the City of Example, Any State, as of June 30, 20X1, and the respective changes in financial position and, where applicable, cash flows thereof for the year then ended in conformity with accounting principles generally accepted in the United States of America.*

The [*identify accompanying required supplementary information, such as management's discussion and analysis and budgetary comparison information*] on pages XX through XX and XX through XX are not a required part of the basic financial statements but are supplementary information required by accounting principles generally accepted in the United States of America. We have applied certain limited procedures, which consisted principally of inquiries of management regarding the methods of measurement and presentation of the required supplementary information. However, we did not audit the information and express no opinion on it.

Our audit was conducted for the purpose of forming opinions on the financial statements that collectively comprise the City of Example's basic financial statements. The [*identify accompanying supplementary information, such as the introductory section, combining and individual nonmajor fund financial statements, and statistical section*] are presented for purposes of additional analysis and are not a required part of the basic financial statements. The [*identify relevant supplementary information, such as the combining and individual nonmajor fund financial statements*] have been subjected to the auditing procedures applied in the audit of the basic financial statements and, in our opinion, are fairly stated in all material respects in relation to the basic financial statements taken as a whole. The [*identify relevant supplementary information, such as the introductory section and statistical sections*] have not been subjected to the auditing procedures applied in the audit of the basic financial statements and, accordingly, we express no opinion on them.

[*Signature*]
[*Date*]

---

*If a government presents required budgetary comparison information as basic financial statements instead of as required supplementary information, the opinion paragraph would be replaced with the following: "In our opinion, the financial statements referred to above present fairly, in all material respects, the respective financial position of the governmental activities, the business-type activities, the aggregate discretely presented component units, each major fund, and the aggregate remaining fund information of the City of Example, Any State, as of June 30, 20X1, and the respective changes in financial position and cash flows, where applicable, thereof and the respective budgetary comparison for the [indicate the major governmental funds involved] for the year then ended in conformity with accounting principles generally accepted in the United States of America."

Source: American Institute of Certified Public Accountants, Audit and Accounting Guide, *State and Local Governments* (New York: AICPA, 2005), App. 14A, Example A-1.

called the opening or introductory paragraph. In the first sentence of that paragraph, the auditor specifies the financial statements on which the opinion is being expressed. GASB standards (*Codification,* Sections 1200.112 and 2200.102) state that *basic financial statements* must be presented for conformity with generally accepted accounting principles (GAAP). The comprehensive annual financial report (CAFR) should include the basic financial statements as well as required supplementary information (such as the MD&A and budgetary comparison information), combining statements for nonmajor funds and nonmajor discretely presented component units, and individual fund statements and schedules (GASB, *Codification,* 2200.105). However, note that in the auditor's report shown in Illustration 11–2, the auditor accepts responsibility for auditing only the basic financial statements, not the additional information. This is also clear from the first sentence of the fourth and fifth paragraphs of the auditor's report. The auditor does apply certain limited procedures to the supplementary information and may state that they are fair "in relation to" the basic financial statements, but this is not the same as expressing an opinion on them. If the government officials desire an audit report on combining statements, that fact should be made explicit in the written engagement letter before the start of the audit so the auditor can modify the scope of the examination appropriately. The opening paragraph also states that the statements are the responsibility of management.

The first sentence of the second or *scope paragraph* of the auditor's report (Illustration 11–2) states that the examination was made "in accordance with auditing standards generally accepted in the United States of America." That phrase has a definite meaning to professional auditors—a meaning they have been trying for many years to communicate to clients, bankers, judges, legislators, and every other group with a need to understand what an auditor's report means.

The scope paragraph also includes a statement that GAAS require that the auditor plan and perform the audit to obtain reasonable assurance about whether the financial statements are free of material misstatement. In addition, the scope paragraph includes a statement that an audit includes (1) examining, on a test basis, evidence supporting the amounts and disclosures in the financial statements, (2) assessing the accounting principles used and significant estimates made by management, and (3) evaluating the overall financial statement presentation. Finally, the scope paragraph includes a statement that the auditor believes that the audit provides a reasonable basis for the opinion rendered.[3]

The third paragraph of the auditor's report (Illustration 11–2) is referred to as the *opinion paragraph.* In that paragraph, the financial statements on which the auditor is expressing an opinion are identified as presenting fairly, in conformity with accounting principles generally accepted in the United States of America, the financial position of the governmental activities, the business-type activities, the aggregate discretely presented component units, each major fund, and the aggregate remaining fund information of the City of Example, Any State, as of June 30, 20X1, and the respective changes in financial position and, where applicable, cash flows.

The fourth and fifth paragraphs, known as the *explanatory paragraphs,* explain (1) that supplemental information is not part of the basic financial statements, (2) whether the auditors applied auditing procedures or certain limited procedures to that information, and (3) whether the auditors express an opinion on that information. Auditors may apply auditing procedures to combining and individual nonmajor fund financial statements and, if engaged to do so, express an opinion as to the fairness of that information. They may also apply certain limited procedures to information required by the GASB, such as the MD&A and budgetary comparison information, but since such information is not audited, no opinion is offered on that information. Other supplementary information in a CAFR, such as the introductory section and statistical section, are not subjected to auditing procedures and, accordingly, do not have an opinion expressed on them.

Types of Opinions

If the auditor determines that the financial statements contain a departure from GAAP, the effect of which is material, or there has been a material change between periods in accounting principles, or in the method of their application, the auditor may not express

[3] American Institute of Certified Public Accountants, Inc., *Professional Standards,* AU 508.08 (New York: AICPA, 2005).

ILLUSTRATION 11–3 **Report on Basic Financial Statements That Includes a Qualified Opinion on Major Governmental Funds Because of a GAAP Departure***

Independent Auditor's Report

[Same first and second paragraphs as in Illustration 11–2.]

Management has not adopted a methodology for reviewing the collectibility of taxes receivable in the [*indicate the affected major governmental funds*] and, accordingly, has not considered the need to provide an allowance for uncollectible amounts. Accounting principles generally accepted in the United States of America require that an adequate allowance be provided for uncollectible receivables, which would decrease the assets and fund balances, and change the revenues in the [*indicate the affected major governmental funds*]. The amount by which this departure would affect the assets, fund balances and revenues of the [*indicate the affected funds*] is not reasonably determinable.**†

In our opinion, except for the effects of not providing an adequate allowance for uncollectible taxes receivable for the [*indicate the affected major governmental funds*] as described in the preceding paragraph, the financial statements referred to above present fairly, in all material respects, the respective financial position of the [*indicate the affected major governmental funds*] of the City of Example, Any State, as of June 30, 20X1, and the respective changes in financial position thereof for the year then ended in conformity with accounting principles generally accepted in the United States of America.

In addition, in our opinion, the financial statements referred to above present fairly, in all material respects, the respective financial position of the governmental activities, the business-type activities, the aggregate discretely presented component units, [*indicate the major funds not affected by the qualification*], and the aggregate remaining fund information of the City of Example, Any State, as of June 30, 20X1, and the respective changes in financial position and where applicable, cash flows thereof for the year then ended in conformity with accounting principles generally accepted in the United States of America.

[Signature]
[Date]

---

*Paragraph A-l (of Appendix A-l of the Audit and Accounting Guide *State and Local Governments*) describes conditions that may make modifications to this report necessary, such as when the financial statements include information from a prior period or when the auditor is reporting on RSI (required supplementary information) or SI (supplementary information).

**Depending on the nature and magnitude of the GAAP departure, it is possible that the auditor's opinion on the governmental activities also would be qualified, as illustrated in Example A-10 (of Appendix A-l of the Audit and Accounting Guide *State and Local Governments*). Further, the same GAAP departure in the nonmajor governmental funds could affect the auditor's opinion on the aggregate remaining fund information. This example assumes that the auditor has concluded that the GAAP departure is not material to the governmental activities opinion unit or to the aggregate remaining fund information opinion unit. Another auditor could make a different professional judgment. (See paragraphs 14.07 and 14.08 of the Audit and Accounting Guide *State and Local Governments*). If a GAAP departure is material to more than one opinion unit, the explanatory paragraph should explain the nature and effect of the departure on each affected opinion unit.

†If a government presents budgetary comparison information as basic financial statements instead of as required supplementary information, the explanatory paragraph also should explain the effect of the GAAP departure on the budgetary comparison information. This example assumes that the government budgets on a cash basis, and thus the GAAP departure would not affect the budgetary comparison information if it were presented as a basic financial statement.

Source: American Institute of Certified Public Accountants, Audit and Accounting Guide, *State and Local Governments* (New York: AICPA, 2005), App. 14A, Ex. A-5.

---

an *unqualified opinion.* One example that precludes an unqualified opinion is a stand-alone consolidated report that some governments have issued on an experimental basis. If an audit opinion is to be rendered on such a report, it must be an *adverse opinion* stating the report does not present fairly in conformity with GAAP.[4] It is also possible that the auditor cannot express an unqualified opinion because the scope of the examination was affected by conditions that precluded the application of one or more auditing procedures the auditor considered necessary in the circumstances. If it is not appropriate for the auditor to express an unqualified opinion, the auditor should consult relevant authoritative pronouncements to determine whether a *qualified opinion* (see Illustration 11–3)

[4] Because consolidated reports are based on different accounting principles than are used for basic financial statements, the auditor must render an adverse opinion. Auditors may, however, issue a restrictively worded report that certain summary information of the type published by some governments in "popular reports" is fairly presented in relation to the basic financial statements from which it has been derived. The auditor must have audited the basic financial statements and must refer to that audit in the "in relation to" report on the summary information. Source: American Institute of Certified Public Accountants, Audit and Accounting Guide, *State and Local Governments* (New York: AICPA, 2005), par. 14.71.

ILLUSTRATION 11–4   GAAP Hierarchy Summary

	Nongovernmental Entities	State and Local Governments	Federal Governmental Entities
	Established Accounting Principles		
Category (a)	FASB Statements and Interpretations, APB Opinions, and AICPA Accounting Research Bulletins	GASB Statements and Interpretations, plus AICPA and FASB pronouncements if made applicable to state and local governments by a GASB Statement or Interpretation	FASAB Statements and Interpretations, plus AICPA and FASB pronouncements if made applicable to federal governmental entities by a FASAB Statement or Interpretation
Category (b)	FASB Technical Bulletins, AICPA Industry Audit and Accounting Guides, and AICPA Statements of Position, if cleared by the FASB	GASB Technical Bulletins, and the following pronouncements if specifically made applicable to state and local governments by the AICPA (and cleared by the GASB): AICPA Industry Audit and Accounting Guides and AICPA Statements of Position	FASAB Technical Bulletins and the following pronouncements if made applicable to federal governmental entities by the AICPA and cleared by the FASAB: AICPA Industry Audit and Accounting Guides and AICPA Statements of Position
Category (c)	Consensus positions of the FASB Emerging Issues Task Force and AICPA Practice Bulletins	Consensus positions of the GASB Emerging Issues Task Force* and AICPA Practice Bulletins if specifically made applicable to state and local governments by the AICPA (and cleared by the GASB)	AICPA AcSEC Practice Bulletins if specifically made applicable to federal governmental entities and cleared by the FASAB as well as Technical Releases of the Accounting and Auditing Policy Committee of the FASAB
Category (d)	AICPA accounting interpretations, "Qs and As" published by the FASB staff, as well as industry practices widely recognized and prevalent	Implementation guides ("Qs and As") published by the GASB staff, as well as industry practices widely recognized and prevalent	Implementation guides published by the FASAB staff, as well as practices that are widely recognized and prevalent in the federal government
	Other accounting literature (not detailed here)		

*As of the date of this section, the GASB had not organized such a group.

Source: American Institute of Certified Public Accountants, *Statement on Auditing Standards No. 91, An Amendment to Statement on Auditing Standards No. 69, The Meaning of Present Fairly in Conformity with Generally Accepted Accounting Principles in the Independent Auditor's Report,* vol. 1, AU sec. 411 (New York: AICPA, 2005).

should be issued, or whether an opinion should be *disclaimed.* Expanded discussion of the nature of each of these types of opinions and the conditions that would warrant the use of each is beyond the scope of this text. Interested readers are referred to current collegiate auditing texts and to the pronouncements of the AICPA.[5]

To determine what is GAAP for various entities, the auditor must first identify the sources of literature describing accounting principles for the type of entity being audited and then assess the weight of authority to give different pronouncements and writings. The AICPA provides guidance in this process through the **GAAP hierarchy** shown in Illustration 11–4. This chart ranks four categories of literature for each of three types of entities: nongovernmental (i.e., businesses or not-for-profit organizations), state or local government, or federal government.

[5] A convenient source of information on currently effective pronouncements is a publication of the American Institute of Certified Public Accountants: *AICPA Professional Standards.*

Before any audit work is done, there should be a clear understanding of the scope of each engagement by all interested parties. A written memorandum of the engagement, or **engagement letter,** specifying the scope of the work to be done should be prepared in advance and copies retained by both the auditor and auditee. A written record of the agreement is essential for the protection of both parties. The need for specific, written memorandums of the scope of engagements was forcefully pointed out to independent public accountants by a number of well-known liability cases.

Governments often engage more than one audit firm to conduct annual audits. Some component units such as airports, hospitals, and utilities may have their own governing boards and select their own auditor, yet meet the criteria discussed in Chapters 2 and 9 for inclusion in the governmental reporting entity. The principal auditor for the primary government must in this case decide whether to make reference to the other auditor in his or her audit report or to assume responsibility for the work performed by the other auditor without reference in the audit report. If reference is made to the other auditor, the principal auditor's report should disclose the magnitude of the portion of the financial statements audited by the other auditor. An audit report making reference to another auditor is not a qualified report unless some other reason exists for qualification.

Auditing procedures deemed particularly applicable to audits of state and local governments by independent CPAs are published in the AICPA Audit and Accounting Guide, *State and Local Governments*. The audit guide and other authoritative auditing literature provide guidance to all auditors, not just independent CPAs, whose function it is to examine financial statements, and the underlying records, for the purpose of determining whether the statements present fairly the financial position as of a certain date, changes in financial position, and cash flows for a fiscal period, in conformity with generally accepted accounting principles.

The audit guide emphasizes the importance of testing for compliance with laws and regulations that may have a material effect on the determination of financial statement amounts. The guide notes that the auditor is required to design the audit to provide reasonable assurance that the financial statements are free of material misstatement resulting from violations of laws and regulations, error, or fraud.[6]

Materiality

Determining the potential for misstatements on the financial statements to adversely impact a user's evaluation of the entity's financial condition is an important part of the auditing process. Auditors refer to **materiality** to indicate, in their judgment, the level at which the quantitative or qualitative effects of misstatements will have a significant impact on user's evaluations. The AICPA's Audit and Accounting Guide, *State and Local Governments* provides important guidance for auditors in determining materiality for *GASBS 34* financial statements. The guide requires auditors to make separate materiality determinations for each opinion unit. **Opinion units** in the *GASBS 34* reporting model are (1) governmental activities, (2) business-type activities, (3) aggregate discretely presented component units, (4) each major governmental and enterprise fund, and (5) the aggregate remaining fund information (nonmajor governmental and enterprise funds, the internal service fund type, and the fiduciary fund types). The auditor's report, then, will contain an opinion regarding each opinion unit or assertions

---

[6] American Institute of Certified Public Accountants, Audit and Accounting Guide, *State and Local Governments* (New York: AICPA, 2005), pars. 4.39–4.48.

to the effect that an opinion on one or more opinion units cannot be expressed. Specific guidance for evaluating materiality is in Chapter 14 of the Audit and Accounting Guide (pars. 14.04–14.11).

Required Supplementary Information

Auditors render an opinion on the fairness of the basic financial statements and, if engaged to do so, on the combining and individual fund presentations. Required supplementary information (RSI), such as the MD&A and budgetary comparison schedules, are outside the scope of the financial statement audit. Auditors apply certain limited procedures in connection with RSI to provide assurance that they are fairly presented *in relation to* the basic financial statements. These procedures include inquiries about the methods used to prepare RSI and comparison of RSI to information in the audited financial statements. The auditor may also perform a limited review of the Introductory and Statistical sections of a Comprehensive Annual Financial Report (CAFR) and other supplementary information, although the level of responsibility for this material is much less than for RSI.[7] As part of its conceptual framework project, the GASB issued Concepts Statement No. 3, *Communication Methods in General Purpose External Financial Reports That Contain Basic Financial Statements.*[8] This statement discusses factors to consider in determining whether information should be "displayed" on the face of the financial statements, "disclosed" in the notes to the statements, or considered RSI or "supplementary information (SI)." The statement is primarily a tool for standards setters; however, preparers and auditors will find it useful in understanding the conceptual framework on which generally accepted accounting principles are built.

GOVERNMENT AUDITING STANDARDS

Audit standards that are to be followed by auditors of federal organizations, programs, activities, functions are much broader in scope than the audit standards discussed in the first section of this chapter. The Government Accountability Office (formerly the General Accounting Office) under the direction of the Comptroller General of the United States has developed government auditing standards. **Generally accepted government auditing standards (GAGAS)** are set forth and explained in the publication *Government Auditing Standards;* because of the color of its cover, the document is generally referred to as the *yellow book.* Generally accepted auditing standards (GAAS), shown in Illustration 11–1, are used as a basis for governmental auditing standards. Reasons that the standards established by the AICPA were deemed to be too narrow in

[7] See John H. Engstrom and Donald E. Tidrick, "Audit Issues Related to GASB Statement No. 34," *Public Budgeting and Finance,* Fall 2001, pp. 63–78 for a discussion of auditor's responsibilities for required supplementary information and other supplementary information, as well as American Institute of Certified Public Accountants, Audit and Accounting Guide, *State and Local Governments,* 2005, pars. 14.49–14.56.

[8] Government Accounting Standards Board. Concepts Statement No. 3., *Communication Methods in General Purpose External Financial Reports That Contain Basic Financial Statements.* (Norwalk, CT: GASB, April 2005).

scope for audits of recipients of public funds are expressed in the introduction of the yellow book:

> The concept of accountability for public resources is key in our nation's governing processes. Legislators, other government officials, and the public want to know whether (1) government resources are managed properly and used in compliance with laws and regulations, (2) government programs are achieving their objectives and desired outcomes, and (3) government services are being provided efficiently, economically, and effectively. Managers of these programs are accountable to legislative bodies and the public. Auditors of these programs, when they adhere to GAGAS, provide reports that enhance the credibility and reliability of the information that is reported by or obtained from officials of the audited entity.[9]

The first edition (1972) of the yellow book presented a single set of auditing standards that were similar to the AICPA statement of generally accepted auditing standards. Subsequent revisions of the yellow book in 1981, 1994, 1999, and 2003 developed a progressively broader set of standards, reflecting the need to provide standards for performance audits and attestation engagements in addition to financial audits. The broader standards also reflect the unique auditing and operating environments of government and not-for-profit organizations. Government auditing standards now differ so much from GAAS that the term *generally accepted government auditing standards* (GAGAS) is typically used to distinguish the yellow book standards from GAAS.[10]

Types of Audits and Engagements

The yellow book describes audits and engagements that cover a broad range of financial or nonfinancial objectives. The GAGAS framework includes three types of government audits and services: financial audits, attestation engagements, and performance audits. Illustration 11–5 lists the objectives and characteristics of these auditor services. Performance audits are often performed by internal auditors or state audit agencies. An engagement letter between the auditor and the organization should clearly specify what type of audit is to be performed and which auditing standards will be followed.

Financial audits are all audits covered under GAAS, such as financial statement audits, special reports (e.g., SAS 99 fraud reports), reviews of interim financial information, letters to underwriters, compliance audits, and service organization audits. In financial audits, the auditors express an opinion on the fairness of an entity's financial statements as well as whether the statements conform to GAAP. **Attestation engagements** include services related to providing various levels of assurance on other financial or nonfinancial matters, such as internal control, compliance, MD&A presentation, allowability and reasonableness of proposed contract amounts, final contract costs, and reliability of performance measures. **Performance audits** or operational audits are independent assessments of the performance and the management of the entity, program, service, or activity against objective criteria. Objectives include assessing effectiveness and results, economy and efficiency, and internal controls and compliance with laws and regulations.

---

[9] Comptroller General of the United States, *Government Auditing Standards, 2003 Revision* (Washington, DC: U.S. General Accounting Office, 2003, par. 1.11).

[10] Another acronym often used to denote government auditing standards is GAS, which is the abbreviation for the publication *Government Auditing Standards.* These terms are used interchangeably; however, the term GAGAS is used in this text.

ILLUSTRATION 11–5   **Types of Governmental Audits and Other Engagements**

Financial Audits

- Provide an independent report on whether an entity's financial information is presented fairly in accordance with recognized criteria.
- Inform users whether they can rely on that information.
- When performed in accordance with GAGAS, also provide information about internal control and compliance with laws and regulations as they relate to financial transactions, systems, and processes.

Attestation Engagements

- Examinations, reviews, or an agreed-upon procedures report on the subject matter or on an assertion about the subject matter that is the responsibility of another party.
- Can cover a broad range of financial or nonfinancial objectives.
- Provide various levels of assurance about the subject matter or assertion dependent upon the user's needs.

Performance Audits

- Provide an independent assessment of the performance and management of government programs against objective criteria or an assessment of best practices and other information.
- Provide information to improve program operations and facilitate decision making by parties with responsibility to oversee or initiate corrective action and improve public accountability.
- Include work sometimes classified as program evaluations, program effectiveness and results audits, economy and efficiency audits, operational audits, and value-for-money audits.

Source: *Government Auditing Standards* (Washington, DC: GAO, 2003), pars. 1.12.–1.14.

As indicated by Illustration 11–6, GAGAS expands on standards issued by the AICPA through GAAS and statements of standards for attestation engagements (SSAE), and addresses performance audits. Differences between GAAS and GAGAS exist even in standards addressing the same concept. For example, competence, addressed in the first general standard in GAAS, is "the audit is to be performed by a person or persons having adequate technical training and proficiency as an auditor."[11] However, the third general standard in GAGAS is "the staff assigned to perform the audit or attestation engagement should collectively possess adequate professional competence for the tasks required."[12]

This language from the yellow book places responsibility on audit organizations to ensure that assignments are performed by staff that collectively have the knowledge, skills, and experience for the assignment; see GAGAS (par. 3.42). A specific GAGAS requirement to ensure that auditors conducting audits under GAGAS maintain their professional competence is that each auditor should complete every two years at least 80 hours of continuing professional education that directly contribute to the auditor's professional proficiency to perform such work (par. 3.45). At least 20 of these hours should be completed in each year of the two-year period. A technical amendment to the CPE requirements in 2005 includes partial exemptions for auditors who are only involved in performing field work, expanding the list of topics that satisfy the requirements, and clarifying that CPE programs should have learning objectives.[13]

[11] AICPA, *Professional Standards,* Vol. 1, Sec. AU 210.01.

[12] *Government Auditing Standards,* par. 3.39.

[13] Government Accountability Office, *Government Auditing Standards: Guidance on GAGAS Requirements for Continuing Professional Education* (GAO-05-568G, April 2005).

ILLUSTRATION 11–6 A Comparison of Standards and Services by Issuer (AICPA or GAO)

	Financial Audits		Attestation Engage-ments		Performance Audits	
	GAAS	GAGAS	GAAS	GAGAS	GAAS*	GAGAS
GENERAL STANDARDS	3	4	5	5	0	4
FIELD WORK STANDARDS	3	7	2	7	0	4
REPORTING STANDARDS	4	11	4	9	0	4
Totals	10	22	11	21	0	12

*Note: Although the AICPA does not have standards for performance audits *per se,* it does have standards for consulting services; see AICPA, *Professional Standards* Vol. 2, Sec. CS .01–.10.

To further ensure the quality of government audits, the fourth general standard in GAGAS requires each audit organization to have an "appropriate internal quality control system" and undergo an external peer review at least once every three years by an audit organization independent of the audit organization being reviewed.[14]

The field work standards for financial audits contained in GAGAS emphasize the importance of audit follow-up on prior audit findings; detection and reporting of irregularities, illegal acts, and other instances of noncompliance with laws and regulations; and understanding and testing of internal controls. Six of the GAGAS field work standards are also required by GAAS, either by the three field work standards listed in Illustration 11–1 or by various *Statements on Auditing Standards.*

Similarly, GAGAS reporting standards for financial audits incorporate the four GAAS reporting standards shown in Illustration 11–1. Additional reporting standards cover reporting on compliance, required communications, internal controls, report distribution, and irregularities and illegal acts. The yellow book permits auditors to exclude reporting certain *privileged and confidential information;* eliminates the requirement for written reports, allows oral comments to be equally acceptable as written comments; and recognizes the timeliness standard as an element of report quality.

The GAGAS field work and reporting standards for performance audits are unique in that the objective of performance audits is to provide evidence to assess performance of a governmental organization, program, activity, or function rather than to render a professional opinion. Thus, testing for compliance with laws and regulations, although of critical importance in a financial audit, may be relatively less so if the

[14] Ibid., pars. 3.49–3.53.

audit objective in a performance audit is to assess the efficiency and effectiveness of a program and there are no laws and regulations that would have a material effect on the program.

Independence Standards

The Government Accountability Office (GAO) amended the yellow book independence standards in 2002. This action may appear to be a response to high-profile business failures and congressional review of auditing and accounting standards-setting, but, in fact, the GAO independence standard had been in exposure draft form for quite some time before its issuance in final form. The demand for quality audits was greater than ever, and independence, the cornerstone of the auditing profession, is one of the strongest determinants of audit quality. The second general standard in both the AICPA and GAO auditing standards is:

> GAAS, AICPA: "In all matters relating to the assignment, an independence in mental attitude is to be maintained by the auditor or auditors."[15]
> GAGAS, GAO: "In all matters relating to the audit work, the audit organization and the individual auditor, whether government or public, should be free both in fact and appearance from personal, external, and organizational impairments to independence."[16]

The GAO substantially changed the independence standard to ensure that the highest degree of integrity and objectivity is maintained by any auditor (CPA, non-CPA, government financial auditor, and performance auditor) performing audits of federal, state, and local governments and not-for-profit entities that receive federal financial assistance so that the public is best served. The standard primarily addresses independence issues when nonaudit work is performed for audited entities. **Nonaudit work** is that solely for the benefit of the entity requesting the work and does not provide for a basis for conclusions, recommendations, or opinions as would a financial audit, attestation engagement, or performance audit.

The GAO independence standard uses an engagement-team focus, as does the AICPA in its Code of Professional Conduct, but also articulates a principles-based approach with two overarching principles supplemented by seven safeguards. The principles follow:

1. Auditors should not perform management functions or make management decisions.

2. Auditors should not audit their own work or provide nonaudit services in situations where the nonaudit services are significant to the audit subject matter.

In general, providing routine advice or methodologies to assist management is normal, so no safeguards need to be in place. Examples of routine services are participating on committees in an advisory capacity; providing advice on establishing internal controls; answering technical questions and providing training; and providing tools, such as best practices guides, benchmarking studies, and internal control assessment methodologies that are then used by management. Certain nonaudit services are prohibited, such as maintaining the basic accounting records, posting transactions to the entity's financial records, recommending a single individual for a specific position, conducting an executive search, operating or supervising the information technology system, and preparing the indirect cost proposal when the costs to be recovered exceed $1 million.[17]

---

[15] American Institute of Certified Public Accountants, Inc., *Professional Standards,* AU 220.01 (New York: AICPA, 2004).

[16] General Accounting Office, *Government Auditing Standards* (Washington, DC: GAO, 2003), par. 3.03.

[17] Office of Management and Budget, Circular A–133, Section 305(b).

Nonaudit services are permitted if *all* of the following safeguards are in place:

1. Preclude nonaudit personnel from planning, conducting, or reviewing the audit work related to the nonaudit service.

2. Do not reduce the scope and extent of the audit work beyond the level that would be appropriate if the nonaudit work were performed by another unrelated party.

3. Document consideration of the nonaudit service and rationale that providing the nonaudit service does not violate the two overarching principles.

4. Establish and document an understanding with the audited entity regarding the objectives, scope of work, and product of the nonaudit service and management's responsibility for the substantive outcomes of the work before the work is begun.

5. Include policies and procedures in the auditor's quality control system to ensure compliance with the independence requirements including management's written understanding and compliance with its specific responsibilities.

6. Avoid nonaudit services that by their nature impair independence (e.g., operating the auditee's accounting system) and communicate to the management of the audited entity that this work would impair the auditor's independence in performing subsequent audit work.

7. Make all nonaudit services documentation related to an audit available for peer review.

Examples of permitted nonaudit services with appropriate safeguards are preparing draft financial statements based on management's trial balance, preparing draft notes to the financial statements based on information provided by management, maintaining depreciation schedules for which management has determined the key elements in the calculations, proposing adjusting and correcting entries that management accepts, providing limited payroll services, preparing routine tax filings, assisting management in evaluating potential candidates for employment, providing limited advice on information technology, and reviewing the work of a specialist who has provided appraisals or valuation services. Long-standing practice is that auditors should not serve on governing boards, make policy decisions, or supervise or maintain custody of an entity's assets.

Guidance from the GAO in the form of 92 questions and answers provides that auditors should consider "substance over form" in the nature and significance of the nonaudit services provided to an audit entity and avoid those engagements where reasonable, well-informed people would conclude that that auditor is not independent.[18]

SINGLE AUDITS

Federal grants-in-aid to state and local governments grew from $2.2 billion in 1950 to $385.7 billion in 2003. Although grants-in-aid originate from more than 1,000 different programs administered by more than 50 federal departments and agencies, about 91 percent of the grants-in-aid in 2003 were made by five departments: the Department of Health and Human Services (57.3 percent), Department of Transportation (10.1 percent), Department of Housing and Urban Development (10.2 percent), Department of Agriculture (5.7 percent), and the Department of Education (7.6 percent).[19]

[18] GAO-02-870G. Available at http://www.gao.gov/govaud/d02870g.pdf.

[19] U.S. Census Bureau, U.S. Dept. of Commerce, "Federal Aid to States for Fiscal Year 2003," September 2004, www.census.gov/prod/2004pubs/03fas.pdf, Figure 2.

History of the Single Audit

Until the mid-1980s each federal agency established accounting, reporting, and auditing requirements for each program it administered, and these requirements differed from agency to agency. Furthermore, each agency had the right to make on-site audits of grant funds and often did so. Since even a relatively small local governments might have several dozen active federal grants (each with different accounting, reporting, and auditing requirements), the amount of time spent keeping track of conflicting requirements and providing facilities for a succession of different groups of auditors became extremely burdensome. Efforts were made in the 1960s to standardize grant accounting, reporting, and auditing requirements but with only modest success. In 1979, the Office of Management and Budget (OMB) issued Attachment P, *Audit Requirements,* OMB Circular A–102, *Uniform Administrative Requirements for Grants-in-Aid to State and Local Governments,* to ensure that audits were made on an organizationwide basis, rather than on a grant-by-grant basis. This concept is called the **single audit**.

Experience with Attachment P led to the enactment of the Single Audit Act of 1984. The purposes of the act were to

(1)   Improve the financial management of state and local governments with respect to federal financial assistance programs,

(2)   Establish uniform requirements for audits of federal financial assistance provided to state and local governments,

(3)   Promote the efficient and effective use of audit resources, and

(4)   Ensure that federal departments and agencies, rely upon and use audit work done pursuant to the Single Audit Act.

In 1985, OMB issued Circular A–128, *Audits of State and Local Governments,* to provide administrative guidance to federal program managers, state and local government recipients of federal financial assistance, and auditors in implementing and complying with the Single Audit Act. Each state and local government that received federal financial assistance equal to or in excess of $100,000 in any of its fiscal years was required to have an audit for such fiscal year in accordance with the provisions of the Single Audit Act and OMB Circular A–128. The 1984 Act applied only to state and local governments, even though a large amount of federal assistance was also being provided to not-for-profit organizations, particularly institutions of higher education. In order to extend the benefits of the single audit to not-for-profit organizations, the OMB issued in 1990 Circular A–133, *Audits of Institutions of Higher Education and Other Nonprofit Institutions,* which administratively required single audits for institutions of higher education and other not-for-profit organizations.

Subsequent studies by the GAO found that the Single Audit Act of 1984 and OMB Circular A–133 had improved accountability over federal assistance, strengthened the financial management of state and local governments and not-for-profit organizations, and reduced the overall audit burden. However, thousands of single audits were being imposed on small entities that in aggregate represented only a small percentage of total federal assistance.

Single Audit Act Amendments of 1996

Recognizing the need to further improve the Single Audit Act, Congress passed the Single Audit Act Amendments of 1996 (P.L. 104–156). These amendments include one additional purpose: to reduce audit burdens on state and local governments, Indian tribes, and not-for-profit organizations.

The 1996 amendments also:

1. Raised the threshold for a single audit from $100,000 to $300,000.
2. Extended the statutory requirement for single audit coverage to not-for-profit organizations.
3. Established a risk-based approach for selecting programs for audit testing.
4. Improved the contents and timeliness of single audit reporting.
5. Increased administrative flexibility by giving OMB the authority to revise certain audit requirements periodically without seeking further amendments to the Single Audit Act.

The 1996 amendments essentially replaced the 1984 Act. A 1997 revision to Circular A–133, *Audits of States, Local Governments, and Non-Profit Organizations,* provides uniform guidance for administering and conducting all single audits and thus replaces OMB Circular A–128. The 2003 revision to OMB Circular A–133 raised the threshold for a single audit to $500,000 of federal funds expended.[20]

Who Must Have a Single Audit?

Illustration 11–7 provides a flowchart to determine whether an entity must have a single audit or other type of audit. As Illustration 11–7 shows, nonfederal entities that expend $500,000 or more in a year in federal awards must have a single audit or a **program-specific audit** for that year. The election of a program-specific audit applies when an auditee expends federal awards under only one program or a cluster of related programs, and the program's (cluster's) laws, regulations, or grant agreements do not require an entitywide financial statement audit. A program-specific audit is usually performed on the financial statements of the particular program and examines matters related to the program such as internal controls and compliance with pertinent laws, regulations, and agreements. In many cases a program-specific audit guide will be available to provide detailed audit guidance for conducting the program-specific audit.

Nonfederal entities that expend less than $500,000 of federal awards during the fiscal year generally are exempt from federal audit requirements for that year. Nonetheless, any federal awarding agency may conduct or arrange for additional audits it deems necessary. Such additional audits should be rare, should build upon work performed for other audits, and should be paid for by the federal agency conducting or requesting the audit. Some states have voluntarily adopted federal GAGAS and single audit requirements that may apply under state audit mandates, even if federal awards expended are less than $500,000 and no other federal audit requirement exists. In other states that do not mandate their own requirements for GAGAS audits or single audits, annual audits of local governments and not-for-profit organizations, when required, will be performed in conformity with AICPA GAAS, discussed earlier in this chapter.

Circular A–133 defines a *nonfederal entity* as a state or local government, or nonprofit organization. *Federal awards* are defined as:

> Federal financial assistance [defined by OMB as grants, loans, loan guarantees, property, cooperative agreements, interest subsidies, insurance, food commodities, direct appropriations, and other assistance] and federal cost-reimbursement contracts that nonfederal entities receive directly from federal awarding agencies or indirectly from pass-through entities. It does not include procurement contracts, under grants or

---

[20] The OMB revises its *Compliance Supplement* regularly (e.g., March 2004). See http://www.whitehouse.gov/OMB/circulars).

ILLUSTRATION 11–7 **Determining Applicability of the Single Audit**

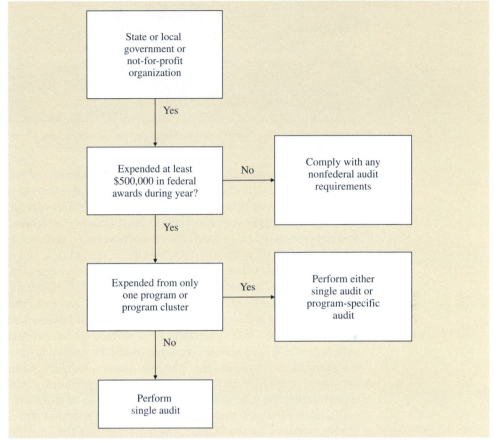

contracts, used to buy goods or services from vendors. Any audits of such vendors shall be covered by the terms and conditions of the contract. Contracts to operate federal government owned, contractor operated facilities are excluded from the requirements of this part, as are payments for Medicare services provided.[21]

An important change made by the 1996 amendments is that the required audit threshold is now based on federal awards *expended* rather than *received,* as was previously the case. Unfortunately, calculating federal awards expended is not as straightforward as it might seem. The basic rule is that a federal award has been expended at the point in time when the awarding agency has become at risk and the nonfederal recipient has become accountable for how the award is being used. Risk exposure and a duty of accountability normally arise when activity occurs that requires the nonfederal entity to begin complying with laws, regulations, or contractual provisions relating to the award. Typical examples are expenditure/expense transactions (such as incurring labor costs, purchasing or using supplies, and paying utility bills) associated with grants, cost-reimbursement contracts, cooperative agreements, and direct appropriations; disbursement of funds by a pass-through entity to a subrecipient; the receipt of property; the receipt or use of program income (such as

---

[21] Office of Management and Budget, OMB Circular No. A–133, *Audits of States, Local Governments, and Non-Profit Organizations* (Washington, DC: OMB, 2003), § _____ .105.

ILLUSTRATION 11–8   Determining Federal Awards Expended for a Hypothetical Direct Loan Program

Loan Activity	Amounts	Highest Balance
Balance, beginning of year	$400,000	
New loans during year	150,000	
		$520,000*
Loans repaid during year	(100,000)	
Balance, end of year	$450,000	

*$520,000 is assumed to have been the highest loan balance outstanding at any point during the year. Because the federal government was at risk at one point during the year for $520,000, that is the amount of federal awards deemed to have been expended.

charges to program beneficiaries for services rendered and rental from program facilities); and the distribution or consumption of food commodities. Amounts expended would normally be determined using the entity's basis of accounting. Thus, either an expenditure or expense may enter into the calculation of federal awards expended. Federal noncash assistance received such as free rent (if received by a nonfederal entity to carry out a federal program), food stamps, commodities, and donated property should be valued at fair value at the time of receipt or the assessed value provided by the awarding federal agency.

If federal awards involve loan, loan guarantee, and insurance programs, the federal award expended is the amount to which the federal government is at risk for the loans. Generally this will be the amount of loans made (or received) during the year, plus any loan balances from previous years for which the federal government imposes continuing compliance requirements, plus any interest subsidy, cash, or administrative cost allowance received.[22] To the extent that new and previously issued loans may have been repaid during the year, adjustments would need to be made. This is so because the federal awards expended under a loan or insurance program represent the highest amount of risk exposure for the federal government during the year. Thus, if the total loan balance varies during the year, the highest loan balance outstanding at any point during the year is the amount of federal awards expended.

Illustration 11–8 provides an example of how federal awards expended would be calculated for a hypothetical direct loan program administered by a local government or not-for-profit organization. Although neither the beginning nor ending loan balances exceed the $500,000 single audit threshold, it is assumed that at one point during the year, the loan balance reached $520,000. Because at that point in time the federal government was at risk for $520,000 and the nonfederal entity had compliance duties for the $520,000 in loans outstanding, federal awards are deemed to have been expended in the same amount. If this was the only federal program for which awards were received during the year, the entity may have the option of having a single audit or a program-specific audit.

What Does the Single Audit Require?

The 1996 amendments to the Single Audit Act of 1984 mandate the following audit requirements for the single audit:

1. An annual audit must be performed encompassing the nonfederal entity's financial statements and schedule of expenditures of federal awards.
2. The audit must be conducted by an independent auditor in accordance with generally accepted government auditing standards (GAGAS) and cover the operations of

[22] Ibid., § ____ . 205(b).

the entire nonfederal entity. Alternatively, a series of audits that cover departments, agencies, and other organizational units is permitted if the series of audits encompasses the financial statements and schedule of expenditures of federal awards for each such department, agency, or other organizational unit, which in aggregate are considered to be a nonfederal entity. *Independent auditor* means an external federal, state, or local auditor who meets the GAGAS independence standards or an independent public accountant.

3. The auditor must determine whether the financial statements are presented fairly in all material respects with GAAP and whether the schedule of federal financial awards is presented fairly in relation to the financial statements taken as a whole.

4. For each major program, the auditor must obtain an understanding of the internal controls pertaining to the compliance requirements for the program, assess control risk and perform tests of controls, unless the controls are deemed to be ineffective. (*Note:* OMB Circular A–133 requires the auditor to obtain an understanding of and conduct testing of internal controls to support a low assessed level of control risk; that is, as if high reliance will be placed on the internal controls.) In addition, for each major program the auditor shall determine whether the nonfederal entity has complied with laws, regulations, and contract or grant provisions pertaining to federal awards of the program. Auditors test compliance by determining if requirements listed for each program in the A–133 *Compliance Supplement* published by the OMB have been met. Auditors are required to use the *Compliance Supplement,* which details compliance auditing requirements for many federal programs, listed by *Catalog of Federal Domestic Assistance* (CFDA) title and number.

5. Circular A–133 assigns certain responsibilities to federal awarding agencies and nonfederal entities that act as "pass-through" agents in passing federal awards to subrecipient nonfederal entities.

Compliance Audits

As noted in item (4) above, Circular A–133 requires the auditor to express an opinion that the auditee complied with laws, regulations, and grant or contract provisions that could have a direct and material effect on each major program. To gather sufficient evidence to support his or her opinion in such **compliance audits,** the auditor tests whether each major program was administered in conformity with administrative requirements contained in OMB Circular A–102, *Uniform Administrative Requirements for Grants and Cooperative Agreements with State and Local Governments* or OMB Circular A–110, *Uniform Administrative Requirements for Grants and Other Agreements with Institutions of Higher Education, Hospitals, and Other Nonprofit Organizations,* as appropriate. The auditor also tests for compliance with the detailed *compliance* requirements for major programs provided in the A–133 *Compliance Supplement* or other guidance provided by federal awarding agencies. The *Compliance Supplement* identifies 14 generic compliance requirements, although not all the requirements apply to every major program. Moreover, there are additional compliance requirements specified for some programs. Generally, compliance requirements relate to matters such as allowed and unallowed activities; allowed and unallowed costs; eligibility of program beneficiaries; responsibilities of the nonfederal entity regarding matching, level of effort, and earmarking; management of equipment and real property acquired from federal awards; and required reporting.

Auditee Responsibilities

OMB Circular A–133 also details the responsibilities of auditees (nonfederal entities). Auditees are responsible for identifying all federal awards received and expended, and the federal programs under which they were received. Identification of the federal program includes the CFDA title and number, award number and year, and name of the federal agency. In addition, auditees are responsible for maintaining appropriate internal controls and systems to ensure compliance with all laws, regulations, and contract or grant provisions applicable to federal awards. Finally, auditees must prepare appropriate financial statements and the schedule of expenditures of federal awards, ensure that audits are properly performed and submitted when due, and follow up and take appropriate corrective action on audit findings. The latter requirement includes preparation of a summary schedule of prior audit findings and a corrective action plan for current year audit findings.

How Are Programs Selected for Audit?

Illustration 11–9 shows the procedures and criteria for selecting major programs for audit as described in Chapter 9 of the AICPA Audit Guide *Government Auditing Standards and Circular A–133 Audits.* A **major program** is a federal award program

ILLUSTRATION 11–9   **Risk-Based Approach for Selecting Major Programs for Audit**

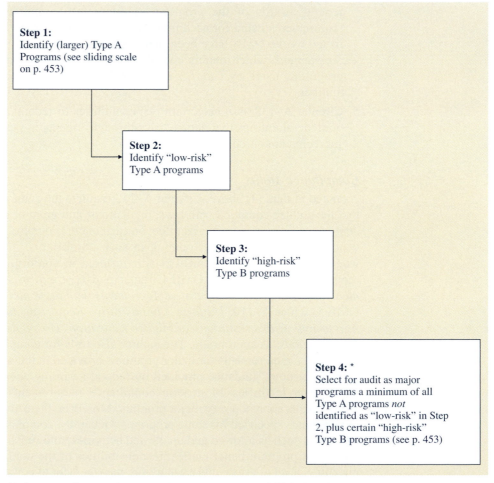

Step 1:
Identify (larger) Type A Programs (see sliding scale on p. 453)

Step 2:
Identify "low-risk" Type A programs

Step 3:
Identify "high-risk" Type B programs

Step 4: *
Select for audit as major programs a minimum of all Type A programs *not* identified as "low-risk" in Step 2, plus certain "high-risk" Type B programs (see p. 453)

*Audit as many major programs as necessary to ensure that at least 50% of all federal awards expended during the year are audited.

selected for audit using the procedures described below and shown in Illustration 11–9 or by request of a federal awarding agency. Use of a **risk-based approach** for selecting major programs for audit ensures that audit effort is concentrated on the highest risk programs. The risk-based approach is applied as follows:

1. Identify the "larger" federal programs and analyze them according to the Type A criteria. Programs not meeting Type A criteria are identified as Type B programs. Type A programs are determined using the following sliding scale:

Federal Awards Expended	Threshold for Type A Program
$300,000 to $100 million	Larger of $300,000 or 3% (.03) of total federal awards expended
More than $100 million to $10 billion	Larger of $3 million or .3% (.003) of total federal awards expended
More than $10 billion	Larger of $30 million or .15% (.0015) of total federal awards expended

2. Identify low-risk Type A programs: programs previously audited in at least one of the two most recent audit periods as a major program, with no audit findings in the most recent audit period; programs with no significant changes in personnel or systems that would have significantly increased risk; and programs that, in the auditor's professional judgment, are low risk, after considering such factors as the inherent risk of the program, the level of oversight exercised by federal awarding agencies and pass-through agencies, and the phase of a program in its life cycle. New programs, for example, tend to be more risky than more mature programs.

3. Identify Type B programs that, based on the auditor's professional judgment and criteria discussed above, are high risk. The auditor is not expected to perform risk assessments on relatively small federal programs. Risk assessments are performed only for those Type B programs that are (*a*) $100,000 or .3% (.003) of total federal awards expended when total federal awards expended are less than or equal to $100 million or (*b*) $300,000 or .03% (.0003) of total federal awards expended when total federal awards expended are more than $100 million.

4. At a minimum, audit as major programs all Type A programs *not* identified as low risk and certain high-risk Type B programs, using one of the following options:
   (*a*) audit at least half of the high-risk Type B programs but not required to audit more Type B than Type A programs identified as low risk; or
   (*b*) audit one high-risk Type B program for each Type A program identified as low risk.

The *percentage of coverage rule* requires auditing of as many major programs as necessary to ensure that at least 50 percent of total federal awards expended are audited. In addition to the possibility of reduced audit coverage resulting from individual Type A programs being classified as low risk, A–133 also provides that the auditee itself can be classified as low risk and thereby receive even greater reduction in audit coverage.[23] An auditee that meets the rather stringent criteria prescribed in Circular A–133 to be a low-risk auditee needs to have audited a sufficient number of major programs to encompass only 25 percent of total federal awards expended.

---

[23] An auditee is considered "low risk" if unqualified opinions have been received on annual single audits with no deficiencies in internal control and no audit findings.

What Reports Are Required for the Single Audit?

The 1996 amendments require that all auditors' reports for the single audit be submitted to the federal clearinghouse designated by the OMB within the earlier of 30 days after receipt of the auditor's report(s) or nine months after the end of the audit period.[24] Both the auditee and auditor have responsibilities for particular reports that comprise the reporting package.

The reporting package consists of:

1. Financial statements and schedule of expenditures of federal awards.
2. Summary schedule of prior audit findings.
3. Auditors' reports.
4. Corrective action plan.

The auditee is responsible for preparing all documents described in items (1), (2), and (4) above. The auditor is responsible for preparing the various auditors' reports in item (3) and for following up on prior year audit findings, including testing the accuracy and reasonableness of the summary schedule of prior audit findings. In addition, both the auditee and auditor have responsibilities for completing and submitting the comprehensive data collection form that accompanies the reporting package to the clearinghouse. In general, the form provides for extensive descriptive data about the auditee, the auditor, identification of types and amounts of federal awards and major programs, types of reports issued by the auditor, and whether the auditor identified internal control deficiencies or significant noncompliance with laws, regulations, and grant provisions. Both a senior-level representative of the auditee and auditor must sign the data collection form, certifying its accuracy and completeness.

Auditor's Reports

OMB Circular A–133 specifies several reports that the auditor must submit for each single audit engagement. These reports can be in the form of separate reports for each requirement or a few combined reports. The auditor's report on the financial statements should indicate that the audit was conducted in accordance with GAAS and GAGAS. Other auditor's reports required by the single audit should indicate the audits were conducted in accordance with GAAS, GAGAS, and provisions of Circular A–133. The required single audit reports, whether made as separate reports or combined, must include:

1. An opinion (or disclaimer of opinion) as to whether the financial statements are presented fairly in conformity with GAAP and whether the schedule of expenditures of federal awards is presented fairly in relation to the financial statements taken as a whole.
2. A report on internal controls related to the financial statements and major programs.
3. A report and an opinion on compliance with laws, regulations, and provisions of grant or contract agreements that could have a material effect on the financial statements. The report must also include an opinion on compliance matters related to major programs audited that could have a direct and material effect on each major program. Where applicable, include findings of noncompliance in the separate schedule of findings and questioned costs, described in item (4) below.

---

[24] A three-page data collection form (SF-SAC) is sent electronically to the Federal Audit Clearinghouse, Bureau of the Census, Department of Commerce. See http://harvester.census.gov/fac.

ILLUSTRATION 11–10 Required Auditor's Reports

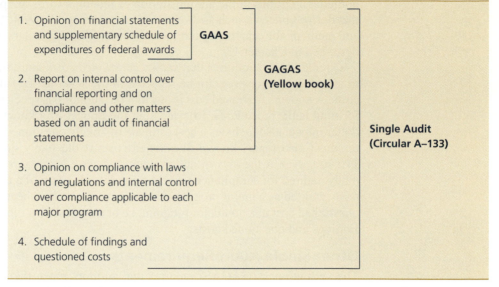

Source: Adapted from Table 12.1, AICPA Audit Guide, "*Government Auditing Standards and Circular A–133 Audits*" (New York: AICPA, 2005).

4. A schedule of findings and questioned costs, containing the following:
   (*a*) A summary of the auditor's results, including such information as type of opinion rendered on the financial statements, reportable conditions relating to internal control weaknesses, material noncompliance affecting the financial statements, major programs audited, type of opinion on compliance for major programs and reportable conditions in internal control affecting major programs, and a statement as to whether the auditee qualified as low risk.
   (*b*) Findings related to the audit of the financial statements required to be reported by the yellow book (GAGAS). These relate primarily to the auditor's responsibility to ensure adequate communication of material irregularities and illegal acts.
   (*c*) Audit findings and questioned costs. Audit findings are discussed next.

Illustration 11–10 shows the relationship of the required auditor's reports under GAAS, GAGAS, and the Single Audit (OMB Circular A–133).

Reporting Audit Findings

As listed in item (4) above, auditors must prepare a schedule of findings and questioned costs. **Audit findings** reported in the schedule provide detail on matters such as internal control weaknesses, instances of noncompliance, questioned costs, fraud and illegal acts, material violations of contract and grant agreements, and material abuse.

Regarding reporting on internal controls, item (4a) above uses the term **reportable condition.** This term is used in AICPA authoritative audit publications and has been adopted in the yellow book and Circular A–133. In the context of GAGAS audits, a reportable condition is a significant deficiency in the design or operation of internal control that could adversely affect the entity's ability to administer a federal award program in accordance with laws and regulations. A **material weakness** is a reportable condition of such magnitude that the internal control components do not reduce the risk of material noncompliance to an acceptably low level.

A **questioned cost** arises from an audit finding, generally relating to noncompliance with a law, regulation, or agreement, whose costs are either not supported by adequate documentation or appear unreasonable. Cost principles to be followed by nonfederal entities in the administration of federal awards are prescribed by circulars that define concepts such as direct and indirect costs, allowable and unallowable costs, and methods for calculating indirect cost rates. These circulars and cost principles are described in Chapter 13.

Circular A–133 requires that *known questioned costs* more than $10,000 identified in auditing a major program be reported in the schedule of findings and questioned costs. A known questioned cost is one that the auditor has specifically identified in performing audit procedures. In evaluating the impact of a known questioned cost, the dollar impact also includes a best estimate of "likely questioned costs." Thus, the auditor must also report known questioned costs if the likely questioned costs exceed $10,000, even if the known dollar amount is zero. Nonmajor programs are not normally audited for compliance (except for audit follow-up of a program that was previously audited as a major program); however, if the auditor becomes aware of a known questioned cost in a nonmajor program, he or she must also report it in the schedule of findings and questioned costs.

Other Single Audit Requirements

The yellow book (GAGAS) requires that auditors make their audit working papers available to other auditors and to oversight officials from federal awarding agencies and cognizant agents for quality review purposes. Federal agency access also includes the right to obtain copies of the working papers, which should be retained for a minimum of three years.

OMB Circular A–133 provides that a **cognizant agency for audit responsibilities** will be designated for each nonfederal entity expending more than $50 million a year in federal awards. The cognizant agency will be the federal awarding agency that provides the predominant amount of direct funding unless the OMB specifically designates a different cognizant agency. Among the cognizant agency's responsibilities are providing technical audit advice and liaison to auditees and auditors, obtaining or conducting quality control reviews of selected audits made by nonfederal auditors, communicating to affected parties the deficiencies identified by quality control reviews (including, when necessary, referral of deficiencies to state licensing agencies and professional bodies for possible disciplinary action), and promptly communicating findings of irregularities and illegal acts to affected federal agencies and appropriate federal law enforcement agencies. Nonfederal entities expending less than $50 million in federal awards are assigned an **oversight agency.** The oversight agency is the agency that makes the predominant amount of direct funding to the nonfederal entity. An oversight agency has responsibilities similar to a designated cognizant agency, but less extensive.

IMPACT OF SOX ON GOVERNMENTS

The Sarbanes-Oxley (SOX) Act of 2002, Congress's response to corporate accounting scandals of the late 1990s and early 2000s, applies to publicly held companies, their public accounting firms, and other issuers.[25] However, governments and not-for-profit organizations (NPOs) are feeling the effects of this legislation as well. Provisions of the

[25] For more detailed information, students are directed to the Act itself (P.L. 107–204), as well the AICPA Web site (www.aicpa.org/sarbanes/index.asp), and the Public Company Accounting Oversight Board (PCAOB) Web site (www.pcaobus.org).

act that could be made applicable to public and not-for-profit sector entities are (1) the document retention provisions in Title VIII of SOX (the Corporate and Criminal Fraud Accountability Act of 2002) that establish penalties for destroying documents in contemplation of a federal investigation, and (2) protection for "whistle-blowers" who disclose employer information in court proceedings involving fraud. SOX indirectly affected governmental accounting standards setting by establishing the Public Company Accounting Oversight Board (PCAOB) and altering the funding for the GASB and FASB.

Some states, such as California, have passed SOX-type regulations for not-for-profit entities, and Congress is considering increased reporting requirements of NPOs. Many governments and NPOs are exploring "best practices" in the SOX legislation that can strengthen the organization before being required to do so by an oversight body. Three such practices are discussed next.

Best Practices—Audit Committees

The SOX legislation requires audit committees of public companies, subsets of the board of directors, to (1) appoint and oversee the auditor, (2) resolve disagreements between management and its auditor, (3) establish procedures to receive complaints from employees who "blow the whistle" on those responsible for fraud, (4) ensure auditor independence, and (5) review the audit report and other written communications. A state or local government or not-for-profit organization that establishes an audit committee, at a minimum, signals to the public that the auditors report to the board that hired them, not to management.[26]

Best Practices—Independence

The GAO issued more stringent independence standards in its 2002 amendment to the yellow book *(Government Auditing Standards—GAS)* before the PCAOB or AICPA issued similar guidance. As discussed earlier in this chapter, there are two overarching independence principles in GAS: Auditors should neither make management decisions nor audit their own work. These GAS principles go beyond AICPA rules in that they require certain safeguards when an auditor performs nonaudit services. The SOX independence regulations may appear more restrictive in that they list restricted services, but it seems fair to say that in the last few years, all of the bodies responsible for providing guidance to auditors have tightened up their regulations to ensure that the public can depend on auditors to be independent of the client they are auditing not only in appearance but in fact.

Best Practices—Internal Controls

Section 404 of SOX requires managers of publicly traded companies to accept responsibility for the effectiveness of the entity's internal control system. The act of "certifying" requires that management present a written assertion not only that they have adopted some framework for internal controls, but also that they test these controls and can document the effectiveness of the internal control system. The OMB reexamined its internal control requirements for federal agencies in light of the Sarbanes-Oxley Act of 2002 and revised OMB Circular A–123 *Management's Responsibility for Internal Control.* This circular "provides guidance to Federal managers on improving the accountability and effectiveness of Federal programs and operations by establishing, assessing, correcting, and reporting on internal control."[27]

---

[26] The AICPA produced a *Government Audit Committee Toolkit* to provide guidance for governments in establishing and working with audit committees, available at www.aicpa.org.

[27] OMB Circular A–123 revised, *Management's Responsibility for Internal Control* (Washington, DC: OMB), December 21, 2004, effective for fiscal year 2006.

Managers of government and not-for-profit entities could benefit from voluntarily adopting certain requirements of the Sarbanes-Oxley Act, such as creation of an audit committee, monitoring the independence of auditors, and certification of internal controls and financial statements by the chief executive or financial officer of the entity.

Key Terms

Attestation
  engagements, *442*
Audit findings, *455*
Cognizant agency for
  audit responsibilities,
  456
Compliance audit, *451*
Engagement letter, *440*
Financial audits, *434*
GAAP hierarchy, *439*

Generally accepted
  auditing standards
  (GAAS), *434*
Generally accepted
  government auditing
  standards
  (GAGAS), *441*
Major programs, *452*
Materiality, *440*
Material weakness, *455*

Nonaudit work, *445*
Opinion units, *440*
Oversight agency, *456*
Performance audits, *442*
Program-specific
  audit, *448*
Questioned cost, *456*
Reportable condition, *455*
Risk-based approach, *453*
Single audit, *447*

Selected References

American Institute of Certified Public Accountants. Audit and Accounting Guide. *State and Local Governments.* New York: AICPA, 2005.

_____. Audit Guide. *Government Auditing Standards and Circular A–133 Audits.* New York: AICPA, 2005.

_____. Audit Risk Alert. *State and Local Governmental Developments—2005.* New York: AICPA, 2005.

Comptroller General of the United States. *Government Auditing Standards.* Washington, DC: Superintendent of Documents, U.S. Government Printing Office, 2003.

Office of Management and Budget. *Circular A–133,* "Audits of States, Local Governments, and Nonprofit Organizations." Washington, DC: Superintendent of Documents, U.S. Government Printing Office, 2003.

_____. OMB Circular A–133, *Compliance Supplement.* Washington, DC. Superintendent of Documents, U.S. Government Printing Office, March 2004.

Questions

11–1. What assurance does the independent auditor's report provide users of financial statements of governmental and not-for-profit entities?

11–2. What is the meaning of the term *unqualified opinion* as used in auditing literature? Why might a governmental entity receive a *qualified opinion?*

11–3. Define *GAGAS,* and describe how GAGAS differs from GAAS.

11–4. What are the major types of auditor services described in the Government Accountability Office's *Government Auditing Standards* (the yellow book, as revised in 2003), and how do they differ?

11–5. Explain the independence standard established by the GAO to ensure that auditors are independent when providing nonaudit services to governmental or not-for-profit organizations that they audit.

11–6. Describe the single audit concept set forth in the Single Audit Act of 1984, the 1996 amendments, and OMB *Circular A–133.*

11–7. Explain how federal award programs are selected for audit under the risk-based approach.

11–8. Distinguish between the terms *reportable condition* and *material weakness* in reporting internal control findings.

11–9. Describe the audit reports that auditors must submit upon completion of a single audit. What documents compose the single audit reporting package that must be sent to the federal clearinghouse?

11–10. What are the benefits of having an audit committee?

Cases

11–1 Single Audit. Background. Mountain Lake Mental Health Affiliates, a nongovernmental not-for-profit organization, has contacted Bill Wise, CPA, about conducting an annual audit for its first year of operations. The governing board wishes to obtain an audit of the financial statements and, having received favorable information about Mr. Wise's ability to conduct such audits, has decided not to issue a request for proposals from other audit firms. Cybil Civic, president of the board, heard from a friend associated with a similar organization that $5,000 is an appropriate price for such an audit and has offered Mr. Wise the audit for that price. Although Mr. Wise agrees that $5,000 would be reasonable for a typical financial statement audit of an organization of Mountain Lake's type and size, he refuses to contract for the audit at that price until he is able to estimate the extent of audit work that would be involved.

Facts. In discussions with Mountain Lake's controller, Mr. Wise obtains the following information about the organization for the year just ended:

1. Mountain Lake received a $200,000 grant from the City of Mountain Lake, of which 50 percent was stated as being from federal sources. Of this amount, $150,000 was expended during the year, equally from federal and nonfederal sources.

2. Unrestricted gifts of $50,000 were received from private donors; $40,000 was spent during the year.

3. The organization received $300,000 from Medicare for mental health services rendered during the year.

4. A building owned by the U.S. Department of Health and Human Services is occupied by Mountain Lake for rent of $1 per year. The fair value of the rental has been appraised at $30,001.

5. Mountain Lake carried out a program with the Federal Bureau of Prisons to provide alcohol and drug abuse counseling services for prisoners at a nearby federal prison. Services are provided on a "units of service" reimbursement basis. Each unit of service is reimbursed at the rate of $100 and the contract provides for maximum reimbursement of $400,000. Actual units of service for the year were 4,400. Direct costs incurred for these services amounted to $250,000 in total.

Required

a. Based on the foregoing facts, is Mountain Lake Mental Health Affiliates required to have a single audit? Explain your answer.

b. Should Mr. Wise accept the audit engagement for a $5,000 fee? Why or why not?

    c. Would Mr. Wise be considered independent according to *Government Auditing Standards* if he also prepares routine tax filings for the organization? Why or why not?

(*Note:* The authors are indebted to James Brown, a partner with Baird, Kurtz & Dobson in Springfield, Missouri, for providing the example on which Case 11–1 is based.)

11–2 Single Audit and Major Programs. Trenton City expended federal awards from the following programs during its most recent fiscal year.

Program	Amount Expended
1. Community Service Block Grants	$ 500,000
2. Solid Waste Management Assistance	600,000
3. Emergency Federal Law Enforcement Assistance	250,000
4. Low Income Home Energy Assistance	200,000
5. Community Economic Adjustment Planning Assistance	250,000
6. Air Pollution Control Program	50,000
Total	$1,850,000

Other Information. The auditor has rendered an unqualified report on the financial statements and found no reportable conditions or material weaknesses in internal control at the financial statement level. In addition, the auditor has given an unqualified opinion on the Schedule of Expenditures of Federal Awards, from which the preceding information was obtained. Next the auditor must determine which major federal award programs require internal control evaluation and compliance testing.

    Following the risk-based approach, the auditor, with the concurrence of the oversight agency, has classified programs 2 and 4 as low risk. Program 6 was not assessed as to risk due to its small size.

Required

a. Which programs should the auditor audit as major programs for the year just ended? Explain your rationale.

b. How would your answer to requirement *a* differ if program 2 had not been classified as low risk?

11–3 Internet Case. The City of Belleview receives pass-through funds from the state's Department of Housing to assist in administering the federally funded Supportive Housing Program for the elderly. At the request of the state's Department of Housing, the city has engaged you to perform a program-specific audit of its expenditures of federal awards for the Supportive Housing Program for the elderly. Although you are unfamiliar with the particular program, you have extensive experience in governmental auditing and have audited many other federal programs.

Required

Utilize the Internet to answer the following questions about this program.

a. What is the Catalog of Federal Domestic Assistance (CFDA) number for this program? (Relevant Web site is http://www.cfda.gov.)

b. Describe the program's purpose and its eligible beneficiaries.

c. Which of the 14 compliance items (A through N) listed in the A–133 *Compliance Supplement* are applicable to auditing compliance for this program? (*Hint:* Access Parts, 2, 3, and 4 of the *Compliance Supplement* at http://www.whitehouse.gov/OMB/circulars.)

11–4 Internet Case. Authoritative Auditing Guidance. You are a junior accountant in a local public accounting firm that recently decided to perform audits of small governmental clients. Your audit manager has asked you to use the Internet to locate the most current resources available to provide guidance in performing generally accepted government auditing standards audits of these entities, including single audits. In particular, he would like to know if there is a compliance supplement from the Office of Management and Budget for OMB *Circular A–133* (see http://www.whitehouse.gov/omb), an audit and accounting guide on *State and Local Governments* from the American Institute of CPAs (see http://www.aicpa.org), implementation guides from the Governmental Accounting Standards Board for the *GASBS 34* reporting model (see http://www.gasb.org), and any questions and answers on the independence standards from the GAO (see http://www.gao.gov).

Required

Identify which of these documents can be downloaded from the Internet and which can only be ordered in print form. What is the date of the most current version of each?

11–5 Audit Committees. The city council members of Laurel City are considering establishing an audit committee as a subset of the council. Several members work for commercial businesses that have recently established such committees in response to the Sarbanes-Oxley Act of 2002. They have asked your advice as a partner in the public accounting firm that audits the city's annual financial statements. They are especially interested in whether the benefits of such a committee outweigh any costs to establishing one.

Required

a. What resources are available to the city to help them use this audit committee efficiently and effectively?

b. Provide a short report to the council that lists the benefits and costs of establishing an audit committee. Explain what qualifications would be expected of council members who sit on this committee and the tasks in which they would be engaged.

Exercises and Problems

11–1 Examine the CAFR. Using the CAFR you obtained for Exercise 1–1, answer the following questions:

a. Auditors. Was this CAFR audited by external certified public accountants (CPAs) or by state or local governmental auditors?

b. Audit Opinion. What type of opinion did this entity receive? If it was qualified, what reason was given? Was an opinion expressed on the supplementary information as well as the basic financial statements?

c. Auditing Standards. Did the auditor use generally accepted auditing standards (GAAS), generally accepted governmental auditing standards (GAS or GAGAS), or both?

d. Paragraphs. How many paragraphs are there in the auditor's report? Can you identify the introductory, scope, opinion, and any explanatory paragraphs?

e. Single Audit. Can you tell whether this entity was required to have a single audit? If so, are the required single audit reports contained within the cover of the CAFR that you are examining? If the entity does receive federal financial assistance but you see no mention of the single audit in the auditor's report, where do you expect that single audit report to be?

11–2 Multiple Choice. Choose the best answer.

1. Which of the following activities would always indicate that an auditor's independence has been impaired?
   a. Providing advice on establishing an internal control system.
   b. Posting adjusting journal entries into the client's accounting records.
   c. Providing benchmarking studies to be used by management.
   d. Preparing draft financial statements based on management's trial balance.

2. An adverse opinion is most likely to be rendered when:
   a. Fund financial statements are presented along with government-wide statements in the basic financial statements.
   b. There is a violation of generally accepted accounting principles that does not cause the basic financial statements to be materially misstated.
   c. The auditor is not independent of the government being audited.
   d. The government issues a stand-alone consolidated report.

3. Which of the following is a true statement about the relationship between generally accepted government auditing standards (GAGAS) and generally accepted auditing standards (GAAS)?
   a. GAGAS and GAAS provide standards for financial audits, attestation engagements, and performance audits.
   b. GAGAS encompasses GAAS and supplements certain GAAS.
   c. Single audits must be performed using GAGAS and GAAS.
   d. GAGAS is promulgated by the Government Accountability Office and GAAS is promulgated by the Government Accounting Standards Board.

4. One of the overarching principles in the GAO's standard on *independence* is:
   a. Auditors should never provide payroll or tax services to audit clients.
   b. Auditors should document an understanding with the audited entity regarding the objectives, scope of work, and product of the nonaudit service.
   c. Auditors should not perform management functions or make management decisions.
   d. Auditors should not perform nonaudit work for audit clients.

5. The goal of a performance audit is to:
   a. Provide information to improve program operations and facilitate decision making by management.
   b. Determine whether government programs and activities are meeting their stated goals and objectives.
   c. Determine whether governments are performing their duties in the most economic and efficient manner possible.
   d. All of the above.

6. Under the *GASBS 34* reporting model, materiality is determined:
   a. For *opinion units*.
   b. At the government-wide level.
   c. At the fund level.
   d. For governmental and business-type activities and the aggregate discretely presented component units only.

7. Single audits performed pursuant to OMB *Circular A–133:*
   a. Apply to all entities that receive $500,000 or more in a fiscal year.
   b. Result in the same number of reports as a generally accepted government auditing standards (GAGAS or yellow book) audit.

      c. Must be performed in accordance with generally accepted government auditing standards.

      d. Result in a reporting package that is submitted to the Office of Management and Budget.

8. The single audit concept:

      a. Dates back to 1979 and was codified in 1984 and amended in 1996.

      b. Requires that all audits of entities receiving federal financial assistance be audited by GAO auditors.

      c. Means that each federal grant that an entity receives is audited as a single unit.

      d. Requires that all large grants and half of the small grants be audited without regard to risk.

9. OMB *Circular A–133* and the related *Compliance Supplement* provide guidance for auditors in:

      a. Conducting a financial audit of governmental entities.

      b. Conducting financial audits, attestation engagements, and performance audits of governmental entities.

      c. Conducting a single audit of a government that has expended more than $500,000 in federal financial assistance.

      d. None of the above.

10. The auditor's responsibility for required supplementary information (RSI) is:

      a. The same as with the basic financial statements.

      b. To perform certain limited procedures to ensure that RSI is fairly presented in relation to the audited financial statements.

      c. The same as for all information in the financial section of a Comprehensive Annual Financial Report.

      d. To render an opinion as to the fairness of the RSI and whether it conforms to generally accepted accounting principles.

11–3 Qualified Audit Opinion. On August 23, 2008, the CPA firm of Ross and Mahoney completed its audit of the City of Kawkawlin's basic financial statements for the year ended June 30, 2008. The city presents its financial position, changes in financial position, and cash flows using the financial statements prescribed by generally accepted accounting principles. However, Ross and Mahoney believe that the Kawkawlin Cultural Center, a theater for the performing arts and financially subsidized by the city, meets the criteria specified by the GASB for inclusion as a component unit in Kawkawlin's basic financial statements. Kawkawlin's finance director has steadfastly refused to include the cultural center in Kawkawlin's basic financial statements on the basis that it would cause the financial statements to be misleading. Ross and Mahoney feel compelled to issue an "except for" qualified audit opinion to bring attention to this departure from GAAP, although they believe the financial statements present fairly in all other respects. Ross and Mahoney have determined that the effect of including the cultural center in Kawkawlin's basic financial statements would have been to increase the reported assets and revenues of the enterprise funds by $545,000 and $182,000, respectively, and increase the excess of revenues over expenses in that fund type by $8,200 for the year ended June 30, 2008.

Required
Prepare the qualified audit report that Ross and Mahoney, CPAs, should render on the City of Kawkawlin's basic financial statements for the year ended June 30, 2008.

11–4 **Single Audit.** Tri-States Community Service Agency expended federal awards during its most recent fiscal year in the following amounts for the programs shown:

Program 1	$ 450,000
Program 2	350,000
Program 3	140,000
Program 4	60,000
Total	$1,000,000

Additional information: Programs 1 and 2 were audited as major programs in each of the two preceding fiscal years, with no audit findings reported. Although neither Program 1 nor 2 is considered inherently risky, a new manager, recently graduated from the state university, was appointed during the current year to manage activities related to Program 2.

Required

a. Assuming the auditor classifies Programs 2 and 3 as high risk and Program 1 as low risk, which programs would be audited as major programs? Explain.

b. Explain what audit work would be required to audit the major programs.

11–5 **Auditor's Opinion.** Catalpa City's Balance Sheet as of December 31, 2008, is shown below. The *Annual Report for 2008* also includes a statement of changes in cash for that year and an operating statement for that year. No auditor's report is associated with these three financial statements.

CATALPA CITY
Balance Sheet
As of December 31, 2008

Assets		
Cash		$ 155,155
Accounts receivable		
Current-year property taxes		58,792
Prior-year property taxes		2,921
Other taxes		514
Municipal services—usage		71,861
Municipal services—tap fees		9,077
Toll bridges		30,598
School district		5,242
Other		173
Total current assets		$ 334,333
Property, plant, and equipment:		
Library—building and equipment		16,550
Storage shed		14,742
Public Safety Dept.—building and equipment		266,317
Municipal Services Dept.—land, building, and equipment		2,325,893
Highway Department		28,755
Cemetery		21,595
Town office—equipment		4,369
Land		12,000
Toll bridges		22,500
Total property, plant, and equipment	2,712,721	
Less: Accumulated depreciation	(283,357)	2,429,364
Total assets		$2,763,697

Liabilities and Equity

Accounts payable	$ 1,725	
Tax anticipation notes	250,000	
Current portion—long-term debt:		
Bonds	85,000	
Notes	84,304	
Due to school district	46,089	
Total current liabilities	467,118	
Long-term debt:		
Bonds	1,395,000	
Notes	373,416	
Total liabilities		$2,235,534
Equity	850,421	
Less: Wind recovery costs	(322,258)	528,163
Total liabilities and equity		$2,763,697

Required

Assuming you conducted an audit for 2008 and found no material errors in the amounts presented in the statements, could you express the opinion that the statements present fairly the financial position of the city at December 31, 2008 and the changes in financial position for the year then ended in conformity with accounting principles generally accepted in the United States? Why or why not? Be explicit.

11–6 **GAO Independence Standards.** Indicate which of the following activities performed by an auditor for a governmental client are (a) allowable, (b) permitted if safeguards are in place, or (c) prohibited.

1. Serving on the building committee of the board in an advisory capacity.
2. Preparing the indirect cost proposal expected to be $3,000,0000.
3. Searching for a new finance director and recommending the best candidate.
4. Preparing draft financial statements based on the client's adjusted trial balance.
5. Proposing adjusting journal entries that management accepts and records.
6. Maintaining the client's general ledger.
7. Providing routine advice on how to determine the percentage of taxes receivable that may not be collected.
8. Maintaining depreciation schedules for which management has determined useful lives and residual values.
9. Providing appraisals and valuation of property held by the government.
10. Preparing annual tax forms, such as sales and use tax to the state and payroll taxes to the federal government.

11–7 **Conformity with GAAP.** You are auditing the accounts of the clerk-treasurer of the Town of Belton. You find, in the ledger, accounts for the General Fund, the Street Fund, and the Capital Projects Fund. The legally approved budget for the Street Fund for the year you are examining consisted of the following three appropriations only:

Labor	$60,000
Materials	66,000
Equipment	24,000

In the appropriation and disbursement ledger accounts, you find the record of transactions for the Street Fund shown as follows:

LABOR ACCOUNT

Date	Description	Warrant	Appropriation	Disbursements	Appropriation Balance
Jan. 1	From advertised budget		$60,000		$60,000
31	Street labor	115–142		$6,000	54,000
Feb. 28	Street labor	219–241		7,000	47,000
Mar. 31	Street labor	252–263		6,000	41,000
Apr. 30	Street labor	274–294		5,000	36,000
June 30	Labor on municipal parking lots	371–388		8,000	28,000
Aug. 31	Street labor	400–424		10,000	18,000
Oct. 31	Street labor	510–523		10,000	8,000
Dec. 31	Street labor	600–621		8,000	–0–

MATERIALS ACCOUNT

Date	Description	Warrant	Appropriation	Disbursements	Appropriation Balance
Jan. 1	From advertised budget		$66,000		$66,000
20	Asphalt mix for street repair	109		$ 6,000	60,000
Feb. 21	Repair of truck used on streets	217		2,000	58,000
Mar. 12	Purchased used truck for street department	268		12,000	46,000
Apr. 15	Auditor of State, gasoline tax distribution		4,920		50,920
May 31	Gas and oil for street trucks	301		3,000	47,920
June 6	Tile	367		4,000	43,920
July 14	Concrete for building fireplaces in park	425		6,900	37,020
Aug. 7	Street lights (utility bill)	451		7,220	29,800
Sep. 29	Refund received on tile purchased by warrant 367		100		29,900
Oct. 18	Labor on streets	524–532		12,000	17,900
Nov. 2	Reimbursement for cutting weeds on private property		640		18,540
Dec. 11	To contractor for paving street	622		20,000	(1,460)
31	Additional appropriations as advertised on this date		1,460		–0–

EQUIPMENT ACCOUNT

Date	Description	Warrant	Appropriation	Disbursements	Appropriation Balance
Jan. 1	From advertised budget		$24,000		$24,000
9	Grading equipment			$16,000	8,000
Feb. 10	Fire hydrants	189		6,000	2,000
19	Shovels, picks, and hand tools	208		1,420	580

Required

a. Comment on whether accounting for the Street Fund appears to be in conformity with generally accepted accounting principles. Explain fully.

b. As the auditor, would you be able to render an unqualified opinion on the financial statements of the Town of Belton? Would your answer depend on whether the Street Fund is a "major fund" within the governmental funds?

Chapter Twelve

Accounting and Reporting for the Federal Government

Learning Objectives

After studying this chapter, you should be able to:

1. Describe the financial management structure of the federal government.
2. Describe the process for establishing generally accepted accounting principles for federal agencies.
3. Explain the concepts underlying federal agency accounting and financial reporting.
4. Describe government-wide financial reporting for the federal government.
5. Identify the financial statements required of federal agencies.
6. Contrast and compare budgetary accounting with proprietary accounting.
7. Record budgetary and proprietary journal entries and prepare financial statements for federal agencies.
8. Contrast and compare accounting for state and local governments with federal agencies.

The federal government of the United States of America is the largest reporting entity in the world and is growing. Total outlays of all federal agencies were $107 billion in 1962, $2.3 trillion in 2004, and are projected to be $3 trillion in 2010.[1] Accountability for public revenues raised to meet the outlay or cost of government services has always been a responsibility of elected and appointed officials. An accounting structure has been provided for the U.S. federal government by statutes since 1789. The professional accounting consultants to the first and second Hoover Commissions generally are given credit for being among the first to provide direction to the effort to improve federal government accounting in the late 1940s to mid-1950s.

Major institutional change in the last two decades is providing the impetus for even greater change in federal accounting. Among these changes are the Chief Financial Officers Act (CFO) of 1990, the creation of the Federal Accounting Standards Advisory

[1] A history of federal outlays and other budget information by agency is available at www.whitehouse.gov/omb/budget/FY 2006.

Board (FASAB) in 1990, the Government Performance and Results Act of 1993 (GPRA), the Government Management Reform Act of 1994 (GMRA), the Federal Financial Management Improvement Act of 1996, the Reports Consolidation Act of 2000, and the Accountability of Tax Dollars Act (ATDA) of 2002.

Readers will notice that federal accounting standards are similar in some respects to those used by private sector entities, and in other respects are like those developed for state and local governments, as discussed in Chapters 1–9 of this text. Important differences do exist, however. This chapter first focuses on reporting for the federal government as a whole, and then on the unique aspects of accounting for federal agencies.

FEDERAL GOVERNMENT FINANCIAL MANAGEMENT STRUCTURE

The U.S. government is a complex set of branches, offices, and departments, as can be seen in Illustration 12–1, as well as independent establishments and government corporations, such as the U.S. Postal Service, Securities and Exchange Commission, and the Central Intelligence Agency (not shown). The United States Code (31 U.S.C. §3512) requires the head of each executive agency to establish, evaluate, and maintain adequate systems of accounting and internal control. Despite this requirement, many federal agencies have found it difficult to establish effective financial management systems. To help ensure that federal agencies correct their deficient accounting and reporting systems, Congress enacted the **Federal Financial Management Improvement Act of 1996 (FFMIA).** The act states:

> To rebuild the accountability and credibility of the Federal Government, and restore public confidence in the Federal Government, agencies must incorporate accounting standards and reporting objectives established for the Federal Government into their financial management systems so that all the assets and liabilities, revenues, and expenditures or expenses, and the full costs of programs and activities of the Federal Government can be consistently and accurately recorded, monitored, and uniformly reported throughout the Federal Government.[2]

The FFMIA further requires that each agency "shall implement and maintain financial management systems that comply substantially with federal financial management systems requirements, applicable federal accounting standards, and the U.S. Government Standard General Ledger at the transaction level."[3] At the present time, 24 major agencies of the federal government must submit two reports annually to the Office of Management and Budget: (1) the audited financial statements, required by the CFO Act of 1990 (P.L. 101-576) as amended by the GMRA of 1994, and (2) performance and accountability reports (PARs) that provide financial and performance information useful in assessing the agency's performance relative to its mission. For agencies not covered by the CFO Act, the Accountability of Tax Dollars Act of 2002 (P.L. 107-289), requires those entities to submit performance and accountability reports to the OMB. The Reports and Consolidation Act of 2000 (P.L. 106-531) permits agencies to combine these reports, if both are required, to be efficient.[4]

[2] Public Law 104-208, 104th Congress, Federal Financial Management Improvement Act of 1996, Sec. 802(a)(5).

[3] Ibid., Sec. 803(a).

[4] Office of Management and Budget *Circular A–136, Financial Reporting Requirements,* December 2004.

ILLUSTRATION 12–1 The United States Government

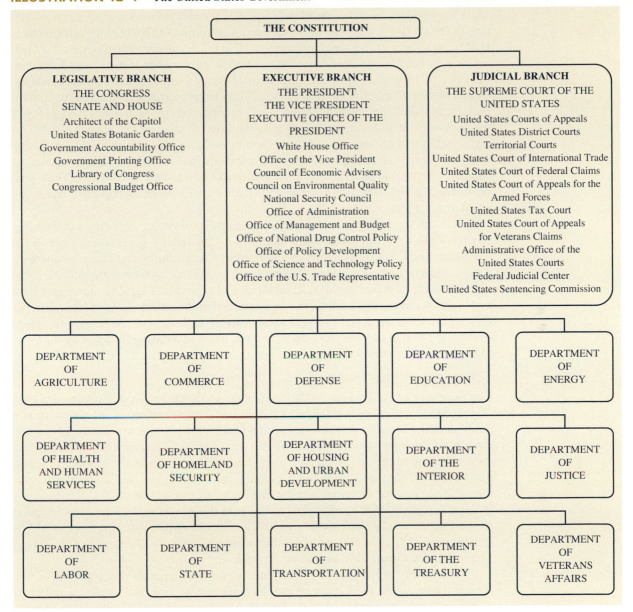

Federal statutes assign responsibility for establishing and maintaining a sound financial management structure for the federal government as a whole to three principal officials: the Comptroller General, the Secretary of the Treasury, and the Director of the Office of Management and Budget (OMB). Responsibilities assigned to each of these officials, as well as the Director of the Congressional Budget Office, are discussed briefly, after which recent cooperative efforts of these officials to enhance the quality of federal financial management under the auspices of the Joint Financial Management and Improvement Program (JFMIP) will be examined.

Comptroller General

The Comptroller General of the United States is the head of the Government Accountability Office (previously called the General Accounting Office but still referred to as GAO), an agency of the legislative branch of the government. The Comptroller General is appointed by the President with the advice and consent of the Senate for a term of office of 15 years. Since 1950, the United States Code (31 U.S.C. §3511) has assigned to the Comptroller General responsibility for prescribing the accounting principles, standards, and related requirements to be observed by each executive agency in the development of its accounting system. The Chief Financial Officers Act of 1990 assigns significant responsibility for establishing policies and procedures for approving and publishing accounting principles and standards (particularly as regards agency financial reporting) to the Director of the Office of Management and Budget. Thus, both under the law and in fact, the responsibility for prescribing accounting principles and standards is a joint responsibility.

Just as the appropriational authority of state and local governments rests in their legislative bodies, the appropriational authority of the federal government rests in the Congress. The Congress is, therefore, interested in determining that financial and budgetary reports from executive, judicial, and legislative agencies are reliable; that agency financial management is timely and useful; and that legal requirements have been met by the agencies. Under the assumption that the reports of an independent audit agency would aid in satisfying these interests of the Congress, the GAO was created as the audit arm of the Congress itself. The standards of auditing followed by the GAO in financial and performance audits are discussed in some detail in Chapter 11.

Secretary of the Treasury

The Secretary of the Treasury is the head of the Department of the Treasury, a part of the executive branch of the federal government. The Secretary of the Treasury is a member of the Cabinet of the President, appointed by the President with the advice and consent of the Senate to serve an indefinite term of office. The Department of the Treasury was created in 1789 to receive, keep, and disburse monies of the United States, and to account for them. From the beginning, the word *receive* was construed as *collect,* and the Internal Revenue Service, Bureau of Customs, and other agencies active in the enforcement of the collections of revenues due the federal government are parts of the Department of the Treasury, as are the Bureau of the Mint, the Bureau of Engraving and Printing, the Bureau of Public Debt, the Office of Treasurer of the United States, and the Financial Management Service.

The Secretary of the Treasury is responsible for the preparation of reports that will inform the President, the Congress, and the public on the financial condition and operations of the government (31 U.S.C. §3513). An additional responsibility of the Secretary of the Treasury is the maintenance of a system of central accounts of the public debt and cash to provide a basis for consolidation of the accounts of the various executive agencies with those of the Department of the Treasury.

The Department of the Treasury's Financial Management Service (FMS) maintains the U.S. Government Standard General Ledger, subject to the approval of the OMB. Originally published by the OMB in 1986, the Standard General Ledger is intended to (1) provide an accounting structure that will standardize financial information accumulation and processing, (2) enhance financial control, and (3) support budget reporting and external financial reporting. Implementation of the Standard General Ledger has enhanced the ability of central agencies to more accurately consolidate accounting data derived from individual agency accounting records. The chart of accounts presented

in the Standard General Ledger is based on a standardized 4-digit coding system for assets (1000), liabilities (2000), net position (3000), budgetary (4000), revenue and other financing sources (5000), expenses (6000), and gains/losses/miscellaneous items (7000) with flexibility so that agency-specific accounts may be incorporated.[5] Accounting for typical transactions of a federal agency illustrated in a later section of this chapter is based on the Standard General Ledger structure.

Director of the Office of Management and Budget

The Director of the Office of Management and Budget is appointed by the President and is a part of the Executive Office of the President. As the direct representative of the President with the authority to control the size and nature of appropriations requested of each Congress, the Director of the OMB is a powerful figure in the federal government.

Congressional requirements for the budget have a number of accounting implications in addition to the explicit historical comparisons that necessitate cooperation among the OMB, the Department of the Treasury, and the GAO. Implicit in the requirements for projections of revenues and receipts is the mandate that the OMB coordinate closely with the Council of Economic Advisers in the use of macroeconomic (the study of the economic system in its aggregate) and **macroaccounting** (accounting for the economy in the aggregate) forecasts. Macroaccounting is beyond the scope of this text, yet the subject is of increasing importance in the financial management of the federal government.

The OMB is assigned major responsibilities under the Chief Financial Officers Act of 1990 for establishing policies and procedures for approving and publishing financial accounting principles and standards to be followed by executive branch agencies and prescribing the form and content of financial statements. Pursuant to the Act, an Office of Federal Financial Management has been established within the OMB, headed by a controller appointed by the President. The Act also authorizes each major department or agency of the federal government to have a Chief Financial Officer (CFO) and a deputy CFO. Under the Act, the Director of the OMB is required to prepare and update each year a five-year financial plan for the federal government. The OMB issues circulars and bulletins relating to the financial reporting and management of federal agencies.

Director of the Congressional Budget Office

The Congressional Budget and Impoundment Control Act of 1974 established House and Senate budget committees, created the Congressional Budget Office (CBO), structured the congressional budget process, and enacted a number of other provisions to improve federal fiscal procedures. The Director of the CBO is appointed to a four-year term by the Speaker of the House of Representatives and the President *pro tempore* of the Senate. The CBO gathers information for the House and Senate budget committees with respect to the budget (submitted by the executive branch), appropriation bills, and other bills providing budget authority or tax expenditures.[6] The CBO also provides the Congress information concerning revenues, receipts, estimated future revenues and receipts, changing revenue conditions, and any related information-gathering and analytic functions assigned to the CBO; its director is responsible for

[5] Financial Management Service, *United States Standard General Ledger (USSGL),* June 30, 2005. See www.fms.treas.gov.
[6] A *tax expenditure* is a revenue loss attributable to provisions of federal tax laws that allow special exclusion, exemption, or deduction from gross income, or that provide a special credit, a preferential rate of tax, or a deferral of tax liability.

working with the Comptroller General, the Secretary of the Treasury, and the Director of the Office of Management and Budget in developing central files of data and information to meet the recurring requirements of the Congress.

GENERALLY ACCEPTED ACCOUNTING PRINCIPLES FOR FEDERAL AGENCIES

Although accounting principles and standards were prescribed for many years by *Title 2* of the *General Accounting Office Policy and Procedures Manual for Guidance of Federal Agencies,* not all federal agencies complied with that guidance. The diverse financial systems used among and within federal departments and agencies made it difficult to achieve uniform financial reporting and to educate and train federal financial managers. To establish an improved and more generally accepted structure for setting accounting principles and standards, the three principal sponsors of the JFMIP signed a memorandum of understanding in October 1990, creating the **Federal Accounting Standards Advisory Board (FASAB)**. The nine-member board utilizes a due process similar to that of FASB and GASB. Initially, the board had six federal members and three public members; however, effective June 30, 2002, that composition is reversed in order to increase public input on federal accounting and reporting standards. The members may serve two five-year terms.

According to OMB *Circular A–134,* "Financial Accounting Principles and Standards" (par. 2):

> The role of the FASAB is to deliberate upon and make recommendations to the Principals on accounting principles and standards for the Federal Government and its agencies. The MOU [memorandum of understanding] states that if the Principals agree with the recommendations, the Comptroller General and the Director of OMB will publish the accounting principles and standards.

Since its inception, the FASAB has issued four Statements of Federal Financial Accounting Concepts (SFFAC), 30 Statements of Federal Financial Accounting Standards (SFFAS), and several reports, technical releases, and interpretations. These statements collectively provide general and specific accounting and financial reporting standards on a variety of topics, including assets; liabilities; inventory and related property; property, plant, and equipment; revenues and other financial sources; direct loans and loan guarantees; managerial cost accounting concepts; and supplementary stewardship reporting. This chapter provides only an overview of these standards; detailed discussion of the many complex issues covered by these standards is beyond the scope of this text.[7] The authoritative status of SFFASs is made clear by OMB *Circular A–134* (par. 5.b):

> SFFASs shall be considered generally accepted accounting principles (GAAP) for Federal agencies. Agencies shall apply the SFFASs in preparing financial statements in accordance with the requirements of the Chief Financial Officers Act of 1990. Auditors shall consider SFFASs as authoritative references when auditing financial statements.

Hierarchy of Accounting Principles and Standards

Additional recognition of the authoritative status of FASAB standards as "federal GAAP" came in April 2000 when the American Institute of Certified Public Accountants

---

[7]Students who desire information about current FASAB projects, including exposure drafts of possible new standards, should consult FASAB's Web site at www.fasab.gov.

expanded its GAAP hierarchy to include the federal government and its agencies in Rule 203 of the Code of Professional Conduct.[8] *SAS No. 91* identifies the following as federal GAAP hierarchy.

Category

a. FASAB Statements and Interpretations, plus AICPA and FASB pronouncements if made applicable to federal governmental entities by a FASAB Statement or Interpretation.

b. FASAB Technical Bulletins and the following pronouncements if specifically made applicable to federal governmental entities by the AICPA and cleared by the FASAB: AICPA Industry Audit and Accounting Guides and AICPA Statements of Position.

c. AICPA AcSEC Practice Bulletins if specifically made applicable to federal governmental entities and cleared by the FASAB and Technical Releases of the Accounting and Auditing Policy Committee of the FASAB.

d. Implementation guides published by the FASAB staff and practices that are widely recognized and prevalent in the federal government, as well as other accounting literature.

The federal government concurs with this hierarchy; the language is repeated in OMB *Bulletin 0l-09,* par. 1.2.[9]

CONCEPTUAL FRAMEWORK

Accounting standards recommended by the FASAB and issued by the Comptroller General and the OMB for federal agencies are intended to be consistent with a conceptual framework the FASAB is developing. In this respect, the FASAB is following the general pattern established by the FASB, which attempts to issue standards consistent with its several Statements of Financial Accounting Concepts; and the GASB, which looks to its *Concepts Statement No. 1,* "Objectives of Financial Reporting" (see Chapter 1 of this text).

Concepts Statements

To date, the FASAB has issued four concepts statements: *Statement of Federal Financial Accounting Concepts (SFFAC) No. 1,* "Objectives of Federal Financial Reporting"; *SFFAC No. 2,* "Entity and Display"; *SFFAC No. 3,* "Management's Discussion and Analysis"; and *SFFAC No. 4,* "Intended Target Audience and Qualitative Characteristics for the Consolidated Financial Report of the United States Government."

Objectives

SFFAC No. 1 is considerably broader in scope than either the FASB's or GASB's concepts statements on objectives. The FASAB, for example, intends to set standards for internal management accounting and performance measurement, as well as for external financial reporting. *SFFAC No. 1* identifies four objectives of federal financial reporting, all of which rest on the foundation of accountability. The objectives in brief are

---

[8] *Statement on Auditing Standards No. 91,* "Federal GAAP Hierarchy" (New York: American Institute of Certified Public Accountants, April 2000).
[9] OMB, *Bulletin No. 01-09,* "Formats and Instructions for the Form and Content of Agency Financial Statements" (Washington, DC: September 2001), par. VIII.

to assist report users in evaluating *budgetary integrity, operating performance, stewardship,* and *adequacy of systems and controls. Budgetary integrity* pertains to accountability for raising monies through taxes and other means in accordance with appropriate laws, and expenditures of these monies in accordance with budgetary authorization. Accountability for *operating performance* is accomplished by providing report users information on service efforts and accomplishments: how well resources have been managed in providing services efficiently, economically, and effectively in attaining planned goals. *Stewardship* relates to the federal government's accountability for the general welfare of the nation. To assess stewardship, report users need information about the "impact on the country of the government's operations and investments for the period and how, as a result, the government's and the nation's financial conditions have changed and may change in the future" (par. 134). Finally, financial reporting should help users assess whether financial management *systems and controls* (internal accounting and administrative controls) "are adequate to ensure that (1) transactions are executed in accordance with budgetary and financial laws and other requirements, are consistent with the purposes authorized, and are recorded in accordance with federal accounting standards, (2) assets are properly safeguarded to deter fraud, waste, and abuse, and (3) performance measurement information is adequately supported" (par. 146).

Unlike the FASB and the GASB, which focus their standards on external financial reporting, the FASAB and its sponsors are concerned with both internal and external financial reporting. Accordingly, the FASAB has identified four major groups of users of federal financial reports: citizens, Congress, executives, and program managers. Given the broad role the FASAB has been assigned, future standards recommended by the board may focus on cost accounting systems and controls, the use of financial information in service efforts and accomplishments measures, and on the principles of financial accounting and reporting.

Reporting Entity

SFFAC No. 2, "Entity and Display," provides additional conceptual guidance for federal agency financial reporting. *SFFAC No. 2* specifies the types of entities that should provide financial reports, establishes guidelines for defining each type of reporting entity, identifies the types of financial statements each type of reporting entity should provide, and suggests the types of information each type of statement should convey.[10]

As discussed in Chapter 9 for state and local governments, accountability reporting is facilitated by including as part of the reporting entity all separate entities for which there is financial accountability or financial interdependence. *SFFAC No. 2* discusses three perspectives from which the federal government can be viewed for accounting and reporting purposes: organizational, budget, and program. From the *organizational perspective,* the government is viewed as a collection of departments and agencies that provide governmental services. From the *budget perspective,* the government is viewed as a collection of expenditure (appropriations or funds) or receipt budget accounts. **Budget accounts** are generally quite broad in scope and are not the same as the Standard General Ledger accounts used for accounting purposes. A budget account may cover an entire organization, or a group of budget accounts may aggregate to cover an organization. From the *program perspective* the government is viewed as an aggregation of programs (or functions) and activities.

---

[10] Paraphrased from FASAB, *Report Number 1,* Reporting Relevant Financial Information, "Overview of Federal Financial Accounting Concepts and Standards" (Washington, DC: 1996), p. 11.

Most programs are financed by more than one budget account, and some programs are administered by more than one organization. Similarly, some organizations administer multiple programs. Thus, in defining the reporting entity, it is necessary to consider the interacting nature of the perspectives. *SFFAC No. 2* also addresses the nature of the financial statements that should be included in the financial report of a reporting entity and the recommended format and content of the financial statements. Thus, it provides clear and strong direction to the FASAB and its three sponsoring agencies in setting accounting and reporting standards for the federal government; it also leaves little discretion to go down a different path.

Management's Discussion and Analysis

SFFAC No. 3 provides guidance for the MD&A included in the general purpose federal financial report (GPFFR). The MD&A is described as an "important vehicle for (1) communicating managers' insights about the reporting entity, (2) increasing the understandability and usefulness of the GPFFR, and (3) providing accessible information about the entity and its operations, service levels, successes, challenges, and future."[11] One difference between the FASAB's concept statement on the MD&A and the GASB's MD&A requirement in *Statement No. 34* is that federal agencies should address the reporting entity's performance goals and results in addition to financial activities.

Target Audience

SFFAC No. 4 expands the audiences for the consolidated financial report of the U.S. government described in *SFFAC No. 1*: (1) citizens, (2) citizen intermediaries, (3) Congress, (4) federal executives, and (5) program managers. The FASAB suggests the first two, citizens and their intermediaries, are the primary audiences. This statement indicates that the consolidated financial report should be "general purpose"—directed to external users and made available on a timely basis.

Funds Used in Federal Accounting

FASAB's standards do not focus on fund accounting, but Congress regularly passes laws that create, define, and modify funds for various purposes. Fund accounting is needed for federal agencies to demonstrate compliance with requirements of legislation for which federal funds have been appropriated or otherwise authorized to carry out specific activities and for financial reporting.

Two general types of funds are found in federal government accounting: (1) those used to account for resources derived from the general taxation and revenue powers or from business operations of the government and (2) those used to account for resources held and managed by the government in the capacity of custodian or trustee. Six kinds of funds are specified within the two general types:

1. Funds derived from general taxing and revenue powers and from business operations.
   General Fund
   Special funds
   Revolving funds
   Management funds
2. Funds held by the government in the capacity of custodian or trustee.
   Trust funds
   Deposit funds

---

[11] *Statement of Federal Financial Accounting Concepts No. 3,* "Management's Discussion and Analysis," Federal Accounting Standards Advisory Board, April 1999, p. i.

General Fund

The General Fund is credited with all receipts that are not dedicated by law and is charged with payments out of appropriations of "any money in the Treasury not otherwise appropriated" and out of general borrowings. Strictly speaking, there is only one General Fund in the entire federal government. The Financial Management Service of the Department of the Treasury accounts for the centralized cash balances (as it receives and disburses all public monies), the appropriations control accounts, and unappropriated balances. On the books of an agency, each appropriation is treated as a fund with its own self-balancing group of accounts; these agency "appropriation funds" are subdivisions of *the* General Fund.

Special Funds

Receipt and expenditure accounts established to account for receipts of the government that are earmarked by law for a specific purpose but that are not generated from a cycle of operations for which there is continuing authority to reuse such receipts (as is true for revolving funds) are classified as *special funds* in federal usage. The term and its definition are very close to that of the classification "special revenue funds" used in accounting for state and local governments.

Revolving Funds

A revolving fund is credited with collections, primarily from other agencies and accounts, that are earmarked by law to carry out a cycle of business-type operations in which the government is the owner of the activity. This type of fund is quite similar to internal service funds.

Management (Including Working Funds)

These are funds in which there are merged monies derived from two or more appropriations in order to carry out a common purpose or project but not involving a cycle of operations. Management funds include consolidated working funds that are set up to receive (and subsequently disburse) advance payments, pursuant to law, from other agencies or bureaus.

Trust Funds

Trust funds are established to account for receipts that are held in trust for use in carrying out specific purposes and programs in accordance with agreement or statute. In distinction to revolving funds and special funds, the assets of trust funds are frequently held over a period of time and may be invested in order to produce revenue. For example, the assets of the Social Security and Medicare Funds are invested in U.S. securities.

The corpus of some trust funds is used in business-type operations. In such a case, the fund is called a *trust revolving fund.* Congress uses the term "trust fund" to describe some funds that in state and local governmental accounting would be called special revenue funds. An example is the Highway Trust Fund. Other federal trust funds, such as those used to account for assets that belong to Native Americans, are true trust funds.

Deposit Funds

Combined receipt and expenditure accounts established to account for receipts held in suspense temporarily and later refunded or paid to some other fund or receipts held by the government as a banker or agent for others and paid out at the discretion of the owner are classified within the federal government as deposit fund accounts. They are similar in nature to the agency funds established for state and local governments.

REQUIRED FINANCIAL REPORTING—U.S. GOVERNMENT-WIDE

In FY 1997, the Department of the Treasury began issuing an annual *Financial Report of the United States Government* that follows FASAB standards and is audited by the Government Accountability Office. Prototype "Consolidated Financial Statements" had been issued since the early 1980s; however, the Government Performance and Results Act of 1993 expanded the requirements of the Chief Financial Officers Act of 1990 and required that 24 federal agencies be audited and comprehensive government-wide financial statements be prepared within three years. Not surprisingly, the first eight years of audits of the U.S. government's Consolidated Financial Statements resulted in a disclaimer of opinion by the Comptroller General of the United States. The most recent disclaimer (p. 34) read as follows:

> Because of the federal government's inability to demonstrate the reliability of significant portions of the U.S. government's accompanying consolidated financial statements for fiscal years 2004 and 2003, principally resulting from the material deficiencies, and other limitations on the scope of our work, described in this report, we are unable to, and we do not, express an opinion on such financial statements.[12]

Major challenges facing federal agencies include property, plant, and equipment and inventories of the Department of Defense (DOD); environmental liabilities; and intragovernmental activity and balances.

Given the difficulties that agencies have experienced in complying with newly developed federal GAAP, it may be surprising that 18 of 24 agencies *did* receive unqualified opinions and 22 agencies reported by the targeted date. The Comptroller General states (p. 2):

> Since Treasury issued the first audited government-wide report for fiscal year 1997, we have made great strides in accelerating the timeliness of government financial reporting and improving its reliability. By accelerating the issuance of this year's report to December 15, just 75 days after the end of the fiscal year, we have made much progress towards matching the timeliness of private sector financial reporting. This acceleration is notable this year because 22 of the 24 major departments and agencies completed their audited financial statements by November 15, within 45 days of the end of the fiscal year. In addition, Treasury has just implemented a new reporting system, which compiles information from agency financial statements and is designed to ensure consistency in reporting and compliance with generally accepted accounting principles.[13]

So, although federal accounting is improving at a rapid rate, attributed in part to congressional mandate and increasingly high professional skills and dedication of governmental accountants, auditors, and agency managers, there are serious financial management issues in the federal agencies, departments, and government corporations that "roll up" into the consolidated, government-wide financial statements of the U.S. government. Keeping in mind that the comptroller general was not able to render an opinion on the federal government's consolidated financial statements, it is helpful to see the "big picture" in the government-wide statements before studying GAAP and reporting for federal agencies. The comparative balance sheets for the United States government for FY 2003 and FY 2004, as shown in Illustration 12–2, report a $7.7 trillion deficit in net position on September 30, 2004. The cost of government operations in FY 2004 exceeded revenues for the year by $616 billion, as seen in the Statement of

---

[12] FY 2004 Consolidated Financial Report of the United States Government is available at www.fms.treas.gov/fr/index.html.

[13] Ibid.

ILLUSTRATION 12–2

UNITED STATES GOVERNMENT
Balance Sheets
as of September 30, 2004, and September 30, 2003

(In billions of dollars)	2004	2003
Assets:		
Cash and other monetary assets	$ 97.0	$ 119.6
Accounts receivable, net	35.1	33.8
Loans receivable, net	220.9	221.1
Taxes receivable, net	21.3	22.9
Inventories and related property, net	261.5	252.7
Property, plant, and equipment, net	652.7	658.2
Other assets	108.8	97.1
Total assets	1,397.3	1,405.4
Liabilities:		
Accounts payable	60.1	62.2
Federal debt securities held by the public and accrued interest	4,329.4	3,944.9
Federal employee and veteran benefits payable	4,062.1	3,880.0
Environmental and disposal liabilities	249.2	249.9
Benefits due and payable	102.9	100.0
Loan guarantee liabilities	43.1	34.6
Other liabilities	260.3	228.0
Total liabilities	9,107.1	8,499.6
Contingencies and commitments*		
Net position	(7,709.8)	(7,094.2)
Total liabilities and net position	$1,397.3	$1,405.4

The notes (not shown here) are an integral part of these financial statements.
*Described in notes, no amount reported here.

Operations in Illustration 12–3, which led to the increase in the net position deficit from the prior year. Students are directed to the GAO's resource for understanding the U.S. Government's annual financial report (see references at the end of this chapter).

REQUIRED FINANCIAL REPORTING—GOVERNMENT AGENCIES

OMB *Bulletin No. 01-09* specifies the form and content of financial statements for 24 major executive departments and agencies that have been designated as reporting entities. OMB *Bulletin No. 01-09* specifies that the general purpose federal financial report of a reporting entity consists of (1) Management's Discussion and Analysis (MD&A), (2) basic statements and related notes, (3) required supplemental stewardship information (RSSI), and (4) required supplemental information (RSI). These requirements are discussed briefly in the following paragraphs.

Management's Discussion and Analysis

SFFAS No. 15 (April 1999) requires that an MD&A be included in a federal agency's general purpose federal financial report as required supplementary information. The conceptual basis for the role and importance of this statement was described earlier in the chapter with the discussion of the four FASAB concepts statements. This standard requires the MD&A to address the entity's mission and organizational structure;

ILLUSTRATION 12–3

UNITED STATES GOVERNMENT
Statements of Operations and Changes in Net Position
for the Years Ended September 30, 2004, and September 30, 2003

(In billions of dollars)	2004	2003
Revenue:		
Individual income tax and tax withholdings	$ 1,512.3	$ 1,481.3
Corporation income taxes	183.8	128.2
Unemployment taxes	36.8	31.2
Excise taxes	72.5	67.6
Estate and gift taxes	24.8	21.9
Customs duties	21.0	19.0
Other taxes and receipts	47.7	39.8
Miscellaneous earned revenues	13.8	7.0
Total revenue	1,912.7	1,796.0
Less net cost of Government operations	2,524.9	2,488.1
Unreconciled transactions affecting the change in net position	(3.4)	24.5
Net operating cost	(615.6)	(667.6)
Net position, beginning of period	(7,094.2)	(6,820.2)
Change in accounting principle	—	383.1
Prior period adjustments	—	10.5
Net operating cost	(615.6)	(667.6)
Net position, end of period	$(7,709.8)	$(7,094.2)

The notes (not shown here) are an integral part of these financial statements.

performance goals and results; financial statements; systems, controls, and legal compliance; and forward-looking information regarding the possible effects of currently known demands, risks, uncertainties, and trends.

Basic Financial Statements

OMB *Bulletin No. 01-09* specifies essentially the same financial statements recommended by *SFFAC No. 2.* It also provides detailed descriptions and instructions for completing each part of each statement. These statements include the following:

1. Balance sheet
2. Statement of net cost
3. Statement of changes in net position
4. Statement of budgetary resources
5. Statement of financing
6. Statement of custodial activity

Each of these statements is discussed briefly in the following paragraphs. The FY 2004 principal financial statements of the U.S. Department of the Interior are presented in Illustrations 12–4 through 12–9. This department was featured in the 2004 Financial Report of the United States Government as a way to acquaint the reader with one of the U.S. government's many missions. The statements consolidate the various units of the Department of the Interior, such as the Bureau of Indian Affairs, the National Park Service, the U.S. Fish and Wildlife Service, the Bureau of Land Management, the

ILLUSTRATION 12–4

U.S. DEPARTMENT OF THE INTERIOR
Consolidated Balance Sheet
as of September 30, 2004 and 2003
(dollars in thousands)

	FY 2004	FY 2003
ASSETS		
Intragovernmental Assets:		
Fund Balance with Treasury	$30,866,144	$28,698,208
Investments, Net	6,187,329	5,609,992
Accounts and Interest Receivable, Net	348,034	387,169
Other		
Advances and Prepayments	1,211	3,624
Total Intragovernmental Assets	37,402,718	34,698,993
Cash	1,081	1,094
Investments, Net	191,844	182,637
Accounts and Interest Receivable, Net	1,347,641	1,226,984
Loans and Interest Receivable, Net	227,514	233,656
Inventory and Related Property, Net	324,319	338,714
General Property, Plant, and Equipment, Net	17,154,211	16,955,915
Other		
Advances and Prepayments	126,579	126,866
Other Assets, Net	170,371	201,544
Stewardship Assets		
TOTAL ASSETS	$56,946,278	$53,966,403
LIABILITIES		
Intragovernmental Liabilities:		
Accounts Payable	$ 76,826	$ 67,838
Debt	1,304,879	1,364,452
Other		
Accrued Payroll and Benefits	171,092	185,437
Advances and Deferred Revenue	1,754,256	1,236,739
Deferred Credits	2,745	19,326
Custodial Liability	671,478	763,387
Aquatic Resource Amounts Due to Others	420,896	389,762
Judgment Fund	178,878	179,725
Other Liabilities	157,889	143,961
Total Intragovernmental Liabilities	4,738,939	4,350,627

continued

Bureau of Land Reclamation, the U.S. Geological Survey, the Minerals Management Services, and the Office of Surface Mining. The department received an unqualified audit opinion from the public accounting firm KMPG for FY 2004.

Balance Sheet

The U.S. Department of the Interior's Balance Sheet for FY 2004 that follows OMB *Bulletin No. 01-09* is presented in Illustration 12–4. Agencies have considerable latitude regarding the level of aggregation to be used in preparing the financial statements. Agencies can use either a single-column (consolidated) format or a multicolumn format displaying financial information for component units or lines of business. If consolidated reporting is used, *Bulletin No. 01-09* (p. 9) requires a separate column presenting the intraentity transactions (for example, eliminations of intercomponent unit receivables

ILLUSTRATION 12–4 *(Continued)*

	FY 2004	FY 2003
Accounts Payable	1,024,845	965,509
Loan Guarantee Liability	60,081	52,185
United States Park Police Pension Actuarial Liability	604,640	—
Federal Employees Compensation Act Liability	664,855	712,250
Environmental Cleanup Costs	101,808	116,086
Other		
Accrued Payroll and Benefits	535,277	434,225
Advances and Deferred Revenue	125,024	137,497
Deferred Credits	690,785	498,545
Contingent Liabilities	781,453	776,546
Other Liabilities	644,014	410,068
TOTAL LIABILITIES	9,971,721	8,453,538
Commitments and Contingencies*		
Net Position		
Unexpended Appropriations	4,080,359	3,929,302
Cumulative Results of Operations	42,894,198	41,583,563
Total Net Position	46,974,557	45,512,865
TOTAL LIABILITIES AND NET POSITION	$56,946,278	$53,966,403

The notes (not shown here) are an integral part of these financial statements
*Described in notes, no amount reported here.

and payables) in the *consolidating* statements underlying the consolidated statements. As shown, when consolidated financial information is provided, comparative totals for the prior year must be presented for the balance sheet, the statement of budgetary resources, and the statement of custodial activity.

Assets   A streamlined format is required in which *entity assets* are combined with *nonentity assets* but *intragovernmental assets* are reported separately from *governmental assets*. **Entity assets** are those the reporting entity has authority to use in its operations, whereas **nonentity assets** are held by the entity but are not available for the entity to spend. An example of a nonentity asset is federal income taxes collected by the Internal Revenue Service for the U.S. government. Nonentity assets should be disclosed in the notes. **Intragovernmental assets (liabilities)** are claims by (against) a reporting entity that arise from transactions among federal entities. **Governmental assets (liabilities)** arise from transactions of the federal government or an entity of the federal government with nonfederal entities.

SFFAS No. 1 provides specific standards relating to Cash, Fund Balance with Treasury, Accounts Receivable, Interest Receivable, and various other asset categories. In most federal agencies *Fund Balance with Treasury* is used rather than *Cash* to indicate that the agency has a claim against the U.S. Treasury on which it may draw to pay liabilities. Only a few large federal departments and agencies, such as the Department of Defense, are authorized to write and issue checks directly against their balances with the Treasury. Most departments and agencies must request that the Treasury issue checks to pay their liabilities. If a federal agency does have the right to maintain one or more bank accounts, bank balances would be reported as *Cash*.

Consistent with the manner in which business entities report inventories, *SFFAS No. 3*, "Accounting for Inventory and Related Property," distinguishes inventory from consumable supplies. Inventory is defined as "tangible personal property that is (1) held for sale, (2) in the process of production for sale, or (3) to be consumed in the production of goods for sale or in the provision of services for a fee" (p. 4). Inventory may be valued at either historical cost or latest acquisition cost. Supplies to be consumed in normal operations are reported as *operating materials and supplies. SSFAS No. 3* also defines several additional types of inventory or related property: (1) stockpile materials, (2) seized and forfeited property, (3) foreclosed property, and (4) goods held under price support and stabilization programs. Discussion of these other types is beyond the scope of this text.

Several *SSFASs* establish standards for property, plant, and equipment (PP&E). Included in this term are several items. **General PP&E** are used to provide general government goods and services, as well as military weapon systems and space exploration equipment. **Heritage assets** are multi-use heritage assets and **stewardship land.** These include PP&E, such as the Washington Monument, that possess educational, cultural, or natural characteristics, and national parks.

Early *SFFASs,* such as No. 6, "Accounting for Property, Plant & Equipment" (1998), No. 11, "Amendments to Accounting for PP&E—Definitions" (1999) and No. 16, "Amendments to Accounting for PP&E—Multi-Use Heritage Assets" (2000) addressed general accounting and reporting of PP&E as well as the unique aspects of national defense PP&E, heritage assets, and stewardship land. More recent *SFFASs* reflect the evolution of FASAB deliberations and conclusions that information about these assets is essential to the fair presentation of the financial position of a federal agency and should be reclassified into categories that are well defined in the professional accounting literature and familiar to report users. *SFFAS No. 23,* "Eliminating the Category National Defense Property, Plant, and Equipment" (2003), does just what its title implies and reclassifies these assets as general PP&E that is capitalized and depreciated (except for land, of course). *SFFAS No. 29,* "Heritage and Stewardship Land" (2005), requires that these assets be accounted for as basic financial information with a note on the balance sheet that discloses information about them, but without any asset dollar amount shown. The notes will disclose information such as a description of major categories of heritage, multi-use heritage, and stewardship land; physical units added and withdrawn during the year; methods of acquisition and withdrawal; and condition information.

Liabilities *SSFAS No. 1* and *SSFAS No. 2* provide specific accounting standards for Accounts Payable, Interest Payable, and Other Current Liabilities. OMB *Bulletin No. 01-09* provides additional guidance on reporting liabilities. For example, liabilities covered by budgetary resources (funded) and liabilities not covered by budgetary resources (unfunded) are combined on the face of the balance sheet. *Liabilities covered by budgetary resources* are those for which monies have been made available either through congressional appropriations or current earnings of the entity. *Liabilities not covered by budgetary resources* result from the receipt of goods or services in the current or prior periods but for which monies have not yet been made available through congressional appropriations or current earnings of the entity. Examples of the latter are liabilities for accrued leave, capital leases, and pensions. These should be disclosed in the notes.

SFFAS No. 5, "Accounting for Liabilities of the Federal Government," establishes standards for liabilities not covered in *SFFAS No. 1* and *No. 2.* The statement defines a *liability* as "a probable future outflow or other sacrifice of resources as a result of past transactions or events" (par. 19). *SFFAS No. 5* provides the following recognition criteria for liabilities arising from the transactions or events indicated:

1. *Exchange transactions.* Recognize the liability when one party receives goods or services in exchange for a promise to provide money or other resources in the future.
2. *Nonexchange transactions* (for example, grants and entitlements). Recognize a liability for any unpaid amounts due at the end of the fiscal period.

3. *Government-related events* (nontransactions-based events that involve interaction between federal entities and their environment; for example, damage to private property). Recognize a liability when the event occurs if the future outflow of resources is probable and measurable.

4. *Government-acknowledged events* (events for which the government *chooses* to acknowledge responsibility. For example, damage from a natural disaster). Recognize liability when the government formally acknowledges responsibility for an event and a nonexchange or exchange transaction has occurred.

5. *Contingencies.* Generally disclosed in the notes or in some cases such as contingencies related to government-acknowledged events, not disclosed at all.

6. *Capital leases.* Criteria for a capital lease are essentially the same as those specified by the FASB for commercial entities and the GASB for state and local governmental entities (see Chapter 5 of this text). A liability should be recognized in the amount of the present value of the rental and other minimum lease payments.

7. *Federal debt* (for example, U.S. Treasury bonds). Recognize a liability when an exchange transaction occurs between involved parties. Original issue premiums and discounts are amortized using the effective interest method.

8. *Pensions, other retirement benefits, and other postemployment benefits.* Recognize an expense at the time employees' services are rendered. Any unfunded portion of cost calculated using the "Aggregate Entry Age Normal Cost" method should be reported as a liability.

9. *Insurance and guarantee programs* (other than social insurance and loan guarantee programs). Recognize a liability for unpaid claims incurred as a result of insured events that have already occurred. (*Note:* Loan guarantee program liabilities are covered by *SFFAS No. 2.* Reporting of social insurance programs is discussed later in this chapter.)

SFFAS No. 5 also requires disclosure in the notes to the financial statements of the condition and estimated cost to remedy deferred maintenance on PP&E. In addition, it provides standards for measurement and recognition of expenses and liabilities related to environmental cleanup and closure costs from removing general PP&E from service.

Net Position   OMB *Bulletin No. 01-09* requires that the fund balances of the entity's funds be reported in the balance sheet as **net position.** The components of net position are **unexpended appropriations,** the amount of the entity's appropriations represented by undelivered orders and unobligated balances, and **cumulative results of operations,** the net difference between expenses/losses and financing sources, including appropriations, revenues, and gains, since the inception of the activity. Cumulative results of operations would also include any other items that would affect the net position, including, for example, the fair market value of donated assets and assets (net of liabilities) transferred to or from other federal entities without reimbursement.

Statement of Net Cost

Illustration 12–5 presents the Department of the Interior's consolidated statement of net cost. This statement shows the components of the net cost of the reporting entity's operations, both for the entity as a whole and for each of its responsibility centers or segments. Responsibility segments should align directly with the major goals and outputs described in the entity's strategic plans required by the Government Performance and Results Act. If the reporting entity has a complex organizational structure, it may need to provide supporting schedules in the notes to the financial statements to provide net cost information for its major programs and activities.

ILLUSTRATION 12–5

U.S. DEPARTMENT OF THE INTERIOR
Consolidated Statement of Net Cost
for the years ended September 30, 2004 and 2003
(dollars in thousands)

	Resource Protection	Resource Use	Recreation	Serving Communities	Reimbursable Activity and Other	FY 2004
Cost—Services Provided to the Public	$2,941,070	3,384,911	2,138,937	6,398,034	381,059	$15,244,011
Revenue Earned from the Public	511,134	941,325	238,306	407,603	109,317	2,207,685
Net Cost of Services to the Public	2,429,936	2,443,586	1,900,631	5,990,431	271,742	13,036,326
Cost—Services Provided to Federal Agencies	105,593	145,001	21,535	383,874	1,893,020	2,549,023
Revenue Earned from Federal Agencies	100,128	140,931	20,647	366,267	1,898,327	2,526,300
Net Cost (Revenue) of Services Provided to Federal Agencies	5,465	4,070	888	17,607	(5,307)	22,723
Net Cost of Operations	$2,435,401	2,447,656	1,901,519	6,008,038	266,435	$13,059,049

	Protect the Environment and Preserve Our Nation's Natural & Cultural Resources	Provide Recreation for America	Manage Natural Resources for a Healthy Environment and a Strong Economy	Provide Science for a Changing World	Meet Our Trust Responsibilities to Indian Tribes and Our Commitments to Island Communities	Reimbursable Activity and Other	Costs Not Associated with Programs	FY 2003
Cost—Services Provided to the Public	$4,306,918	2,113,487	3,632,240	1,264,688	2,420,119	216,330	—	$13,953,782
Revenue Earned from the Public	462,597	171,275	862,284	166,654	117,692	38,273	—	1,818,775
Net Cost of Services to the Public	3,844,321	1,942,212	2,769,956	1,098,034	2,302,427	178,057	—	12,135,007
Cost—Services Provided to Federal Agencies	118,870	31,197	130,943	186,508	204,025	1,394,950	—	2,066,493
Revenue Earned from Federal Agencies	114,846	29,723	127,841	176,478	201,491	1,392,827	—	2,043,206
Net Cost (Revenue) of Services Provided to Federal Agencies	4,024	1,474	3,102	10,030	2,534	2,123	—	23,287
Costs Not Associated with Programs	—	—	—	—	—	—	81,100	81,100
Net Cost of Operations	$3,848,345	1,943,686	2,773,058	1,108,064	2,304,961	180,180	81,100	$12,239,394

The notes (not shown here) are an integral part of these financial statements.

Statement of Changes in Net Position

The Department of the Interior's consolidated statement of changes in net position is shown in Illustration 12–6. The purpose of this statement is to communicate all changes in the reporting entity's net position: cumulative results of operations and unexpended appropriations. Net cost of operations is obtained from the bottom of the consolidated statement of net cost (see Illustration 12–5) and includes gross costs less any exchange (earned) revenues. Further additions or deductions, as appropriate, of prior-period adjustments (due to material errors or accounting changes), change in cumulative results of operations, and unexpended appropriations compose the total change in net position.

ILLUSTRATION 12–6

U.S. DEPARTMENT OF THE INTERIOR
Consolidated Statement of Changes in Net Position
for the years ended September 30, 2004 and 2003
(dollars in thousands)

	FY 2004	FY 2003
UNEXPENDED APPROPRIATIONS		
Beginning Balances, as adjusted	$ 3,929,302	$ 3,846,318
Budgetary Financing Sources		
Appropriations Received, General Funds	10,061,570	9,610,818
Appropriations Transferred In/Out	89,861	81,820
Appropriations—Used	(9,871,434)	(9,519,709)
Other Adjustments	(128,940)	(89,945)
Total Budgetary Financing Sources	151,057	82,984
Ending Balance—Unexpended Appropriations	$ 4,080,359	$ 3,929,302
CUMULATIVE RESULTS OF OPERATIONS		
Beginning Balances, as adjusted	$41,583,563	$39,908,117
Cumulative Effect of Change in Accounting	(649,300)	—
Beginning Balances, as adjusted	40,934,263	39,908,117
Budgetary Financing Sources		
Appropriations—Used	9,871,434	9,519,709
Royalties Retained	3,491,208	2,582,663
Transfers In/Out without Reimbursement	(40,424)	127,338
Non-Exchange Revenue		
Tax Revenue	717,364	659,217
Abandoned Mine Fees	286,160	282,411
Donations and Forfeitures of Cash and Cash Equivalents	29,710	39,833
Other Non-Exchange Revenue	153,466	130,544
Other Budgetary Financing Sources and Adjustments	2,422	13,361
Other Financing Sources		
Imputed Financing From Costs Absorbed by Others	519,171	570,544
Transfers In/Out without Reimbursement	(27,222)	(57,643)
Donations and Forfeitures of Property	15,695	46,863
Total Financing Sources	15,018,984	13,914,840
Net Cost of Operations	(13,059,049)	(12,239,394)
Ending Balance—Cumulative Results of Operations	$42,894,198	$41,583,563

The notes (not shown here) are an integral part of these financial statements.

ILLUSTRATION 12–7

U.S. DEPARTMENT OF THE INTERIOR
Combined Statement of Budgetary Resources
for the years ended September 30, 2004 and 2003
(dollars in thousands)

	FY 2004		FY 2003	
	Total Budgetary Accounts	**Non-Budgetary Credit Program Financing Accounts**	**Total Budgetary Accounts**	**Non-Budgetary Credit Program Financing Accounts**
Budgetary Resources:				
Budget Authority:				
Appropriations Received	$14,712,390	—	$14,003,754	—
Borrowing Authority	—	$ 8,625	—	$18,906
Net Transfers, Current Year Authority	(139,167)	—	(70,350)	—
Unobligated Balance:				
Beginning of Fiscal Year	4,905,271	67,678	4,478,411	55,779
Net Transfers, Unobligated Balance, Actual	25,980	—	(29,833)	—
Spending Authority From Offsetting Collections:				
Earned				
Collected	4,722,696	26,240	4,784,999	8,322
Receivable From Federal Sources	(4,537)	—	(146,516)	(475)
Change in Unfilled Customer Orders				
Advance Received	547,677	—	517,626	—
Without Advance From Federal Sources	28,869	—	(159,721)	—
Subtotal: Spending Authority From Offsetting Collections	5,294,705	26,240	4,996,388	7,847
Recoveries of Prior Year Obligations	393,579	26	304,691	137
Temporarily Not Available Pursuant to Public Law	(2,249)	—	—	—
Permanently Not Available	(177,829)	(6,189)	(207,623)	2,487
Total Budgetary Resources	**$25,012,680**	**$96,380**	**$23,475,438**	**$85,156**

continued

Statement of Budgetary Resources

The statement of budgetary resources for the Department of the Interior (see Illustration 12–7) presents the availability of budgetary resources and the status of those resources at year-end. OMB *Circular A–34,* "Instructions on Budget Execution," provides the definitions and guidance for budgetary accounting and reporting. As shown in Illustration 12–7, the equation for this statement is Budgetary resources = Status of budgetary resources. Available **budgetary resources** include new budgetary authority for the period plus unobligated budgetary authority carried over from the prior period and offsetting collections, if any, plus or minus any budgetary adjustments. The *Status of Budgetary Resources* section consists of obligations incurred (that is, budget authority expended and amounts reserved for undelivered orders) plus any current budgetary authority that is still available to finance operations of the current period or those of prior periods. The lower portion of the statement of budgetary resources reconciles obligations incurred during the period to total budgetary outlays for the period, after adjusting for offsetting collections and budgetary adjustments, and the change in obligations during the year is carried forward.

ILLUSTRATION 12–7 *(Continued)*

	FY 2004		FY 2003	
	Total Budgetary Accounts	Non-Budgetary Credit Program Financing Accounts	Total Budgetary Accounts	Non-Budgetary Credit Program Financing Accounts
Status of Budgetary Resources:				
Obligations Incurred:				
Direct	$14,667,176	$19,544	$14,035,601	$17,478
Reimbursable	5,136,048	—	4,534,566	—
Total Obligations Incurred	19,803,224	19,544	18,570,167	17,478
Unobligated Balance:				
Apportioned	5,072,733	76,836	4,738,941	66,160
Exempt From Apportionment	39,444	—	41,349	—
Unobligated Balance not Available	97,279	—	124,981	1,518
Total Status of Budgetary Resources	$25,012,680	$96,380	$23,475,438	$85,156
Relationship of Obligations to Outlays:				
Obligations Incurred	$19,803,224	$19,544	$18,570,167	$17,478
Obligated Balance, Net, Beginning of Fiscal Year	5,740,974	8,063	4,953,205	11,601
Obligated Balance, Net, End of Fiscal Year:				
Accounts Receivable	326,657	—	331,195	—
Unfilled Customer Orders From Federal Sources	552,221	—	523,353	—
Undelivered Orders	(6,288,774)	(3,952)	(5,345,138)	(8,063)
Accounts Payable	(1,359,920)	(3,823)	(1,250,384)	—
Total Obligated Balance, Net, End of Fiscal Year	(6,769,816)	(7,775)	(5,740,974)	(8,063)
Less: Spending Authority Adjustments	(417,910)	(26)	1,546	338
Outlays:				
Disbursements	18,356,472	19,806	17,783,944	21,354
Collections	(5,270,374)	(26,240)	(5,302,624)	(8,322)
Subtotal	13,086,098	(6,434)	12,481,320	13,032
Less: Offsetting Receipts	(4,269,067)	—	(3,661,729)	—
Net Outlays	$ 8,817,031	$ (6,434)	$ 8,819,591	$13,032

The notes (not shown here) are an integral part of these financial statements.

Statement of Financing

Another required statement is the statement of financing (see Illustration 12–8). This statement reconciles the Department of the Interior's budget-based information in the statement of budgetary resources to the accrual-based *net cost of operations* information in the statement of net costs. Total budgetary and nonbudgetary resources available to fund current-period operations are reported in the upper section, Resources Used to Finance Activities. The section Resources Used to Finance Items not Part of the Net Cost of Operations essentially deducts items that were included in sources or uses of budgetary resources but were not included as part of the net cost of operations on the accrual basis. The third section, Components of the Net Cost of Operations That Will Not Require or Generate Resources in the Current Period, includes items that would have been included in the measurement of the net cost of operations but that did not require financing. This section would typically be required for an increase in unfunded liabilities, such as

ILLUSTRATION 12–8

U.S. DEPARTMENT OF THE INTERIOR
Consolidated Statement of Financing
for the years ended September 30, 2004 and 2003
(dollars in thousands)

	FY 2004	FY 2003
Resources Used to Finance Activities:		
Budgetary Resources Obligated:		
Obligations Incurred	$19,822,768	$18,587,645
Less: Spending Authority From Offsetting Collections/Recoveries	(5,714,550)	(5,309,063)
Obligations Net of Offsetting Collections and Recoveries	14,108,218	13,278,582
Less: Offsetting Receipts	(4,269,067)	(3,661,729)
Net Obligations	9,839,151	9,616,853
Other Resources:		
Donations and Forfeitures of Property	15,695	46,863
Transfers In/Out Without Reimbursement	(27,222)	(57,643)
Imputed Financing From Costs Absorbed by Others	519,171	570,544
Net Other Resources Used to Finance Activities	507,644	559,764
Total Resources Used to Finance Activities	10,346,795	10,176,617
Resources Used to Finance Items Not Part of the Net Cost of Operations:		
Change in Budgetary Resources Obligated for Goods, Services, and Benefits Ordered but Not Yet Provided	(391,696)	(47,223)
Resources That Fund Expenses Recognized in Prior Periods	131,102	(264,012)
Budgetary Offsetting Collections and Receipts That Do Not Affect Net Cost of Operations:		
Credit Program Collections Which Increase Liabilities for Loan Guarantees or Allowances for Subsidy	17,193	15,408
Offsetting Receipts Not Part of the Net Cost of Operations	2,832,565	2,547,888
Resources That Finance the Acquisition of Assets	(819,203)	(870,147)
Other Resources or Adjustments to Net Obligated Resources That Do Not Affect Net Cost of Operations	37,256	(20,454)
Total Resources Used to Finance Items Not Part of the Net Cost of Operations	1,807,217	1,361,460
Total Resources Used to Finance the Net Cost of Operations	12,154,012	11,538,077

continued

unfunded annual leave. An accrual for annual leave would have been included in the net cost of operations but not as an obligation incurred for budgetary purposes. Of course, this item would be deducted in a future period when the leave is funded as Resources Used to Finance Items not Part of the Net Cost of Operations.

Statement of Custodial Activity

OMB *Bulletin No. 01-09* requires entities that "collect nonexchange revenue for the General Fund of the Treasury, a trust fund, or other recipient entities" prepare a statement of custodial activity (see Illustration 12–9). As shown in Illustration 12–9, the Department of the Interior's statement of custodial activity essentially reports on

ILLUSTRATION 12–8   (*Continued*)

	FY 2004	FY 2003
Components of Net Cost of Operations That Will Not Require or Generate Resources in the Current Period:		
Components Requiring or Generating Resources in Future Periods:		
Increase (Decrease) in Annual Leave Liability	17,922	12,013
Increase (Decrease) in Environmental and Disposal Liability	(15,777)	(102,365)
Upward/Downward Reestimates in Credit Subsidy Expense	(335)	1,510
Increase (Decrease) in Exchange Revenue Receivable From the Public	(1,166)	(10,978)
Other	53,487	(115,399)
Total Components of Net Cost of Operations That Will Require or Generate Resources in Future Periods	54,131	(215,219)
Components Not Requiring or Generating Resources:		
Depreciation and Amortization	460,946	455,939
Revaluation of Assets or Liabilities	44,791	81,100
Components of Net Cost of Operations Related to Transfer Accounts Where Budget Amounts are Reported by Other Federal Entities	358,936	367,938
Other	(13,767)	11,559
Total Components of Net Cost of Operations That Will Not Require or Generate Resources in the Current Period	850,906	916,536
Total Components of Net Cost of Operations That Will Not Require or Generate Resources	905,037	701,317
Net Cost of Operations	$13,059,049	$12,239,394

The notes (not shown here) are an integral part of these financial statements.

the agency's fiduciary responsibility to report on how much has been collected and accrued and how the monies were distributed.

Required Supplemental Information

OMB *Bulletin No. 01-09* requires that the costs related to stewardship PP&E be recognized on the face of the statement of net costs or be disclosed in the notes to the financial statements. Disclosures about deferred maintenance for both general and stewardship PP&E are also required. Information about *stewardship investments,* such as the amount of annual investments and description of major programs related to these investments, must also be disclosed. **Stewardship investments** are beneficial investments of the government in items such as nonfederal physical property (property financed by the federal government but owned by state or local governments), human capital, and research and development. In addition, pursuant to applicable federal accounting standards, *Bulletin No. 01-09* discusses the required disclosures about environmental cleanup costs, detail of budgetary resources and obligations, and incidental amounts of custodial collections and distributions that may not warrant separate reporting in a statement of custodial activity.

Accounting for Social Insurance

Accounting for federal social insurance programs—Social Security, Medicare and Supplementary Medical Insurance (Part B), Railroad Retirement benefits, Black Lung benefits, and Unemployment Insurance is, not surprisingly, very complex. In general,

ILLUSTRATION 12–9

U.S. DEPARTMENT OF THE INTERIOR
Consolidated Statement of Custodial Activity
for the years ended September 30, 2004 and 2003
(dollars in thousands)

	FY 2004	FY 2003
Revenues on Behalf of the Federal Government		
Mineral Lease Revenue		
Rents and Royalties	$7,498,235	$6,716,830
Offshore Lease Sales	560,225	485,841
Strategic Petroleum Reserve	1,191,284	1,044,350
Total Revenue	$9,249,744	$8,247,021
Disposition of Revenue		
Distribution to Department of the Interior		
National Park Service Conservation Funds	$1,049,000	$1,049,000
Bureau of Reclamation	924,486	753,374
Minerals Management Service	1,300,525	1,070,294
Bureau of Land Management	16,216	72,843
Fish and Wildlife Service	737	2,909
Distribution to Other Federal Agencies		
Department of the Treasury	4,375,632	4,208,092
Department of Agriculture	25,232	22,920
Department of Energy	1,191,284	1,044,350
Distribution to Indian Tribes and Agencies	93,892	79,544
Distribution to States and Others	75,777	65,488
Change in Untransferred Revenue	196,963	(121,793)
Total Disposition of Revenue	$9,249,744	$8,247,021

The notes (not shown here) are an integral part of these financial statements.

SFFAs No. 17 requires a liability to be recognized when payments are due and payable to beneficiaries or service providers, and supplementary stewardship information is required to facilitate assessing long-term sustainability of programs and the nation's ability to raise resources from future program participants to pay for benefits proposed to present participants.

The FASAB acknowledges that although *SFFAS No. 17* was a major step forward in federal financial reporting, there is much more work to do in properly accounting for social insurance. Social insurance is a unique blend of nonexchange transactions, such as annual governmental assistance programs, and exchange transactions, such as long-term pension programs. The FASAB decided in earlier studies on liabilities (*SFFAS No. 5*) and supplementary stewardship reporting (*SFFAS No. 8*) that social insurance programs were unique enough to require a separate project. Required supplementary information includes long-range cash-flow projections, projections of the ratio of amounts paid into and out of the programs, and actuarial values of benefits and contributions/income from or on behalf of participants (both current and future).

SFFASs No. 25, "Reclassification of Stewardship Responsibilities and Eliminating the Current Services Assessment," and. *No. 26,* "Presentation of Significant Assumptions of the Statement of Social Insurance: Amending SFFAS 25," further address significant assumptions for a statement of social insurance, but the effective dates of these two standards are deferred by *SFFAS No. 28,* "Deferral of the Effective Date of Reclassification of the Statement of Social Insurance: Amending SFFAS 25 and 26," until fiscal years beginning after September 30, 2005. Aspects of the social insurance liability project that are on FASAB's 2005 technical agenda include the application of the definition of a liability to social insurance programs; determining the obligating event of a social insurance liability; and other recognition, measurement and display issues.

DUAL-TRACK ACCOUNTING SYSTEM

Financial reports of federal agencies must be based on historical costs to indicate whether an entity has complied with laws and regulations (e.g., 31 U.S.C. §1341). Congressional policy as expressed in 31 U.S.C. §3512 and the Federal Financial Management Improvement Act of 1996 calls for using cost information in budgeting and in managing operations. This law also provides for using cost-based budgets, at such time as may be determined by the President, in developing requests for appropriations. All departments and agencies, therefore, should have budget and accounting systems that have the capability to produce cost-based budgets. In this context, cost is the value of goods and services used or consumed by a government agency within a given period, regardless of when they were ordered, received, or paid. In any given year, the obligations incurred may be less than, equal to, or greater than the costs recognized for that period due to changes in inventories, obligations, and so on. At the completion of a program, however, obligations and costs are identical.

The accounting system of a federal agency must provide information needed for financial management as well as information needed to demonstrate that agency managers have complied with budgetary and other legal requirements. Accordingly, federal agency accounting is based on a *dual-track system,* one track being a self-balancing set of *proprietary* accounts intended to provide information for agency management and the other track being the self-balancing set of *budgetary accounts* needed (1) to ensure that available budgetary resources and authority are not overexpended or overobligated and (2) to facilitate standardized budgetary reporting requirements. The dual-track system is not likely to change in the near future since the FASAB's role specifically excludes budgetary accounting. Illustration 12–10 summarizes key differences between budgetary and proprietary track accounting in terms of the timing of the recognition of events and transactions. The use of the dual-track system is illustrated in the next section.

Illustrative Transactions and Entries

The basic budgetary authority for a federal agency can come from many different sources. Only one of those sources is illustrated here—basic operating appropriations.[14] The flow of budgetary authority generally follows a sequence of events described as follows:

1. The Congressional **appropriation** is enacted into law and provides budget authority to fund an agency's operations for the year.

---

[14] The illustrative journal entries shown in this section are modeled on the account titles prescribed by the U.S. Government Standard General Ledger except that we have added fiscal year designations after certain accounts for instructional purposes. The financial statements that follow are based on those specified by OMB *Bulletin No. 01-09.*

ILLUSTRATION 12–10   Summary of Key Differences between Budgetary and Proprietary Accounting in Recognition of Events That Constitute Transactions

Budgetary Accounting	Proprietary Accounting
Entries are made for commitment of funds in advance of preparing orders to procure goods and services.	Entries are not made for commitments.
Entries are made for obligation of funds at the time goods and services are ordered.	Entries are not made for obligations.
Entries are made to expend appropriations when goods and services chargeable to the appropriation are received, regardless of when they are used and regardless of when they are paid.	Goods and services that will last more than a year and otherwise meet the criteria to qualify as assets are capitalized and expensed when consumed, regardless of what appropriation funded them and when they are paid.
Entries are only made against an appropriation for transactions funded by the appropriation.	Goods and services consumed in the current period for which payment is to be made from one or more subsequent appropriations is recognized as an expense in the current period.
Entries are not made against an appropriation for transactions not funded by the appropriation.	Goods and services consumed in the current period but paid for in prior periods are expensed in the current period.

Source: U.S. General Accounting Office, *GAO Accounting Guide: Basic Topics Relating to Appropriations and Reimbursables* (Washington, DC: GAO, 1990), p. 3–2.

2. An **apportionment,** usually quarterly, is approved by the Office of Management and Budget and may be used by the agency to procure goods and services for the quarter.

3. The head of the agency or his or her designee authorizes an **allotment** of the apportionment for procurement of goods and services.

4. Authorized agency employees reserve allotted budget authority in the estimated amount of an order as a **commitment** prior to the actual ordering of goods and services.

5. **Obligation** of the allotment occurs when a formal order for acquisition of goods and services is placed, charging the allotment with the latest estimate of the cost of goods or services ordered.

6. An **expended appropriation** occurs when goods or services have been received.

It should be noted that the term *expended appropriation* means that the budget authority has been used and is no longer available to provide for goods and services. It does not necessarily mean that cash has been disbursed; it may be that only a liability has been incurred. A *commitment* (item 4) does not legally encumber an appropriation, but its use is recommended for effective planning and fund control. Some agencies, however, use commitments only for certain spending categories.

As shown in Illustration 12–11, the full amount of an agency's appropriation for the year is reported as a budgetary resource that, at a given point during the period, is distributed among the budgetary accounts shown under status of resources. As discussed earlier and in the following illustrative transactions, budgetary authority normally flows down the accounts, culminating ultimately in the expending of authority. If the agency whose September 30, 2007, post-closing trial balance is shown in Illustration 12–12 receives from Congress a one-year appropriation for fiscal year

ILLUSTRATION 12–11   Relationship among Budgetary Accounts

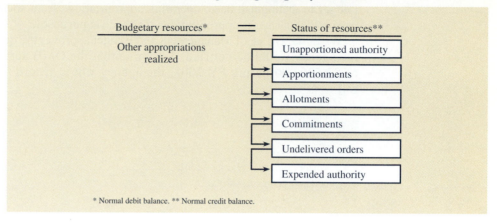

* Normal debit balance. ** Normal credit balance.

2008 (FY 2008) in the amount of $2,500,000, the Treasury's Bureau of Government Financial Operations would prepare a formal notice to the agency after the appropriation act has been signed by the President. The following entries would be made in the agency accounts:

		Debits	Credits
1a.	*Budgetary:*		
	Other Appropriations Realized—2008	2,500,000	
	Unapportioned Authority—2008		2,500,000
1b.	*Proprietary:*		
	Fund Balance with Treasury—2008	2,500,000	
	Unexpended Appropriations—2008		2,500,000

ILLUSTRATION 12–12

FEDERAL AGENCY
Post-Closing Trial Balance
As of September 30, 2007

	Debits	Credits
Proprietary Accounts:		
Fund Balance with Treasury—2007	$ 675,000	
Operating Materials and Supplies	610,000	
Equipment	3,000,000	
Accumulated Depreciation on Equipment		$ 600,000
Accounts Payable		275,000
Unexpended Appropriations—2007		400,000
Cumulative Results of Operations		3,010,000
	$4,285,000	$4,285,000
Budgetary Accounts:		
Other Appropriations Realized—2007	$ 400,000	
Undelivered Orders—2007		$ 400,000
	$ 400,000	$ 400,000

The *Other Appropriations Realized* account is used in the U.S. Standard General Ledger to distinguish basic operating appropriations from specific appropriation authority that earmarks appropriations for specific purposes.

When the Office of Management and Budget approves the quarterly apportionment, the agency would be notified. Assuming that the OMB approved apportionments of $2,500,000 during FY 2008, the agency would record the apportionments as follows:[15]

		Debits	Credits
2.	*Budgetary:*		
	Unapportioned Authority—2008	2,500,000	
	Apportionments—2008		2,500,000

If, during FY 2008, the agency head allotted to subunits within the agency the entire apportionment, the event would be recorded in the agency accounts in the following manner:

		Debits	Credits
3.	*Budgetary:*		
	Apportionments—2008	2,500,000	
	Allotments—2008		2,500,000

All three entries—for the annual appropriation, for the apportionment by the OMB, and for the agency allotments—would be made as of October 1, the first day of fiscal year 2008. Although journal entries are made the first day of the fiscal year, in some years the appropriation bill might not have actually been enacted by that date. The substance of the three entries is that agency managers had obligational spending authority for the year totaling $2,500,000 to finance agency operations. As discussed in Chapters 3 and 4 for state and local government accounting, federal agencies are legally constrained to manage the activities of the agency so obligational authority is not exceeded. It should also be noted that if the OMB should withhold any portion of the annual appropriations, that amount would not be available to the agency. Furthermore, for single-year appropriations, any apportionments and allotments not expended or obligated ordinarily must be returned to the U.S. Treasury at the end of the fiscal year.

Commitments were recorded during FY 2008 in the amount of $1,150,000. Operations of the example agency for FY 2008 are summarized in the following journal entries:

		Debits	Credits
4.	*Budgetary:*		
	Allotments—2008	1,150,000	
	Commitments—2008		1,150,000

[15] OMB ordinarily does not have authority to withhold apportionments. If OMB does withhold a portion of an apportionment, special accounts would be used. This requirement is beyond the overview scope of our coverage here.

Purchase orders and contracts for goods and services were issued in the amount of $1,144,000 during the year.

		Debits	Credits
5.	*Budgetary:*		
	Commitments—2008	1,144,000	
	Undelivered Orders—2008		1,144,000

Checks for Accounts Payable as of October 1 were requested from the Treasury. The Accounts Payable were for materials received in fiscal year 2007 in the amount of $90,000 and equipment received in the amount of $185,000. This event does not reduce the agency's Fund Balance with Treasury until the checks are actually issued by the Treasury. Instead, most agencies would credit the account *Disbursements in Transit* until notified by the Treasury that the requested checks have been issued. Disbursements in Transit is a current liability account since liabilities to vendors and creditors cannot be considered settled until the checks have actually been issued. If this agency had been one of the few with authority to issue checks directly, then Fund Balance with Treasury would have been credited immediately. Since this agency is not assumed to have check-writing authority, the following entry would be made:

6.	*Proprietary:*		
	Accounts Payable	275,000	
	Disbursements in Transit—2007		275,000

The agency received notification from the Treasury that the checks requested in Transaction 6 had been issued. This notification would be recorded as follows:

7.	*Proprietary:*		
	Disbursements in Transit—2007	275,000	
	Fund Balance with Treasury—2007		275,000

Goods and equipment ordered in FY 2007 (prior fiscal year) are reported in Illustration 12–12 in the net position account, Unexpended Appropriations—2007, a proprietary account, as amounting to $400,000. A budgetary account Undelivered Orders—2007 also exists in the same amount, as does its offsetting account Other Appropriations Realized—2007. (All other budgetary accounts for 2007 were closed at the end of that fiscal year because all unobligated appropriation authority expired at year-end.) Assuming that all the goods and equipment ordered in 2007 were received during the first quarter of FY 2008, one entry is necessary in the budgetary accounts to show that fiscal 2007 obligations are now liquidated and that the prior-year appropriation is expended in the same amount. Entries in proprietary accounts are required to record the debit to Unexpended Appropriations—2007 and the offsetting credit to the Appropriations Used account, as well as debits to asset accounts and a credit to Accounts Payable. These entries follow:

		Debits	Credits
8a.	*Budgetary:*		
	Undelivered Orders—2007	400,000	
	Expended Authority—2007		400,000
8b.	*Proprietary:*		
	Operating Materials and Supplies	150,000	
	Equipment	250,000	
	Accounts Payable		400,000
	Unexpended Appropriations—2007	400,000	
	Appropriations Used		400,000

Operating materials and supplies were received from suppliers during FY 2008 at an actual cost of $1,010,000, for which Undelivered Orders—2008 had been recorded in the estimated amount of $1,005,000. Budgetary track and proprietary track entries for these transactions are shown in Entries 9a and 9b. Because the actual cost of materials and supplies exceeded the estimated amount recorded previously as Undelivered Orders—2008, the $5,000 excess must be debited to Allotments—2008 to record the additional expenditure of obligational authority.

9a.	*Budgetary:*		
	Undelivered Orders—2008	1,005,000	
	Allotments—2008	5,000	
	Expended Authority—2008		1,010,000
9b.	*Proprietary:*		
	Operating Materials and Supplies	1,010,000	
	Accounts Payable		1,010,000
	Unexpended Appropriations—2008	1,010,000	
	Appropriations Used		1,010,000

Payrolls for FY 2008 amounted to $1,188,000. Utilities in the amount of $120,000 were also approved for payment during the year. (The agency does not record commitments for payrolls and other recurring operating expenses.) Checks totaling $1,308,000 were requested from the Treasury for these expenses. The debit in the first proprietary track entry is to the control account Operating/Program Expenses. Obviously, each agency would have a subsidiary expense ledger or more detailed expense accounts in its general ledger tailored to its specific needs. The required entries are:

10a.	*Budgetary:*		
	Allotments—2008	1,308,000	
	Expended Authority—2008		1,308,000
10b.	*Proprietary:*		
	Operating/Program Expenses	1,308,000	
	Disbursements in Transit—2008		1,308,000
	Unexpended Appropriations—2008	1,308,000	
	Appropriations Used		1,308,000

Materials and supplies used in the operating activities during FY 2008 amounted to $1,620,000. The entries would be:

		Debits	Credits
11.	*Proprietary:*		
	Operating/Program Expenses	1,620,000	
	Operating Materials and Supplies		1,620,000

Accounts Payable in the amount of $1,410,000 (see Entries 8b and 9b) were approved for payment and checks were requested from the Treasury. Of this amount, $400,000 will be charged against the FY 2007 Fund Balance with Treasury and $1,010,000 against the FY 2008 Fund Balance with Treasury. The required entry is:

12.	*Proprietary:*		
	Accounts Payable	1,410,000	
	Disbursements in Transit—2007		400,000
	Disbursements in Transit—2008		1,010,000

The Treasury notified the agency that checks in the amount of $2,718,000 (including $400,000 for Accounts Payable arising from fiscal year 2007—see Entry 12) had been issued during FY 2008. Of the $2,318,000 charged against the FY 2008 Fund Balance with Treasury, $1,010,000 was for operating materials and supplies (see Entry 9b), $1,188,000 was for payrolls, and $120,000 was for utilities expense.

13.	*Proprietary:*		
	Disbursements in Transit—2007	400,000	
	Disbursements in Transit—2008	2,318,000	
	Fund Balance with Treasury—2007		400,000
	Fund Balance with Treasury—2008		2,318,000

Adjusting Entries

To prepare accrual-based financial statements, the following items were taken into account: (1) payroll accrued for the last week of the fiscal year is computed to be $27,000 and (2) invoices or receiving reports for goods received but for which payment has not yet been approved totaled $105,000, of which $36,000 worth has been used in operations and $69,000 is in ending inventory. Because the obligations for the items in (1) and (2) have become certain in amount and relevant expense accounts or inventory accounts can be charged, as illustrated as follows, the amounts should be shown in the financial statements as current liabilities. It is assumed that the goods received had been previously obligated in the amount of $105,000, but no commitment or obligation had been recorded for the accrued payroll. The required entries are:

		Debits	Credits
14a.	*Budgetary:*		
	Allotments—2008	27,000	
	Undelivered Orders—2008	105,000	
	Expended Authority—2008		132,000
14b.	*Proprietary:*		
	Operating/Program Expenses	63,000	
	Operating Materials and Supplies	69,000	
	Accounts Payable		105,000
	Accrued Funded Payroll and Benefits		27,000
	Unexpended Appropriations—2008	132,000	
	Appropriations Used		132,000

Depreciation of equipment was computed as $300,000 for FY 2008. Inasmuch as depreciation is not an expense chargeable against the appropriation, the accrual of depreciation expense does not affect any of the appropriation, allotment, or obligation accounts. However, it is recorded as in business accounting to measure the cost of activities on an accrual basis. The credit to Accumulated Depreciation reduces the book value of the equipment.

15.	*Proprietary:*		
	Depreciation and Amortization	300,000	
	Accumulated Depreciation on Equipment		300,000

Although not illustrated here, federal agencies also accrue some expenses such as accrued annual leave that will be funded by future-period appropriations. These unfunded accrued expenses require entries in the proprietary track but require no entries in the budgetary track. The effect of these unfunded expenses is to reduce the balance of Cumulative Results of Operations since the expenses are not offset by a financing source.

Illustrative Financial Statements

After entries just illustrated have been made, the federal agency balance sheet at the end of FY 2008 and the other required statements can be prepared. As discussed earlier in this chapter, OMB *Bulletin No. 01-09* prescribes the form and content of financial statements required to be prepared by most executive agencies and departments. The content of each agency's *annual financial statement* and examples of the basic financial statements were provided as Illustrations 12–4 through 12–9 earlier in this chapter.

Basic financial statements are shown in Illustrations 12–14 through 12–17 for the simple federal agency whose transactions were just discussed. These statements are a balance sheet, statement of changes in net position, statement of budgetary resources, and a statement of financing. Since the example federal agency used in this chapter had no material custodial activities, no statement of custodial activities is needed. Also, no supplemental financial and management information is provided. In the case of an actual federal entity, such as the Department of Defense, for example, there would be numerous funds, programs, and organizational units and thus the need for consolidating and consolidated financial statements, as well as required supplemental information.

Prior to preparing the illustrative financial statements, as of and for the fiscal year ended September 30, 2008, lapsed budgetary authority should be closed and a pre-closing general ledger trial balance should be prepared such as that presented in Illustration 12–13. Note that it is standard practice to prepare the U.S. Standard General Ledger *pre-closing* trial balance after the expended and withdrawn budgetary authority accounts have been closed but before the other temporary proprietary accounts are closed. Closing of expended and withdrawn budgetary authority is discussed here.

Total credits to the Expended Authority—2008 account (Entries 9a, 10a, and 14a) amounted to $2,450,000. Thus, the total *unexpended* budgetary authority at the end of FY 2008 is $50,000 ($2,500,000 − $2,450,000). Of the $50,000 unexpended amount, $34,000 is *reserved* in the Undelivered Orders—2008 for goods or services still on order at year-end. However, the $6,000 balance in Commitments—2008 and $10,000 in Allotments—2008 have not been reserved and must be returned to Treasury. The

ILLUSTRATION 12–13

FEDERAL AGENCY
Pre-Closing Trial Balance
As of September 30, 2008

	Debits	Credits
Proprietary accounts:		
Fund Balance with Treasury—2008	$ 166,000	
Operating Materials and Supplies	219,000	
Equipment	3,250,000	
Accumulated Depreciation on Equipment		$ 900,000
Disbursements in Transit—2008		0
Accounts Payable		105,000
Accrued Funded Payroll and Benefits		27,000
Unexpended Appropriations—2008		34,000
Cumulative Results of Operations		3,010,000
Appropriations Used—2007		400,000
Appropriations Used—2008		2,450,000
Operating/Program Expenses	2,991,000	
Depreciation and Amortization	300,000	
	$6,926,000	$6,926,000
Budgetary accounts:		
Appropriations Realized but Withdrawn—2008	$ 16,000	
Other Appropriations Realized—2008	34,000	
Unapportioned Authority—2008		$ 0
Apportionments—2008		0
Allotments—2008		0
Commitments—2008		0
Undelivered Orders—2008		34,000
Restorations, Writeoffs, and Withdrawals—2008		16,000
	$ 50,000	$ 50,000

following journal entries are needed to record the lapse of obligational authority for the $16,000 not obligated or reserved by fiscal year-end. As the first entry in Entry 16a shows, unused commitments and allotments (as well as apportionments if there had been a year-end balance) are closed to Other Appropriations Realized—2008, as is the amount of appropriations that was expended. In addition, the $400,000 balance in Expended Authority—2007 is closed to Other Appropriations Realized—2007, which also has a $400,000 balance prior to closing. To establish a record of withdrawn appropriations, the second budgetary entry that follows should also be made. In addition, temporary proprietary accounts would be closed as shown in Entry 16b.

		Debits	Credits
16a.	*Budgetary:*		
	Commitments—2008	6,000	
	Allotments—2008	10,000	
	Expended Authority—2007	400,000	
	Expended Authority—2008	2,450,000	
	Other Appropriations Realized—2007		400,000
	Other Appropriations Realized—2008		2,466,000
	Appropriations Realized but Withdrawn—2008	16,000	
	Restorations, Write-Offs, and Withdrawals—2008		16,000
16b.	*Proprietary:*		
	Unexpended Appropriations—2008	16,000	
	Fund Balance with Treasury—2008		16,000

Accounting procedures also exist to reverse the second entry under Entry 16a to the extent that the actual cost of goods or services received early in FY 2009 exceeds the $34,000 estimated in Undelivered Orders. Essentially, a portion of the budgetary authority that was withdrawn in Entry 16a would be *restored* in this case. These accounting procedures are well beyond the scope of the limited coverage presented in this chapter.

Temporary proprietary accounts should be closed to update the net position accounts so the end-of-period balance sheet can be prepared. The necessary closing entry would be:

17.	*Proprietary:*		
	Appropriations Used	2,850,000	
	Cumulative Results of Operations	441,000	
	Operating/Program Expenses		2,991,000
	Depreciation and Amortization		300,000

The balance sheet for the example federal agency whose pre-closing trial balance is shown in Illustration 12–13 is presented in Illustration 12–14. More complex agencies usually prepare a consolidated balance sheet like the one shown in Illustration 12–4. The example federal agency is assumed to have only entity assets (those that can be used for the agency's operations) and, except for Fund Balance with Treasury, the remaining assets are governmental. All liabilities (Accounts Payable and Accrued Funded Payroll and Benefits) are assumed to be governmental. Furthermore, all liabilities are covered by budgetary resources. As discussed earlier in this chapter, the *net position* consists of only two items, Unexpended Appropriations ($34,000 reserved for goods and services on order at year-end) and Cumulative Results of Operations.

ILLUSTRATION 12–14

FEDERAL AGENCY
Balance Sheet
As of September 30, 2008

Assets

Intragovernmental:	
Fund Balance with Treasury	$ 166,000
Governmental:	
Operating materials and supplies	219,000
Equipment (net of accumulated depreciation of $900,000)	2,350,000
Total assets	$2,735,000

Liabilities

Governmental liabilities:	
Accounts payable	$ 105,000
Accrued funded payroll and benefits	27,000
Total liabilities	132,000

Net Position

Unexpended appropriations	34,000
Cumulative results of operations	2,569,000
Total net position	2,603,000
Total liabilities and net position	$2,735,000

A consolidating statement of net cost for a major federal agency was presented in Illustration 12–5. Because the federal agency used in our example is assumed to have a simple organizational structure and no earned revenues, its statement of net cost would be very simple; net cost would be the same as gross cost. Moreover, since the agency's net suborganization or program costs are reported on the first line of the statement of changes in net position presented in Illustration 12–15, a statement of net cost would convey little additional information. Therefore, we do not include one here. While the statement of changes in net position is quite simple, it is informative nonetheless.

The example federal agency would also have to prepare a statement of budgetary resources (see Illustration 12–16). The astute reader will note that the equation applicable to this statement is Budgetary resources = Status of budgetary resources. Budgetary resources in this case is $2,884,000, consisting of current-year appropriations of $2,500,000 less expired appropriations of $16,000 plus $400,000 carried forward from prior-year appropriations to cover undelivered orders at the end of the prior year. Since there are no unobligated appropriations that can be carried forward at year-end, the *status of budgetary resources* in this case is simply the amount of budgetary resources expended ($2,850,000) plus $34,000 obligated for goods on order at the end of FY 2008 that had not yet been expended. Outlays are reported in the bottom section of the statement of budgetary resources and are the same as the total amount expended during the year, or $2,850,000 ($2,450,000 chargeable to the current-year appropriation and $400,000 chargeable to the prior-year appropriation).

The final statement presented for the simple federal agency illustrated in this chapter is the statement of financing (see Illustration 12–17). This statement is intended to reconcile the budgetary basis expenditure or obligation of budgetary resources (obligations incurred) with the accrual basis net cost of operations. As shown in Illustration 12–17, certain resources affect budgetary resources but do not affect the net cost of operations.

ILLUSTRATION 12–15

FEDERAL AGENCY
Statement of Changes in Net Position
For the Year Ended September 30, 2008

	Cumulative Results of Operations	Unexpended Appropriations
Beginning balances	$3,010,000	$ 400,000
Prior period adjustments	0	0
Beginning balances, as adjusted	3,010,000	400,000
Budgetary financing sources:		
Appropriations received		2,484,000
Appropriations used	2,850,000	(2,850,000)
Other financing sources		
Total financing sources	5,860,000	34,000
Net cost of operations (+ −) Note A	3,291,000	
Ending balances	$2,569,000	$ 34,000

Note A: These amounts are taken from the bottom line of the statement of net costs, which is not included here for sake of brevity.

These include the net change in the amount of goods, services, or benefits ordered (in this case, the change in Undelivered Orders from the beginning to the end of the year) and the net change in assets capitalized on the balance sheet. As explained in Note C to the statement, $250,000 of equipment purchases were capitalized during the year, but the balance of Operating Materials and Supplies decreased by $391,000, resulting in a net decrease in capitalized assets of $141,000. The lower section of the statement

ILLUSTRATION 12–16

FEDERAL AGENCY
Statement of Budgetary Resources
For the Year Ended September 30, 2008 (Note A)

Budgetary resources:	
Budgetary authority (Note B)	$2,484,000
Status of budgetary resources:	
Obligations incurred (Note C)	$2,484,000
Total status of budgetary resources	$2,484,000
Relationship of obligations to outlays:	
Obligated balance, net—beginning of period	400,000
Obligated balance, net—end of period	(139,000)
Outlays:	
Obligations incurred	$2,484,000
Net outlays (Disbursements)	$2,745,000

Note A: Comparative totals should also be presented for the prior year. Those totals are omitted in this example.
Note B: Total budgetary resources were $2,500,000 appropriations less $16,000 of expired appropriations at year-end.
Note C: Expended authority of current year of $2,450,000 is added to $34,000 obligated budgetary authority for undelivered goods at year-end.

ILLUSTRATION 12–17

FEDERAL AGENCY **Statement of Financing** **For the Year Ended September 30, 2008**	
Resources used to finance activities:	
Budgetary resources obligated:	
Obligations incurred (Note A)	$2,484,000
Resources used to finance items not part of the net cost of operations:	
Change in budgetary resources obligated for goods, services, and benefits ordered but not yet provided (Note B)	366,000
Resources that finance the acquisition of assets capitalized on the balance sheet (Note C)	141,000
	507,000
Components not requiring or generating resources:	
Depreciation and amortization	300,000
Net cost of operations	$3,291,000

Note A: Obligations incurred consist of $2,450,000 expended from the FY 2005 appropriations plus $34,000 obligated for goods on order at the end of FY 2008.
Note B: The change in goods and services on order is a decrease of $366,000 ($400,000 − $34,000).
Note C: Equipment acquisition is capitalized at $250,000 minus a net decrease in operating materials and supplies of $391,000. Thus, there was a net decrease in capitalization of $141,000. This amount should be added in reconciling the use of budgetary resources to the net cost of operations.

shows an addition for depreciation expense since it had not been included in obligations incurred but is a part of the net cost of operations.

SUMMARY OF ACCOUNTING AND REPORTING FOR FEDERAL GOVERNMENT AGENCIES

Illustration 12–18 provides a summary comparison of budgetary and proprietary accounting procedures for state and local governments as compared with federal agencies. Although some similarities exist, there are areas specific to each level of government. As shown in Illustration 12–18, state and local governments do not account for apportionments and most do not account for allotments. Federal agency accounting takes into consideration certain accruals (supplies used and depreciation) generally ignored in state and local government accounting, although as mentioned in several earlier chapters, the *GASBS 34* reporting model requires the use of accrual accounting by state and local governments at the government-wide level.

The head of each agency in the executive branch of the federal government has the statutory responsibility for the establishment and maintenance of systems of accounting and internal control in conformity with principles, standards, and requirements established by the Comptroller General, the Secretary of the Treasury, and the Director of the OMB. Federal agency accounting is directed at providing information for intelligent financial management of agency activities and programs to the end that they may be operated with efficiency and economy, as well as providing evidence of adherence to legal requirements. As emphasized by the headings of Illustration 12–18 and by the discussions in earlier chapters, accounting for governmental funds presently focuses on legal compliance. The focus of federal agency accounting, in contrast, is broadened to include information needed for the management of agency resources (the

ILLUSTRATION 12–18 **Comparison of Accounting for State and Local Governmental Fund Types and Accounting for Federal Agencies (journal entries)**

Item	State and Local Government Funds Compliance Track Only	Federal Agency	
		Budgetary Track	Proprietary Track
1. Passage of appropriations (and for state and local governments, revenue) bills	Estimated Revenues 　Appropriations 　Fund Balance	Other Appropriations Realized 　Unapportioned Authority	Fund Balance with Treasury 　Unexpended Appropriations
2. Revenues accrued (at expected collectible amount)	Taxes Receivable 　Estimated Uncollectible 　Taxes Revenues	No equivalent for taxes; user charges, if any, recognized as billed	Taxes Receivable 　Allowance for Uncollectible Taxes 　Earned Income from the Public
3. Apportionment by OMB	No equivalent	Unapportioned Authority 　Apportionments	No entry
4. Allotment by agency head	No equivalent*	Apportionments 　Allotments	No entry
5. Budget authority reserved prior to ordering goods or services	No equivalent	Allotments 　Commitments	No entry
6. Goods or services ordered	Encumbrances 　Reserve for 　Encumbrances	Commitments 　Undelivered Orders†	No entry
7. Goods or services received	Reserve for Encumbrances 　Encumbrances Expenditures 　Accounts Payable	Undelivered Orders 　Expended Authority	Expense or asset account 　Accounts Payable Unexpended Appropriations 　Appropriations Used
8. Liability paid (expenditure recorded in 7)	Accounts Payable 　Cash	No entry	Accounts Payable 　Fund Balance with Treasury‡
9. Supplies used	No entry	No entry	Operating/Program Expenses 　Inventory for Agency Operations
10. Physical inventory (consumption method assumed for state and local governments)	Inventory 　Expenditures Fund Balance 　Reserve for Inventory	No entry	Entry for (7) assumes perpetual inventory; would need entry for (10) if physical inventory and book inventory differed
11. Depreciation computed	No entry (computation used for cost reimbursements and management information)	No entry (Not an expenditure of appropriations; will never require a check to be drawn on U.S. Treasury)	Depreciation and Amortization 　Accumulated Depreciation 　(on general property, plant, and equipment but not certain military assets and stewardship assets)
12. Closing entries	Appropriations Revenues 　Estimated Revenues 　Encumbrances 　Expenditures 　Fund Balance	Expended Authority 　Other Appropriations Realized; (Also must close any budgetary accounts associated with expired budget authority)	Cumulative Results of Operations 　Operating/Program Expenses Appropriations Used 　Cumulative Results of Operations

*As discussed in Chapter 3, some local governments utilize allotment accounting. In such cases, the credit in Entry 1 would be to Unallotted Appropriations, and an Entry 4 would be necessary to record the debit to that account and the credit to Allotments.

†As illustrated by Entry 4 earlier in this chapter, and by Entry 5, some agencies opt to use the interim account Commitments to improve planning for procurement of goods and services. If commitments are not recorded in advance of placing orders, the debit for the budgetary track would be to Allotments.

‡As indicated in this chapter, the account credited here might be Disbursements in Transit rather than Fund Balance with Treasury.

proprietary track) as well as for compliance with fund control requirements (the *budgetary* track). However, as discussed in Chapters 1–9 of this text, the authors have introduced dual-track accounting for state and local government accounting to meet the full accrual accounting needs at the government-wide level while continuing to focus on legal compliance within the governmental funds.

Key Terms

Allotment, *492*
Apportionment, *492*
Appropriation, *491*
Budget accounts, *474*
Budgetary
  resources, *486*
Commitment, *492*
Cumulative results of
  operations, *483*
Entity assets, *481*
Expended appropriation
  (authority), *492*

Federal Accounting
  Standards Advisory
  Board (FASAB), *472*
Federal Financial
  Management
  Improvement Act of
  1996 (FFMIA), *468*
General property, plant,
  and equipment, *482*
Governmental assets
  (liabilities), *481*
Heritage assets, *482*

Intragovernmental assets
  (liabilities), *481*
Macroaccounting, *471*
Net position, *483*
Nonentity assets, *481*
Obligation, *492*
Stewardship
  investments, *489*
Stewardship land, *482*
Unexpended
  appropriations, *483*

Selected References

Government Accountability Office. *Understanding the Primary Components of the Annual Financial Report of the United States Government,* GAO-05-9585P, September 2005.
Office of Management and Budget. *U.S. Government Standard General Ledger,* 2005.
———. *Bulletin No. 01-09,* "Form and Content of Agency Financial Statements." 2001.
———. *Circular A–134,* "Financial Accounting Principles and Standards." 1993.
Tierney, Cornelius E. *Federal Accounting Handbook: Policies, Standards, Procedures, Practices.* New York: Wiley, 1999.

Questions

12–1. Identify the principals of the Joint Financial Management and Improvement Program (JFMIP) and explain in which branch of the federal government each operates. What contribution has the JFMIP made to the federal accounting standards-setting process?

12–2. Describe the institutional process for establishing generally accepted accounting principles for the federal government.

12–3. Discuss the conceptual framework of accounting for federal agencies and compare it to the conceptual framework established by the GASB for state and local governments.

12–4. Explain the differences among these accounts: (1) *estimated revenues* used by state and local governments, (2) *other appropriations realized* used by federal agencies in their budgetary track, and (3) *fund balance with Treasury* used by federal agencies in their proprietary track.

12–5. Describe the funds used by a federal agency. Explain whether state and local governments use similar funds.

12–6. "The FASAB sets standards for federal agencies that relate to external financial reporting, much like the GASB sets standards for state and local governments for external financial reporting. Do you agree or disagree with this statement?" Explain.

12–7. Describe financial reporting of the consolidated activities of the U.S. government. Has the federal government received an unqualified audit opinion on its consolidated financial statements? If not, provide some reasons that it has not.

12–8. Describe the dual-track system used in federal agency accounting. Compare this to the system by the same name used in the discussion of state and local government reporting under *GASBS 34* in Chapters 1–9.

12–9. Identify the budgetary accounts used in federal agency accounting and explain the sequential flow of budgetary authority through the accounts in your own words.

12–10. Name the financial statements that should be prepared for each federal agency in conformity with OMB *Bulletin No. 01-09*.

Cases

12–1 OMB Press Release. The following press release from the Office of Management and Budget was issued December 2, 2004.

EXECUTIVE OFFICE OF THE PRESIDENT
OFFICE OF MANAGEMENT AND BUDGET
WASHINGTON, D.C. 20503

FOR IMMEDIATE RELEASE
December 2, 2004

2004-17

Majority of Federal Agencies Receive Clean Audits on Accelerated Financial Statements

17 of the record 22 Federal agencies that completed their Performance and Accountability Reports just 45 days after the end of the 2004 fiscal year have received unqualified audit opinions on their FY 2004 financial statements, maintaining the high performance levels of previous years while accelerating their financial reporting dramatically.

"A significant milestone has been achieved in Federal financial management. Major Federal agencies were able to maintain a comparable number of unqualified audit opinions to the prior year while accelerating their reporting (after accounting for prior year revisions). This continues progress made to ensure that the Federal Government is accounting for the taxpayers' money in a timely and accurate manner," said Linda Springer, Controller for OMB's Office of Federal Financial Management.

Of the 24 major Federal agencies, one agency—the Small Business Administration (SBA)—received a qualified opinion, five agencies—the Departments of Defense, Homeland Security, Housing and Urban Development, Justice and the National Aeronautics and Space Administration—received disclaimers and one agency—the Department of Health and Human Services—has not yet issued an audit report. Increased audit work surfaced issues at several agencies not receiving an unqualified opinion that could not be resolved in time to meet the accelerated reporting deadline.

Noteworthy progress was made at SBA whose audit opinion improved from a disclaimer to a qualified opinion in fiscal year 2004. The improvements made by SBA over the past year have positioned it well for receiving an unqualified opinion in the future.

For more information please contact OMB Communications at 202-395-7254 or visit http://www.whitehouse.gov/omb/financial/2004AuditOpinionsDecldraft.pdf for a listing of audit opinions for all CFO Act agencies.

Source: www.whitehouse.gov/omb/pubpress/index 2004.html.

Required
Choose a federal agency of the U.S. government and locate its annual financial report for the most recent fiscal year from its agency Web site or a government

site such as www.fedworld.gov or www.firstgov.gov. Answer the following questions.

   a. Did this agency receive an unqualified opinion for the most recent fiscal year? If not, can you determine why?

   b. Examine the statements of net cost and changes in net position and determine the amount of operations that was funded by appropriations for this fiscal year. Did the agency report a positive or negative change in net position? Which elements of this financial statement were significantly different from those of the prior year and might have contributed most to the change in net position?

   c. Does the agency integrate accountability reports with performance reports produced under the Government Performance and Results Act?

12–2 Internet Case—FASAB. At the cutoff date for publication of this edition of the text, 30 Statements of Federal Financial Accounting Standards (SFFASs) had been issued. In addition, OMB *Bulletin No. 01-09* provided authoritative guidance for the form and content of federal agency financial statements.

Required

Using the Internet, explore the FASAB (www.fasab.gov) and OMB (www.whitehouse.gov/omb) Web sites and determine whether:

   a. Any additional SFFASs have been issued. If so, list them by name and provide a short synopsis along with their effective dates.

   b. Has the OMB replaced *Bulletin No. 01-09* with a later one? If so, how do the financial statements required by the later bulletin compare to those required by *Bulletin No. 01-09,* as described and illustrated in this chapter? (*Note:* Preceding OMB bulletins on form and content of agency financial statements were *Bulletins Nos. 97-01* and *94-01.* Thus, the OMB may not intend to make frequent changes in its reporting guidance.)

12–3 U.S. Government-wide Annual Report. Obtain the most recent audited annual financial report of the U.S. government. It is available from the Government Accountability Office (GAO) either in print (see the Government Printing Office at www.access.gpo.gov) or on the Internet at www.gao.gov.

Required

   a. Did the U.S. Government have a surplus or deficit for this year?

   b. Was there an increase or decrease in the net position of the U.S. government? How does that compare to last year?

   c. Did the GAO give the federal government an unqualified, qualified, adverse, or disclaimer of opinion?

   d. What weaknesses or deficiencies did the Comptroller General of the GAO note in his report?

   e. What federal agencies received an unqualified opinion for this fiscal year? (*Hint:* Read page 1 of the Management's Discussion and Analysis.)

Exercises and Problems

12–1 Multiple Choice. Choose the best answer.

  1. Federal statutes assign responsibility for establishing and maintaining a sound financial structure for the federal government to which of the following:

   a. Comptroller General of the United States.

   b. Secretary of the Treasury and the Comptroller General.

   c. Comptroller General, Secretary of the Treasury, and Director of the Office of Management and Budget.

   d. Federal Financial Accounting Standards Board.

2. The process for establishing generally accepted accounting principles (GAAP) for federal agencies includes:
   a. A recommendation of the Federal Accounting Standards Advisory Board (FASAB) to the three principals of the JFMIP to issue a statement.
   b. A vote of the six federal and three nonfederal members of the FASAB.
   c. Approval by the American Institute of CPAs and the Governmental Accounting Standards Board.
   d. All of the above.

3. The hierarchy of accounting principles and standards for federal government entities is described in:
   a. The FASB's pronouncements, both statements and technical bulletins.
   b. The FASAB's concept statements and statements of federal financial accounting standards (SFFAS).
   c. The GASB's *Statement No. 34.*
   d. The AICPA's *Statement of Auditing Standards No, 91* that amends *SAS No. 69.*

4. Objectives that are identified by Statement of Federal Financial Accounting Concepts (SFFAC) No. 1 for federal financial reporting include all of the following except:
   a. Budgetary integrity.
   b. Operating performance.
   c. Stewardship.
   d. Transparency.

5. When closing entries are made, the Cumulative Results of Operations account will be affected by which of the following transactions or events that occurred during the year?
   a. Expiration of budget authority.
   b. Purchase of property, plant, and equipment.
   c. Depreciation of property, plant, and equipment.
   d. Both b and c are correct.

6. Assuming that an agency's unused appropriations expire at year-end but appropriations continue in effect for obligated amounts (purchase orders, etc.), which of the following budgetary accounts would likely be found in the agency's post-closing trial balance at year-end?
   a. Undelivered Orders and Other Appropriations Realized.
   b. Commitments and Other Appropriations Realized.
   c. Expended Authority and Undelivered Orders.
   d. Commitments and Undelivered Orders.

7. Which of the following is a correct mathematical relationship among proprietary account balances?
   a. Net position equals Total assets minus Total liabilities.
   b. Fund Balance with Treasury equals Unexpended Appropriations.
   c. Cumulative Results of Operations equals Revenues and Financing Sources minus Operating/Program Expenses.
   d. Disbursements in Transit equals Fund Balance with Treasury minus Accounts Payable and Other Current Liabilities.

8. Which of the following is required by OMB *Bulletin No. 01-09* in the basic financial statements for a federal entity?
   a. Statement of net assets.
   b. Statement of changes in net position.

    c. Statement of revenues, expenditures, and changes in fund balances.

    d. Statement of activities.

9. Which of the following is a true statement about the difference between accounting and reporting for federal government agencies versus state and local governments?

    a. The federal government uses a dual-track method of accounting for proprietary accounts and budgetary accounts; state and local governments do not use budgetary accounting.

    b. State and local governments use accrual accounting in the government-wide statements as well as proprietary and fiduciary funds; federal agencies use only the cash basis of accounting.

    c. The budget is recorded in the general ledger of a state or local government, but not in a federal agency.

    d. State and local governments do not account for apportionments and most do not account for allotments.

10. Which of the following statements is true about the United States government-wide financial report?

    a. Since 1997, the financial statements of the U.S. government as a whole have been audited by an external certified public accounting firm.

    b. The Comptroller General of the United States has rendered a disclaimer of opinion on the U.S. government's Consolidated Financial Statements for as long as that office has audited these statements.

    c. The majority of the 24 major federal agencies required to be audited have received unqualified audit opinions by the OMB.

    d. None of the above statements are true.

12–2 **Fund Balance with U.S. Treasury.** One amount is missing in the following trial balance of proprietary accounts, and another is missing from the trial balance of budgetary accounts of a certain agency of the federal government. This trial balance was prepared before budgetary accounts were adjusted, such as returning unused appropriations. The debits are not distinguished from the credits.

FEDERAL AGENCY
Pre-closing Trial Balance
September 30, 2008

Proprietary accounts:	
Accounts Payable	$ 2,100,000
Accumulated Depreciation—Plant and Equipment	2,600,000
Appropriations Used	4,000,000
Fund Balance with Treasury—2008	?
Operating Materials and Supplies	2,700,000
Cumulative Results of Operations—10/1/07	7,700,000
Operating/Program Expenses	4,150,000
Depreciation and Amortization	1,150,000
Plant and Equipment	8,900,000
Unexpended Appropriations—2008	2,100,000
Budgetary accounts:	
Other Appropriations Realized—2008	?
Expended Authority—2008	4,000,000
Undelivered Orders—2008	1,500,000
Apportionments—2008	600,000

Required

a. Compute each missing amount in the pre-closing trial balance.

b. Compute the net additions (or reductions) to assets other than Fund Balance with Treasury during fiscal year 2008. Clearly label your computations and show all work in good form.

12–3 Federal Agency Financial Statements. Using the data from Problem 12–2, prepare the following:

a. In general journal form, entries to close the budgetary accounts as needed and to close the operating statement proprietary accounts.

b. In good form, a balance sheet for the federal agency as of September 30, 2008. (*Note:* Assume that all assets are *entity assets,* Fund Balance with Treasury is an *intragovernmental asset,* and all other assets are *governmental.*)

12–4 Federal Agency Transactions and Financial Statements. The Balance Sheet of the Rural Assistance Agency of the federal government for the year ended September 30, 2007, is provided as follows:

RURAL ASSISTANCE AGENCY
Balance Sheet
As of September 30, 2007

Assets	
Intragovernmental:	
Fund Balance with Treasury	$ 3,165,000
Governmental:	
Property, plant, and equipment, net of accumulated depreciation of $1,790,000	6,835,000
Operating materials and supplies	325,000
Total assets	$10,325,000
Liabilities	
Accounts payable	$ 240,000
Accrued funded payroll and benefits	55,000
Accrued unfunded liabilities	340,000
Total liabilities	635,000
Net Position	
Unexpended appropriations	1,869,000
Cumulative results of operations	7,821,000
Total net position	9,690,000
Total liabilities and net position	$10,325,000

Additional information follows:

1. Total appropriations for the fiscal year ending September 30, 2008, were $15,513,000.

2. Accounts Payable reported on the balance sheet as of September 30, 2007, in the amount of $240,000 were paid early in fiscal year 2008.

3. Materials and supplies in the amount of $1,869,000 ordered in fiscal 2007 were received in early fiscal year 2008; this is the same amount as reported for Unexpended Appropriations on the balance sheet as of September 30, 2007. All materials and supplies are credited to Accounts Payable upon receipt.

4. Additional materials and supplies were ordered and received during Fiscal Year 2008 in the amount of $2,050,000. Property, plant, and equipment in the amount of $400,000 was also purchased during Fiscal Year 2008. Upon the agency's request, the Treasury paid $400,000 for the property, plant, and equipment. (*Note:* The $2,050,000 for purchases of materials and supplies was credited to Accounts Payable.)

5. Operating/program expenses for Fiscal Year 2008 totaled $15,076,000. This amount excluded depreciation expense of $450,000 on property, plant, and equipment but included accruals at fiscal year-end in the amounts of $60,000 for accrued payroll and benefits and $10,000 for accrued annual leave. (*Note:* Credit to Accrued Unfunded Liabilities for the accrued leave. Notice that accrued annual leave is unfunded and therefore does not reduce the balance of Unexpended Appropriations, nor does it increase Appropriations Used. The total FY 2008 appropriations used amounted to $11,162,000: $15,076,000 for FY 2008 expenses minus $3,904,000 of materials and supplies consumed minus $10,000 for expenses that will be funded in future years.) Except for materials and supplies in the amount of $3,904,000 consumed in operations and the two accrued items, all other operating/program expenses were paid by checks drawn on the Treasury during the fiscal year.

6. Accounts payable in the amount of $3,654,000 were paid during the year. In addition, early in FY 2008, the $55,000 reported as accrued funded payroll and benefits on the September 30, 2007, balance sheet was paid by charging Fund Balance with Treasury.

7. No property, plant, or equipment was sold or otherwise disposed of during fiscal year 2008.

Required

a. Prepare all necessary *proprietary* journal entries only for the Rural Assistance Agency (ignore *budgetary* entries) for fiscal year 2008. For simplicity, assume that there is one Fund Balance with Treasury account rather than one for each year.

b. Prepare a comparative balance sheet for the Rural Assistance Agency as of September 30, 2007 and 2008.

c. Prepare a statement of changes in net position for the Rural Assistance Agency for the year ended September 30, 2008.

12–5 **Statement of Budgetary Resources.** The trial balance of the Federal Science Administration, as of August 31, 2008, follows:

	Debits	Credits
Budgetary Accounts		
Other Appropriations Realized—2008	$4,894,855	
Unapportioned Authority—2008		$ 200,000
Apportionments—2008		150,000
Allotments—2008		600,000
Commitments—2008		150,000
Undelivered Orders—2008		664,131
Expended Authority—2008		3,130,724
Total Budgetary Accounts	$4,894,855	$4,894,855

Required

Prepare a statement of budgetary resources for the 11 months ended August 31, 2008, assuming that goods on order at the end of the prior year amounted to $1,210,210.

12–6 **Transaction Analysis and Statements.** Congress authorized the Flood Control Commission to start operations on October 1, 2008.

Required

a. Record the following transactions in general journal form as they should appear in the accounts of the Flood Control Commission. Record all expenses in the Operating/Program Expenses account.

   (1) The Flood Control Commission received official notice that the one-year appropriation passed by Congress and signed by the President amounted to $7,000,000 for operating expenses.

   (2) The Office of Management and Budget notified the Commission of the following schedule of apportionments: first quarter, $2,000,000; second quarter, $2,000,000; third quarter, $1,500,000; and fourth quarter, $1,500,000.

   (3) The Flood Control Commissioner allotted $1,000,000 for the first month's operations.

   (4) Obligations were recorded for salaries and fringe benefits, $400,000; furniture and equipment, $270,000; materials and supplies, $250,000; rent and utilities, $50,000. The Commission does not record commitments prior to recording obligations.

   (5) Payroll for the first two weeks in the amount of $170,000 was paid.

   (6) Invoices approved for payment totaled $395,000; of the total, $180,000 was for furniture and equipment, $175,000 for materials and supplies, and $40,000 for rent.

   (7) Liability was recorded for the payroll for the second two weeks, $160,000, and for the employer's share of FICA taxes for the four weeks, $23,000. (*Note:* Credit to Accrued Funded Payroll and Benefits.)

   (8) Accounts payable totaling $189,000 were paid, which included liabilities for materials and supplies, $149,000, and rent, $40,000. Accrued Funded Payroll and Benefits in the amount of $183,000 were paid.

   (9) Accruals recorded at month-end were salaries, $30,000, and utilities, $10,000. Materials and supplies costing $60,000 were used during the month. Depreciation of $2,500 was recorded on furniture and equipment for the month. (*Note:* In practice, this would likely be done in worksheet form for monthly reporting purposes.)

   (10) Necessary closing entries were prepared as of October 31, 2008. (*Note:* Again, for monthly statements, this would be a worksheet entry only.)

b. Prepare the Balance Sheet of the Flood Control Commission as of October 31, 2008, assuming that all of the Commission's assets are entity assets, Fund Balance with Treasury is intragovernmental; and all other assets are governmental.

c. Prepare the Statement of Changes in Net Position of the Flood Control Commission for the month ended October 31, 2008.

d. Prepare the Statement of Budgetary Resources of the Flood Control Commission for the month ended October 31, 2008.

e. Prepare the Statement of Financing of the Flood Control Commission for the month ended October 31, 2008.

12–7 DOT Audit Report and Transmittal Letter. The following excerpt is from the Inspector General's transmittal letter to the Secretary of the Department of Transportation (DOT).

U.S. DEPARTMENT OF TRANSPORTATION
Office of the Secretary of Transportation Office of Inspector General

Date: November 15, 2004

Subject: ACTION: Report on Consolidated Financial
Statements for Fiscal Years 2004 and 2003, DOT FI-2005-009

From: Kenneth M. Mead, JA-20 Inspector General

To: The Secretary

I respectfully submit the Office of Inspector General report on the Department of Transportation (DOT) Consolidated Financial Statements for Fiscal Years (FY) 2004 and 2003. This report is required by the Chief Financial Officers Act of 1990, as amended by the Government Management Reform Act of 1994.

UNQUALIFIED OPINION

This audit report concludes that DOT's Consolidated Financial Statements are presented fairly, in all material respects, in conformity with U.S. generally accepted accounting principles. This is the fourth fiscal year in a row—2001, 2002, 2003, and 2004—that DOT has achieved an unqualified or "clean" opinion. The clean audit opinion signals to users of the financial statements that they can rely on the information presented. This occurred as the Department completed its transition to a new, commercial off-the-shelf accounting system, called Delphi. According to DOT officials, DOT is the first cabinet-level agency to have implemented, Department-wide, a modern commercial off-the-shelf accounting system.
…

The Department made progress correcting the internal control deficiencies we reported last year. The Department made sufficient progress correcting two of the material weaknesses—the Department's information security program and FAA's oversight of cost-reimbursable contracts—that we are not reporting them as material weaknesses this year.
…

The Federal Aviation Administration, the Highway Traffic Administration agencies, the Department's Office of Financial Management, and the auditors had to exert extraordinary efforts to overcome significant financial management deficiencies in order to meet the accelerated due date for audited financial statements. These deficiencies were due to weaknesses in internal controls, which are the policies, procedures, and practices that need to operate effectively to produce reliable and timely financial information. We categorized the problems we identified into four material weaknesses and four reportable conditions. Responding to a draft of this report, DOT agreed with these findings and committed to taking timely corrective action.
…

Source: http://www.dot.gov/perfacc2004/opinion.htm

Required

a. Explain the role of an inspector general within a federal agency. Is an opinion from this person considered an *independent* auditor's opinion?

b. Describe how long it typically takes for financial statements to be made available to the public and where these can be found. Did the DOT present all the financial statements required by OMB *Bulletin No. 01-09* on time?

c. Look at the full text of the Inspector General's report at the Web site indicated at the bottom of the excerpt. Did the Department of Transportation have any material weaknesses in internal controls or reportable conditions? If so, did they result in a qualified or adverse audit opinion for the department? Discuss.

Chapter **Thirteen**

Budgeting and Costing of Government Services

Learning Objectives

After studying this chapter, you should be able to:

1. Explain the objectives of budgeting and cost determination in relation to measuring performance.
2. Explain the implications of *GASBS 34* for public budgeting
3. Explain the differences among various budgeting approaches.
4. Identify the procedures involved in specific types of budgets including appropriation budgets, revenue budgets, cash budgets, and capital budgets.
5. Describe budgeting for performance:
   Total quality management (TQM).
   Service efforts and accomplishments (SEA).
6. Explain unique aspects of costing government services:
   Federal contracts and grants.
   Activity-based costing (ABC).
   Cost accounting and expenditure accounting.

Legislators authorize government managers to raise and expend resources to provide services to citizens by approving an annual budget. Budget legislation also specifies what legal sanctions will be imposed if managers overspend appropriations. Along with budgeting, determining the cost of public services has long been a critical task in governments, particularly those governments that receive federal or other restricted funds. This chapter expands on the discussion presented in Chapter 3 on General Fund budgeting and on the discussion in Chapter 4 on reporting the cost of governmental activities by function on the government-wide statement of activities.

In recent years, preparers of government reports and accounting standards setters have taken on the challenge of how best to report on the quality of government services provided to citizens. Unlike a business for which the financial "bottom-line" is a well-accepted measure of performance, there is no comparable single performance measure for governments. In this chapter we continue the discussion of financial analysis presented in Chapter 10 by integrating the concepts of budgeting and costing of government services with assessing financial and operational performance.

OBJECTIVES OF BUDGETING

The GASB *Budgeting, Budgetary Control, and Budgetary Reporting Principle* provides that:

a. An annual budget(s) should be adopted by every government.
b. The accounting system should provide the basis for appropriate budgetary control.
c. Budgetary comparison schedules should be presented as required supplementary information for the general fund and for each major special revenue fund that has a legally adopted annual budget. The budgetary comparison schedule should present both (a) the original and (b) the final appropriated budgets for the reporting period as well as (c) actual inflows, outflows, and balances, stated on the government's budgetary basis.[1]

The *Budgeting Principle* is directly related to the *Accounting and Reporting Capabilities Principle,* which specifies that a governmental accounting system must make it possible for a government (1) to prepare financial reports in conformity with generally accepted accounting principles (GAAP) and (2) to determine and demonstrate compliance with finance-related legal provisions. Chapter 3 is concerned with budgets as legal documents binding on the actions of administrators and with budgetary accounting needed to make it possible to prepare budgetary reports to demonstrate legal compliance. It is also concerned with budgetary comparisons required for the General Fund and major special revenue funds in conformity with the *GASBS 34* reporting model.

Budgeting is also an important tool for achieving efficient and effective management of resources. Because of public demand for improved government performance, innovative performance measurement systems are being developed at all levels of government. Since 1997, federal agencies have submitted strategic plans to Congress, developed annual performance plans (since FY99), reported annually on the results achieved in those performance plans, and integrate *accountability reports* with the Government Performance and Results Act (GPRA) performance reports (in 2002).[2]

In 1998, the National Advisory Council on State and Local Budgeting, a cooperative of organizations, issued a document that describes nearly 60 *best* budget practices covering the planning, development, adoption, and execution phases of the budget process.[3] This document recognizes that budgeting is one of the most important activities undertaken by state and local governments in allocating scarce resources to programs and services.

Implications of *GASBS 34* for Public Budgeting

GASB does not set budget principles for state and local governments; however, the budget has always played a role in general purpose external financial reports through the required budget-to-actual comparison statements for those funds that have a legally approved budget. *GASBS 34* continues to require this supplementary information but allows governments to choose whether they present a budgetary comparison schedule

[1] Governmental Accounting Standards Board, *Codification of Governmental Accounting and Financial Reporting Standards,* as of June 30, 2005 (Norwalk, CT: GASB, 2005), Sec. 1100.111.

[2] See Chapter 12 for more discussion of the GPRA and performance reporting.

[3] See www.gfoa.org, "Recommended Practices."

after the notes to the financial statements as required supplementary information (RSI) or a more traditional statement that compares budgeted to actual operating performance within the basic financial statements. According to *GASBS 34,* the original budget as well as the final amended budget must be presented, using whatever budgetary basis is adopted by the government. *GASBS 34* also retains the requirement to reconcile the budgetary basis to generally accepted accounting principles (GAAP) basis, if different.

GASBS 34 has a number of implications for budgeting as discussed in an article by Dr. James Chan. They include (1) emphasizing the long-term perspective in budgeting, (2) stressing budgets as a tool for demonstrating public accountability, (3) considering the government as a whole, (4) activating the debate about accrual accounting, (5) raising the need to project financial position, and (6) critically appraising budget practices.[4] It remains to be seen whether *GASBS 34* will result in government financial managers supplying budgets for operational performance of the government as a whole and whether the public and other financial statement users will demand such budgets.

Interrelation of Planning, Budgeting, and Performance Measurement

The concept of "managing for results" has taken hold in many governments as a commonsense way to focus the activities of employees toward the needs that the government is trying to address. These goals might include safe highways, healthy children, plentiful employment opportunities, and a culturally diverse citizenry. When planning, budgeting, and performance measurement are related, and good performance is rewarded, then public employees' behaviors will change. Highway patrol officers who are judged on accident rates for their highway beat, rather than on their output of tickets written or miles covered, have changed their behavior, writing tickets strategically to slow down drivers on the most hazardous stretches of roads, and reporting potholes that cause accidents to maintenance departments more often.[5]

Illustration 13–1 is a graphic representation of the interrelations among the processes of policy setting through a strategic plan, budgeting the resources needed to deliver services that accomplish the goals of the plan, monitoring operations and reporting on performance, and assessing performance as it relates to the strategic plan. Once a government identifies the public needs it is trying to address, then it needs to develop an overall strategic plan for addressing those needs; devise policies, programs, and services to meet those needs; implement budgeting, accounting, and management systems that support the strategic plan; and track cost and performance data that allows the government to gauge its progress in reaching its goals.[6] While framing budgeting tasks within a "managing for results" philosophy may seem new, over the years, governments have experimented with various approaches to budgeting intended to lead to results. These approaches are described

---

[4] James L. Chan, "The Implications of GASB Statement No. 34 for Public Budgeting," *Public Budgeting & Finance* (Fall 2001), p. 80.

[5] James Fountain, Wilson Campbell, Terry Patton, Paul Epstein, Mandi Cohn, *Special Report: Reporting Performance Information: Suggested Criteria for Effective Communication* (Norwalk, CT: GASB), August 2003, p. 13.

[6] Ibid.

ILLUSTRATION 13–1 **Managing for Results Process**

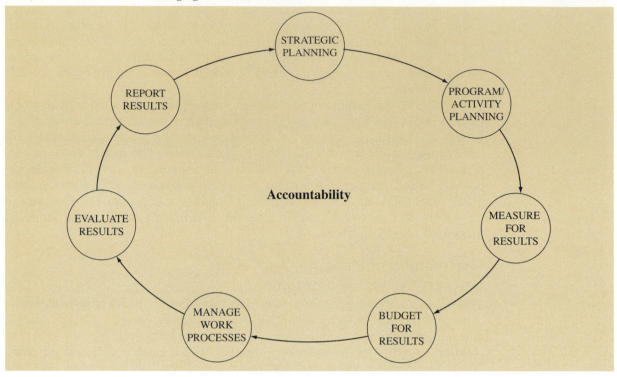

Source: Adapted from James Fountain, Wilson Campbell, Terry Patton, Paul Epstein, Mandi Cohn, *Special Report: Reporting Performance Information: Suggested Criteria for Effective Communication* (Norwalk, CT: GASB), August 2003, p. 14.

in the next section, and budgeting for performance is further discussed later in this chapter.

BUDGETING APPROACHES

The legalistic view is that a budget is a plan of financial operation embodying an estimate of proposed expenditures for a given period of time and the proposed means of financing them. In a much more general sense, budgets may be regarded as devices to aid management in operating an organization more effectively. Budgets are the financial expression of plans prepared by managers for operating an organization during a time period and for changing its physical facilities and its capital structure. In this sense, the budget is a tool for management and for communication.[7]

As the budget process evolved from a control orientation to improving the management of operations and the assignment of priorities to public problems, so have the basic formats of budgets evolved. Governments use a variety of budgeting approaches in developing annual budgets. Some of these budget approaches are briefly discussed next.

[7] Robert L. Bland and Irene S. Rubin, *Budgeting: A Guide for Local Governments.* (Washington, DC: International City/County Management Association, 1997), p. v.

Types of Budgeting

Incremental Budgeting

A simplistic and often used approach to budgeting is called **incremental budgeting.** In essence, an incremental budget is derived from the current year's budget by adding amounts expected to be required by line items. Examples include salary and wage increases, increases in the cost of supplies and equipment, decreases that would result from shrinkage in the scale of operations forced by pressures such as spending limitations mandated by the electorate (for example, California's Proposition 13 in 1978), and cuts in capital equipment purchases. Incremental budgeting focuses largely on controlling resource inputs and typically uses the *line-item* budget format in which the focus is on departmental expenditures for specified purposes or objects, such as personnel, supplies, equipment, and travel.

Incremental budgeting is often contrasted with *rational* budgeting approaches, which stress the relation of inputs to outputs (amounts of work accomplished) and outcomes (impacts on goals and objectives). Rational budgeting approaches, as they have evolved, attempt to identify fundamental objectives of the government, estimate future-year costs and benefits, and systematically analyze alternative ways of meeting the government's objectives. Approaches commonly described as rational are performance budgeting and program-based budgeting. Variations of these approaches are discussed next.[8]

Performance Budgeting

The evolution of the concept of a budget from "an estimate of proposed expenditures and the proposed means of financing them" to an "operating plan" was a natural accompaniment to the development of the concept of professional management. In public administration, as in business administration, the concept of professionalism demanded that administrators or managers attempt to put the scarce resources of qualified personnel and money to the best possible uses. The legal requirement that administrators of governments submit appropriate requests to the legislative bodies in budget format provided a basis for adapting required budgetary estimates of proposed expenditures to broader management use. The legislative appropriation process has traditionally required administrators to justify budget requests. A logical justification of proposed expenditures is to relate the proposed expenditures of each governmental subdivision to the programs and activities to be accomplished by that subdivision during the budget period. The type of budgeting in which input of resources is related to output of services is sometimes known as **performance budgeting.** Performance budgeting is linked conceptually with *performance auditing* as defined in Chapter 11 of this text. Performance budgeting is a plan for relating resource inputs to the efficient production of outputs; performance auditing is the subsequent evaluation to determine that resources were in fact used efficiently and effectively in accordance with the plan.

Performance budgeting historically focused on the relation between inputs and outputs of each organizational unit rather than programs. The use of performance budgeting in governments received significant impetus from the work of the first Hoover Commission for the federal government. Its report, presented to the Congress in 1949, led to the adoption in the federal government of budgets then known as *cost-based budgets* or *cost budgets*. The use of these designations suggests that a government

---

[8] More details about these specific budgeting techniques and their application to industries, such as service, not-for-profit, higher education, and health care, can be found in William R. Lalli, ed., *Handbook of Budgeting,* 5th ed. (New York: John Wiley & Sons, 2003, with 2005 Supplement).

desiring to use performance budgeting must have an accrual accounting system rather than a cash accounting system in order to routinely ascertain the costs of programs and activities. The recommendations of the second Hoover Commission led to the statutory requirement of both accrual accounting and cost-based budgeting for agencies of the executive branch of the federal government. Federal statutes also require the synchronization of budgetary and accounting classifications and the coordination of these with the organizational structure of the agencies. Subsequently, it was realized that the planning and programming functions of federal agencies were not performed by the same organizational segments that performed the budgeting and accounting functions and that plans and programs were thus often not properly related to appropriation requests.

Program Budgets

Program budgeting is a term sometimes used synonymously with performance budgeting. However, the term is more generally used to refer to a budget format that discloses the full costs of programs or functions without regard to the number of organizational units that might be involved in performing the various aspects of the program or functions. Program budgets address the fundamental issues of whether programs should exist at all and how to allocate scarce resources among competing programs.

Planning-Programming-Budgeting System

The integration of planning, programming, budgeting, and accounting has considerable appeal to persons concerned with public administration because an integrated system should, logically, provide legislators and administrators with much better information for the management of governmental resources than has been provided by separate systems. In the late 1960s, there was a concentrated effort to introduce a **planning-programming-budgeting system,** called PPBS, throughout the executive branch of the federal government, and to adapt the concept to state and local governments and other complex organizations.

Zero-Based Budgeting

In the 1970s, the wave of interest in PPBS receded and was replaced by widespread discussion of another approach to wedding the legally required budget process to a rational process of allocating scarce resources among alternative uses: **zero-based budgeting,** or ZBB. As the name indicates, the basic concept of ZBB is that the very existence of each activity as well as the amounts of resources requested to be allocated to each activity be justified each year.

Many governments of various sizes have experimented with performance budgeting, program budgeting, PPBS, ZBB, and mixed approaches to rational budgeting. Successful implementation of these approaches requires formulation of the government's fundamental objectives and identification and evaluation of alternative ways of achieving the objectives. Techniques used to evaluate alternatives are sometimes referred to as *systems analysis, cost/benefit analysis,* and *cost-effectiveness analysis.* Techniques for "productivity measurement" or "productivity evaluation" are also often utilized by administrators who use the budgeting process as an aid in the allocation of scarce resources among competing demands for services. Quantitative techniques such as model building and simulation studies are utilized as aids in evaluating alternative allocations of governmental resources just as they are for evaluating business alternatives.

However simple or sophisticated the methods used to develop information to aid in the resource allocation process, any method can produce useful output only if the data input are sufficiently reliable. Chapters 2 through 9 are intended to provide the reader with the background needed to understand data produced in conformity with GASB standards. Modifications that would facilitate rational budgeting are discussed later in this chapter.

BUDGETING PROCEDURES

Budgeting Governmental Appropriations

Appropriations budgets are an administration's requests for authorization to incur liabilities for goods, services, and facilities for specified purposes. In practice, the preparation of appropriations budgets for any one year is related to the administration's budget of revenues since the revenues budget is the plan for financing the proposed appropriations. If the program or performance budget concept is followed, appropriations budgets are prepared for each existing and continuing work program or activity of each governmental subdivision; for each program authorized or required by action of past legislative bodies but not yet made operative; and for each new program the administration intends to submit to the legislative body for approval.

In business budgeting, each ongoing program should be subjected to rigorous management scrutiny at budget preparation time to make sure there is a valid reason for continuing the program at all: This is the fundamental idea of zero-based budgeting. If the program should be continued, management must decide whether the prior allocation of resources to the program is optimal or changes should be made in the assignment of personnel, equipment, space, and money. In a well-managed government, the same sort of review is given to each continuing program. The mere fact that the program was authorized by a past legislative body does not mean that the administration may shirk its duty to recommend discontinuance of a program that has ceased to serve a real need. If, in the judgment of the administration, the program should be continued, the appropriate level of activity and the appropriate allocation of resources must be determined; this determination takes far more political courage and management skill than the common practice of simply extrapolating the trend of historical activity and historical cost.

If the administration is convinced that a program should be continued and the prior allocation of resources is reasonable, the preparation of the appropriations budget is delegated to the persons in charge of the program. In the case of a new program, the administration states the objectives of the program and sets general guidelines for the operation of the program and then delegates budget preparation to individuals who are expected to be in charge of the program when legislative authorization and appropriations are secured. State laws or local ordinances typically require that certain steps be followed in the budgeting process and may prescribe dates by which each step must be completed. These requirements are referred to as the **budget calendar.** A budget calendar for a small city is presented in Illustration 13–2. The budget calendar for most large governments will likely span a 12- to 18-month period. Many governments are implementing multiyear budgeting to enhance long-range planning, decrease staff time, and improve program evaluation.[9] In these cases, the budget calendar should span the two-year period (or appropriate time frame) and refer to dates when mid-period forms and reports are due.

[9] Andrea Jackson, "Taking the Plunge: The Conversion to Multi-Year Budgeting," *Government Finance Review* (August 2002), p. 24; and the International City/County Management Association, *Service Report: Multiyear Budgeting* (June 1999). See also www.icma.org.

ILLUSTRATION 13–2

	SAMPLE CITY **Budget Calendar** **Year Ending September 30**	
Date	**Event**	**Requirement or Action**
July 20	1st Budget Workshop	Departments'/Programs' goals due. Budget forms issued.
August 4	2nd Budget Workshop	Draft budget and documentation including revenue projections.
August 11	Regular Council Meeting/ 3rd Budget Workshop	Long-term General Fund projections, capital outlay and analysis of budget increases.
August 25	Regular Council Meeting/ 4th Budget Workshop	Budget presentations by County Health District, Chamber of Commerce, and other related organizations.
September 1	Special Council Meeting/ 5th Budget Workshop	Water/Sewer budget presentation. Call for public hearing to be held September 8.
September 3	Newspaper Publication	Publish notice of public hearing on budget to be held on September 8.
September 8	Regular Council Meeting	Public hearing on proposed budget.
September 15	Special Council Meeting	First reading of budget ordinance.
September 22	Regular Council Meeting	Second reading and vote on adoption of budget ordinance.

To ensure that administrative policies are actually used in budget preparation and that the budget calendar and other legal requirements are met, it is customary to designate someone in the central administrative office as budget officer. In addition to the responsibilities enumerated, the **budget officer** is responsible for providing technical assistance to the operating personnel who prepare the budgets. The technical assistance provided may include clerical assistance with budget computations as well as the maintenance of files for each program containing (1) documents citing the legal authorization and directives, (2) relevant administrative policies, (3) historical cost and workload data, (4) specific factors affecting program costs and workloads, and (5) sources of information to be used in projecting trends.

Budgets prepared by departmental administrators should be reviewed by the central administration before submission to the legislative branch because the total of departmental requests frequently exceeds the total of estimated revenues, and it is necessary to trim the requests in some manner. Central review may also be necessary to make sure that enough is being spent on certain programs. Good financial management of the taxpayers' dollars is a process of trying to determine the optimum dollar input to achieve the desired service output, not a process of minimizing input. Even though the appropriations budget is a legally prescribed document, the administration should not lose sight of its managerial usefulness.

It should be emphasized that governmental budgets submitted to the legislative branch for action must be made available for a certain length of time for study by interested citizens, and one or more public hearings must be held before the legislative branch takes final action. Ordinarily, few citizens take the trouble to study the proposed budgets in detail; however, newspaper and television reporters often publicize proposed appropriations, especially those for programs, activities, and functions deemed particularly newsworthy. News reporters also publicize increases in taxes and fees

ILLUSTRATION 13–3   **Sources of Conflict in the Budget Process**

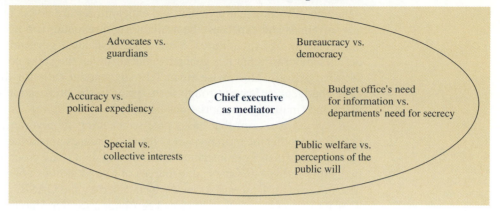

proposed to finance budgeted appropriations. Representatives of organizations such as the state or local Chamber of Commerce and League of Women Voters analyze the budgets in detail and furnish analyses to their members, the public, and news media.

Generally, such broadly based organizations attempt to be evenhanded in their budget analyses. In many instances, however, members of special interest groups also sift through the proposed budget to determine the proposed allocation of resources to the programs, activities, and functions of interest to the groups they represent. Budget analyses by special interest groups are not intended to be evenhanded. If the proposed budget does not meet the interests of the groups as well as they think it should, the groups may be counted on to attempt to influence the members of the legislative branch to change the budget before it is enacted into law. Thus, it is evident that the governmental process involves political and social considerations and, at higher levels of government, aggregate economic considerations, all of which may be more important to many voters, administrators (bureaucrats), and legislators (politicians) than are financial considerations.

In public budgeting there is natural tension among these stakeholders that must be mediated by the government's chief executive officer or financial manager. Illustration 13–3 shows sources of conflict that will arise during a budget process that serves to air community concerns and build consensus about which public services should be provided with available levels of public resources. For example, department heads and interest groups may advocate for more funding than they know the guardians in the budget office will approve. Citizen participation that symbolizes a democracy may seem inefficient to a bureaucrat. The budget office may demand information that a department prefers to keep secret. The public may want something different than officials believe is needed. Special interest groups may command a louder voice than the collective interests of the whole. Public administrators may have a concern for realism in the budget when politicians prefer a positive budget picture.[10] All these conflicts make the budget process a political one in which the budget emerges to communicate the plan of elected officials and bureaucrats to meet the demands of its citizens subject to economic and other constraints.

[10] Bland and Rubin, *Budgeting: A Guide for Local Governments*, pp. 11–19.

Budgeting Governmental Revenues

Although governmental revenues and expenditures are not as interdependent as business revenues and expenses, the availability of revenues is a necessary prerequisite to the incurring of expenditures. Some states and local governments may operate at a deficit temporarily, but it is generally conceded that they may not do so for several consecutive periods. Thus, wise financial management calls for the preparation of revenues budgets, at least in rough form, prior to the preparation of detailed operating plans and finalizing appropriations budgets.

Revenues is a term that has a precise meaning in governmental accounting. The GASB states that the term *revenues* "means increases in (sources of) fund financial resources other than from interfund transfers and debt issue proceeds."[11] For purposes of budgeting inflows of financial resources of a fund, it does not seem particularly valuable to distinguish among revenues, as defined by the GASB, interfund transfers, and debt issue proceeds, other than to keep budgeting terminology consistent with accounting and financial reporting terminology.

Sources of revenue and other financial inflows available to a given local government are generally closely controlled by state law; state laws also establish procedures for the utilization of available sources and may impose ceilings on the amount of revenue a local government may collect from certain sources. Sources generally available for financing routine operations include property taxes, sales taxes, income taxes, license fees, fines, charges for services, grants or allocations from other governments, and revenue from the use of money or property. Chapter 3 of this text describes revenue sources and discusses revenue accounting in some detail. The present discussion is, therefore, limited to the broad aspects of governmental revenue budgeting.

Within the framework set by legal requirements and subject to the approval of the legislative body (which, in turn, reacts to the electorate), the determination of revenue policy is a prerogative of the administration. Major considerations underlying the policy formulation are set forth in the preceding section of this chapter. After policies have been established, the technical preparation of the revenues budget is ordinarily delegated to the budget officer. To facilitate budget preparation, experienced budget officers generally keep for each revenue source a file containing (1) a copy of legislation authorizing the source and any subsequent legislation pertaining to the source; (2) historical experience relative to collections from the source, including collections as a percentage of billings, when applicable; (3) relevant administrative policies; and (4) specific factors that affect the yield from the source, including for each factor the historical relationship of the factor to revenue procedures to be used in projecting the trend of factors affecting yield and factors affecting collections. Graphic presentations of these factors are also frequently included in the file. Finance officers of large governments use more sophisticated statistical and econometric methods of revenue forecasting, particularly to evaluate alternative assumptions, but the method described here is generally used for preparation of a legal revenues budget.

Budgeting Capital Expenditures

Accounting principles for business enterprises and for proprietary funds of governments require the cost of assets expected to benefit more than one period to be treated as a balance sheet item rather than as a charge against revenues of the period. No such

---

[11] GASB, *Codification*, Sec. 1800, 114.

distinction exists for governmental fund types. Expenditures for long-lived assets to be used in the general operations of a government are treated in the appropriations process in the same manner as are expenditures for salaries, wages, benefits, materials, supplies, and services to be consumed during the accounting period. Accounting control over long-lived assets used in governmental activities is established at the government-wide level.

Effective financial management requires the plans for any one year to be consistent with intermediate- and long-range plans. Governmental projects such as the construction or improvement of streets; construction of bridges and buildings; acquisition of land for recreational use, parking lots, and future building sites; and urban renewal may require a consistent application of effort over a span of years. Consequently, administrators need to present to the legislative branch and to the public a multiyear capital improvements program, as well as the budget for revenues, operating expenditures, and capital outlays requested for the forthcoming year.

Effective financial management also requires nonfinancial information such as physical measures of capital assets, their service condition, and their estimated replacement cost. Nonfinancial information of these types is useful for purposes of forecasting future asset repair and replacement schedules, repair and replacement costs, and financing requirements, and is required for certain eligible infrastructure assets.

Budgeting Cash Receipts

Revenues and expenditures budgets would best be prepared on the same basis as the accounts and financial reports: modified accrual, in the case of governmental funds—particularly the General Fund and special revenue funds. Although it is highly desirable for persons concerned with the financial management of governments (or any other organization) to foresee the effects of operating plans and capital improvement plans on receivables, payables, inventories, and facilities, it is absolutely necessary to foresee the effects on cash. An organization must have sufficient cash to pay employees, suppliers, and creditors the amounts due at the times due, or it risks labor troubles, an unsatisfactory credit rating, and consequent difficulties in maintaining its capacity to render services at levels acceptable to its residents. An organization that maintains cash balances in excess of needs fails to earn interest on temporary investments; therefore, it is raising more revenues than would otherwise be needed or failing to offer services.

In Chapter 4 it was noted that in a typical government, cash receipts from major sources of revenues of general and special revenue funds are concentrated in a few months of each fiscal year, whereas cash disbursements tend to be approximately level month by month. Under the heading "Tax Anticipation Notes Payable" in Chapter 4, reference is made to cash forecasting done by the treasurer of the Town of Brighton in order to determine the amount of **tax anticipation notes** to be issued. The cash forecasting method illustrated in that chapter is quite crude but often reasonably effective if done by experienced persons. Sophisticated cash budgeting methods used in well-managed governments require additional data, such as historical records of monthly collections from each revenue source including percentage of billings where applicable. In addition to the historical record of collections, the budget files should contain analyses of the factors affecting the collections from each source so that adjustments to historical patterns may be made, if needed, for the budget year.

Property taxes are often the largest recurring cash receipt in a government; however, all other expected cash receipts must be included in the cash budget. More difficult to project are self-assessed taxes, such as income taxes; nonrecurring receipts, such as those from the sale of assets; and income earned on **sweep accounts,** arrangements by which a bank automatically "sweeps" cash that exceeds the target balance into short-term cash investments.

Budgeting Cash Disbursements

Except for modified accrual provisions regarding expenditures of debt service funds, the expenditures of all other governmental funds (and of all proprietary funds) are to be recognized and budgeted on the accrual basis for governments that follow GAAP for budgeting. Therefore, the conversion of the approved appropriations budget into a cash disbursements budget involves the knowledge of personnel policies, purchasing policies, and operating policies and plans, which should govern the timing of expenditures of appropriations and the consequent payment of liabilities. Information as to current and previous typical time intervals between the ordering of goods and contractual services, their receipt, and the related disbursements should be available from the appropriation expenditures ledgers and cash disbursement records. In the case of salaries and wages of governmental employees, the cash disbursements budget for each month is affected by the number of paydays that fall in the month rather than that number of working days in the month.

Monthly cash receipts budgets are prepared for all sources of revenues of each fund, and cash disbursements budgets are prepared for all organizational units. Management should then match the two in order to determine when and for how long cash balances will rise to unnecessarily high levels or fall to levels below those prudent management would require. Note that the preceding sentence concerns cash receipts and disbursements of all funds of a government, not of a single fund. There is no reason for bank accounts and fund cash accounts to agree, except in total. Effective cash planning and control suggests that *all* cash be put under control of the treasurer of the government.

As shown in Illustration 13–4, cash receipts for the Town of Brighton are highest in April, May, and November, presumably when taxes are collected. Disbursements are fairly constant across the year, except for January, which may be when capital assets are acquired. The pattern of short-term borrowing, repayment, and investment seems to indicate that the city's cash and investment policies include (1) a target monthly cash balance of at least $425,000, (2) new borrowing made in increments of $5,000, and (3) cash exceeding the target used to repay short-term borrowing; any remaining excess is invested. A very small government that has few receipts and infrequent disbursements may be able to plan temporary investments and short-term borrowings on the basis of cash budgets for periods longer than one month, perhaps quarterly or semiannually. Conversely, a government with considerable cash activity involving large sums might need to budget cash receipts and cash disbursements on a daily basis to maintain adequate but not excessive cash balances.

Budgeting, by definition, involves planning on the basis of assumptions about economic conditions, salary levels, numbers of employees at each salary level, prices of supplies and capital acquisitions, and other factors that cannot be foreseen with great accuracy. Accordingly, it is necessary at intervals throughout the year to compare actual receipts with budgeted receipts, source by source, and actual disbursements with budgeted disbursements for each organizational unit, function and object. This provides for control of the budget and, if necessary, revision of the budget in light of new knowledge about economic conditions, salary, price levels, and other factors affecting collections and disbursements.

ILLUSTRATION 13–4

TOWN OF BRIGHTON

Budgeted Cash Receipts and Disbursements for FY 2008

(000 omitted)

	January	February	March	April	May	June	July	August	September	October	November	December
Balance first of month	$ 610	$425	$425	$425	$ 425	$425	$425	$427	$427	$427	$ 427	$425
Expected receipts during month	165	250	295	570	1,096	134	280	370	285	270	892	116
Cash available	775	675	720	995	1,521	559	705	797	712	697	1,319	541
Expected disbursements during month	1,050	240	280	325	320	320	508	325	315	335	320	455
Provisional balance at end of month	(275)	435	440	670	1,201	239	197	472	397	362	999	86
Less: Temporary investments purchased	—	—	—	—	346	—	—	—	—	—	454	—
Less: Repayment of short-term borrowings	—	10	15	245	430	—	—	45	—	—	120	—
Add: Temporary investments sold	—	—	—	—	—	186	160	—	—	—	—	340
Add: Short-term borrowings	700	—	—	—	—	—	70	—	30	65	—	—
Balance at end of month	$ 425	$425	$425	$425	$ 425	$425	$427	$427	$427	$427	$ 425	$426

527

BUDGETING FOR PERFORMANCE

During the last several decades, growth in service demands and cutbacks in unrestricted federal funding forced numerous state and local governments to increase taxes and user fees. Meanwhile, taxpayers have become increasingly frustrated with paying higher taxes for what they perceive as bloated, inefficient government bureaucracies. Fiscal reform has thus become a popular platform for politicians aspiring to key elective offices. Even though, as discussed previously in this chapter, many governments have experimented with so-called rational budgeting approaches, most of these experiments seem to have had little real impact on improving the efficiency and effectiveness of service delivery. Given their limited success with prior budgeting approaches, political leaders and government managers are experimenting with management innovations in the private sector that might improve the efficiency of government operations and reduce the need for higher taxes.

Many state and local governments are well along in their efforts to link performance measurement systems with budgeting and strategic planning and many have improved their budgeting practices in the past decades. A major impetus for this improvement has been the Government Finance Officers Association's Distinguished Budget Presentation Awards Program. Voluntary applications for this award increased from 113 in 1984, the year the program was initiated, to 1,027 in 2004. About 90 percent of the applicants have received the award, and many of the unsuccessful applicants have received confidential reviewer suggestions that permitted them to subsequently qualify for the award.[12] Some states have passed legislation that requires performance measures, both financial and nonfinancial, to be reported by local governments and public institutions, such as colleges and universities.

Strategies being employed by many governments to measure and improve performance of the organization are total quality management, customer relationship management, and service efforts and accomplishments.

Total Quality Management

Total quality management (TQM) is attractive to many government officials because it links customer (taxpayer and other resource provider) satisfaction to improvements in the operating systems and processes used to provide goods and services. TQM seeks to continuously improve the government's ability to meet or exceed customer demands for customers who might be external, such as taxpayers and service recipients, or internal, such as the customers of an internal service fund. Central to TQM is using customer data to identify and correct problems. Individual governments have tailored their TQM structures to meet their unique requirements, but most incorporate a majority of the following elements:

1. Support and commitment of top-level officials.
2. Customer orientation.
3. Employee involvement in productivity and quality improvement efforts.
4. Employees rewarded for quality and productivity achievement.
5. Training provided to employees in methods for improving productivity and quality.
6. Reduction of barriers to productivity and quality improvement.

[12] See "Annual Report—Distinguished Budget Presentation Awards Program" of the GFOA, available at www.gfoa.org/services/awards.shtml.

7. Productivity and quality measures and standards that are meaningful to the government.

8. Written vision or mission statements that are linked directly to team-established targets or goals.[13]

The elements of TQM are obviously consistent with those of the rational budgeting approaches (particularly PPBS) previously discussed. Thus governments that have implemented one of the rational budgeting approaches or a mixed approach may find it less costly to implement a TQM structure. On the other hand, few governments possess adequate data on customer satisfaction. Moreover, the traditional emphases of government on line-item budgeting, rigid personnel classifications, restrictive procurement regulations, and so on, tend to reduce management autonomy and thus may be inconsistent with the need under TQM to empower employees to be "entrepreneurial" in improving processes and meeting customer demand. It should also be noted that the objective of TQM is not necessarily to reduce cost but to increase "value for the dollar." Insofar as a TQM program successfully adds value, it has the potential to improve the public perception of government in addition to improving service delivery.

Element 7 from the preceding list of TQM elements requires that the government develop meaningful standards for and measures of performance in terms of productivity and quality. In the government and not-for-profit context, the analogous performance terms more typically used are *efficiency* and *effectiveness,* the former relating efforts (resource inputs) to outputs of a service process and the latter relating efforts to outcomes or the results produced by service.

Customer Relationship Management

Customer relationship management (CRM) systems, developed in the 1990s for businesses, have great potential for governments as they provide services to their customers—citizens. CRM systems create an integrated view of a customer to coordinate services from all channels of the organization with the intent to improve the long-term relationship the organization has with its customer.

At first glance, it would seem that the high cost of CRM technology that would allow citizens to interact with their government electronically for public services, and the traditional government culture where information resides in departments or agencies that often do not share data, might seem like insurmountable obstacles for governments in establishing a CRM system. However, a 2001 Accenture study found that government managers were realistic about the challenges and interested and eager to put CRM principles to work as they strive to become more effective and efficient at providing public services.[14] Examples some governments have tried include obtaining licenses and making tax payments through a government Web site. Choosing to apply CRM to strategically selected narrow projects with modest goals may be the most realistic way for governments to realize benefits from this innovative business tool.[15]

[13] Adapted from James J. Kline, "Total Quality Management in Local Government," *Government Finance Review,* August 1992, p. 7. See also International City/County Management Association, MIS Report: Performance Measurement for Accountability and Service Improvement, September 1997.

[14] Accenture, *Customer Relationship Management—A Blueprint for Government,* November 2001, pp. 6–13; see www.accenture.com.

[15] Darrell K. Rigby and Dianne Ledingham, "CRM Done Right," *Harvard Business Review,* November 2004, p. 2.

Service Efforts and Accomplishments (SEA)

GASB's accountability reporting objective includes reporting on the efficient and effective use of resources. GASB *Codification* Appendix B, *Concepts Statement 1,* Par. 77c. states:

> Financial reporting should provide information to assist users in assessing the service efforts, costs, and accomplishments of the governmental entity.

The lack of a bottom-line measure of performance for a governmental entity, such as "profit" for a business, means that *nonfinancial* measures of **service efforts and accomplishments** (SEA) and related costs are necessary for informed decision making by citizens, elected officials, appointed officials, investors and creditors, and others having an interest in the government's performance. The GASB has sponsored and conducted extensive research on SEA measures for several service areas, including, among others, elementary and secondary education, higher education, fire departments, police departments, and hospitals, as well as public health, mass transit, road maintenance, and sanitation collection and disposal organizations.

Based on the research to date, GASB issued in 1994 *Concepts Statement No. 2,* which identified three broad categories of SEA measures: (1) measures of service efforts, (2) measures of service accomplishments, and (3) measures that relate efforts to accomplishments.[16] Measures of service efforts, or **input measures,** relate to the amount of financial and nonfinancial resources (such as money and materials) used in a program or process.[17] Measures of service accomplishments are of two types: outputs and outcomes. **Output measures** are quantity measures that reflect either the quantity of a service provided, such as the number of lane-miles of road repaired, or the quantity of service provided that meets a specified quality requirement, such as the number of lane-miles of road repaired to a specified minimum condition. **Outcome measures** gauge accomplishments, or the results of services provided, such as the percentage of lane-miles of road in excellent, good, or fair condition. Such measures are particularly useful when compared with established objectives or norms or with results from previous years. Finally, measures that relate efforts to accomplishments are essential to assessing efficiency and effectiveness. **Efficiency measures** relate the quantity or cost of resources used to unit of output (e.g., cost per lane-mile of road repaired). Measures that relate resource costs to outcomes are useful in evaluating how effectively service objectives are being met and at what cost (e.g., the cost per lane-mile of road maintained in excellent, good, or fair condition). Additional quantitative and narrative explanation may be necessary to help users fully assess the entity's performance. **Effectiveness measures** relate costs to outcomes; for example, cost for each percentage reduction in traffic accidents or percentage increase in citizens who report feeling safe in the neighborhood.

Illustration 13–5 shows recommended SEA indicators for fire departments. The input measures indicate quantities and dollar amounts of resources used in providing fire suppression services. The output and outcome indicators collectively indicate service accomplishments when outputs indicate quantities of work done on particular activities (such as number of fire calls answered) and outcomes indicate the results of activities in achieving desired objectives (such as minimizing fire damage).

---

[16] Governmental Accounting Standards Board, *Concepts Statement No. 2,* "Service Efforts and Accomplishments Reporting" (Norwalk, CT: April 1994).

[17] The discussion of SEA measures in this paragraph is paraphrased from the discussion in *Concepts Statement No. 2,* pars. 50–53.

ILLUSTRATION 13–5 **Recommended SEA Indicators for Fire Departments: Fire Suppression**

Indicator	Rationale for Selecting Indicator
Inputs:	
Personnel	
Full-time personnel	Provide information on labor resources used
Part-time and volunteer personnel	
Total human-hours worked	
Total operating expenditures	Provide information on resources committed to
Total capital expenditures	suppression activity
Human-hours in training programs	
Percentage of fire fighters reaching an	Provide information on preparedness
NFPA-recommended certification level	
Outputs:	
Number of fire calls answered	Measures suppression workload, readily available
Outcomes:	
Water supply	
Minimum water volume available	
Minimum water flow available	Measures availability of water needed to
Population with access to adequate	suppress fires—a measure of fire fighting
water supply	readiness
Response time	
Average response time	Measures success in delivering timely service;
Percentage of responses in under	currently measured by fire departments
5 minutes	
Average time to control fires	
Single-alarm, residential	
Single-alarm, industry	
Two-alarm, industry	
Percentage of fires spread limited to X%	Measures success in minimizing fire damage
Square feet on arrival	
Single-alarm, residential	
Single-alarm, industry	
Two-alarm, industry	
Efficiency:	
Operating expenditures per capita	Provide per capita cost of service information for operations
Capital expenditures per capita	Provide per capita cost of capital investment
Operating expenditures per $100,000 of property protected	Relate operating cost information to value of property protected
Capital expenditures per $100,000 of property protected	Relate capital investment to value of property protected

Source: Government Accounting Standards Board, *Research Report: Service Efforts and Accomplishments Reporting: Its Time Has Come* (Norwalk, CT: GASB, 1990), Exhibit 5–2.

In 2003, GASB published 16 suggested criteria for use in preparing reports on service efforts and accomplishment measures presented in three broad categories. Illustration 13–6 shows these measures and categories. It is important to note that these are criteria that suggest characteristics of performance reports and measures that are

ILLUSTRATION 13–6 **Suggested Criteria and Purpose for Reporting Performance Information**

Category I: The External Report on Performance Information

1. *Purpose and scope:* To inform users of the intent of the report and to identify the programs and services that are included.
2. *Statement of major goals and objectives:* To provide users with the goals and objectives and their source so users can determine how they were established.
3. *Involvement in establishing goals and objectives:* To help users identify who established goals and objectives and whether that includes those responsible for achieving results.
4. *Multiple levels of reporting:* To allow specific users to find the appropriate level of detail performance information for their needs.
5. *Analysis of results and challenges:* To present performance results with a discussion of challenges facing the organization.
6. *Focus on key measures:* To ensure that reports provide users with enough (and not too much) information to develop their own conclusions about the organization's performance.
7. *Reliable information:* To assist users in assessing the credibility of the reported performance information.

Category II: What Performance Information to Report

8. *Relevant measures of results:* To ensure that performance measures reflect the degree to which those goals and objectives have been accomplished.
9. *Resources used and efficiency:* To facilitate an assessment of resources used and the efficiency, cost-effectiveness, and economy of programs and services.
10. *Citizen and customer perceptions:* To ensure that a more complete view of the results of programs and services results than is captured in other "objective" measures of outputs and outcomes.
11. *Comparisons for assessing performance:* To provide a clear frame of reference for assessing the performance of the organization, its programs, and its services.
12. *Factors affecting results:* To help users understand the factors that might have an effect on performance, including relevant conditions in the state, region, or community.
13. *Aggregation and disaggregation of information:* To provide performance information that is not misleading and is relevant to users with different interests and needs.
14. *Consistency:* To allow users to compare an organization's performance from period to period and to better understand changes in measures and reasons why measures changed.

Category III: Communication of Performance Information

15. *Easy to find, access, and understand:* To ensure that a broad group of potential users can access, understand, and use various forms of performance reports to reach conclusions.
16. *Regular and timely reporting:* To ensure that organizations report performance information on a regular and timely basis to be useful in decision making.

Source: James Fountain, Wilson Campbell, Terry Patton, Paul Epstein, and Mandi Cohn, *Special Report: Reporting Performance Information: Suggested Criteria for Effective Communication* (Norwalk, CT: GASB), August 2003, pp. 36–39.

expected to lead to their usefulness by users. There is no suggestion as to what values of these measures would be considered good or bad.

Since these suggested criteria were published, several state and local governments have experimented with issuing performance information and reports. In July 2005, the GASB issued *Government Service Efforts and Accomplishments Performance Reports: A Guide to Understanding* that provides users and preparers with a basis for understanding and using an SEA performance report. Included in this user guide are several excerpts from performance reports issued by local governments, including one from the Prince William County, Virginia's *FY 2004 Service Efforts and Accomplishments Report.* Illustration 13–7 presents a graphic of what Prince William County calls its Results Oriented Government System. As can be seen, this county builds its system

ILLUSTRATION 13–7   **Prince William County (PWC), Virginia, Results Oriented Government System**

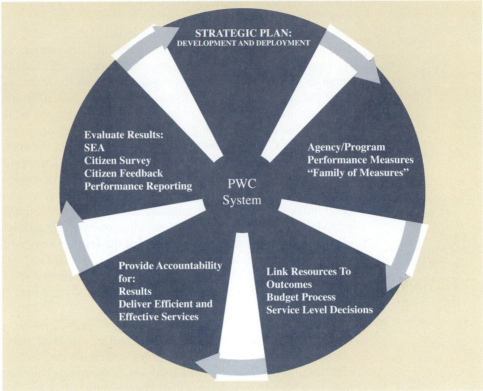

Source: Prince William County, VA, *FY 2004 Service Efforts & Accomplishments Report,* p. XVI. See www.pwcgov.org/accountability.

on the characteristics of an accountability model presented earlier in this chapter in Illustration 13–1.

Budgeting for performance requires sophisticated cost accounting systems to determine the full cost of programs or functions. Better managed state and local governments are therefore actively developing improved cost accounting systems. One innovative costing approach being implemented by some governments is activity-based costing (ABC), discussed in the next section along with key concepts about costs as they relate to budgets.

COSTING OF GOVERNMENT SERVICES

The explosive increase in demand for government services, relative to the increase in resources, has forced the adoption of the techniques of good financial management, including better cost accounting. The use of cost as a measure of the input of resources into a program, as an element of the budget, and as a basis to assess performance has been discussed earlier in this chapter.

The GFOA added a recommended practice on *costing government services* to its set of recommended practices that calls for governments to calculate the full cost of the different services they provide. Full costs should include all direct and indirect costs related to that service. The GFOA further calls for governments to use full cost data appropriately, for example, considering only *avoidable costs,* not the *unavoidable costs,* when discussing privatization of an activity.[18] This section discusses the role of costs in a system that integrates management, budgeting, and costing for a governmental or not-for-profit organization.

Cost accounting, as discussed in standard college texts, is obviously applicable to business operations of governments and health care entities, but its application to nonbusiness activities of a government, not-for-profit organizations, or colleges and universities is not as immediately obvious. However, the same tasks of segregating direct from indirect costs, variable from fixed costs, standard from actual costs, and incremental from sunk costs are as important in capturing the total cost of delivering governmental or not-for-profit program services as they are in private-sector companies. Another similarity with traditional cost accounting in the context of for-profit organizations is that **job order cost** accounting may be appropriate for some tasks (i.e., recording costs chargeable to specific grants, programs, projects, activities, or departments), and for others **process cost** accounting is more appropriate (i.e., recording continuous activities of governments, health care entities, and universities for a time period). In any organization, predetermination of overhead rates involves budgeting the overhead costs that should be incurred at the level of activity chosen as a basis for determination of the rate. Governments and not-for-profit organizations can use **flexible budgeting** to budget costs at different levels of activity and then compare costs that were actually incurred in a period with costs that should have been incurred to achieve that level of output.

The next section presents two other cost accounting issues with special significance to governmental and not-for-profit organizations. The first, acceptance of federal grants and sponsored agreements, brings with it the duty to comply with particular regulations on allowable costs and methods of spending. The second, activity-based costing, has been adopted by some governments as a key element of performance evaluation systems. Such systems are enhanced by designing accounting systems to provide as much activity-based cost data as possible, even though the need for some statistical cost data outside of the accounting system is inevitable.

Federal Grants and Sponsored Agreements

State and local governments and not-for-profit entities, particularly colleges and universities, have found grants from and sponsored agreements with the federal government important, although diminishing, sources of financing. The United States Office of Management and Budget has issued a series of circulars to set forth *cost principles* to govern payments by the federal government under grant programs, contracts, and other agreements, to state and local governments (OMB *Circular A–87*), educational institutions (OMB *Circular A–21*), and other not-for-profit organizations (OMB *Circular A–122*). The wording of the three circulars is similar in many respects. They provide that the total cost of a program or contract is the sum of the allowable direct costs incident to its performance, plus its allocable portion of allowable indirect costs, less applicable credits. The terms *allowable costs, direct costs,* and *indirect costs,* among others, are defined in the circulars.

Administrative requirements describing *how* federal expenditures are made are also detailed in OMB circulars (for example, maintaining a financial management system and competitive bidding for procuring supplies and property). Illustration 13–8 shows

---

[18] Government Finance Officers Association, *Measuring the Cost of Government Services,* 2002; see www.gfoa.org.

ILLUSTRATION 13–8   OMB Grants Management Circulars

	Cost Principles	Administrative Requirements
State and local governments	*Circular A–87* "Cost Principles for State, Local and Indian Tribal Governments" (revised 5/10/04)	*Circular A–102* "Grants and Cooperative Agreements with State and Local Governments" known as the **"Common Rule"** (revised 1994, amended 8/29/97)
Educational institutions	*Circular A–21* "Cost Principles for Educational Institutions" (revised 5/10/04)	*Circular A–110* "Uniform Administrative Requirements for Grants and Other Agreements with Institutions of Higher Education, Hospitals, and Other Non-Profit Organizations" (revised 1993, amended 9/30/99)
Not-for-profit organizations	*Circular A–122* "Cost Principles for Non-Profit Organizations" (revised 5/10/04)	*Circular A–110* (same as above)

Source: All Circulars are available from the Office of Management and Budget (Washington, DC: Superintendent of Documents, U.S. Government Printing Office) or www.whitehouse.gov/omb.

the relationship of these circulars to the organizations they cover. Just as the OMB combined *Circulars A–128* and *A–133* (as discussed in Chapter 11), there is a movement toward a combined circular for cost principles and another for administration requirements covering all types of organizations receiving federal funds. An organization accepting federal funds must follow *all* relevant OMB circulars.

Allowable Costs

To be an **allowable cost,** a cost must meet the following general criteria:

a. Be necessary and reasonable for proper and efficient performance and administration of federal awards.
b. Be allocable to federal awards under provisions of *Circular A–87.*
c. Be authorized or not prohibited under state or local laws or regulations.
d. Conform to any limitations or exclusions set forth in *Circular A–87,* federal laws, terms and conditions of the federal award, or other governing regulations as to types or amounts of cost items.
e. Be consistent with policies, regulations, and procedures that apply uniformly to both federal awards and other activities of the government.
f. Be accorded consistent treatment. Consequently, a cost may not be assigned to a federal award as a direct cost if any other cost incurred for the same purpose in like circumstances has been allocated to the federal award as an indirect cost.
g. Except as otherwise provided for *in Circular A–87,* be determined in accordance with generally accepted accounting principles.
h. Not be included as a cost or used to meet cost sharing or matching requirements of any other federal award in either the current or a prior period, except as specifically provided by federal law or regulation.
i. Be determined net of all applicable credits.
j. Be adequately documented.[19]

[19]OMB, *Circular A–87,* Attachment A, C-1.

Each circular provides standards for determining the allowability of selected items of cost. Certain items of cost are generally allowable whether or not mentioned specifically in a grant, contract, or other agreement document. Certain other cost items are allowable only if specifically approved by the grantor agency, and certain other cost items are unallowable. *Circular A–87* lists 43 selected cost items ranging alphabetically from advertising to travel costs. Of the 43 cost items, most are allowable whether direct or indirect to the extent of benefits received by federal awards.[20] Depreciation and use allowances are included in the allowable cost items. As explained in Chapter 5, even though governmental funds do not record depreciation expense, it is reported for general capital assets at the government-wide level in the *GASBS 34* reporting model. Moreover, although public colleges and universities formerly did not report depreciation expense, they report it now as a business-type activity under *GASBS 35*. Consequently, both governments and public colleges and universities will find it relatively easy to charge depreciation to federal grants and contracts.

Several of the allowable items are allowable under highly restrictive conditions and generally require the explicit approval of the grantor agency. An example is advertising costs that are allowable only for such items as recruitment of personnel, procurement of goods and services, and disposal of scrap or surplus materials related to the performance of a federal award. Some of the cost items are *unallowable,* including items such as alcoholic beverages, bad debt expenses, contributions and donated services, fund-raising and investment management costs, entertainment, general expenses of the state or local government (e.g., salaries of the chief executive, legislatures, judicial department officials), and lobbying. Similar prohibitions apply to colleges and universities under the provisions of *Circular A–21*.

Direct Costs

Direct costs are those that can be identified specifically with a particular cost objective.[21] A **cost objective,** in federal terminology, is an organizational unit, function, activity, project, cost center, or pool established for the accumulation of costs. A final, or ultimate, cost objective is a specific grant, project, contract, or other activity (presumably one of interest to the federal agency that provides resources for the activity under a grant, contract, or other agreement). A cost may be direct with respect to a given function or activity but indirect with respect to the grant or other final cost objective of interest to the grantor or contractor. Typical direct costs chargeable to grant programs include compensation of employees for the time and efforts devoted specifically to the execution of grant programs; cost of materials acquired, consumed, or expended specifically for the purpose of the grant; and other items of expense incurred specifically to carry out the grant agreement. If approved by the grantor agency, equipment purchased and other capital expenditures incurred for a certain grant or other final cost objective would be considered direct costs.

Indirect Costs

Indirect costs, according to *Circular A–87,* are those (1) incurred for a common or joint purpose benefiting more than one cost objective and (2) not readily assignable to the cost objectives specifically benefited without effort disproportionate to the results achieved.[22] The term *indirect costs* applies to costs originating in the grantee department

---

[20] OMB, *Circular A–87,* Attachment B.
[21] Ibid., Attachments A, E.
[22] Ibid., Attachments A, F.1.

as well as to those incurred by other departments in supplying goods, services, and facilities to the grantee department. To facilitate equitable distribution of indirect expenses to the cost objectives served, it may be necessary to establish a number of "pools" of indirect cost within the grantee department. Indirect cost pools should be distributed to benefited cost objectives on bases that produce an equitable result in consideration of relative benefits derived. In certain instances, grantees may negotiate annually with the grantor a predetermined fixed rate for computing indirect costs applicable to a grant or a lump-sum allowance for indirect costs, but generally grantees must prepare a cost allocation plan that conforms with instructions issued by the U.S. Department of Health and Human Services. Cost allocation plans of local governments will be retained for audit by a designated federal agency. (Audit of federal grants is discussed in some detail in Chapter 11 of this text.)

Activity-Based Costing

Activity-based costing (ABC) was developed for use by manufacturing companies when it became apparent that traditional cost accounting systems were producing distorted product costs. Thus, some products that were thought to be profitable were, on closer inspection, found to be unprofitable, and vice versa. Two Harvard University professors, Robin Cooper and Robert S. Kaplan, made convincing arguments that typical cost accounting systems often understate profits on high-volume products and overstate profits on low-volume specialty items.[23] This problem is attributable, in part, to greater product diversity, shorter product life cycles, shift in production technology from labor to automation, more diverse distribution channels, and greater quality demands, all of which are driven by the need to more effectively compete in the global marketplace. The net effect of these trends (which are also applicable to government, at least to some extent) is to create a larger infrastructure of "production support" activities and, thus, to shift costs from direct cost categories to indirect cost, or overhead, categories. Because a larger proportion of these costs is allocated to products, product cost distortions become a larger problem and may result in poor product decisions.

ABC essentially attempts to determine the cost of specific process-related activities, the "drivers" of those costs (e.g., labor-hours, machine-hours, or units of material) and the consumption of cost drivers in producing outputs of goods or services. Emphasis is placed on tracing the specific activities performed to specific outputs of goods or services rather than on allocating average costs to units of output as is done in conventional cost accounting systems.

Determining the amount of each activity that is consumed in each product or service utilizes materials usage records, observation, and timekeeping systems, but is often augmented with estimates obtained through employee interviews and other means. The cost of designing a system that totally eliminates the need for overhead allocation is likely to be prohibitive. If allocation of "residual" unassigned costs is not potentially distortive, it may be more cost effective to focus ABC design on major activities and cost drivers and to allocate any remaining costs on an appropriate basis.

State-of-the-art approaches, such as total quality management (TQM) and service efforts and accomplishments (SEA) measures, implemented by some governments to improve performance, require timely information on the full cost of resources consumed in providing service outputs. To calculate the full cost of services, however,

[23] Robin Cooper and Robert S. Kaplan, "Measure Costs Right: Make the Right Decisions," *Harvard Business Review,* September–October 1988, pp. 96–103.

ILLUSTRATION 13–9 **Identification of Components in an Activity-Based Costing System: Grahamston Revenue Collection Program**

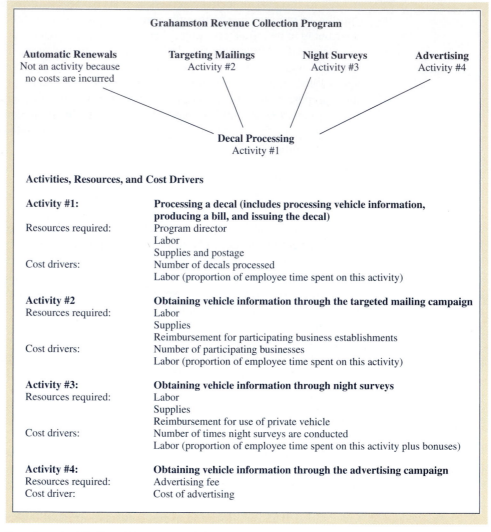

Grahamston Revenue Collection Program

Automatic Renewals
Not an activity because
no costs are incurred

Targeting Mailings
Activity #2

Night Surveys
Activity #3

Advertising
Activity #4

Decal Processing
Activity #1

Activities, Resources, and Cost Drivers

Activity #1:	**Processing a decal (includes processing vehicle information, producing a bill, and issuing the decal)**
Resources required:	Program director
	Labor
	Supplies and postage
Cost drivers:	Number of decals processed
	Labor (proportion of employee time spent on this activity)
Activity #2	**Obtaining vehicle information through the targeted mailing campaign**
Resources required:	Labor
	Supplies
	Reimbursement for participating business establishments
Cost drivers:	Number of participating businesses
	Labor (proportion of employee time spent on this activity)
Activity #3:	**Obtaining vehicle information through night surveys**
Resources required:	Labor
	Supplies
	Reimbursement for use of private vehicle
Cost drivers:	Number of times night surveys are conducted
	Labor (proportion of employee time spent on this activity plus bonuses)
Activity #4:	**Obtaining vehicle information through the advertising campaign**
Resources required:	Advertising fee
Cost driver:	Cost of advertising

Source: International City/County Management Association, Service Report: *Introduction to Activity-Based Costing,* February 1998. Reprinted with permission of ICMA. All rights reserved.

requires careful allocation of indirect costs such as the clerical and administrative costs of general government functions (e.g., chief executive's office, finance department, legal department). The use of inappropriate allocation bases may produce distorted cost estimates for some service outputs in much the same manner that conventional cost systems produce distorted product costs. It is not surprising then that some governments have adopted ABC for key service functions. An article by Bridget Anderson explains the objectives of ABC in a governmental environment as follows:

> The objectives of ABC are to preserve, at a minimum, the present quality and availability of core services but to acknowledge that some of the forces for greater expenditures have not been controlled. It seeks to reduce the costs of service outcomes by:
>
> • reducing the number of service units through program redesign,
> • finding lower cost alternatives,

ILLUSTRATION 13–10   **Cost Analysis of Revenue Collection Program**

Activity	1 Decal Processing	2 Sending Targeted Mailings	3 Night Surveys	4 Advertising	Total
Program director	$ 40,000				$ 40,000
Labor	89,600	$19,200	$19,200		128,000
Employee bonuses for night work			6,000		6,000
Employee reimbursement for use of their personal vehicles			600		600
Supplies and postage	6,000	1,500	500		8,000
Annual advertising costs				$ 500	500
Reimbursements for participating businesses		4,800			4,800
Total annual costs	$135,600	$25,500	$26,300	$ 500	$187,900
Divided by number of decals processed as a result of this activity	15,300	2,700	1,260	540	
Equals cost per decal	$ 8.86	$9.44	$ 20.87	$0.93	
Additional cost of Activity 1		8.86	8.86	8.86	
Total cost per decal by activity	$ 8.86	$ 18.30	$ 29.73	$9.79	

Source: International City/County Management Association, Service Report: *Introduction to Activity-Based Costing,* February 1998. Reprinted with permission of ICMA. All rights reserved.

- making volume increases dependent on cost reductions, and
- understanding and controlling the delivery/program design interaction.[24]

A simplified diagram of an ABC cost model used by the City of Grahamston for its revenue collection process for personal property taxes on vehicles is shown in Illustration 13–9. This program involves four activities that identify vehicle owners who need to renew their auto registration: (1) sending a mailing by which owners can automatically renew their auto registration, (2) mailing information requests to car dealers and repair shops, (3) having officers put flyers on cars during a night patrol, and (4) placing ads in the local paper and at community events. The resources required and cost drivers associated with each of these activities are also presented in Illustration 13–9.

A quick review of the total cost per registration by activity (shown in Illustration 13–10) suggests that night surveys are the most expensive way to identify residents who have not registered their vehicles and, therefore, represent the greatest potential for cost-cutting measures. The costs associated with this activity appear to be all variable; that is, if surveys are conducted less frequently, costs would be reduced proportionately. Advertising is the least expensive method of collecting revenue for personal property taxes on vehicles. Although it is tempting to shift resources to increase this activity, the advertising campaign will likely not reach all residents contacted through other approaches. The targeted mailings, while twice as costly as the advertising

[24] Bridget M. Anderson, "Using Activity-Based Costing for Efficiency and Quality," *Government Finance Review,* June 1993, pp. 7–9.

approach, are probably effective because correspondence is sent personally addressed to the resident whose address was obtained by a participating car dealer or repair shop.

Activity-based costing is a managerial tool that can enhance decision making by creating a clearer picture of the costliest activities of a service. However, ABC only supplements traditional accounting systems; it does not replace them.

Administrative Costs

A very large part of governmental expenditures are incurred for administrative services of a general nature (such as the costs of the chief executive's office, costs of accounting and auditing, and costs of boards and commissions), which are somewhat remote from the results any given subdivision is expected to accomplish. Furthermore, in smaller units of government, many offices or departments perform such a variety of services that separating their costs is practically impossible under their present schemes of organization.

Given the importance and magnitude of key administrative offices, government officials should attempt to measure the efficiency and effectiveness of the activities of these offices just as it would other service activities. The primary difference is that many of these activities, such as those of the finance and legal departments for example, mainly serve customers within the government rather than the general public. Activity-based costing would seem to be a useful tool for measuring the cost of such activities. Possible activities and cost drivers for selected offices follow.

Office	Activities	Cost Drivers
Tax collector	Preparing tax bills.	Number of bills prepared.
	Collecting tax bills.	Number of bills collected.
	Preparing receipts.	Number of receipts prepared.
	Mailing receipts.	Number of receipts mailed.
	Preparing deposits.	Number of deposits prepared.
Accounting	Recording revenues.	Number of revenue transactions.
	Recording expenditures.	Number of expenditure transactions.
	Processing payroll.	Number of employees.
	Recording purchase orders.	Number of orders.
Public recorder	Recording documents.	Number of documents or number of lines.

This table is intended to be illustrative of the types of activities and cost drivers that might apply to certain administrative offices. Obviously, the list is incomplete, but, insofar as the activities and drivers are appropriate for a particular office, costs accumulated by activity could be useful both for internal performance review and pricing services to other offices. As an example of pricing services rendered, the costs of accounting services could be priced to other departments on the basis of the amount of accounting activities other departments consume. For example, assume that the Public Works department generates 30 percent of all purchase requisitions processed by the Accounting department. Arguably, Public Works should then be charged for 30 percent of the total cost of recording purchase orders in the accounting function. Similarly, the costs of recording expenditures could be charged to departments proportionate to the expenditures they make. Although an activity-based costing approach to costing central services seems technologically feasible, much additional research is needed to determine whether the benefits would warrant the considerable costs involved.

CONCLUSION

In spite of difficulties presented in this chapter, rational allocation of resources requires the best available information as to benefits expected to result from a proposed program to be matched with the best available information as to costs of the same program. Anticipated benefits from a program must be stated in monetary or quantitative terms or at least in explicit and operational terms to be of value in the management process. There is a crucial link among these benefits or performance measures, the government's budgetary process, and the cost of government services. A debate among governmental professional associations is whether performance measures are inherently budgetary and managerial in character and, as such, out of the purview of accounting and financial reporting standards setting as conducted by the Governmental Accounting Standards Board.[25]

An entity that integrates its strategic planning, budgeting, and cost/benefit analysis with the management of the resources with which it is entrusted can more effectively document performance than if these financial management functions stand alone. The statement of anticipated benefits from a proposed program, activity, or grant should follow from a statement of objectives for it. The statement of objectives should be expanded into a plan of action to achieve the objectives, which in turn serves as a basis for planning costs to be incurred. Unless this course is followed, administrators and legislators will not be able to allocate resources of the governmental unit wisely, nor will administrators be able to manage resources committed to approved programs. Legislators and the public have a right to expect this integration of long-range analysis and fiscal period planning, so that they may evaluate the actions of the administrators in following the plan as well as the success of the programs in achieving the stated objectives. Cost accounting takes on an even more important role in long-range fiscal planning as organizations evaluate the benefits of privatizing and outsourcing traditional functions.

[25] Timothy Grewe, "The GASB's Mission and Performance Measurement," *Government Finance Review*, October 2001, pp. 4–5.

Key Terms

Activity-based costing (ABC), *537*
Allowable costs, *535*
Budget calendar, *521*
Budget officer, *522*
Common Rule, *535*
Cost objective, *536*
Direct costs, *536*
Effectiveness measures, *530*
Efficiency measures, *530*

Flexible budgeting, *534*
Incremental budgeting, *519*
Indirect costs, *536*
Input measures, *530*
Job order cost, *534*
Outcome measures, *530*
Output measures, *530*
Performance budgeting, *519*
Planning-programming-budgeting system (PPBS), *520*

Process cost, *534*
Program budgeting, *520*
Service efforts and accomplishments, *530*
Sweep accounts, *526*
Tax anticipation notes, *525*
Total quality management, *528*
Zero-based budgeting, *520*

Selected References

Bland, Robert L. and Irene S. Rubin. *Budgeting: A Guide for Local Governments.* Washington, DC: International City/County Management Association, 1997.
Epstein, Paul, James Fountain, Wilson Campbell, Terry Patton, and Kimberly Keaton. *Government Service Efforts and Accomplishments Performance Reports: A Guide*

to Understanding. Norwalk, CT: Government Accounting Standards Board, July 2005.

Fountain, James, Wilson Campbell, Terry Patton, Paul Epstein, and Mandi Cohn. *Special Report: Reporting Performance Information: Suggested Criteria for Effective Communication.* Norwalk, CT: Government Accounting Standards Board, August 2003.

Government Finance Officers Association. *Best Practices in Public Budgeting.* Chicago, IL: GFOA, 2000 (on CD-ROM) at www.gfoa.org.

Lalli, William, ed., *Handbook of Budgeting,* 5th ed. New York: John Wiley & Sons, 2005, with 2005 Supplement.

Meyers, Roy T. *Handbook of Government Budgeting.* San Francisco, CA: Jossey-Bass, 1998.

National Advisory Council on State and Local Budgeting. *Recommended Budget Practices: A Framework for Improved State and Local Government Budgeting.* Chicago, IL: NACSLB, 1998.

Questions

13–1. Explain the interrelation among the processes of strategic planning, budgeting, service delivery, and performance assessment that should exist in a government's accountability system.

13–2. If governmental budgets should be prepared to facilitate management of resources, why should the budget documents be subjected to study by individual taxpayers, reporters, public interest groups, and legislative bodies?

13–3. Explain the costs and benefits of performance budgeting compared with incremental budgeting.

13–4. What advantages does total quality management (TQM) offer compared with rational budgeting approaches? Is it fundamentally a budgeting approach?

13–5. What are some of the factors to be taken into account in preparing revenue estimates for inclusion in a budget?

13–6. Why is a good cost accounting system an important component of rational budgeting?

13–7. If governments, educational institutions, and not-for-profit health care entities exist to provide services needed by the public or a segment of the public but are not concerned with the generation of net income, why should they be interested in the determination of costs? Explain your answer.

13–8. The finance officer of a small city has heard that certain items of cost may be allowable under federal grants and contracts, even though they were not incurred specifically for the grant or contract. To what source could the finance officer go to determine what costs are allowable under federal grants and contracts?

13–9. What are the three broad categories of service efforts and accomplishment (SEA) measures? Explain the GASB's role in developing standards for SEA reporting.

13–10. Explain why conventional cost accounting systems have become less useful in both the business and government setting. How does activity-based costing (ABC) reduce the problems created by conventional cost accounting systems?

Cases

13–1 Activity-Based Costing. Frumerville Hospital has always determined the full cost of serving patients by accounting for the direct and indirect costs of all hospital operations. The hospital uses the step-down method of allocating indirect costs: The costs of nonrevenue producing departments are allocated in sequence to departments they serve, whether or not these produce revenue. Once the costs of a department have been allocated, the costing process for that department is closed, and it receives no further charges. A new CFO has recently joined the hospital after a distinguished career in the manufacturing industry. In that capacity, he initiated activity-based costing (ABC), which resulted in a documented savings to the business. As an accounting assistant, you have been asked to meet with the CFO to discuss the issues involved in implementing ABC in this hospital. A copy of the hospital's most recent step-down expense distribution is presented on the following page.

Required

In preparation for the meeting, answer the following questions by examining the expense distribution:
a. What "activities" do you consider most appropriate in describing the operations of the hospital?
b. What are the cost drivers of these programs?
c. What particular problems do you expect to face in implementing ABC in this hospital?

13–2 Indirect Costs. As a cost reimbursement accountant in a large public research university, you are aware that federal agencies have increased auditing efforts in the area of federal research grants to higher education institutions. In particular, OMB *Circular A–21* detailing allowable costs for colleges and universities receiving federal funds has been revised. The administration has asked you whether it is appropriate to include certain overhead costs in the pool of indirect costs (facilities and administrative costs) that are recovered in most federal research awards. Items include (1) holiday lights put on the president's university-owned home, (2) library books in the research section of the undergraduate library, (3) cost of a large boat used by higher administration in meeting with faculty and outside researchers for social events, (4) advertising new graduate programs in the large urban newspaper, (5) clerical salaries in the academic departments where a large amount of research is conducted, and (6) utility bills in the research wing of one of the buildings.

Required

Write a short professional memo to the administration giving your opinion about whether these costs would be allowable "indirect costs" to be recovered in part by federal research grants. Defend your position.

13–3 Internet Case. Use the Internet to identify and then list as many governments (in the state in which the college or university you are attending is located) as you can that have received the Government Finance Officers Association Distinguished Budget Award since its inception in 1984 until today. Information may be available on the GFOA's Web site (www.gfoa.org) or the individual city's Web site or by searching the Internet using key words such as *governmental budgeting.* Identify the particular strengths of their budgets for which they were recognized.

FRUMERVILLE HOSPITAL
Step-Down Method—Expense Distribution
Year Ended April 30, 20—

	Direct Costs	Maintenance of Plant	Operation of Plant	Housekeeping	Laundry and Linen	Cafeteria	Administration	Medical Supplies	Medical Records	Nursing Service	Dietary	Total Costs
General services:												
Maintenance of plant	$ 252,000	$(252,000)	—	—	—	—	—	—	—	—	—	—
Operation of plant	354,600	113,400	$(468,000)	—	—	—	—	—	—	—	—	—
Housekeeping	357,000	2,520	2,340	$(361,860)	—	—	—	—	—	—	—	—
Laundry and linen service	216,000	10,080	16,848	7,236	$(250,164)	—	—	—	—	—	—	—
Cafeteria	23,640	756	14,508	7,236	1,251	$(47,391)	—	—	—	—	—	—
Administration	844,800	7,560	28,548	25,332	249	6,918	$(913,407)	—	—	—	—	—
Medical supplies	480,000	2,520	6,084	1,809	501	1,707	39,276	$(531,897)	—	—	—	—
Medical records	132,000	2,520	4,680	10,857	—	1,137	25,575	—	$(176,769)	—	—	—
Nursing service	1,800,000	1,764	7,020	2,532	6,504	20,709	466,752	—	—	$(2,305,281)	—	—
Dietary	657,000	10,080	19,188	10,857	3,003	4,596	103,215	—	—	—	$(807,939)	—
Special services:												
Operating rooms	482,460	25,200	28,548	3,618	41,778	3,459	77,640	79,785	—	—	—	$ 742,488
Delivery rooms	141,000	15,120	14,508	10,857	21,015	1,422	31,968	53,190	—	—	—	289,080
Radiology	300,000	10,080	14,508	14,475	3,003	1,707	29,276	—	—	—	—	383,049
Laboratory	381,000	7,560	16,848	14,475	3,003	3,459	77,640	—	—	—	—	503,985
Blood bank	219,000	2,016	3,744	5,427	249	570	12,789	—	—	—	—	243,795
Cost of medical supplies sold	—	—	—	—	—	—	—	265,947	—	—	—	265,947
Routine Services:												
Medical and surgical	144,000	25,200	219,024	218,202	138,339	—	—	79,785	137,880	1,959,489	807,939	3,729,858
Nursery	13,500	3,024	23,868	7,236	18,762	—	—	26,595	8,838	345,792	—	447,615
Outpatient clinic	192,000	12,600	47,736	21,711	12,507	1,707	39,276	26,595	30,051	—	—	384,183
Totals	$6,990,000	$ 0	$ 0	$ 0	$ 0	$ 0	$ 0	$ 0	$ 0	$ 0	$ 0	$6,990,000

**Exercises
and Problems**

13–1 Examine the Budget. Obtain a copy of a recent operating budget document of a government.* Familiarize yourself with the organization of the operating budget document; read the letter of transmittal or any narrative that accompanies the budget.

Budgetary practices may differ from the GAAP reporting model as to *basis, timing, perspective,* and *entity.* GASB standards (*Codification,* Section 2400. 110–199) define these differences as:

1. *Basis* differences arising through the employment of a basis of accounting for budgetary purposes that differs from the basis of accounting applicable to the fund type when reporting on the operations in accordance with GAAP.
2. *Timing* differences that can result in significant variances between budgetary practices and GAAP may include continuing appropriations, project appropriations, automatic reappropriations, and biennial budgeting.
3. *Perspective* differences resulting from the structure of financial information for budgetary purposes. The perspectives used for budgetary purposes include fund structure, and organizational structure, or program structure. In addition, some subsidiary perspective, such as nature of revenue source, special projects, or capital and operating budgets, may also be used. The fund structure and individual fund definitions establish which assets, liabilities, equities, and revenue and expenditure/expense flows are recorded in a fund. In the traditional view, budgeting, accounting, financial reporting, and auditing would follow the fund perspective.
4. *Entity* differences occur when "appropriated budget" either includes or excludes organizations, programs, activities, and functions that may or may not be compatible with the criteria defining the governmental reporting entity.

Required

Answer the following questions, which aid in assessing the quality of the budget document you are reviewing.†

Policy Document. Does the operating budget you are reviewing include a coherent statement of organizationwide financial and programmatic policies and goals that address long-term concerns and issues? Does the operating budget document describe the organization's short-term financial and operational policies that guide budget development for the upcoming year? Does the budget document include a coherent statement of goals and objectives of organizational units? Does the document include a budget message that articulates priorities and issues for the budget for the new year? Does the message describe significant changes in priorities from the current year and the factors producing those changes?

Financial Plan. Does the operating budget document include and describe all funds that are subject to appropriation? Does the document present a summary of major revenues and expenditures as well as other financing sources and uses? Does the document include summaries of revenues, other resources, and expenditures for prior-year actual, current-year budget and/or estimated current-year

*The footnote of Exercise 1–1 suggested that you attempt to obtain an operating budget document from the entity whose CAFR you analyzed for Exercises 1–1 through 10–1. If this was not possible, contact the budget officer of the city, town, or county of your choice and request a copy of the most recent available operating budget document.
†These questions are paraphrased from the awards criteria established by the Government Finance Officers Association for its Distinguished Budget Presentation Awards Program.

actual, and proposed budget year? Are major revenue sources described? Are the underlying assumptions for revenue estimates and significant revenue trends explained? Does the document include projected changes in fund balances for governmental funds included in the budget presentation, including all balances potentially available for appropriation?

Does the budget document include budgeted capital expenditures and a list of major capital projects (even if these are authorized in a separate capital budget)? Does the document describe whether, and to what extent, capital improvements or other major capital spending will impact the entity's current and future operating budget? Are financial data on current debt obligations provided, describing the relationship between current debt levels and legal debt limits, and explaining the effects of existing debt levels on current and future operations? Is the basis of budgeting explained for all funds, whether GAAP, cash, modified accrual, or some other basis?

Operations Guide. Does the operating budget document describe activities, services, or functions carried out by organizational units? Are objective methods (quantitative and/or qualitative) of measuring of results provided by unit or program? (Information on results should be provided for prior-year actual, current-year budget and/or estimate, and budget year.) Does the budget document include an organizational chart for the entire organization? Is a schedule(s) or summary table(s) provided giving personnel or position counts for prior, current, and budget years, including descriptions of significant changes in levels of staffing or reorganizations planned for the budget year?

Communication Device. Does the operating budget document provide summary information, including an overview of significant budgetary issues, trends, and resource choices? Does the budget document explain the effect, if any, of other planning processes (e.g., strategic plans, long-range plans, capital improvement plans) on the budget and budget process? Is the process used to prepare, review, adopt, and amend the budget explained? If a separate capital budget is prepared, is a description provided of the process by which it is prepared and how it relates to the operating budget? Are charts and graphs used, where appropriate, to highlight financial and statistical information? Is narrative information provided when the messages conveyed by the charts and graphs are not self-evident? Does the document provide narrative, tables, schedules, crosswalks, or matrices to show the relationship between different revenue and expenditure classifications (e.g., funds, programs, organization units)? Is a table of contents provided to make it easy to locate information in the document? Is there a glossary to define terms (including abbreviations and acronyms) that are not readily understood by a reasonably informed lay reader? Does the document include statistical and supplemental data that describe the organization and the community or population it serves and provide other pertinent background information related to services provided? Finally, is the document printed and formatted in such a way as to enhance understanding and utility of the document to a lay reader? Is it attractive, consistent, and oriented to the reader's needs?

13–2 Multiple Choice. Choose the best answer.

1. Which of the following budgeting approaches focuses mainly on relating work activity outputs to resource inputs?
   a. Incremental (line-item) budgeting.

    b. Program budgeting.

    c. Performance budgeting.

    d. PPBS.

2. Which of the following steps would *not* usually be part of the budgeting process?

    a. Heads of operating departments prepare budget requests.

    b. Budget officer and other central administrators review and make adjustments to departmental requests.

    c. One or more public budget hearings are held.

    d. The chief executive (mayor or city manager, as appropriate) formally adopts the budget, thus giving it the force of law.

3. Which of the following budgeting approaches is most consistent with total quality management (TQM)?

    a. Incremental (line-item) budgeting.

    b. Performance budgeting.

    c. Program budgeting.

    d. Planning-Programming-Budgeting System (PPBS).

4. Measurement of *efficiency* requires that:

    a. Inputs be related to outcomes.

    b. Inputs be related to outputs.

    c. Outputs be related to outcomes.

    d. Dollar cost of inputs be related to quantities of inputs.

5. Which of the following is the central focus of a TQM system?

    a. Measuring productivity and quality improvement.

    b. Rewarding employees for productivity and quality achievement.

    c. Obtaining the support and commitment of top-level officials.

    d. Continuously meeting or exceeding customer expectations.

6. Which of the following cost items would be unallowable by a federal grantor agency?

    a. Depreciation on buildings and equipment.

    b. Advertising expense.

    c. Alcoholic beverages for a holiday party.

    d. All of the above.

7. Service efforts and accomplishments (SEA) refers to

    a Linking customer satisfaction to improvements in the operating systems and processes used to provide goods and services.

    b. Determining the cost of specific process-related activities, the "drivers" of those costs, and the consumption of cost drivers in producing outputs of goods or services.

    c. Comparing financial and nonfinancial measures of inputs, outputs, and efficiency.

    d. None of the above.

8. Which of the following statements about activity-based costing is true?

    a. It is intended to reduce the probability of distorted unit costs that may adversely affect management decisions.

    b. It eliminates the need for allocation of indirect costs.

    c. It permits measuring the true cost of every unit of output (i.e., cost measures that are free from subjective estimates).

    d. All of the above.

9. A good cost accounting system facilitates a type of budgeting in which the costs associated with different levels of activity are planned. Such a form of budget is referred to as:
   a. Incremental budgeting.
   b. Fixed budgeting.
   c. Rational budgeting.
   d. Flexible budgeting.

10. Determining the cost of depreciation related to the general capital assets of a government for purposes of charging the cost to a federal grant, or for internal costing of services, is complicated by which of the following factors?
    a. The method of depreciation used does not correspond with actual patterns of asset consumption.
    b. Some capital assets are used for many activities and records of such use may not be adequate.
    c. Depreciation is not recorded in any governmental fund type for such assets, nor is depreciation recorded in the governmental activities accounts.
    d. Both *b* and *c* are correct.

13–3 General Fund Budget. A portion of the General Fund operating budget for Southwest City's Street Department follows here and on subsequent pages.

Required

After reading and evaluating the budget information for the Street Department of Southwest City, answer the following questions:
   a. Does Southwest City appear to be using program budgeting? If not, what form of budgeting is the city using?
   b. Does the budget provide information useful for evaluating the performance of the Street Department's management?
   c. Do the goals established for the Street Department appear appropriate? How could they be improved?

SOUTHWEST CITY

Annual Budget	**General Fund**
FY 2007–2008	**Description**
Department Description	**Streets**

The Street Department is responsible for maintaining all city-owned streets, alleys, and parking lots, keeping them in serviceable condition to ensure the safety and welfare of the public. Activities include repairing damage caused by waterline breaks; repairing potholes and patching utility cuts; repairing base failures; preparing street driving surfaces for annual seal coating program; reconstructing streets to upgrade driving surface and drainage to meet increased traffic volumes; cleaning and repairing drainage ditches and structures; inspecting and making repairs to city bridges and sidewalks; performing annual crack sealing to prevent water damage to driving surface of streets; performing traffic counts on an as-needed basis; installing and maintaining traffic control signs and paving markings; responding to emergency conditions by barricading, sandbagging, clearing fallen trees and debris from streets and drainage structures, and sanding streets during icing conditions; mowing rights-of-way and maintaining street and alley shoulders; installing and maintaining street name signs; and assisting other departments as needed.

SOUTHWEST CITY

Annual Budget				General Fund
FY 2007–2008				Description
Department Description *(continued)*				Streets
Expenditure Summary				

Classification	2005–2006 Actual	2006–2007 Budget	2006–2007 Estimated	2007–2008 Budget
Personnel	$206,135	$226,748	$227,273	$250,000
Supplies	10,649	11,714	11,818	13,000
Maintenance	70,624	77,686	66,367	73,000
Services	73,768	81,145	60,909	67,000
Capital outlay	31,927	2,500	34,000	3,000
Total	$393,103	$399,793	$400,367	$406,000

Staffing

Position	Number
Superintendent	1
Assistant superintendent	1
Crew leader	2
Equipment operator	6
Total	10

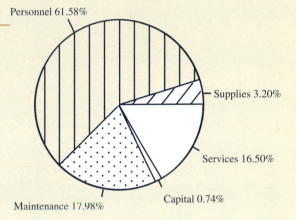

Personnel 61.58%
Supplies 3.20%
Services 16.50%
Capital 0.74%
Maintenance 17.98%

Department Goals

Increase the number of repairs for old utility cuts, upgrade the street driving surface, and prevent future water damage.

Pursue an aggressive weed and grass control program within street gutters and rights-of-way and behind curbs.

Increase miles of street shoulder repairs to prevent pavement breaking and erosion.

Replace existing noncompliance yield signs with stop signs.

Increase work-hours spent on trimming overhanging limbs and brush in and over streets.

Indicators

Measurement	2005–06 Actual	2006–07 Estimated	2007–08 Proposed
Traffic and street signs	84	159	175
Miles of streets maintained	66	70	70
Square yards of seal coating	42,500	44,800	42,500
Number of utility cuts	136	155	250
Miles of right-of-way mowing	34	172	172
Tons of asphalt for potholes	84	102	175
Tons of asphalt for street leveling	66	40	100
Feet of drainage ditches cleared	3,350	3,750	4,250
Feet of street shoulder bladed	4,150	5,275	6,000
Square yards of sidewalks repaired	40	65	150
Feet of weed control on streets	12,500	16,750	18,000
Miles of streets cleaned	10	19	76

SOUTHWEST CITY

Annual Budget
FY 2007–2008
Department Description *(concluded)*

General Fund
Description
Streets

Streets

Account Number	Account Description	FY 2006 Actual	FY 2007 Budget	FY 2007 Estimated	FY 2008 Budget
02-13-00-0101	Salaries—Administrative	$ 4,827.90	$ 4,910.00	$ 4,910.00	$ 4,910.00
02-13-00-0102	Salaries—Operations	27,445.47	29,834.00	29,834.00	36,617.00
02-13-00-0103	Salaries—Supervisory	67,951.32	70,081.00	59,231.00	58,577.00
02-13-00-0104	Salaries—Skilled	42,957.99	42,944.00	55,175.00	69,443.00
02-13-00-0107	Salaries—Overtime	6,584.77	6,854.00	7,604.00	6,500.00
02-13-00-0108	Part-time and hourly	0	1,800.00	0	0
02-13-00-0116	TMRS retirement	12,159.21	11,847.00	12,169.00	11,665.00
02-13-00-0117	Employer's FICA	11,249.99	1,581.00	11,208.00	11,707.00
02-13-00-0118	Hospitalization insurance	12,203.21	13,532.00	13,090.00	15,544.00
02-13-00-0119	Workers' compensation	20,351.76	32,987.00	33,941.00	33,941.00
02-13-00-0120	Unemployment compensation	403.38	378.00	111.00	1,096.00
	Total personnel	$206,135.00	$226,748.00	$227,273.00	$250,000.00
02-13-00-0210	Chemical supplies	$ 760.95	$ 250.00	$ 0	$ 1,500.00
02-13-00-0220	Clothing supplies	1,638.28	2,164.00	1,520.00	1,600.00
02-13-00-0260	General office supplies	14.79	50.00	6.00	25.00
02-13-00-0270	Janitorial supplies	143.43	50.00	72.00	75.00
02-13-00-0280	Minor tools	609.32	300.00	496.00	400.00
02-13-00-0285	Fuel and vehicle supplies	6,938.49	8,500.00	8,861.00	8,900.00
02-13-00-0290	Other supplies	543.74	400.00	863.00	500.00
	Total supplies	$ 10,649.00	$ 11,714.00	$ 11,818.00	$ 13,000.00
02-13-00-0302	Building maintenance	$ 0	$ 50.00	$ 93.00	$ 50.00
02-13-00-0304	Street maintenance	17,520.75	20,950.00	20,950.00	18,950.00
02-13-00-0305	Seal coating and overlays	37,457.21	35,488.00	24,481.00	35,275.00
02-13-00-0306	Sidewalks	5,085.75	1,048.00	1,048.00	1,000.00
02-13-00-0307	Street sweeping	0	10,500.00	10,500.00	9,575.00
02-13-00-0401	Heating and air conditioning maintenance	60.00	50.00	225.00	50.00
02-13-00-0420	Machine tools maintenance	1,928.05	1,500.00	1,978.00	1,500.00
02-13-00-0430	Motor vehicle maintenance	5,000.00	5,000.00	5,000.00	3,500.00
02-13-00-0460	Radio maintenance	0	100.00	0	100.00
02-13-00-0480	Signs	3,572.24	3,000.00	2,092.00	3,000.00
	Total maintenance	$70,624.00	$77,686.00	$66,367.00	$73,000.00

13–4 Police Department Budget. The police chief of the Town of Meridian submitted the following budget request for the police department for the forthcoming budget year 2008–09.

Item	Actual FY 2007	Budget FY 2008	Forecast FY 2008	Budget FY 2009
Personnel	$1,051,938	$1,098,245	$1,112,601	$1,182,175
Supplies	44,442	61,971	60,643	64,450
Maintenance	47,163	45,310	46,139	47,422
Miscellaneous	34,213	36,272	32,198	37,723
Capital outlay	65,788	69,433	67,371	102,210
Totals	$1,243,544	$1,311,231	$1,318,952	$1,433,980

Upon questioning by the newly appointed town manager, a recent masters graduate with a degree in public administration from a nearby university, the police chief explained that he had determined the amounts in the budget request by multiplying the prior year's budget amount by 1.04 (to allow for the expected inflation rate of 4 percent). In addition, the personnel category includes a request for a new uniformed officer at an estimated $40,000 for salary, payroll expenses, and fringe benefits. Capital outlay includes a request for a new patrol vehicle at an estimated cost of $30,000. The amount of $300 was added to the maintenance category for estimated maintenance on the new vehicle. The police chief is strongly resisting instructions from the town manager that he justify the need not only for the new uniformed position and additional vehicle but also for the existing level of resources in each category. The town manager has stated she will not request any increase in the police department's budget unless adequate justification is provided.

Required

a. Evaluate the strengths and weaknesses of the police chief's argument that his budget request is reasonable.

b. Are the town manager's instructions reasonable? Explain.

c. Would the town council likely support the town manager or the police chief in this dispute, assuming the police chief might take his case directly to the town council?

d. What other improvements could be made to the town's budgeting procedures?

13–5 Allowable Costs. Compensation for personal services rendered during the period of performance under the grant agreement is an allowable cost under OMB *Circular A–87,* as are employee benefits such as vacation leave, sick leave, or employer's contributions to retirement and health plans, and so on, if "the cost thereof is equitably allocated to all related activities, including grant programs."

During 2008, John Burt, an employee of Green City, was paid an annual salary of $68,000. He took three weeks' paid vacation plus one-week paid sick leave. The employer's contributions to retirement and health plans amounted to 25 percent of Burt's annual salary. During 2008, Burt worked 12 weeks on HHS Grant No. 9227. Compute the appropriate charge to that grant for Burt's salary and fringe benefits (round to the nearest dollar).

13–6 Total Program Costs. On the basis of the following data, prepare a statement for the Town of Chippewa for the year ended June 30, 2008, showing the total cost of solid waste removal and the cost per ton of residential solid waste removed or cubic yard of commercial solid waste removed (carry unit costs to three decimal places).

	Residential	Commercial
By town employees:		
Salaries and wages	$702,000	$481,000
Materials and supplies	$ 39,000	$ 36,090
Equipment use	$300,840	$201,470
Tons collected	165,000	—
Cubic yards collected	—	248,000
Labor-hours	90,000	68,000
By contractors:		
Cost	$ 78,900	$ 48,000
Tons collected	23,000	—
Cubic yards collected	—	30,000

Overhead for town collection of residential solid waste is $0.948 per labor-hour; for commercial solid waste collection it is $0.924 per labor-hour. Overhead for contract residential solid waste collection is 20 percent of cost (exclusive of overhead); for commercial solid waste collection it is 15 percent of cost (exclusive of overhead).

13–7 **Allocating Administrative Costs.** When the county commission of Copper County questioned the county treasurer about his request for additional appropriations, he claimed the large number of tax bills prepared and collected was responsible for the heavy expenses of his office. Since the duties of the treasurer's office are rather uniform and of limited range, it was decided to attempt a cost study in an effort to determine the reasonableness of the treasurer's request. Because tax bills are numbered serially, it is possible to determine accurately the number prepared and collected. It was decided to divide the activities of the office into general administration, billing, and collecting. General administration consists of supervising the office and providing information to taxpayers, attorneys, and others. It would be measured on the basis of thousands of dollars of collections. Preparing bills and collecting would be measured on the basis of number of bills prepared and collected, respectively. The following information is available about the costs of the office:

1. The salary of the treasurer is $4,000 per month. His time is devoted to general administration except that during approximately three months of each year, he spends practically all his time on collections.
2. Each of two regular deputies receives $1,800 per month. Their time is divided approximately four months to billing, four months to collections, and the remainder to general administration.
3. During the year, the office spent $12,000 for extra help, of which two-thirds was chargeable to billing and one-third to collecting.
4. The office collected $240,000 of delinquent taxes, interest, and penalties during the year, of which the treasurer retained 4 percent to be credited equally to administration and collection.
5. Utility bills, stationery and stamps, repairs to office equipment, retirement contributions, and so on totaled $81,480 for the year. This was distributed to administration, billing, and collection on the basis of total salaries chargeable to those operations except that $20,600 spent for stamped envelopes was chargeable in total to collections.

6. The number of tax bills prepared during the year was 51,280, of which 740 were unpaid at the end of the year. The $240,000 of delinquent taxes collected during the year was on 625 bills.
7. Collection of current taxes during the year amounted to $3,000,000.

Required

a. Prepare a schedule showing the allocation of the treasurer's office costs to general administration, billing, and collecting.
b. Prepare a schedule showing the computation of the unit costs for each activity. (The basis for measuring each activity is given. Carry unit costs to the third decimal place.)

13–8 Activity-Based Costing in a Government. The midsize City of Orangeville funds an animal control program intended to minimize the danger stray dogs pose to people and property. The program is under scrutiny because of current budgetary constraints and constituency pressure.

An animal control warden responds to each complaint made by citizens about dogs running loose. Approximately one in six complaints results in the capture of a dog. When a dog is caught, the warden must drive it to a kennel 20 miles from the center of the city. Donna's Kennels, a privately owned animal boarding establishment, is under contract with the city to board, feed, and care for the impounded dogs. It is a no-kill shelter (i.e., it does not euthanize healthy animals), and dogs remain there until they are claimed by their owners or adopted. The program's complaint and impoundment data for the past four years follow:

	Year 1	Year 2	Year 3	Year 4
Complaints	2,330	2,410	2,540	2,730
Impoundments	376	398	414	440
Impound rate	16.1%	16.5%	16.3%	16.1%

Costs of Orangeville's animal control program are as follows. The city employs two animal control wardens, a clerk, and a program director. The task of the wardens is to respond to complaints, drive to the site, search for the dog, and deliver it (if it is found) to Donna's Kennels. The clerk is responsible for issuing licenses to dogs that are returned to their owners or are adopted, as well as tracking correspondence between Donna's Kennels and the city. The clerk also tracks program statistics and provides support to the program director.

The city owns and operates two vehicles specially designed for impounding and transporting stray dogs. For $10 per dog per day, Donna's Kennels provides shelter, food, and routine veterinary care. On average, 60 percent of impounded dogs are returned to their owners in seven days. The other 40 percent stay at Donna's Kennels for an average of 14 days before being adopted. Summarized program costs follow:

Salaries (annual):	
Program director	$40,000
Animal wardens (2)	$56,000 ($28,000 × 2)
Clerk	$27,000
Vehicles:	
Cost	$48,000 ($24,000 × 2)
Expected life	7 years
Operating costs	$0.30 per mile

Dog care:	
Shelter, food, medical care	$10 per dog per day (according to the contract)
Revenues:	
Fees received for adoptions	$35 per adoption
Fees received from owners:	
Fines	$75 per dog
Boarding expense reimbursement	$10 per dog per day

Critics of the animal control program argue that it costs too much to drive to the distant kennel to deliver an impounded dog. They have suggested that the city convert a vacant building within the city limits into an animal shelter to save on transportation costs. Prompted by the need to cut the city budget and address the public outcry, city officials are reviewing the budget proposal for the animal control program and are looking for ways to reduce the program's costs.

Required

a. Prepare a diagram that identifies (1) the activities related to the animal control program, (2) the relationship among each of the activities, (3) the resources required for each activity, and (4) the cost drivers for each activity. Use the format of Illustration 13–9.

b. Calculate the cost of each activity. Show your work. Use the format of Illustration 13–10.

c. Interpret the results of the activity based-costing example.

This problem is taken from the International City/County Management Association *Service Report: Introduction to Activity-Based Costing*, February 1998, pp. 9–13.

Chapter **Fourteen**

Accounting for Not-for-Profit Organizations

Learning Objectives

After studying this chapter, you should be able to:

1. Distinguish not-for-profit organizations (NPOs) from entities in the governmental and commercial sectors of the U.S. economy.
2. Identify the authoritative standards-setting body for establishing GAAP for nongovernmental NPOs.
3. Explain financial reporting and accounting for NPOs.

   Required financial statements.

   Classification of net assets.

   Accounting for revenue, gains, and support.

   Accounting for expenses.

   Accounting for assets.
4. Identify the unique accounting issues of financially interrelated organizations.
5. Describe optional fund accounting.
6. Describe accounting information systems for NPOs.
7. Prepare financial statements using *SFAS No. 117*.

DEFINING THE NOT-FOR-PROFIT SECTOR

In the United States the not-for-profit sector has more than 1.6 million entities of which 1.2 million serve a public purpose and receive an estimated $665 billion in revenue and support each year.[1] The Independent Sector (an NPO itself) estimates that the not-for-profit sector has combined annual budgets of $934 billion, assets of nearly $3 trillion, and employs 11 million people.[2] This diverse sector includes organizations that may be tax exempt or taxable, charitable or mutually beneficial, a public charity or a private foundation. Not-for-profit organizations (NPOs)[3] are characterized

[1] The *New Nonprofit Almanac & Desk Reference* (Washington, DC: Independent Sector and the Urban Institute, 2001).

[2] Independent Sector. *2004 Annual Report,* p.16, available at www.independentsector.org.

[3] The AICPA prefers the term *not-for-profit organizations.* Abbreviations for nongovernmental, not-for-profit entities include NPO, NFP entity, ONPO (other nonprofit organizations), and NGO (nongovernmental organizations, a term used in an international context). The abbreviation NPO and the term not-for-profit are used in this text.

by the absence of owners and dependence on contributions, dues, charges for services, and investment income for revenue, rather than taxes. The definition of a **not-for-profit organization** articulated by the AICPA[4] and FASB[5] is an entity that possesses the following characteristics that distinguish it from a business enterprise.

1. Contributions of significant amounts of resources from resource providers who do not expect commensurate or proportionate pecuniary return.
2. Operating purposes other than to provide goods or services at a profit.
3. Absence of ownership interests like those of business enterprises.

Not-for-profit organizations have the preceding characteristics in varying degrees. NPOs include **voluntary health and welfare organizations (VHWO)** or **human service organizations** (those that receive contributions from the public at large and provide health and welfare services for a nominal or no fee), such as the American Cancer Society, Girl Scouts, and Boy Scouts. There is a variety of other not-for-profit organizations, such as cemetery organizations, civic organizations, fraternal organizations, labor unions, libraries, museums, cultural institutions, performing arts organizations, political parties, private schools, professional and trade associations, social and country clubs, research and scientific organizations, and religious organizations. These organizations are classified by Internal Revenue Code Sections (discussed further in Chapter 15). The National Center for Charitable Statistics (NCCS) of the Urban Institute developed a National Taxonomy of Exempt Entities (NTEE) that divides that largest set of tax-exempt entities, Internal Revenue Code Sec. 501(c)(3) and (c)(4) organizations, into 10 functional categories (arts, culture, and humanities; education; environment/animals; health; human services; international/foreign affairs; public/society benefit; religion related; mutual/membership benefit; and others) and 26 major group areas.[6]

Illustration 14–1 shows various organizational forms that comprise the not-for-profit sector of the U.S. economy. The terms *public* and *private* that appear in illustration 14–1 can be confusing; For example, *public* charities are in the not-for-profit sector, *public* schools are in the governmental sector, and *publicly* traded companies are in the for-profit sector of our economy. Distinguishing between for profit, not-for-profit, and *governmental/nongovernmental* is more useful.

Organizations that provide dividends, lower costs, or other economic benefits directly and proportionately to their owners, members, or participants (e.g. mutual insurance companies, credit unions, farm and rural electric cooperatives, and employee benefit plans) are not-for-profit because they do not have residual interest owners; however, they do not meet the criteria stated previously for a not-for-profit organization.[7] They operate essentially as commercial businesses and are covered under separate AICPA industry audit guides.

There are also "governmental" not-for-profit organizations that may receive tax revenue or be controlled by a government but are not governments.[8] Examples of entities that

---

[4] American Institute of Certified Public Accountants, Audit and Accounting Guide, *Not-for-Profit Organizations* (New York, 2005), par. 1.01.

[5] Financial Accounting Standards Board, *Statement of Financial Accounting Standards No. 116,* "Accounting for Contributions Received and Contributions Made" (Norwalk, CT, 1993), App. D.

[6] This set of organizations, representing 75 percent of all tax-exempt organizations, is sometimes referred to as the *independent sector* because it includes private, self-governing organizations founded to serve a public purpose and foster volunteerism and philanthropy.

[7] Ibid.

[8] See pp. 5–6 for the definition of a governmental entity.

ILLUSTRATION 14–1 **Organizational Forms**

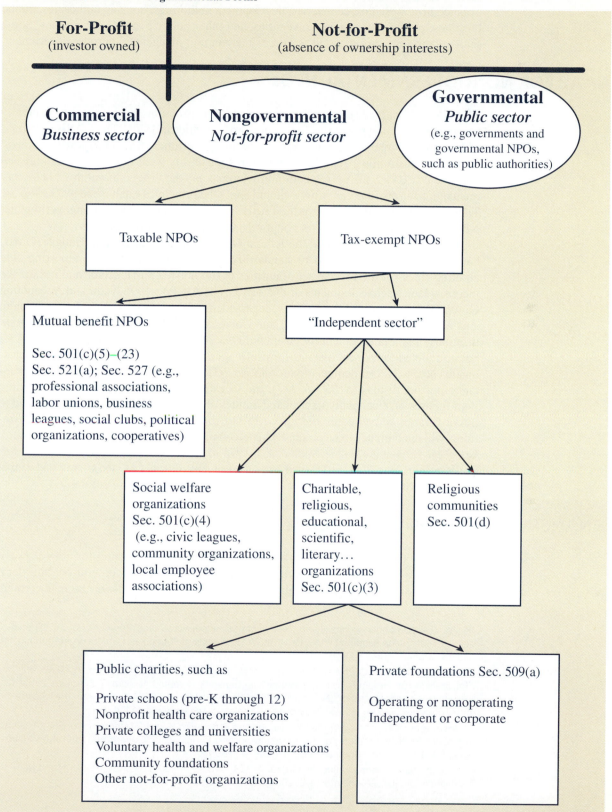

receive special tax revenue include libraries and transportation authorities. Governments often control museums, cemeteries, development authorities, housing authorities, public hospitals, public colleges and universities, and other public benefit corporations. Some such organizations are reported as a department or unit of a general purpose government.

GAAP FOR NONGOVERNMENTAL NPOs

The FASB assumed primary responsibility for providing guidance on generally accepted accounting principles for not-for-profit entities in 1979.[9] The GASB is responsible for governmental organizations including governmental not-for-profit organizations (see Illustration 1–1). These lines of responsibility were most clearly established with the AICPA's *SAS No. 69,* commonly known as "the GAAP hierarchy."[10] Governmental not-for-profit organizations should apply the principles established by *GASBS 34.* They are not permitted to adopt the FASB's standards applicable to nongovernmental NPOs.[11] This chapter focuses on nongovernmental not-for-profit entities.

The AICPA, the FASB, and the federal Office of Management and Budget (OMB) have made a concerted effort to standardize the accounting, financial reporting, and auditing rules for the diverse set of entities in the not-for-profit sector and reduce the inconsistencies across segments of this sector. The AICPA's 1996 Audit and Accounting Guide, *Not-for-Profit Organizations,* superseded three audit guides (Voluntary Health and Welfare Organizations, Colleges and Universities, and Certain Not-for-Profit Organizations) and four statements of Position (*SOPs 74-8, 78-10, 87-2,* and *94-2*). The FASB has completed four of its five not-for-profit agenda items designed to reduce inconsistencies across NPOs: depreciation (*SFAS No. 93*), contributions (*SFAS No. 116*), financial reporting display (*SFAS No. 117*), and investments (*SFAS No. 124*). The remaining item focuses on financially interrelated entities and was separated into issues related to intermediaries addressed in *SFAS No. 136* and combinations of not-for-profit organizations, which continues to be on the FASB's technical agenda (at the time of publication). Congress revised the Single Audit Act in 1996 to cover both governmental and not-for-profit entities, and the OMB issued a revision of *Circular A–133* (see Chapter 11)[12] that includes governments, not-for-profit organizations, and health care entities.

FINANCIAL REPORTING AND ACCOUNTING

As stated in Chapter 1, the FASB's objectives of financial reporting for not-for-profit agencies are to provide information useful in (1) making resource allocation decisions, (2) assessing services and ability to provide services, (3) assessing management

---

[9] Financial Accounting Standards Board, *Statement of Financial Accounting Standards No. 32,* "Specialized Accounting and Reporting Principles in AICPA Statements of Position and Guides on Accounting and Auditing Matters" (New York, 1979).

[10] American Institute of Certified Public Accountants, *Statement of Auditing Standards (SAS) No. 69,* "The Meaning of 'Present Fairly in Conformity with Generally Accepted Accounting Principles' in the Independent Auditor's Report" (New York, 1992). The FASB rescinded *SFAS No. 32* upon the issuance of this guidance. *SAS No. 69* was amended by *SAS No. 91;* see Illustration 11–4.

[11] Most paragraphs of Governmental Accounting Standards Board, *Statement No. 29,* "The Use of Not-for-Profit Accounting and Financial Reporting Principles by Governmental Entities" (Norwalk, CT, 1996) were superseded by *GASBS 34* (1999).

[12] Office of Management and Budget, *Circular A–133,* "Audits of States Local Governments and Non-Profit Organizations" (Washington, DC, 2003).

stewardship and performance, and (4) assessing economic resources, obligations, net resources, and changes in them.[13] Common phrases heard today when speaking of financial reporting of any organization include accountability and transparency to stakeholders. Stakeholders of NPOs that use not-for-profit financial statements include donors, grantors, members, lenders, consumers, and others who provide resources to NPOs.

Financial Reporting

FASB *Statement No. 117* requires NPOs to present financial statements showing an aggregate view of the entity.[14] This approach effectively moved not-for-profit financial reporting away from the disaggregated, traditional method of fund-based reporting and toward the commercial for-profit model of financial reporting. Not all users welcomed this change, but more than a decade later preparers and users alike appear to accept this integrated not-for-profit financial reporting model.

FASB *Statement No. 117* established minimum standards for general purpose external financial statements for NPOs by requiring a statement of financial position, statement of activities, and statement of cash flows, along with notes to the financial statements. Voluntary health and welfare organizations must also present a statement of functional expenses. Although the information specified by *SFAS No. 117* is to be presented for the entity as a whole, the statement permits additional display of disaggregated information, such as fund-based information that may be useful for management of the entity and accountability to donors and others. Comparative statements are encouraged, but not required. Illustrative financial statements for the Community Family Service Agency, Inc., a voluntary health and welfare organization, are presented in Illustrations 14–2 through 14–5, although alternative financial statement formats are allowed by *SFAS No. 117*.[15] The amounts shown in the financial statements reflect the illustrative transactions and journal entries presented at the end of this chapter.

Statement of Financial Position

This statement, also known as a balance sheet, shows total assets, total liabilities, and the difference, **net assets**, for the organization as a whole. As seen in Illustration 14–2, net assets for this organization are categorized into the three classes required by *SFAS No. 117:* unrestricted net assets, temporarily restricted net assets, and permanently restricted net assets. **Unrestricted net assets** arise from contributions for which either no donor restrictions exist or the restrictions have expired, revenues for services provided, and most investment income. Unrestricted net assets can be further segregated into board-designated and residual available for operations. **Board-designated net assets** are those unrestricted net assets appropriated or set aside by the governing board rather than an external donor and are sometimes subtitled "investments" and "net equity in capital."

Temporarily restricted net assets result from contributions on which the donor imposes restrictions as to purpose (how the asset may be used) or time (when the asset may be used). When the restrictions are met, these net assets are "released from

---

[13] Financial Accounting Standards Board, *Statement of Financial Accounting Concepts No. 4,* "Objectives of Financial Reporting by Nonbusiness Organizations" (Norwalk, CT, 1980), pp. 19–23.

[14] Financial Accounting Standards Board, *Statement of Financial Accounting Standards No. 117,* "Financial Statements for Not-for-Profit Organizations" (Norwalk, CT, 1993).

[15] Further guidance is provided by the National Assembly of Health & Human Service Organizations in "The Black Book," *Standards of Accounting and Financial Reporting for Voluntary Health & Welfare Organizations"* (Dubuque, IA: Kendall/Hunt Publishing Company, 1998), first published by the United Way.

ILLUSTRATION 14-2

COMMUNITY FAMILY SERVICE AGENCY, INC.
Statement of Financial Position
December 31, 2008, and 2007

	2008	2007
Assets:		
Cash	$ 28,953	$ 58,711
Short-term investments, at fair value	22,000	22,000
Accounts receivable (net)	1,150	2,350
Contributions receivable (net)	6,061	5,165
Supplies, at lower of cost or market	19,100	23,095
Prepaid expense	3,600	3,917
Assets restricted:		
For land, buildings, and equipment:		
Investments, at fair value	15,000	20,000
Contributions receivable (net)	982	10,182
For endowment:		
Cash	100,000	
Investments, at fair value	226,000	230,000
Land, buildings, and equipment, less allowance for accumulated depreciation of $17,961 and $13,776	104,763	103,948
Long-term investments	14,000	17,000
Total assets	$541,609	$496,368
Liabilities:		
Accounts payable and accrued expenses	$ 44,147	$ 25,911
$8\frac{1}{4}$% mortgage payable, due 2020	48,500	55,000
Total liabilities	92,647	80,911
Net assets:		
Unrestricted	26,377	97,302
Temporarily restricted	96,585	88,155
Permanently restricted	326,000	230,000
Total net assets	448,962	415,457
Total liabilities and net assets	$541,609	$496,368

restrictions" and reported as increases in unrestricted net assets. **Permanently restricted net assets** are assets for which the donor stipulates that the assets be held in perpetuity but allows the organization to spend any income earned by investing those assets. These gifts are also called **endowments** and are nonexpendable. Endowments may take the form of *pure* endowments, *term* endowments, or *quasi-*endowments. Term endowments are classified as temporarily restricted net assets because as the term expires, the assets can be used at the discretion of the NPO. Quasi-endowments or "funds functioning as endowments" are those in which the board designates that funds be set aside; however, since the board can reverse that decision, this form of endowment is classified as an unrestricted net asset. Permanently restricted net assets may also be in the form of artwork, land, or other assets that must be used for a certain purpose and may not be sold. Information on temporarily and permanently restricted net assets can be reported on the face of the statement of financial position or in the notes to the financial statements.

SFAS No. 117 recommends that NPOs list assets and liabilities in order of liquidity similar to the manner in which business enterprises list them. The nature of assets and any restrictions should be disclosed. In general, restrictions apply to net assets, not to specific assets. However, if cash or other assets received are designated for long-term purposes or have donor-imposed restrictions that limit their use, they should be segregated on the financial statement, as seen in Illustration 14–2, or disclosed in the notes.

Statement of Activities

The statement of activities is an operating statement that presents, in aggregated fashion, all changes in unrestricted net assets, temporarily restricted net assets, permanently restricted net assets, and total net assets for the reporting period. These changes take the form of revenues, gains, support, expenses, and losses. As seen in Illustration 14–3, a section titled "Net Assets Released from Restrictions" indicates the reclassification of temporarily restricted support to unrestricted support in the year in which the donor stipulations were met. Reclassifications are made for (1) satisfaction of program or purpose restrictions, (2) satisfaction of equipment acquisition restrictions, sometimes measured by depreciation expense, and (3) satisfaction of time restrictions, either actual donor or implied restrictions.

NPOs have considerable flexibility in presenting financial information as long as it is useful and understandable to the reader. *SFAS No. 117* does not preclude the NPO from using additional classifications, such as operating and nonoperating, expendable and nonexpendable, earned and unearned, and recurring and nonrecurring. An alternative format is presented later in Illustration 14–9.

Although some NPOs may use the cash basis as a simple method of internal accounting, external financial statements must be prepared on the accrual accounting basis to be in conformity with GAAP. In general, revenues and expenses should be reported at their gross amounts. Exceptions include activities peripheral to the entity's central operations and investment revenue, which may be reported net of related expenses, if properly disclosed. Although revenues are categorized into three classes, all expenses are reported as reductions of unrestricted net assets. In addition, expenses must be reported by their functional classification (e.g., program or supporting) either in this statement or in the notes to the financial statements. Gains and losses on investments and other assets are reported as changes in unrestricted net assets unless their use is temporarily or permanently restricted.

Statement of Cash Flows

SFAS No. 117 requires a statement of cash flows by amending *SFAS No. 95* to extend its coverage to not-for-profit organizations.[16] As Illustration 14–4 shows, cash flows are reported in three categories: operating, investing, and financing. The direct or indirect method may be used. If the direct method is used, a reconciliation showing the change in total net assets from the statement of activities to net cash used for operating activities must be prepared.

Donor-imposed restrictions are not separately reported in the cash flows statement; however, the statement does have some unique aspects. Unrestricted gifts are

---

[16] Financial Accounting Standards Board, *Statement of Financial Accounting Standards No. 95,* "Statement of Cash Flows" (Norwalk, CT, 1987).

ILLUSTRATION 14–3

COMMUNITY FAMILY SERVICE AGENCY, INC.
Statement of Activities
For the Year Ended December 31, 2008

	Unrestricted	Temporarily Restricted	Permanently Restricted	Total 2008
Revenues, gains and other support:				
Contributions	$401,396	$36,500	$100,000	$537,896
Special events		10,250		
Less: Direct costs		3,000		
Net special events		7,250		7,250
Program service fees	55,000			55,000
Membership dues	1,000			1,000
Sales to the public (net)	100			100
Investment income	15,680	1,390		17,070
Miscellaneous	1,500			1,500
Net assets released from restrictions:				
Satisfaction of program requirements	27,400	(27,400)		
Satisfaction of equipment acquisition restrictions	4,185	(4,185)		
Expiration of time restrictions	5,125	(5,125)		
Total revenues, gains, and other support	511,386	8,430	100,000	619,816
Expenses and losses:				
Program services:				
Counseling	185,513			185,513
Adoption	69,560			69,560
Foster home care	172,531			172,531
Special outreach project	62,870			62,870
Total program expenses	490,474			490,474
Support expenses:				
Management and general	53,085			53,085
Fund-raising	27,178			27,178
Total support expenses	80,263			80,263
Unrealized loss on investments	3,000		4,000	7,000
Payments to affiliated organizations	8,574			8,574
Total expenses and losses	582,311		4,000	586,311
Change in net assets	(70,925)	8,430	96,000	33,505
Net assets, December 31, 2007	97,302	88,155	$230,000	415,457
Net assets, December 31, 2008	$ 26,377	$96,585	$326,000	$448,962

included with the operating activities, whereas the receipt of temporarily and permanently restricted net assets given for long-term purposes are included in the financing activities section, as is the related income. The financing activities section also includes the issuance and repayment of long-term debt. Noncash gifts or in-kind contributions (discussed later) are disclosed as noncash investing and financing activities in a separate section.

ILLUSTRATION 14–4

COMMUNITY FAMILY SERVICE AGENCY, INC.
Statement of Cash Flows
Year Ended December 31, 2008

Cash flows from operating activities:	
Cash received from contributors	$345,300
Cash collected on contributions receivable	68,500
Cash received from service recipients	57,200
Cash collected from members	1,000
Investment income	15,680
Miscellaneous receipts	1,750
Cash paid to employees and suppliers	(530,164)
Cash paid to affiliated organizations	(8,574)
Interest paid	(4,540)
Net cash used for operating activities	(53,848)
Cash flows from investing activities:	
Purchase of equipment	(5,000)
Proceeds from sale of investments	5,000
Net cash used by investing activities	0
Cash flows from financing activities:	
Proceeds from contributions restricted for:	
Investment in plant	13,200
Future operations	16,000
Endowments	100,000
Other financing activities:	
Interest and dividends restricted for plant acquisition	1,390
Repayment of long-term debt	(6,500)
Net cash provided by financing activities	124,090
Net increase (decrease) in cash	70,242
Cash, December 31, 2007	58,711
Cash, December 31, 2008 (Note A)	$128,953
Reconciliation of Changes in Net Assets to Net Cash Used for Operating Activities:	
Change in net assets	$ 33,505
Adjustments to reconcile changes in net assets to net cash provided by operating activities:	
Depreciation	4,185
Decrease in accounts receivable, net	1,200
Decrease in contributions receivable, net	8,304
Decrease in supplies	3,995
Decrease in prepaid expenses	317
Increase in accounts payable and accrued expenses	18,236
Gifts, grants, and bequests restricted for long-term investment	(129,200)
Interest restricted for long-term investment	(1,390)
Unrealized loss on investments	7,000
Cash used for operating activities	$ (53,848)

Note A: Includes regular operating cash and cash restricted for endowment.

Notes to the Financial Statements

As with financial statements for all entities, the notes are an integral part of the financial statements of NPOs. Disclosures include principles applicable to for-profit entities unless there is a specific exemption for not-for-profit organizations. Examples of required disclosures are those relating to financial instruments; commitments; contingencies; extraordinary items; prior-period adjustments; changes in accounting principles; employee benefits; and credit risks. In addition, the nature and amounts of unrestricted, temporarily restricted, and permanently restricted net assets must be disclosed if not displayed on the face of the financial statements. Notes are encouraged to report the detail of reclassifications, investments, and promises to give. Policy statements regarding whether restricted gifts received and expended in the same period are reported first as temporarily restricted must also be disclosed.

Statement of Functional Expenses

VHWOs must prepare a statement of functional expenses along with their other financial statements. Illustration 14–5 shows a format with functional expenses reported in the columns and the natural classification of expenses shown as rows. *Functional expenses* are those that relate to either the program or mission of the organization (*program expenses*) or the management and general and fund-raising expenses required to operate the programs (*support expenses*). The natural classification of expenses, or object of expense, includes salaries, supplies, occupancy costs, interest, and depreciation among other categories the organization considers useful to the readers. Watchdog agencies, donors, and others often use the ratio of program expenses to total expenses as a measure of an NPO's performance. Natural expenses that apply to more than one function must be allocated across program, general and administrative, and fund-raising using a systematic method. Allocation of fund-raising costs is discussed later in this chapter, and performance measurement is discussed in Chapter 15.

Accounting for Revenues, Gains, and Support

Not-for-profit organizations have traditionally distinguished revenues, gains, and support. **Revenues** represent increases in unrestricted net assets arising from bilateral **exchange transactions** in which the other party to the transaction is presumed to receive direct tangible benefit commensurate with the resources provided. Examples are membership dues, program service fees, sales of supplies and services, and investment income. **Gains,** such as realized gains on investment transactions and gains on sale or disposal of equipment, are increases in net assets that relate to peripheral or incidental transactions of the entity and often are beyond the control of management. **Support** is an increase in net assets arising from contributions of resources or **nonexchange transactions** and includes only amounts for which the donor derives no tangible benefits from the recipient agency. Membership dues may be part revenue and part contribution if the value received by the member is less than the dues payment. A government grant is usually considered support unless it is essentially a purchase of services, in which case the recipient is considered a vendor and the grant is classified as revenue. Often organizations present one section in the statement of activities for revenues, gains, and support, in which case these distinctions are less important. Revenues, gains, and support generally should be recognized on the accrual basis and reported at gross amounts to be in conformity with GAAP, although some NPOs (e.g., colleges and universities) report certain revenues net of certain deductions. Revenue that is restricted by an agreement, such as fees or dues dedicated for a specific purpose, is reported in unrestricted net assets because it does not arise from a restricted gift by a donor.

ILLUSTRATION 14–5

COMMUNITY FAMILY SERVICE AGENCY, INC.
Statement of Functional Expenses
Year Ended December 31, 2008
(with comparative totals for 2007)

	Program Services					Supporting Services			Total Program and Supporting Services Expenses	
	Counseling	Adoption	Foster Home Care	Special Outreach Project	Total	Management and General	Fund-Raising	Total	2008	2007
Salaries	$ 87,720	$36,559	$ 83,610	$13,738	$221,627	$35,153	$ 8,220	$43,373	$265,000	$232,170
Employee benefits	16,882	7,036	16,091	2,644	42,653	6,765	1,582	8,347	51,000	47,035
Payroll taxes	6,720	2,801	6,405	1,051	16,977	2,693	630	3,323	20,300	11,400
Total salaries and related expenses	111,322	46,396	106,106	17,433	281,257	44,611	10,432	55,043	336,300	290,605
Professional fees	25,107	3,929	11,643	18,143	58,822	1,178	—	1,178	60,000	54,600
Supplies	4,049	2,167	4,747	3,950	14,913	790	592	1,382	16,295	8,500
Telephone	3,897	1,430	3,350	190	8,867	600	333	933	9,800	9,610
Postage and shipping	2,840	1,073	2,402	908	7,223	684	210	894	8,117	6,750
Occupancy	8,772	1,415	8,078	2,586	20,851	2,468	581	3,049	23,900	24,600
Rental and maintenance of equipment	3,669	1,520	3,511	—	8,700	—	—	—	8,700	8,750
Printing and publications	2,761	1,420	1,352	1,462	6,995	940	1,565	2,505	9,500	7,200
Travel	7,700	1,500	7,500	5,000	21,700	300	—	300	22,000	24,000
Conferences, conventions, meetings	3,450	887	4,436	4,436	13,209	591	—	591	13,800	13,700
Specific assistance to individuals	9,000	1,000	16,100	3,900	30,000	—	—	—	30,000	28,500
Membership dues	234	187	93	93	607	93	—	93	700	677
Awards and grants to National Headquarters	—	5,500	—	—	5,500	—	—	—	5,500	5,000
Fee to United Way	—	—	—	—	—	—	13,200	13,200	13,200	—
Uncollectible accounts expense	—	—	—	—	—	104	—	104	104	—
Miscellaneous	1,744	843	1,891	4,144	8,622	118	—	118	8,740	5,200
Total before depreciation	184,545	69,267	171,209	62,245	487,266	52,477	26,913	79,390	566,656	487,692
Depreciation of buildings and equipment	968	293	1,322	625	3,208	712	265	977	4,185	4,200
Total expenses	$185,513	$69,560	$172,531	$62,870	$490,474	$53,189	$27,178	$80,367	$570,841	$491,892

Contributions

Not-for-profit organizations, in particular voluntary health and welfare organizations, depend on contributions for their operations. A **contribution** is an unconditional transfer of cash or other asset to the entity (or a settlement or cancellation of its liabilities) in a voluntary, nonreciprocal transfer by another entity acting other than as an owner. *SFAS No. 116* provides guidance on contributions when the reporting entity is a donor or donee; however, it does not apply when the entity is acting as an agent, trustee, or intermediary or to tax exemptions, incentives, or abatements.[17]

Donors may restrict the period in which the gift can be used or its purpose, or make the contribution without restrictions. In general, *SFAS No. 116* requires that both unrestricted and restricted gifts be recognized as support and at fair value at the time of the gift. Restricted support increases either temporarily or permanently restricted net assets, depending on whether the restriction is temporary or permanent. In the absence of donor-imposed restrictions, unrestricted net assets are increased. If the provisions of a temporarily restricted contribution are met in the period of the gift, the revenue and expenses *may* be reported in the unrestricted category. The discerning reader will recognize that documenting the donor's intentions in writing at the time of the contribution is critical for proper accounting and reporting.

Promises to give assets to an organization (commonly called *pledges*) can be conditional or unconditional. A **conditional promise to give** depends on the occurrence of a specified future and uncertain event to bind the promissor, such as obtaining matching gifts by the recipient. A conditional promise to give is *not* recognized as support until the conditions on which it depends have been substantially met. An **unconditional promise to give** depends only on the passage of time or demand by the promisee for performance. These promises are recorded as support in the year made. Unconditional promises to give that will not be received until future periods must be reported as temporarily restricted net assets unless explicit donor stipulations or the circumstances surrounding the promise make it clear that the donor intended the contribution to support activities of the current period. The contribution is measured at the present value of future cash flows. Any difference in previously recorded temporarily restricted support and the current value when the period arrives is recorded as unrestricted contribution revenue, not interest income.

Promises may require the establishment of an allowance for estimated uncollectible pledges, inasmuch as pledges may not be enforceable under law. A description of promises and their terms must be disclosed in the notes to the financial statements. Pledges or intentions to give are not recorded until they have the characteristics of an unconditional promise to give, for example, a written document, partial payment, or a public announcement by the donor.

These *nonexchange* transactions can take the form of cash, securities, capital assets, materials, or services. Cash contributions require that a strong system of internal controls over the safeguarding of this asset be in place; however, they pose no unusual accounting or reporting problems. Donated securities may be received for any purpose, although generally they are received as a part of the principal of an endowment. They are recorded at their fair value at the date of the gift, and the same valuation rule is applied to capital assets received either as a part of an endowment or for use in the operations of the organization. Donations of capital assets, such as land, buildings, or works of art, may be temporarily or permanently restricted. If the donor does not stipulate how the asset should be used, the gift is classified as unrestricted. If the donor

---

[17] FASB, *SFAS No. 116,* par. 4.

does impose restrictions, such as how long the asset must be used as a building, or if the NPO has a policy implying a time restriction over the useful life of the asset, the contribution is classified as temporarily restricted. For buildings and equipment, an amount equal to annual depreciation expense is typically reclassified from temporarily restricted to unrestricted net assets each year to reflect that the cost of "using up" the asset's service potential satisfies the donor's imposed restriction.[18]

Donated Materials and Services

One of the basic characteristics that distinguishes not-for-profit organizations from commercial organizations is their reliance on noncash contributions or **gifts in kind.** Sheltered workshops for persons with disabilities often depend heavily on donations of clothing and furniture, thrift shops receive their inventory from donations, and health agencies may obtain contributions of drugs from pharmaceutical firms. Office space may be furnished rent free; and television, radio, and periodicals may publicize fund drives, special events, or the general work of NPOs at no charge. *SFAS No. 116* requires that all unconditional gifts, including material amounts of donated materials, be reported as both a contribution, measured at fair value on the date of the gift, and an expense or a noncash asset. An objective, clearly measurable basis for fair value can be established by proceeds from resale by the organization, price lists, market quotations, or appraisals.[19] Donated materials used or consumed in rendering services should be reported as part of the cost of the services rendered.

The services of unpaid workers may well make the difference between an effective organization and one that fails to achieve its objectives. Voluntary health and welfare organizations typically rely on the efforts of volunteer workers to supplement the efforts of paid employees. *SFAS No. 116* requires recognition of contributed services at their fair value if the services received (1) create or enhance nonfinancial assets or (2) require specialized skills, are provided by individuals possessing those skills, and typically would need to be purchased if not provided by donation (e.g., accountants). Although *SFAS No. 116* does not provide an example of the first criterion, a logical example would be recognition of support for donated architectural, legal, or carpentry services related to construction of a building addition. In this example, a capital asset account rather than a program or support expense would be debited. In general, nonfinancial assets are assets other than cash and assets readily convertible into cash, such as consumable supplies and capital assets. The second criterion is quite restrictive and results in many donated services not being recognized.

Donated Land, Building, and Equipment

If a donor makes a contribution of real estate or equipment to an NPO without any restrictions on its use, the contribution may be reported as unrestricted or temporarily restricted, depending on the policy of the organization. This policy should be clearly stated in the notes to the financial statements. The donor may stipulate that the gift is temporarily or permanently restricted. In any case, the donation should be recorded at the fair value at the date it is made. If an NPO receives the use of a building for a reduced rate, the difference between the rent paid and the fair market rental value should be reported as a contribution. If the organization receives donations that it intends to sell rather than use, then these contributions should be reported as increases in unrestricted net assets.

[18] American Institute of Certified Public Accountants, Audit and Accounting Guide, *Not-for-Profit Organizations,* with conforming changes May 1, 2005 (New York) par. 9.08.
[19] *SFAS No. 116,* par. 19.

Split-Interest Gifts

Donors may arrange to divide the interest in a gift among several beneficiaries, including an NPO. In these cases, one party may receive the gift's investment income as an asset and the other party has the right to the gift's principal at some point in time (such as the donor's death). These complex legal agreements, often involving charitable lead and remainder trusts, as well as deferred (planned) giving programs and gifts of life insurance, are discussed in greater detail in Chapter 16.

Special Events

Special events are fund-raising activities in which something of tangible value is offered to donor participants or designees for a payment that includes a contribution adequate to yield revenue for the sponsoring agency over and above direct expenses. Dinners, dances, golf outings, bazaars, card parties, fashion shows, and sales of candy, cookies, cakes, or greeting cards are typical "special events." The special events category of support is reserved for those events sponsored by the voluntary organization or by an organization over which it has control. If a completely independent organization sponsors an event for the voluntary agency's benefit, the amount given to the agency should be reported as contributions.

Special events may give rise to incidental revenue, such as advertising programs; incidental revenue is properly reported in the special events category of support. NPOs have traditionally netted direct costs of special events (such as the cost of dinner, rental of ballroom, or cost of prizes) against the gross proceeds of the special event. FASB *Statement No. 117,* par. 138, requires that all special event revenue and direct costs, except those of a peripheral or incidental nature, be reported at their gross amounts. If desired, NPOs can provide more detailed reporting of support categories, either on the face of the statement of activities or in the notes to the financial statements.

Expenses of promoting and conducting special events, such as expenses of printing tickets and posters, mailings, fees and expenses of public relations and fund-raising consultants, and salaries of employees of the voluntary agency attributable to planning, promoting, and conducting special events are treated as fund-raising expenses and are not charged against special events support.

Accounting for Expenses

Generally accepted accounting principles require that all expenses of NPOs be measured on the accrual basis and be reported as decreases in unrestricted net assets on the statement of activities. Depreciation of capital assets, including contributed capital assets, used in the operation of the organization is required by *SFAS No. 93.*[20] Depreciation of art and historical collections is discussed later in this chapter.

Functional Expenses

NPOs have long been required to report some degree of functional expenses, that is, segregation of expenses incurred for operating the *programs* from expenses incurred for *supporting* the programs (e.g., fund-raising or management and general expenses). Depreciation expense should be allocated to programs as well as to support function expenses. Illustration 14–6 presents a chart that shows the relationship between functional and natural or object classifications of expenses (also called line-item expenses). The human service organization used in the illustration operates three programs:

[20] Financial Accounting Standards Board, *Statement of Financial Accounting Standards No. 93,* "Recognition of Depreciation by Not-for-Profit Organizations" (Norwalk, CT, 1987).

ILLUSTRATION 14–6 **Functional Basis Financial Package of a Not-for-Profit Human Service Organization**

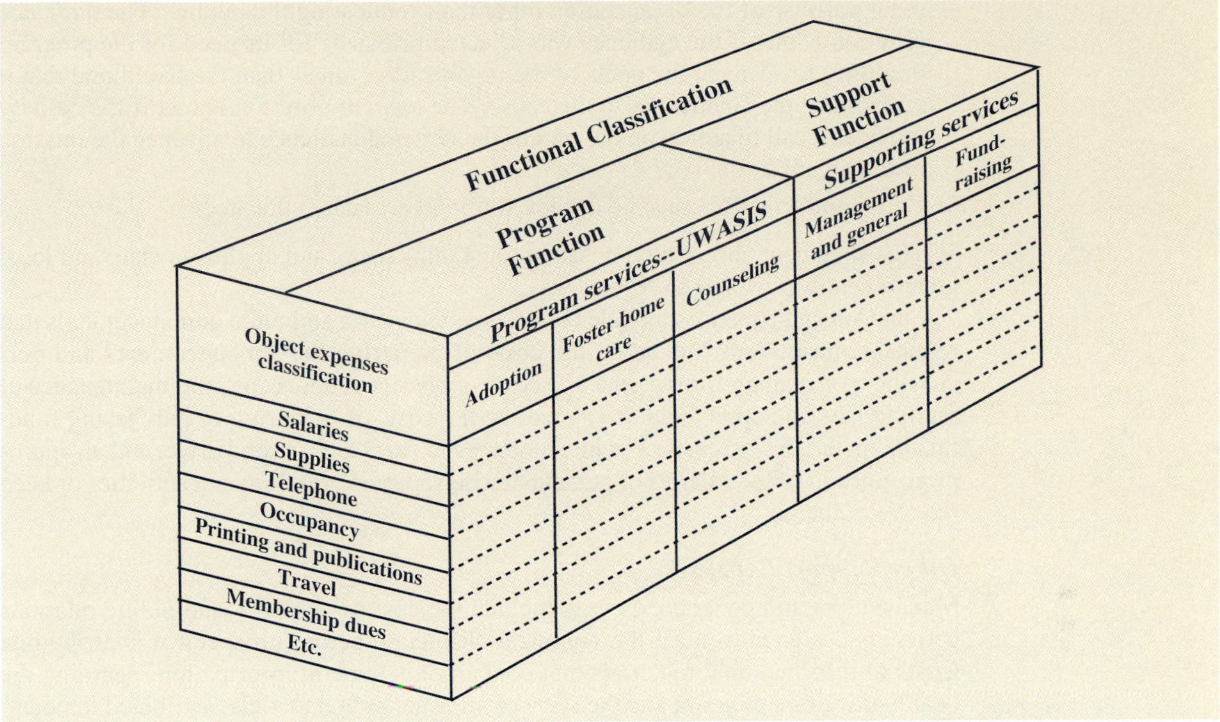

Source: United Way of America, *Accounting and Financial Reporting: A Guide for United Ways and Not-for-Profit Human Service Organizations* (Alexandria, VA, 1989), p. 159. Note: No longer in print.

adoption, foster home care, and counseling. A local fund-raising organization, such as the United Way, that is intended to allocate most of its inflows to participating agencies rather than to engage directly in offering program services to the public may find it desirable to present "allocating and agency relations" or "planning and evaluation" as well as management and general, and fund-raising categories.

Allocation of Costs with a Fund-Raising Appeal

Not-for-profit organizations often conduct an activity that combines a program purpose and a fund-raising purpose. An example is a door-to-door campaign to educate the public on its mission *and* solicit contributions. In the past, the cost of this joint activity often was reported entirely as functional program expenses, such as *Advocacy Costs,* with no allocation to the functional support expense of "fund-raising." AICPA *Statement of Position 98-2* revises *SOP 87-2* on joint costs and makes it more difficult to allocate "educating the public" or "advocacy" costs to program expenses. *SOP 98-2* provides the following:

1. The total cost of activities that include a fund-raising appeal should be reported as fund-raising costs unless a *bona fide* program or management and general function has been conducted in conjunction with the appeal for funds.

2. The joint costs of a bona fide program or management and general function should be allocated between those cost objectives and fund-raising using an equitable allocation base.

3. Criteria of purpose, audience, and content must be met in order to conclude that a bona fide program or management and general function has been conducted in conjunction with the appeal for funds.

The *purpose* criterion is met if the activity accomplishes a program or management purpose of the organization other than "educating the public." The *audience* criterion is met if the audience was selected primarily for its need for the program or ability to advance the goals of the organization rather than the likelihood that it will contribute financially to the cause. The *content* criterion is met if the activity includes a call to action on the part of the targeted audience to advance the mission of the organization.

4. Certain information must be disclosed if joint costs are allocated.[21]

This statement covers total costs, not just joint costs, and applies to state and local governments, as well as to NPOs.

Fund-raising expenses include the costs of television and radio announcements that request contributions, including the costs of preparing the announcements and purchasing or arranging for the time; the costs of postage, addressing, and maintenance of mailing lists and other fund drive records; the costs of preparing or purchasing fund-raising materials; the costs of public meetings to "kick off" a fund drive; and an appropriate portion of the salaries of personnel who supervise fund-raising activities or keep records of them.

Other Support Expenses

Management and general expenses include the cost of publicity and public relations activities designed to keep the organization's name before prospective contributors. Costs of informational materials that contain only general information regarding the health or welfare program and the costs of informational materials distributed to potential contributors, but not as a part of a fund drive, are considered management and general expenses. The costs of budgeting, accounting, reporting, legal services, office management, purchasing, and similar activities are examples of expenses properly classifiable as management and general expenses.

Accounting for Assets

Assets that have different treatment by NPOs than by for-profit entities include investments and collection items.

Investments

SFAS No. 124 provides guidance to NPOs on accounting for investments in a manner similar to *SFAS No. 115* for businesses and removes the inconsistencies in investment accounting across the various audit guides for not-for-profit entities.[22] *SFAS No. 124* requires that not-for-profit organizations mark all investments in equity securities that have readily determinable values and all debt securities to market or *fair value* rather than reporting them at original cost, amortized cost, or lower of cost or market. This statement is simpler than *SFAS No. 115* in that there is no requirement that NPOs classify their investments into trading, available-for-sale, and held-to-maturity categories. It does not apply when accounting for investments in securities under the equity

---

[21] AICPA, Audit and Accounting Guide, *Not-for-Profit Organizations* (New York: AICPA), 2005, par. 13-41–13-60.

[22] Financial Accounting Standards Board, *Statement of Financial Accounting Standards No. 124,* "Accounting for Certain Investments Held by Not-for-Profit Organizations" (Norwalk, CT, 1995), and *Statement of Financial Accounting Standards No. 115,* "Accounting for Certain Investments in Debt and Equity Securities" (Norwalk, CT, 1994).

method; consolidated subsidiaries; or investments with no readily determinable market value, such as real estate mortgages, oil and gas interests, and limited partnerships without a publicly traded market value.

Gains and losses are measured as the changes in fair value of the investments. Fair values are determined by quoted market prices, if available; selling price of similar securities; or valuation techniques, such as discounted cash flows. All realized and unrealized gains and losses on investments, as well as investment income (i.e., interest and dividends), are reported in the current period's statement of activities. Income and gains (losses) are reported as increases (decreases) in unrestricted net assets, unless their use is restricted by the donor or legally restricted by state law.[23] If restrictions on income exist, income is reported as an increase in either temporarily or permanently restricted net assets, depending on the nature of the restriction, and gains and losses are reported in the same manner as the income. When the restriction is satisfied in the same period in which the income or gain is earned, the investment income and gains may be reported as increases in unrestricted net assets as long as the organization has a similar policy for reporting contributions received, reports consistently from period to period, and discloses its accounting policy.

Endowments pose some additional accounting problems. If the donor requires that a specific investment security be held in perpetuity, the gains and losses on that security are also permanently restricted. However, if the NPO can choose suitable investments, gains on those investments are reported as increases in unrestricted net assets unless the income was restricted. The donor may stipulate that part of the net appreciation value (unrealized gain) is restricted, which is often done to protect the endowment from the effects of inflation. In this case, gains are reported as permanently restricted net assets until the required net appreciation value is reached, and then the remainder is reported as unrestricted. Losses on endowments are more complicated, in part, because the donor is often silent regarding any loss. *SFAS No. 124* requires that endowment losses reduce unrestricted net assets if the net appreciation requirement has been reached; otherwise, endowment losses decrease temporarily restricted net assets. In subsequent years, gains that restore the fair value of the endowment assets to the required level are reported as increases in unrestricted net assets.

SFAS No. 124 also requires extensive disclosures such as: (1) composition of investment return, (2) a reconciliation of investment return to amounts reported in the statements of activities, (3) the aggregate carrying amount of investments by major types (e.g., equity securities, U.S. Treasury securities, mutual funds, corporate debt securities, real estate), (4) the basis for determining the carrying amount for investments not covered by this standard, (5) the method(s) and significant assumptions used to estimate the fair values of investments other than financial instruments if those other investments are reported at fair value, (6) the aggregate amount of deficiencies for all donor-restricted endowment funds for which the fair value of the investment at the reporting date is less than the level required by donor stipulation or law, and (7) the nature of and carrying amount for each individual investment or group of investments that represents a significant concentration of market risk.

---

[23] Most states have adopted some version of the Uniform Management of Institutional Funds Act (UMIFA) (1970s) and some have adopted the Uniform Prudent Investors Act (1994), which describes standards of care, portfolio theory, and delegation of investment authority.

NPOs must follow the disclosure guidance in *SFAS No. 133* as amended by *SFAS No. 138* as it relates to derivative instruments and hedging activities.[24]

Collection Items

Certain not-for-profit organizations, particularly museums and libraries, have significant collections. *SFAS No. 116* defines **collections** as works of art, historical treasures, or similar assets that are

1. Held for public exhibition, education, or research in furtherance of public service rather than financial gain.
2. Protected, kept unencumbered, cared for, and preserved.
3. Subject to an organizational policy that requires the proceeds of items that are sold to be used to acquire other items for collection.[25]

An NPO may adopt the policy of recognizing collections as assets or not recognizing them; however, selective capitalization is not allowed. Implementation of *SFAS No. 116* required organizations to either retroactively capitalize their collections, prospectively capitalize the collections, or not capitalize at all.

If an NPO capitalizes its collections, it should recognize them as assets in the period in which they are acquired, either at cost or fair market value, if contributed. If contributed, collections should be recorded in the appropriate net asset category, depending on any restrictions placed on the contribution by the donor. If the organization chooses not to capitalize, it should provide note disclosure of its collections.

SFAS No. 93 states that works of art or historical treasures do not need to be depreciated so long as their economic benefit is used up so slowly that their estimated useful lives are extraordinarily long. This characteristic exists if (1) the assets individually have cultural, aesthetic, or historic value that is worth preserving perpetually and (2) the holder has the technological and financial ability to protect and preserve essentially undiminished the service potential of the asset and is doing that.[26]

FINANCIALLY INTERRELATED ENTITIES

Not-for-profit organizations may *have control over* or be *financially interrelated with* another entity, such as a for-profit entity, another NPO, or a related public institution. At issue is whether the financial statements of the two entities should be combined and whether disclosure is adequate to provide the decision maker with the fairest picture of the overall organization. AICPA *SOP 94-3* provides guidance to NPOs on reporting affiliated entities and makes uniform the previous guidance in the three former industry audit guides (Colleges and Universities, VHWO, and Certain Not-for-Profit Organizations).[27] In general, the nature of the relationship between the entities should drive the decision to consolidate the financial information of two entities, display one entity as a component unit of another or disclose information if statements are not consolidated.

[24] Financial Accounting Standards Board, *Statement of Financial Accounting Standards No. 133,* "Accounting for Derivative Instruments and Hedging Activities" (Norwalk, CT, 1998); and *Statement of Financial Accounting Standards No. 138,* "Accounting for Certain Derivative Instruments and Certain Hedging Activities—an Amendment of FASB Statement No. 133" (Norwalk, CT, 2000).

[25] AICPA, Audit and Accounting Guide, *Not-for-Profit Organizations,* par. 7.05; and FASB, *SFAS No. 116,* Appendix D.

[26] FASB, *SFAS No. 93,* par. 6.

[27] AICPA, *Statement of Position 94-3,* "Reporting of Related Entities by Not-for-Profit Organizations" (New York, 1994).

Investments in For-Profit Entities

If an NPO has a controlling financial interest through direct or indirect ownership of a majority voting interest in a for-profit entity, it should consolidate that entity's financial information with its own if conditions of *ARB No. 51* and *SFAS No. 94* are met and the control is not expected to be temporary.[28] If an entity owns less than a controlling interest, but has significant influence over a for-profit entity, it should use the equity method to report investments in that entity if the guidelines in *APB Opinion No. 18* are met.[29] If the entity does not exert influence, the investment should be reported at fair value, according to *SFAS No. 124*.

Financially Interrelated NPOs

In the case of financially interrelated not-for-profit organizations, an NPO should consolidate another NPO in which it has a controlling financial interest and an economic interest. Control exists if one organization can determine the direction of management policies through ownership, contract, or otherwise. Evidence of control might be majority membership on the board, a charter granting the ability to dissolve the other organization, or contracts assigning oversight responsibility. An **economic interest** exists if the other entity holds or utilizes significant resources that must be used for the purposes of the NPO; or the reporting organization is responsible for the liabilities of the other entity. Examples of economic interests include:

1. Other entities solicit funds in the name of the reporting organization, and the solicited funds are intended by the contributor to be transferred to the reporting organization or used at its discretion.
2. A reporting organization transfers significant resources to another entity whose resources are held for the benefit of the reporting organization.
3. A reporting organization assigns certain significant functions to another entity.
4. A reporting organization provides funds for another entity or guarantees its debt.

If either control *or* an economic interest—but not both—exists, related party disclosures required in *SFAS No. 57* should be made, as well as disclosures that identify the other organization and the nature of the relationship. Contributions made to an organization by its governing board members, officers, or employees need not be disclosed if the contributors do not receive a reciprocal economic benefit in consideration for the contribution. Reasonable amounts of salaries, wages, employee benefits, and reimbursement of expenses incurred in connection with a contributor's duties are not considered reciprocal benefits. If a national or international not-for-profit organization has local organizations that determine their own program activities, are financially independent, and control their own assets, consolidated financial statements are not required.

Funds Received as an Intermediary

Community, federated fund-raising, and foundations related to universities asked the FASB to clarify paragraph 4 of *SFAS No. 116,* which declared that the statement did not apply to transfers of assets in which the reporting entity was acting as an agent, trustee, or intermediary, rather than as a donor or donee. In June 1999, the FASB issued *SFAS No. 136* to clarify that an organization that receives financial assets

[28] *Accounting Research Bulletin (ARB) No. 51,* "Consolidated Financial Statements" (New York: AICPA, 1959), and FASB, *SFAS No. 94,* "Consolidation of All Majority-Owned Subsidiaries" (Stamford, CT, 1987).
[29] *Accounting Principles Board (APB) Opinion No. 18,* "The Equity Method of Accounting for Investments" (New York, 1971).

from a donor and agrees to transfer them (and/or the return on investment of those assets) to a specified "unaffiliated" beneficiary should recognize the fair value of the gift as an asset and a liability. Under this rule, most federated fund-raising foundations, such as United Way organizations, are treated as agents when they receive such gifts.

However, if the donor grants the recipient organization **variance power** to redirect the assets to another beneficiary or if the recipient organization and the specified beneficiary are "financially interrelated" organizations, the gift is recognized as an asset and as contribution revenue. Captive fund-raisers, such as institutionally related foundations, then, are not considered agents. This statement also provides guidance on the definition of financially interrelated, revocable or reciprocal transfers, required disclosures, and when a beneficiary NPO should recognize its rights to the assets held by another NPO.[30]

Funds Held in Trust by Others

Beneficial interests in perpetual trusts held in trust by third parties under a legal trust instrument created by a donor to generate income for an NPO should not be included in the balance sheet of the not-for-profit organization if it has no control over the actions of the trustee and if the organization is not the remainderman under the trust. The existence of the trust may be disclosed either parenthetically in the balance sheet or in notes to the financial statements. Income from such trusts, if significant, should be reported separately in the statement of activity.

Combinations of NPOs

Because of the unique issues involved with many NPO combinations, the FASB chose not to make *SFAS No. 141,* "Business Combinations," applicable to not-for-profit entities. For example, many combinations of NPOs do not involve an exchange of consideration and have been accounted for as a pooling of interests, a method that the FASB recently prohibited for businesses. Therefore, the FASB established a separate agenda item on these combinations. For now, NPOs will continue to follow the guidance in *APB Opinion No. 16,* "Business Combinations," and *APB Opinion No. 17,* "Intangible Assets," until a final statement on NPO combinations is issued.

Component Units of Governmental Entities

Certain not-for-profit organizations are created for the sole purpose of raising and holding economic resources for the direct benefit of a government. For example, public universities often are instrumental in creating a separate legal entity, collectively referred to as *institutionally related foundations,* for fund-raising, managing businesslike activities or endowment assets, conducting medical or other research, promoting athletics, or interacting with alumni of the university. Other governmental entities, such as hospitals, libraries, museums, parks, and school districts may also have affiliated organizations. If all of the following criteria are met, a tax-exempt nongovernmental entity should be discretely presented as a component unit of the related governmental entity even if the reporting public entity is not accountable for the financial and capital resources of the not-for-profit entity:

- The economic resources received or held by the separate organization are entirely or almost entirely for the direct benefit of the primary government, its component units, or its constituents.

[30] Financial Accounting Standards Board, *Statement of Financial Accounting Standards No. 136,* "Transfers of Assets to a Not-for-Profit Organization or Charitable Trust That Raises or Holds Contributions for Others" (Norwalk, CT, 1999). This statement incorporates and supersedes the 1996 FASB *Interpretation No. 42* with a similar title.

- The primary government or its component units are entitled to or have the ability to otherwise access a majority of the economic resources received or held by the separate organization.
- The economic resources received or held by an individual organization that the specific primary government or its component units are entitled to or have the ability to otherwise access are significant to that primary government.[31]

Certain relationships between primary governments and other organizations that do not meet each of the criteria just listed should still be blended or discretely displayed in the reporting entity's financial statements if it would be misleading to exclude them.[32]

OPTIONAL FUND ACCOUNTING

Fund accounting was defined and illustrated in Chapters 1 through 9 for governments as a method of segregating assets, liabilities, and fund balances into separate accounting entities associated with specific activities, donor-imposed restrictions, or obligations. Similarly, a fund accounting system makes it possible to determine compliance with laws, regulations, and agreements and to demonstrate that the NPO is meeting its stewardship responsibility to resource providers. Many NPOs still use this accounting method for internal management and grant-reporting purposes. As mentioned previously, *SFAS No. 117* permits not-for-profit organizations to also present disaggregated data classified by fund groups as long as the aggregated net asset statements are also presented. Fund categories described in the AICPA Audit and Accounting Guide, *Not-for-Profit Organizations,* follow:

- Unrestricted current or operating, or general funds.
- Restricted current or operating, or specific purpose funds.
- Plant funds (or land, building, and equipment funds).
- Loan funds.
- Endowment funds.
- Annuity and life income funds or split-interest funds.
- Agency funds (or custodian funds).[33]

All NPO funds are self-balancing sets of accounts that are both accounting entities and fiscal entities maintained on the full accrual basis except the agency funds, which report only assets and liabilities. The residual difference between total assets and total liabilities in a fund is labeled fund balance. Net assets also represent residual interests, but net assets are not the same as fund balances, in part because all expenses reduce unrestricted net assets under *SFAS No. 117* and in a fund accounting system, operating funds reflect both revenues and expenses.

Unrestricted current funds are used to account for all resources that may be used at the discretion of the governing board for carrying on the operations of the organization, including assets designated by the board for specific purposes. Restricted current funds

---

[31] Governmental Accounting Standards Board, *Statement No. 39,* "Determining Whether Certain Organizations Are Component Units" (Norwalk, CT, 2002) amends GASB *Statement No. 14.*

[32] Governmental Accounting Standards Board, *Statement No. 14,* "The Financial Reporting Entity" (Norwalk, CT, 1991).

[33] AICPA, Audit and Accounting Guide, *Not-for-Profit Organizations,* pars. 16.01–16.20

account for resources that may be used for operations but have been *restricted* by the stipulations of donors or grantors. Current liabilities are recorded in the appropriate fund depending on which funds will be used to pay them.

Plant funds are used to account for land, buildings, and equipment used by not-for-profit organizations in the conduct of their operations; liabilities relating to the acquisition or improvement of plant assets; and cash, investments, or receivables contributed specifically for acquiring, replacing, or improving the plant. Loan funds account for loans made to students, employees, and other constituents; consequently, they appear most often in accounting for colleges and universities.

The principal amounts of gifts and bequests that must, under the terms of agreements with donors, be maintained intact in perpetuity or until the occurrence of a specified event or for a specified time period are accounted for as endowment funds. Other gifts may take the form of split interests in which donors retain some of the gift (either the income or principal) for a period of time, sometimes until their death. Annuity funds are used when the donor specifies an amount of income to be paid to the donor or to a designated third party for a specified period. A life income fund is used when the donor stipulates that all income will be paid to the donor or a designated third party, with the principal reverting to the NPO upon the donor's death or some other specified time.

Agency or custodian funds are established to account for assets received by an organization to be held or disbursed only on instructions of the person or organization from whom they were received. Assets of a custodian fund belong to donors, and are not assets of the organization; income generated from the assets is added to the appropriate liability account. For these reasons, neither the receipt of assets to be held in custody nor the receipt of income from those assets should be reported by the not-for-profit organization as revenue or support. Assets of custodian funds and the offsetting liabilities should not be combined with assets and liabilities of other funds.

NPOs that use fund accounting recognize revenues and expenses for current operating funds. This practice makes it relatively easy for NPOs to prepare the aggregated entitywide financial statements required by FASB *Statement No. 117.* Unrestricted current fund balance is reported as unrestricted net assets, restricted current fund balances as temporarily restricted net assets, and *pure* endowment fund balance as permanently restricted net assets. The remaining fund balances can contain elements of each category, and the terms of their existence must be examined for donor restrictions. All interfund receivables and payables must be eliminated in preparing entitywide statements. Fund accounting for not-for-profit entities is not illustrated in this chapter.

ACCOUNTING INFORMATION SYSTEMS FOR NOT-FOR-PROFIT ORGANIZATIONS

Not-for-profit organizations, such as voluntary health and welfare organizations (VHWOs), differ from governments in part because VHWOs rely on grants and contributions in the operation of distinct programs rather than on taxes or user charges. Grants may be received from governments, other not-for-profit organizations, or foundations; contributions also come from individual donors. Either type of funding may be given to support specified programs or the organization as a whole. Grants are characterized by proposed budgets, authorized direct and indirect costs, grant periods, and

ILLUSTRATION 14–7   **Relationship of Programs and Grantors in Nonprofit Organizations**

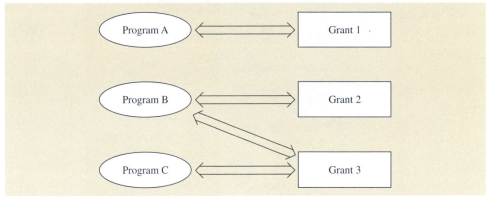

periodic reports to the grantor by the recipient agency. The accounting challenge in being accountable to the grantor is to capture total costs of each program and to match actual to budgeted costs for each grant. Difficulties arise because shared costs must be allocated across programs, grantors have different fiscal years, and terminology often differs across granting sources. For example, federal government grants may approve *telephone and printing costs,* but a local government grant covers *communication costs.* Further complications come when there are multiple grantors for one program and multiple programs supported by one grantor as seen in Illustration 14–7. A computerized accounting information system can help meet this reporting challenge, if properly designed.

Small organizations use commercial accounting software packages designed for business entities. Larger NPOs can afford to purchase higher priced software designed for not-for-profit entities. Whatever the decision, the creation of a chart of accounts is a critical step that must be taken in the beginning stages of the organization and revised each time the organization changes software or has other structural changes in its operation. The chart of accounts provides the framework used to classify transactions that affect programs and granting sources. All decision makers who are expected to use the reports generated by the accounting information system (for example, management, program directors, the board of directors, grantors, and donors) should be considered in the process of creating the chart of accounts so that the accounting system captures information that is useful, relevant, and reliable.

Illustration 14–8 shows a simple chart of accounts for a VHWO that advocates for school-age students at-risk. The agency has seven programs funded, in part, by 12 grantors. Natural expenses (i.e., objects of expenditures or line items) are called *costs* when associated with programs and *expenses* when related to general and administrative or fund-raising activities.

To report on activities effectively for various decision makers, the chart of accounts must allow for costs to be characterized by program, grant, and natural line item. Some accounting software facilitates this reporting by allowing reports to be prepared based on a range of account numbers in which fields of the account number are *masked* to focus on the distinguishing field in the account number. For the example agency in Illustration 14–8, which has a six-digit account number, a report for the Community Impact program could be generated by printing all revenues and costs for the A program; that is, the range of accounts used in the report would be 4**A** and

ILLUSTRATION 14–8 **Chart of Accounts for a Not-for-Profit Organization**
Account Number (X)–(XX)–(X)–(XX)

Type of Account X	Object XX	Program X	Funding Source XX

1 = Assets	10 = Cash
	20 = Accounts receivable
	30 = Inventory
	40 = Prepaid expenses
	50 = Investments
	60 = Property, plant, and
	   equipment
	70 = Accumulated
	   depreciation		

2 = Liabilities	10 = Accounts payable 20 = Accrued payroll 30 = Other accrued liabilities		
3 = Net assets	10 = Unrestricted net assets 20 = Unrestricted, designated net assets 30 = Temporarily restricted net assets 40 = Permanently restricted net assets		

4 = Revenues	10 = Contributions
	20 = Grants
	30 = Charges for services
	40 = Dues
	50 = Investment income
	60 = Special events
	70 = Miscellaneous
		A = Community Impact
		B = Youth Commission
		C = Juvenile Court Advocacy
		D = Student Outreach
		E = Safe Schools
		F = Parent Effectiveness
		   Training
		G = Advocacy
			01 = Federal grant
			02 = Community development
			   block grant
			21 = State grant
			22 = County grant
			23 = City grant
			24 = City Housing
			   Commission grant
			30 = Ford Foundation grant

5 = Cost of programs
6 = Expenses (general
   and administrative;
   fund-raising)
	11 = Salaries and wages
	12 = Fringe benefits and
	   payroll taxes
	20 = Travel
	30 = Supplies, phone, postage, printing
	40 = Occupancy costs
	60 = Equipment maintenance
	61 = Depreciation
	70 = Legal and professional services
	80 = Miscellaneous
			31 = Kellogg Foundation grant
			32 = Smith Foundation grant
			33 = Brown Foundation grant
			43 = Universal Church
			50 = United Way

5**A** where the * is used as a *wild card* to indicate all numbers. Similarly, if the agency wants a report on the federal grant, it can obtain it by selecting 4***01 and 5***01 accounts. Other software may produce the same result by allowing each revenue or cost to be characterized and consequently sorted by another item; for example, programs may be considered *classes* or *jobs* and funding sources may be treated as *customers.* Not surprisingly, more expensive software programs written specifically with not-for-profit agencies and their needs in mind may be more efficient in producing specialized reports. Whatever software is chosen, the critical step is to create a chart of accounts that contains enough detail in accounts to properly report to stakeholders with varying degrees of need for financial information.

ILLUSTRATIVE TRANSACTIONS—VOLUNTARY HEALTH AND WELFARE ORGANIZATIONS

Preceding sections of this chapter point out the fact that there are many differences among NPOs regarding the kinds of program services provided and the sources of support and revenue utilized. Accordingly, the transactions and accounting entries presented in this section should be taken as illustrative of those considered appropriate for an organization that offers counseling, adoption, and foster home care but is not necessarily typical of other NPOs. The transactions illustrated in this section are assumed to pertain to the year 2008 of a hypothetical organization called the Community Family Service Agency, Inc. The trial balance of the Community Family Service Agency, Inc., as of December 31, 2007, is shown next.

COMMUNITY FAMILY SERVICE AGENCY, INC.
Trial Balance
As of December 31, 2007

	Debits	Credits
Cash	$ 58,711	
Short-term Investments—Unrestricted	22,000	
Short-term Investments—Temporarily Restricted—Plant	20,000	
Accounts Receivable	2,485	
Allowance for Uncollectible Accounts Receivable		$ 135
Contributions Receivable—Unrestricted	5,424	
Allowance for Uncollectible Contributions—Unrestricted		259
Contributions Receivable—Temporarily Restricted	10,470	
Allowance for Uncollectible Contributions—Temporarily Restricted		288
Supplies	23,095	
Prepaid Expense	3,917	
Land—Temporarily Restricted	16,900	
Building—Temporarily Restricted	58,000	
Allowance for Depreciation—Building		4,640
Equipment—Temporarily Restricted	42,824	
Allowance for Depreciation—Equipment		9,136
Long-term Investments—Unrestricted	17,000	
Long-term Investments—Permanently Restricted	230,000	
Accounts Payable and Accrued Expenses		25,911
Mortgage Payable		55,000
Unrestricted Net Assets—Undesignated—Available for Operations		67,302
Unrestricted Net Assets—Designated for Special Outreach Project		30,000
Temporarily Restricted Net Assets—Programs		3,900
Temporarily Restricted Net Assets—Plant		79,130
Temporarily Restricted Net Assets—Time		5,125
Permanently Restricted Net Assets		230,000
Totals	$510,826	$510,826

The trial balance as of December 31, 2007, indicates that the capital assets (land, building, and equipment) are temporarily restricted, either explicitly by the donor or by an organization policy implying that donated capital assets will be restricted for the term of their useful life. An amount equal to depreciation expense is reclassified from temporarily restricted to unrestricted net assets each year. The donors of temporarily restricted gifts for the programs, the plant, or future periods have also restricted the specific asset or investments. Donors are more likely to restrict these assets than cash.

Contributions received in 2007 but specified by donors for unrestricted use in 2008 were transferred from the temporarily restricted to the unrestricted net asset class, as shown by Entry 1.

		Debits	Credits
1.	Net Assets Released—Expiration of Time Restrictions—Temporarily Restricted	5,125	
	Net Assets Released—Expiration of Time Restrictions— Unrestricted		5,125

Pledges receivable resulting from the 2008 fund drive were recorded. Pledges of $69,500 were unrestricted; in addition, pledges of $16,500 were donor restricted for a special outreach project to be undertaken in 2008.

2a.	Contributions Receivable—Unrestricted	69,500	
	Contributions—Unrestricted		69,500
2b.	Contributions Receivable—Temporarily Restricted	16,500	
	Contributions—Temporarily Restricted—Program		16,500

Cash collected for unrestricted pledges totaled $68,500; collection of accounts receivable amounted to $2,200. Cash collected for restricted pledges made this year totaled $16,500. Cash in the amount of $9,200 was collected for pledges given during a building fund drive in the preceding year.

3a.	Cash	70,700	
	Contributions Receivable—Unrestricted		68,500
	Accounts Receivable		2,200
3b.	Cash	16,500	
	Contributions Receivable—Temporarily Restricted		16,500
3c.	Cash	9,200	
	Contributions Receivable—Temporarily Restricted		9,200

The organization sponsored a bazaar to raise funds for the Special Outreach Project. Direct costs of $3,000, not considered peripheral or incidental in nature, incurred for this event were paid in cash; the event yielded cash contributions of $10,000.

		Debits	*Credits*
4a.	Cash	10,000	
	Contributions—Temporarily Restricted—Program		10,000
4b.	Direct Costs—Special Outreach Project—Program	3,000	
	Cash		3,000

The FY 2008 allocation from the United Way of Fairshare Bay amounted, in gross, to $317,000. Related fund-raising expenses to be borne by the Community Family Service Agency totaled $13,200; the net allocation was received in cash.

5.	Cash	303,800	
	Fund-Raising Support Expenses	13,200	
	Contributions—Unrestricted		317,000

Salaries expense for the year totaled $265,000, employee benefits expense totaled $51,000, and payroll taxes expense was $20,300. As of year-end, $15,100 of these expenses were unpaid; the balance had been paid in cash.

6.	Salaries Expense	265,000	
	Employee Benefits Expense	51,000	
	Payroll Taxes Expense	20,300	
	Cash		321,200
	Accounts Payable and Accrued Expenses		15,100

Expenses incurred for the Special Outreach Project were professional fees, $17,000; supplies, $4,500; and printing and publications, $1,600. All amounts were paid in cash.

7.	Professional Fees Expense	17,000	
	Supplies Expense	4,500	
	Printing and Publications Expense	1,600	
	Cash		23,100

Expenses for program services and supporting services were professional fees, $43,000; supplies, $7,800; telephone, $9,800; postage and shipping, $7,800; occupancy, $23,900; rental and maintenance of equipment, $8,700; printing and publications, $7,900; travel, $22,000; conferences, conventions, and meetings, $13,800; specific assistance to individuals, $30,000; membership dues, $700; awards and grants to national headquarters, $5,500; costs of sales to the public, $900; and miscellaneous, $4,200. All expenses were credited to accounts payable and accrued expenses.

		Debits	Credits
8.	Professional Fees Expense	43,000	
	Supplies Expense	7,800	
	Telephone Expense	9,800	
	Postage and Shipping Expense	7,800	
	Occupancy Expense	23,900	
	Rental and Maintenance of Equipment Expense	8,700	
	Printing and Publications Expense	7,900	
	Travel Expense	22,000	
	Conferences, Conventions, and Meetings	13,800	
	Specific Assistance to Individuals	30,000	
	Membership Dues	700	
	Awards and Grants to National Headquarters	5,500	
	Cost of Sales to the Public	900	
	Miscellaneous Expense	4,200	
	Accounts Payable and Accrued Expenses		186,000

Unrestricted support and revenue were received in cash during 2008 from the following sources: legacies and bequests, $15,000; membership dues from individuals, $1,000; program service fees, $55,000; investment income, $2,900; and miscellaneous, $1,500. In addition, $250 of net incidental revenue was collected in cash from advertisers for the Special Outreach Project.

		Debits	Credits
9.	Cash	75,650	
	Contributions—Unrestricted		15,000
	Membership Dues		1,000
	Program Service Fees		55,000
	Investment Income—Unrestricted		2,900
	Miscellaneous Revenue		1,500
	Contributions—Temporarily Restricted—Program		250

Sales to the public amounted to $1,000 gross for the year. None of this amount was collected by year-end.

		Debits	Credits
10.	Accounts Receivable	1,000	
	Sales to the Public		1,000

Accounts payable and accrued expenses paid in cash during 2008 totaled $182,864.

		Debits	Credits
11.	Accounts Payable and Accrued Expenses	182,864	
	Cash		182,864

Contributions received in cash in 2008 but specified by donors for use in 2009 amounted to $20,000.

		Debits	Credits
12.	Cash	20,000	
	Contributions—Temporarily Restricted—Time		10,000
	Contributions—Temporarily Restricted—Program		6,000
	Contributions—Temporarily Restricted—Plant		4,000

Interest of $4,540 and $6,500 on the principal of the mortgage were paid in cash. Short-term investments that were restricted for the plant were sold at par, $5,000; the proceeds were used to purchase equipment. The Agency's policy is that there is an implied restriction on plant assets and that this restriction is satisfied as the assets are used (measured by depreciation expense).

		Debits	Credits
13a.	Miscellaneous Expense	4,540	
	Mortgage Payable	6,500	
	Cash		11,040
13b.	Cash	5,000	
	Short-Term Investments—Temporarily Restricted—Plant		5,000
13c.	Equipment—Temporarily Restricted	5,000	
	Cash		5,000

Interest received in cash on short-term investments restricted for the plant amounted to $1,390. Interest received in cash on investments of endowment funds amounted to $12,780. This income was not restricted by the donor.

		Debits	Credits
14a.	Cash	1,390	
	Investment Income—Temporarily Restricted—Plant		1,390
14b.	Cash	12,780	
	Investment Income—Unrestricted		12,780

The Community Family Service Agency paid its national affiliates in accord with the affiliation agreements; the amount of the payment in 2008 was $8,574.

		Debits	Credits
15.	Payments to Affiliated Organizations	8,574	
	Cash		8,574

At the end of the year, a local family donated $100,000 in cash to be held in perpetuity with any investment income or gains and losses (realized or unrealized) to be used at the discretion of management.

		Debits	Credits
16.	Cash	100,000	
	Contributions—Permanently Restricted		100,000

End-of-the-Year Adjusting Journal Entries

A physical count of supplies, valued at the lower of cost or market, indicated the proper balance sheet value should be $19,100. Prepaid expenses at year-end were $3,600; the decrease is chargeable to postage and shipping expense.

		Debits	Credits
17a.	Supplies Expense	3,995	
	Supplies		3,995
17b.	Postage and Shipping Expense	317	
	Prepaid Expense		317

An analysis of the investment accounts indicated that the fair value of the long-term investments had decreased. The long-term investments for endowment have a fair value of $226,000 at the end of the year, and the unrestricted long-term investments are valued at $14,000. Short-term investments and investments for land, building, and equipment did not change.

18.	Unrealized Loss on Investments	7,000	
	Long-Term Investments—Permanently Restricted		4,000
	Long-Term Investments—Unrestricted		3,000

The allowance for uncollectible accounts receivable appeared adequate and not excessive, but the allowance for uncollectible unrestricted pledges should be increased by $104. This adjustment relates to current period unrestricted contributions (see Entry 2a).

19.	Contributions—Unrestricted	104	
	Allowance for Uncollectible Contributions—Unrestricted		104

Depreciation on buildings and equipment belonging to the Community Family Service Agency is recorded in the amounts shown in Entry 20. Since the depreciation reduced the carrying value of the capital assets, a reclassification is made for the net assets temporarily restricted for plant released from restriction.

20a.	Depreciation of Buildings and Equipment	4,185	
	Allowance for Depreciation—Building		1,145
	Allowance for Depreciation—Equipment		3,040
20b.	Net Assets Released—Satisfaction of Plant Restrictions—		
	Temporarily Restricted	4,185	
	Net Assets Released—Satisfaction of Plant Restrictions—		
	Unrestricted		4,185

End-of-the-Year Reclassification Journal Entries

Miscellaneous expenses for mortgage interest (in Entry 13a) and depreciation expense (in Entry 20a) were allocated to program services and supporting services. The allocation is assumed to be as shown in Entry 21.

		Debits	Credits
21.	Counseling Program Expenses	2,480	
	Adoption Program Expenses	990	
	Foster Home Care Program Expenses	2,510	
	Special Outreach Project Program Expenses	2,050	
	Management and General Support Expenses	530	
	Fund-Raising Support Expenses	165	
	Miscellaneous Expense		4,540
	Depreciation of Buildings and Equipment		4,185

The natural classification of expenses in Entry 7 were allocated to the Special Outreach Project.

22.	Special Outreach Project Program Expenses	23,100	
	Professional Fees Expense		17,000
	Supplies Expense		4,500
	Printing and Publications Expense		1,600

The remaining natural classification of expenses (in Entries 6, 8, and 17b) were allocated to the various program and support categories in the assumed amounts shown in Entry 23, except Costs of Sales to the Public (Entry 8), which will be netted with Sales to the Public.

23.	Counseling Program Expenses	183,033	
	Adoption Program Expenses	68,570	
	Foster Home Care Program Expenses	170,021	
	Special Outreach Project Program Expenses	37,720	
	Management and General Support Expenses	52,555	
	Fund-raising Support Expenses	13,813	
	Salaries Expense		265,000
	Employee Benefits Expense		51,000
	Payroll Taxes Expense		20,300
	Professional Fees Expense		43,000
	Supplies Expense		11,795
	Telephone Expense		9,800
	Postage and Shipping Expense		8,117
	Occupancy Expense		23,900
	Rental and Maintenance of Equipment		8,700
	Printing and Publications Expense		7,900
	Travel Expense		22,000
	Conferences, Conventions, and Meetings		13,800
	Specific Assistance to Individuals		30,000
	Membership Dues		700
	Awards and Grants to National Headquarters		5,500
	Miscellaneous Expense		4,200

Unrestricted net assets that were designated by the board of the Special Outreach Project were deemed no longer necessary; the board authorized the return of the amount, $30,000, to unrestricted net Assets—undesignated. Temporarily restricted funds of $27,400 ($3,900 + $23,500) were spent on the programs this year.

		Debits	Credits
24.	Unrestricted Net Assets—Designated for Special Outreach Project	30,000	
	Unrestricted Net Assets—Undesignated— Available for Operations		30,000
	Net Assets Released—Satisfaction of Program Restrictions— Temporarily Restricted	27,400	
	Net Assets Released—Satisfaction of Program Restrictions—Unrestricted		27,400

End-of-the-Year Closing Journal Entries

The following closing journal entries are made: (*a*) reclassifications for net assets released are closed into the appropriate categories of net assets, (*b*) unrestricted support and revenue are closed to unrestricted net assets, (*c*) program and support expenses as well as payments to affiliated organizations are closed to unrestricted net assets, (*d*) temporarily restricted support for programs, plant, and time are closed to temporarily restricted net assets, and (*e*) permanently restricted support is closed to permanently restricted net assets, if any.

25a.	Temporarily Restricted Net Assets—Time	5,125	
	Net Assets Released—Expiration of Time Restrictions— Unrestricted	5,125	
	Net Assets Released—Expiration of Time Restriction— Temporarily Restricted		5,125
	Unrestricted Net Assets—Undesignated— Available for Operations		5,125
	Temporarily Restricted Net Assets—Plant	4,185	
	Net Assets Released—Satisfaction of Plant Restrictions— Unrestricted	4,185	
	Net Assets Released—Satisfaction of Plant Restrictions— Temporarily Restricted		4,185
	Unrestricted Net Assets—Undesignated— Available for Operations		4,185
	Temporarily Restricted Net Assets—Program	27,400	
	Net Assets Released—Satisfaction of Program Restrictions— Unrestricted	27,400	
	Net Assets Released—Satisfaction of Program Restrictions— Temporarily Restricted		27,400
	Unrestricted Net Assets—Undesignated— Available for Operations		27,400

		Debits	Credits
25b.	Contributions—Unrestricted	401,396	
	Sales to the Public	1,000	
	Membership Dues—Individuals	1,000	
	Program Service Fees	55,000	
	Investment Income—Unrestricted	15,680	
	Miscellaneous Revenue	1,500	
	Unrestricted Net Assets—Undesignated—Available for Operations		475,576
25c.	Unrestricted Net Assets—Undesignated—Available for Operations	580,211	
	Counseling Program Expenses		185,513
	Adoption Program Expenses		69,560
	Foster Home Care Program Expenses		172,531
	Special Outreach Project Program Expenses		62,870
	Cost of Sales to Public		900
	Management and General Support Expenses		53,085
	Fund-Raising Support Expenses		27,178
	Payments to Affiliated Organizations		8,574
25d.	Contributions—Temporarily Restricted—Program	32,750	
	Contributions—Temporarily Restricted—Time	10,000	
	Contributions—Temporarily Restricted—Plant	4,000	
	Investment Income—Temporarily Restricted—Plant	1,390	
	Temporarily Restricted Net Assets—Program		29,750
	Temporarily Restricted Net Assets—Plant		5,390
	Temporarily Restricted Net Assets—Time		10,000
	Direct Costs—Special Outreach Project—Program		3,000
25e.	Contributions—Permanently Restricted	100,000	
	Permanently Restricted Net Assets		100,000
25f.	Permanently Restricted Net Assets	4,000	
	Unrestricted Net Assets—Undesignated—Available for Operations	3,000	
	Unrealized Loss on Investments		7,000

The effects of the preceding journal entries are reflected in Illustrations 14–2 through 14–5. Illustration 14–9 presents the Statement of Activities for Community Family Service Agency, Inc., prepared according to Format A in *SFAS No. 117,* a single column that is most useful for multiyear comparisons. *SFAS No. 117* also displays Format C, which reports information in two statements: The first summarizes detailed changes in unrestricted net assets to focus attention on operating activities, and the second reconciles changes in all three categories of net assets. That format is not illustrated in this chapter.

NPOs other than VHWOs may have transactions not illustrated here. For example, deferred revenue arises from exchange transactions, such as subscriptions in a performing arts organization, and long-term debt from a construction project may exist in larger not-for-profit organizations.

ILLUSTRATION 14–9

COMMUNITY FAMILY SERVICE AGENCY, INC.
Statement of Activities
Year Ended December 31, 2008

Changes in unrestricted net assets:	
Revenues and gains:	
Contributions	$401,396
Program service fees	55,000
Membership dues	1,000
Sales to public (net)	100
Investment income	15,680
Miscellaneous	1,500
Total unrestricted revenues and gains	474,676
Net assets released from restrictions:	
Satisfaction of program requirements	27,400
Satisfaction of equipment acquisition restrictions	4,185
Expiration of time restrictions	5,125
Total net assets released from restrictions	36,710
Total unrestricted revenues, gains, and other support	511,386
Expenses and losses:	
Program services:	
Counseling	185,513
Adoption	69,560
Foster home care	172,531
Special outreach project	62,870
Total program services	490,474
Supporting services:	
Management and general	53,085
Fund-raising	27,178
Total supporting services	80,263
Unrealized loss on investments	3,000
Payments to affiliated organizations	8,574
Total expenses and losses	582,311
Decrease in unrestricted net assets	(70,925)
Changes in temporarily restricted net assets:	
Contributions	36,500
Special events	10,250
Less: Direct costs	3,000
Net special events	7,250
Investment income	1,390
Net assets released from restrictions	(36,710)
Increase in temporarily restricted net assets	8,430
Change in permanently restricted net assets	96,000
Increase in net assets	33,505
Net assets, December 31, 2007	415,457
Net assets, December 31, 2008	$448,962

Key Terms

Board-designated net assets, *559*
Collections, *572*
Conditional promise to give, *566*
Contribution, *566*
Economic interest, *573*
Endowment, *560*
Exchange transactions, *564*
Gains, *564*

Gifts in kind, *567*
Human service organization, *556*
Net assets, *559*
Nonexchange transactions, *564*
Not-for-profit organization, *556*
Permanently restricted net assets, *560*
Promise to give, *566*

Revenue, *564*
Support, *564*
Temporarily restricted net assets, *559*
Unconditional promise to give, *566*
Unrestricted net assets, *559*
Variance power, *574*
Voluntary health and welfare organizations, *556*

Selected References

American Institute of Certified Public Accountants. Audit and Accounting Guide, *Not-for-Profit Organizations.* New York: AICPA, 2005.
————. *Not-for-Profit Organizations Industry Developments.* New York: AICPA, 2005.
Berger, Steven. *Understanding Nonprofit Financial Statements,* 2nd ed. Washington, DC: BoardSource, 2003.
Financial Accounting Standards Board. *Statement of Financial Accounting Standards No. 116,* "Accounting for Contributions Received and Made." Norwalk, CT: FASB, 1993.
————. *Statement of Financial Accounting Standards No. 117,* "Financial Statements of Not-for-Profit Organizations." Norwalk, CT: FASB, 1993.
————. *Statement of Financial Accounting Standards No. 136,* "Transfers of Assets to a Not-for-Profit Organization or Charitable Trust That Raises or Holds Contributions for Others." Norwalk, CT: FASB, 1999.
Gross, Jr., Malvern J., John H. McCarthy, and Nancy E. Shelmon. *Financial and Accounting Guide for Not-for-Profit Organizations,* 7th ed. New Jersey: John Wiley & Sons, 2005.
National Assembly of Health & Human Service Organizations, and National Health Council. *Standards of Accounting and Financial Reporting for Voluntary Health and Welfare Organizations ("The Black Book"),* 4th ed. Dubuque, IA: Kendall/Hunt Publishing Company, 1998.

Questions

14–1. Identify the key characteristics of an organization in the not-for-profit sector that distinguish it from an organization in the public sector or for-profit business sector. Provide an example of an entity in each sector.

14–2. Distinguish between *public support* and *revenue.* What type of organization would likely have a high proportion of total support and revenue from each of the following sources: (*a*) contributions, (*b*) charges for services, and (*c*) investment income?

14–3. Under what conditions should donated services be recognized in the financial statements of a not-for-profit organization as contributions and as expenses, assuming that the organization is subject to FASB jurisdiction?

14–4. Distinguish between the accounts *board designated net assets* and *temporarily restricted net assets?* Give an example of each.

14–5. Distinguish between *program services* and *supporting services* as the terms are used in financial reports recommended for use by not-for-profit organizations. How would you classify the salary of the executive director of a not-for-profit organization?

14–6. Why is a statement of functional expenses considered an important financial statement for a voluntary health or welfare organization? How does a statement of functional expenses relate to a statement of activities?

14–7. A not-for-profit organization that operates a summer camp for disadvantaged urban youth conducted a door-to-door information campaign. Volunteers canvassed a wealthy neighborhood and distributed pamphlets that describe the organization's mission and an envelope in which to mail donations. Would the cost of this campaign be considered a program expense or a fund-raising expense?

14–8. Not-for-profit organizations may not use fund accounting systems under *SFAS No. 117.* Do you agree or disagree with this statement? Why?

14–9. Describe how a not-for-profit museum accounts for its collections of works of art and historical treasures.

14–10. How does a not-for-profit fund-raising foundation account for a gift intended for the benefit of a particular charity when the donor stipulates that the fund-raising foundation may use its discretion to make the gift available to a different charity?

Cases

14–1 Institutionally Related Foundations. Compass State University Foundation (CSUF) was incorporated as a not-for-profit organization to support a public university in its fund-raising efforts and the management of its endowment. The foundation has a self-perpetuating board, one-third of whose members are selected by the university's president. Under a joint operating agreement, the university agrees to provide staff, computers, mail service, and office space to the foundation and to pay the foundation management fee based on a formula that incorporates a percentage of the endowment balance, cash gifts received, dollars raised, and donor records maintained. In addition, the university transferred its $8 million endowment to the foundation to manage. Since the inception of the foundation, the endowment has grown to $30 million.

Required
a. From an accounting (not legal) point of view, is the foundation a separate entity or a component unit of the related public university? What guidance is provided in *GASBS 39,* "Determining Whether Certain Organizations Are Component Units" (*GASB, 2002*) to address this financial reporting issue?
b. Who are the stakeholders in the foundation and what are their accountability concerns?
c. Assume the role of the president of the university and discuss the advantages and disadvantages of transferring $8 million of the university's endowment funds to the foundation.

This case is based on S. Ravenscroft and S. Kattelus, "Compass State University: Managerial Accounting Issues in a Nonprofit Entity," *Issues in Accounting Education* 13, no. 3 (1998).

14–2 Terms of Gift. The Shelter Association of Gogebic County receives the majority of its funding from the local chapter of the United Way. That federated fund-raising organization has this policy: If a member agency reports unrestricted net assets in excess of one year's budgeted revenues and support, the excess will be deducted from its allocation for next year. The association's reporting year ends December 31, and unrestricted net assets are just about equal to last year's revenues and support.

On December 30, Bill Olson contacts the Shelter Association about making a large contribution. It is important to Bill to make the gift in the current calendar year so that he can deduct the charitable contribution on his personal federal income tax return. However, Bill has heard that the treasurer of the association and several board members recently resigned after allegations of financial mismanagement were made. He is considering restricting his gift for the direct purposes of acquiring food, clothing, and supplies for the homeless over the next several years so that management could use none of the money for overhead expenses.

Required

Take the position of the association's certified public accountant.

a. Do you recommend that the association advise Mr. Olson to make the gift unrestricted or restricted? Give your reasons.

b. Mr. Olson asks you how he can be sure that the association spends his contribution as he intends, assuming that he restricts the purpose of his gift, as well as efficiently and effectively. Explain to Mr. Olson what kind of public information is available to him. Do you consider that information adequate to assess whether the not-for-profit agency was efficient and effective in its use of public donations?

14–3 Accountability Standards. The BBB Wise Giving Alliance has established *Standards for Charity Accountability* (see its Web site at www.give.org). Choose a not-for-profit organization in your home town. Obtain information from the NPO's Web site, if one exists, that helps you assess how well the organization measures up to the BBB Wise Giving Alliance's 20 standards of accountability. Interview the executive director of the organization and obtain additional information that would help you assess how well the NPO has complied with these accountability standards.

Required

a. Prepare a report to the executive director of the not-for-profit organization you investigated that summarizes your findings on each of the twenty standards for charity accountability established by the BBB Wise Giving Alliance.

b. Include in your report an explanation of any standard for which the not-for-profit organization is not in compliance. What steps could the organization take to improve its performance for each of these standards?

Exercises and Problems

14–1 Multiple Choice. Choose the best answer.

1. Which of the following is a distinguishing characteristic of an organization in the not-for-profit sector as opposed to one in the business sector?

    a. Operating purposes designed to accomplish the mission of the organization while efficiently using the scarce resources available to it.

    b. Contributions from resource providers in nonexchange transactions.

c. Importance of human capital in the form of employees and board members.

d. Use of generally accepted accounting principles in the preparation of annual financial statements to be audited by external CPAs.

2. Generally accepted accounting principles for nongovernmental, not-for-profit organizations are promulgated by the:
   a. Governmental Accounting Standards Board.
   b. American Institute of Certified Public Accountants.
   c. Office of Management and Budget.
   d. Financial Accounting Standards Board.

3. The FASB's *SFAS No. 117* requires a statement of functional expense for which of the following groups of not-for-profit organizations:
   a. Health care organizations.
   b. Mutual benefit not-for-profit organizations.
   c. Voluntary health and welfare organizations.
   d. All not-for-profit organizations.

4. Which of the following statements is designed primarily to report the balances in unrestricted, temporarily restricted, and permanently restricted net assets at the end of a reporting period?
   a. Statement of financial position.
   b. Statement of activities.
   c. Statement of functional expenses.
   d. Statement of cash flows.

5. Houses for Homeless, a well-established not-for-profit organization, received a $250,000 pledge in fiscal year 2008 that was restricted to cover operating expenses. The gift was paid in two installments, $100,000 in the first year and $150,000 in the second year. The following table reflects the cash received as well as cash spent on operating the organization.

	June 30, 2008	June 30, 2009
Gifts received	$100,000	$150,000
Camp operating expenses	$ 90,000	$170,000

How much should Houses for Homeless report as *Support from Contributions* for the year ended June 30, 2009?
   a. $0.
   b. $150,000.
   c. $170,000.
   d. $250,000.

6. Using the same data as in question 5, what should the camp report as *Net Assets Released from Restrictions* on the statement of activities for the fiscal year ended June 30, 2009?
   a. $150,000.
   b. $160,000.
   c. $170,000.
   d. $250,000.

7. Which of the following statements is true about *SFAS No. 124,* the FASB statement that provides guidance to not-for-profit organizations on accounting for investments?
   a. Not-for-profit organizations follow the same reporting requirements for investments as do businesses under *SFAS No. 115.*
   b. Debt securities for not-for-profit organizations are reported at amortized cost.
   c. NPOs and businesses classify their investments into trading, available-for-sale, and held-to-maturity categories.
   d. Investments in equity securities that have a readily determinable value must be marked to market or fair value at the end of the year.

8. For not-for-profit organizations that choose to use fund accounting for internal purposes, all of the following are appropriate funds *except:*
   a. Unrestricted current funds.
   b. Endowment funds.
   c. Private-purpose trust funds.
   d. Agency or custodian funds.

9. If a not-for-profit entity owns less than a controlling interest, but has significant influence over a for-profit entity, then it should:
   a. Use the equity method to report investments in that entity, if the guidelines in *APB Opinion No. 18* are met.
   b. Report the interest at fair value, according to *SFAS No. 124.*
   c. Consolidate that entity's financial information with its own if the conditions of *ARB No. 51* and *SFAS No. 94* are met and the control is not expected to be temporary.
   d. None of the above.

10. The Friends of the Sports Arena received contributions in cash in 2008 of $40,000 that were specified by donors for use in 2009. Of this total, $25,000 was unrestricted as to purpose; $9,000 was for restricted program purposes; and $6,000 was for the purchase of equipment. The journal entry required to record this transactions is 2008 is:

	Debits	Credits
a. Cash	40,000	
Contributions—Temporarily Restricted—Time		40,000
b. Cash	40,000	
Contributions—Temporarily Restricted—Time		25,000
Contributions—Temporarily Restricted—Program		15,000
c. Cash	40,000	
Contributions—Temporarily Restricted—Time		25,000
Contributions—Temporarily Restricted—Program		9,000
Contributions—Temporarily Restricted—Plant		6,000

   d. No entry should be recorded until 2009, when the contributions may be spent.

14–2 Joint Activities with a Fund-Raising Appeal. Consider the following scenarios relating to activities that include a fund-raising appeal:

1. The Green Group's mission is to protect the environment by increasing the portion of waste recycled by the public. The group conducts a door-to-door canvass of communities that recycle a low portion of their waste. The canvassers share their knowledge about the environmental problems caused by not recycling with households, asking them to change their recycling habits. The canvassers also ask for charitable contributions to continue this work, although these canvassers have not participated in fund-raising activities before.

2. Central University's mission is to educate students in various academic pursuits. The political science department holds a special lecture series in which prominent world leaders speak about current events. Admission is priced at $250, which is above the $50 fair value of other lectures on campus, resulting in a $200 contribution. Invitations are sent to previous attendees and donors who have contributed significant amounts in the past.

3. The mission of Kid's Camp is to provide summer camps for economically disadvantaged youths. It conducts a door-to-door solicitation campaign for its camp programs by sending volunteers to homes in upper-class neighborhoods. The volunteers explain the camp's programs and distribute leaflets explaining the organization's mission. Solicitors say, "Although your own children most likely are not eligible to attend this camp, we ask for your financial support so that children less fortunate can have this summer camp experience."

Required
Determine for each scenario whether its purpose, audience, and content meet the criteria described in *AICPA,* Audit and Accounting Guide, *Not-For-Profit Organizations* (Chapter 13 of this guide) so that the joint costs can be allocated between programs and support expenses. Explain your reasons.

14–3 Statement of Functional Expenses. The following statement of functional expenses of the NPO Support Organization for the year ended September 30, 2008 (along with other required financial statements), was presented to its board of directors. This organization supports other NPOs by renting building space, training boards, and providing training, among other services.

Required
a. As the accountant of the NPO Support Organization, prepare a brief report (professionally written and in good form) to the board that explains the generally accepted accounting principles followed in preparing this statement, as well as its relationships to the other required financial statements.
b. If the NPO Support Organization approached you as a potential contributor and presented this statement as evidence of its merit for your contribution, what would be your reaction and why?

NPO SUPPORT ORGANIZATION
Statement of Functional Expenses
For the Year Ended June 30, 2008

	Program Services									Supporting Services			
	Education and Training	Information Systems and Support	Building Management	Advocacy and Outreach	Consulting	Board	Technology	Publications	Total Program Services	Management and General	Fundraising	Total Supporting Services	2008
Payroll expenses:													
Wages	$ 68,634	$38,018	$ 50,050	$14,146	$25,947	$35,681	$24,431	$7,303	$264,210	$ 66,155	$ 7,500	$ 73,655	$337,865
Payroll taxes	7,330	2,832	3,698	1,109	2,148	2,670	—	539	20,326	11,585	2,901	14,486	34,812
Employee benefits	3,962	795	3,814	—	1,483	128	364	—	10,546	2,949	1,226	4,175	14,721
Total payroll expenses	79,926	41,645	57,562	15,255	29,578	38,479	24,795	7,842	295,082	80,689	11,627	92,316	387,398
Other expenses:													
Office supplies	549	358	3,198	—	—	444	—	70	4,619	5,852	—	5,852	10,471
Program expenses	3,897	—	—	—	3,563	—	—	—	7,460	—	—	—	7,460
Telephone	1,069	963	535	—	963	642	749	—	4,921	428	—	428	5,349
Postage	3,681	201	—	32	218	126	41	6	4,305	1,102	—	1,102	5,407
Postage—tenant reimbursable	—	—	12,941	—	—	—	—	—	12,941	—	—	—	12,941
Janitorial	—	—	9,874	—	—	—	—	—	9,874	—	—	—	9,874
Utilities	—	—	30,505	—	—	—	—	—	30,505	—	—	—	30,505
Rent	—	—	300	—	—	—	—	—	300	—	—	—	300
Travel and conferences	25	89	37	—	382	308	—	—	841	1,454	—	1,454	2,295
Training	—	—	—	—	—	—	—	—	—	—	—	—	—
Dues and subscriptions	—	2,164	—	—	—	5,500	—	—	7,664	2,294	—	2,294	9,958
Insurance	—	—	2,511	—	—	—	—	—	2,511	4,265	—	4,265	6,776
Meals and entertainment	3,363	—	—	—	38	145	—	—	3,546	135	82	217	3,763
Copying and printing	7,995	—	—	—	98	—	—	—	8,093	2,030	—	2,030	10,123
Repairs and maintenance	—	—	7,554	—	—	—	—	—	7,554	5,194	—	5,194	12,748
Contract services	4,176	1,200	10,612	—	—	1,350	9,435	200	26,973	7,200	—	7,200	34,173
Professional fees	—	—	—	—	—	—	—	—	—	4,400	—	4,400	4,400
Donated services	81,443	—	—	—	—	—	5,550	—	86,993	10,787	—	10,787	97,780
Marketing and promotion	9,126	316	281	—	179	386	100	2,250	12,638	7,049	—	7,049	19,687
Miscellaneous	62	—	381	—	290	—	250	—	693	8,303	—	8,303	8,996
Bad debt	—	—	—	—	—	—	—	—	290	—	—	—	290
Loss on disposal	—	—	—	—	—	—	—	—	—	6,675	—	6,675	6,675
Allocation of occupancy costs	14,396	3,942	(37,259)	518	3,804	5,033	2,644	1,164	(5,758)	5,758	—	5,758	—
Total expenses before depreciation	209,708	50,878	99,032	15,805	39,113	52,413	43,564	11,532	522,045	153,615	11,709	165,324	687,369
Depreciation	23	3,656	25,111	—	535	—	—	—	29,325	5,196	—	5,196	34,521
Total expenses	$209,731	$54,534	$124,143	$15,805	$39,648	$52,413	$43,564	$11,532	$551,370	$158,811	$11,709	$170,520	$721,890

14–4 Prepare Financial Statements. The Children's Counseling Center was incorporated as a not-for-profit voluntary health and welfare organization 10 years ago. Its adjusted trial balance as of June 30, 2008, follows.

	Debits	Credits
Cash	$126,500	
Pledges Receivable—Unrestricted	41,000	
Estimated Uncollectible Pledges		$ 4,100
Inventory	2,800	
Investments	178,000	
Furniture and Equipment	210,000	
Accumulated Depreciation—Furniture and Equipment		160,000
Accounts Payable		13,250
Unrestricted Net Assets		196,500
Temporarily Restricted Net Assets		50,500
Permanently Restricted Net Assets		100,000
Contributions—Unrestricted		338,820
Contributions—Temporarily Restricted		48,100
Investment Income—Unrestricted		9,200
Net Assets Released from Restrictions—Temporarily Restricted	22,000	
Net Assets Released from Restrictions—Unrestricted		22,000
Salaries and Fringe Benefit Expense	286,410	
Occupancy and Utility Expense	38,400	
Supplies Expense	6,940	
Printing and Publishing Expense	4,190	
Telephone and Postage Expense	3,500	
Unrealized Loss on Investments	2,000	
Depreciation Expense	21,000	
Totals	$942,740	$942,740

1. Salaries and fringe benefits were allocated to program services and supporting services in the following percentages: counseling services, 40%; professional training, 15%; community service, 10%; management and general, 25%; and fund-raising, 10%. Occupancy and utility, supplies, printing and publishing, and telephone and postage expense were allocated to the programs in the same manner as salaries and fringe benefits. Depreciation expense was divided equally among all five functional expense categories. Unrealized loss on investments was charged to the management and general function.

2. The organization had $153,314 of cash on hand at the beginning of the year. During the year, the Center received cash from contributors: $310,800 that was unrestricted and $48,100 that was restricted for the purchase of equipment for the Center. It had $9,200 of income earned and received on long-term investments. The Center spent cash of $286,410 on salaries and fringe benefits, $22,000 purchase of equipment for the Center, and $86,504 for operating expenses. Other pertinent information follows: Net pledges receivable increased $6,000, inventory increased $1,000, accounts payable decreased $100,594, and there were no salaries payable at the beginning of the year.

Required

a. Prepare a statement of financial position as of June 30, 2008, following the format in Illustration 14–2.

b. Prepare a statement of functional expenses for the year ended June 30, 2008, following the format in Illustration 14–5.

c. Prepare a statement of activities for the year ended June 30, 2008, following the format in Illustration 14–3.

d. Prepare a statement of cash flows for the year ended June 30, 2008, following the format in Illustration 14–4.

14–5 Statement of Activities. The Green Museum recently hired a new controller. His experience with managerial accounting and strong communication skills were extremely attractive. The new controller sent each member of the Board of Trustees' Finance Committee a set of the monthly financial statements one week before the monthly meeting for their review. The set included the following statement of activities.

THE GREEN MUSEUM
Statement of Activities
For the Eleven Months Ended February 28, 2008
(in hundreds of dollars)

	Public Exhibits	Abstract Exhibit	Mgt. & General	Total
Revenues:				
Contributions	$ 61,400	$50,000	$ 0	$111,400
Charges for services	478,800	0	0	478,800
Interest income	0	0	2,500	2,500
Total revenues	540,200	50,000	2,500	592,700
Expenses:				
Salaries and wages	381,900	24,700	44,200	450,800
Occupancy costs	38,100	12,000	14,900	65,000
Supplies	7,100	2,300	8,300	17,700
Equipment	5,000	0	6,500	11,500
Travel and development	2,800	0	6,900	9,700
Depreciation	12,000	1,500	6,300	19,800
Interest	0	0	3,700	3,700
Total variable expenses	456,900	40,500	90,800	588,200
Allocated management and general expenses	85,300	5,500	(90,800)	0
Total costs	542,200	46,000	0	585,700
Excess of revenues over expenses	$ (2,000)	$ 4,000	$ 2,500	$ 4,500

Other information: The management and general expenses are first allocated to the programs to which they directly relate; for example, the executive director's salary is allocated to the Public Exhibit Program according to the percentage of time spent working on the program. Remaining unallocated management and general expenses are allocated to the programs as indirect costs based on the relative amount of salaries and wages to total salaries and wages for the programs.

Required

As a member of The Green Museum's Board of Directors Finance Committee, review this statement and answer the following questions:

a. Is the statement in proper form according to *SFAS No. 117?*

b. What questions do you have for the controller?

c. The Green Museum would like to open an Impressionists exhibit. If its operating expenses are expected to be similar to that of the Abstract Exhibit, how much should the organization solicit in contributions or grants to operate the full cost of the program?

d. If you were a potential contributor to The Green Museum, do you think you have enough information from this statement on which to base your decision to donate?

14–6 Notes on Net Assets. The following items are taken from the financial statements of the Kids Clubs of America for the years ending December 31, 2008 and 2007, with related notes.

KIDS CLUBS OF AMERICA
Statement of Financial Position (selected items)
For the Years Ended December 31, 2008 and 2007

	2008	2007
Net assets:		
Unrestricted		
Undesignated	$ 878,901	$ 882,912
Board designated (Note 11)	66,540,051	57,479,525
Temporarily restricted (Note 9)	74,789,227	47,668,565
Permanently restricted (Note 9)	18,675,644	16,183,950
Total net assets	$160,883,823	$122,214,952

Note 9: Restricted Net Assets

Temporarily restricted net assets at December 31, 2008 and 2007, are available for the following purposes or periods:

	2008	2007
Gifts and other unexpended revenues available for on-site assistance to member clubs and establishment of new clubs	$ 4,469,136	$ 5,266,823
Gifts and other unexpended revenues available for leadership training, development, and support of youth programs	35,864,678	27,915,087
Gifts available for future periods	34,455,413	14,486,655
	$74,789,227	$47,668,565

Permanently restricted net assets consist of the following at December 31, 2008 and 2007:		
Endowments	$18,675,644	$16,183,950

Note 11: Unrestricted Net Assets—Board Designated
Board-designated net assets consist of the following at December 31, 2008 and 2007:

	2008	2007
Reserve fund (functioning as quasi-endowment)	$44,762,573	$39,203,909
Gains on endowments	12,051,815	10,678,020
Land, buildings, and equipment	9,010,568	6,924,643
Other board designated	715,095	72,953
	$66,540,051	$57,479,525

The authors would like to thank Michelle Richards of the Center for Empowerment and Economic Development, Ann Arbor, MI, for sharing the model on which this statement is built.

Required

a. Explain what the term *board-designated, unrestricted net assets* means. What does the board plan to do with these net assets? Can board members change their minds in future years?

b. Describe the types of restrictions that donors have placed on net assets. How much of those gifts are restricted for a period of time as opposed to purpose?

c. If an unexpected need arises, can the board of directors decide to spend donor-restricted funds in ways other than the donor indicated when the contribution was made?

14–7 Accounting for Volunteers. The following excerpt is taken from the FY 2004 audited financial statements for Habitat for Humanity International, Inc.

Habitat for Humanity International, Inc.
Notes to Consolidated Financial Statements

2. Summary of Significant Accounting Policies (continued)

Contributed Services

A substantial number of volunteers have made significant contributions of their time to Habitat's program and supporting services. The value of this contributed time is not reflected in the financial statements since it does not require a specialized skill. However, certain other contributed services that require specialized skills, where provided by individuals possessing those skills and otherwise needing to be purchased if not provided by donation, are recognized as revenue and expense. Such amounts, which are included in the accompanying Statements of Activities and Changes in Net Assets, totaled $848,923 and $1,124,569 for the years ended June 30, 2004 and 2003, respectively.

Required

a. Provide some examples of contributed services that might be included in the amounts recognized for FY 2004 and FY 2003 as revenue and expense. Explain how these services meet the criteria required by FASB.

b. This organization had a change in unrestricted net assets of ($4,315,726) for FY 2004. Explain what effect contributed services had on this decrease in unrestricted net assets.

Chapter **Fifteen**

Not-for-Profit Organizations— Regulatory, Taxation, and Performance Issues

Learning Objectives

After studying this chapter, you should be able to:

1. Identify oversight bodies and the source of their authority over not-for-profit organizations (NPOs).
2. Describe how and why states regulate NPOs and describe the following:
   Not-for-profit incorporation laws.
   Registration, licenses, and tax exemption.
   Lobbying and political influence.
3. Identify how the federal government regulates NPOs and describe the following:
   Tax-exempt status—public charities and private foundations.
   Unrelated business income tax.
   Restricting political activity.
   Intermediate sanctions.
   Reorganization and dissolution.
4. Describe governance issues of NPO Boards including incorporating documents and board membership.
5. Identify how benchmarks and performance measures can be used to evaluate NPOs.

OVERSIGHT AUTHORITY

Demand for the services of not-for-profit charitable organizations continues to grow, especially in times of national and international tragedies, such as September 11, 2001, in New York City, Washington D.C., and Pennsylvania; the December 26, 2004, tsunami in south Asia and east Africa; and Hurricane Katrina on August 29, 2005, with subsequent floods in New Orleans and the Gulf Coast area. Fortunately, the compassion and generosity of people supplies charities with tremendous amounts of resources to meet the demand, particularly in the early days after such tragedies. Although new organizations are created to meet the health and welfare needs of people in crisis, more often donors provide resources to large and well-established not-for-profit organizations that have proven track records of effective and efficient delivery of services to the needy, such as the American National Red Cross (established in 1881) and the Salvation Army (established in 1878).

Charitable not-for-profit organizations, such as the ones just described, are just a subset of the broad-based not-for-profit sector, as shown in Illustration 14–1. Increased vigilance by the media and watchdog agencies over all types of not-for-profit organizations ensures that the public is more aware than ever of the times when managers of these organizations perform well and other times when they engage in abuse, fraud, and other acts of financial impropriety.

NPOs are accountable to the state government that grants them their legal existence, the federal government for granting them tax-exempt status, their own governing board, individual donors and grantors, consumers of their services, and the public at large. It is important to note that churches, while certainly part of the nongovernmental, not-for-profit sector, do not require states and the federal government to grant them legal and tax-exempt status because of the historic constitutional separation of church and state in the United States. However, many activities in which churches engage are subject to state and federal regulations.

Accountants and auditors play a critical role in assuring stakeholders that all not-for-profit organizations have complied with applicable laws and regulations, and, in the process, have efficiently and effectively used the assets with which they were entrusted. The purpose of this chapter is to provide an overview of regulations affecting NPOs by oversight bodies, such as state governments, the federal government, and governing boards. Many of these topics have complex legal aspects that are beyond the scope of this book. For the interested reader, additional references are provided at the end of the chapter.

STATE REGULATION

Oversight responsibility derives from a state's power to give legal life to a not-for-profit organization. In the absence of stockholders, the state monitors NPO managers whom the public entrusts with funds and grants economic privileges, such as exemption from taxes. The state has responsibility to represent public beneficiaries of charities and contributors and to detect cases when managers or directors have mismanaged, diverted, or defrauded the charity and the public.

Legislation regulating NPOs varies greatly across states. However, there are some common methods used by states and sometimes adopted by local governments to ensure that the public good is protected as NPOs solicit charitable contributions and conduct business. The audited annual financial statements are not always sufficient to satisfy the oversight body that the NPO complied with laws. The accountant often serves the NPO client in preparing specialized reports required by the oversight body.

Nonprofit Incorporation Laws

A group of individuals who share a philanthropic or other vision may operate as an unincorporated association if it is small or if they expect the endeavor to have a limited life; however, organizers are treated as partners and share liability for any debts incurred by the association. If the organization plans to grow into a long-lived operation, organizers may choose to file articles of incorporation with a state under the not-for-profit corporation statutes or charitable trust laws to create a legal entity and limit the liability of the incorporators and directors. These laws differ across the 50 states, but states generally have built into the not-for-profit corporation laws the requirement that organizers (1) choose a name that is not misleading or in use by another corporation, (2) designate a resident agent and address, (3) state a clear purpose for the entity, (4) appoint a board of directors, (5) write by-laws that delineate board responsibilities and operating structure, (6) call at least one board meeting a year, and (7) require management to report on financial condition and operations at least once a year. Not-for-profit incorporation statutes also state the extent to which directors are individually liable for the misapplication of assets through neglect or failure to exercise reasonable care and prudence in administration of the affairs of the corporation. Upon conferring the NPO legal status separate from the incorporators, the state bears oversight responsibility for the NPO.

Registration, Licenses, and Tax Exemption

State regulation of not-for-profit corporations has increased since the State of New York established an Office of Charitable Registration in 1955 to administer fund-raising regulations for NPOs.[1] Some states require NPOs to register with a specified department of the state (e.g., Attorney General, Secretary of State, Consumer Affairs, Regulatory Affairs, or Commerce) or apply for a license in order to solicit funds, hold property, do business in the state, or lobby. For the most part, state and local governments require fees to accompany registration and licenses in order to defray the cost of regulation and monitoring. Failure to file required reports may result in automatic dissolution of the NPO.

License to Solicit Contributions

Some states protect citizens from competitive fund-raising requests by requiring the NPO to obtain a license to solicit charitable contributions. **Charitable solicitation** is the direct or indirect request for money, credit, property, financial assistance, or other things of value on the representation that these assets will be used for a charitable purpose. The Model Act Concerning the Solicitation of Funds for Charitable Purposes was promulgated in 1986 by the National Association of Attorneys General, the National Association of State Charity Officials, and a private-sector advisory group to guide states in designing this type of legislation. Although the Act has been challenged by some charities that argue soliciting is protected free speech, most legislation stands as an efficient way to protect the public from fraud.

States granting licenses usually impose annual compliance reporting on NPOs. A few states require audited annual financial reports to be filed when the level of public support exceeds a certain threshold, such as $250,000. Some states require a license when an NPO compensates someone for fund-raising, such as a professional fund-raiser or solicitor, and a fee may be required of the organization for the right of each fund-raiser to solicit. Many states also require specific disclosures be put on all written materials mailed to potential donors to indicate that financial information about the organization may be on file with the state. In addition to the state, local governments

[1] Seth Perlman, *State Fund-Raising Regulations: Registration Forms, Requirements, and Procedures* (New York: John Wiley & Sons, 2001).

may regulate charitable solicitation, although sometimes more for its fee revenue potential than for regulatory purposes.

Other Licenses

States or local governments may require a not-for-profit organization to get a license or permit for bingo, raffles, and charity games with maximum prizes. Often licenses or permits are granted for one-day beer, wine, and liquor sales for events.

Taxes

NPOs are often exempted from the taxes levied by state and local governments, such as sales, real or personal property, transfer, employment, or excise taxes. Of course, this privilege varies across the country and, in the case of property taxes, is being challenged by interest groups suspicious of some NPOs' charitable mission and defended by not-for-profit coalitions. To be relieved from the tax, the NPO may have to file for specific tax exemption and document that the property is *in use* for charitable purposes. Fund-raising events often give rise to sales tax reporting, both collection of tax from customers and exemption from sales tax paid on the purchase of goods. Often overlooked by the NPO are the excise taxes on telephone and utility bills for which they may not be liable and could recover by filing for a refund.

Lobbying and Political Influence

Some NPOs, organized specifically as a political party, campaign committee, or political action committee, are discussed later in the chapter in a section on IRC Section 527 organizations. For the most part, however, a not-for-profit organization cannot be organized primarily to attempt to influence legislation or participate in any political campaigns. Two primary ways that states regulate lobbying and political activity for all organizations are through lobbying acts and campaign finance acts. These laws require organizations to register with the state and then account for lobbying or campaign financing activities. The NPO must determine whether it, or someone it hires, is a lobbyist or lobbyist agent and, consequently, subject to these regulations. **Lobbying** is communicating directly with a public official in either the executive or legislative branch of the government for the purpose of influencing legislation. **Influencing** means to promote, support, affect, modify, oppose, or delay by any means. In one state, the amount of money spent on lobbying each year determines whether the NPO must register with a specified state agency. For example, if more than $1,825 is spent on lobbying or more than $475 is contributed to any single public official in any 12-month period, the NPO must register, file annual reports detailing its lobbying activity, and specify the amounts contributed to public officials. In addition to registering and reporting, certain prohibitions may exist. For example, there may be prohibitions stating that compensation of lobbyists cannot be contingent upon certain legal outcomes; no gifts or honorariums can be paid to public officials; and no contributions can be made to campaigns to support (or defeat) ballot questions.

The impact of excessive political activity on NPOs can be significant due to the harsh sanctions for violating these laws, as well as negative publicity that may harm future fund-raising efforts. The ultimate penalty is revocation of exemption from taxes, but more often fines are imposed for engaging in prohibited behavior.

Illustration 15–1 presents a chart that summarizes typical regulation of nongovernmental not-for-profit organizations at the state and local levels.

ILLUSTRATION 15–1   **Regulations over Not-for-Profit Organizations (varies by state)**

State and/or Local Government Regulations
Application to operate under an assumed name
Application to incorporate as a not-for-profit corporation or a charitable trust
Annual compliance reporting
Special licenses with particular state departments to operate a health care facility (public health), housing corporation (housing authority), residential care facility (social service), or school (education), or to handle food
Application for exemption from income, franchise, sales, use, real and personal property taxes
Employer registration including payroll tax returns, withholding of state taxes, and unemployment
License to solicit charitable contributions
Registration of political lobbyists, lobbying agents, or lobbying activities
License for one-day beer, wine, and liquor sales
License to conduct charitable games (e.g., bingo, raffles, millionaires parties)
Policies on conflict of interest and self-dealing with directors
License to collect sales and use taxes as a vendor
Freedom of Information Act (FOIA) (if a substantial amount of funds are public)
Open Meetings Act (if governmental in nature)
Notice of plans to merge with another agency
Notice of plans to dissolve, including tax clearance

FEDERAL REGULATION

Because charities serve the common good, the federal government has encouraged not-for-profit associations and charitable contributions since the first revenue act in 1894 . The public, then, expects the federal government to monitor those organizations receiving tax benefits to ensure that these privileges are not abused. Of course, NPOs must follow general laws that govern businesses (such as fair labor standards, older workers' benefits protection, equal employment opportunities acts, disabilities acts, civil rights laws, drug-free workplace laws, immigration laws, antidiscrimination and harassment laws, and veterans and whistleblowers' protection) unless they are specifically exempted. This section describes federal laws that are unique to NPOs.

Illustration 15–2 is a chart depicting how a public charity interacts with the IRS during its existence.

Tax-Exempt Status

Even though a state may have conferred not-for-profit corporation status on an organization, that NPO must still apply to the Internal Revenue Service (IRS) for exemption from federal income tax.[2] As shown in Illustration 14–1, not all not-for-profit organizations are tax exempt. A common reason that an NPO is not exempt from income taxes is that its mission is primarily to influence legislation. The stated purpose of the NPO and the services it will perform determine under which section of the Internal Revenue Code (IRC) of 1986 the NPO requests exemption. Illustration 15–3 shows some of the more than 25 classifications of statutory exemptions under which tax-exempt organizations fall. The

[2] Application for income tax exemption is made on Form 1023 for public charities and Form 1024 for all other organizations. NPOs may also qualify for exemption from certain federal excise taxes (e.g., communications, manufacturers, diesel, and motor fuels taxes). See also IRS Pub. 557 *Tax-Exempt Status for Your Organization.*

ILLUSTRATION 15–2 Life Cycle of a Public Charity

Starting Out
- Articles, Trust, or Charter
- By-Laws
- Employer Identification Number (EIN)
- Charitable Solicitation
- Help from the IRS

Applying to IRS
- Application Forms (Form 1023 and 1024)
- IRS Processing
- Help from the IRS

Annual Filings
- Annual Exempt Organizations Return
- Unrelated Business Income Tax (UBIT)
- Help from the IRS

Ongoing Compliance
- Jeopardizing Exemption
- Intermediate Sanctions
- Employment Taxes
- Substantiation and Disclosure (e.g, noncash contributions)
- Public Disclosure Requirements
- Charitable Contributions—What's Deductible?
- *Charitable Contributions. Substantiation and Disclosure Requirements* (Pub. 1771)
- Help from the IRS
- Customer Account Services
- Compliance Guide (Pub. 4221)
- *Tax-Exempt Status for Your Organization* (Pub. 557)

Significant Events
- Notifying the IRS (e.g., mergers)
- Private Letter Ruling
- Audits of Exempt Organizations
- Termination of an Exempt Organization
- Help from the IRS

Source: Internal Revenue Service "Life Cycle of a Public Charity" with examples and links to appropriate forms, available at www.irs.ustreas.gov/charities/charitable/article/0,,id= 122670,00.html.

most common classification under IRC Section 501 is Sec. 501(c)(3), which is an organization operated for philanthropic, educational, or similar purposes. The **organizational test** for tax-exempt status is that the articles of incorporation must limit the organization's purposes to those described in the categories in IRC Sec. 501 and must not empower it to engage in activities that are not in furtherance of those purposes. Alternatively, some not-for-profit organizations, such as hospitals, have been criticized for not providing an adequate amount of free services as a benefit to society, as stated in their application for tax-exempt status.

An individual can receive a charitable contribution deduction by making a donation to a Sec. 501(c)(3) organization (and certain other exempt organizations) but only if the gift is used for charitable purposes. Many categories of tax-exempt organizations, such as business leagues, social clubs, and cooperatives, cannot offer donors the advantage of a charitable deduction from income taxes because they operate primarily for the benefit of members, not the public at large. Another advantage of tax exemption under

ILLUSTRATION 15–3 **Tax-Exempt Status According to the Internal Revenue Code (selected)**

Section of 1986 Internal Revenue Code	Description of Organization and Its Activities
501(c)(1)	Corporations organized under acts of Congress, such as Federal Deposit Insurance Corporation
501(c)(2)	Title-holding corporation for exempt organizations
501(c)(3)	Charitable, religious, scientific, literary, educational, testing for public safety
501(c)(4)	Civic leagues, social welfare organizations, local employee associations, community organizations
501(c)(5)	Labor unions, agricultural and horticultural organizations, farm bureaus
501(c)(6)	Business leagues, trade associations, chambers of commerce, real estate boards
501(c)(7)	Social and recreational clubs, hobby clubs, country clubs
501(c)(8)	Fraternal beneficiary society and associations; lodges providing for payment of insurance benefits to members
501(c)(9)	Voluntary employees' beneficiary associations to provide insurance benefits to members
501(c)(13)	Cemetery companies; burial activities
501(c)(14)	State-chartered credit unions, mutual reserve fund
501(c)(17)	Supplemental unemployment benefit trusts
501(c)(19)	Veterans' organizations or armed forces members' posts
501(c)(20)	Group legal service plans provided by a corporation for its members
501(d)	Religious and apostolic associations; religious communities
501(e)	Cooperative hospital service organization
501(f)	Cooperative service organization of operating educational organizations
501(k)	Child care organizations
521(a)	Farmers; cooperative associations
527	Political parties, campaign committees, political action committees
529	Qualified state tuition programs

Sec. 501(c)(3) is the opportunity to apply for grants from foundations and government agencies, which often limit funding to public charities. An organization that is not a Sec. 501(c)(3) organization must disclose to donors that contributions are *not* tax deductible. Independent charitable organizations may voluntarily join together as a **federated fund-raising organization** to raise and distribute money among themselves. Examples of such federations are the United Way and community chests.

Annual Compliance Reporting

Form 990 is the primary tool the federal government uses to collect information about the NPO and its activities. The IRS expands the form as Congress requires more information to be furnished by tax-exempt organizations. The form must be made available to the public for three years.[3] Failure to file this form brings significant penalties,

---

[3] Public disclosure regulations issued in 1999 require that tax-exempt organizations provide a copy of their three most recently filed Form 990s and exempt application immediately upon personal request or within 30 days for a written request. Penalties for not doing so are $20 per day up to a maximum of $10,000 but can be avoided if the organization makes these forms widely available on the Internet [Treas. Reg. §1.6104]. Similar regulations were passed for private foundations and their Form 990–PFs in 2000.

ILLUSTRATION 15–4 **Parts of the IRS Form 990**

Top of Page 1	Descriptive information: name, address, employer identification number (EIN), type of organization, accounting method
Part I	Statement of revenue, expenses, and changes in net assets or fund balances
Part II	Statement of functional expenses with joint costs
Part III	Statement of program service accomplishments
Part IV	Balance sheets (for two years) with reconciliation of revenue and expenses to audited statements
Part V	List of officers, directors, trustees, and key employees (with compensation)
Part VI	Other information (e.g., amount of political expenditures, compliance with other regulations, location of the books)
Part VII	Analysis of income-producing activities
Part VIII	Relationship of activities to the accomplishment of exempt purposes
Part IX	Information regarding taxable subsidiaries
Part X	Information regarding transfers associated with personal benefit contracts
Schedule A	
Part I	Compensation of the five highest paid employees other than officers, directors, and trustees
Part II	Compensation of the five highest paid independent contractors for professional services
Part III	Statement about activities (e.g., political activity, leasing, making grants)
Part IV	Reason for non-private foundation status (and four-year support schedule)
Part V	Private school questionnaire
Part VI	Lobbying expenditures by electing and nonelecting public charities
Part VII	Information regarding transfers to and transactions and relationships with noncharitable exempt organizations
Schedule B	Schedule of contributors

unless an extension is granted. Annual reporting requirements do not apply to federal agencies, churches and their affiliates, and NPOs with gross receipts less than $25,000.

Form 990 provides useful information for donors, grantors, regulators, and researchers. Included in the information on Form 990 is identification of the four largest program services; a list of directors and officers and their compensation; a report of expenses segregated into the functional categories of unrelated business income, program, and support; and a list of major contributors, although the latter item need not necessarily be public information. Illustration 15–4 delineates information that is required on the annual reporting Form 990.

Public Charities versus Private Foundations

Tax-exempt status brings with it potential liability for penalties in the form of excise taxes, such as those for certain activities of private foundations, unrelated business income, some activity of feeder organizations, and excess lobbying. IRC Sec. 501(c)(3) encompasses private foundations and public charities. A **private foundation** is one that receives its support from a small number of individuals or corporations and investment income rather than from the public at large; it exists to make grants to public charities. These tax-exempt organizations file an annual Form 990-PF and are subject to several excise taxes (1) for failure to take certain actions (such as distribute a minimum amount to public charities), (2) for prohibited behavior (such as speculative investing, self-dealing transactions with disqualified persons, and excess business holdings), and (3) on net investment income (this tax is then used to support the costs of auditing tax-exempt organizations.) Donors should be aware that they are limited in the amount of charitable deductions that can be taken when giving to a private foundation. A tax-exempt organization is presumed to be a private foundation unless it meets a specific exclusion allowing it to be considered a public charity.[4]

Public charities receive preferential tax treatment over private foundations because they are funded, operated, and monitored by the public at large rather than by a limited number of donors. An IRC Sec. 501(c)(3) organization is considered to be a public charity if it notifies the IRS that it meets one of the exclusions to the private foundation definition: For example, it is broadly supported by the public, government, or other public charities; it operates to support another public charity; or it tests products for public safety.

Two parts of the *broad public support test* must be satisfied. The **external support test** is met if at least one-third of the organization's total revenue comes from the government, general public (e.g., individuals, private foundations, corporations), or other public charities in the form of contributions, grants, membership dues, charges for services, or sales of merchandise. If gross receipts from any person or governmental agency exceed $5,000 or 1 percent of the organization's support for the taxable year, the excess is not counted in public support for the purposes of the external support test. Investment income and gains from sales of capital assets are *not* considered public support. Private foundations try not to give a grant to a not-for-profit organization that might cause the public charity to fail the support test and be reclassified as a private foundation. If that happens, the foundation must exercise **expenditure responsibility** and monitor whether the grant was used exclusively for the purpose for which it was made. The private foundation can require the grantee to provide assurance that the grant will not *tip* the grantee into private foundation status before it is granted. The **internal support test** requires that the NPO *not* receive more than one-third of its total support from investment income and unrelated business income. Classification as a public charity must be redetermined each year.

Unrelated Business Income Tax

Owners of small businesses have long complained that NPOs compete with them in businesslike activities with the unfair advantage of lower costs due to exemption from income taxes. For example, college bookstores sell clothing, credit unions operate travel agencies, YMCAs run health clubs, and universities operate veterinary clinics.[5] In 1950 Congress passed the first unrelated business income tax (UBIT), which assesses tax at corporate rates on income that NPOs derive from activities not substantially related to their charitable or tax-exempt mission.[6] UBIT requirements apply to all not-for-profit organizations and public colleges and universities except federal corporations and certain charitable trusts.

The IRS is primarily interested in how the unrelated business income was earned, not in how it is used, even if it is used to further the organization's tax-exempt purpose. **Unrelated business income** (UBI) is calculated as the gross income from an unrelated trade or business engaged in on a *regular* basis less directly connected expenses, certain net operating losses, and qualified charitable contributions. The first $1,000 of net unrelated business income is excluded from taxation. Unrelated trade or business activities are those that are *substantially* unrelated to carrying out the organization's

---

[4] IRC Sec. 509(a).

[5] See www.irs.gov/charities, then search for "UBIT" for general rules and current developments.

[6] IRC Secs. 511–513. Unrelated business income is also subject to the alternative minimum tax.

exempt purpose. The activities that must be carefully examined include sponsorships, advertising, affinity credit card arrangements, sale of mailing lists, travel tour services, and fund-raising events.

To determine whether the business activity is substantially related to the organization's exempt purpose, the relationship between the business activity and the exempt purpose is examined. Unrelated business income does not include dividends, interest, royalties, fees for use of intangible property, and gains on the sale of property (unless that property was used in an unrelated trade or business), or income from activities in which substantially all of the work is done by volunteers, income from the sale of donated merchandise, income from legally conducted games of chance, rents from real property, or when the trade is conducted primarily for the convenience of its members, such as a laundry in a college dorm. However, rents from debt-financed property, rents based on a percentage of net income rather than gross income, and rents on personal property are considered to be unrelated business income. Excluded from UBI is income from advertising done in the form of corporate sponsorships for particular events if (1) the corporate sponsor does not get any substantial benefit in return for its payment other than the promotion of its name, (2) the display does not advertise the company's products or services, and (3) the amount of payment is not contingent on the level of attendance at the event.[7] Corporate sponsorships that appear in regularly published periodicals are still UBI. Special rules apply to bingo and distribution of low-cost items, such as pens or stickers.

Feeder Organizations

NPOs may control a **feeder organization** that is organized to carry on a trade or business for the benefit of the exempt organization and remit its profits to the NPO. The income passed from the feeder to the not-for-profit organization in the form of interest, rents, royalties, and annuities is subject to unrelated business income tax. In 1997, Congress redefined *control* as more than 50 percent of the voting stock of a feeder organization, down from 80 percent, effectively classifying more income of NPOs as unrelated. Some activities not subject to the feeder organization rules are those that (1) generate rental income that would be excluded from rent for UBIT, (2) use volunteers for substantially all the work, and (3) sell merchandise that was substantially all received as contributions.

Unrelated Debt-Financed Income

If an NPO has income from an asset that is mortgaged or **debt-financed income,** for example, rental of real estate, that income is UBI. The unrelated business income is the total income times the proportion to which the property is financed by debt. There are many exceptions to this general rule, such as property that is substantially used to achieve the organization's exempt purpose.

Political Activity

Early legislative attempts at restricting political activity of public charities were intended to deny a charitable contribution income tax deduction for a selfish contribution made merely to advance the personal interests of the donor. If any of the activities of the NPO consists of participating in any political campaign on behalf of (or in opposition to) any candidate for public office, the organization will not qualify for tax-exempt status. This includes publishing or distributing political statements. However, the facts and circumstances on the amount of money, time, and energy spent on each case determine

---

[7] This change came about in the Taxpayer Relief Act of 1997 and was a codification of proposed IRS regulations from prior years.

whether the organization can be tax-exempt. For example, certain voter education activities or public forums conducted in a nonpartisan manner may not be considered prohibited political activity. The key is whether the activities encouraged people to vote for or against a particular candidate, even if that was not the intent of the NPO.

Legislative Activities

While the political activities described above are absolutely barred for charitable entities, a different set of rules applies to lobbying or legislative activities, and these rules are different at the federal and state levels. The general rule is that no substantial part of a charity's activities may involve conducting propaganda or otherwise attempting to influence legislation. **Propaganda** is information skewed toward a particular belief with a tendency to have little or no factual basis. **Legislation** is generally action by Congress, a state legislative body, or a local council to establish laws, statutes, and ordinances.

If an organization passes the "no *substantial* amount of propaganda or influencing legislation" hurdle and is granted tax-exempt status, it still faces limitations on the amount of political activity it can conduct. The severest penalty is loss of tax-exempt status. Less extreme is a tax on excessive political expenditures.[8] An exempt organization other than a church is allowed to make limited expenditures to influence legislation if properly elected on Form 5786.[9] A permissible amount of **direct lobbying** (i.e., testifying at legislative hearings, corresponding or conferring with legislators or their staffs, or publishing documents advocating specific legislative action) is allowed, up to a ceiling calculated to allow for **grass-roots lobbying** (i.e., an appeal to the general public to contact legislators or to take other action regarding a legislative matter), but not to exceed $1 million in any one year. "Influencing legislation" does not include distributing nonpartisan studies, providing technical advice to a governmental body, opposing legislation that negatively affects the organization, exchanging information among organization members, and communicating on routine matters with governmental officials. The annual Form 990 provides a significant amount of information on legislative and political activities. Federal penalties for excess political activity are in addition to those that might be assessed by a state for lobbying.

Sec. 527 Political Organizations

Political action committees (PACs), political parties, and campaign committees for candidates for government office are considered **political organizations** and are subject to special reporting and disclosures requirements. In 2000, Congress passed P.L. 106-230 as part of campaign financing reform, which imposes three requirements on political organizations: (1) provide an initial notice to the IRS that an organization is to be treated as an IRC Sec. 527 organization, (2) make periodic reports with the names and addresses of persons contributing more than $200 and persons receiving expenditures of more than $500, and (3) file other modified annual returns including an expansion of organizations required to file Form 1120-POL. The IRS implemented a voluntary compliance program to promote disclosure and reporting by these Sec. 527 organizations.[10]

Intermediate Sanctions

The preceding sections identified sanctions for specific prohibited or excessive activities by exempt organizations, but until recently, the only sanction for excessive economic

---

[8] IRC Sec. 4955.

[9] IRC Sec. 501(h).

[10] IRS Notice 2004–110, August 19, 2004.

benefits received by officers of NPOs was revocation of the organization's tax-exempt status. This drastic measure was seldom used. In 1996 Congress gave the IRS a new weapon in the Taxpayer Bill of Rights 2.[11] **Intermediate sanctions** for private inurement resulting from excess economic benefit transactions are penalties assessed when a transaction confers a substantial benefit on a disqualified person. A **disqualified person** is one who has substantial influence over the organization's affairs. Examples of **excess benefit transactions** include unreasonable compensation, sales of assets at bargain prices, and lease arrangements.[12] The law applies to public charities but may be extended to other classifications of exempt organizations. The first-tier penalty is a tax of 25 percent of the excess benefit on the disqualified person in addition to repayment of the excess benefit. If the organization's managers are aware the transaction is improper, the NPO is assessed a tax of 10 percent of the excess benefit (up to a maximum of $10,000 per transaction). A second-tier penalty of 200 percent of the excess benefit is assessed on the disqualified person if the transaction is not corrected within the taxable period. Careful structuring of management compensation contracts along with documentation of comparable salaries of similar positions is critical in avoiding intermediate sanctions.

Reorganization and Dissolution

If an NPO finds that the societal needs initially described in the tax-exemption application are no longer met, it may redefine its mission, merge, or choose to dissolve the organization. It is not unusual for not-for-profit entities, particularly in the health care industry, to merge with other NPOs or associate with for-profit organizations. Mergers may be to achieve optimal **economic size** (i.e., the minimum possible size to be able to provide services without long-term damage to its financial base) or to integrate services. Many grantors fund only pilot programs, which results in NPOs looking for financial resources after the start-up phase of the organization.[13] Accounting issues involved in a reorganization include the merging of two information systems, measuring costs and benefits, **due diligence** (i.e., the formal disclosing and discovery of all relevant information, particularly about risks), and the surviving audit firm's reliance on the work of the former auditor. Accountants along with legal and financial consultants play a key role in the process of reorganizing or dissolving an NPO.

The accounting issues involved in a dissolution include ensuring that (1) all creditors are paid, (2) all federal, state, and local taxes are paid, and (3) all assets are appropriately transferred (e.g., to another tax-exempt organization). If the incorporating documents are silent about the distribution of assets, state law or IRS regulations dictate. The IRS has said that if an NPO liquidates, dissolves, or terminates, its assets have to be distributed for another exempt purpose or be given to the federal or a state or local government.[14] Involuntary dissolution may come for failure to file an annual report or as a result of a state attorney general's determination of fraud or unlawful conduct.

Emerging Issues

In testimony to Congress in 2004, the IRS commissioner declared that one of the service's four enforcement initiatives was related to enforcing regulations in the tax-exempt

---

[11] U.S. Congress, H.R. 2337, July 30, 1996.

[12] IRC Sec. 4958.

[13] David LaPiana, *The Leaders' Guide to Considering, Negotiating and Executing a Merger* (Washington, D.C.: Boardsource), 2000.

[14] Rev. Proc. 82-2, 1982-1 CB 367.

sector. Among the governance failures that the IRS is investigating in its oversight role are business contracts with related parties, unreasonably high executive compensation, loans to executives, and credit counseling organizations. Joint efforts between federal (e.g., IRS) and state agencies (e.g., National Association of State Charity Officers) to enforce existing regulations are expected to reduce abusive transactions on the part of not-for-profit managers. Often these breaches of ethics and conflicts of interest arise in an organization with weak internal controls and ineffective oversight by governing bodies.[15]

In 2005 Congress was considering other legislation that would require increased reporting and disclosure on the part of tax-exempt entities. The stated rationale for increasing federal attention on the not-for-profit, tax-exempt sector is often framed in extending the Sarbanes-Oxley Act of 2002, which requires publicly traded corporations to improve internal controls and accountability on the part of corporate managers and boards. NPOs essentially receive a public subsidy to operate programs when granted an exemption from federal income tax, and, as such, are held to a high standard of accountability by Congress and the IRS.

GOVERNANCE

Managers of tax-exempt, not-for-profit organizations are directly accountable to the board of the organization, which in turn is ultimately responsible to the public and governmental oversight bodies. This relationship is not different from that among corporate managers, boards of directors, and stockholders. What is different, however, is the importance of incorporating documents that define the philanthropic or not-for-profit mission of the organization and the (sometimes underestimated) responsibilities of board members who may be invited to serve on the board, without compensation, more for their fund-raising ability than their financial management expertise.

Incorporating Documents

The incorporating documents include the articles of incorporation, which have an external focus and describe the purpose of the organization without being too restrictive, and the by-laws, which have an internal focus and describe the functional rules of the organization. Other important documents to the accountant include minutes of board meetings (i.e., the legal history of the organization) and written policies. They establish the charitable or exempt purpose for which the organization was organized and for which it should be held accountable. Expectations of resource providers, such as donors and grantors, as well as federal and state governments requiring reporting on the financial management of assets devoted to the exempt purpose, are revealed in these documents. State laws may govern the type of information that must be included in some of these documents; for example, the articles of incorporation are required to list name, purpose, organizational activities, registered office, and the incorporators.

Not-for-profit corporations can take the form of (1) membership in which there is voting or nonvoting stock (for example, property owners association) or (2) directorship when the board is self-perpetuating (i.e., it elects itself). In the case of a directorship there is little threat of removal by the membership at large. The significance of the form of the not-for-profit corporation for accountants is that the stakeholders or

---

[15] Testimony to the Committee on Finance, U.S. Senate: Hearing on Charitable Giving Problems and Best Practices, by Mark W. Everson, Commissioner of Internal Revenue, IR-2004-81, June 22, 2004.

users of financial information and their needs may differ depending on the organizational form.

Board Membership

Board members are responsible for all authorized activities generating financial support on the organization's behalf.[16] They set policy and provide fiscal guidance and ongoing governance. Characteristics of a quality board include diversity, leadership, sensitivity, direction, and, probably the most important, the ability of each member to contribute and attract funds. Treasurers of boards have specific duties articulated in the incorporating documents that require them to have custody of corporate funds and securities, keep full and accurate records of all receipts and disbursements, and deposit money and valuables in designated depositories until funds are authorized to be disbursed. Internal board members, managers, and employees of the organization may have competing objectives from those of external board members who are outside the daily operations of the organization and who have no financial stake in the organization. Board members may carry errors and omissions insurance and require that indemnification clauses be included in the articles of incorporation to protect them from lawsuits.

To satisfy its fiduciary responsibilities, the board should require managers to regularly summarize the activities of administering the entity. It should regularly review the organization's policies, programs, and operations. Incentive performance contracts can be made with managers to encourage certain goals and outcomes. By-laws or policies may call for continuous quality improvement so boards can assess performance against benchmarks and predetermined performance goals.

BENCHMARKING AND PERFORMANCE MEASURES

Oversight bodies, such as boards of directors, not-for-profit watchdog agencies, and an increasing number of states, are tracking performance measures of exempt organizations. Financial and operational results are compared to specified performance targets as well as benchmarked to comparable organizations in the industry. Not-for-profit agencies collecting information about entities in the not-for-profit sector include the BBB Wise Giving Alliance, the American Institute of Philanthropy, the Tax-Exempt/Government Entities (TE/GE) Division of the IRS, Independent Sector, and the Urban Institute among other regional associations supporting NPOs.[17] These organizations are likely to provide standards for charitable solicitation useful for donors, but information necessary to benchmark one NPO to its peer organizations or other organizations is just at the early stages of development in the not-for-profit sector.

Generally, NPOs need to demonstrate accountability to their stakeholders for effective and efficient operations, compliance with laws and regulations, financial management (short and long-term), fiduciary responsibility of managers and board members, sustainability of the organization over time, and community impact or "making a difference." Illustration 15–5 shows some financial ratios that can be computed from

---

[16] Boardsource, *Twelve Principles of Governance That Power Exceptional Boards* (Washington, D.C.: Boardsource), 2005.

[17] The respective Web sites of these organizations are http://www.give.org, www.charitywatch.org, www.irs.gov, www.independentsector.org, and www.nccs.urban.org. One regional organization that provides much information for users and preparers of NPO financial information is the Maryland Association of Nonprofit Organizations at http://www.standardsforexcellence.org.

ILLUSTRATION 15–5   **Performance Indicators**

Type of Ratio	Indicator	Ratio
Liquidity	Can the organization pay its current debts?	$\dfrac{\text{Current assets (cash, A/R, inventory)}}{\text{Current liabilities}}$ $\dfrac{\text{Quick assets (cash and A/R)}}{\text{Current liabilities}}$
Going concern	Are revenues sufficient to cover expenses?	$\dfrac{\text{Revenues}}{\text{Expenses}}$
	How many months of operating expenses can be covered by unrestricted net assets?	$\dfrac{\text{Unrestricted net assets}}{\text{Operating expenses}}$
Capital structure	Does the organization rely more on debt or equity to finance its operations?	$\dfrac{\text{Debt}}{\text{Total assets}}$ $\dfrac{\text{Debt}}{\text{Net assets}}$
Program effectiveness	Is an appropriate amount spent on accomplishing the NPO's goals?	$\dfrac{\text{Program expenses}}{\text{Total expenses}}$
Efficiency	Is the cost per achieved outcome decreasing over time?	$\dfrac{\text{Program expenses}}{\text{Number of clients served}}$
Leverage and debt coverage	Is the debt service expense adequately covered by income?	$\dfrac{\text{Revenue, support, gain plus interest and depreciation expense}}{\text{Annual debt service expense}}$
Fund-raising efficiency	Are contributions received appropriately higher than the cost of raising those funds?	$\dfrac{\text{Public support}}{\text{Fund-raising expenses}}$
Investment performance	Are earnings on investments (unrealized and realized gains and losses and investment income) on target?	$\dfrac{\text{Budgeted total return on investments}}{\text{Actual total return on investments}}$

financial statement information and used as performance indicators that can be tracked over time and shared with stakeholders.

Several limitations of financial ratio analysis should be considered. For instance, donors may incorrectly assume that federal and state laws govern the percentage of annual revenue that a charity must spend on its programs or that there are limits on the percentage of revenue that is spent on fund-raising. Another limitation is the lack of benchmarks for comparable not-for-profit organizations that provide generally accepted targets for fund-raising efficiency, debt coverage, and capital structure, among other financial ratios. The percentage of total expenses spent on the program, rather than supporting the program, is such a well-publicized measure of effectiveness that organizations are quite careful to allocate as much to the program category as possible. At issue has been the joint costs of advocacy or educational materials that have a fund-raising appeal. As explained in Chapter 14, the AICPA's *SOP 98-2* restricts the amount of such costs that can be classified as program expenses. Another way to increase the proportion of program expenses to total expenses is to recognize the fair value of **gifts in kind** (i.e., contributions of tangible items) and contributed services used in the operations of the program as expenses. Generally accepted accounting principles do require that this type of gift be recognized as both income and expense if fair value can be objectively determined, expenses would have been incurred even without the donation, nonfinancial assets are enhanced or specialized skills are required, and amounts are material.[18] At issue is whether fair market value is objective, particularly

[18] AICPA, Accounting and Audit Guide, *Not-for-Profit Organizations,* pars. 5.39–5.46.

ILLUSTRATION 15–6   **Ten Largest NPOs and Selected Performance Measures (2003)**

R a n k		Size = Total Revenue (in millions)	Size = Public Support (in millions)	Program Spending as a Percent of Total Income	Program Spending as a Percent of Total Expenses	$ of Public Support Raised for every $1 of Fund-raising Expense
1	YMCAs in the United States	$4,657	$ 757	76%	82%	$ 9.90
2	American Red Cross	3,019	587	101	91	4.78
3	Catholic Charities USA	2,859	473	79	89	14.48
4	Salvation Army	2,846	1,217	39	84	9.85
5	United Jewish Communities	2,276	1,779	82	85	8.68
6	Goodwill Industries International	2,215	360	84	88	31.25
7	Shriners Hospitals for Children	1,389	286	35	92	18.53
8	Boys & Girls Club of America	1,151	501	77	83	9.95
9	American Cancer Society	836	794	73	71	6.72
10	Gifts in Kind International	791	787	100	99	4,706.86

Source : "The NPT Top 100," *The Nonprofit Times,* November 2004, www.nptimes.com.

for corporate contributions of obsolete inventory. If it is overstated, the public interest is not served.

Form 990 provides a substantial amount of information that can be used in evaluating tax-exempt entities; however, this information is not audited. In addition to financial information, the form asks questions about self-dealing by key officers and for a description of significant program service accomplishments in the charity's own words. Illustration 15–6 provides several performance measures for some of the nation's largest public charities based on total revenues.

As the federal government requires outcome and performance measures of its agencies, we should expect those agencies to require the same information from the organizations that receive public funds. Many NPOs are voluntarily reporting some type of service efforts and accomplishments in their annual reports. As this practice becomes more widespread, NPOs are expected to report similar statistics to stay competitive for charitable gifts.

SUMMARY

This chapter provides a general description of tax laws and other state and federal regulations so that accountants and decision makers using financial information are familiar with the environment within which tax-exempt organizations operate. It should be clear that a thorough understanding of current case law about exempt organizations is also important but outside the scope of this text. More specific details are available in Internal Revenue Service literature available on its Web site (www.irs.ustreas.gov) and books on taxation of tax-exempt organizations. In the future, NPOs can expect increased scrutiny and accountability for performance outcomes as a more well-informed public demands it and as technology enables government agencies, such as the IRS, to audit and monitor tax-exempt organizations.

Key Terms

Charitable solicitation, *603*
Debt-financed income, *610*
Direct lobbying, *611*
Disqualified person, *612*
Due diligence, *612*
Economic size, *612*
Excess benefit transaction, *612*
Expenditure responsibility, *609*

External support test, *609*
Federated fund-raising organization, *607*
Feeder organization, *610*
Gifts in kind, *615*
Grass-roots lobbying, *611*
Influencing, *604*
Intermediate sanctions, *612*
Internal support test, *609*
Legislation, *611*

Lobbying, *604*
Organizational test, *606*
Political organization, *611*
Private foundation, *608*
Propaganda, *611*
Public charity, *609*
Unrelated business income, *609*

Selected References

Accounting Aid Society. *Michigan Nonprofit Management Manual,* 4th ed. Detroit, MI: Accounting Aid Society, 2004.

Gross, Malvern J. Jr., John H. McCarthy, and Nancy E. Shelmon. *Financial and Accounting Guide for Not-for-Profit Organizations.* 7th ed. New York: John Wiley & Sons, 2005.

Internal Revenue Service, Department of Treasury. *Application for Recognition of Exemption under Sec. 501(c)(3) of the Internal Revenue Code.* Package 1023.

_____. Pub. 557. *Tax-Exempt Status for Your Organization.*

_____. Pub. 78. *Cumulative List of Exempt Organizations.*

Lampkin, Linda M., and Thomas H. Pollak. *The New Nonprofit Almanac and Desk Reference.* Washington, DC: The Urban Institute Press, 2002.

Ober Kaler. *The Nonprofit Legal Landscape.* Washington, D.C.: Boardsource, 2005.

Perlman, Seth. *State Fund-Raising Regulation: Registration Forms, Requirements, and Procedures.* New York: John Wiley & Sons, 2001.

Periodicals

Chronicle of Philanthropy. http://philanthropy.com.
Journal of Nonprofit Management and Leadership, Jossey-Bass.
Nonprofit Sector and Voluntary Quarterly, Association for Research on Nonprofit Organizations and Voluntary Action (ARNOVA).
The Exempt Organization Tax Review. Tax Analysts.
The Nonprofit Times. http://www.nptimes.com.

Questions

15–1. Why should an auditor understand the laws and regulations that apply to the activities of not-for-profit organizations?

15–2. Why does a state have regulatory authority over a not-for-profit organization? Name some of the activities of a not-for-profit organization that a state regulates.

15–3. Why is a not-for-profit organization accountable to the federal government? What are some of the federal laws that govern not-for-profit organizations, and how does an NPO demonstrate compliance with these laws?

15–4. Under which statutory authority are the following public charities most likely to be exempt from federal income tax? (*Hint:* Use Illustration 15–3 as a guide in answering this question.)
   a. Association of Professional Bus Drivers.
   b. American Allergy Association.

    c. Evergreen Country Club.

    d. Perpetual Light Cemetery.

    e. Idaho Credit Union.

    f. Greenville City Civic League.

15–5. Is a public charity in the public sector? Why or why not? Describe the basic differences between public charities and private foundations. Which of these two types of tax-exempt entities receives the most preferential tax treatment under federal laws? Why?

15–6. Describe the limitations on political activity and lobbying that are placed on tax-exempt organizations by the federal government. What is the purpose of an IRC Sec. 527 organization?

15–7. How can a not-for-profit museum ensure that its gift shop activities will not result in an unrelated business income tax liability?

15–8. Why are the "intermediate sanction" regulations an important tool for the IRS to use in curbing abuses such as excessive management compensation?

15–9. Describe information that tax-exempt entities provide to the IRS on the annual Form 990. How can a potential donor obtain this information to use in evaluating an organization when making a donation decision?

15–10. What incorporating documents should an auditor examine in conducting an audit or preparing an annual Form 990 tax-return of a not-for-profit organization? What information in these documents is most useful to stakeholders external to the not-for-profit organization?

Cases

15–1 Establishing a Not-for-Profit Organization. As a certified public accountant, you have been asked by a group of local citizens to assist in establishing a not-for-profit organization for the purpose of raising funds to keep their neighborhood safe and clean. These people are concerned about the growing crime rate and increased amount of trash and traffic in their community. They believe that a collaborative effort is needed to address these problems.

Required

a. Prepare a memo to the group that outlines the process involved in creating a tax-exempt not-for-profit entity. Be sure to point out particular alternative strategies, including the advantages and disadvantages you believe the incorporating officers should spend time considering.

b. What resources are available on the Internet to help this group understand the regulatory, taxation, and performance measure issues that they will face as officers of a tax-exempt, not-for-profit organization?

15–2 Unrelated Business Income Tax. Dan Smith is a certified human resource manager who serves on the board of a local professional association of human resource managers. The association puts on an annual conference for its members at which there are educational workshops, keynote speakers, and a display of vendors that serve the needs of human resource managers. This year, the association has decided to allow vendors to advertise in the annual meeting publication for a fee. Mr. Smith is unsure whether the benefits of allowing this advertising outweigh the potential costs if this income is subject to unrelated business income tax. As a result, Mr. Smith has asked your assistance, as an accounting student, in analyzing the costs and benefits of this proposal.

Required

a. Create a list of questions to pose to the executive director of the association about the proposed advertising so that the board has all the relevant facts on hand.

b. What resources are available to investigate whether income from advertising is subject to unrelated business income tax?

c. Prepare a memo to Mr. Smith that outlines the key issues involved in the proposal and suggest an approach to analyzing whether the proposal is in the best interests of the professional association.

15–3 Internet Case—Performance Measures. Go to the Internet Web sites of five of the largest charitable organizations listed in Illustration 15–6 and search for financial information and performance measures they may disclose on their Web sites.

Required

a. Locate a comparable organization for each of these five NPOs, perhaps a competitor. From information provided on the Web sites, calculate the amount that each organization spent on its program (as a percentage of income and of total expenses) as well as the number of dollars it raised for each dollar spent on fund-raising.

b. Select other financial performance measures from Illustration 15–5, calculate those measures, and compare pairs of organizations. Where could you get other useful information?

c. Prepare a table showing the five charities, their counterparts, and performance measures for each. Which charity would you consider the most efficient and effective? Why?

15–4 Charitable Giving in Times of Crises. Tragic events in the recent past, including September 11, 2001, the tsunami of 2004, and Hurricane Katrina in 2005, brought billions of charitable contributions into not-for-profit human service agencies in a short period of time. In the aftermath of such tragedies, the public expects a high level of accountability by these NPOs for the use of these charitable funds. The accounting systems and internal controls in place in these NPOs can be severely taxed in accounting for a large supply and demand of charitable funds over a relatively short time period.

Required

a. Review the Web sites of the major human service agencies that respond to the needs of victims of natural and man-made disasters. Do you see evidence of strong internal controls over the receipt and use of charitable funds that are received by these organizations in response to a crisis? Discuss.

b. Investigate the Charities & Non-Profits section of the IRS Web site (www.irs.ustreas.gov) and locate not-for-profit organizations that were formed specifically to help victims in certain tragedies. (*Hint:* Search the online version of Publication 78, *Cumulative List of Exempt Organizations.*) Go to the Web site of one or two of these organizations and see whether they describe their processes for ensuring accountability over the restricted contributions that they receive. Discuss the life expectancy of these organizations that were created with a narrow purpose.

Exercises and Problems

15–1 Multiple Choice. Choose the best answer.

1. The incorporating documents that have an external focus and describe the legal structure of the organization are called
   a. By-laws.
   b. Policies and procedures.

    c. Minutes of the board meetings.

    d. Articles of incorporation.

2. Which of the following is a true statement about IRS Form 990?

    a. All not-for-profit organizations must prepare one.

    b. It is an information return prepared by all tax-exempt not-for-profit organizations.

    c. It is required of all organizations exempt under IRC Sec. 501 that have gross receipts of more than $25,000 and that do not fall into an exception category.

    d. All of the above are correct.

3. Which term best describes the set of tax laws that allows the IRS to assess penalties against NPO managers who benefit excessively from certain transactions?

    a. Unrelated business income tax.

    b. Intermediate sanctions.

    c. Excess benefits excise tax.

    d. Tax-exempt penalties.

4. A measure of performance that would indicate that the organization is effectively accomplishing its mission is

    a. Program expense as a percent of total expenses.

    b. Current ratio.

    c. Return on investment.

    d. Number of contribution dollars raised as a percentage of fund-raising dollars spent.

5. A tax-exempt organization that receives its support primarily from a small number of individuals or corporations and a large percentage from investment income is called a

    a. Public charity.

    b. Private foundation.

    c. Public foundation.

    d. Voluntary health and welfare organization.

6. Which of the following is a reason that a charitable NPO might fail to qualify for tax-exempt status?

    a. Its officers are paid excessive wages.

    b. It is operated primarily for the benefit of its members.

    c. It has unrelated business income.

    d. Its primary purpose is to promote the passage of legislation favorable to institutions of higher learning.

7. Which of the following organizations is most likely to qualify for tax-exempt status as a not-for-profit organization under IRC Sec. 501(c)(3)?

    a. Association of Behavioral Therapists.

    b. Beta Gamma Omega fraternity.

    c. City of Westland.

    d. Tiny Tot Pre-School.

8. Which of the following is a characteristic of public charities but *not* private foundations?

    a. They are exempt from federal income taxes under IRC Sec. 501(c)(3).

    b. They are supported by a broad set of donors and organized to meet the public good.

   c. They are subject to excise taxes on certain prohibited transactions, such as self-dealing.

   d. They may not participate in any political campaign on behalf of a candidate for public office.

9. Which of the following is an important reason that board members of a not-for-profit agency should be familiar with the laws and regulations that impact the organization?

   a. They have a fiduciary responsibility to ensure that the not-for-profit organization complies with all laws and regulations.

   b. They have a legal responsibility to ensure that the not-for-profit organization complies with all laws and regulations.

   c. They have a responsibility to management to provide on-going fiscal governance as well as direction.

   d. All of the above.

10. Form 990, the annual reporting form that an exempt entity submits to the IRS, must contain which of the following information items?

    a. Compensation of the five highest paid independent contractors.

    b. Home addresses of the officers and directors.

    c. Statement of cash flows.

    d. None of the above.

15–2 Public Charity. The Kids Club of Washtenaw County is a public charity under IRC Sec. 501(c)(3). It had total support last year of the following:

United Way support	$ 80,000
Grant from Washtenaw County	70,000
Contributions	350,000
Investment income	75,000
	$575,000

Of the $350,000 received from contributors, $250,000 came from five contributors, each of whom gave more than $5,000; the other $100,000 came from small individual contributors.

Required

a. Calculate the total amount of support that qualifies as "public support" in meeting the external support test to escape private foundation status.

b. Is the organization considered a public charity or a private foundation? Why?

c. If the organization had received an additional $140,000 grant from one individual during the year, would the NPO still be classified the same as your response to part *b* (assuming that the previous five gifts still represent more than 1 percent of the new total)?

15–3 Lobbying Expenses. EarthFriendly, Inc., an IRC Sec. 501(c)(3) organization, incurred lobbying expenses of $150,000 and exempt purpose expenditures of $1.2 million in carrying out its exempt mission.

Required

a. What are the tax consequences if the organization does not elect to participate in lobbying activities on a limited basis?

b. Discuss the factors involved in the association's decision to elect to participate in lobbying activities under IRC Sec. 501(h).

15–4 Unrelated Business Income Tax. The Lewis and Clark Association has a mailing list of 15,000 members, donors, catalog purchasers, and other supporters of the association and its mission, which is to educate the public about the historic expedition to the West from the eastern United States in the early 1800s. Revenue from the sale of this list to for-profit companies for use in their promotional activities previously averaged $5,000. This year, because of a television special about the historic journey, revenue from sales of the list jumped to $86,000. The accountant recently attended a workshop on tax issues for not-for-profit organizations and learned about unrelated business income tax. She is now concerned that this revenue is subject to that tax.

Required
a. Consider the facts of this case and the unrelated business income tax rules. Is the association liable for unrelated business income tax?
b. What if next year the revenue from sales of the mailing list increases to $286,000? Would the association then have unrelated business income?

15–5 Gift Shop UBIT. A local exempt organization that trains at-risk youth for employment has an annual operating budget of $300,000, which includes revenue from operating a gift shop in a nearby hotel lobby. Gift shop sales result in a profit of $15,000. The organization has $6,500 of endowment income that it earns on permanently restricted net assets. The income from both the gift shop and the endowment is used to support the organization's exempt purpose. The balance of $278,500 required for annual operations is provided through public support and charges for services.

Required
a. Calculate the UBIT if the corporate tax rate is 15 percent on the first $50,000 of net income and 25 percent on the next $25,000 of income.
b. Assume that the endowment income is reinvested rather than being used to support annual operations. Calculate the amount of unrelated business income.

15–6 Intermediate Sanctions. For each of the following independent situations, determine whether the organization is at risk for receiving intermediate sanctions from the Internal Revenue Service for conferring excess economic benefits on disqualified persons. If so, indicate how the organization can minimize those sanctions.
1. Jane is president of an IRC Sec. 501(c)(3) public charity and personally owns a building that she has decided to sell to the not-for-profit organization. The appraisal value is $200,000, and the agreed-upon selling price is $250,000.
2. A large public charity is very happy with its president's performance and offers him a new compensation agreement for the coming year. He will receive a base salary plus a percentage of the increase in the gross revenues of the organization with no limitation as to the maximum amount.
3. Ann is a member and the director of a symphony association. She receives 20 free admission tickets as a member of the organization.
4. The local chapter of the United Way recently hired Joe Curtis as its new president at a salary of $200,000. The outgoing president was paid $150,000. Mr. Curtis had other offers that ranged from $95,000 to $190,000. The minutes of the meeting reflected that he was exceptionally talented and would not have accepted the position for a lower salary.

15–7 Mergers. Two not-for-profit organizations that serve disabled and disadvantaged individuals with housing needs have been collaborating for several years and are now considering a legal merger. They believe they can significantly reduce support expenses, such as general and administrative and fund-raising expenses, resulting in more funds available to meet the needs of the populations they serve. What financial and accounting issues should they consider in their decision to either dissolve one entity or merge the two?

15–8 Performance Measures. Information from the consolidated Form 990 for the American National Red Cross (including its constituent chapters and branches) for the fiscal year ending June 30, 2004, follows. The full text of the Form 990 is available at www.redcross.org or www.guidestar.org.

Required

a. Compute the following performance measures using Form 990 data presented in this exercise and comment on what information they convey to a potential donor without comparing them to prior years or other comparable agencies.
   1. Current ratio—liquidity.
   2. Revenues/expenses—going concern.
   3. Program expenses/total expenses—program effectiveness.
   4. Public support/fund-raising expenses—fund-raising efficiency.
   5. Investment performance.
b. Obtain the audited annual financial statement for the American National Red Cross for fiscal year 2004 from www.redcross.org. Calculate the same ratios listed in requirement a. Comment on any differences. Note: Use the most recent year for which both audited financial statements and Form 990 are readily available.
c. Discuss the advantages of analyzing financial performance using audited annual financial statement information versus IRS Form 990 information.

AMERICAN NATIONAL RED CROSS
AND ITS CONSTITUENT CHAPTERS AND BRANCHES

Form **990**	**Return of Organization Exempt From Income Tax**	OMB No. 1545-0047
	Under section 501(c), 527, or 4947(a)(1) of the Internal Revenue Code (except black lung benefit trust or private foundation)	**2004**
Department of the Treasury Internal Revenue Service	▶ The organization may have to use a copy of this return to satisfy state reporting requirements.	**Open to Public Inspection**

A For the 2004 calendar year, or tax year beginning _____, 2004, and ending _____, 20____

B Check if applicable:
- ☐ Address change
- ☐ Name change
- ☐ Initial return
- ☐ Final return
- ☐ Amended return
- ☐ Application pending

Please use IRS label or print or type. See Specific Instructions.

C Name of organization

Number and street (or P.O. box if mail is not delivered to street address) | Room/suite

City or town, state or country, and ZIP + 4

D Employer identification number

E Telephone number ( )

F Accounting method: ☐ Cash ☐ Accrual ☐ Other (specify) ▶

● Section 501(c)(3) organizations and 4947(a)(1) nonexempt charitable trusts must attach a completed Schedule A (Form 990 or 990-EZ).

G Website: ▶

J Organization type (check only one) ▶ ☐ 501(c) ( ) ◀ (insert no.) ☐ 4947(a)(1) or ☐ 527

K Check here ▶ ☐ if the organization's gross receipts are normally not more than $25,000. The organization need not file a return with the IRS; but if the organization received a Form 990 Package in the mail, it should file a return without financial data. Some states require a complete return.

H and **I** are not applicable to section 527 organizations.
- **H(a)** Is this a group return for affiliates? ☐ Yes ☐ No
- **H(b)** If "Yes," enter number of affiliates ▶ _____
- **H(c)** Are all affiliates included? ☐ Yes ☐ No (If "No," attach a list. See instructions.)
- **H(d)** Is this a separate return filed by an organization covered by a group ruling? ☐ Yes ☐ No
- **I** Group Exemption Number ▶
- **M** Check ▶ ☐ if the organization is **not** required to attach Sch. B (Form 990, 990-EZ, or 990-PF).

L Gross receipts: Add lines 6b, 8b, 9b, and 10b to line 12 ▶

Part I Revenue, Expenses, and Changes in Net Assets or Fund Balances (See page 18 of the instructions.)

1	Contributions, gifts, grants, and similar amounts received:			
a	Direct public support	1a	393,218,246	
b	Indirect public support	1b	163,835,709	
c	Government contributions (grants)	1c	60,642,338	
d	**Total** (add lines 1a through 1c) (cash $ 577,993,145 noncash $ 39,703,148)	1d		617,696,293
2	Program service revenue including government fees and contracts (from Part VII, line 93)	2		2,311,183,621
3	Membership dues and assessments	3		0
4	Interest on savings and temporary cash investments	4		135,756
5	Dividends and interest from securities	5		54,223,306
6a	Gross rents	6a	5,915,905	
b	Less: rental expenses	6b	3,172,849	
c	Net rental income or (loss) (subtract line 6b from line 6a)	6c		2,743,056
7	Other investment income (describe ▶)	7		0

		(A) Securities		(B) Other	
8a	Gross amount from sales of assets other than inventory	243,782,757	8a	16,432,640	
b	Less: cost or other basis and sales expenses	235,796,621	8b	4,668,134	
c	Gain or (loss) (attach schedule)	7,986,136	8c	11,764,506	
d	Net gain or (loss) (combine line 8c, columns (A) and (B))		8d		19,750,642

9	Special events and activities (attach schedule). If any amount is from **gaming,** check here ▶ ☐			
a	Gross revenue (not including $ 0 of contributions reported on line 1a)	9a	45,547,942	
b	Less: direct expenses other than fundraising expenses	9b	17,262,700	
c	Net income or (loss) from special events (subtract line 9b from line 9a)	9c		28,285,242
10a	Gross sales of inventory, less returns and allowances	10a	0	
b	Less: cost of goods sold	10b	0	
c	Gross profit or (loss) from sales of inventory (attach schedule) (subtract line 10b from line 10a)	10c		0
11	Other revenue (from Part VII, line 103)	11		31,523,440
12	**Total revenue** (add lines 1d, 2, 3, 4, 5, 6c, 7, 8d, 9c, 10c, and 11)	12		3,065,541,356

Expenses				
13	Program services (from line 44, column (B))	13		2,891,973,863
14	Management and general (from line 44, column (C))	14		170,345,765
15	Fundraising (from line 44, column (D))	15		111,178,153
16	Payments to affiliates (attach schedule)	16		0
17	**Total expenses** (add lines 16 and 44, column (A))	17		3,173,497,781

Net Assets				
18	Excess or (deficit) for the year (subtract line 17 from line 12)	18		(107,956,425)
19	Net assets or fund balances at beginning of year (from line 73, column (A))	19		2,166,816,327
20	Other changes in net assets or fund balances (attach explanation)	20		142,121,456
21	Net assets or fund balances at end of year (combine lines 18, 19, and 20)	21		2,200,981,358

For Privacy Act and Paperwork Reduction Act Notice, see the separate instructions.   Cat. No. 11282Y   Form **990** (2004)

Note: Selected information reproduced here.

624

AMERICAN NATIONAL RED CROSS
AND ITS CONSTITUENT CHAPTERS AND BRANCHES

Part II **Statement of Functional Expenses**　All organizations must complete column (A). Columns (B), (C), and (D) are required for section 501(c)(3) and (4) organizations and section 4947(a)(1) nonexempt charitable trusts but optional for others. (See page 22 of the instructions.)

	Do not include amounts reported on line 6b, 8b, 9b, 10b, or 16 of Part I.		**(A)** Total	**(B)** Program services	**(C)** Management and general	**(D)** Fundraising
22	Grants and allocations (attach schedule) . . (cash $ _____ noncash $ _____)	22	0			
23	Specific assistance to individuals (attach schedule)	23	118,433,399	118,433,399		
24	Benefits paid to or for members (attach schedule).	24	0	0		
25	Compensation of officers, directors, etc. . .	25	2,505,152	2,243,129	173,054	88,969
26	Other salaries and wages	26	1,251,368,525	1,120,483,525	86,443,495	44,441,505
27	Pension plan contributions	27	31,974,844	29,594,282	1,493,795	886,767
28	Other employee benefits	28	199,169,482	175,618,345	16,240,156	7,310,981
29	Payroll taxes	29	107,378,536	98,102,807	5,863,844	3,411,885
30	Professional fundraising fees	30	8,297,013	0	0	8,297,013
31	Accounting fees	31	5,494,556	2,348,263	2,928,997	217,296
32	Legal fees	32	12,556,828	11,463,155	1,045,782	47,891
33	Supplies	33	531,613,789	517,103,823	4,328,295	10,181,671
34	Telephone	34	31,377,373	28,566,707	1,619,664	1,191,002
35	Postage and shipping	35	54,797,755	48,132,335	1,063,413	5,602,007
36	Occupancy	36	94,617,735	91,284,761	1,305,448	2,027,526
37	Equipment rental and maintenance	37	28,892,621	25,059,031	2,968,858	864,732
38	Printing and publications	38	16,918,575	12,386,819	1,231,575	3,300,181
39	Travel	39	60,908,211	55,607,311	3,552,718	1,748,182
40	Conferences, conventions, and meetings .	40	5,098,749	3,389,270	1,038,007	671,472
41	Interest	41	34,598,563	31,554,552	2,707,767	336,244
42	Depreciation, depletion, etc. (attach schedule)	42	95,235,096	78,873,464	13,764,650	2,596,982
43	Other expenses not covered above (itemize): **a**	43a		0	0	0
b	**Minor Equipment**	43b	26,571,358	24,473,480	1,659,229	438,649
c	**Auto Rental & Maintenance**	43c	31,550,082	30,974,496	437,325	138,261
d	**Other Contractual Services**	43d	415,663,642	380,222,213	19,076,328	16,365,101
e	**Other Assistance**	43e	8,475,897	6,058,696	1,403,365	1,013,836
44	Total functional expenses (add lines 22 through 43). *Organizations completing columns (B)-(D), carry these totals to lines 13—15* .	44	3,173,497,781	2,891,973,863	170,345,765	111,178,153

Joint Costs. Check ▶ ☐ if you are following SOP 98-2.
Are any joint costs from a combined educational campaign and fundraising solicitation reported in **(B)** Program services? . ▶ ☐ **Yes** ☐ **No**
If "Yes," enter **(i)** the aggregate amount of these joint costs $_____; **(ii)** the amount allocated to Program services $_____;
(iii) the amount allocated to Management and general $_____; and **(iv)** the amount allocated to Fundraising $_____

Part III **Statement of Program Service Accomplishments** (See page 25 of the instructions.)

What is the organization's primary exempt purpose? ▶ --

	Program Service Expenses (Required for 501(c)(3) and (4) orgs., and 4947(a)(1) trusts; but optional for others.)
All organizations must describe their exempt purpose achievements in a clear and concise manner. State the number of clients served, publications issued, etc. Discuss achievements that are not measurable. (Section 501(c)(3) and (4) organizations and 4947(a)(1) nonexempt charitable trusts must also enter the amount of grants and allocations to others.)	
a .... (Grants and allocations　$　　　　　)	
b .... (Grants and allocations　$　　　　　)	
c .... (Grants and allocations　$　　　　　)	
d .... (Grants and allocations　$　　　　　)	
e Other program services (attach schedule)　(Grants and allocations　$　　　　　)	
f **Total of Program Service Expenses** (should equal line 44, column (B), Program services). . . . . ▶	

Note: Selected information reproduced here.

AMERICAN NATIONAL RED CROSS
AND ITS CONSTITUENT CHAPTERS AND BRANCHES

Part IV	**Balance Sheets** (See page 25 of the instructions.)					

	Note: *Where required, attached schedules and amounts within the description column should be for end-of-year amounts only.*			**(A)** Beginning of year		**(B)** End of year
Assets	**45** Cash—non-interest-bearing			157,731,882	**45**	117,193,945
	46 Savings and temporary cash investments			578,520,602	**46**	544,882,723
	47a Accounts receivable	**47a**	241,261,621			
	b Less: allowance for doubtful accounts	**47b**	6,984,922	239,218,332	**47c**	234,276,699
	48a Pledges receivable	**48a**	132,759,992			
	b Less: allowance for doubtful accounts	**48b**	1,763,078	140,659,982	**48c**	130,996,914
	49 Grants receivable			0	**49**	0
	50 Receivables from officers, directors, trustees, and key employees (attach schedule)			0	**50**	0
	51a Other notes and loans receivable (attach schedule)	**51a**	0			
	b Less: allowance for doubtful accounts	**51b**	0	0	**51c**	0
	52 Inventories for sale or use			170,920,391	**52**	169,353,654
	53 Prepaid expenses and deferred charges			89,567,004	**53**	74,297,120
	54 Investments—securities (attach schedule) ▶ ☐ Cost ☐ FMV			0	**54**	0
	55a Investments—land, buildings, and equipment: basis	**55a**				
	b Less: accumulated depreciation (attach schedule)	**55b**			**55c**	0
	56 Investments—other (attach schedule)			1,026,460,817	**56**	1,101,546,685
	57a Land, buildings, and equipment: basis	**57a**	1,794,300,918			
	b Less: accumulated depreciation (attach schedule)	**57b**	792,380,425	930,109,637	**57c**	1,001,920,493
	58 Other assets (describe ▶ _____)				**58**	
	59 **Total assets** (add lines 45 through 58) (must equal line 74)			3,333,188,647	**59**	3,374,468,233
Liabilities	**60** Accounts payable and accrued expenses			371,792,965	**60**	365,254,173
	61 Grants payable			0	**61**	0
	62 Deferred revenue			0	**62**	0
	63 Loans from officers, directors, trustees, and key employees (attach schedule)			0	**63**	0
	64a Tax-exempt bond liabilities (attach schedule)			223,291,949	**64a**	220,616,743
	b Mortgages and other notes payable (attach schedule)			197,125,402	**64b**	222,703,331
	65 Other liabilities (describe ▶ **Postretirement benefits, other liabilities**)			374,162,004	**65**	364,912,628
	66 **Total liabilities** (add lines 60 through 65)			1,166,372,320	**66**	1,173,486,875
Net Assets or Fund Balances	**Organizations that follow SFAS 117, check here ▶ ☒** and complete lines 67 through 69 and lines 73 and 74.					
	67 Unrestricted			1,292,937,231	**67**	1,359,126,009
	68 Temporarily restricted			470,273,486	**68**	412,800,255
	69 Permanently restricted			403,605,610	**69**	429,055,094
	Organizations that do not follow SFAS 117, check here ▶ ☐ and complete lines 70 through 74.					
	70 Capital stock, trust principal, or current funds				**70**	
	71 Paid-in or capital surplus, or land, building, and equipment fund				**71**	
	72 Retained earnings, endowment, accumulated income, or other funds				**72**	
	73 **Total net assets or fund balances** (add lines 67 through 69 **or** lines 70 through 72; column (A) **must** equal line 19; column (B) **must** equal line 21)			2,166,816,327	**73**	2,200,981,358
	74 **Total liabilities and net assets / fund balances** (add lines 66 and 73)			3,333,188,647	**74**	3,374,468,233

Form 990 is available for public inspection and, for some people, serves as the primary or sole source of information about a particular organization. How the public perceives an organization in such cases may be determined by the information presented on its return. Therefore, please make sure the return is complete and accurate and fully describes, in Part III, the organization's programs and accomplishments.

Chapter **Sixteen**

Accounting for Colleges and Universities

Learning Objectives

After studying this chapter, you should be able to:

1. Distinguish between generally accepted accounting principles for public and private colleges and universities.
2. Describe financial reporting for governmentally owned colleges and universities.
3. Discuss accounting and reporting issues for all colleges and universities, such as:
   Accounting for assets, liabilities, and net assets.
   Accounting for revenues and expenses.
   Accounting for cash flows.
4. Journalize transactions for private colleges and universities following *SFAS No. 116* and *SFAS No. 117*.
5. Prepare financial statements for governmentally owned colleges and universities following *GASBS 35.*
6. Prepare financial statements for private colleges and universities following *SFAS No. 117.*
7. Discuss managerial, auditing, and reporting issues, such as:
   Performance measures.
   Auditing.
   Federal financial assistance.
   Related entities.

Institutions of higher learning have long been dichotomized into public colleges and universities, which are governmental in nature, and private colleges and universities, which are nongovernmental not-for-profit organizations. In comparison, public institutions receive a significant share of their total revenues from state appropriations and research grants, whereas private institutions depend to a larger extent on student tuition and fees, private gifts, and research grants. Also governmental in nature, community colleges are supported in large part by local property tax assessments. More recently, a few for-profit corporations have joined the higher education market. The National Center for Education Statistics estimates that in 2001 there were more than 4,182 institutions of higher learning with $177 billion of current operating revenue and enrollment of 15.9 million students in the United States.[1]

[1] National Center for Education Statistics (NCES), *Digest of Education Statistics* (Washington, DC: Department of Education, 2003).

ACCOUNTING AND FINANCIAL REPORTING STANDARDS

For most of the 20th century, the majority of institutions in the higher education industry, without regard to their sources of financing, followed a single set of accounting and financial reporting standards. This guidance was described in the AICPA Audit Guide *Audits of Colleges and Universities* and included standards set by the American Institute of Certified Public Accountants (AICPA) in cooperation with committees of the National Association of College and University Business Officers (NACUBO) and task forces of groups related to the U.S. Department of Education.

In 1984, the GASB was given jurisdiction over accounting and financial reporting standards for public colleges and universities, as well as state and local governments and public schools. The FASB retained jurisdiction over accounting and financial reporting standards for private colleges and universities, and for for-profit businesses providing higher education. In 1991, the GASB issued a statement that allowed public colleges and universities to continue using the AICPA college guide model until comprehensive studies of governmental reporting models were completed.[2] The AICPA college guide model included six fund groups: current funds (unrestricted and restricted), loan funds, endowment and similar funds, annuity and life income funds, plant funds (composed of four subgroups), and agency funds.

Until 1993, with the exception that private colleges and universities were required by FASB *Statement No. 93* to report depreciation of their plant assets, most colleges and universities, both public and private, used the AICPA college guide model. The issuance of FASB *Statement No. 116,* "Accounting for Contributions Received and Contributions Made," and FASB *Statement No. 117,* "Financial Statements of Not-for-Profit Organizations," in 1993, marked a significant divergence in the accounting and reporting standards applicable to public and private colleges and universities.

Statement Nos. 116 and *117* require private colleges and universities to report on the net assets of the entity as a whole rather than reporting on fund groups as prescribed in the AICPA college guide model. This change was made to standardize the way all nongovernmental not-for-profit entities report to the public and to make them report more like businesses and less like governments. An important presumption was that decision makers would find this format more useful, even though comparability between public and private universities would be made more difficult.[3]

After much due process that included a Research Report (1988), Invitation to Comment (1994), public hearings, user focus groups, task forces, mail surveys, Preliminary Views (1995), and two Exposure Drafts (1997 and 1999), the GASB issued *GASBS 35,* "Basic Financial Statements—and Management's Discussion and Analysis—for Public Colleges and Universities," in November 1999.[4] This statement amends *GASBS 34* to include public colleges and universities as special-purpose governments and possibly enterprise funds or component units of another governmental entity. Comparability between public and private entities is again possible as a result of *GASBS 34* and *35*'s added emphasis on accrual accounting and net assets. Due to the changes in college and university accounting brought about by FASB and GASB standards, the

[2] GASB, *Codification,* Sec. Co5.101.

[3] John H. Engstrom and Connie Esmond-Kiger, "Different Formats, Same User Needs: Do the FASB and GASB College and University Reporting Models Meet User Needs?" *Accounting Horizons* 11 (September 1997), pp. 16–34.

[4] See Appendices A and B in *GASBS 35* for details on the due process and other background information, pars. 13–20.

AICPA no longer issues a separate audit guide for colleges and universities, instead the relevant guidance is in the AICPA Audit and Accounting Guides, *Not-for-Profit Organizations* and *State and Local Governments.*

Many of the accounting and financial reporting requirements for private colleges and universities were addressed in Chapter 14, while many of the accounting and financial reporting requirements for public colleges and universities were addressed in Chapter 7. Therefore, in this chapter those accounting and reporting issues unique to the higher education industry are addressed.

Public Colleges and Universities

GASBS 35 requires that all public colleges and universities follow the *GASBS 34* financial reporting model used by state and local governments (and described in Chapters 2–9) for their separately issued financial statements. This reflects the GASB's decision that adopting the existing *GASBS 34* for colleges and universities was preferable to creating a precedent of setting standards on an industry-by-industry basis. *GASBS 35/34* permit colleges and universities to use the guidance for special purpose governments engaged only in business-type activities, engaged only in governmental activities, or engaged in both, for their stand-alone reports. A management's discussion and analysis (MD&A) is required, and infrastructure assets must be reported. The accrual basis of accounting must be used, and depreciation must be reported on capital assets. A statement of cash flows using the direct method is required.

Most public colleges and universities follow the model for public institutions engaged only in business-type activities. The basic financial statements for Midwest University, a hypothetical public university reporting as a business-type activity are presented in Illustrations 16–1, 16–2, and 16–3. These statements include the statement of net assets (Illustration 16–1), statement of revenues, expenses, and changes in net assets (Illustration 16–2), and the statement of cash flows (Illustration 16–3). Since the reporting model is that used by business-type activities, the statements are similar in format to Illustrations 7–6, 7–7, and 7–8 for proprietary funds. If a college or university has a component unit, such as a university hospital, it is presented discretely from the primary institution.

Some public higher education institutions, such as community colleges, have "taxing authority," the power to assess special taxes on local residents. These institutions may elect to report as "engaged in governmental-type activities only" or "engaged in both governmental and business-type activities." The basic financial statements are the same as those discussed for state and local governments in Chapters 1 through 9 and shown in Illustrations 1–4 through 1–14 using revenue and expenditure/expense classifications appropriate to colleges and universities. These institutions would use fund accounting, based on the authoritative guidance provided by *GASBS 34.*

Private Colleges and Universities

The FASB requires private colleges and universities to report on the changes in unrestricted, temporarily restricted, and permanently restricted net assets of the entity as a whole, the same as the nongovernmental not-for-profit organizations described in Chapter 14. The reader is directed to that chapter for more information on the definitions of net asset classifications and the considerable discretion that is allowed by *SFAS No. 117* in presenting financial information, including optional display of supplementary fund accounting information, if desired. Illustrations 16–4, 16–5, and 16–6 present the statement of financial position, statement of activities, and statement of cash flows, respectively, for Valley College, a hypothetical private not-for-profit college. These statement formats are generally the same as those illustrated in Chapter 14.

ILLUSTRATION 16–1

MIDWEST UNIVERSITY
Statement of Net Assets
June 30, 2008
(in thousands)

	Primary Institution	Component Unit Hospital
Assets		
Current assets:		
Cash and cash equivalents	$ 1,568	$ 98
Short-term investments	428	225
Accounts receivable, net	110	953
Inventories	95	127
Deposits with bond trustee	373	—
Prepaid expenses	29	47
Total current assets	2,603	1,450
Noncurrent assets:		
Endowment investments	10,450	—
Loans receivable, net	613	—
Long-term investments	7,063	646
Capital assets, net of depreciation	63,440	3,260
Total noncurrent assets	81,566	3,906
Total assets	84,169	5,356
Liabilities		
Current liabilities:		
Accounts payable and accrued liabilities	274	291
Deferred revenue	35	—
Deposits held in custody for others	350	—
Annuities and income payable	1,855	—
Long-term liabilities—current portion	1,050	99
Total current liabilities	3,564	390
Noncurrent liabilities:		
Notes payable	600	
Bonds payable	24,000	220
Total noncurrent liabilities	24,600	220
Total liabilities	28,164	610
Net Assets		
Invested in capital assets, net of related debt	37,790	2,941
Restricted for:		
Nonexpendable:		
Scholarships and fellowships	10,496	—
Expendable:		
Research	1,459	228
Instructional department uses	3,417	—
Loans	756	—
Capital projects	2,185	91
Debt service	430	15
Unrestricted	(528)	1,471
Total net assets	$56,005	$4,746

Source: Adapted from *GASBS 35*, App. D.

ILLUSTRATION 16–2

MIDWEST UNIVERSITY
Statement of Revenues, Expenses, and Changes in Net Assets
For the Year Ended June 30, 2008
(in thousands)

	Primary Institution	Component Unit Hospital
Operating Revenues		
Tuition and fees (net)	$ 2,690	
Patient services (net)		$4,629
Federal grants and contracts	35	747
Auxiliary activities	2,300	—
Other operating revenues	—	43
Total operating revenues	5,025	5,419
Operating Expenses		
Salaries and wages	5,346	2,699
Benefits	998	775
Scholarships and fellowships	135	—
Utilities	1,211	912
Supplies and other services	215	734
Depreciation	3,000	297
Other operating expenses	302	—
Total operating expenses	11,207	5,417
Operating income (loss)	(6,182)	2
Nonoperating Revenues (Expenses)		
Federal appropriations	438	—
State appropriations	4,170	—
Gifts	1,621	32
Investment income	975	49
Change in fair value of investments	189	—
Interest expense	(1,850)	(3)
Net nonoperating revenues	5,543	78
Income before changes in capital assets and endowments	(639)	80
Capital grants and gifts	220	71
Additions to permanent endowments	2,186	—
Increase in net assets	1,767	151
Net Assets		
Net assets—beginning of year	54,238	4,595
Net assets—end of year	$56,005	$4,746

(*Note:* Operating expenses are displayed here using object classification; however, expenses could be shown using functional classification as in Illustration 16–5.)

Source: Adapted from *GASBS 35,* App. D.

Some of the major differences that do exist between the financial statements of private and public institutions of higher education are in the areas of classification of net assets, format of the operating statement, cash flows statement, investments, pension disclosures, and compensated absences. Several of the accounting and reporting differences are discussed in the next section of this chapter.

ILLUSTRATION 16–3

MIDWEST UNIVERSITY
Statement of Cash Flows
For the Year Ended June 30, 2008
(in thousands)

	Primary Institution	Component Unit Hospital
Cash Flows from Operating Activities		
Cash received from students for tuition and fees	$ 2,775	—
Research grants and contracts	35	—
Cash received from auxiliary activities	2,300	—
Cash received from patients and third-party payors	—	$1,858
Cash received from Medicaid and Medicare	—	3,164
Payments to suppliers and others	(1,322)	(1,308)
Payments to students—scholarships	(135)	—
Payment to employees	(6,344)	(3,299)
Payment to annuitants	(250)	—
Other payments	(447)	(100)
Net cash provided (used) by operating activities	(3,388)	315
Cash Flows from Noncapital Financing Activities		
Federal appropriations	438	—
State appropriations	4,170	—
Gifts and grants received for endowment purposes	4,192	—
Net cash flows provided by noncapital financing activities	8,800	—
Cash Flows from Capital and Related Financing Activities		
Capital grants and gifts received	220	71
Proceeds from capital debt	500	—
Purchase of capital assets	(1,490)	(195)
Principal paid on capital debt	(550)	(13)
Interest paid on capital debt	(1,850)	(3)
Net cash used by capital and related financing activities	(3,170)	(140)
Cash Flows from Investing Activities		
Proceeds from sales and maturities of investments	2,664	284
Investment income	975	7
Loans	(163)	—
Purchase of investments	(4,825)	(454)
Net cash provided (used) by investing activities	(1,349)	(163)
Net Increase in Cash and Cash Equivalents	893	12
Cash and cash equivalents—beginning of year	675	86
Cash and cash equivalents—end of year	$ 1,568	$ 98
Reconciliation of Net Operating Revenues (Expenses) to Net Cash Provided (Used) by Operating Activities		
Operating income (loss)	$(6,182)	$ 2
Adjustments to reconcile net income (loss) to net cash provided (used) by operating activities:		
Depreciation expense	3,000	297

ILLUSTRATION 16–3   **Continued**

	Primary Institution	Component Unit Hospital
Change in assets and liabilities:		
Receivables, net	70	33
Inventories	(15)	(16)
Short-term investments	(128)	—
Deposit with bond trustee	(23)	—
Prepaid expenses	(9)	8
Accounts payable	119	(8)
Deferred revenue	15	—
Deposits held in custody for others	15	—
Annuities payable	(250)	(1)
Net cash provided (used) by operating activities	$(3,388)	$ 315

Source: Adapted from *GASBS 35,* App. D.

Fund Accounting

Many private and public colleges and universities may continue to use fund accounting for internal purposes. For these institutions, a worksheet can then be used to convert fund accounting information to institution-wide information necessary for the basic financial statements. Fund information may also be included as supplementary information in the financial report. In this chapter, our focus is on basic external financial reporting for the majority of colleges and universities expected to report as "engaged in business-type activities only"; consequently, there is little discussion of fund accounting in this chapter.

ACCOUNTING AND REPORTING ISSUES

Because *GASBS 34* primarily focuses on state and local governments, we can expect public colleges and universities to rely on industry guidance, such as NACUBO's *Financial Accounting and Reporting Manual for Higher Education (FARM),* and its Accounting Principles Council that studies issues and publishes guidance in the form of implementation guides. Private colleges and universities follow the guidance in *SFAS Nos. 116, 117,* and *FARM.* It might be helpful during the following discussion of selected elements of the financial statements to refer periodically to the illustrative financial statements for Midwest University (Illustrations 16–1 through 16–3), a hypothetical public university, and to those of Valley College (Illustrations 16–4 through 16–6, shown later), a hypothetical private college. Differences between generally accepted accounting principles for public and private institutions will be noted where applicable.

Statement of Net Assets or Financial Position

Illustration 16–1 presents a statement of net assets for a public university, and Illustration 16–4 presents a statement of financial position (or balance sheet) for a private college. Some of the accounting issues related to assets, liabilities, and net assets of colleges and universities are discussed next.

Unrestricted and Restricted Assets

Resources available for use in carrying out operations directly related to the institution's educational objectives arise from the instruction, research, and public service activities of a college or university as well as from residence halls, food services, intercollegiate athletics, student stores, and other auxiliary activities. Assets that are available for all purposes of the institution at the discretion of the governing board are *unrestricted*. Assets that are not available for current operating purposes (i.e., have a long-term purpose) due to limitations placed on them by persons or organizations outside the institution are considered restricted or limited as to use. The FASB indicates that such assets should be identified separately from current assets and reported on the face of the financial statement or disclosed in the notes. For public colleges and universities, the GASB indicates that restrictions that limit the ability of assets to pay current liabilities should be disclosed either in the noncurrent asset section of the financial statement or the financial statement notes.

Investments

Investments, under both FASB and GASB standards, are to be reported at fair value as of the end of the reporting period. Unrealized gains and losses arising from reporting investments at fair value are reported on the statement of activities for both public and private colleges and universities.

Capital Assets

The general sources of capital assets are resources from external agencies, student fees and assessments for capital acquisition purposes, borrowings from external sources, investment income, and gifts restricted for plant, property, and equipment. Long-lived assets are carried at cost or at fair value at the date of acquisition in the case of assets acquired by gift. In the absence of historical cost records, the assets may be stated at historically based appraised values. The basis of valuation should be disclosed in the notes to the financial statements.

GASBS 35 requires that long-lived assets, including infrastructure assets (e.g., roads, bridges, tunnels, drainage systems, water and sewers, and lighting systems), be capitalized and depreciated. Under *GASBS 34/35* public colleges and universities may elect not to depreciate certain eligible infrastructure assets by adopting the "modified approach." In these cases, if the government uses an asset management system and documents that the eligible assets are being preserved at the level established in that system, all expenditures incurred to preserve the eligible infrastructure assets at that level are expensed in the period incurred. See Chapter 5 for further discussion on capital assets and depreciation for governmental entities.

Disclosures about capital assets should be provided in the notes to the financial statements. The GASB indicates that disclosures should include a schedule showing beginning of the year balances, additions, retirements, and end-of-year balances of land; infrastructure; buildings; furniture, fixtures, and equipment; library materials; capitalized collections; and related accumulated depreciation. Disclosures under FASB include the amount of depreciation expense for the year, accumulated depreciation, depreciation method, and liquidity of property, plant, and equipment (such as pledged, collateralized, or restricted). The FASB does not recognize an infrastructure category.

Collections

Many colleges and universities have historical archives, libraries, and museums containing valuable works of art, historical treasures, and similar assets. Both FASB *Statement No. 116* and *GASBS 34* provide for note disclosure of such assets rather than reporting them on the balance sheet; however, both standards permit nonrecognition only if the donated items are added to **collections** that meet these conditions:

a. Are held for public exhibition, education, or research in furtherance of public service rather than financial gain.

b. Are protected, kept unencumbered, cared for, and preserved.

c. Are subject to an organizational policy that requires the proceeds from sales of collection items to be used to acquire other items for collections.

The clear intent of the authoritative guidance is to allow nonrecognition of contributions of valuable collections *only* if the collection is to be maintained to serve the public interest, not to achieve financial gain from trading in collectible items.

Liabilities

FASB and GASB require that short-term and long-term liabilities be reported. Long-term liabilities include leases, bonds payable, compensated absences, and pension obligations. For private colleges and universities disclosures are the same as those for corporate entities; however, public colleges and universities should disclose additions, reductions, the current portion of long-term liabilities, and segments (identified in part by debt issues) in the notes to the financial statements.

Net Assets

Three categories of net assets should be reported in the statement of financial position for private colleges and universities: unrestricted, temporarily restricted, and permanently restricted. Public colleges and universities also report three categories of net assets, but those categories are unrestricted, restricted, and invested in capital assets, net of related debt. For public institutions the restricted category should be divided according to purpose into expendable or nonexpendable.

Restrictions on net assets may arise from donors or resource providers stipulating that funds be used for scholarships and fellowships, research, instructional department uses, loans, capital projects, debt service, or other reasons. Accounts and reports must be in sufficient detail to demonstrate that the donor's restrictions and any board policies are being met. The next three topics, loan assets, endowments, and split-interest agreements, are examples of restricted net assets commonly found in colleges and universities.

Loan Assets

Assets that are loanable to students, faculty, and staff of an educational institution are provided by gifts, grants, and income from endowments and, in some cases, from loans made to the institution for that purpose. The intent is that the loan activities be operated on a self-sustaining basis: Repayment of loans and interest received on the loans are deposited and are then available for lending to other eligible persons. Interest earned on loans and interest earned on temporary investments of loan assets are expected to offset wholly or partially the cost of administration of loan activities and the loss from uncollectible loans. Interest on loans should be credited on the full accrual basis to appropriate revenue accounts. Costs of administration of loan activities, losses on investments of loan assets, provision for losses on loans (either estimated or actual), and related expenses and losses serve to reduce loan net asset balances.

Endowments

Gifts whose principal is nonexpendable as of the date of reporting and is invested, or is available for investment, for the purpose of producing income are referred to as *endowments. Pure endowments* are gifts for which donors or other external agencies have stipulated, as a condition of the gift, that the principal is to be maintained intact in perpetuity. The principal is invested in order to earn income. The use of the income may be restricted by the donor; if so, the income is considered as an addition to restricted net assets. If the use of the income is unrestricted, the income is considered to increase unrestricted net assets. **Term endowments** are defined in the same manner as pure endowments with the exception that the conditions of the gift provide that the assets be released from inviolability to permit all or a part of them to be expended on the happening of a particular event or the passage of a stated period of time. **Quasi-endowments** are assets segregated for endowment by the governing board of the institution to account for assets to be retained and invested. Since they are board designated, the principal as well as the income may be utilized at the discretion of the board; therefore, quasi-endowments, or *funds functioning as endowments,* are unrestricted.

Traditionally, the investment objective of most educational institutions has been the preservation of principal and the production of dividend and interest income. More recently, a broadened concept of return on investments has developed that assumes that changes in market value of portfolio securities are also a part of return on assets. This concept is known as **total return,** the sum of net realized and unrealized appreciation or shrinkage in portfolio value plus dividend and interest yield. Total return has another aspect; this is the determination of **spending rate,** the proportion of total return that may prudently be used by an institution for current purposes. The adoption of total return as a policy requires the approval of legal counsel and formal approval of the governing board. The total return concept appears to be used by an increasing number of colleges and universities.

Split-Interest Agreements

Colleges and universities are often parties to **split-interest agreements,** such as charitable lead and remainder trusts, charitable gift annuities, and pooled life income agreements. In these cases the institution shares either the income from an investment or the investment itself with the donor and sometimes other beneficiaries. These gifts may be established as trusts with the assets held by a third party. If the institution has an interest in an irrevocable split-interest agreement, the assets received should be recorded at their fair value when received, or the present value of the interest in future income or assets should be recorded. Any liabilities accepted, such as to pay the donor-stipulated amounts of an annuity agreement, should also be recorded at the time of the agreement. Any difference between assets and liabilities is either a restricted or unrestricted net asset, depending on the agreement with the donor.

Split-interest agreements are common forms of planned giving to colleges and universities by donors, who are often alumni. **Annuity agreements** are used to account for assets given to an institution under conditions that bind the institution to pay stipulated amounts periodically to the donors or other designated individuals for a period of time specified in the agreements or for the lifetime of the donor or other designated individual. **Life income agreements** are used to account for assets given to an institution under agreements that bind the institution to pay periodically to the donors or other designated individuals the total income earned by the donated assets for a period of time, usually the lifetimes of the income beneficiaries.

The acceptance of annuity funds by a not-for-profit organization is subject to regulation by the Internal Revenue Service and, in many jurisdictions, by agencies of the appropriate state government. The Internal Revenue Code and regulations state the conditions under which (for IRS purposes) an annuity trust may be established and administered. State agencies may specify the types of investments in which annuity assets may be invested.

It is possible to have an annuity agreement in which liabilities exceed initial assets. Entering into an annuity agreement that has initial deficit net assets would not appear to be in the institution's best interests. Agreements with potential donors of annuities should be carefully drawn by competent attorneys in consultation with accountants and investment managers in order to protect the interests of the receiving institution as well as the donor. The definition of *income* is one of the matters needing most careful attention. From the accounting point of view, *income* should be defined in accrual terms. It is also in the interest of the institution that an equitable allocation of indirect administrative expenses be permitted as well as a deduction for direct expenses of administering each annuity.

Annuity payments are debited to a liability account that was created when the agreement was initiated. Periodically, an adjustment is made between the liability and restricted net assets to record the actuarial gain or loss due to recomputation of the liability based on revised life expectancy and anticipated return on investments. On termination of an annuity agreement, the principal of the annuity is transferred to the net asset category specified in the agreement; if the agreement is silent on the point, the principal of the terminated annuity fund should be transferred to unrestricted net assets and identified so readers of the financial statements will not infer that a new gift has been received.

Life income agreements differ from annuity agreements. The primary difference is that the life income agreement provides that the income earned by the donated assets will be paid to the donors over a specified period rather than to a stipulated amount. Since the amount to be paid periodically varies from period to period as the income produced by the life income assets varies, it is not practicable or necessary to compute the present value of the stream of unknown future payments. Accordingly, the liabilities of life income agreements consist of life income payments currently due and any indebtedness against the life income assets. With this exception, accounting for life income agreements is similar to annuity agreements.

The Internal Revenue Code and regulations provide for three variations of the life income "unitrust": straight, net income, and net plus makeup. In order to qualify for, and maintain tax-exempt status, private colleges must comply with the technicalities of income tax law concerning life income agreements. It is not possible in this brief treatment of life income funds to do more than alert the interested reader to the existence of IRS requirements.

Statement of Revenues, Expenses, and Changes in Net Assets

Revenues

Colleges and universities should recognize revenues on the accrual basis. Revenue accounts provided in the NACUBO chart of accounts include these:

Tuition and Fees
Federal Appropriations
State Appropriations
Local Appropriations
Federal Grants and Contracts

State Grants and Contracts

Local Grants and Contracts

Private Gifts

Investment Income

Sales and Services of Educational Activities

Sales and Services of Auxiliary Activities

Other Sources

All of the account titles listed are control accounts and should be supported by appropriately named subsidiary accounts. For example, Tuition and Fees may be supported by subsidiary accounts for the regular session, summer school, extension, continuing education, and any other accounts providing useful information for a given educational institution. Gross tuition and fees should be recorded as a revenue even though some will be offset by fee remissions, scholarships, and fellowships. Actual refunds should be charged against the Tuition and Fees account. The AICPA Guide *Not-for-Profit Organizations,* which applies to private colleges and universities, requires that tuition revenue be reported net of tuition discounts and scholarships.[5] *GASBS 34* also indicates that tuition and fees be reported at a net amount.

Also with regard to Tuition and Fees, it should be noted that because college fiscal years and academic years rarely coincide, it is common for tuition and fees collected near the end of a fiscal year to relate in large portion to services to be rendered by the institution during the ensuing fiscal year. *GASBS 35* requires that institutions use full accrual principles, recognizing the revenue in the period in which it is available and earned. NACUBO indicates that determining when an institution earns tuition revenue is a matter of professional judgment.[6] Therefore, recognition of such tuition revenues may vary by institution.

The GASB requires that revenues be shown net of any estimated uncollectible amounts. Public colleges and universities can use a contra-revenue account, such as Provision for Bad Debts (see Chapter 7), to account for estimated uncollectible tuition and fees. NACUBO indicates that colleges and universities should show tuition and fees net of any estimated uncollectible amounts, directly adjusting the revenue account for the estimate.[7]

SFAS No. 117 allows colleges and universities the option of identifying operating revenues (and expenses) separately from non-operating revenues (and expenses). *GASBS 34,* however, requires the identification of operating and non-operating activity on the face of the financial statement.

Nonexchange Transactions

GASBS 33 (discussed in Chapter 4), and *SFAS No. 116* (discussed in Chapter 14) provide guidance to public and private colleges and universities, respectively, when they are the recipients of gifts and grants in nonexchange transactions. Private colleges and universities may depend more on contributions from alumni and other supporters to keep tuition costs reasonable than do public institutions that receive relatively more state funding. However, this distinction is becoming less evident as public universities

---

[5] AICPA, Audit and Accounting Guide, *Not-for-Profit Organizations* (AAG-NPO) (New York: AICPA, 2005), 12.05 and 13.07.

[6] NACUBO, *FARM,* Sec. 309.

[7] Ibid., Sec. 311.

recognize the benefits of increasing endowments to decrease reliance on volatile state funding and constrained tuition support. Endowments are permanently restricted net assets that result from nonexchange transactions.

GASBS 33, SFAS No. 116, and the AICPA Audit and Accounting Guide *Not-for-Profit Organizations* distinguish between (1) nonexchange transactions, such as contributions in which the donor does not expect anything of value in return, and (2) exchange transactions in which there is quid pro quo or expectation by each party that goods or services will be exchanged between the parties at fair values. Contributions by donors are considered nonexchange transactions as long as the donor does not receive any direct benefits from the donation. Public colleges and universities recognize contributions as revenue when any eligibility requirements and time restrictions have been met. However, contributions with a purpose restriction but no eligibility requirement are recognized as revenue and reported as restricted net assets. Private colleges and universities recognize contributions as income in the period in which they are made and report increases as either unrestricted, temporarily restricted, or permanently restricted net assets, depending on the stipulation of the donor. This also applies to promises to give, even though they may not be legally enforceable.

If a contribution to a private or public college or university is contingent upon a future event, such as obtaining matching funds, the university waits until the condition has been met before recording the contribution revenue. *Intentions to give,* such as naming a university in a will, are not recognized as revenue or considered a promise because the potential donor can change the will at any time.

Grants, Awards, and Scholarships

Grants and other assistance given by governments, foundations, or corporations may be nonexchange or exchange transactions, depending upon whether the resource provider directly benefits by receiving something of value through the transaction. The facts and circumstances of each award should be examined. For example, a federal research grant given to a university in which the value received by the agency is incidental to the public benefit from using the assets transferred is considered a *nonexchange* transaction; consequently, it is recognized as revenue in the period in which the contribution is made and classified as an increase in expendable restricted net assets by a public college or university or as temporarily restricted net assets by a private college or university. On the other hand, if a federal agency enters into a contract in which the university tests a product and any patent or other results of the activity are retained by the federal agency, that transaction is considered an exchange transaction, not a contribution; consequently, this transaction results in an increase in unrestricted net assets because only donors in nonexchange transactions can restrict net assets.[8] Colleges and universities should not report grants as exchange transactions or operating revenue without careful consideration of the terms of the grant.

Gifts in Kind

Contributions of noncash, tangible assets to a college or university are called **gifts in kind.**[9] If these gifts can be used or sold by the institution, they should be recorded in the period received at their fair value. If the donor has stipulated that the assets

---

[8] AICPA, AAG-NPO, par. 5.16; GASB, *Codification,* Sec. N50.902.

[9] AICPA, AAG-NPO. pars. 5.06–5.08.

should be distributed to a third party and the school does not have discretion over the disposition of the assets, the university is acting as an agent, and the gift should not be recorded as a contribution. The university may also receive items, such as tickets or merchandise, that are to be given to the ultimate resource provider at a fund-raising event, for example, an auction for the university's public radio station. In these cases, the value of the contribution to be recognized is initially the fair value of the gift in kind plus any additional amount paid by the ultimate donor (i.e., the contributor to the radio station). If the item is auctioned off for less than its initial fair value, the contribution revenue should be decreased for the difference between the ultimate amount paid and the fair value at the date of the gift to the university.

Contributed Services

Although contributed service by unpaid volunteers is generally less important for colleges and universities than for other not-for-profit organizations, such as service organizations and hospitals, some colleges and universities do utilize volunteers extensively for fund-raising and other activities, and, in the case of religious colleges, for instruction. *Statement No. 116* permits recognition of contributed services at their fair value if the services received create or enhance a nonfinancial asset (e.g., property and equipment) or (1) need to be purchased by the organization, (2) require specialized skills, and (3) are provided by professionals with those skills. If these criteria are met, the fair value of the services should be reported as both a contribution and as a salary expense. In any case, reporting the fair value of contributed services is encouraged, if practicable.[10] GASB standards are silent on the issue of reporting revenues and expenses relating to contributed services. This issue is relevant to public colleges and universities that have executives and/or artists-in-residence who teach courses.

Expenses

Expenses should be recognized on the full accrual basis and can be classified on a natural basis (as seen in Illustration 16–2) or on a functional basis (as demonstrated later in Illustration 16–5). Recall from Chapter 14 that the FASB requires that not-for-profit organizations, such as private colleges and universities, identify expenses by function. Functional classifications provided in the NACUBO chart of accounts for educational and general expenses include the following:

Instruction
Research
Public Service
Academic Support
Student Services
Institutional Support
Operation and Maintenance of Plant
Scholarships and Fellowships

Functional expense accounts are also provided for auxiliary activities.

Within each of the functional expense account categories just listed, accounts are kept by organizational unit, project, or other classification that provides useful information

[10] Ibid., pars. 5.39–5.40.

for internal or external users of the financial statements. A third level of analysis of expenses is provided by an object classification—personnel compensation and supplies expense are suggested as object classifications in the NACUBO chart of accounts. Further detail under each of these object classifications is usually kept to facilitate planning and control. For example, personnel compensation may be subdivided into salaries, other personnel services, and personnel benefits, with each of these further subdivided as desired by the administrators of a given college or university.

The AICPA Audit and Accounting Guide, *Not-for-Profit Organizations,* pertinent to private colleges and universities, also requires that expenses that relate to more than one function, such as occupancy costs, and interest and other expenses, be allocated to the programs or functional expenses to which they pertain.[11] It is not difficult to assign direct expenses, such as travel, to various functions; however, in order to allocate indirect expenses, such as occupancy costs or interest expense, a reasonable allocation basis must be employed. That basis may be square footage of space occupied by each program or personnel costs. There appears to be a difference of opinion as to whether CPA firms consider the language in the AICPA Audit and Accounting Guide prescriptive or suggestive. For example, some institutions reported plant and interest costs as separate line or object items rather than allocating them across programs in their audited financial statements.

Statement of Cash Flows

GASBS 34, applicable to public colleges and universities, requires a statement of cash flows to be prepared using the direct method. Private colleges and universities have the option of preparing the statement using either the direct or indirect method, according to *SFAS No. 117,* as described in Chapter 14. Illustration 16–3 shows a statement of cash flows for the sample public university while Illustration 16–6 provides a private college example. Note that state appropriations are reported as nonoperating revenues in Illustration 16–2 and as cash flows from noncapital financing activities in Illustration 16–3.

Segment Reporting

GASBS 35/34 require that public institutions that use business-type reporting present segment information in the notes to the financial statements. A segment is an identifiable activity for which one or more revenue bonds or other revenue-backed debt instruments are outstanding, for example, revenue bonds for residence halls or bookstores. Required disclosures include a condensed statement of net assets; statement of revenues, expenses, and changes in net assets; and statement of cash flows. *SFAS No. 131* exempts private colleges and universities from segment reporting.[12]

ILLUSTRATIVE TRANSACTIONS FOR PRIVATE COLLEGES AND UNIVERSITIES

This section presents journal entries for selected illustrative transactions for Valley College, a hypothetical private college. This information is then summarized in the financial statements presented in Illustrations 16–4 through 16–6. The account balances as of July 1, 2007, the beginning of Valley College's fiscal year, are provided in the following trial balance.

[11] Ibid., pars. 13.42–13.45.
[12] FASB, *SFAS No. 131*, pars. 115–118.

VALLEY COLLEGE
Post-Closing Trial Balance
As of June 30, 2007

	Debits	Credits
Cash and Cash Equivalents	$ 675,000	
Tuition and Fees Receivable	298,000	
Allowance for Doubtful Accounts		$ 18,000
Pledges Receivable	800,000	
Allowance for Doubtful Pledges		50,000
Discount on Pledges Receivable		100,000
Loans Receivable	460,000	
Allowance for Doubtful Loans		10,000
Inventories	80,000	
Deposits with Trustees	350,000	
Prepaid Expenses	20,000	
Long-Term Investments	16,163,000	
Property, Plant, and Equipment	85,745,000	
Accumulated Depreciation		21,795,000
Accounts Payable		140,000
Accrued Liabilities		15,000
Deposits Held in Custody for Others		335,000
Deferred Revenue		350,000
Annuities and Income Payable		1,720,000
Notes Payable		700,000
Bonds Payable		25,000,000
Net Assets—Unrestricted		37,158,000
Net Assets—Temporarily Restricted		2,200,000
Net Assets—Permanently Restricted		15,000,000
Total	$104,591,000	$104,591,000

During the fiscal year ended June 30, 2008, the following revenue items were recorded:

Receivables:	
Tuition and fees	5,990,000
Federal grants and contracts	1,075,000
Pledges	
Unrestricted	4,850,000
Temporarily restricted	1,000,000
Cash revenue items:	
Investment Income	
Unrestricted	700,000
Temporarily restricted	280,000
Auxiliary enterprises	2,300,000

In addition, student scholarships in the amount of $450,000 were awarded, reducing the amount of the receivable and creating a contra-revenue account. Deferred revenues in the amount of $350,000 reported in the beginning trial balance is reclassified as Tuition and Fees because that amount was collected in the preceding year from students for summer classes offered in the current year. The pledges are temporarily restricted since they will be collected over the five succeeding fiscal years. As a result the pledges collected in year's two through five must be discounted to present value. The amount of the discount on pledges receivable is $74,000. Entry 1 records the recognition of this revenue.

		Debits	Credits
1.	Cash	3,280,000	
	Tuition and Fees Receivable	5,540,000	
	Grants Receivable	1,075,000	
	Pledges Receivable	5,850,000	
	Deferred Revenue	350,000	
	Tuition and Fees Discounts and Allowances	450,000	
	Tuition and Fees—Unrestricted		6,340,000
	Federal Grants and Contracts—Unrestricted		1,075,000
	Contributions—Unrestricted		4,850,000
	Contributions—Temporarily Restricted		926,000
	Discount on Pledges Receivable		74,000
	Investment Income—Temporarily Restricted		280,000
	Investment Income—Unrestricted		700,000
	Auxiliary Enterprises—Unrestricted		2,300,000

Entry 2 records the collections of cash for tuition and fees receivable amounting to $5,650,000, grants receivable of $1,075,000, and $4,945,000 in pledges receivable. For those pledges collected from prior periods, $14,000 of the Discount on Pledges Receivable was amortized and recorded as unrestricted contributions.

2.	Cash	11,670,000	
	Discount on Pledges Receivable	14,000	
	Tuition and Fees Receivable		5,650,000
	Grants Receivable		1,075,000
	Pledges Receivable		4,945,000
	Contributions—Unrestricted		14,000

Entry 3 records operating expenses incurred in accomplishing the goals of the college. In addition, operating expenses for auxiliary enterprises are recorded.

3.	Instruction Expense	4,321,000	
	Public Service Expense	1,123,460	
	Academic Support Expense	129,630	
	Student Services Expense	2,592,600	
	Institutional Support Expense	2,872,170	
	Auxiliary Enterprises Expense	2,116,000	
	Accounts Payable		3,936,500
	Accrued Liabilities		9,218,360

Accounts payable and accrued liabilities were paid in the amounts of $4,003,500 and $9,133,900, respectively. Refunds of students' deposits amounted to $10,000.

		Debits	Credits
4.	Accounts Payable	4,003,500	
	Accrued Liabilities	9,133,900	
	Deposits Held in Custody for Others	10,000	
	Cash		13,147,400

Inventories and prepaid expenses increased during the year in the amounts shown in Entry 5. These increases reduced expenses in instruction and institutional support, as shown.

5.	Inventories	15,000	
	Prepaid Expenses	9,000	
	Instruction Expense		13,200
	Institutional Support Expense		10,800

Contributions restricted for the purpose of research were received.

6.	Cash	1,109,000	
	Contributions—Temporarily Restricted		1,109,000

Expenses for the restricted research purposes described in Entry 6 were incurred during the period in the amount of $1,025,000.

7a.	Research Expense	1,025,000	
	Accrued Liabilities		10,000
	Cash		1,015,000
7b.	Net Assets Released from Restrictions—		
	Temporarily Restricted	1,025,000	
	Net Assets Released from Restrictions—		
	Unrestricted		1,025,000

Entry 8 records the receipt of state grants that are temporarily restricted for student loans.

8.	Cash	208,000	
	State Grants and Contracts—Temporarily Restricted		208,000

Loans were made to students during the year in the amount of $260,000, and other student loans were repaid in the amount of $95,000 with an additional amount of

$7,000 received as interest revenue on these loans. There are no imposed stipulations on the interest earned. Entries 9a and 9b record the loan transactions.

		Debits	Credits
9a.	Loans Receivable	260,000	
	Cash		260,000
9b.	Cash	102,000	
	Loans Receivable		95,000
	Investment Income—Unrestricted		7,000

During the year, cash of $500,000 for construction of a new laboratory building was received from a private foundation and 8 percent term bonds maturing in five years were issued in the amount of $2,000,000.

10.	Cash	2,500,000	
	Bonds Payable		2,000,000
	Contributions—Temporarily Restricted		500,000

During the year, the new laboratory building was completed at a cost of $2,000,000. Equipment costs amounted to $350,000. Renovations to the old laboratory building totaled $250,000; however, none of the renovations met the criteria for capitalization.

11a.	Buildings	2,000,000	
	Equipment	350,000	
	Research Expense	250,000	
	Cash		2,600,000
11b.	Net Assets Released from Restrictions— Temporarily Restricted	500,000	
	Net Assets Released from Restrictions— Unrestricted		500,000

Valley College received endowment gifts during the year in the amount of $2,186,000. In addition, the college has annuity agreements (split-interest agreements) with some contributors. For the year, $487,000 was received from annuity contributors. The actuarial liability related to the annuity contributions is $385,000 with the difference between the contribution and the liability permanently restricted until the annuity term expires. Entry 12 records the effect of the endowment and annuity gifts.

12.	Cash	2,673,000	
	Contributions—Permanently Restricted		2,288,000
	Annuities and Income Payable		385,000

Long-term investments were made using $2,200,000 from the endowment and $300,000 from the annuity contributions.

		Debits	Credits
13.	Long-Term Investments	2,500,000	
	Cash		2,500,000

Entry 14 records the interest and principal payments on outstanding bonds and notes. The interest is allocated to the instruction function.

14.	Instruction Expense	1,850,000	
	Bonds Payable	500,000	
	Notes Payable	50,000	
	Cash		2,400,000

Valley College acts as an agent for a number of student groups. These groups deposited $130,000 with the college; $110,000 in withdrawals were made, as shown in Entries 15a and 15b.

15a.	Cash	130,000	
	Deposits Held in Custody for Others		130,000
15b.	Deposits Held in Custody for Others	110,000	
	Cash		110,000

As shown in Entry 16, distributions related to annuity agreements was $250,000.

16.	Annuities and Income Payable	250,000	
	Cash		250,000

Near the end of the current fiscal year, the college collected tuition and fees in the amount of $350,000 for classes that will be held in the following fiscal year. The college recognizes a deferred revenue liability since the fees are related to educational programs conducted in the following fiscal year.

17.	Cash	350,000	
	Deferred Revenue		350,000

Adjusting Entries

Entry 18 records the accrual of instructional and public service expenses at June 30, 2008, in the amounts shown.

		Debits	Credits
18.	Instruction Expense	51,000	
	Public Service Expense	21,000	
	Accounts Payable		65,000
	Accrued Liabilities		7,000

At the end of the year, a pre-audit review of the loans receivable and pledges receivable indicates that the balances in the allowance accounts are sufficient. However, the Allowance for Doubtful Accounts related to tuition and fees is increased for expected write-offs in the amount of $2,000.

19.	Tuition and Fees—Unrestricted	2,000	
	Allowance for Doubtful Accounts		2,000

As of June 30, 2008, the fair value of long-term investments increased by $7,800 from the value reported in the college's financial records. The gain is permanently restricted.

20.	Long-Term Investments	7,800	
	Unrealized Gain on Investments		7,800

Capital assets are depreciated as shown in Entry 21. For simplicity, the total expense is charged to instruction.

21.	Instruction Expense	300,000	
	Accumulated Depreciation		300,000

Closing Entries

All revenue and expense accounts were closed to the appropriate net asset accounts.

22a.	Tuition and Fees—Unrestricted	6,338,000	
	Federal Grants and Contracts—Unrestricted	1,075,000	
	Contributions—Unrestricted	4,864,000	
	Investment Income—Unrestricted	707,000	
	Auxiliary Enterprises—Unrestricted	2,300,000	
	Net Assets—Unrestricted	1,793,860	
	Instruction Expense		6,508,800
	Public Service Expense		1,144,460
	Academic Support Expense		129,630
	Student Services Expense		2,592,600
	Institutional Support Expense		2,861,370
	Auxiliary Enterprises Expense		2,116,000
	Research Expenses		1,275,000
	Tuition and Fees Discounts and Allowances		450,000

		Debits	Credits
22b.	Contributions—Temporarily Restricted	2,535,000	
	State Grants—Temporarily Restricted	208,000	
	Investment Income—Temporarily Restricted	280,000	
	Net Assets—Temporarily Restricted		3,023,000
22c.	Contributions—Permanently Restricted	2,288,000	
	Unrealized Gain on Investments	7,800	
	Net Assets—Permanently Restricted		2,295,800

Net assets released from restrictions are closed in the following entry:

		Debits	Credits
23.	Net Assets—Temporarily Restricted	1,525,000	
	Net Assets Released from Restrictions—Unrestricted	1,525,000	
	Net Assets—Unrestricted		1,525,000
	Net Assets Released from Restrictions— Temporarily Restricted		1,525,000

The financial statements for Valley College are presented in Illustrations 16–4, 16–5, and 16–6 for the fiscal year ended June 30, 2008.

OTHER ACCOUNTING ISSUES

Performance Measures

The performance of the organization is monitored by decision makers, such as internal management (e.g., administrators), oversight bodies (e.g., governing boards, accrediting agencies), funding sources (e.g., governments, donors, grantors, investors), and constituents with a beneficial interest in the school (e.g., students, faculty, alumni, and staff). The extent to which these stakeholders use financial information to make their decisions and the most useful form of financial reporting continue to be accounting research questions. The objective of audited annual financial statements is to ensure that statements conform to generally accepted accounting principles and are fairly presented, not to document whether the organization performed efficiently. Consequently, other methods of measuring and reporting performance are being developed.

Public colleges and universities are encouraged to present nonfinancial and non-quantitative information, such as service efforts and accomplishments, that document how well the organization accomplished its mission.[13] However, many accrediting agencies, and a few states, are requiring assessment of student outcomes, sometimes as a determining factor in funding levels. Some states are requiring standardized norm-based objective exams, although more often the institution is allowed to develop its own measure of outcomes based on mission-based objectives. This approach recognizes that the mission of higher education institutions differs in the weight each one places on instruction, research, and service. Outputs, for example, might be faculty

---

[13] Governmental Accounting Standards Board, *Concepts Statement No. 2,* "Service Efforts and Accomplishments" (Norwalk, CT: GASB, 1994).

ILLUSTRATION 16–4

VALLEY COLLEGE
Statement of Financial Position
June 30, 2008

Assets

Cash and cash equivalents	$ 414,600
Tuition and fees receivable, less allowance for doubtful accounts of $20,000	168,000
Pledges receivable, less allowance for doubtful pledges of $50,000 and a discount of $160,000	1,495,000
Loans receivable, less allowance for doubtful loans of $10,000	615,000
Inventories, at average cost	95,000
Prepaid expenses	29,000
Deposits with trustees	350,000
Long-term investments, at fair value, cost of $18,663,000	18,670,800
Property, plant and equipment, net of accumulated depreciation of $22,095,000	66,000,000
Total assets	$87,837,400

Liabilities and Net Assets

Liabilities:

Accounts payable	$ 138,000
Accrued liabilities	116,460
Deposits held in custody for others	345,000
Deferred revenue	350,000
Annuities and income payable	1,855,000
Notes payable	650,000
Bonds payable	26,500,000
Total liabilities	29,954,460

Net Assets:

Unrestricted	36,889,140
Temporarily Restricted	3,698,000
Permanently Restricted	17,295,800
Total net assets	57,882,940
Total liabilities and net assets	$87,837,400

productivity, number of graduates, or job placements.[14] Outcomes differ from outputs in that they measure the benefits derived by constituents, such as increased knowledge of students. NACUBO, as well as many universities, have projects on benchmarking for process improvement. The best measures are those that capture the "value added" to the student through the educational process. Although doing so is difficult, many universities are measuring the knowledge and skills of students through pretesting upon entering school, posttesting as the student reaches graduation, and regularly surveying alumni.[15] There is more discussion about performance evaluation in Chapter 13.

[14] Ken Brown and Mary Fischer, "Assessment Measures: Management's Yardstick," *Assessment and Evaluation in Higher Education* 19, no. 3 (1994), pp. 163–74.

[15] J. Gainen and P. Locatelli, *Assessment in the Accounting Curriculum* (Sarasota, FL: AAA, 1995).

ILLUSTRATION 16–5

VALLEY COLLEGE
Statement of Activities
Year Ended June 30, 2008

	Unrestricted	Temporarily Restricted	Permanently Restricted	Total
Revenues and gains:				
Student tuition and fees (net)	$ 5,888,000			$ 5,888,000
Government grants and contracts	1,075,000	$ 208,000		1,283,000
Investment income	707,000	280,000		987,000
Contributions	4,864,000	2,535,000	$ 2,288,000	9,687,000
Auxiliary enterprise sales and services	2,300,000			2,300,000
Gain on investments			7,800	7,800
Net assets released from restrictions	1,525,000	(1,525,000)		0
Total revenues and gains	16,359,000	1,498,000	2,295,800	20,152,800
Expenses and losses:				
Educational and general expenses:				
Instruction	6,508,800			6,508,800
Public service	1,144,460			1,144,460
Academic support	129,630			129,630
Research	1,275,000			1,275,000
Student services	2,592,600			2,592,600
Institutional support	2,861,370			2,861,370
Total educational and general expenses	14,511,860			14,511,860
Auxiliary enterprises	2,116,000			2,116,000
Total expenses and losses	16,627,860			16,627,860
Total change in net assets	(268,860)	1,498,000	2,295,800	3,524,940
Net assets, beginning of the year	37,158,000	2,200,000	15,000,000	54,358,000
Net assets, end of the year	$36,889,140	$3,698,000	$17,295,800	$57,882,940

The financial community, through bond rating agencies, financial analysts, underwriters, and investors, has always evaluated financial performance and the creditworthiness of institutions that issue debt. Some key ratios they use to evaluate viability, return, and leverage are (1) expendable resources to debt, (2) unrestricted resources to operations, (3) expendable resources to total net assets, (4) total resources per full-time-equivalent student, and (5) maximum debt service coverage.[16]

Auditing Colleges and Universities

Most colleges and universities, whether private or public, publish audited financial statements, more and more on their Web sites. At a minimum, audits of colleges and universities are performed in conformity with the generally accepted auditing standards (GAAS) promulgated by the AICPA, as discussed in Chapter 11. Additionally, many colleges and universities, as a condition of accepting federal financial awards,

---

[16] See Engstrom and Esmond-Kiger, "Different Formats," pp. 24–25.

ILLUSTRATION 16–6

VALLEY COLLEGE
Statement of Cash Flows
Year Ended June 30, 2008

Cash Flows from Operating Activities	
Increase in net assets	$ 3,524,940
Adjustments to reconcile increase in net assets to net cash provided by operating activities:	
Depreciation	300,000
Increase in pledges receivable (net)	(845,000)
Decrease in tuition and fees receivable (net)	112,000
Increase in accounts payable and accrued expenses	99,460
Increase in deposits and agency funds	10,000
Increase in annuities payable	135,000
Increase in prepaid expenses	(9,000)
Increase in inventories	(15,000)
Gains restricted for long-term purpose	(7,800)
Contributions restricted for long-term investment	(2,673,000)
Net cash provided for operating activities	631,600
Cash Flows from Investing Activities	
Purchases of investments	(2,500,000)
Purchases of property, plant, and equipment	(2,350,000)
Loans to students and faculty	(260,000)
Collections of loans to students and faculty	95,000
Net cash used for investing activities	(5,015,000)
Cash Flows from Financing Activities	
Proceeds from contributions restricted for long-term investment	2,673,000
Issuance of long-term debt	2,000,000
Repayment of long-term debt	(550,000)
Net cash provided by financing activities	4,123,000
Net decrease in cash and cash equivalents	(260,400)
Cash and cash equivalents, beginning of year	675,000
Cash and cash equivalents, end of year	$ 414,600

are audited under the auditing standards established by the U.S. Government Accountability Office in its publication *Government Auditing Standards* (GAS), also known as the "yellow book," as discussed in Chapter 11. Specifically, if a college or university expends $500,000 or more in federal awards in a given fiscal year, it must have a "single audit" in accordance with the provisions of Office of Management and Budget (OMB) *Circular A–133,* "Audits of States, Local Governments and Nonprofit Organizations." Since the audit requirements for the single audit are described in considerable detail in Chapter 11, they need not be reiterated here.

Due to the large number of dollars involved and decentralized controls an item of special concern in auditing colleges and universities is ensuring that only costs allowable under OMB *Circular A–21,* "Cost Principles for Educational Institutions," are charged, either as direct costs or indirect costs, to federal grants or contracts. Since

1993, the federal government has devoted an increasing amount of resources to auditing educational institutions that receive federal assistance, in particular their compliance with OMB *Circular A–21,* as well as unrelated business income. The cost principles and administrative requirements under OMB *Circular A–110* are discussed more fully in Chapter 13. The tax issues involving unrelated business income are discussed in Chapter 15. As with single audits of state and local governments, *Circular A–133* audits place heavy emphasis on evaluating the system of internal controls and compliance with applicable laws and regulations in addition to the traditional audit of the financial statements.

Federal Financial Assistance

The federal government, as well as state governments occasionally, support institutions of higher learning in the form of research grants and student loan funds. As mentioned in the previous section on auditing issues, acceptance of federal funds requires reporting to the grantor and conformance with various cost accounting rules as well as administrative requirements.

Sponsored Research Funds

Research funds received from the federal government are most likely to be in the form of contracts and grants in which the government is expecting periodic activity reports and a report at the end of the grant period as to how the funds were used. In some instances, the organization may contract with the federal government for a specific product for the funds paid. The terms of the grant or contract are critical factors in determining whether it is an exchange or a nonexchange transaction. Some universities may have a policy to classify all federal grants as exchange transactions, but the facts and circumstances of each grant should be examined.

Student Grants and Loans

Student assistance takes various forms: loans or grants, subsidized or unsubsidized, held by the institution or given directly to the student. A Pell Grant is one in which the federal government provides funds to the institution, which then selects the recipient.[17]

Related Entities

Public and private colleges and universities can be complex in their organizational structure including majority-owned subsidiaries for intellectual property and businesslike enterprises; clinical and research facilities; financing corporations; and controlled affiliates for fund-raising, alumni relations, and management of assets. At issue is whether there is sufficient control of one organization over another to combine their financial information under one reporting entity.

Most institutionally related fund-raising, clinical, and athletic foundations are legally separate organizations independent of the university they serve. However, it may be misleading to exclude the foundation from the university's financial report if the foundation operates essentially as an agent of the university. GASB *Statement No. 39* (May 2002) provides guidance for public universities in determining whether certain organizations such as those just described are component units of the

---

[17] Catalog of Federal Domestic Assistance (CFDA) #84.063. See: http://www.cfda.gov.

university.[18] The statement says that organizations that raise and hold economic resources for the direct benefit of a governmental unit, are legally separate, tax-exempt entities, and meet *all* of the following criteria should be discretely presented as component units:

1. The economic resources received or held by the separate organization are entirely or almost entirely for the direct benefit of the primary government, its component units, or its constituents.
2. The primary government or its component units are entitled to or have the ability to otherwise access a majority of the economic resources received or held by the separate organization.
3. The economic resources received or held by an individual organization that the specific primary government or its component units are entitled to or has the ability to otherwise access are significant to that primary government.

If a university has a relationship with an organization that does not meet each of these criteria and for which it is not financially accountable, professional judgment should be exercised to determine whether exclusion would render the financial statements of the reporting entity misleading or incomplete.[19] At a minimum, note disclosures of the existence of these affiliated organizations should be made in the public university's financial report. Private colleges and universities, although less likely to have independent fund-raising foundations, often have affiliated organizations that should be disclosed in the notes to the financial statements.

It should be noted that many public universities are related to not-for-profit foundations whose objective is to obtain contributions and endowments. In those cases, discrete presentation as a component unit or note disclosure should report the existence of those foundations and the amount of investment income or other monies received from them, depending on the degree of financial interdependence between the two organizations.

[18] Government Accounting Standards Board, *Statement No. 39,* "Determining Whether Certain Organizations Are Component Units" (Norwalk, CT: GASB, 2002).
[19] Government Accounting Standards Board, *Statement No. 14,* "The Financial Reporting Entity" (Norwalk, CT: GASB, 1991).

Key Terms

Annuity agreements, *636*
Collections, *635*
Gifts in kind, *639*
Life income agreements, *636*

Quasi-endowments, *636*
Spending rate, *636*
Split-interest agreements, *636*

Term endowments, *636*
Total return, *636*

Selected References

American Institute of Certified Public Accountants. Audit and Accounting Guide. *Not-for-Profit Organizations.* New York: AICPA, 2005.
Financial Accounting Standards Board. *Statement of Financial Accounting Standards No. 116,* "Accounting for Contributions Received and Contributions Made." Norwalk, CT, 1993.

_____. *Statement of Financial Accounting Standards No. 117,* "Financial Statements of Not-for-Profit Organizations." Norwalk, CT, 1993.

Goldstein, Larry. *College and University Budgeting*: *An Introduction for Faculty and Academic Administrators,* 3rd ed. Washington, DC: NACUBO, 2005.

Governmental Accounting Standards Board. *Codification of Governmental Accounting and Financial Reporting Standards as of June 30, 2005.* Norwalk, CT, 2005.

National Association of College and University Business Officers. *Financial Accounting and Reporting Manual for Higher Education* (*e-FARM*). Washington, DC. In electronic form.

Periodicals:

Business Officer. Washington, DC: NACUBO.

The Chronicle of Higher Education. Washington, DC.

Higher Education Director. Falls Church, VA: Higher Education Publications, Inc.

Questions

16–1. Many colleges and universities are governmentally owned; others are privately supported not-for-profit organizations. What bearing does this situation have on the determination of authoritative financial reporting standards for colleges and universities?

16–2. Explain how restricted gifts and grants are reported by a public college or university. How would such restricted gifts and grants be recorded and reported by a private college or university that follows FASB *Statement Nos. 116* and *117?*

16–3. Private colleges and universities report temporarily and permanently restricted net assets. What, if any, comparable reporting is provided by public universities?

16–4. What are some of the accounting and reporting differences between endowments and split-interest agreements?

16–5. "Endowments of public colleges and universities should be accounted for in the same manner as permanent trust funds of state and local governments." Do you agree? Why or why not?

16–6. "Under FASB standards applicable to private colleges and universities, *all* contributions must be recognized as revenues or gains in the period received." Do you agree? Why or why not?

16–7. Explain the conditions that must exist for a public or private college or university to avoid accounting recognition of the value of its collections of art, historical treasures, and similar assets.

16–8. List the financial statements required by the FASB for private colleges and universities with those required for public colleges and universities.

16–9. How are segments reported under the FASB standards? GASB standards?

16–10. Describe some measures of performance that can be used in assessing whether a university operates effectively.

Cases

16–1 Component Units. The following is a section taken from the Notes to the Comprehensive Annual Financial Report of the State of Michigan for the fiscal year ended September 30, 2004.

Note 1—Summary of Significant Accounting Policies

A. *Reporting Entity* (selected)

Ten of the State's public universities are considered component units because they have boards appointed by the primary government. Their balances and operating results are included with the other discretely presented components units on the government-wide statements. The ten universities included in these statements are: Central Michigan University, Eastern Michigan University, Ferris State University, Grand Valley State University, Lake Superior State University, Michigan Technological University, Northern Michigan University, Oakland University, Saginaw Valley State University, and Western Michigan University. Michigan State University, the University of Michigan, and Wayne State University are not included in the State's reporting entity because they have separately elected governing boards and are legally separate. The State provides significant funding to support these institutions; however, under the GASB Statement No. 14 criteria, they are considered fiscally independent, special-purpose governments.

Required

a. Which criteria under GASB *Statement No. 14* do you expect that the three universities *not* included in the State of Michigan's CAFR fail to meet? (*Hint:* Review the GASB *Statement No. 14* criteria in Chapter 9.)

b. What other relationships among states and their public institutions of higher learning might you expect to find (for example, between the State of California and the University of California and California State University systems)?

c. How useful is the *discrete* method of presenting college and university component units (as opposed to *blending* component units with the state's financial information) if the column in the government-wide financial statements Component Units includes the 10 institutions of higher learning and authorities for the bridges, state parks, housing development, and higher education student loans?

16–2 **Comparison of Public and Private Universities.** You have recently been hired as the financial manager of Marywood University, a private university in an urban area. Your previous experience was with Southern State University, a public university in the area. To familiarize yourself with the differences between the audited financial statements of this private university, which follows *SFAS No. 117,* and the public university, which follows *GASBS 35,* you are comparing Marywood University's Statement of Activities to Southern State University's Statement of Revenues, Expenses, and Changes in Net Assets shown on the following pages. Student enrollment at the private university is approximately 4,100 and at the public university approximately 23,000.

Required

a. List some of the differences in the formats of the two operating statements for the year that are immediately evident.

b. What proportion of the total revenues of Marywood University come from tuition and fees versus state appropriations versus other income? How does that compare to those for Southern State University?

c. What proportion of all of Marywood University's private gifts, grants, and contracts are in the form of endowments? How does that compare to those for the public university? Can you tell how much each institution earns on its endowments?

d. What proportion of all of Marywood University's expenses are spent for the educational programs as opposed to that spent on supporting the programs (e.g., general and administrative and fund-raising expenses)? How does that compare with those for the public university?

e. Which university appears to have had a better year from the perspective of financial operations? Why?

MARYWOOD UNIVERSITY
Statement of Activities
Year Ended June 30, 2008
(in thousands)

	Unrestricted	Temporarily Restricted	Permanently Restricted	Totals
Revenues, gains, and other support:				
Tuition and fees (net of scholarships of $805,113)	$15,359	$ —	$ —	$15,359
State appropriation	525	—	—	525
Government grants and contracts	748	—	—	748
Private gifts, grants, and contracts	952	630	257	1,839
Pledges	40	458	63	561
Investment income	1,196	3	—	1,199
Realized gain from investments	3,310	—	—	3,310
Auxiliary enterprises	689	—	—	689
Other sources	384	93	—	477
Net assets released from restrictions	1,643	(1,632)	(11)	—
Total revenues and other support	24,846	(448)	309	24,707
Net appreciation on investments	314	—	—	314
Total revenues, gains, and other support	25,160	(448)	309	25,021
Expenses and losses:				
Instruction	9,391	—	—	9,391
Public service	86	—	—	86
Academic support	2,301	—	—	2,301
Student services	2,056	—	—	2,056
Management and general	2,388	—	—	2,388
Fund-raising	442	—	—	442
Auxiliary enterprises	448	—	—	448
Operations and maintenance of plant	2,768	—	—	2,768
Repairs and renovations	992	—	—	992
Retirement of plant	152	—	—	152
Interest	253	—	—	253
Other	15	—	—	15
Total expenses and losses	21,292	—	—	21,292
Change in net assets	3,868	(448)	309	3,729
Net assets, beginning of year	41,422	891	3,548	45,861
Net assets, end of year	$45,290	$ 443	$3,857	$49,590

SOUTHERN STATE UNIVERSITY
Statement of Revenues, Expenses, and Changes in Net Assets
For the Year Ended June 30, 2008
(in thousands)

Operating Revenues

Student tuition and fees	$ 87,563
Scholarship allowances	(11,867)
Net student tuition and fees	75,696
Federal grants and contracts	4,584
Federal financial aid	9,377
State grants and contracts	973
State financial aid	2,818
Nongovernmental grants and contracts	7,879
Departmental activities	5,093
Auxiliary activities, less internal service billings	31,760
Other	3,191
Total operating revenues	141,371

Operating Expenses

Instruction	76,517
Research	3,730
Public service	13,414
Academic support	19,881
Student services	20,926
Institutional support	28,269
Scholarships and fellowships	10,153
Operation and maintenance of plant	15,815
Auxiliary activities, less internal service billings	27,733
Depreciation	13,356
Capital additions, net	(4,742)
Other	596
Total operating expenses	225,648
Operating (Loss) Income	(84,277)

Nonoperating Revenues (Expenses)

State appropriations	86,280
Gifts	2,318
Investment income	4,359
Investment expense	(5,471)
Other	489
Net nonoperating revenues (expenses)	87,975
Income before other revenues, expenses, gains, or losses	3,698
Capital appropriation	2,547
Capital gifts	8,550
Increase in net assets	14,795

Net Assets

Net Assets—beginning of year	232,023
Net Assets—end of year	$246,818

16–3 Chart of Accounts and Enterprise Systems—Internet Case. Assume you are a newly hired accountant in the Office of Financial Operations of a large public university. In the coming year, you will be involved in a major initiative to revise the university's chart of accounts in preparation for conversion of the university's fund accounting information system to an ERP (enterprise resource planning) or ES (enterprise system) accounting information system.

Required

a. What type of information is available on the Internet to assist you in understanding the chart of accounts of a public university? For example, look at the NACUBO Web site under "University Accounting."

b. Locate information that will be helpful in understanding the impact of converting to an enterprise system. For example, see one university's Web site (http://bannertrain.emich.edu) that provides guidance and links to helpful resources for staff implementing the enterprise system.

c. Prepare a one-page outline for your supervisor that summarizes the key issues of converting from a disaggregated fund accounting information system to an enterprise system.

Exercises and Problems

16–1 Multiple Choice. Choose the best answer.

1. Under *GASBS 34* and *35,* public colleges and universities engaged only in business-type activities present all of the following statements in their stand-alone reports except a:
   a. Statement of net assets.
   b. Statement of revenues, expenses, and changes in net assets.
   c. Statement of revenues, expenditures, and changes in fund balances.
   d. Statement of cash flows.

2. Private colleges and universities must report on:
   a. Changes in fund balances.
   b. Changes in net assets.
   c. Cash flows from operating, financing, and investing activities.
   d. Both changes in net assets and cash flows from operating, financing, and investing activities.

3. Which of the following is a true statement about tuition revenue in a college or university?
   a. Scholarships should always be reported as expenses.
   b. Tuition receivables estimated to be uncollectible should be reported as an operating expense.
   c. Refunds should be reported as deductions from gross revenue.
   d. All of these statements are true.

4. Depreciation is a cost of using long-lived assets and must be recorded by which type of college or university?
   a. Public colleges and universities.
   b. Private colleges and universities.
   c. Both private and public colleges and universities.
   d. Neither private nor public colleges and universities.

5. Funds that the governing board of a public university has set aside and designated only the income earned on the assets as expendable are called:
   a. Term endowments.
   b. Designated, unrestricted net assets.

   c. Life income agreements.

   d. Permanently restricted net assets.

6. If a college or university expends more than $500,000 in federal awards, such as research grants, it is required to:

   a. Have a single audit in accordance with the provisions of OMB *Circular A–133.*

   b. Follow OMB *Circular A–21,* "Cost Principles for Educational Institutions."

   c. Follow federal uniform administrative requirements under OMB *Circular A–110.*

   d. Do all of the above.

7. Accounting for public colleges and universities and private colleges and universities differs in that:

   a. Net assets are classified differently.

   b. Depreciation is reported differently.

   c. Collections are reported differently.

   d. Only private colleges and universities report investments at fair value.

8. Under generally accepted accounting principles applicable to public universities, the monies resulting from a new library construction fund drive would be recorded as increases to:

   a. Unrestricted net assets.

   b. Permanently restricted net assets.

   c. Restricted assets.

   d. Restricted net assets.

9. Funds received from an external donor that are to be retained and invested, with the related earnings restricted to purchase library books would be accounted for as an increase to:

   a. Temporarily restricted net assets in a private university.

   b. Nonexpendable, restricted net assets in a public university.

   c. Unrestricted net assets in either a public or private university.

   d. Permanently restricted net assets in a public university.

10. A statement of cash flows is required for

	Public Colleges and Universities	Private Colleges and Universities
a.	Yes	Yes
b.	Yes	No
c.	No	Yes
d.	No	No

16–2 Private College Transactions. Elizabeth College, a small private college, had the following transactions in fiscal year 2008.

1. Billings for tuition and fees totaled $5,600,000. Tuition waivers and scholarships of $61,500 were granted. Students received tuition refunds of $101,670.

2. During the year the college received $1,891,000 cash in unrestricted private gifts, $575,200 cash in temporarily restricted grants, and $1,000,000 in securities for an endowment.

3. A pledge campaign generated $626,000 in unrestricted pledges, payable in fiscal year 2009.

4. Auxiliary enterprises provided goods and services that generated $94,370 in cash.

5. Collections of tuition receivable totaled $5,380,000.

6. Unrestricted cash of $1,000,000 was invested.

7. The college purchased computer equipment at a cost of $10,580.

8. During the year the following expenses were paid:

Instruction	$3,866,040
Academic support	1,987,000
Student services	87,980
Institutional support	501,130
Auxiliary enterprises	92,410

9. Instruction provided $450,000 in services related to the temporarily restricted grant recorded in transaction 2.

10. At year-end, the allowance for uncollectible tuition and fees was increased by $7,200. The fair value of investments had increased $11,540, of this amount, $3,040 was allocated to permanently restricted net assets, the remainder was allocated to unrestricted net assets. Depreciation on plant and equipment was allocated $34,750 to instruction, $41,000 to auxiliary enterprises, and $12,450 to academic support.

11. All nominal accounts were closed.

Required

a. Prepare journal entries in good form to record the foregoing transactions for the fiscal year ended June 30, 2008.

b. Prepare a statement of activities for the year ended June 30, 2008. Assume beginning net asset amounts of $7,518,000 unrestricted, $200,000 temporarily restricted, and $5,000,000 permanently restricted.

16–3 **Public University Transactions.** The Statement of Net Assets of Baraga State University, a governmentally owned university, as of the end of its fiscal year June 30, 2007, follows.

BARAGA STATE UNIVERSITY
Statement of Net Assets
June 30, 2007

Assets		
Cash		$ 340,000
Accounts receivable (net of doubtful accounts of $15,000)		370,000
Prepaid expenses		40,000
Investments		210,000
Capital assets	$1,750,000	
Accumulated depreciation	275,000	1,475,000
Total assets		2,435,000
Liabilities		
Accounts payable		105,000
Accrued liabilities		40,000
Deferred revenue		25,000
Bonds payable		600,000
Total liabilities		770,000

Net Assets

Invested in capital assets, net of related debt	875,000
Restricted	215,000
Unrestricted	575,000
Total net assets	$1,665,000

The following information pertains to the year ended June 30, 2008:

1. Cash collected from students' tuition totaled $3,000,000. Of this $3,000,000, $362,000 represented accounts receivable outstanding at June 30, 2007; $2,500,000 was for current-year tuition; and $138,000 was for tuition applicable to the semester beginning in August 2008.

2. Deferred revenue at June 30, 2007, was earned during the year ended June 30, 2008.

3. Accounts receivable in the amount of $13,000 were determined uncollectible and were written off against the allowance account. At June 30, 2008, the allowance account balance should be $10,000.

4. During the year, an unrestricted appropriation of $60,000 was made by the state. This state appropriation was to be paid to Baraga sometime in August 2008.

5. Equipment for the student computer labs was purchased for cash in the amount of $225,000.

6. During the year, unrestricted cash gifts of $80,000 were received from alumni. Baraga's board of trustees allocated $30,000 of these gifts to student loans.

7. Interest expense on the bonds payable in the amount of $48,000 was paid.

8. During the year, investments with a carrying value of $25,000 were sold for $31,000. Investments were purchased at a cost of $40,000. Investment income of $18,000 was earned and collected during the year.

9. General expenses of $2,500,000 were recorded in the voucher system. At June 30, 2008, the accounts payable balance was $75,000.

10. Accrued liabilities at June 30, 2007, were paid.

11. One-quarter of the prepaid expenses at June 30, 2007, expired during the current year; they pertained to general education expense. There was no addition to prepaid expenses during the year.

12. Depreciation expense on the capital assets in the amount of $90,000 was recorded.

Required

a. Prepare journal entries in good form to record the foregoing transactions for the year ended June 30, 2008, including closing the nominal accounts.
b. Prepare a statement of net assets for the year ended June 30, 2008.

16–4 Financial Statements—Private University. The following is the pre-closing trial balance for Horton University as of June 30, 2008. Additional information related to net assets and the statement of cash flows is also provided.

HORTON UNIVERSITY
Pre-Closing Trial Balance
June 30, 2008

	Debits	Credits
Cash and Cash Equivalents	$1,516,600	
Investments	3,200,000	
Tuition and Fees Receivable	372,400	
Allowance for Doubtful Accounts		$ 75,600
Pledges Receivable	223,000	
Allowance for Doubtful Pledges		79,000
Property, Plant and Equipment	1,996,160	
Accumulated Depreciation		658,720
Accounts Payable		103,000
Accrued Liabilities		37,500
Deposits Held in Custody for Others		17,570
Bonds Payable		792,000
Deferred Revenue		62,150
Liabilities Under Split-Interest Agreements		40,510
Net Assets—Unrestricted		4,051,410
Net Assets—Temporarily Restricted		200,600
Net Assets—Permanently Restricted		980,000
Net Assets Released from Restrictions—Temporarily Restricted	26,850	
Net Assets Released from Restrictions—Unrestricted		26,850
Tuition and Fees		290,750
Tuition and Fees Discounts and Allowances	98,000	
Contributions—Unrestricted		310,200
Contributions—Temporarily Restricted		77,000
Grants and Contracts—Unrestricted		324,000
Grants and Contracts—Temporarily Restricted		121,800
Investment Income—Unrestricted		11,500
Other Revenue		13,250
Auxiliary Enterprise Sales and Services		53,560
Unrealized Gain on Investments		280,400
Instruction Expense	629,750	
Research Expense	269,600	
Academic Support Expense	100,400	
Student Services Expense	46,500	
Institutional Support Expense	68,910	
Auxiliary Enterprise Expenses	58,700	
Loss on Sale of Equipment	500	
Total	$8,580,520	$8,580,520

Additional information:

Net assets released from temporary restrictions totaled $26,850. There were no restrictions on the investment income earned. Twenty percent of the unrealized gain is related to permanently restricted net assets, 10 percent is related to temporarily restricted net assets, with the remainder related to unrestricted net assets.

The difference between the beginning and ending balances were as follows:

Tuition and Fees Receivable increased by $10,230, while Pledges Receivable decreased by $1,560. The Allowance for Doubtful Accounts was increased by $770 to allow for an increase in estimated uncollectible tuition and fees (the bad debt was netted against Tuition and Fees). No adjustment was made to the Allowance for Uncollectible Pledges. Accounts Payable decreased by $2,900, and Accrued Liabilities decreased by $1,120. There was an increase of $6,200 in deferred revenues. For the period, depreciation expense was $30,070. Cash was used to retire $100,000 in bonds. Investments were sold for $1,500,000 and others were purchased for $1,250,000.

Required

a. Prepare a statement of activities for the year ended June 30, 2008.

b. Prepare a statement of financial position for June 30, 2008.

c. Prepare a statement of cash flow for the year ended June 30, 2008.

16–5 Institutionally Related Foundations. Review each of the following cases that describe a public university and a foundation related to it (i.e., an institutionally related foundation). Explain whether the criteria in GASB *Statement No. 39,* "Determining Whether Certain Organizations Are Component Units," are met so that the organizations should be discretely presented in the financial statements of the public university. If the criteria are not met, explain why.

1. *University Alumni Association.* KMH University Alumni Association was established as a legally separate, tax-exempt organization to support both KMH University and its students. Generally, when the university awards a scholarship to a student who meets the criteria established by the Alumni Association, the university requests funds from the Alumni Association's resources. Normally, the Alumni Association honors the request and transfers the funds to the university. In the current year, the Alumni Association has endowed a chair and financed 14 scholarships for the KMH University School of Business and has donated funds for these purposes to KMH University. The funds donated directly to the university and the resources held by the association are significant to the university's financial statements.

2. *University Fund-Raising Foundation.* CCB University Foundation is a legally separate, tax-exempt organization whose bylaws state that it exists solely to provide financial support to CCB University. The foundation regularly makes distributions directly to the university and pays certain maintenance expenses by making payments directly to vendors and contractors rather than the university. Separately, the direct cash payments to the university and the maintenance expenses of the university paid by the foundation are not significant to the university; however, they are significant when combined. The economic resources of the foundation that are restricted for the benefit of the university are significant.

3. *University Research Foundation.* Ten years ago, the State University Research Foundation was established as a legally separate, tax-exempt organization to provide the buildings, laboratory facilities, and administrative support necessary for the faculty of State University to competitively attract and carry out research grants, principally from the federal government and corporations. The foundation's total research and administrative costs were significant to the university in the current year. The foundation occupies two buildings that it constructed on campus on land leased from the university. A significant

portion of instructional faculty in the School of Engineering, Science, and Technology carry out research at the foundation, and the annual university performance evaluations and merit increases of these faculty are based to a certain extent on the research they perform at the foundation.

The completion of a research grant typically results in the submittal of a report of research findings and recommendations to the grantor, and often the publication of results in academic and professional journals. This research activity is deemed integral to the duties of faculty and is consistent with the university's mission.

A formal agreement between the university and the foundation requires the foundation to make its general lecture and meeting rooms available, upon request, to the university, and to make certain research laboratories available for special lectures and seminars. The university's personnel office provides administrative support for hiring foundation personnel, including research technicians who typically are selected by faculty committees. The relationship between the university and the foundation is disclosed in a brochure for prospective faculty of the university.

Students enrolled in university graduate courses work at the foundation as research assistants. They are compensated through stipends paid by research grants through financial aid work-study programs administered by the university. Faculty are required to periodically report their research, instructional, and other efforts through a reporting system administered jointly by the foundation and the university. Faculty working on research grants typically receive a portion of their compensation from grant funds.

Note: The preceding cases were taken from Appendix C of *GASBS 39*.

16–6 Financial Statements—Public University. The following balances come from the trial balance of Big Horn State University as of the end of the 2008 fiscal year. Accounts are listed in alphabetical order.

Academic Support Expenses	$ 17,054,226
Accounts Payable and Accrued Liabilities	33,615,927
Accounts Receivable	6,202,298
Additions to Permanent Endowments	2,436,702
Auxiliary Activities Expenses	18,475,126
Auxiliary Activities Revenue	23,729,637
Capital Appropriations	5,298,182
Capital Assets, Net of Accumulated Depreciation	288,882,469
Capital Grants and Gifts	19,079,213
Cash and Cash Equivalents	12,670,760
Deferred Revenue	7,798,417
Depreciation Expense	9,340,062
Endowment Investments	39,735,741
Gain on Disposal of Plant Assets	871,026
Gifts	4,666,959
Government Grants and Contracts Revenue	14,414,080
Institutional Support Expenses	10,277,381
Instruction Expenses	69,767,112
Interest on Capital Asset-Related Debt	3,923,062
Inventory	1,795,231
Investment Income (Net of Investment Expense)	2,152,407
Loan Administrative Fees and Collection Costs	289,669

Long-term Liabilities—Current Portion	4,669,830
Long-term Liabilities—Noncurrent Portion	81,456,504
Net Assets—Invested in Capital Assets, Net of Related Debt	208,351,923
Net Assets—Restricted for Nonexpendable—Scholarships & Academic Support	15,342,683
Net Assets—Restricted for Expendable—Scholarships & Academic Support	16,034,683
Net Assets—Restricted for Expendable—Capital Projects	16,405,221
Net Assets—Restricted for Expendable—Loans	10,797,539
Net Assets—Unrestricted	??
Nongovernmental Grants Revenue	277,682
Operation and Maintenance—Plant Expenses	14,123,470
Other Assets—Noncurrent	1,252,509
Other Long-Term Investments	16,811,243
Other Operating Revenues	5,133,584
Pledges Receivable—Current	5,319,067
Pledges Receivable—Noncurrent	10,878,556
Prepaid Expenses & Other	1,138,157
Public Service Expenses	9,063,014
Research Expenses	1,794,503
Restricted Cash & Cash Equivalents	1,016,245
Restricted Short-Term Investments	13,279,961
Sales and Services of Educational Activities	3,737,481
Scholarships and Related Expenses	5,182,992
Short-Term Investments	23,707,181
State Appropriation Receivable	21,822,389
State Appropriations	60,688,422
Student Notes Receivable—Current Portion	2,303,000
Student Notes Receivable—Net of Allowance—Noncurrent	8,043,530
Student Services Expenses	14,043,915
Student Tuition and Fees (Net of Scholarship Allowances)	69,456,040

Other information follows:

Cash and Cash Equivalents at the Beginning of the Year	$ 3,221,231

Cash Flows from Capital and Related Financing Activities

Bond issue costs paid on new debt issue	553,675
Capital appropriations	10,959,667
Capital grants and gifts received	10,083,302
Interest paid on capital debt	3,365,408
Principal paid on capital debt	3,355,000
Proceeds from capital debt	36,475,000
Proceeds from sale of capital assets	955,806
Purchases of capital assets and construction	58,698,119

Cash Flows from Investing Activities

Investment income	2,044,992
Proceeds from sales and maturities of investments	69,000,425
Purchase of investments	82,433,705

Cash Flows from Operating Activities

Auxiliary activities charges	23,435,232
Collection of loans from students	11,022,203
Grants and contracts	13,014,446
Loans issued to students	10,901,362
Other receipts	7,785,394
Payments for benefits	20,519,694
Payments for scholarships and fellowships	4,418,546

Payments for utilities	5,244,151
Payments to employees	81,353,053
Payments to suppliers	42,975,054
Sales and service of educational activities	4,293,735
Tuition and fees	70,252,353
Cash Flows from Noncapital Financing Activities	
Charitable annuities receipts, net of payments	1,535,724
Federal direct loan lending disbursements	42,636,345
Federal direct loan receipts	42,680,945
Gifts and grants for other than capital purposes	3,802,250
Private gifts for endowment purposes	2,436,702
State appropriations	57,141,710
Net assets at the beginning of the year	288,710,776

Required

a. Prepare a statement of revenues, expenses, and changes in net assets for the year ended June 30, 2008, in good form. See Illustration 16–2; however, display expenses using functional classifications as shown in Illustration 16–6.

b. Prepare a statement of net assets as of June 30, 2008, in good form. See Illustration 16–1.

c. Prepare a statement of cash flows for the year ended June 30, 2008, in good form. See Illustration 16–3.

Chapter Seventeen

Accounting for Health Care Organizations

Learning Objectives

After studying this chapter, you should be able to:

1. Identify the different organizational forms and the related authoritative accounting literature for health care organizations.
2. Describe financial reporting for health care organizations.
3. Explain unique accounting and measurement issues in health care organizations including accounting for revenues, assets, expenses, and liabilities.
4. Journalize transactions and prepare the basic financial statements for not-for-profit and governmental health care organizations.
5. Describe other accounting issues in the health care industry:

   Budgeting and costs.

   Auditing.

   Taxation and regulation.

   Prepaid health care services.

   Continuing care retirement communities.
6. Explain financial and operational analysis of health care organizations.

HEALTH CARE INDUSTRY

The health care industry in the United States changed dramatically in the last century. In the early 1900s health care was provided primarily by not-for-profit hospitals affiliated with communities or religious organizations, major projects were funded by donations, and hospital managers had little financial expertise and faced few regulations. Today, health care organizations are complex entities that cross the private, public, and not-for-profit sectors; spiraling costs outpace inflation, capital construction requires extensive financing, and professional managers face increasing public scrutiny and government oversight. Technological advances brought dramatic changes in the delivery and quality of health care services but also contributed greatly to rising costs. Health care spending in 2003 was $1.7 trillion, representing 15.3 percent of gross domestic product.[1]

---

[1] National Coalition on Health Care. *Health Insurance Cost.* www.nchc.org.

Political, social, and economic factors explain the tremendous change in the health care industry. For example, in the 1940s and 1950s, health insurance coverage became a common employee fringe benefit, and health care providers began to look to employers and third parties for payment for services. The Hill Burton Program in 1944 encouraged growth in the industry by making federal funds available for the construction of health care facilities.[2] The initiation of entitlement programs, such as Medicare and Medicaid in the 1960s, reflected public policy efforts to make health care a basic right to be regulated at the federal level. In the 1980s, employers and insurance companies initiated managed care systems in an attempt to bring down the cost of providing health care coverage. In the 1990s, comprehensive health care reform became a political issue at the federal level.

Health care continues to be a political issue in the first decade of the 21st century, with soaring health care costs exceeding four times the rate of inflation in 2003 alone.[3] Today, roughly half of *hospital* health care is provided by not-for-profit organizations, although most *providers* of health care are for-profit groups of medical professionals who are associated with governmental or not-for-profit health care organizations. Illustration 17–1 shows classifications of health care organizations by legal structure as well as by the nature of services they provide. This chapter focuses on the financial reporting and accounting issues of primarily not-for-profit and governmental organizations that charge patients or third parties for the services provided. Voluntary health and welfare organizations, which are nonbusiness oriented and provide more general social services funded primarily by contributions and grants rather than charges for services, are discussed in Chapter 14.

GAAP FOR HEALTH CARE PROVIDERS

Generally accepted accounting principles (GAAP) for hospitals and other health care organizations have evolved through the efforts of the American Hospital Association (AHA), the Healthcare Financial Management Association (HFMA), and the American Institute of Certified Public Accountants (AICPA). More recently, statements of the Financial Accounting Standards Board and the Governmental Accounting Standards Board have directly impacted accounting and reporting for health care providers. The AICPA Audit and Accounting Guide *Health Care Organizations* applies to health care organizations that are either (1) investor-owned businesses, (2) not-for-profit enterprises that, although they have no ownership interests, are essentially business oriented and self-sustaining from fees charged for goods and services, or (3) governmental entities. These organizations are often classified by the nature of the services provided, as listed in Illustration 17–1. Since 1990, the AICPA Audit and Accounting Guide has covered *all* providers of health care services, not just hospitals. The guide covers *governmental* providers that use proprietary accounting, as well as private and not-for-profit health care organizations.[4]

---

[2] The Hospital Survey and Construction Act of 1946 (P.L. 79-725).

[3] National Coalition on Health Care. *Health Insurance Cost.* www.nchc.org.

[4] American Institute of Certified Public Accountants, Audit and Accounting Guide, *Health Care Organizations* (AAG-HCO) (New York: AICPA, 2004).

ILLUSTRATION 17–1 **Classification of Health Care Organizations**

Sponsorship or Legal Structure

For-profit (Proprietary)   Not-for-profit: Business oriented   Governmental: Public

For-profit (Proprietary)

Are:

– Investor owned

Not-for-profit: Business oriented

Are:

– Community based

– Religion affiliated

– Private university sponsored

Governmental: Public

Are:

– Federal

– State

– County

– City

– Public university sponsored

Types of Health Care Organizations

Clinics, medical group practices, individual practice associations, individual practitioners, and other ambulatory care organizations

Continuing care retirement communities (CCRCs)

Health maintenance organizations (HMOs) and similar prepaid health care plans

Home health agencies

Hospitals

Nursing homes that provide skilled, intermediate, and a less-intensive level of health care

Drug and alcohol rehabilitation centers and other rehabilitation facilities

Parent companies and other organizations that primarily plan, organize, and oversee health care services

Source: Adapted from the American Institute of Certified Public Accountants, Audit and Accounting Guide, *Health Care Organizations* (New York: AICPA, 2005), Preface.

Governmental hospitals and health care providers are considered special purpose governments, that is, legally separate entities that may be either component units of another government or stand-alone governmental entities. *GASBS 34* provides guidance for organizations that may be engaged in either governmental or business-type activities or both. The AICPA Audit and Accounting Guide is considered category (b) authority for both governmental and nongovernmental entities, which means that GASB and FASB statements

ILLUSTRATION 17–2   GAAP for Health Care Entities in Different Sectors

Accounting and Reporting Issue	Health Care Providers		
	Investor Owned	Not-for-Profit	Governmental
Reporting entity	APB *Opinion No. 18*, *SFAS No. 94*	AICPA *SOP 94-3*	GASB *Statement Nos. 14* and *39*
Contributions and financial statement display	*SFAS No. 116*	*SFAS Nos. 116* and *117*	GASB *Statement Nos. 33* and *34*
Cash flows	*SFAS No. 95*	*SFAS No. 95*	GASB *Statement No. 9*
Deposits with financial institutions	*SFAS No. 105*	*SFAS No. 105*	GASB *Statement Nos. 3* and *40*
Investments	*SFAS No. 115* and AAG-HCO, Chapter 4	*SFAS No. 124*	GASB *Statement Nos. 3, 28, 31*, and *40*
Operating leases	*SFAS No. 13*	*SFAS No. 13*	GASB *Statement No. 13*
Prepaid health care arrangements and self-insurance programs	AAG-HCO, Chapters 8 and 14	AAG-HCO, Chapters 8 and 14	GASB *Statement No. 10*
Compensated absences	*SFAS Nos. 43* and *112*	*SFAS Nos. 43* and *112*	GASB *Statement No. 16*
Debt refundings	APB *Opinion No. 26, SFAS Nos. 4* and *125*	APB *Opinion No. 26, SFAS Nos. 4* and *125*	GASB *Statement Nos. 7* and *23*
Pensions	*SFAS No. 87* and *132* (revised)	*SFAS Nos. 87* and *132* (revised)	GASB *Statement No. 27*
Risks and uncertainties	AICPA *SOP 94-6*	AICPA *SOP 94-6*	GASB *Statement Nos. 10* and *30*
Post retirement benefits	*SFAS Nos. 106* and *132* (revised)	*SFAS Nos. 106* and *132* (revised)	GASB *Statement No. 45*

Source: Adapted from the AICPA, *Audit Risk Alert, Health Care Industry Developments—2001/02* (New York: AICPA, 2002), par. 121.

take precedence.[5] Consequently, even though there is only one audit guide for all health care entities, accounting and reporting rules may differ, depending on whether the health care provider is legally structured as an investor-owned, not-for-profit, or governmental organization. Some of the differences relate to accounting and reporting for contributions and financial reporting display, cash flows, and investments, as seen in Illustration 17–2. This chapter illustrates financial accounting and reporting for not-for-profit health care organizations, the largest segment of the in-patient health care industry, and points out differences unique to governmental health care providers. The reader is directed to Chapter 14 for a more thorough discussion of *SFAS Nos. 116* and *117* for not-for-profit organizations, and to Chapter 7 for a discussion of business-type enterprises of government.

FINANCIAL REPORTING

The financial statements of a health care entity serve a broad set of users and consequently include: (1) balance sheet (statement of financial position) or statement of net assets; (2) statement of operations or statement of revenues, expenses, and changes in net assets; and (3) statement of cash flows, as well as notes to the financial statements.

[5] American Institute of Certified Public Accountants, *SAS No. 69*, "The Meaning of 'Present Fairly in Conformity with Generally Accepted Accounting Principles' in the Independent Auditor's Report" (New York: AICPA, 1991), as amended by *SAS No. 91*, "Federal GAAP Hierarchy," 2001.

ILLUSTRATION 17–3

BLOOMFIELD HOSPITAL
Balance Sheet
As of September 30, 2008

Assets		Liabilities and Net Assets	
Current assets:		Current liabilities:	
Cash	$ 172,100	Accounts payable	$ 259,000
Accounts and notes receivable, net of		Accrued expenses payable	173,500
allowance for uncollectibles of $135,000	353,000		
Pledges receivable, net of allowance for			
uncollectibles of $114,300	548,700		
Accrued interest receivable	44,000		
Inventory	160,000		
Prepaid expenses	8,000		
Short-term investments	1,778,000		
Total current assets	3,063,800	Total current liabilities	432,500
Assets limited as to use:		Long-term debt:	
Internally designated for capital		Mortgages payable	6,000,000
acquisition—cash	6,500	Total liabilities	6,432,500
Internally designated for capital			
acquisition—investments	778,000		
Total assets limited as to use	784,500	Net assets:	
Long-term investments	146,000	Unrestricted—undesignated	8,536,600
Property, plant, and equipment:		Unrestricted—designated	784,500
Land	1,080,000	Temporarily restricted	2,417,700
Buildings, net of accumulated		Permanently restricted	178,000
depreciation of $1,365,000	9,685,000	Total net assets	11,916,800
Equipment, net of accumulated			
depreciation of $1,702,000	3,590,000		
Total property, plant, and equipment	14,355,000		
Total assets	$18,349,300	Total liabilities and net assets	$18,349,300

Additionally, proprietary and not-for-profit entities prepare a statement of changes in equity (net assets), which can be issued as a separate statement or combined with the statement of operations. The FASB and AICPA allow considerable flexibility in displaying financial information.

A health care organization may choose to use fund accounting for internal purposes, in part, to account for revenues and expenses associated with grants (or because it is a governmental entity). For organizations using fund accounting, the fund structure should include general unrestricted funds and donor-restricted funds (e.g., specific purpose, plant replacement and expansion, and endowment). Comparative statements for a hypothetical not-for-profit hospital are presented in Illustrations 17–3 through 17–5.

Balance Sheet or Statement of Net Assets

The balance sheet presented in Illustration 17–3 is for Bloomfield Hospital, a hypothetical not-for-profit health care entity. Not-for-profit organizations are

ILLUSTRATION 17–4   **Illustration of a Two-Part Statement of Operations**

BLOOMFIELD HOSPITAL
Statement of Operations
Year Ended September 30, 2008

Unrestricted revenues, gains, and other support:		
Net patient service revenue		$ 9,161,000
Other revenue		48,800
Contributions		297,900
Investment income		36,100
Total revenues and gains		9,543,800
Expenses and losses:		
Nursing services	$4,667,500	
Other professional services	1,311,620	
General services	2,056,260	
Fiscal and administrative services	1,332,320	
Total expenses		9,367,700
Loss on disposal of equipment		1,500
Total expenses and losses		9,369,200
Excess of revenue and gains over expenses and losses		174,600
Net assets released from restrictions:		
Satisfaction of equipment acquisition restrictions		100,000
Increase in unrestricted net assets		$ 274,600

Statement of Changes in Net Assets
Year Ended September 30, 2008

Unrestricted net assets (see Part 1 above):	
Total unrestricted revenues, gains, and other support	$ 9,543,800
Net assets released from restrictions	100,000
Total unrestricted expenses and losses	(9,369,200)
Increase in unrestricted net assets	274,600
Temporarily restricted net assets:	
Contributions	25,000
Investment income	77,000
Increase in provision for uncollectible pledges	(66,300)
Loss on sale of investments	(26,000)
Net assets released from restrictions	(100,000)
Decrease in temporarily restricted net assets	(90,300)
Permanently restricted net assets:	
Contributions	24,000
Increase in permanently restricted net assets	24,000
Increase in net assets	208,300
Net assets at beginning of year	11,708,500
Net assets at end of year	$11,916,800

ILLUSTRATION 17–5   **Illustration of Statement of Cash Flows—Not-for-Profit Organizations**

BLOOMFIELD HOSPITAL
Statement of Cash Flows
Year Ended September 30, 2008

CASH FLOWS FROM OPERATING ACTIVITIES	
Cash received from patients and third-party payors	$ 8,842,000
Other receipts from operations	48,800
Interest received on assets limited as to use	36,100
Receipts from unrestricted gifts	297,900
Cash paid to employees and suppliers	(8,014,200)
Interest paid	(160,000)
Net cash provided by operating activities	1,050,600
CASH FLOWS FROM INVESTING ACTIVITIES	
Purchase of property and equipment	(400,000)
Purchase of long-term investments	(737,000)
Proceeds from sale of securities	59,000
Proceeds from sale of equipment	500
Net cash used by investing activities	(1,077,500)
CASH FLOWS FROM FINANCING ACTIVITIES	
Proceeds from contributions restricted for:	
Investment in plant	292,000
Future operations	5,000
	297,000
Other financing activities:	
Interest and dividends restricted to endowment	69,000
Repayment of long-term debt	(400,000)
	(331,000)
Net cash used by financing activities	(34,000)
Net increase (decrease) in cash	(60,900)
Cash and cash equivalents, September 30, 2007	239,500
Cash and cash equivalents, September 30, 2008	$ 178,600

Reconciliation of Changes in Net Assets to Net Cash
Provided by Operating Activities

Changes in net assets	$ 208,300
Adjustments to reconcile change in net assets to net cash provided by operating activities:	
Depreciation	783,000
Loss on disposal of equipment	1,500
Increase in patient accounts receivable, net	(139,000)
Increase in supplies	(80,000)
Increase in accounts payable and accrued expenses	306,500
Decrease in prepaid expenses	4,000
Gifts, grants, and bequests restricted for long-term investment	(49,000)
Interest restricted for long-term investment	(77,000)
Loss on sale of investments	26,000
Increase in provision for uncollectible pledges	66,300
Net cash provided by operating activities	$ 1,050,600

required to present information about the liquidity of their assets and liabilities. The net asset section of a not-for-profit organization balance sheet should classify net assets into unrestricted, temporarily restricted, and permanently restricted categories, as described in Chapter 14. Governmental organizations classify net assets into invested in capital assets, restricted, and unrestricted, as illustrated in Chapters 1 through 9. The equity section of an investor-owned health care provider should show stockholders' equity separated into capital stock and retained earnings.

Operating Statement

The principal sources of revenue for a health care organization are (1) patient service revenue, (2) premium revenue derived from **capitation fees,** which are fixed fees per person paid periodically, regardless of services provided, by a health maintenance organization, (3) resident service revenue, such as maintenance or rental fees in an extended care facility, and (4) other revenue or gains. Service revenue is shown net of contractual adjustments, discussed later in this chapter. Other revenue includes sales (e.g., medical supplies and cafeteria meals), fees (e.g., for educational programs or transcripts), rental of facilities other than to residents, investment income and gains, contributions, and grants. Additionally, some governmental health care organizations may be supported, at least in part, by taxes or intergovernmental revenue. Research grants or contracts may be considered exchange transactions or nonexchange transactions (i.e., contributions), as discussed in Chapters 14 and 16. Not-for-profit health care entities show net assets released from temporary restrictions as increases to unrestricted net assets, and also indicate how the restriction was met, such as passage of time or through acquisition of equipment. Bloomfield Hospital, as shown in Illustration 17–4, reports some of these sources of income.

Considerable flexibility is allowed not-for-profits in displaying the results of operations, such as identification by such classes as operating and nonoperating, earned and unearned, or recurring and nonrecurring. FASB concepts statements provide guidance on distinguishing operating items (i.e., those arising from ongoing major activities, such as service revenue) from nonoperating items (i.e., those arising from transactions peripheral or incidental to the delivery of health care, such as investment income and unrestricted contributions).[6] Unlike not-for-profits, governmental health care entities are required to display operating and nonoperating activity on the operating statement.

As required, this not-for-profit hospital reports all expenses as decreases in unrestricted net assets. Functional expenses must be displayed or disclosed in the notes and can be as simple as distinguishing between health care services and support services, such as general/administrative expenses. If functional expenses are displayed, all natural expenses (e.g., depreciation, interest, and provision for bad debts) should be allocated to the functional expenses.

Not-for-profit health care organizations should include a **performance indicator** to report the results of operations. The principal components of a performance indicator are unrestricted revenues, gains, and other support; expenses; and other income. Examples include excess of revenues over expenses, revenues and gains over expenses and losses, earned income, and performance earnings. Investment income, realized gains and losses, and unrealized gains and losses on trading securities should be

[6] Financial Accounting Standards Board, *Concepts Statement No. 6,* "Elements of Financial Statements" (Norwalk, CT: FASB, 1985).

reported in the performance indicator; however, the following items should be reported separately from the performance indicator:

- Transactions with owners acting in that capacity.
- Equity transfers involving other related entities.
- Receipt of temporarily and permanently restricted contributions.
- Contributions of (and assets released from donor restrictions related to) long-lived assets.
- Unrealized gains and losses on investments other than trading securities.
- Investment returns restricted by donors or by law.
- Other items that are required by GAAP to be reported separately, such as extraordinary items, the effect of discontinued operations, or the cumulative effect of accounting changes.[7]

Statement of Changes in Net Assets

Illustration 17–4 shows increases and decreases in the three classes of net assets for a not-for-profit organization: unrestricted, temporarily restricted, and permanently restricted. Net assets released from restrictions increase unrestricted net assets and decrease temporarily restricted net assets. Net gains on permanently restricted endowments are shown as increases to the permanently restricted net assets in Illustration 17–4; however, the accounting treatment of net gains will depend on donor stipulations, state law, and organizational policy. Note that this statement may be combined with the statement of activities or operations. Governmental health care entities do not have a statement comparable to the statement of changes in net assets.

Statement of Cash Flows

The statement of cash flows in Illustration 17–5 is that required by *SFAS No. 95* (as amended).[8] The direct method is presented with a reconciliation of changes in net assets to net cash provided by operating activities, although the indirect method is also acceptable. Note that Illustration 17–6, presented later in this chapter, shows the statement of cash flows required by GASB standards for a governmental health care organization. That statement includes a fourth section, cash flows from noncapital financing activities. The FASB statement can be prepared using either the direct method or the indirect method, but under *GASBS 34,* governmental entities must use the direct method.[9] The statements differ primarily in terms of which cash flows are reported as part of each activity. In the GASB statement, interest paid and interest received are reported as investing activities, whereas the same items are reported as operating activities in the FASB statement except for investment income added to temporarily or permanently restricted net assets. Such restricted income is reported in the FASB statement as a financing activity. Acquisitions of property and equipment are reported as capital and related financing activities in the GASB statement but as investing activities in the FASB statement. Unrestricted gifts are reported as cash flows from noncapital financing activities in the GASB statement but as cash flows from operating activities in the FASB statement. A final, and major, difference is that the reconciliation

[7] AAG-HCO, pars. 4.06, 10.19.

[8] Financial Accounting Standards Board, *Statement No. 95,* "Statement of Cash Flows" (Norwalk, CT: FASB, 1987), as amended by *SFAS No. 117,* "Financial Statements of Not-for-Profit Organizations" (Norwalk, CT: FASB, 1993), par. 30.

[9] GASB, *Statement No. 34,* par. 105.

schedule in the GASB statement reconciles operating income (loss) to cash flows from operating activities, whereas in the FASB statement the schedule reconciles changes in net assets to cash flows from operating activities. In preparing either cash flow statement, the worksheet or T-account approaches explained in most intermediate accounting texts may be useful.

ACCOUNTING AND MEASUREMENT ISSUES

Revenues

Sources of Revenue

Health care organizations receive the majority of their revenue in the form of fees for services. These fees may come from the patient; the government in the form of Medicare or Medicaid payments; third-party payors, such as Blue Cross/Blue Shield or other private insurance companies; or contracts with other private health care companies. This service revenue is recorded at the gross amount when services are rendered. **Contractual adjustments (or allowances)** are recorded as contra-revenue accounts (i.e., reductions of revenue and receivables) for the difference between the gross patient service revenue and the negotiated payment by third-party payors in arriving at net patient service revenue. Prepaid health care plans that earn revenues from *agreements to provide* services record revenue at the point that agreements are made, not when services are rendered. The variety of payment plans with third-party payors makes accounting for patient service revenue a complicated accounting task. For example, payments can be made on a per case, per service performed, per diem, or per person (capitated) basis. In addition, interim payments are often received with final settlement at a later point in time.

Charity Service

Tax-exempt entities are expected to provide **charity care,** services to persons with a demonstrated inability to pay. Since charity service is never expected to result in cash flows, it is neither recognized as revenue nor receivables nor bad debt expense.[10] If the health care organization does not pursue collection of amounts determined to qualify as charity care, they are not reported as revenue. In practice, it is often difficult to distinguish bad debt expense from charity service. However, it is important to disclose management's charity care policies and the level of care provided for several reasons. The Hill-Burton Act of 1946 requires that hospitals receiving federal assistance for construction projects perform some charity care. The IRS and local tax authorities question the tax-exempt status of some not-for-profit health care providers that do not appear to deliver an adequate amount of charity service to justify their tax exemption, although regulations do not specify levels of adequacy. Some third-party payors reimburse for a portion of bad debts but not charity service.

Third-Party Payors

Contracts with Medicare, Medicaid, Blue Cross and other insurance companies, and state and local welfare agencies customarily provide for payment by **third-party payors** according to allowable costs or a predetermined (prospective) contractual rate rather than paying the service rates billed by the health care provider. For example, under Medicare's **Prospective Payment System (PPS),** payments are based on allowable

[10] AAG-HCO, par. 10.03.

service costs for medical procedures within the same diagnosis-related group (DRG), explained later in this chapter, rather than on the length of the patient's hospital stay or actual cost of services rendered. Some payment methods, such as capitation fees in prepaid health care plans, shift a considerable amount of risk to the provider. That is, the fixed amount of revenue received per patient may not cover the costs of providing the service.

Other Revenue and Support

Services donated to a not-for-profit health care entity and noncash assets donated to a not-for-profit or governmental health care entity generally are recorded at their fair value when received. This presumes that the criteria described in Chapter 14 and the AICPA Audit and Accounting Guide are met.[11] Noncash assets could be supplies used in operations or long-lived items, such as land, buildings, or equipment. Donors may make cash or noncash gifts unrestricted or restricted. Restricted gifts to not-for-profit entities must be identified as temporarily restricted or permanently restricted. As indicated in Chapter 4, governmental health care entities defer recognition of unrestricted or restricted nonexchange transactions, such as gifts, until any related eligibility requirements are met.

Assets

Assets Limited as to Use

The phrase **assets limited as to use** is associated with not-for-profit entities and refers to unrestricted assets whose use is limited by the governing board or contracts or agreements with outside parties other than donors or grantors.[12] Examples include proceeds of debt issues; funds deposited with a trustee; self-insurance funding arrangements, such as medical malpractice funding arrangements; and statutory reserve requirements (i.e., those required under state law for health maintenance organizations). An example of a limitation placed on the assets by the board of directors or trustees would be for capital acquisition. Information about significant contractual limits should be disclosed in the notes to the financial statements. Internally designated funds should be reported separately from externally designated funds on the face or in the notes to the financial statements.[13] Assets that are held in trust by other parties are not reported on the balance sheet of the health care entity; however, their existence should be disclosed in the notes. Notice that assets limited as to use differs from restricted assets as discussed in Chapter 16.

Investments

Generally, health care organizations report their investments at fair value, although exact treatment of specific assets depends on the legal structure of the organization, as seen in Illustration 17–2. Not-for-profit organizations follow *SFAS No. 124,* which requires that all investments in equity securities with readily determinable values and all debt securities be reported at fair value with the realized and unrealized gains and losses reported as changes in net assets. Governmental entities follow *GASBS 31,* which requires that changes in the fair value of certain investments be reported in the statement of revenues, expenses, and changes in net assets. Investor-owned entities follow *SFAS No. 115,* which is the most complicated set of rules in that investments

[11] Ibid., pars. 10.08–10.12.
[12] Ibid., par. 9.03.
[13] Ibid., par. 1.30.

are separated into three categories and the accounting treatment differs for each category.[14]

Receivables

Amounts due from patients and third-party payors result in several asset and contra-asset accounts on the balance sheet: Accounts Receivable, Allowance for Uncollectible Accounts, Allowance for Contractual Adjustments, Clearing accounts, Interim Payments, and Settlement accounts. **Settlement accounts** are the receivables (or payables) arising from differences between original payment estimates by third-party payors, cash received and paid, and final determinations.

The rate-setting process in the health care industry is complex and beyond the scope of this text. However, an understanding of the relationship between accrual accounting revenue recognition principles and alternative payment methods, such as prospective and retrospective, is critical in properly accounting for revenues and receivables in a health care organization. These organizations may also have pledges receivable that arise from donations and loans receivable that result from loans to employees or physicians' groups.

Expenses

All health care providers use full accrual accounting, and the accrual of expenses is generally the same as for any business organization. An exception is that the GASB requires governmental health care organizations to recognize bad debts as an adjustment to revenue instead of as an expense. Other health care organizations (nongovernmental) recognize bad debts as an expense. All organizations record depreciation on capital assets other than land, including donated buildings and equipment. Expenses can be reported using either a natural presentation (e.g., salaries, supplies, and occupancy costs) or a functional presentation (e.g., inpatient services, ancillary outpatient services, and fiscal and administrative services). Functional expenses, if reported, should be based on full cost allocations.

Liabilities

Commitments and Contingencies

Contingencies that are common for health care providers arise from malpractice claims, risk contracting, third-party payor payment programs, obligations to provide uncompensated care, and contractual agreements with physicians. Other commitments and contingencies found in most business enterprises also apply to health care organizations, such as those that arise from construction contracts, pension plans, operating leases, purchase commitments, and loan guarantees. The cost of these claims against the health care organization should be accrued if they can be reasonably estimated, and it is probable they will have to be paid.[15] Accruals should be made for unasserted claims at the best estimates based on industry experience.

Long-Term Debt

The high cost and critical nature of facilities and equipment in the delivery of health care lead to significant amounts of long-term debt. Very often, health care providers

---

[14] Financial Accounting Standards Board, *Statement No. 115,* "Accounting for Certain Investments in Debt and Equity Securities" (Norwalk, CT: FASB, 1993); and *Statement No. 124,* "Accounting for Certain Investments Held by Not-for-Profit Organizations" (Norwalk, CT: FASB, 1996), p. 1; GASB, *Statement No. 31,* "Accounting and Financial Reporting for Certain Investments and for External Investment Pools" (Norwalk, CT: GASB, 1996).

[15] Financial Accounting Standards Board, *SFAS No. 5,* "Accounting for Contingencies" (Norwalk, CT: FASB, 1975); Financial Accounting Standards Board, *Interpretation No. 14,* "Reasonable Estimation of the Amount of a Loss" (Norwalk, CT: FASB, 1976); and GASB, *Codification,* Sec. C50.

are entitled to financing assistance through tax-exempt debt or governmental financing authorities, such as the federal Health and Education Financing Authority, without regard to their legal structure. Financing agreements often include requirements to set aside funds for repayment of the interest on and principal of the debt. These funds are reported as *assets limited as to use* (not-for-profit) or restricted (governmental).

ILLUSTRATIVE CASE FOR A NOT-FOR-PROFIT HEALTH CARE ORGANIZATION

The illustrative transactions provided in this section are for a hypothetical not-for-profit hospital, Bloomfield Hospital. Hospitals continue to be the dominant form of health care organization and usually exhibit a greater range of operating activities and transactions than other forms of health care organizations. Typical hospital transactions are illustrated for Bloomfield Hospital following the post-closing trial balance as of September 30, 2007, the end of its fiscal year.

BLOOMFIELD HOSPITAL
(A Not-for-Profit Organization)
Post-Closing Trial Balance
As of September 30, 2007

	Debits	Credits
Cash	$ 233,000	
Short-Term Investments	1,480,000	
Accrued Interest Receivable	36,000	
Accounts and Notes Receivable	300,000	
Allowance for Uncollectible Receivables		$ 86,000
Pledges Receivable	960,000	
Allowance for Uncollectible Pledges		73,000
Inventory	80,000	
Prepaid Expenses	12,000	
Assets Limited as to Use—Cash	6,500	
Assets Limited as to Use—Investments	400,000	
Long-Term Investments	146,000	
Land	1,080,000	
Buildings	11,050,000	
Equipment	4,920,000	
Accumulated Depreciation—Buildings		1,050,000
Accumulated Depreciation—Equipment		1,260,000
Accounts Payable		110,000
Accrued Expenses Payable		16,000
Mortgages Payable		6,400,000
Net Assets—Unrestricted, Undesignated		8,640,000
Net Assets—Unrestricted, Designated		406,500
Net Assets—Temporarily Restricted—Plant		2,508,000
Net Assets—Permanently Restricted		154,000
	$20,703,500	$20,703,500

During fiscal year 2008, the gross revenues for patient services from all responsibility centers totaled $9,261,000. It is the practice of Bloomfield Hospital to debit receivable accounts for the gross charges for all services rendered to patients except for charity care patients. The following entry should be made:

		Debits	Credits
1.	Accounts and Notes Receivable..........................	9,261,000	
	Patient Service Revenue.................................		9,261,000

The preceding entry recorded the revenues the hospital would have earned if all services rendered to each patient (other than charity care patients) were to be collected from the patients or third-party payors as billed. Customers of profit-seeking businesses do not all pay their bills in full, and neither do hospital patients or patients' insurance companies. The variety of third-party payment policies makes estimation of net patient service revenue difficult but obviously necessary for sound financial management and proper financial reporting. For the FY 2008, it is assumed the estimated provision for bad debts is $180,000 and actual contractual adjustments from third-party payors is $100,000. The entry to record this information is:

2.	Provision for Bad Debts.................................	180,000	
	Contractual Adjustments	100,000	
	Allowance for Uncollectible Receivables		180,000
	Accounts and Notes Receivable		100,000

Provision for Bad Debts is another name for Bad Debts Expense and is reported as an operating expense. Contractual Adjustments, however, is deducted from Patient Service Revenue and only the net amount is reported as revenues of the period.

Examples of *other revenues* for hospitals include tuition from nursing students, interns, or residents; cafeteria and gift shop revenues; parking fees; fees for copies of medical records; and other activities related to the ongoing major or central operations of the hospital. Similarly, unrestricted gifts, grants, and endowment income restricted by donors to finance charity care would appropriately be classified as other revenue of a hospital. If a total of $48,800 was received in cash during FY 2008 from sources classified as other revenue, Entry 3 is appropriate:

3.	Cash..	48,800	
	Other Revenue		48,800

Apart from items previously described, hospitals may receive unrestricted donations of money or services. Ordinarily, such donations should be classified as nonoperating gains rather than revenues. Hospitals often receive donated medicines and other materials. If such medicines and materials would otherwise have to be purchased, it is appropriate to record these donations at fair value as other revenue. Hospitals also routinely receive benefits from the services of volunteer workers; however, the value of such services is recorded only rarely as a revenue or gain (and as an expense) since the restrictive conditions required by the FASB standards for recognition are seldom met. (See related discussions in Chapters 14 and 16.)

Assume that total contributions were received in cash in the amount of $297,900 and unrestricted endowment income was $8,100.

		Debits	Credits
4.	Cash	306,000	
	Contributions—Unrestricted		297,900
	Investment Income—Unrestricted		8,100

One piece of capital equipment, which had a historical cost of $28,000 and a book value of $2,000 as of September 30, 2007, was sold early in the 2008 fiscal year for $500 cash. The entry to record the disposal of the asset at a loss is:

5.	Cash	500	
	Loss on Disposal of Equipment	1,500	
	Accumulated Depreciation—Equipment	26,000	
	Equipment		28,000

New capital equipment costing $400,000 was purchased during FY 2008 by Bloomfield Hospital, $100,000 with temporarily restricted net assets and $300,000 with unrestricted net assets. The entries should be:

6a.	Equipment	400,000	
	Cash		400,000
6b.	Net Assets Released from Restrictions—Temporarily		
	Restricted—Plant	100,000	
	Net Assets Released from Restrictions—Unrestricted		100,000

During the year, the following items were recorded as accounts payable: the $16,000 accrued expenses payable as of September 30, 2007; nursing services expenses, $4,026,000; other professional services expenses, $947,200; general services expenses, $1,650,000; fiscal and administrative services expenses, $1,124,000; and supplies added to inventory, $400,000. The following entry summarizes that activity:

7.	Accrued Expenses Payable	16,000	
	Nursing Services Expenses	4,026,000	
	Other Professional Services Expenses	947,200	
	General Services Expenses	1,650,000	
	Fiscal and Administrative Services Expenses	1,124,000	
	Inventory	400,000	
	Accounts Payable		8,163,200

Collections on accounts and notes receivable during the year amounted to $8,842,000; accounts and notes receivable totaling $131,000 were written off:

		Debits	Credits
8.	Cash..	8,842,000	
	Allowance for Uncollectible Receivables	131,000	
	Accounts and Notes Receivable..........................		8,973,000

The following cash disbursements were made during FY 2008: accounts payable, $8,014,200; a principal payment in the amount of $400,000 was made to reduce the mortgage liability; and interest amounting to $160,000 on mortgages was paid:

		Debits	Credits
9.	Accounts Payable	8,014,200	
	Mortgages Payable....................................	400,000	
	Interest Expense	160,000	
	Cash..		8,574,200

Supplies issued during the year cost $320,000 ($20,000 of the total was for use by fiscal and administrative services; $120,000 for use by general services; and the remainder by other professional services):

		Debits	Credits
10.	Other Professional Services Expenses.......................	180,000	
	General Services Expenses...............................	120,000	
	Fiscal and Administrative Services Expenses..................	20,000	
	Inventory..		320,000

Accrued expenses as of September 30, 2008, included $160,000 interest on mortgages; fiscal and administrative service expenses, $8,700; and other professional services expenses, $4,800. Prepaid expenses, consisting of general services expense items, declined $4,000 during the year:

		Debits	Credits
11.	Interest Expense	160,000	
	Fiscal and Administrative Service Expenses	8,700	
	Other Professional Services Expenses......................	4,800	
	General Services Expenses..............................	4,000	
	Accrued Expenses Payable.............................		173,500
	Prepaid Expenses....................................		4,000

Depreciation of plant and equipment for FY 2008 was in the amounts shown in the following journal entry:

		Debits	Credits
12.	Depreciation Expense	783,000	
	Accumulated Depreciation—Buildings		315,000
	Accumulated Depreciation—Equipment		468,000

The hospital received cash of $28,000 for interest on investments held in the Assets Limited as to Use—Investments account. Entry 13 records the receipt of cash and the corresponding credit.

13.	Cash	28,000	
	Investment Income—Unrestricted.		28,000

The $28,000 received in cash for interest (see Entry 13) was reinvested in investments to be held for eventual use for expansion of facilities; the hospital governing board decided to purchase an additional $350,000 of investments for the same purpose. Entries 14a and 14b reflect the purchase of the investments and the increase in unrestricted designated net assets.

14a.	Assets Limited as to Use—Investments	378,000	
	Cash		378,000
14b.	Net Assets—Unrestricted, Undesignated	378,000	
	Net Assets—Unrestricted, Designated		378,000

Individual philanthropists and civic and charitable groups have donated money and securities to Bloomfield Hospital subject to the restriction that the assets may be utilized only for plant replacement and expansion. Cash was received during FY 2008 from the following sources: interest on marketable securities (including the amount accrued at the end of the 2007 fiscal year), $69,000; collections of pledges receivable, $292,000;

15.	Cash	361,000	
	Pledges Receivable		292,000
	Accrued Interest Receivable		36,000
	Investment Income—Temporarily Restricted—Plant		33,000

Marketable securities carried in the accounts at $85,000 were sold for $59,000. The proceeds were reinvested in marketable securities, and $300,000 additional marketable securities were purchased from cash received during the year. The $26,000 loss on sale of investments reduces the amount available for acquisition of plant and will be closed at year-end to Net Assets—Temporarily Restricted—Plant.

		Debits	Credits
16a.	Cash	59,000	
	Loss on Sale of Investments—Temporarily Restricted—Plant	26,000	
	Short-Term Investments		85,000
16b.	Short-Term Investments	359,000	
	Cash		359,000

A review of pledges receivable indicated pledges restricted for plant acquisition in the amount of $25,000 should be written off, and the allowance for uncollectible pledges should be increased by $66,300.

17a.	Allowance for Uncollectible Pledges	25,000	
	Pledges Receivable		25,000
17b.	Provision for Uncollectible Pledges	66,300	
	Allowance for Uncollectible Pledges		66,300

The fair values of short-term investments and assets limited as to use have not changed during the year. At the end of FY 2008, the amount of interest accrued on marketable securities is computed to be $44,000. This amount is temporarily restricted for plant acquisition.

18.	Accrued Interest Receivable	44,000	
	Investment Income—Temporarily Restricted—Plant		44,000

Bloomfield Hospital did not have any net assets temporarily restricted for programs as of September 30, 2007. In September 2008, however, a civic organization donated $5,000 to the hospital to be used to augment the physician residency program. The organization pledged an additional sum of $20,000 to be paid in the coming year for the same purpose.

19.	Cash	5,000	
	Pledges Receivable	20,000	
	Contributions—Temporarily Restricted—Programs		25,000

The governing board and administration of Bloomfield Hospital expect the civic organization to honor its pledge; therefore, no Allowance for Uncollectible Pledges is created. Because the gift was received shortly before the end of FY 2008, no expenses for the program were incurred during the year.

The hospital endowment consists of donated assets, the principal of which must be retained intact. The income from hospital endowment assets is expendable as the donor directed either for general operating purposes or for named items or projects. The discussion in Chapters 8 and 16 concerning problems involved in distinguishing between principal and income are relevant also to hospital endowments. In order to be able to show that the terms of each endowment have been met, it is desirable to keep records for each separate endowment. As of September 30, 2007, Bloomfield Hospital is assumed to have only one endowment.

During FY 2008, the hospital received marketable securities with a market value of $24,000 at the date of the gift. The securities are to be held for the production of income; the income from these securities is for unrestricted use. The endowment may be recorded as shown in the following entry:

		Debits	Credits
20.	Short-Term Investments	24,000	
	Contributions—Permanently Restricted		24,000

Natural expenses of depreciation, interest, and provision for bad debts were allocated to the functional expenses based on an allocation basis established by the hospital.

		Debits	Credits
21.	Nursing Services Expenses	641,500	
	Other Professional Services Expenses	179,620	
	General Services Expenses	282,260	
	Fiscal and Administrative Services Expenses	179,620	
	Provision for Bad Debts		180,000
	Depreciation Expense		783,000
	Interest Expense		320,000

The pre-closing trial balance for Bloomfield Hospital as of September 30, 2008, is shown here. Financial statements reflecting the preceding transactions for Bloomfield Hospital were shown earlier in this chapter as Illustrations 17–3, 17–4, and 17–5.

BLOOMFIELD HOSPITAL
Pre-Closing Trial Balance
As of September 30, 2008

	Debits	Credits
Cash	$ 172,100	
Short-Term Investments	1,778,000	
Accrued Interest Receivable	44,000	
Accounts and Notes Receivable	488,000	
Allowance for Uncollectible Receivables		$ 135,000
Pledges Receivable	663,000	
Allowance for Uncollectible Pledges		114,300
Inventory	160,000	
Prepaid Expenses	8,000	
Assets Limited as to Use—Cash	6,500	
Assets Limited as to Use—Investments	778,000	
Long-Term Investments	146,000	
Land	1,080,000	
Buildings	11,050,000	

	Debits	Credits
Equipment	5,292,000	
Accumulated Depreciation—Buildings		1,365,000
Accumulated Depreciation—Equipment		1,702,000
Accounts Payable		259,000
Accrued Expenses Payable		173,500
Mortgages Payable		6,000,000
Net Assets—Unrestricted, Undesignated		8,262,000
Net Assets—Unrestricted, Designated		784,500
Net Assets—Temporarily Restricted—Plant		2,508,000
Net Assets—Permanently Restricted		154,000
Patient Service Revenue		9,261,000
Contractual Adjustments	100,000	
Other Revenue		48,800
Contributions—Unrestricted		297,900
Contributions—Temporarily Restricted—Programs		25,000
Contributions—Permanently Restricted		24,000
Investment Income—Unrestricted		36,100
Investment Income—Temporarily Restricted—Plant		77,000
Net Assets Released from Restrictions—Unrestricted		100,000
Net Assets Released from Restrictions—Temporarily Restricted	100,000	
Nursing Services Expenses	4,667,500	
Other Professional Services Expenses	1,311,620	
General Services Expenses	2,056,260	
Fiscal and Administrative Services Expenses	1,332,320	
Loss on Disposal of Equipment	1,500	
Provision for Uncollectible Pledges	66,300	
Loss on Sale of Investments—Temporarily Restricted—Plant	26,000	
	$31,327,100	$31,327,100

End-of-the-Year Closing Journal Entries

Unrestricted revenues and expenses that pertain to FY 2008 are closed to the Net Asset—Unrestricted, Undesignated account as follows:

		Debits	Credits
22.	Patient Service Revenue	9,261,000	
	Other Revenue	48,800	
	Contributions—Unrestricted	297,900	
	Investment Income—Unrestricted	36,100	
	Contractual Adjustments		100,000
	Nursing Services Expenses		4,667,500
	Other Professional Services Expenses		1,311,620
	General Services Expenses		2,056,260
	Fiscal and Administrative Services Expenses		1,332,320
	Loss on Disposal of Equipment		1,500
	Net Assets—Unrestricted, Undesignated		174,600

Restricted revenues that pertain to FY 2008 are closed to the restricted net asset accounts as shown:

		Debits	Credits
23.	Contributions—Temporarily Restricted—Programs	25,000	
	Contributions—Permanently Restricted	24,000	
	Investment Income—Temporarily Restricted—Plant	77,000	
	Net Assets—Temporarily Restricted—Plant	15,300	
	Provision for Uncollectible Pledges		66,300
	Loss on Sale of Investments—Temporarily Restricted—Plant		26,000
	Net Assets—Temporarily Restricted—Programs		25,000
	Net Assets—Permanently Restricted		24,000

Net assets released from restrictions are closed out in the following entry:

24.	Net Assets Released from Restrictions—Unrestricted	100,000	
	Net Assets—Temporarily Restricted—Plant	100,000	
	Net Assets Released from Restrictions—		
	Temporarily Restricted—Plant		100,000
	Net Assets—Unrestricted, Undesignated		100,000

FINANCIAL REPORTING FOR A GOVERNMENTAL HEALTH CARE ORGANIZATION

GASBS 34 indicates the required content of the annual financial report and provides guidance for governmental health care organizations that may be engaged in either governmental activities (i.e., financed through taxes, intergovernmental revenues, and other nonexchange revenues) or business-type activities (i.e., financed in whole or in part by fees charged to external users), or both.[16] Governmental health care activities that are part of a larger primary government are reported in governmental funds and internal service funds, and business-type activities are reported in enterprise funds. Governmental health care organizations that are legally separate from the primary government (e.g., component units) are required to provide an MD&A, basic financial statements for governmental activities or business-type activities, as applicable, and other required supplementary information (RSI).

If a governmental health care organization is engaged in more than one governmental program or has both governmental and business-type activities, it should provide both fund financial statements and government-wide financial statements. For these organizations, all requirements for basic financial statements and RSI apply. Separately issued financial statements of a component unit hospital or other health care provider should acknowledge that it is a component unit of another government, for example "Sample County Hospital, a component unit of Sample County." In addition, the notes to the financial statements should identify the primary government in

---

[16] *GASBS 34,* Appendix D, describes changes that are codified into Section Ho5 on Hospitals and Other Health Care Providers.

ILLUSTRATION 17–6 **Illustration of Statement of Cash Flows—GASB Jurisdiction**

BLOOMFIELD HOSPITAL
Statement of Cash Flows
Year Ended September 30, 2008

CASH FLOWS FROM OPERATING ACTIVITIES	
Cash received from patients and third-party payors	$ 8,842,000
Cash paid to employees and suppliers	(8,014,200)
Other receipts from operations	48,800
Net cash provided by operating activities	876,600
CASH FLOWS FROM NONCAPITAL FINANCING ACTIVITIES	
Unrestricted gifts and income from endowments	306,000
Gifts restricted for future operations	5,000
Net cash provided by noncapital financing activities	311,000
CASH FLOWS FROM CAPITAL AND RELATED FINANCING ACTIVITIES	
Purchase of property and equipment	(400,000)
Principal paid on mortgage	(400,000)
Interest paid	(160,000)
Collection of pledges receivable	292,000
Proceeds from sale of equipment	500
Net cash used for capital and related financing activities	(667,500)
CASH FLOWS FROM INVESTING ACTIVITIES	
Proceeds from sale of securities	59,000
Interest received on assets limited as to use	28,000
Interest received on donor-restricted assets	69,000
Cash invested in assets limited as to use	(378,000)
Cash invested in donor-restricted assets	(359,000)
Net cash used by investing activities	(581,000)
Net increase (decrease) in cash	(60,900)
Cash and cash equivalents, September 30, 2007	239,500
Cash and cash equivalents, September 30, 2008	$ 178,600

Reconciliation of Operating Income to Net Cash
Provided by Operating Activities

Operating income (loss)	$ (157,900)
Adjustments:	
Depreciation	783,000
Increase in patient accounts receivable, net	(139,000)
Increase in inventory	(80,000)
Increase in accounts payable	149,000
Increase in accrued expenses	157,500
Decrease in prepaid expenses	4,000
Interest paid in cash (Note 1)	160,000
Net cash provided by operating activities and gains and losses	$ 876,600

Note 1: Interest was classified as an operating expense on the income statement but as cash flows from capital and related activities on the cash flows statement prepared in conformity with GASB standards.

whose financial reporting entity it is included and describe its relationship with the primary government.

Fewer differences exist between not-for-profit and governmental health care organizations than did prior to *GASBS 34.* One difference that remains is that the statement of cash flows prepared by a governmental entity will have four sections, an additional section relating to cash flows from noncapital financing activities, such as unrestricted gifts, investment income, and gifts restricted for future periods, as shown in Illustration 17–6. The statement of net assets (or balance sheet) and statement of revenue, expenses, and changes in net assets required for governmental health care organizations that follow proprietary fund accounting—the most common case—are similar to the balance sheet and operating statements illustrated for not-for-profit health care organizations in Illustrations 17–3 and 17–4. Thus, these statements are not illustrated in this chapter. The interested reader should refer to Chapter 7 for illustrations of the formats of proprietary fund statements.

RELATED ENTITIES

Health care organizations have long been associated with separate fund-raising foundations, medical research foundations, auxiliaries, and guilds. More recently, organizations are networking with other organizations in an effort to integrate health care services, control costs, increase efficiency, and ultimately improve the quality of health care. Some independent organizations combine for a specific purpose, for example, to obtaining financing, in which case they become an **obligated group.** These joint ventures include every combination of legal structure: for-profit, not-for-profit, and governmental organizations. Financial reporting guidance comes from the FASB in existing statements on consolidations and affiliated organizations and from the GASB in statements on the reporting entity and affiliated organizations. If one entity controls another, the financial statements of the two organizations should be consolidated in order to be most useful to the decision maker. At a minimum, any economic interest between the organizations should be disclosed in each other's notes to the financial statements. At issue are working definitions of *control* and *agency.* The FASB is expected to provide further guidance as part of its consolidations project.[17]

OTHER ACCOUNTING ISSUES

Budgeting and Costs

Governmental and not-for-profit hospitals and other health care organizations, even though they are service institutions, must have an inflow of funds at least equal to their outflow of funds. Since this is the case, prudent management will attempt to forecast the outlays for a definite period and forecast the income for the same period. Most hospitals use comprehensive budgets for managerial purposes but do not incorporate the budgetary provision in the accounts. Other hospitals, principally governmental hospitals, do record their budgets in the ledger. Nevertheless, it is important that every hospital and other health care organization have an annual budget and that the budget be administered intelligently. For a hospital or any other enterprise, good financial management requires outlays to be evaluated in terms of results achieved. Insistence on

---

[17] When the FASB completes its projects on consolidations, the authors will make an update bulletin available to adopters of this book.

rigid adherence to a budget not related to actual workload (as is the case in some governmental agencies) tends to make the budget useless as a management tool. Budgetary accounts are used only if required by law.

Until the 1980s, it was customary for hospitals to determine costs of services rendered during a fiscal year by rearranging financial accounting data generated during that year. Although never satisfactory for financial management purposes, the procedure for cost determination was acceptable for purposes of reporting costs to third-party payors, which reimbursed hospitals on a retrospective (after-the-fact) basis. Since 1983, however, the largest purchaser of hospital services, Medicare, in an attempt to establish better control over hospital costs, has utilized a system of prospective payment. The Medicare system pays health care providers standardized rates for services rendered to patients in each **diagnosis-related group (DRG).** In addition, many other third-party payors negotiate services and rates with health care providers. Health care providers, therefore, have an incentive to determine actual costs of services rendered, to keep their costs commensurate with payments for services. It is now common for most hospitals to have sophisticated systems to capture costs by procedure.

The DRG is a case-mix classification scheme that is used to determine the payment provided to the hospital for inpatient services, regardless of how much the hospital spends to treat a patient. For example, the DRG for maternity patients may provide payment at 0.8 relative to a norm of 1.0, while the DRG for a heart transplant patient may provide 1.3 times the average payment. These relative numbers are multiplied by the federal standard rate as determined by the Centers for Medicare & Medicaid Services (CMS).

Auditing

Auditing issues of particular significance to the health care industry relate to contingencies, third-party payors, related entities, and restructuring. Renewed efforts on the part of the federal government to curb health care fraud and illegal acts also affect auditors and their clients. Congress instituted new civil and criminal penalties in the Health Insurance Portability and Accountability Act (HIPAA) of 1996, False Claims Act, and Stark Laws I and II that are designed to penalize individuals and organizations that contribute to the estimated $100 billion losses due to fraud and abuse in the health care industry. Investigations center on improper billing and coding, improper care, and kickbacks. Health care providers should have written compliance policies and designate a *compliance officer* who has the authority to implement the compliance program.[18] Auditors must also understand OMB *Circular A–133* and its application to hospitals and health care organizations that receive federal financial assistance, as described in Chapter 11 of this text.

Taxation and Regulatory Issues

Since a large number of health care providers are legally structured as tax-exempt organizations under IRC Sec. 501(c)(3), the regulations and activities of the Internal Revenue Service should be of concern to the accountant working with health care organizations. For example, the penalties for private inurement or excess economic benefits to individuals, introduced in the Taxpayer Bill of Rights 2 of 1996 (see Chapter 15 of this text), apply to health care administrators and persons with substantial

[18] AICPA, Audit Risk Alert, *Health Care Industry Developments 2001–02* (New York: AICPA, 2002), p. 10; AICPA, *Statement of Position 00-1*, "Auditing Health Care Third-Party Revenues and Related Receivables" (New York: AICPA, 2000).

influence over the organization. The IRS has increased its review of physician recruiting incentives, joint operating agreements for exemption applications, unrelated business income (such as hospital pharmacy sales to the general public), private-activity bonds, and independent contractor (versus employee) status. Congressional and public scrutiny over the accountability for assets of not-for-profit organizations and the amount of charity care provided by tax-exempt hospitals is at a high point. Sanctions are economically significant and may involve loss of tax-exempt status or eligibility for tax-exempt financing. Health care providers may also be regulated by states that have laws governing the granting of licenses and scope of services to be rendered.

Prepaid Health Care Plans

Prepaid health care plans, such as **health maintenance organizations (HMOs)** and **preferred provider organizations (PPOs),** function as brokers between the consumer or patient demanding the services and the providers of health care, such as health care professionals or hospitals. Contractual arrangements among these parties, including employers, are complex and varied. If the premium revenue from contracts is not expected to cover the agreed-upon health care costs, the prepaid plan may transfer some of its risk to an insurance company under *stop-loss insurance,* or a risk contract. In any case, the costs of future services to be rendered, net of anticipated revenue, should be recorded as a liability if it meets the criteria of a contingent liability. Certain contract acquisition costs, such as commissions paid to agents based on new enrollments or subscriber contracts, should be expensed as incurred, although there is some theoretical support for deferring these costs.[19]

Continuing Care Retirement Communities

There are more than 1,000 **continuing care retirement communities (CCRCs)** in the United States that are operated primarily by not-for-profit organizations. CCRCs provide residential care in a facility, along with some level of long-term medical care that is less intensive than hospital care. There are many ways to structure contracts between the patient/resident and the CCRC; however, most plans require advance payment of an entrance fee and periodic fees to cover operating costs in exchange for current use of the facilities and the promise to provide some level of health and residential services in the future. The advance fee may be refundable if certain future events occur, such as the death of the resident. Accounting issues, such as refundable and nonrefundable advance fees, the obligation to provide future services, and the costs of acquiring initial continuing care contracts,[20] are beyond the scope of this text.

FINANCIAL AND OPERATIONAL ANALYSIS

The goal of financial and operational analysis depends, of course, on the needs of the decision maker. For example, managers are directly accountable for performance, financial analysts determine the creditworthiness of organizations issuing debt, and third parties determine appropriate payment based on costs. Consumers may want nonfinancial performance and quality measures, such as the success rate for various procedures or the value received for money spent.

Health care entities are evaluated using a variety of ratios and benchmarks, some of which are unique to hospitals and others that are similar to those applied to

---

[19] AAG-HCO, Sec. 13.10.
[20] Ibid., Sec. 14.22–33.

other businesses. These analyses can be categorized into those that measure the following:

1. Patient volume (e.g., occupancy rate or daily census and average length of stay).
2. Patient and payout mix (e.g., Medicare, Medicaid, commercial, self-pay, and other).
3. Productivity and efficiency (e.g., full-time-equivalent personnel per average daily census or overhead expenses as a percentage of operating expenses).
4. Debt covenant ratios.

Once ratios are computed, they are compared to industry benchmarks, both for financial decision making and to improve performance. Hospitals are compared based upon bed size, geographic location, and teaching designation. Further analysis is performed according to the type of patient care. Organizations that accumulate information about health care norms include the American Hospital Association (AHA); the Institute for Health Care Improvement (IHI); bond-rating agencies, such as Moody's and Standard & Poor's; Health Care Investment Analysts, Inc. (HCIA); and the Center for Health Care Industry Performance Studies (CHIPS).

CONCLUSION

A single chapter on accounting for health care organizations can touch on only the most fundamental features. Variations in the reporting and accounting procedures for individual health care entities exist due to the variety in the type and size of health care providers, the range of services offered, the dependence of these entities on third-party payors, and the financial sophistication of the governing board, administrator, and finance director. For further information, the references cited in the Selected References section are recommended.

Key Terms

Assets limited as to use, *677*
Capitation fees, *674*
Charity care, *676*
Continuing care retirement communities (CCRCs), *691*
Contractual adjustments (or allowances), *676*
Diagnosis-related groups (DRGs), *690*
Health maintenance organization (HMO), *691*
Obligated group, *689*
Performance indicator, *674*
Preferred provider organization (PPO), *691*
Prospective Payment System (PPS), *676*
Settlement accounts, *678*
Third-party payor, *676*

Selected References

American Institute of Certified Public Accountants. Audit and Accounting Guide, *Health Care Organizations.* New York, 2004.
Financial Accounting Standards Board. *Statement No. 116,* "Accounting for Contributions Received and Contributions Made." Norwalk, CT, 1993.
_____. *Statement No. 117,* "Financial Statements of Not-for-Profit Organizations." Norwalk, CT, 1993.
Governmental Accounting Standards Board. *Codification.* "Section Ho5." Norwalk, CT, 2005.

Periodicals
Healthcare Financial Management. The journal of the Healthcare Financial Management Association, Oak Brook, IL.
Hospital Progress. The journal of the Catholic Hospital Association, St. Louis, MO.
Hospitals. The journal of the American Hospital Association, Chicago, IL.

Questions

17–1. Under what circumstances would a provider of health care services use fund accounting?

17–2. What are the required financial statements for (*a*) a not-for-profit health care entity and (*b*) a governmental health care entity reporting only business-type activities?

17–3. What is an example of a performance indicator and to what would it compare in investor-owned financial reporting?

17–4. How do the accounting treatments for charity services, patient discounts, contractual adjustments, and provision for bad debts differ in terms of their effects on patient service revenues and related receivables? Explain any differences between not-for-profit and governmental recognition.

17–5. What is the difference in accounting for investments among investor-owned, not-for-profit, and governmental health care organizations?

17–6. Breyer Memorial Hospital received a $100,000 gift that was restricted by the donor for heart research. At fiscal year-end Breyer had incurred $25,000 in expenses related to this project. Explain how these transactions would be reported in Breyer's balance sheet and operating statement under the independent assumptions that Breyer is (*a*) a government hospital and (*b*) a not-for-profit hospital. Would your answer change if the gift was based on cost-reimbursement as opposed to a purpose restriction?

17–7. What are *assets limited as to use* and how do they differ from restricted assets?

17–8. What contingent liabilities arise from a health care organization's relations with third-party payors?

17–9. Explain the importance of diagnosis-related groups (DRGs) in the cost accounting systems of a health care provider.

17–10. What are some particular issues in auditing health care organizations?

Cases

17–1 Charity Care. The local newspaper of a large urban area printed a story titled "Charity Care by Hospitals Stirs Debate." The story quotes one legislator who wants "to ensure that the state's nonprofit hospitals are fulfilling their obligation; that is to provide charity care at least equal to the tax exemption they receive as a nonprofit entity." The following table is provided:

Comparison of Selected Factors in Three Nonprofit Hospitals
(dollars in millions)

	Hope Hospital	St. Pat's Hospital	Capitol Hospital
Estimated taxes the hospitals would pay if they were not tax exempt	$6.8	$2.2	$4.5
Charity and other uncompensated care	$17.8 of which $3.8 is bad debts	$3.1 not including bad debts	$6.7
Community service programs*	$1.6	$1.0	n.a.
Unpaid cost of Medicaid and Medicare	$3.4	$0.6	n.a.
Nonreimbursed research and graduate medical education	$2.0	$0.7	n.a.

n.a. = Not available.
*Including such programs as activity sponsorships, playground equipment, neighborhood outreach, and scholarships for at-risk students.

Required

a. What are the obligations of IRC Sec. 501(c)(3) organizations to provide charity care?

b. Do you agree that the hospitals are not fulfilling their obligations? Why or why not?

c. What additional information would you like to have? Do you expect to find this information in the audited annual financial statements?

17–2 Purchase of a Health Care Organization. You are an accountant with a large public hospital. The hospital board recently decided to horizontally integrate by purchasing other health care organizations that provide specialized services. You have been asked to review Arbor Community Hospital's Statement of Operations (presented below) in order to determine if it is a financially sound organization. It is a not-for-profit hospital with a self-perpetuating board composed of community leaders. Arbor Community offers specialized services including an inpatient headache clinic and a substance abuse clinic.

Required

a. Write a concise, professional report to your superior identifying some ratios you find relevant from the statement of operations that support your position as to whether the hospital is financially sound.

b. What other factors do you consider critical in a decision to purchase an existing health care facility?

c. What other financial information would you like to review in order to form an opinion as to the performance of this hospital?

ARBOR COMMUNITY HOSPITAL
Statements of Operations
Years Ended December 31

	2008			2007		
	Unrestricted	Temporarily Restricted	Total	Unrestricted	Temporarily Restricted	Total
Revenue, gains, and other support:						
Net patient service revenue	$39,408,595	—	$39,408,595	$36,655,677	—	$36,655,677
Other revenue	2,701,284	—	2,701,284	2,411,442	—	2,411,442
Investment income	980,244	$ 32,752	1,012,996	514,844	$ 14,183	529,027
Net assets released from restrictions used for operations	44,034	(44,034)	—	20,086	(20,086)	—
Total revenue, gains, and other support	43,134,157	(11,282)	43,122,875	39,602,049	(5,903)	39,596,146
Expenses:						
Inpatient nursing services	5,035,376	—	5,035,376	5,219,917	—	5,219,917
Outpatient and ancillary services	18,468,238	—	18,468,238	16,236,239	—	16,236,239
Physician offices	1,928,224	—	1,928,224	1,933,725	—	1,933,725
General services	5,692,281	—	5,692,281	5,677,606	—	5,677,606
Fiscal services	1,585,042	—	1,585,042	1,621,436	—	1,621,436
Administrative services	4,967,417	—	4,967,417	4,381,216	—	4,381,216
Interest	809,895	—	809,895	510,008	—	510,008
Depreciation and amortization	2,752,519	—	2,752,519	2,459,604	—	2,459,604
Bad debts	994,506	—	994,506	858,790	—	858,790
Total expenses	42,233,498	—	42,233,498	38,898,541	—	38,898,541

	2008			2007		
	Unrestricted	Temporarily Restricted	Total	Unrestricted	Temporarily Restricted	Total
Excess of revenue, gains, and other support over (under) expenses:	900,659	(11,282)	889,377	703,508	(5,903)	697,605
Net gain on investments reported at fair value	48,674	—	48,674	433,446	—	433,446
Contributions	952	158,068	159,020	4,566	135,267	139,833
Net assets released from restrictions used for purchase of property and equipment	36,540	(36,540)	—	488,524	(488,524)	—
Change in net assets before extraordinary item	986,825	110,246	1,097,071	1,630,044	(359,160)	1,270,844
Extraordinary loss on refinancing of debt	—	—	—	(140,129)	—	(140,129)
Increase (decrease) in net assets	$ 986,825	$110,246	$ 1,097,071	$ 1,489,915	$(359,160)	$ 1,130,755

17–3 Internet Case. The federal government through the Medicare and Medicaid programs is one of the largest providers of patient service revenues to health care organizations. Information concerning these programs is available through the Department of Health and Human Services Web site.

Required

Accessing the Web site at www.cms.hhs.gov answer the following questions:
a. Who are the recipients of Medicare and Medicaid program benefits?
b What were the annual outlays (expenditures) for each program for the most recent year?
c. What is CMS?
d. What is the National Program on Integrity and what are the objectives of its program reviews?
e. What factors do you believe contribute to fraud in Medicare and Medicaid programs?

17–4 Internet Case. Because of the high cost of health care, providers, payors, and users of health care systems are all concerned about controlling costs while providing efficient and effective care. Several organizations are devoted to addressing such concerns.

Required

a. Locate the Web site for the New York State Health Accountability Foundation and identify its purpose and the type of information available through its Web site.
b. Locate the Web site for the American Health Quality Association and identify its purpose. What success stories is it reporting for your state?
c. Locate Web sites for consumer information related to health care organizations in your state (frequently these are maintained by state government agencies). What information is available?

Exercises and Problems

17–1 Multiple Choice. Choose the best answer.
1. Not-for-profit health care organizations are typically sponsored by:
    a. Community organizations.
    b. Religious organizations.
    c. Universities.
    d. Any of the above.

2. Revenue from the gift shop of a hospital would normally be included in:
   a. Nonoperating Gains.
   b. Other Revenue.
   c. Patient Service Revenue.
   d. Professional Services Revenue.

3. Donated medicine that normally would be purchased by a skilled care facility should be recorded at fair market value and should be credited directly to:
   a. Other Revenue.
   b. Nonoperating Gains.
   c. Unrestricted Net Assets.
   d. Deferred Revenue.

4. A not-for-profit hospital that follows FASB standards and the AICPA Audit and Accounting Guide *Health Care Organizations* should report investment income from endowments that is restricted to a specific operating purpose as:
   a. General Fund revenue.
   b. An increase in permanently restricted net assets.
   c. An increase in unrestricted net assets.
   d. An increase in temporarily restricted net assets.

5. A $50,000 donation is held by a bank in an independent permanent trust with the investment income dedicated for use by a hospital for operating purposes. The $50,000 principal should be:
   a. Reported as an asset limited as to use by the hospital.
   b. Reported as nonoperating revenue of the hospital.
   c. Reported as a permanently restricted net asset of the hospital.
   d. Disclosed in notes to the financial statements of the hospital.

6. Restricted funds of a not-for-profit nursing home are:
   a. Not available unless the board of directors removes the restrictions.
   b. Restricted as to use by the donor, grantor, or other source of the resources.
   c. Not available for current operating use; however, the income earned on the funds is available.
   d. Restricted as to use only for board-designated purposes.

7. Depreciation should be recognized in the financial statements of:
   a. Proprietary (for-profit) hospitals only.
   b. Both proprietary (for-profit) and not-for-profit hospitals.
   c. Governmental and not-for-profit hospitals only if they are affiliated with a college or university.
   d. All hospitals as a memorandum entry not affecting the statement of revenues and expenses.

8. Charity care provided by a health care organization would:
   a. Be recorded in a contra-revenue account.
   b. Be recorded as an operating expense.
   c. Be recorded as a loss on services.
   d. Not be recorded.

9. Contractual adjustments arising from third-party payor contracts are:
   a. Recorded in a contra-revenue account.
   b. Recorded as an operating expense.
   c. Recorded as a loss on services.
   d. Not recorded.

10. A possible contingency that might have to be disclosed in the notes to the financial statements of a health care organization is:

a. An agreed-upon settlement between a third-party payor and the health care provider.

b. Premiums received for prepaid health care by a health maintenance organization.

c. An uncertain result of ongoing negotiations for payment with a third-party payor for services rendered to patients.

d. None of the above.

17–2 Not-for-Profit Hospital. The Gonzalez Community Hospital Balance Sheet as of December 31, 2007, follows.

GONZALEZ COMMUNITY HOSPITAL
Balance Sheet
December 31, 2007

Assets			Liabilities and Net Assets		
Current:			Current:		
Cash		$ 65,000	Accounts payable		$ 65,000
Accounts and notes receivable	$ 140,000		Accrued payroll		110,000
Less: Allowance for uncollectibles	12,000	128,000			
Inventory		71,000			
Total current assets		264,000	Total current liabilities		175,000
Assets limited as to use:					
Cash	11,500		Long-term debt:		
Investments	210,000		Mortgage payable		3,500,000
Total assets limited as to use		221,500	Total liabilities		3,675,000
Property, plant, and equipment:			Net assets:		
			Unrestricted, undesignated		1,782,000
Land		208,000	Unrestricted, designated for plant replacements		221,500
Buildings, at cost	4,516,000		Total net assets		2,003,500
Less: Accumulated depreciation	1,506,000	3,010,000			
Equipment, at cost	2,871,000				
Less: Accumulated depreciation	896,000	1,975,000			
Total property, plant, and equipment		5,193,000			
			Total liabilities and net assets		$5,678,500
Total assets		$5,678,500			

Required

a. Record in general journal form the effect of the following transactions during the fiscal year ended December 31, 2008, assuming that Gonzalez Community Hospital is a not-for-profit hospital.

(1) Summary of revenue journal:

Patient services revenue, gross	$3,584,900
Adjustments and allowances:	
Contracting agencies	123,000

(2) Summary of cash receipts journal:

Interest on investments in Assets Limited as to Use	7,350
Unrestricted grant from United Fund	200,000
Collections of receivables	3,575,600

(3) Purchases journal:

Administration	167,900
General services expenses	181,200
Nursing services expenses	278,800
Other professional services expenses	263,100

(4) Payroll journal:

Administration	253,700
General services expenses	179,200
Nursing services expenses	559,200
Other professional services expenses	422,400

(5) Summary of cash payments journal:

Interest expense	280,000
Payment on mortgage principal	500,000
Accounts payable for purchases	936,800
Accrued payroll	1,479,500
Transfer to Assets Limited as to Use	30,000

(6) The following additional information relates to assets limited as to use:

(*a*) $10,000 in CDs matured on which $590 in interest was earned.
(*b*) $30,000 was reinvested in CDs.
(*c*) $12,300 in equipment was purchased.

(7) Depreciation charges for the year amounted to $117,000 for the buildings and $128,500 for equipment.

(8) Other information:

(*a*) Provision for uncollectible receivables was increased by $3,800.
(*b*) Supplies inventory:

	12/31/2007	12/31/2008
Administration	$ 8,000	$ 7,300
General services expenses	8,700	9,000
Nursing services expenses	17,000	16,800
Other professional services expenses	37,300	40,000
Totals	$71,000	$73,100

(*c*) Portion of mortgage payable due within one year, $500,000.

(9) Assume that there was no change in fair value of investments at year-end.

(10) Provisions for bad debts, interest expense, and depreciation expense were allocated to functional expense accounts in proportion to their preallocation balances. Nominal accounts were closed.

(11) Reflecting the net increase in Assets Limited as to Use of $25,640 (see transactions 2, 5, and 6), record the increase in Net Assets—Unrestricted, Designated for Plant Replacement.

b. Prepare a balance sheet as of December 31, 2008.

c. Prepare a statement of operations for the year ended December 31, 2008.

17–3 Restricted Contribution. The following transactions occurred at Jackson Hospital:
1. Under the will of Samuel H. Samuels, a bequest of $100,000 was received for research on gerontology. Because the principal of the bequest, as well as any earnings on investments, is expendable for the specified research purpose, the bequest should be reported as temporarily restricted.
2. Pending the need for the money for the designated purpose, part of the bequest was invested in $95,000 of par value City of Jackson 6 percent bonds at 103 and accrued interest of $823.
3. An interest payment of $2,850 was received on the City of Jackson bonds.
4. The bonds were sold at 104 and accrued interest of $443.
5. The income from the Samuels gift was used for the stipulated purpose.

Required
Make journal entries for these transactions assuming that this is a not-for-profit hospital.

17–4 Third-Party Payors. The following transactions took place at Whitworth Memorial Hospital during the fiscal year 2008.
1. Gross revenues of $83,850,000 were earned for service to Medicare patients.
2. Expected contractual adjustments with Medicare, a third-party payor, total $44,450,000; the Allowance for Contractual Adjustments account is used to record these contractual adjustments.
3. Medicare "cleared charges" of $75,465,000 with payments of $35,469,000 and contractual allowances of $39,996,000.
4. Interim payments received from Medicare amounted to $2,600,000.
5. The hospital made a lump-sum payment of $1,000,000 back to Medicare. The hospital uses an interim payments account to keep track of the payments made between Medicare and the hospital until final settlement is determined.

Required
a. Record the transactions in the general journal.
b. Calculate the amount of net patient service revenue.
c. What is the net cash flow from transactions with Medicare?
d. What adjustments must be made at the end of the year to "settle" up with Medicare and properly report the net patient service revenue after this settlement?

17–5 Not-for-Profit Financial Statements. ClearView Drug Rehabilitation Center uses fund accounting for internal purposes. Presented is the December 31, 2008 balance sheet prepared from the funds the center uses.

Required
The controller asks that you prepare an aggregated balance sheet in accordance with current financial reporting standards using *SFAS No. 117* and the AICPA Audit and Accounting Guide *Health Care Organizations*. Based on additional information provided, you determine that
1. The cash and investments of the plant are restricted under the terms of several gifts to use for plant expansion, with income from plant fund investments restricted to the same purpose.
2. Income from endowment fund investments may be used at the discretion of the center's governing board.

CLEARVIEW DRUG REHABILITATION CENTER
Balance Sheet
As of December 31, 2008

Assets			Liabilities and Fund Balances		
OPERATING FUND					
Cash		$ 120,000	Accounts payable		$ 516,000
Short-term investments		500,000	Accrued expense—payable		96,000
Accounts receivable	$ 137,000				
Less: Allowance for uncollectible accounts	27,000	110,000	Total liabilities		612,000
Inventory of supplies		74,000	Fund balance		192,000
Total		$ 804,000	Total		$ 804,000
PLANT FUND					
Cash		$ 53,800	Mortgage bonds payable		$ 950,000
Investments		871,200			
Land		400,000			
Buildings	$2,750,000				
Less: Accumulated depreciation	525,000	2,225,000	Fund balance: Investment in plant		2,621,000
Equipment	1,380,000		Reserved for plant improvement and replacement		925,000
Less: Accumulated depreciation	434,000	946,000	Total fund balance		3,546,000
Total		$4,496,000	Total		$4,496,000
ENDOWMENT FUND					
Cash		$ 6,000	Fund balance—		
Investments		1,260,000	income unrestricted		$1,266,000
Total		$1,266,000	Total		$1,266,000

17–6 Governmental Hospital. During 2008, the following selected events and transactions were recorded by City General Hospital.
1. Gross charges for hospital services, all charged to accounts and notes receivable, were as follows:
   Patient service revenues $1,364,900
2. After recording patient service revenues, it was determined that $53,500 related to charity care.
3. Additional information relating to current-year receivables and revenues is as follows:
   Contractual adjustments $318,000
   Provision for bad debts   20,400
4. During the year, the hospital received unrestricted cash contributions of $50,000 and unrestricted cash income from endowment investments of $6,500.
5. A federal cost reimbursement research grant of $350,000 was awarded. As of the end of the year, $200,000 in expenses related to the grant had been made. (Hint: see Chapter 4 for eligibility requirements.)

6. New equipment costing $39,000 was acquired from donor-restricted cash. An X-ray machine that cost $31,000 and had an undepreciated cost of $2,400 was sold for $500 cash.

7. Vouchers totaling $1,339,800 were issued for the following items:

Fiscal and administrative services expenses	$241,800
General services expenses	253,100
Nursing services expenses	585,000
Other professional services expenses	185,600
Inventory	67,500
Expenses accrued at December 31, 2007	6,800

8. Collections of accounts receivable totaled $1,159,000. Accounts written off as uncollectible amounted to $11,900.

9. Cash payments on vouchers payable (paid to employers and suppliers) during the year were $1,031,200.

10. Supplies of $68,000 were issued to nursing services.

11. On December 31, 2008, accrued interest income on investments was $800.

12. Depreciation of buildings and equipment was as follows:

Buildings	$44,000
Equipment	73,000

13. On December 31, 2008, closing entries were made in the general journal.

Required

a. Show in general journal form the entries that should be made for each of the transactions and the closing entries in accordance with the standards for a governmental health care entity that follows proprietary fund accounting, as discussed in this chapter and Chapter 7.

b. Using the available information, calculate the net patient service revenue that would be reported on the statement of revenues, expenses, and changes in net assets.

17–7 Governmental Hospital Financial Statement Analysis. Examine the financial statements for City College Hospital for the years ended June 30, 2007 and 2008.

Required

a. From the presentation of the financial statements it does not appear that City College Hospital followed the GASB standards for proprietary fund financial reporting. Identify areas of non-conformance with GASB standards.

b. What additional information would you expect to find in the notes to the financial statements about major classifications of assets and net assets?

c. Describe how net patient service revenue likely differs from gross patient service revenue.

d. Discuss whether the hospital had a profitable year, and its performance relative to the prior year.

e. What is the best explanation for the change in cash for the most recent year? For the previous year?

CITY COLLEGE HOSPITAL
Balance Sheets
For Years Ended June 30
(in thousands)

Assets	2008	2007	Liabilities and Net Assets	2008	2007
Current assets:			Current liabilities:		
Cash and cash equivalents	$ 6,340	$ 12,169	Accounts payable and		
Accounts receivable from			accrued expenses	$ 28,027	$ 21,742
patient care services, less			Accrued compensation	44,962	48,972
allowance for uncollectible			Payable to other		
accounts of $35,763 in 2008			College units	50,997	43,936
and $38,079 in 2007	203,988	154,571	Estimated third-		
Other accounts receivable	4,449	5,708	party payables	16,364	36,180
Inventory and other			Current portion of		
current assets	24,833	15,198	long-term debt	5,215	5,580
Total current assets	239,610	187,646	Total current liabilities	145,565	156,410
Noncurrent assets:					
Properties:			Long-term debt	327,604	332,534
Land and land improvements	42,628	42,610			
Buildings and building			Payable to other		
improvements	664,480	640,155	College units	66,500	30,000
Equipment	413,447	357,052	Accrued malpractice		
Accumulated depreciation	(609,304)	(539,970)	expense	3,161	10,950
	511,251	499,847	Total liabilities	542,830	529,894
Construction in progress	46,224	30,079	Net assets	1,127,891	1,215,167
Net properties	557,475	529,926			
Investments	852,878	1,014,918			
Other assets	20,758	12,571			
Total noncurrent assets	1,431,111	1,557,415			
Total assets	$1,670,721	$1,745,061	Total liabilities and net assets	$1,670,721	$1,745,061

CITY COLLEGE HOSPITAL
Statements of Operations
For Years Ended June 30
(in thousands)

	2008	2007
Revenue		
Net patient service revenue	$ 814,205	$ 939,679
Other revenue	10,944	9,959
Total revenue	825,149	949,638
Expenses		
Salaries, wages and staff benefits	408,820	403,895
Medical School faculty services	48,214	171,720
Depreciation	72,805	67,499
Interest	14,543	16,186
Supplies, services and other	276,501	266,726
Total expenses	820,883	926,026

	2008	2007
Income before adjustments, settlements and investment income	4,266	23,612
Prior period adjustments and settlements	3,000	36,400
Investment income including unrealized gains on investments	85,300	112,981
Excess of revenue over expenses	92,566	172,993
Transfers to other College units	(179,842)	(25,208)
	(87,276)	147,785
Net assets, beginning of year	1,215,167	1,067,382
Net assets, end of year	$1,127,891	$1,215,167

CITY COLLEGE HOSPITAL
Statements of Cash Flow
For Years Ended June 30
(in thousands)

	2008	2007
Operating Activities:		
Income before settlements and investment income	$ 4,266	$23,612
Adjustments to reconcile to net cash provided by (used in) operating activities:		
Depreciation and amortization	73,574	68,490
Third-party settlements received (paid)	(2,073)	33,944
Increase in accounts receivable	(64,161)	(10,533)
Increase in other assets	(8,200)	(1,225)
Change in accounts payable, accrued expenses and compensation	255	(8,901)
Decrease in accrued malpractice expense	(5,704)	(8,043)
Net cash provided by (used in) operating activities	(2,043)	97,344
Investing Activities:		
Investment income received	46,591	45,785
Decrease (increase) in noncurrent investments	200,828	(48,884)
Decrease (increase) in long-term receivables	(8,669)	510
Net cash provided by (used in) investing activities	238,750	(2,589)
Capital and Related Financing Activities:		
Purchase of property and equipment	(101,611)	(48,026)
Repayment of long-term debt	(5,580)	(4,510)
Net cash used in capital and related financing activities	(107,191)	(52,536)
Non-Capital Financing Activities:		
Payments to other College units	(135,345)	(30,192)
Net cash used in non-capital financing activities	(135,345)	(30,192)
Increase (decrease) in cash and cash equivalents	(5,829)	12,027
Cash and cash equivalents at beginning of year	12,169	142
Cash and cash equivalents at end of year	$ 6,340	$12,169

17–8 Not-for-Profit Hospital Financial Statement Analysis. Examine the financial statements for Oak Valley Hospital for the years ended December 31, 2007 and 2008.

Required

Prepare a short answer to address each of the following questions.

a. Discuss the relative importance of different classifications of assets to total assets. What additional information would you expect to find in the notes to the financial statements about major classification of assets?

b. Describe how net patient service revenue likely differs from gross patient revenue.

c. Did this hospital have a profitable year? Why or why not?

d. What is the best explanation for the change in cash for the most recent year? For the previous year?

OAK VALLEY HOSPITAL
Consolidated Balance Sheets
December 31
(in thousands)

Assets			Liabilities and Net Assets		
	2008	**2007**		**2008**	**2007**
Current assets:			Current liabilities:		
Cash and cash equivalents	$ 15,289	$ 623	Accounts payable and		
Marketable securities	6,963	11,776	accrued expenses	$ 53,041	$ 69,009
Patient accounts receivable,			Salaries, wages, and		
less allowance for doubtful			amounts withheld	11,009	7,295
accounts	42,438	66,314	Accrued vacation and sick pay	15,013	16,397
Current portion of funds held			Current portion of		
by Trustee	1,023	2,712	long-term debt	7,205	6,906
Inventories	8,846	8,344			
Prepaid expenses and other					
current assets	16,530	17,550			
Total current assets	91,089	107,319	Total current liabilities	86,269	99,607
Assets with limited use:					
Capital expansion fund	167,298	150,121	Deferred revenue and deposits	18,589	18,617
Board designated	92,170	98,046	Accrued compensation	21,830	17,100
Funds held by Trustee	207	30,068	Claims liability	69,442	74,457
Investments	27,657	23,562	Long-term debt, less		
	287,332	301,797	current portion	377,591	386,652
Other assets:			Unrestricted net assets	298,457	363,740
Investments	80,280	141,315			
Deferred bond issue costs, less					
accumulated amortization of					
$4,783,225 in 2008 and					
$3,868,295 in 2007	14,429	15,423			
Investment in affiliates	13,065	11,723			
Pledges receivable	2,963	3,801			
Other	13,867	17,896			
	124,604	190,158			

	2008	2007		2008	2007
Property and equipment:					
Land	15,157	16,038			
Buildings and improvements	304,856	318,465			
Equipment	332,685	282,762			
Construction in progress	33,599	23,854			
	686,297	641,119			
Accumulated depreciation	(317,144)	(280,220)			
	369,153	360,899			
Total assets	$872,178	$960,173	Total liabilities and net assets	$872,178	$960,173

OAK VALLEY HOSPITAL
Consolidated Statements of Operations and Changes in Net Assets
Year Ended December 31
(in thousands)

	2008	2007
Unrestricted revenue, gains and other support:		
Net patient service revenue	$553,152	$555,579
Other revenue	72,800	75,867
Total revenue	625,952	631,447
Expenses:		
Salaries and wages	297,248	283,800
Employee benefits	52,071	54,845
Services, supplies and other	215,719	206,097
Bad debts	43,329	32,096
Depreciation and amortization	46,141	39,859
Interest	20,592	21,020
Impairment and restructuring	28,725	
Total expenses	703,825	637,718
Operating loss	(77,873)	(6,271)
Nonoperating gains (losses):		
Investment income	23,537	19,308
Interest expense	—	(410)
Share of net income (loss) of affiliates	377	(77)
Excess of (expenses over revenue)	(53,959)	12,548
Other changes in net assets:		
Change in unrealized appreciation in fair value of investments	(11,326)	16,466
(Decrease) increase in net assets, before extraordinary item	(65,283)	29,015
Extraordinary loss from extinguishment of debt	—	(1,032)
(Decrease) increase in net assets	(65,283)	27,983
Net assets, beginning of year	363,740	335,757
Net assets, end of year	$298,457	$363,740

OAK VALLEY HOSPITAL
Consolidated Statements of Cash Flows
Year Ended December 31
(in thousands)

	2008	2007
Operating Activities:		
(Decrease) increase in unrestricted net assets	$(65,282)	$ 27,983
Adjustments to reconcile (decrease) increase in unrestricted net assets to net cash provided by operating activities and nonoperating gains and losses:		
Extraordinary loss from extinguishment of debt	—	1,032
Depreciation and amortization	46,141	39,859
Impairment of long-lived assets	24,940	2,000
Change in unrealized depreciation (appreciation) in fair market value of investments	11,330	(16,466)
Decrease in accounts receivable	23,872	5,211
(Increase) decrease in inventories	(501)	170
Decrease (increase) in other current assets	1,019	(7,361)
Decrease in pledges receivable	836	418
(Decrease) increase in accounts payable and other accrued expenses	(15,966)	13,629
Increase in accrued compensation and amounts withheld	7,058	32
(Decrease) increase in deferred revenue	(29)	1,005
(Decrease) increase in claims liability	(5,014)	1,425
Share of net (gain) loss in equity transactions of affiliate	(383)	77
Cash provided by operating activities and nonoperating gains and losses	28,022	69,017
Investing activities:		
Purchase of property and equipment	(78,421)	(58,082)
Decrease (increase) in investments, marketable securities with limited use	70,676	(63,726)
Increase in investment in affiliates	(958)	(4,097)
Decrease (increase) in other assets	4,109	(2,425)
Cash used in investing activities	(4,594)	(128,331)
Financing activities:		
Proceeds form issuance of long-term debt	—	124,472
Payments and refunding of long-term debt	(8,762)	(66,886)
Cash (used in) provided by financing activities	(8,762)	57,586
Increase (decrease) in cash and cash equivalents	14,666	(1,728)
Cash and cash equivalents at beginning of year	623	2,351
Cash and cash equivalents at end of year	$ 15,289	$ 623

Glossary

Some of these definitions were adapted from publications of the Government Finance Officers Association. Others were taken from specialized publications cited in the text; the remainder were supplied by the authors. The letters *q.v.* signify "which see"; that is, the preceding word is defined elsewhere in the glossary.

A

Abatement   A complete or partial cancellation of a levy imposed by a government. Abatements usually apply to tax levies, special assessments, and service charges.

Accountability   Being obliged to explain one's actions, to justify what one does; the requirement for government to answer to its citizenry—to justify the raising of public resources and expenditure of those resources. Also, in the GASB's view, the obligation to report whether the government operated within appropriate legal constraints; whether resources were used efficiently, economically, and effectively; whether current-year revenues were sufficient to pay for the services provided in the current year; and whether the burden for services previously provided will be shifted to future taxpayers.

Accounting Period   A period at the end of which and for which financial statements are prepared. See also Fiscal Period.

Accounting System   The total structure of records and procedures that discover, record, classify, and report information on the financial position and operations of a government or any of its funds, and organizational components.

Accounts Receivable   Amounts owing on open account from private persons, firms, or corporations for goods and services furnished by a government. Taxes Receivable and Special Assessments Receivable are recorded separately. Amounts due from other funds or from other governments should be reported separately.

Accrual Basis   The basis of accounting under which revenues are recorded when earned and expenditures (or expenses) are recorded as soon as they result in liabilities for benefits received, notwithstanding that the receipt of cash or the payment of cash may take place, in whole or in part, in another accounting period. See also Accrue and Levy.

Accrue   To record revenues when earned and to record expenditures (or expenses) as soon as they result in liabilities for benefits received, notwithstanding that the receipt of cash or payment of cash may take place, in whole or in part, in another accounting period. See also Accrual Basis, Accrued Expenses, and Accrued Revenue.

Accrued Expenses   Expenses incurred during the current accounting period but not payable until a subsequent accounting period. See also Accrual Basis and Accrue.

Accrued Income   See Accrued Revenue.

Accrued Interest on Investments Purchased   Interest accrued on investments between the last interest payment date and the date of purchase.

Accrued Interest Payable   A liability account that represents the amount of interest expense accrued at the balance sheet date but not due until a later date.

Accrued Revenue   Revenue earned during the current accounting period but not to be collected until a subsequent accounting period. See also Accrual Basis and Accrue.

Accrued Taxes Payable   A liability for taxes that have accrued since the last payment date.

Accrued Wages Payable   A liability for wages earned by employees between the last payment date and the balance sheet date.

Accumulated Depreciation   See Allowance for Depreciation.

Acquisition Adjustment   Difference between amount paid by a utility for plant assets acquired from another utility and the original cost (q.v.) of those assets less depreciation to date of acquisition.

Activity   A specific and distinguishable line of work performed by one or more organizational components of a government for the purpose of accomplishing a function for which the government is responsible. For example, food inspection is an activity performed in the discharge of the health function. See also Function, Subfunction, and Subactivity.

Activity-Based Costing (ABC)   A cost accounting system that identifies specific factors (cost drivers) that drive the costs of service or production activities and tracks the consumption of cost drivers in producing outputs of goods or services. See also Cost Determination.

Activity Classification   A grouping of expenditures on the basis of specific lines of work performed by organization units. For example, sewage treatment and disposal, solid waste collection, solid waste disposal, and street cleaning are activities performed in carrying out the function of sanitation, and the segregation of the expenditures made for each of these activities constitutes an activity classification.

Actuarial Accrued Liability (AAL)   A liability arising from past unfunding and ad hoc changes in pension plan provisions. AAL is determined by using any of several generally accepted actuarial methods, for example, entry age method.

Actuarial Basis   A basis used in computing the amount of contributions to be made periodically to a fund so that the total contributions plus the compounded earnings thereon will equal the required payments to be made out of the fund. The factors taken into account in arriving at the amount of these contributions include the length of time over which each contribution is to be held and the rate of return compounded on such contribution over its life. A trust fund for a public employee retirement system is an example of a fund set up on an actuarial basis.

Actuarial Present Value of Total Projected Benefits   A component of the annual required contribution that allows for projected salary increases and additional statutory or contractual agreements.

Actuarial Value of Assets   The value of a pension plan's assets used by an actuary for purposes of determining annual required contributions and other actuarial aspects of a defined benefit pension plan.

Ad Valorem Property Taxes   In proportion to value. A basis for levy of taxes on property.

Advance Refunding   The issuance of debt instruments to refund existing debt before the existing debt matures or is callable.

Agency Funds   Funds consisting of resources received and held by the government as an agent for others; for example, taxes collected and held by a municipality for a school district. *Note:* Sometimes resources held by a government for other organizations are handled through an agency fund known as a *pass-through agency fund.*

Allocate   To divide a lump-sum appropriation into parts that are designated for expenditure by specific organization units and/or for specific purposes, activities, or objects. See also Allocation.

Allocation   A part of a lump-sum appropriation that is designated for expenditure by specific organization units and/or for special purposes, activities, or objects. In federal usage, a transfer of obligational authority from one agency to another. See also Allocate.

Allot   To divide an appropriation into amounts that may be encumbered or expended during an allotment period. See also Allotment and Allotment Period.

Allotment   A part of an appropriation (or, in federal usage, parts of an apportionment) that may be encumbered (obligated) or expended during an allotment period. See also Allot and Allotment Period.

Allotment Period   A period of time less than one fiscal year in length during which an allotment is effective. Bimonthly and quarterly allotment periods are most common. See also Allot and Allotment.

Allotments Available for Commitment/Obligation   The portion of a federal agency's allotments not yet obligated by issuance of purchase orders, contracts, or other evidence of commitment.

Allowable Costs   Costs that meet specific criteria determined by the resource provider, generally used in the context of federal financial assistance.

Allowance for Amortization   The account in which the amounts recorded as amortization (q.v.) of the intangible asset are accumulated.

Allowance for Depreciation   The account in which the amounts recorded as depreciation (q.v.) of the related asset are accumulated.

Amortization   (1) Gradual reduction, redemption, or liquidation of the balance of an account according to a specified schedule of times and amounts. (2) Provision for the extinguishment of a debt by means of a debt service fund (q.v.).

Annual Pension Cost   The annual expense to an employer for a pension plan, which is a function of annual required contribution (ARC), net pension obligation (NPO), interest, and adjustments.

Annual Required Contribution (ARC)   An actuarially determined amount that the employer should contribute each year to a defined benefit pension plan to ensure full actuarial funding of the plan.

Annuities Payable   A liability account that records the amount of annuities due and payable to retired employees in a public employee retirement system.

Annuity   A series of equal money payments made at equal intervals during a designated period of time. In governmental accounting, the most frequent annuities are accumulations of debt service funds for term bonds and payments to retired employees or their beneficiaries under public employee retirement systems.

Annuity, Amount of   The total amount of money accumulated or paid during an annuity period from an annuity and compound interest at a designated rate.

Annuity Agreements   Funds established to account for assets given to an organization subject to an agreement that binds the organization to pay stipulated amounts periodically to the donor(s).

Annuity Period   The designated length of time during which an amount of annuity is accumulated or paid.

Annuity Serial Bonds   Bonds for which the amount of annual principal repayments is scheduled to increase each year by approximately the same amount that interest payments decrease.

Apportionment   A distribution made of a federal appropriation by the Office of Management and Budget into amounts available for specified time periods.

Appropriation   An authorization granted by a legislative body to incur liabilities for purposes specified in the Appropriation Act (q.v.). *Note:* An appropriation is usually limited in amount and as to the time when it may be expended. See, however, Indeterminate Appropriation.

Appropriation Act, Bill, Ordinance, Resolution, or Order   A legal action giving the administration of a government authorization to incur on behalf of the government liabilities for the acquisition of goods, services, or facilities to be used for purposes specified in the act, ordinance, or so on, in amounts not to exceed those specified for each purpose. The authorization usually expires at the end of a specified term, most often one year.

Appropriation Expenditure   See Expenditures.

Appropriations Budget   Appropriations requested by departments or by the central administration of a government for a budget period. When the appropriations budget has been adopted in accord with procedures specified by relevant law, the budget becomes legally binding on the administration of the government for which the budget has been adopted.

Appropriations Used   An account used in federal government accounting to indicate resources provided by current- or prior-period appropriations that were consumed during the current fiscal period.

Arbitrage   Earning a higher interest rate from investing borrowed funds than is applicable to the entity's tax-exempt debt. Federal tax regulations require governments to rebate the investment earnings in excess of that permitted. See also Arbitrage Rebate.

Arbitrage Rebate   Required repayment to the federal government arising from the arbitrage rules that prohibit the government from investing bond proceeds at interest rates higher than that applicable to the entity's tax-exempt debt.

Assess   To value property officially for the purpose of taxation. *Note:* The term is also sometimes used to denote the levy of taxes, but such usage is not correct because it fails to distinguish between the valuation process and the tax levy process.

Assessed Valuation   A valuation set on real estate or other property by a government as a basis for levying taxes.

Assessment   (1) The process of making the official valuation of property for purposes of taxation. (2) The valuation placed on property as a result of this process.

Asset Impairment   A significant, unexpected decline in the service utility of a capital asset (q.v.).

Assets   Probable future economic benefits obtained or controlled by a particular entity as a result of past transactions or events.

Assets Limited as to Use   Assets whose use is limited by contracts or agreements with outside parties (such as proceeds of debt issues, funds deposited with a trustee, self-insurance funding arrangements, and statutory reserve requirements) other than donors or grantors. The term also includes limitations placed on assets by the board of directors or trustees.

Attestation Engagements   Services related to internal control, compliance, MD&A presentation, allowability and reasonableness of proposed contract amounts, final contract costs, and reliability of performance measures.

Audit   The examination of documents, records, reports, systems of internal control, accounting and financial procedures, and other evidence for one or more of the following purposes:

1. To determine whether the financial statements or other financial reports and related items are fairly presented in accordance with generally accepted accounting principles or other established or stated criteria.

2. To determine whether the entity has complied with laws and regulations and other specific financial compliance requirements that may have a material effect on the financial statements or that may affect other financial reports or the economy, efficiency, or effectiveness of program activities.

3. To determine whether the entity is acquiring, protecting, and using its resources economically and efficiently.

4. To determine whether the desired program results or benefits established by the legislature or other authorizing body are being achieved.

Audit Committee   A committee of the governing board whose function it is to help select the auditor, monitor the audit process, review results of the audit, assist the governing board in understanding the results of the audit, and participate with both management and the independent auditor in resolving internal control or other deficiencies identified during the audit.

Audit Findings   Items identified by the auditors in the course of the audit, such as internal control weaknesses, instances of noncompliance, questioned costs, fraud, and material misrepresentations (by the auditee).

Auditor's Opinion or Report   A statement signed by an auditor stating that he or she has examined the financial statements in accordance with generally accepted auditing standards (with exceptions, if any) and expressing his or her opinion on the financial condition and results of operations of the reporting entity, as appropriate.

Authority   A government or public agency created to perform a single function or a restricted group of related activities. Usually such governments are financed from service charges, fees, and tolls, but in some instances they also have taxing powers. An authority may be completely independent of other governments, or in some cases it may be partially dependent on other governments for its creation, its financing, or the exercise of certain powers.

Authority Bonds Bonds payable from the revenues of a specific authority. Since such authorities usually have no revenue other than charges for services, their bonds are ordinarily revenue bonds (q.v.).

Auxiliary Enterprises Activities of a college or university that furnish a service to students, faculty, or staff on a user-charge basis. The charge is directly related but not necessarily equal to the cost of the service. Examples include college unions, residence halls, stores, faculty clubs, and intercollegiate athletics.

Available Collectible within the current period or soon enough thereafter to be used to pay liabilities of the current period.

B

Balance Sheet A statement that reports the balances of assets, liabilities, reserves, and equities of a fund, government, or not-for-profit entity at a specified date, properly classified to exhibit financial position of the fund or unit at that date.

Basic Financial Statements Term used in *GASBS 34* to describe required government-wide and fund financial statements.

Basis of Accounting The standard(s) used to determine the point in time when assets, liabilities, revenues, and expenses (expenditures) should be measured and recorded as such in the accounts of an entity. See Accrual Basis, Cash Basis, and Modified Accrual Basis.

Bearer Bond A bond that requires the holder to present matured interest coupons or matured bonds to the issuer or a designated paying agent for payment. Payments are made to the bearer since the issuer maintains no record of current bond ownership. *Note:* Federal law requires that all tax-exempt bonds issued since June 15, 1983, must be in registered form (see also Registered Bonds). However, some long-term bearer bonds remain outstanding.

Benchmarking The method of identifying a number that represents a target to which actual results are compared, or a basis for comparison; for example, industry averages.

Betterment An addition made to or change made in a capital asset that is expected to prolong its life or to increase its efficiency over and above that arising from maintenance (q.v.) and the cost of which is therefore added to the book value of the asset. *Note:* The term is sometimes applied to sidewalks, sewers, and highways, but these should preferably be designated as improvements or infrastructure assets (q.v.).

Blended Presentation The method of reporting the financial data of a component unit in a manner similar to that in which the financial data of the primary government are presented. Under this method the component unit data are usually combined with the appropriate fund types of the primary government and reported in the same columns as the data for the primary government except General Funds. See Discrete Presentation.

Block Grants Federal monies given to state or local governments with the discretion to administer for many projects and to many recipients and for which no matching requirement exists.

Board-Designated Funds Funds created to account for assets set aside by the governing board of an organization for specified purposes.

Board-Designated Net Assets Unrestricted net assets that the not-for-profit organization's board decided to set aside or "designate" for specific purposes.

Bond A written promise to pay a specified sum of money, called the *face value* or *principal amount,* at a specified date or dates in the future, called the *maturity date(s),* together with periodic interest at a specified rate. *Note:* The difference between a note and a bond is that the latter runs for a longer period of time and requires greater legal formality.

Bond Anticipation Notes (BANs) Short-term interest-bearing notes issued by a government in anticipation of bonds to be issued at a later date. The notes are retired from proceeds of the bond issue to which they are related. See also Interim Borrowing.

Bond Discount The excess of the face value of a bond over the price for which it is acquired or sold. *Note:* The price does not include accrued interest at the date of acquisition or sale.

Bond Indenture The contract between an entity issuing bonds and the trustees or other body representing prospective and actual holders of the bonds.

Bond Ordinance or Resolution An ordinance (q.v.) or resolution (q.v.) authorizing a bond issue.

Bond Premium The excess of the price at which a bond is acquired or sold over its face value. *Note:* The price does not include accrued interest at the date of acquisition or sale.

Bonded Debt That portion of indebtedness represented by outstanding bonds. See Gross Bonded Debt and Net Bonded Debt.

Bonded Indebtedness See Bonded Debt.

Bonds Authorized and Unissued Bonds that have been legally authorized but not issued and that can be issued and sold without further authorization. *Note:* This term must not be confused with the terms *margin of borrowing power* or *legal debt margin,* either one of which represents the difference between the legal debt limit of a government and the debt outstanding against it.

Book Value   Value (q.v.) as shown by the books of account. *Note:* In the case of assets subject to reduction by valuation allowances, *book value* refers to cost or stated value less the appropriate allowance. Sometimes a distinction is made between *gross* book value and *net* book value, the former designating value before deduction of related allowances and the latter after their deduction. In the absence of any modifier, however, the term *book value* is understood to be synonymous with net book value.

Budget   A plan of financial operation embodying an estimate of proposed expenditures for a given period and the proposed means of financing them. Used without any modifier, the term usually indicates a financial plan for a single fiscal year.

Budget or Budgetary Accounts   Accounts used in federal agencies that are broad in scope, for which appropriations are made, and that are not the same as the standard general ledger accounts used for accounting purposes. Budget accounts may cover an entire organization, or a group of budget accounts may be aggregated to cover an organization.

Budget Calendar   A schedule of certain steps to be followed in the budgeting process and the dates by which each step must be completed.

Budget Document   The instrument used by the budget-making authority to present a comprehensive financial program to the appropriating body. The budget document usually consists of three parts. The first part contains a message from the budget-making authority with a summary of the proposed expenditures and the means of financing them. The second consists of schedules supporting the summary. These schedules show in detail the information as to past years' actual revenues, expenditures, and other data used in making the estimates. The third part is composed of drafts of the appropriation, revenue, and borrowing measures necessary to put the budget into effect.

Budget Message   A general discussion of the proposed budget as presented in writing by the budget-making authority to the legislative body. The budget message should contain an explanation of the principal budget items, an outline of the government's experience during the past period and its financial status at the time of the message, and recommendations regarding the financial policy for the coming period.

Budget Officer   A person, usually in the central administrative office, designated to ensure that administrative policies are actually used in budget preparation and that the budget calendar and other legal requirements are met.

Budgetary Accounts   Those accounts that reflect budgetary operations and condition, such as estimated revenues, appropriations, and encumbrances, as distinguished from proprietary accounts. See also Proprietary Accounts.

Budgetary Control   The control or management of a government or enterprise in accordance with an approved budget for the purpose of keeping expenditures within the limitations of available appropriations and available revenues.

Budgetary Resources   A term that includes new budgetary authority for the period plus unobligated budgetary authority carried over from the prior period and offsetting collections, if any, plus or minus any budgetary adjustments in a federal agency.

Buildings   A capital asset account that reflects the acquisition value of permanent structures used to house persons and property owned by a government. If buildings are purchased or constructed, this account includes the purchase or contract price of all permanent buildings and fixtures attached to and forming a permanent part of such buildings. If buildings are acquired by gift, the account reflects their appraised value at time of acquisition.

Business-Type Activities   Commercial-type activities of a government, such as public utilities (e.g., electric, water, gas, and sewer utilities), transportation systems, toll roads, toll bridges, hospitals, parking garages and lots, liquor stores, golf courses, and swimming pools.

C

Callable Bond   A type of bond that permits the issuer to pay the obligation before the stated maturity date by giving notice of redemption in a manner specified in the bond contract. Also called optional bond.

Capital Assets   Assets of a long-term character that are intended to continue to be held or used, such as land, buildings, machinery, furniture, and other equipment. *Note:* The term does not indicate the immobility of an asset, which is the distinctive character of "fixture" (q.v.). Also called *fixed assets.*

Capital Budget   A plan of proposed capital outlays and the means of financing them for the current fiscal period. It is usually a part of the current budget. If a capital program is in operation, it will be the first year thereof. A capital program is sometimes referred to as a capital budget. See also *capital program.*

Capital Expenditures   See Capital Outlays.

Capital Improvements Fund   A fund to accumulate revenues from current taxes levied for major repairs and maintenance to capital assets of a nature not specified at the time the revenues are levied. Appropriations of this fund are made in accord with state law at the time specific projects become necessary.

Capital Lease   A lease that substantively transfers the benefits and risks of ownership of property to the lessee. Any lease that meets certain criteria specified in applicable accounting and reporting standards is a capital lease. See also Operating Lease.

Capital Outlays   Expenditures that result in the acquisition of or addition to capital assets.

Capital Program   A plan for capital expenditures to be incurred each year over a fixed period of years to meet capital needs arising from a long-term work program or otherwise. It sets forth each project or other contemplated expenditure in which the government is to have a part and specifies the full resources estimated to be available to finance the projected expenditures.

Capital Projects Fund (CPF)   A fund created to account for all resources to be used for the construction or acquisition of designated capital assets by a government except those financed by proprietary or fiduciary funds. See also Bond Fund.

Capitation Fee   Fixed dollar amount of fees per person paid periodically by a third-party payor to a health care organization, regardless of services provided.

Cash   Currency, coin, checks, money orders, and bankers' drafts on hand or on deposit with an official or agent designated as custodian of cash and bank deposits. *Note:* All cash must be recorded as a part of the fund to which it belongs. Any restrictions or limitations as to its availability must be indicated in the records and statements. It is not necessary, however, to have a separate bank account for each fund unless required by law.

Cash Basis   The basis of accounting under which revenues are recorded when received in cash and expenditures (or expenses) are recorded when cash is disbursed.

Cash Discount   An allowance received or given if payment is completed within a stated period of time.

Cash Equivalents   Short-term, highly liquid investments that are both readily convertible into known amounts of cash and so near their maturity that they present insignificant risk of changes in value due to changes in interest rates.

Certificate of Participation (COP)   A long-term debt instrument authorized for construction of municipal facilities, typically issued by a quasi-independent authority but secured by a long-term lease with a general purpose local government.

Character   A basis for distinguishing expenditures according to the periods they are presumed to benefit. See also Character Classification.

Character Classification   A grouping of expenditures on the basis of the fiscal periods they are presumed to benefit. The three groupings are (1) current expenditures, presumed to benefit the current fiscal period, (2) debt service, presumed to benefit prior fiscal periods primarily but also present and future periods, and (3) capital outlays, presumed to benefit the current and future fiscal periods. See also Activity, Activity Classification, Function, Functional Classification, Object, Object Classification, and Expenses.

Charitable Solicitation   The direct or indirect request for money, credit, property, financial assistance, or other things of value on the representation that these assets will be used for a charitable purpose.

Charity Care   Service provided by a health care organization to persons with a demonstrated inability to pay.

Check   A bill of exchange drawn on a bank and payable on demand; a written order on a bank to pay on demand a specified sum of money to a named person, to his or her order, or to the bearer, from money on deposit to the credit of the maker. *Note:* A check differs from a warrant in that the latter is not necessarily payable on demand and may not be negotiable. It differs from a voucher in that the latter is not an order to pay.

Clearing Account   An account used to accumulate total charges or credits for the purpose of distributing them later among the accounts to which they are allocable or for the purpose of transferring the net differences to the proper account. Also called suspense account.

Cognizant Agency for Audit Responsibilities   The federal awarding agency that provides the predominant amount of direct funding to a nonfederal entity expending more than $25 million in federal awards, as provided by OMB *Circular A–133,* unless the OMB designates a different cognizant agency.

Collateralized   Secured with the pledge of assets to minimize the risk of loss. Deposits, investments, or loans are often required to be collateralized.

Collections   Works of art, historical treasures, or similar assets that are (1) held for public exhibition, education, or research in furtherance of public service rather than financial gain, (2) protected, kept unencumbered, cared for, and preserved, and (3) subject to an organizational policy that requires the proceeds of items that are sold to be used to acquire other items for collection.

Combined Financial Statement   A single financial statement that displays the combined financial data for various fund types and, if applicable, discretely presented component units in separate adjacent columns eliminated by *GASBS 34.* See Combining Financial Statement.

Combining Financial Statement   A financial statement that displays the financial data for the funds of a given fund type (e.g., special revenue funds) in columns with totals that agree with those reported in the combined financial statements. See Combined Financial Statement.

Commitment   In federal government usage, a reservation of an agency's allotment in the estimated amount of orders for goods or services, prior to actually placing the orders. See also Obligations.

Common Rule Term given to OMB *Circular A–102* that describes administrative requirements that must be met by a state or local government receiving federal financial assistance.

Compliance Audit An audit designed to provide reasonable assurance that a government has complied with applicable laws and regulations. Required for every audit performed in conformity with generally accepted governmental auditing standards.

Component Unit A separate government, agency, or not-for-profit corporation that, pursuant to the criteria in the GASB *Codification,* Section 2100, is combined with other component units to constitute the reporting entity (q.v.).

Comprehensive Annual Financial Report (CAFR) A government's official annual report prepared and published as a matter of public record. In addition to the general purpose external financial statements, the CAFR should contain introductory material, schedules to demonstrate legal compliance, and statistical tables specified in the GASB *Codification.*

Conditional Promise to Give A promise to make a contribution to an organization that depends on the occurrence of a specified future and uncertain event to bind the promisor, such as obtaining matching gifts by the recipient.

Construction Work in Progress The cost of construction work that has been started but not yet completed.

Consumption Method A method of recording supplies as inventory when purchased and as expenditures when used or consumed. The alternative method is called the *purchases method.*

Contingency Fund Assets or other resources set aside to provide for unforeseen expenditures, anticipated expenditures, or uncertain amount(s).

Contingent Liabilities Items that may become liabilities as a result of conditions undetermined at a given date, such as guarantees, pending lawsuits, judgments under appeal, unsettled disputed claims, unfilled purchase orders, and uncompleted contracts. Contingent liabilities of the latter two types are disclosed in balance sheets of governmental funds as Reserve for Encumbrances; other contingent liabilities are disclosed in notes to the financial statements.

Continuing Appropriation An appropriation that, once established, is automatically renewed without further legislative action, period after period, until altered or revoked. *Note:* The term should not be confused with *indeterminate appropriation* (q.v.).

Continuing Care Retirement Communities (CCRCs) A facility that provides residential care along with some level of long-term nursing or medical care, generally to elderly or retired persons.

Contractual Adjustments (or Allowances) The difference between the gross patient service revenue and the negotiated payment by third-party payors in arriving at net patient service revenue.

Contributions Amounts given to an individual or to an organization for which the donor receives no direct private benefits. Contributions may be in the form of pledges, cash, securities, materials, services, or capital assets.

Control Account An account in the general ledger in which is recorded the aggregate of debit and credit postings to a number of identical or related accounts called *subsidiary accounts.* For example, the Taxes Receivable account is a control account supported by the aggregate of individual balances in individual property taxpayers' accounts.

Cost The amount of money or money's worth exchanged for property or services. *Note:* Costs may be incurred even before money is paid, that is, as soon as a liability is incurred. Ultimately, however, money or money's worth must be given in exchange. Again, the cost of some property or service may, in turn, become a part of the cost of another property or service. For example, the cost of part or all of the materials purchased at a certain time will be reflected in the cost of articles made from such materials or in the cost of services provided using such materials.

Cost Accounting The branch of accounting that provides for the assembling and recording of all elements of cost incurred to accomplish a purpose, to carry on an activity or operation, or to complete a unit of work or a specific job.

Cost Determination The use of statistical procedures to determine or estimate the cost of goods or services as opposed to accumulating such costs in a formal cost accounting system.

Cost Objective In federal terminology, an organization unit, function, activity, project, cost center, or pool established for the accumulation of costs.

Cost Unit A term used in cost accounting to designate the unit of product or service whose cost is computed. These units are selected for the purpose of comparing the actual cost with a standard cost or with actual costs of units produced under different circumstances or at different places and times. See also Unit Cost and Work Unit.

Coupon Rate The interest rate specified on interest coupons attached to a bond. The term is synonymous with nominal interest rate (q.v.) for coupon bonds.

Credit Risk The risk that a debt issuer will not pay interest and principal when due. See also Default.

Cumulative Results of Operations A term generally used in federal agencies to refer to the net difference between expenses/losses and financing sources, including appropriations, revenues, and gains, since the inception of the activity.

Current   A term applied to budgeting and accounting that designates the operations of the present fiscal period as opposed to past or future periods.

Current Assets   Those assets that are available or can be made readily available to meet the cost of operations or to pay current liabilities. Some examples are cash, temporary investments, and taxes receivable.

Current Financial Resources   Cash or items expected to be converted into cash during the current period or soon enough thereafter to pay current period liabilities.

Current Fund   In governmental accounting sometimes used as a synonym for General Fund.

Current Funds   Funds whose resources are expended for operating purposes during the current fiscal period. Colleges and universities and voluntary health and welfare organizations often use fund types called Current Fund—Unrestricted and Current Funds—Restricted for internal purposes.

Current Liabilities   Liabilities payable within a relatively short period of time, usually no longer than a year. See also Floating Debt.

Current Resources   Resources (q.v.) to which recourse can be had to meet current obligations and expenditures. Examples are estimated revenues of a particular period not yet realized, transfers from other funds authorized but not received, and, in the case of certain funds, bonds authorized and unissued.

Current Revenue   Revenues of a government available to meet expenditures of the current fiscal year. See Revenue.

Current Special Assessments   (1) Special assessments levied and becoming due during the current fiscal period from the date special assessment rolls are approved by the proper authority to the date on which a penalty for nonpayment is attached. (2) Special assessments levied in a prior fiscal period but becoming due in the current fiscal period from the time they become due to the date on which a penalty for nonpayment is attached.

Current Taxes   (1) Taxes levied and becoming due during the current fiscal period from the time the amount of tax levy is first established to the date on which a penalty for nonpayment is attached. (2) Taxes levied in the preceding fiscal period but becoming due in the current fiscal period from the time they become due until a penalty for nonpayment is attached.

Current-Year's Tax Levy   Taxes levied for the current fiscal period.

Customer Advances for Construction   Amounts required to be deposited by a customer for construction projects undertaken by the utility at the request of the customer.

Cycle Billing   A practice to bill part of the customers each working day during a month instead of billing all customers as of a certain day of the month. It is followed by utilities, retail stores, and other organizations with a large number of credit customers.

D

Data Processing   (1) The preparation and handling of information and data from source media through prescribed procedures to obtain specific end results such as classification, problem solution, summarization, and reports. (2) Preparation and handling of financial information wholly or partially by use of computers.

Debt   A liability resulting from the borrowing of money or from the purchase of goods and services. Debts of governments include bonds, time warrants, notes, and floating debt. See also Bond, Notes Payable, Time Warrant, Floating Debt, Long-Term Debt, and General Long-Term Debt.

Debt-Financed Income   Income from property that is subject to debt, such as rental income from a building that has been financed with a mortgage.

Debt Limit   The maximum amount of gross or net debt that is legally permitted.

Debt Margin   The difference between the amount of the debt limit (q.v.) and the net amount of outstanding indebtedness subject to the limitation.

Debt Service Fund (DSF)   A fund established to finance and account for the payment of interest and principal on all tax-supported debt, serial and term, including that payable from special assessments.

Default   Failure of a debtor to pay interest or repay the principal of debt when legally due.

Defeasance   A transaction in which the liability for a debt is substantively settled and is removed from the accounts, even though the debt has not actually been paid. See also Legal Defeasance and In-Substance Defeasance.

Deferred Revenues or Deferred Credits   In governmental accounting, items that may not be recognized as revenues of the period in which received because they are not "available" until a subsequent period.

Deferred Serial Bonds   Serial bonds (q.v.) in which the first installment does not fall due for two or more years from the date of issue.

Deficiency   A general term indicating the amount by which anything falls short of some requirement or expectation. The term should not be used without qualification.

Deficit   (1) The excess of liabilities and reserved equity of a fund over its assets. (2) The excess of expenditures over revenues during an accounting period or, in the case of enterprise and internal service funds, of expense over revenue during an accounting period.

Defined Benefit Plan   A pension plan that provides a specified amount of benefits based on a formula that may include factors such as age, salary, and years of employment.

Defined Contribution Plan A pension plan that specifies the amount or rate of contribution, often a percentage of covered salary, that the employer and employees must contribute to the members' accounts.

Delinquent Special Assessments Special assessments remaining unpaid on and after the date on which a penalty for nonpayment is attached.

Delinquent Taxes Taxes remaining unpaid on and after the date on which a penalty for nonpayment is attached. Even though the penalty may be subsequently waived and a portion of the taxes may be abated or canceled, the unpaid balances continue to be delinquent taxes until abated, canceled, paid, or converted into tax liens. *Note:* The term is sometimes limited to taxes levied for the fiscal period or periods preceding the current one, but such usage is not entirely correct. See also Current Taxes, Current-Year's Tax Levy, and Prior-Years' Tax Levies.

Deposit Warrant A financial document prepared by a designated accounting or finance officer authorizing the treasurer of a government to accept for deposit sums of money collected by various departments and agencies of the government.

Deposits Money deposited with a financial institution that must be released upon the "demand" of the depositor; for example, demand deposits (checking) and time deposits (savings accounts). These funds are generally insured by the Federal Deposit Insurance Corporation (up to a limit) and are distinguished from investments.

Depreciation (1) Expiration of the service life of capital assets other than wasting assets attributable to wear and tear, deterioration, action of the physical elements, inade-quacy, and obsolescence. (2) The portion of the cost of a capital asset other than a wasting asset that is charged as an expense during a particular period. *Note:* In accounting for depreciation, the cost of a capital asset, less any salvage value, is prorated over the estimated service life of such an asset and each period is charged with a portion of such cost. Through this process, the cost of the asset less salvage value is ultimately charged off as an expense.

Derived Tax Revenues A classification of nonexchange transactions, such as income or sales taxes.

Designated A term that describes assets or equity set aside by action of the governing board; as distinguished from assets or equity set aside in conformity with requirements of donors, grantors, or creditors.

Diagnosis-Related Groups (DRGs) A case-mix classification scheme instituted by Congress in 1983 in relation to the Medicare program that is used to determine the reim-bursement received by a hospital for inpatient services. Payment is made based on the patient's diagnosis regardless of how much the hospital spends to treat a patient.

Direct Cost A cost incurred because of some definite action by or for an organization unit, function, activity, project, cost center, or pool; a cost identified specifically with a cost objective (q.v.).

Direct Debt The debt that a government has incurred in its own name or assumed through the annexation of territory or consolidation with another government. See also Overlapping Debt.

Direct Expenses Those expenses that can be charged directly as a part of the cost of a product or service or of a department or operating unit as distinguished from overhead and other indirect costs that must be prorated among several products or services, departments, or operating units.

Direct Lobbying Testifying at legislative hearings, corresponding or conferring with legislators or their staffs, and publishing documents advocating specific legislative action.

Disbursements Payments in cash.

Discount on Taxes A cash discount offered to taxpayers to encourage early payment of taxes.

Discrete Presentation The method of reporting financial data of component units in a column(s) separate from the financial data of the primary government.

Disqualified Person A person who has substantial influence over the affairs of a not-for-profit organization, such as an officer or manager.

Donated Assets Noncash contributions (q.v.) that may be in the form of securities, land, buildings, equipment, or materials.

Donated Materials See Donated Assets.

Donated Services The services of volunteer workers who are unpaid or are paid less than the market value of their services.

Double Entry A system of bookkeeping that requires that for every entry made to the debit side of an account or accounts an entry for a corresponding amount or amounts to the credit side of another account or accounts be made. *Note:* Double-entry bookkeeping involves maintaining a balance between assets on the one hand and liabilities and equities on the other.

Due Diligence Formal disclosure and discovery of all relevant information about a transaction or organization, particularly about risks.

E

Earnings See Income and Revenue.

Economic Condition A composite of a government's financial health and its ability and willingness to meet its financial obligations and its commitments to provide services.

Economic Interest   An interest in another organization because it holds or utilizes significant resources that must be used for the purposes of the reporting organization or the reporting organization is responsible for the liabilities of the other entity.

Economic Resources Measurement Focus   Attention on measuring the total economic resources that flow in and out of the government rather than on measuring *current financial resources* only.

Economic Size   The minimum possible size to be able to provide services without long-term damage to the organization's financial base.

Effective Interest Rate   The rate of earning on a bond investment based on the actual price paid for the bond, the maturity date, and the length of time between interest dates, in contrast with the nominal interest rate (q.v.).

Eligibility Requirements   Specified characteristics that program recipients must possess or reimbursement provisions and contingencies tied to required actions by the recipient.

Encumbrances   Accounts used to record the estimated amount of purchase orders, contracts, or salary commitments chargeable to an appropriation. The account is credited when goods or services are received and the actual expenditure of the appropriation is known.

Endowment   A gift whose principal must be maintained inviolate but whose income may be expended.

Engagement Letter   Written agreement between an auditor and the audited entity that describes the scope of work to be completed, among other things.

Enterprise Debt   Debt that is to be retired primarily through the earnings of governmentally owned and operated enterprises. See also Revenue Bonds.

Enterprise Fund (EF)   A fund established to finance and account for the acquisition, operation, and maintenance of governmental facilities and services that are entirely or predominantly self-supporting by user charges; or for when the governing body of the government has decided periodic determination of revenues earned, expenses incurred, and/or net income is appropriate. Governmentally owned utilities and hospitals are ordinarily accounted for by enterprise funds.

Entitlement   The amount of payment to which a state or local government is entitled as determined by the federal government pursuant to an allocation formula contained in applicable statutes.

Entity Assets   Those assets of a federal agency that the reporting entity has authority to use in its operations as opposed to holding but not available to spend.

Entitywide Perspective   A view of the net assets of the organization as a whole, rather than as a collection of separate funds.

Entry   (1) The record of a financial transaction in its appropriate book of account. (2) The act of recording a transaction in the books of account.

Equipment   Tangible property of a more or less permanent nature (other than land, buildings, or improvements) that is useful in carrying on operations. Examples are machinery, tools, trucks, cars, furniture, and furnishings.

Equity Transfer   Nonrecurring or nonroutine transfers of equity between funds. Also referred to as residual equity transfer (q.v.). *GASBS 34* eliminates this term from usage. See Interfund Transfers.

Escheat Property   Private property that reverts to government ownership upon the death of the owner if there are no legal claimants or heirs.

Estimated Expenditures   The estimated amounts of expenditures included in budgeted appropriations. See also Appropriations.

Estimated Other Financing Sources   Amounts of financial resources estimated to be received or accrued during a period by a governmental or similar type fund from interfund transfers or from the proceeds of noncurrent debt issuance.

Estimated Other Financing Uses   Amounts of financial resources estimated to be disbursed or accrued during a period by a governmental or similar type fund for transfer to other funds.

Estimated Revenue   For revenue accounts kept on an accrual basis (q.v.), this term designates the amount of revenue estimated to accrue during a given period regardless of whether or not it is all to be collected during the period. For revenue accounts kept on a cash basis (q.v.), the term designates the amount of revenue estimated to be collected during a given period. Under the modified accrual basis (q.v.), estimated revenues are those that are measurable and available. See also Revenue, Revenue Receipts, Cash Basis, Accrual Basis, and Modified Accrual Basis.

Estimated Revenue Receipts   A term used synonymously with estimated revenue (q.v.) by some governments reporting their revenues on a cash basis. See also Revenue and Revenue Receipts.

Estimated Uncollectible Accounts Receivable (Credit)   That portion of accounts receivable that it is estimated will never be collected. The account is deducted from the Accounts Receivable account on the balance sheet in order to arrive at the net amount of accounts receivable.

Estimated Uncollectible Current Taxes (Credit)   A provision out of tax revenues for that portion of current taxes receivable that is estimated will never be collected.

The amount is shown on the balance sheet as a deduction from the Taxes Receivable—Current account in order to arrive at the net taxes receivable.

Estimated Uncollectible Delinquent Taxes (Credit)
That portion of delinquent taxes receivable that it is estimated will never be collected. The account is shown on the balance sheet as a deduction from the Taxes Receivable—Delinquent account to arrive at the net delinquent taxes receivable.

Estimated Uncollectible Interest and Penalties on Taxes (Credit) That portion of interest and penalties receivable that is estimated will never be collected. The account is shown as a deduction from the Interest and Penalties Receivable account on the balance sheet in order to arrive at the net interest and penalties receivable.

Estimated Uncollectible Tax Liens That portion of tax liens receivable that it is estimated will never be collected. The account is shown as a deduction from the Tax Liens Receivable account on the balance sheet in order to arrive at the net amount of tax liens receivable.

Excess Benefit Transaction A transaction that results in unfair benefits to a person who has substantial influence over a not-for-profit organization, for example, unreasonable compensation, sales of assets at bargain prices, and lease arrangements.

Exchange Transactions Transactions in which each party receives direct tangible benefits commensurate with the resources provided, for example, sales between a buyer and a seller.

Exchange-like Transactions A transaction in which the values exchanged, though related, may not be quite equal or in which the direct benefits may not be exclusively for the parties to the transaction, unlike a "pure" exchange transaction.

Exemption A statutory reduction in the assessed valuation of taxable property accorded to certain taxpayers, such as senior citizens and war veterans.

Exhibit (1) A balance sheet or other principal financial statement. (2) Any statement or other document that accompanies or is a part of a financial or audit report. See also Schedules and Statements.

Expendable Assets and resources may be converted into cash and used in their entirety for purposes of the fund.

Expended Appropriation Authority A charge against an appropriation for the actual cost of items received; the appropriation is no longer available to acquire additional goods and services.

Expenditure Disbursements A term sometimes used by governments operating on a cash basis (q.v.) as a synonym for expenditures (q.v.). It is not recommended terminology.

Expenditure Responsibility The responsibility of one public charity over another to which it has given a grant to ensure that the grant was used exclusively for the purpose for which it was made.

Expenditures Expenditures are recorded when liabilities are incurred pursuant to authority given in an appropriation (q.v.). If the accounts are kept on the accrual basis (q.v.) or the modified accrual basis (q.v.), this term designates the cost of goods delivered or services rendered, whether paid or unpaid, including expenses, provision for debt retirement not reported as a liability of the fund from which retired, and capital outlays. When the accounts are kept on the cash basis (q.v.), the term designates only actual cash disbursements for these purposes. *Note:* Encumbrances are not expenditures.

Expenses Charges incurred, whether paid or unpaid, for operation, maintenance, interest, and other charges presumed to benefit the current fiscal period.

External Investment Pool Centrally managed investment portfolios (pools) that manage the investments of participants (e.g., other governments and not-for-profit organizations) outside the reporting entity of the government that administers the pool.

External Support Test One of two parts of the broad public support test to determine if an organization is a public charity rather than a private foundation. It is met if at least one-third of the organization's total revenue comes from the government or general public in the form of contributions, grants, membership dues, charges for services, or sales of merchandise.

Extraordinary Items Unusual and infrequent material gains or losses.

F

Face Value As applied to securities, the amount of liability stated in the security document.

Facilities and Administrative Costs (F&A) Costs that are not readily assignable to one program or cost objective in a college or university but are incurred for a joint purpose. These costs are called *indirect costs* in some OMB circulars. See also Indirect Costs.

Fair Value The amount at which a financial instrument could be exchanged in a current transaction between willing parties other than in a forced or liquidation sale.

Federal Financial Management Improvement Act of 1996 (FFMIA) Act of Congress in 1996 that requires each federal agency to maintain a financial management system that applies federal accounting standards and provides the information necessary to report whether the agency is in compliance with those standards.

Federated Fund-Raising Organization An organization composed of independent charitable organizations that have voluntarily joined together to raise and distribute money among themselves.

Feeder Organization An entity controlled by a not-for-profit organization and formed to carry on a trade or business for the benefit of an exempt organization and remit its profits to the exempt organization.

Fidelity Bond A written promise to indemnify against losses from theft, defalcation, and misappropriation of public finds by government officers and employees. See also Surety Bond.

Fiduciary Activity Activity in which the government acts in a fiduciary capacity either as an agent or trustee for parties outside the government, for example in the collection of taxes or amounts bequeathed from private citizens, as well as assets held for employee pension plans.

Fiduciary Funds Any fund held by a government in a fiduciary capacity for an external party, ordinarily as agent or trustee. Also called *trust and agency funds.*

Financial Accountability (Financially Accountable) The obligation of a government to justify the raising of public resources and the expenditure of those resources. See Accountability.

Financial Audit One of the two major types of audits defined by the U.S. Government Accountability Office (see Performance Audit for the other major type). A financial audit provides an auditor's opinion that financial statements present fairly an entity's financial position and results of operations in conformity with generally accepted accounting principles or that other financial reports comply with specified finance-related criteria.

Financial Condition The probability that a government will meet its financial obligations as they become due and its service obligations to constituencies, both currently and in the future. See Financial Position.

Financial Position The adequacy of cash and short-term claims to cash to meet current obligations and those expected in the near future. See Financial Condition.

Fiscal Accountability Current-period financial position and budgetary compliance reported in fund-type financial statements of governments. See also Financial Accountability.

Fiscal Agent A bank or other corporate fiduciary that performs the function of paying, on behalf of the government, or other debtor, interest on debt or principal of debt when due.

Fiscal Capacity A government's ongoing ability and willingness to raise revenues, incur debt, and meet its financial obligations as they become due.

Fiscal Period Any period at the end of which a government determines its financial position and the results of its operations.

Fiscal Year A 12-month period of time to which the annual budget applies and at the end of which a government determines its financial position and the results of its operations. For example, FY06 refers to the year that ends in 2006 (e.g., 7-1-05 to 6-30-06).

Fixed Assets See Capital Assets.

Fixed Charges Expenses (q.v.) the amount of which is set by agreement. Examples are interest, insurance, and contributions to pension funds.

Fixtures Attachments to buildings that are not intended to be removed and that cannot be removed without damage to the latter. *Note:* Those fixtures with a useful life presumed to be as long as that of the building itself are considered a part of the building; all others are classed as equipment.

Flexible Budgeting Budgeting method that provides for alternative levels of activity, such as separate budgets for high, medium, and low levels of activity.

Floating Debt Liabilities other than bonded debt and time warrants that are payable on demand or at an early date. Examples are accounts payable, notes, and bank loans. See also Current Liabilities.

Force Account Construction The determination of the cost of construction of buildings and improvements by some agency of the government.

Forfeiture The automatic loss of cash or other property as a punishment for not complying with legal provisions and as compensation for the resulting damages or losses. *Note:* The term should not be confused with *confiscation.* The latter term designates the actual taking over of the forfeited property by the government. Even after property has been forfeited, it cannot be said to be confiscated until the government claims it.

Franchise A special privilege granted by a government permitting the continuing use of public property, such as city streets, and usually involving the elements of monopoly and regulation.

Full Accrual Basis See Accrual Basis.

Full Cost The total cost of providing a service or producing a good; the sum of both direct costs (q.v.) and indirect costs (q.v.).

Full Faith and Credit A pledge of the general taxing power for the payment of debt obligations. *Note:* Bonds carrying such pledges are usually referred to as *general obligation bonds.*

Function A group of related activities aimed at accomplishing a major service or regulatory responsibility for which a government is responsible. For example, public health is a function. See also Subfunction, Activity, Character, and Object.

Functional Classification   A grouping of expenditures on the basis of the principal purposes for which they are made. Examples are public safety, public health, and public welfare. See also Activity, Character, and Object Classification.

Fund   A fiscal and accounting entity with a self-balancing set of accounts recording cash and other financial resources together with all related liabilities and residual equities or balances, and changes therein, which are segregated for the purpose of carrying on specific activities or attaining certain objectives in accordance with special regulations, restrictions, or limitations.

Fund Accounting   An accounting system organized on the basis of funds, each of which is considered a separate accounting entity. Accounting for the operations of each fund is accomplished with a separate set of self-balancing accounts that comprise its assets, liabilities, fund equity, revenues, and expenditures, or expenses, as appropriate. Resources are allocated to and recorded in individual funds based upon purposes for which they are to be spent and the means by which spending activities are controlled. Fund accounting is used by states and local governments and internally by not-for-profit organizations that need to account for resources the use of which is restricted by donors or grantors.

Fund Balance   The portion of fund equity (q.v.) available for appropriation.

Fund Balance Sheet   A balance sheet for a single fund. See Fund and Balance Sheet.

Fund Balance with Treasury   An asset account of a federal agency representing cash balances held by the U.S. Treasury upon which the agency can draw. The Treasury will disburse cash on behalf of and at the request of the agency to pay for authorized goods and services.

Fund Equity   The excess of fund assets and resources over fund liabilities. A portion of the equity of a governmental fund may be reserved (q.v.) or designated (q.v.); the remainder is referred to as *fund balance.*

Fund Financial Statements   A category of the basic financial statements that assist in assessing fiscal accountability.

Fund Type   A classification of funds that are similar in purpose and character.

Funded Debt   Same as Bonded Debt, which is the preferred term.

Funded Deficit   A deficit eliminated through the sale of bonds issued for that purpose. See also Funding Bonds.

Funded Ratio   The ratio of actuarial value of assets to actuarial accrued liability (AAL) of a pension plan.

Funding   The conversion of floating debt or time warrants into bonded debt (q.v.).

Funding Bonds   See Refunding Bonds.

Funds Functioning as Endowments   Funds established by the governing board of an institution, usually a college or university, to account for assets to be retained and invested. Also called *quasi-endowment funds.*

G

GAAP Hierarchy   The chart from *SAS No. 69* amended by *SAS No. 91* that shows the relative weight to be placed on authoritative and other material for nongovernmental entities, state and local governments, and federal governmental entities.

Gains   Increases in net assets from peripheral or incidental transactions of an entity.

General Capital Assets (GCA)   Those capital assets of a government that are not recognized by a proprietary or fiduciary fund.

General Fund   A fund used to account for all transactions of a government that are not accounted in another fund. *Note:* The General Fund is used to account for the ordinary operations of a government that are financed from taxes and other general revenues.

General Long-Term Debt or Liabilities   Long-term debt legally payable from general revenues and backed by the full faith and credit of a governmental entity. See Long-Term Debt.

General Obligation (GO) Bonds or Debt   Bonds for whose payment the full faith and credit of the issuing body is pledged. More commonly, but not necessarily, general obligation bonds are considered to be those payable from taxes and other general revenues. In some states, these bonds are called *tax-supported bonds.* See also Full Faith and Credit.

General Obligation Special Assessment Bonds   See Special Assessment Bonds.

General Property, Plant, and Equipment   Property, plant, and equipment used to provide general government goods and services in a federal agency.

General Purpose Financial Statements   The term used prior to *GASBS 34* to describe the five combined financial statements of a reporting entity that were required for conformity with generally accepted accounting principles.

General Purpose Governments   Governments that provide many categories of services to their residents, such as states, counties, municipalities, and townships.

General Revenues   Revenues that are not directly linked to any specific function or do not produce a net revenue.

Generally Accepted Accounting Principles (GAAP)
The body of accounting and financial reporting standards, conventions, and practices that have authoritative support from standards-setting bodies such as the Governmental Accounting Standards Board and the Financial Accounting Standards Board, or for which a degree of consensus exists among accounting professionals at a given point in time. Generally accepted accounting principles are continually evolving as changes occur in the reporting environment.

Generally Accepted Auditing Standards (GAAS)
Standards prescribed by the American Institute of Certified Public Accountants to provide guidance for planning, conducting, and reporting on audits by certified public accountants.

Generally Accepted Government Auditing Standards (GAGAS)   See Government Auditing Standards.

Gifts in kind   Contributions of tangible items to a tax-exempt organization.

Government Auditing Standards (GAS)   Auditing standards set forth by the Comptroller General of the United States to provide guidance for federal auditors, state and local governmental auditors, and public accountants who audit federal organizations, programs, activities, and functions. Also referred to as *generally accepted government auditing standards (GAGAS).*

Government-Mandated Nonexchange Transactions   A category of nonexchange transactions, such as certain education, social welfare, and transportation services mandated and funded by a higher level of government.

Governmental Accounting   The composite activity of analyzing, recording, summarizing, reporting, and interpreting the financial transactions of governments and agencies. The term generally is used to refer to accounting for state and local governments rather than the U.S. federal government.

Governmental Activities   Core governmental services, such as protection of life and property (e.g., police and fire protection), public works (e.g., streets and highways, bridges, and public buildings), parks and recreation facilities and programs, and cultural and social services. Also includes general administrative support, such as data processing, finance, and personnel.

Governmental Assets (Liabilities)   Assets (or liabilities) that arise from transactions of the federal government or an entity of the federal government with nonfederal entities.

Governmental Funds   A generic classification used by the GASB to refer to all funds other than proprietary and fiduciary funds. The General Fund, special revenue funds, capital projects funds, debt service funds, and permanent funds are the types of funds referred to as *governmental funds.*

Government-wide Financial Statements   Two statements prescribed by *GASBS 34* designed to provide a highly aggregated overview of a government's net assets and results of financial activities.

Grant   A contribution by one entity to another, usually made to aid in the support of a specified function (for example, education), but sometimes for general purposes or for the acquisition or construction of capital assets.

Grants in Aid   See Grant.

Grass-Roots Lobbying   An appeal to the general public to contact legislators or to take other action regarding a legislative matter.

Gross Bonded Debt   The total amount of direct debt of a government represented by outstanding bonds before deduction of any assets available and earmarked for their retirement. See also Direct Debt.

Gross Revenue   See Revenue.

Gross Tax Levy   The amount of the tax bill sent to the taxpayer without regard for any estimate of uncollectible taxes.

H

Health Maintenance Organization (HMO)   A prepaid health care plan that functions as a broker of health care between the consumer/patient requiring services and health care providers. HMOs differ depending, in part, on whether or not the health care provider is an employee of the HMO. Similar to *preferred provider organizations (PPOs).*

Heritage Assets   Federal capital assets (q.v.), such as the Washington Monument, that possess educational, cultural, or natural characteristics.

Historical Cost   The amount paid or liability incurred by an accounting entity to acquire an asset and make it ready to render the services for which it was acquired.

Human Service Organizations   See Voluntary Health and Welfare Organizations.

I

Imposed Nonexchange Revenues   A category of nonexchange revenue, such as property taxes and most fines and forfeitures.

Improvements   Buildings, other structures, and other attachments or annexations to land that are intended to remain so attached or annexed, such as sidewalks, trees, drives, tunnels, drains, and sewers. *Note:* Sidewalks, curbing, sewers, and highways are sometimes referred to as *betterments,* but the term *improvements other than buildings* is preferred. *Infrastructure assets* is also a term used.

Improvements Other than Buildings   A capital asset account that reflects the acquisition value of permanent improvements, other than buildings, that add value to land. Examples of such improvements are fences and retaining walls. If the improvements are purchased or constructed, this account contains the purchase or contract price. If improvements are obtained by gift, it reflects fair value at time of acquisition.

Income A term used in accounting for governmental enterprises to represent the excess of revenues earned over the expenses incurred in carrying on the enterprise's operations. It should not be used without an appropriate modifier, such as operating, nonoperating, or net. See also Operating Income, Nonoperating Income, and Net Income. *Note:* The term *income* should not be used in lieu of *revenue* (q.v.) in nonenterprise funds.

Income Bonds See Revenue Bonds.

Incremental Budgeting A budgeting approach that is simply derived from the current-year's budget by multiplying by a factor (i.e., an incremental increase equal to inflation) or by adding amounts expected to be required by salary and other cost increases and deducting expenses not needed when the scope of operations is reduced.

Indenture See Bond Indenture.

Indeterminate Appropriation An appropriation that is not limited to any definite period of time and/or to any definite amount. *Note:* A distinction must be made between an indeterminate appropriation and a continuing appropriation. A continuing appropriation is indefinite only as to time, an indeterminate appropriation is indefinite as to both time and amount. Even indeterminate appropriations that are indefinite only as to time are to be distinguished from continuing appropriations in that such indeterminate appropriations may eventually lapse.

Indirect Cost A cost incurred that cannot be identified specifically with a cost objective (q.v.) but benefits multiple cost objectives (e.g., a hospital cafeteria, central data processing department, and general management costs).

Indirect Expenses Those expenses that are not directly linked to an identifiable function or program.

Industrial Aid Bonds Bonds issued by governments, the proceeds of which are used to construct plant facilities for private industrial concerns. Lease payments made by the industrial concern to the government are used to service the bonds. Such bonds may be in the form of general obligation bonds (q.v.) or revenue bonds (q.v.). Also called *industrial development bonds (IDBs)*.

Influencing Promoting, supporting, affecting, modifying, opposing, or delaying by any means. Often used in the context of "influencing" legislation or political candidates.

Infrastructure Assets Roads, bridges, curbs and gutters, streets, sidewalks, drainage systems, and lighting systems installed for the common good. See also Improvements.

Input Measures Measures of service efforts, or financial and nonfinancial resources used in a program or process.

In-Substance Defeasance A transaction in which low-risk U.S. government securities are placed into an irrevocable trust for the benefit of debtholders, and the liability for the debt is removed from the accounts of the entity even though the debt has not been repaid. See Defeasance and Legal Defeasance.

Inter-Activity Transactions Interfund loans or transfers that occur between a governmental fund (or internal service fund) and an enterprise fund.

Interest and Penalties Receivable on Taxes The uncollected portion of interest and penalties due on taxes.

Interest Receivable on Investments The amount of interest receivable on investments, exclusive of interest purchased. Interest purchased should be shown in a separate account.

Interest Receivable—Special Assessments The amount of interest receivable on unpaid installments of special assessments.

Interfund Accounts Accounts in which transactions between funds are reflected. See Interfund Transfers.

Interfund Loans Loans made by one fund to another.

Interfund Transfers Amounts transferred from one fund to another. See Equity Transfers and Operating Transfers.

Intergovernmental Revenue Revenue from other governments. Grants, shared revenue, and entitlements are types of intergovernmental revenue.

Interim Borrowing (1) Short-term loans to be repaid from general revenues during the course of a fiscal year. (2) Short-term loans in anticipation of tax collections or bonds issuance. See Bond Anticipation Notes, Tax Anticipation Notes, and Revenue Anticipation Notes.

Interim Statement A financial statement prepared before the end of the current fiscal year and covering only financial transactions during the current year to date. See also Statements.

Intermediate Sanctions Penalties imposed by the IRS in the form of excise taxes on private inurement to disqualified persons resulting from excess economic benefit transactions. For example, excessive salaries paid to a manager of a not-for-profit organization or rents higher than fair market value paid to a board member who owns the building the organization occupies.

Internal Control A plan of organization under which employees' duties are so arranged and records and procedures so designed as to make it possible to exercise effective accounting control over assets, liabilities, revenues, and expenditures. Under such a system, the work of employees is subdivided so that no single employee performs a complete cycle of operations. For example, an employee handling cash would not post the accounts receivable records. Moreover, under such a system, the procedures to be followed are definitely laid down and require proper authorizations by designated officials for all actions to be taken.

Internal Exchange Transactions   A term (coined by the authors) that captures both the interfund and interactivity nature of reciprocal exchange transactions within an entity (formerly called *quasi-external transactions*).

Internal Service Fund (ISF)   A fund established to finance and account for services and commodities furnished by a designated department or agency to other departments and agencies within a single government or to other governments. Amounts expended by the fund are restored thereto either from operating earnings or by transfers from other funds, so that the original fund capital is kept intact. Formerly called a *working capital fund* or *intragovernmental service fund.*

Internal Support Test   One of two tests of broad public support to determine if an organization is a public charity rather than a private foundation. The test is met if the not-for-profit organization does not receive more than one-third of its total support from investment income and unrelated business income.

Interperiod Equity   A term coined by the Governmental Accounting Standards Board indicating the extent to which current-period revenues are adequate to pay for current-period services.

Intra-Activity Transactions   Transactions that occur between two governmental funds (or between a governmental fund and an internal service fund) or between two enterprise funds.

Intra-Entity Transactions   Exchange or nonexchange transactions between the primary government and its blended or discretely presented component units.

Intragovernmental assets (liabilities)   Claims by or against a reporting entity that arise from transactions between that entity and other reporting entities.

Inventory   A detailed list showing quantities, descriptions, and values of property and frequently units of measure and unit prices.

Invested in Capital Assets, Net of Related Debt   One of the three categories of net assets reported by governments. It is the net capital assets less the debt relating to the acquisition or construction of the capital assets.

Investment Trust Fund   Fund used to account for the assets, liabilities, net assets, and changes in net assets corresponding to the equity of the external participants.

Investments   Securities and real estate held for the production of income in the form of interest, dividends, rentals, or lease payments. The term does not include capital assets used in governmental operations.

Irregular Serial Bonds   Bonds payable in which the total principal is repayable, but the repayment plan does not fit the definitions of regular serial bonds, deferred serial bonds, or term bonds.

J

Job Order Cost   Cost accounting system most appropriate for recording costs chargeable to specific jobs, grants, programs, projects, activities, or departments.

Judgment   An amount to be paid or collected by a government as the result of a court decision, including a condemnation award in payment for private property taken for public use.

Judgment Bonds   Bonds issued to pay judgments (q.v.). See also Funding.

Judgments Payable   Amounts due to be paid by a government as the result of court decisions, including condemnation awards in payment for private property taken for public use.

L

Land   A capital asset account that reflects the carrying value of land owned by a government. If land is purchased, this account shows the purchase price and costs such as legal fees and filling and excavation costs that are incurred to put the land in condition for its intended use. If land is acquired by gift, the account reflects its appraised value at time of acquisition.

Lapse   (Verb) As applied to appropriations, to terminate an appropriation. *Note:* Except for indeterminate appropriations (q.v.) and continuing appropriations (q.v.), an appropriation is made for a certain period of time. At the end of this period, any unexpended and unencumbered balance thereof lapses unless otherwise provided by law.

Leasehold   The right to the use of real estate by virtue of a lease, usually for a specified term of years, for which a consideration is paid.

Legal Defeasance   A transaction in which debt is legally satisfied based on certain provisions in the debt instrument (e.g., third-party guarantor assumes the debt) even though the debt has not been repaid. See also Defeasance and In-Substance Defeasance.

Legal Investments   (1) Investments that public employee retirement systems, savings banks, insurance companies, trustees, and other fiduciaries (individual or corporate) are permitted to make by the laws of the state in which they are domiciled or under the jurisdiction of which they operate or serve. The investments that meet the conditions imposed by law constitute the legal investment list. (2) Investments that governments are permitted to make by law.

Legal Opinion   (1) The opinion, as to legality, of an official authorized to render it, such as an attorney general or city attorney. (2) In the case of municipal bonds, the opinion of a specialized bond attorney as to the legality of a bond issue.

Legislation   Action by Congress, a state legislative body, or a local council to establish laws, statues, and ordinances.

Levy   (Verb) To impose taxes, special assessments, or service charges for the support of governmental activities. (Noun) The total amount of taxes, special assessments, or service charges imposed by a government.

Liabilities   Probable future sacrifices of economic benefits arising from present obligations of a particular entity to transfer assets or provide services to other entities in the future as a result of past transactions or events. *Note:* The term does not include encumbrances (q.v.).

Life Income Agreements   Funds, ordinarily of colleges and universities and not-for-profit organizations, established to account for assets given to the organization subject to an agreement to pay to the donor or designee the income earned by the assets over a specified period of time.

Limited Obligation Debt   Debt secured by a pledge of the collections of a certain specified tax (rather than by all general revenues).

Limited Purpose Governments   See Special Purpose Governments.

Line Item Budget   A detailed expense or expenditure budget, generally classified by object within each organizational unit and often classified within each object as to authorized number of employees at each salary level within each job classification, and so on.

Loans Receivable   Amounts that have been loaned to persons or organizations, including notes taken as security for such loans.

Lobbying   Communicating directly with a public official in either the executive or legislative branch of the state government for the purpose of influencing legislation.

Local Education Agency (LEA)   A broad term that is used to include school districts, public schools, intermediate education agencies, and school systems.

Local Improvement Fund   See Special Assessment Fund.

Local Improvement Tax   See Special Assessment.

Long-Term Budget   A budget prepared for a period longer than a fiscal year, or, in the case of some state governments, a budget prepared for a period longer than a biennium. If the long-term budget is restricted to capital expenditures, it is called a *capital program* (q.v.) or a *capital improvement program.*

Long-Term Debt   Debt with a maturity of more than one year after the date of issuance.

Losses   Decreases in net assets from peripheral or incidental transactions of an entity.

Lump-Sum Appropriation   An appropriation made for a stated purpose or for a named department without specifying further the amounts that may be spent for specific activities or for particular objects of expenditure. An example of such an appropriation would be one for the police department that does not specify the amount to be spent for uniform patrol, traffic control, and so on, or for salaries and wages, materials and supplies, travel, and so on.

M

Machinery and Equipment   See Equipment.

Macroaccounting   Accounting for the economy of the federal government in the aggregate.

Maintenance   The upkeep of physical properties in condition for use or occupancy. Examples are the inspection of equipment to detect defects and the making of repairs.

Major Fund   A fund is classified as major if it is significantly large with respect to the whole government. A fund is "major" if

(a) total assets, liabilities, revenues, or expenditures/expenses of the individual governmental or enterprise fund are at least 10 percent of the corresponding total of assets, liabilities, revenues, or expenditures/expenses for all funds of that category or type (total governmental or total enterprise funds), and

(b) total assets, liabilities, revenues, or expenditures/expenses of the individual governmental fund or enterprise fund are at least 5 percent of the corresponding total for all governmental and enterprise funds combined.

Major Programs   All federal programs identified by the auditor through a risk-based process that will be audited as part of a single audit.

Management's Discussion and Analysis (MD&A)   Narrative information, in addition to the basic financial statements, in which management provides a brief, objective, and easily readable analysis of the government's financial performance for the year and its financial position at year-end. An MD&A is required by *GASBS 34* for state and local governments and by FASAB's *SFFAC No. 3* for federal agencies.

Market Risk   The risk of loss arising from increases in market rates of interest or other factors that reduce market value of securities.

Material Weakness   A reportable condition of such magnitude that the internal control structure elements do not reduce the risk of material noncompliance to an acceptably low level.

Materiality   An auditor's judgment as to the level at which the quantitative or qualitative effects of missstatements will have a significant impact on user's evaluations.

Matured Bonds Payable   Bonds that have reached their maturity date but remain unpaid.

Matured Interest Payable   Interest on bonds that has matured but remains unpaid.

Measurable   Capable of being expressed in monetary terms.

Measurement Focus   The nature of the resources, claims against resources, and flows of resources that are measured and reported by a fund or other entity. For example, governmental funds currently measure and report available financial resources, whereas proprietary and fiduciary funds measure and report economic resources.

Modified Accrual Basis   Under the modified accrual basis of accounting, required for use by governmental funds (q.v.), revenues are recognized in the period in which they become available and measurable, and expenditures are recognized at the time a liability is incurred pursuant to appropriation authority.

Modified Approach   An approach that allows the government to elect *not* to depreciate certain eligible infrastructure assets provided certain requirements are met.

Modified Cash Basis   Sometimes same as Modified Accrual Basis, sometimes a plan under which revenues are recognized on the cash basis but expenditures are recognized on the accrual basis.

Mortgage Bonds   Bonds secured by a mortgage against specific properties of a government, usually its public utilities or other enterprises. If primarily payable from enterprise revenues, they are also classed as revenue bonds. See also Revenue Bonds.

Municipal   In its broadest sense, an adjective that denotes the state and all subordinate units of government. As defined for census statistics, the term denotes a city, town, or village as opposed to other units of local government.

Municipal Bond   A bond (q.v.) issued by a state or local government.

Municipal Corporation   A body politic and corporate established pursuant to state authorization for the purpose of providing governmental services and regulations for its inhabitants. A municipal corporation has defined boundaries and population and is usually organized with the consent of its residents. It usually has a seal and may sue and be sued. Cities and towns are examples of municipal corporations. See also Quasi-Municipal Corporations.

Municipal Improvement Certificates   Certificates issued in lieu of bonds for the financing of special improvements. *Note:* As a rule, these certificates are placed in the contractor's hands for collection from the special assessment payors.

N

Net Assets   The difference between total assets and total liabilities.

Net Bonded Debt   Gross bonded debt (q.v.) less cash or other assets available and earmarked for its retirement.

Net Income   A term used in accounting for governmental enterprises to designate the excess of total revenues (q.v.) over total expenses (q.v.) for an accounting period. See also Income, Operating Revenues, Operating Expenses, Nonoperating Income, and Nonoperating Expenses.

Net Pension Obligation (NPO)   A component of annual pension cost that comprises (1) the transition pension liability (or asset), if any, and (2) the cumulative difference from the implementation date of *GASBS 27* to the current balance sheet date between the annual pension cost and the employer's actual contributions.

Net Position   Net assets of a federal agency.

Net Profit   See Net Income.

Net Revenue   See Net Income.

Net Revenue Available for Debt Service   Gross operating revenues of an enterprise less operating and maintenance expenses but exclusive of depreciation and bond interest. *Net revenue* as thus defined is used to compute "coverage" of revenue bond issues. *Note:* Under the laws of some states and the provisions of some revenue bond indentures, net revenues used for computation of coverage are required to be on a cash basis rather than an accrual basis.

Nominal Interest Rate   The contractual interest rate shown on the face and in the body of a bond and representing the amount of interest to be paid, in contrast to the effective interest rate (q.v.). See also Coupon Rate.

Nonaudit Work   Work that is solely for the benefit of the entity requesting the work and does not provide for a basis for conclusions, recommendations, or opinions.

Nonentity Assets   Those assets of a federal agency that the reporting entity is holding but are not available for the entity to spend.

Nonexchange Revenue   See Derived Tax Revenues, Imposed Nonexchange Revenues, Voluntary Nonexchange Transactions, and Government-Mandated Nonexchange Transactions.

Nonexchange Transactions   Transactions in which the donor derives no direct tangible benefits from the recipient agency, for example, a contribution to or support for a government or not-for-profit organization.

Nonexpendable   The principal and sometimes the earnings of a gift that may not be expended. See also Endowment Fund.

Nonexpenditure Disbursements   Disbursements not chargeable as expenditures; for example, a disbursement made for the purpose of paying a liability previously recorded on the books.

Nonoperating Expenses   Expenses (q.v.) incurred for nonoperating properties or in the performance of activities not directly related to supplying the basic service by a governmental enterprise. An example of a nonoperating expense is interest paid on outstanding revenue bonds. See also Nonoperating Properties.

Nonoperating Income   Income of governmental enterprises that is not derived from the basic operations of such enterprises. An example is interest on investments or on bank time deposits.

Nonoperating Properties   Properties owned by a governmental enterprise but not used in the provision of basic services for which the enterprise exists.

Nonoperating Revenue   Revenue arising from transactions peripheral or incidental to the delivery of basic operations, including investment income, gains and losses, and unrestricted contributions.

Nonrevenue Receipts   Collections other than revenue (q.v.), such as receipts from loans whose liability is recorded in the fund in which the proceeds are placed and receipts on account of recoverable expenditures. See also Revenue Receipts.

Normal Cost   The present value of benefits allocated to the current year by the actuarial cost method being used.

Not-for-Profit (Nonprofit) Organizations   An entity that is distinguished from a business enterprise by these characteristics: (1) contributions by providers who do not expect commensurate returns, (2) operating purposes other than to earn a profit, and (3) absence of ownership interests. The AICPA prefers the term *not-for-profit* over *nonprofit*.

Notes Payable   In general, an unconditional written promise signed by the maker to pay a certain sum in money on demand or at a fixed or determinable time either to the bearer or to the order of a person designated therein. See also Temporary Loans.

Notes Receivable   A note payable held by an entity.

O

Object   As used in expenditure classification, this term applies to the article purchased or the service obtained (as distinguished from the results obtained from expenditures). Examples are personal services, contractual services, materials, and supplies. See also Activity, Character, Function, and Object Classification.

Object Classification   A grouping of expenditures on the basis of goods or services purchased, for example, personal services, materials, supplies, and equipment. See also Functional Classification, Activity Classification, and Character Classification.

Objects of Expenditure   See Object.

Obligated Group   A group of independent organizations that have joined together for a specific purpose, for example, to obtain financing in which case all parties are obligated in some way to repay the debt.

Obligations   Generally amounts that a government may be required legally to meet out of its resources. They include not only actual liabilities but also unliquidated encumbrances. In federal usage, obligation has essentially the same meaning as encumbrance in state and local government accounting.

Obsolescence   The decrease in the value of capital assets resulting from economic, social, technological, or legal changes.

Operating Budget   A budget that applies to all outlays other than capital outlays. See Budget.

Operating Cycle   The cycle of an organization that includes forecasting cash flows; collecting revenues; investing excess cash; tracking the performance and security of investments; making disbursements for various purposes; and monitoring, evaluating, and auditing cash flows.

Operating Expenses   (1) As used in the accounts of governmental enterprises, those costs that are necessary to the maintenance of the enterprise, the rendering of services, the sale of merchandise, the production and disposition of commodities produced, and the collection of enterprise revenues. (2) Sometimes used to describe expenses for general governmental purposes.

Operating Fund   The fund used to account for all assets and related liabilities used in the routine activities of a hospital. Also sometimes used by governments as a synonym for General Fund.

Operating Income   Income of a governmental enterprise derived from the sale of its goods and/or services. For example, income from the sale of water by a municipal water utility is operating income. See also Operating Revenues.

Operating Lease   A rental-type lease in which the risks and benefits of ownership are substantively retained by the lessor, and thus do not meet the criteria defined in applicable accounting and reporting standards for a capital lease (q.v.).

Operating Revenues   Revenues derived from the primary operations of governmental enterprises of a business character.

Operating Statement   A statement summarizing the financial operations of a government for an accounting period as contrasted with a balance sheet (q.v.) that shows financial position at a given moment in time.

Operating Transfers   Legally authorized interfund transfers (from a fund receiving revenue to the fund that is to make the expenditures). This term was eliminated by

GASBS 34. Instead, operating transfers are now one type of interfund transfers. See also Equity Transfers and Interfund Transfers.

Operational Accountability   Information useful in assessing operating results and short- and long-term financial position and the cost of providing services from an economic perspective reported in entitywide financial statements.

Order   A formal legislative enactment by the governing body of certain local governmental entities that has the full force and effect of law. For example, county governing bodies in some states pass orders rather than laws or ordinances.

Ordinance   A formal legislative enactment by the council or governing body of a municipality. If it is not in conflict with any higher form of law, such as a state statute or constitutional provision, it has the full force and effect of law within the boundaries of the municipality to which it applies. *Note:* The difference between an ordinance and a resolution (q.v.) is that the latter requires less legal formality and has a lower legal status. Ordinarily, the statutes or charter will specify or imply those legislative actions that must be by ordinance and those that must be by resolution. Revenue-raising measures, such as the imposition of taxes, special assessments, and service charges, universally require ordinances.

Organization Unit   Units or departments within an entity, such as police department or city attorney department.

Organizational Test   A not-for-profit organization meets the organizational test if its articles of incorporation limit the organization's purposes to those described in IRC Sec. 501 and does not empower it to engage in activities that are not in furtherance of those purposes.

Original Cost   The total of assets given and/or liabilities assumed to acquire an asset. In utility accounting, the original cost is the cost to the first owner who dedicated the plant to service of the public.

Other Appropriations Realized   A budgetary account used in federal government accounting to record an agency's basic operating appropriations for a fiscal period.

Other Comprehensive Basis of Accounting (OCBOA)   A term used to encompass bases of accounting that are not GAAP (q.v.). Bases included are cash, modified cash, regulatory basis, income tax basis, and substantial support criteria basis. The cash, modified cash, and regulatory basis apply to governments.

Other Financing Sources   An operating statement classification in which financial inflows other than revenues are reported, for example, proceeds of long-term debt and transfers in.

Other Financing Uses   An operating statement classification in which financial outflows other than expenditures are reported, for example, transfers out.

Other Post-Employment Benefits (OPEB)   Benefits, other than pensions, provided to employees subsequent to employment. Included would be items such as health care and life insurance.

Other Stand-Alone Government   A legally separate governmental organization that does not have a separately elected governing body and is not a component unit.

Outcome Measures   Accomplishments, or the results of services provided.

Outlays   Sometimes synonymous with disbursements. See also Capital Outlays.

Output Measure   A quantity measure reflecting either the total quantity of service provided or the quantity of service provided that meets a specified quality requirement.

Overdraft   (1) The amount by which checks, drafts, or other demands for payment on the Treasury or on a bank exceed the amount of the credit against which they are drawn. (2) The amount by which requisitions, purchase orders, or audited vouchers exceed the appropriation or other credit to which they are chargeable.

Overhead   Those elements of cost necessary in the production of an article or the performance of a service that are of such a nature that the amount applicable to the product or service cannot be determined accurately or readily. Usually they relate to those objects of expenditure that do not become an integral part of the finished product or service, such as rent, heat, light, supplies, management, or supervision.

Overlapping Debt   The proportionate share of the debts of local governments located wholly or in part within the limits of the government reporting entity that must be borne by property within each government. *Note:* Except for special assessment debt, the amount of debt of each unit applicable to the reporting unit is arrived at by (1) determining what percentage of the total assessed value of the overlapping jurisdiction lies within the limits of the reporting unit and (2) applying this percentage to the total debt of the overlapping jurisdiction. Special assessment debt is allocated on the basis of the ratio of assessments receivable in each jurisdiction that will be used wholly or in part to pay off the debt to total assessments receivable that will be used wholly or in part for this purpose.

Oversight Agency   The federal agency that makes the predominant amount of direct funding to the nonfederal entity receiving less than $25 million in federal awards. An oversight agency's responsibilities are similar to those of a cognizant agency but are less extensive.

P

Pay-As-You-Go Basis   A term used to describe the financial policy of a government that finances all of its capital outlays from current revenues rather than by borrowing. A government that pays for some improvements from current revenues and others by borrowing is said to be on a *partial* or *modified pay-as-you-go basis.*

Pay-In Warrant   See Deposit Warrant.

Payment Warrant   See Warrant.

Penalty   A legally mandated addition to a tax on the day it became delinquent (generally, the day after the day the tax is due).

Pension Trust Fund (PTS)   See Public Employee Retirement Systems.

Performance Audit   One of the two major types of audits defined by the U.S. Government Accountability Office (see Financial Audit for the other type). A performance audit provides an auditor's independent determination (but not an opinion) of the extent to which government officials are efficiently, economically, and effectively carrying out their responsibilities.

Performance Budget   A budget format that relates the input of resources and the output of services for each organizational unit individually. Sometimes used synonymously with program budget (q.v.).

Performance Indicator   A measure of how well a health care organization performed. Examples include "excess of revenues over expenses," "revenues and gains over expenses and losses," "earned income," and "performance earnings."

Permanent Fund   The governmental-type fund used to account for public-purpose trusts for which the earnings are expendable for a specified purpose, but the principal amount is not expendable (i.e., an endowment).

Permanently Restricted Net Assets   A term used in accounting for not-for-profit organizations indicating the amount of net assets whose use is permanently restricted by an external donor. See Endowment and Net Assets.

Perpetual Inventory   A system whereby the inventory of units of property at any date may be obtained directly from the records without resorting to an actual physical count. A record is provided for each item or group of items to be inventoried and is so divided as to provide a running record of goods ordered, received, and withdrawn, and the balance on hand, in units and frequently also in value.

Petty Cash   A sum of money set aside for the purpose of making change or paying small obligations for which the issuance of a formal voucher and check would be too expensive and time consuming. Sometimes called a *petty cash fund,* with the term *fund* here being used in the commercial sense of earmarked liquid assets.

Planning-Programming-Budgeting System (PPBS)   A budgeting approach that integrates planning, programming, and budgeting into one system; most popular in the federal government during the 1960s.

Plant Acquisition Adjustment   See Acquisition Adjustment.

Political Organization   Entities described in IRC Sec. 527, such as political action committees, political parties, and campaign committees for candidates for government office.

Pooled Investments   Investments that may be pooled or merged to simplify portfolio management, obtain a greater degree of investment diversification for individual endowment or trusts, and reduce brokerage, taxes, and bookkeeping expenses.

Postaudit   An audit made after the transactions to be audited have taken place and have been recorded or have been approved for recording by designated officials if such approval is required. See also Preaudit.

Posting   The act of transferring to an account in a ledger the data, either detailed or summarized, contained in a book or documentary of original entry.

Preaudit   An examination for the purpose of determining the propriety of proposed financial transactions and financial transactions that have already taken place but have not yet been recorded, or, if such approval is required, before the approval of the financial transactions by designated officials for recording.

Preferred Provider Organization (PPO)   See Health Maintenance Organization.

Prepaid Expenses   Expenses entered in the accounts for benefits not yet received. Prepaid expenses differ from deferred charges in that they are spread over a shorter period of time than deferred charges and are regularly recurring costs of operations. Examples of prepaid expenses are prepaid rent, prepaid interest, and premiums on unexpired insurance.

Prepayment of Taxes   The deposit of money with a government on condition that the amount deposited is to be applied against the tax liability of a designated taxpayer after the taxes have been levied and such liability has been established. See also Taxes Collected in Advance, and Deferred Revenues.

Primary Government   A state government or general purpose local government. Also, a special purpose government that has a separately elected governing body, is legally separate, and is fiscally independent of other state or local governments.

Prior-Years' Encumbrances   See Reserve for Encumbrances—Prior Year.

Prior-Years' Tax Levies   Taxes levied for fiscal periods preceding the current one.

Private Foundation   An organization exempt from federal income taxes under IRC Sec. 501(a) that (1) receives its support from a small number of individuals or corporations and investment income rather than from the public at large and (2) exists to make grants to public charities.

Private-Purpose Trust Fund   Contributions received under a trust agreement in which the investment income of an endowment is intended to benefit an external individual, organization, or government.

Private Trust Fund   A trust fund (q.v.) that will ordinarily revert to private individuals or will be used for private purposes, for example, a fund that consists of guarantee deposits.

Pro Forma   For form's sake; an indication of form; an example. The term is used in conjunction with a noun to denote merely a sample form, document, statement, certificate, or presentation, the contents of which may be either wholly or partially hypothetical, actual facts, estimates, or proposals.

Process Cost   Cost accounting system most appropriate for recording costs of continuous activities or processes, such as governmental services, health care services, or higher education.

Program Budgeting   A budget wherein inputs of resources and outputs of services are identified by programs without regard to the number of organizational units involved in performing various aspects of the program. See also Performance Budget and Traditional Budget.

Program Revenue   Revenue linked to a specific function or program and reported separately from general revenues on the government-wide statement of activities.

Program-Specific Audit   An audit of one specific federal program as opposed to a single audit of the whole entity.

Programs   Activities, operations, or organizational units grouped together because they share purposes or objectives.

Project   A plan of work, job, assignment, or task. Also refers to a job or task.

Promise to Give   A pledge or promise to make a contribution that may be unconditional or conditional.

Propaganda   Information that is skewed toward a particular belief with a tendency to have little or no factual basis.

Property Assessment   A process by which each parcel of taxable real and personal property owned by each taxpayer is assigned a valuation.

Property Taxes   Taxes levied by a legislative body against agricultural, commercial, residential, or personal property pursuant to law and in proportion to the assessed valuation of said property, or other appropriate basis. See Ad Valorem Property Taxes.

Proprietary Accounts   Those accounts that show actual financial position and operations, such as actual assets, liabilities, reserves, fund balances, revenues, and expenditures, as distinguished from budgetary accounts (q.v.).

Proprietary Fund   Sometimes referred to as *income-determination, business-like,* or *commercial-type* funds of a state or local government. Examples are enterprise funds and internal service funds.

Prospective Payment System (PPS)   Medicare's system in which payments are based on allowed service costs for medical procedures within the same diagnosis-related group rather than on the length of the patient's hospital stay or actual cost of services rendered.

Public Authority   See Authority.

Public Charity   An organization exempt from taxes under IRC Sec. 501(a) that receives its support from the public at large rather than from a limited number of donors. Most often public charities are exempt from federal income taxes under IRC Sec. 501(c)(3).

Public Corporation   See Municipal Corporation and Quasi-Municipal Corporation.

Public Employee Retirement Systems (PERS)   The organizations that collect retirement and other employee benefit contributions from government employers and employees, manage assets, and make payments to qualified retirants, beneficiaries, and disabled employees.

Public Enterprise Fund   See Enterprise Fund.

Public Improvement Fund   See Special Assessment Fund.

Public-Purpose Trust   Contributions received under a trust agreement in which the investment income or an endowment must be used to benefit a public program or function or the citizenry.

Public Trust Fund   A trust fund (q.v.) whose principal, earnings, or both, must be used for a public purpose, for example, a pension or retirement fund.

Purchase Order   A document that authorizes the delivery of specified merchandise or the rendering of certain services and the making of a charge for them.

Purchases Method   A method of recording supplies as Expenditures when purchased. If inventory levels have risen at the end of the month, the asset Supplies Inventory is debited and Fund Balance—Reserve for Inventory is credited. An alternative method is called the *consumption method.*

Purpose Restrictions   Specifications by resource providers of the purposes for which resources are required to be used.

Q

Quasi-Endowments   See Funds Functioning as Endowments.

Quasi-External Transaction   See Internal Exchange Transactions.

Quasi-Municipal Corporation   An agency established by the state primarily for the purpose of helping to carry out its functions, for example, a county or school district. *Note:* Some counties and other agencies ordinarily classified as quasi-municipal corporations have been granted the powers of municipal corporations by the state in which they are located. See also Municipal Corporations.

Questioned Cost   A cost identified by an auditor in an audit finding that generally relates to noncompliance with a law, regulation, or agreement, when the costs are either not supported by adequate documentation or appear unreasonable. OMB cost circulars identify, for different kinds of organizations, which costs are allowable and unallowable.

R

Rate Base   The value of utility property used in computing an authorized rate of return as authorized by law or a regulatory commission.

Realize   To convert goods or services into cash or receivables. Also to exchange for property that is a current asset or can be converted immediately into a current asset. Sometimes applied to conversion of noncash assets into cash.

Rebates   Abatements (q.v.) or refunds (q.v.).

Receipts   This term, unless otherwise qualified, means cash received.

Recoverable Expenditure   An expenditure made for or on behalf of another government, fund, or department or for a private individual, firm, or corporation that will subsequently be recovered in cash or its equivalent.

Refund   (Noun) An amount paid back or credit allowed because of an overcollection or the return of an object sold. (Verb) To pay back or allow credit for an amount because of an overcollection or because of the return of an object sold; to provide for the payment of a loan through cash or credit secured by a new loan.

Refunding Bonds   Bonds issued to retire bonds already outstanding. The refunding bonds may be sold for cash and outstanding bonds redeemed in cash, or the refunding bonds may be exchanged with holders of outstanding bonds.

Registered Bond   A bond the owner of which is registered with the issuing government and that cannot be sold or exchanged without a change of registration.

Registered Warrant   A warrant that is registered by the paying officer for future payment on account of present lack of funds and that is to be paid in the order of its registration. In some cases, such warrants are registered when issued; in others, they are registered when first presented to the paying officer by the holders. See also Warrant.

Regular Serial Bonds   Bonds payable in which the total principal is repayable in a specified number of equal annual installments.

Regulatory Accounting Principles   The accounting principles prescribed by federal or state regulatory commissions for investor-owned and some governmentally owned utilities. Also called *statutory accounting principles (SAP)*. RAP or some SAP may differ from GAAP.

Reimbursement   Cash or other assets received as a repayment of the cost of work or services performed or of other expenditures made for or on behalf of another government or department or for an individual, firm, or corporation.

Replacement Cost   The cost as of a certain date of a property that can render similar service (but need not be of the same structural form) as the property to be replaced. See also Reproduction Cost.

Reportable Condition   A significant deficiency in the design or operation of the internal control structure that could adversely affect the entity's ability to administer federal financial assistance programs in accordance with laws and regulations.

Reporting Entity   The primary government and all related component units, if any, combined in accordance with GASB *Codification* Section 2100 constitute the governmental reporting entity.

Reproduction Cost   The cost as of a certain date of reproducing an exactly similar new property in the same place.

Repurchase Agreement   An agreement wherein a government transfers cash to a financial institution in exchange for securities and the financial institution agrees to repurchase the same securities at an agreed-upon price.

Required Supplementary Information (RSI)   Information that is required by generally accepted accounting principles to be included with the audited annual financial statements, usually directly following the notes to the general purpose external financial statements.

Requisition   A written demand or request, usually from one department to the purchasing officer or to another department, for specified articles or services.

Reserve   An account that records a portion of the fund equity that must be segregated for some future use and that is, therefore, not available for further appropriation or expenditure. See Reserve for Inventory or Reserve for Encumbrances.

Reserve for Encumbrances   A segregation of a portion of fund equity in the amount of encumbrances outstanding. See also Reserve.

Reserve for Encumbrances—Prior Year Encumbrances outstanding at the end of a fiscal year are designated as pertaining to appropriations of a year prior to the current year in order that related expenditures may be matched with the appropriations of the prior year rather than an appropriation of the current year.

Reserve for Inventory A segregation of a portion of fund equity to indicate that assets equal to the amount of the reserve are invested in inventories and are, therefore, not available for appropriation.

Reserve for Noncurrent Interfund Loans Receivable A reserve that represents the segregation of a portion of a fund equity to indicate that assets equal to the amount of the reserve are invested in a long-term loan to another fund and are, therefore, not available for appropriation.

Reserve for Revenue Bond Contingency A reserve in an enterprise fund that represents the segregation of a portion of net assets equal to current assets that are restricted for meeting various contingencies, as may be specified and defined in the revenue bond indenture.

Reserve for Revenue Bond Debt Service A reserve in an enterprise fund that represents the segregation of a portion of net assets equal to current assets that are restricted to current servicing of revenue bonds in accordance with the terms of a bond indenture.

Reserve for Revenue Bond Retirement A reserve in an enterprise fund that represents the segregation of a portion of net assets equal to current assets that are restricted for future servicing of revenue bonds in accordance with the terms of a bond indenture.

Reserve for Uncollected Taxes A reserve equal to the amount of taxes receivable by a fund. The reserve is deducted from Taxes Receivable, thus effectively placing the fund on the cash basis of revenue recognition.

Residual Equity Transfer Nonrecurring or nonroutine transfers of equity between funds (e.g., transfers of residual balances of discontinued funds to the General Fund or a debt service fund). This term was eliminated by *GASBS 34*. See also Equity Transfer and Interfund Transfers.

Resolution A special or temporary order of a legislative body; an order of a legislative body requiring less legal formality than an ordinance or statute. See also Ordinance.

Resources Legally budgeted revenues of a state or local government that have not been recognized as revenues under the modified accrual basis of accounting as of the date of an interim balance sheet.

Restricted Assets Assets (usually of an enterprise fund) that may not be used for normal operating purposes because of the requirements of regulatory authorities, provisions in bond indentures, or other legal agreements, but that need not be accounted for in a separate fund.

Restricted Fund A fund established to account for assets the use of which is limited by the requirements of donors or grantors. Hospitals may use three types of restricted funds for internal purposes: specific purpose funds, endowment funds, and plant replacement and expansion funds. The governing body or administration cannot restrict the use of assets; they may only designate the use of assets. See Board-Designated Funds.

Restricted Net Assets The portion of the residual of assets and liabilities (i.e., net assets) that has been restricted in purpose or time by parties external to the organization.

Retirement Allowances Amounts paid to government employees who have retired from active service or to their survivors. See Annuity.

Retirement Fund A fund out of which retirement annuities and/or other benefits are paid to authorized and designated public employees. The accounting for a retirement fund is the same as that for a pension trust fund (q.v.).

Revenue The inflow of economic resources resulting from the delivery of services or activities that constitute the organization's major or central operations rather than from interfund transfers (q.v.) and debt issue proceeds.

Revenue Anticipation Notes (RANS) Notes issued in anticipation of the collection of revenues, usually from specified sources, and to be repaid upon the collection of the revenues.

Revenue Bonds Bonds whose principal and interest are payable exclusively from earnings of a public enterprise. In addition to a pledge of revenues, such bonds sometimes contain a mortgage on the enterprise's property and are then known as *mortgage revenue bonds.*

Revenue Receipts A term used synonymously with *revenue* (q.v.) by some governments that account for their revenues on a cash basis (q.v.). See also Nonrevenue Receipts.

Revenues Budget A legally adopted budget authorizing the collection of revenues from specified sources and estimating the amounts to be collected during the period from each source.

Revenues Collected in Advance A liability account that represents revenues collected before they are earned.

Revolving Fund See Internal Service Fund.

Risk-Based Approach This approach, used by auditors to determine which programs will be audited as part of the single audit, is a five-step process designed to select federal programs that are relatively large as well as likely to have problems. The auditors can use their professional judgment to classify programs that have been audited recently without audit findings, have had no significant changes in personnel or systems, or have a high level of oversight by awarding agencies as "low risk."

Risk Contract An insurance policy used to protect a prepaid health care plan from losses arising from excess of actual cost of providing health care over the fixed (capitation) fee.

S

Schedules (1) The explanatory or supplementary statements that accompany the balance sheet or other principal statements periodically prepared from the accounts. (2) The accountant's or auditor's principal work papers covering their examination of the books and accounts. (3) A written enumeration or detailed list in orderly form. See also Exhibit and Statements.

Scrip An evidence of indebtedness, usually in small denomination, secured or unsecured, interest bearing or noninterest bearing, stating that the government, under conditions set forth, will pay the face value of the certificate or accept it in payment of certain obligations.,

Securities Bonds, notes, mortgages, or other forms of negotiable or nonnegotiable instruments. See also Investments.

Self-Supporting or Self-Liquidating Debt Debt obligations whose principal and interest are payable solely from the earnings of the enterprise for the construction or improvement of which they were originally issued. See also Revenue Bonds.

Serial Annuity Bonds Serial bonds in which the annual installments of bond principal are so arranged that the combined payments for principal and interest are approximately the same each year.

Serial Bonds Bonds the principal of which is repaid in periodic installments over the life of the issue. See Serial Annuity Bonds and Deferred Serial Bonds.

Service Capacity A government's ongoing ability and willingness to supply the capital and human resources needed to meet its commitments to provide services.

Service Efforts and Accomplishments (SEA) A conceptualization of the resources consumed (inputs), tasks performed (outputs), goals attained (outcomes), and the relationship among these items in providing services in selected areas (e.g., police protection, solid waste garbage collection, and elementary and secondary education).

Shared Revenue Revenue levied by one governmental unit but shared, usually on a predetermined basis, with another unit of government or class of governments.

Shared Tax See Shared Revenue.

Short-Term Debt Debt with a maturity of one year or less after the date of issuance. Short-term debt usually includes floating debt, bond anticipation notes, tax anticipation notes, and interim warrants.

Single Audit An audit prescribed by federal law for state and local governments and not-for-profit organizations that expend federal financial assistance above a specified amount. Such an audit is to be conducted in conformity with the Office of Management and Budget *Circular A–133*. Such an audit is conducted on an organizationwide basis rather than on the former grant-by-grant basis. The Single Audit Act of 1984, as amended in 1996, and the circular cited impose uniform and rigorous requirements for conducting and reporting on single audits.

Sinking Fund See Debt Service Fund.

Sinking Fund Bonds Bonds issued under an agreement that requires the government to set aside periodically out of its revenues a sum that, with compound earnings thereon, will be sufficient to redeem the bonds at their stated date of maturity. Sinking fund bonds are usually also term bonds (q.v.).

Special Assessment A compulsory levy made against certain properties to defray part or all of the cost of a specific improvement or service that is presumed to be a general benefit to the public and of special benefit to such properties.

Special Assessment Bonds Bonds payable from the proceeds of special assessments (q.v.). If the bonds are payable only from the collections of special assessments, they are known as *special-special assessment bonds*. If, in addition to the assessments, the full faith and credit of the government is pledged, they are known as *general obligation special assessment bonds*.

Special Assessment Liens Receivable Claims that a government has on properties until special assessments (q.v.) levied against them have been paid. The term normally applies to those delinquent special assessments for the collection of which legal action has been taken through the filing of claims.

Special Assessment Roll The official list showing the amount of special assessments (q.v.) levied against each property presumed to be benefited by an improvement or service.

Special District An independent unit of local government organized to perform a single governmental function or a restricted number of related functions. Special districts usually have the power to incur debt and levy taxes; however, certain types of special districts are entirely dependent on enterprise earnings and cannot impose taxes. Examples of special districts are water districts, drainage districts, flood control districts, hospital districts, fire protection districts, transit authorities, port authorities, and electric power authorities.

Special District Bonds Bonds issued by a special district. See Special District.

Special Fund Any fund that must be devoted to some special use in accordance with specific regulations and restrictions. Generally, the term applies to all funds other than the General Fund (q.v.).

Special Items   Operating statement items that are either unusual or infrequent and are within management control.

Special Purpose Governments   Governments that provide only a single function or a limited number of functions, such as independent school districts and special districts. Formerly called *limited purpose governments.*

Special Revenue Fund (SRF)   A fund used to account for revenues from specific taxes or other earmarked revenue sources that by law are designated to finance particular functions or activities of government. After the fund is established, it usually continues year after year until discontinued or revised by proper legislative authority. An example is a motor fuel tax fund used to finance highway and road construction.

Special-Special Assessment Bonds   See Special Assessment Bonds.

Spending Rate   The proportion of total return that may prudently be used by an institution for current purposes.

Split-Interest Agreements   Forms of planned giving by donors who divide the rights to investment income on assets and assets themselves with intended beneficiary organizations in a predetermined manner.

Statements   (1) Used in a general sense, all of those formal written presentations that set forth financial information. (2) In technical accounting usage, those presentations of financial data that show the financial position and the results of financial operations of a fund, an entire governmental reporting entity, or a component unit thereof for a particular accounting period. See also Exhibit and Schedule.

Statute   A written law enacted by a duly organized and constituted legislative body. See also Ordinance, Resolution, and Order.

Statutory Accounting Principles   See Regulatory Accounting Principles.

Stewardship Investments   Beneficial investments of the federal government in items such as nonfederal physical property (property financed by the federal government but owned by state or local governments), human capital, and research and development.

Stewardship Land   Federal land other than that included in general property, plant, and equipment (e.g., national parks).

Stores   Materials and supplies on hand in storerooms subject to requisition and use.

Straight Serial Bonds   Serial bonds (q.v.) in which the annual installments of a bond principal are approximately equal.

Subactivity   A specific line of work performed in carrying out a governmental activity. For example, replacing defective street lamps would be a subactivity under the activity of street light maintenance.

Subfunction   A grouping of related activities within a particular governmental function. For example, police is a subfunction of the public safety function.

Subsidiary Account   One of a group of related accounts that support in detail the debit and credit summaries recorded in a control account, for example, the individual property taxpayers' accounts for taxes receivable in the general ledger. See also Control Account and Subsidiary Ledger.

Subsidiary Ledger   A group of subsidiary accounts (q.v.) the sum of the balances of which is equal to the balance of the related control account. See also Control Account and Subsidiary Account.

Subvention   A grant (q.v.).

Support   The increase in net assets arising from contributions of resources or nonexchange transactions and includes only amounts for which the donor receives no direct tangible benefits from the recipient agency.

Surety Bond   A written promise to pay damages or to indemnify against losses caused by the party or parties named in the document through nonperformance or through defalcation. An example is a surety bond given by a contractor or by an official handling cash or securities.

Surplus   Now generally obsolete in accounting usage. See Fund Balance.

Surplus Receipts   A term sometimes applied to receipts that increase the balance of a fund but are not a part of its normal revenue, for example, collection of accounts previously written off. Sometimes used as an account title.

Suspense Account   An account that carries charges or credits temporarily pending the determination of the proper account or accounts to which they are to be posted. See Suspense Fund and Clearing Account.

Suspense Fund   A fund established to account separately for certain receipts pending the distribution or disposal thereof. See also Agency Fund.

Sweep Accounts   Arrangements in which a bank automatically "sweeps" cash that exceeds the target balance into short-term cash investments.

Syndicate, Underwriting   A group formed for the marketing of a given security issue too large for one member to handle expeditiously after which the group is dissolved.

T

Tax Anticipation Notes (TANs)   Notes (sometimes called *warrants*) issued in anticipation of collection of taxes usually retirable only from tax collections and frequently only from the proceeds of the tax levy whose collection they anticipate.

Tax Anticipation Warrants   See Tax Anticipation Notes.

Tax Certificate   A certificate issued by a government as evidence of the conditional transfer of title to tax-delinquent property from the original owner to the holder of the certificate. If the owner does not pay the amount of the tax arrearage and other charges required by law during the special period of redemption, the holder can foreclose to obtain title. Also called *tax sale certificate* and *tax lien certificate* in some jurisdictions. See also Tax Deed.

Tax Deed   A written instrument by which title to property sold for taxes is transferred unconditionally to the purchaser. A tax deed is issued on foreclosure of the tax lien (q.v.) obtained by the purchaser at the tax sale. The tax lien cannot be foreclosed until the expiration of the period during which the owner may redeem his or her property through paying the delinquent taxes and other charges. See also Tax Certificate.

Tax Expenditure   A revenue loss attributable to provisions of federal tax laws that allow a special exclusion, exemption, or deduction from gross income or that provide a special credit, a preferential rate of tax, or a deferral of tax liability.

Tax Increment Debt   Debt secured by an incremental tax earmarked for servicing the debt, such as a half-cent sales tax, or payable from taxes derived from incremental growth in the tax base that was financed by the tax increment debt.

Tax Levy   See Levy.

Tax Levy Ordinance   An ordinance (q.v.) by means of which taxes are levied.

Tax Liens   Claims that governments have on properties until taxes levied against them have been paid. *Note:* The term is sometimes limited to those delinquent taxes for the collection of which legal action has been taken through the filing of liens.

Tax Liens Receivable   Legal claims against property that have been exercised because of nonpayment of delinquent taxes, interest, and penalties. The account includes delinquent taxes, interest, penalties receivable up to the date the lien becomes effective, and the cost of holding the sale.

Tax Notes   See Tax Anticipation Notes.

Tax Rate   The amount of tax stated in terms of a unit of the tax base, for example, 25 mills per dollar of assessed valuation of taxable property.

Tax Rate Limit   The maximum rate at which a government may levy a tax. The limit may apply to taxes raised for a particular purpose or to taxes imposed for all purposes and to a single government, a class of governments, or all governments operating in a particular area. Overall tax rate limits usually restrict levies for all purposes and of all governments, state and local, having jurisdiction in a given area.

Tax Roll   The official list showing the amount of taxes levied against each taxpayer or property. Frequently, the tax roll and the assessment roll are combined but even in these cases the two can be distinguished.

Tax Sale Certificate   See Tax Certificate.

Tax Supplement   A tax levied by a local government that has the same base as a similar tax levied by a higher level of government, such as a state. The local tax supplement is frequently administered by the higher level of government along with its own tax. A locally imposed, state-administered sales tax is an example of a tax supplement.

Tax-Supported Debt   All debt secured by pledges of tax revenues.

Tax Title Notes   Obligations secured by pledges of the government's interest in certain tax liens or tax titles.

Taxable Property   All property except that which is exempt from taxation; examples of exempt property are property owned by governments and property used by some religious and charitable organizations.

Taxes   Compulsory charges levied by a government for the purpose of financing services performed for the common benefit. *Note:* The term does not include either specific charges made against particular persons or property for current or permanent benefits such as special assessments or charges for services rendered only to those paying such charges as, for example, sewer service charges.

Taxes Collected in Advance   A liability for taxes collected before the tax levy has been made or before the amount of taxpayer liability has been established.

Taxes Levied for Other Governments   Taxes levied by the reporting government for other governments, which, when collected, are to be paid over to these governments.

Taxes Paid in Advance   Same as Taxes Collected in Advance. Also called *prepaid taxes.*

Taxes Receivable—Current   The uncollected portion of taxes that a government has levied but that are not yet delinquent.

Taxes Receivable—Delinquent   Taxes remaining unpaid on and after the date on which a penalty for nonpayment is attached. Even though the penalty may be subsequently waived and a portion of the taxes may be abated or canceled, the unpaid balances continue to be delinquent taxes until paid, abated, canceled, or converted into tax liens.

Temporarily Restricted Net Assets   A term used in accounting for not-for-profit organizations indicating the amount of net assets temporarily restricted by an external donor for use in a future period or for a particular purpose. See Net Assets.

Temporary Loans   Short-term obligations representing amounts borrowed for short periods of time and usually evidenced by notes payable (q.v.) or warrants payable (q.v.). They may be unsecured or secured by specific revenues to be collected. See also Tax Anticipation Notes.

Term Bonds   Bonds the entire principal of which matures on one date.

Term Bonds Payable   A liability account that records the face value of general obligation term bonds issued and outstanding.

Term Endowment   Assets for which donors or other external agencies have stipulated, as a condition of the gift, that the principal is to be maintained intact for a stated period of time (or term).

Termination Benefits   Benefits provided to employees as a result of the voluntary or involuntary termination of employment.

Third-Party Payor   Term used in health care organizations to refer to the entity other than the patient/client that pays for services such as an insurance company or federal insurance program.

Time Requirements or Restrictions   Requirements that relate to the period when resources are required to be used or when use may begin.

Time Warrant   A negotiable obligation of a government having a term shorter than bonds and frequently tendered to individuals and firms in exchange for contractual services, capital acquisitions, or equipment purchases.

Time Warrants Payable   The amount of time warrants outstanding and unpaid.

Total Quality Management (TQM)   A management approach in which an organization seeks to continuously improve its ability to meet or exceed customer demands, where *customer,* in government or not-for-profit organization usage, may be broadly defined to include such parties as taxpayers, service recipients, students, and members.

Total Return   A comprehensive measure of rate of investment return in which the sum of net realized and unrealized appreciation or shrinkage in portfolio value is added to dividend and interest yield.

Traditional Budget   A term sometimes applied to the budget of a government wherein appropriations are based entirely or primarily on objects of expenditure. The focus of a traditional budget is on input of resources rather than on the relationship between input of resources and output of services. For budgets focusing on the latter, see Program Budget and Performance Budget.

Transfers   See Interfund Transfers, Operating Transfers, and Residual Equity Transfers.

Trial Balance   A list of the balances of the accounts in a ledger kept by double entry (q.v.), with the debit and credit balances shown in separate columns. If the totals of the debit and credit columns are equal or their net balance agrees with a control account, the ledger from which the figures are taken is said to be "in balance."

Trust and Agency Funds   See Agency Fund, Trust Fund, and Fiduciary Fund.

Trust Fund   A fund consisting of resources received and held by the government as trustee, to be expended or invested in accordance with the conditions of the trust. See also Endowment Fund, Private-Purpose Trust Fund, and Public-Purpose Trust Fund.

U

Unallotted Balance of Appropriation   An appropriation balance available for allotment (q.v.).

Unamortized Discounts on Bonds Sold   That portion of the excess of the face value of bonds over the amount received from their sale that remains to be written off periodically over the life of the bonds.

Unamortized Premiums on Bonds Sold   An account that represents that portion of the excess of bond proceeds over par value and that remains to be amortized over the remaining life of such bonds.

Unapportioned Authority   The amount of a federal appropriation made by the Congress and approved by the President but not yet apportioned by the Office of Management and Budget. See Other Appropriations Realized and Apportionments.

Unbilled Accounts Receivable   An account that designates the estimated amount of accounts receivable for services or commodities sold but not billed. For example, if a utility bills its customers bimonthly but prepares monthly financial statements, the amount of services rendered or commodities sold during the first month of the bimonthly period would be reflected in the balance sheet under this account title.

Unconditional Promise to Give   A promise to make contributions to an organization that depends only on the passage of time or demand by the promisee for performance.

Underwriting Syndicate   See Syndicate, Underwriting.

Undistributed Change in Fair Value of Investments   An account used by a cash and investment pool to accumulate realized and unrealized gains and losses on sales of investments pending distribution to pool participants. See Undistributed Earnings.

Undistributed Earnings   An account used by a cash and investment pool to accumulate investment earnings pending distribution to pool participants. See also Reserve for Change in Fair Value of Investments.

Unearned Income   See Deferred Revenues.

Unencumbered Allotment   That portion of an allotment not yet expended or encumbered.

Unencumbered Appropriation   That portion of an appropriation not yet expended or encumbered.

Unexpended Allotment   That portion of an allotment not yet expended.

Unexpended Appropriations   The equity of a federal agency provided by an appropriation that has not yet been expended.

Unfunded Actuarial Liability See Actuarial Accrued Liability.

Unit Cost A term used in cost accounting to denote the cost of producing a unit of product or rendering a unit of service, for example, the cost of treating and purifying a thousand gallons of sewage.

Unliquidated Encumbrances Encumbrances outstanding.

Unrealized Revenue See Accrued Revenue.

Unrelated Business Income Gross income from trade or business regularly carried on by a tax-exempt organization less directly connected expenses, certain net operating losses, and qualified charitable contributions that is not related to its exempt purpose. If more than $1,000, the income is subject to federal income tax at corporate tax rates.

Unrestricted Assets Assets that may be utilized at the discretion of the governing board of a not-for-profit entity.

Unrestricted Funds Funds established to account for assets or resources that may be utilized at the discretion of the governing board.

Unrestricted Net Assets The portion of the excess of total assets over total liabilities that may be utilized at the discretion of the governing board of a governmental or not-for-profit entity. See Net Assets, Temporarily Restricted Net Assets, and Permanently Restricted Net Assets.

User Charge A charge levied against users of a service or purchasers of a product.

Utility Fund See Enterprise Fund.

Utility Plant Acquisition Adjustment An account that captures the premium paid on a utility plant purchased by a government. Similar to goodwill except that the premium is the difference between the purchase price and the depreciated original cost of the utility rather than the difference between the purchase price and fair value.

V

Value As used in governmental accounting, this term designates (1) the act of describing anything in terms of money or (2) the measure of a thing in terms of money. The term should not be used without further qualification. See also Book Value and Face Value.

Variance Power The unilateral power of an organization to redirect donated assets to a beneficiary different than the third party initially indicated by the donor.

Voluntary Health and Welfare Organization Not-for-profit organizations that receive contributions from the public at large and provide health and welfare services for a nominal or no fee. Also known as *human service organizations.*

Voluntary Nonexchange Transactions A category of nonexchange transaction that includes certain grants and entitlements and most donations.

Voucher A written document that evidences the propriety of transactions and usually indicates the accounts in which they are to be recorded.

Voucher Check A document combining a check and a brief description of the transaction covered by the check.

Voucher System A system that calls for the preparation of vouchers (q.v.) for transactions involving payments and for the recording of such vouchers in a special book of original entry (q.v.), known as a *voucher register,* in the order in which payment is approved.

Vouchers Payable Liabilities for goods and services evidenced by vouchers that have been preaudited and approved for payment but not been paid.

W

Warrant An order drawn by the legislative body or an officer of a government on its treasurer, directing the latter to pay a specified amount to the person named or to the bearer. It may be payable on demand, in which case it usually circulates the same as a bank check, or it may be payable only out of certain revenues when and if received, in which case it does not circulate as freely. See also Registered Warrant and Deposit Warrant.

Warrants for Disbursements A formal certification of the validity of the debt, with authorization or direction to a financial agent to pay the debt. One step beyond a voucher in the payment process.

Warrants Payable The amount of warrants outstanding and unpaid.

Work Order A written order authorizing and directing the performance of a certain task and issued to the person who is to direct the work. Among the items of information shown on the order are the nature and location of the job, specifications of the work to be performed, and a job number that is referred to in reporting the amount of labor, materials, and equipment used.

Work Program A plan of work proposed to be done during a particular period by an administrative agency in carrying out its assigned activities.

Work Unit A fixed quantity that will consistently measure work effort expended in the performance of an activity or the production of a commodity.

Working Capital Fund See Internal Service Fund.

Y

Yield Rate See Effective Interest Rate.

Z

Zero-Based Budgeting (ZBB) A budget based on the concept that the very existence of each activity as well as the amounts of resources requested to be allocated to each activity, must be justified each year.

Governmental and Not-for-Profit Organizations

AAA — **American Accounting Association**   An organization of accounting educators and practitioners involved in education whose objectives are to contribute to the development of accounting theory, to encourage and sponsor accounting research, and to improve the quality of accounting education.

ACE — **American Council on Education**   A not-for-profit organization founded in 1918 with members from institutions of all sectors of higher education and other education-related organizations. It provides leadership and advocacy on adult and higher education issues, represents the views of the higher education community to policy makers, and offers services to its members.

AFGI — **Association of Financial Guaranty Insurors**   The trade association of the insurers and reinsurers of municipal bonds and asset-backed securities.

AGA — **Association of Government Accountants**   An association formed in 1950 to serve the professional interests of governmental financial managers by providing education, encouraging professional development, influencing governmental financial management policies and practices, and serving as an advocate for the profession.

AHA — **American Hospital Association**   An association organized in the early 1900s by hospital administrators to promote economy and efficiency in hospital management. Its current mission is to take a leadership role in public policy, representation and advocacy, and health services.

AICPA — **American Institute of Certified Public Accountants**   The professional organization to which certified public accountants (CPAs) belong. In addition to providing educational and lobbying services on behalf of its members, the AICPA is responsible for promulgating auditing standards applicable to private companies, governments, and not-for-profit organizations.

APPA — **American Public Power Association**   The national trade association representing state and local government-owned electric utilities.

ABFM — **Association for Budgeting and Financial Management**   A section of the American Society for Public Administration that advances the science, processes and art of public administration as it relates to budgeting and financial management.

ASBOI — **Association of School Business Officials International**   A professional association that provides programs and services to employees of public and private schools (including community and junior colleges and state departments of education) that promote the highest standards of school business management practices, professional growth, and the effective use of educational resources.

BBB   **BBB Wise Giving Alliance**   A 2001 merger of the National Charities Information Bureau and the Philanthropic Advisory Service of the Council of Better Business Bureaus Foundation.

BMA   **Bond Market Association**   An association that represents securities firms and banks that underwrite, trade, and sell debt securities, including municipal bonds, U.S. Treasury securities, federal agency securities, and other asset-backed securities.

CBO   **Congressional Budget Office**   An office of the legislative branch of the federal government established in 1974 that gathers information for the House and Senate budget committees with respect to the budget submitted to the executive branch, appropriations bills, other bills providing budget authority, tax expenditures, and other analysis.

CSG   **Council of State Governments**   An association of state financial officers formed in 1933 to assist states with multistate and regional solutions to problems.

FAF   **Financial Accounting Foundation**   The organization that finances and appoints members of the Financial Accounting Standards Board and Governmental Accounting Standards Board.

FASAB   **Federal Accounting Standards Advisory Board**   The nine-member standards-setting body that recommends federal governmental accounting and financial reporting standards to the U.S. Comptroller General, Secretary of the Treasury, and Director of the Office of Management and Budget.

FASAC   **Financial Accounting Standards Advisory Council**   The council that advises the Financial Accounting Standards Board on policy matters, agenda items, project priorities, technical issues, and task forces.

FASB   **Financial Accounting Standards Board**   An independent, nongovernmental, privately funded entity that is responsible to the public at large and the public accounting profession for developing concepts, standards, and guidance on financial accounting and reporting for commercial entities as well as nongovernmental, not-for-profit organizations. The organization was established in 1973 and replaced the Accounting Principles Board.

GAO   **Government Accountability Office**   An agency of the legislative branch of the federal government responsible for prescribing accounting principles for federal agencies; the auditing arm of Congress.

GASAC   **Governmental Accounting Standards Advisory Council**   The council that advises the Governmental Accounting Standards Board on policy matters, agenda items, project priorities, technical issues, and task forces. Its members are broadly representative of preparers, attestors, and users of financial information.

GASB   **Governmental Accounting Standards Board**   The independent agency established under the Financial Accounting Foundation in

1984 as the official body designated to set accounting and financial reporting standards for state and local governments.

GFOA — **Government Finance Officers Association**   A professional association of government finance managers founded in 1906 (formerly the Municipal Finance Officers Association) to help establish uniformity in state and local government accounting practices. The GFOA administers the Certificate of Achievement program to reward excellence in financial reporting, budgeting, and other areas.

GRA — **Governmental Research Association**   A national organization, founded in 1914, of individuals professionally engaged in governmental research.

HFMA — **Healthcare Financial Management Association**   A not-for-profit organization of financial management professionals employed by hospitals and other health care providers established in 1946 to provide professional development opportunities, influence health care policy, and communicate information and technical data.

ICMA — **International City/County Management Association**   An organization founded in 1914 (formerly International City Management Association) that is the professional and educational association of appointed administrators serving cities, counties, other local governments, and regional entities around the world.

NACo — **National Association of Counties**   An organization created in 1935 by county officials to provide legislative, research, technical, and public affairs assistance to members, and ensure that the concerns of over 3,000 counties in the United States are heard at the federal level of government.

NACUBO — **National Association of College & University Business Officers**   A not-for-profit professional organization founded in 1962 representing chief administrative and financial officers at colleges and universities whose mission is to promote sound management and financial practices at institutions of higher education.

NASACT — **National Association of State Auditors, Comptrollers, and Treasurers**   An organization formed in 1915 to represent the states' views on financial management issues and to provide leadership and training in meeting state fiscal and financial management challenges in order to improve the financial management of state government.

NASBO — **National Association of State Budget Officers**   The professional membership organization for state finance officers through which the states have collectively advanced state budget practices for more than 50 years.

NASRA — **National Association of State Retirement Administrators**   An organization comprised of the administrators of the state retirement systems for the 50 states, the District of Columbia, and U.S. territories.

NCGA — **National Council on Governmental Accounting**   The body that established accounting and financial reporting standards for state and local governments prior to the formation of the Governmental Accounting Standards Board.

NCSL	**National Conference of State Legislatures** A national association of state legislatures that includes many sections offering services to member legislatures, such as the NCSL Leadership Staff Section for leaders and party caucuses and the National Legislative Services and Security Association, which produces a manual to enable legislatures to cope with the problems of maintaining order and normal operations.
NFMA	**National Federation of Municipal Analysts** An association chartered in 1983 to promote professionalism in municipal credit analysis and furthering the skill level of its members through educational programs and industry communication.
NGA	**National Governors' Association** A bipartisan national organization of the nations' governors founded in 1908 through which the governors identify priority issues and deal collectively with issues of public policy and governance at both the national and state levels.
NLC	**National League of Cities** An organization founded in 1924 (formerly the American Municipal Association) by state municipal leagues to serve and represent municipal governments by establishing unified policy positions, advocating these policies, and sharing information that strengthens municipal government throughout the nation.
OMB	**Office of Management and Budget** An office of the executive branch of the federal government that has responsibility for establishing policies and procedures for approving and publishing financial accounting principles and standards to be followed by executive branch agencies. It also has the authority to control the size and nature of appropriations requested of each Congress.
PCIE	**President's Council on Integrity and Efficiency** A federal agency established by executive order that is comprised of all presidentially appointed Inspectors General, as well as other federal agency members. Its charge is to conduct interagency and interentity audits, and inspection and investigation projects in order to effectively and efficiently deal with governmentwide issues of fraud, waste, and abuse.
SEC	**Securities and Exchange Commission** An independent, quasi-judicial federal agency formed in 1934 to protect investors in publicly traded securities by ensuring that there is full and fair disclosure of all material facts concerning securities offered for sale across state lines.
USCM	**U.S. Conference of Mayors** A nonpartisan organization established in 1932 representing U.S. cities with populations of 30,000 or more. The conference aids the development of effective national urban policy, strengthens federal–city relationships, ensures that federal policy meets urban needs, and provides mayors with leadership and management tools of value in their cities.

For the address, phone number, fax number, Internet address, and journal of each of these organizations, see one of the authors' Web sites: http://people.emich.edu/skattelus under "Government and Nonprofit Resources."

Index

A

Account structure, federal, 475
Accountability, 6
  fiscal, 8
  operational, 8
Accounting, governmental; *see* Fund
  accounting
Accounting principles, regulatory, 283
Accounts
  budgetary, described, 67, 474
  classification of
    expenditures, 72–73
    expenses, 60–62
    revenues, 62–63, 75
Accrual basis
  full accrual, 36
  modified, 41
Activity, defined, 73
  business-type, 34
  fiduciary, 34
  governmental, 34
Activity-based costing, 537
Actuarial accrued liability, 328
Actuarial present value of total projected
  benefits, 332
Actuarial value of assets, 328
Ad valorem property taxes, 75
Agency fund, 45
  accounting for, 304
  characteristics of, 304
  "pass-through funds," 311
  tax agency funds, 305–311
Allotments
  federal, definition of, 492
  state and local accounting
    for, 85
Allowable costs; *see* Costs
Allowance for Funds Used During
  Construction (AFUDC), 284
American Institute of Certified Public
  Accountants, Audit and
  Accounting Guides
    on health care organizations, 692
    on not-for-profit organizations, 589
    on state and local governments,
      458
Anderson, Bridget M., 539
Annual pension cost, 333
Annual required contribution
  (ARC), 328
Annuity agreements, 636
Annuity serial bonds, 219; *see* Bonds

Apportionments, 492
Appropriations, defined,
  69, 491
Arbitrage rebate, 190
Assessed valuation, 76
Assessments, property, 75
Assets
  entity, 481
  governmental, 481
  impairment, 175
  limited as to use, 677
  nonentity, 481
Attestation engagements, 442
Audits
  cognizant agent for audit
    responsibilities, 456
  committee, 457
  compliance, 451
  financial audits, 434
  findings, 455
  government audit standards, 441
  independence, 445
  performance audits, 442
  program-specific, 448
  published audit guides
    Health Care Organizations, 692
    Not-for-Profit Organizations, 589
    State and Local Governments, 458
  single audit, defined, 447
Available, defined, 41

B

Balance sheets
  combining, 39
  interim, 121
Basic financial statements, 8
Basis of accounting
  full accrual, 36
  modified accrual, 41
Benchmarking, 410
Berne, Robert, 398
Bland, Robert K., 541
Blended presentation, 351
Blending, 35
Board-designated net assets, 559
Bond anticipation notes, 188
Bond premium, discount and accrued
  interest, 185, 218
Bonds
  general obligation, 274
  refunding, 234–235

  repayments of long-term, 220–221
  revenue, 273
  serial
    annuity, 219
    deferred, 219
    irregular, 219
    regular, 219
    term, 224
Broder, John R., 396
Brown, Ken, 649
Budgetary accounts, 67, 474
Budgetary resources, 486
Budgetary solvency; *see* Solvency
Budgeting
  appropriations, 521
  capital expenditures, 524
  flexible, 534
  incremental, 519
  revenues, 524
Budgets
  adoption, 68
  amendments, 69
  calendar, 521
  cash disbursements, 526
  cash receipts, 525
  incremental, 519
  as legal documents, 516
  officer, 522
  performance, 519
  program, 520
Buildings, defined, 169
Business-type activities, 34

C

CAFR; *see* Comprehensive Annual
  Financial Report
Campbell, Wilson, 517, 541–542
Capital assets, 163
Capital grants, 62
Capital improvement funds, 177
Capital lease, 172
Capital projects funds
  accounting for capital leases, 172
  general nature of, 41, 164
  judgments payable, 188
  legal requirements, 178
  multiple period and project bond
    funds, 190
  premiums, discounts, and accrued
    interest on bond entries, 185
  re-establishment of encumbrances, 191

retained percentages, 187
statements, 184
Capitation fee, 674
Carpenter, Francis H., 377
Cash
disbursements, 526
equivalents, 526
solvency; *see* Solvency
Cash and investment pools, 317
Cash flows, statement of
health care entities, 675
not-for-profit organizations, 561
proprietary funds, 255
Chan, Sewell, 395
Chaney, Barbara A., 417
Character, meaning of, 73
Charitable solicitation, 603
Charity care, 676
Chief Financial Officer (federal
government) Act of 1990, 467
Classification, by activity, 73
character, 73
function or program, 72
fund, 72
general fund expenditures, 72–74
general fund revenues, 74–79
object, 74
source, 75
Codification; *see* GASB Codification
Cognizant agency, 456
Cohn, Mandi, 517
Collection
current taxes, 116
delinquent taxes, 118
Collections, 572, 635
College and university accounting
procedures
assets
restricted, 633
unrestricted, 633
depreciation, 634
Financial Accounting and
Reporting Manual for
Higher Education, 654
statements of
activities, 637
cash flows, 641
net assets, 633
Commercial and governmental
accounting compared, 3
Commitment, 492
Common rule, 535
Comparison of local government and
federal agencies, 504
Compliance audit; *see* Audits
Component unit, 35, 349
Comprehensive Annual Financial
Report, 9
defined, 9
financial section, 9

introductory section, 9
statistical section, 21
Comptroller General
audits by, 442
responsibilities of, 470
Conditional promise to give, 566
Congressional Budget Office, 471
Construction Work in Progress
general capital assets, 170
utilities, 272, 284
Consumption method, 129
Continuing care retirement community
(CCRC), 691
Contractual adjustments (or
allowances), 674
Contribution, 566
Cooper, Robin, 537
Correction of errors, 124
Costs
allowable, 535
direct, 536
indirect, 536
job order cost accounting, 534
objective, 536
process cost accounting, 534
Crawford, Michael A., 382
Crawford and Associates, 407, 410
Cumulative results of operations, 483
Current financial resources, 41
Current fund; *see* General fund
Customers' advances for
construction, 273
Customers' deposits, 273
Cycle billing, 270

D

Debt
defeasance, 235
limit, 212
long-term, 207
margin, 213
statements of
direct and overlapping
debt, 215
legal debt margin, 213
Debt-financed income, 610
Debt service funds
budgeting, 218
capital lease payments, 233
debt refunding, 234
deferred serial bond accounting
procedure, 228
note disclosures, 209
number of, 217
purpose of, 39
regular serial bonds accounting
procedures, 219
sinking funds, 218

term bonds accounting
procedures, 224
types of serial bonds, 219
Defeasance
in-substance, 235
legal, 235
Deferred serial bonds; *see* Bonds
Defined benefit plan, 324
Defined contribution plan, 324
Definitions of governmental and not-for-
profit accounting terms, 707
Delinquent taxes, 117
Depreciation, general capital
assets, 166
Derived tax revenues, 121
Diagnosis-related groups (DRGs), 690
Direct costs (expenses), definition,
60, 536
Direct lobbying, 611
Director of the Congressional Budget
Office, 471
Director of the Office of Management
and Budget, 471
Discrete presentation, 35, 351
Disqualified person, 612
Donated materials, 547
Donated services, 567
Due diligence, 612

E

Economic condition, 399
Economic interest, 573
Economic resources measurement
focus, 36
Economic size, 612
Educational institutions; *see* College and
university accounting procedures
Effectiveness measures, 530
Efficiency measures, 530
Eligibility requirements, 138
Encumbrances
accounting for, 82
described, 69
re-establishment, 125
Endowments
college and university, 635
health care organizations, 671
not-for-profit organizations, 560
Engagement letter, 440
Engstrom, John H., 441, 628
Enterprise funds
accounting for non-utility
enterprises, 285
balance sheet items
construction work in progress, 272
current and accrued assets, 270
current liabilities, 273
customer deposits, 273

Enterprise funds—*Cont.*
   balance sheet items—*Cont.*
      long-term liability, 273
      plant acquisition adjustment, 284
      restricted assets, 271
   original cost, 284
   purpose of, 44
   required segment information, 287
   statements
      cash flows, 281
      net assets, 279
      revenues, expenses, and changes in
         net assets, 281
Entity assets, 481
Epstein, Paul, 542
Escheats, 34, 79
Esmond-Kiger, Connie, 628
Estimated other financial sources, 69
Estimated other financial uses, 69
Estimated revenues, 69
Excess benefit transaction, 612
Exchange-like transactions, 115, 147
Exchange transactions, 115, 564
Expended appropriation, 492
Expenditure responsibility, 609
Expenditures, 43
Expenses, 43
External investment pool, 313
External support test; *see* Support test
Extraordinary items, 63

F

Fair value, 231, 314
FASB; *see* Financial Accounting
   Standards Board
Federal Accounting Standards Advisory
   Board, 5, 472
Federal Energy Regulatory
   Commission, 271
Federal Financial Management
   Improvement Act of 1996
   (FFMIA), 468
Federal Power Commission; *see* Federal
   Energy Regulatory Commission
Federated fund-raising organizations, 607
Feeder organizations, 610
FICA (Federal Insurance Contribution
   Act) taxes, 112
Fiduciary activities, 34
Fiduciary funds, 303
   agency funds, 304
      reporting
         cash and investment pool, 317
         tax agency fund, 305
   pass-through agency funds, 311
   Public Employee Retirement
      Systems, 325
   trust funds, 312

Financial accountability, 349
Financial Accounting Standards Board, 3
Financial audits; *see* Audits
Financial condition, defined, 398
Financial position, 398
Financial reporting entity, 398
Financial resources focus, 41
Financial section, CAFR, 9
Financially interrelated
   organizations, 573
Fines and forfeits, 79
Fiscal accountability, 8
Fiscal capacity, 399
Fischer, Mary L., 649
Fixed assets; *see also* Capital assets
   basis of accounting for, 164
   buildings and improvements other
      than buildings, 169
   construction work in progress, 170
   cost
      after acquisition, 174
      reduction of, 174
   equipment, 170
   general, 163
   infrastructure, 170
   land, 169
   leased assets, 172
   machinery and equipment, 170
Flexible budgeting; *see* Budgeting
Fountain, James, 517
Force account, 170
Functions, defined, 72
Fund, defined, 38
Fund accounting, 37
   federal
      entries, 491
      statements of, 478
      structure, 475
   types of funds used by not-for-
      profits, 575
   types of funds used by state and local
      governments
      agency, 304
      capital projects, 164
      debt service, 217
      enterprise, 269
      fiduciary, 303
      general, 64
      governmental, 39
      internal service, 256
      investment trust, 313
      pension trust, 324
      permanent, 142
      private-purpose trust, 323
      special revenue, 137
Fund balance, 41
Fund balance with Treasury, 481
Fund equity, 41
Fund financial statements, 8
Funded ratio, 328

G

GAAP Hierarchy, 439
Gainen, J. 649
Gains, 564
GASB; *see* Governmental Accounting
   Standards Board
GASB codification, 3
General capital assets; *see also* Fixed
   assets, 163
General fund
   actual and estimated revenues, 74
   adjusting entries, 129
   characteristics, 64
   closing entries, 133
   expenditures accounting, 72
   fund balance, appropriations or
      reservations of, 83
   illustrative entries, 107–121
   interfund transfers, 108, 141
   inventories, procedures for
      recognition of, 129–130
   purposes, 39
   statements of
      balance sheet
         interim, 122
         year-end, 134
      revenues, expenditures and
         changes in fund balance, 135
         budget and actual, 136
General long-term debt liabilities, 207
   capital lease obligations, 216
   claims, judgments, 188
   debt limit, 212
   debt margin, 213
   overlapping debt, 213
   statements of
      direct and overlapping debt, 215
      legal debt margin, 213
General obligation bonds, 274
General property, plant and
   equipment, 482
General purpose government, 2
General revenues, 62
Generally accepted accounting principles
   (GAAP), 5
   hierarchy, 439
Generally accepted auditing standards,
   (GAAS), 434
Generally accepted government auditing
   standards (GAGAS), 441
Gifts-in-kind, 567, 615, 639
Gimenez, Carlos A., 395
Government Accountability Office,
   audits by, 441
Government-mandated non-exchange
   transactions, 148
Government Performance and Results Act
   of 1993, 468
Government-wide financial statements, 8

Governmental Accounting Standards
  Board, on
    accounting and reporting, 3
    capital lease agreements, 172
    claims and judgments payable, 188
    defining the governmental reporting
      entity, 34, 348
    intergovernmental revenue, 78
    objectives of accounting and financial
      reporting, 6
    public employee retirement system
      accounting, 325
    recognition of revenue from property
      taxes, 115
Governmental activities, 34
Governmental assets, 481
Governmental funds, 39
Governmental liabilities, 481
Governments
  general purpose, 2
  special purpose, 2
Grant, definition, 78
Grant revenues, governmental funds, 78
Grass roots lobbying; *see* Lobbying
Grew, Timothy, 541
Gross, Malvern, J., Jr. 617
Gross tax levy, 115

H

Health care entities
  accounting, 676
  assets limited as to use, 677
  diagnosis-related group, 690
  financial statements of
    balance sheet, 671
    cash flows, 675
    change in net assets, 675
    operations, 674
Health maintenance organization
  (HMO), 691
Heritage assets, 482
Hill-Burton Act of 1946, 668
Historical cost, 165, 284
Hoover Commission, 520
Human service organizations; *see*
  Voluntary health and welfare
  organizations

I

Imposed nonexchange revenues,
  116, 149
Income; *see* Revenue accounting
Incremental budgeting; *see* Budgeting
Indirect costs or expenses, 60, 536
Influencing, 604
Infrastructure assets, 170

Input measures, 530
In-substance defeasance, 235
Inter-activity transactions, 142
Interest and penalties receivable on
  property taxes
    accounting for, 117
    revenue classified as "taxes," 117
Interest charged to construction
  capital projects funds, 181
  enterprise funds, 273
Interfund transactions
  entries, 142
  loans and advances, 140
  transfers, 141, 183
Intergovernmental revenue, 78
Interim financial reports, 121, 352
Intermediate sanctions, 612
Internal exchange transactions, 128
Internal investment pool, 313
Internal service funds, 44
  accounting and financial
    reporting, 256
  assets acquired under lease
    agreements, 266
  closing entries, 262
  dissolution of, 268
  establishment of, 259
  as financing devices, 267
  illustrative entries, 259
  statements of
    cash flows, 264
    net assets, 263
    revenues, expenses, and changes in
      net assets, 263
Internal support test; *see* Support test
Interperiod equity, 6
Intra-activity transactions, 142
Intra-entity transactions, 142
Intragovernmental assets (liabilities), 481
Intragovernmental service funds; *see*
  Internal service funds
Inventories, internal service
  funds, 260–261
Investment trust fund, 45, 313
Irregular serial bonds; *see* Bonds

J

Jackson, Andrea, 521
Job order cost; *see* Costs
Joint venture, 349
Jointly governed organizations, 349
Judgments payable, 188

K

Kaplan, Robert S., 537
Kattelus, Susan C., 590
Kleine, Robert, 411

Kline, James, J., 529
Kloha, Philip, 411

L

Lambkin, Linda M., 617
Land, described, 169
LaPiana, David, 612
Leases
  capital, 172
  operating, 173
Ledgers
  expenditures, 83
  revenue, 80
Ledingham, Dianne, 529
Legal defeasance, 235
Legally separate organizations, 349
Legislation, 611
Letter of transmittal, 9
Licenses and permits, 78
Life income agreements, 636
Loan assets, 635
Lobbying, 604
  direct, 611
  grass-roots, 611
Locatelli, P., 649
Long-run solvency; *see* Solvency

M

Macroaccounting, 471
Major funds, 21, 38
Major programs, 452
Management's discussion and analysis, 8,
  355–364
Material weakness, 455
Materiality, 440
McCarthy, John H., 617
Mead, Dean Michael, 89, 397, 417
Measurable, 49
Measurement focus, governmental
  funds, 49
Meyers, Roy T., 542
Miscellaneous revenue, 79
Modified accrual basis, 13, 41
Modified approach, 171
Municipal solid waste landfills, accounting
  for, 285

N

National Association of Regulatory
  Utility Commissioners, 271
National Center for Education
  Statistics, 627
Net assets, 559
Net pension obligation, 333
Net position, 483

Nollenberger, Karl, 398
Nonaudit work, 445
Nonentity assets, 481
Nonexchange revenue, 116
Nonexchange transactions, 121, 564
Normal cost, 332
Not-for-profit organizations
    categories, 557
    distinguishing characteristics, 556
    financial reporting objectives, 558
Notes payable
    bond anticipation, 188
    tax anticipation, 120

O

Object, classification by, 74
Objectives of financial reporting
    by federal governmental
        agencies, 473
    by not-for-profit entities, 558
    by state and local governmental
        reporting entities, 6
Obligated group, 689
Obligation, federal definition, 492
Office of Management and
    Budget, 471
Operating lease, 173
Operational accountability, 8
Opinion units, 440
Organizational test, 606
Organizational unit, 73
Original cost, utilities, 284
Other comprehensive basis of
    accounting, 377
Other financing sources, 65
Other financing uses, 65
Other post-employment benefits, 335
Other stand-alone governments, 349
Outcome measures, 530
Output measures, 530
Overlapping debt, 213
Oversight agency, 456

P

Patton, Terry K., 517, 542
Penalty, 77
Pension funds; *see* Retirement funds
Pension plan
    defined benefit, 324
    defined contribution, 324
Pension trust funds, 45
Performance audits; *see* Audits
Performance budget, 519
Performance indicator, 674
Perlman, Seth, 603, 617
Permanent fund, 45, 142

Permanently restricted net
    assets, 560
PERS; *see* Retirement funds
Peters, Jeremy, 396
Planning-programming-budget
    system, 520
Plant acquisition adjustment, 284
Political organization, 611
Pollak, Thomas H., 617
Pooled investments, external, 313
Popular reporting, 377
PPBS; *see* Planning-programming-
    budget system
Preferred provider organization
    (PPO), 691
Primary government, 35, 349
Private foundation, 608
Private-purpose trust, 45, 142
Proceeds of debt issue, 185–186
Process cost; *see* Costs
Program budgets, 520
Program classification, 72
Program revenue, 62
Program services (expenses), 564
Program specific audit; *see* Audits
Programs, 72
Promise to give, 566
Propaganda, 611
Property, plant, equipment
    general, 164
    stewardship, 489
Property assessment, 75
Property taxes
    ad valorem, 75
    assessment, 75
    collections of
        current, 116
        delinquent, 118
    exemptions, 77
    interest and penalties, 77
    recording levy, 115
    revenue determination from taxes,
        77, 115
    write-off of uncollectibles, 119
Proprietary funds, 43, 254; *see also*
    enterprise funds and internal
    service funds
Prospective payment system
    (PPS), 676
Public charity, 609
Public employee retirement system; *see*
    Retirement funds
Public improvements fund; *see* Special
    assessments
Public-purpose trust, 142, 323
Public schools
    expenditures, classification, 89–90
    revenues, classification of, 90–92
Purchases method, 129
Purpose restrictions, 148

Q

Quasi-endowments, 636
Questioned cost, 456

R

Ravenscroft, Susan, 590
Regular serial bonds; *see* Bonds
Regulatory accounting principles, 283
Reimbursement, 148
Reportable condition, 455
Reporting entity, 34
Reports published, governmental
    Comprehensive Annual Financial
        Report (CAFR), 9
Required supplementary information
    (RSI), 8
Reserve accounts, 109
Reserve for encumbrances
    defined, 109
    reclassification, 110
Restricted funds, 575
Restricted net assets
    permanently restricted, 560
    temporarily restricted, 559
Retained percentages, 187
Retirement funds (PERS)
    accounting for, 325
    illustrative case, 328
    requirements for government
        employers financial reporting, 331
    requirements for PERS financial
        reporting, 325
Revenue, 564
Revenue accounting, general fund,
    classifications
        charges for services, 78
        fines and forfeits, 79
        intergovernmental, 78
        licenses and permits, 78
        miscellaneous, 79
        taxes, 75
Revenue bonds, 273
Revenue ledger accounts, 75
Revolving funds; *see* Internal
    service funds
Reyes, David, 395
Rigby, Darrell K., 529
Risk-based approach, 453
Risk contract, 691
Rubin, Irene S., 541

S

Schermann, Kenneth, 417
Schools; *see* Public Schools
Serial bonds; *see* Bonds

Service capacity, 399
Service efforts and accomplishments, 24, 530
Service-level solvency; *see* Solvency
Settlement accounts, 678
Sharp, Florence C., 377
Shelmon, Nancy E., 617
Single audit, 447
Single Audit Act Amendments of 1996, 447
Sinking funds, 218
Social Security taxes; *see* FICA taxes
Solvency
    budgetary, 398
    cash, 398
    long-run, 398
    service-level, 398
Soybel, Virginia E., 395
Special assessments, 192
    bonds, reporting of, 208
Special items, 63
Special purpose governments, 2
Special revenue funds, 39
Spending rate, 636
Split interest agreements, 636
Statements; *see references to various kinds of funds or other topics to which the statements may be related*
Statistical section, 21
Stewardship investments, 489
Stewardship land, 482
Stop-loss insurance, 691
Subsidiary records
    appropriations, 83
    encumbrances, 83
    estimated revenues, 80
    expenditures, 83
    revenues, 80
Summary Statement of Governmental Accounting and Financial Reporting Principles, 47–50
Supplies funds; *see* Internal service funds
Support, 564
Support test
    external, 609
    internal, 609
Sweep accounts, 523

T

Tax agency fund, 305–311
Tax anticipation notes, 120, 525
Tax rate, 115
Tax-supported debt, 208
Taxable property, 77
Taxes; *see also* Property taxes
    accounting for
        accrual of interest and penalties, 117
        collection of current taxes, 116
        correction of errors, 124
        FICA, 112
        payroll taxes, 112
        recording property tax levy, 115
        write-off of uncollectible delinquent taxes, 119
    ad valorem, 75
Temelo, Judy W., 418
Temporarily restricted net assets, 559
Term bonds; *see* Bonds
Term endowment funds, 636
Termination benefits, 335
Terminology, 707
Third-party payor, 676
Tidrick, Donald E., 441
Time requirements, 138
Total quality management, 528
Total return, 636
Transactions
    exchange, 147
    nonexchange, 147
Transfers, 141
Treasury, Secretary of, responsibilities of, 470
Trust funds; *see also* Endowments
    objective of, 312
    private-purpose, 323
    public-purpose, 142

U

Uncollectible taxes, 117
Unconditional promise to give, 566
Unexpended appropriations, 483

Unfunded actuarial liability, 332
United Way of America, 569
University accounting; *see* College and university accounting procedures
Unrelated business income, (UBI), 609
Unrestricted net assets, 559
Utility funds; *see* Enterprise funds
Utility plant acquisition adjustment, 284

V

Variance power, 574
Voluntary health and welfare organizations, 556
    program services and supporting services, 568–569
Voluntary nonexchange transactions, 138

W

Walsh, Mary Williams, 396
Weissert, Carol S., 411
Wilgoren, Jodi, 396
Work in progress; *see* Construction work in progress
Working capital funds; *see* Internal service funds

Z

Zero-based budgeting (ZBB), 520